证据理论与科学

——第四届国际研讨会论文集

常林 张中◎主编

 中国政法大学出版社

2014·北京

图书在版编目（CIP）数据

证据理论与科学:第四届国际研讨会论文集/常林,张中主编. —北京:中国政法大学出版社，2014.12

ISBN 978-7-5620-5686-7

Ⅰ.①证… Ⅱ.①常…②张… Ⅲ.①证据－理论研究－国际学术会议－文集 Ⅳ.①D915.130.1-53

中国版本图书馆CIP数据核字(2014)第279482号

出版者　中国政法大学出版社

地　址　北京市海淀区西土城路25号

邮寄地址　北京100088信箱8034分箱　邮编100088

网　址　http://www.cuplpress.com（网络实名：中国政法大学出版社）

电　话　010-58908524(编辑部)　58908334(邮购部)

承　印　固安华明印业有限公司

开　本　787mm×1092mm　1/16

印　张　53

字　数　1200千字

版　次　2014年12月第1版

印　次　2015年3月第2次印刷

定　价　136.00元

Preface

前 言

为促进证据理论与科学的国际学术交流和跨学科研究，中国政法大学证据科学研究院于2007年9月、2009年7月、2011年7月成功举办了第一、二、三届证据理论与科学国际研讨会。2013年7月20~21日，由司法文明协同创新中心、国际证据科学协会主办，中国政法大学证据科学研究院承办，法庭毒物分析公安部重点实验室协办的第四届证据理论与科学国际研讨会在北京隆重召开。来自中国大陆和台湾地区的代表一百三十余人，以及来自美国、英国、西班牙、意大利、荷兰、匈牙利、瑞士、澳大利亚、韩国等国家的二十余人，共一百五十余位证据法学家和法庭科学家齐聚一堂，围绕证据理论与科学展开了深入的研讨。

第四届证据理论与科学国际研讨会的主题为“证据科学与司法文明”，下设4个专题：①证据法如何推动司法文明；②证据法与社会和谐；③法庭科学与司法公正；④法庭科学与事实发现。本次国际研讨会的会期共两天，日程分为两个阶段：第一天上午由五位中外专家就证据法学、法庭科学的最新研究进展作大会主题报告；随后的一天半中，会议分为证据法学和法庭科学两个分会场进行相关主题交流。在每个专题中，均由来自国内外的4~6位学者围绕一个主题进行发言，与会专家再就发言和研讨主题进行深入讨论。

国际证据科学协会主席、美国西北大学威格莫尔特座教授罗纳德·J. 艾伦在致辞中代表国际证据科学协会对会议对各位参会者表述感谢。他指出，证据法对于法制和文明意义重大，理性和人类文化的共同点，普世的人类状逻辑和知识连贯性，使得世界各国的证据法研究具有共性。证据法已经成为中国法制建设的重要领域，但是目前证据问题的研究还不够，此次国际研讨会的召开非常重要。在主旨演讲中，艾伦教授就《证据改革的框架》、瑞士洛桑大学的克里斯托弗·山普教授就《在DNA转移问题上对DNA证据和专家意见的理解》、北京大学的陈瑞华教授就《新法定证据主义》、意大利帕维亚大学的米歇尔·塔鲁弗教授就《证据、事实与法制》进行了深入研讨和交流，四川大学龙宗智教授介绍了《我国非法口供排除的“痛苦规则”及相关问题》，并从证据学的角度对聂树斌案件做了法理研判。

20日下午开始，会议分为证据法学和法庭科学两个分会场，与会代表围绕各自的主题进行了深入交流。在证据法学分会场，中外代表证据法学理论和实务中的热点问题进行了主题发言，并回答了其他代表的发言。在法庭科学分会场，法庭科学家围绕法医学、物证技术等领域的问题做了分会场发言，并和与会代表进行了讨论。经过一天半的议程，代表之间就证据科学中的一些焦点问题达成了共识，并对争议问题交换了意见。

21日下午，国际证据科学协会第一届理事会第二次全体会议举行，会议将讨论过去两年来协会的工作，吸收了3位新理事，并对2015年第五届国际研讨会的筹备工作进行了讨论。

在两天的会议中，不同国家、地区的学者对于证据科学领域的前沿问题展开了理论和实践方面的讨论，分享着各自的经验、知识和思考；不同学科的研究者对相同的问题提供了不同角度的思考路径和研究方法，为问题的深入研究和解决方案提供了更多的参考依据。可以说，证据理论与科学国际研讨会已成长为一个比较成熟的证据科学国际论坛，成为全世界证据法学家和法庭科学家开展跨学科交流的一个重要平台，各国专家通过会议能够达到发现问题、增加共识、协调差异的目的，这既推动了学术和思想的碰撞，也加深了各国学者的相互理解和友谊。

论文集出版是证据理论与科学国际研讨会的重要成果。为了让广大学界同仁更多地了解第四届证据理论与科学国际研讨会的会议情况和学术成果，大会组委会决定出版本次国际研讨会论文集。本次会议共收到投稿论文157篇，其中证据法学论文50篇，法庭科学论文75篇（其中9篇仅有英文摘要），英文论文32篇。大会组委会邀请相关专家对投稿论文进行匿名评审，共录用中文论文141篇，其中证据法学35篇，法庭科学74篇；英文论文32篇，其中证据法学9篇，法庭科学23篇。研讨会结束后，组委会逐一与参会者联系，获得作者将论文编入论文集出版的授权，并要求作者根据会议情况修改论文后发回，进行编辑加工，最终呈现在各位读者面前。

本次证据理论与科学国际研讨会的成功举行，得益于司法文明协同创新中心、国际证据科学协会、法庭毒物分析公安部重点实验室的鼎力相助。本次会议的成功举行，得益于中国政法大学证据科学研究院的诸多教师，以及该院2010级、2011级法律硕士研究生付出的巨大努力。本届论文集的顺利出版，中国政法大学证据科学院褚福民、汪诸豪、郝红霞、连园园等老师，以及中国政法大学出版社编辑们付出了很多辛劳。在此一并表示感谢！

编　者

2014年3月

Contents

目 录

Ⅱ 法 庭 科 学

The Framework for the Reform of Evidence

Ronald J. Allen *

Thank you for those kind words of introduction. It is a great pleasure to be addressing you today, and a distinct honor. I have been working with the faculty of CUPL and other Chinese Universities for over a decade now, and this is my fifteenth trip to China to do lectures and meet with colleagues concerning matters of mutual interest. What began for me as a somewhat exotic excursion into the law of another nation has now become a part of the fabric of my life. And as a teacher and scholar, it is particularly gratifying to see the great progress that has been made in China through the contributions of the many Chinese scholars I have been privileged to have study with at Northwestern University, and with whom I have interacted over the years in China and the United States.

The general title of this conference may appear a bit audacious. It is not often that a field of study implies through the title of its conferences that the scholars of that field believe that their efforts have contributed to the rule of law and the progression of civilization. Lest anyone think that the Chinese scholars who have organized this conference have belied their normal humility, I should hasten to point out that I was the one who suggested the title. The reason I suggested it is that it hints at a great and significant truth, in fact two truths really. First, that the field of evidence is critical to the rule of law. Second, that the rule of law is critical to the progression of society. I would go further and say that the single most important field of study to the rule of law is evidence, and that society can only progress within the rule of law.

You in China have confirmed these truths with a natural and in my opinion regrettable experiment that we in the West call the Cultural Revolution. Among the many things that occurred during that lamentable time was the essential shutting down of the legal system, and the shutting of all but one of the law schools, I believe. This had the predictable effect of devastating the economy and causing a horrific drop in the gross domestic product of China. This natural experiment, though, continued after the end of the Cultural Revolution when your government liberalized the economy. At first there was a great burst of productivity, but it quickly began to subside, and the reason is precisely that a functioning legal system is an absolute requirement of a productive society. The creation of wealth depends on trade, but trade will not occur except

* Ronald J. Allen, John Henry Wigmore Professor of Law, Northwestern University, U. S. A; President, Board of Foreign Advisors, Evidence Law and Forensic Sciences Institute; Fellow, Procedural Law Research Center, CUPL.

I am indebted to Jiang Yujia, a second year law student at Northwestern University, for her research assistance.

through barter within a functioning legal system. It was the recognition of this fact that led your government to begin the long process of reestablishing a functioning legal system, a process that continues to this day.

As I will talk about in a few minutes, at the heart of that process is indeed the law of evidence, and thus I will say again what I have said before in China: Those of you in this room who are studying and furthering knowledge about the field of evidence, and its handmaiden procedural fields, are the single most important part of your country's continuing progress. Without you and your efforts, or without the continuing improvement of evidence and procedure, the economy will be retarded in its growth and rights will be meaningless; without the production of wealth, the aspirations of modern societies cannot be realized. More importantly, without accurate fact finding rights essentially have no significance whether those are economic, human, or political rights. These are the things that I want to talk with you about today, and I will begin with the rule of law.

There is great interest today in China and the world at large in the rule of law. The phrase "the rule of law" can mean many different things, however. What I mean by the phrase, and what all countries interested in the twin aims of stability and progress should mean by the phrase is, first, that there are generally agreed upon determinants of what makes a demand, command or order binding upon a certain set of people. H. L. A. Hart referred to this as the "rule of recognition," by reference to which a person can determine what is authoritative within a society.[1] As Hart pointed out, more is needed, including rules that allow a society to change its authoritative commands, its "law," in light of changed circumstances that the evolution of society invariably brings. These are often located in modern times in constitutions, such as that of China and the United States, that create certain institutions with such power. Yet, as Hart further pointed out, more is needed still, including a means of enforcing authoritative commands and resolving disputes about them. This again in modern times typically falls to courts and forms of adjudication. There is much more to be said about the philosophical basis of "the rule of law," of course, including the mechanisms for enforcement of commands emphasized by John Austin,[2] the hierarchical nature of law emphasized by Hans Kelsen[3], and the relationship between law and morality that has driven the Har – Dworkin debate that has occupied a good deal of modern western jurisprudence for the last forty years, but I will put aside for today's purposes these deep and interesting questions and simply focus on the prerequisites for the rule of law identified by Hart, for they capture the conventional meaning of "the rule of law" as it is being used in conventional discourse, I believe.

The attractions of the Hartian view, and why so many people around the world are calling for reform that takes societies in that direction, are as profound as they are obvious. Law in the

---

〔1〕 H. L. A. Hart, The Concept of Law.

〔2〕 John Austin, *Lectures on Jurisprudence, or The Philosophy of Positive Law*, Two Vols., R. Campbell (Ed.), 4th edition, rev., London: John Murray; Reprint, Bristol: Thoemmes Press, 2002.

〔3〕 Hans Kelsen, The Pure Theory of Law (1934).

Hartian sense is part of the glue that holds society together peacefully. It provides the means by which rights and obligations can be known in advance, and negotiated around. I own something. You want it. You need to negotiate with me over its price rather than just seize it arbitrarily. There is thus a critical sense in which the law, rather than being restrained, is liberating. It channels the ways in which people can construct their lives and pursue their livelihoods and removes the risk of arbitrary and unpredictable intrusions into their personal spheres, whether from governments or other individuals.

In this social dynamic, it is conventional to attribute the values of the rule of law primarily to the articulation of rights and their reciprocal obligations. There is some important truth to this view, but it obscures something equally profound, which is that without accurate resolution of disputes—without accurate fact finding, in other words—rights and obligations are meaningless. I have made this point to you many times in my lectures in China, but let me remind you once again, for the point cannot be emphasized enough, that facts are prior to and determinative of rights and obligations. Without accurate fact finding, rights and obligations are meaningless. Consider the simple case of ownership of the clothes you are wearing. Your ownership of those clothes allows you the "right" to possess, consume, and dispose of those assets, but suppose I demand that you return "my" clothes. That is, I insist that the clothes that you are wearing actually belong to me. What will you do? You will search for a decision - maker to whom you will present evidence that you bought, made, found, or were given the clothes in question, and, if successful in this effort, the decision - maker will indeed grant you those rights and impose upon me reciprocal obligations. The critical point is that those rights and obligations are dependent upon what facts are found and are derivative of them. The significance of this point cannot be overstated. Tying rights and obligations to true states of the real world anchors rights and obligations in things that can be known and are independent of whim and caprice. This is why the ideas of relevance and materiality are so fundamentally important to the construction of a legal system. They tie the legal system to the bedrock of factual accuracy. This point is truly universal. On the one hand, neither rights nor obligations nor policy choices can be pursued in the absence of knowledge of the actual, relevant states of affairs. On the other hand, tying rights to facts gives them solidity and stability so that they cannot be removed arbitrarily.

As many of you know, often when I emphasize the importance of facts, I use property rights as the example. Let me give another example, this time of a human right. At this point in events like this, most people normally expect an American to be critical of the Chinese record on human rights, but that is not the example I wish to discuss. Instead, it is the spying by the American government on its own citizens, foreigners, and even foreign sovereigns that has been disclosed by Edward Snowden. I am not sure whether I think Mr. Snowden should be treated as a hero or a traitor, but I am confident that without his disclosures I and my countrymen would have been completely oblivious to the massive violations of our rights that have taken place during the Obama administration. Without that knowledge, there is simply no way I or anyone else could have vindicated our rights. Without the facts, one can almost say that no violations occurred.

Thus, it is not just adjudication in the Hartian triumvirate that matters, but accurate adjudication. Again as I've said many times in China, that is why those of you who are studying and advancing knowledge about evidence, procedure, and the structure of legal systems, and bringing that knowledge to bear to reform your law are absolutely fundamental to the continuing progression of your country. As you have moved from a less arbitrary to more predictable legal system, your prosperity and ability to flourish have improved commensurately. I commend you for your astonishing achievements, am humbled to have played a small role in them, and charge you to continue in these efforts.

There are thus aspects of the law structuring dispute resolution—evidence and procedure—that have universal aspects. And of course accurate dispute resolution involves rational people deliberating upon reliable evidence, which introduces more universal attributes into the mix. However, structuring dispute resolution is not just a matter of optimizing these universal aspects of the enforcement of rights and the meaning of rationality. It also has a heavily contextualized component. Here there are three critically important points to comprehend. The first point is that all rules that structure the process of proof, are derived from and implement a theory of dispute resolution. The dominant theory of dispute resolution in the United States is the adversarial process, but this is not universal. The second and related point is that theories of dispute resolution, such as the adversarial system or continental (sometimes called the inquisitorial) system, are themselves derived from underlying conceptions of the appropriate role of government in the resolution of disputes between private individuals in civil cases and in the prosecution of criminal cases. In the Anglo American tradition, the role of the government in private dispute resolution has been largely facilitative. The government provides a fair and disinterested forum for the impartial resolution of private disputes, and that is essentially all the government has an obligation, or even a right, to do. In an extraordinary way, this conception of dispute resolution affects criminal cases as well. The government prosecutes cases, but the government is conceived of as analogous to a private party that stands on equal footing with the other private party, the defendant, before the courts. The courts are neutral, in other words, and are not part of the organs of government structured to further the government's specific policy interests in the particular trial; indeed, as is well known, the courts in the United States are famous for obstructing the policy objectives of the government through such things as exclusionary rules. Again, this is not a universal characteristic of legal systems. The third preliminary point is at a deeper conceptual level. The judiciary and the other branches of government are all designed to further the political aspirations reflected in the founding documents and traditions of the country, such as the United States Constitution and the Chinese Constitution. This injects another contingency into the analysis, because not all countries have commensurate political theories. For example, the central political problem of governing in the United States is a principal – agent problem: The Government is the agent of the people, and the primary problem is how the principal—the people—can control its agent—the Government. This concern about controlling and limiting the central government out of fear of its tendency to concentrate power in itself is what explains the two defining features of the political structure of the United States, federalism and separation of powers. This stands in stark contrast with numerous eastern sovereigns in particular. For example, you have long had a theory of unitary political power located in the Communist Party, and thus the central political problem is the efficient implementation of the policy objectives of Government. These differences plainly affect the legal systems that are constructed in their reflection. One would predict that the Chinese government will tend to exercise more power and control in the dispute resolution process in order to efficiently implement its policy goals. In contrast, in the United States the government has more limited power and the courts are primarily a disinterested forum.

These two distinctions between types of legal systems and theories of government do not necessarily involve stark contrasts but come in many different shades. For example, the conception of the role of the government in the resolution of disputes is not uniform even in representative democracies that otherwise share many traits. In many Western European countries, for example, disputes are not "private" matters to the extent that they are in the United States, and the government plays a much more active role in virtually all phases of litigation. The government often is more actively involved in investigation, and the trial process is controlled more by the court than is true in the United States. This reflects the view that disputes between citizens have a public feature, and thus that the resolution of disputes is a matter of collective concern. In the United States, by contrast, private disputes are not understood to be matters of social concern for the most part, and the government plays a much less active role. The parties are responsible for investigating and preparing the case for trial, and in large measure controlling the presentation of evidence at trial. Similarly, appellate courts often purport to decide cases based only on the arguments presented to them by the parties, thus generating the possibility that cases with virtually identical facts will be decided differently due to the legal arguments advanced. The critical point to understand is that the obligation of the court extends to deciding the case correctly based on what the parties have put forth rather than to decide it "correctly" for all purposes.

The structure of legal systems is also affected by two additional variables. The first involves legal epistemology, which refers to beliefs concerning how effective different forms of dispute resolution are in producing accurate verdicts. In the United States, it is generally although not universally believed that adversarial investigation and presentation of evidence is more likely to yield a verdict consistent with the truth than is a process more dominated by a tribunal. The parties know their case better than anyone else and have the proper incentives to invest the optimal resources in dispute resolution. A government bureaucracy normally would be a poor substitute for the more thorough knowledge and more finely calibrated incentives of the parties. Those who favor more inquisitorial systems emphasize that control by a disinterested tribunal will lead to less abuse and manipulation of the evidence, which they believe may increase the chance that verdicts consistent with the truth will emerge.

The pursuit of truth is not the only social good, however, and there are disagreements about how that particular social good interacts with others, such as privacy. In the United States, the general view is that in civil cases the parties should have essentially unfettered access to all the pertinent information concerning a dispute before the trial begins. The process of obtaining that information is called discovery, and its robustness is one of the defining features of the American legal system. The idea is that trial should truly be an epistemological event and not full of either surprises or road blocks. However, all countries compromise the pursuit of truth by favoring from time to time other values, as I have discussed in various lectures here in China. What values outweigh truth again is quite socially contingent.

The last important preliminary point to mention is the effect that juries or lay assessors have on the structure of a legal system. In the United States, juries are at once revered and simultaneously treated as alien intruders into the otherwise professional world of the law who must be regulated and controlled. A considerable part of the law of evidence and procedure in the United States is driven by the judge – jury divide. It should be looked at to inform the structure of evidence law in other countries only with this point well in mind.

To sum up, as we think about the structure or reform of evidence law, we must keep in mind these five points:

(1) Rules of evidence (and procedure) are part of a theory of litigation.

(2) Theories of litigation are themselves part of a theory of government.

(3) Theories of government vary dramatically.

(4) Dispute resolution involves fact finding, and there are disagreements about the most efficient and effective way to get to the truth, and relatedly the value of truth when it competes with other social goods.

(5) The presence of lay fact finders such as jurors may affect how the litigation process is otherwise structured.

The various issues that we have discussed above illuminate the depth and profundity of the conceptual foundations and implications of evidence, and together create the framework for the structure and reform of the law of evidence. What I have said so far may be conceptually useful, interesting, and perhaps even correct, but it is not very programmatically useful, is it? It situates the field of evidence in its larger context, but does not provide any sort of roadmap for the reformer of the law of evidence to follow. In what follows, I try to extract from the complex considerations referred to above the general considerations that must be attended to by the reformer of the law of evidence. The reformer of the law of evidence faces five general issues, or what I call "problems".

The Organizational Problem. The law of evidence is a critical mechanism to regulate the interactions of the various participants in the legal system: trial judge, jurors and other lay assessors, attorneys, parties, and witnesses (both lay and expert). The law of evidence constructs the framework for a trial. It allocates both power and discretion to each of the actors. However, the general framework for trials and the role individuals play within that framework can be highly socially contingent. Thus, the reform of the law of evidence must ask not just what makes most conceptual sense, but also and equally important, what are the social expectations of the various participants? These two variables interact, of course. Sometimes the reformer should defer to social expectations and sometimes not. A good example of this is the increasing use in your various evidence enactments and proposals of what we in the United States call discovery. Robust discovery is somewhat new to China, and by advancing these proposals your reformers are slowly conditioning people to accept them, I believe. This point should be generalized, however, and throughout the law of evidence is woven the issue of the best analytical structure and what is socially expected or feasible.

The Epistemological Problem. How one constructs trials, and thus the rules of evidence one fashions to facilitate trials, is a function of beliefs concerning one of the fundamental questions of human thought—what does it mean to know something? A trial is an epistemological event at which claims of knowledge are advanced, considered, rejected, or accepted. The question of knowledge just discussed leads to another fundamental question: what is the purpose or purposes of trials? The typical response has much to do with accurate fact finding, and as we have tried to make clear that typical response has enormous significance. But, are trials like science in its pursuit of truth, and more importantly should they be? How do scientific and legal decision making differ? Unlike scientific pursuits, legal decision – making cannot defer judgment until more information is collected. Also, the judgment to be made is what actually happened rather than what the underlying universal laws might be. Most tellingly, perhaps, there is no organized body of knowledge that is applicable to the typical case, as there is in science. To the contrary, the fact finder has to import the necessary background knowledge for a decision. If, on reflection, trials do not seem a lot like science (at least some types of science), are they like history? The focus of history is on facts, but as a means, generally, of greater understanding. At trials, understanding is largely irrelevant (except as a matter of persuasion). Or is that not accurate? Should trials be the means by which social peace is restored and preserved regardless of any considerations of what "actually" happened? Whether, and to what extent, one thinks a scientific truth or a deep understanding of historical facts is obtainable will affect one's view of particular evidence rules.

In my opinion, the epistemological issue is critically important for Chinese reformers to concentrate on. You tend to refer to "evidence science". To be sure, there is much knowledge about evidence, the law of evidence, and the significance of both. But constructing legal systems and their constituent parts, such as the law of evidence, requires knowledge of a different sort rather than the aspiration of the hard sciences. It requires the weighing and balancing of numerous issues, and the accommodation of very diverse utility functions of many different people. Very little within the field of law is subject to controlled experiments of the sort that are the hallmark of the hard sciences, and one should not conflate the different types of pursuit of knowledge. Moreover, the law can and does adjust as social issues unfold. Much of what the reformer does is driven by reasonable compromises and responses to changed conditions rather than absolute truth.

Perhaps the most important issue here is one I touched upon above, which is knowledge about social disputes can be obtained in different ways. One can put the burden on the litigants or on some governmental organ, and the critical question in any society is which model is more likely to foster efficient truth – seeking? To what extent should trials look like free markets; to what extent should the government regulate them? To some extent the answer to such questions comes from universal laws of nature and human nature, but at the same time will be informed by the contingencies of social practices and expectations. This leads to the next "problem".

The Social Problem. Trials may serve many other purposes in addition to accurate fact finding. They serve very important economic interests, quite apart from their effect on the parties. In addition to the parties, the lawyers, the judges, the court reporters, and all the court personnel have vested economic interests in trials. There are in addition potential symbolic and political purposes to trial. Both institutions and individuals make statements through the means of trials, and actually impart lessons of various kinds. There is, in short, an extraordinarily complex set of issues that inform the nature of trials, and the reformer must at least ask whether any of them should influence the law of evidence.

There is another deep question here, and that is whether trials are the ideal or instead are perverse. Is the legal system designed to encourage trials or settlement? What should it be designed for? Societies differ in their willingness to tolerate disputes, and there is a direct correlation between the structure of trials and the encouragement of private dispute resolution. How that balance is structure should be thought about carefully by the reformer. A good example of how this directly intersects evidence law is the law of privileges. Robust privileges can protect relationships and privacy, but they also increase the cost of litigating, making it a less attractive option for resolving disputes.

The Governance Problem. Evidence law does not just structure fact finding; it also create incentives of various kinds. I just mentioned a very general incentive—how much individuals will be encouraged to litigate. But the law of evidence can create, and in most countries does, incentives for various primary behaviors. Privileges, which I just mentioned, are one example, but there are many others. They range from rape relevancy rules that are designed to encourage the bringing of sexual assault cases to things like the repair rule that are designed to encourage individuals to reduce the risk of harm by eliminating dangerous situations. Accurate fact finding is important, but the deep question here is how accurate fact finding competes with other social values.

The Enforcement Problem. Many times in my trips to China, I have reminded you of the distinction between the law on the books and the law in action. It is one thing to write laws and rules; it is another to enforce them in the way anticipated by the drafter of those provisions. The drafter of an evidence code may think that allocating discretion to someone, whether trial judge or attorney, makes sense, but he will have in mind an approach to exercising that discretion that might not be shared by those being regulated by the rule. More generally, it is hard to enforce complex codes in social events such as trials. The event itself, the trial, is often fluid and unpredictable, and in any event it would be impossible to have every decision made at trial second guessed by some other authority.

Again, there is another deep question lurking here, which involves first the relationship between evidence law and procedural law, and in addition the relationship between both of them and substantive law. What evidence law giveth, procedural law can taketh away. And there is a similarly complex interaction between evidence and procedure on the one hand, and substantive law on the other. One can have a procedural context that makes litigation easy to bring, but substantive definitions of causes of action that are essentially impossible to ever prove. And the opposite can be true: There can be broad definitions of rights, but procedural contexts that are essentially impossible to employ.

So, to sum up, the reformer of the law of evidence has to consider the implications of:

The Organizational Problem,

The Epistemological Problem,

The Social Problem,

The Governance Problem, and

The Enforcement Problem.

You have kindly listened to me for some considerable time, and thus I will bring these remarks to an end. I will do so by returning to where I began. You people in this room and across China who are so assiduously studying the law of evidence and procedure in good measure carry the hope for the rule of law and the progression of society on your shoulders. Neither will occur without your continuing efforts. At the same time, those efforts will involve all the complexities that I have just briefly alluded to today. I have come to know many of you well over the ten years or so I have been involved with your country, and I have seen how ably you have begun to discharge these difficult tasks. The road away will be long and complicated, but I am confident that the tremendous progress that has already occurred will be exceeded by even greater progress in the future. I look forward to seeing that happen hopefully continuing to play a small role in the process.

Evidence, Truth and the Rule of Law

Michele Taruffo *

1. *Fact and law*

The expression "rule of law" has a variety of meanings even within the common law systems; other problems deal with its correspondence or equivalence with similar concepts used in other legal cultures, such as "principio di legalità", "princípio de legalidad", "estado de derecho", "stato di diritto", *Rechtsstaat*, and so forth. However, and notwithstanding the difficulty of defining analytically all these concepts, they have in common a basic core: it is the principle according to which the law has to be applied and enforced when the truth of the facts to which the legal rule involved refers has been duly established.

In general terms it may be said that the law performs its function of regulating the people's behaviors, and of preventing conflicts, on the basis of a sort of presumption (or of a reasonable forecast) that if necessary the law will be applied and enforced when - and only when - the relevant facts actually occurred and their truth will be duly established. It seems rather clear that without sucha presumption, or such a forecast, the law would lose its meaning and would not perform its regulatory function. In such a case, the general principle of the "rule of law" would be deprived of any value.

Such a statement may be better understood by referring to the classic Hans Kelsen's theory according to which any legal rule has a conditional logical structure and is composed by the combination of two statements: the former establishes a *condition* (or *protasis*) and is the statement referring to a *type* of facts, i. e. to a kind of factual occurrence defined in general terms (since rules usually are expressed in "general and abstract" words). The German doctrine speaks of *abstrakteTatbestand* in order to underline that the content of this part of the rule is "factual" (*Tatbestand*; Hare talked of the *frastic*part of the rule) and is stated in general terms. The latter statement is the *consequence* (the *apodosis*) and deals with the legal consequences that the rule provides for the case in which the condition occurred. Then the rule sounds as anything like: when (and only when) a fact "f" corresponding to the general definition of fact F (i. e. a *token* of the *type* provided by the rule) occurred, *then* the effect "e" (i. e. a *token* of the *type* E) may be acknowledged as existing in the specific case. This is an extremely simplified and sketchy idea of the structure of a legal rule, but - besides the fame of its author - it is very useful in order to show that legal rules do not apply *in vacuo*. Legal

* Professor at University of Pavia (Italy) Càtedra de Cultura Jurídica, Girona (Spain), Email: taruffo@ unipv. it.

effects (rights, obligations, and so forth) are not ascribed at random, and hence that facts are the real and unavoidable premises for the correct enforcement of any legal rule.

And, it is well known in the general theory of law and interpretation that while it is the reference to the factual condition of the rule that determines the selection of the legally relevant facts, the facts of the case are the main factor that determines the interpretation of the rule, in a *dialectic* or even *circular* proceeding that may come to an end when a *konkreteTatbestand* (i. e. a legally relevant specific fact) is found as corresponding to a proper meaning (among the several possible meanings) of the *abstrakteTatbestand* defined by the rule. Once again: the facts are the real factor that determines when and how the rule may be correctly enforced in specific cases, that is: in the real life of the legal system.

2. *Theories of justice*

Kelsen's is not the only theoretical approach to the way how a legal system works, but it has the advantage of showing in clear terms the connection existing between facts and law. This advantage becomes especially significant when one looks at a legal system from the point of view of the administration of justice, taking in special consideration what happens in the judicial context, civil or criminal.

However, from this standpoint one has to take into account the existence of several ideologies concerning the function and the aims of judicial proceedings. A detailed analysis of such ideologies cannot be developed here, but some examples can be considered and some general remarks can be made.

If, for instance, one shares the general and very common idea that the function and the aim of a judicial process is just that of dispute resolution, *and nothing more*, he has to accept the consequence that *any solution* of the dispute has to be approved, provided it is efficient and effective, that is: provided the conflict between the parties actually comes to an end. If this is considered to be the real and only purpose of the procedural machinery, it may be achieved in many ways according with the social, moral and cultural context in which such a machinery works. Then, an efficient dispute resolution may be achieved by means of illegal decisions, by judgments based upon false or wrong reconstruction of the facts in issue, by choices made at random, by casting dices, by duel or ordalic proofs, and so on. One could even say that not enforcing the fundamental rights of the parties would be fine, provided it is economically efficient, that is: provided that time and money may be spared.

This lack of consideration for the content and the quality, and mainly for the lawfulness, of the outcome of the judicial machinery, is common to various ideas of the judicial process that are widely shared within the current legal culture. For instance, it is inherent with the adversarial theory of justice that is still dominating in the USA, according to which a trial is a sort of individual competition (remember Roscoe Pound's idea of the "fight theory of justice"). In such a competition, where the judge is just a passive umpire, of course the winner will be the stronger and the smarter of the fighters, no matter whether he was right or wrong from a legal point of view. Things are roughly the same with the *ritualistic* or *procedural* theories of judicial process, according to which it is the "ritual", or the "procedure", that *legitimizes* the final decision to the eyes of the public. In other words, the procedural ritual sends to the surrounding society the message that the decision should be accepted just because it came out from that procedure, independently from the contents and the legal quality of such a decision. Once again, it may be the outcome of a gross violation of the law, or of a dramatic error about the facts, but it may be accepted by the public if the "judicial theater" worked well in representing at least the appearance of a fair proceeding.

It seems quite clear that if one of these perspectives is shared, the principles of the rule of law come to an unhappy end: if the law is irrelevant as a standard for decision – making, talking of the rule of law while speaking of the judicial administration of justice sounds very odd, as something that has nothing to do with the way how disputes should be solved by courts. *A fortiori*, talking of the search of truth in judicial contexts may sound even stranger and – at least – irrelevant and not interesting. Actually the most coherent theorization of the American adversarial system says that the search of truth is of no interest for anyone, and therefore it should be avoided as a waste of time, of money and of judicial activities.

Things change completely if a different ideology of judicial decision – making is adopted. The point is not to deny that judicial proceedings are aimed at resolving disputes: this is so obvious that does not deserve any further discussion. The relevant point is *how* disputes should be resolved. The principle of the rule of law requires that each dispute be resolved according to the law, i. e. by applying the legal rule that regulates the facts in issue. "Applying" means "applying correctly" and – in its turn – "applying correctly" means that the rule has to be interpreted "in the light" of the facts of the case, and – moreover – that such facts should be properly reconstructed as "true" . As Justice Frank once said, no just decision can be made upon wrong facts.

Such a shift of perspective has several relevant consequences. A very important one is that the search of the truth about the facts, far from being something that should be carefully avoided, is a necessary aspect of judicial proceedings. Another important consequence is that the justice of the decision (i. e. the correctness of the application of the law in the specific case) *depends* directly on the truthfulness of the reconstruction of the facts in issue. A true determination of the facts is not the only sufficient condition for the justice of the decision, since a proper interpretation of the legal rule and a fair trial are also required, but it is a *necessary condition* for the justice of the decision. So to say, a decision is just insofar as it is based upon a truthful reconstruction of the facts in issue. It means that the principle of the rule of law is infringed when a dispute is decided without establishing the truth of such facts.

3. *About truths*

This line of argument raises a further problem. Actually to state that in judicial proceedings the truth of the facts should be established means to presuppose that such a truth *can* be discovered. However, just such a presupposition is not generally admitted.

Sometimes it happens as a consequence of general philosophical options. For instance, an important trend of German philosophy in the XX century, going from Nietsche to Gadamerand passing through Heidegger, denied any meaning to the concept of truth (whatever they intended for it, which is far from being clear). In a similar way, the so-called postmodern philosophers tried to de-construct several general concepts, including the concept of truth. It is clear that if one shares one of these theories, or follows Richard Rorty in saying that discussing of truth is just a waste of time, to talk of truth in the administration of justice would be just nonsense.

However, the range of philosophical options is not so narrow, fortunately. Actually, while the Nietschean and the Heideggerian fashions are vanishing, and the postmodern style of thought is coming to an end, in the last years philosophy and epistemology are experiencing what could be called a "return to the truth". Several authors, such as Bernhard Williams, Michel Lynch, Franca D' Agostini and many others, share the idea that truth is a fundamental value not only in the philosophy of knowledge and science, but also in social and political contexts.

This shift is very complex and extremely interesting, but unfortunately it cannot be examined here as it would deserve. Suffice it to say that this new trend includes the choice in favor of a "new critical realism" in ontology, that is: the belief in the existence of the real world and of empirical facts, and in favor of an "epistemological rationalism", that is: the belief in the possibility of achieving a reliable and truthful knowledge of facts.

Therefore, it seems that in the current days one may have good philosophical reasons to believe that the discovery of a truthful knowledge of a fact is at least possible by rational means (although in many cases not easy).

However, a philosophically ignorant lawyer (as the Twining's "hard – nosed practitioner") could still take another way to say that talking of truth in the administration of justice is nonsense. A very common argument in this direction says that in a judicial proceeding that are so many and so strict constraints to the search of truth (such as: rules excluding relevant evidence, methods for the presentation of evidence, res judicata, and so forth), that in the end what can be achieved is a sort of "formal" or "procedural" truth (that is: not the "real" truth), while the "true truth" could be achieved only out of the judicial process.

This kind of argument is very popular among lawyers, but it is wrong. On the one hand, one has to consider that there are many types of proceedings: some are oriented at facilitating the discovery of truth, while others are oriented in the opposite sense and include various anti – epistemic technical rules. Then the question of whether or not a proceeding allows or prevents the search of truth has no general solutions: all this depends on the political and systemic choices made by the procedural lawgiver in any place and time. Bentham's ideal system of justice, for instance, was a procedure in which all the relevant evidence should have been admitted, with no rules of exclusion, since admitting all the relevant evidence is a basic condition to achieve the truth of the facts.

On the other hand, there is no reason to think that the kind of knowledge that can be discovered in an epistemically - oriented judicial proceeding is *ontologically* different from the kind of knowledge that one achieves in the ordinary daily life. It is easy to see, in fact, that every day and dozens of times we look for the truth of facts, using exactly the same means that are used in judicial proceedings, such as documents, testimonial statements, inspections, experts' opinions, circumstantial evidence, and so forth. Besides, one may observe that many times in a judicial proceeding the use of these means is often more careful, more controlled, more efficient and therefore more reliable if compared with what people usually do, even when important decisions need to be taken (for instance, a cross examination well performed in a trial is usually considered, following Wigmore, as "the best legal engine ever invented for the search of truth"). Even time limits or other constraints (such as lack of money) usually compel people (including scientists) to be satisfied with truths that are qualitatively not better than "judicial" truths.

4. *Which truth*

While talking of truth, and specifically of "judicial truth", one would need to define what he means with words as "true", "truthful", "truth", and so forth. Actually the market of the ideas about truth is very rich (one could say: exceedingly rich), as it used to be historically but is much more in these current days. People speak of truth as coherence (narrative or logical), of truth as consent (of a few people, of many, or even of the universal public), of truth as plausibility or persuasiveness of a story, of truth as probability (or as one of the various concepts of probability), of absolute truths, of relative truths, of subjective truths, and so on in a long series of variations. Such an infinitely complex topic, that in the Western culture is discussed at least beginning with Aristoteles, cannot be seriously analyzed herein its general terms. However, some words can be said about what we might take as a correct idea of truth when we are thinking of the search of truth in a judicial context.

The starting point is that in the administration of justice, as in any other human enterprise, there is no "absolute" truth to be discovered by intuition or by miracles. But this does not mean - as some popperian disappointed absolutists tend to do - that *then* in the judicial context there cannot be any truth at all. It simply means that in such a context we are thinking of non - absolute truths, that is of *relative* truths. After all, the epistemologists tell us that *any* truth, including scientific truths, is relative, at least because its cognitive value depends on the set of information available and on the method used to process such information. If, therefore, all truths are (objectively, not subjectively) relative, no wander that judicial truths are also relative.

Moreover, the standard of truth cannot be - as some "narrativists" or "story - tellers" say - anything like the *narrative coherence* of the stories told about the facts in issue. A judicial proceeding is not a sort of literary competition in which the victory goes to the narratively most coherent and most persuasive or plausible story. After all, a perfectly coherent story could be completely false, as it normally happens with novels. Even judicial stories could be false, and rather frequently they actually are false, even when they appear to be narratively coherent.

The fact is that the administration of justice is interested in discovering what actually occurred in the real world of facts and behaviors, since it is to such facts and behaviors that the rule of law has to be applied by the judge in his final decision. As abovementioned, the law is correctly enforced if, and only if, it is applied to the facts to which specific legal consequences are ascribed. Then these facts need to have actually occurred and to be established in a truthful way.

This being the proper perspective in which the concept of truth can be defined with reference to the basic function of a judicial proceeding, then we may made some basic assumptions, starting from the premise that we are talking of the truth of the statements concerning the facts in issue:

a) At the level of philosophical assumptions, the existence of the external world, that is of empirical facts and actual behaviors of people, deserves to be assumed.

b) At the epistemological level, the best choice is to refer to a concept of truth as *correspondence* of factual statements to the real facts that are described by these statements. This is not to share old – styled and naïf ideas of knowledge. It corresponds to the much more sophisticated and up – to – date ideas of the "new realism", according to which when a proposition refers to a real fact, it is the reality of this fact that determines whether or not this proposition is true. Then a judicial "story" can be taken as truthful if – and only if – there are good reasons to believe that it corresponds to the realty of the facts that the story narrates.

It may be said that actually such a "truth as correspondence" to the reality will never be achieved in judicial proceedings in an absolute way, and such a remark would make sense. But this does not imply that such a concept of truth is meaningless in a judicial context. Rather, "alethic" truth works as a "regulatory ideal", that is: as a reference point toward which the concrete search of truth should be oriented. In a sense, it is like the North: one may never actually reach the North Pole, but its existence and the knowledge of where it is, are necessary in order to determine the direction of a journey.

5. *Nature and function of evidence*

The preceding remarks show that a judicial trial, if considered with reference to the rule of law, may be interpreted also as a sort of epistemic enterprise aimed at discovering and establishing the truth of a story told about the facts in issue.

Within this framework the nature and the function of evidence may be properly understood.

As in happens in science (as epistemologists tell us) but also in any kind of rational knowledge of any fact in the ordinary experience of life, evidence is the means (or – better – the set of means) by which a subject collects the information he needs in order to achieve a truthful conclusion about that fact. This is especially true for the evidence collected in a judicial proceeding, since a general principle says that the trier of fact (judge or juror) is obliged to build up his judgment on the facts in issue *only* by taking into account the evidence that was presented at trial. It means that he *cannot* rely on the "private" knowledge that for any reason he might have of the facts in issue or of any circumstantial fact. Actually he may take the so-called "judicial notice" only of facts that are "notorious" in the general culture of that place and time, and of common sense generalizations (or more generally: the stock of knowledge) that people use to interpret the world. But nothing else. The specific information that is needed for the reconstruction of the facts in issue may be provided *only* by evidence.

Then the epistemic function of evidence, as the only possible means to achieve the knowledge and then to establish the truth of the facts in issue, should be clear. However, there are some further problems deserving to be shortly discussed.

5. 1. *Rhetorical evidence*?

One of these problems concerns just the nature and function of evidence. It derives from an idea that is rather common among lawyers, according to which evidence would not be an epistemic device, but only a *persuasive* technique. In other words, evidence would perform nothing else that a *rhetoric* function, and would be aimed only at creating in the mind of the trier of fact a *belief*, i. e. a psychological state, about the fact in issue. Such a belief would have nothing to do with the truth or falsehood of the narration describing the fact, since a belief is a state of mind, not an epistemic statement. Then one might have a strong subjective belief about absurd and dramatically false stories. Examples of it are thousands, from the flat form of the Earth (that was a very strong belief shared by millions of people for centuries) to the outcome of advertising or of political propaganda.

This idea about the function of evidence does not fit with the conception of the judicial process as an epistemic machinery aimed at discovering the truth about the facts in issue, but it is not completely absurd. Rather, it interprets rather well the way how *lawyers* try to use the evidence at trial. As it is well known, lawyers are not interested in the search of truth since their main interest and duty is to defend their client with all the (hopefully) legal means. Then their aim in the presentation of evidence is *not* to help the trier of fact to find out the truth, but to persuade him to reach a decision in favor of their client (even, and moreover, when they know that the truth would determine the client's defeat). One could say that this aspect is even more important when the trier of fact is a lay juror, since the judicial rhetoric arguments is probably less effective for a professional judge.

However, the use that lawyers tend to make of evidence may be understood from *their* perspective, but it does not determine the function that evidence performs from the point of view of the decision on the facts. If, as abovementioned, such a decision has to be based upon a truthful reconstruction of such facts, and if evidence is the only means to discover the truth, the consequence is that - notwithstanding the possible persuasive aspects - the essential function of evidence is epistemic. After all, and just to take an example among many, it would be very odd to consider the outcome of a DNA test as a persuasive rhetorical argument rather than as a reliable information to be used in order to establish a fact as the match between two genetic profiles.

5.2. *Olistic stories?*

The reference to the jury leads to a further question that is worth discussing here, i. e. the question whether the evidence should be considered *analytically* or *holistically*. The origin of the problem is in some studies developed in the area of social psychology, according to which jurors do not take into account the single items of evidence one by one, with the aim of establishing the probative weight of such items with reference to every specific factual statement. On the opposite, such studies say that jurors tend to evaluate all the evidence together, as a homogeneous whole (hence the term "holistic") and to refer this "whole" to the whole story concerning all the facts of the case. Then they orient their preference in favor of the "whole" story that seems to be supported by the "whole" set of evidence. Here the problem is not to establish whether this picture of how juries behave describes faithfully what jury actually do (if it were so, as probably is, one should reflect seriously over the pros and the cons of a jury system). Rather, the point is whether or not a "holistic" method is the best way to appreciate the epistemic probative value of the evidence at hand, or whether an "analytical" consideration of the evidence would work better as a way to establish the truth of the facts in issue.

There are several good reasons to prefer the analytical approach. One reason is that it is not clear at all what it may be to appreciate the "whole" evidence in one single shot, without establishing which information, how reliable, how relevant and how useful, is provided by each specific item of evidence. For instance, is far from clear which could be the outcome of all the testimonies presented at trial without appreciating the credibility of each witness and the reliability of his answers. The "holistic" appreciation should not distinguish between truthful and false testimonies?

Another reason is that in order to determine whether or not a story is true as a description of what happened, one would need to establish whether or not each factual statement included in the story is true or not (that is: has been or has not been proved). It seems rather obvious that if a story is (as it usually is) a narration of a chain of events, it is true if and only if all the events connected actually occurred. If one or some rings of the chain are doubtful, or simply were not proved at all, the story cannot be considered as truthful in its whole, since the persuasive force of a chain is equal to the force of its weakest ring. Deciding that the whole story is true or false without knowing whether its parts (i. e. the statements concerning single events) are true or false, seems to be nonsense, since if one or some links of a chain are lacking, the chain simply does not exist as a chain.

The main point here is that the "holistic" trier of fact may be inclined to prefer a story of the facts in issue not because it was completely proved as true in all its parts, but just because the whole story seem to be coherent, narratively good, and then "persuasive". But here the danger is that the trier of fact may take as true fact that may not have happened, and may not consider relevant fact that may have actually occurred. Once again, at this point we are reasoning as if the judicial process were something like a literary competition, not an epistemic enterprise aimed at finding out the truth of the facts in issue.

5.3. *Standards of proof*

A final topic that is worth briefly considering while talking of evidence and proof of relevant facts is that of the so-called *standards of proof*. In rough terms a standard of proof is the *degree* at which the truth of a factual statement should be confirmed by the available evidence, as a condition for considering such a statement as *proved* and then as *true* in that context.

However, and notwithstanding the fact that the notion of the standard of proof is fundamental in any theory of evidence, actually a general definition of how a standard of proof should be determined does not exist. Definitions of standards of proof are context-laden, since in any judicial context a specific standard can be established according to various criteria, with the aim of determining at which degree a statement of fact should be confirmed by the evidence in order to be "taken as true" in that context. The American procedural system provides very useful examples of this variety. The standard of the proof of culpability "beyond any reasonable doubt" is applied (whatever it means, which is far from clear) only in criminal cases. In civil cases the usual standard is that of the "preponderance of evidence" (whatever it means, which once again is far from clear), but in some special cases the reference is to a "higher" standard of the "clear and convincing evidence" (or something alike). Establishing the meanings of such different standards is a very difficult problem that cannot be solved here (mainly considering that such a problem has no satisfactory solution even in the large literature existing in common law systems). But the American example is useful to show that establishing one or more (and higher or lower) standards of proof in different judicial situations is not a philosophical or an epistemic problem. Rather, it is a *policy* problem that may be solved in various different ways by the lawgiver or by courts, depending on the degree of approximation to the truth (that is: the distance from the North) that is considered as adequate in each procedural context.

Such a "relativity" of the standards of proof does not contradict what has been said above about the epistemic function of evidence and the nature of judicial truth. Just the opposite: the epistemic function of evidence is performed because evidence provides with the cognitive basis that is needed to establish the truth of the statements about the facts in issue, but - on the other hand - such a truth is relative to the amount and the quality of the information provided by the evidence. The standard of proof is - so to say - the measure of the evidentiary confirmation that is necessary and sufficient, for a rational trier of fact, to consider a factual statement as true in its proper judicial context.

Selected bibliography

Allen, *The Nature of Juridical Proof*, in *Cardozo L. Rev.* 1991, 413.

Factual ambiguity and theory of evidence, in 88 *Northw. Un. L. Rev.* 1994, 604.

Blackburn, *Truth. A Guide*, Oxford 2005.

Celano, *La teoria del diritto di Hans Kelsen*, Bologna 1999.

Chase, *Law, Culture and Ritual. Disputing Systems in Cross-Cultural Context*, New York-London 2005.

Clermont, *Death of Paradox: The Killer Logic Beneath the Standards of Proof*, in 88 *Notre*

Dame L. Rev. 2012, 1.

D'Agostini, *Introduzioneallaverità*, Milano 2011.

(*The*) *Dynamics of Judicial Proof. Computation, Logic, and Common Sense*, M. MacCrimmon and P. Tillers eds., Heidelberg – New York 2002.

Engisch, *LogischeStudienzurGesetzesanwendung*, 2. Aufl., Heidelberg 1960.

Estándares de prueba y prueba científica. Ensayos de epistemología jurídica, Carmen Vásquez ed., Madrid – Barcelona – Buenos Aires – São Paulo 2013.

Ferrer Beltran, *La valoración racional de la prueba*, Madrid – Barcelona – Buenos Aires 2007.

Goldman, *Knowledge in a Social World*, Oxford 1999.

Haack, *Evidence and Inquiry. A Pragmatist Reconstruction of Epistemology*, 2nd ed., Amherst, NY, 2009.

Ho, *A Philosophy of Evidence Law. Justice in the Search for Truth*, Oxford 2008.

Hruschka, *Die Konstitution des Rechtsfalles*, Berlin 1965.

Kagan, *Adversarial Legalism. The American Way of Law*, Cambridge, Mass. – London 2001.

Lynch, *True to Life. Why Truth Matters*, Cambridge, Mass., 2004.

Pardo, *Pleadings, Proof, and Judgment: A Unified Theory of Civil Litigation*, in 51 *Boston College L. Rev.* 2010, 1451.

Pardo – allen, *Juridical Proof and the Best Explanation*, in27 *Law and Philosophy* 2008, 223.

Taruffo, *La provadeifattigiuridici*, Milano 1992.

Taruffo, *La sempliceverità. Ilgiudice e la costruzionedeifatti*, Bari 2009.

Taruffo, *La prueba*, Madrid – Barcelona – Buenos Aires, 2008.

Taruffo, *Evidence*, in *International Encyclopedia of Comparative Law*, vol. XVI, Hamburg 2009.

Twining, *Rethinking Evidence. Exploratory Essays*, 2nd ed., Cambridge 2006.

Williams, *Truth and Truthfulness. An Essay in Genealogy*, Princeton – Oxford 2002.

The Evaluation of Evidence from a Historical Aspect

Miklós Kengyel *

1. *The historical evolution of evaluation methods*

Statutory rules relating to evidence usually constitute a uniform logical system and express legislative intentions that vary according to era - often pointing beyond the direct purpose of evidence. Therefore, the system of evidence does not only mean the totality of statutory rules relating to evidence, but it also directly expresses the purpose of evidence and, on the other hand, it defines the scope of action provided for the judge by legislation to achieve this purpose. The extent of the judge's scope of action concerning the evidence and, in particular, the assessment of evidence depends mainly on whether the legislator endeavours to exclude arbitrary judicial power from the administration of justice or to help the truth prevail under any circumstances. While in the first case the legislator is satisfied with formal truth, in the latter case he expects the judge to reveal the objective truth. A generally accepted classifying criterion of systems of evidence is the extent of judicial discretion, based on which one may distinguish between regulated (statutory, formal) and free (material) systems of evidence. This distinction is always relative in the sense that there is no absolutely regulated or absolutely free system of evidence, since there is no regulated system of evidence that does not provide the judge with freedom in any respect, neither is there a free system of evidence that contains no regulated elements.

The historical development of systems of evidence is characterized by alternations between judicial discretion and statutory restrictions from era to era. In the historical development of the law of evidence Enrico Ferri distinguished five stages: ①the primitive stage, where the demonstration of evidence took place based on personal impressions; ②the religious period: the era of ordeals, trial by battle and different others trials; ③the statutory period, where means of evidence and their probative force are determined by statute; ④the emotional period, where the demonstration of evidence is governed by the judge's inner conviction; ⑤the scientific period, which was defined by Ferri at the turn of the 19th and 20th centuries as the future system of evidence and in which evidence is supplied by expert opinions prepared on the basis of scientific results.[1] The historical roots of the free system of evidence go back to the early stage of

---

* Professor at University of Pécs, Email: kengyel. miklos@ ajk. pte. hu.

[1] E. Ferri, *La sociologie criminelle*, Paris, 1905. pp. 515 - 516.

development of the state and law, when the parties involved in a controversy could choose their judges themselves, who could act without being restricted by any rules, based on their life experiences and conscience. The gradual increase in the power of the state and the evolution of state administration of justice led to the adoption of rules restricting judicial discretion. This course of development is well – illustrated by the history of the Roman law of court procedure as well.[2]

The German law of court procedure characterized by judicial combat, ordeal and other supernatural means of evidence was just the opposite of Roman procedural law built on rational foundations. In the judgment about evidence the judge prescribed which party was to prove what, by which means of evidence and within what time limit. By the classification of evidence and the determination of the probative force of evidence, German procedural law achieved a high level of the formal demonstration of evidence, which conformed to the social, economic and religious conceptions of the era.[3]

The law relating to evidence within the canon law of procedure, which exerted a significant influence on Western – and Central – European laws of procedure in the 14th and 15th centuries, combined the elements of Roman and German procedure in a peculiar way, but as a result of scholasticism and the teaching of the Catholic Church, it developed into an independent system of evidence. It was to no avail that canon law stressed judicial discretion, in practice the judge was bound by rules that obligatorily prescribed for him with regard to specific cases when he should be "convinced".

Under the influence of canon law, late medieval secular laws of procedure also developed a system of statutory evidence. The Constitutio Criminalis Carolina – the great code issued by Charles V in 1532 – meant the beginning of this era already. The clearest manifestations of the regulated system of evidence can be found in the codes of this era.

2. *The regulated system of evidence*

The regulated system of evidence sets statutory limits for the judge's conviction by predetermining the weight and amount of evidence in the case of which the judge is obliged to establish the existence of the alleged fact and, on the contrary, by laying down that the judge cannot establish the existence of a fact in the lack of the required evidence regardless of his possible conviction to the contrary. Therefore, the law predetermines the force of the individual types of evidence, in other words, the court only adds up the total force of the pieces of evidence having a predetermined force. The law determines a priori perfect and non – perfect, full and not full evidence, which may be divided proportionally further into half –, quarter –, eighth – etc. evidence. This system is intended to eliminate the judge's arbitrary power, but instead of this, it deprives the judge of the freedom which is indispensible for practising his profes-

[2] M. Kaser, *Das römische Zivilprozessrecht*, München, 1966. p. 84.

[3] H. Nagel, *Die Grundzüge des Beweisrechts im Europäischen Zivilprozess*, Eine rechtsvergleichende Studie, Baden – Baden, 1967. p. 154.

sion. The demonstration of evidence is not aimed at convincing the judge, but at producing means of evidence that comply with such statutory requirements based on which the judge is obliged to accept the existence of a fact in spite of his conviction, while in the case of non-compliance with such statutory requirements, he cannot establish the existence of a fact in spite of his best conviction. The statutory system of evidence means prescriptions primarily with regard to the method of proof, partly concerning the assessment of evidence and partly concerning the use of evidence.

The "record" of the mechanical evaluation of witness evidence was set by Bentham's scale. The description of the "testionometric method" can be found in his work entitled "Rationale of Judicial Evidence" published in 1817, which was highly recognized in his era. He was the first author to apply the achievements of contemporary psychology to the examination of the truth or falsity of witness statements. Since he did not find the language suitable for expressing the different shades of conviction, he constructed a scale the positive part of which expressed the levels of persuasion of the existence of the fact to be proved and the negative part of which indicated persuasion about the non-existence of the fact. He divided both parts of the scale into ten units respectively, adding that the division of the scale could be increased even to one hundred or thousand units if necessary. The zero point of the scale denotes the situation when both the affirmative and the negative, the existence or non-existence of the fact to be proved seem probable or improbable to the same extent. Accordingly, the witness expresses himself not by words, but by numbers, saying "my persuasion is at 9 affirmative". The accuracy of this method can be compared - in the opinion of its inventor - to that of a barometer or thermometer. (In spite of this, the scale was not applied in practice.) Bentham's controversial experiment exemplifies the turn away from English historical law and a search for solutions based on rational law.[4]

3. *Judicial discretion and the French revolution*

In Europe the principle of the free evaluation of evidence was first introduced by the French revolutionary legislature. In 1791 the French Legislative Assembly rejected the formal theory of evidence and provided that jurors were to make a decision solely based on their inner conviction arrived at during the oral hearing (conviction intime).

After the fall of the revolution Napoleonic legislature did not restore the formal system of evidence. Napoleon himself is alleged to have criticized the principle "unus testis nullus testis" in the following way: "So, according to this, it is not possible to convict a villain based on the testimony of one honest man, but an honest man may be convicted based on the testimony of two villains."[5] Although the French Act of 1806 on Civil Procedure did not eliminate the formalism of procedure and, in particular, of evidence, which had been inherited from the canonical procedural law, it established the conditions for the renewal of European procedural law by

---

〔4〕 Cited by L. Nagy, *Tanúbizonyítás a polgári perben*, Budapest, 1966. p. 437.

〔5〕 F. Gorphe, *L'apprécation des preuves en justice*, *Paris*, 1947. p. 35.

emphasizing the principles of oral hearing, publicity and judicial discretion.

For the free system of evidence to become spread over Europe another century was needed. As a result of the Napoleonic conquest, the French law of civil procedure invaded Italy, Spain, the Netherlands and Belgium as well as some German states. It proved to have a lasting influence, which did not cease even after Napoleon's defeat. Out of the basic principles of French civil procedure - consecrated by the revolution - it was the principles of publicity and oral hearing that aroused the interest of the European bourgeoisie the most, since they could directly be used by them during their battles against the feudal administration of justice. The demand for the publicity of proceedings and oral hearings - which was lent a taint of natural law in the first half of the 19th century - diverted attention from the urging need for a reform of the law of evidence. It was also under French influence that the principle of the free evaluation of evidence was incorporated into the Italian and Spanish codes of civil procedure of 1865 and 1881 respectively. The codification of the unified German Code of Civil Procedure of 1877 testified to the full triumph of the principles of oral hearing, publicity and judicial discretion. The ZPO explained its recommendation about the introduction of the free system of evidence by pointing out that judges must be freed from the chains of statutory rules of evidence.

4. *The free system of evidence*

In the free system of evidence the judge is not restricted by law either in the use of the means of proof or the evaluation of evidence. Therefore, on the one hand, the judge may use any means of proof (evidence) that is suitable for shaping his conviction and, on the other hand, he may evaluate the result of proof, the probative force of the evidence based on his own conviction without any statutory restrictions.

It is well-known that every free system of evidence necessarily contains some regulated elements. Thus, for example, in French law the provisions relating to the execution of the demonstration of evidence are rather formalistic. The most widely known rule is Article 1341 of the Code Civil, pursuant to which witness evidence in itself is not sufficient in the case of civil law transactions exceeding a specific amount (800 at present), instead a deed or, at least, some "substantiating documentary evidence" is required. The Code Civil and the Nouveau Code de Procédure Civile of 1975 *define* the value of some procedures/means of evidence *directly* as well: On the one hand, they contain statutory provisions relating to public documents, private documents, admissions, parties' statements and oaths; on the other hand, persons unsuitable to act as witnesses are excluded from the list of witnesses.[6] In other cases the judge *evaluates* the evidence *freely*. Although it is not possible to exclude a certain hierarchy with regard to the different types of evidence, there is no set ranking of the individual means of evidence based on their probative force. Nevertheless, if during the evaluation of evidence the judge disregards one piece of evidence or attributes greater importance to one piece of evidence over another, he is obliged to explain on what basis he has become convinced of the existence of the (given) fact.

[6] G. Rouhette, *Frankreich*, In Nagel/Bajons, Beweis-Preuve-Evidence, Baden-Baden, 1967. pp. 182-182.

The Spanish Act on Civil Procedure of 1881 did not contain any reference to the fact that evidence should be evaluated based on inner conviction. In accordance with Article 658, the judge shall evaluate the probative force of a witness statement with sound criticism (sana crítica), while he shall evaluate expert opinions in accordance with the rules of common sense. Judges had no discretion concerning the evaluation of the probative force of documents.[7] The new Spanish Act on Civil Procedure is also characterised by the principle of freedom of proof. Under the Ley de Enjuiciamiento Civil of 2000, the judge's judgment is based on his own conviction, but he is bound by the rules of logic and practical experience. The new Act does not define a general principle either, but it gives detailed guidance how to evaluate the particular means of evidence. The judge freely evaluates the statements made by the parties and witnesses as well as expert opinions, the probative force of private documents, physical evidence and other documents. As opposed to this, concerning documentary evidence it is laid down what probative force shall be attributed to commercial (business) books for example. Similarly to French law, in matters involving sums of money exceeding a certain value proof by witness evidence is excluded.[8]

Pursuant to the Italian Act on Civil procedure (Codice di procedura civile of 1940), the judge shall weigh the evidence presented by the parties in order to shape his conviction about the existence of the facts. He may base his decision only on evidence introduced by the parties, his conviction cannot be founded on sources of information that were brought to his knowledge outside the adversarial hearing (Article 115). The judge has discretion to shape his conviction freely to the extent that he evaluates the evidence freely, or in the formulation of the Act, he subjects it to "prudent appraisal" (prudente apprezzamento) (Article 116). The principle of the free evaluation of evidence is limited by the statutory rules of evidence that define the probative force of the individual means of evidence.[9]

Pursuant to § 286 (1) of the German Code of Civil Procedure (Zivilprozessordnung) - which had a great influence on Central - European legal development - the court is to decide, at its discretion and conviction, and taking account of the entire content of the hearings and the results obtained by evidence being taken, if any, whether an allegation as to fact is to be deemed true or untrue. The judgment is to set out the reasons informing the conviction of the judges. The judge is not bound by statutory rules of evidence; therefore, he can freely evaluate the probative force of the individual pieces of evidence, including the presentations of the parties, witness statements and expert opinions. The Act makes exceptions only in some cases, when it regulates the probative force of the records of oral hearings (ZPO § 165), documents (§ 195) and the facts of the case as established by the judgment (ZPO § 314).[10]

An essentially similar provision is contained in the Austrian Code of Civil Procedure of

---

[7] L. Prieto - Castro y Ferrándiz, *Derecho Procesal Civil*, Pamplona, 1985. p. 466.

[8] F. Ramos Méndez, *Derecho Procesal Civil*, Madrid, 1989. p. 599.

[9] S. Patti, Italien in In Nagel/Bajons, *Beweis - Preuve - Evidence*, Baden - Baden, 1967. p. 269.

[10] L. Rosenberg/ K. H. Schwab/ P. Gottwald: *Zivilprozessrecht*. 17. Aufl. 2010. pp. 631 - 632.

1895 as well. Pursuant to § 272 (1), unless the Act provides otherwise, the court has discretion to decide, based on its own conviction and carefully taking into account the results of all the hearings and the taking of evidence, whether it will accept the existence of a fact or not. Discretion with regard to the evaluation of evidence means that the judge shall act to the best of his knowledge and in accordance with his conscience, his practical experience and knowledge of human character. The judge's objectivity is mainly ensured by the requirement that in the reasons given for his decision he is to specify the circumstances and aspects he regarded as determinant in shaping his conviction [öZPO § 272 (3)].[11]

In the beginning, the possibility of the free evaluation of evidence was hindered by the rigid application of the principle of adversarial hearing, since only the parties could supply the court with the evidence required for deciding the legal dispute. However, the rigidity of the adversarial principle became gradually dissolved by judicial practice and legal development. The conspicuous enhancement of the judge's position increased the demand for the revelation of the true facts of the case as corresponding to reality. Proceedings became centred on this aim. Parallel to this, there was a growing interest in procedural science as well toward the basic problems of evidence, including questions relating to the limitation and impossibility of limitation of judicial discretion.

Socialist civil procedural laws accepted the principle of the free assessment of evidence as the method of evaluation of evidence. Judicial discretion was retained even during the *great changes* that took place after 1990. As an example, one may refer to the Yugoslavian Code of Civil Procedure of 1976, which has been retained by the majority of the successor states without any significant change. Pursuant to Article 8 of *Zakon o parničnom postupku*, the question as to when a fact should be regarded as proven must be decided by the court in accordance with its own conviction, on the basis of the individual pieces and the totality of evidence as well as the result of the hearings. According to the dominant position, the free evaluation of evidence emphasizes the responsibility of the trial judge and conditions the decision on the experience and the human and moral qualities of the person entrusted to administer law. Free evaluation does not mean arbitrary judicial power, the judge is bound by past experience and the rules and regularities of rational thinking and he is to provide reasons for his establishment of facts.[12]

The Hungarian Code of Civil Procedure (HCCP), which was renewed after 1990, also adopted the provisions of the Act of 1952 relating to the freedom of proof and the free evaluation of evidence. Unless otherwise provided for by law, in civil proceedings the court shall not be bound by formal requirements relating to the taking of evidence, or to specific procedures for the performance of taking of evidence or to the use of specific means of proof, and may freely

---

[11] W. H. Rechberger/ A - D. Simotta, *Zivilprozessrecht. Erkenntnisverfahren.* 7. Aufl. Wien, 2009. pp. 389 - 390.

[12] Triva/Belajec/Dika, *Gradjansko parnicno procesno pravo.* Zagreb, 1986. § 28 Nr. 5.; *A. Uzelac*: Kroatien in In Nagel/Bajons, Beweis - Preuve - Evidence, Baden - Baden, 1967. p. 341.

use the arguments of the parties, as well as any other evidence deemed admissible for ascertaining the relevant facts of the case [HCCP, § 3 (5)]. This general principle is supplemented by § 206 of the HCCP relating to the assessment of evidence. Pursuant to this, the court shall ascertain the relevant facts of a case upon weighing the arguments of the parties against the evidence obtained by the performance of taking of evidence. The court shall evaluate the evidence as a whole, and shall rule relying on its conviction. Just like every free system of evidence, the Hungarian HCCP also contains some *regulated elements* as a matter of course.[13]

The possibility of the free evaluation of evidence does not mean the absolute lack of restrictions for the judge. The regulated elements that are the necessary concomitants of the free system of evidence can be classified in two groups depending on whether they are connected with the use of means of proof (evidence) or the assessment of evidence. The restrictions belonging in the first group constitute general or specific instructions addressed to the judge relating to what means of proof may be used by him in the specific case and what means of proof must be disregarded by him.

The second group consists of regulations laying down the probative force of the individual means of evidence and, therefore, directly restricting judicial discretion. They include, for example, provisions relating to proof by documentary evidence, statutory presumptions or the effect of a criminal judgment. Mention should also be made here of the judge's obligation to state the reasons for his judgment, which constitutes an indirect restriction of judicial discretion.

[13] M. Kengyel, *Magyar polgári eljárásjog*. 11. ed. Budapest, 2012, pp. 328 – 330.

Evidence Law and Judicial Civilization

Omar Sumaria Benavente *

"Each age has a predilection for a mode of proof." The Christian Middle Ages had a preference for the ordeal and the oath. The Ancien Régime developed the document and the confession involving torture. Our age has a predilection for the expert evidence. "Certainly the confession, testimony, the document or the oath continue to be used, but the means of proof wich attracts, responds to our expectations, and arouses discussion is expert evidence" [1]

INTRODUCTION:

Although the term "judicial culture" is not well defined and is somewhat vague and indeterminate plays an important role in the appreciation of the different procedural systems (Taruffo, over the borders, Writings on civil justice, 2006). Thus, in principle can be understood "judicial culture" as the relationship between each village with the rule of law and the position of the right front of the real and the individuals who form the people (Garapon & Papadopoulos, 2006). "Judicial culture" can also be understood in three aspects or dimensions. In a first appearance as the sum of different sets of knowledge and approaches, constituted by the sum of theories, philosophies and legal doctrines elaborated by jurists and philosophers of law in a certain historical stage; in a second appearance, legal culture integrates the set of ideologies, models of Justice and ways of thinking about the right to own the professional legal professionals, judges, legislators or administrators; and in a third aspect you understand common sense concerning the right and each legal institution operational and widespread in a given society (Ferrajoli, legal culture and constitutional paradigm. The Italian experience of the 20th century, 2010). "Legal culture" also can be defined as the set of presentation techniques and interpretative techniques that deal right, both practical and theoretical, and the set of ideologies concerning the function of the law that such technical thought (Tarello, 2002).

As a result, there are different meanings of the term "judicial culture", but to overview it can be understood as the set of doctrines and conceptual systems developed by the lawyers, or the set of models of reasoning used by the jurists in the jurisprudence both doctrinal function, or the set of interpretations and practices provided by legal operators related to the daily application of the normative textsmaking accuracy which not only refers to law as the expression leg-

* Professor at Inca Garcilaso de la Vega University.

islators but to the foundational regulatory text which seems to begin around him, a sort of large text that condenses all ancient legal wisdom and time and which is intended to provide clarity, conciseness, consistency and authority, permanence, universality and which is incarnated the ideal of Justice called code of HammurabiTen Commandments, law of the XII tables, code of Justinian, code of Napoleon, Universal Declaration of the rights of man, etc. (Talavera, 2006)

In this way the concept "judicial culture" is generated at various levels that communicate, interact and feed each other in a certain context where "judicial culture" is, at least, in part and for a limited historical period and a specified scenario.

In this sense, the law is framed as a social phenomenon and its analysis or study not be limited only to its structural or technical order, which is the reflection of a theory or the material expression of a given context, but, that warns a triple level of analysis. A third level is the goal legal aspect or know theoretical, which is reviewed and is critical if adopted theory and is consistent with other systems side of society and the State, and other States both the political, economic, social and cultural. A second level of analysis is the systematic aspect, or know systematic internal, which is the policy analysis, based on the qualities of belonging and consistency that determines the validity of the forms. And, a first level of analysis that correspond to the pragmatic or practical, order because of that law as abstraction that is born before the alteration of reality and tries to rebuild it or correct it, creating their own space, in which judges, lawyers, litigants involved.

I. e. , the construction of judicial culture occurs in the relationship of these three levels of analysis that communicate with each other, in reciprocal and sometimes contrary, flows that are not isolated, but interdependent and often with frictions and contradictions, then in a sistematizador effort, but understanding the mutual influence of these areas or areas to the other. You must descend the paradise of the concepts to the purgatory of the rules and then to hell of procedural acts. "But the journey from paradise to hell is of back and forth and with a forced passage through purgatory." (Gómez Lara, 2006, p. 132)

This concept of "judicial culture" is built through different organizational logics that are produced in the tension and adequacy of basic social relational dichotomies between the "autonomy and integration, or accession", in a micro dimension, i. e. in relations individual - community, the "separation and accommodation" for politico - civil and religious - cultural relations in a dimension macro (Sánchez - Bayonm, anual of American legal sociology. The power, the sacred and the freedom in Western modernity, 2009) which determine a model or organizational logic.

The organizational logic is in turn the result of Assembly capabilities, i. e. the collective productions of the company and whose development requires, and construction, competition and conflict and whose utilities are of different value because they depend on the relational systems in which they operate. It is this aspect, the capacities are understood as attributes of the individual and the community, values, beliefs, etc. , that determine the social, political, economic and legal structures and will evolve as society develops. (Sassen, 2010)

1. *Judicial process, conflict resolution and "judicial culture" institutionalized mechanisms*

In this respect the judicial process or any institutionalized mechanism for resolving disputes is a catalyst for the tension of these basic relational dichotomies either accelerating or stabilising relations between the individual and the community and between the competence of the powers that be, connecting the practices and uses, as the right values for given historical social context as it is justice, i. e. institutionalized dispute settlement mechanism becomes a factor for Assembly of the capabilities in the production of the organizational logic.

The product of this transformation and Assembly of the relation "State - jurisdiction" proposes a matrix through the identification of capabilities, turning points and organisational logics and is inferred from them the construction of the institutionalized model of conflict resolution. Variables or this Assembly capabilities make it the concepts of legitimacy of the authority and the exercise of legitimate not only power but also cash which are decisive (Bobbio, 2006), the social structure, the economic mode of production and the political model, developed in different tipping points such as old age, modern age, contemporary age and new information age that develops from a logical organizational centripetal based on dominant norms of the State to become in a centrifugal organizational logic based on a multiform and partial regulations.

Then, the key to understanding the functioning of the institutionalized system of conflict resolution in a given context depends on harmonious play of their basic relational dichotomies, among them the trajectory and Assembly of the relationship "Status - jurisdiction", which are not simple attributes but complex, autonomous institutions that are constituted by specific processes and emerge from the struggles and conflicting interests. They are interdependent and at the same time specific, conditioned by the level of formalisation and institutionalisation, assembled in concrete structures at different places and times, varying, therefore the model of judicial process or mechanism of institutionalized dispute settlement through which this relationship 'State - jurisdiction' is built, inserted and materialized.

I. e., verifying the "cultural context" given stage of evolution of mankind can be seen different forms of mechanisms of institutionalized or formal dispute originating in the logic of the trajectory of the relationship State, jurisdiction, making present the passage of a stadium of evolution towards another not always presented so segmented and continued, but rather means progress and setbacks with unique, different paths in intensity and dynamics in different regions in which this development occurs.

It should be noted that the Assembly of this relationship society – State – jurisdiction can be analyzed through different organizational logics that is performed, however, these different organizational logics are conceptual separations rather than historical, because it may be that in a same time and territory different organisational logics are developed simultaneously.

Assembly of organisational logics have resulted in institutionalized method of conflict resolution. However, the "logical genesis" of building a system, in this case of the judicial process or institutionalized mechanism of conflict resolution, is not a reconstruction of the historical "genesis". "Logical genesis" is the reconstruction of the concept of the idea of articulating reality that enters this reality, while it is in contact with the "historical genesis", should not be confused, because they have different structure and they obey different theoretical interests (Habermas, 2010), the historical periods are not univocal but multifaceted (Sassen, 2010), therefore the use of certain specific historical junctures mentioned do not points to chronology nor historical evolutions, essential and constitutive elements are, but this analysis translates into a conceptual and theoretical preparation for the understanding of the judicial process or institutionalized mechanism of conflict resolution in a given organizational logic.

Put another way, the process jurisdictional or institutionalized mechanisms of conflict resolution are presented as mechanisms calibrators or modulating the tension of these relational dichotomies Basic, serving as a communicative code essential for the understanding of the individuals of the community or the community of communities. Becoming in this way the judicial process and the institutionalized mechanisms of conflict resolution in a space of encounter between the social and legal, in a social field where relations and performances continuously updated according to the specific contexts of significance of each society. (López Ayllon)

In this perspective, making a relationship between socio – economic organization in pre – industrial societies and formal dispute settlement mechanisms, are determining verification of different variables that indicate whether we have a system of formal conflict resolution with regard to the degree of complexity of this society, in consequence, to greater social complexity arise as many variables which establishes the formality and institutionalizing social referral system of resolution of conflicts. The variables to be determined are: (a) the use of a neutral third party that resolves; (b) the requirement of social call that third neutral; (c) the authority of the decision of the third; (d) the centralization of decision that resolves the conflict; (e) the existence of various judicial instances (NEWMAN, 1983). It is so the process or institutionalized method of conflict resolution responds to certain logic and rationality according to the organisational logic, wherein, test a role always rational in relation to specific mechanism for resolving disputes in such a context, being always the test subject one of the axes of the judicial process which becomes the space between the social and legal, a public space in which there is a contradictory debate on a socially significant fact (López Ayllon), and therefore are the product of the culture and society are in (2011 Chase).

In this respect, the test, as rational support of the judicial process or the institutionalized mechanism of conflict resolution in a given organizational logic has played diverse and various formal functions in relation to the conceptual stages – historical society, but always the same function of content determine the truth. In modern dispute resolution procedures as well as in a modern process and test pre society play a similar role, provide a source and a link to the cultural knowledge valid, ensuring to litigants and society in general, neutrality, consistency and the legitimacy of the result. In this sense, an Oracle or the judge incorporated into its activity predominant hierarchical conventions based on beliefs that holds the group, turning in a case the logic of magic as an explanation of the phenomena of the world and on the other by applying the law and valuing the test (2011 Chase), but in both situations, a double "magic" making relive what opera is not living. It is spent and done to revive the consciousness of the judgement of someone who was totally absent and strange to him, to the experience that you want to relive. (Spinelli, 1975) It is pointed out, that while the process plays a role in ritualistic for acceptance or social acceptability of the decision, it also plays a role of content and quality of decisions based on the correct determination of the facts. (Taruffo & Cavallone, Verifobia. A dialogue on truth and proof, 2012)

Thus, for example, in the world modern in its own organizational logic characterised by the uncertainty of the right scientific testing becomes a staple for the current procedural models either for a process as a result of implementation of policy or a process of conflict resolution (Damaska, 1986), which are aimed on the one hand the confrontation of two versions ago publicly succeed the most plausible story, and on the other hand, the search of the substance of the truth to establish an official story, but both cases end the mode of production of the truth, meanwhile, activity is performed in the articulation of the fact and the law "on the borders of a legal order when an abstract rule must grasp life, put it in form and meaning". (Garapon & Papadopulos, 2006, p. 114)

2. *Evidence law, process and organizational logic*

The evaluation of the test in the *Civil Law* aims to establish the final connection between the presented evidence and truth and falsehood of the statements on the facts at issue, pretending to establish through the judge if the available evidence to support any conclusion about the statements and to what degree (Taruffo, proof, 2008). So considering that the purpose of the test is the search for truth, without distinguishing it, or relativize, been explained traditionally three well – known rating systems:

(1) The legal test or assessed test system by which the legislator gives a value specific to each test regardless of the conviction of the judge.

(2) System of free conviction or the intimate conviction, that as opposed to the previous assessment of the test depends on the degree of conviction that the judge granted her.

(3) System healthy criticism or appreciation, which test the judge to arrive at the conviction that causes should apply the rules of the "healthy criticism".

However, this traditional "so – called systems of assessment evidence" classification tends to indicate a level of development in terms of mechanisms for this purpose, which apparently evolutionary from the irrational to the rational, from the informal to the formal (Weber, 2000) decontextualizing and analyzing the valuation system, only in relation to the search for truth, and not in relation to its functionality in the process.

This line proposes a different classification in relation to the function of the test in the process on the basis of a religious character towards the construction of a substantive right to be tested as part of a fundamental right of access to the jurisdiction or jurisdictional tutelage, constitutionally recognized in the majority of countries of the *Civil Law*, and the test in this way becoming a rational basis for the jurisdictional decision. This classification contextualized historical thread of the question points to a cycle upward, helical, recognizing marches and setbacks, advances and setbacks (Alvaro de Oliveira, 2007), which would go in phases or stages according to the time, in relation to the functioning of the test in the process.

2. 1 *The logic of the justification of the rule*: "*Process*" *and* "*Community*"

In the first stage, which coincides with the ancient age, the concept of legitimacy of authority was supported by the concept of "force" that justified the domination. The economic mode of production was based on slavery which in turn would determine the social status, as a result, freedom was the constituent element of the policy in the city (Schiavone, 2009, p. 90). Political organization was based on the concept of "community," the city, "*civitas*", "*community of citizens*", which was composed of all subjects who enjoyed the special status "freedom" which is the fundamental separation between the two categories of human beings which constitute the ancient society. "*Citizens*", "*free*" *men can or will not participate in the Government of the city. This is less* "*free*". (Grimal, 1998, p. 12)

The perception of wealth now mark a difference among members of the group who are superior to the rest generating individualism, the division of labor for its ability and differs according to their occupation or profession, and thus people who have greater scope to develop more functional and vital activities and thus take more of the wealth of the group. In this context the war takes another dimension, for the purposes of this were the taking of prisoners to convert them into slaves and get work of cheap hand (Núñez, political power, Constitution and State, 2009).

In political terms, it is the exercise of anonymous power on the basis of a unilinear structure, residence and the social structure which is initially in the clan[2]. This social unit is the political base and unit auto sustainable, depositary of the ownership of the land and with the faculty of warfare, where highlights the absence of a custom holder of political power, taking decisions within the group individually or by group but according to temporal and spatial circumstances horizontally.

This same impulse invaded and disciplining relations of equal reciprocity between the heads of the family[3]; and the land of the *ius*, would have been a field that the Roman mentality would have never identified fully with the powers of the King, to book into action somehow sovereign of the *patres*, dependent on direct only links religious do not coincide with the area of royalty. "It's originally – the generative nucleus – germ of the autonomous disciplining of aprivate plot[4] of community life where family and heritage budgets of citizenship, irreducibly different political order were made". (Schiavone, 2009, pp. 72 – 3)

In sequel aspect legal develops the idea of Justice under the conception primary revenge where he responds aggression for aggression, and then at a more advanced stage will decide to move that justice to an authority responsible for applying it, thinking more in the interest of the group rather than in the interest of the individual, to which is added then repair economic damage caused by anti – social behaviour you were looking for the transaction between the offender and the victim. In this way the form of dispute settlement was through the private revenge, which in one way or another was later regulated and subsequently absorbed by the economy of the test system. In this sense "*the formalism of the procedures based on the ordeals gradually yields the place to increasingly less formalist techniques, but also more flexible and effective discovery of truth of the facts*". (Taruffo, simply the truth, 2010, p. 24)

From this results the community became the public space which is airing the conflict where the settlement of the conflict in a "process" does not validate the result but the performance before the community. (Schiavone, 2009, p. 85)

Vertical relations between gods and men, were drawn up on the basis of the same culture, they reflected the same behaviors, where, the ritualistic propensity and verbal caution dominated both glided from one field to another. Thus, the contractual relations with the divine ceremonial, rites, concerning sacrifices or not, as guarantee of his wrath insured got formulaic symmetries in relationships and networks of reciprocity for gestural and verbal behaviors aimed to achieve the same goal. Then, with supernatural harmony and conviviality were essential values in a community where the balances were always precarious "*in the background, the same pattern was repeated: there was no peace, nor theological, not social, but in the fulfilment of the ritual. Outside always stalked the imminent shadow of devastating violence*". (Schiavone, 2009, p. 89)

Just around the need to exorcise the violence and instability, probably the first mental horizon of the city ever built. For example, in the XII tables emerges a world suspended between religiosity, magic and early secular prescription which is reflected in their procedures. His goal was the replace the physical confrontation between the contenders for its ritual staging, and so peaceful and symbolic.

In the "process" the opposing claims were subjected to formulas rigidly established, put into scene before the watchful eye of the magistrate, officiating the ceremony, where parties are trusted to a sort of commitment that would have determined the loser to give the community an important remedy. Once this rite have been met, the controversy would not exist rather than in terms of its symbolic Transfiguration: the contenders, with the whole of the own reasons and of own force, social and physical, had become the actors of a ritual, where played symmetrically opposing roles. The possibility of violence had been in this remote way and maintained outside the community once more (Schiavone, 2009, p. 126).

The result of the intervention of the magic or the Divinity in the solution of Bates and the creation of new standards is strictly formal character of any primitive legal procedure, these media only serve to resolve properly the question correctly submitted.

In this way, the process arises as the most ancient "legal business" since it is based on a contract (litis contestatio, contract of Atonement, etc.), hence the same principle is applicable to private legal businesses whose celebration, strict Roman law, both at the dawn of the middle ages, required solemn forms and each alteration, although small, the magic formula of efficiency originates the invalidity of the Act.

Originally it offered no evidence to prove the truth or falsity of a fact, it is initially to investigate which parts and how can or have to raise issues affecting "legally" them with magical powers. (Weber, 2000, p. 519) The formal character of the process coexists with the quite irrational decision means. However, it may be inadequate distinction between rational and "non – rational" test because the belief in an intervention divine or supernatural can be so consistent or rational as legitimate and reasonable is claiming otherwise. Perhaps, more appropriate would be to speak of a para – racionalidad. As a result, the test you can be irrational substantially (an Oracle) but formally rational (the rational development of test medium), but the Romanists have used the qualifier of irrational without considering if it is the more accurate term to describe a reality that responds to a different mentality in the supernatural interpretation of natural facts and the way to respond to them. (Piquer Mari, 2010)

Thus, the truth of the fact doesn't matter so much, but strengthening the right claimed. Then it can be said that Roman evidentiary law was delayed by the abstract material law (Wilhem Hedemann, 1931). But rigid adherence to form hand responds to a mechanism to appease the passions in the claims, which would be done through the formula, however, more important would be the function to act as a control to avoid the "natural justice" and submit the individual case to the common judgment. As a result, though it may be paradoxical one might speak of a "free rating system", which would be inaccurate, insofar as the test, did not mean the truth of the facts, but to establish the correspondence between the formula and the right.

The evolution of the "legis actiones" to the "extraordinary cognitio", going through the process "form" shows a progressive increase of the State authority that would determine the reduction of the influence of the formula in the process, as that grows and intensifies the power and the discretion of the judge, also decreases the formalism, correlate element's containment of this power.

At this stage with regard to the assumption and valuation of the test the "iudex" enjoyed wider freedom of conscience and nothing linked their personal belief, however, the burden of proof was a exclusive parties. Register the fullness of orality, due to the intimate and deep test function. However, this freedom of belief does not come from a mature procedural awareness, the phenomenon only reflects the lack of interest of the State and of the law in relation to the judgment in fact, basically because the "*iudex*" was not a State body but a simple citizen, acting more as an instrument of the parties as to subject of the process.

The situation begins to change in the classic post process of the "cognitio", overriding gradually freedom of appreciation, giving rise to a normed assessment procedure. The oath plays a more important role, creates the general duty of witnessing, introduces rules on the number of witnesses required and the probative value of the documents are privileged. (Alvaro de Oliveira, 2007, pp. 56 – 7)

This development was origin confrontation or conflict of two institutional assumptions and power. The first model in question had its Center in the restoration of an uncompromising Primate by old gentilicios groups. The second project would have contrasted the patricia preeminence, and projecting more force on the political scene to the plebeian masses.

Then the city was found facing two different regulatory organization and social regulation hypotheses. One founded in the paradigm, specifically Roman *ius*; as a product of a civil knowing deeply integrated in the body of the *civitas* that is organized according to specific criteria or expression "*Juris prudentia*"; and the other on the other hand, in the Greek and Mediterranean *lex* (Schiavone, 2009, pp. 107 – 9) linked to its original meaning, showing an act of political power Empire citizen, a power that was in a plane other than the religious disciplining, destined to act at a different level of community life, only human or citizen equipped with the strength of a coercive penalty. A loaded term of ideology which indicated a paradigm of sovereignty forming an inseparable triad – law, writing, secularism – able to oppose the certainty of the knowable and the stability at the mercy of a religious or customary, manipulable rule to your liking by those who held power, "*the excarnacion of the obligation through its graphical representation, presupposed in fact, the breakdown of the figure of the priest King, guarantor and mystical founder, through his person, of every social rule*". (SCHIAVONE, 2009, p. 111)

I am divided as well to the tasks of the *ius* and *lex*, as civil disciplinary and rule policy, a job that is transferred to the process or procedure that was on the one hand based on the rule and on the other hand allowed elasticity to find the formulation that would qualify the claims opposite in terms that currently an *juris dictio* exercise most suitable to the reality of the needs.

2. 2. *The logic of the justification of coercion: "Process" and "State"*

The second turning point, corresponds to the second stage of the evolution of humanity, which coincides with the middle ages. The concept of legitimation of authority varies from the "force" to "God" for this way justify coercion, punishment of sin, or disobedience to authority that obtains the power of divinity as a particular good, "*which since its origins, difference to Christian penance in confession and purification processes extended the primitive religions, although of course of them persist traces even in our days, it is the legal importance of the penitential process*". (Prodi, 2008, p. 34)

Arises the phenomenon of the formation of States as a result of the separation of the political authority of the community, which will concentrate power, and therefore replaced revenge private by the transfer of the decision on authority for the specific case based on equity, i. e., through jurisprudence. Coover warns it is this aspect that the "*State becomes central in the process not why this well prepared for the creation of the right, nor because the why cultural grant meant to standard setting processes cease in the presence of the State. The State acquired a central place only because it is an act of commitment that is the central aspect of the legal meaning. And the violence represents a measure and a test extremely commitment*". (Coover, 2000, p. 25)

Politically, the feudalism arises from the disbandment of the Roman Empire and the fragmentation of power in the hands of various individuals, who exercised it in small Territories, filling the power vacuum left by the old state of Rome. Relations who lived in slavery were replaced by easements between the Lord and his servants through the "feudal bargain" giving rise to a new social organization structure. The law on land was decisive to define social status and political power.

On the other hand, the Catholic Church was developed gaining a preponderance of political and territorial, as a unified and disciplined organization with its own economic and cultural resources, as well as a huge influence on the beliefs and behaviors of all persons. Well aware of the existence of two parallel powers, one earthly and the other religious, in relationships of competition, conflict or cooperation according to the short – term political needs. This online justice took a more private character due to the existence of dispersed through various ccTLD powers. This situation gave rise to the theory of the two swords. On one side the ecclesiastical theory defending the predominant power of the Church over the State, based on its universal character and Christian and their predominance in the world, as part of the designs of God which was its Organizer why should having a right and consistent with this Government, and on the other side were those who advocated the superiority of the power of the State on the other powers within the spiritual head of the Church. In other cases arose as a collaboration between both powers, giving the State management of earthly interests and the Church it would handle matters relating to the spiritual. But ultimately the problem ended on who would be appointed the monarch or Supreme ruler in each case. (Núñez, political power, Constitution and State, 2009)

The medieval universe is characterized by expressing an incomplete political power, meaning that not only the lack of effectiveness, but also by the absence of a tote, all – inclusive project. In other words, the political power is not intended to control all areas of society. It is characterized by a substantial disregard for areas of society – wide and even sweeping – that do not interfere directly with the Government of the public thing (Grossi, 2003), where autonomous society translates into thousands of combinations from the political to the economic of the estates to professional, religious family, proposing different corporate figures, tied to a collective psychology appealed by insecurity general and designated by the humility of its individuals-developing through two main characters on the one hand the nature and on the other hand the community as niche essential for the development of the individual as an abstraction within the network of relations offered.

The right arises as historical reality that is born in the society, not being tied to the political power. It is sufficient "plastic" community organization which was born and towards which goes in deep and lasting levels of this, fusing, as the legal dimension that can not be intended as a world of pure forms or simple mandates separated a social reality and therefore rooted in this.

To not emanate from individual political authority, the right has an ontic reality, belongs to an objective order, the nature of things, where you can and you should discover, and therefore is conceived as interpretation, in the work of a community of lawyers, which on the basis of authorized texts, reading the signs of the times, from a subjective dimension to an objective dimension.

Function sort, such as limit to freedom, is identified with the reason as cognitive activity prevalent on the volitional activity which materializes in the *lex*, but is not only form and mandate, but a substantial content and reading of reality with a truth contained in which is inserted the order planned and acted by the divinity. (Grossi 2003)

The Middle Ages was a period of complex interactions that are marked by the multiplicity of forms of territorial attachment, the absence of an exclusive territorial authority, the existence of various overlapping jurisdictions in view that territorial attachment to become exclusive authority and enforcement of rights to certain kinds of people rather than territorially exclusive units. Feudalism is characterized as a system marked by the multiplicity of units, the economy in kind and the emergence of personal ties.

In this same land socio – economic marked by the end of the middle ages feudalism is the separation between the *civil law* and the *common law*. Van Caenegem indicates that "*until the 12th century English law and continental were notably to a single legal, Germanic feudal family, both the substantive and the procedural*". (Van Caenegem, 2011, p. 124) Roman law and Roman canonically procedure transformed the continent, while in England emerged a native and law common to the entire Kingdom, creating a common feudal right in these courts so that the need for Roman neo Model felt. In this sense, while the continent was an urban revolution for the modernization of law in England a rural revolution for this same purpose, gave it that the dessert was giving the fundamental characteristics between these two systems.

The law of the *common law* is based on the idea of the "relationship" and the legal consequences that they depend on, warranties, duties, incidents having as original model the feudal institution of the right of the *Land Lord and Tenant* (Lord of the Earth and holder of the same). While on the right of the *civil law* it relies on legal business as agreement of wills as an act voluntarily directed to produce results which the law recognizes as the effect desired by the parties, it plays a corner stone, as an institution created in a *civitas* of families patriarchal with a system of rules designed to safeguard peace between their chiefs (Pound).

I. e. the "relation" and "will" are opposing axes in which is based the development of both systems, but this was possible only because the strategy of modernization of law in two socio economic aspects are different, one that had the rural agricultural sector such as polo and the other which attaches the urban development, in which bourgeois sector is aligned with the Roman law in its function of interest as has elaborate theories about private property and the media to ensure contractual compliance.

In brief, the medieval legal order is a combination of Canon law, the law "vulgar romano" and the usual, with elements of customary law, phenomena that are the formalization of the nobility and with the passage of time in a variety of orders legal individuals, with variable results of this combination especially in areas that received distinct influence of Rome and which were more affected by the Germanic invasions that it is due to the different economic political cultures that develop from the rise of the cities as organizations territorial but conceived as a system of dispersed territorialities, inserted in a field larger and more diffuse with jurisdictions overlapping, ranking cities as a central space of a local economy, as a network of translocal of cities and capital circulation, and in other cases such as formations, potentially subject to a State power of territorial character, being this last dimension that would set the course for the nation State. (Sassen, 2010, p. 87)

In this first stage the phenomenon to perceive is the relationship Estado – jurisdiccion – process which is reflected during the middle ages determines a unique form of mechanisms for resolving disputes in which prevails the decision on how, through a process of type "*isonomico*", so called because it is built on the basis of the principle of the contradictory and the equality of parties before the political phenomenon of the absence of unity of jurisdiction product of social relations and in that time. The key to the medieval procedure solved in a regulation of the dialogue claiming reciprocity and equality to the parties, whereas as a methodology to reach the truth, representing the instrument for the dialectical pursuit of a "likely truth", which conforms to the topical way between the reciprocal discrepancy by parties.

The "contradictory" constituted the important structure in relation to the subject of proof, because no proof can be put as a foundation for the trial if it has not been previously subjected to critical scrutiny of the parties. It guaranteed equality between rulers and rule, between the judge and the parties and between the same parties. The judge was professional and non – bureaucratic, and assumed a neutral position, as the choice, at the contradictory of the parties, between two argumentative hypothesis.

This is why the "*ordo iudiciaris*" was based on the "*dialectic*" in opposition to the "*apodictic*", there's nothing scientific or rigorous because in the field of the law we are faced with a reality in motion things that may change with human choice, develops a common language, stops at the origin and etymology of the wordanalyzes proposed definitions that are confronted with "*common opinions*" and choose definitions that are resistant to the "*fire of the discrepancy*" in the light of the dialectic.

Useful practical problems are analyzed to guide the conduct of the judge and the parties in the process. It is a collection of points of view, in the form of doctrinal and jurisprudential quotes. But the case is not oriented to make obvious or to clarify principles or pre – established rules, in the reasoning part of the "*sensus communis*" the precedent is used as an example used the argumentative procedures "topical" tradition, and from this angle the litigators of the time interest was oriented to the evidentiary procedure and the study of the pathology of argumentation to discover the error and abuse. (Picardi, 2009, p. 296) In this sense, M. Cappelletti designates which "*priori ideology and formalistica, the scholastic abstracismo of the time, were in short in the medieval process the most impressive and most faithful mirror*". (Cappelletti, *Process*, *Ideology and Society*, 1974, p. 6)

2. 3 *The logic of the justification of the law*: "*Process*" *and* "*Law*"

In the third stage, the concept of emerging territorial State is strengthened in a context where national unity is still far from being achieved and their own authority is weak that eventually they merged under the control of a sovereign national units or in process of being governed by a sovereign with absolute authority. The abstract forms of authority are distinguished from the concrete forms of material power.

The concept of sovereignty is essential to the existence of the national State. The specific political economy of urban territory which establishes the possibility of a unitary system with a citizenry that demands and makes civil liberties at the same time developing forms of secular governments. We can say that the history of the formation of the State is the history of the French monarchy from the 12th to the 17th which deals with the strengthening of the Prince and his increasingly more accurate perception of the importance of the right in the State project, and in consequence of the increasingly felt need to manifest themselves as legislator. (Grossi, 2003, p. 33)

Then, the old pluralism was replaced by a rigid monism, the link between law and society, between rights and emerging social economic facts, is cut off, while operating a sort of centralization and channeling obliged, giving the politicization and formalization of the legal dimension. Thus, the right is transformed into a system of authoritarian rules, mandates designed and abstract and inelastic, incriticable in its content, since his authority comes not from its own quality but attribute of the legislator idea which is reinforced between the enforced coincidence between the legislative will and the general will (Grossi, 2003, p. 34), therefore the reduction of the role of the judge to mere "application of the law" and the legal process as a formal tool for this objective.

The development of the territorial authority is essential to explain how influenced the construction of the State - nation and national capitalism worldwide originated from the 16th century. The State bureaucracy arises for the obtaining of income, above all by the ability to impose increasingly standardized assessments, and contributed to the State became the main economic actor during that period and to act as the main organizer of the economic operations worldwide.

The strengthening of the State occurred even in cases in which national unity had failed, as well the development of State capabilities and global scale emerges as a key element for the consolidation of the territorial unit. (Sassen, 2010, p. 42)

The secular character of the urban right located urban governments out of the ecclesiastical hierarchy and allowed that each city developed its own variant of urban law. With the latter being just a Variant among various non - religious legal orders (the royalist, the feudal, the noble, the commercial), so none could be attributed the exclusivity over the cities, which in turn strengthened the alternative of secularizing the urban government. (Sassen, 2010, p. 100)

The political economy of urban territory stands out for the urban settlements of the middle ages did not constitute separate legal and political units, and the productivity gained generated rapid growth of agricultural surplus, creating an offer for an urban population whose livelihood was no longer in the field, producing the incentive for political and economic innovations. It would determine the growth of cities in quantity and economic importance, constituting the city a set of social structures that promote the social uniqueness and innovation, creating the conditions that push merchants, artisans, leaders and the city's inhabitants to innovate in the political sphere.

The new kind of authority that is set in this period, with specific and formalized historical character, embodies the territorial jurisdiction and the exclusive authority over the territory. The limits of sovereignty become geographic that supposes the existence of a mutual agreement for the recognition of a spatial demarcation of the political authority, emerging the legal equivalence principle (Sassen, 2010, p. 121) with the development of a "legitimate" system of laws and norms that concentrating the productive capital.

Urban law thus enables the growth and change, and the romano – canonico law was useful for developing new ideas and legal principles that meet these needs in a systematic way. The burghers were placed on side of the rulers who protect the right to private property and eliminate the coming judicial duel of Germanic law.

The villages and the boroughs propelled a judicial system focused on principles, in the presentation of evidence and the functioning of courts, more than in the arbitrary exercise of power by part of the Kings and feudal lords. Resulting favourable to their interests than the right will change in a field of professionals who place them in a systemic totally different position of the nobility with respect to the right. Because of its own interests, the bourgeois materialized a shift towards rational and instrumental thinking in terms of property rights and legal proceedings. (Sassen, 2010, p. 98)

The legislation thus becomes the instrument of domination to "assimilate" estates feudal society through a political hegemony of the legislative power which first used a speech or social policy to ensure socially a system of domination "*super State*", through the destruction of the feudal institutions like the division of the large property through inheritancethe prohibition of personal servitude and the introduction of a civil concept of property, which tended to destroy the stately relations and create a liberalized ownership society, which should be capable of producing military and financial yields for the expansion of the State, which carries an externality or value – added trade in relation to the power of the State. But the ideologization of the reform programme in order to "moral conquests" was not hidden that this program was motivated by the politics of power. (Fehrenbach, 1980, p. 236)

Can be seen, therefore, that with the phenomenon of revolutions bourgeois caused by the confrontation of an impoverished noble class and a bourgeois class emerging by the new form of industrial production and accumulation of wealth, being the "autonomous" State the resulting from material conflicts between the bourgeoisie and the aristocracy (Wallerstein, 2005, p. 355), which are distributed the quotas of political power, and the law becomes the concept of legitimation of authority resulting in the formation of national States. Affirming J. Merryman to "*nationalism was another aspect of the glorification of the State. The goal was a national legal system that would articulate the national ideals and the unity of the culture of the nation. Such national law should express themselves in a national language and should include institutions and national concepts*" (Merryman, 1989, p. 45), and the way to solve disputes is through the application of the law through the forms provided for this purpose, called the procedure.

In this period the procedural model is developed "*sincretista*", praxista or procedural named for confusion between substantive and procedural levels of State Management (Dinamarco C. R. , 2009, p. 25). "*knowledge were purely empirical, without any awareness of principles, concepts and the definition of a method. The process itself, as the reality of experience facing the trials and courts, was seen only in its external physical reality and was perceptible to the senses: the mere procedure was confused when they defined it as a succession of acts, while they say nothing about the legal relationship that exists between their subjects (procedural legal relationship), or on political expediency to leave the way open for the participation of the litigants (contradictory)*". (Dinamarco R. C. , 2003, p. 58)

The jurisdiction is faced as a system for the protection of the subjective rights of individuals, and this is their main purpose; the action was conceived as an extension of the subjective right and simple process procedure. (Mitidiero, 2009, p. 42) conception that responded to the ideology of the French Revolution by which the single declaration of law implied its existence, being subordinate his jurisdictional performance.

Thus, the Mission of the magistrate is exclusively reduced to the application of the law, since the right is hardly the originary freedom of man that the law will imitate, nor the right will be a category to be determined by the judge who, being a quality and not quantity, will be out of any secure, indisputable definition. (Baptista da Silva, 2005, p. 175)

2. 4 *The logic of the justification of the legitimacy*: "*Process*" *and* "*Right*"

The route which ends with the first half of the 19th century attends the final triumph of positive law and the constitutions as a domestic guarantees of the State and of the encoding systems, but still far the great debates that are open to century about the relationship between positive law and Constitution, and is not yet envision on the horizon the great dangers that will become apparent with the first world war and totalitarian deviations, but the system of the rule of law, with their constitutions and their codes, have already been delineated. (Prodi, 2008, p. 399)

So the history of fundamental rights is linked to the emergence of the constitutional State as organization form of power and a system of representation of a new system of rulers and ruled, that arises as a response to the excesses of the absolutist State, whose thought is due to the change of thinking about the role of the State and the place of the people within the State Organization. (Carbonell, 2010, pp. 55 - 60)

At the end of the 19th century the dynamics of the development of industrial capitalism would be the formation of the working class and the rise of the new ruling class. Each of these classes is a combination of different social groups, although in the long run is a group that represents the majority or dominant runs (Sassen, 2010, p. 158). In that regard, the framers of the Constitution were concerned by the existence of factions and especially by the possibility that poor aglutinaran in a faction which would lead to political moves to impose the distribution of wealth. Therefore, placed matters relating to property and the market in a supra - political sphere: that of private law.

Thus such matters were constituted as matters of law and not politics (Sassen, 2010, p. 166), generating the emergence of a new legal concept of privacy, with an interest for the protection of the personality and the personality prominently. It also detects a transformation of "civil rights" they are born as guarantees of free people, but then set up a collective Declaration of rights, and finally become the social rights of the welfare State in its early stages and constitute an indispensable part of the new balance struck by the liberal State in the pursuit of public order and the protection of private liberties.

Thus, interpretations on this period is dominated by the notion of an exceptional development marked by the struggle of certain State institutions to set up the future welfare State powerful opposite other institutions obstructing that process contingent on the interests of large companies.

While the importance of the constitutionalization for modern civil rights is well documented, there are other fundamental elements for the constitutional legal development that have been comparatively relegated as legal positivism, administrative law and executive power to act the social order (Sassen, 2010, p. 179). In this last aspect coincides Gregorio Peces – Barbas, quoted by M. Carbonell, who indicates that "without prior efforts centralized, strengthening of the unitary and indivisible sovereignty of the State, not have been possible historically fundamental rights". (Carbonell, 2010, p. 58)

As a result, this process of evolution initially revolves around the old question of the legitimacy of the power of the State. Constitutional law replaced the civil law as the maximum of legitimacy of the power authority State, but not necessarily as a source of law, which was given later.

In short, the era of the hyper nationalism which starts at the end of the 19th century and during much of the 20th century is the complex result of the construction of the national capitalism in a world of great powers that compete and interact while it is being born the world economy of the 20th century, competition that leads to the emergence and multiplication of international conflicts, of the colonization processes that occur in the framework of the expansion of such capitalism, of economic internationalism of cartels and market, backed by the interstate coordination is oriented towards the construction of national Capitalisms, which requires recognition of the demands of national economic actors, including the population and the labor force of the country, from which it derives the granting of rights to workers and consumers by investing in the domestic consumption, which then translates into a Constitution, to thus legitimize the exercise of power.

While the contradictions between positive law and that natural in its primordial elements consist of individual freedom to ensure the best forms of action, pursuant to the deliberative capacity, beyond respecting freedoms; property rights, as a substrate of exchanges and as condition of free initiative and independence of individuals, to choose the best goals in the use of the freedom, represent lost opportunities of welfare and therefore end up manifesting in unrest, breakdown of the social fabric, break the harmony between its components and possible violent confrontation.

Therefore social change would be in a process of positive natural laws, through the predominance of reason or violence, in variable combination of these elements, according to the circumstances (caves, p. 72), being the origin of the appearance of fundamental rights, their subsequent re – elevation in a Constitution and source of legitimation of the State and law translationwhich ultimately would be the germ of the theory of human rights.

In this way, the evolution towards the contemporary age, the phenomenon of the constitutionalization of the right and therefore constitutions boom, and this is the concept that legitimates the authority through the constitutional States, that as mentioned by J. Merryman "constitutions are the hostel in new individual rights, and the clash of constitutional litigation in the duct of its definition and execution. The emergence of constitutionalism is therefore an additional way of decoding: civil codes do not already play a constitutional role. As we have said before, that function has been moved from the more private sources of private law – civil code – to the most public of the sources of public law: the Constitution". (Merryman, 1989, p. 292)

The process as a conflict resolution mechanism is valued through the category of a constitutional guarantee of the people versus the development of jurisdictional activity as legitimate role of the State, focusing on this stage the study of procedural law towards the development of the judicial function.

With the formation of the modern States germinated and stated the principle of the statehood of the process, claiming in the hands of the sovereign monopoly of the procedural legislation, whose procedural from 18th – century laws not only operated on the methodology they had various developments at the cultural level, covering the legal education, the judicial system and process, and assuming a character efficientist, with remarkable presence of the State, through the judge producing a change in the process "*of order isonomico*" which based on the authority, hierarchy and bureaucratic logic.

Therefore, there is common agreement that this stage of scientific procedural law begins in Germany in the mid – 19th century in two key points established in the so – called controversy between B. Winschaid and T. Muther (1856), which established the public character and the autonomy of the right of action, and the work of O. Bülow (1868) which defined the concept of procedural legal relationship other than the material relationship, and became the cornerstones of the procedural right future.

However, the so – called controversy of Winschaid – Muther, is actually a discussion justifying the expropriation of the possibility of private revenge toward the State, making it a right to request the State jurisdictional activity either for the settlement of the conflict between individuals (specific theories of liberal character) or for the solution of the conflict as social evil (abstract theories of the Welfare State), and thus justify the presence and existence of the authority of the State in private relations, as it had been mentioned is reconciliation between "freedom and necessity" throughout the State.

This transformation of procedural "syncretism" to its "autonomy" means all radical changes in the way of perceiving the procedural phenomenon. Seated so the basis for the further development.

However, in their longing to rediscover the value of the process and to scientific contours to the civil procedural law, ended up exceeding its mission. The intention of purging the civil process of contamination with the substantial right to the imposed by the legal tradition of the 19th century, led to the doctrine initiated by Chiovenda to erect the foundations of a completely carefree civil litigation by the material law, about the abstract concept of "action" as methodological polo and would have relationship only with the procedural law defined based on criteria only procedural and unable to give meaning to the jurisdictional provision.

2. 5 *The logic of the crisis of the State*: "*Process*" *and* "*Constitution*"

The exhaustion of the regime of capitalist accumulation and microeconomic type keynesians strategies, the crisis of existing paradigms (Mosterín, 2006) and the assertion of scientific - technical paradigms articulated around the new technologies of the information and the unstoppable advance of the globalization process, appear as central deep mutations that affected the world in recent decades. In this context, a new scenario whose coordinates social, economic, political, cultural, institutional, regional, differ substantively which had consolidated in the heyday of the capitalist development of the post - war years has been configured.

To this new scenario has been consolidating, generated a new dynamic of inclusion therein, that leads Governments to deal with different emphasis and depth the application of strategies of economic, political and social restructuring, noting multiple transformations that affect all the dimensions of social life, and that the right cannot be oblivious to these changes. (De Mattos, Hernaux, & Restrepo Botero, 1998, p. 7)

The first phase of the industrial revolution occurred in a market economy, in a hierarchical structuring of the company. The second took the concentration and monopoly to the functional hierarchical structure specialized, functional services joint, but what happens that comes to be called the third phase of the industrial revolution, mounted on nuclear energy and electronics, gives singular embossing to intellectual tasks and gives rise to the AutoCorrect, mechanical works and servicesat the same time that it causes the concentration, programming, the "management by objectives" and imposes work on computer, on a network communicative and informative (Goytizolo Vallet, 1969, p. 78), scenario proposed in accordance with the "world system" analysis, in a total history, contextualized. (Brea, 2007)

In this new dynamic insertion in this new scenario on the basis of the construction of a territory you can just think in entering the global world.

This way, we talk about a new era, digital ones, to other space or computing, where a new concept legitimate authority that are human rights. This ideology used to justify and to stabilize the political groups who are in power or for those who want to achieve power. In this sense designates G. Robles to "*the concept of* '*human rights*' *is a political concept and not technical*, *and cannot be anything else. And as such a concept is based on the political struggle*: *serve or it can be used to try to transform the reality or to try to keep it*". (Oaks, 1982, p. 54)

However, this new ideology of human rights leads to a crisis of sovereignty and State, because there is a transfer from domestic sources of law to external sources of law (Ferrajoli, rights and guarantees. The law of the weakest, 2002, p. 16), thus validating the thesis of M. Serra Dominguez on the absolute nature of the jurisdiction which designates "*jurisdiction is not resolved in a State function that exists independently of the State, being only a few historical circumstances the determinants that at the present time the State has been obtained for himself the monopoly of jurisdiction*". (Serra Dominguez, 2008, p. 19) In this way jurisdictio of the State is spreading, and shown the formation of supra – national courts which oblige States to comply with their decisions to a new "one – dimensionality" standard, in which be confounded again "moral and right" increasingly vigilant and rigorous.

And on the other hand the expansion of trade relations in this global scenario constitutes a new jurisdiction without State through alternative mechanisms for resolving disputes such as arbitration or negotiation with more flexible rules and a target more focused finalist in the re – establishment of the relationship and less symbolic content not being its purpose the affirmation of the sovereignty and authority of the State.

Globalization as a general trend becomes one of the most important factors of the current legal culture directly related to the globalization of the world economy, but the questions are globalization of what, for whom? And consequently what the globalization of procedural justice can give? Understanding that you apart from the commercial issues becomes more sensitive to other issues such as environmental law and respect for fundamental rights at a national and supranational, with the possibility to refer to the case law and precedents of other national or international courts mainly when the decisions subject matter has to do with the interpretation and the implementation fundamental rights (Taruffo, a proposal for the harmonisation of the civil process, 2011, pp. 29 ~ 45).

Then, the "State monopoly of jurisdiction" has notably, fractured where the jurisdiction is not an exclusive feature of the State; the bodies to which the jurisdictional functions are entrusted are not always State organs. In this new space the State and not state courts are interconnected among themselves and are tendentially expendable, and correlatively brings "the crisis of the monopoly of the procedural legislation" compelling, but well to the standardization, to harmonisation and mutual integration between jurisdictions at the vertical level, as at the horizontal level, with a logic of cooperation or other times with a control logic emerging the need of an extra State Foundation for jurisdiction (Picardi, 2009), whose function would be now born in the bosom of the community or society.

In conclusion, the mode of production occurs through globalization, and the new wealth is based on the possession of the technology and information, where the State loses presence in the partnership relations. Raising the range of basic guarantees of the process right, makes a new object of study of procedural law does not conflict resolution mechanism, but the study of the content of this fundamental right, either the right to judicial protection or due process, in accordance with this new ideology of DD. HH.

C. Magris mentioned law must adapt its rules to hit new forms of violence that may arise, the new challenges that may be created, and the legal experience has been extremely fruitful and innovative. It has ventured into new territories, has produced new guardianships and has defined new subjects, traditionally "weak" in the societies of the past and present, such as women, minors, the disabled, new immigrants (Magris, 2008, p. 68) resulting in a more plastic process to meet these new needs.

Today this problem is particularly alive in an era when globalization that assails the world also implies to the right, i. e. , the ways with which should protect people, exposed to the forces of a mechanism removed all experience direct and subject to a power or powers that often it is difficult not only to control, but anyways.

3. *The function of the test in the current law: the test as part of the constitutional right of the probative right and the rationality of the scientific proof*

An increasingly complex society creates new relationships between men, lawful or unlawful new forms, of confrontation, and therefore, possibly, of conflict; and where there is a conflict, so it is only potential, there should be a law that regulate it and mediate it in a civil manner. But a new reality can be involved along with the advantages, new dangers, that need to be addressed (Magris, 2008, p. 60).

Outlines from the right to the process, as a fundamental right of postwar constitutions (Spain, 1978, Italy, 1947, Bonn 1949 Federal law, Portugal 1979, Colombia 1991), and the right to test becomes a substantial right of constitutional connotation which enables the citizen to claim and obtain guarantees of adequate protection.

Probationary due process, gives rise to the right to try and discussions, being the guarantor judge that parties have any possibility of Defense. On the other hand the proper evidentiary process can be understood also as the right to a clean contradictory that "*corresponds to all the rights and guarantees which should be observed in the confrontation and discussion of the evidence*" (Ramirez Carvajal, the trade test. "A perspective to the civil Dialogic process", 2009), that includes the contribution from all the test that are considered necessary, the right to a technical defense, prohibition of self – incrimination evidentiary and the right to discussion any test that is alleged against him, as well as guaranteeing the absolute nullity of the evidence obtained in violation of due process or any other fundamental right. Thus the contradictory clean corresponds to the right to due evidentiary process, which develops at least three principles: the right of defense, the law of contradiction and the full annulment of the test when it is obtained in violation of the due process.

As regards the assessment of the test the principle of "healthy criticism" which is presented to appreciate the evidence the judge must justify its decision on the basis of the rules of reason, experience, etc. The problem of it, that although it looks like an intermediate system between the legal assessment and the free conviction, is to establish "rules" of reason and experience, it is an undetermined field and lead inevitably to the discretion of the judge and the private knowledge, and be fully established would be a return to a legal trial system.

That a more current look is why some authors develop the theme of the test through a cognitive process, in which what is tested are statements on the facts. Michelle Taruffo, notes, "*in these sectors is a common conceptual schema can be called of" evidence and inference "and who relies on contributions from different fields for the purpose of offering General instruments for the formulation and the rational control of the inferences that underlie assertions on facts. In this context, emerges a general notion of 'proof' as confirmation of conclusions concerning assertions on facts or as a premise of inferences to substantiate conclusions consistent assertions on facts*". (Taruffo, test, 2008, p. 237)

However, it points out that the ability of the courts to assess the evidence is a cause of concern predominantly in the Western legal system today, that apparently, crosses and cut the traditional division between Anglo – American Legal system and the legal systems European continental. The main way in which highlights this concern is the discussion of the bias of the expert or experts. However, bias, of course is something that is not only applicable to experts or experts, and is very likely that the testimony may be partial, and it is always possible that the judge may also be biased.

Therefore, different legal systems have dealt with these problems in different ways: some jurisdictions may exclude the testimony of the civil parties, defendants or those who maintain certain relations with them and others can leave the question of partiality of the witness to be evaluated with the ruling; the judicial partiality, on the other hand, may be recusal, or settled in the second instance.

However, the possibility of bias in the testimony of experts is a problem for the Court in a different way to form of partiality in the testimony of the witnesses, and that cannot be addressed, as in the case of the judges, in the second instance, and only rarely through the challenge. (Dwyer, 2008, p. 1)

4. *The evaluation of the test as a matrix system*

Some part of the doctrine that deals with tests and judicial determination of the facts is to present an opposition between the judge and the scientist to deny that there is a significant analogy (Taruffo, test, 2008, p. 330). However, resort to the appeal of the model or scientific method for the estimation of the test it is a modern trend that is formed as a response to the problems posed by the use of common sense for the estimation of the test.

Norbert Wiener (Wiener, 1969), devoted a long chapter to the right, explaining these two central ideas, finding a relationship between law and cybernetics:

(a) That legal problems are by nature of problems of communication and cybernetics, i. e. relating to regular monitoring and critical, repeatable.

(b) The theory and practice of law consist of two sets of problems: those of its general purpose, focused on the concept justice, and the technique, using, which are those ideas.

Thus, there is a notorious expansion apply knowledge resource or scientific investigations or scientific methods to check the facts provided to the process, instead of referring to the uncertain common sense notions.

This guidance has been developed through two general lines. The first one that tends to the "scientific" of the evidential reasoning and includes several directions of research aimed to develop models of evidentiary reasoning inspired schemes or scientific principles, among which is the development of probabilistic models to apply to the analysis and assessment of the evidence, based on calculations of probability based on Bayes theorem, or based on the quantitative probability calculation. Another group, draws on logical probability models and which are based on inferential evidential reasoning structure analysis, and a second line that propose the application of logical schemes of the artificial intelligence to problems arising in the judicial reasoning in general, and in particular in the area of judgment in fact. (Taruffo, over the borders. Writings on civil justice, 2006, p. 132)

It is to that end, proposed a change of perspective on the problem of the assessment of the test, getting away a little of its natural horizon established by the "search for truth", defining the test as a data matrix that develops inside the process.

4. 1 *The fact as datum*

The data word has its etymology in the Latin term "datum", which means "given". However, strictly speaking, in the field of scientific research, as said Gil Flores, "*most of the authors assume that the investigator plays an active role with respect to the data: the data is the result of a development process, i. e. , the data must be build it*" (Gil Flores, 1994). Such a statement is perfectly applicable to the fact presented in the process, since only occurs the affirmation of something made in the past and that will not be repeated, still the process mechanism to rebuild the last fact.

That is, there is a transportation of the fact of the real plane passed to the legal flat present, therefore, the notion of "data" is defined as information extracted from the reality that has to be registered in some physical or symbolic support, which implies a conceptual elaboration and in addition that can be expressed through some form of language, with the following components: ①a conceptual elaboration; ②an information content; ③a recording on physical media; and ④the expression in any form of language, either numerically or non – numerical.

It holds Galtung that all data has a structure composed of three elements: analysis units, variables and values. Lugo, any "data" consist of: ①a unit of analysis; ②in a variable it will assume; ③A certain value.

So, what constitutes a fact, for this author, would be these three elements considered jointly through the relationships that keep each other.

It should be noted, that J. Samaja, contrary to what Galtung indicates, says that the general structure of the scientific data has four components, which are related to the four functions that meet the descriptive statements, namely: ①analysis unit, which corresponds to the "argument" (x) component; ②Variables, which corresponds to the same function (F); ③Values, which coincides with the value of the function (and); ④Indicators, which corresponds to operations that is built and that used to calculate the value of the function.

4.2 *The proof as a matrix system*

Following this methodological framework we refer back to the proposition function as opposed to the silogistica proposition. A functional system of the test as opposed to a holistic system, this translates into an array of data, consisting of the following elements and where: unit of analysis. AU (fact), Variable. V (medium evidence), inference. = (evidentiary procedure) and result. R (rating), with the following structure: $R = V * UA$.

Where it moves to the evidentiary process, is not the entire array, but only the AU (fact), by the Variable (between probative). Being that in the evidentiary process will establish the inference and the result (estimation).

The highlight of the function type proposition, is that your applications have as a result the construction of a "universe of facts", with a hierarchical structure that, in many respects, evokes the complexity of an ecological system. The body of descriptive statements is not organized flat, chaining the facts one next to another, but in a more complex way in which constitute one from others. The need for the construction and interpretation of the test system, aims to achieve "transduction" the real flat fact passed to the ideal flat (legal) present.

For Michelle Taruffo (Taruffo, proof of the facts, 2005), not the judicial process a scientific enterprise, it is not necessary to establish "absolute truths", being sufficient to establish "relative truths" that offer a reasonable basis established for the decision, being this a key issue for discussion about issues relating to testing and determining the facts, which would only be possible to establish a relative truth as to the means of knowledge and the context. Thus, it then introduces the idea of degrees or measures of knowledge, according to which every factual hypothesis deserves a double confirmation that graduation they will in a first direction from 0 to 1 (where 0 ignorance and 1 truth), the probative value as specific of each means of proof with respect to the factual hypothesis, and in a second sense on a scale from 0 to ∞, which indicates different media test set probative value in relation to the hypothesis about the fact. With this theoretical support acceptability of a hypothesis problem translates into the assessment concerning the degree of confirmation that the hypothesis has received on the basis of the evidence provided. If the grade is considered sufficient then the hypothesis is acceptable and can, therefore, be taken into account as the basis for the decision.

In this assessment, what the author has done is a "vector sum", vectors are objects that have the characteristics of movements and represent magnitudes, direction and sense, and their combination represent a vector sum. These quantities define the dimensions of the object and define the object of study, thus when you mentioned that the test as a whole has a value from 0 to ∞, it is that the fact has been appreciated in all its magnitude, and returned to rebuild.

The matrix of test system character allows a reconstruction of the real made past according to their magnitude, each one relative to the other, and not make partial insights, then allowing their signal transduction to the legal theoretical, which reconstructs the entire discourse or narration based on all the facts. Here is how to make a representation in 3D from the fact, then in a complete narrative performance with other facts appreciated altogether and make a multimedia representation.

Although of seemingly complicated languagethe case is very simple and takes us to approach reality with the truth you are looking for, for which only requires that in a universe of matrices only has only two real variable types: ①the arrays that tend to have unit roots; and② The matrices which do not tend to have unit roots or are intermingled (in this case what is happening that the matrix is not defined well in the case variables that tend to have unit roots are that lead us to find the truth and which do not have unit roots are false).

For which the matrix must comply with the following requirements: ①that the variables tend to be unitary; ②The matrix (X) "n" variable (tests) must be invertible; ③That the matrix (X) "n" variable have a tendency to be likely that comes close to the unit and that this matrix for its degree of certainty (probability) be affirmative or comes close to the truth or the reason because of this between 0.5 to 1 and when the probability of this matrix in 0 to 0.5 means that obtained tests dont give you no certainty ensure a sentence; ④To the matrix (X) have covariance; ⑤That the probability of the matrix (X) tends to 1 the more is closer to 1 real and true will have the tests. The operative part is simple, the important thing is that I have to have very clear concepts and their interpretation.

Bibliography

Alvaro de Oliveira, C. (2007), *Of the formalism to the civil process (proposal of an evaluative formalism)*. (J. J. Palacios, Trad.) Lima: Palestra.

Baptista da Silva, O. A. (2005), *Jurisdiction and execution in the roamno tradition – canonical.* Lima: Palestra.

J. Barragan, (2009), *Strategies and law*, Mexico D. F.: Ediciones Miguel Angel Porrúa.

Barrio de Angelis, D. (2005), *Theory of the process* (Second ed.). Montevideo: IBDF.

N. Bobbio, (2006), *State, Government and society. For a general theory of policy*, (J. F. Santillan, Trad.) Mexico D. F.: Fondo de Cultura Econ6mica.

J. L. IT Annoys, (2007), *Does. Mutations of the culture in the era of electronic distribution*, Barcelona: Gedisa.

M. Cappelletti, (1974), *Process, ideology and society*, (S. S. Melendo, Trad.) Buenos Aires: EJEA.

M. Caarbonell, (2010), *To understand the rights. Brief history of their key moments*, Lima: Palestra.

O. G. Chase, (2011), *Law, culture and ritual*, Madrid: Marcial Pons.

P. Clastres, (2000), *Archaeology of violence. The war in primitive societies* (2nd ed.), (L Padilla, Trad.) Buenos Aires: Fondo de Cultura Econ6mica.

R. Coover, (2000), *Law, narrative and violence*, Barcelona: Gedisa.

H. Cuevas, economic theory of the State. In H. caves (Ed.), *legal and economic theories of the State.* Bogotá: Universidad Externado de Colombia.

H. Cuevas, (Ed.). (2002), *State economic and legal theories*, Bogotá: Universidad

Externado de Colombia.

M. Damaska, (1986), *The faces of Justice and State power. Comparative analysis of the legal process*, (D. Accatino, Trad.) Santiago de Chile: law Publishing House of Chile.

C. Mattos, N. Hernaux & D. Restrepo Botero, (1998). *Globalization and territory. Impacts and perspectives.* Santiago de Chile: Fondo de Cultura Económica.

C. R. Dinamarco, (2009), *The process of instrumentality*, Lima: Communitas.

R. C. Dinamarco, (2003), *Institutions of Civil procedural law*, Sao Paulo: Malheiros.

D. Dwyer, (2008), *The Judicial Assemet of the expert evidence*, Cambridge: Cambridge University Press.

E. Fehrenbach, (1980), *Traditional society and modern law. The reception of the Code Napoleon in the States of the Federation of Rhenish*, (A. Calderon, Trad.) Buenos Aires: Alpha.

L. Ferrajoli, (2010), *Legal culture and constitutional paradigm. The Italian experience of the 20th century*, (A. d. held, Trad.) Lima: Palestra.

L. Ferrajoli, (1995), *Right and reason. The do theory*, (A. P. Ibañez, Trad.) Madrid: Trotta.

L. Ferrajoli, (2002), *Rights and guarantees. The law of the weakest* (2nd ed.). (A. P. Ibañez, Trad.) Madrid: Trotta.

A. Garapon & I. Papadopoulos, (2006), *Judge in France and in the United States. UU. French legal culture and Common Law*, Bogota: Legis.

C. Geertz, (1988), *The interpretation of cultures*, Barcelona: Gedisa.

J. Gil Flores, (1994), *Analysis of qualitative data. The educational research application.* Barcelona: Editorial PPU.

C. Gomez Lara, (2006), *Procedural Systematics*, Mexico D. F.: Oxford University Press.

P. Grimal, (1998), *The loss of freedom* (Second ed.), (A. Bixio, Trad.) Barcelona: Gedisa.

P. Grossi, (2003), *Legal mythology of modernity*, (M. M. Neira, Trad.) Madrid: Trotta.

J. Habermas, (2010), *Actuality and validity. On the right and the democratic rule of law and terms of discourse theory* (Sixth Edition ed.), (M. J. round, Trad.) Madrid: Editorial Trotta.

O. Hoffe, (2008), *Intercultural right*, (R Seville, Trad.) Barcelona: Gedisa.

G. Kantorowicz, (1949), The struggle for a science of law. Savigny Kirchman, Zitelmann, & Kantorowicz, *The science of law* (W. Goldschmidt, Trad.). Buenos Aires: Editorial Losada.

P. Khan, (2001), *Cultural analysis of the law*, Barcelona: Gedisa.

S. López Ayllon, (n. d.). Retrieved 11 – 12 2012, http://biblio. juridicas. unam. mx/libros/2/645/12. pdf.

D. Lopez Medina, (2005), *Impure theory of law. The transformation of Latin American legal culture.* Bogota: Legis.

C. Magris, (2008), *Literature and law before the law.* (M. T. Meneses, Trad.) Madrid: Ediciones sixth floor.

J. H. Merryman, (1989), *The Roman legal tradition – canonical* (Second ed.), (C. Sierra, Trad.) Mexico D. F.: Fondo de Cultura Económica.

D. Mitidiero, (2009), *Cooperation in civil*, Lima: Communitas.

J. Mosterín, (2006), *Crisis of paradigms in the 21st century*, Lima: Fondo Editorial of the Universidad Inca Garcilaso de la Vega.

K. Newman, (1983), *Economics and law organization*, Cambridge: Cambridge University Press.

J. Snow Fenoll, (2009), *Jurisdiction and process*, Madrid: Marcial Pons.

R. Núñez, (2009), Politician, Constitution and State power. In AA. VV, *theories juridical and economic state.* Bogotá: Universidad Externado de Colombia.

F. Ost, (2005), *At the right time.* (M. G. Torres, Trad.) Mexico D. F.: Century XXI Editores.

N. Picardi, (2009), *The jurisdiction at the dawn of the third millenium*, (J. J. Palacios, Trad.) Lima: Communitas.

J. M. Piquer Mari, (2010), "*Non – rational*" *tests in Rome. AB Urbi condita until the end of the Republic*, Madrid: Editorial DYKINSON, S. L.

R. Pound, *The spirit of the "Common Law"*, (J. P. Brutau, Trad.) Barcelona: Bosch.

P. Prodi, (2008), *A history of Justice*, (L Padilla, Trad.) Buenos Aires: Katz.

D. Ramirez Carvajal, (2009), *Trade test. "A perspective to the civil Dialogic process"*, Bogotá: Universidad Externado de Colombia.

D. Ramirez Carvajal, (2009), The procedural claim contemporary perspective. In AA. VV, *knowledge, test, Pretension and orality*, Lima: ARA.

E. Redenti, (1957), *Civil procedure*, Buenos Aires: EJEA.

G. Robles, (1982), *Epistemology and right*, Madrid: Ediciones pyramid.

A. Sanchez – Bayón, (2010), *Studies of culture policy – legal. Tolerance to liberty and its current quarantine.* Madrid: Editorial – Delta.

A. Sanchez – Bayón, (2009), *Manual of American legal sociology. Power, the sacred and the freedom in Western modern* (2nd ed.), Madrid: Delta publications.

S. Sassen, (2010), *Territory, authority, rights. Medieval assemblies to the assemblies golobales.* (M. V. Rodil, Trad.) Buenos Aires: Katz.

A. Schiavone, (2009), *IUS. The invention of the right in the West*, (G Prosperi, Trad.) Buenos Aires: Adriana Hidalgo Editora.

M. Serra Dominguez, (2008), *Jurisdiction, action and process*, Barcelona: Atelier.

M. Spinelli, (1975), *Civil evidence*, (T. A. Banzhaf, Trad.) Buenos Aires: Ediciones legal Europe – America.

P. Talavera, (2006), *Law and literature*, Granada: Editorial Comares.

G. Tarello, (2002), *Legal culture and policy of law*, Granada: Comares.

M. Taruffo, (2008), *Test*, (J. F. Beltrán, Trad.) Madrid: Marcial Pons.

M. Taruffo, (2005), *The proof of the facts* (Second Edition ed.), (J. F. Beltrán, Trad.) Madrid: Editorial Trotta.

M. Taruffo, (2010), *Simply the truth*, (D. Accatino, Trad.) Madrid: Marcial Pons.

M. Taruffo, (2006), *Over the borders. Posted on civil justice*, (B. Quintero, Trad.) Bogota: Temis.

M. Taruffo, (2011), A proposal for the harmonization of the civil process, In AA. VV, *jurisdiction and the international protection of the law.* Medellín: Seal Publishing House of the University of Medellin.

M. Taruffo & B. Cavallone, (2012), *Verifobia. A dialogue on test and truth*, (M. Aramburu, Trad.) Lima: Palestra.

J. Vallet de Goytizolo, (1969), *Masses and law societies*, Madrid: Taurus.

R. Van Caenegem, (2011), *Judges, legislators and professors. Phases of European legal history.* Lima: Palestra.

I. Wallerstein, (2005), *Analysis of the world system. An introduction*, (C. D. Schoroeder, Trad.) Mexico D. F.: Century XXI Editores.

M. Weber, (2000), *Economy and society*, (J. Medina, Trad.) Mexico: Fondo de Cultura Económica.

N. Wiener, (1969), *Cybernetics and society*, (J. N. Hill, Trad.) Buenos Aires: Editorial Sudamericana.

J. Wilhem Hedemann, (1931), *The presumptions in the law*, (L A. Seral, Trad.) Madrid: Journal of private law.

L. Zolezzi, (2011), *Law in context*, Lima: Fondo Editorial of the Pontifical Catholic University of Peru.

[1] Cadiet, Loui. (Ed.) *Dictonarie of justice.* Press Universitàries de France, 2004. p. 503. Quoted by: DWYER, Deirdre. The Judicial assessment of the expert evidence. Cambridge University Press, Cambridge, 2008. p. 1.

[2] Form making inroads to the dawn of Imperial Rome

[3] (already in the first iron age '*par*' is a monosyllabic archaic, probably of Etruscan origin, indicating the equality of every member within the community of farmers – warriors)

[4] (*privus is also an archaic Word*)

实体真实与人权保障

樊崇义 * 夏 红**

引 言

“在已实行的犯罪与刑罚之间，实际上有一场‘诉讼’（proces），这就是刑事诉讼（proces penal）。”[1] 帕卡教授1963年在分析刑事诉讼的犯罪控制（Crime Control）和正当程序（Due Process）两种模式时就明确指出：两种模式其实质是代表了两种截然不同的价值观。不同的历史阶段，两种模式所代表的价值观此消彼长。[2] 虽然其是以美国为例进行的分析，但是结论同样适用于中国的刑事司法状况。我国长期以来关于刑事诉讼惩罚犯罪与保障人权二元目的的冲突与协调问题[3] 也与帕卡的观点有着惊人的暗合性。

我国长期以来一直关注人权问题。1991年，中国国务院新闻办公室发表《中国的人权状况》白皮书，首次系统地回顾了中国人权事业的发展和现状。1997年中国共产党第十五次全国代表大会又将“人权”概念写入了党代会的政治报告。2004年，将“国家尊重和保障人权”写入宪法修正案。2006年《国民经济和社会发展十一五规划纲要》中明确提出要“尊重和保障人权”。2007年，党的十七大将“尊重和保障人权”写入《中国共产党章程》。2011年，在《国民经济和社会发展十二五规划纲要》“全面推行法制建设”一章中强调“加强人权保障，促进人权事业全面发展”。2012年党的十八大明确将“人权得到切实尊重和保障”作为全面建成小康社会的重要指标。“尊重和保障人权是政治承诺，是国家立场，更是坚实行动，发展归宿。”[4]

我国的刑事诉讼法律制度也随着社会的变迁不断地进行着调整。2012年3月14日十一届全国人大五次会议表决通过了《关于修改刑事诉讼法的决定》。修改后的《刑事诉讼法》将“尊重和保障人权”明确写入了总则。这是“尊重和保障人权”这7个字

---

* 樊崇义，中国政法大学教授，博士研究生导师。

** 夏红，辽宁师范大学法学院教授。

〔1〕［法］卡斯东·斯特法尼、乔治·勒瓦索、贝尔纳·布洛克：《法国刑事诉讼法精义》（上），罗结珍译，中国政法大学出版社1999年版，第1页。

〔2〕 Hebert L. Packet，(1964)“Two Models of The Criminal Process”，*University of Pennsylvania Law Review*，113 (11). pp. 1～68.

〔3〕 我国对刑事诉讼目的的论著颇多，多言及二者的关系。参见宋英辉：《刑事诉讼目的论》，中国人民公安大学出版社1995年版；宋英辉：“刑事诉讼目的论”，载《政法论坛》1992年第2期；郝银钟：“刑事诉讼目的双重论之反思与重构”，载《法学》2005年第8期；陈建军、喻永红：“论我国刑事诉讼目的、价值的定位及其实现条件”，载《河北法学》2004年第1期，等等。

〔4〕 王石川：“尊重和保障人权是国家的发展归宿”，http：//opinion. cntv. cn/renquanluntan516/index. shtml，访问日期：2013年5月8日。

在2004年写入宪法修正案后，再次明确写入法典。“尊重和保障人权”既是具有宣示意义的表述，同时也是具有实质意义的法律规则和行动指南。全国人大常委会副委员长王兆国在对《刑事诉讼法修正案（草案）》的说明中指出：“尊重和保障人权是我国宪法确立的一项重要原则，体现了社会主义制度的本质要求。刑事诉讼法在程序设置和具体规定中都贯彻了这一宪法原则。考虑到刑事诉讼制度关系公民的人身自由等基本权利，将‘尊重和保障人权’明确写入刑事诉讼法，既有利于更加充分地体现我国司法制度的社会主义性质，也有利于司法机关在刑事诉讼程序中更好地遵循和贯彻这一宪法原则。”〔5〕接下来的问题是，如何在刑事诉讼法执行的过程中贯彻“尊重和保障人权”。

在以三段论为典型逻辑的法律适用过程中，事实认定是基础。如何认识和判断案件事实，既与被追诉人相关，也与被害人相关；既与个人相关，也与公共利益、国家利益相关；既与犯罪的惩罚相关，也与人权的保障相关。可谓是牵一发而动全身的根本性问题。2012年的修订，在将“尊重和保障人权”写入《刑事诉讼法》之时，亦在程序的许多方面规定了具体的尊重和保障人权的程序措施，特别是对被追诉人权利的保障规则，如在多个程序中保障辩方的知情权、讯问时的录音录像制度、证据收集时的不得强迫自证其罪规则，等等。如果概要式地将刑事诉讼过程看做是个人和国家之间的对抗的话，那么这些修改，无疑为被追诉人的权利保障提供了更多的便利和机会，相应地，就为刑事追诉设置了更多的障碍，案件事实的发现势必更加困难。如果按照这样的逻辑推演下去，惩罚犯罪和人权保障真的就成为两种非此即彼的选择。人权保障多了，实体真实就难以发现，犯罪的惩治力度就不可避免地被削弱；要增强犯罪的惩治力度，就要更迅速有效地发现实体真实，那就必须以牺牲对个人权利的承认和保障为代价。对此，日本律师也曾指出：“与实体真实主义相比，过分重视尊重人权主义和程序公正时，就要考虑实体真实会受到什么损害，损害到什么程度的问题。”〔6〕

在高高扬起“尊重和保障人权”的大旗的同时，我们也不禁要认真思忖一下“尊重和保障人权”和实体真实的发现到底是怎样的关系？“尊重和保障人权”真的阻滞了案件事实的发现吗？能否正视并回答这些问题，决定了刑事司法的发展方向。

一、实体真实主义解读

在大陆法系的传统中，一直都非常重视事实。德国联邦宪法法院将追求实体真实当作是刑事程序的“中心任务”。〔7〕德国学者认为“确定事实是刑事诉讼程序的目的与德国刑事诉讼强调发现实体真实（materielle Wahreit）是一致的”。〔8〕之所以如此，正如台湾学者蔡墩铭教授所言，“刑事诉讼既在于决定国家刑罚权是否存在，则应以真实之事实为裁判之依据，稗对于犯罪者科以应得之刑罚，并避免罚及无辜，是以实质

〔5〕《全国人大第二次全体会议 王兆国作刑事诉讼法修正案草案的说明》，http：//www.china.com.cn/v/zhuanti/2012lh/2012－03/08/content_ 24841932.htm，上传时间：2012年3月8日，访问日期：2012年4月20日。

〔6〕［日］五十岚二叶：“论有罪答辩制度的引进”，载《季刊刑事辩护》1999年第20号，第23页，转引自［日］田口守一：《刑事诉讼的目的》（增补版），张凌、于秀峰译，中国政法大学出版社2010年版，第9页。

〔7〕BverfG NStZ 1987，419；BGH NJW 1956，1647. 转引自［日］田口守一：《刑事诉讼的目的》（增补版），张凌、于秀峰译，中国政法大学出版社2010年版，第31页。

〔8〕［德］托马斯·魏根特：《德国刑事诉讼程序》，岳礼玲、温小洁译，中国政法大出版社2005年版，第16页。

真实之发见，向被认为刑事诉讼之目的。因之，所谓实质真实主义遂成为刑事诉讼之原理，而与职权主义发生密切关系”。[9]

深受德国法学体系理论影响的日本也非常注重发现真相。以真实为基准的原理，叫做实体真实主义（也称为实体真实发现主义，真实主义）。[10] 正如松尾浩也教授所言：日本的旧刑事诉讼法属于重视解明真相的刑事诉讼法，其基本原理为实体真实主义（Prinzip der materiellen Wahrheit）以及职权审理主义（Untersuchungsgrundsztz）。[11] 日本刑事诉讼法关于刑事诉讼目的的规定，可以简要地概况为“在正当法律程序中实现实体真实主义”。[12] 这个看起来完美的刑事诉讼目的，在遇到具体冲突时，往往存在难以调和的矛盾，势必面临取舍选择。关于这一冲突，较早的理论认为，“刑事诉讼始终是由实体真实主义支配的”，这是因为，实体真实主义（实体真实发现主义）是刑法中最重要的指导理念。发现实体真实是进行正确审判的前提。[13] 最初的实体真实主义是与形式真实主义相对的概念，而且，诚如前述论证的那样，在初期，人们往往将这两种真实主义与不同的诉讼模式进行一一对应。由于这一时期程序工具主义价值观占主导地位，刑事诉讼中实体真实主义强调的是实体真实、绝对真实、真正真实。以积极发现实体犯罪行为的绝对、真正真相为指向，以将犯罪绳之以法为目标。最初的实体真实主义其实质就是偏重于积极方面的实体真实主义。

但是“实体真实主义的观念也是历史发展的产物。现在出现了新的变化，已经开始从古典的呆板的实体真实主义概念向灵活的实体真实主义的观念转变”。[14] 现在日本的实体真实主义是“被缓和了的实体真实主义”，“并不是查明绝对真实的固有原理，而是受到各种界限和制约的复杂的原理”。[15]

日本学者普遍认为实体真实主义包括积极和消极两个方面。“一方面透过查明犯罪事实而不使有罪的人逃脱刑罚制裁作用（积极的实体真实主义）中表现出来。因为实现刑罚权的效果，与其在实体法上实行重刑，倒不如在刑事程序法上无遗漏地准确处罚更为有益。但是，也不得因此而处罚无罪者。因此，在另一方面，实体真实主义在追求不得错误地认定犯罪事实而将无罪者认定成有罪这一消极方面作用（消极的实体真实主义）中表现出来。‘宁可错放一百，也不错杀一个无辜’的古谚，就是消极的实体真实主义理念的体现。”[16] 积极的实体真实主义意指有罪者一定要受到惩罚。从正面而言，其强调犯罪一定能被发现并处罚；从反面而言，其旨在表明毫无遗漏地处罚

---

〔9〕 蔡墩铭：《刑事诉讼法论》，五南图书公司2002年版，第26页。

〔10〕［日］田口守一：《刑事诉讼法》（第5版），张凌、于秀峰译，中国政法大学出版社2010年版，第14页。

〔11〕［日］松尾浩也：《日本刑事诉讼法》（上卷），丁相顺译，中国人民大学出版社2005年版，第13页。

〔12〕 李心鉴、莫晓芙：“实体真实与法律程序的冲突及选择”，载《中外法学》1990年第4期，第60页。

〔13〕［日］团藤重光：“実体的真実主義”，现代法律学演習講座刑事訴訟法5頁以下。转引自吉利用宣：刑事裁判における真実主義序説——戦後日本の当事者主義に関する覚書（2）。

〔14〕《九州工業大学研究報告（人文·社会科学）》，第35，41~82页，http://ci.nii.ac.jp/naid/110000151947.

［日］田口守一：《刑事诉讼的目的》（增补版），张凌、于秀峰译，中国政法大学出版社2010年版，第67页。

〔15〕［日］田口守一：《刑事诉讼的目的》（增补版），张凌、于秀峰译，中国政法大学出版社2010年版，第53页。

〔16〕［日］土本武司：《日本刑事诉讼法要义》，董璠舆、宋英辉译，五南图书出版公司1998年版，第15页。

犯罪。积极的实体真实主义是以必罚主义为哲学基础的刑事诉讼目的观。消极的实体真实主义则以确保无罪的人不受处罚为旨趣，其以不罚主义为基本出发点，更加注重程序规则的功能和作用。[17] 如今，对于实体真实主义的理解逐渐由积极的实体真实主义向消极的实体真实主义转变。

不管是为了制裁有罪者，还是为了保护无辜者，其根本点均在于发现案件真实情况。积极的实体真实主义和消极的实体真实主义在这一点上并无特异。其迥异性主要表现在达成这一终极目标的过程上。在积极惩罚有罪者过程中，不以确保无罪者无虞为底线，对于追诉的方法，查明的手段等不加任何限制，一概以目的正当性蔽之，故而难保不形成瓜连无辜的恶果。恰如松尾浩也教授所言，“如果在理念上过分向解明真相倾斜的话，在实际运用上就会出现下列不足：（1）侦查过于严酷，侵害相关人员的权利；（2）审判追随侦查的结果，或者法官过于积极作为反倒会产生误判的危险”。[18]

凸显消极实体真实主义的目的在于寻求个人利益和国家利益，发现真实与尊重和保障人权之间的平衡。“无限制地‘宁失不经’，则不仅恐难维持社会治安，且使实体真实发现主义从其根本而瓦解”。[19] 现代刑事诉讼的基本理念在于经由正当程序实现个体及社会的公正。因此，对于刑事犯罪的追诉而言，以程序法所允许的方式发现真实是消极实体真实主义最低限度的要求和内涵。

二、诉讼视域中的实体真实：“法律真实”

“实体真实”在不同的学科、领域、甚至不同的语境下均呈现出不同的面相。具体在诉讼的视域中，“实体真实”到底是怎样的呢？笔者尝试以马克思主义认识论的基本原理为工具，从三个方面进行分析：

从认识的主观性与客观性的原理的角度来看，认识活动是联系主客观的纽带。认识的对象具有客观性，是不以人的主观意志为转移的；认识的结果是主观感知客观事物后在头脑中的反映。因此，所谓认识是将客观事物成像于主观意识的过程和结果，兼具主观性和客观性的双重特征。具体到诉讼中，认定案件事实，必须以证据为根据，是经由证据对于已经过去的案件情况的认识。也正因为是一种历史性的回溯认识，客观事物在主观意识中的成像永远不可能是对客观事物的简单摹写。“强调案件事实可以被认识，意味着办案人员应当努力地做到自己的主观认识与案件客观事实一致。当然，这种一致并不是完全的一样，只要与裁判有关的事实特别是主要事实一致就可以。在有些情况下裁判所认定的事实与案件事实会出现部分不一致甚至完全不一致；但是这种不一致不应当成为一种普遍的情况，否则司法公正无法实现，司法裁判不会为民众认同，司法权威也将受到严重损害。”[20] 所以，刑事诉讼中的认识，无法达到“绝对真实”的程度。诉讼中的“实体真实”不是“绝对真实”。

从认识的相对性和绝对性的原理的角度来看，人类认识活动是相对性和绝对性的统一，是由无数个具有相对性的认识不断发展，日益趋向绝对性的认识的历程。认识

〔17〕 参见［日］能势弘之：《刑事诉讼法25讲》，青林书院1987年版，第7~8页；http：//ameblo.jp/kentarou1177/entry－11159919028.html，访问日期：2013年5月12日。

〔18〕［日］松尾浩也：《日本刑事诉讼法》（上卷），丁相顺译，中国人民大学出版社2005年版，第13页。

〔19〕 黄东熊、吴景芳：《刑事诉讼法论》，三民书局2002年版，第19页。

〔20〕 陈光中、李玉华、陈学权：“诉讼真实与证明标准改革”，载《政法论坛》2009年第2期，第7页。

的绝对性是对认识进行历史考察的结果。诉讼中对于案件事实的认识，是在特定时空片段内的认识，因此其只能是一种相对性的认识，即案件事实并非是“绝对真实”。这种“相对真实”中蕴含着绝对真实的要素。证据必须经过查证属实，才能作为定案根据的要求即表明构成相对“真实”的素材的质的规定性。对此，卡尔·拉伦茨陈述了类似的观点：在判决的事实部分出现的“案件事实”，是作为陈述的案件事实，它与实际上发生的案件事实不同，前者既要与后者一致，又要在后者的基础上作进一步的选择和加工。[21] 同时，这种“相对真实”不是随意性的“真实”。“相对真实”的框架和内容是由法律规定的，法定的要求包括两个方面，实体法如刑法关于犯罪构成要件的规定，程序法如关于证明标准的规定。因此，诉讼视域中的“实体真实”是“相对真实”，是“法律真实”。

从认识的真理性和正当性的原理的角度来看，人类的一般认识活动会将认识的真理性放在第一位，“在认知行为的领域中，人类行为的目的是而且仅仅是发现客观实在的事实之真，因此，如果违背了实事求是或客观真实性原则，就无法达到认识的目的”[22]。但是，这一原则一旦进入诉讼领域，则必须要受到认识正当性的约束，即合法性约束。正当性（合法性）原则作为司法领域中至上性原则，意味着司法活动不能毫无保留地服从认识的真理性指向。诉讼活动的特质将价值评价（合法性评价）标准引入到事实认识的过程中来，“在司法领域中，由合法性原则所代表的法律之善总是具有主导地位。当司法活动服从实事求是和客观真实性原则的要求，有利于实现和促进法律之善时，服从就是必要的；反之，就不存在服从的必要性，而只存在限制或者超越的必要性”[23]。因此，对于诉讼中的认识而言，正当性是第一位的，真理性是第二位的，诉讼中的“实体真实”是兼具正当性和相对真理性的事实，是法律程序创造的“事实”（诉讼各方实际上都参与了事实的发现或者创造），是“法律事实”。

诉讼中的“实体真实”的实质是“法律真实”。诉讼中的“实体真实”是诉讼认识的结果。从范畴上而言，诉讼认识也是一种认识，但与一般意义上的认识活动相比较而言，其具有鲜明的特征。

第一，诉讼认识的个别性。诉讼认识与科学认知不同，其并非旨在发现具有普遍适用意义的客观规律或者真理。诉讼请求是诉讼认识的起点，诉讼请求的特质决定了诉讼认识必然是以特定诉讼主体、诉讼标的为对象的。这种认识活动即便是在同一类型的诉讼请求认定中也不具有可复制性。

第二，诉讼认识过程的限定性。诉讼认识是一种个别认识，所有的诉讼认识都是在特定时空条件下的具体认识活动，在这一时空节点上，人类当时的认识能力以及认识水平是一定的，有限的。在这样有限条件下的诉讼认识活动，还要受到诉讼运行期限、诉讼发展条件、诉讼进行规则等多方面的制约，这使得诉讼过程具有限定性特征。

第三，诉讼认识目的多元性。刑事司法中发现真相对于正确适用法律有重要的积

---

〔21〕［德］卡尔·拉伦茨：《法学方法论》，陈爱娥译，商务印书馆2004年版，第160页及以下。

〔22〕郑成良：“法律之善优于事实之真”，载樊崇义主编：《部门法学哲理化研究》，中国人民公安大学出版社2007年版，第22页。

〔23〕郑成良：“法律之善优于事实之真”，载樊崇义主编：《部门法学哲理化研究》，中国人民公安大学出版社2007年版，第24页。

极意义。但是发现真相并非是刑事司法的唯一目的。美国学者贝勒斯指出："与纯科学不同，法律的目的并不在于发现真相，并不在于发现全部真相，并不纯粹在于发现真相。这不但代价过高，而且往往与解决争执的目的不沾边"。[24] 因此即便出现案件事实真伪不明的状态，司法机关也需要承担裁决义务，此时，需要运用证明责任分配原理来解决问题。刑事司法的目的不仅仅在于发现真相，同时也在于能够定纷止争，恢复被犯罪行为破坏的社会关系，诉讼认识目的的多元化已经成为一种事实。

第四，诉讼认识的职能分化性。诉讼中的认识不仅受特定场域的限制，而且有明确的分工划分，此种职能划分是诉讼原理的基本要求。诉讼中的认识能力和认识方法的选用与其诉讼职能和在诉讼中的地位紧密相关，而和个人的认识意愿及能力无关。如根据《刑事诉讼法》的规定，辩护律师经证人或者其他有关单位和个人同意，可以向他们收集与本案有关的材料。而非律师辩护人则无此项诉讼权利。当公检法机关收集证人证言时，则无征询同意的程序要求。又如，技术侦查手段是只能由公安和检察机关在符合法定条件的情况下采用的侦查措施，其他诉讼主体则无权采用。

第五，诉讼认识手段法定性。虽然在通常情况下，诉讼认识也是朝着最大限度地查明案件事实真相努力的，但是这种努力并非是为了真相不惜采用一切手段，不惜牺牲一切代价。刑事诉讼法中对查明案件事实的方法有明确的规定，对不同方法适用的条件、步骤及要求也都有清晰的规定。程序法本身具有限制权力和保障权利的双重属性。刑事诉讼法中明令禁止采用刑讯逼供、威胁、引诱、欺骗等非法手段发现案件事实，一旦采用，通过非法方法获取的证据也将作为非法证据而被予以排除，即从正反两个方面反映了诉讼认识手段严格法定性的特质。诉讼认识手段的限定性是诉讼利益选择的结果，这个结果也是司法文明化、人道化映射在诉讼中的必然反映。

第六，诉讼认识检验标准的非绝对性。《刑事诉讼法》规定，刑事诉讼证明应当达到证据确实、充分的程度。具体而言，证据确实、充分包括：定罪量刑的事实都有证据证明；据以定案的证据均经法定程序查证属实；综合全案证据，对所认定事实已排除合理怀疑。从这个证明标准中可以看到，证明的范围限定于跟犯罪有关的定罪和量刑两个方面的事实；证明的过程要求经法定程序审查，并要确认其属实；证明的指标达到排除合理怀疑的程度即可。因此，检验刑事诉讼认识的标准从认识范围到认识程度上均具有强烈的法律规定性，而非绝对性。

综上，刑事诉讼中所追求的真实首先是"诉讼上的真实"，只有依据证据法所认定的"诉讼上"的事实，才是"真实"；其次是"实体上的真实"，是"尽可能接近于真相的事实"，而非绝对的真正的真实（wahre Wirklichkeit），或者全部的真实（ganze Wahreit）。实体的真实是在必要限度内所追求的"中间目的"（Zwischenziel）。[25] 这一"中间目的"即为"法律真实"，是在法律空间内经多方共同努力探明的"真实"，是

---

〔24〕［美］迈克尔·D. 贝勒斯：《法律的原则——一个规范的分析》，中国大百科全书出版社1996年版，第23页。

〔25〕参见［日］田口守一：《刑事诉讼法》（第5版），张凌、于秀峰译，中国政法大学出版社2010年版，第14页；［日］田口守一："刑事诉讼目的序说"，载《西原春夫先生古稀祝贺论文集》（第4卷），成文堂1998年版，第51页，转引自［日］田口守一：《刑事诉讼的目的》（增补版），张凌、于秀峰译，中国政法大学出版社2010年版，第68页。

受到法律规则约束和限制的“真实”，是在法律价值选择影响下的“事实”，是消极的实体真实主义。

三、实体真实的实现的前提：人权保障

积极的实体真实主义将落脚点放在发现“真实”上，而消极的实体真实主义则将重点放在发现真实的“方法”上。现代刑事诉讼要求协调发现真实和人权保障两个方面的目的指向。“如果考虑到作为人权保障的宪法规范的重要性，消极的真实主义的观念是妥当的。法院积极追求真实的活动并非总是积极的真实主义。‘积极’地对被起诉的犯罪事实进行严密的批判，这才是消极的真实主义所追求的核心。”即将人权保障作为实体真实实现的前提和基础。

人权保障是宪法化权利在刑事诉讼中的具体体现，我国于2004年将体现社会主义法制本质要求的“尊重和保障人权”写入宪法修正案。此次刑事诉讼法修正案中重申该项宪法原则，一方面反映了宪法和刑事诉讼二者之间的紧密关系，同时也表明了在刑事诉讼中将“尊重和保障人权”精神实质贯彻到底的决心和信心。对于案件事实的发现，以及对于犯罪的惩罚均应当符合人权保障的精神和要求，按照正当程序进行，这一精神应渗透到刑事诉讼的各个程序中。

刑事诉讼中的人权保障首先体现在对追诉程序的规范上。如果将刑事诉讼程序整体看作是追诉犯罪的机器的话，对于这部机器的约束和限制越少，其追诉的成功率及效率就会越高。20世纪80年代的“严打”可谓是按照这个逻辑实践的典型样本。1983年9月2日全国人大常委会颁布了《关于严惩严重危害社会治安的犯罪分子的决定》和《关于迅速审判严重危害社会治安的犯罪分子的程序的决定》。前者规定对一系列严重危害社会治安的犯罪，“可以在刑法规定的最高刑以上处刑，直至判处死刑”；后者则规定在程序上，对严重犯罪要迅速及时审判，上诉期限也由刑事诉讼法规定的10天缩短为3天。这其中，不仅刑事程序蜕变为单纯服务于实体结果的工具，而且被追诉人的程序性权利和实体权利均在“从重从快”的战役式推进中被冲击得支离破碎。历史的事实告诉我们，不仅对于程序独立价值的尊重要求注重刑事诉讼中的人权保障，对于实体公正的追求同样要求认真践行人权保障的程序规则。毕竟，刑事裁决是经由刑事程序运行才得以产生的。

刑事诉讼中的人权保障也体现在对实体真相的探求上。以犯罪嫌疑人供述和辩解的获取为例。现行刑事诉讼法对此进行了详尽的规定：原则上，不得强迫被追诉人自证其罪。具体程序上，侦查中讯问应当由侦查人员2人以上进行（主体资格、数量）；通常讯问的地点应在看守所内（地点）；讯问时提问的先后次序（逻辑顺序）、讯问笔录的制作、讯问时的录音、录像制度（讯问记录）；对特殊主体讯问的特殊要求（未成年人、聋哑人），等等。同时，刑事诉讼法中还规定禁止采用刑讯逼供等非法方法获得犯罪嫌疑人供述。若发生此类行为，不仅辩护方有权提请排除该供述，同时各专门机关均负有排除该项证据的义务，并且特别明确了非法证据排除的具体程序和相关规则。口供具有很强的证明力，其“证据之王”的地位也并非妄言。如果秉承积极的实体发现主义，只有不受限制地获取证据才是与其目的性相匹配的。但法律的文本的规则很显然不是这样的，上述对于讯问犯罪嫌疑人程序的所有规定，均旨在规范及限制讯问主体讯问权力的行使，其全部的目的皆在于对犯罪嫌疑人的基本权利给予尊重和保障。

“通过宣布违反程序的取证行为无效，来迫使国家执法人员严格遵守法定程序，并在法定程序的约束下选择理性的替代方法去发现案件的真相。”〔26〕对于发现真实的方法的重视，正是消极的实体真实主义的旨趣所在。

刑事诉讼对于人权的保障在各个诉讼程序中均有明确且详细的规定。“我们不能为了社会的利益而牺牲个人的利益。如果说，司法正义的要求是：一切犯罪人始终应当受到惩罚，但同时也强调受到追诉的人享有自我辩护的一切可能（辩护权）。受到追诉的人，只有当其责任与‘当受惩罚性’经法官全完认定时，才能被剥夺自由或者受到某种制裁。”〔27〕我国将立案作为独立的诉讼程序，同时采用书面宣告主义的立案方式，立案是刑事诉讼程序的开始。强制侦查行为只能在立案后才能进行。旨在防止无准入条件情况下刑事程序对个人权利的恣意和威胁。在刑事侦查程序中，严格贯彻侦查法定主义，非侦查机关无权进行侦查。有侦查权的机关也必须在法定的侦查措施中选用恰当的方法开展侦查活动，侦查措施的适用应当符合法定的条件，取得必要的令状（如搜查、扣押、查封物证书证、技术侦查手段的采用等都需要履行审批手续，获得授权），遵循法定的步骤、方法，同时受到一定的监督。公诉阶段，一旦发现案件超过法定追诉时效，不管案件事实是否已经查明，都应当作出不起诉决定，不再追诉。此时，程序规则适用优于对案件事实的法律判断，对个人权利的保障优于对“实体真实”的探求。在审判阶段，《刑事诉讼法》第187条第3款规定：“公诉人、当事人或者辩护人、诉讼代理人对鉴定意见有异议，人民法院认为鉴定人有必要出庭的，鉴定人应当出庭作证。经人民法院通知，鉴定人拒不出庭作证的，鉴定意见不得作为定案的根据。”很显然，鉴定意见不能作为定案根据并非是因为其不能证明案件事实，而是因为其没有符合程序规则的要求。《刑事诉讼法》第227条规定：“第二审人民法院发现第一审人民法院的审理有下列违反法律规定的诉讼程序的情形之一的，应当裁定撤销原判，发回原审人民法院重新审判：（一）违反本法有关公开审判的规定的；（二）违反回避制度的；（三）剥夺或者限制了当事人的法定诉讼权利，可能影响公正审判的；（四）审判组织的组成不合法的；（五）其他违反法律规定的诉讼程序，可能影响公正审判的。”此时的发回重审，也并非因为第一审法院对于案件实体事实的判断错误或者存在误差，而是由于违反了程序法规则，这些程序规则中包含着被追诉人的基本诉讼权利。

综上，实体真实的实现要以人权保障为前提。以人权保障为前提，就能够克服积极实体真实主义中过度必罚主义倾向，在促进对实体真实追求的同时，不损逆法治的精髓。消极的实体真实主义体现了人权保障和实体真实主义两个方面的价值需求，调和了二者之间的对立和冲突。二者协调表现在程序法中即为正当程序，“所谓的正当程序，就是真实主义与人权保障之间实现了适度平衡的程序。”〔28〕在尊重和保障人权的基础上发现的实体真实就是“法律真实”。

---

〔26〕张建伟：《司法竞技注意——英美诉讼传统与中国庭审方式》，北京大学出版社2005年版，第193页。

〔27〕［法］卡斯东·斯特法尼、乔治·勒瓦索、贝尔纳·布洛克：《法国刑事诉讼法精义》（上），罗结珍译，中国政法大学出版社1999年版，第3页。

〔28〕［日］田口守一：《刑事诉讼法》（第5版），张凌、于秀峰译，中国政法大学出版社2010年版，第18页.

四、实体真实的相对性

实体真实主义在当前诉讼中是以消极的实体真实主义面目出现的，其在具体的诉讼中可以表达为“法律真实”。但是在刑事诉讼中，“实体真实”或者说“法律真实”也并不总是以一成不变的面目示人，其具有相对性。

首先，实体真实的探求要受到追诉意愿的局限。按照不告不理的原理，没有起诉就没有审判，同时审判的对象也是由起诉所决定的。现行刑事诉讼法确定了对未成年犯罪嫌疑人的附条件不起诉制度。未成年犯罪嫌疑人即便符合起诉条件，但是其涉嫌犯罪为刑法分则第四章、第五章、第六章规定的罪名并且可能判处一年有期徒刑以下刑罚，有悔罪表现的，人民检察院可以行使起诉裁量权，从而作出附条件不起诉的决定。若未成年犯罪嫌疑人遵守相关规定，考验期满后则检察院将作出不起诉决定。此时，追诉者追诉意愿的放弃阻隔了探求实体真实的勇往直前的脚步。程序的阻隔使得追诉成为不可能。这是实体真实相对性的客观方面。

其次，实体真实要受到主体判断的影响。诉讼的进程是个动态的连续锁链系统，程序之间彼此勾连，一个程序既为前一程序的结果，同时又是后续程序的基础和前提。这个系统是由多个诉讼主体的诉讼行为共同作用的结果。我国刑事诉讼程序由立案开始，达到有犯罪事实，需要追究刑事责任的条件就可以立案；达到犯罪事实清楚，证据确实充分，需要追究刑事责任，法律手续完备条件的，侦查程序终结；进入审查起诉阶段后，判断达到提起公诉条件的案件，由人民检察院起诉到人民法院。在这一连续的过程中，相关主体的判断是至关重要的环节，虽然他们所做的判断也是以案件事实为指向，以证据为基础的，但是这些对于案件事实的判断都不是裁判者的判断，是程序意义上的事实判断，以这些事实判断为基础所进行的法律判断，也只具有程序意义。只有裁判者依法进行的事实判断才能成为具有法律意义的实体裁决的基础。此乃实体真实主义相对性的主观方面。

最后，实体真实主义在刑事诉讼过程的不同阶段、不同种类的刑事诉讼程序也存在差异性。“即使在个案中，也有不同形态——或者说不同层次——的真相。”[29]

不同种类的诉讼中，对于“真实”要求是不同的。通常情况下，民事诉讼中的纷争利益是私人权益，以意思自治和当事人处分主义为核心的民事法律中，允许当事人运用自认的方式判断争议的法律关系，这种“形式真实主义”并不以客观上一定存在自认陈明的状况为前提。此种“形式真实主义”在我国自诉案件和刑事附带民事诉讼中也有所体现。《最高人民法院关于适用〈中华人民共和国刑事诉讼法〉解释》第155条第4款规定，附带民事诉讼当事人就民事赔偿问题达成调解、和解协议的，赔偿范围、数额不受第2款、第3款规定的限制。即不受赔偿范围及数额的限制，民事赔偿问题本质上仍属于附带民事诉讼当事人有权处分的空间，适用民事法律规则。我国刑事诉讼法规定，自诉案件允许和解、调解、撤诉及反诉。其中意思自治和处分原则体现得与民事诉讼无异，“形式真实主义”亦可作为纷争解决的基础。

但是在纯粹的刑事领域，即定罪和量刑领域，刑事诉讼则对此种“形式真实主义”

---

〔29〕［美］亚伦·德肖维茨：《合理的怀疑——从辛普森案批判美国司法体系》，高忠义、侯荷婷译，法律出版社2010年版，第31页。

持否定态度。我国《刑事诉讼法》第53条明确规定:“对一切案件的判处都要重证据,重调查研究,不轻信口供。只有被告人供述,没有其他证据的,不能认定被告人有罪和处以刑罚;没有被告人供述,证据确实、充分的,可以认定被告人有罪和处以刑罚。”“实体真实主义”是刑事领域,特别是刑事公诉案件中的主流理论。但在具体适用中,其程度也存在差异性。

在刑事公诉案件的第一审程序中,若被告人不认罪或者辩护人作无罪辩护,法庭要在查明定罪事实的基础上,查明有关量刑的事实。在公诉案件第一审程序中,若被告人认罪,则法庭调查可以主要围绕量刑和其他有争议的问题进行。达到案件事实清楚,证据确实、充分,依据法律认定被告人有罪的,应当作出有罪判决。显然,虽然二者均是适用第一审的普通程序,但是被告人认罪案件的审理程序对定罪事实部分探明有所简化,该类型案件的“实体真实”程度显然要逊色于前者(不认罪的案件审理程序)。

适用简易程序审理的案件以被告人承认自己所犯罪行,对指控的犯罪事实没有异议为条件。庭审中,对控辩双方无异议的证据,可以仅就证据的名称及所证明的事项作出说明;对控辩双方有异议,或者法庭认为有必要调查核实的证据,应当出示,并进行质证;控辩双方对与定罪量刑有关的事实、证据没有异议的,法庭审理可以直接围绕罪名确定和量刑问题进行。显见,与前述被告人认罪案件的第一审普通程序相比,适用简易程序审理的案件,只要是没有异议,与定罪和量刑有关的事实及证据的调查及辩论均可以省略,是更加略式的“实体真实”。

我国上诉一审程序和再审程序均实行全面审查原则,允许提出新的证据和新的事实,因此,可以认为是在原有一审基础上,对案件事实探明的进一步深化和确认。田口守一教授将第二审程序中的真实称为“最严密的实体真实”,将再审程序中的认定的事实称为“最终极的实体真实”。[30] 笔者认为,如果“最终极”这几个字是从程序先后次序的意义上讲的,再审“真实”具有最后性是无可厚非的。但是如果“最终极”是从与“绝对真实”的接近程度上而言的话,在我国的刑事诉讼程序中则没有出死刑裁判之右者。《关于办理死刑案件审查判断证据若干问题的规定》详细规定了办理死刑案件,认定犯罪事实和量刑事实的条件要求。对被告人犯罪事实的认定,必须达到证据确实、充分。证据确实、充分是指:“(一)定罪量刑的事实都有证据证明;(二)每一个定案的证据均已经法定程序查证属实;(三)证据与证据之间、证据与案件事实之间不存在矛盾或者矛盾得以合理排除;(四)共同犯罪案件中,被告人的地位、作用均已查清;(五)根据证据认定案件事实的过程符合逻辑和经验规则,由证据得出的结论为唯一结论。办理死刑案件,对于以下事实的证明必须达到证据确实、充分:(一)被指控的犯罪事实的发生;(二)被告人实施了犯罪行为与被告人实施犯罪行为的时间、地点、手段、后果以及其他情节;(三)影响被告人定罪的身份情况;(四)被告人有刑事责任能力;(五)被告人的罪过;(六)是否共同犯罪及被告人在共同犯罪中的地位、作用;(七)对被告人从重处罚的事实。人民法院认定被告人的量刑事实,除审查

〔30〕[日]田口守一:《刑事诉讼法》(第5版),张凌、于秀峰译,中国政法大学出版社2010年版,第16页。

法定情节外，还应审查以下影响量刑的情节：（一）案件起因；（二）被害人有无过错及过错程度，是否对矛盾激化负有责任及责任大小；（三）被告人的近亲属是否协助抓获被告人；（四）被告人平时表现及有无悔罪态度；（五）被害人附带民事诉讼赔偿情况，被告人是否取得被害人或者被害人近亲属谅解；（六）其他影响量刑的情节。既有从轻、减轻处罚等情节，又有从重处罚等情节的，应当依法综合相关情节予以考虑。不能排除被告人具有从轻、减轻处罚等量刑情节的，判处死刑应当特别慎重。”可见，死刑案件对于“实体真实”的要求远高于非死刑案件。1984 年联合国经济与社会理事会第 1984/50 号决定附录中《关于保护面对死刑的人的权利的保障措施》第 4 条中更是基于死刑的严酷性及不可挽回性，将死刑案件的证明标准规定为“明确和令人信服且对事实没有其他解释的余地”，并且针对死刑案件定罪量刑的证据均应当符合：每个证据都是清晰的，无瑕疵的；证据本身及证据的形成的结论令人信服；所有证据均指向同一个结论，没有得出其他结论的可能性。

五、刑事诉讼目的与实体真实

“真相的发现虽然是刑事审判的一个重要目的，但绝非唯一目的。……有罪的条件必须达到‘排除一切合理怀疑’的证明。这与客观真相的追求有所不同，因为这明显偏好某种特定的真相。所偏好的真相，是认定嫌犯并未犯案，同时我们要求陪审团必须宁可错放，即使在某些案子中，被告似乎真的有罪。”[31] 按照我国目前的主流观点，刑事诉讼具有双重目的，即惩罚犯罪和保障人权。这一目的对证据和证明标准的要求就是既要查明事实真相又要保障人权，诉讼目的的变革，要求理论和实务工作者在证明标准上，必须厘清实体真实与正当程序的关系。修改后刑事诉讼法贯彻法律正当程序精神，刑事诉讼不仅以查明案件真实为目的，而且把尊重和保障人权作为刑事诉讼的目的，要求实体真实与人权保障协调一致。

长期以来，我国司法实践中将刑诉法视为保证刑法实施的工具，导致在诉讼中不择手段，非法取证，刑讯逼供盛行，执行“有罪必罚”的方针，对违法取得的证据也承认它的证据力，在立法上也没有确立非法证据排除规则。传统的诉讼目的观，决定着对积极的实体真实主义的追求。修改后刑事诉讼法将“尊重和保障人权”、“不得强迫自证其罪”、“非法证据排除规则”、“侦查讯问全程录音录像”等一系列法律正当程序的理念、原则、措施写进了法典。这一新变化，昭示着刑事诉讼法的概念和内涵，刑事诉讼的目的、任务等基本问题都发生了重大变革。

修改后的刑事诉讼法关于证明标准的规定，已经从积极的实体真实转向了消极的实体真实，或曰相对的实体真实。这一观念的转变，对“综合全案证据，对所认定的事实已排除合理怀疑”的把握和运用十分重要。其一，明确刑事诉讼法的目的，既惩罚犯罪又保障人权。其二，消除积极的实体真实，即必罚主义的影响，沿着法律正当程序的要求严格依法收集和审查判断证据，以实现相对的实体真实或曰消极的实体真实主义为归宿，完成证明的任务。其三，办案人员是人不是神，人的认识是有局限性的。但是，办案人员必须以法治的思维，严格执行法定的程序，收集和审查证据，用

[31] [美] 亚伦·德肖维茨：《合理的怀疑——从辛普森案批判美国司法体系》，高忠义、侯荷婷译，法律出版社 2010 年版，第 25~26 页。

程序来保障案件的质量，用程序让当事人和人民群众看得见摸得着“公平正义”，案结事了，完成刑事诉讼的任务。

结 论

实体真实主义在大陆法系国家，特别是在日本的转变历程，从一个层面描摹了职权主义诉讼程序在认识和发现实体真实问题上的变化轨迹，这个轨迹恰与刑事诉讼价值及刑事诉讼目的的变化曲线具有相同的频率。近来，越来越多的研究成果表明，不仅大陆法系对“真实”情有独钟，即便是在普通法传统的刑事司法体系中，也都在自觉地探讨发现真实的问题。由于诉讼理念、诉讼构造等诸多方面的差异性，导致两大法系在发现真实的方法和制度层面也显现出不同，这些差异只是技术手段选择层面的问题。在协调处理发现“实体真实”与“尊重和保障人权”的关系问题上，两大法系面临同样的难题，都需要进行一定取舍。在大陆法系的话语体系中，解决这一问题的立场在于将人权保障理念和程序规则嵌入实体真实主义（积极的实体真实主义），将其改造（发展）成为消极的实体真实主义。在英美法系的话语体系中，由于本初的逻辑是程序先于权利的程序正义，因此在后续的发展中，逐步加入了对于程序自身的实质性考量，正当程序的概念和理念深入人心。在我国，经过多年对客观真实主义的反思，对重实体、轻程序惯性思维的纠偏，法律真实已经成为理论和实务界认同的概念。“法律真实”是大陆法系的消极实体真实主义和英美法系的正当程序的中国式表达，是解决和克服绝对实体真实关键的核心。只有坚持“法律真实”才能达到实体真实与人权保障的完美融合，完成刑事诉讼任务，实现刑事法治。

“不得强迫自证其罪”的价值及立法不足

姜小川 *

2012年3月，反映国家和民族文明程度，体现国家法制发展水平，具有小宪法之称的《刑事诉讼法》再次修改，将2004年宪法规定的“尊重和保障人权”的原则载入其中，并实现了“不得强迫自证其罪”从无到有的跨越[1]，但是，仔细研究整部法律，便会发现这一法律规定尚有欠缺。

一、“不得强迫自证其罪”之价值

（一）强化犯罪嫌疑人、被告人的诉讼权利，确保言词证据的合法性

国家作为刑事追诉权的主体，不仅占有雄厚的财力、人力和制度资源，而且享有法律赋予的大量诉讼权力，使得作为被追诉方的犯罪嫌疑人、被告人在强大的国家机器面前显得十分渺小和单薄。控辩双方实力对比的悬殊，往往导致弱势一方无法有效行使法律赋予的各种权利，有碍程序的正义。为此，一方面要对诉讼中国家专门机关的权限和行为方式加以限制和规范；另一方面要提高犯罪嫌疑人、被告人的诉讼地位，并赋予其相应的诉讼权利以提高其对抗的能力。不得强迫犯罪嫌疑人、被告人自证其罪的权利，通过举证责任的分配加以体现，要求追诉方承担证明犯罪嫌疑人、被告人有罪的责任，而不得转嫁由被追诉方承担，从而增加了被追诉方与追诉方对抗的筹码，有利于诉讼权利的平衡。

合法性是证据的前提和保障，而言词证据对合法性的要求更高。言词证据缺乏实物证据的有效客观实物载体，且主观性较强，这就使得言词证据容易受取证方式和供述意愿的影响。侦查人员如果通过合法手段获取能够反映犯罪嫌疑人、被告人自主供述意志的真实的言词证据，那将对案件的侦破起到极大的推动作用；反之，言词证据的真实性就大打折扣，因为程序违法将使证据失去可采性。在不得强迫自证其罪的法律保护之下，犯罪嫌疑人、被告人没有义务证明自己有罪，证明其有罪的举证责任完全转移到追诉方，这时基于犯罪嫌疑人和被告人的自愿而作出的供述其真实性将大大提升。而且，不得强迫自证其罪的规定也有助于预防非法讯问活动的发生。根据非法证据排除规则，在违背犯罪嫌疑人、被告人供述意志的情况下获取的供述，将不能作为定罪量刑的证据使用。即便供述的内容是真实的，也将因程序违法而被排除。从而导致强迫自证其罪的行为归于无用功，侦查人员还可能因此将自己陷于不利之地。这就有助于侦查人员在讯问之初便打消非法取供的动机，达到法律的预防作用。

---

* 姜小川，法学博士、中央党校政法部教授、博士研究生导师。Email：jiangxiaochuan@126.com。

[1]《刑事诉讼法》第50条规定：“审判人员、检察人员、侦查人员必须依照法定程序，收集能够证实犯罪嫌疑人、被告人有罪或者无罪、犯罪情节轻重的各种证据。严禁刑讯逼供和以威胁、引诱、欺骗以及其他方法收集证据，不得强迫任何人证实自己有罪。”

（二）规范警察行为，提升侦查能力

按照不得强迫自证其罪的规定，犯罪嫌疑人、被告人享有不被强迫自证其罪的权利，除非出于自愿，否则侦查人员将很难取得口供等言词证据，从而迫使侦查人员摆脱对口供的过分依赖，转而向其他证据发力。在传统的侦查活动中，口供被认为是获取犯罪线索和证据的来源。对口供的过分依赖，导致刑讯逼供的泛滥，警察权力的滥用，不仅严重侵犯犯罪嫌疑人、被告人的人权，而且使口供的可信性大大降低，导致了冤假错案的发生。解决刑讯逼供问题“首先要把严禁刑讯逼供同贯彻‘不得强迫自证其罪’结合起来，赋予犯罪嫌疑人、被告人反对刑讯逼供的权利。”[2] 不得强迫自证其罪，意味着侦查人员也要告别原始、野蛮的非法取证方式，坚持“重证据，不轻信口供”的原则，实现由“口供中心主义”向“证据中心主义”的转变。这不仅为犯罪嫌疑人、被告人诉讼权利的保障提供了防线，也为侦查机关转变破案模式、提升侦查能力，规范自身执法行为提供了良好的机遇。

（三）提高刑事诉讼效率

许多人对不得强迫自证其罪的法律规定能否提高刑事诉讼效率予以质疑，认为不得强迫自证其罪不仅使口供的获取更加困难，而且只能投入更多的资源去收集口供以外的其他证据，这将大大降低刑事诉讼的效率。然而，当我们从宏观层面考察时结论将会不同。

刑事诉讼成本应当包含三个方面：侦查资源的投入成本、错案与翻供成本和司法诚信成本。首先，应该肯定，不得强迫自证其罪的规定将使口供的获取难度加大、成本上升，从而迫使侦查人员降低对口供的依赖而转向用更多的成本投入去获取其他证据。从这个方面看确实成本上升，刑事诉讼效率降低。但是，任何一项制度的运行都需要其他制度的配套，不得强迫自证其罪的良好运行也离不开其他制度与之配套。如美国刑事诉讼程序的严谨为众人称道，号称“世纪审判”的辛普森案件，对程序和证据要求之苛刻更是成为了美国刑事诉讼制度下案件审判的典范，然而我们也要看到，在美国每年都有大量的案件是通过辩诉交易方式结案的。正是辩诉交易制度成功分流了大量的刑事诉讼案件，使得司法机关能够节约大量的刑事诉讼资源，从而投到了辛普森案式的严格程序之中。不得强迫自证其罪要在我国刑事诉讼体系中发挥其应有的作用，同样需要建立起与之相适应的相关程序。其次，不得强迫自证其罪的规定将大大降低因错案和翻供产生的成本。用刑讯逼供及其他非法方法获取的口供，其真实性将大打折扣，近年来披露的层出不穷的冤假错案足以说明这个问题。而对案件的重新侦查、取证，因时过境迁和错判的作出而大大增加了办案成本。在不得强迫自证其罪规定的保护下，犯罪嫌疑人拥有供述与否的选择权，真实性因此大大提高，从而提高了整个刑事诉讼的效率。最后，不得强迫自证其罪将大大提高司法诚信，从而提高刑事诉讼效率。刑讯逼供等非法取证方式极大地损害了司法机关的形象，给司法机关带来了极大的被动，对法律的权威性也是极大的损害。法律本是正义的化身，司法机关更应是正义的践行者和守护者，而司法人员权力行使不当，却可能使这些化为泡影。

---

〔2〕 胡石庆：“完善‘严禁刑讯逼供’法律制度——兼谈‘不得强迫自证其罪’”，载《法学杂志》2007年第1期。

没有犯罪嫌疑人、被告人的配合，没有广大群众的理解和支持，刑事诉讼效率又从何谈起。不得强迫自证其罪的规定，使犯罪嫌疑人、被告人免受非法取证之害，供述的真实成为可能，司法权威有了得以树立的基础。

（四）使国内法符合国际人权公约的规定

“不得强迫自证其罪”既是世界主要国家的法律，也是国际人权等公约对被刑事指控者最低限度的保证。英国国会1641年通过禁止强迫自证其罪的法律；1791年，《美国联邦宪法第五修正案》规定：“在任何刑事案中，不得强迫任何人证明自己犯罪”。[3] 德国、日本、法国的《刑事诉讼法》也分别对不得自证其罪予以了规定。[4] 我国政府于1998年10月签署加入的1966年联合国《公民权利与政治权利国际公约》第14条第3款（庚）规定：“在判定对他提出的任何刑事指控时，人人完全平等地有资格享受以下的最低限度的保证：不被强迫作不利于他自己的证言或强迫承认犯罪”[5]；我国政府签署并于1992年3月生效的1989年联合国《儿童权利公约》第40条第2款（b）规定：“所有被指称或指控触犯刑法的儿童至少应得到下列保证……（四）不得被迫作口供或认罪”。与此相对应的公约还有《世界人权宣言》，以及我国于1982年签署并于1988年11月正式生效的《禁止酷刑和其他残忍不人道或有辱人格的待遇或处罚》，等等。我国修改后的刑事诉讼法对于“不得强迫自证其罪”的肯定，实现了国内法与国际公约的一致，有利于对犯罪嫌疑人、被告人权利的保护。

二、“不得强迫自证其罪”立法之不足

（一）“不得强迫自证其罪”只是“法律规则”而非“法律原则”

“不得强迫自证其罪”在西方法治发达国家乃至国际社会处于公民的一项基本权利和刑事诉讼法的一项基本原则的地位，而我国仅将其作为一项收集口供的法律规则，在《刑事诉讼法》第50条的证据内容中予以了原则性的规定[6]。按照我国刑事诉讼法的立法体例，总则部分第一章“任务和基本原则”中的法律规定对整部法律的制定具有统领和指导作用，其中的各项法律原则是整部法律的灵魂，贯穿于整部法律之中。由此可见，“不得强迫自证其罪原则”在刑诉法修改中只是作为一项法律规则被规定在刑诉法总则第五章证据部分，作为规范言词证据取证过程中的举证责任分配和取证方式的具体法律规则。显然，这与“不得强迫自证其罪”的法律基本原则的法律地位差距甚大，其在法律中的低位及由此反映的问题可见一斑。

理论上讲，不得强迫自证其罪是一项法律原则，法律原则具有高度的概括性、普遍适用性、抽象性和体系性特点。其往往能够统摄一个或者多个部门法，而不是专属

---

〔3〕 后来美国联邦最高法院将此解释为“沉默权”。

〔4〕 德国《刑事诉讼法》第136条规定：“首次讯问被告人时……要告知他对于控诉有答辩的权利，也有权不予答辩。”日本《刑事诉讼法》147条规定：“任何人可因自己被可能被追究刑事责任或被处有罪判决而拒绝作证。”法国《刑事诉讼法》114条规定：被告人首次出庭时，负责侦查的预审法官应“通知他有不作供述的自由”。

〔5〕 该条约还对刑讯（酷刑）等问题予以了相应的规定。该条约第7条规定：“对任何人不得加以酷刑或施以残忍的、不人道或侮辱性的待遇或处罚”；第10条规定：“所有被剥夺自由的人应给予人道及尊重固有的人格尊严的待遇”。

〔6〕 中国法学会办公室宣传处：“中国刑事诉讼法学研究会2012年年会综述”（摘编），载《中国法学会》2013年第2期。

于某一法律体系内的制度或程序阶段；而且其往往衍生出许多具体化的制度安排和程序设计，细化为众多的法律条款。不得强迫自证其罪具有丰富的内涵，包括被追诉人有权拒绝回答归罪性提问、有权获得律师帮助、不得采取强迫性提问方式、举证责任分配、取证方式等等。这些内容分散在整个刑事诉讼法律体系之中，贯穿刑事诉讼的全过程。由于法律规则和法律原则在法律体系中的地位悬殊，具体的法律规则在司法实践中更容易被规避。受限于当前的立法技术和立法现实，我国法律规定普遍具有过于笼统的特点，在具体的法律适用过程中，往往需要借助司法机关的司法解释。法律原则不仅对整部法律具有指导性作用，对法律解释活动同样具有指导意义，而法律规则却只能成为法律解释的对象。“不得强迫任何人证实自己有罪”的法律规定存在着被法律解释规避的风险。

“不得强迫自证其罪原则”在美国等许多国家都将其作为宪法性原则规定在宪法之中，以统摄整个国家法律体系，贯穿于所有具体法律制度和法律规定之中。如果仅将其作为一条普通法律条文规定在证据部分，其地位和分量明显不足，势必影响其价值的体现以及在诉讼法中的定位和作用的发挥。笔者认为应当考虑将这一法律规定上升为法律原则，规定在开篇的“任务和基本原则”中，以便贯穿于整部法律体系之中。只有如此，才能避免被规避的命运，才能避免法律体系内部条文之间的冲突，才能将犯罪嫌疑人、被告人权利保障落到实处，才能真正发挥不得强迫自证其罪原则的诉讼价值。

与上述问题相关的是，“法律规则”而非“法律原则”的规定，还反映出立法者对待公民权利与公权力义务的态度和关系的处理。在西方法治发达国家，不得强迫自证其罪往往是从公民享有权利的角度进行规定和具体制度设计的。而我国却将不得强迫自证其罪作为公权力机关的义务的角度进行规定。虽然权利与义务是对立统一的，但是从立法技术角度研究却有着明显的区别，二者在举证责任、举证难度上有着明显的区别。按照著名法学家西塞罗的观点，正义就是“使每个人获得其应得的东西的人类精神取向”[7]。为此，当赋予公民某项权利时，相关制度设计是围绕权利的行使和保障进行的，确保权利有效实施；当规定公权力履行某项义务时，制度设计是围绕公权力的义务履行和监督进行的，二者制度设计的可操作性和实际效果是有明显区别的。如此次修改的刑诉法中“不得强迫自证其罪”的规定是以侦查机关的义务形式引入的，义务履行与否的监督措施是讯问全程录音录像。但是通过部分地区的实践表明，讯问过程全程录音录像也非铜墙铁壁，被规避的情形也有很多。在缺乏第三方制约的前提下，一旦出现规避情形，犯罪嫌疑人、被告人往往很难举证，规定也就形同虚设。

（二）“不得强迫自证其罪”与“如实供述”的矛盾

修改后的刑事诉讼法在将“不得强迫任何人证实自己有罪”纳入怀中的同时，基于各种原因，立法者仍然在第118条同时保留了“犯罪嫌疑人对侦查人员的提问，应当如实回答”的规定。如此的法律规定，难免让人对不得自证其罪规定的实现感到忧虑。

---

〔7〕［美］博登海默：《法理学：法律哲学与法律方法》，邓正来译，中国政法大学出版社2004年版，第277页。

一方面规定不得强迫任何人证实自己有罪，另一方面又要求“应当”如实回答。无论怎样解释，都难掩二者之间的矛盾和冲突，二者不能共生于同一部法律之中，否则必有一方难逃被规避的命运。“不得强迫任何人证实自己有罪”意味着犯罪嫌疑人、被告人对归罪性的提问有权拒绝回答，而不承担不利性后果，讯问人员不得以任何方式强迫其回答，此处之“强迫”应包括肉体强迫、精神强迫和法律强迫；而“犯罪嫌疑人对侦查人员的提问，应当如实回答”中的“应当”二字表明，“如实回答”是一项法律义务，即将证实自己有罪的举证责任分配给被追诉人，而拒绝如实回答将作为酌定的量刑情节要求被追诉者承担不利的法律后果。更何况“如实回答”的法律规定曾一度被视为刑讯逼供泛滥的根源。如果我们承认“不得强迫任何人证实自己有罪”，那被追诉人就拥有拒绝回答归罪性提问的权利，那么“如实回答”的法律规定就是对犯罪嫌疑人、被告人进行法律强制，用法律手段强迫被追诉人回答归罪性提问，这显然与我们的前提相矛盾；如果我们仍然坚持犯罪嫌疑人、被告人有“如实回答”的义务，那“不得强迫任何人证实自己有罪”就意味着对“严禁刑讯逼供和以威胁、引诱、欺骗以及其他非法方法收集证据”法律规定的否定，这样的法律修改显然失去了应有的意义。

其实，二者之间的矛盾远非字面意义所能解释，其背后是两种对立的法律价值的冲突：一方面，二者矛盾的源头是无罪推定和有罪推定之间的冲突，“不得强迫自证其罪原则”是无罪推定的自然延伸，正是基于无罪推定的假设，法律才要严格保护犯罪嫌疑人、被告人的权利，严禁强迫犯罪嫌疑人、被告人证实自己有罪[8]；而“如实回答”却是“有罪推定”的产物，正是基于犯罪嫌疑人、被告人有罪的假设，才要求其如实回答侦查人员的提问，如实供述。无罪推定和有罪推定是两种对立的法律思想的产物，二者之间的矛盾不可调和。另一方面，二者之间的矛盾是刑诉法目的之争的具体体现，刑诉法的首要目的是打击犯罪还是保障人权，二者之间如何平衡是刑诉法立法者必须要面对的问题。我们国家长期以来的立法规定和司法实践都是重打击轻保护，而以保障人权为先还是以打击犯罪为先是两种不同的立法理念的冲突。这种法律规定的矛盾冲突，势必影响法律的实施，影响法律修改目的的实现，对法律的权威性造成伤害。

由此可见，“如实回答”义务与“不得强迫任何人证实自己有罪”的冲突极大地损害了法律的统一性和权威性，是法制改革不彻底的产物。“如实回答”义务作为有罪推定的产物早已被世界法治发达国家所抛弃，也与我国的法治进步大趋势格格不入，只有彻底摒弃“如实回答”这一有罪推定思想的产物，用“不得强迫自证其罪原则”统领整个犯罪嫌疑人和被告人权利保障体系，才能维护法制的统一和法律的权威。

（三）“不得强迫自证其罪”与“坦白从宽”之困惑

“坦白从宽”在本次刑诉法修改中被纳入第118条：“侦查人员在讯问犯罪嫌疑人的时候，应当告知犯罪嫌疑人如实供述自己罪行可以从宽处理的法律规定”。至此，“坦白从宽、抗拒从严”刑事政策完成了法律化构造，“坦白从宽”被纳入法律，而“抗拒从严”法律对此没有进一步规定，似乎意味着其退出了历史的舞台。由于“坦白

---

〔8〕 参见卫跃宁：“无罪推定原则的确立与口供制度的完善”，载《证据科学》2008年第6期。

从宽、抗拒从严”刑事政策长期以来都是与“如实供述”相伴生的，二者之间从刑事政策和法律两个方面相互配合，一度成为打击刑事犯罪的利器。而“如实供述”义务是有罪推定的产物，因此“坦白从宽、抗拒从严”刑事政策也就具有了鲜明的有罪推定特色。而有罪推定正与“不得强迫自证其罪原则”格格不入，作为事关侦查讯问程序的两项重要刑事诉讼制度“不得强迫自证其罪原则”与“坦白从宽”是否可以共生，让人困惑。

要解决此困惑必须先找到导致困惑的根源，即“坦白从宽”是否为有罪推定的产物。“坦白从宽、抗拒从严”刑事政策要求犯罪嫌疑人、被告人如实回答自己的犯罪事实，对坦白者给予从宽处罚，而拒不供述的将受到从严惩处，显然政策的出发原点就认为犯罪嫌疑人、被告人是有罪的。[9] 但是本次刑诉法修改，事实上抛弃了“抗拒从严”的提法，只规定了“坦白从宽”，而摆脱了“抗拒从严”的“坦白从宽”其含义只是对坦白的犯罪嫌疑人给予从宽处理。前提是犯罪嫌疑人对自己的犯罪事实作出如实供述，其只是对如实供述行为的法律后果确认，因此不涉及对犯罪嫌疑人供述前有罪与否的界定，也就不存在有罪推定的问题。既然不存在冲突，二者之间制度配合的实现就成为可能。不得强迫自证其罪保护的是犯罪嫌疑人拒绝供述时享有不被强迫的权利，并不否认犯罪嫌疑人也可以基于自己的意志选择供述的自由。虽然口供一直以来广受诟病，但是犯罪嫌疑人的如实供述对案件侦破和取证的重要性是显而易见的。我们禁止强迫自证其罪，但是鼓励和引导犯罪嫌疑人自愿供述，只有二者制度设计相互协调，我们才能真正在尊重和保障人权的同时有效地打击刑事犯罪，提高刑事诉讼效率。

“坦白从宽、抗拒从严”的刑事政策从新中国成立到现在经历了从备受推崇到质疑动摇再到重生的历程，其间一度面临被废止的窘境。“坦白从宽”从刑事政策到法律制度，经受了司法实践的检验，有其合理内核，将其纳入法律规定具有合理性，只是民众对此并无感受。因此法律在予以规定的同时应该予以必要的说明，这种法律知识的普及对于被追诉一方来讲至关重要。

（四）缺乏“不得自证其罪”配套制度和措施的法律规定

法律是一个制度体系，有着完整的逻辑结构，任何具体制度的有效运行都需要一系列制度措施与之配套，否则制度难逃被规避的命运。不得强迫自证其罪规定能否有效运行关键看四个方面：其一，侦查机关执行制度规定的主动性，主动性取决于原则对侦查工作的冲击力度和侦查机关是否有替代措施选择空间。我国侦查机关长期以来对口供都具有很强的依赖性，刑讯逼供等非法讯问措施屡见不鲜，不得强迫自证其罪规定如若实施必定会对讯问工作带来极大的冲击，侦查机关对这一原则具有本能的抵制倾向。替代措施选择方面，在美国，有辩诉交易制度与严格的侦查程序进行配套；在我国台湾地区，也有侦查交易制度为侦查机关提供替代性选择；而当前我国刑事诉讼法并没有做出合理的制度设计，缺乏必要的制度创新。只有为侦查机关提供合法的、并且能够有效地获取犯罪嫌疑人、被告人口供的制度渠道，才能降低侦查机关对不得强迫自证其罪原则的抵制心理。其二，讯问过程是否处于实时、有效、可控状态。讯

---

〔9〕 参见宋世杰：《举证责任论》，中南工业大学出版社1996年版，第125页。

问过程是一个侦查人员与犯罪嫌疑人、被告人的交锋过程，侦查人员在这一过程中采取非法讯问措施时，犯罪嫌疑人很难举证，而警方举证也容易流于形式，不得强迫自证其罪规定要有效实施，必须建立起对讯问过程的实时有效控制。2012 年刑诉法修改将讯问过程全程录音录像纳入法律规定，这在一定程度上实现了对讯问过程的实时监控，但是实践中被规避的情形也已经出现。由于当前我国看守所隶属于公安机关，无法确保讯问活动只在讯问室内进行，一旦讯问场所变动，讯问过程将失去控制。侦查讯问律师在场权在本次修法前呼声很高，但是最终未能采纳。仔细研究本次修法，法律并没有设计出有效的制度来实现对讯问过程的实时有效控制。其三，违反规定获取的犯罪嫌疑人口供能否切实有效地予以排除。获取口供是侦查讯问人员的直接动力，如果非法获取的口供能够切实有效地予以排除，那将从源头上打消侦查讯问人员非法讯问的动力。因此，不得强迫自证其罪落实的关键是非法证据排除规则的保障机制。但是，与 2010 年“两高”非法证据排除规定相比，刑诉法对非法证据排除的修改并没有太大进步。首先，修改后的刑事诉讼法对非法言词证据排除的规定仅限于“刑讯逼供等非法手段获得的证据”，并非所有通过“强迫”手段获取的言词证据[10]。其次，2010 年非法证据排除的规定，为律师进行程序性辩护提供了契机，但是实施两年多来效果并不尽如人意。证据能力实质审查的缺失、举证责任分配的虚置等，严重限制了非法证据排除规则作用的发挥，而刑事诉讼法对此几乎未予修改。其四，制度执行规则设计缺失。此次刑诉法修改只是在第 50 条宣言性地引入了不得强迫自证其罪，而具体制度执行规则缺失，如规定的引用情形、“强迫”的界定、违反规定的法律后果、举证责任分配、权利救济等。法律只是宣言性地规定了侦查机关的这一义务，却没有制定具体制度执行规则或者赋予犯罪嫌疑人、被告人具体的权利来监督和制衡公权力机关履行义务。

法律的生命在于实施，要想将“不得强迫任何人证实自己有罪”这一法律条文付诸实施，就需要其他法律制度的协调，如果配套制度不健全或者不严密，同样难逃被规避或虚置的命运。虽然 2012 年刑诉法修改用 5 个法律条文对非法证据排除规则进行了系统性规定，为排除违反不得强迫自证其罪原则获取的非法言词证据提供了法律支持和操作程序。但是，法律还需对“强迫”进行准确定义，对违反原则的讯问行为的举证责任以及证明标准进行界定。如果法律只是规定“不得强迫任何人证实自己有罪”，却没有具体的实践路径，没有告诉我们当我们的权利受到侵犯的时候我们该如何行动，我们就有充分的理由怀疑其为“空头支票”。

三、“不得强迫自证其罪”立法不足之原因

（一）传统的刑事诉讼理念的禁锢

受历史因素的影响，我国刑事诉讼法具有浓厚的专政色彩，“重打击、轻保护”，“重实体、轻程序”等传统的刑事诉讼理念严重地制约我国刑事诉讼法的发展。我国传统的刑事诉讼理念可谓根深蒂固。首先，我国法律受苏联法治思想影响深厚。苏联法律带有浓厚的阶级斗争色彩，受极左思想毒害，检察强权，刑事审判军事化，暴力革

---

〔10〕 中国法学会办公室宣传处：“中国刑事诉讼法学研究会 2012 年年会综述”（摘编），载《中国法学会》2013 年第 2 期。

命、阶级斗争的许多东西都渗透进整个法律体系。因此我国法律同样具有浓厚的阶级斗争色彩。打击犯罪、维护社会主义的统治秩序是第一位的，保护犯罪嫌疑人、被告人的合法权益永远都是第二位的，是次要的。其次，受1978年宪法的影响。现行的1979年刑事诉讼法最初是根据1978年的宪法制定的。由于1976年我国文化大革命刚刚结束，1978年整个国家的政治生活还没有走向正轨，所以匆忙制定的1978年宪法仍然受到极左思想的深厚影响。依据该宪法制定的刑事诉讼法，自根源上就受其影响。最后，我国现行的司法程序实际上是近代清末变法修律结果的延续，如何将西方的法律制度与中国的传统法律文化和现实国情相结合，如何处理本土与借鉴的关系，至今理论不清，实践难免盲目。

（二）立法缺陷导致对言词证据的过度依赖

立法是司法的前提，其对司法的影响显而易见。我国刑法学研究中，犯罪构成理论长期以来都坚持四要件论，即犯罪主体、主观方面、犯罪客体和犯罪客观方面，受此影响，我国刑法立法中许多罪名的确立都包含着对犯罪嫌疑人、被告人主观方面的认识和态度。而在具体犯罪证明过程和证明标准中，犯罪的主观方面是很难通过客观证据证明的，有些甚至只有犯罪嫌疑人自己内心才知道。为了完善证据体系，达到犯罪证明标准，完成举证责任，侦查机关势必要获取犯罪嫌疑人的口供。如果口供拿不到，轻则犯罪嫌疑人、被告人被降格起诉，严重的将因证据不足而无法达到证明标准，犯罪嫌疑人将因此逃脱法律的制裁。另外，由于口供在获取线索和证据方面的天然优势和实物证据获取的困难，使得侦查人员在长期的办案实践中形成了"口供中心主义"的办案模式。不得强迫自证其罪原则必然导致口供获取难度的增加，使得不得强迫自证其罪原则立法遭遇检察系统和公安系统的强大阻力。

（三）部门利益博弈在立法层面的具体体现

2012年刑诉法修改对"不得强迫自证其罪"的引入有支持和反对两个阵营，支持一方主要是全国人大法工委、最高法院、学者、律师，而反对一方前台是公安部和最高检，背后则还有中纪委、中央政法委和安全部，因此双方的交锋异常激烈。双方对立法权和话语权的争夺实质上是观念和利益的交锋。一方面，近些年来不断曝出的冤假错案和司法实践中刑讯逼供的泛滥，引起社会各界的强烈关注，刑讯逼供成为众矢之的，根治刑讯逼供的呼声不断高涨。打击刑讯逼供呼声最高的是一部分刑诉法学家，他们基于大量的理论研究和实证研究，提出了一系列的根治措施，不得强迫自证其罪、沉默权、全程录音录像、律师在侦查阶段的介入、侦查讯问的律师在场权、非法言词证据排除等等，他们对不得强迫自证其罪原则入律起到了至关重要的作用。律师队伍则对刑讯逼供的危害感受最深，他们在日常办案过程中接触到大量的刑讯逼供案例。由于现行法律缺乏有效的保护制度，使得犯罪嫌疑人、被告人无法有效对抗侦查机关的刑讯，即使受到了刑讯逼供也很难取证，出于对当事人利益的保护，律师必然成为推动不得强迫自证其罪原则入律的天然同盟。传统观点认为公、检、法三机关"分工负责、互相配合、互相制约"，三机关配合有余制约不足，但是本次刑诉法修改法院系统却明确支持遏制刑讯逼供。究其原因，近年来冤假错案层出，错案责任追究首先就是法院。由于我国当前的司法体制，法院在案件的审判上受到大量的来自外界的干扰，有许多案件存在问题，可仍然要判。一旦启动错案追究机制，法院却要承担错判的责任，明显有代人受过的成分，所以法院对遏制刑讯逼供、非法证据排除的态度非常明确。另一方面，由于传统和现实的原因，讯问在侦查机关破案中具有举足轻重的作用，任何对讯问活动的限制都将对侦查机关的办案带来极大的挑战。公安机关对讯问的依赖由来已久，与讯问相关的法律修改必然会招致公安机关的极大关注。检察机关自侦案件对讯问的依赖性更大，由于我国现在并未建立起完善的官员财产申报制度和严密的金融监管机制，贪污贿赂案件具有很大的隐蔽性，取证比较困难。不得强迫自证其罪原则的引进，沉默权的赋予以及取消“如实供述”的义务将会给职务犯罪侦查带来非常大的困难。因此，检察机关对上述法律修改也同样持反对态度。而中央政法委、中纪委和国家安全部在办案过程中也面临相同的问题。双方都从本位出发，坚持自身的利益，最终的法律修改只能是妥协的产物，也就出现了种种矛盾和不足。

（四）法治发展自身的客观规律所决定

与一个国家的政治制度，经济发展水平，社会犯罪形势，人们的法治观念以及法律从业者的素质密切相关，法治发展有其自身的客观规律。而一项法律制度的确立也必然要考虑众多的因素，远非简单的线性逻辑。不得强迫自证其罪作为刑事诉讼法律体系一项重要的基础性的法律制度，其确定对整部刑事诉讼法更是牵一发而动全身，势必会遇到各种问题。其一，经历改革开放三十多年的经济腾飞，我国当前的经济社会与三十年前发生了巨大变化，而犯罪形势也相当严峻。赶超式的发展，使西方社会几百年遇到的社会问题，在我国改革开放的三十年中全部爆发出来，各种社会问题纠缠在一起，使打击犯罪、维护社会治安压力相当巨大，所以任何法制改革都必须考虑当前打击犯罪的承受能力。其二，我国当前侦查能力的发展现状尚无法满足民众对犯罪嫌疑人、被告人权利保障的过高要求。由于受经费投入、刑事科技发展水平、警察数量、侦查人员的素质等多方面的影响，我国当前大部分地区的侦查水平尚有不足，过高的权利保障标准，会给侦查机关的侦查破案带来极大的压力。其三，法治的进步与社会的法治观念息息相关，伴随着经济社会的发展，我国民众的法治观念觉醒，人权保障的意识不断提高。在前几年一系列冤假错案的刺激下，人们对刑讯逼供的认识越来越深刻，遏制刑讯逼供已经在全社会形成了共识。但是，在遏制刑讯逼供是否非要赋予犯罪嫌疑人、被告人沉默权、取消如实回答的义务等问题上各方的意见仍未达成一致。所以立法中也就出现了两种相互矛盾、相互冲突的法律制度同时存在的问题，而要进一步完善不得强迫自证其罪原则必然需要法制观念的进一步统一。其四，法律是一个制度体系，其中任何一个制度都不能脱离其他配套制度独立运行。不得强迫自证其罪原则要有效运行，也离不开其他制度与之配套。而这套配套制度在我国的形成尚需时日。其五，法制的发展从来就不是一蹴而就的，都需要经历一个漫长的过程。西方法治发达国家经历了几百年的时间才有今天的法制成果，我们国家的法制进步也势必要经历一个漫长的过程。

任何法律制度的确立，都不可能一蹴而就，虽然“不得强迫自证其罪原则”仍然存在些许不足，但是其巨大的进步性毋庸置疑，其必将在司法实践中不断地得到完善和发展。

证据法的运行机制与社会控制功能

郑　飞*

一、引言：社会失范与证据规则的缺位

随着中国经济、社会的快速发展，诸多社会失范现象也频繁出现在各种现代传媒中，成为公众讨论的话题。如冤假错案频发，司法腐败严重，社会公德丧失，等等。在我们这个急剧转型的社会中，这些失范现象的发生有着非常复杂的政治、经济、社会和文化原因。本文无意于分析这些社会失范现象的深层次成因，而是想思考这样一个问题：我们的法律制度——具体而言，证据法律制度——是否对某些社会失范现象做出了必要的回应？证据法本身的运行机制，能否发挥某些社会调控功能，对解决这些社会失范问题有所助力？

法律制度应当致力于解决同时代的社会问题，对社会失范现象作出回应，推动法制和伦理秩序的恢复或重建。证据法作为规制司法审判事实认定过程的规范体系，与其他实体法和程序法律部门一样，应当在其功能限度内，发挥调整社会行为和关系的作用，实现法律预设的价值目标。然而，当前中国证据制度的不完善，尤其是某些规则的缺位，导致其不仅难以很好地回应某些社会失范现象，甚至还加剧了事态的严重性。以近年来频发的刑事冤案问题为例，从佘祥林案、杜培武案、聂树斌案到赵作海案，再到今年的张辉和张高平叔侄案、梅吉祥和梅吉杨案以及李怀亮案，这些冤假错案的发生固然主要是因为“司法行政化”〔1〕问题，使法官背离了正当法律程序和证据裁判的要求，而按照上级指示进行裁判。但我国证据制度的不完善实际上又进一步加剧了司法行政化。我们都知道，在证据法中，诸多证据规则和原则（比如相关性规则、直接言词原则、辨认、鉴真和鉴定规则、交叉询问规则、最佳证据规则、传闻证据规则、意见证据规则、品性与倾向证据规则等）的主要功能都是促进事实真相的发现，使事实认定者免受偏见和情绪的干扰，从而作出理性的事实裁决。然而在我国现行立法中，鉴真规则、传闻规则和品性与倾向证据规则〔2〕等依然没有确立，最佳证据规则

---

* 郑飞，中国政法大学博士研究生，美国西北大学联合培养博士研究生。

本文是北京市优秀博士学位论文指导教师人文社科项目（项目名称：证据科学与司法文明；项目编号：20121005301）的阶段性成果。

〔1〕关于司法行政化导致冤假错案的论述，参见张保生：“证据制度建设是司法改革首要任务”，载《中国改革》2011年第9期。

〔2〕1984年4月26日发布的《最高人民法院、最高人民检察院、公安部关于当前办理强奸案件中具体应用法律的若干问题的解答》规定，“在认定是否违背妇女意志时，不能以被害妇女作风好坏来划分。强行与作风不好的妇女发生性行为的，也应定强奸罪。”尽管在该规定中已经出现了排除品性与倾向证据的萌芽，但与英美法系的品性与倾向证据规则仍然相去甚远。

和意见证据规则[3]也不够完善；在司法实践中，证人出庭率非常低，直接言词原则无法得到贯彻，当事人的对质权也无法得到保障。这些证据规则的缺失和不完善，实际上给司法证明留下了很大的规范空白，既无法防止法官对事实认定裁量权的滥用，也无法给法官提供防止外界不当因素干扰的屏障。最终，现有的证据法律制度无法保证事实裁判的作出是理性证据评价的结果，从而为司法行政化（行政命令的干扰）提供了很大的空间，必然会造成冤假错案频发。

与司法行政化相联系的另一个问题是司法腐败。从辽宁高院原院长田凤歧受贿案、广东高院原院长麦崇楷受贿案到湖南高院原院长吴振汉受贿案，再到最高人民法院原副院长黄松有受贿案，司法官员的腐败大大降低了司法的公信力。这些司法腐败案件也昭示着法官职权的滥用，尤其是对审判权力的滥用。作为事实认定者的法官的司法权与行政官员的审批权有着很大的不同，法官的司法权在事实认定阶段主要表现为采纳和排除证据的权力，它总是与滥用纠缠在一起。"例如，一个受贿的法官只要擅自排除一个重要证据，就可以使判决结果发生实质性改变。根据这个特点，司法反腐必须依靠完善的证据制度，用精致的证据规则对事实认定各个环节和法官的司法行为加以规范。"[4] 但遗憾的是，我国证据规则的粗疏为法官滥用事实认定裁量权留下了过大的空间，不足以规制法官的司法行为；从而，也为司法腐败留下了很大的空间。

另外一个证据制度不完善加剧社会失范的例子是，"不得用以证明过错或责任"的这类证据规则的缺位。2011年"小悦悦事件"之后，《中国青年报》社会调查中心曾通过中国网和新浪网做过一个在线民意调查，调查结果显示：造成社会冷漠的首要原因是"'南京彭宇案'等案例暗示公众做好事可能会吃亏（65.7%）"。[5] 彭宇案之所以成为众矢之的，是因为本案的一审法官采用了这样一种常理推断：将"被告把原告扶起并送往医院，且垫付医药费的行为"作为被告应负过错责任的不利证据。[6] 从日常生活经验来说，被告救助被害者并且支付医药费，与被告的侵权事实之间确实存在一定的相关性（尽管这种相关性非常微弱），即：被告积极救助原告并垫付医药费，倾向于支持被告撞倒了原告这一事实主张。从这个角度来看，一审法官的推理尽管过高地评估了基于这种相关性的证据的证明力，但其逻辑并无错误。不过，将被告的救助行为作为对其不利的证据，会带来这样一种后果：降低人们在社会中做出这些行为的动力。因为诸如事后救助及垫付医药费等有益社会的行为，很有可能被作为以后可能提起的诉讼中的不利证据，使自己承担侵权赔偿责任。因此，基于不降低人们从事有益社会之行为的动力的考虑，在英美证据法中存在这样一类规则：事后补救措施、提议和解和谈判、支付医药费用或类似费用、购买责任保险等行为，不得作为证明行为人侵权或应当承担责任的证据使用。这类规则被概括为"不得用以证明过错或责任的

---

〔3〕《最高人民法院、最高人民检察院、公安部、国家安全部和司法部关于办理死刑案件审查判断证据若干问题的规定》（以下简称《死刑案件证据规定》）第8条和第12条，初步建立了最佳证据规则和意见证据规则。

〔4〕张保生："证据制度建设是司法改革首要任务"，载《中国改革》2011年第9期。

〔5〕其他原因还有："社会安全感不够，人们自保心态重"（64.1%）、"现在社会怨气太重，缺少温暖"（49.4%）、"自利主义盛行，人们只关心自己的小利益"（45.1%）、"许多人自身利益常受侵害，无暇顾及他人"（37.2%）等。参见记者向楠："76.3%受访者承认小悦悦的死让自己反思"，载《中国青年报》2011年10月27日，第7版。

〔6〕参见南京市鼓楼区人民法院民事判决书（2007）鼓民一初字第212号。

证据规则”。[7] 该类规则从法律上切断了从行善行为到过错责任的自然推理链条，消除了人们因增加败诉风险而不敢做好事的后顾之忧，从而保护了人们积极从事对社会有益之行为的动机。但中国目前却尚未确立这类规则，所以我们看到彭宇案经过媒体放大之后，给人们相互之间的救助行为带来了抑制效应，加剧了道德滑坡。[8]

从以上分析可以看出，至少对于某些与司法审判紧密相关的社会失范问题而言，中国当前的证据制度并未作出有效回应。而且证据规则的缺位，实际上为社会失范现象提供了空间，加剧了社会失范问题的严重性。因此，本文将基于对证据法运行机制的分析，论证证据法所可能具有的社会控制功能，从而呼吁通过证据立法对某些社会失范现象作出回应，以提供解决这些问题的一个切入点。

二、证据法的规范体系与价值追求

证据法的运行机制实际上是由它的独特规范体系——证据排除规则体系决定的，排除规则决定了证据法的作用方式或者说调整方式。而证据法基于其独特的运行机制所能够发挥的社会控制功能，又取决于证据法的价值追求，因为它是其内在价值目标的客观实现方式。因此，在分析证据法的运行机制和社会控制功能之前，有必要概述其规范体系和价值追求。

（一）证据法的规范体系

因为大陆法系国家并不存在独立的部门法典意义上的证据法，因此，本文在界定证据法的规范体系时将首先以英美证据法为参照，而后再扩展到对大陆法系同类法律规则的概括。英美证据法在很大程度上是英美学者对普通法中零散的证据规则进行融贯性研究和体系化梳理的结果。在经过了几次并不成功的尝试后[9]，现代英美证据法基本上沿袭了19世纪著名证据法学家塞耶（Thayer）所确立的框架。根据塞耶的理论，证据法的规范体系奠定在两项基本原则之上：“（1）逻辑上不相关的或者被认为是不相关的东西不可采，且不存在任何例外；（2）逻辑上相关的东西都可采，但存在许多例外和限制”。[10] 因此，英美证据法实际上主要是各类证据排除规则的集合。正如英美证据法学家塞耶所论述的：

---

〔7〕 这一类规则可见于美国《联邦证据规则》规则407、408、409、411。罗纳德·J. 艾伦将该类证据规则命名为“不得用以证明过错或责任的规则”。参见Ronald J. Allen, Richard B. Kuhns and Eleanor Swift, *Evidence: Text, Problems, and Cases* (5th ed.), New York: Wolters Kluwer Law & Business, 2011, p. 327.

〔8〕 彭宇案经过媒体放大之后产生了三种极其恶劣的影响：其一，它产生了一种阻却人们做好事的效应，它暗示人们做好事可能会吃亏，导致人们因怕掉入陷阱再也不敢做好事。因此，彭宇案之后，全国各地都出现了“老人摔倒无人敢扶，小孩被撞无人敢救，最终因救治不及时而身亡”的现象。其二，这种新的“社会规范”的产生，使得少部分自己摔倒的老人在子女和金钱等压力下，诬告做好事者为肇事者。尽管有部分做好事者因为有证人作证或其善行被公共摄像头等设备记录而得以清白，但仍有部分案件因缺少证人等原因而事实不清。其三，更有甚者利用这种新的“社会规范”来牟利，通过“职业碰瓷”来讹诈好心人。这些现象的出现，进一步恶化了整个社会风气。参见维基百科：http://zh.wikipedia.org/wiki/%E5%8D%97%E4%BA%AC%E5%BD%AD%E5%AE%87%E6%A1%88，访问日期：2013年4月8日。

〔9〕 按照威廉·特文宁教授等人的观点，在英美证据法研究史上曾先后出现过四种具有代表性的为证据规则提供统括性原则的尝试：吉尔伯特的最佳证据规则、边沁的“反规范论”、斯蒂芬的相关性原则、塞耶的可采性原则。参见Terence Anderson, David Schum and William Twining, *Analysis of Evidence* (*Second Edition*), Cambridge University Press, 2005, p. 290.

〔10〕 James Bradley Thayer, *A Preliminary Treatise on Evidence at the Common Law*, Boston: Little Brown, 1898. From Peter Murphy, *Evidence, Proof, and Facts*, Oxford University Press, 2003, pp. 32 ~ 33.

"在现实中，除了逻辑相关性之外，还有其他的可采性检验标准。一些东西因为其意义微乎其微而被排除，或由于具有太多的推测性和遥远的联系而被排除；有些东西因为它们对陪审团有影响而具有危险性，而且可能被那个团体误用或高估而被排除；有些东西，由于不合时宜，或因公共原因不安全而被排除；有些东西，完全是因为没有先例而被排除。正如我前面所说，正是这一类的事情——实际上具有证明力的东西根据这样或者那样的实践理由而被排除——构成了证据法中的典型内容。"[11]

无论是系统编纂的成文证据法典（美国《联邦证据规则》就是一个典范），还是分布在先例中的普通证据法规则，其主要内容都是规范证据的采纳与排除。

以证据排除规则为核心的英美证据法，在大陆法系也是可以找到某些对应物的。观察大陆法系证据制度（一般是作为诉讼法典的章节），也能找到实际上发挥着证据排除功能的规则，如某些证人也享有特免权，[12] 违反法定程序收集的证据不得作为定案根据（在德国被称为证据禁止制度）等。因此有学者指出，将排除规则视为英美证据法的特色，是明显夸大了，"因为排除规则中只有一小部分真正是英美法系所特有的。……为了与事实真相的追求无关的诸多价值而排除有证明力之信息的诸多规则显然不是英美法系所特有的"。[13] 实际上，如果超越英美证据法的语境，从广义的视角观之，证据排除规则在不同法域中是普遍存在的，只是因为程序环境、价值诉求等差异而呈现出不同的特征。如果将司法审判中的事实认定看作一个决策过程，那么允许哪些信息进入决策者的视野就具有了重要意义，而这正是证据排除规则的功能所在。现代的任何法律制度都不会完全放任法庭决策过程，必然会基于各种各样的理由进行适度管制，或多或少、以此种或彼种方式排除证据，预先筛选所输入的信息，[14] 尽管它们可能不将这类规则称为"证据排除规则"。正如罗纳德·J. 艾伦教授所言："任何诉讼或争端解决制度都有大量的排除规则。实际上，所有证据规则和许多程序规则都规定了什么能够在法庭上出示。所有这类规则都区分了什么可采和不可采以及证据排除的可能后果。"[15]

因此，本文在使用证据法这一部门法概念时，指代的是以证据排除规则为核心的

---

〔11〕 James Bradley Thayer, *A Preliminary Treatise on Evidence at the Common Law*, pp. 264～266 (1898). 转引自［美］罗纳德·J. 艾伦等：《证据法：文本、问题和案例》，张保生、王进喜、赵滢译，满运龙校，高等教育出版社 2006 年版，第 148 页。

〔12〕 德国法关于特免权的类似规定参见德国《刑事诉讼法典》第 55 条，类似的规定还存在于奥地利（《刑事诉讼法典》第 152 条）、瑞士的许多自治区以及采用德国民事诉讼和刑事诉讼模式的那些中欧国家。转引自［美］米尔建·R. 达马斯卡：《漂移的证据法》，李学军等译，中国政法大学出版社 2003 年版，第 16 页。

〔13〕 ［美］米尔建·R. 达马斯卡：《漂移的证据法》，李学军等译，中国政法大学出版社 2003 年版，第 16 页。

〔14〕 冯俊伟博士将证据规则定性为"约束裁判信息的程序机制"。参见冯俊伟：《欧盟证据法一体化趋势研究》，中国政法大学出版社 2012 年版。

〔15〕 ［美］罗纳德·J. 艾伦："排除规则的困难"，郑飞、强卉译，张保生校，载《证据科学》2012 年第 6 期。

一系列规范的集合。[16] 虽然主要以英美证据法的体系为参照，但也涵盖了大陆法系中所存在的那些规范证据采纳与排除问题的规则。因此，本文所要分析的也就是以证据排除规则为核心的证据法体系，所具有的独特运行机制与社会控制功能。

（二）证据法的价值追求

与实体法和程序法相比，以排除规则为主体规范的证据法，在调整对象和价值诉求上有所不同。实体法面对的是裁决性风险问题，调整的是公民之间实体权利义务的分配；程序法面对的是参与性风险问题，调整的是诉讼参与人的参与性权利/权力的分配；而证据法则不同，它面对的是信息性风险问题，调整的是诉讼活动中信息性风险的分配。[17] 当然，三者之间也有着紧密的联系：因为实体法是调整公民日常生活中的权利和义务关系的法律，它直接影响和控制着人们的日常行为；而程序法则是规制审判过程和步骤的法律，证据法是规制法庭审判中运用证据进行事实认定的法律，二者结合起来共同调整着审判中诉讼参与人的诉讼行为，而诉讼行为的最终目的又是间接影响和控制人们的日常行为。[18] 因此，只有实体法、程序法和证据法的紧密协作，才能更好地调整社会秩序，实现“通过法律的社会控制”[19]。但在作为社会控制规则系统的法律体系中，证据法基于其规范结构和调整对象的独特性，必然在所追求的价值目标上表现出特殊性。

司法审判的过程分为两个阶段：事实认定和法律适用。而证据法正是规制前一阶段的证据运用和事实认定的法律规范。证据法的首要目标是促进事实真相的发现，即求真；但这不是其唯一目标，它同时还维护着众多的社会普遍价值，即求善。[20] 因此在司法实践中，求真与求善常常具有竞争关系：“求真的目的与其他目的——诸如经济性、保护某些自信、助长某些活动、保护一些宪法规范——相互竞争”[21]。当鱼与熊掌不可兼得时，证据法往往会牺牲求真的目标以追求某种更为重要的善。世界各国的法律和国际公约中有许多证据规则都反映了这种价值权衡：如美国《联邦证据规则》403 规定的一个平衡检验标准，反映了在某种特定情况下，求真的目标将让位于公正、

---

〔16〕 实际上，在英美法的语境中，证据排除规则与证据法也不能完全等同。有些规定排除证据的规则往往被划入实体法或程序法的范围中，如非法证据排除规则、未经开示的证据不得当庭提出的规则等；另一方面，证据法也并非完全局限于排除规则，而是也包含一些其他种类的规则，如关于证明责任和证明标准的规则，关于法官指示的规则等。但英美证据法范围的形成，尤其是其与程序法的分界，实际上有着独特的历史成因。本文不局限于英美证据法语境，因此在使用证据法一词时，指代的是在不同法系可能都存在的那类以规范证据采纳与排除问题为核心的规则，包括在英美法系往往被划入宪法性刑事诉讼法的非法证据排除规则。

〔17〕 See Alex Stein, “Constitutional Evidence Law”, *Vanderbilt Law Review*, Vol. 61, 2008.

〔18〕 关于证据法、程序法和实体法三者之间的关系，以及它们对诉讼行为和日常行为的影响，参见［美］罗纳德·J. 艾伦：“证据法、程序法和实体法的关系”，张保生、张月波和汪诸豪译，载《证据科学》2010 年第 6 期。

〔19〕 “通过法律的社会控制”这一理念的提出，参见［美］罗斯科·庞德：《通过法律的社会控制》，沈宗灵等译，商务印书馆 2010 年版。

〔20〕 以“求真”和“求善”概括证据法的价值选择，并将证据法的价值目标概括为准确、公正、和谐与效率四个价值支柱，参见张保生：“证据规则的价值基础和理论体系”，载《法学研究》2008 年第 2 期。

〔21〕 ［美］波斯纳：《法理学问题》，苏力译，中国政法大学出版社 1994 年版，第 261 页。

效率等价值;[22] 美国诸多特免权规则的设置则是为了保护诸如律师-委托人、医生-患者、牧师-忏悔者、夫妻等被社会珍视的各种特殊社会关系，他们认为通过破坏这些特殊关系而获得查明事实真相的价值，不及牺牲查明事实真相而维护这些关系的价值;[23] 联合国《禁止酷刑公约》第15条的规定反映了在某些情况下，求真的目标应该让位于人权保护这一法治社会的最高价值;[24] 我国新《刑事诉讼法》第195条的规定也反映了在证据不足的情况下，求真的目标将让位于保障人权的"无罪推定原则";[25]《最高人民法院关于民事诉讼证据的若干规定》(以下简称《民事证据规定》)第68条规定的排除规则也同样反映了其他社会价值与求真目标的权衡，[26] 等等。这种有关价值权衡的证据规则不胜枚举，价值选择问题在证据法中几乎是随处可见。正如美国德博拉·琼斯·梅里特(Deborah Jones Merritt)教授所言，整部美国《联邦证据规则》都在试图平衡各种相互竞争的政策(或价值)，[27] 这一点集中体现在规则102所述的美国《联邦证据规则》的立法目的中。[28]

三、证据法运行机制的类型化分析

从上文的分析可以看出，证据法既致力于促进对事实真相的发现，也致力于促进与事实真相发现无关的其他目标：降低司法程序的成本、保护人权、保护某些社会关系、保护隐私权和保护人们做出有益于社会之行为的动机等。相对于发现真相是司法证明程序的直接或内在目的而言，其他目标则是外在于司法证明程序的，因此可以概述为"外部政策"。[29] 那么，证据法又是通过怎样的运行机制来促进对事实真相的发现和对外部政策的保护的呢？在一般的语境中，"运行机制"一词指的是"事物在进行某种具有周而复始形式的运动的过程中，其运动各阶段或者各组成部分之间相互作用的过程、方式和机理，及其在这一过程中所体现出来的规律或原理"。[30] 相应地，在法律语境中，当讨论某一规则体系的运行机制时，也就是在讨论该规则系统的"运动

---

〔22〕 参见美国《联邦证据规则》403："如果相关证据的证明价值为以下一个或者多个危险所严重超过，则法院可以排除该证据：不公平损害、混淆争点或者误导陪审团、不当拖延、浪费时间或者不必要地出示重复证据。"

〔23〕 See John Henry Wigmore, *Evidence* §2285, John T. McNaughton rev. 1961, p. 527.

〔24〕 参见联合国《禁止酷刑公约》第15条："每一缔约国应确保在任何程序中，不得援权业经确定系以酷刑取得的口供为证据，但这类口供可用做被控施酷刑者刑讯逼供的证据。"

〔25〕 参见我国新《刑事诉讼法》第195条："证据不足，不能认定被告人有罪的，应当作出证据不足，指控的犯罪不能成立的无罪判决。"

〔26〕 参见《最高人民法院关于民事诉讼证据的若干规定》第68条："以侵害他人合法权益或者违反法律禁止性规定的方法取得的证据，不能作为认定案件事实的依据。"

〔27〕 See Deborah Jones Merritt, Ric Simmons. Learning Evidence: From the Federal Rules to the Courtroom. Thomson/Reuters, 2009, p. 21. 此外，美国 Alex Stein 也有类似论述，See Alex Stein, *Foundations of Evidence Law*, Oxford University Press, 2005, pp. 25~31.

〔28〕 参见美国《联邦证据规则》规则102："目的"。对本证据规则的解释，应当保证在每个程序中司法公平，消除不合理的耗费与迟延，促进证据法的发展，从而实现查明真相与公正判决之宗旨。

〔29〕 通常，英美学者在概述证据法的价值目标时，"外部政策"一词不包括降低程序成本。例如罗纳德·艾伦将"对证明过程加以管制的正当理由"分为：发现真相、降低成本、保护外部政策。参见[美]罗纳德·J. 艾伦等：《证据法：文本、问题和案例》，张保生、王进喜、赵滢译，满运龙校，高等教育出版社2006年版，第136页。但本文认为，降低效率与保护隐私权、保护人权等目标一样，实际上也并非司法证明程序的直接、内在目的。换言之，它也是外在于发现真相目标的，因此也可以划入外部政策的范畴。

〔30〕 翟继光："论经济法的运行机制"，载《安徽大学法律评论》2005年第5卷第1期。

各阶段或者各组成部分之间相互作用的过程、方式和机理，及其在这一过程中所体现出来的规律或原理”。[31] 因此，证据法的运行机制也就是指它在司法审判事实认定过程中，规制取证、举证、质证和认证等各阶段的证据规则之间相互作用的过程、方式和机理，及其在求真与求善的价值权衡过程中所体现出来的规律或原理。根据证据法发挥规制作用的客观方式的不同，本文将证据法的运行机制区分为证据筛选、举证激励、行为制裁、动机保护等四种基本的运行机制，以及辅助性的证据裁定救济机制。证据法正是通过这些运行机制促进着具体的求真与求善之价值目标，发挥着对社会的控制功能。

（一）证据筛选机制

证据法首先是一种证据信息的过滤、筛选机制。并非所有携带案件信息的潜在证据材料都被允许提交到法庭上，成为事实认定的推论前提。“可采性和证据能力虽然都以鼓励采纳证据为主旨，但它们同时也对证据采纳具有限制功能，起着某种‘过滤器’或‘安全阀’的作用。因此，我们在两大法系都看到一种以排除规则来贯彻可采性和证据能力规则的相似情况。”[32] 携带案件信息的资料具有相关性，能够起到证明案件事实的作用，但一部分这样的资料却被排除规则阻挡在事实认定者进行决策的法庭之外。传闻规则、意见证据规则、品性与倾向证据规则、最佳证据规则（文书原件规则）等都在发挥着这样的功能。之所以对诉讼双方所提交的证据进行预先的筛选，是因为考虑到这些证据的潜在危险性：事实认定者可能被这些证据所误导，过高地评价其证明力；或者，这些证据会引起不公正的偏见。[33] 例如，对于传闻证据而言，由于难以通过交叉询问程序质证，所以很难保证其可信性；对于品性证据而言，用某个人的品格特征证明他在特定场合的行为，证明力很微弱，并且可能带来“坏人”偏见——陪审团可能会仅仅因为某人是“坏人”而惩罚他。此外，美国《联邦证据规则》规则403还赋予了法官排除证据的自由裁量权：“如果相关证据的证明价值为以下一个或者多个危险所严重超过，则法院可以排除该证据：不公平损害、混淆争点或者误导陪审团、不当拖延、浪费时间或者不必要地出示重复证据”。因此，证据排除规则实际上建立起了一种信息隔离机制，将某些被认为具有认知危险性的信息阻隔在事实认定者（尤其是陪审团）的视野之外。这种预先筛选机制在证据法的诸多运行机制中处于核心的地位。通过这样一种预先筛选的方式，证据法致力于优化供法庭决策的信息。

（二）举证激励机制

证据法促进对事实真相的发现，并不仅仅是通过预先筛选证据信息的方式实现的。除了对证据进行预先的过滤筛选，证据法实际上还有激励诉讼双方提交最佳证据的功能。诉讼双方所提交的供法庭决策的证据，应当是最大程度上有利于发现真相的证据，即“最佳证据”。正如18世纪的英国法学家吉尔伯特所言：“有关证据的首要也是最显著的规则是，一个人必须提出事实的性质所能允许的最佳的证据。”[34] 以文书原件规

---

〔31〕 翟继光：“论经济法的运行机制”，载《安徽大学法律评论》2005年第5卷第1期。

〔32〕 张保生主编：《证据法学》，中国政法大学出版社2009年版，第25页。

〔33〕 Lisa Dufraimont, *Evidence Law and the Jury: A Reassessment*, 53 McGill L. J. 199 (2008).

〔34〕 Geoffrey Gilbert, The Law of Evidence, 1754, pp. 3～4. 转引自易延友：“最佳证据规则”，载《比较法研究》2011年第6期。

则为例。为了证明一份文件（如合同）的内容，最佳的证据是这份文件的原件。复印件或者证人的描述（如证人曾看过这份文件，于是该证人在法庭上针对这份文件的内容作证）的证明力相对于原件而言较低。原件被假定为“最佳”，因为它可以减少其他证据的欺诈、错误和疏漏风险。[35] 因此，在证据法中有一条历史悠久的规则：为了证明文书的内容，需要提交该文书原件。[36] 这样一条规则实际上为诉讼双方提供了一种激励机制：胜诉的欲望必然促使诉讼双方提交证据支持己方事实主张，但原件（在美国《联邦证据规则》中还包括例外情形下的复制件）之外的其他证据对于证明文书内容而言，将不被采纳。因此诉讼双方有足够的动因提交原件。除了文书原件规则，传闻规则也体现了激励举证的功能，促使诉讼双方的证人出庭作证。

（三）行为制裁机制

很多情况下，证据法要求排除证据，实际上是提供了一种行为制裁机制：某些诉讼行为因为侵犯了诉讼参与人的权利或者侵害了其他司法政策目标，而被视为“不正当”。因此，需要通过排除证据这种方式对这样的行为施加制裁。这被中国学者总结为“程序性制裁”原理。[37] 通过制裁，证据法提供了反向激励机制。关于排除规则制裁不当诉讼行为，最明显的例子就是非法证据排除规则。[38] 如果警察在收集证据的过程中使用了侵犯宪法权利的手段，那么所获得的证据将被排除。这显然不是为了优化法庭决策的信息，因为通过非法手段获取的证据往往具有很大的证明力。排除非法证据的制度逻辑在于，如果非法获取的证据不具有可采性，那么警察就不会有动力从事非法取证行为，因为它对于控方所追求的诉讼结果来说，不会产生任何收益。对于违法取证行为，当然可以追究行为人的实体责任，如构成刑法上的暴力取证罪等。但如果放任非法取证行为产生其所追求的法律效果，将不足以消除警察实施不当行为的动机。所以，还需要“剥夺违法者违法所得的利益”，“令违法行为不发生预期的法律效果”[39]。排除规则对不当诉讼行为的反向激励功能还可见于民事诉讼中的举证期限规

---

〔35〕 关于最佳证据规则的法理基础，吉尔伯特认为在于防止欺诈，威格摩尔认为，不仅在于防止欺诈，还在于防止不小心导致的错误、遗漏。See John Henry Wigmore, *Evidence in Trials at Common Law*, Revised by Peter Tillers, Vol. IV, Boston: Little Brown and Company, 1983, p. 1180.

〔36〕 在美国《联邦证据规则》（规则 1002）中，文书原件规则被表述为：“除非本法或联邦制定法另有规定，否则，为了证明其内容，必须提交文书、录制品和照片的原件”。基于对现代复印技术的认可，该规则承认了复印件原则上也可采。关于美国《联邦证据规则》2011 年风格重塑后的条文表述及相关分析，参见王进喜：《〈美国联邦证据规则〉（2011 年重塑版）条解》，中国法制出版社 2012 年版。

〔37〕 “所谓‘程序性制裁’，其实是指警察、检察官、法官违反法律程序所要承受的一种程序性法律后果。与那种通过追究办案人员的行政责任、民事责任甚至刑事责任来实施的‘实体性制裁’措施不同，程序性制裁是通过宣告无效的方式来追究程序性违法者的法律责任的。”参见陈瑞华：《刑事诉讼的前沿问题》，中国人民大学出版社 2005 年版，第 288 页。

〔38〕 在美国刑事诉讼中，排除非法证据的依据是被告人的两项宪法权利：宪法第四修正案所规定的免受无理搜查和扣押的权利、宪法第五修正案所规定的免于强迫自证其罪的权利。参见［美］罗纳德·J. 艾伦：“美国证据排除规则”，郑飞、王磊译，载《证据科学》2012 年第 1 期。美国的非法证据排除规则并不规定在《联邦证据规则》中，实际上，非法证据排除规则并不属于英美证据法中的可采性规则，而属于刑事诉讼法中对被告人权利进行保护的规则。参见易延友：《证据法的体系与精神——以英美法为特别参照》，北京大学出版社 2010 年版，第 36 页。但这并不妨碍本文的讨论，因为它仍然属于证据排除规则这个范畴。

〔39〕 参见陈瑞华：《刑事诉讼的前沿问题》，中国人民大学出版社 2005 年版，第 313 页。

定。在民事诉讼中，出于诉讼效率的考虑，当事人超过举证期限提交的证据[40]和违反证据交换规则的证据[41]都将面临被法官排除的风险；而《民事证据规定》第68条所规定的排除规则，则是出于防止以侵害他人合法权益或者违反法律禁止性规定的方法收集证据的考虑。[42]

（四）动机保护机制

有些排除规则意味着“制裁”，但有些排除规则却意味着“保护”，旨在保护行为人从事某些行为的动机。这主要体现在两大类规则上：一类是各种作证特免权规则，另一类是“不得用以证明过错或责任的证据”规则。设置特免权的理由包括两类，一类是传统的功利主义理由，认为特免权主要是用来保护各种职业关系中作出的交流。“这些交流需要由国家政策加以鼓励，否则这些职业关系将不能顺利开展。”[43]威格摩尔是这种观点的积极拥护者。另一类是隐私权保护的理由，“社会中某些秘密性的利益需要用特权加以保护，不管这些特权能否对它所保护的关系中的行为产生影响”[44]。这对于婚内交流特免权、配偶之间的秘密交流特免权有明显的解释力度。不管作何种解释，特免权规则都是一种动机保护机制：如果没有特免权规则，那么人们在建立某种家庭或职业关系的过程中披露给对方的一些个人信息，在日后可能成为法庭上对自己不利的证据；这不仅会降低人们建立这种关系的动机，也会导致人们对已经建立的关系失去信心。对于“不得用以证明过错或责任的证据规则”而言，它最重要的目的在于保护人们积极从事对社会有益之行为的动机。从功利主义的角度来看，之所以排除事后补救措施、提议和解和谈判、支付医疗费和类似费用以及是否购买了责任保险的证据，防止其用来证明行为人有过错或责任，最重要的原因乃是基于“被立法机关或法院视为社会得以存在的原则和标准”[45]之社会政策的考量。因为如果不排除此类证据将有可能暗示人们“做好事可能会吃亏或掉入陷阱”，从而产生一种阻却效应，即人们可能不敢再积极从事这些对社会有益的行为——比如在事故发生后积极采取补救措施促进进一步的安全；在纠纷发生后努力寻求私人和解降低社会成本；在事故发生

---

〔40〕2012年修订的《民事诉讼法》第65条规定：“当事人对自己提出的主张应当及时提供证据。人民法院根据当事人的主张和案件审理情况，确定当事人应当提供的证据及其期限。……当事人逾期提供证据的，人民法院应当责令其说明理由；拒不说明理由或者理由不成立的，人民法院根据不同情形可以不予采纳该证据，或者采纳该证据但予以训诫、罚款。”据此，在民事诉讼中实行的是“证据限时提出主义”，其背后的理由是提高诉讼效率、防止证据偷袭等。当事人超过举证期限提交的证据，可能被法官排除，这是对举证迟延的制裁。参见樊传明：“论证据排除规则的激励功能”，载《证据科学》2013年第1期。

〔41〕最高人民法院2002年4月1日实施的《关于民事诉讼证据的若干规定》第38条规定：“人民法院组织当事人交换证据的，交换证据之日举证期限届满。”因此，在证据交换之日前没有提交的证据可能会因举证期限届满而被排除。通过排除证据的威胁督促当事人交换证据，背后的政策目标包括防止证据偷袭、保障庭审顺利进行、实现当事人阅卷权、增加庭审对抗实质性、提高诉讼效率、促成当事人庭前和解等。参见樊传明：“论证据排除规则的激励功能”，载《证据科学》2013年第1期。

〔42〕最高人民法院2002年4月1日实施的《关于民事诉讼证据的若干规定》第38条规定：“以侵害他人合法权益或者违反法律禁止性规定方法取得的证据，不能作为认定案件事实的依据。”

〔43〕［美］约翰·W. 斯特龙主编：《麦考密克论证据》（第5版），汤维建等译，中国政法大学出版社2003年版，第150页。

〔44〕［美］约翰·W. 斯特龙主编：《麦考密克论证据》（第5版），汤维建等译，中国政法大学出版社2003年版，第150页。

〔45〕Black's Law Dictionary, 8th, Thomson West, 2004, p. 1196.

后积极采取垫付医药费等救助行为，避免受害人遭受进一步的损害；积极购买责任保险以促进社会互助，等等。然而法律并不想担此恶名，因此规定排除此类证据防止其用来证明行为人有过错或责任，从而保护了人们积极从事对社会有益之行为的动机。

（五）证据裁定救济机制

证据筛选、举证激励、行为制裁和动机保护是证据法的四种基本运行机制，但这几种机制的发挥有赖于法官作出采纳或排除证据的裁定。如果法官的裁定是错误的，背离了证据法的精神，那么它将会扭曲这四种机制的良好运行。因此，现代证据法还确立了一种救济机制来纠正法官的错误证据裁定。我们都知道，案件事实是过去发生的，它具有不可逆性；而事实认定者又不具有亲身知识，因此他只能通过“证据之镜”去努力“折射”（还原）出案件事实，但证据又常常是不完整的，这就导致了对事实的逆向认知具有很大的模糊性和不准确性;〔46〕加之司法审判具有很高的时效性，要求必须在规定诉讼期间作出事实认定裁判，故而，司法审判中的事实认定必然存在着错误风险。如果司法实践中发生了错误事实认定，那么证据法又如何对错误事实认定进行救济呢？这主要通过“错误裁定后果规则”来实现，即法官采纳或排除证据的裁定，如果使当事人的实质权利受到影响，就属于错误裁定，它将成为一种法定的上诉理由。这在美国被称为“为上诉之错误保全”或“为上诉而保全证据争点”。〔47〕尤其是排除证据的错误裁定，属于一种适用法律错误，上诉法院可以撤销原判、发回重审。但是，证据法的这种救济机制要想得到实现，还必须建立和完善认证理由公开制度，要求法院的“判决书、裁定书中应当写明诉讼各方对证据提出的异议，以及审判人员予以支持或者驳回的认证及理由”〔48〕。只有法官的认证理由公开，当事人才能知晓法官对证据的采纳或排除是否存在错误，才能保证该错误裁定后果规则在司法实践中不被架空，以达到救济错误事实认定的最终目的。

四、通过证据法的社会控制

综上，以证据排除规则为核心的证据法拥有证据筛选、举证激励、行为制裁和动机保护等四种基本的运行机制，以及辅助性的证据裁定救济机制。正是通过这些机制的有效运行，证据法才能在其价值追求的引导下，发挥对社会的良好控制功能。证据法对社会的控制功能可以区分为两个不同的方面。首先，证据法直接规制司法审判中的事实认定活动，因此对于诉讼中的参与主体（法官和控辩双方）有直接的约束力，对于诉讼活动所直接涉及的社会利益关系具有调节作用。这是证据法的直接社会控制功能，包括降低错案风险、抑制司法腐败、保障被追诉者人权等。其次，证据法作为

---

〔46〕关于“证据之镜原理”的详细阐述，请参见张保生主编：《证据法学》，中国政法大学出版社2009年版，第15～16页。

〔47〕“为上诉之错误保全”或“为上诉而保全证据争点”体现在美国《联邦证据规则》103。参见［美］罗纳德·J. 艾伦等：《证据法：文本、问题和案例》，张保生、王进喜、赵滢译，满运龙校，高等教育出版社2006年版，第123～125页。

〔48〕具体内容请参见《人民法院统一证据规定》司法解释建议稿第10条（证据认证理由的说明）。（张保生主编：《〈人民法院统一证据规定〉司法解释建议稿及论证》，中国政法大学出版社2008年版）；另参见最高人民法院《关于民事诉讼证据的若干规定》第79条：“人民法院应当在裁判文书中阐明证据是否采纳的理由。对当事人无争议的证据，是否采纳的理由可以不在裁判文书中表述。”最高人民法院《关于行政诉讼证据若干问题的规定》第72条：“……人民法院应当在裁判文书中阐明证据是否采纳的理由。”

一种行为激励机制，它所带来的行为调节作用不限于诉讼过程中，而且还借助诉讼中的事实认定程序这样一个“杠杆”，对诉讼外的社会关系和行为具有调控作用。这是证据法的间接社会控制功能，包括保护社会关系、增进社会福利等。当然，证据法作为一个以排除规则为核心的法律规范体系，在发挥社会控制功能方面并不是万能的。因此，本文将分析指出，证据法可以通过它的直接控制功能和间接控制功能，推动解决我国当下社会中的某些社会失范问题。

（一）直接控制功能

1. 降低错案风险

根据上文的分析，证据法通过两种运行机制促进事实认定的准确性：一方面，通过信息筛选机制，对法官或陪审团所能够接触到的证据进行预先的筛选，将可能被高估证明力或者引起不公正偏见的材料排除。这在客观上优化了法庭决策信息。另一方面，通过举证激励机制，对作为证据搜集和提交主体的诉讼双方提供激励。某些证据因为对于发现案件事实而言并非最佳证据，因此法律将它们排除，从而促使诉讼双方搜集并提交更有利于证明案件事实的证据。证据筛选机制着眼于排除规则对事实认定者的直接影响；而举证激励机制则着眼于对诉讼双方的直接影响，进而间接影响到事实认定者，因为诉讼双方的举证是为事实认定者提供据以裁决的信息。

通过这两种机制，证据法促进了事实认定的准确性。当然，基于司法证明的认识论性质，对案件事实的认定无法达到百分之百的准确性。因为“事实认定是一个概率推论过程，所得到的‘思想产品’是概率真理，达不到绝对的确定性，却存在着出错的巨大危险性。”[49] 但是，证据筛选机制和举证激励机制，提高了决策信息的质量，为事实认定者的裁判活动提供了信息上的保障。因此，客观上具有降低事实认定错误风险的功能，对于防范刑事冤案具有重要意义。尤其是在刑事诉讼中，证据法在理论上区分了两种错案：一是错判有罪（将无辜者定罪），二是错判无罪（将有罪者释放）。“从一项法律推理的结果来看，如果对无罪者治罪就等于经济成本加上道德成本，其成本更高；而如果是未对有罪者治罪只等于经济成本。”[50] 所以，证据法尤其偏重于降低错判有罪（即刑事冤案）的风险。这不仅仅体现在刑事诉讼的控方需要承担将犯罪事实证明到“排除合理怀疑”或者“确信无疑”的高度标准，[51] 也体现在许多排除规则在宗旨上更倾向于保护刑事被告，提高定罪的难度。例如，传闻规则在当代的理论基础之一就是被告人对质权，[52] 它要求指控被告的证人必须到庭接受交叉询问。

〔49〕 张保生：“刑事错案及其纠错制度的证据分析”，载《中国法学》2013年第1期。

〔50〕 参见［美］迈克尔·D. 贝勒斯：《法律的原则》，张文显、宋金娜、朱卫国、黄文艺译，中国大百科全书出版社1996年版，第29、32页。转引自张保生：“刑事错案及其纠错制度的证据分析”，载《中国法学》2013年第1期。

〔51〕 “排除合理怀疑”是英美法系的刑事诉讼有罪证明标准；“确信无疑”是大陆法系的刑事诉讼有罪证明标准。

〔52〕 依据美国宪法第六修正案，在所有的刑事起诉中，被告人应当有权同反对他的证人对质。但联邦最高法院并没有对此做极端的解释，而是认为“对质条款禁止使用某些而不是全部传闻证据来反对刑事被告人”。“大多数立法者、法院、律师和评论者都赞同，刑事被告人在人身自由方面的权益分量更重一些，因而要求检控方提供当场证人。”参见［美］罗纳德·J. 艾伦等：《证据法：文本、问题和案例》（第3版），张保生、王进喜等译，高等教育出版社2006年版，第659、681页。

这是实现被告方弹劾控方证人的重要保障。再比如，品性证据规则是为了防止“坏人”偏见，而这一“坏人”偏见最容易出现在刑事被告身上。因此，很多排除规则看似给控辩双方提供了平等的对抗制武装，但实际上在价值上和实际功能上更倾向于保护被告。进而，尤为强调降低错判有罪的风险，以防止刑事冤假错案的产生。

2. 抑制司法腐败

祛除司法行政化以保持法院和法官的司法独立固然是司法公正得以实现的重要保障，但是权力天生就容易被滥用。只呼吁司法独立和自由裁量而不讲对司法权的约束，实际上会加大司法腐败的风险。因此，必须设置合理的规则，在保障法官独立裁判和自由裁量的同时，还需防止和纠正法官对司法裁判权的滥用。根据上文对社会失范现象的描述，经常滋生司法腐败的一个领域就是法官对证据的排除——通过不正当地排除证据而交换贪腐利益。[53] 因此有必要对法官排除证据的自由裁量权进行合理的规制，以防止司法腐败和司法不公的产生。

张保生教授认为，证据制度预防司法腐败和司法不公的功能，主要是依靠上文所述的“错误裁定后果规则”来实现的。[54] 但与美国“错误裁定后果规则”相比，目前中国的上级法院往往忽视审查下级法院采纳或排除证据方面的错误，致使一些法官在判决书中随意或恣意排除证据或不排除非法证据，甚至在逻辑上错误百出，上诉法院却视而不见；更有甚者在判决书中直接有意无意地忽略当事人在庭审中提出的证据或者证据异议。这种自由裁量权不受约束的滥用，是产生司法腐败和司法不公的主要原因之一。因此，《非法证据排除规则》、新《刑事诉讼法》和刚刚出台的《最高人民法院关于适用〈中华人民共和国刑事诉讼法〉的解释》（以下简称新《刑事诉讼法解释》）第 101 条初步建立了有关“错误裁定后果”的证据规则：对一审没有审查排除非法证据的申请且该证据作为定案依据的，以及诉讼双方不服一审有关证据收集合法性的调查结论等情形，都可以作为抗诉和上诉的理由，二审法院应当对证据收集的合法性进行审查。但这一规定与美国“错误裁定后果规则”相比还十分不完善，例如对法官在判决书中没有对当事人在庭审中提出的证据或证据异议作任何分析处理的情况，我国法律就没有十分明确的规定。此外，正如上文所述，该规定要想实现在赋予法官采纳和排除证据权力的同时，为其施加必要的义务，避免法官在证据排除规则的运用中滥用自由裁量权的目的，还必须建立和完善认证理由公开制度。因为“法官必须为排除证据的认证提供法律理由和正当理由，这是证据法治的本义，也是法官必须履行的一项强制性义务，逃避这种义务就会导致司法腐败。”[55] 而认证理由公开制度最重要的功能在于它能够保障当事人对采纳或排除证据的错误裁定的上诉权，保证错误裁定后果规则在司法实践中不被架空，从而激励法官细致、认真和公正地审理案件，达

---

〔53〕 笔者从参与的几个案件中发现：因为我国的实体法逐渐完善，所以法官在接到上级的不当指示或受到外部的不当干扰后，一般都很难在实体法的适用范围内将“黑的写成白的”，于是就只能打事实认定的主意，通过混淆事实的方式（例如，在判决书中直接有意无意地忽略当事人在庭审中提出的证据或者证据异议）来完成领导指示或达到外部干扰因素的要求。

〔54〕 张保生：“证据制度建设是司法改革的首要任务”，载常林、张中主编《证据理论与科学——第三届国际研讨会论文集》，中国政法大学出版社 2012 年版，第 14 页。

〔55〕 张保生：“证据制度建设是司法改革首要任务”，载《中国改革》2011 年第 9 期。

到排除非法证据、遏制刑讯逼供和保障人权等立法目的。

3. 保障被追诉者人权

证据法通过规制刑事追诉权（侦查权和检察权）以保障被追诉者的人权，这主要是通过非法证据排除规则这种行为制裁机制来实现的。“警察向来以破案为首要目标，为防止警方不择手段取得证据，法律上可以采取多种手段来吓阻。但司法实践表明，从程序上排除非法证据的使用，最能发挥功效。非法证据可以被采纳，是警察甘愿冒险进行违法取证的最大诱因，而非法证据的排除，则把其违法的成本上升到最大。如果警察通过违法搜查、扣押获得的证据若最终被法院排除，警察违法取证就没有任何意义，徒浪费时间与人力。”[56] 非法证据排除规则对于中国来说是个舶来品，从2010年《非法证据排除规定》在中国正式确立非法证据排除规则以来，其实施效果并不理想，并未达到抑制侦查权和检察权对公民权利的侵害的立法初衷，主要表现在三个方面：其一，在许多案件中，即使有证据证明存在刑讯逼供，法院也最终没有启动非法证据排除程序，这在涉嫌组织、领导黑社会性质组织罪的樊奇航一案中表现得淋漓尽致；其二，部分案件虽然启动了非法证据排除程序，但侦查人员很少出庭作证，而且很少排除涉嫌非法取证的证据；其三，即使在非法证据排除程序中排除了部分证据，最终也因为诸多外部因素的影响而很少作出无罪判决。[57] 由此可见，非法证据至今仍难以在我国司法审判实践中被排除，它无法对警察的违法取证起到吓阻作用，因此刑讯逼供现象依然没有得到明显改善。那为什么舶来的非法证据排除规则能够在国外很好地规制侦查权和检察权对公民权利的侵犯，而在中国却仍然仅仅是停留在纸面上的法律呢？除了中国非法证据规则自身存在的诸多内部缺陷——比如补正问题、侦查人员出庭作证问题和非法证据排除的波及效力问题等[58] ——的原因之外，外部运行环境问题也是制约中国非法证据排除规则实施效果的主要原因。尽管新《刑事诉讼法》和新《刑事诉讼法解释》已经修正了该规则的部分内部结构问题，但未来如果不对司法证明模式、司法体制和社会民众理念等外部运行环境因素进行相应地改革，那么舶来的非法证据排除规则将很难在中国生根发芽，[59] 非法证据排除规则抑制侦查权和检察权对公民权利的侵犯的功能也注定将得不到彰显。

（二）间接控制功能

证据法的社会控制功能不仅直接体现在对诉讼中的主体行为和社会关系的调控和约束上，而且还体现在它可以通过对诉讼案件的直接规制而间接作用于诉讼外的日常行为和社会关系。证据法的间接社会控制功能主要是通过上文所分析的动机保护机制来实现的。

1. 保护社会关系

在证据法中，大多数证据规则和证据原则的主要目标都是为了促进事实真相的发

---

〔56〕 张保生主编：《证据法学》，中国政法大学出版社2009年版，第274页

〔57〕 关于这三种情形的实证分析，参见郑飞、樊传明：“论中国非法证据排除规则的未来——以内部结构和运行环境为切入点”，载《西北大学学报（哲学社会科学版）》2013年第4期。

〔58〕 关于非法证据排除规则的内部结构问题，参见郑飞、樊传明：“论中国非法证据排除规则的未来——以内部结构和运行环境为切入点”，载《西北大学学报（哲学社会科学版）》2013年第4期。

〔59〕 参见郑飞、樊传明：“论中国非法证据排除规则的未来——以内部结构和运行环境为切入点”，载《西北大学学报（哲学社会科学版）》2013年第4期。

现，“但创设证据特免权的规则与此不同。从总体上看，它们排除具有相关性的证据，这是为了促进与准确事实认定无关的外部政策。它们的主要目的，是保护法庭世界之外的特定关系和利益，这些关系和利益被认为具有充分的重要性，值得司法程序以失去有用证据的方式来承担这些成本”〔60〕。例如，家庭关系尤其是近亲属之间的关系，对于一个人的生活是至关重要的。但假如某人涉嫌犯罪，而他或她的配偶、父母、子女等知道某些案件信息，于是出庭作证指控他或她。那么，必然导致对家庭关系的极大破坏。因此，夫妻特免权、父母—子女特免权规则要求排除配偶或父母、子女的不利证言，以保护这几类近亲属关系。值得一提的是，中国 2012 年修改的《刑事诉讼法》第 188 条规定：“经人民法院通知，证人没有正当理由不出庭作证的，人民法院可以强制其到庭，但是被告人的配偶、父母、子女除外”。该条规定了配偶、父母、子女可以免于强制出庭作证，虽然与特免权规则还有很大差距，但在价值取向和功能上类似于近亲属之间的作证特免权规则，有利于对这些社会关系的保护。除了近亲属之间的特免权，“律师—委托人”〔61〕和“医生—患者”特免权等也同样是在保护某些特定的社会关系。它们主要是保护特定职业关系中的秘密交流，“这些交流需要由国家政策加以鼓励，否则这些职业关系将不能顺利开展”〔62〕。

2. 增进社会福利

前文分析已经阐明，正是因为我国没有移植不得用以证明过错与责任的证据规则，才导致彭宇案中的一审法官将“被告把原告扶起并送往医院，且垫付医药费的行为”作为认定彭宇对该事故负有过错责任的不利证据；也正是因为这种从行善行为到过错责任的自然推理链条，导致了人们因害怕自己吃亏或落入陷阱而不敢再积极从事有益于社会的行为，从而使得整个社会的公德进一步恶化。而美国不得用以证明过错或责任的证据规则，则“通过切断这些善意行为与行为责任之间的因果关系，使行为者无需担心自己的善意行为被反过来成为自己承担责任的陷阱，在行善之时也就无需瞻前顾后，”〔63〕从而激励人们敢于积极从事对社会有益的行为，使得美国整个社会也因此受益。但在我国，彭宇案的自然推理链条和价值权衡已经形成了一种不良的“社会规范”，导致社会更加冷漠，使得“老人摔倒无人敢扶，小孩被撞无人敢救，最终因救治不及时而身亡”的现象更加普遍。面对岌岌可危的社会公德，我国毋庸置疑应该尽快移植此类规则，充分发挥证据法对社会道德的正确引导作用，从而促进整个社会道德风尚向有益于全社会的方向发展。但遗憾的是，“调解优先”的司法政策导致彭宇案的

---

〔60〕 Allen, Ronald J., Kuhns, Richard B., Eleanor Swift, and Schwartz, David S., Pardo, Michael S., *Evidence, Text, Problems, and Cases*, New York: Wolters Kluwer Law & Business, 2011. p. 793.

〔61〕 中国《律师法》和《刑事诉讼法》也初步确立了律师—委托人特免权。参见《中华人民共和国律师法》第 38 条：“律师对在执业活动中知悉的委托人和其他人不愿泄露的有关情况和信息，应当予以保密。但是，委托人或者其他人准备或者正在实施危害国家安全、公共安全以及严重危害他人人身安全的犯罪事实和信息除外。”《中华人民共和国刑事诉讼法》第 46 条：“辩护律师对在执业活动中知悉的委托人的有关情况和信息，有权予以保密。但是，辩护律师在执业活动中知悉委托人或者其他人，准备或者正在实施危害国家安全、公共安全以及严重危害他人人身安全的犯罪的，应当及时告知司法机关。”

〔62〕［美］约翰·W. 斯特龙主编：《麦考密克论证据》（第 5 版），汤维建等译，中国政法大学出版社 2003 年版，第 150 页。

〔63〕 吴洪淇：“挽救社会公德法律亦有可为”，载《法制日报》2011 年 10 月 12 日，第 10 版。

二审最后以秘密和解撤诉告终，而没有通过正式判决的方式对一审法院这种有违道德原则和公正原则的所谓“常理推断”作出明确否定。因此，我们应该改变“调解优先”的司法政策，恢复法院应有的审判角色，让证据规则的激励机制能够通过司法审判的方式得以有效发挥，并通过司法审判活动的教育示范功能来改变人们“打官司就是打关系”的观念，从而在社会上树立起“打官司就是打证据”的理念，进而影响人们的日常行为。

五、结语：认真对待证据法

我国冤假错案频发，司法腐败严重，社会公德丧失等社会失范现象，呼唤法律制度特别是证据制度改革能够对此作出必要的回应。但目前我国证据制度中的规则缺位，不仅导致其难以很好地回应这些社会失范问题，甚至还加剧了事态的严重性。作为规制司法审判事实认定过程的证据法，应当具备促进事实真相发现和维护社会普遍价值的双重功能。正是在求真与求善的价值权衡过程中，证据法对于解决中国的某些社会失范现象将有所助力。因为通过证据筛选、举证激励、行为制裁和动机保护等四种基本的运行机制，以及辅助性的证据裁定救济机制，证据法能够发挥降低错案风险、抑制司法腐败和保障被追诉者人权的直接社会控制功能，以及保护社会关系和增进社会福利的间接社会控制功能。因此，完善的证据制度将有助于解决我国当下社会中那些因为证据规则缺位和不完善而造成的司法不公、司法腐败和社会公德丧失等社会失范问题。

然而，当前我国对证据制度建设却缺乏统一系统的规划，这导致了法律制度特别是证据制度无法对以上这些社会失范问题作出有效的回应，致使这些社会失范现象存在进一步恶化的趋势。因此，我们必须认真对待证据法，必须进一步改革和完善我国的证据制度，以增强法律制度对社会失范现象的社会控制。当然，关于具体如何完善我国的证据制度，是分别完善三大诉讼证据制度；还是从完善三大诉讼证据制度的宏观视角去构建我国统一的证据制度，这又是另外一个非常重要而宏大的问题了。它已经超出了本文的写作范围，需要我国证据法学界同仁的共同努力才能实现。

新法定证据主义

——一种以限制证据证明力为核心的证据理念

陈瑞华 *

一、引　言

从比较法和法律史的角度来看，刑事诉讼中的证明制度曾先后出现过法定证据和自由心证两种模式。一般认为，法定证据制度曾长期存在于中世纪欧洲各国法律之中，它建立在纠问式诉讼制度的基础之上，使法官同时行使刑事追诉和司法裁判的职能，不承认被告人的诉讼主体地位，将被告人口供奉为证据之王，承认酷刑取证的合法性。[1] 在法定证据制度下，每一种证据的证明价值都是由法律明文确定的，法官没有自由评判的自由，也不能根据其内心确信和良知意识作出认定。刑事案件只要存在那种"符合法定证明力要求"的证据，法官即应作出有罪判决。[2]

随着纠问式诉讼制度逐渐退出历史舞台，法定证据制度也最终受到抛弃，取而代之的是自由心证的证据制度。根据这一制度，对于证据的证明力或证据价值问题，法律不作任何限制性的规定，而由法官、陪审员根据经验、理性和良心，进行自由评价和判断。[3] 自由心证所适用的对象是证据的证明力问题，而不是证据能力问题。当然，自由心证原则也有一些例外。

我国法学界对于法定证据制度基本上持否定的态度，认为这一制度对证据的证明力作出了不科学的限制，是非理性的；这一制度将口供视为证据之王，认同酷刑取证的合法性，因此也是不人道的。但是，围绕着自由心证应否成为我国证据法基本原则的问题，法学界却存在着激烈的争论。无论是赞同者还是反对者，几乎都从应然的角度，对自由心证及其所蕴含的证明方式进行了价值评价，也对中国未来的证据立法提出了理论构想。例如，一些学者在承认这一原则"历史进步意义"的同时，也认为自由心证为法官的主观擅断打开了方便之门，在认识论上具有明显的局限性。[4] 也有一些学者出于澄清自由心证真实含义的考虑，从比较法上对这一原则的制度制约机制进行了全面的分析，认为这一原则与法官独立审判机制有着密切的关系，与直接和言词原则的贯彻不可分割，而诸如较为发达的证据能力规则的确立、裁判理由充分说明以

---

* 陈瑞华，法学博士、北京大学法学院教授、教育部长江学者奖励计划特聘教授。

〔1〕 参见［法］卡斯东·斯特法尼等：《法国刑事诉讼法精义（上）》，罗结珍译，中国政法大学出版社1998年版，第75页以下。

〔2〕 参见［法］贝尔纳·布洛克：《法国刑事诉讼法》，罗结珍译，中国政法大学出版社2008年版，第79页。

〔3〕 参见［美］弗洛伊德·菲尼、［德］约阿希姆·赫尔曼、岳礼玲：《一个案例 两种制度——美德刑事司法比较》，郭志媛译，中国法制出版社2006年版，第350页。

〔4〕 参见樊崇义主编：《证据法学》，法律出版社2001年版，第36页以下。

及上诉审机制的相对完善等，则构成了保障自由心证原则正常运转的制度前提。而在中国尚未建立这些制度制约机制的情况下，确立自由心证原则可能会带来一些新的问题。〔5〕还有些学者将证明制度划分为“法定证明模式”和“自由证明模式”，认为我国现行法律规定的证据制度属于自由证明制度，鉴于目前法官的总体素质不容乐观，而且这一现状不可能在短时间内得到改善，因此，未来中国的证据制度应当确立“以法定证明为主、以自由证明为辅”的模式。〔6〕

在这种以价值评判和制度构建为主的应然研究之外，法学界也对我国现行的证明制度进行了经验研究。有学者将中国的刑事诉讼证明模式概括为“印证证明模式”，认为这一证明模式仍然属于“自由心证体系”，属于自由心证的一种“亚类型”。但与自由心证不同的是，这一模式注重证据之间的相互印证，强调对犯罪事实的证明需要达到最高的证明标准。〔7〕也有学者对法学界普遍反对证明力规则的现象进行了反思，强调证明力规则在中国诉讼制度中具有一定的合理性。我们与其断然否定证明力规则的正当性，倒不如从证据立法的现实出发，认真分析这些规则出现的原因和背景。〔8〕

随着我国最高司法机关相继确立旨在规范证据审查判断的规则，也随着诉讼制度的逐步完善，我国初步结束了在证据运用领域无法可依的局面。尤其是2012年颁布实施的两个刑事证据规定〔9〕，更是确立了大量的排除性规则，其中很多可以被归入“非法证据排除规则”的范畴。与此同时，这两部证据规定也确立了不少旨在限制各类证据证明力的规则。无论是在对物证、书证、视听资料、电子证据的审查过程中，还是在对证人证言、被告人供述、鉴定意见、勘验检查笔录、辨认笔录的评判过程中，两个证据规定都对法官提出了审查证据证明力的具体要求和方法。而对于证人证言出现自相矛盾、被告人供述出现翻供的情况，证据规定也确立了具体的采信标准。与此同时，对于原始证据与传来证据、直接证据与间接证据的证明力问题，两个证据规定也建立了一般性的采信规则。这显示出，在对单个证据的证明力大小强弱做出评价的问题上，两个证据规定设定了明确的限制性规则。不仅如此，对于何谓“事实清楚、证据确实、充分”的证明标准，对于只有间接证据的案件如何认定被告人达到有罪的标准，以及对于被告人有罪供述的补强等问题，两个证据规定也做出了明确的规定。〔10〕这也足以说明，在对全部证据是否形成“完整的证明体系”的问题上，两个证据规定也确立了旨在限制证明力评判的规则。而这些旨在规范法官认定案件事实的“法定证明标准”，在立法部门2012年通过的刑事诉讼法中又得到了明确的强调。

在此之前，一些高级法院曾颁行过地方性证据规则，最高法院也曾就民事证据和

---

〔5〕参见王亚新：“刑事关于自由心证原则历史和现状的比较法研究——刑事诉讼中发现案件真相与抑制主观随意性的问题”，载《比较法研究》1993年第2期。

〔6〕参见何家弘、刘品新：《证据法学》，法律出版社2004年版，第92页以下。

〔7〕参见龙宗智：“印证与自由心证——我国刑事诉讼证明模式”，载《法学研究》2004年第2期。

〔8〕参见李训虎：“证明力规则检讨”，载《法学研究》2010年第2期。

〔9〕2010年6月，最高人民法院、最高人民检察院、公安部、国家安全部、司法部联合发布了《关于办理死刑案件审查判断证据若干问题的规定》和《关于办理刑事案件排除非法证据若干问题的规定》。对这两个证据规定的权威解释，可参见张军主编：《刑事证据规则理解与适用》，法律出版社2010年版，第1页以下。

〔10〕对于上述问题的分析，可参见陈瑞华：《刑事证据法学》，北京大学出版社2012年版，第163、165、182、254、334页。

行政诉讼证据的审查判断问题颁行过具有司法解释效力的证据规则，而这些证据规则也对各类证据的证明力大小强弱作出了一系列的规定。因此，我们据此可以断定，两个证据规定对证据的证明力所作的法律限制，延续了中国证据立法的传统。而这种以限制证据的证明力为核心的理念，在相当长的时间内一直影响着中国的证据立法，并逐渐成为支撑中国证据立法的指导性原则。

本文认为，中国证据立法遵循了一种以限制证据的证明力为核心的基本理念，也就是“新法定证据主义”的理念。本文拟通过与法定证据制度和自由心证制度的比较分析，界定“新法定证据主义”的基本内涵，分析这一证据理念出现的原因，讨论这一证据理念的利弊得失，并对这一立法理念的未来走向作出评估。在笔者看来，“新法定证据主义”作为一种对中国证据立法理念的总结，对证据立法和司法实践中的很多问题具有一定的解释力。假如我们抛弃泛政治主义和泛道德主义的立场，而以社会科学的方法研究证据问题的话，那么，对“新法定证据主义”的全面清理，将是绕不开的理论课题。

二、新法定证据主义的基本特征

根据现代证据法的基本假定，证据法所要规范的主要是证据的法律资格和司法证明的基本方式，而对于单个证据的证明力大小强弱以及法官对案件事实内心确信的标准，法律则一般不作限制性的规定，而交由法官进行自由评判。法官根据自己通过法庭审理所形成的直观印象，根据经验、理性和良心，来对证据的证明力和案件事实作出裁判。这也就是一般意义上的自由心证原则。[11]

但是，中国证据法在规范证据的法律资格并构建各种证据排除规则的同时，还对证据的证明力问题作出了明确的法律限制。一方面，几乎所有证据规则都对单个证据的证明力大小强弱作出了区分，甚至在证明同一案件事实的不同证据出现矛盾的情况下，还就不同种类证据的证明力确立了优先采信的标准。另一方面，证据规则还对法官对案件事实的内心确信确立了明确、具体的标准，特别是在刑事证据规则中，对于何谓“事实清楚”、“证据确实、充分”、“证据不足”甚至“仅仅依据间接证据如何定案”等问题，都作出了近乎繁琐的规定。这充分显示出，中国证据法不仅仅满足于对证据法律资格的规范和限制，而且还对单个证据的证明力和案件证据的综合评判都确立了明确的限制性规则。这说明，中国证据法所确立的并不是真正意义上的自由心证原则，而是带有法定证据制度色彩的特殊证据制度。

当然，将中国的证据制度称为“法定证据制度”，这也是不符合客观情况的。尤其是在中国的刑事诉讼制度中，司法与行政相分离，国家追诉犯罪的职能与司法裁判职能发生了分离，被告人具有当事人地位，可以在律师帮助下行使辩护职能。刑事诉讼的整体构造已经与纠问制不可同日而语了。与此同时，被告人有罪供述已经不再被视为证据之王，而是一种受到严格法律限制的普通证据。没有口供，其他证据确实充分的，可以对被告人定罪；只有被告人供述，没有其他证据的，不得对被告人定罪。这种口供补强规则的确立，显示出对被告人供述的慎重使用态度。不仅如此，法律严禁刑讯逼供和以威胁、引诱、欺骗等非法手段获取证据，对于通过刑讯逼供等非法手段

〔11〕 参见［德］罗科信：《刑事诉讼法》，吴丽琪译，法律出版社2003年版，第117页以下。

所获取的被告人有罪供述，法院应当作出“强制性的排除”。[12] 这种非法证据排除规则的确立，也显示出对被告人供述进行合法取证的重要性。凡此种种，都说明那种与纠问制相伴而生的法定证据制度，已经不可能确立在中国刑事证据法之中了。

欧洲中世纪的法定证据制度已经成为历史，但是，其作为一种旨在对证据的证明力作出法律限制的立法理念，却并没有完全消失。按照通常的看法，即便在当代大陆法国家的证据制度中，那种针对被告人口供所确立的补强规则，以及那种“疑问时做有利于被告人的推定”的法律要求，在一定程度上体现了法定证据主义的理念，成为自由心证原则的例外。[13] 但是，尽管存在着这些法定证据制度的残余物，我们仍然将大陆法系国家的证据制度称为“自由心证制度”。这是因为，大陆法系国家的证据规则并不对证据的证明力大小强弱作出明确的法律限制，对于法官对犯罪事实的“内心确信无疑”也不设定明确的标准。对于这些证明力领域的事项，大陆法系国家的证据法都交由法官进行自由判断。

中国证据法的情况就完全不同了。在确立疑罪从无、口供补强等规则方面，中国证据法与大陆法系国家的证据法尽管大体是一致的，但是，由于存在着对单个证据证明力的普遍法律限制，也由于存在着对案件事实认定标准的一般法律规则，因此，我们认为中国证据立法贯彻了一种带有法定证据制度色彩的理念。为了与欧洲中世纪曾普遍实行的法定证据制度进行区分，我们将这种旨在限制证明力的证据立法理念，称为“新法定证据主义”。当然，这里所说的“新法定证据主义”，属于一种对中国证据制度进行类型化分析的理论总结，它并不必然与那些重视口供、允许刑讯逼供的纠问式诉讼制度具有必然的联系。假如我们不再持一种泛政治化或泛道德化的立场，那么，从中国证据法对证明力的法律限制这一角度来看，用“新法定证据主义”来概括这种证据立法理念，或许是既直观形象而又准确贴切的。

那么，作为一种证据立法理念，“新法定证据主义”究竟具有哪些基本特征呢？在以下的讨论中，笔者将结合近年来中国证据立法的发展情况，以最高法院颁布的证据规则以及立法机关通过的法律为样本，对这一证据立法理念作出简要的实证分析。笔者所要解释的主要是新法定证据主义理念的特征，至于这一理念对司法实践的影响，则不是本文所要讨论的主要问题。

（一）对不同证据证明力的区分

本来，根据自由心证原则，法律不应对不同证据证明力大小强弱作出限制和约束，而应交由法官根据庭审中所形成的印象作出自由评价。当然，根据经验法则，法官可以根据案件的具体情况，对不同证据的证明力作出一定的区分，这是无可厚非的，也属于法官行使自由裁量权的内在应有之义。但是，中国证据法却对不同证据的证明力明确确定了大小强弱的标准，并使之上升到法律规范的层次，使之具有普遍的法律效力。这与法定证据制度下将不同证据的证明力区分为三六九等的情况，就具有了一定的相似性。例如，在法定证据制度下，被告人自白的证明力要明显大于证人证言；两

---

〔12〕 关于中国的非法证据排除规则，可参见陈瑞华：“非法证据排除规则的中国模式”，载《中国法学》2010 年第 6 期。

〔13〕 参见宋冰编：《读本：美国与德国的司法制度及司法程序》，中国政法大学出版社 1998 年版，第 377 页。

份证人证言的证明力要大于一份证人证言；间接证据的证明力要小于直接证据。

中国现行的证据规则尽管并不推崇被告人供述的证明力，也没有将不同证据的证明力作出数量化的区分，却对不同证据的证明力确定了优先顺序。例如，根据2001年最高法院有关民事证据问题的司法解释〔14〕，“原始证据的证明力一般大于传来证据”；“直接证据的证明力一般大于间接证据”。而根据该法院次年就行政诉讼中证据运用问题所作的司法解释〔15〕，“国家机关以及其他职能部门依职权制作的公文文书优于其他书证”；“鉴定结论、现场笔录、勘验笔录、档案材料以及经过公证或者登记的书证优于其他书证、视听资料和证人证言”；“出庭作证的证人证言优于未出庭作证的证人证言”。很显然，这两个证据规则都对“数个证据对同一事实的证明力”作出了大小强弱的区分，以指导法官对其做出优先选择。

在2005年前后，一些地方的高级法院曾出现过制定证据规则的高潮。迄今为止，北京、江苏、上海、湖北、四川、广东等地的高级法院仍然在实施当时颁行的刑事证据规则。而在这些地方性证据规则中，对于“数个证据对同一事实的证明力”作出明确的区分，属于法官所要遵循的评判证据证明力的基本规则。尽管在条文表述上可能有所差异，但这些证据规则都承认了原始证据、直接证据的证明力分别大于传来证据、间接证据，同时还明确规定，“实物证据的证明力大于言词证据”；“与被告人有亲属关系的证人所提供的证言，其证明力要低于其他证言”；“在同等条件下，多名证人的证言证明力大于单一证人就同一事实的证言”，等等。〔16〕

2010年由最高法院参与制定的两个证据规定，尽管没有将上述有关“数个证据对同一事实的证明力”规则全部确立下来，但也吸收了其中的一些规定。例如，对于没有直接证据证明犯罪事实但间接证据确实、充分的案件，该规定虽然规定“可以认定被告人有罪”，但是，“判处死刑应当特别慎重”。〔17〕这体现出一种间接证据证明力低于直接证据的观念。又如，对于与被告人有亲属关系的证人所作的有利于被告人的证言，以及对于与被告人有利害冲突的证人所作的不利于被告人的证言，该规定要求“慎重使用”，采信的前提是“有其他证据印证”，这也明显体现了对这类证言证明力

---

〔14〕最高法院在2001年颁布的《关于民事诉讼证据的若干规定》中，对若干证据的证明力确立一些限制性的规则。例如，法院就“数个证据对同一事实的证明力”，可以依照下列原则认定：①国家机关、社会团体依职权制作的公文书证的证明力一般大于其他书证；②物证、档案、鉴定结论、勘验笔录或者经过公证、登记的书证，其证明力一般大于其他书证、视听资料和证人证言；③原始证据的证明力一般大于传来证据；④直接证据的证明力一般大于间接证据；⑤证人提供的对与其有亲属或者其他密切关系的当事人有利的证言，其证明力一般小于其他证人证言。参见最高人民法院《关于民事诉讼证据的若干规定》第77条。

〔15〕最高法院2002年颁布的《关于行政诉讼证据若干问题的规定》，在限制证据的证明力问题上确立了一些证据规则。例如，证明同一事实的数个证据，其证明效力一般可以按照下列情形分别认定：①国家机关以及其他职能部门依职权制作的公文文书优于其他书证；②鉴定结论、现场笔录、勘验笔录、档案材料以及经过公证或者登记的书证优于其他书证、视听资料和证人证言；③原件、原物优于复制件、复制品；④法定鉴定部门的鉴定结论优于其他鉴定部门的鉴定结论；⑤法庭主持勘验所制作的勘验笔录优于其他部门主持勘验所制作的勘验笔录；⑥原始证据优于传来证据；⑦其他证人证言优于与当事人有亲属关系或者其他密切关系的证人提供的对该当事人有利的证言；⑧出庭作证的证人证言优于未出庭作证的证人证言；⑨数个种类不同、内容一致的证据优于一个孤立的证据。参见最高人民法院《关于行政诉讼证据若干问题的规定》第63条。

〔16〕对这些地方性证据规则的分析和评论，可参见房保国：“现实已经发生——论我国地方性刑事证据规则”，载《政法论坛》2007年第3期。

〔17〕参见张军主编：《刑事证据规则理解与适用》，法律出版社2010年版，第26页。

不信任的态度。

（二）对证据相互印证规则的确立

与中世纪的法定证据制度偏重证据的相关性不同，中国现行的证据规则更加重视证据的真实性，并确立了一些旨在保证证据真实性的证据规则。前面所说的对不同证据证明力的法律区分，就是以证据的真实性为主要标准来设定的。而对证据真实性的强调，还直接促成了证据相互印证规则的确立。

所谓“证据相互印证”，是指两个以上的证据由于同时包含着相同或相似的事实信息，因此其真实性得到了其他证据的验证，而它们所共同包含的证据事实都得到了证明。[18] 作为一项证据规则，“证据相互印证”既是对单个证据真实性的客观验证，又是对法官正确认定案件事实的制度保障。本来，根据自由心证原则，法官对于证据的真实性以及对案件事实的认定，应当根据其从法庭审理中所获得的直观印象，依据经验、理性，作出自由评判，而不受法律规则的限制。但在中国证据制度中，法官通过法庭审理，固然对证据的真实性和案件事实形成了一些印象，但仅凭这些印象来作出裁判还是远远不够的。法官无论是确认证据的真实性还是认定案件事实，都必须遵循一些带有客观性的评价标准。其中，“证据相互印证”就属于最为重要的标准。假如没有达到“证据相互印证”的程度，法官即使相信证据的真实性，也不能作此认定。

例如，根据两个证据规定，证据之间具有内在的联系，共同指向同一待证事实，且能合理排除矛盾的，才能作为定案的根据。这里所表达的就是证据相互印证的状态。又如，被告人推翻庭前供述，而改作无罪辩解的，法官仍然可以采信庭前供述的真实性，但前提之一是该庭前供述“与其他证据能够相互印证”。再如，证人当庭证言与庭前证言相互矛盾，或者未出庭证人的书面证言出现矛盾的，法官对庭前证言的采信标准，仍然是该证言是否“有相关证据印证”。

（三）法官内心确信标准的法定化

根据自由心证原则，法官对于案件事实的认定需要达到内心确信无疑的程度。对于何谓“内心确信无疑”，法律只要求法官根据自己从法庭审理中形成的直观印象，依据经验、理性、良心来作出自由判断；而在法官内心存在合理怀疑，无法形成内心确信时，则作有利于被告人的解释，直接作出无罪之宣告。在自由心证原则的作用下，法律对于法官的内心确信无疑并不作出明确的法律规定。[19]

但中国的证据规则对于法官认定案件事实的标准却作出了明确规定。尤其是对于证明被告人有罪的标准，也就是“证据确实、充分”，作出了明确的界定。例如，根据2012年《刑事诉讼法》的规定，“证据确实、充分”需要同时符合以下三个要求：一是定罪量刑的每一事实都有证据证明；二是据以定案的每一证据都经法定程序查证属实；三是综合全案证据，对所认定的事实已经排除合理怀疑。又如，最高法院2010年参与颁行的《关于办理死刑案件审查判断证据若干问题的规定》（以下简称《办理死刑案件证据规定》），对死刑案件事实的证明确定了五项具体标准，如证据与证据之间、

---

〔18〕 关于证据相互印证规则的讨论，可参见陈瑞华：“论证据相互印证规则”，载《法商研究》2012年第1期。

〔19〕 参见林钰雄：《严格证明与刑事证据》，法律出版社2002年版，第86页。

证据与案件事实之间“不存在矛盾或者矛盾得以合理排除”，“由证据得出的结论为唯一结论”，等等。再如，根据江苏省高级法院颁行的刑事证据规则，刑事案件具备以下情形之一的，应当视为“证据不足”：一是据以定案的证据不真实、不可靠；二是作为犯罪构成要件的案件事实没有必要的证据加以证明；三是据以定案的证据与待证事实之间、证据与证据之间存在重大矛盾无法排除。

这种对法官内心确信标准所确立的法律规则，显示出证据法对法官认定事实标准的严格控制。如同对单个证据的证明力所确立的认定标准一样，对于定罪标准的法律限制，也为法官作出有罪裁决设定了外在的要求。换言之，法官通过庭审即便对被告人构成犯罪的事实形成了内心确信，也还要满足这些外在“客观标准”。因此，法官仅凭自己的主观确信，是不能认定案件事实成立的。这就与中世纪的法定证据制度有一些相似之处。例如，根据那一时期出现的《卡洛琳娜法典》，被告人自白具有“全部证明力”，可以成为法官唯一的定罪根据；而一份证人证言则只具有50%的证明力，法官只有根据两份以上的证言，才能作出有罪裁决。[20] 而中国证据规则就法官认定案件事实的标准所作的法律限定，也体现了这种严格限定全案证据证明力的判断标准的理念。

（四）间接证据证明体系的法定化

按照自由心证的原则，对于证据的证明力以及案件事实的认定，法律都不作明确的限制，而交由法官根据庭审中形成的印象进行自由判断。无论是对直接证据还是对间接证据，法律都不对其证明力大小强弱加以区分，而由法官根据经验法则和逻辑法则进行评判。但中国的证据规则则不仅确立了“直接证据证明力大于间接证据”的规则，而且对法官根据间接证据定案作出了更为严格的法律限制。

根据最高法院参与颁行的《办理死刑案件证据规定》，法官运用间接证据定案要符合更为严格的条件。例如，“据以定案的间接证据之间相互印证，不存在无法排除的矛盾和无法解释的疑问”；“据以定案的间接证据已经形成完整的证明体系”；“依据间接证据认定的案件事实，结论是唯一的，足以排除一切合理怀疑”，等等。这些对间接证据定案的法律要求，较之根据直接证据定案的要求而言，显得更为严格和苛刻，显示出规则制定者对间接证据持有一种慎重甚至不信任的态度。

其实，中世纪欧洲国家的法定证据制度，就曾对间接证据的运用作出过限制性的规定。例如，根据法国中世纪曾颁行过的《刑事裁判法令》，证据依据其证明力大小可分为“完全证据”、“半证据”和“不完全证据”，被告人自白和两份证人证言，构成“完全证据”，法官凭此可以直接定罪；一个证言或者两份间接证据，则属于“半证据”，法官凭此可以做出实施刑讯的命令；而一份间接证据则属于“不完全证据”，法官凭此既不能定罪，也不能做出刑讯的命令。[21]

当然，根据司法实践的经验，直接证据所包含的事实信息较多，尤其是可以证明犯罪构成要件的事实；而间接证据则只能证明案件事实的某一环节或片段，法官无法根据某一个间接证据认定案件主要事实，而必须将若干个间接证据结合起来，通过逻

---

〔20〕 参见林钰雄：《严格证明与刑事证据》，法律出版社2002年版，第85页。

〔21〕 参见王亚新：“刑事关于自由心证原则历史和现状的比较法研究——刑事诉讼中发现案件真相与抑制主观随意性的问题”，载《比较法研究》1993年第2期。

辑推理，来认定案件事实的成立。经验还表明，通常情况下，根据直接证据定案的法官可以形成完全的内心确信，而仅仅依靠间接证据定案的法官则很难达到完全确信的程度，而往往会有一些疑问。但是，对于这些经验，法律一旦将其上升为证据规则的高度，法官就要在所有案件中都要遵循了。这些产生于个案之中的经验一旦被转化为对所有案件都具有规范作用的法律准则，那么，这就有可能出现一种形式化的证据判断标准。

（五）积极的法定证据主义与消极的法定证据主义

无论是对于单个证据证明力的限制，还是对案件事实证明标准所确立的法律规则，中国证据法都从两个角度体现了法定证据主义的理念。其中之一是，在满足证明力要求的前提下，对某一证据具有证明力以及犯罪事实得到证明所作的肯定的判断。例如，符合“印证规则”的证人证言、被告人供述，可以成为定案的证据；对于精神上有缺陷或者与被告人有利害关系的证人所作的证言，有其他证据印证的可以采信，等等。又如，在对于几对证据证明力的采纳问题上，证据法要求法院优先将直接证据、原始证据、出庭作证的证人证言、经过公证的书证或者无利害关系人的证言等采纳为定案（定罪）的根据。再如，对于从被告人口供中提取到“隐蔽性较强的书证、物证”，并且证据之间相互印证的，可以“认定被告人有罪”。这些例子足以显示，法官可以将那些符合形式要件的证据采纳为定罪的证据，也可以根据那些满足了法定规格的证据来认定被告人有罪。对于这种旨在积极地确定证据证明力和证明标准的理念，我们可以称之为“积极的法定证据主义”。

相反，法律对于那些尚未达到法定证明力要求的案件，要求法官不得采信某一证据，或者不得作出有罪判决。例如，未出庭作证证人的书面证言出现矛盾，不能排除矛盾且无证据印证的，不能作为定案的根据。又如，被告人庭前供述出现反复，庭审中不供认，且无其他证据与庭前供述印证的，不能采信庭前供述。再如，仅仅依靠间接证据来认定犯罪事实的案件，法官在适用死刑方面应当“特别慎重”，等等。这些例子足以说明，证据法对某些证据的证明力采取了限制使用的态度，而对不符合特定证据规格的证据，则确立了不能认定被告人有罪的规则。对于这种证据理念，我们可以称之为“消极的法定证据主义”。

三、新法定证据主义兴起的原因

新法定证据主义理念的实质，在于将一些本来适用于个案的经验法则，上升为证据法律规范，使之具有普遍的法律效力。按照这一理念，证据法在对证据的法律资格作出规范的同时，还要为法官评判证据的证明力确定限制性规则，并且为法官认定案件事实设置约束性的标准。

中国证据法为什么要将这些模棱两可、模糊不定的“经验法则”上升为法律规则呢？为什么在中国证据法中，有关规范证据证明力的规则竟然占据如此重要的地位呢？通过确立如此多的“证明力规则”，使法官在采信证据和认定事实方面受到诸多方面的法律限制，证据法究竟要实现什么样的立法目标呢？对于这些问题，有些学者已经进行过分析，并提出了一些观点。[22] 在以下的分析中，笔者将以刑事证据规则为范例，

---

〔22〕 参见李训虎：“证明力规则检讨”，载《法学研究》2010年第2期。

重点讨论新法定证据主义兴起的原因。

（一）对证据真实性的优先考虑

在欧洲中世纪的法定证据制度中，法律固然对证据的证明力作出了法律规定，甚至进行了数量化的区分，但是，这种法律规定更多属于对证据相关性的规范。其实，被告人口供之所以被视为“证据之王”，属于“完全证据”或者具有全部证明力，主要是因为该类证据具有较强的相关性；而一份证言之所以被视为“半证据”或者“具有50%的证明力”，而一份间接证据被视为“不完全证据”，也是因为这类证据相关性较弱。[23] 但是，同样是对证据证明力作出法律限制，中国的新法定证据主义理念却更加重视证据的真实性，而对证据的相关性则没有给予明显的强调。可以说，“新法定证据主义”理念在中国的兴起，与证据规则的制定者高度关注证据的真实性问题有着密切的关系。

通常说来，任何一项证据要转化为定案的根据，必须同时具备证据能力和证明力；证据能力是法律问题，是证据法对证据所提出的法律资格要求，而证明力则属于事实问题，一个证据只有同时具备真实性和相关性，才具有证明力，而一个证据相关性的大小则直接决定了证明力的强弱。在证据制度中，对证据法律资格的漠视，往往导致有关证据能力的规则极为欠缺；而对证据真实性和相关性的强烈关注，则必然带来证明力规则的兴盛不衰。

按照中国刑事证据规则制定者的解释，之所以要对死刑案件率先确立证据规则，是考虑到“死刑案件人命关天，质量问题尤为重要，在认定事实和采信证据上绝对不容许出任何差错”，为此就需要首先“对死刑案件采用更为严格的证明标准”[24]。

最高法院一位大法官认为，制定刑事证据规则的主要目的在于“从源头和基础工作上切实把好事实关、证据关，切实保障死刑案件的质量”。按照他的说法，“据统计，近三年来，每年仍有相当数量的死刑案件因事实、证据问题而不核准，即便是核准的死刑案件，也有相当的数量是在复核阶段经补查、完善证据后予以核准的，高级法院在二审审理中因证据问题发回重审的案件就更多，有的甚至占死刑二审案件的50%左右。这些问题的存在，严重影响死刑案件的复核质量和效率，甚至埋下发生冤假错案的隐患。近年来发生的多起刑事错案，主要是在事实认定、证据审查和运用方面出了差错，其中又多与刑讯逼供直接相关……”[25]

在两个证据规定的制定过程中，包括云南杜培武案件、河北李久明案件、湖北佘祥林案件、河南赵作海案件在内的一系列“冤假错案”，受到强烈的关注，并成为两个证据规定出台的重要背景。在最高法院的法官看来，这些错案发生的一个重要原因在于，刑事证据制度“不健全、不完善”，“办案人员素质不高，责任心不强，证据收集和审查违规违法”。[26]

这种基于防止“冤假错案”的考虑而对证据真实性的强烈关注，势必会对一系列旨在限制证明力的证据规则的确立产生影响。无论是证人改变证言或者证言出现“前

---

〔23〕 参见林钰雄：《严格证明与刑事证据》，法律出版社2002年版，第85页。

〔24〕 参见南英：“大力夯实刑事案件审理的证据基础”，载《人民法院报》2010年6月30日。

〔25〕 参见南英：“大力夯实刑事案件审理的证据基础”，载《人民法院报》2010年6月30日。

〔26〕 参见张军主编：《刑事证据规则理解与适用》，法律出版社2010年版，第1页以下。

后不一致”，还是被告人的供述和辩解“出现反复”，甚至当庭翻供，都涉及对证人证言和被告人供述的真实性的评判问题。两部证据规定为此确立了“合理解释”规则和“印证”规则，以解决这一在司法实践出现频率较高的证据运用难题。根据“合理解释”规则，证人改变证言、被告人推翻原有供述的，法官要采纳改变后的证言或者翻供后的辩解，都需要证人、被告人对其翻证、翻供提供合理的解释，否则，后来的证言、辩解一般不予采信。而根据“印证”规则，无论是证人证言还是被告人供述，一旦出现翻证、翻供问题，都需要有其他证据与其相互印证，也就是对证言、供述的真实性加以佐证，令人产生信服，否则，该项证言、供述也不得转化为定案的根据。很显然，这种针对翻证、翻供现象所确立的证据规则，无一不是为了确保证据的真实性而建立起来的。不仅如此，两个证据规定所提出的诸如“排除矛盾”、“排除一切合理怀疑”、“排除其他可能性”、“得出唯一的结论”等方面的定罪标准，也是在这种注重证据真实性的立法理念下得以确立的。

那些对不同证据的证明力划分“三六九等”的证明力规则，也被赋予维护证据真实性的功能。例如，在原始证据与传来证据之间，优先选择原始证据，显示出对传来证据真实性的怀疑；在有被告人供述这一直接证据的案件中，强调供述只要得到其他证据的补强，就可以作出有罪裁决，而在那种只有间接证据的案件中，即便达到了定罪的条件，也要慎用死刑，这体现了对间接证据定案能否达致真实的怀疑；对于那些有利害关系的证人所提供的证言，强调要“慎重使用”，而且要有其他证据印证，甚至在认定被告人的年龄时不予使用，这也体现了对这类证人证言的可靠性的深深不信任……

（二）对法官自由裁量权的约束

规范和约束法官自由裁量权的使用，已经成为我国刑事司法改革的重要课题。自21世纪初以来，最高法院一直倡导“量刑规范化改革”，并将其纳入两个“五年改革纲要”之中，其中的重要考虑就是规范法官的自由裁量权。〔27〕而在证据立法领域，规范和约束法官的自由裁量权也成为重要的指导性理念。

表面看来，法院的独立审判权经常难以得到保障，刑事法官更是无法对案件的实体裁判结果拥有独立裁决权。但实际上，由于没有证据规则的有效约束，刑事法官在采纳证据和认定案件事实方面往往拥有太大的自由裁量权。例如，对于同一证人的证言前后存在矛盾的，法官在采纳哪份证言方面可以自由裁断；对于被告人在庭审前和法庭上推翻原来的有罪供述的，法官也可以较为随意地决定采纳供述或辩解；对于证据之间存在矛盾、证明体系存在合理怀疑的，法官也可以自行决定案件是否达到“事实清楚、证据确实、充分”的程度……而法官在进行上述证据评判过程中竟然享有完全的自由，而不必在裁判文书中提供采纳证据的理由。在这种背景下，中国的刑事证据立法就需要解决一个极为特殊的问题：证据法不可能只是对证据的法律资格作出限制性规定，而不对证据的证明力大小强弱作出一定程度的规范，以防止法官在采信证据和认定案件事实方面任意裁断，而不受有效的节制。

如果说法律对证据的法律资格所作的规范属于“外在证据规范”的话，那么，法

〔27〕 参见胡云腾：“构建我国量刑程序的几个争议问题”，载《法制日报》2009年6月18日。

律对法官采信证据的标准和要求所作的规范则属于“内在证据规范”。中国刑事证据法长期以来没有建立较为完善的“外在证据规范”，使得任何证据都可以畅通无阻地进入法庭，成为控辩双方举证、质证和辩论的对象。在“重实体、轻程序”的传统难以消除的制度中，在程序法的有效实施难以得到保证的背景下，那些代表着证据之“程序要求”的证据能力规则，可能在短时间内难以建立起来，或者即便建立起来，也很难得到有效的实施。在这种情况下，那些旨在限制法官评判和采纳证据证明力的“内在证据规范”，就有了得以发育的条件和空间。毕竟，法官在采纳证据和认定事实方面经常会出现错误，而这些错误的发生又与法官滥用自由裁量权有关，而要解决这一问题，就要建立较为完善的证据规则。而既然有关证据能力的规则无法建立起来，那么，人们就会尝试构建规范法官采信证据的规则，从而有效地约束法官采信证据、认定事实的过程。这或许是“新法定证据主义”得以兴起的重要原因，

（三）刑事诉讼构造的纠问化

一般说来，法定证据制度与纠问式诉讼制度具有一种共生关系，纠问式诉讼制度的存在，为法定证据制度的产生提供了重要的制度环境。而纠问式诉讼之所以成为滋生法定证据制度的土壤，是因为在这种诉讼制度中，法官集调查证据、发动诉讼和作出裁判的权力于一身，很容易在采纳证据甚至认定事实方面独断专行。而法定证据制度对证据的证明力所作的有约束力的规定，主要用意在于对法官采纳证据的权力加以限制，以防止法官恣意擅断。[28] 不仅如此，法官之所以容易出现司法擅断，还跟纠问式诉讼所具有的书面的、间接的审判方式有着密切的联系。在法庭审判之前，调查官员将其秘密调查所得的结果都制作成书面的案卷笔录。法院在开庭审理中，不再对证据进行任何实质上的调查，而是通过宣读调查官员移交的证据笔录，来完成对被告人犯罪事实的认定。由于法院的判决直接建立在调查官员书面记录的基础上，因此，纠问式诉讼所实行的就是一种书面审理和间接审理相结合的原则。[29]

中国现行的刑事诉讼制度自然是与纠问式诉讼制度不可同日而语的。但是，现行的“公、检、法三机关分工负责、相互配合、相互制约”的司法体制，造就出一种侦查中心主义的纵向诉讼构造，而那种源自西方的以司法裁判为中心的诉讼构造还远没有在中国刑事诉讼中形成。结果，侦查成为刑事诉讼的中心环节，是搜集证据、认定案件事实的关键阶段。对于侦查机关所搜集的证据材料，法庭所要做的无非只是形式上的审查而已，而放弃了实质上的证据调查和质证程序；对于侦查机关所认定的案件事实，法庭一般也只是对其予以接纳和确认而已，而不再责令公诉方提出证据加以证明。不仅如此，法官在公诉方的证明体系存在缺陷、对案件事实存有疑问的情况下，还可以直接进行庭外调查核实证据的工作，从而对公诉方的证据进行拾遗补漏，从而最终促成对被告人定罪活动的完成。

在中国，侦查中心主义的诉讼构造与案卷移送主义的起诉方式有着密切的联系。我国 1979 年颁布的《刑事诉讼法》首次确立了检察机关提起公诉时移送全部案卷的制度。立法机关在 1996 年刑事诉讼法修订过程中曾限制检察机关庭前移送案卷的范围，

---

〔28〕 参见［德］罗科信：《刑事诉讼法》，吴丽琪译，法律出版社 2003 年版，第 117 页。

〔29〕 参见陈瑞华：《刑事审判原理论》第 2 版，北京大学出版社 2003 年版，第 161 页以下。

只允许移送“主要证据的复印件”、“证据目录”和“证人名单”，以防止法官庭前全面了解公诉方的证据材料，避免形成先入为主的预断。但是，在这次刑事诉讼法修订完成后不久，检察机关就被要求在庭审结束后移送全部案卷材料，使得法官在开庭审理结束后获得全面阅卷的机会。结果，1979 年的庭前移送案卷制度就演变成了 1996 以后的庭后移送案卷制度，法院依然是根据公诉方的案卷来认定案件事实，法庭审理依然是流于形式的。2012 年，立法机关通过再次修订刑事诉讼法，废止了 1996 年的制度设计，恢复了 1979 年的案卷移送制度，检察机关在提起公诉时可以将全部案卷材料移送法院。至此，法官庭前阅卷制度得到全面恢复。[30]

在案卷移送制度的影响下，“公、检、法三机关”的刑事诉讼活动带有“接力比赛”的性质，而最初由侦查机关制作的案卷笔录则成为三机关先后交接的“接力棒”。在法庭审理过程中，法官将各种证据笔录作为法庭调查的对象，对证据笔录的当庭阅读、出示成为主要的调查方式，而证人的出庭作证、接受当庭盘问则成为十分罕见的例外。对于证人证言、鉴定意见、被害人陈述，被告人及其辩护人一般无法进行交叉询问，而只能通过指出前后不一致、证据相互间有矛盾或者违背常理等方式，来进行形式上的“质证”。被告方的这种质证活动一般很难削弱公诉方的证明体系。基本上，法官如果对公诉方提交的证据笔录不持异议，就可以直接以此为根据形成对案件事实的认定。

可以说，在侦查中心主义的诉讼构造和案卷笔录中心主义的审判方式的双重影响下，中国刑事诉讼制度具有挥之不去的纠问化倾向。为避免这种消极后果的出现，刑事证据法就只得对证据的证明力大小强弱作出一些限制性的规定，对法官所形成的内心确信设置法定的标准。可以说，这些带有法定证据主义色彩的证据规则，无一不体现了立法者对法官滥用自由裁量权的担忧，也显示出一种通过限制法官内心确信的标准来加强制度控制的立法思路。

（四）司法裁判的行政决策机制

在中国刑事审判制度中，主持审判的无论是独任法官还是合议庭，都并不真正享有独立自主的审判权。特别是在合议庭审判之外，还存在着一系列带有行政审批色彩的决策机制。诸如庭长、院长的行政审批，审判委员会的秘密讨论，以及下级法院向上级法院的内部请示报告等程序，就属于这种行政决策机制的有机组成部分。[31] 这些秘密的审批、讨论或内部批示，几乎都绕开了正式的法庭审判程序，规避了诸如审判公开、回避、辩护、当庭质证、评议等制度安排，变成一种越来越普遍的“潜规则”。另一方面，中国上下级法院的组织关系，也使得那种“两审终审”的审级制度受到规避，无论是上诉审还是死刑复核都带有明显的行政审批性质。这是因为，二审法院和死刑复核法院都将阅卷作为进行司法复审的首要途径，也都带有对下级法院的裁判进行行政复审的意味，而无论是公诉方还是辩护方，对这两类法院在认定案件事实方面的影响力都很微弱。二审法院对于大多数上诉案件都不开庭审判，而死刑复核法院则

---

〔30〕 有关案卷笔录移送制度的演变问题，可参见陈瑞华：“案卷移送制度的演变与反思”，载《政法论坛》2012 年第 5 期。

〔31〕 有关中国法院在司法裁判中的行政审批机制，可参见江必新：“论合议庭职能的强化”，载《人民法院报》2002 年 9 月 18 日。另参见蒋慧岭：“审判活动行政化之弊端分析”，载《人民司法》1995 年第 9 期。

完全实行那种“调查讯问式”的复核方式。

无论是法院内部的行政审批机制，还是上级法院带有行政化色彩的“复审”体制，都不可避免地带有对合议庭或者下级法院的事实裁判进行全面审查的性质。而要进行全面审查，避免事实误判，就需要建立一种带有客观性的裁判标准。这种裁判标准既包括证据采纳的标准，也包括事实认定的尺度。这些标准和尺度最好是可操作的，甚至具有公式化的特点，能够为司法裁判的行政决策者和上级法院所容易掌握，也能够为合议庭和下级法院所接受。这样，在法庭审判流于形式、控辩双方对司法裁判形成过程的参与可有可无的情况下，决策者和上级法院也能有一些具体的审查标准。例如，在单个证据的审查判断上，被告人的近亲属被认为“不会做不利于被告人的证言”，与被告人有利害冲突的证人被认为“不会做有利于被告人的证言”，而“前后自相矛盾”的证人证言、被告人供述则经常被视为不可靠的证据，等等。这些简明扼要的证明规则，就足以成为决策者和上级法院评判的标准。又如，在证明标准的确定上，诸如“证据相互之间能够得到印证”、“间接证据是否形成完整的证明体系”、“被告人口供是否得到了其他证据的补强”等方面的标准，也可以成为行政审批者确定原来的事实裁判能否成立的尺度。

假如刑事证据法不设置任何可操作的证明力规则，也不确立明确的证明标准，而是像大陆法系国家那样赋予法官“自由评判证明力”的权力，那么，这种法院内部的行政审批方式和上级法院的行政化复审机制，就将失去存在的基础。因为道理很简单：“自由心证”的事实裁判方式注定是与法官独立审判的制度联系在一起的，而行政审批机制则构成了对法官独立审判的外部干预；“自由心证”的事实裁判方式也赋予法官不对事实裁判结论陈述理由的权威，而上级法院在下级法院对其事实裁判不说明理由的情况下，也是无法进行“客观”的事实复审的。刑事司法的经验表明，法官越是拥有独立自主的事实裁判权，刑事证据法就越不需要设置过于繁杂的证明力规则和证明标准。相反，越是对法官的行政控制较为严格，法官的事实裁判权受到诸多干涉的制度，刑事证据法就需要建立越加严密的证明力规则，并将法官内心确信的标准予以法定化。可以说，对法官认定事实的外部控制力量的大小，是与法官认定事实法律标准的明确化成正比例的。

四、对新法定证据主义的理论反思

对新法定证据主义的成因进行理论解释，并不意味着要对这一证据理念的正当性加以承认。其实，任何现存的制度或理念都有其存在的原因，也都可以发挥一定的积极功能。例如，新法定证据主义理念的贯彻对于在个案中有效规范法官的自由裁量权、确保法官自由心证的客观性、减少事实误判，确实具有一定的积极意义。不仅如此，任何制度和理念的存在也都有其制约性条件，离开了这些制约性条件，该制度或理念可能就不具有存在的现实基础了。例如，新法定证据主义的理念在很大程度上受制于中国现行的司法体制和诉讼制度，在这种体制和制度不发生实质变化的情况下，要指望这一证据理念发生变化，将是非常困难的。

尽管如此，从新法定证据主义发生作用的实际效果来看，我们认为也有必要对这一证据理念进行深刻的反思。在这一方面，笔者不赞同那种过分实用主义的立场，以为“存在的都是合理的”。其实，存在的制度或理念固然有其存在的原因，但在价值评价层面，它们却未必是公正的或者好的。在以下的讨论中，笔者拟从上述后一角度出发，对新法定证据主义进行全面的理论反思。

（一）证明力与证据能力的混淆

两部刑事证据规定确立了大量排除性的证据规则，大都采用了“不得作为定案的根据”的表述方式。但在那些被纳入排除规则适用范围的证据中，除了那些在取证主体、取证方式、取证程序等方面存在违法情形的证据以外，还有不少证据属于在真实性、相关性方面存在问题的证据。例如，在对证人证言的审查判断方面，法官遇有应当依法出庭而没有出庭作证的证人证言，“经质证无法确认的”，不能将其作为“定案的根据”。未出庭作证证人的书面证言出现矛盾，不能排除矛盾且无证据印证的，不能作为“定案的根据”。很显然，有关不出庭的证人所作书面证言应被排除的规定，属于对证人证言的证据能力所作的限制；而对那种前后矛盾且无法印证的证人证言的排除，则带有对其证明力加以否定的意味。又如，法官对以下两种视听资料都不得作为“定案的根据”：一是经审查或鉴定无法“确定真伪”的视听资料；二是在制作和取得的时间、地点、方式上存有异议的视听资料。后一情形属于在证据保管链条方面存在程序违法的证据，属于证据能力存在缺陷的证据，前一情况则属于因欠缺真实性而不具有证明力的证据。

应当说，法官对证据的“审查判断”确实包含着两个证据评价过程：一是对证据合法性的评判，也就是对证据是否具有证据能力的判断；二是对证据之真实性有无、相关性大小强弱的评价，也就是对证据证明力的判断。证据法对证据的证据能力作出法律上的限制，并对那些不具有证据能力作出排除性的规定，这确实无可厚非，也是证据立法的应有使命之所在。但是，按照新法定证据主义的证据立法思路，证据法将各种证据的证明力作为法律规范的对象，对于法官评判证据证明力的活动施加了诸多方面的法律限制。这就明显混淆了证据能力和证明力的概念。

当然，对特定证据的证明力作出适度的限制，这在不少国家的证据立法中都是存在的，也都有一定的合理性。例如，英美证据法就有一些关于证据相关性的限制性规则；大陆法国家的诉讼法也对诸如口供的证明力确立了“补强规则”。但是，这些针对证据证明力的法律规范，通常都是排除性的证据规则，而极少有从积极角度确认证明力、肯定定罪条件的证据规则。相反，我国的证据规则却确立了不少确定性的证明力规则，肯定性的定罪标准规则。例如，在认定被告人是否年满18周岁问题的认定上，法官可以采信无利害关系人的证言；在运用间接证据认定犯罪事实问题上，案件只要达到了法定的定罪条件，法官就可以作出有罪裁判……这种从积极的角度认可有罪证据的证明力、确定定罪标准的立法方式，不是在限制证据证明力的使用，而是对公诉方证据以及证明体系在审查判断上确立了过宽的标准，有可能带来控方证据不受严格审查、控方证明体系不受有效限制的后果。

（二）经验法则和逻辑法则的滥用

法官应当遵循经验法则和逻辑法则，对各种证据的证明力进行审查判断。这本身是无可厚非的，也是自由评价证据证明力原则的基本要求。但是，我国最高司法机关颁布的一些司法解释，却有着一种将经验法则一般化、逻辑法则规范化的立法倾向，使得大量本属于经验和逻辑层面的证据评价规则，上升为普遍的法律规范。作为重要法律渊源的司法解释，竟然不在规范证据的证据能力方面作出一些突破性的努力，却热衷于“总结司法实践的经验”，对证据的证明力大小强弱作出限制性规定。例如，直接证据的证明力被认为大于间接证据；原始证据的证明力被认为大于传来证据；有利害关系的证人提供的证言在证明力上被认为小于“无利害关系人的证言”……

将所谓的“经验法则”和“逻辑法则”上升为普遍的法律规范，固然有一定的合理性，却可能带来不可低估的风险。毕竟，这些“根据司法实践的经验”所总结的规则，尽管在大多数案件中是可以成立的，却通常不具有普遍适用价值，有些规则甚至有明显的例外。例如，有利害关系的证人有时候可能提供真实可靠的证言，而无利害关系的人则是完全可能做伪证的；作为直接证据的被告人供述经常是虚假的，而作为间接证据的物证则完全可能是真实无误的；一份书证的原件（原始证据）可能受到了伪造或篡改，但它在被伪造、篡改前形成的复印件（传来证据）却可能是可靠的……事实上，大多数经验法则、逻辑法则都是成立的，这并不能推导出这些规则普遍成立的结论。在不同的案件中，同一经验法则和逻辑法则的运用经常受制于诸多方面的制约条件，甚至可以得出不同的结论。而这也恰恰属于一种更广泛意义上的“经验法则”。

还有些“经验法则”或“逻辑法则”因为具有太大的局限性，而带有“伪经验法则”或“伪逻辑法则”的性质。法官运用这些规则对特定的证据进行审查判断，或许有一定的合理性，但它们一旦被转化为法律规范，就失去了存在的正当性，甚至会给刑事司法活动带来负面的影响。例如，被告人庭前供述一致，法庭上推翻供述的，法官这时面临着对庭前供述和庭审中辩解的选择问题。根据司法实践的“经验”，如果被告人不能合理说明翻供理由，而庭前供述与其他证据能够相互印证的，法官可以采信被告人庭前供述，而否定庭审中辩解的证明力。然而，即便被告人无法“合理解释翻供的理由”，其庭审中的辩解仍然可能是正确的；即便被告人的供述在形式上有其他证据加以“印证”，这些供述的真实性也不一定就是真实可靠的。这种针对言词证据的证明力所确立的“印证规则”，作为否定某一言词证据的证明力的依据，或许有一定的合理性，但在确认某一言词证据的证明力方面，却带有明显的局限性。其实，司法实践的另外一些“经验”恰恰表明，言词证据即便得到其他证据的形式上的“印证”，它仍然可能是不真实、不可靠的，其证明力也未必就得到了验证。

（三）证据采纳和事实认定的形式化

最高司法机关为证据的采纳和事实的认定确立证据规则，这本身是无可厚非的。毕竟，在缺乏证据规则的情况下，要指望刑事司法活动不出现“冤假错案”，这确实是不切实际的幻想。但是，一种成文化的司法解释，假如将法官评价各种证据证明力的过程都加以规范，甚至将法官认定犯罪事实的过程都施加明确的限制，那么，法官的自由裁量权就会受到彻底的剥夺，他们根据经验、理性和良心来评价证据证明力的能力也受到了否定。我国证据规则的制定者仿佛对所有法官都持不信任的态度，认为只要在证据证明力和定罪标准上确立明确的规则，就等于设置了明确的“证据公式”，法官只要将案件的证据套用到这些公式上面，就可以直接得出结论了。

例如，围绕着证人改变证言、被告人翻供问题所确立的“印证规则”，就体现了这种为法官设立“证据公式”的立法精神。规则制定者以为只要这些庭外言词笔录“得到了其他证据印证”，而证人改变证言、被告人翻供又都不能得到合理解释的，法官就应当予以采信。其实，这种证据评价过程纯粹是流于形式的活动，而对于这些言辞证据的证明力缺乏实质性的审查评判。

又如，根据被告人供述提取了“隐蔽性很强的物证、书证”，且与其他证据相互印证，并“排除串供、逼供、诱供等可能性的”，法官就可以认定有罪。[32] 这种带有“定罪公式”色彩的证据规则，将法官塑造成一种僵化的司法机器，只需要将有关证据套入公式之中，就足以完成定罪的过程。但是，案件的证据情况都是千差万别的，即便案件存在这样的物证、书证，即便相关证据与被告人供述能够相互印证，即便排除了非法取证的可能性，法官在认定被告人有罪问题上仍然具有一些不确定的因素。在司法实践中，一名对他人犯罪事实了如指掌的无辜者，完全可以做出有罪供述，然后提供有关物证、书证的线索，然后使其他证据对被告人供述形成“形式上的印证”。这种依据形式化的印证标准所进行的定罪活动，很可能会造成刑事误判。

（四）自由裁量权滥用的新隐患

表面看来，在新法定证据主义影响下所确立的诸多“证明力规则”，其主要用意在于规范法官在认定事实方面的自由裁量权，避免法官对证据的证明力任意取舍，防止法官任意出入认罪。但实际上，在这些抽象的证明力规则的指引下，法官对各种证据的证明力进行区分，对案件是否达到定罪的标准做出评价，恰恰可能带来更为隐蔽的滥用自由裁量权问题。

新法定证据主义所确立的一些证明力规则，要求法官在证据满足某种形式化要件的情况下，就可以做出不利于被告人的判断，甚至将某一证据直接采纳为定罪的根据。例如，被告人庭前供述一致，庭审中翻供，但被告人不能说明翻供理由，而庭前供述与其他证据相互印证的，可以采信被告人庭前供述。两个证据规定对于证人证言也有类似的规定。考虑到我国目前很难做到证人出庭作证，法庭大都通过宣读证言笔录来审查证人证言；而我国目前被告人在庭审前大都被迫作出了有罪供述，因此，这种允许法官在满足形式化要件的情况下就可以采信供述或证言的规定，无疑给了法官较大的自由裁量权。法官完全可以因为满足一些形式上的证明力要件，而对被告人、证人采取某种有强迫性的取证手段。

新法定证据主义所确立的一些证明标准规则，要求法官在案件符合某种形式化要件的情况下，可以直接认定“案件事实清楚”，甚至直接作出有罪裁判。例如，在没有直接证据的案件中，法官根据几个形式化要件就可以“认定被告人有罪”；在被告人作出有罪供述的情况下，根据供述提取了“隐蔽性很强的物证、书证”，且与其他证据相互印证，并排除了非法取证的可能性的，法官“可以认定有罪”。其实，在司法实践中，案件要满足这些法定的形式化要件，有时并不困难。但是，具有了这些形式化要件，法官就必须作出有罪认定吗？法官要不要根据自己的经验和理性，来对案件是否形成完整的证明体系进行判断呢？假如法官只知道遵守这些形式要件，而根本不考虑社会生活的经验法则和逻辑法则，甚至不考虑一些基本的正义理念，那么，满足这些

〔32〕 对口供补强规则的分析和评论，可参见张军主编：《刑事证据规则理解与适用》，法律出版社2010年版，第256页以下。

形式要件的案件有时恰恰可能是冤假错案。

无论是杜培武案件、佘祥林案件还是赵作海案件，都显示出当初的有罪判决至少在形式上并不违背新法定证据主义的理念。[33] 例如，被告人的翻供“得不到合理的解释”，原来的有罪供述笔录得到了“其他证据的印证”，证据之间的矛盾“得到了合理的排除”……但是，在“真相大白”——也就是“真正的犯罪人”归案——之后，人们才发现，这些形式上的证明力规则和定罪标准，其实是靠不住的。

五、新法定证据主义的未来

尽管新法定证据主义的盛行具有前述所说的诸多隐患，其运用也可能带来诸多方面的负面影响，但是，在这一立法理念所赖以存在的原因消除之前，要指望将这一理念从证据立法中彻底抛弃，却是不切实际的。因为只要支撑一种制度存在的理由仍然发挥着作用，那么，这一制度就将难以得到真正的废除。在这一方面，研究者与其充当一种变革者的角色，倒不如做一个实实在在的观察者和评估者，尽可能树立价值无涉或价值中立的观念，对新法定证据主义的理念进行一种科学的考察。

在那种阶级分析观念非常盛行的年代，自由心证制度曾经在政治上受到过武断的否定。后来在泛政治主义的迷雾逐渐消散之后，法学界开始平心静气地看待自由心证以及与其相关联的诸多证据规则。在将自由心证与法定证据制度放置在一个平面上进行历史考察和比较分析之后，一种否定法定证据制度、肯定自由心证制度的观点也逐渐出现。不少人甚至将自由心证与审判独立、无罪推定、直接和言词原则相提并论，认为确立这些基本原则将是刑事证据制度走向现代化的主要标志。结果，我们在送走泛政治主义之后，却发现一种泛道德主义的思维方式逐渐产生了影响力。

21 世纪初先后生效实施的民事证据规则和行政诉讼证据规则，以一种较为隐晦的表述方式，吸收了自由心证的一些理念。[34] 根据前一规则，“审判人员应当依照法定程序，全面、客观地审核证据，依据法律的规定，遵循法官的职业道德，运用逻辑推理和日常生活经验，对证据有无证明力和证明力大小进行独立判断，并公开判决的理由和结果”。而根据后一规则，“法庭应当对经过庭审质证的证据和无需质证的证据进行逐一审查和对全部证据综合审查，遵循法官职业道德，运用逻辑推理和生活经验，进行全面、客观和公正地分析判断，确定证据材料与案件事实之间的证明关系，排除不具有关联性的证据材料，准确认定案件事实”。上述两部证据规则尽管表述不同，但都承认自由心证原则的核心内容：裁判者对证据有无证明力和证明力大小可以进行独立评价和判断，遵循逻辑推理和生活经验。当然，这两部证据规则都没有强调法律不对证据是否具有证明力以及证明力大小作出明确的限定，也没有要求法官、陪审员根据自己从法庭审理过程中对案件事实得出的内心确信，来对案件事实作出判定。这显然说明，它们所确立的是一种不完整的自由心证原则。

但具有讽刺意味的是，这两部证据规则在表述了自由心证的理念之后，又随即确立了诸多旨在限制证据证明力的“证据规则”。这些“证明力规则”要么对数个证据

---

〔33〕 有关这些冤假错案的理论分析，可参见陈永生：“我国刑事误判问题透视——以 20 起震惊全国的刑事冤案为样本的分析”，载《中国法学》2007 年第 3 期。

〔34〕 参见最高人民法院《关于民事证据的若干规定》第 64 条，最高人民法院《关于行政诉讼证据若干问题的规定》第 54 条。

就同一事实的证明价值进行了明确的区分，要么对不同证据的“证据效力”作出了优劣评价。在这样的证明力规则的约束和规范下，裁判者怎么能做到对证明力进行“独立判断”呢？对于这些“证明同一事实的数个证据”，司法解释既然对其证明力大小强弱作出了明确的界定，那么，法官可能就不得不机械地适用那些“证明力公式”，而哪里有证据评判上的自由呢？

不难看出，法律即便明确表述了自由心证的部分理念，也无法将新法定证据主义从证据规则中驱逐出去。新法定证据主义在证据规则中不仅实际存在着，而且还发挥着有效的影响力。那么，自由心证究竟应否在中国证据法中得到确立呢？

在笔者看来，自由心证的确立不是一个法律道德问题，而是有无现实制度保障的问题。一方面，作为自由心证的适用前提，法官、陪审员必须拥有独立的审判权，他们对证据证明力的评判和对案件事实的认定不应受到外在的干涉和压力；在裁判者的资格和组成方面，法官必须具有精深的法律素养和深厚的社会阅历，陪审员必须具有适当的生活经验和理性思维能力，并经由一种随机的程序遴选出来，而不能受到人为的掌控，合议庭一经组成，就应集体庭审、集体评议和集体决策，最终按照多数裁决原则形成裁判结论；在法庭审理方面，法庭应当按照直接和言词审理原则调查证据，接触所有证据的最原始形式，听取控辩双方对证据的质证和对证人的当庭盘问，不受公诉方案卷笔录的预先影响，从而对各项证据的证明力作出当庭评判……另一方面，为避免裁判者滥用自由心证，法律也应要求在裁判文书中详细地说明裁判理由，对其评判证明力的过程做出合乎经验和理性的说明；负责上诉审查的法院也应对下级法院采纳证据、认定事实的情况进行全面审查，对那些有违经验法则、逻辑法则和良心法则的裁判结论及时加以纠正……

自由心证无疑是一项非常美妙的证据评判原则，也是对法定证据主义的合理扬弃。但是，在上述诸多方面的制度前提和程序保障都不具备的情况下，它具有得到确立和实施的条件吗？

两部刑事证据规定在规范证据的法律资格方面做出了幅度较大的制度突破。无论是对实物证据还是对言词证据，新的刑事证据规则都确立了大量旨在限制证据能力的规则。针对违法程度不同的“非法证据”，刑事证据规则分别确立了“强制性的排除”和“自由裁量的排除”原则，针对那些违法程度最低的“程序瑕疵”，证据规则确立了“可补正的排除规则”。根据粗略的统计，两个证据规定所确立的带有排除后果的非法证据和瑕疵证据总计不下 30 种。要知道，这两部刑事证据规则并没有自由心证的表述，而且还确立了多项证明力规则，明确体现了新法定证据主义的理念。但是，对证据的法律资格和证据能力提出越来越详尽的要求，并对那些非法证据确立明确的排除性后果，这本身就对法官在采纳证据上的自由裁量权作出了严格限制。更何况，对各种证据的证据能力提出更加严格的要求，肯定有助于减少刑讯逼供、暴力取证等非法取证行为的发生，可以避免诸如非法形成鉴定意见、随意确认辨认结果、任意采纳来源不明的实物证据等一系列侦查程序违法现象，这对于减少虚假证据的出现、避免冤假错案的发生都是富有成效的制度保障。

新的刑事证据规则尽管不可能对诉讼程序和证据制度做出重大的调整，虽然很难带来司法制度的实质变革，但这种对规范证据法律资格所作的积极尝试，无疑会使证据的法庭准入资格受到越来越严格的限制，那些严重违反法律程序所获取的非法证据，要想顺利地通过法庭上的程序审查机制，也将变得更加困难。这种证据立法努力或许会带来一个人们所始料未及的效果：随着刑事证据法对证据能力作出更加严格的法律限制，那些旨在限制证据证明力的规则所发挥的积极功效会有所降低，其负面作用也会得到越来越充分的暴露；等到刑事证据法更加完备的时候，那些对不同证据的证明力划分三六九等的证据规则，以及那些明确限定定罪标准的“证明规则”也就逐渐失去其存在的价值。这或许是我们可以期待的一种渐进结果。

当然，即便有关证据能力的规则逐渐得到完善，新法定证据主义也可能会长期存在下去。这种建立在限制法官自由裁量权基础上的证据理念，在那种行政化的司法审批机制、书面化的法庭审理方式以及以口供为中心的事实认定模式下，确实有其存在的现实基础。为了防止法官对被告人有罪供述偏听偏信，也为了避免冤假错案的发生，证据法对证据的证明力大小强弱作出一定的限制，并对认定事实的证明标准作出明确的界定，的确是有其必要性和合理性的。当然，那些带有“积极的法定证据主义”色彩的证据规则，动辄强调法官可以将某一证据“采纳为定案（定罪）的根据”，或者要求法官可以在符合某种证明要求的情况下“认定被告人有罪”，这都是不合情理，也是非常危险的，容易造成法官定罪权的滥用。相反，新法定证据主义的理念对于限制定罪证据的证明力，或者对那些没有满足法定证明标准的案件作出不构成犯罪的裁判结论，这确实是有益无害的。例如，在被告人前后翻供、证人推翻证言的情况下，被告人口供、证人证言没有得到其他证据印证的，法官不得将有关口供、证言作为定案（定罪）的根据。又如，在案件主要证据相互之间存在重大矛盾，且无法相互印证，或者根据全案证据无法得出唯一的结论或者难以排除其他可能性的，法官应作出事实不清、证据不足的无罪判决。这些已经成为现行证据法所确立的证据规则，属于带有“消极的法定证据主义”色彩的证据规则，又恰恰具有一定的生命力。

新形式证据观

——论证据裁判原则下的证据 *

张 中 **

证据是法治的基石，是实现司法公正的基石。在刑事诉讼中，证据则是刑事诉讼的基石，对于准确定罪量刑，防止冤假错案的发生具有关键作用。[1] 但对于“证据是什么”这个证据法最基本问题的争论在证据法学界和诉讼法学界一直存在，形成了多种学说，10 年前就有学者将其概括为“十四种学说”。[2] 由于这个问题关系到对证据本质的认识问题，也关系到整个证据制度的根基问题，并直接影响到诉讼制度的建设和发展，属于“牵一发而动全身”的问题，我们必须有正确的认识和理解。2012 年《刑事诉讼法》修改时对证据的概念做了重新定义，即证据是“可以用于证明案件事实的材料”。据资料显示，这一修改是经过立法机关、司法实务部门和法学家们反复讨论、深思熟虑的结果，是实践理性的产物，因而可以说是适当的，也是正确的。[3] 刑事诉讼法对于证据概念的重新定义标志着证据观念的根本转变，即由过去的实质证据观转向形式证据观，这对于整个证据制度的完善来说，具有非常重要的标志性意义。

一、从“事实”到“材料”：证据观的转变

对于证据的概念，1979 年《刑事诉讼法》第 31 条第 1 款和 1996 年《刑事诉讼法》第 42 条第 1 款均规定：“证明案件真实情况的一切事实，都是证据”。据此，证据被视为事实，因而都应当是客观的、真实的。但上述两个条文的第 3 款又规定：“证据必须经过查证属实，才能作为定案的根据。”按照这一要求，证据是否属实只有经过法定程序审查后才能确定。也就是说，公安机关收集的证据以及控辩双方向法庭提交的证据不一定都是真实的，也不一定都会被司法机关采纳作为定案的根据。事实上，证据有真有假，而且经常处于真假混杂的状态。[4] 这不仅指收集的证据有真有假，真假混杂，而且作为判决根据的证据也同样有真有假，真假混杂。司法实践中，相当一部分冤假

---

* 本文得到了教育部新世纪优秀人才计划项目及中国政法大学青年教师学术创新团队项目的资助。

** 张中，中国政法大学研究院（证据科学教育部重点实验室）副教授兼副院长。

〔1〕 最高人民法院研究室编：《新刑事诉讼法司法解释理解与适用》，法律出版社 2013 年版，第 21 页。

〔2〕 关于证据概念的“十四种学说”包括：“事实说”、“根据说”、“统一说”、“定案证据说”（又称为“狭义说”）、“两义说”（又称为“事实和材料说”、“双重含义说”）、“材料说”（又称为“广义证据说”）、“方法说”（又称为“手段说”）、“结果说”、“原因说”、“证明说”、“反映说”、“信息说”、“综合说（事实和方法说）”、“多义说”等。参见高家伟、邵明、王万华：《证据法原理》，中国人民大学出版社 2004 年版，第 3 页。

〔3〕 2011 年 8 月 30 日，中国人大网（www. npc. gov. cn）全文公布了《中华人民共和国刑事诉讼法修正案（草案）》，并向社会公开征集意见，截止日期为 2011 年 9 月 30 日。经过一个月的征求意见，全国人大法律草案征求意见系统共征集到 78 000 条建议。参见《刑事诉讼法草案征求意见结束 共获近 8 万条建议》，载《新京报》2011 年 10 月 1 日。

〔4〕 刘金友主编：《证据法学（新编）》，中国政法大学出版社 2003 年版，第 84 页。

错案就是因证据被伪造、被篡改造成的。也正是基于这个原因，才决定了证据审查的必要性。

2012 年《刑事诉讼法》第 48 条第 1 款把证据定义为：“可以用于证明案件事实的材料”。按照这一规定，结合本条第 2 款的规定，证据的概念至少包括以下三层含义：①证据是以法律规定形式表现出来的某种材料，如刀具、文件、书面证词、音像资料等，在证据种类上被称作物证、书证、证人证言、视听资料等。②证据与案件事实存在某种相关性，可以用来揭示、推断即证明案件事实。③证据是内容和形式的统一体，即证据的内容是证据所反映的案件事实，证据的形式是证据赖以存在的载体。因此，在刑事诉讼中，证据是指以某种形式表现出来的可以用于证明案件情况的材料。

证据概念的新定义，一方面，使证据回到了它的汉语本义。从汉语的字词结构来理解，证据就是证明的根据。如《辞海》对证据的解释就是：“法律用语，据以认定案情的材料。”这是对证据一词最简洁最准确的解释，也是人们在日常生活中普遍接受的证据基本含义。另一方面，消除了旧法条中的逻辑矛盾，既符合实际，又有利于防止先入为主的偏见，同时减少“结果定格”的错误。[5] 因为证据是不是事实，能不能证明案件事实，能不能作为定案的根据，只有经过法庭查证核实以后才能确定，在未经法庭查证之前，证据尚未核实，又怎知其能否证明案件真实情况呢？实际上还有相当一部分证据经法庭查证“属实”以后，还存在被推翻、被否定的情况。当然，新《刑事诉讼法》对于证据的重新定义并不是意味着虚假的材料可以作为定案的根据使用，也不是说公安机关在收集证据材料时不分真假材料通通收集。无论如何，在人民法院对案件最终作出处理时，必须依据能够反映案件真实情况的证据材料。[6]

在理论上，关于证据的概念，学界存在着“事实说”、“信息说”、“材料说”等多种学说，其中“事实说”影响最大。该说认为，证据是一种客观存在的事实，即“能够证明案件真实情况的客观事实”。[7] 事实属于客观范畴，既然证据是事实，证据也必然属于客观范畴。由于事实是实质性的东西，因此有些学者把“事实说”称为“实质证据观”，甚至把实质证据观视为唯一科学的证据观。[8] 该说提出，应当从实质上理解和把握证据，并把体现着实质的事实直接看作证据。[9] 这种观点由于过于强调证据的实质内容而忽视了证据的表现形式，从而难以回答虚假证据的法律属性问题。

一般来说，实质证据观是相对于形式证据观而言的。形式证据观的代表性理论被认为是证据概念的“反映说”。该说认为，证据总是以充当事实论据的判断形式出现的，它不是客观事实的本身，而是客观事实在人的意识中的反映。[10] 该说认为，证据在总体上属于主观范畴，主张应从反映形式上理解和把握证据，即把反映事实的形式

---

〔5〕 梁玉霞：“什么是证据——反思性重塑”，载何家弘主编：《证据学论坛》（第 3 卷），中国检察出版社 2001 年版，第 360 页。

〔6〕 陈光中主编：《〈中华人民共和国刑事诉讼法〉修改条文释义与点评》，人民法院出版社 2012 年版，第 48 页。

〔7〕 江伟主编：《证据法学》，法律出版社 1999 年版，第 206 页。

〔8〕 裴苍龄：“证据观念的大转变——论实质证据观”，载《法律科学》2006 年第 3 期。

〔9〕 裴苍龄：《新证据学论纲》，中国法制出版社 2002 年版，第 9 页。

〔10〕 吴家麟：“论证据的主观性与客观性”，载《法学研究》1981 年第 6 期。

直接看成了证据。[11] 形式证据观认识到了证据与事实的关系及其差别，但由于过于强调证据的主观性而受到客观主义理论的批判，认为“形式证据观是把证明当证据”，因而是不正确的。[12]

新《刑事诉讼法》用“材料”取代“事实”，标志着一种新的证据观念的确立，我们将之称为“新形式证据观”。一方面，它与以“事实说”代表的实质证据观有着本质区别。实质证据观的最基本立场是“证据是事实”。[13] 其主要论据首先就是我国1979年颁布的《刑事诉讼法》第31条第1款的规定，论者认为该款确立了证据是事实的观点，从而意味着“在中华大地上树起了实质证据观的大旗”。但随着新《刑事诉讼法》的颁行，实质证据观的依据便不复存在了。事实上，正是由于认识到了“事实是证据”这一提法在逻辑和实践中都存在问题，刑事诉讼法修正案在定义证据概念时才用“材料”取代“事实”的。[14]

实质证据观认为证据具有客观性和关联性两种属性，并认为证据的客观性指的是事实的客观性，证据的关联性指的也是事实的关联性。[15] 该论把证据等同于事实，明显混淆了证据与事实的概念。实质证据观认为证据只有三种，即物证、书证、人证，认为物证是客观存在的，书证是被“书”记载的，人证是被人感知的。这种证据分类明显有违形式逻辑。按照论者的逻辑，证据是事实，事实是客观存在的，证据也是客观存在的，书证、人证也都是客观存在的。如果人证是被人感知的，这种证据就成了实质证据观所竭力批判的“反映论”了。实质证据观提出证据有四大功能，即证据是认识的基础、证明的根据、检验的标准、思想的指南，并强调“证据的四大功能就是事实的四大功能”。这明显把证据与事实混为一谈了。虽然事实在一定条件下能构成证据，[16] 或者说在有些情况下一个事实可以成为另一个事实的证据，[17] 但在特定的证明关系中，事实与证据处于证明关系的两端，作为认定事实依据的证据毕竟不是事实本身，如果说事实是一个需要论证的命题，[18] 那么证据就是论证这个命题的依据。因此，事实与证据的关系，在逻辑上可以说是一种命题与论据的关系。总之，实质证据观是一种把证据理解为客观范畴、存在范畴的证据理论。

与实质证据观从实质内容上理解和把握证据不同，新形式证据观更看重证据的形式。一份材料，不管其内容如何，只要可以用于证明案件事实，都应该作为证据呈献给事实认定者。就像英国学者摩菲所说，“能够说服法官认定某个案件事实真实或者可能的任何材料”都应被视作证据。[19] 即使在证据被伪造的场合，未经查证属实或者最终确定为不实之前，由于该材料在形式上与案件事实存在某种关联，我们无法否定该

---

〔11〕 裴苍龄：《新证据学论纲》，中国法制出版社2002年版，第9页。

〔12〕 裴苍龄：“证据观念的大转变——论实质证据观”，载《法律科学》2006年第3期。

〔13〕 裴苍龄：“证据学的大革命——再论实质证据观”，载《法律科学》2010年第3期。

〔14〕 王尚新、李寿伟主编：《〈关于修改刑事诉讼法的决定〉释解与适用》，人民法院出版社2012年版，第40页。

〔15〕 裴苍龄：“形式证据观的终结——四论实质证据观”，载《河北法学》2013年第5期。

〔16〕 裴苍龄：“证据学的大革命——再论实质证据观”，载《法律科学》2010年第3期。

〔17〕 张保生等：《证据法学》，高等教育出版社2013年版，第15页。

〔18〕 张继成：“事实、命题与证据”，载《中国社会科学》2001年第5期。

〔19〕 何家弘、刘品新：《证据法学》，法律出版社2007年版，第107页。

材料的证据性质。如某人作证说他目击了被告人实施犯罪的过程，但后经法庭调查证明该证人为陷害被告人作伪证。毫无疑问，该份证言不能作为定案根据，但它在证据法上仍然属于证人证言。

另一方面，与“反映说”所代表的形式证据观相比，新形式证据观不仅看重证据对事实的依赖关系，更强调证据的自身形式。按照实质证据观的说法，形式证据观不是把事实看作证据，而是把人对事实做出的反映看作证据。[20] 我们认为，把事实看作证据是不对的，把人对事实做出的反映看作证据也是不准确的。因为证据不是人对事实做出的反映，而是作为证据的材料对事实的反映。就像有的学者所说的事实与证据的关系，在某些方面，类似于本质与现象、内容与形式的关系。[21] 按照这种理解，证据是对案件事实的直接反映，而不是人对事实做出的反映。但从认识论的角度看，证据与事实的关系离不开认识主体的介入，尤其是在证据法语境下，如果没有人的介入，证据与事实是不会发生关系的，尽管我们无法否认事实发生之时必然会产生证据。从这个角度看，把人对事实做出的反映看作证据的观点似乎又是成立的。但是，我们必须看到，证据对事实的反映以及人对证据的认识都是相对的。在法庭上，控辩双方出示的证据材料在很多情况下能够反映案件事实，但有时候并不一定能够证明案件事实，如品性证据。同样的道理，人们对于同样的证据，得出的结论也可能是不同甚至相反的。也就是说，人对证据的认识并不一定是证据对事实的反映。

相对于形式证据观，新形式证据观更强调证据对于事实的独立性以及证据对于事实证明的相对性。证据对于事实的独立性意味着证据具有独立品格。换句话说，证据并不必然是事实的反映，更不是事实本身。这就可以解释伪造证据以及无关证据的存在问题了，从而也就可以区分采纳用作定案根据的证据与不予采纳的证据了。证据对于事实证明的相对性意味着认识了证据并不等于认识了事实。换句话说，有证据不一定有事实。这也就可以解释悬案、疑案存在的必然性了。就像有的学者所说，通过证据来认定事实，就像做“拼图”游戏，能否完整地拼出过去的事实，取决于能够获得多少证据“片段”，以及证据真假的程度。[22]

新形式证据观要求我们要正确区分用于证明案件事实的证据和作为认定案件事实根据的证据。对于前者，不应有太多的要求和限制，尽可能地将所有证据材料都呈献给法官，以便其作出更理性、更正确的判断；但对于后者，即证据裁判原则下的证据，从保证事实认定的准确性考虑，用作定案根据的证据应当具有真实性、相关性和合法性。

二、从证据客观性到证据真实性

新形式证据观的确立意味着人们证据认识的根本性转变。证据不再是一种客观事实。按照证据的新定义，传统的证据客观性理论将受到严峻挑战，学界必然会就证据的客观性问题进行新的讨论。事实上，学界对证据客观性的质疑从来就未间断过，认为证据的客观性理论不符合辩证唯物主义的认识规律，也有悖于法官对证据的认定

---

〔20〕 裴苍龄：“形式证据观的终结——四论实质证据观”，载《河北法学》2013年第5期。

〔21〕 张保生等：《证据法学》，高等教育出版社2013年版，第15页。

〔22〕 张保生等：《证据法学》，高等教育出版社2013年版，第16页。

权,[23] 甚至有人提出了“客观性理论的终结”的论断。[24]

按照实质证据观，客观性是证据的天然属性，甚至把证据客观性理论同证据是事实的观点看作是人类认识证据新时代的标志，甚至是人类智力发展新时代的标志。[25] 在实质证据观论者看来，证据是客观存在的事实或者客观上真实发生过的事实，是不以人的意志为转移的客观存在。很显然，证据的客观性理论是以证据概念的“事实说”为理论基础的，其形式逻辑是，证据是事实，事实是客观的，因而证据必然具有客观性。对此，有学者指出，证据客观性在司法实践中会造成这样一种悖论：即使法官对证据真实性的判断结论可能并不符合客观真实（事实上这种“不”的状况是无意且难以避免的)，也应当从法律上认可这种“判断”结论，而这种被“判断”过、且可能不符合客观真实的证据最终成了认定案件事实的根据，亦即依证据的客观性不能成为证据的却事实上或在法律上成为了证据。[26] 还有学者从事实分层的角度来批判证据的客观性理论，即将诉讼中的案件事实分为客观事实、证据事实和法律事实三个层次，认为证据既与客观事实不同，也不是法律事实，而只能作为建立一定的证据事实的素材，唯此才符合证据在诉讼中的合理定位。[27] 实践是检验真理的标准。从司法实践情况看，要求法官用以认定案件事实的证据必须符合客观真实是不可能完全做到的，因而应从理论上舍弃证据的客观性特征。

一般来说，证据的存在并不以人们的主观意志为转移，但对证据的认识以及证据的应用却离不开人的主观意识。更直接地说，控辩双方向法庭提供的证据材料，并非都是纯客观的真材实料，诸如虚假的供述、证人所作的伪证以及伪造的书面材料等，均不能否定它们的证据资格。虽然经过法定程序查证属“假”，不能作为定案根据，但这属于证据的审查判断和采纳与否的问题，而不是证据资格问题。因此，应当把证据与定案根据区分开来，我们不赞成把客观性作为证据的本质特征，但也不反对把真实性作为证据的法律属性。

“求真”是证据法的基本价值之一。证据法追求“事实真相”的价值，因为当事人的权利和义务取决于准确的事实认定。“没有准确的事实认定，权利和义务就变得毫无意义。”[28] 事实上，我国立法一直把“准确查明犯罪事实”作为刑事诉讼法的主要任务，而证据的真实性则是完成这一任务的保障。在立法层面，我们发现最新的有关司法解释开始使用“真实性”术语，强调审查证据的真实性。如最高人民法院《关于适用〈中华人民共和国刑事诉讼法〉的解释》第 78 条第 3 款规定：“经人民法院通知，证人没有正当理由拒绝出庭或者出庭后拒绝作证，法庭对其证言的真实性无法确认的，该证人证言不得作为定案的根据。”第 104 条第 1 款规定：“对证据的真实性，应当综

---

〔23〕 张晋红、易萍：“证据的客观性特征质疑”，载《法律科学》2011 年第 4 期。

〔24〕 姜涛：“证据的客观性质疑”，载何家弘主编：《证据学论坛》（第 6 卷），中国检察出版社 2003 年版，第 408 页。

〔25〕 裴苍龄：“证据观念的大转变——论实质证据观”，载《法律科学》2006 年第 3 期。

〔26〕 张晋红、易萍：“证据的客观性特征质疑”，载《法律科学》2011 年第 4 期。

〔27〕 姜涛：“证据的客观性质疑”，载何家弘主编：《证据学论坛》（第 6 卷），中国检察出版社 2003 年版，第 401 页。

〔28〕 ［美］罗纳德·J. 艾伦：“刑事诉讼的法理和政治基础”，张保生等译，载《证据科学》2007 年 1、2 期合刊。

合全案证据进行审查。”最高人民检察《人民检察院刑事诉讼规则（试行）》第73条规定了对犯罪嫌疑人、被告人供述的真实性进行审查，第310条第2款则规定了对讯问笔录真实性等产生疑问的应当如何处理。

上述规定表明，证据的真实性对于证据材料具有重要意义，它是证据审查不可回避的一个问题，它是决定证据材料能否被采纳为证据的一个重要因素。不过，也有学者指出，证据本身无所谓真伪，证据反映的内容或说事实才谈得上真伪。从而否定客观性的同时连带否定证据的真实性。[29] 我们认为，证据是存在真假的，否则，就不存在查证属实的问题了，也就没有伪证的概念了。之所以出现这种情况，主要是混淆了真实与真实性的概念。对于真实的涵义，亚里士多德曾说，“凡以不是，是为不是者，这就是假的；凡以是为是，以假为假者，这就是真的”。[30] 据此，真实与否的判断标准不在于判断对象自身的真假，而在于人们对它的判断与其是否相符。对于一份文书，经过审查判断，如果能够认定它是被伪造的，那么，这份文书就可以被断定是不真实的。这份文书是客观存在的，但它是不真实的。就此意义而言，客观性不同于真实性，客观存在的不一定是真实的。对于这份文书，经过审查判断，如果不能认定它是被伪造的，那么，这份文书就可以被断定是真实的，也可能出现一种悬疑状态：不能确定它是真的还是假的。对于这种情况，我们可以说这份文书具有较大的真实性。因此，真实性不是非真即假的问题，它是一个度的问题，即证据材料反映的事实与案件事实的契合程度。

此外，真实性的概念除了能反映出证据自身存在状况外，还能反映它的内容情况。事实上，任何一份证据材料都含有丰富的内容，同一份证据材料，有的内容完全是真的，有的内容完全是假的。如目击证人的证人证言，某证人作证说被告人拿刀捅了被害人，经现场录像核实，这与案件事实完全符合，但证人说该被告人当时上身穿的是蓝色T恤，经核实，被告人当时穿的T恤是黑色的。那么，这就产生证言的真实性问题。也就是说，证据的真实性本身涵盖了证据内容的真假问题，审查证据的真实性，就是审查证据存在的真假问题和证据内容真假程度。一般来说，实物证据的真实性比较高，而言词证据的真实性较低。

三、从实质相关性到形式相关性

证据的相关性，又称证据的关联性，被誉为“所有现代证据法律制度的基本原则”，[31] 其基本含义是，证据有助于证明事实存在可能的属性。证据相关性的门槛并不高，所提供的证据只要与待证事实有任何逻辑联系，有助于事实认定者对事实存在的可能性作出判断就够了。[32] 所以，有学者把相关性解释为“证据对其所要求证明的事实具有必要的最小限度的证明能力”。[33] 对于相关性的经典表述，首推美国《联邦

---

〔29〕 姜涛：“证据的客观性质疑”，载何家弘主编：《证据学论坛》（第6卷），中国检察出版社2003年版，第401页。

〔30〕 亚里士多德：《形而上学》，吴寿彭译，商务印书馆1959年版，第79页。

〔31〕［美］罗纳德·J. 艾伦等：《证据法：文本、问题和案例（第3版）》，张保生等译，高等教育出版社2006年版，第147页。

〔32〕 张保生等：《证据法学》，高等教育出版社2013年版，第16页。

〔33〕［日］我妻荣编：《新法律学辞典》，中国政法大学出版社1991年版，第249页。

证据规则》401的规定，即“‘相关证据’是指使任何事实的存在具有任何趋向性的证据，即对于诉讼裁判的结果来说，若有此证据将比缺乏此证据时更有可能或更无可能”。[34] 这一规定充分显示了美国联邦证据规则在遣词造句和语法规则上的晦涩臃肿，经过我国学者的解读，在评估证据是否具有相关性时，可以按照两步进行：首先，提出证据者应当确定所提出的证据所要证明的“具有重要意义的事实”；其次，要确定该证据是否会使得与没有该证据相比，具有重要意义的事实更可能存在或者更不可能存在。[35] 也就是说，如果一项证据对于案件中的实质问题具有证明作用，不管它是肯定还是否定其存在的可能性，它都具有相关性。

在我国证据理论中，对于相关性的阐述，很多学者习惯使用“关联性”一词。在实质证据观看来，关联性是证据最本质的属性，证据与案件事实的关系应当是一种客观的、内在的、必然的联系。首先，证据的关联性是以客观性为前提的。[36] 换句话说，证据的相关性是一种客观联系，即证据事实与案件事实之间的联系是客观存在的，其联系是不以办案人员的主观意志为转移的。[37] 在实质证据观看来，证据同案件事实之间的联系之所以是客观的，是因为证据是一种客观事实，案件事实也是一种客观事实，前一事实就是人们用来证明后一事实存在的证据，这两种事实具有相同的性质，它们之间的关联就是一种客观联系。[38] 其次，证据的关联性是一种内在联系，即一个证据与案件事实之间存在某种关系，无论这种关系是直接的还是间接的，也无论这种关系远近强弱，证据发出的信息总能够在案件事实中找到联结点。[39] 证据的关联性是由案件事实决定的，案件事实的发生在客观世界留下了一定的痕迹，这些痕迹被人们所感知，就能成为证明案件事实的证据。证据与案件事实之间有本质的、内在的联系，这样证据才有关联性。[40] 既然证据的关联性是一种内在联系，证据与案件事实之间的表面联系则被不可避免地被抛弃了，哪怕看起来是对案件事实具有证明作用的证据。最后，证据的关联性是一种必然联系。在实质证据观看来，证据与案件事实的联系意味着一个已知的事实必然地导致了案件中的某个事实情节的发生，或者一个事件的发生必然地产生了某种痕迹、孳生物。如果并不必然导致，那么这二者之间就没有关联性。[41] 按照这种说法，看一项证据是否具有关联性，不在于它能证明什么，而是在于它证明力的确定性。也就是说，如果一项证据能够直接证明案件中的某个情节或者环节，哪怕仅仅是一个细节、一个情节的某个方面，那么，它与案件之间就具有了必然联系，就可能成为该案中的证据。应当说，以上实质证据观对于证据相关性的理解是有失偏

---

〔34〕［美］罗纳德·J. 艾伦等：《证据法：文本、问题和案例（第3版）》，张保生等译，高等教育出版社2006年版，第148~149页。

〔35〕王进喜：《美国〈联邦证据规则〉（2011年重塑版）条解》，中国法制出版社2012年版，第57页。

〔36〕陈一云主编：《证据学（第4版）》，中国人民大学出版社2010年版，第62页。

〔37〕陈光中主编：《刑事诉讼法》，北京大学出版社、高等教育出版社2002年版，第130页；卞建林主编：《证据法学》，中国政法大学出版社2002年修订版，第53页。

〔38〕裴苍龄：“论证据的关联性”，载《政治与法律》1992年第4期。

〔39〕吕萍：“证据的关联性思考”，载《理论学刊》2007年第2期。

〔40〕陈光中主编：《中华人民共和国刑事证据法专家拟制稿（条文、释义与论证）》，中国法制出版社2004年版，第138页。

〔41〕吕萍：“证据的关联性思考”，载《理论学刊》2007年第2期。

颇的。

在证据法理论上，证据的相关性存在两种相关性概念，一是逻辑相关性，二是法律相关性。如果一项证据在逻辑上具有证明某个命题的任何趋势，我们可以说该证据具有逻辑上的相关性。如果一项证据的证明力足以支持在考虑该证据时带来的延迟、耗费、损害或者混淆的正当性，则我们就可以说该证据具有法律上的相关性。[42] 在本质上，法律相关性是价值权衡或者是基于某项政策的结果，是为了防止某些证据被不适当地使用，而通过证据规则来限制某些证据的法律资格，如传闻、品性证据等。因此，真正意义上的相关性通常指的是逻辑相关性。正如美国学者塞耶所言，相关性是一个经验逻辑问题，而完全不是法律问题。相关性的检验标准是证据与它所要证实的最终事实结论之间的逻辑关系是否存在。[43] 这一观点得到了西蒙勋爵的支持，他也认为，如果证据在逻辑上对待证事实的存在与否具有证明作用，该证据就具有关联性。[44] 既然如此，证据是否具有相关性将就看它在逻辑上是否能够推断出它要证明的事实，或者否定该事实的存在。从诉讼认识论的角度看，证据与案件事实的逻辑关系更多的是一种经验证明，而不是一种客观自在的关联性。证据的关联性是以假定证据的真实性为前提的，它并不涉及证据的真假和证明价值，对证据真假及证明力大小的判断是即证据相对于证明对象是否具有实质性和证明性。[45] 需要特别指出的是，这里的实质性并不是说证据与证明对象之间的关联是一种实质关联，而是指证据的证明对象是属于待证事实，也就是对解决法律争议具有重要意义的事实。正如有的学者所说，一个证据拟证明的事项是否具有实质性，必须根据该诉讼所涉及的实体法来判断。[46] 为了消除歧义，2011 年重塑版的美国《联邦证据规则》401 用 of consequence（具有重要意义）一词取代了普通法传统使用的 material（实质性）这个词，避免了术语意思含混所带来的不严谨性。[47] 此外，证据的相关性是一种可能性或者倾向性，而非必然性。用美国学者华尔兹的话说，“相关性必然涉及某种情况下的盖然性”。[48] 从《联邦证据规则》401 使用的 probable 一词来看，相关性表明了证据与证明对象之间的非确定性关系，可以说是“从很小的可能性到 100% 的确定性”。[49]

新《刑事诉讼法》在定义证据时强调“可以用于证明案件事实”。从字面上看，“可以用于”意味着证据与案件事实的关系更多的是一种形式上的证明关系。至于证据能否证明案件事实，只有经过审查判断以后才能确定。换个角度看，如果某项材料在形式上与待证事实毫不相干，就意味着不可以用于证明案件事实，从而可以认为它不具有相关性。按照美国学者摩根的逻辑相关性理论，如果某个证据在推论上无合理的

---

〔42〕 王进喜：《美国〈联邦证据规则〉(2011 年重塑版) 条解》，中国法制出版社 2012 年版，第 57 页。

〔43〕 [美] 格雷厄姆·利利：“证据的相关性”，载《法学译丛》1984 年第 2 期。

〔44〕 Adrian Keane, *The Modern law of Evidence*, 4th ed., Butterworth, London, Dublin, Edinburgh, 1996, p. 19. 转引自汤维建、卢正敏：“证据‘关联性’的涵义及其判断”，载《法律适用》2005 年第 5 期。

〔45〕 卞建林主编：《证据法学》，中国政法大学出版社 2002 年版，第 53 页。

〔46〕 易延友：《证据法的体系与精神——以英美法为特例参照》，北京大学出版社 2010 年版，第 100 页。

〔47〕 王进喜：《美国〈联邦证据规则〉(2011 年重塑版) 条解》，中国法制出版社 2012 年版，第 57 页。

〔48〕 [美] 乔恩·R. 华尔兹：《刑事证据大全》(第 2 版)，何家弘等译，中国人民公安大学出版社 2004 年版，第 81 页。

〔49〕 Bryan A. Garner, *A Dictionary of Modern Legal Usage*, 2nd ed., 1985, p. 694.

可能，无阐明案件疑难之处的可能，无助于发现案件真实情况之可能或无发现待证事之可能，均无逻辑上的关联，不可作为证据使用。[50] 因此，按照证据的新定义，相关性更多的是指证据对于案件事实形式意义上的证明关系。

四、从实质合法性到形式合法性

证据的合法性，又称证据的法律性，主要是指证据必须具有法律规定的形式和由法定人员依照法定程序收集和运用。[51] 在我国证据法理论上，对于合法性能否作为证据的属性问题一直存在争议，甚至曾一度形成“两性说”和“三性说”论战的局面。可能是为了避免这种争议，1996 年《刑事诉讼法》颁布后出版的部分权威教材开始使用“证明力”和“证据能力”来阐述证据的特性。[52] 但从对证据能力的解释来看，它指的是证据资料在法律上允许其作为证据的资格，这实际上就是我国传统证据理论上的合法性，在英美法系国家则称之为可采性。令人不解的是，对于证据的证据能力或者可采性，学界基本没有争议，但一说起合法性，有部分学者认为，它是人为强加给证据的，而不是它本身所固有的特征。[53]

事实上，我国证据理论上的合法性与英美等国证据法上的可采性是有差异的。按照通常理解，可采性的主旨是“容许性”，即鼓励采纳证据。[54] 也就是说，只要证据为法律所容许，就可用于证明案件的待证事实。按照美国《联邦证据规则》401 确定的“最小相关性检验标准”，如果一个证据对事实认定者评估要件事实存在的可能性有所帮助，它就是相关的，法官就应当采纳。也就是说，可采性规则是鼓励法官尽可能采纳相关证据的规则，它体现了“倾向于采纳并依靠所有信息的联邦政策”。[55] 不过，有时候出于其他政策或者特殊利益的考虑，有的证据即使是与待证事实有关联，也可能被排除。[56] 合法性的主旨则是“限定性”，即防止非法证据进入诉讼程序。据此，证据必须由法定人员依照法定程序以合法的方法收集，证据必须具有合法的形式，证据必须具备合法的来源，证据必须经法定程序查证属实。[57] 如果证据属非法证据，则会被依法排除。限制非法证据的目的很明显，就是为了遏制刑讯逼供和其他非法收集证据的行为，维护司法公正和刑事诉讼参与人的合法权利。[58]

从字面上看，新《刑事诉讼法》对于证据的定义从来就不包括合法性的特征，但从相关条款的内容看，合法性则似乎又是证据的属性。如对证据的法律种类作了明确规定，很难想象不符合法定形式的证据材料会作为证据被使用。再如《刑事诉讼法》对于证据的收集和审查判断程序作了明确规定，并强调证据必须经过法定程序查证属实后才能作为定案根据。尤其重要的是，新《刑事诉讼法》对于非法证据排除规则的

---

〔50〕［美］摩根：《证据法之基本问题》，李学灯译，世界书局 1982 年版，第 198 页。

〔51〕樊崇义主编：《刑事诉讼法学》，中国政法大学出版社 2002 年版，第 152 页。

〔52〕陈光中主编：《刑事诉讼法学（新编）》中国政法大学出版社 1996 年版，第 148 ~ 154 页。

〔53〕刘金友主编：《证据法学（新编）》，中国政法大学出版社 2003 年版，第 96 页。

〔54〕张保生等：《证据法学》，高等教育出版社 2013 年版，第 24 页。

〔55〕［美］罗纳德·J. 艾伦等：《证据法：文本、问题和案例（第 3 版）》，张保生等译，高等教育出版社 2006 年版，第 147 页。

〔56〕郭志媛：《刑事证据可采性研究》，中国人民公安大学出版社 2004 年版，第 24 页。

〔57〕樊崇义主编：《刑事诉讼法学》，中国政法大学出版社 2002 年修订版，第 152 ~ 153 页。

〔58〕参见“王兆国关于刑事诉讼法修正案草案的说明”，载中国网 2012 年 3 月 8 日。

完善，凸显了证据合法性的意义。在这里，需要说明的是，证据法上的证据是诉讼证据，而非一般意义上的证据，从它进入诉讼领域那一刻起，就要受法律规范的调整和规制，从而具有明显的法律色彩。此外，强调合法性能够彰显证据的法治意义，通过对非法证据的否定，可以促使公安司法人员对于法律的服从和遵守。

一般来说，证据的合法性可分为实质合法性和形式合法性。前者是以正当性为基础，追求的是证据对案件事实的实际证明价值；后者是以法治为基础，强调证据本身的规范性。在我国证据理论上，主张合法性是证据本质属性的学者，大都不否定证据的客观性，因而这种合法性理论在本质上属于实质证据观范畴。受这种理论的影响，我国非法证据排除的范围长期被限制在部分言词证据上，对于物证、书证等实物证据，即使是刑讯逼供获得的，也被用来作为定案的根据，虽然新《刑事诉讼法》对此做了修改，但从其限制条件上看，“不符合法定程序”，“可能严重影响司法公正”、“不能补正或者作出合理解释”这三个条件必须同时具备才可能排除相关证据。事实上，这种情况基本上不会出现。此外，像视听资料、电子数据等被认为证明价值较大的证据，根本没有被纳入非法证据排除的范围。为何实践中刑讯逼供屡禁不止，是因为口供的“证据之王”地位没有发生根本改变，办案人员太看重口供的证明价值了。新形式证据观主张形式合法性，它视法律为生命，只要证据本身不合法，不管它有多大的证明价值，均不能用来作为定案的根据。当然，形式合法并不意味着必然是正当的、合理的，如刑事诉讼法关于证据种类即证据表现形式的规定，虽然抛弃了那种完全封闭列举式规定，但“证据包括：……”这种“开放列举式”的规定在很大程度上限制了新的证据材料成为新的证据种类的可能性。但不管怎样，形式合法性要求证据应当符合法律规定的表现形式，否则，不具有证据资格，不能作为认定事实的依据。此外，我们也反对采用刑讯逼供等暴力手段、威胁、引诱、欺骗甚至盗窃等不正当手段获得的证据作为认定事实的依据，否则，受到伤害的不仅仅是当事人，也是对整个法治的破坏。

五、结论：以证据为根据

《关于办理死刑案件审查判断证据若干问题的规定》第2条规定：“认定案件事实，必须以证据为根据。”这被认为是我国立法上第一次明文确立了证据裁判原则。《最高人民法院关于适用〈中华人民共和国刑事诉讼法〉的解释》第61条重申了这一原则。按照比较权威的解释，该条的基本含义是“通过证据来认定案件事实，即将证据作为实事裁判的根据”。[59] 在刑事诉讼中，坚持证据裁判原则，就必须做到认定案件事实应有相应的证据予以证明，一切都要靠证据说话，没有证据不得认定犯罪事实，更不得认定被告人有罪。证据裁判原则的确立，意味着法官认定案件事实必须以证据为根据，有效限制了法官的恣意擅断，为法官心证的形成提供了证据基础，保障了自由心证的合理性，解决了法官“拍脑袋”断案的问题。

新《刑事诉讼法》对于证据概念的重新定义，标志着证据观念的重大转变。用“材料”取代“事实”，标志着“新形式证据观”的确立。与实质证据观从实质内容上理解和把握证据不同，新形式证据观更看重证据的形式；与以“反映说”为代表的形式证据观相比，新形式证据观不仅看重证据对事实的依赖关系，更强调证据的自身形

---

〔59〕 张军主编：《刑事证据规则理解与适用》，法律出版社2010年版，第38页。

式。新形式证据观与证据裁判原则具有内在的一致性。根据新形式证据观，用以证明案件事实的证据与作为认定案件事实根据的证据是不同的。控辩双方提供的证据可能有真有假或者真假混杂，但作为认定案件事实根据的证据必须是经过法定程序查证属实的，即经过法庭举证、质证等程序，被确定为具有真实性，在形式上具有相关性和合法性。

通讯监听证据可采性研究 *

尚 华 **

一、通讯监听证据的相关性

通讯监听，也称为通讯检查，是“指以感官、录音机、录影机、电子器械或其他设计物，截取他人之秘密通讯之行为”。[1]该侦查措施的对象是秘密通讯内容，具体包括对有线通讯的截取、电子通讯的截取和口头会话的截取等。通讯监听可以同步、动态地锁定犯罪事实，其所获取的证据可以有效发现案件真相。鉴于通讯监听具有重要的侦查犯罪的作用，已被越来越多地运用于各国侦查实践中。但实践中通讯监听如果缺乏严格规范，也容易带来损害当事人通讯自由、隐私权的风险，各国立法和实践都很关注通讯监听证据能否被采纳作为定案根据。

一项证据具有可采性，其必要前提是具有相关性。正如美国《联邦证据规则》第402条的规定，相关证据一般具有可采性；不相关的证据不可采，即“除《美国宪法》、国会立法、本证据规则或最高法院依据法定权限制定的其他规则另有规定外，所有相关证据均具有可采性。不具有相关性的证据不可采”[2]。简言之，证据相关性是可采性的必要但不充分条件。因而，认定通讯监听证据是否具有可采性，首先需要分析该证据的相关性，其次，对通讯监听证据进行关于可采性的“平衡检验”，评判该证据的证明价值是否超过使用该证据可能带来的负面影响。

证据的相关性，又称“关联性”，或“相关证据”。在美国证据法中有一个“最小相关性检验标准”，《联邦证据规则》401把相关性定义为“使任何事实的存在具有任何趋向性（any tendency）……更有可能或更无可能”，“如果一个证据对事实认定者评估要件事实存在的可能性有所帮助，那么它就是相关的”[3]。通讯监听证据对于认定案件事实意义重大，通讯监听往往是在监听对象不知情的前提下进行，更可能反映案件的真实情况，监听对象一般不会基于各种主观考虑而故意说谎，因而该截取内容往往具有重要的证据价值。此外，有些犯罪信息及证据的形成可能稍纵即逝。如果不及时同步截取，可能就难以获得。特别对一些重大的“无明显被害人案件”，通讯监听与传统证据收集方式相比，具有明显的及时性和有效性。

---

* 本文系国家2011计划司法文明协同创新中心研究成果，同时是2012年北京市优秀博士学位论文指导教师人文社科项目“证据科学与司法文明”（张保生教授主持，项目编号：20121005301）、2012年国家社科基金项目（编号：12CFX043）、2013年中国博士后科学基金（编号：2013M530850）阶段性成果。

** 尚华，北方工业大学讲师，中国社科院法学所流动站、最高人民法院中国应用法学研究所博士后。

〔1〕 林富郎：“通讯监察法制化之研究”，载台湾《司法研究年报》第21辑第12篇，第7页。

〔2〕 ［美］罗纳德·J. 艾伦等：《证据法：文本、问题和案例》，张保生、王进喜、赵滢译，满运龙校，高等教育出版社2006年版，第149页。

〔3〕 张保生主编：《证据法学》，中国政法大学出版社2009年版，第20页以下。

需要注意的是，通讯监听与传统搜查、扣押措施相比，具有实施时间较长、对象不特定的特殊性。传统搜查、扣押的实施对象在实施时就特定化，针对特定的人或物，但通讯监听不同，需要从不特定的通讯信息中寻求与案件有关的特定对象。实践中通讯监听往往持续较长时间，在该时间内截取的通讯信息内容较为丰富，其中有些通讯信息对证明案件事实非常有用，但也必然会存在一些与案件无关的信息内容。鉴于此，通讯监听证据的相关性评估，需要结合截取信息内容与案件待证事实的关系，具体问题具体分析。

为了确保通讯监听证据的相关性，在实施通讯监听时需要坚持相关性原则，即通讯监听的实施应当与特定案件事实有关，一般围绕特定的犯罪嫌疑人及其实施犯罪有关的特定对象进行。这种做法在一些国家的立法中得以确立。例如，德国《刑事诉讼法典》第100条a5规定："命令监视、录制电讯往来时，只允许针对被指控人，或者针对基于一定事实可以推断他们为被指控人代收或者转送他所发出信息的人员，或者针对被指控人在使用他们的电话线的人员作出命令。"〔4〕美国的《综合控制犯罪与街道安全法》规定监听的实质条件之一是：有合理的根据相信三种事项：①某个人正在实施、已经实施或即将实施《美国法典》规定的属于监听范围内的犯罪（其中包括贿赂犯罪）；②通过监听可以获得有关该犯罪的特定通讯；③准备监听通讯的设备或场所正在或即将用于与实施上述犯罪有关的活动，或者被个人租用或登记在其名下或通常由他使用，但法律另有规定的除外。〔5〕日本将通讯监听适用对象限定为正在实施犯罪或有犯罪倾向的人。

在中国，新《刑事诉讼法》增设了技术侦查措施，并明确了通讯监听所获材料的证据资格，但这并不意味着所有通讯监听材料都必然具有可采性。只有与案件事实有关的通讯材料才具有相关性，才有可能被采纳作为定案根据。实践中，应当避免对与案件事实无关的通讯内容予以截取，因为这些通讯信息不具有证据的相关性，也不具有可采性，不能作为认定案件事实的根据，而且这些通讯信息的截取还很容易侵犯他人的通讯自由和隐私权。只有将通讯监听的实施严格限定在与案件事实有关的人和事，才可能确保通讯监听所截取的信息具有证据相关性，从而为其具有可采性奠定必要性条件。

二、通讯监听证据可采性的"平衡检验"

证据具有相关性只是其可采的必要前提，并非必然具有可采性。通讯监听所截取的信息，不仅应当具有证据的相关性，还需要通过可采性的"平衡检验"，即该证据的证明价值超过使用该证据可能带来的负面影响。美国《联邦证据规则》403条规定了以偏见、混淆或费时为由排除相关证据，即"相关的证据，如果具有不公正偏见、混淆争议或误导陪审团的危险，或对其过分拖延、浪费时间或无需出示累积证据的考虑，在实质上超过其证明价值时，亦可被排除，不予采用"。〔6〕为了正确评价通讯监听证据的可采性，需要对该证据的证明价值与其可能带来的负面效应予以平衡和取舍。

---

〔4〕《德国刑事诉讼法典》，李昌珂译，中国政法大学出版社1995年版，第33页。

〔5〕孙长永：《侦查程序与人权》，中国方正出版社2000年版，第136～137页。

〔6〕［美］罗纳德·J. 艾伦等：《证据法：文本、问题和案例》，张保生、王进喜、赵滢译，满运龙校，高等教育出版社2006年版，第165页。

毋庸置疑，在符合相关性原则下的通讯监听对于侦查重大疑难案件作用明显，其截取的通讯信息也具有证据的相关性，但其最大的负面影响就是可能侵犯公民的秘密通讯自由和隐私权。不容否认，通讯监听的信息往往是受监听人不愿公开的秘密通讯内容，部分内容可能会涉及监听对象隐私权保护的范围。这必然会涉及侦查的有效性与相对人的权益保障之间的冲突和平衡。可以说，通讯监听已经成为各国司法机关既钟爱又担忧的侦查措施。

从域外立法和实践来看，尽管一些国家在实践中存在较多争议，但大多肯定了通讯监听证据的可采性。在美国，通讯监听证据的可采性经历了较长时间的争议。美国1934年《联邦通讯法》制定后，在1937年Nardone v. United States案和1939年Nardone v. United States案的裁判中，最高法院的态度是“禁止监听和泄露电话通讯”，因此监听证据或任何直接从监听中衍生而来的证据都不得在审判中使用。在随后的Goldman v. U. S. 案、On Lee v. U. S. 案、Silverman v. U. S. 案、Lopez v. U. S. 案、Berger v. New York案中，最高法院在判断监听证据是否可采时主要围绕“对宪法第四修正案的搜查扣押是否包括声音这个‘无形物’以及是否伴有‘物理侵入’私人领域而形成”。[7] 1967年Katz v. U. S. 案是一个里程碑式的转折性案例，该案将监听证据的可采性与隐私权保护密切联系起来。为了进一步有效解决监听证据的可采性与隐私权保护之间的冲突，美国国会于1968年制定了《综合犯罪控制和街道安全法》，有关联邦监听的法律程序与证据问题集中体现在该法典的第三篇。该法明确了通讯监听证据在符合法定条件时具有可采性。

在欧洲，监听法律的制定和完善与欧洲人权公约关系密切。在英国，欧洲人权法院就Malone v. the United Kingdom案的判决对英国通讯监听立法起到了重要的推动作用，制定了《通讯监听法》。此后，2000年7月28日，英国制定了《2000年侦查权规制法》，并取代了《通讯监听法》。通讯监听证据经历了从无规则限制的可采到绝对排除，再到有限可采的过程。在法国，通讯监听也经历了一个由无规则到有规则的发展过程。这其中欧洲人权法院起到了重要的推动作用。在通讯监听无规则时期，法国通讯监听行为多次受到欧洲人权法院的质疑和批评。在1990年“哈维格与克拉斯林诉法国”案的判决作出后，法国迫于国内外压力，于1991年7月10日在刑事诉讼法中增加了“电讯的截留”一节，明确规范了通讯监听行为及其证据的可采性。在德国，1975年刑事诉讼法修改增加了“监视电信通讯”内容，对通讯监听行为予以严格规范，并明确了通讯监听证据的有条件可采。

虽然各国对于通讯监听证据的可采性存在争议，但基本的做法和趋势是有条件地确认其可采性。正如德国刑事诉讼法学家托马斯·魏根特所言：“当立法机关试图引入电话监听这一措施时，它必须在受保护的个人利益和执法利益之间寻求妥协，根据法院做出的解释，这种妥协明显偏向于执法利益。”[8] 正如哈耶克指出：“证明任何特定法律规则是否具有正当性，所依据一定是该规则所具有的功效——即使这种功效有可

---

〔7〕 李明：《监听制度研究》，法律出版社2008年版，第70页。

〔8〕 ［德］托马斯·魏根特：《德国刑事诉讼程序》，岳礼玲、温小洁译，中国政法大学出版社2003年版，第122页。

能无法通过理性的论证得到确证，但是它仍可以为人们所知，这是因为这一特定规则在实践中能够证明自己比其他手段更为适宜。”[9] 当然，为了确保通讯监听证据可采的正当性，需要立法严格规范通讯监听的实施条件和程序，从而将其负面影响降至最低。

一些国际公约也确认了通讯监听证据的可采性，例如，《联合国反腐败公约》第50条第1款的规定：“为有效地打击腐败，各缔约国均应当在其本国法律制度基本原则许可的范围内并根据本国法律规定的条件在其力所能及的情况下采取必要措施，允许其主管机关在其领域内酌情使用控制下交付和在其认为适当时使用诸如电子或者其他监视形式和特工行动等其他特殊侦查手段，并允许法庭采信由这些手段产生的证据。”可见，通讯监听对于侦查一些特定类型的重大犯罪而言，其侦查取证的有效性已经超过其可能带来的负面影响。

在中国，学界关于监听证据的可采性或证据能力，存在两种基本观点。一是肯定监听证据的可采性，认为监听证据“可以直接进入审判程序，而不需要什么转化过程。只要公诉机关能够证明其真实性，就可以作为定案的根据”[10]。二是否定其可采性，认为“只能在分析案情时使用，不能在审判中直接作为证据使用。如果要在法庭上作为证据使用，需要在此前一定时间内告知有关案件各方秘密取证的信息，将其公开化后方能作为合法证据使用”[11]。从立法的角度看，《宪法》第40条规定：“中华人民共和国公民的通信自由和通信秘密受法律的保护。除因国家安全或者追查刑事犯罪的需要，由公安机关或者检察机关依照法律规定的程序对通信进行检查外，任何组织或者个人不得以任何理由侵犯公民的通信自由和通信秘密。”可见，公民的通信自由和通信秘密并非绝对，有关司法机关可以根据刑事侦查需要依法实施通讯检查。中国立法关于通讯监听证据的可采性，经历了一个发展过程。中国《国家安全法》和《人民警察法》都提到“技术侦察措施”，但并未明确所获证据的可采性。直至2010年5月30日，最高人民法院、最高人民检察院、公安部、国家安全部、司法部联合颁布了《关于办理死刑案件审查判断证据若干问题的规定》，该规定第35条明确了包括通讯监听在内的特殊侦查措施所获材料的证据资格。2012年中国修改后的《刑事诉讼法》第152条进一步明确规定了通讯监听所获材料的证据资格，在符合法律规定情形下通讯监听证据可以被采纳为定案根据。这一规定是在充分考虑通讯监听证据的证明价值与其可能带来的负面影响之后的平衡和选择，符合中国刑事司法的价值追求和实践需要。

三、违法通讯监听的证据排除

（一）非法通讯监听证据排除的模式和程序

各国关于非法通讯监听证据排除的模式不尽相同，这主要与各国不同的法律传统和非法证据排除的一般模式有关。例如，美国坚持审判中心和法官自由裁量原则，因而违法通讯监听所获的材料并不必然被排除，而是由法官根据具体案件情况，综合考

---

〔9〕［英］弗里德利希·冯·哈耶克：《自由秩序原理》（上），邓正来译，生活·读书·新知三联书店1997年版，第198页。

〔10〕杨迎泽、李麟：“电话监听证据研析”，载《证据学论坛（第1卷）》，中国检察出版社2000年版，第395页。

〔11〕何家弘：《证据调查》，法律出版社1997年版，第306页。

虑和平衡司法利益，自由裁量排除。在英国，通讯监听所获材料只是有限可采，但在司法实务中基于英国法官自由裁量排除的传统，对非法通讯监听所获材料的排除问题，一般由法官自由裁量。德国现行立法并未明确规定非法通讯监听的证据排除，主要依据证据禁止理论予以排除，包括违反宪法原则的排除和违反一般法律的排除问题。但在司法实践中，“德国判例采用了一种有限排除的做法，即只排除那些完全违反相应法律规定的非法监控行为或只有当对法律的违反是故意所为时才使用非法证据排除规则。德国法院在对待秘密监控的非法证据时，采用一种利益权衡的做法，需要综合考虑秘密监控手段侵犯的个人利益与所追求的执法利益，这种权衡没有预先确定的结论”。〔12〕意大利对于非法通讯监听证据排除，采用刚性的法定排除模式，对法律规定的违法通讯监听行为所获材料一律予以排除。

各国在非法通讯监听证据排除的模式上存在区别，其排除程序也不尽相同。例如，在美国，一般并不由法官主动启动证据排除，而是由当事人申请启动排除。这主要与对抗制及法官角色定位有关。《美国法典》第2518条第10款第1项规定，任何受到损害的人可以依据以下理由提出排除监听内容及其派生证据的动议：①通讯是被非法监听的；②授权或认可的监听令状明显不适当；③监听行为与授权或认可监听令状规定不一致的。这种申请必须在审判、听证或其他程序开始前提出，除非没有提出的机会或者申请人当时还不知道申请理由的。〔13〕但是，在德国法中，“排除不可采的证据原则上不需要一方当事人提出动议”。〔14〕也就是说，负责案件审理的法庭在一定的情况下，可以主动发动排除非法证据的程序。

在中国，根据新《刑事诉讼法》第56条规定，审判人员可以依职权对证据的合法性予以调查，当事人及其辩护人、诉讼代理人也可以申请人民法院对以非法方法收集的证据依法予以排除。这符合中国诉讼模式和法官定位，中国法官享有较大的权力，在必要时可以依职权对案件相关事实、证据进行审查。因而负有职权探知功能的法官可以对有非法嫌疑的证据予以审查。基于中国司法实践状况，需要进一步强化当事人及其辩护人、诉讼代理人的证据排除申请权，同时也需要保留法官主动排除的权力。关于非法通讯监听证据排除的时间，根据中国《关于办理刑事案件排除非法证据若干问题的规定》（以下简称《非法证据排除规定》）第5条规定，中国刑事诉讼中排除非法证据既可以在开庭审理前，也可以在庭审中。

（二）非法通讯监听证据排除的内容

1. 非法通讯监听证据排除的一般内容

通讯监听应当严格遵循法定程序进行，但监听程序违法并不必然导致其所截取的通讯资料被排除。实践中，往往需要结合所违反程序的性质及其重要程度，具体情况具体分析。不同国家非法通讯监听的证据排除内容存在一定的区别。

美国对非法通讯监听证据的排除采用较为灵活的态度，并非所有违反法定程序所获的材料都要排除。在U. S. v. Chavez案，最高法院认为未能完全履行Title Ⅲ之要件并

---

〔12〕 程雷：《秘密侦查比较研究》，中国人民公安大学出版社2008年版，第532页。

〔13〕 李明：《监听制度研究》，法律出版社2008年版，第192页。

〔14〕 ［德］托马斯·魏根特：《德国刑事诉讼程序》，岳礼玲、温小洁译，中国政法大学出版社2003年版，第201页。

非必然会导致有线或口头通讯之截取成为违法之行为。在 U. S. v. Giordano 案，美国联邦最高法院认为，违法通讯监听证据排除的前提是：所违反的程序应当“在法律程序框架中具有核心作用”〔15〕，因而实践中并非任何违反监听法定程序的非法监听资料都需要排除，“只有那些违反监听法规定的程序要件，将无法达成立法者限制‘监听在真正需要情况下始得实施’的目的时，违法监听所得的证据始得加以排除”〔16〕。

在欧洲，德国对通讯监听行为予以严格规范，非法通讯监听的证据排除范围较宽。“对于合法取得监听录音可以作为证据使用，但无法官授权所取得录音资料不得作为证据使用，在合法的监听措施中，发现有违法行为，但此行为并非法定如监听之范围，所取得的录音资料也不得作为证据使用。如果用此窃听资料非难被窃听之人而取得其陈述，其陈述仍不得作为证据之用。对合法取得的监听资料，如仅片断或总结性地播放或朗读该内容，则属违法，也为判例所禁止。”〔17〕 法国刑事诉讼法对于非法监听材料排除未有明确规定，只对一些特殊对象（国民议会议员、律师）的非法监听材料排除予以具体规定，强调对于这些特殊对象的违法监听所获得的资料应当排除。实践中一般要求通讯监听应当具有目的正当性，有判例认为，通讯监听“不可有积极挑逗诱发电话通讯，否则有失光明正大，而所得证据自亦失其合法性”〔18〕。在意大利，如果窃听是在法律允许的情况以外进行的或者未遵守法律规定的程序，所获得的材料不得加以使用。〔19〕

在中国，立法并未专门规定非法监听所获资料的排除问题。新《刑事诉讼法》第54条规定非法收集的言词证据应当予以排除。对于物证、书证，其收集不符合法定程序，可能严重影响司法公正的，应当予以补正或者作出合理解释；不能补正或者作出合理解释的，对该证据应当予以排除。本文认为，应当参照中国非法证据排除的一般规定，并结合通讯监听的特殊性予以判断。下文将结合几个具体程序违法问题展开分析。

2. 违反授权主体和程序的证据排除

通讯监听极易侵犯公民的秘密通讯自由和隐私权，所以各国立法都严格规定通讯监听的审批权限和程序，大多将通讯监听的批准权授予法官或检察官。对于违反批准权限和程序所得到的通讯信息，法院应当予以排除，不能作为认定案件事实的根据。违反通讯监听审批权限的行为属于明显且十分重大的违法行为，对于其所截取的通讯信息，应当严格地予以排除。

在美国，违反授权规范的通讯监听属于违反“具有核心作用”的程序规范，所获的材料应当予以严格排除。在1974年的 U. S v. Giordano 案，最高法院认为，为了在令状签发前对监听进行控制，有关授权申请人资格等规定在监听程序中扮演“核心作用”，本案并未遵守此规定，因而所获证据应当予以排除。〔20〕 在德国，违反授权规范

---

〔15〕 U. S. v. Giordano, 416U. S. 505, (1974).

〔16〕 江舜明：“监听在刑事程序方法上之理论与实务”，载《法学丛刊》1998年第5期，第106页。

〔17〕［德］克劳斯·罗科信：《刑事诉讼法》，吴丽琪译，法律出版社第2003年版，第335页。

〔18〕 刁荣华主编：《比较刑事证据法各论》，汉林出版社1984年版，第292页。

〔19〕《意大利刑事诉讼法典》，黄风译，中国政法大学出版社1994年版，第92页。

〔20〕 U. S. v. Giordano, 416U. S. 505, (1974).

所获的材料不得作为定案根据，需要予以排除。意大利对于非法通讯监听证据排除较为严格，违反授权规范所获材料应当予以排除。我国台湾地区采取与美国相似做法，“未经检察官或法官授权而实施搜索，因违反授权原则，致搜索有遭执法人员滥用之情事，而侵害宪法保障之基本权利，故所取得之证据应予以排除”。[21]

在中国，新《刑事诉讼法》第 148 条只规定“根据侦查犯罪的需要，经过严格的批准手续，可以采取技术侦查措施”。但并未具体规定由谁批准授权、如何批准，也没有明确规定违反批准授权规范所获材料的排除问题。本文认为，遵守授权程序规范是通讯监听纳入法治轨道的基本要求，对于违反批准授权规范取得的通讯材料应当予以排除，不能作为定案的根据。同时，立法应当进一步完善具体批准授权主体和程序。

3. 违反授权书内容的证据排除

通讯监听的实施应当严格依据签发的授权书内容，禁止违反法定程序和批准的令状内容而实施通讯监听。对此，各国法律大多予以严格规范。但对于违反该内容所获的通讯材料是否应当排除，各国实践做法并不一致。美国实践中并非一律排除，而是由法官根据具体案情予以裁量排除。例如，对于被监听人的身份，在 1974 年 U. S. v. Kahn 一案中，最高法院认为，为了提高监听侦查效果，对于令状未明确监听对象的身份所获证据材料并不需要排除。在 U. S. v. Donovan 一案中，梅尔欧和劳尔的名字并没有被监听令状列入监听对象目录，对其监听所获通讯材料也并不需要排除。也有国家对此予以严格排除，意大利刑事诉讼法就明确规定：对违反法定前提条件和形式所取得的监听资料不得作为证据使用。

在中国，新《刑事诉讼法》第 149 条规定“批准决定应当根据侦查犯罪的需要，确定采取技术侦查措施的种类和适用对象。批准决定自签发之日起 3 个月以内有效。对于不需要继续采取技术侦查措施的，应当及时解除；对于复杂、疑难案件，期限届满仍有必要继续采取技术侦查措施的，经过批准，有效期可以延长，每次不得超过 3 个月”。第 150 条第 1 款规定“采取技术侦查措施，必须严格按照批准的措施种类、适用对象和期限执行。”立法并未明确有关证据排除问题。

本文认为，对于违反授权书记载内容所获的通讯材料是否排除，需要结合具体情况予以分析。其一，对于违反批准的种类和期限所获材料需要排除。其二，对于适用对象的不一致不能一概排除，需要结合当时具体情况予以判断，因为通讯监听不同于传统搜查、扣押，搜查、扣押在决定之初适用对象就已经特定化，而通讯监听有可能在决定之初对象不确定，在实施过程发现一些极为有用的通讯资料，如果绝对排除就会影响侦查工作的顺利进行。其三，对于其他形式问题或瑕疵，可以予以补正或合理解释，只有在无法补正或合理解释的情况下，才需要法官予以裁量排除。这不仅符合中国新《刑事诉讼法》和《非法证据排除规定》的立法精神和做法，也符合实践情况。中国实践中通讯监听的批准一般由公安、检察内部决定，并未严格纳入司法令状的范畴。

4. 违反保密和销毁规定的证据排除问题

通讯监听作为一种较为特殊的侦查措施，较易侵犯公民的秘密通讯自由和隐私权，

---

〔21〕 林富郎：“通讯监察法制化之研究”，载台湾《司法研究年报》第 21 辑第 12 篇，第 254 页。

因而对其截取的通讯证据需要遵循严格的保存、保密和销毁程序。实践中，通讯监听一般会持续较长时间，所截取的通讯材料也可能涉及多方面内容，有些与案件事实有关，有些通讯材料与案件事实无关。这些无关的通讯材料既对侦查和追诉犯罪没有意义，又存在侵犯公民秘密通讯自由和隐私权的危险，因而需要及时销毁这些与犯罪无关的通讯材料。法国《刑事诉讼法典》第100条第6款规定："登记册根据共和国检察官或检察长的要求在公诉时效期间届满时销毁。"[22] 德国《刑事诉讼法典》也规定："追诉不再需要以措施得来的材料时，应当在检察院监督下不迟延地将它销毁。"[23] 意大利《刑事诉讼法典》第269条第2款规定："当诉讼不需要有关材料时，关系人可以为维护其隐私权要求曾经批准或者认可窃听工作的法官将其销毁。"[24] 日本法律也严格规定应当对通讯监听资料保密。

中国新《刑事诉讼法》第150条第2款规定：侦查人员对采取技术侦查措施过程中知悉的国家秘密、商业秘密和个人隐私，应当保密；对采取技术侦查措施获取的与案件无关的材料，必须及时销毁。但这并不意味违反该规定的证据需要排除。本文认为，对于违反保密和销毁规定，所获的证据一般不需排除，可以作为定案的根据。"至于销毁之规定，系为免监察所得资料泄露影响到受监察人之隐私权而设之行政管理上之防备措施，从未确实遵守，亦仅堪认系行政管理上有所缺失，其与人民隐私权之保障虽难谓无关联，然究无必要之关系，故虽有违反，对所取得之证据亦无予以排除法则之必要。"[25] 保密和销毁规定并不影响通讯监听结果的真实性，对通讯截取过程没有直接影响，只是后续资料管理中的规范，没有必要予以排除。

---

〔22〕《法国刑事诉讼法典》，余叔通、谢朝华译，中国政法大学出版社1997年版，第52页。

〔23〕《德国刑事诉讼法典》，李昌珂译，中国政法大学出版社1995年版，第34页。

〔24〕《意大利刑事诉讼法典》，黄风译，中国政法大学出版社1994年版，第91页。

〔25〕林富郎：《通讯监察法制化之研究》，台湾司法研究年报第21辑第12篇，第258页。

证据法视野下谎言的相关性分析

李小恺 *

说谎是一种非常普遍的社会现象，在信息交流过程中时常会存在谎言。谎言影响传递信息之真伪，同时更深入地影响人与人之间的信任关系。谎言是难以识别和判断的，经常会有人被他人欺瞒，将谎话信以为真；人们即便对所听之言产生些许怀疑，也常常无法确证。

证据活动必须建立在各种信息交流的基础上，因此难以避开谎言的身影。在事实中可能混杂着谎言，让人难以辨清也无从认定；证据的内容中可能存在谎言，证人证言、当事人陈述甚至各类笔录中都常见混淆是非的企图。在取证、举证、质证和认证这一系列过程中，谎言的层出不穷给司法程序带来各种不公正的风险。证据活动是受法律约束的司法活动，与日常经验法则相比，这种特殊性决定了在证据活动中对待谎言的态度和要求必定有其自身的特点。在证据法视野下对谎言的相关性进行分析，将有助于进一步研究谎言对证明活动所产生的各种影响以及相应对策。

一、证据法中与谎言有关的概念

（一）谎言与假话的区别

谎言的内容是否一定为假？在谎言概念中，这是最具争议也最易被混淆的问题。日常生活中，人们对谎言的怀疑也会直接着眼在所述内容的真实性上。考勒曼（Coleman）和凯（Kay）从原型语义学的角度分析，认为一段陈述若为谎言，需要满足三个条件：①表达者认为该陈述是假的；②表达者做出该陈述的目的是为了欺骗接收者；③事实证明该陈述是假的。[1] 其中也将“事实证明该陈述是假的”视作谎言的基本条件。而实际上，谎言未必就是假的或不真实的。人的认识能力、记忆能力和表达能力都有局限性，在事实发生后，很难有人可以百分之百准确地再现全部事实。对信息的感知错误、理解歪曲、记忆混乱等现象，可能导致人对事实整体的认识与事实本身截然相反。在此基础上，将错误的认识再次歪曲而成的谎言，很难将它与事实的本来面目相对比，它是真是假已无从判断。我们更不能以某段话是谎言作为理由，直接认定与其内容相反的便为真实。因为谎言与真假之间，还隔着一层谎者的认识。

不妨在谎言与假话之间作个比较。“言”与“话”没有作区分的意义，重点就在“谎”与“假”之间的差异。“假”是与“真”相对的，这是一个形容词，用来形容事物的不真实。而“谎”不仅可以作为形容词，它还是一个动词，代表一种行为。作为一个行为或者行为的产物，谎言的概念中必然包含其行为特征及该行为的主体因素。

说谎、撒谎都是“谎”的行为，与一般陈述行为相比具有特殊性。克劳斯

---

* 李小恺，中国政法大学博士研究生。Email：lixiaokai1111@gmail.com。

〔1〕 羊芙葳：《谎言的识别研究》，华中科技大学2010年博士学位论文，第17页。

(Krauss)把说谎界定为“一种企图在另一人身上建立欺骗认为是错误的信任或理解的行为。”[2] 艾克哈曼给说谎下的定义是:“事先没有对自己的意图作任何交代而有意识地蒙骗别人的行为。”[3] 潘清泉等的定义说“说谎是个体有意识地对事实进行隐瞒、歪曲或凭空编造假信息以误导他人的行为。”[4] 这些定义都是在将“谎”视作行为进行描述。在这些定义中总结出一点共识,即带有欺骗他人的企图,这是“谎”的行为特征。

行为的主体因素也是谎言概念的重要组成部分。按照因果关系,行为主体通过“谎”的行为,才会产生谎言和谎话的结果。谎者要隐瞒自己的想法,达到误导他人的目的。那么作为这种带有欺骗企图之行为的产物,谎言势必与其头脑中的认识不一致。Coleman 和 Kay 在归纳出谎言的三个必要条件后也表示,这其中第一个条件是谎言最重要的特征,即表达者认为该陈述是假的。[5] 由此可见,若表达者“信以为真”的假话则不具备这样的特征,纵然陈述内容与事实不符,也不能称之为谎言。

总而言之,谎言与假话有着本质上的区别。在与假话的对比分析中,笔者总结出谎言应当具备的两个基本特征,以此作为谎言的概念:其一,表达者企图利用该表述欺骗他人;其二,表达者认为其表述内容为假。

(二)事实性谎言与证据性谎言的关系

信息在诉讼的各阶段里一般扮演着两种不同的角色:一种是成为证明的对象,即作为待证事实出现;另一种则是与待证事实具有相关性,可能作为证据使用,在证明活动中发挥对待证事实的证明力。在证据法视野下,谎言也有事实性谎言和证据性谎言的区分。

所谓事实性谎言,即以谎言作为待证事实或者待证事实中的一部分。在很多法律关系中,是否构成谎言是对事实定性的标准。例如,伪证罪需要证明证人在作证中撒谎;[6] 合同条款存在欺诈,也需要证明签订合同的一方当事人存在对另一方当事人说谎的行为;[7] 商品责任中,商家是否构成虚假宣传,也要证明是否在宣传中对消费者

---

〔2〕［英］Albert Vrij.:《说谎心理学》,郑红丽译,中国轻工业出版社2005年版,第7页。

〔3〕［美］Paul Ekman:《识破谎言——如何识破政界、军界、商界及婚姻中的骗局》,刘文荣、今夫译,广西民族出版社1992年版,第71页。

〔4〕潘清泉,周宗奎:“说谎判断研究新发展”,载《理论月刊》2009年第6期,第123页。

〔5〕第1条在某种意义上与第3条产生逻辑上的矛盾,因为“陈述者认为”与“事实证明”之间并不是同一个概念,但Coleman和Kay认为第1条是谎言最重要的特征。

〔6〕在很多有关伪证罪的法律规定中,证人撒谎或者进行达到撒谎效果的行为均是犯罪构成的一部分。例如《中华人民共和国刑法》第305条规定:“在刑事诉讼中,证人、鉴定人、记录人、翻译人对与案件有重要关系的情节,故意作虚假证明、鉴定、记录、翻译,意图陷害他人或者隐匿罪证的,处3年以下有期徒刑或者拘役;情节严重的,处3年以上7年以下有期徒刑。”《美国加州刑法典(PENAL CODE)》第118条(a)款规定:“Every person who, having taken an oath that he or she will testify, declare, depose, or certify truly before any competent tribunal, officer, or person, in any of the cases in which the oath may by law of the State of California be administered, willfully and contrary to the oath, states as true any material matter which he or she knows to be false, and every person who testifies, declares, deposes, or certifies under penalty of perjury in any of the cases in which the testimony, declarations, depositions, or certification is permitted by law of the State of California under penalty of perjury and willfully states as true any material matter which he or she knows to be false, is guilty of perjury.”

〔7〕比如《中华人民共和国刑法》第224条中对合同诈骗罪的定义:“合同诈骗罪是指以非法占有为目的,在签订、履行合同过程中,采取虚构事实或者隐瞒真相等欺骗手段,骗取对方当事人财物数额较大的行为。”

说谎。[8] 在这些例子中，如何界定其行为的性质，关键就在如何证明特定陈述是否可定性为谎言。

所谓证据性谎言，即将谎言作为证据以证明其他事实。谎言并非孤立存在，它与很多事实具有相关性。至少根据谎言的基本特征来看，谎言能够表明谎者有欺骗他人的企图，也能表明谎言的内容在谎者看来是虚假的。由于这种相关性的存在，可以将谎言作为证据来证明相关的待证事实。在很多时候，诉讼中的一方指出另一方说谎，或者指出证人在说谎，其目的是要证明其所述事实为虚假，甚至是要证明与谎言内容相反的情况才是事实真相。

对事实性谎言与证据性谎言的区分有重要的意义。

对于前者，证据法关注的重点应当是怎样完成对谎言的证明。在日常生活中，人们捕捉到陈述者目光闪烁、张口结舌等各种蛛丝马迹，可能就会主观认定其说谎。轻则对其所述内容之真实性大打折扣，重则直接给其冠以不诚实的评价。而根据证据法的要求，任何一方提出的主张必须有证据证明，并且需达到相应的证明标准，否则所主张之事实不能成立，更不能对法律关系产生任何影响。因此，若要证明谎言成立，首先要求主张者提出符合可采性要求的证据；同时，这些证据还要有足够的证明力以满足证明标准的要求。

对于后者，证据法关注的重点则是谎言的证明力问题。欺骗他人、隐瞒真相，这些显现出的企图可以反映出谎者撒谎的原因和谎者的真实想法；内容令人生疑、矛盾丛生，这些也给发现真相提供了反面的模板；各种不良品性、曾经的撒谎行为，这些也会或多或少影响到陈述者的可信性。但是，影响谎言的因素有很多，仅谎言的动机就五花八门，事实究竟与谎言有多大的出入？这只有在弄清其全部内在关系之后才能给出准确的答案。那么在模糊不清时，谎言与证明对象之间相关性的有无以及程度的大小将会成为影响证据证明力的核心问题。而对于可信性而言，这本就是证明力问题。证据的内容、证据提出者的动机和品性甚至证据的获取程序，这其中一旦出现令人怀疑的污点，则证据的可信性就会动摇。其表现就是令事实认定者对证据的证明力打折扣。至于折扣的多少，则要视谎言对可信性影响之大小来决定。

当然，事实性谎言与证据性谎言在很多时候是联袂出现的。要利用谎言证明待证事实，首先就需要证明该陈述是否确为谎言，此时的谎言就是作为证明对象出现的；同样，在大多数情况下，完成对一个事实性谎言的证明之后，随之而来的就是要利用这一结论来进一步完成对其他事实的证明。从逻辑角度来看，要先完成对一个谎言的证明，才能够利用谎言去说明其他问题。而对这一谎言存在与否的事实证明到何种程度，则将直接影响到谎言在之后所要发挥的证明力。

二、谎言与待证事实的相关性

不论何种形式的谎言，其本质都是人的意思表示，来源于人的意识。而意识的形成必须依赖客观存在的事实。谎言一定是某些信息的载体，与特定事实之间具有逻辑上的相关性。在证据法视野下，因谎言而引起关注的事实主要有两个：一是谎者的动

---

〔8〕 比如《中华人民共和国反不正当竞争法》第4条规定：广告不得含有虚假的内容，不得欺骗和误导消费者。

机，二是谎言内容所涉及的事实真相。

（一）说谎与谎者的动机

没有动机，即没有欺骗他人的企图，也就不能制造谎言。经验常识也表明，在面对重要事务时，没有足够的动机就不会有谎言。在不必要的时候，人是不会舍弃实话而说谎的。从谎言的概念上看，谎者主观上是要欺骗他人。然而，“欺骗”仅仅是采取说谎行为时业已形成的企图。那么究竟是什么使谎者产生了这种企图？这才是谎者动机的深层内容，也是揭露谎言所掩藏之真相的关键事实。

产生谎言的原因有很多种，其根源来自于人的各种需要。有些人为了获得更多的利益，如广告中充斥的虚假宣传、诈骗犯口中的种种许诺等；有些人为了逃避惩罚而撒谎，如交通事故的肇事者隐瞒行踪、商人隐瞒产品的瑕疵、打破碗的小孩在父母面前沉默不语等；有些人是为了摆脱尴尬的境地而撒谎，如同性恋者隐瞒自己曾与其他同性相处、有夫之妇隐瞒自己私会情人等；有些人为了摆脱当前困境或者避免不必要的麻烦而撒谎，如被刑讯逼供的无辜者为避免再受皮肉之苦而承认自己有罪、了解其他亲友间债务纠纷的人为避免恶化感情而三缄其口谎称不知情等；还有些人是为了善意的目的选择撒谎，如对患了绝症之人谎称其只是小毛病、为了博情人一笑而编造不存在的滑稽故事。各种不同的需要，使谎言在谎者看来具有使用价值，因此可能促使其选用谎言以欺骗他人。

在证据法视野下，证据具有可采性的前提是要与事实之间具有逻辑的相关性。具有上述意图的陈述者都可能编造谎言以实现其目的，因此这些反应陈述者意图的信息均与谎言存在之事实具有逻辑上的相关性。这是一种依据经验常识得出的因果关系，具备特定动机可以用来表明存在说谎的可能性。

然后在某些情况下，推理的过程并不是以动机来证明谎言。很多时候是主张陈述者撒谎以证明该谎者具有某种特定动机，并进一步将这一动机与谎者可能从事的其他行为建立相关性。那么，如果将上述的因果关系反过来，假如证明了说谎的事实可能成立或者确实成立，那么是否也能够从谎言中大胆得出谎者是属于何种动机的结论呢？多种意图可能产生同一种行为，这属于“多因一果”的因果关系，只要其中一个原因满足，得出“谎言成立”之结论的可能性就很大。但是，以“谎言”为起点，可能产生谎言的每一种原因都可能成为推论的终点。在没有其他证据加以佐证时，谎言与动机间的相关性会因为被各种可能性均分而大为削弱，从谎言到任意一个动机的推论都变得十分不可靠。因此，虽然谎言与谎者动机之间是具有相关性的，但是在挖掘该相关性的证明作用时，如何建构推论的逻辑关系会使相关性的强弱产生巨大的差异。

（二）谎言的内容与事实真相

谎言的内容一定是以事实信息为蓝本的。事实一旦发生就不再重现，之后的事实认定过程，都只能依据事实发生时被各种载体所俘获的信息片段。作为一种重要的信息载体，人通过感知能力可以获得大量的事实信息，这些信息形成人对事实的记忆和认识。当人陈述某个事实的时候，其陈述的内容就源自这些材料。谎言的本质是谎者所作的陈述，因此，谎言的内容也一定不会凭空出现，必然是以各种事实信息为来源。可以说，谎言的内容与事实真相之间具有天然的相关性。

然而，谎言的内容与事实真相之间的相关性是间接的，二者之间无法直接建立联系。与一般的陈述行为一样，陈述主体是陈述内容的直接来源，其中的信息来自于人的记忆和认识。另外，谎言还有其自身的特点。根据谎言的基本特征，谎者一定是认为谎言的内容为假。这说明，在谎者看来，谎言的内容应当是与其对事实信息的记忆和认识不相符的。换言之，在谎者编制谎言内容的时候，一定需要对原本存在其头脑中的信息进行伪造、变造、添加、删除等加工处理。这种加工处理有“度”的差异。可能是对其中全部信息都进行改动，也可能只是部分性修改；可能是与原来的意思表示完全相反，也可能只是稍微有所偏离。此时如果要从谎言的内容反向推论出事实真相，必须以两个重要信息为基础：其一，谎者的记忆和认识是否符合事实真相；其二，谎者是对其记忆和认识中的信息做了何种方式以及何种程度的改动，才使其最终形成谎言的内容。这两个信息均为谎者的主观因素，这种主观因素阻断了谎言的内容与事实真相之间的相关性。因此，谎言内容与事实真相之间是间接的联系。在评价其相关性程度时，一定无法回避谎者主观因素所产生的影响。究竟谎者为什么要说谎？他希望谎言达到什么样的效果？只有在得到这两个答案之后，方能进一步弄清谎言的内容与事实真相之间的真实关系。

三、谎言与证言的可信性

证言的可信性问题是证据法的一个重要命题。证言是否可信、可信程度几何，这些都会影响证言的证明力。此外，可信性非常差的证言还可能会带来强烈的误导性。如果这种误导性对公正审判产生的风险超过了其相关性所带来的证明价值，此时就会导致证言被排除在证据大门之外。然而很多时候，事实认定者在判断证言是否可信时，更多地考虑证人是否诚实。英美法系对证人的可信性进行弹劾的方法主要有五种：第一种是证明证人自相矛盾；第二种是证明证人因情感或经济利益的影响，对一方证人有所偏袒；第三种是证明证人的品性不可信；第四种是证明在重要事实上该证人的证言与其他证人的证言之间存在矛盾；第五种是证明证人的感知、回忆和表述能力存在缺陷。前四种方法主要是针对证人的诚实性而使用的。[9]

何谓诚实？说谎的人必然不诚实，而诚实的人则不会说谎。因此，评价证言的可信性，实际上是在评判证人说谎的可能性。如何识别、评价和认定谎言对确定证言的可信性至关重要。

识别、评价或者认定谎言的过程中，谎言处于待证事实的地位。对事实性谎言的认定应当是一个证明过程，各种证据的运用应当满足证据法的各项要求。比如，证明证人说谎的证据必须满足可采性要求，提出证据的责任应当按照相应规则加以分配，所需要达到的证明标准也应当符合相关要求。一般情况下，证明证人说谎或者证言中存在谎言的途径有以下三种：

第一，结合各种信息对比判断证言内容的真实性。判断所接收信息之真实性，是辨别谎言的最常用的方式。虽然假信息不等于证人的谎言，这一点在前文中已经有所论述。但是一般的经验常识认为，如果陈述的内容不属实，那么证人说谎的可能性则较大。因此，如果与真实信息直接作比较，那么假信息立时显现本色，证人证言为谎言也就具有了可能性。在诉讼过程中，通常对一个待证事实会使用多项证据加以证明，

---

〔9〕 参见王进喜：《刑事证人正言论》，中国人民公安大学出版社2002年版，第194页。

这些不同来源的证据都能够给事实认定者提供对比的参照物。此外，事实认定者都具有一定生活经验，形成了所谓的“常理”，陈述内容是否符合常理，这也是判断证言内容真实性的依据。然而，一个事实能够留下的信息总量在事实发生后就已经确定下来，不会再有所增加，只会随着时间的推移以及各种行为的影响而不断减少。能否有足够数量和质量的参照信息出现，这一点无从保证。因此，对于真实性，这只能是一个盖然性或者倾向性的概念。因为，所谓“真实”的信息不是绝对的真实，只能是相关程度或者说服力强弱的问题。“三人成虎”的典故[10]就是这种过分依赖经验做法而对谎言判断失误的经典例子。虽然内容上是否矛盾的判断是挖掘证言内容真实性的最直接的途径，但是在通常情况下，这种做法既有实现难度，也存在出错的风险。

第二，挖掘证人说谎的潜在动机。要证明证言是谎言，如果不能在证言的内容上入手，那么另一个途径就是从证言的主体因素入手。在很多时候，人们认为有说谎动机的人比没有撒谎动机的人更可能撒谎。因为在一定动机的驱使下，主体的行为更具倾向性。在诉讼中，经常可以见到一方结合各种因素，对导致证人说谎的理由进行深入论证，试图说服事实认定者相信证人极具说谎的可能性。比如利用证人与案件最终结果有利害关系、证人与当事人有与案件无关的其他利益关系、证人自身经历导致对该案件或者某一方当事人有偏激的看法[11]等证人存在偏见的可能性。根据前文对谎言与谎者动机之间相关性的分析，动机与谎言之间逻辑上的联系确实存在。但是，出现动机就一定会说谎吗？存在动机也许能够说明存在说谎的可能性，但是这种动机能否转化为制造谎言的意图还有待确认。此外，即便陈述者具备了“谎者的意图”也未必就会真的成为“谎者”，还需要将这种意图践行为与其认识不符的谎言内容。主观上产生了谎言的意图，客观上采取行动时也需要表现这种意图，这才构成一个完整的说谎行为。从动机到谎言的最终出现，这是一个客观影响主观、再由主观指导实际行为的系列过程，这其中每个环节都会影响最终谎言成立的可能性。

第三，例举证人的不良品性。品性证据一直是证据法学研究的一项重点。一般认为，品性证据具有两种类型的相关性，即与“争点”的相关性和与“可信性”的相关性。[12] 对于前者，品性证据矛头直指被指控的事实，一般采用“过去类似行为”的证据来证明被告做出某种行为的可能性更大还是更小。而对于后者，品性证据则大多用来弹劾证言的可信性，意图用证人的不良品性来表明证人更可能说谎，其证言不足为信。在这里，品性一般是指证人诚实与否的名声，或者是否说谎成性、曾经多次说谎。但有时也会使用其他事实来弹劾可信性，比如证人过往的犯罪记录。这背后的理论是：任何犯罪的定罪判决都与证人的可信性有关，因为人们认为这揭示了该人的伦理品质。[13] 无论是直接与说谎行为有关的品性，还是通过其他伦理品质间接反映诚实性的

〔10〕 三人成虎，我国古代成语，出自《韩非子》，原意指三个人谎报集市里有老虎，听者就信以为真。比喻谣言多人重复述说，就能使人信以为真。

〔11〕 例如种族歧视、证人自身曾经是与案件类似事件的受害者等。

〔12〕［英］Christopher Allen：《英国证据法实务指南》，王进喜译，中国政法大学证据科学研究院2012年8月印，第214页。

〔13〕［英］Christopher Allen：《英国证据法实务指南》，王进喜译，中国政法大学证据科学研究院2012年8月印，第214页。

品性，具有这些品性的人说谎的可能性的确相对较大，这是日常生活经验归纳出的规律。但是，在考察这种相关性的时候，还要注意两个问题：首先，品性只是对某人一般品质或者行为之倾向性的归纳，对于特定案件中的特定陈述而言，品性对谎言的驱动力恐怕比不上当前情况所产生的说谎动机。如前文所述，动机的存在只能在一定程度上提高证人说谎的可能性，那么品性最多也不过如此，它并不能达到足以认定的程度。其次，社会普遍的价值观决定了大多数人厌恶品性不良之人，那么品性不良的证据势必增加了事实认定者以及公众对证人持排斥态度，这种个人情绪往往与案件事实并无相关性，但是却在很多时候使事实认定者倾向于相信证人在说谎，最终影响到对证言可行性的评估。这种来源于感情因素的“相关性”，会带给弹劾证据不恰当的证明力。

通过对以上三种途径的分析，可以得出这样的结论：评估证言的可信性，实际上就是在评价证人之陈述为谎言的可能性，而与之相关三种途径都存在对相关性运用得不准确或者不恰当的风险。这些风险的出现，给事实认定的准确与公正带来了极大的挑战。

四、谎言的相关性与可采性和证明力的关系

研究谎言的相关性，是为了进一步探讨证据法视野下，这种相关性对证据发挥证明效果的影响。谎言的相关性与证明力和可采性这两个概念的关系，就是这种影响的具体表现。

（一）谎言的相关性与可采性

可采性和证明力一样，都与相关性有密切的关系。一般情况下，有无相关性决定证据是否具有可采性，相关性的程度影响证明力的大小。《美国联邦证据规则》第403条中最后一句的表述为：“……不相关的证据不可采。”[14] 可见，相关性是可采性的最低要求，这一点无需过多阐述。

然而在很多情况下，虽然证据与事实之间具有相关性，但是微弱的或者极具误导性的相关性，其在证明力方面作出的贡献可能比不上其对公正审判带来的风险。此时，证据法就要在证据可采性问题上加以限制。[15] 在与谎言有关的问题上，这种限制有三类比较典型的体现：

第一，对品性证据的排除。正如前文所述，品性证据有多种用途，但更多的是用在弹劾证人的诚实性，即表明其更可能撒谎这一事实。这样的证据具有一定的相关性，但有时相关性很微弱，并且会带来更大的不公正的风险。最典型的就是对检控方提出刑事被告品性不良的证据加以排除。刑事被告本身就处于道德上的劣势，人们在惩罚犯罪行为的同时，也对犯罪行为的主体施加道德上的谴责。刑事被告由于有为自己脱

---

〔14〕 此条原文为：Relevant evidence is admissible unless any of the following provides otherwise：the United States Constitution；a federal statute；these rules；or other rules prescribed by the Supreme Court. Irrelevant evidence is not admissible.

〔15〕 如《美国联邦证据规则》第403条规定：如果相关证据的证明价值为以下一个或者多个危险所严重超过，则法院可以排除该证据：不公平损害、混淆争点或者误导陪审团、不当拖延、浪费时间或者不必要地出示重复证据。参见王进喜：《美国〈联邦证据规则〉（2011年重塑版）条解》，中国政法大学证据科学研究院2012年印，第57页。

罪的动机，其诚实性本身就已经处于受质疑的地位。检控方提出被告不良证据，意在说明被告说谎的可能性。此类证据一方面可以削弱被告证明自己无罪之证言的证明力，而与此同时，也很可能促使事实认定者加深对被告可能以说谎来脱罪的质疑。这等于是在弹劾被告证言可信性的同时，附加了一个本不存在的、相当于有罪证据的证明力。

第二，对识谎手段的限制。识谎就是对陈述是否为谎言或者陈述者是否在撒谎进行识别。由于追求真相之内在动力的趋势，识谎一直是诉讼中的主要内容之一，并产生了多种识谎的手段。在中国古代西周时期的审判活动中，就产生了“五听”之法，即辞听、色听、气听、耳听、目听。这些手段是司法官吏在审理案件时观察当事人心理活动的五种方法，其主要任务就是判断当事人是否在撒谎，是否如实进行陈述。大陆法系证据法原则中的直接言词原则与英美法系的传闻证据排除规则，其产生和存在的重要理由之一，也是保证事实认定者能够在证人作证时，对证人的神态、语气和表情等表征进行直接的观察，这也是事实认定者判断证人是否如实陈述的一个重要途径。这些方法都与证人说谎时的心理和生理活动有关，可以具有一定的证明力。但是具有类似作用的方法未必都具有可采性，特别是对以“测谎仪器”为代表的测谎领域的科学证据，证据法上普遍都对其可采性作出限制。如果从相关性角度分析，专业的测谎技术也是依据人撒谎时的生理指标来进行判断，这与之前的几种方法并无差别；同时，心理学对人撒谎时的心理活动与生理指标之间的相关性已经按照科学的方法作出大量研究，测谎技术在归纳的严谨性上理应不差于之前几种依据日常经验法则的判断方式。但是，无论是测谎技术还是“五听法”，它们与谎言之间的相关性并非十分稳定，因为同样的生理指标很可能并非由说谎的心理活动而导致。因此，即便有证明力，其证明力的程度也并不是很高，一般只能作为辅助证明使用。而对于测谎技术，由于它带有心理学所赋予的科学色彩，“相对严谨”的归纳形式和“科学”的外表可能会给事实认定者增加过度的信任感。本是证明力一般的证据，却很可能直接带来对谎言的“终审判决”。这产生不公正的风险超过了它可能带来的证明价值，因此，法律要对其加以排除。

第三，对使用谎言所获取的证言的排除。谎言并不一定只存在于证据之中，谎言也可能存在于证言的获取过程中，影响获取证言的真实性。比如，刑事案件中，侦查人员在获取证据时欺骗犯罪嫌疑人，谎称如果供认所指控事实，则可以当即释放不予追究。这种情况下，侦查人员的谎言给犯罪嫌疑人提供了“摆脱当前困境”的契机，如果无辜的犯罪嫌疑人被骗了，那么这种契机很可能就转化为说谎的动机，获取的证据是真是假无从保证。除了真实性以外，使用谎言获取证据，特别是司法人员参与此类事件，将成为司法形象的直接威胁。司法形象直接影响到各种司法裁决在社会中的公信力。如果取证程序中也存在谎言，司法人员也采用欺骗手段，那么公众如何相信这个过程？如何确定自己不会成为被欺骗的对象？当司法不再有公信力时，司法判决的效力及其权威性将会受到严重的削弱，公平和正义也将无从谈起。

（二）谎言的相关性与证明力

证据具有可采性并不说明证据所主张的事实业已证明成立，而是该证据可以成为事实认定者赋予证明力的对象。待证事实是否存在，这尚且是一个可能性的概念，可能性大小由事实认定者依据经验理性进行判断，依据其被说服的程度进行抉择，确定赋予证据多少证明力。这一过程在对谎言的判断中表现得尤为突出。

在前文的各种相关性分析中，能够得出这样的结论：谎言与主观和客观方方面面的事实都具有一定的相关性，特别是几乎每个诉讼都必然包括对证人诚实性的判断；同时，谎言与各种事实间的逻辑关系又都带有不确定性，多种可能因素无法证实也无法排除才使得谎言愈加难于确证，更多的时候只是停留在特定主体有说谎的可能性上。如何评估这种可能性？这在日常生活中是个难题，在证明活动中也是一大挑战。

在证明和事实认定的过程中，人们的思维方式总是沿着由一个信息之存在而推理出另一个信息也存在的模式进行，这种推理的基础就是前后两个信息之间存在的相关性。事物之间是普遍联系的，并且这种联系客观存在——这是哲学上的相关性。而逻辑上的相关性是人们认识事物的手段和依据，它来源于人们对已知世界中各种随机事物之间关系所进行的归纳。归纳的目的是抽象出相对稳定的规律，再依据这种规律来判断事物之间待定的关系。越是谨慎的归纳，抽象出的规律越准确、可靠，对所判断的关系得出的结论也就越贴近事实真相；反之，则得出的规律适用性较差，所得判断结论不符合事实真相的可能性也很大。

因此，如何正确地运用经验的归纳来解读谎言的相关性，将对与谎言有关的各种证据的证明力评价产生重要影响。这也是在证据法视野下，谎言给证明的公正性带来的最大风险来源。对于谎言，人们迫于交往的实际需要，作出归纳的机会很多，胆子也很大。归纳越是大胆，证据的证明力可能就越大，但是大胆归纳的麻烦是，与小心谨慎的归纳相比，它们更不可能是真的。[16] 如果任由生活经验所带来的各种不严谨的归纳在证据领域中被滥用，将很可能因不恰当赋予证明力而带来风险。因此在证明活动中，对于证据的相关性需要最为谨慎的归纳，这种苛刻的要求与生活经验的灵活自如形成鲜明对比：

首先，证明力不是某一证据单独出现时的可信性，而是综合考虑全部证据之后，在待证事实存在与否的可能性问题上被说服的程度。这里包含两个层次的问题。第一是对证人说谎的怀疑程度与其证言对待证事实之证明力的区别问题。只要证人的陈述在动机、表现等方面流露出说谎的可能性，那么就存在对证言为谎言的合理怀疑。但是这种怀疑只是影响证言证明力的待定因素，在与其他证据一起进行综合分析时，产生怀疑的因素可能减少也可能增加，怀疑的程度也会发生变化。因此，究竟其对待证事实存在与否的说服程度有多少，需要结合其他证据进行综合判断，孤证的可信性与其产生的证明力并非同一概念。第二个问题是证明标准的问题，这是“说服力”在事实认定过程中与日常生活中的本质区别。不同的案件、不同的证明对象有不同的法定证明标准，对证人诚实性心存怀疑不能直接导致对证言的不采信或者对其所支持之主张的不认可，必须要考虑内心确信的程度是否符合法律的要求。如果怀疑的程度并未使证明力减损至证明标准之下，则不能任由疑惑肆意膨胀，依然要凭借理性与良知作出公正的裁判。

其次，从证据到结论的推论过程要受到法律的约束。在法定证据制度时期，为了

---

〔16〕［英］Christopher Allen：《英国证据法实务指南》，王进喜译，中国政法大学证据科学研究院 2012 年 8 月印，第 22 页。

防止法官在证明力判断时的恣意，不同主体的证言会被预设不同的证明力。随着法定证据制度逐渐退出历史舞台，自由心证取而代之。这并不意味着对证明力的评价就是任意行为。证明力不再由法律预先设定，但是如何依据相关性形成正确的归纳形式以产生证据到待证事实的合理推论，这些依然需要遵循证据法基本原则，即依据相关性所采用的归纳形式不能够对事实认定产生不公正的风险。在谎言问题上，这种风险甚为严重。例如前文所述，从动机到谎言与从谎言到动机的两种推论模式的可靠性有天壤之别，然而这种推论又是人们根据日常生活经验不由自主便会形成的归纳形式。为了防止此类风险，有的做法是采用证明力指导性的规则，在风险发生时，起到警示与重审证据法原则的做用。〔17〕 而对于证据存在的风险大大超出其具有的证明价值时，则存在通过证据排除的手段来规避不公正损害的做法。〔18〕

---

〔17〕 例如 *Rv Lucas* [1981] QB 720 案中确立的规则：英国法官在陪审团面对刑事被告的谎言时，会被要求向陪审团作出裁量性的注意警告，指示陪审团应当考虑的谎言的各种动机之可能性，避免陪审团过分加大被告有罪的证明力。参见［英］Christopher Allen：《英国证据法实务指南》，王进喜译，中国政法大学证据科学研究院 2012 年 8 月印，第 168 页。

〔18〕 例如美国《联邦证据规则》第 403 条规定："如果相关证据的证明价值为以下一个或者多个危险所严重超过，则法院可以排除该证据：不公平损害、混淆争点或者误导陪审团、不当拖延、浪费时间或者不必要地出示重复证据。"详细规则解释参见王进喜：《美国〈联邦证据规则〉(2011 年重塑版) 条解》，中国政法大学证据科学研究院 2012 年印，第 60 页。

论“情况说明”的证据效力*

高同丽*

情况说明并不是一个严格的法律术语，在我国的刑事法律及司法解释中并没有关于这一词语的明确定位，然而在刑事案件证据卷宗中却存在多种办案情况说明，本文所要探讨的情况说明则专指侦查或检察机关的侦查部门就其侦查行为合法性所出具的证明材料。虽然情况说明在立法及司法解释中并没有明确的定位，但是不得不说，这种材料却早已在司法实践中大有用武之地，并呈滥用之势，只要辩护方提出侦查人员取证行为违法的抗辩意见，侦查机关基本都会出具情况说明。更为可怕的是法院通常都会对这种情况说明不加审查而采纳，并在情况说明与被告人当庭供述相矛盾时优先确认情况说明的证明力。本文探讨了情况说明大量存在的原因，并分析了以情况说明证明侦查行为合法的危害，学者们以情况说明不符合证据的三性而否定情况说明的证据能力，笔者在驳斥了这一论点的同时，认为情况说明在性质上系侦查人员就对其取证合法的质疑而提出的辩解，与犯罪嫌疑人、被告人辩解性质相同，情况说明与案件的程序性事实相关，应当具有证据能力。在情况说明上加盖公章的行为并不能强化其真实性，法官不应因其加盖了公章而赋予其过高的证明力。情况说明作为证据使用应当要与其他证据相互印证，并适用补强规则，经过庭审质证后才能作为定案的根据。

一、情况说明在司法实践中的现状

（一）大量存在，几乎每案必有情况说明

有学者在研究中指出，情况说明并没有统一的名称，司法实践中除大量使用“关于……的情况说明”外，还有“工作记录”、“工作情况说明”、“工作说明”、“工作情况”、“说明”等名称[1]，笔者以以上几个名称作为关键词在北大法宝的司法案例版中搜索，在从2001年到2013年总数为307 305的刑事案件中得到如下结果：

称　谓	案件数量	所占比重（%）
情况说明	36 614	11.91
说　明	19 186	6.24
工作记录	7290	2.37

* 本文系国家2011计划司法文明协同创新中心研究成果，同时是2012年北京市优秀博士学位论文指导教师人文社科项目“证据科学与司法文明”（张保生教授主持，项目编号：20121005301）、2012年国家社科基金项目（编号：12CFX043）、2013年中国博士后科学基金（编号：2013M530850）阶段性成果。

* 高同丽，中国政法大学硕士研究生。Email：sunlightdaisy@ sina. cn。

〔1〕 张少林：“刑事案件中的‘情况说明’之我见”，载《贵州职业警官学院学报》2008年第5期。

续表

称　谓	案件数量	所占比重（%）
工作情况说明	1841	0.60
工作说明	1741	0.57
总　计	66 672	21.70

这种搜索方法可能不甚准确，但从中至少可以窥见情况说明在刑事审判中数量之多，分量之重。还有学者选择以刑事判决书作为考察对象，在西部某中级人民法院2007～2009年间的一审判决书中，每年随机选取50份，共计150份为抽样分析，得到了54%的案件都有情况说明，平均每个案件有2.15份情况说明的惊人结果〔2〕。这说明在总体上，刑事审判中将情况说明作为证据采用的现象非常普遍。

（二）不经质证，情况说明具有天然的可采性

我国刑事诉讼法及相关司法解释规定了法庭对被告人审判前供述取得的合法性有疑问时，经依法通知，讯问人员应当出庭作证。但由于没有规定拒不出庭作证的法律后果和强制措施，所以侦查人员出庭作证的几率极小。针对辩护方当庭提出的侦查人员存在刑讯逼供的辩护意见，控诉机关往往提供由侦查人员出具的情况说明来否定刑讯逼供或其他违法取证行为的存在。情况说明本质上就是侦查人员违规取证的补正品，侦查人员不出庭作证的替代品。〔3〕而法院既不会传唤相关证人、侦查人员出庭作证，也不宣读新的书面材料，更不会对侦查人员是否存在违法取证的问题进行任何形式的调查，几乎完全采信侦查人员出具的情况说明。这说明，在中国的刑事法官眼中，侦查人员出具的情况说明具有天然的可采性。

（三）不经审查，优先接受情况说明的证明力

如前所述，情况说明在刑事案件中非常普遍，几乎每个案件中都至少有1～2个情况说明，但是法庭却不会对情况说明的可采性及证明力进行审查。当被告人的当庭供述与侦查机关出具的情况说明存在矛盾时，法院会优先采纳情况说明，并以此否定被告人的当庭供述，这说明，法院在对待公诉方的证言和被告人的证言间实行差别待遇。笔者从北大法宝的司法案例中随机抽取了2个案例的裁判文书，摘取了部分片段如下：

案例一：黄畅胜等贩卖毒品案〔4〕

“另查明，公安民警在侦查阶段未对上诉人黄畅胜进行胁迫诱供。

上述事实，有经一审、二审庭审举证、质证的下列证据证实，足以认定：

……

〔2〕周维平、马明亮：“论‘办案说明’在刑事审判中的运用——以刑事判决书为样本的考察”，载《全国法院系统第二十二届学术讨论会论文集》2011年第1期。

〔3〕周维平、马明亮：“论‘办案说明’在刑事审判中的运用——以刑事判决书为样本的考察”，载《全国法院系统第二十二届学术讨论会论文集》2011年第1期。

〔4〕该案由海口市中级人民法院于2013年3月12日做出终审裁定。参见该院（2013）海中法刑终字第44号刑事裁定书，载北大法宝“司法案例”版。

13. 情况说明，证实：海口市公安局琼山分局刑警大队民警在办案过程中，无刑讯逼供或者以威胁、引诱、欺骗以及其他非法方法收集证据。

14. 在押人员入所笔录，证实：上诉人黄畅胜、原审被告人王和财在入所时未被刑讯、体罚过。

本院认为，上诉人黄畅胜、原审被告人王和财贩卖毒品氯胺酮6.7641克、甲基苯丙胺0.0812克，其二人的行为均已构成贩卖毒品罪，依法应予惩处。对上诉人黄畅胜提出其在侦查阶段被胁迫的意见，经查，黄畅胜在讯问笔录中证实笔录的内容与其所说的相符，且出庭检察员在二审庭审时出示的情况说明、在押人员入所笔录和在押人员体格检查表相互印证，证实黄畅胜在侦查阶段未受到威胁、引诱，或者欺骗，故上述意见与本院查明的事实不符，不予采信。……"

案例二：卢海超等盗窃、掩饰、隐瞒犯罪所得案〔5〕

"上述事实，有公诉机关提供，并经法庭质证、认证的下列证据予以证实：

……

11. 平南县公安局的情况说明证实，上渡派出所在办理卢海超、罗××涉嫌盗窃案中没有刑讯逼供行为。

本院认为，被告人卢海超伙同他人以非法占有为目的，采取秘密手段，多次窃取公民财物，数额较大，其行为已触犯刑律，构成盗窃罪，依法应受刑罚处罚。……被告人卢海超辩解公诉机关指控的第三单盗窃其没有参与，其只是帮销赃且在上渡派出所讯问时被打。平南县公安局调查后的情况说明可以证实，上渡派出所在侦查卢海超、罗××涉嫌盗窃案中没有刑讯逼供行为；……"

以上两个案件中，被告人无一例外地都在庭审过程中提出侦查人员曾对其刑讯逼供，其有罪供述是在刑讯逼供下作出的，面对这种抗辩，法院通常也会休庭，责令公诉方对被告人辩称的"刑讯逼供"问题进行调查。但在庭审恢复之后，法院却允许公诉方当庭宣读侦查人员就侦查行为的合法性问题所作的"情况说明"，并在"听取被告人、辩护人意见后"，当庭采纳这种材料，裁断"刑讯逼供的事实并不存在"。〔6〕这种贸然以情况说明为依据来确定侦查行为合法性的做法，显示了法院没有对侦查行为的合法性进行独立自主的判断，更反映了公诉方提供的情况说明在证据能力上是强力推定的〔7〕，在证明力上是优先选择的。

二、追根溯源：形成这种现状的原因探讨

冰冻三尺，非一日之寒。情况说明作为一种没有"名分"的书面材料竟然在司法实践中应用得如此普遍，法庭对其证据能力如此不加怀疑，并当情况说明与被告人的当庭陈述相矛盾时优先选择前者，这是多种因素综合作用的结果。笔者在此试图从制度环境上探讨成因。

---

〔5〕 该案由广西壮族自治区平南县人民法院于2012年12月23日做出。参见该院（2012）平刑初字第344号刑事判决书，载北大法宝"司法案例"版。

〔6〕 杨子良："论翻供的处理"，载《刑事审判要览》（总第1辑），法律出版社2003年版，第98页。

〔7〕 陈瑞华：《刑事诉讼的中国模式》，法律出版社2008年版，第133～143页。

（一）证据概念的修改为情况说明提供了生存空间

1979 年及以前的《刑事诉讼法》在证据概念上都采取封闭式的规定，如“证明案件真实情况的一切事实，都是证据。证据有下列七种…”，列举了七种证据种类，这种封闭式的概念将“情况说明”排除在法定证据种类之外，为寻找其存在的正当性，学界们大多将其归属为证人证言〔8〕，而实务界为获得较高的证明效力倾向于将其归为书证〔9〕，甚至作为公文书证对待。〔10〕2012 年《刑事诉讼法》在修改时将证据概念改为“可以用于证明案件事实的材料，都是证据。证据包括……”这样一种开放立法模式，意味着只要相关材料能够证明案件事实，都可以作为证据使用，扩大了证据的可采范围，这就为情况说明的存在提供了法律依据。

（二）司法解释为情况说明的存在提供了直接依据

《关于办理刑事案件排除非法证据若干问题的决定》（以下简称《非法证据排除规定》）第 7 条第 3 款规定：“公诉人提交加盖公章的说明材料，未经有关讯问人员签名或者盖章的，不能作为证明取证合法性的依据。”此规定在规范层面上确认了证明侦查行为合法性的情况说明的证据能力，并规定了基本的形式要件。2012 年随着《刑事诉讼法》的修改，各有权机关陆续出台了司法解释，如《人民检察院刑事诉讼规则（试行）》（以下简称《高检规则》）第 72 条规定：“人民检察院认为存在以非法方法收集证据情形的，可以书面要求侦查机关对证据收集的合法性进行说明。说明应当加盖单位公章，并由侦查人员签名”。最高人民法院《关于适用〈中华人民共和国刑事诉讼法〉的解释》第 72、73、77 条都规定对于物证、书证、证人证言的收集、调取程序存在瑕疵的，法院可以要求公诉机关“补正或者作出合理解释”，由于没有同时限定补正或作出合理解释的方式，聪明的侦查机关大都选择出具情况说明这种简单高效的方式来补正或作出合理解释。

（三）侦查机关自由裁量的结果

情况说明之所以能够在司法实践中大量存在，很大一部分是因为其制作简单，法律对其内容、格式、制作主体、制作程序等都没有规定，所以说，在情况说明的行文格式上，侦查机关享有绝对的自由裁量权。《非法证据排除规定》规定了法庭对被告人审前供述取得的合法性有疑问的，公诉人应当向法庭提供询问笔录、原始的讯问过程录音录像等证据，并首次提出了讯问人员就供述取得合法出庭作证的要求。《刑事诉讼法》第 57 条也规定侦查人员就证据收集的合法性问题有出庭作证的义务。但实际上，由于侦查机关对口供的严重依赖〔11〕，通过刑讯逼供迅速获取口供已成为侦查人员的共识，如果按照法律要求播放讯问过程录音录像，那么其获取的证据很可能被作为非法

〔8〕 郭晶：“刑事诉讼‘情况说明’证据能力之再思考——以‘两个证据规定’和 2013 年《刑事诉讼法》为背景”，载《研究生法学》2012 年第 27 卷第 5 期；孙琳：“刑事案件情况说明应当规范使用”，载《检察日报》2012 年 11 月 12 日。

〔9〕 黄婕：“‘情况说明’的证据学属性分析——兼论侦查人员出庭作证制度之构建”，载《中国刑事法杂志》2010 年第 5 期。

〔10〕 唐艳，姚明平：“刑事案件办案情况说明：从功能背离到制度规范——以西部某法院近三年司法运行情况为实证蓝本”，载《建设公平正义社会与刑事法律适用问题研究——全国法院第 24 届学术讨论会获奖论文集》（下册）。

〔11〕 吴纪奎：“口供供需失衡与刑讯逼供”，载《政法论坛》2010 年第 4 期。

证据排除，再者，《刑事诉讼法》对录音录像的规定也不是普遍强制性的，仅在重罪案件中才是“应当”对讯问过程录音或者录像[12]；而侦查人员对法院或者被告人的出庭作证要求带有某种程度的抵触和反感，并且检察机关也没有足够的动力和权威监督侦查人员出庭作证[13]，由此，播放录音录像和侦查人员出庭作证两种方式的可行性不强，侦查人员基于成本收益的权衡，宁愿选择一纸证明力极高的情况说明回应对其侦查行为合法性的质疑，既除去了证据被排除的风险，又能大大提高诉讼效率。

（四）以侦查为主导下诉讼模式的结果

长期以来，我国的刑事法官已经习惯于通过查阅、研读检察机关移送的案卷笔录来展开庭前准备活动，对于证人证言、被害人陈述、被告人供述等言词证据也普遍通过宣读案卷笔录的方式进行法庭调查，法院在判决书中甚至普遍援引侦查人员所制作的案卷笔录，并将其作为判决的基础，中国刑事审判中实际存在着一种以案卷笔录为中心的裁判模式。[14] 由于辩护方一般无从查阅全套侦查案卷材料，但是控诉方却掌握绝大部分证据资料并能自由选择向法庭出示哪些证据材料，实际演变成了公诉方通过侦查案卷主导整个法庭调查程序的模式，对法官而言，这种以侦查案卷为依据的宣读笔录式的调查方式，使得法庭在采纳证据、认定事实方面几乎完全丧失了独立自主性，法官几乎完全依据公诉方的案卷笔录来形成其对案件事实的内心确信。[15] 即使被告人当庭作出了与先前供述笔录不一致的陈述，并提出其有罪供述是在刑讯逼供下作出的抗辩，在绝大多数情况下，法院都会以辩护方“没有提出相关事实和证据为由”，断然拒绝辩护方有关排除非法证据的请求。这说明法院在推定公诉方案卷笔录合法性上是毋庸置疑的，潜意识中对辩护方提供排除非法证据的相关线索或者材料施加了过高的证明标准。同时法院这种仅依据案卷笔录或书面材料为依据来确定侦查行为合法性的做法，显示出法院并没有对侦查行为的合法性进行任何独立自主的判断[16]，是一种以侦查为主导的诉讼模式的直接反映。

（五）官本位思想强化了情况说明的真实性

受儒家文化的影响，我国传统政治文化和政治实践几千年来的集中体现之一就是官本位思想[17]，在这种思想的影响下，控诉机关和被告人的地位不平等，法院特别重视公诉人员的权力，将其看成是一个战壕里的战友，对其出具的材料也是“另眼相待”，而轻视被告方的权利。诚如有学者所言，人们心中长期膜拜权力，社会推行官本位体制，因而在司法过程中对于权力的设置与制约一贯比较关注，似乎只要官员严格履行了职责正确行使权力就可以公正地处理案件。[18] 面对辩护方提出诸如侦查人员存在刑讯逼供问题的辩护意见，即使被告人提供了侦查人员存在刑讯逼供或者其他违法

[12] 《刑事诉讼法》第121条第1款规定：“侦查人员在讯问犯罪嫌疑人的时候，可以对讯问过程进行录音或者录像；对于可能判处无期徒刑、死刑的案件或者其他重大犯罪案件，应当对讯问过程进行录音或者录像。”可见，我国立法对于全程录音录像制度的规定不具有普遍的强制性。

[13] 陈瑞华：“论侦查人员的地位”，载《暨南学报》（哲学社会科学版）2012年第2期。

[14] 陈瑞华：“案卷笔录中心主义——对中国刑事审判方式的重新考察”，载《法学研究》2006年第4期。

[15] 陈瑞华：《刑事诉讼的中国模式》，法律出版社2008年版，第119～121页。

[16] 陈瑞华：《刑事诉讼的中国模式》，法律出版社2008年版，第131～135页。

[17] 朱岚：“中国传统官本位思想生发的文化生态根源”，载《理论学刊》2005年第11期。

[18] 宋世杰：《证据学新论》，中国检察出版社2002年版，第7页。

取证的线索，法院还是会相信公诉方加盖了公章的一纸情况说明。《高检规则》、最高人民法院的《关于适用〈中华人民共和国刑事诉讼法〉的解释》以及《非法证据排除规定》都要求“证明取证行为合法性的说明材料要加盖公章并由侦查人员签名”[19]，难道加盖了公章就真的能保证侦查人员出具的情况说明是真实的吗？侦查人员会因为加盖公章这一要求心生敬畏进而如实陈述侦查过程吗？答案显然是否定的，在这里，公章的形式效应大于实质作用。反过来，若是由辩护方出具一份证实刑讯逼供存在的情况说明，法官是断然不会不加审查而采纳的。所以说，法官之所以赋予侦查人员出具的情况说明以天然可采性，很大一部分是由于官本位思想在作祟。

（六）检法间既配合又制约的矛盾关系难辞其咎

审判中立是保证审判公正的先决条件，也是正当程序的基本要求。控、辩任何一方与审判者有某种利害关系，都会对公正裁判产生消极影响[20]。而在我国，检察机关既承担控诉职能，同时又作为法律监督机关，对法院的审判活动进行监督。这就在某种程度上对法院的审判形成了一种制约，如果允许一个专司控诉职能的公诉人同时还附带承担一定的庭审监督职能，就意味着检察官可能拥有比辩方更多的影响法官的权力，意味着检察官可以对法官的行为进行裁决，这将使法官难以在控辩双方之间保持中立。[21] 若不采纳控诉机关提供的情况说明、否定其证据能力，转而展开对侦查人员取证行为合法性的实质调查，将不仅加大检察机关的抗诉以及上级法院改判的风险，还要承受检察机关对他的个人生活以及其他审判活动进行监督调查的风险。并且，我国宪法和刑事诉讼法共同确立了公检法之间分工负责、相互配合、相互制约的协作模式，但实际上，公检法之间相互配合是主要的、相互制约是次要的，配合制约原则实质上是“配合”原则。[22] 在长期形成的配合协作关系下，法官基于现实主义的考量，不敢轻易排除对他的个人前途起到制约作用的检察机关提供的情况说明。

三、现实考量：以情况说明证明侦查行为合法性的危害

侦查行为的合法性判断是一个极为重要的问题，关涉到据以定罪量刑的证据是否能够作为非法证据被排除，进而关涉针对被告人的有罪控诉是否成立。对于侦查人员出具的情况说明，假如法院一律不加审查就采纳的话，法院在事实认定方面就会发生一定的风险。

首先，情况说明不能保证侦查人员提供的情况真实。通过查阅大量案卷资料显示，当辩护方提出存在刑讯逼供的辩护意见时，侦查人员所出具的情况说明几乎无一例外是“侦查行为是合法的，不存在刑讯逼供行为”，试想一下，为维护公诉机关的荣誉和权威，以及出于个人职业前途的考虑，侦查人员会在一份他可以自由撰写的文书上承认自己取证过程违法吗？当然不会。情况说明的问世没有受到法律的实质约束，其真实性无法得到保障；在法庭调查阶段，由于侦查人员普遍不出庭，被告人丧失了通过对质来揭露其虚假性的机会。而法院采纳这种情况说明并以此为依据驳回辩护方对取

---

〔19〕 分别参见《高检规则》第66条、最高法《关于适用〈刑事诉讼法〉若干问题的解释》第101条、《非法证据排除规定》第7条。

〔20〕 徐阳：“公检法三机关分工、制约、配合原则评析”，载《河北法学》2002年第20卷第2期。

〔21〕 陈卫东、李奋飞：“论刑事诉讼中的控审不分问题”，载《中国法学》2004年第2期。

〔22〕 陈卫东、李奋飞：“论刑事诉讼中的控审不分问题”，载《中国法学》2004年第2期。

证合法性的质疑，客观上将导致法官对案件关键事实的审理建立在情况说明的真实性推定之上，放弃了对案件事实的独立判断，这就使侦查权游离于法庭之外，极易导致冤假错案的产生。近些年不断暴露出来的佘祥林案、赵作海案、杜培武案，以及杭州叔侄强奸案凸显了有效防范和治理非法审讯尤其是刑讯逼供的重要性和迫切性。这些冤案无一例外都是因刑讯逼供等非法手段获取证据所造成的。

其次，情况说明作为证明取证合法性的证据使用，降低了控方取证合法性的证明标准，弱化了非法证据排除的威慑效力，纵容了侦查机关的违法取证行为。作为非法证据的异议主体，被告人要通过提供相关线索或者材料启动非法证据的排除程序，而作为控诉方则对非法证据的证明承担主要的证明责任。《刑事诉讼法》第 57 条第 1 款明确了控诉方应当对证据收集的合法性承担证明责任[23]，从各地的实践来看，当辩护方对侦查机关的取证存在合法性质疑时，控诉机关也确实在承担这一举证责任，但问题的关键是一纸情况说明是否足以证明取证的合法性？控方的证明标准是什么？

我国 2010 年两部三高《非法证据排除规定》第 11 条对检察机关证据合法性的证明标准提出了明确的要求，即“对被告人审判前供述的合法性，公诉人不提供证据加以证明，或者已提供的证据不够确实、充分的，该供述不能作为定案的根据”，同时在第 12 条也规定了二审法院应当对被告人审判前供述取得的合法性进行审查，检察人员不提供证据或已提供的证据不够确实、充分的，被告人的供述不能作为定案的根据。由此可见，目前我国控诉方在非法证据排除上的证明标准应当是“确实、充分”。侦查机关出具的一份不经法庭审查、剥夺了被告方质证权的情况说明显然很难形成法官的内心确信，这无疑擅自降低了控诉机关的证明标准。如此低的证明标准将使得非法证据被排除的几率大大降低，减少了侦查机关违法取证的成本，弱化了非法证据排除的威慑效力。

四、侦查行为合法性的证明标准

证明标准主要解决“证明到何种程度”的问题，即证明主体履行证明责任所要达到的程度或要求。[24] 按照证明对象的重要性不同，证明标准可分为严格证明与自由证明。按照德国刑事诉讼法的规定，“对于攸关认定犯罪行为之经过、行为人之责任及刑罚之高度等问题的重要事项，法律规定需以严格之方式提出证据”即为严格证明，有关被告人、证人、鉴定人、勘验及文书证件的证据需严格证明”，“对裁判只具诉讼上之重要性之事实认定，例如有权提起告诉之人知悉犯罪行为及行为人之时间或者对证人年龄之认定”，“法院得以一般实务之惯例以自由证明之方式调查之，亦即可不拘任何方式来获取可信性，在许多案例中对此只需有纯粹的可使人相信之释明程度即已足”，“如果一项事实有双重之重要性时，亦即同时对罪责及刑罚之问题及诉讼上之问题均同具重要性时，则适用严格证明程序”。[25] 在日本，对于以被告人的罪责为基础的实体法上的事实，即犯罪事实和不存在违法阻却事由、责任阻却事由的事实需严格证明，量刑情节只通过自由证明即可。但是，对于倾向于加重被告人刑罚的情节事实

〔23〕 刑事诉讼法第 57 条第 1 款原文表述如下：在对证据收集的合法性进行法庭调查的过程中，人民检察院应当对证据收集的合法性加以证明。

〔24〕 陈光中主编：《证据法学》，法律出版社 2011 年版，第 288 页。

〔25〕［德］克劳思·罗科信：《刑事诉讼法》，吴丽琪译，法律出版社 2003 年版，第 208 页。

需要严格证明。[26] 从国外的立法实例来看，对证据合法性的证明标准并未形成统一。多数意见认为证明标准应确定为优势可信，即能够让裁判者相信所提出的事情存在的可能大于不存在的可能。少数意见认为对证据合法性的证明标准应以排除合理怀疑为宜。[27]

近些年，随着两个证据规定的陆续出台，我国在非法证据排除方面有了较大地进步，新修订的《刑事诉讼法》又规定了非法证据排除规则的范围、方式、法律后果，进一步完善了我国的非法证据排除规定，体现了我国刑事法律对被告人人权的尊重和重视。对于我国严格证明和自由证明对象的划分，规范制定者认为，对于所有犯罪构成要件事实和倾向于加重被告人刑罚甚至适用死刑的量刑事实的证明，必须采用严格证明的方式；对于有利于被告人的量刑事实和大部分程序法事实的证明，可以采用自由证明的方式。[28] 严格证明与自由证明的划分实质上是刑事诉讼兼顾实体公正和效率的结果。鉴于我国刑讯逼供屡禁不止，已成为侵蚀我国司法公正的一大顽疾和毒瘤这一现状，如若对言词证据合法性这一证明事项仍按照一般的程序事项采取任意性自由证明的话，那么侦查取证程序的合法性将被随意证明，导致非法证据排除的虚化[29]，纵容了侦查机关的违法取证行为，致使冤假错案的产生几率大大增加，悖离了刑事诉讼打击犯罪、保障人权的初衷。对控诉方降低非法证据排除规则的证明标准必然导致客观上由被告方承担证明责任，刑事诉讼法所规定的“确实、充分”的定罪标准将失去存在的基础，在司法实践中则无法杜绝因采纳以刑讯逼供等非法手段取得的口供而将疑案错误地作为留有余地不判处死刑立即执行的案件降格处理的做法。[30]

五、情况说明的证据能力探讨

从《高检规则》第 72 条、最高法《关于适用〈中华人民共和国刑事诉讼法〉的解释》第 101 条以及《非法证据排除规定》第 7 条的规定来看，只要证明取证程序合法的说明材料加盖公章并由侦查人员签名，就具有证据能力，可以作为证据使用。这说明我国在立法层面上确认了情况说明的证据能力。实践中法院对其证据能力也不做评价，而是通过简单的书面审查之后直接援引作为判决的依据。对此，有学者表示失望：“表明过去司法实践中长期存在的以侦查机关及其人员用以自证清白的所谓说明材料仍然具有证明取证合法性的证据能力，这里面包含着对于侦查人员群体人性的充分信任，认为只要有关讯问人员签名或者盖章的，说明材料的内容就具有真实性——这也是长期以来司法实践中的惯常做法，这一做法使辩护方无数试图揭破证据合法性假面的努力归于失败。”[31]

证明侦查行为合法的情况说明是否可以作为证据采纳，即情况说明是否具有证据能力，在这一问题上，鲜有专门系统的论述，有学者从证据的三性出发，认为情况说

---

〔26〕［日］田口守一：《刑事诉讼法》，张凌、于秀峰译，中国政法大学出版社 2010 年版，第 220 页。

〔27〕胡波：“论我国刑事证据合法性推定的建立”，载《法治论坛》2011 年第 2 期。

〔28〕张军：《刑事证据规则理解与适用》，法律出版社 2010 年版，第 279 页。

〔29〕郭晶：“刑事诉讼‘情况说明’证据能力之再思考——以‘两个证据规定’和 2013 年《刑事诉讼法》为背景”，载《研究生法学》2012 年第 27 卷第 5 期。

〔30〕张军：《刑事证据规则理解与适用》，法律出版社 2010 年版，第 336 页。

〔31〕张建伟：“纸面上的法与行动中的法——排除非法证据规定引发的一点思考”，载《西部法学评论》2010 年第 5 期。

明由于附加了侦查人员的主观推测而不符合证据的客观性及关联性，并由于没有依照法定程序收集、不符合法定形式而不合法，由此认定情况说明没有证据能力，是对非法证据排除的僭越。[32] 笔者认为，探讨证据能力首先要从证据的概念入手，2012 年《刑事诉讼法》在证据制度上的最大突破就是将证据内涵由原来的“事实说”改为现在的“材料说”，由“封闭列举式”的姿态改为现在的“开放接纳式”，证据材料在法庭审判之前不再区分真伪，证据种类也不再局限于法条列举的几类，只要出具的材料能够证明案件事实，都可以作为证据使用。在新刑事诉讼法生效前，以情况说明不属于法定证据种类而否定其证据能力的理由尚能成立，但随着新刑事诉讼法的生效，这一理由已经不能成立。笔者同样认为那种认为情况说明不具有关联性的观点不能成立，情况说明实质上应该是侦查人员针对其侦查行为违法的质疑所提出的辩解，它虽与案件的实体性事实关联性不大，但却关乎案件的程序性事实，在程序正义的理念日益得到凸显的今天，程序性事实的重要性丝毫不亚于实体性事实。针对辩方提出的侦查行为存在刑讯逼供行为的抗辩意见，侦查机关以出具书面情况说明的形式作出了反驳，旨在否定这种质疑，在性质上应当是一种辩解，与犯罪嫌疑人、被告人辩解性质相同。这一辩解与案件的程序性事实相关联，符合证据的关联性。至于那种认为情况说明附加了侦查人员的主观猜测而不具有证据的客观性的说法更是站不住脚的，詹姆斯·艾伦告诉我们，证据的另一概念其实是符号（sign）或记号（token），证据学其实是符号学（semiology），[33] 我们用证据认定案件事实的过程其实就是用我们所观察到的符号来推测还原我们不曾直接观察到的、已经发生了[34] 的事件的过程，这是一个主观认识客观的过程，所以不可避免地要带有人的主观因素，无论对物证、书证的解读，还是对证人证言的呈现都掺杂了人的主观因素，所以说再以纯粹的客观性作为证据属性、评判证据能力的观点已不合时宜。

《美国联邦证据规则》在考察一份材料是否可以作为证据使用时，有两项标准：相关性和可采性。“如果证据具有使得对确定诉讼具有重要意义的事实更可能存在或者更不可能存在的任何趋向（any tendency），则该证据具有相关性。”[35] 它不需要达到“比不可能更可能”（more probable than not）的高度，仅仅是“比没有它更可能（more probable than before）”，其规定了最低限度的相关性要求，将最大限度地容纳证据。具有相关性的证据一般都具有可采性，除非相关证据的证明价值为“不公平损害、混淆争点或者误导陪审团、不当拖延、浪费时间或者不必要地出示重复证据”所严重超过时，[36] 这些证据不可采。可以看出美国证据的准入口径是较为宽松的，具有相关性的材料都有证据能力，只有当它对案件事实的证明价值被采纳它的危险严重超过时，才否定其证据能力。我国刑事诉讼法对于证据概念的修改也在某种程度上反映了立法者

---

〔32〕 王丹：“‘情况说明’的证据越位——对《非法证据排除规定》第七条第三款的检讨”，载《人大研究》2011 年第 6 期。

〔33〕 ［美］David A. Schum：“关于科学证据的思考”，王进喜译，载《科学证据》2009 年第 17 卷第 1 期。

〔34〕 具体参见张中：“无证据，不事实——论证据裁判原则下的事实认定”，载常林、张中主编：《证据理论与科学——第三届国际研讨会论文集》，中国政法大学出版社 2012 年版，第 62 页。

〔35〕 王进喜：《美国〈联邦证据规则〉条解》（2011 年重塑版），法制出版社 2012 年版，第 55 页。

〔36〕 王进喜：《美国〈联邦证据规则〉条解》（2011 年重塑版），法制出版社 2012 年版，第 56 ~ 65 页。

接纳证据的姿态，所以将具有辩解性质的情况说明作为证据使用并没有违反立法本意，经过当庭质证的情况说明应当具有证据能力。

六、情况说明的证明力问题

前已提及，情况说明实质上是侦查人员针对辩护方对其侦查行为合法性的质疑而提出的辩解，在性质上相当于犯罪嫌疑人、被告人辩解，立法及司法解释的修改为情况说明作为证据使用提供了法律依据。《高检规则》、最高法的《关于适用〈中华人民共和国刑事诉讼法〉的解释》以及《非法证据排除规定》都对证明取证程序合法的情况说明提出了相同的形式要求：加盖公章并由侦查人员签名，只要符合了这些要求，情况说明作为证据使用已经不存在法律障碍，各地法院在判决中采纳侦查人员出具的情况说明不存在违法之嫌。造成情况说明滥用的根源不在于情况说明的证据能力问题，而是法院高估了情况说明的证明力，将情况说明请上了神坛，以为只要盖上了公章就成了公文书证，在证明力上高出其他证据一筹。

在我国，证据的证明力判断问题已不完全属于法官自由裁量的范围，为避免法官滥用自由裁量权，我国最高司法机关规范证据的审查判断时，确立了证据相互印证规则，[37] 即“对证据的证明力，应当根据具体情况，从证据与待证事实的关联程度、证据之间的联系等方面进行审查判断”。这就要求法官在综合考察各种证据的证明力基础上，排除证据间的矛盾之处，做到证据间相互印证。情况说明既然在性质上属于侦查人员的辩解，属于言词证据的范畴，就应该和犯罪嫌疑人、被告人辩解、证人证言等其他言词证据处于同等地位，法官就不应该在情况说明没有经过当庭质证并且和被告人当庭有罪供述相矛盾的情况下优先采纳情况说明而拒绝采纳被告人供述。

相比于《高检规则》和《非法证据排除规定》，最高法的《关于适用〈中华人民共和国刑事诉讼法〉的解释》在赋予情况说明以证据能力的同时，又紧接着规定了情况说明的补强规则，“上述说明材料不能单独作为证明取证过程合法的根据”，补强规则的确立说明最高人民法院已经认识到侦查人员针对其取证过程合法性所出具的说明材料在证明力上是薄弱的，需要有其他证据予以证实才可以作为定案根据。

经过前文的讨论可知，侦查人员出具的情况说明要加盖公章并由侦查人员签名才能作为证明取证合法的依据，但是加盖公章的形式要求并不能强化情况说明的证明力，仅证明了侦查人员的身份，所以，法院不能将加盖了公章的情况说明作为公文书证对待，在情况说明与被告人当庭供述及其他证明侦查行为违法的证据间存在矛盾时优先选择情况说明。情况说明既然在性质上是侦查人员的辩解，就应当同所有的证据一样接受当庭质证、认证，否则不能作为定案的根据。

七、结　论

情况说明在司法实践中的滥用既有立法方面的原因，也与我国的以侦查为主导的诉讼模式、法检之间既制约又配合的矛盾关系，以及我国官本位思想的盛行有关。情况说明在性质上应当属于侦查人员就其侦查行为合法性所做的辩解，是对案件程序性事实所作的辩解，与犯罪嫌疑人、被告人的辩解性质相同，在情况说明上加盖公章的行为不足以强化情况说明的真实性，法官不应过高评价情况说明的证明力。侦查行为

---

〔37〕 具体参见陈瑞华：“以限制证据证明力为核心的新法定证据主义”，载《法学研究》2012 年第 6 期。

合法性的判断关涉非法证据能否被排除的问题，进而关涉针对被告人的有罪控诉是否成立的问题，属于严格证明的事项，应当达到“确实、充分”的证明标准，实践中以情况说明证明取证过程不存在违法行为的做法实际上降低了这一标准，纵容了侦查机关的违法行为。法院不经任何实质审查即优先选择情况说明的证明力的做法，意味着侦查行为的合法性可以不经过任何法庭审查即为法院所确认，这就使侦查权游离于法庭之外，极易导致冤假错案的产生。立法及司法解释都确认了情况说明的证据能力，遏制情况说明滥用的关键在于加强庭审质证，落实相互印证规则和补强规则，将情况说明请下证据的神坛，与其他言词证据同等对待。

我国非法口供排除的“痛苦规则”及相关问题

龙宗智 *

口供在我国刑事证据体系中占有特殊地位，且实践证明非法获取口供是导致冤假错案的主要原因，因此，《刑事诉讼法》就非法证据排除、规制的重点是非法获取口供。“两高”司法解释，对非法口供的范围作了界定，将刑事诉讼法的原则性规定具体化为可操作的证据规则，本文拟对司法解释确立的口供排除规则以及相关问题进行分析，以帮助实务界正确理解和适用刑事诉讼法及其解释性规范，同时力图弥补解释性规范中的缺漏与不足。

一、司法解释确立的关于非法口供的证据规则——“痛苦规则”

修改后的《刑事诉讼法》的第50条规定：“……严禁刑讯逼供和以威胁、引诱、欺骗以及其他非法方法收集证据，不得强迫任何人证实自己有罪。”第54条规定：“采用刑讯逼供等非法方法收集的犯罪嫌疑人、被告人供述和采用暴力、威胁等非法方法收集的证人证言、被害人陈述，应当予以排除。收集物证、书证不符合法定程序，可能严重影响司法公正的，应当予以补正或者作出合理解释；不能补正或者作出合理解释的，对该证据应当予以排除。”

比较上引两条规定，可以看出刑事诉讼法就证据收集方法限制，采取了可称为“宽禁止、严排除”的立法模式。即第50条规定禁止使用的非法方法列举范围较宽，威胁、引诱、欺骗均属法律“严禁”的取证方法，但排除方法限制较严。如就口供，仅列举“刑讯逼供”一种方法，其余即以“等”字概括。而就证言和被害人陈述，则列举“暴力”、“威胁”两种方法，其余亦以“等”字概括。采取这种立法模式的原因，是“威胁、引诱、欺骗”的方法与侦查审讯的“谋略”容易发生混淆，因此不宜不加区别地一律作为非法证据予以排除。[1]

“刑讯逼供”获取的口供应当排除，此无疑义，但“等”字如何理解，则是颇有争议的问题。2012年3月《刑事诉讼法》修正案通过后，对“等”字的解释大致三种意见。一是“等”就等同于、等效于“刑讯逼供”。这是实务界相当一部分人士的观点。意在严格限制排除范围，避免排除范围较宽而妨碍打击犯罪。二是“等”系其他“残忍、不人道、有辱人格的方法”，以及法律所禁止的“威胁、引诱、欺骗”的方法

---

* 龙宗智，四川大学法学院教授。

〔1〕 笔者在十多年前提出威胁、引诱、欺骗的方法可能是侦查审讯谋略的要素，并非一律非法，而应区别对待（参见拙著：“威胁、引诱、欺骗的方法是否违法”，载《法学》2000年第3期；“欺骗与刑事司法行为的道德界限”，载《法学研究》2002年第4期）。这种观点后来得到普遍认可，刑诉法修改时立法机关也考虑做出限制，并在刑事诉讼法修改草案中将严禁的范围修改为“严禁刑讯逼供和以其他非法方法收集证据”，不再明确列举威胁、引诱、欺骗的方法。但在社会讨论时反对声音较强，认为是法制的倒退，不利于保障人权。因此，修正案仍保留原法的规定。但在排除非法证据的条款中以“等”字作概括性处理。

收集的证据。这是部分学者的看法。即以联合国《反酷刑公约》相关规范和《刑事诉讼法》第50条关于证据方法禁止的规定为依据，强调维护取证程序的正当性。三是"等"系其他严重违法，包括违法实施"威胁、引诱、欺骗等非法方法"收集证据的行为。是介于前两种观点之间的折中主张。

在2012年底出台的最高人民法院与最高人民检察院关于实施刑诉法的司法解释，对排除非法口供作了严格限制其范围的解释。如《最高人民法院关于适用〈中华人民共和国刑事诉讼法〉的解释》第95条规定："使用肉刑或者变相肉刑，或者采用其他使被告人在肉体上或者精神上遭受剧烈疼痛或者痛苦的方法，迫使被告人违背意愿供述的，应当认定为刑事诉讼法第54条规定的'刑讯逼供等非法方法'。"[2] 两高解释精神一致，略有区别。鉴于法院是对证据合法性问题做出最终确认的裁判机关，这里主要根据最高法院的解释分析职务犯罪侦查中的非法取证禁止问题。

根据最高法院上述规定，就非法口供排除，提出了三个要件：一是采用肉刑或者变相肉刑，或者采用其他与其相当的非法方法。这是非法口供的客观要件。二是使被告人在肉体上或精神上遭受剧烈疼痛和痛苦。这是非法口供的主观要件。三是迫使被告人违背意愿供述。这是非法口供的意志要件，也属主观要件。

把握上述三要件的关系，应当注意：其一，除肉刑或变相肉刑外的其他非法方法，不是一切不规范的审讯方法，而是限于与肉刑或者变相肉刑相当的非法方法，即这些方法必须达到"使被告人在肉体或精神上遭受剧烈疼痛和痛苦"的程度。而这一程度要求，正是联合国《反酷刑公约》就酷刑所作的解释。[3] 对此，最高检察院《人民检察院刑事诉讼规则（试行）》第65条的解释更为直接：其他非法方法是指违法程度和对犯罪嫌疑人的强迫程度与刑讯逼供或者暴力、威胁相当而迫使其违背意愿供述的方法。可见，非法取供的认定，不论其采用何种方法，关键在于具有使嫌疑人、被告人剧烈的疼痛和痛苦的效应。其二，供述的自愿性虽列为认定要件，但其认定前提仍然是，使嫌疑人肉体上或精神上剧烈疼痛或痛苦。刑讯（酷刑）是为了逼供，由此获得口供当然是"违背意愿"的。如果没有采用达到剧烈疼痛或痛苦程度的方法，即使非自愿供述，也不能界定为"非法证据"。可见，供述自愿性依附于酷刑方法。因此，在司法实践的规范适用上并无独立判断意义，从而缺乏实际功用。这与国外将自白任意性即有罪供述的自愿性作为排除非法口供的标准有重要区别。[4] 形成这种区别的一个原因，是作为口供排除规则基础的权利规则是否确立。自白任意性规则，以嫌疑人的

---

〔2〕 最高人民检察院《人民检察院刑事诉讼规则（试行）》第65条的解释为："刑讯逼供是指使用肉刑或者变相使用肉刑，使犯罪嫌疑人在肉体或者精神上遭受剧烈疼痛或者痛苦以逼取供述的行为。其他非法方法是指违法程度和对犯罪嫌疑人的强迫程度与刑讯逼供或者暴力、威胁相当而迫使其违背意愿供述的方法。"

〔3〕 我国于1986年签署、1988年批准生效的联合国《禁止酷刑和其他残忍、不人道或有辱人格的待遇或处罚公约》（简称反酷刑公约）第1条第1款规定："'酷刑'是指为了向某人或第三者取得情报或供状，为了他或第三者所作或涉嫌的行为对他加以处罚，或为了恐吓或威胁他或第三者，或为了基于任何一种歧视的任何理由，蓄意使某人在肉体或精神上遭受剧烈疼痛或痛苦的任何行为，而这种疼痛或痛苦是由公职人员或以官方身份行使职权的其他人所造成或在其唆使、同意或默许下造成的。纯因法律制度制裁而引起或法律制裁所固有或附带的疼痛或痛苦不包括在内。"简言之，"酷刑"为"蓄意使某人在肉体或精神上遭受剧烈疼痛或痛苦的任何行为"。

〔4〕 张建伟教授曾就我国刑事诉讼法的口供排除，注重刑讯逼供等外部行为，忽略引诱、欺骗等非法方法，未采用自白任意性规则的问题，作了有意义的分析并提出调整建议。参见张建伟："自白任意性规则的法律价值"，载《法学研究》2012年第6期。

沉默权为基础，凡是侵犯或实质上侵犯沉默权获得的口供属于非自愿口供而不能作为定案依据。而在我国刑事诉讼法，虽然已经确立了“不得强迫自证其罪”的一般法律原则，但并无具体实施规范，反而仍然保留了“犯罪嫌疑人对侦查人员的提问，应当如实回答”的规定。对这条规定如何理解，以及该规定与不强迫自证其罪的原则是否存在冲突，刑诉法修改后一直有不同的看法。但新刑事诉讼法在保留上述“如实回答”的规范之后，还保留规定，与本案无关的问题，嫌疑人有“拒绝回答的权利”。依此逻辑，与案件有关的问题，嫌疑人应不享有拒绝回答的权利。因此，称我国目前确立了沉默权，即使是所谓“默示的沉默权”，也是易受质疑的，而且在实践中因有碍于打击犯罪也会受到抵制。可见，在这样的规范背景中，自白任意性，难以作为判定是否为非法口供的独立标准或主要标准。

以上分析说明，嫌疑人“在肉体上或精神上遭受剧烈疼痛或痛苦”的标准，才是判定口供非法并予排除的关键，而方法要件与意志要件都依附于这一涉及人体感受的主观要件。而这一标准，也正是联合国《反酷刑公约》（《禁止酷刑和其他残忍、不人道或有辱人格的待遇或处罚公约》）对“酷刑”所设定的判断标准。因此，相对于国外排除非法口供是以供述的任意性（自愿性）为中心建立的排除规则，即“自白任意性规则”，我国排除非法口供的证据规则，可以概括称为“痛苦规则”,〔5〕或“酷刑规则”。

二、“痛苦规则”的理解和适用

“自白任意性规则”与“痛苦规则”是不同的非法口供排除规则。前者是以当事人的意志自由为基础，以自白的任意性即自愿性为中心进行评判；后者则是以当事人对于痛苦的耐受性为基础，以侵权的严重性为中心进行评判。前者强调的是“内心自由”的“内在标准”，后者重视的是形成痛苦源的肉刑、变相肉刑等方法的应用，即“外部的标准”。比较而言，“痛苦规则”的可操作性较强。因为外在标准比较容易辨识。而内在标准，即自由意志的妨碍较难判断。刑事审讯必然带有一定的对抗性与谋略性，被告认罪及做出供述通常都有不情愿甚至被迫的因素。〔6〕这种被迫性与自白任意性之间的关系如何把握，界限如何划分，常常是司法实践中的难题。在操作上，通常也需求诸是否采用了人身强制、言语胁迫等外部标准来作辨识。但自白任意性规则的合理性在于，一方面，它体现了尊重人权，即尊重涉案公民与外界沟通的选择权而不是将其作为客体予以强迫的人道主义原则和法治精神；另一方面，它因固守人的“意志内核”，更能反映现代刑事司法制度中非法口供的本质和核心，因而能够比较适应排除不同性质、不同形式非法口供的需要。例如采用威胁、引诱、欺骗，以及除刑讯逼供外的其他残忍、不人道、有辱人格的方法，迫使、诱使被告人违背意愿进行供述，只要达到一定程度，都可以将其判定为违背“自白任意性规则”而予以排除。而“痛苦规则”存在适用面较窄的局限性，即仅限于酷刑，而将其他违法、侵权甚至可能导致虚假供述的非法方法排除于口供排除规则之外。鉴于《刑事诉讼法》第50条列举

---

〔5〕“痛苦”一词，本可涵盖肉体上的疼痛与精神上的痛苦。

〔6〕著名的美国刑事审讯专家弗雷德·英博曾说：“绝大多数罪犯不情愿承认罪行，从而必须从心理角度促使他们认罪，并且不可避免地要通过使用包括哄骗因素在内的审讯方法来实现。”引自弗雷德·英博：《审讯与供述》，何家弘等译，群众出版社1992年版，第275页。

了威胁、引诱、欺骗等非法方法为法律严禁的取证方法，而“痛苦规则”则将口供排除限定于“刑讯逼供”以及“等同于刑讯逼供”的方法，即酷刑方法，实际上限缩了刑事诉讼法规定的非法口供排除的范围。这种限缩性解释的主要原因应当是，重点防范刑讯逼供，避免非法证据界定范围扩大对打击犯罪不利。然而，司法解释限缩立法规范，存在合法性质疑；而非法口供范围界定过窄，给司法实践带来操作上的难题，存在合理性质疑。

不过，考虑到中国刑事司法的体制和现实，排除规则实施比较困难，如排除范围规定较宽，实施起来将更为困难，规则制定者突出防范刑讯逼供的重心，而且是在刑事诉讼法中确立排除规则的初始阶段，这种以“痛苦规则”限缩刑事诉讼法规定的排除范围的做法，也不宜过于苛责。

无论学理上如何争议，一旦司法解释规范确立，实务界与学界应当重点考虑的，就是其理解与实施。由于非法口供的司法解释仍有相当的理解与解释空间，而且解释规范以外的法律与实践问题也需做出回应，作为学者，希望实务界能够在现规范的“所指”与“能指”范围内，对司法解释规范作出不离解释原意同时符合立法精神和司法实践的理解，为此提出一些分析意见。首先是“痛苦规则”适用的具体对象与范围。

根据司法解释确立的“痛苦规则”，在实践中，主要有三种情况属于非法证据排除的对象：

第一，采取肉刑或不让睡眠、长期保持特定姿势、饥渴、寒冷以及长时间浸泡在污秽物中等变相肉刑手段，使嫌疑人在精神和肉体上剧烈疼痛和痛苦，迫使其违背意愿供述的。这一点在解释上较为清楚，实务界理解上的分歧也不大，实践中的主要问题在于把握程度。不应过严把握，将一些主要属于精神压制而非肉体折磨的手段作为刑讯逼供，如偶尔采取的拳打脚踢，意在精神压制而并非使其疼痛、痛苦，一般不应当作为刑讯逼供；也不能把握标准过于宽松，如将某些因个人耐受力较弱，实已达到剧烈疼痛和痛苦程度的非法取供行为不纳入排除范围。这里存在一个疼痛和痛苦的“剧烈性”判定标准问题。操作中，既要考虑一般人的耐受程度即一般标准，更要注重特定环境情形中个体的不同耐受性而产生的特殊标准。个体差异性标准，应当是主要判定标准，同时可以适当参照普通人的一般耐受标准。例如，一般情况下，女士的疼痛耐受力较差，而男士较强，但也因人而异，应当注意这种个体差异。关于联合国有关公约的权威性著述称：“肉体或精神的痛苦是否能被定位‘剧烈的’，还取决于受害者的主观感受。这一定性只能在每一特定的案件中，通过仔细地平衡考虑各种情况，包括受害者自身对疼痛的忍受能力，才能得到确认。”〔7〕欧洲人权法院判例认为，对不人道待遇（广义的酷刑）是否存在，因考虑的相关因素包括：有关待遇的持续时间；它的肉体或精神效果；以及受害者的性别、年龄和健康状况等等。〔8〕

基于无罪推定、有利被告原则，同时鉴于肉刑与变相肉刑反人道主义的野蛮性，

---

〔7〕引自［奥］曼弗雷德·诺瓦克：《民权公约评注——联合国〈公民权利和政治权利国际公约〉》（上），毕小青等译，生活·读书·新知三联书店2003年版，第131～132页。

〔8〕［英］克莱尔·奥维、罗宾·怀特：《欧洲人权法原则与判例（第三版）》，何志鹏、孙璐译，北京大学出版社2006年版，第82页。

对于那些介于二者之间，可上可下的违法取证行为，应当尽量判定为非法而适用证据排除规则。

第二，采取其他残忍、不人道、有辱人格的方法，使嫌疑人在肉体或精神上剧烈疼痛或痛苦，迫使其违背意愿供述的。这主要是指多种方法同时或先后使用，产生叠加效应，使嫌疑人在肉体或精神上剧烈疼痛和痛苦，而被迫认罪并供述的。因为根据联合国《反酷刑公约》，使用任何方法达到使受刑人精神上和肉体上剧烈疼痛和痛苦的程度即为“酷刑”，而根据联合国大会1975年《反酷刑宣言》，酷刑是残忍、不人道、有辱人格的待遇或惩罚的一种“加重形式”。其他残忍、不人道、有辱人格的方法，达不到酷刑的严重程度，否则即为酷刑。然而，肉体折磨以及其他残忍、不人道、有辱人格的多种行为叠加，即可产生酷刑效果。如某职务犯罪案件，辩护方称被告受到“寒冷逼供”、“饥饿逼供”、“亲情逼供”、“传染病逼供”，以及“拳打脚踢”、“不让睡觉”等。虽然这些行为，每一种都没有达到刑讯逼供的程度，但全部违法行为叠加产生的累积性作用，即可产生刑讯逼供的同样效果。如果对这些非法行为查证属实或不能排除其可能性，那么由此获得的口供应当排除。

第三，采取威胁的方法，使嫌疑人精神上剧烈痛苦，被迫做出供述的。虽然《刑事诉讼法》第54条在非法口供排除中未列举威胁方法，而在非法证言排除中则将其列出（“胁迫”），但将达到酷刑效果的威胁，作为非法口供排除的手段行为，有法律、学理和实践依据。其一，刑事诉讼法已将“威胁”作为取证方法禁止的内容，同时新增不得强迫自证其罪规定，而“威胁”是强迫的重要手段，因此可认为对于禁止威胁有进一步的规定。其二，联合国《反酷刑公约》的权威解释以及国际法庭的判例，将威胁包括模拟处死等，作为“酷刑”予以严禁。负责解释并监督执行《反酷刑公约》的联合国人权事务委员会认为，模拟处死等威胁性行为，一般认为达到了酷刑的“剧烈的疼痛或痛苦”的程度。[9] 而“两高”对刑事诉讼法所规定的非法证据的解释，是参照对我国具有国际法约束力的联合国《反酷刑公约》做出的，同时适用该公约的解释，可谓顺理成章符合逻辑。其三，从法理上分析，威胁与暴力具有同质性与同效性。我国刑法关于劫持航空器罪、劫持船只、汽车罪、强奸罪、抢劫罪等七个分则条款，都将胁迫规定为与暴力同等的犯罪手段。其四，从司法实践看，威胁完全可以达到刑讯的逼迫效果。有时甚至更甚。[10]

不过，对于采用威胁方法获取口供，也应作具体分析，只有那种严重的威胁，导致嫌疑人精神上剧烈痛苦，被迫供述，才属于排除范围。刑事审讯，因为涉及嫌疑人及其亲属的重大权益，个别甚至事涉生死，嫌疑人通常不会自愿供述，审讯人员必须采取法律允许的各种方法促其开口。施加精神压力迫使被告认罪，也是审讯的必要手段，只要保持在一个较为合理的限度内，不应当作为法律禁止的“威胁”。实践中如交代政策，以证据确凿拒不认罪将从严处理向嫌疑人宣示，一般不应当作为违法威胁。有些威胁虽然有欠妥当，但尚未达到前述严重程度，也不宜作为排除对象。是否达到

---

〔9〕 参见［奥］曼弗雷德·诺瓦克：《民权公约评注——联合国〈公民权利和政治权利国际公约〉》（上），毕小青等译，生活·读书·新知三联书店2003年版，第132页。

〔10〕 尤其是以近亲属的重大利益如追究刑事责任相威胁，是迫使某些职务犯罪嫌疑人承认犯罪事实的主要方法。

违法的严重威胁的标准，应当根据案件的具体情况判断。主要应参酌威胁的强度、威胁的方式、嫌疑人的耐受性，以及导致口供虚假的可能性等因素判定。如以嫌疑人及其亲属的重大利益相威胁，而且采取清晰、明确的威胁方式，并使嫌疑人感到有实现这种威胁的现实可能性，即可构成作为排除对象的非法威胁。反之，如系笼统的宣称某种不利后果，通常不构成非法威胁。一般情况下，不应当以亲属的重大利益相威胁，而且这种威胁是直接的而嫌疑人认为完全可能实现的。因为由此形成高强度的威逼作用，可能使一个没有犯罪的人为保护亲属而承认犯罪。但也有例外。例如，如果亲属确已构成从属性犯罪（如协助受贿），侦查机关与嫌疑人进行辩诉协商，以不追究其亲属为条件促使嫌疑人交代犯罪事实并以嫌疑人不交代将依法追究其亲属相威胁，如被告人自愿接受条件而认罪并供述，此种方法不宜作为非法获取口供。[11]

三、引诱、欺骗以及其他法律禁止的方法取供如何应对

在根据法律和司法解释规范分析我国非法口供排除的机理和范围后，另一方面的问题随即产生——除上述范围以外，采用其他违背法律的方法获取的口供能否排除，如何排除？例如《刑事诉讼法》第50条严禁的某些取证方法——引诱、欺骗的方法如何应对。又如，实践中导致冤假错案的“元凶”之一——“指供”即“指名指事问供”如何处理。再如，在不合法的时间、地点进行审讯获取的口供是否排除等。这些问题，在司法实践中可能遇到，如何应对，需要进一步分析。

（一）关于引诱、欺骗的方法获取口供

通过引诱、欺骗获取口供，是采用使嫌疑人受意识牵引、精神满足或产生虚假认识的方法获取其供述，此类方法，不具备使嫌疑人“肉体上或精神上剧烈疼痛或痛苦”的特征，因此难以纳入非法证据排除范围。由于司法解释实际上排除了引诱、欺骗方法获取的证据被作为非法证据酌定排除（区别于刑讯逼供的法定排除）的可能性，在这个意义上，应当说司法解释有悖于刑事诉讼法严禁引诱、欺骗等非法方法收集证据的规范精神。

笔者认为，“引诱”、“欺骗”需要作为非法取证方法予以规制，这是因为不适当的引诱、欺骗将损害证据的真实性、取证的正当性，乃至其他合法利益（如司法诚信原则），也被各国刑事诉讼法普遍禁止或限制，我国也早在晚清即已立法（《民刑事诉讼暂行章程》等），禁止采取“诈罔”等非法方法取供。[12] 现行法应当对其作出一定的禁止性规定，并在此基础上确立一种排除规则。

具体分析，引诱取供，可能包括两种情况。一种是诱导性讯问。即诱导嫌疑人按照侦查人员的意图、根据侦查人员的提示做出供述。这实际上为“指供”的一种间接的方式。另一种是利益诱导，即许以好处，嫌疑人以认罪供述换取此种“好处”。学界和实务界讨论“引诱”取证方法，多指“利益诱导”的情况，而将“引供”、“诱供”作为另一类型的行为研究。本文亦循此将引诱限于“利益诱导”，而将诱导讯问纳入后

---

〔11〕 实系一种“辩诉交易”。虽然我国法律并未正式承认辩诉交易，但法律关于坦白从宽的有关规定，以及被告人认罪案件处理的程序规定，为实践中的辩诉交易提供了一定空间。笔者历来认为，在法制和人权保护原则作用下，侦控机关为实现侦查效益和效率，不可避免地需要一定范围内的辩诉交易。这也是我国和其他国家刑事司法的现实。

〔12〕 参见张建伟：“‘威胁、引诱和欺骗’为何不能删除？”，载《检察日报》2012年2月6日，第3版。

面的指供问题分析。对利益诱导，不能一概禁止，但也不能任其实施。如果审讯活动中，以法律允许的利益诱导嫌疑人如实供述，不应作为非法取证处理。[13] 反之，基于错误的判断，以不适当的方法，过度地实施引诱，则为法律所禁止，因为它可能使一个没有犯罪的人承认自己犯罪。而且，利益引诱有时与威胁具有一体两面的关系，从重处罚、恶劣待遇是威胁，不从重从严或允诺从轻从宽即为引诱。实践中二者经常交叉使用，并未截然分开，实践效果并无根本区别。因此，虽然某些严重威胁因其与刑讯逼供的同效性，其实际危害可能大于除刑讯逼供以外的其他非法取证方法，但将威胁与引诱截然分开，在排除规则中只规制威胁不规制引诱不尽合理，也与司法实践不符。

欺骗的方法，也是刑事司法实践中常用的取证方法。在对抗性和斗智攻心的刑事侦讯活动中，欺骗是侦查谋略的重要因素。化装侦查、卧底侦查、诱惑侦查等，均具有一定的欺骗性；审讯中适度利用欺骗，也不应当作为非法行为，因为从总体上不能达到使受审者丧失意志自由，被迫做出供述的程度。但欺骗需有限度以及适当的方式，否则亦应禁止。实践中主要有三种违法实施欺骗的方法。一是违背司法诚信原则。即审讯人员对嫌疑人做出某种从轻、从宽处理的承诺，如不作刑事追究、取保候审、不牵连家属等，但在嫌疑人认罪并作供述后予以反悔，称系审讯谋略、侦查需要等。国家司法机关和司法人员出尔反尔，为个案取胜而破坏诚信原则，损害司法之公信力，因小失大，实为司法之禁忌。二是采取的欺骗的方法损害了其他合法利益，“冲击了社会的良心”。如警察装扮律师或装扮神职人员（对信徒嫌疑人）而获取口供等。三是可能导致虚假供述的过度欺骗。如反复欺骗以至嫌疑人产生错觉，相信侦查人员而作出虚假供述。

对上述非法采用引诱、欺骗方法获取口供应如何应对？由于前述司法解释限制难以援引排除规则予以排除，只能采取其他方式处理。主要的方式，是以《刑事诉讼法》第48条关于“证据必须经过查证属实，才能作为定案的根据”为依据，以客观真实性为由，排除相关口供。这对过度的利益诱导，以及过度的欺骗是能够适用的，因为这些类型的引诱、欺骗其要害在于损害证据的客观性。但就其中某些类型，如违背司法诚信原则及损害其他合法利益的欺骗取供，客观性难以作为排除依据，而应当援引的排除根据是司法的纯洁性、正当性及公信力，但在目前的规范体系中，还缺乏将正当程序的一般规范作为排除非法证据的根据，因此，对这类非法取供行为，通常情况下难以排除其获得的证据。如果违法情节严重、影响恶劣，笔者认为可以避开司法解释，直接援引《刑事诉讼法》第50条和第54条，将其作为“……等非法方法”收集的证据予以排除。由于这样在操作上容易引起争议，因此仅在特殊情况下采用。

（二）关于指供方法获取口供

指供，是指“侦讯人员在讯问被告人时，对未查实的问题向被告人指出具体的人、

---

〔13〕 国外立法例如德国《刑事诉讼法》第136条a就“禁止的讯问方法”规定，“只允许在刑事诉讼法准许的范围内实施强制。……禁止以法律没有规定的利益相许诺”。

时间、地点、情节等让被告人作供述”。[14] 广义的指供，包括间接指供，即诱供和引供。[15] 本文中在此种广义上使用指供概念。

指供是我国刑事审讯实务中比较常见的一种非法讯问方式。其要害是“主客错位”，即口供本应由嫌疑人作为供述主体，但在指控使用的情境下，实际上侦查人员作为提供口供内容的主体——侦查人员按照自己的判断明示或暗示嫌疑人按其要求供述，笔录记载的口供本质上并非嫌疑人的供述，而系侦查人员对事实的认定。这种“主客错位”，是口供出错甚至导致冤假错案的根本原因。

由于指供在实践中较为普遍，而且冤假错案总与指供相关，有的实务工作者认为：“无论是以肉刑为特征的刑讯，还是以语言或行动为传递形式的威胁、引诱以及欺骗，它们在使案件向误区发展过程中只发挥一定的辅助性作用。那么，是什么样的非法讯问方法在导致冤、假、错案形成中起到至关重要的作用呢？笔者认为是指名问供，又称指名指事问供。”[16] 还有人认为：“从核查的一切冤假错案看，引供、诱供、指名指事问供造成的危害不亚于刑讯逼供。”[17] 不能否认，刑事案件出现冤假错案常常是以指供产生虚假口供为直接原因。但是，立法和实践规制的重点之所以是刑讯逼供包括变相刑讯逼供而非指供，这是因为，按照侦查人员的指供作有罪供述，与嫌疑人的利益相悖，而要突破嫌疑人为切身利益设置的心理防线而使其接受指供，通常情况下，需要依托一定的手段，而刑讯通常是实现指供目的最有效也是最恶劣的手段。此外，威胁、引诱、欺骗也常常是指供所依托的手段。因此，如果有效地防治刑讯逼供以及非法实施威胁、引诱、欺骗，则在一定程度上可以防止指供的发生。

然而，指供也有一定的独立性，某些指控并不明显依托刑讯或其他法律禁止的取供方法。例如，部分侦查人员作审讯笔录时曲解原意，甚至代替嫌疑人作供，有意作不利嫌疑人的供述笔录，要求嫌疑人签字，嫌疑人或者明知不是自己的原意勉强签字，或者根本就没有认真看笔录就签了字（这种情况实践中常发生，尤其是文化水平不高的被告），这就形成部分事实，尤其是某些关键情节上的指供。[18] 又如，某些嫌疑人事先知道不按侦查人员的交代过不了关，皮肉受了苦还得认罪，因此没有明显刑讯就按照指供作了供述。再如，诱供、引供等间接指供，以威胁作为指供的依托，但威胁没有达到使嫌疑人精神剧烈痛苦的程度，也属于无法纳入非法证据排除的相对独立的指供。

---

〔14〕 邢福和：“讯问方法与引供、诱供、指名指事问供关系的探讨”，载《公安大学学报》1989年第4期。

〔15〕 例如佘祥林冤案。佘在其申述材料中称：问如何沉的尸，自己只好胡乱交代。审讯人员看说得不对，就提示问是不是袋子装着，当我说是麻袋装的，审讯人员又质问是麻袋装的吗，我即改口为蛇皮袋装石头沉尸。审讯人员问蛇皮袋装了石头总不会直接压在尸体上，总有什么连着吧？我猜不出，一个刑警不耐烦地解下了自己脚上的两根皮鞋带结好，问我多长、多粗，手感如何，看着这样的举动，我猜着说是“用比香烟还细点的尼龙绳”，对方骂道，“你是没吃够亏的原因吧，那是尼龙绳吗？”我于是改口说是麻绳（姜志：“知情法官透漏：政法委‘协调’审判终铸冤案”，载《南方都市报》1995年4月8日）。此案例中侦查人员的引导供述，即为间接指供。

〔16〕 王兆志（时任北京市公安局预审处副处长）：“浅析使用证据与指名问供的界限”，载《公安大学学报》1989年第3期。

〔17〕 邢福和：“讯问方法与引供、诱供、指名指事问供关系的探讨”，载《公安大学学报》1989年第4期。

〔18〕 由于当前基本使用电脑记录口供，实践中出现一种“粘贴式指供”现象。即将某证人或其他嫌疑人的笔录内容，直接在电脑上作块处理，粘贴为该嫌疑人口供。有时甚至人称都未改变，在法庭上被律师指出证据作伪。

刑事诉讼法及司法解释没有针对指供的规范，援引非法证据排除规则排除指供缺乏法律依据。但是指供确系导致冤假错案的重要原因，必须否定此种方法及其所获证据。笔者认为对指供可以区别情况采取三种方式应对：一是以肉刑、变相肉刑以及其他使嫌疑人肉体上或精神上剧烈疼痛或痛苦的方法为依托进行指供，由此获得的口供应以刑讯逼供等非法方法取供为由，适用排除规则将其排除。二是在审讯中采用了诱供、引供等间接性指供，或者在全部审讯笔录中有部分内容采用直接指供的方式产生，则应援引《刑事诉讼法》第48条第3款，以口供不能查证属实为由将其排除或将其中部分内容排除。三是有罪供述的全部内容或主要内容均以直接指供方式产生，或者就是侦查人员按自己的意思写好后让嫌疑人签字，此种口供只是侦查人员对案情的判断甚至臆想而不具备口供的基本要素——记录嫌疑人所说的话。也就是说，如果部分记录不准确，或者供述形成只是含有侦查人员诱导的因素，此类笔录还具备口供的基本要素，因此不否定其存在，而只是以客观性为由将其排除或部分排除；如果其全部或主要内容不是嫌疑人的陈述，那只能认为没有口供。法院可以根据法律行为成立要件不具备的法理，直接否定该口供存在。

（三）在法律不允许的时间或地点审讯形成口供

法律不允许的时间审讯，主要是指违背《刑事诉讼法》第117条第2款、第3款的规定，超过传唤、拘传的法定时限和次数限制的审讯，或拘留、逮捕超期羁押时的审讯；不允许的地点，主要是指违反《刑事诉讼法》第116条第2款关于“犯罪嫌疑人被送交看守所羁押以后，侦查人员对其进行讯问，应当在看守所内进行”的规定，无正当理由将嫌疑人提出看守所在其他地点进行审讯。对超时限及非法定地点审讯获得的口供如何认定其证据能力，诉讼实践中控辩双方常常发生争议，而法律和司法解释对此均无明确规定，法院常常感到难以处理。此类口供一律排除，不仅缺乏规范依据，而且容易引起控方抗议，也妨碍打击犯罪。但不排除，又意味着法院纵容违法侵权，这有悖于法院职责。

笔者认为，在规范缺位的情况下，可以按“相对合理”的思路应对此一问题。对超时限问题，如果超时限的情节不严重，可按可补正与合理解释的瑕疵证据处理；如果情节较严重，如超过12小时或24小时传唤、拘传时间过长，在辩方以侦查人员刑讯逼供等非法方法取证为由，提出证据效力抗辩的前提下，如果控方不能以十分确凿的证据证明其审讯中未使用非法手段，则可用不能排除以非法手段获取口供可能性为由，而将其口供排除。对非法定地点审讯的问题，如无正当理由而违法改变审讯地点，自然产生对侦查人员非法取供的合理怀疑（转移出看守所就是为了规避看守所的监督和看守所审讯室的物理隔离），如果控方不能做出合理解释或对审讯行为合法性缺乏有效证明，则应当适用证据排除规则。

四、“重复自白”问题

“重复自白”，又称“二次自白”，此问题是指在可能采取非法手段获取口供后，再次审讯或而后多次审讯获得了同样内容的口供，但并未涉嫌采用非法手段，那么这些后续审讯所获口供能否作为定案依据。

笔者认为，关于刑事诉讼法的司法解释对“重复自白”问题未作出规定，是关于非法证据规制中最为突出的问题，也是影响最为显著的缺漏。因为几乎每一个辩方要求排除非法证据的案件，法院都会遇到重复自白的采用难题。由于嫌疑人对犯罪事实的供述在案件中总会有多份笔录，[19] 即使侦查人员采用非法手段，也不可能每次讯问时都采用，尤其在看守所的审讯室，或在全程录音录像监控的条件下，非法审讯实施受到限制。因此，侦查、控诉机关常常避开可能引起争议的供述笔录，而以这些审讯与被审讯人之间有物理隔离或有监控条件的审讯笔录作为定案依据。有的案件，控诉方还提出批捕检察官、公诉检察官所作讯问笔录作为佐证，而这些检察官是不需要也不可能同样实施非法手段的。由此可见，如果不排除“重复自白”，排除非法证据的规范就会被规避，排除规则就会丧失其效用。然而，排除“重复自白”并无明确法律依据。“两高”尤其是最高法院的司法解释，本应按照刑事诉讼法关于排除非法证据的立法精神，回应司法实践的规范需求，但司法解释回避了这一问题，这就使排除规则在实践中适用遇到一个很大的难题。[20]

无规范可作依据，但实践中又必须回应，那就只能按照法律的精神寻求一种较为适当的处理方式。

在实践中，“重复自白”有多种类型，包括同一机关同一审讯人员获得的重复自白、同一机关（部门）的不同审讯人员获得的重复自白、不同类型机关（部门）的不同审讯人员获得的重复自白，以及在发现审讯非法的情况下，为解决证据合法性、真实性问题，侦查或批捕审查、公诉机关重新审讯获得的自白等。重复自白证据能力确认的关键，是非法获取的供述与后续供述是否存在因果关系——如果前者效力延及后者，则应否定重复自白的证据能力；如果因果关系阻断，或因自白重复过程中产生“稀释效应”，违法性被稀释到足以容忍，则可确认其证据能力。

如何对待重复自白，学理上有两种主张，一种是严格执行排除规则，认为构成排除条件的口供非法获取，本系取证严重违法，因此产生波及效应，后续同类自白皆不能接纳；[21] 另一种主张是区别对待。即视违法情节严重性，以及阻断因果关系的可能性而定。[22]

笔者曾在探讨“两个证据规定”的规范与执行中的证据问题时，就重复自白问题主张区别对待，参照国外相关法制与法理，设定三个条件。一是取证违法的严重性。如触犯排除规则非法取证，则适用“毒树之果”理论，产生波及效应。原则上侦查、控诉机关的后续口供均以波及效为由予以排除。如属普通违法，则产生稀释效应，“重复自白”可以使用。二是取证主体的改变情况。在实践中，侦查、控诉机关由于受到角色限制，为控诉需要，通常是以巩固原有有罪供述为讯问出发点，因此即使讯问主

---

〔19〕 仅就立案侦查阶段，通常就可能有立案前询问、立案后讯问、逮捕后讯问，以及侦查终结前的综合性、总结性讯问等。而且对主要犯罪事实，为证明其供述稳定以及核实一些具体情节，可能讯问多次。此外，起诉检察官还会进行讯问；根据刑诉法第86条的规定，审查逮捕检察官可以讯问犯罪嫌疑人（遇是否符合逮捕条件有疑问等三种情况，必须讯问嫌疑人）。批捕和起诉检察官讯问时，也会制作讯问笔录。

〔20〕 最高法院在制定刑诉法解释时，曾组织包括笔者在内的几位刑诉法学者讨论该解释草案3天，会上也有学者提出应当解决重复自白问题，但司法解释最终仍未作出规定。可能是制定者认为法律规范不明确，又涉及公、检、法几家关系，最高法院司法解释作出规定有困难。

〔21〕 参见万毅：“论‘反复自白’的效力”，载《四川大学学报（哲学社会科学版）》2011年第5期。

〔22〕 参见张颖：“重复自白的证据能力”，载《中国刑事法杂志》2012年第7期；谢小剑：“重复供述的排除规则研究”，载《法学论坛》2012年第1期。

体变化（公安刑侦部门到检察机关，或纪委到检察机关），但波及效明显，口供笔录虽然维持，但不一定反映嫌疑人、被告人的真实意思。但如法院作为中立主体讯问，在符合讯问要求的情况下，被告仍然承认有罪，这种口供可以作为定罪依据。三是特定的讯问要求。中立的司法机关在讯问时说明其中立客观性，同时说明被讯问人的权利和责任，允许被告人作有罪供述和无罪辩解。此时，波及效可能因此中断，被告所作的有罪供述可以作为定罪依据。[23]

上述观点从学理上讲应该说有一定根据，也是其他有些国家处理重复自白的主导性做法。但提出后有学者提出质疑。如万毅教授称，以取证主体的根本性变化为中心确定的区别对待方式，不一定适应中国刑事诉讼。因为我国公、检、法三机关之间奉行的是“分工负责、互相配合、互相制约”的原则，三机关同质性较高，而且形成“流水线作业式”办案模式，检察官中立性不足，法官亦同，且有重大案件政法委协调办案制度。在这种同质性较高且追诉倾向较强的司法体制和办案模式下，前一阶段（侦查）诉讼主体的行为和结果，很容易为后一阶段（起诉、审判）诉讼主体所认同，单纯变更取证主体，恐无法有效切断先前刑讯逼供行为的影响。而从实践看，在我国司法实践中频频发生的刑讯逼供案，如赵作海、佘祥林等案，均有多次供述，但被告人即使到法庭上也未翻供，盖因已经被“打怕了”。可见，在我国，单纯变更取证主体，无论是由检察官还是由法官来进行讯问，均不能完全抵消原有违法取证行为的消极影响，因而，也不能中断原有的因果关系。[24]

万毅教授的观点持之有据，比较符合我国刑事司法的现实以及冤假错案产生的教训。而且一个新的规范背景是，刑诉法修改后两高司法解释下达，以前述“痛苦规则”实际限缩了由《关于办理刑事案件排除非法证据若干问题的规定》初次界定，并由刑事诉讼法所确认的非法证据排除的范围。也就是说，我国现行非法口供排除，仅适用于采用酷刑，即十分严重的非法取供的情况。这种情况，各国普遍视为必然产生波及效应的情况，并不得以庭审前讯问主体变化为由中断波及作用。考虑到这一点，同时虑及我国刑事司法体制的特点和实践中的教训，笔者认为，凡是确认或不能排除采用使嫌疑人、被告人在肉体上、精神上剧烈疼痛和痛苦的非法方法获取口供的，其后续口供，即使没有继续采用这种方法，也不能使用。而且禁止因非法取供事实存在而重新获取口供的行为，并否定此类重新取供的证据效力。这种情况下，司法机关只能以其他证据证明被告犯罪。

不过，上述排除重复自白原则可以设置两个例外。其一，是被告人在公开的庭审中，在有律师辩护，同时已经获知其如实陈述和进行辩解权利的情况下，仍然承认过去所作自白，这种承认，应当认为具有证据效力。确认此种例外，是因为公开的庭审具有基本的程序保障，即控辩审组合形成的庭审结构、对辩护权的确认与保障、质证与辩论程序，以及公开审判等。这也是对庭审作为刑事诉讼中心环节的尊重。当然，不否认“酷刑”的波及效可能延至庭审甚至庭后阶段，但总的情况看，国家法制在逐步完善，辩护权与公民的权利意识在增强，直到公开庭审时仍有冤不伸的情况也在减

---

〔23〕 龙宗智：“进步与问题——评关于刑事证据的两个规定”，载《中国法学》2010 年第 6 期。

〔24〕 万毅：“论‘反复自白’的效力”，载《四川大学学报（哲学社会科学版）》2011 年第 5 期。

少。这里存在一个利益权衡问题，在庭审这种特殊空间中为波及效中断设置一种例外，可谓相对合理，也使排除重复自白的做法增强一点可行性。其二，根据被告人的供述、指认提取到了隐蔽性很强的物证、书证，且被告人的供述与其他证明犯罪事实发生的证据相互印证，重复自白可以作为定案依据。《最高人民法院关于适用〈中华人民共和国刑事诉讼法〉的解释》第106条规定："根据被告人的供述、指认提取到了隐蔽性很强的物证、书证，且被告人的供述与其他证明犯罪事实发生的证据相互印证，并排除串供、逼供、诱供等可能性的，可以认定被告人有罪。"在符合该规定的情境中，被告人的供述有隐蔽性很强的物证、书证等证据作真实性保障，首次自白如因逼供、诱供等排除，重复自白没有采用这些非法方法，可以认为具有证据能力。这是实体的真实主义与正当程序主义之间的一个协调，在中国目前的刑事司法语境中，应当说还是必要的。

采用上述除例外情况则应排除重复自白的做法，有一个最重要的理由，就是唯其如此，才能使排除范围本已较为狭窄的排除规则真正发挥某种规制性作用，而不至被规避成为虚设。而且由于排除规则的范围已经比较狭窄，真正能适用该规则的，只会是极少数案件，因此，即使排除与之相关的重复自白，对打击犯罪的活动也不会有大的影响。这也是维护法制保障人权同时防治冤假错案必要的，同时可以承受的代价。由于排除重复自白是为了执行法律规定的非法证据排除规则，因此亦应视为有法律依据。当然，为了使这一十分重要的证据排除问题有明确的规范指引，下一步需要通过修改立法或司法解释，明确规定重复自白的排除及其特别例外。

Expert Witness 2012 Update

Harvey Brown *

DAUBERT / EXPERT WITNESS UPDATE

I. INTRODUCTION

Unless there is an objection, an expert does not need to state the basis for the expert opinion for the opinion to be admissible at trial. *United States v. Havvard*, 260 F. 3d 597 (7th Cir. 2001). ("Rule 705 ... allows experts to present naked opinions.") *Arkoma Basin Exploration Co.*, *Inc. v. FMF Assocs.* 1990 – *A*, *Ltd.*, 249 S. W. 3d 380 (Tex. 2008); *see* Tex. R. Evid. 705. One court has commented that "doubts regarding whether an expert's testimony will be useful should generally be resolved in favor of admissibility." *Clark v. Heidrick*, 150 F. 3d 912, 915 (8th Cir. 1998). So while the trial court may be the gatekeeper, it is trial counsel that must ensure that an expert is not allowed to sneak over the wall instead of entering through the gates of admissibility.

All evidence must pass through scrutiny before it is admissible. An expert's opinion must pass through eight particular gates of admissibility, and the analysis under these gates is "rigorous." *Mack Trucks*, *Inc. v. Tamez*, 206 S. W. 3d 572, 579 (Tex. 2006). Moreover, the examination requires "each material part of an expert's theory [to] be reliable". *Whirlpool Corp. v. Camacho*, 298 S. W. 3d 631, 637 (Tex. 2009). *See also Knight v. Kirby Inland Marine*, *Inc.*, 482 F. 3d 347, 355 (5th Cir. 2007).

When one expert relies on another expert as a basis for her opinion, any deficiencies in the opinion of the underlying expert opinion may cause the second expert's opinion to be likewise inadmissible. *Martinez v. San Antonio*? 40 S. W. 3d 587, 594 (Tex. App. —San Antonio 2001, pet. denied). In other words, if one expert relies on another expert and the opinion of the other expert is struck, the second expert's opinion will also be struck.

Helpfulness. *Does the factfinder need an expert to help it understand the issues*? The first gate that expert testimony must pass is the helpfulness gate—it must assist the trier of fact. If the fact – finder is equally competent to examine an issue, the expert's opinion will be struck under this helpfulness standard. The helpfulness gate also undergirds several of the other gates. *See*, *e. g.*, *Jordan v. State*, 928 S. W. 2d 550, 554 (Tex. Crim. App. 1996) (concluding that "unreliable scientific evidence is not helpful to the jury because it frustrates rather than promotes intelligent evaluation of the facts"). If an expert's methodology, reasoning, or

---

* Justice, First Court of Appeal, USA.

foundation is unreliable, the evidence will not assist the trier of fact. *Mack Trucks, Inc. v. Tamez*, 206 S. W. 3d 572, 578 (Tex. 2006).

Qualifications. *Is this particular expert qualified to provide the help the factfinder needs?* Second, an expert witness must pass the qualification gate. The Texas Supreme Court and the federal courts in a number of decisions have now raised this gate (or hurdle) by holding that the expert must be qualified for each separate opinion and that the qualifications for opinions that fall within a field for which subspecialties exist must be tied to the subspecialty in question. *See, e. g., Gammill v. Jack Williams Chevrolet, Inc.*, 972 S. W. 2d 713 (Tex. 1998); *Broders v. Heise*, 924 S. W. 2d 148 (Tex. 1995).

Relevance. *Does the factfinder need this evidence to decide the case?* Third, the United States and Texas Supreme Courts have held that rule 702 of both the Texas and Federal Rules of Evidence imposes on a trial court the obligation to assure that expert evidence is relevant. *Daubert v. Merrell Dow Pharms., Inc.*, 509 U. S. 579 (1993); *E. I. duPont de Nemours v. Robinson*, 923 S. W. 2d 549 (Tex. 1995).

Reliability. The federal rules and courts break the reliability inquiry into three parts, each of which is discussed in detail below. The reliability inquiry on the whole asks: *Does this particular expert testimony actually provide the help the factfinder needs?*

These three reliability challenges are succinctly summarized in *Mack Trucks v. Tamez*:

"The trial court should undertake a *rigorous* examination the facts on which the expert relies, the method by which the expert draws an opinion from those facts, and how the expert applies the facts and methods to the case at hand."

206 S. W. 3d 572 (Tex. 2006); *see also Harris Cnty. Appraisal Dist. v. Houston 8th Wonder Prop., L. P.*, No. 01 - 10 - 00154 - CV, 2012 WL 1757591 (Tex. App. —Houston [1st Dist.] May 17, 2012, no. pet. h.) ("As to reliability, the court must examine the expert's methodology, foundational data, and whether too great an analytical gap exists between the data and methodology, on the one hand, and the expert's opinions, on the other."); *Wilson v. Shanti*, 333 S. W. 3d 909, 913 (Tex. App. —Houston [1st Dist.] 2011, pet. denied). ("The trial court should *undertake a rigorous examination* of the three components of the reliability inquiry—namely, the expert's methodology, foundational data, and whether too great an analytical gap exists as the expert connects the foundational data or methodology with the opinion."); *In re J. B.*, 93 S. W. 3d 609 (Tex. App. — Waco 2002, no pet). *Allstate Texas Lloyds v. Mason*, 123 S. W. 3d 690 (Tex. App. —Fort Worth 2003, no pet) (stating these three tests and adding a fourth test that the expert must rule out other plausible causes). *Cf. State v. Cent. Expressway Sign Assocs.*, 302 S. W. 3d 866, 870 (Tex. 2009) ("to be reliable, the opinion must be based on sound reasoning and methodology").

As part of a general reliability inquiry, it is important to examine expert testimony from the perspective of the expert's particular field. Experts must "employ in the courtroom the same level of intellectual rigor that characterizes the practice of an expert in the relevant field." *Kumho Tire*, 526 U. S. 137 (1999). "The court should ensure that the opinion comports with applicable professional standards outside the courtroom and that it will have a reliable basis in the knowledge and experience of the discipline." *Helena Chem. v. Wilkins*, 47 S. W. 3d 486 (Tex. 2001). In cases involving scientific principles, the reason is that " [l] aw lags science; it does not lead it." *Havner*, 953 S. W. 2d at 714.

Methodological Reliability. Fourth, *Daubert* and *Robinson* require expert evidence to pass the gate of methodological reliability. When the methodology used by an expert is not reliable, the resulting opinion and testimony is not "knowledge" and does not assist the jury. *Robinson*, 923 S. W. 2d at 556; Harvey Brown, *Eight Gates for Expert Witnesses*, 36 Hous. L. Rev. 743, 747 (1999). The reliability requirement applies to all types of expert evidence. *Kumho Tire Co. Ltd. v. Carmichael*, 526 U. S. 137, 149, 119 S. Ct. 1167, 1175, 1177 (1999); *Gammill*, 972 S. W. 2d at 726; *Nenno v. State*, 970 S. W. 2d 549, 560 (Tex. Crim. App. 1998). *Daubert* refers to this reliability test as the "evidentiary reliability" test. *Daubert*, 509 U. S. at 590 n. 9. Because this gate focuses primarily on the reliability of the expert's *methodology*, and other gates focus on other aspects of the reliability of expert *testimony*, this gate is called the methodological - reliability gate. Harvey Brown, *Eight Gates*, 36 Hous. L. Rev. at 748, 778 - 803. This gate examines whether "the testimony is the product of reliable principles and methods". *See Merrell Dow Pharms.*, *Inc. v. Havner*, 953 S. W. 2d 706, 714 (Tex. 1997) (explaining that the opinion is unreliable when an expert uses a "flawed methodology").

Connective Reliability. Fifth, the gatekeeper must ensure that an expert's extrapolation from the basis of the opinion to the expert's conclusion is sound. *Gen. Elec. Co. v. Joiner*, 522 U. S. 136, 118 S. Ct. 512 (1997); *Gammill*, 972 S. W. 2d at 727; *see also Kerr - McGee Corp. v. Helton*, 133 S. W. 3d 245 (Tex. 2004). Expert testimony "is unreliable 'if there is simply too great an analytical gap between the data and the proffered opinion'". *Cooper Tire & Rubber Co. v. Mendez*, 204 S. W. 3d 797, 800 (Tex. 2006).

This test, which I refer to as "connective reliability," focuses on the reasoning used by the expert to lead from certain data or assumptions to the expert's conclusion or opinion, and whether an analytical gap exists between the data and the expert's conclusion. Brown, *Eight Gates*, 36 Hous. L. Rev. at 749, 804 - 10; *Merrell Dow Pharms.*, *Inc. v. Havner*, 953 S. W. 2d 706, 714 (Tex. 1997). As stated in *Whirlpool*, an expert must "connect the data relied on and his or her opinion". 298 S. W. 3d at 642. The court *Havner* explained that "a flaw in the expert's reasoning" makes the opinion unreliable. *Id.* at 714. If the connection between the data and the opinion is only the *ipse dixit* of the expert, it is "fundamentally unsupported". *Gammill*, 972 S. W. 2d at 727. As clarified in FRE 702, a court should examine whether the expert "has applied the principles and methods reliably to the facts of the case". If an expert's methodology or foundational data is sound but the expert's reasoning process applying that methodology or data is not sound or is not demonstrated, the opinion will not be admissible. Connective reliability requires the expert to explain her reasoning.

In *Transcontinental Ins. Co. v. Crump*, 330 S. W. 3d 211 (Tex. Aug. 27, 2010), the Court observed that an expert does not have to eliminate every gap; if a gap is not "too great," it goes to the evidence's weight and not its reliability.

Foundational Reliability. Sixth, *Daubert*, *Joiner*, *Robinson*, and *Havner* require a party to pass the gate of foundational reliability. Tex. R. Evid. 705; *see also* FRE 702 (the expert's testimony must be "based upon sufficient facts or data"). A court must review the reasonableness of the expert's assumptions and the reliability of the data, studies or foundation of the expert's opinion. This rule focuses not on the methodology used by the expert nor the application of the methodology to the facts of the case, but on the reliability of the underlying facts or data upon which the expert's opinion is based. "If the foundational data underlying opinion testimony are unreliable, an expert will not be permitted to base an opinion on that data because any opinion drawn from that data is likewise unreliable." *Havner*, 953 S. W. 2d at 714.

Underlying Inadmissible Evidence. Seventh, Rule 703 of the Texas Rules of Evidence ("TRE") allows an expert to rely on otherwise inadmissible hearsay or other evidence *only if* the underlying facts or data are "of a type reasonably relied upon by experts in the particular field". Generally, the issue of whether the expert's reliance on inadmissible evidence is reasonable goes to the credibility, rather than admissibility, of the evidence. A court may, however, reject an expert's claim that the information is reasonably relied upon by experts in the field. If the court finds that the only data considered by an expert is inadmissible evidence that is not reasonably relied upon by experts in the field, the court may then strike any opinion that is based on that data. If the underlying facts are sufficiently reliable but are normally inadmissible, such as hearsay, a balancing test under TRE 705 (d) and FRE 703 determines whether the jury will hear the inadmissible evidence, both on direct and on cross – examination.

Unfair Prejudice. Finally, *Daubert*, and TRE 403 provide that the expert's opinions must pass the gate of unfair prejudice. TRE 403 has been applied to exclude "prejudicial language", evidence that creates an "aura of scientific infallibility", and "in – court demonstrations or evidence of experiments". Margaret A. Berger, *Evidentiary Framework*, 114 – 16, in Federal Judicial Center's REFERENCE MANUAL ON SCIENTIFIC EVIDENCE (1994). Multiple experts on the same topic are also sometimes excluded by courts as cumulative under TRE or FRE 403. Finally, TRE and FRE 403 are also used as additional support to exclude expert evidence that is unreliable. When the expert's opinion satisfies the reliability standards of TRE or FRE 702, it will be unusual for it to violate TRE or FRE 403.

This paper will first examine each of these eight gates in turn and then turn to briefly explore some procedural issues surrounding *Daubert* challenges.

II. EIGHT GATES OF ADMISSIBILITY

A. First Gate: Helpfulness

The subject matter of an expert's testimony must "assist the trier of fact". Tex. R. Evid. 702; *Holloway v. State*, 613 S. W. 2d 497 (Tex. Crim. App. 1981). The distinction between lay and expert testimony is that lay testimony results from a process of reasoning familiar in everyday life, while expert testimony results from a process of reasoning which can only be mastered by specialists in the field. *United States v. Yanez Sosa*, 513 F. 3d 194, 200 (5th

Cir. 2008) (quoting Fed. R. Evid. 701, advisory committee's not to 2000 amendments). Expert testimony is permitted in those situations where "the expert's knowledge and experience ... are beyond that of the average juror". *Dunnington v. State*, 740 S. W. 2d 896, 898 (Tex. App. —El Paso 1987, writ denied).

The helpfulness gate does not mean that an expert can only testify about something that the jury knows nothing about. An expert may aid the jury in understanding even familiar matters if the expert's experience or training provides a more thorough or refined understanding than ordinary experience provides. *See* Brown, *Eight Gates*, 36 Hous. L. Rev. at 751. It is wrong to apply the standard so stringently that "only evidence completely inaccessible to the jury could come in under Rule 702". *Tyus v. Urban Search Management*, 102 F. 3d 256, 263 (7th Cir. 1996). A trial court is not compelled to exclude expert testimony "just because the testimony may, to a greater or lesser degree, cover matters that are within the average juror's comprehension". *Id.* The helpfulness test considers "whether the untrained layman would be qualified to determine intelligently and *to the best possible degree* the particular issue without enlightenment from those who have a specialized understanding of the subject involved in the dispute". *United States v. Locascio*, 6 F. 3d 924, 936 (2d Cir. 1993) (emphasis added).

Although a court should be cautious in excluding evidence under the helpfulness gate, it should exclude the evidence when a jury can comprehend the information, particularly if the opinion addresses one of the ultimate issues in the case. *Honeycutt v. Kmart*, 24 S. W. 3d 357 (Tex. 2000) (per curiam). For example, a trial court erred in admitting the expert testimony of a clinical psychologist and licensed counselor that the defendant's conduct was "outrageous". *GTE Southwest, Inc. v. Bruce*, 998 S. W. 2d 605, 619 - 20 (Tex. 1999). The testimony would not aid the jurors and the question of whether the defendant's conduct was outrageous was for the jury to determine based on the jurors' general knowledge.

Additionally, in *Honeycutt*, the Texas Supreme Court held that it was proper to exclude the testimony of a human factors and safety expert concerning whether a missing top rail on a grocery cart corral would induce people to sit on the lower railing and whether the lack of the top railing caused the accident. The court noted that an expert's impressive qualifications do not ensure that the expert will aid the jury. Instead it must be shown that "the expert's knowledge and experience are beyond that of the average juror". The Court instructed trial courts to exclude an expert's opinion whenever "the jury is equally competent to form an opinion" on the topic of the expert's testimony.

Applying these rules, the *Honeycutt* Court excluded the expert's opinions. The testimony that the defendant was negligent and that the lack of a top railing served as an invitation to sit on the railing was not helpful because photographs were available of the corral. The jury's "collective common sense" could determine this issue. Additionally, the court cited a number of other cases indicating some skepticism of human factors experts. The expert's causation opinion was not helpful because the causation questions did not involve scientific or technical issues. *Id.* The expert's opinion on the proper use of shopping carts would not aid the jury. Finally, the question of a proper lookout did not require "any special interpretation of the facts" and therefore also did not aid the jury.

Generally speaking, expert testimony on the law is not considered helpful to a jury. *Nat'l Convenience Stores Inc. v. Matherne*, 987 S. W. 2d 145, 149 (Tex. App. —Houston [14th Dist.] 1999, no pet.) ("an expert is not competent to give an opinion or state a legal conclusion regarding a question of law because such a question is exclusively for the court to decide"); *Lyondell Petrochem. Co. v. Fluor Daniel, Inc.*, 888 S. W. 2d 547, 554 (Tex. App. —Houston [1st Dist.] 1994, writ denied) ("An expert witness may not testify to his opinion on a pure question of law.").

An expert's statements of legal opinion are impermissible because such statements would usurp the role of the fact finder at trial. *See* Brown, *Eight Gates*, 36 Hous. L. Rev. at 771, 772. So an expert witness should not offer an opinion on:

(1) the interpretation of an unambiguous lease agreement, *Akin v. Santa Clara Land Co., Ltd.*, 34 S. W. 3d 334, 339 (Tex. App. —San Antonio 2000, pet. denied);

(2) the legal effect of a condominium declaration authorizing a non – judicial foreclosure, *Dickerson v. DeBarbieris*, 964 S. W. 2d 680, 690 (Tex. App. —Houston [14th Dist.] 1998, no pet.);

(3) the construction of a state statute, *Upjohn Co. v. Rylander*, 38 S. W. 3d 600 (Tex. App. —Austin 2000, pet. denied) (but also noting that "an expert may offer an opinion on a mixed question of law and fact as long as the opinion is confined to the relevant issues and based on proper legal concepts"); or

(4) whether OSHA regulations comprise the proper standard of care in a case. *Ledbetter v. Missouri Pac. R. Co.*, 12 S. W. 3d 139 (Tex. App. —Tyler 1999, pet. denied).

However, an expert may testify as to a mixed question of law and facts using legal terminology such as "negligence" provided the expert is given the proper legal definition. *Isern v. Watson*, 942 S. W. 2d 186 (Tex. App. —Beaumont 1997, no writ). In other words, experts must use proper legal definitions. *See Lawrence v. City of Wichita Falls*, 122 S. W. 3d 322 (Tex. App. —Fort Worth 2003, pet. denied).

In some cases, expert testimony will not only aid a jury, it will be necessary. For example, "[q] uestions regarding the reasonableness of a settlement in most personal injury cases are questions upon which the trier of fact must be guided solely by expert testimony". *Amerada Hess Corp. v. Wood Group Prod.*, 30 S. W. 3d 5, 11 (Tex. App. —Houston [14th Dist.] 2000, pet. denied). If uncontroverted and admissible, the expert opinion may defeat the plaintiff's claim as a matter of law. "However, it is the basis of the expert witness's testimony, and not his qualifications or bare opinions alone, that can settle an issue as a matter of law."

Unlike other admissibility gates, appellate courts review a trial court's decision on helpfulness using a de novo standard, not abuse of discretion. *FFE Transp. Servs., Inc. v. Fulgham*, 154 S. W. 3d 84 (Tex. 2004).

The Texas Court of Criminal Appeals has indicated that the fit test helps determine whether the evidence assists the jury. *Morales v. State*, 32 S. W. 3d 862 (Tex. Crim. App. 2000). In this DWI prosecution, the court of appeals remanded for further review the admissibility of the prosecution's expert testimony on the absorption rate of alcohol. The trial court had excluded as irrelevant the testimony on alcohol consumption because the defendant had not been administered a breath test. The court of appeals, however, held that the testimony was relevant because the expert was provided with a hypothetical regarding the rate of alcohol absorption and that the hypothetical contained facts similar to the defendant's case.

The Court of Criminal Appeals observed that the defendant conceded relevance under Rule 401, but contested whether the evidence was helpful:

The reviewing court should, under Rule 702, examine the expert's testimony to assess whether the expert made an adequate effort to tie the relevant facts of the case to the scientific principles about which he testified.

The court of appeals noted one fact that was considered and applied by [the expert] — the passage of time between appellant's last beer and his arrest ... But the court failed to discuss whether this fact alone, as applied to the principles regarding alcohol burn-off, was enough "to be of assistance to the trier of fact" under Rule 702, or whether other facts were and/or should have been considered. The court of appeals' analysis of this question under Rule 702 was inadequate.

Id. at 866 (internal citations omitted).

Interesting or recent cases on Helpfulness

- *Hogan v. Novartis Pharms. Corp.*, No. 06 CIV. 0260 BMC RER, 2011 WL 1533467 (E. D. N. Y. Apr. 24, 2011). In this pharmaceutical claim that the defendant failed to warn of the risk of developing osteonecrosis of the jaw from Zometa, the court observed that "all of plaintiff's experts, to some degree, are being proffered as 'superlawyers' to serve as scientifically informed advocates of conclusions that plaintiff wants the jury to reach and which belong only in summation, not expert testimony." *Id.* at 5. The court, therefore, "cautioned" counsel that the expert "must keep his characterizations of defendant's responses and opinion regarding its conduct to himself".

- *Coble v. State*, 330 S. W. 3d 253, 273 (Tex. Crim. App. 2010). The court stated that in addition to determining whether expert evidence is relevant and reliable, the trial court "must decide whether, on balance, that expert testimony might nonetheless be unhelpful or distracting for other reasons".

- *Rodgers v. State*, 205 S. W. 3d 525, 527 (Tex. Crim. App. 2006) A trial court need not exclude expert testimony simply because the subject matter is within the comprehension of the average jury. If the witness has some special knowledge or additional insight into the field that would be helpful, then the expert can assist the trier of fact to understand the evidence or to determine a fact in issue. An expert "may add precision and depth to the ability of the trier of fact to reach conclusions about subjects which lie well within common experience".

- *Cent. Appraisal Dist. of Taylor Cnty. v. W. AH 406, Ltd.*, 11-10-00115-CV,

2012 WL 1438454 (Tex. App. —Eastland Apr. 26, 2012, no pet. h.). The trial court did not err in sustaining objections to the reliability of an expert's testimony as to a real property appraisal value assessed by the Central Appraisal District of Taylor County. The expert's testimony regarding the land's valuation was based on an incorrect interpretation of a Texas statute.

· *Thompson v. State*, No. 01 – 10 – 00398 – CR, 2012 WL 668937 (Tex. App. — Houston [1st Dist.] March 1 2012, no pet.). The trial court did not err in admitting an expert's interpretation of cell phone records to show the location of the nearest antenna at the time of various phone calls. The phone accessing a particular antenna would be "in the general area of that tower" and would try to "use the most nearby tower", but "not every time will it use the closest possible tower". *Id.* at 5. From this data, the officer then prepared a map showing the location of each antenna at the time of the pertinent events. The court found that this testimony was helpful. Helpfulness is a "threshold determination" that must be satisfied before expert testimony is admissible. "The possibility that [the defendant's] mobile – phone communications could have in fact originated miles away from the antennas does not necessarily render the phone – related testimony unhelpful..... The evidence showed that [his] mobile phone was active in the general vicinity of the murder scene, a location close to neither his home nor his employment, and that after the murder the phone communicated with antennas while travelling along the way to the vicinity of [the defendant's] residence." *Id.* at *9.

· *Diet v. Hill Country Rests., Inc.*, No. 04 – 10 – 00682 – CV, 2011 WL 6206985 (Tex. App. —San Antonio Dec. 14, 2011). The trial court did not abuse its discretion in determining that expert's opinion on dangerousness of walkway would not assist the jury. Following *Honeycutt*, the court stated: "A jury would have been able to observe the photographs of the walkway where the fall took place. A jury would have been able to hear testimony about prior falls or near falls, if any, at the site where the fall took place. A jury would have been able to hear testimony about complaints, if any, about the site where the fall took place. From this evidence, a jury would have been able to form its own conclusion about whether the walkway posed an unreasonable risk of harm."

· *United States v. Whitfield*, 590 F. 3d 325 (5th Cir. 2009). In this case, two Mississippi state judges and a Mississippi trial attorney were found guilty of fraud arising from two bribery schemes involving two civil cases. The district court excluded expert testimony from two attorneys that the two cases were decided correctly. The district court explained that an attorney could not speculate on the mental impressions of the Mississippi Supreme Court, which were better expressed in its written opinion. The Fifth Circuit agreed, explaining that such testimony would not have been helpful to the jury.

· *Wayne v. State*, No. AP – 76, 019, 2010 Tex. Crim. App. LEXIS 1297 (Tex. Crim. App. Oct. 13, 2010). In this capital murder case, Dr. Coons testified about the future dangerousness of the defendant. Although Dr. Coons was a qualified forensic psychiatrist, the record did not reveal what principles of forensic psychiatry Dr. Coons relied upon. Instead, he stated that he relied upon history of violence, attitude toward violence, the crime itself, personality, general behavior, conscience, and where the person will be. The court concluded that these factors sound like "common – sense ones that the jury would consider on its own". Based on this and other problems with Dr. Coons's methodology, the court held that the trial court had abused its discretion in admitting Dr. Coons's expert testimony about future dangerousness.

· *Morris v. State*, No. PD – 0796 – 10, 2011 WL 6057840 (Tex. Crim. App. Dec. 7, 2011). The defendant who was convicted of indecency with a child challenged the trial court's admission of expert testimony on the grooming of children for sexual molestation as a phenomenon. The expert's opinion addressed a legitimate subject of expert testimony, and was useful to jury.

· *Leigh v. Kuenstler*, No. 14 – 08 – 00245 – CV, 2009 WL 3126538 (Tex. App. —Houston [14th Dist.] Oct. 1, 2009, no pet.). The court held that an expert affidavit on duty did not create a fact issue because the existence of a duty is not a question of fact but a question of law for the court.

B. Second Gate: Qualifications

Rule 702 allows expert testimony in scientific, technical or other specialized areas provided the "witness [is] qualified as an expert by knowledge, skill, experience, training, or education". The party presenting an expert witness bears the burden of establishing the witness's expert qualifications. *United Blood Servs. v. Longoria*, 938 S. W. 2d 29, 31 (Tex. 1997).

Trial court judges generally have broad discretion to determine whether a witness may offer expert testimony and the scope of the expert testimony. *Longoria*, 938 S. W. 2d at 30. A trial court's ruling as to whether an expert is qualified can only be reversed for abuse of discretion. *Longoria*, 938 S. W. 2d at 31. The trial court decides the preliminary question of admissibility pursuant to Rule 104 (a) of the Texas Rules of Evidence. *Longoria*, 938 S. W. 2d at 30; *Broders*, 924 S. W. 2d at 151.

The level of "knowledge, skill, experience, training or education" a person must have to be considered an expert on a particular topic is difficult to quantify by "definite guidelines". *Rogers v. Gonzales*, 654 S. W. 2d 509, 513 (Tex. App. —Corpus Christi 1983, writ ref' d n. r. e.). There is no "bright – line" test to determine whether a particular witness is qualified to testify as an expert:

... [S] pecial knowledge of the specific matter about which his expertise is sought, which qualifies a witness to give an expert opinion, may be derived entirely from a study of technical works, specialized education, practical experience, or varying combinations thereof; what is determinative is that his answers indicate to the trial court that he possesses knowledge that will assist the jury in drawing inferences about the fact issues more effectively or reliably than the jury could do unaided.

Agbogun v. State, 756 S. W. 2d 1, 4 (Tex. App. —Houston [1st Dist.] 1988, writ ref' d); *Helena Chem. Co. v. Wilkins*, 18 S. W. 3d 744, 752 – 53 (Tex. App. —San Antonio 2000), *aff' d*, 47 S. W. 3d 486 (Tex. 2001). An expert may be deemed unqualified if the expert equivocates or is ambivalent on qualifications *Gen. Motors Corp. v. Iracheta*, 161 S. W. 3d 462 (Tex. 2005).

In determining the qualifications of an expert, courts may examine how long it has been since the expert actively practiced in the area in question. *Larson v Downing*, 197 S. W. 3d 303 (Tex. 2003). An expert is not disqualified simply because he was not "the best qualified" or "the most appropriate" expert. *Physicians Dialysis Ventures, Inc. v. Griffith*, No. 06 – 2468, 2007 U. S. Dist. LEXIS 78879 (D. N. J. Oct. 24, 2007).

A witness's knowledge, skill, experience, training or education must be separately examined in each area that an opinion is offered. For example, in *Broders v. Heise*, the trial court allowed an emergency room physician to testify about the symptoms of a trauma patient and proper treatment that should have been performed. 924 S. W. 2d 148, 150 – 51 (Tex. 1995). The physician was not permitted, however, to give an opinion concerning what the patient's prognosis would have been had the proper treatment been given because the trial court concluded that he was not competent to testify on that subject.

A unanimous Texas Supreme Court affirmed, holding that although the expert had more knowledge than the general population, his expertise on causation did not meet the requisites of TRE 702 because the plaintiffs failed to establish that his opinions "would have risen above mere speculation to offer genuine assistance to the jury." The possession of a medical degree does not qualify a physician to offer expert testimony on every medical question.

... [G] iven the increasingly specialized and technical nature of medicine, there is no validity, if there ever was, to the notion that every licensed medical doctor should be automatically qualified to testify as an expert on every medical question. Such a rule would ignore the modern realities of medical specialization ... [and] eliminate the trial court's role of ensuring that those who purport to be experts truly have expertise concerning the actual subject about which they are offering an opinion. After all, the proponent of the testimony has the burden to show that the expert "possess [es] special knowledge as to the very matter on which he proposes to give an opinion".

Id. at 152 – 53. In so ruling, the court rejected the general common law rule. Consistent with the liberal rules that an expert is one with knowledge beyond that known by typical jurors, an expert under the common law did not generally need to be a sub – specialist to offer expert testimony in an area of subspecialty; a "general practitioner" in the field was viewed to have more knowledge and experience than a jury and therefore was qualified, and the lack of a subspecialty went to the weight of the opinion rather than its admissibility. Brown, *Eight Gates*, 36 Hous. L. Rev. at 764, 765. According to *Broders*, that an expert possesses more knowledge than the average juror "does not in and of itself mean that such expertise will assist the trier of fact regarding the issue before the court".

The reasoning in *Broders* applies to all experts. *Gammill v. Jack Williams Chevrolet, Inc.*, 972 S. W. 2d 713 (Tex. 1998); *see also* Brown, *Eight Gates*, 36 Hous. L. Rev. at 768. In *Gammill*, the Texas Supreme Court unanimously held that one of the plaintiff's mechanical engineers was qualified to opine that a rear restraint system in an automobile was defective, but the other mechanical engineer was not qualified. Neither expert was qualified to testify on causation, however. Citing *Broders*, the *Gammill* court cautioned that a trial court must review whether the experts have expertise in the particular topic on which they are testifying. "Just as not every physician is qualified to testify as an expert in every medical malpractice case, not every mechanical engineer is qualified to testify as an expert in every products liability case." *Id.* at 719.

Proper qualifications may sometimes require an expert to have experience in a subspecialty. For example, "chemistry is an exceedingly vast science divided into several branches and is far beyond the capacity of one person to master. Tire chemistry .... is a highly specialized field". *Cooper Tire & Rubber Co. v. Mendez*, 204 S. W. 3d 797 (Tex. 2006). General experience in a specialized field is insufficient to qualify a witness as an expert. *Gen. Motors Corp. v. Burry*, 203 S. W. 3d 514, 526 (Tex. App. —Fort Worth 2006, pet. denied).

On the other hand, when a party can show that a subject is substantially developed in more than one field, testimony can come from a qualified expert in any one of those fields. *Broders*, 924 S. W. 2d at 154; *see also Collins v. Pustejovsky*, 280 S. W. 3d 456 (Tex. App. —Fort Worth 2009, no pet.). In criminal cases, the Texas Court of criminal appeals has provided guidance on how to determine whether a witness is a qualified expert. *See Rodgers v. State*, 205 S. W. 3d 525, 527 (Tex. Crim. App. 2006) A trial court need not exclude expert testimony simply because the subject matter is within the comprehension of the average jury. If the witness has some special knowledge or additional insight into the field that would be helpful, then the expert can assist the trier of fact to understand the evidence or to determine a fact in issue. An expert "may add precision and depth to the ability of the trier of fact to reach conclusions about subjects which lie well within common experience". The court offered guidance for appellate courts resolving qualifications challenges:

Appellate courts may consider several criteria in assessing whether a trial court has clearly abused its discretion in ruling on an expert's qualifications. First, is the field of expertise complex? The degree of education, training, or experience that a witness should have before he can qualify as an expert is directly related to the complexity of the field about which he proposes to testify.[10] If the expert evidence is close to the jury's common understanding, the witness's qualifications are less important than when the evidence is well outside the jury's own experience. … Second, how conclusive is the expert's opinion? The more conclusive the expert's opinion, the more important is his degree of expertise. … And third, how central is the area of expertise to the resolution of the lawsuit? The more dispositive it is of the disputed issues, the more important the expert's qualifications are.

Id. at 528. The court also emphasized that the appellate court must review the trial court's ruling in light of what was before that court at the time the ruling was made *Id.* at 528 –29. In this case, the cross – examination revealed problems that had to be considered in ruling on the subsequent motion to strike. *Id.* at 531 –32.

Interesting or recent cases on Qualifications

Federal Courts

· *Larson v. Matter*, 2008 U. S. Dist. LEXIS 63432 (N. D. Texas 2008). In this medical malpractice case against a cardiovascular surgeon for failure to recognize ill effects of using heparin as an anti – coagulant, the trial court excluded a hematologist's testimony about the standard of care, permitted a general surgeon's testimony about the standard of care, and permitted the hematologist and general surgeon to testify about the cause of the plaintiff's injuries. The plaintiff was admitted to a hospital in 2004 with a diagnosis of acute myocardial infarction. The defendant doctor performed coronary artery bypass graft to treat this condition and the plaintiff subsequently developed Heparin Induced Thrombocytopenia ("HIT") and Heparin Induced Thrombosis Syndrome ("HITTS"), which led to multiple amputations, as a result of the plaintiff's exposure to Heparin. The plaintiff offered a hematologist as an expert to testify that the defendant doctor, a cardiovascular surgeon, should have been able to recognize and respond to HIT and HITTS as a result of all the attention HIT and HITTS had received in recent years (2006 - 2008). The hematologist could not testify about the standard of care for a cardiovascular surgeon in 2004 despite advances in the last few years that provide a strong knowledge base for cardiovascular surgeons with regard to anti – coagulants. The trial court noted that plaintiffs' hematologist was unfamiliar with the relevant governing protocols for cardio vascular surgeons in 2004 and that surgeon's knowledge about HIT and HITTS would have been more limited in that time frame. The trial court, however, determined the general surgeon could testify because of his background and his knowledge of the standard of care to which a cardiovascular surgeon would be held during the pertinent time frame.

· *Powell v. Carey Int'l, Inc.*, 483 F. Supp. 2d 1168 (S. D. Fla. 2007). The plaintiffs—limousine drivers—sought overtime pay under the Fair Labor Standards Act. Both plaintiffs and defendants filed summary judgment motions as to the calculation of the overtime hourly wage and a determination of which activities are compensable. In support of their motion, defendants presented expert testimony, and plaintiffs submitted expert rebuttal testimony—which defendants sought to exclude as it neither "fit" the case nor would it assist the trier of fact. In granting the defendants' motion to exclude the expert's testimony, the court found that the expert's qualification extended merely to being a CPA. He had never been hired as an expert, never prepared an expert report, never testified in any litigation, was not an expert on the FLSA or employment law, did not have legal expertise, and did not take employment law courses in conjunction with his accounting degree. Despite his being a CPA, his opinion did not apply accounting principles, other than basic mathematical functions. And furthermore, the court found that the trier of fact could make the factual determination of how many compensable hours for which defendants owed plaintiffs overtime compensation—with a calculator rather than an expert accountant.

· *Morris v. Equifax Info. Servs.*, *LLC*, No. H – 04 – 0423, 2007 WL 1091005, 2007 U. S. Dist. LEXIS 26319 (S. D. Tex. Apr. 10, 2007). The plaintiff had filed suit against Equifax and CSC Credit Services, Inc. in Texas state court, alleging violation of the Fair Credit Reporting Act and libel based on the appearance on his credit report of a delinquent Target charge account, which he argued was his ex – wife's liability. After removal, Equifax moved to strike plaintiff's expert who was designated to testify about "reasonable procedures" in accordance with the requirements of the FCRA. The court recognized that, while the expert was a well – seasoned CPA with extensive ongoing training in his field, was a licensed real estate agent, had been employed as an audit partner at Arthur Young (now Ernst & Young) for at least 14 years, and had served as a CFO of a real estate development corporation, he had no prior education, training, or employment in the credit reporting industry. He first began his study and analysis of the FCRA when he was hired in the case, had never testified at trial, had never conducted a reinvestigation of a consumer dispute under the FCRA, and had never done any research or writing on the credit reporting industry outside of the pending litigation. The court properly determined that, while the expert may be helpful and qualified to testify in certain circumstances, this was not it. His opinions were merely legal conclusions and would not have assisted the jury in understanding what Equifax did in connection with its reinvestigation.

· *Physicians Dialysis Ventures, Inc. v. Griffith*, Civil Action No. 06 – 2468, 2007 U. S. Dist. LEXIS 78879 (D. N. J. Oct. 24, 2007). The plaintiffs filed a deficiency action to recover amounts due on a guaranty of a loan following foreclosure on the assets of the borrower. When the defendants offered an expert to opine on the financial effects of the mismanagement of a dialysis center and critique the plaintiffs' report on the same topic, the plaintiffs moved to exclude the defendants' expert on qualification grounds—arguing that the expert had nothing more than "entry – level" experience in business valuation. *Id.* at * 10. The court rejected this argument, finding the expert had extensive experience in business valuations and appraisals. *Id.* The court specifically noted it would be an abuse of discretion to disqualify an expert simply because the expert was not "the best qualified" or "the most appropriate". *Id.*

Texas Courts

· *Roberts v. Williamson*, 111 S. W. 3d 113, 121 (Tex. 2003). A board – certified pediatrician was qualified to testify not only about the appropriate standard of care for a pediatrician but also about the nature and effect of the newborn's neurological injuries. The pediatrician had studied the effects of pediatric neurological injuries and had "extensive experience advising parents about the effects of those injuries". *Id.* at 122.

· *Thompson v. State*, No. 01 – 10 – 00398 – CR, 2012 WL 668937 (Tex. App. — Houston [1st Dist.] 2012, no pet.). An expert was qualified to interpret cell phone records to show the location of the nearest antenna at the time of various phone calls. The court found that the expert was qualified despite admitting that he was not trained in interpreting phone records. Although the expert admitted that he was not an engineer and could not comment on the science of cellular technology, he interpreted mobile phone records "on a daily basis" for the police department and had "basic knowledge of how the cellular handset is going to communicate with the cellular networks and the cellular antennas. . . ." *Id.* Because the expert had experience in interpreting phone records and the technique of interpreting phone records was relatively simple, the Court concluded that the trial court did not abuse its discretion by qualifying the expert.

· *Lopez – Juarez v. Kelly*, 348 S. W. 3d 10 (Tex. App. —Texarkana 2011, no pet.). In this wrongful death case arising out of a bus accident, a police officer was not qualified to testify as an expert witness regarding accident reconstruction but the trial court's error in allowing the officer to testify as an expert was harmless.

· *U. S. Renal Care, Inc. v. Jaafar*, 345 S. W. 3d 600 (Tex. App. —San Antonio 2011, no pet.). The trial court did not abuse its discretion in finding that a Certified Financial Analyst with a bachelor's degree in finance, a master's degree in business from the University of Texas, accreditation as a "credit senior appraiser", and extensive experience in valuing businesses over the preceding 20 years including several medical related businesses that required a valuation of their accounts receivable was qualified to testify to the value of retained accounts receivable the buyer allegedly owed to the sellers even though he did not have any training or experience concerning insurance practices or healthcare billing, his training was in finance not accounting, and his Ph. D. was from an online university. The court noted that "no bright – line test exists to guide us as to whether a particular witness is qualified to testify as an expert", and therefore courts must focus instead on "whether the expert's expertise goes to the very matter on which he or she is to give an opinion. " *Id.* at 607 (quoting *Broders v. Heise*, 924 S. W. 2d 148, 153 (Tex. 1996)). In this case, his experience did address the very matter in question.

· *Pink v. Goodyear Tire & Rubber Co.* , 324 S. W. 3d 290 (Tex. App. —Beaumont 2010, pet. denied). In this toxic tort lawsuit arising out of a plant workers' claim that benzene exposure caused his renal cell carcinoma, the trial court improperly granted summary judgment because an oncologist's causation opinion was not conclusory and the trial court did not rule on the reliability of the opinion. The court observed that the oncologist might be unqualified to render a causation opinion.

Although the etiology of a disease is often significant to a clinician's care of a patient, as well as to public health issues, and while a clinician may have training and experience in the study of cancer and its etiology, the clinician may nevertheless lack the expertise necessary to present a causation opinion related to a toxic chemical exposure. *Id.* at 296. But the defendant had not made a qualifications objection.

· *In re D. J. R.* , 319 S. W. 3d 759 (Tex. App. —El Paso 2010, pet. denied). In this suit to terminate parental rights as to his three minor children, following the death of one child, the trial court did not abuse its discretion in finding that a board certified forensic pathologist was qualified to testify as an expert concerning the cause of the child's death.

· *In re Commitment of Bohannan*, No. 09 – 09 – 00165 – CV, 2010 WL 2854254 (Tex. App. —Beaumont July 22, 2010, pet. granted). In this case arising from the commitment of an individual because he was a sexually violent predator under Texas law, the court of appeals held that the trial court improperly excluded an expert with a master's degree in counseling and a doctorate in family sciences and family therapy and licenses as a professional counselor and as a sex offender treatment provider. The expert offered sufficient foundation that her opinion would have assisted the jury in determining whether defendant would likely commit a future sexually violent offense. The court had earlier held that the expert also had the necessary qualifications to provide an expert opinion about whether a person had a behavioral abnormality, a determination that is necessary to qualify the person as being a sexually violent predator as those terms are defined by the Legislature.

· *In re McAllen Med. Ctr. , Inc.* , 275 S. W. 3d 458 (Tex. 2008). In a class action involving claims of negligent credentialing against a hospital, the defendant hospital sought to dismiss the claims because the plaintiffs submitted a report by an expert whom the hospital contended was unqualified. The trial court ruled that the plaintiffs' expert on hospital credentialing was qualified to render an opinion. The hospital sought mandamus review of this decision. The Texas Supreme Court ruled that the plaintiffs' expert did not qualify to render opinions on hospital credentialing because she provided an incomplete educational background and failed to show whether she had actively practiced medicine from 1995 - 2008. Additionally, the Court noted that a negligent credentialing claim involves a specialized standard of care and that the plaintiffs' expert report made no reference to those guidelines, nor did the report demonstrate she had any special knowledge, training, or experience about the credentialing process.

· *Menefee v. Ohman*, 323 S. W. 3d 509 (Tex. App. —Fort Worth 2010, no pet.). In this health care liability case, a psychiatrist opined that the defendant doctor (a pediatrician) was negligent for failing to immediately prescribe anticonvulsants to the plaintiff, a sixteen - year - old girl. The trial court excluded this testimony. The court of appeals reversed, holding that the psychiatrist was qualified to render an opinion on the appropriate standard of care for the defendant because although pediatrics was not his area of practice, he was familiar with the appropriate standard of care. The court concluded that the psychiatrist's training and experience in both psychiatric and acute care settings showed that he was qualified to render an expert opinion on the standard of care relevant to the defendant's internal medicine evaluation of the plaintiff.

· *Hayes v. Carroll*, 314 S. W. 3d 494 (Tex. App. —Austin 2010, no pet.). In this health care liability case, Janet Carroll alleged that the physicians and nurses who cared for her while she was unconscious were negligent for tightly bandaging her right leg below the knee and leaving the bandage in place for 28 hours. The bandaging caused necrosis of the skin, muscle, and tendons in her leg which required the amputation of her leg. The trial court denied defendants' motion to dismiss based on various alleged deficiencies in Carroll's expert reports. The court of appeals affirmed. The appellate court concluded that Carroll's expert witnesses, a vascular surgeon and a registered nurse, were qualified to opine on the standard of care that applies to basic medical care in an emergency room because their opinions were not directed at a matter that was unique to a particular medical specialization.

· *Valence Operating Co. v. Anadarko Petroleum Corp.* , 303 S. W. 3d 435 (Tex. App. —Texarkana 2010, no pet.). A certified professional landman who was also an instructor at the American Association of Professional Landmen was qualified to testify regarding "the common understanding of the phrase 'commence work on a proposed operation' in a joint operating agreement even though he was not a driller. The court stated that he was qualified to testify about "the practices in the industry in which he was familiar". The court also held that *Daubert* and its progeny were inapplicable because the case did not involve science or scientific causation.

· *Estorque v. Schafer*, 302 S. W. 3d 19 (Tex. App. —Fort Worth 2009, no pet.). In this medical malpractice case, the court of appeals held that a trial court did not err in concluding that a physician was qualified to testify "on the causal relationship between the physician's failure to refer and the resulting kidney disorders and gynecological cysts". While the injuries may have been specific, the medical care involved the diagnosis and treatment of a patient who exhibit abdominal pain, which did not require expertise in nephrology, urology or gynecology. The physician had treated patients with symptoms similar to the patient's symptoms, was familiar with the complications from such conditions, and stated that a national standard applied to all physicians for treatment of these conditions.

· *Fisher – Riza v. State*, No. 01 – 08 – 00264 – CR, 2009 Tex. App. LEXIS 9769 (Tex. App. —Houston [1st Dist.] Dec. 3, 2009, writ habeas corpus granted May 26, 2010). A police officer who was qualified as an accident reconstruction expert could not testify that Fisher – Riza was acting "psychotic" based on interviews with witnesses because he was not an expert in mental illnesses.

· *Champion v. Great Dane L. P.*, 286 S. W. 3d 533 (Tex. App. —Houston [14th Dist.], 2009, no pet.). In this products liability case, the court of appeals found that the trial court did not err in excluding expert testimony as to a truck trailer's alleged design defect. The court first noted that an expert must be qualified for the specific issue in controversy. "General experience in a specialized field is insufficient to qualify a witness as an expert." *Id.* at 544 [quoting *Gen. Motors Corp. v. Burry*, 203 S. W. 3d 514, 526 (Tex. App. —Fort Worth 2006, pet. denied)]. The court found that the expert was not qualified to testify about any alleged design defects with the trailer's uncovered rear gutter. Although the expert had degrees in industrial engineering and mechanical engineering and was an expert in product safety engineering and manufacturer's engineering, he did not have any specialized knowledge in the design or manufacturing of refrigerated trailers or the rear uncovered gutter of refrigerated trailers.

· *Collini v. Pustejovsky*, 280 S. W. 3d 456 (Tex. App. —Fort Worth 2009, no pet.). In this medical malpractice case, the court reaffirmed that the proper inquiry in assessing a physician's qualifications is not the physician's area of practice but the physician's familiarity with the specific issues involving the claim. The court reasoned that it was insufficient to show that an expert has general background experience in pharmaceutical matters in this case, which involved whether a prolonged use of a particular prescriptive medication caused a particular ailment. The court also reiterated that an expert forming a causation opinion can rely on the opinions of other experts, but those other experts must themselves have been qualified for the specific condition involved in the case.

· *Living v. Montgomery*, 279 S. W. 3d 868 (Tex. App. —Dallas, 2009, no pet.). The parents of an infant sued the treating doctors and nurses for neurological injuries allegedly suffered during the mother's labor and delivery. One question before the court was whether the plaintiff's expert obstetrician/gynecologist was qualified to opine about the cause of the newborn's neurological injuries. The court held that the opinions were admissible because the obstetrician/gynecologist had sufficient knowledge and expertise on hypoxia, the issue directly involved in the case, even though the expert was not a pediatric neurologist.

- *Abilene Independent School District v. Marks*, 261 S. W. 3d 262 (Tex. App. —Eastland 2008, no pet.). This workers' compensation case arose out of a teacher's injury to his left knee. The school district admitted that his torn medial meniscus injury in the left knee was compensable but denied that the chondromalacia in his left patella and left medial femoral condyle was compensable because the chondromalacia was a pre – existing condition and ordinary disease of life. The court of appeals upheld the trial court's ruling that the claimant's treating orthopedic surgeon was qualified to give expert testimony concerning the cause of the claimant's chondromalacia. Even though the physician had changed his opinion about the diagnosis during his care of the teacher, the court concluded that the physician was qualified to offer a causation opinion based on the facts of the case, his findings, his treatment of the teacher, and medical literature.

- *Von Hohn v. Von Hohn*, 260 S. W. 3d 631 (Tex. App. —Tyler, 2008, no pet.). In this divorce case between a lawyer and his wife, the value of the husband's interest in his law firm was the primary issue at trial. The wife had an expert to testify about the value of the husband's interest in the law firm. Before trial, the husband filed a motion to exclude this testimony, arguing that the expert was unqualified and that his methodology was unreliable.

The attack on the expert's qualifications was based primarily on the expert's testimonial admission that he could not recall a specific instance when he had taken specific cases, valued them, and then adjusted the assets of a law firm's balance sheet. Also, he had never used information from patent cases in valuations of law firms. The appellate court found that the trial court did not abuse its discretion in allowing the expert testify. At the pre – trial *Daubert* hearing, the valuations expert testified that he had been performing business valuations for approximately 15 years and had been an expert witness on professional business valuation about 75 to 100 times. He had previously testified in court about valuations of a partnership interest using the income approach. The expert had valued a partnership interest using the income approach, and he had valued a contingency fee attorney's practice by relying on the same type of projections he used in this case. Although he had never used information from a patent case in valuing a law firm, the specific issue in this case was valuation of a partner's interest in a law firm for which the expert had specialized knowledge, skill, experience, training and education.

- *Gainsco Cnty. Mut. Ins. v. Martinez*, 27 S. W. 3d 97 (Tex. App. —San Antonio 2000, pet. dism' d by agr.). In a wrongful death suit arising out of a motor vehicle accident, the trial court erred in admitting a police officer's opinion on vehicle speed and force of impact, when the officer did not have any formal training, had only served on the police force four months, and had not investigated any prior auto fatalities.

· *Praytor v. Ford Motor Co.* , 97 S. W. 3d 237, 242 – 43 (Tex. App. —Houston [14th Dist.] 2002, no pet.). The plaintiff failed to demonstrate that a pulmonologist had specific expertise on the issue of cause in fact for an air bag deployment injury. While he knew more than the general public, that did not show he was an expert on whether an air bag can cause asthma. There was no evidence that the doctor was an expert on toxicity of chemicals released when the bag deployed or was an expert on asthma or the causes of asthma. Similarly, the plaintiff failed to show that an engineer was qualified on the causes of respiratory illnesses. In a summary judgment proceeding, it is the proponent's burden to show the qualifications of the expert's testimony.

· *Yard v. Daimler Chrysler Corp.* , 44 S. W. 3d 238 (Tex. App. —Fort Worth 2001, no pet.). The appellate court affirmed a trial court's decision to strike the plaintiff's expert testimony on causation, and subsequent summary judgment, in a products liability suit brought against the manufacturer and distributor for the injuries and death allegedly caused by a defective airbag. The trial court struck the testimony of a medical physician who would have testified about causation, specifically whether the air bag would have saved the plaintiff's life if it had deployed.

The court of appeals held that the plaintiff failed to satisfy his burden of proving his qualifications. *Id.* at 241. "The offering party must demonstrate that the witness possesses special knowledge as to the very matter on which he proposes to give an opinion." *Id.* The plaintiffs failed to produce evidence that showed that the medical doctor had any "special knowledge about the effects of a deployed or failed airbag on an individual involved in an automobile accident". *Id.* The physician "lacked special training in engineering or in occupant kinematics (the movement of bodies in a vehicle)" and had never consulted on an air bag case. *Id.*

The court of appeals expressed skepticism over a physician gaining knowledge from research performed after his retention in a case. According to the doctor, the deceased's basilar skull fracture was inconsistent with an air bag deploying. He specifically noted that there were no published studies of such an injury with an unrestrained driver whose air bag had properly deployed. The physician conceded, however, that he had only encountered three such fractures during his medical career, and only one had been caused by a car wreck. He could not remember anything about the forces in any of the three prior occasions and did not know the types of forces required to case a basilar skull fracture. Instead, he relied on an article on the amount of forces necessary to cause a fracture. The appellate court held that the physician based his opinions more on his review of the literature than his experience. While his "medical training and experience may have contributed to his ability to understand the published literature, there is no evidence that he had any more specialized knowledge about the effects of deployed or failed air bags in automobile accident than other well – educated individuals with access to the same literature". *Id.* at 242. Therefore, the trial court did not abuse its discretion by excluding his expert testimony.

The plaintiffs' claim that their accident reconstructionist's testimony should have been admitted was waived because they failed to explain his qualifications as an accident reconstruction expert and failed to identify any testimony that he would have offered regarding causation. *Id.* at 243.

• *Pena v. State*, 155 S. W. 3d 238 (Tex. App. —El Paso 2004, no pet.). In this prosecution for use of a deadly weapon and intoxicated manslaughter, the trial court did not err by determining that a police officer was qualified to testify concerning the speed of the defendant's vehicle at the time of the accident in question. The police officer was qualified since he had a variety of training courses in speed reconstruction and had on a number of occasions conducted speed reconstruction. He had been certified twice as an expert in reconstruction by other district courts.

C. Third Gate: Relevance

Like any other evidence, expert testimony must be relevant to be admissible.

Another aspect of relevancy is that the evidence must "fit" the issues in the case. *Daubert*, 509 U. S. at 591; *see also United States v. Downing*, 753 F. 2d 1224, 1242 (3d Cir. 1985) ("An additional consideration under Rule 702—and another aspect of relevancy—is whether expert testimony proffered in the case is sufficiently tied to the facts of the case that it will aid the jury in resolving a factual dispute"). It must be "sufficiently tied to the facts of the case that it will aid the jury in resolving a factual dispute". *Id.* The evidence must have a valid "connection to the pertinent inquiry". *Id.* at 591 - 92. It must be "properly . . . applied to the facts in issue". *Id.* at 591. The Court in *Daubert* observed that "scientific validity for one purpose is not necessarily scientific validity for other, unrelated purposes". *Id.* Thus, the fit requirement requires proof that the expert's entire reasoning process from the beginning to end is valid.

Daubert discusses the fit requirement both under the helpfulness gate and the relevancy gate: "Expert testimony which does not relate to any issue in the case is not relevant and, ergo, non-helpful." 509 U. S. at 591 (citing 3 Weinstein & Berger § 702 [02], p. 702 - 18).

As explained by Judge Becker, the original author of the fit test, the "standard for fit is higher than for relevance". *In re Paoli R. R. Yard PCB Litig.*, 35 F. 3d 717, 745 (3d Cir. 1994). Evidence must speak "clearly and directly to an issue in dispute in the case" to satisfy this element. *In re Breast Implant*, 11 F. Supp. 2d 1217, 1222 (D. Colo. 1998). The expert must connect her reasoning to the facts of the case. If the reasoning is not valid, the opinion is unreliable and inadmissible. Thus, the fit prong is the result of the relevance rules, the assist-the-trier-of-fact language of Rule 702, and the reliability requirement encompassed in Rule 702.

The Texas Court of Criminal Appeals has adopted the fit test as part of its analysis of both helpfulness and relevancy.

Expert testimony that does not relate to a fact in issue is not helpful. This consideration is what the Supreme Court referred to as the "fit" requirement. That is, the proffered testimony must be "'sufficiently tied to the facts of the case that it will aid the jury in resolving a factual dispute.' "

....

Relevance is by nature a looser notion than reliability. Whether evidence "will assist the trier of fact" and is sufficiently tied to the facts of the case is a simpler, more straight – forward matter to establish than whether the evidence is sufficiently grounded in science to be reliable. This is not to say that the relevancy inquiry will always be satisfied. The expert must make an effort to tie pertinent facts of the case to the scientific principles, which are the subject of his testimony. Establishing this connection is not so much a matter of proof, however, as a matter of application.

Jordan v. State, 928 S. W. 2d 550, 554 (Tex. Crim. App. 1996) (internal citations omitted).

Daubert and *Jordan* also indicate that the fit, tie, or connection must be of some significant quantity. *Daubert*, 509 U. S. at 591 (the opinion must be "*sufficiently* tied to the facts of the case that it will aid the jury in resolving a factual dispute") (emphasis added); *Jordan*, 928 S. W. 2d at 556 (the expert's testimony must take "into account *enough* of the pertinent facts to be of assistance to the trier of fact on a fact in issue") (emphasis added).

The Texas Supreme Court has also held that expert evidence must be relevant. *Robinson*, following *Daubert*, held that the rules of evidence restrict scientific expert testimony to relevant evidence. *Robinson* adopted the relevancy test described by Judge Becker in *United States v. Downing*, i. e., that the evidence must be tied to the facts of the case. But the Court did not explicitly adopt the fit language of that case or *Daubert*. Instead, *Robinson* stated that this requirement "incorporates traditional relevancy analysis". 923 S. W. 2d at 556. The court reiterated that expert testimony must be "tied to the facts of the case" so that it aids the jury. *Exxon Pipeline Co. v. Zwahr*, 35 S. W. 2d 705 (Tex. App. —Houston [1st Dist.] 2000), *rev' d*, 88 S. W. 3d 623, 629 (Tex. 2002). If it does not, it is inadmissible under both Rule 701 and Rule 402. *Wolfson v. BIC Corp.*, 93 S. W. 3d 527 (Tex. App. —Houston [1st Dist.] 2002, pet. denied). The Court also recently stated that relevancy requires an expert's opinion to "be based on the facts". *State v. Cent. Expressway Sign Assocs.*, 302 S. W. 3d 866, 870 (Tex. 2009); *see also Wells Fargo Bank Nw.*, *N. A. v. RPK Capital XVI, L. L. C.*, 360 S. W. 3d 691, 711 (Tex. App. —Dallas 2012, no pet.) (same).

While the validity of the expert's reasoning process is a gate for expert testimony, it is less confusing to view the fit analysis as a separate gate because of the broad rules of relevance. The simple relevance standard is a "liberal one". *Daubert*, 509 U. S. at 587.

As recognized in both *Daubert* and *Jordan*, the fit inquiry involves both relevancy and helpfulness. Treating fit as an elevated relevance test is confusing. Instead, the "fit" prong should be treated as a separate test (what this author calls connective reliability). This removes any conflict between the courts in labeling this gate and its rationale. Since *Robinson* did not expressly adopt the fit prong but instead looked solely to the evidence's relevance under this prong and the *Daubert* fit prong requires more than mere relevance, such an analysis is clearer by separately addressing the connective reliability test.

Interesting or recent cases on Relevance

· *Smith v. Bubak*, 643 F. 3d 1137, 1140 (8th Cir. 2011). "To satisfy the relevance requirement, the proponent must show that the expert's reasoning or methodology was applied properly to the facts at issue." The court held that the expert's opinion was properly excluded because it was irrelevant under South Dakota's law on proximate cause, which does not recognize the "loss of chance" doctrine.

· *Tillman v. State*, 354 S. W. 3d 425 (Tex. Crim. App. 2011). In this capital murder case, the trial court excluded testimony from a psychologist on the reliability of using a photo-spread to identify a suspect. The Court of Criminal Appeals held that it was relevant and reliable and therefore admissible. "Relevance is 'a looser notion than reliability' and is 'a simpler, more straight – forward matter to establish'. The relevance inquiry is whether evidence '"will assist the trier of fact" and is sufficiently tied to the facts of the case.'" *Id.* at 438 (citations omitted).

D. Fourth Gate: Methodological Reliability

Unlike many of the other gates, which focus on an expert's conclusion, this gate peels back the curtain to view the methodology used by an expert to reach the conclusion. In three key cases—one decided by the U. S. Supreme Court and two decided by the Texas Supreme Court—this gate has become firmly established in Texas law.

1. *Daubert*

In *Daubert*, the Supreme Court identified four factors as "general observations" for assessing scientific reliability:

(1) Whether the theory "can be (and has been) tested". The Court did not rank the four factors but did indicate that this factor is a "key question".

(2) Whether the theory has been subjected to peer review and publication. "Submission to the scrutiny of the scientific community is a component of 'good science', in part because it increases the likelihood that substantive flaws in methodology will be detected."

(3) What the known or potential rate of error is for any tests or techniques and whether there are standards or controls for the technique's operations. The more errors in the individual applications of the technique or test (e. g. false matches in DNA testing), the less likely the evidence will be considered scientifically reliable.

(4) Whether the theory is generally accepted. *Daubert* maintained the *Frye* standard, but only as one of several factors to be considered. "A 'reliability assessment does not require, although it does permit, explicit identification of a relevant scientific community and an express determination of a particular degree of acceptance within that community' .... Widespread acceptance can be an important factor in ruling particular evidence admissible, and 'a known technique which has been able to attract only minimal support within the community', may properly be viewed with skepticism."

509 U. S. at 593 –94 (citations omitted).

Despite its identification of these factors, the Court stressed that the inquiry envisioned by Rule 702 is a flexible one. *Id.* at 594. "The focus, of course, must be solely on principles and methodology, not on the conclusions that they generate." *Id.* at 594 - 95.

On remand, the Ninth Circuit added another factor for assessing reliability—whether the technique was derived through independent research or was developed for litigation purposes. *See Daubert v Merrell Dow Pharms.*, *Inc.*, 43 F. 3d 1311, 1316 - 17 (9th Cir. 1995) (*Daubert II*). The court noted the expert's bald assurances that the opinions are based on sound scientific techniques was insufficient; the expert had to offer some objective, independent validation of that methodology. *Id.* at 1316.

2. *Robinson and Havner*

The Texas Supreme Court followed the lead of *Daubert* and adopted a reliability test for scientific expert testimony in *E. I. duPont de Nemours v. Robinson*, 923 S. W. 2d 549 (Tex. 1995). *Robinson* was a products liability suit against a fungicide manufacturer. The plaintiffs claimed that the fungicide was contaminated and damaged their pecan orchard. The trial court, after a pre-trial hearing, struck the plaintiffs' causation expert, a horticulturist.

The Texas Supreme Court affirmed. The Court concluded that not only do the rules of evidence themselves restrict scientific expert testimony to *reliable* scientific evidence, but also found two public policy rationales justified the need for restrictions. *See* Brown, *Eight Gates*, 36 Hous. L. Rev. at 795, 796. The Court rejected the argument that requiring a trial judge to act as a gatekeeper would interfere with the jury's right to determine the credibility and weight of the evidence, and observed that an expert may be credible but still give testimony that is not reliable. *Robinson*, 923 S. W. 2d at 558.

Robinson adopted six factors for determining whether the technique or principle is reliable but stressed that the factors are both flexible and non-exhaustive. *Id.* at 557. The factors established by *Robinson* for the reliability inquiry include all four of those identified in *Daubert*, the additional factor identified in *Daubert II*, and the extent to which the technique relies upon the subjective interpretation of the expert. *Id.*

Trial courts may also consider other helpful factors unique to each case. The focus of the inquiry is "solely on the underlying principles and methodology, not on the conclusions they generate". *Id.* at 557 (quoting *Daubert*, 509 U. S. at 595). Trial judges act as gatekeepers who have a "heightened responsibility to ensure that expert testimony shows some indicia of reliability". *Id.* at 553.

One factor that courts have repeatedly examined is whether the expert's theory has been tested. Although testing is not always requested to make an expert opinion reliable, "lack of testing to the extent it was possible, either by the experts or others, is one factor that points toward a determination that an expert opinion is unreliable. If testing of critical aspects of an expert's testimony has not taken place . . . , then an explanation of why it has not is an important consideration in evaluating the expert opinions and determining whether they were substantively more than merely the expert's conclusory, subjective opinion". *Whirlpool*, 298 S. W. 3d at 642 – 43.

Havner reiterated that the *Robinson/Daubert* factors are not the exclusive factors for determining reliability but did not add any new factors or explicitly give one factor more weight than another. *Havner*, 953 S. W. 2d. at 712, 714.

In its application of the *Robinson* factors to the plaintiffs' epidemiological evidence on Bendectin, however, the *Havner* court stressed the importance of peer review and publication. *Id.* at 726 – 27 ("courts must be 'especially skeptical' of scientific evidence that has not been published or subjected to peer review") (quoting *Brock v. Merrell Dow Pharms.*, *Inc.*, 874 F. 2d 307, 313 (5th Cir.), *as modified on reh' g*, 884 F. 2d 166 (5th Cir. 1989)). The expert's opinions had never "been offered outside the confines of a courthouse". *Id.* at 726.

3. *Daubert and Robinson apply to all experts*

The trial court's role as a gatekeeper who examines the reliability of an expert's testimony extends to all experts. A court should normally consider the *Robinson* factors as well as the expert's experience and qualifications in determining the reliability of expert testimony. *Transcont'l Inc. Co. v. Crump*, 330 S. W. 3d 211 (Tex. 2010). But reliability, for both scientific and non – scientific experts, will not *always* require an examination of the *Daubert/Robinson* factors. *See Kumho Co. Ltd. v. Carmichael*, 526 U. S. 137, 119 S. Ct. 1167, 1174 – 75 (1999); *Gammill v. Jack Williams Chevrolet, Inc.*, 972 S. W. 2d 713, 726 (Tex. 1998); *Mack Trucks, Inc. v. Tamez*, 206 S. W. 3d 572, 579 (Tex. 2006); *Nenno v. State*, 970 S. W. 2d 549 (Tex. Crim. App. 1998). The *Robinson* factors do not apply to all expert testimony and a flexible inquiry is necessary. *See Macks Trucks*, 204 S. W. 3d at 579; *Cooper Tire*, 204 S. W. 3d at 801.

The *Robinson* factors "are particularly difficult to apply in vehicular accident cases involving accident reconstruction". *TXI Transp. Co. v Hughes*, 306 S. W. 3d 230, 235 (Tex. 2010). When they do not apply, courts must use other tests for determining reliability. *Id.*

[I] n very few cases will the evidence be such that the trial court's reliability determination can properly be based only on the experience of a qualified expert to the exclusion of factors such as those set out in *Robinson*, or, on the other hand, properly be based only on factors such as those set out in *Robinson* to the exclusion of considerations based on a qualified expert's experience.

Whirlpool Corp. v. Camacho, 298 S. W. 3d 631, 638 (Tex. 2009).

4. *The modified Daubert factors*

Courts and commentators have used numerous other factors for analyzing the reliability of an expert's opinion including the relationship of the expert's technique to established methods, the expert's qualifications, and other relevant factors. *See* Brown, *Eight Gates*, 36 Hous. L. Rev. at 790 – 93, 798 – 801. The Texas Supreme Court has also referred to "*Robinson* – like" and "*Robinson* – type" factors, suggesting other similar factors exist. *Whirlpool*, 298 S. W. 3d at 639 – 40.

Trial courts are granted a great deal of deference in selecting and applying the factors to determine the reliability of expert testimony. *Gen. Elec. Co. v. Joiner*, 522 U. S. 136, 143 (1997). A more stringent review of the trial court's ruling on expert testimony is not necessary when the ruling determines the outcome of the case. *Id.* Indeed, a trial court's exclusion may not be second – guessed by an appellate court unless it rises to an abuse of discretion. *Id.*

This deference was raised to an even higher level in *Kumho Tire*, in which the Court held that even the trial court's selection of the criteria used to evaluate evidentiary reliability must be afforded discretion. 119 S. Ct. at 1175 – 76; *see also Guadalupe – Blanco River Auth. v. Kraft*, 39 S. W. 3d 264 (Tex. App. —Austin 2001) *rev' d on other grounds*, 77 S. W. 3d 805 (Tex. 2002) (Patterson, J. , dissenting) (the trial court's discretion extends to determining which of the *Robinson* factors reasonably measure whether an expert's opinion is reliable, and whether other factors might apply); *United States v. Charley*, 189 F. 3d 1251, 1266 (10th Cir. 1999) ("The trial judge is granted great latitude in deciding which factors to use in evaluating the reliability of expert testimony . . . . "). *City of Tuscaloosa v. Harcros Chem. Inc.* , 158 F. 3d 548 (11th Cir. 1998) (finding an abuse of discretion when court fails to make adequate inquiry into the *Daubert* factors).

A court does not need to address a *Daubert* challenge if the evidence is already in the record through independent evidence or through other reliable evidence. *Center for Economic Justice v. American Ins.* , 39 S. W. 3d 337, 349 (Tex. App. —Austin 2001, no pet.) (when the testimony of four other witnesses established the value of the information contained in quarterly market reports, the appellate court did not need to address whether the expert's testimony met the *Robinson* requirements); *Tarrant Reg' l Water Dist. v. Gragg*, 43 S. W. 3d 609 (Tex. App. —Waco 2001), aff' d 151 S. W. 3d 546 (Tex. , 2004) (trial court could reject *Daubert* challenge to hydrologist's use of computer model because that computer model "was not the sole or even primary basis for the hydrologists' opinions about causation").

Nevertheless, trial judges should normally address the *Daubert* factors or at least explain why they do not apply. *In re J. B.* , 93 S. W. 3d 609 (Tex. App. —Waco 2002, no pet.); *Black v. Food Lion Inc.* , 171 F. 3d 308 (5th Cir. 1999). In *Food Lion*, the Fifth Circuit noted that although *Kumho Tire* gives trial judge broad discretion to select the criteria for determining reliability, "the failure to apply one or another of [the *Daubert* factors] may be unreasonable, and hence an abuse of discretion". *Kumho Tire*, 119 S. Ct. at 1179 (Scalia, J. , concurring). *Kumho Tire*, therefore, does not "grant open season on the admission of expert testimony by permitting courts discretionarily to disavow the *Daubert* factors". *Food Lion*, 171 F. 3d at 311.

Kumho Tire does not require district courts to reinvent the wheel every time expert testimony is offered in court. *Id.* Just as the Supreme Court relied on the *Daubert* factors in *Kumho Tire*, those factors may be used as a starting point for analysis in the usual case. *Id.* In the vast majority of cases, the district court should first decide whether the factors mentioned in *Daubert* are appropriate, then (once it has considered the *Daubert* factors) the court can consider whether other factors, not mentioned in *Daubert*, are relevant to the case at hand. *Id.* at 312.

The Waco Court of Appeals has noted that it is best for a court to attempt to apply the factors first and use its discretion to identify and utilize other factors as it sees necessary to assess the reliability of the expert testimony being offered. *In re J. B.*, 93 S. W. 3d 609, 621 (Tex. App. —Waco 2002, pet. denied). This logic is supported by the Texas Supreme Court in the *Cooper Tire* case when it noted that though the factors, "do not provide a perfect template for evaluating the admissibility of [an expert's] testimony, we turn to them initially for guidance". *Cooper Tire & Rubber Co. v. Mendez*, 204 S. W. 3d 797 (Tex. 2006).

In criminal cases, the court of criminal appeals has distinguished between hard and soft sciences. *Nenno v. State*, 970 S. W. 2d 549, 560 (Tex. Crim. App. 1998). The distinction, while not "rigid," is important because the court adapted a more liberal three – prong reliability test for soft science. *Id.* [using (1) whether the field of expertise is a legitimate one, (2) whether the subject matter of the expert's testimony is within the scope of that field, and (3) whether the expert's testimony properly relies upon and/or utilizes the principles involved in the field.]; *see also State v. Medrano*, 127 S. W. 3d 781 (Tex. Crim. App. 2004) (holding that court would not apply *Kelly* to hypnotically enhanced testimony). *But see Coble v. State*, 330 S. W. 3d 253, 274 (Tex. Crim. App. 2010) (stating " [s] oft science does not mean soft standards. "). Numerous intermediate appellate courts have applied *Nenno* in their opinions.[1]

5. *Beware of catch phrases*

The admissibility of expert testimony is not determined by magic words or catch phrases. *Merrell Dow Pharms.*, *Inc. v. Havner*, 953 S. W. 2d 706, 711 – 12 (Tex. 1997).

For example, in *State Farm & Cas. Co. v. Rodriguez*, 88 S. W. 3d 313 (Tex. App. —San Antonio 2002, pet denied) an expert's "wild – assed guess" was nevertheless admissible because the court looked at the substance of the opinion and found it sufficiently reliable. During a pretrial deposition, an engineering expert characterized any attempt to segregate 100% of foundation damage into smaller percentages attributable to various *potential* causes as a "wild ass guess". Despite the expert's colorful characterization during discovery, the trial court properly admitted his subsequent testimony at trial that 100% of the foundation damage was caused by a plumbing leak. Consideration of the expert's testimony as a whole revealed it to be reliable. The contradiction between the expert's ability to apportion damage to various causes before and during trial went to the weight of the testimony, not its admissibility.

Similarly, in *Welch v. McLean*, 191 S. W. 3d 147 (Tex. App. —Fort Worth 2004, no pet.); the court of appeals held that an expert's opinion that the plaintiff was suffering from pulmonary emboli when she was treated two and one – half months before her eventual death from a massive pulmonary embolism was factually sufficient proof of causation because "the ju-

---

[1] *See, e. g.*, *Taylor v. Tex. Dep't of Prot. & Reg. Servs.*, 160 S. W. 3d 641 (Tex. App. —Austin 2005, pet denied); *In re A. J. L.*, No. 02 – 04 – 050 – CV, 2004 Tex. App. LEXIS 4993 (Tex. App. —Fort Worth, June 3, 2004); *Coastal Tankships, USA, Inc. v. Anderson*, 87 S. W. 3d 591 (Tex. App. —Houston [1st Dist.] 2002, pet. denied); *In re J. B.*, 93 S. W. 3d 609, 621 (Tex. App. —Waco 2002, pet. denied). *But see Bartosh v. Gulf Health Care Ctr. – Galveston*, 178 S. W. 3d 434, 441 n. 3 (Tex. App. —Houston [14th Dist.] 2005, no pet.) (declining to apply *Nenno* in civil case).

ry is authorized to disbelieve expert witnesses". *Id.* at 160. The court noted that experts' use of specific phrases (e. g., "reasonable medical probability", "high probability" and "more likely than not") do not establish causation. *Id.* at 157. "Whether an expert opinion establishes a causal connection based upon reasonable medical probability must be determined by the substance and context of the testimony rather than semantics or the use of a particular term or phrase." *Id.* Although the court had originally held that the expert testimony regarding causation was factually insufficient, in a revised opinion, the court held that the expert testimony was factually sufficient. *Id.* at n. 7. The court explained that a party may generally not establish a vital fact by inference stacking, but medical experts are an exceptions to this rule against inference stacking. *Id.*

Nevertheless, reasonable probability is determined by the substance and context of the opinion and does not turn on semantics or the use of a particular term or phrase. *Id.* at 157; *see also Abilene Indep. School Dist. v. Marks*, 261 S. W. 3d 262, 269 (Tex. App. —Eastland 2008, no pet.)

Although not listed as a separate factor for analyzing the expert's methodology, *Robinson* held that a causation expert must eliminate other potential causes. 923 S. W. 2d at 559. Subsequent Texas courts have struck expert testimony because of the failure to eliminate other potential causes. *Eight Gates*, 36 Hous. L. Rev. at 799 - 899.[2]

---

[2] *See also Wal-mart Stores, Inc. v. Merrell*, 313 S. W. 3d 837 (Tex. 2010) (expert's failure to explain how he eliminated a potential cause of fire makes it conclusory and unreliable); *In re Allied Chem. Corp.*, 227 S. W. 3d 652, 656 (Tex. 2007) (experts "must also exclude other causes with reasonable certainty"); *Mack Trucks, Inc. v. Tamez*, 206 S. W. 3d 572, 581 (Tex. 2006) (stating that the expert "failed to set out any process by which he excluded other sources of ignition of the diesel fuel such as mechanical sparks which could be generated when parts of the truck make contact with the pavement, or ignition of the cargo fuel ..."); *Havner*, 953 S. W. 2d 706, 720 (Tex. 1997) ("[I]f there are other plausible causes of the injury or condition that could be negated, the plaintiff must offer evidence excluding those causes with reasonable certainty."); *Gillie v. Boulas*, 65 S. W. 3d 219 (Tex. App. —Dallas 2001, pet. denied); *Neal v. Dow Agroscis.*, 74 S. W. 3d 468 (Tex. App. —Dallas 2002, no pet.) (testing must be performed to eliminate other potential causes); *Helm v. Swan*, 61 S. W. 3d 493 (Tex. App. —San Antonio 2001, pet. denied) (without testimony to rule out the plaintiff's illness following a surgical procedure as a possible cause, the experts' testimony that complications were caused by a delay in fluid resuscitation is mere speculation); *Martinez v. San Antonio*, 40 S. W. 3d 587, 595 (Tex. App. —San Antonio 2001, pet. denied) (the plaintiffs expert failed to eliminate other potential causes of lead contamination); *Hess v. McLean Feedyard, Inc.*, 59 S. W. 3d 679 (Tex. App. —Amarillo 2000, pet. denied) (expert, testifying in suit against feedyard claiming that runoff contaminated adjoining tract's water supply, failed to rule out the possibility that waste from 4000 head of cattle on the tract had already affected the water quality by the time of the runoff); *Austin v. Kerr-McGee Ref. Corp.*, 25 S. W. 3d 280, 292-93 (Tex. App. —Texarkana 2000, no pet) (finding unreliability when expert could not exclude other possible causes with reasonable certainty); *cf. Nissan Motor Co. Ltd. v. Armstrong*, 145 S. W. 3d 131, 411 (Tex. 2004) (observing that in a products case "other possible cases must be ruled out"); *Ford Motor Co. v. Aguiniga*, 9 S. W. 3d 252, 264 (Tex. App. —San Antonio 1999, pet. denied) (determination that expert opinions about cause of accident were reliable was bolstered by fact that expert "had narrowed the cause [of product failure] to one source"); *Doyle Wilson Homebuilder, Inc., v. Pickens*, 996 S. W. 2d 387, 394 (Tex. App. —Austin 1999, pet. dism' d by agr.) (permitting testimony by the plaintiffs' expert electrical engineer, who while acknowledging that he did not know exactly what caused a fire that destroyed plaintiffs' house, nevertheless narrowed the most likely cause of the fire to defendant's improper installation of electrical wiring and noting that the defendant did not attempt to impeach the witness at trial with any evidence of another cause); *Weiss v. Mech. Associated Servs., Inc.*, 989 S. W. 2d 120, 125 (Tex. App. —San Antonio 1999, pet. denied) (doctors in toxic tort case had not eliminated other potential causes).

On the other hand, disproof of other possible causes does not necessarily prove a particular defect caused an affidavit, *Cooper Tire & Rubber Co. v. Mendez*, 204 S. W. 3d 797, 807 - 08 (Tex. 2006).

The universe of possible causes for the tire failure is simply too large and too uncertain to allow an expert to prove a manufacturing defect merely by the process of elimination. As stated above, even if plaintiffs had eliminated every conceivable reason for the tire failure other than a product defect existing when the tire left Cooper Tire's plant, they did not eliminate the possibility of a design defect.

6. *Specific rules for causation in tort cases.*

Havner and its line of progeny hold that in toxic tort cases, a plaintiff must prove both general and specific causation. *See*, *e. g.* , *Coastal Tankships*, 87 S. W. 2d 591, 601 - 03 (Tex. App. —Houston [1st Dist.] 2002, pet. denied). But it now appears that this rule applies to all personal injury cases. *See*, *e. g.* , *Abilene Indep. School Dist. v. Marks*, 261 S. W. 3d 262, 271 (Tex. App. —Eastland 2008, no pet.) (holding in workers compensation cases that physician's testimony on whether an on – the – job injury caused chondromalcia reliably addressed both general and specific causation and noting that temporal proximity—along with other evidence—supported his causation opinion); *Hackett v. Littlepage & Booth*, 2009 Tex. App. LEXIS 1166, at * 17 – 18 (Tex. App. —Austin Feb. 20, 2009, no pet.) (concluding that trial court did not error err in considering general and specific causation standards of *Havner* in medical malpractice claims).

In *Wal – mart Stores*, *Inc. v. Merrell*, 313 S. W. 3d 837 (Tex. 2010), the Court held that the plaintiff had only proven that a halogen lamp could cause a fire but not that it caused this particular fire. The court that the expert's "specific causation theory amounted to little more than speculation".

The Texas Supreme Court has now "generally" approved the methodology of differential diagnosis used by physicians, although the Court cautioned that the technique will not necessarily be reliable in every case. *Transcont. Ins. Co. v. Crump*, 330 S. W. 3d 211 (Tex. 2010). Unlike the court of appeals, the Court reached this conclusion without rejecting or less strictly applying the *Robinson* factors. Rather the Court found that the differential diagnosis methodology was generally reliable after applying both the *Robinson* factors and the *Gammill* analytical gap analysis. *Id.* at 217. "The mere fact that differential diagnosis was used does not exempt the foundation of a treating physician's expert opinion from scrutiny—it is to be evaluated for reliability as carefully as any other expert's testimony. " *Id.* Turning to the *Robinson* factors, the Court observed that the methodology is generally accepted by the medical community and is used outside the litigation context. It has been subject to peer review and testing. *Id.* Temporal proximity in itself does not prove causation but may be probative in determining causation. *Id.* at n. 3. In some cases, a physician's differential diagnoses may be too dependent upon the physician's subjective guesswork or produce too great a rate of error—for example, when there are several consistent, possible causes for particular set of symptoms. " *Id.* But it is unnecessary for the expert to disprove or discredit every other possible cause of the condition. Instead the other causes must be reliably excluded if they are capable of being disproved with reasonable medical certainty. Turning to the analytical gap test from *Gammill*, the Court also stated that an expert does not have to eliminate every gap; if a gap is not "too great", it goes to its weight and not its reliability. *See Coastal Tankships, U. S. A., Inc. v. Anderson*, 87 S. W. 3d 591 (Tex. App. —Houston [1st Dist.] 2002, pet. denied) (holding that a differential diagnosis method of determining the cause of a disease is reliable if ①general causation is demonstrated, i. e., the cause identified by the expert is reliably shown to be one of the possible causes of the plaintiff's condition or symptoms, and ②the expert utilizes a differential diagnosis procedure properly to eliminate the other most likely causes of the condition).

In *Coastal*, the en banc First Court of Appeals held that the trial court abused its discretion in permitting the plaintiff's medical expert to testify that exposure to the chemical naphtha caused the plaintiff's bronchiolitis obliterans organizing pneumonia (BOOP). The plaintiff's vessel carried naphtha on two occasions and he became so sick that he was transported off the ship. "[A] differential diagnosis by itself, without further scientific evidence that 'rules in' the chemical as a cause, is usually not reliable to prove general causation in the toxic - tort context." *Id.* at 600 n. 16. The opinion adopts for civil cases a "*Daubert/Robinson/Jordan* inquiry" that utilizes a test from the Texas Court of Criminal Appeals for the reliability of "soft" scientific evidence.

The court first stated that the applicability of the *Daubert/Robinson* factors is a flexible requirement. The majority and concurring opinions disagreed concerning the rigidity with which to apply those factors. The majority stated that the concurring opinion's requirement that the expert must address each of the factors was too rigid and had been rejected by *Kumho Tire* and *Gammill. Id.* at 599 n. 15. Quoting from the Court of Criminal Appeals' opinion in *Nenno*, the court stated that the *Daubert* factors do not necessarily apply outside the hard science context. Following the *Nenno* test for "soft sciences", the court stated that the issue for a differential diagnosis is whether the expert properly relied upon and/or utilized the principles involved in the applicable field. The court rejected the holding of the en banc Fifth Circuit in *Moore v. Ashland Chem., Inc.*, 151 F. 3d 269 (5th Cir. 1998) (en banc) concerning the admissibility of a differential diagnosis "to the extent that the opinion rigidly applies the *Daubert* inquiries to a field (clinical diagnosis, not a pure hard science) in which those inquiries are ill - suited". *Id.* at 600 n. 16.

A differential diagnosis is no proof, however, of general causation. The court divided causation "into general causation and specific causation. General causation asks whether a substance is capable of causing a particular injury in the general population; specific causation asks whether that substance caused a particular individual's injury". *Id.* at 601 - 02. The plaintiff must prove both. The plaintiff can prove specific causation by circumstantial evidence. Nevertheless, expert testimony is necessary to prove causation when there are several different possible causes to a condition. The plaintiff must present proof that " 'rule [s] in' the putative cause before ‘ruling out’ other causes”. A differential diagnosis “presumes, but does not solely establish, that the chemical is capable of producing harmful effects generally”. *Id.* at 608. A differential diagnosis, no matter how reliable the trial court finds it, can “at most show specific causation”. *Id.* at 609. Without a showing of general causation, a differential diagnosis is not relevant to show specific causation. *Id.*

General causation cannot be proven from conclusory medical records. The medical records do not constitute expert testimony (which is required for proof of causation) and “show at most specific causation”. Moreover, there was no showing that the records met the *Daubert/Robinson/Jordan* inquiry as to general causation. In the absence of such evidence, the trial court erred in admissible the evidence and there was insufficient evidence to support the jury verdict.

7. *Interesting or recent cases on Methodological Reliability*

Federal Courts

- *United States v. Whitfield*, 590 F. 3d 325 (5th Cir. 2009). In this case, two Mississippi state judges and a Mississippi trial attorney were found guilty of fraud arising from two bribery schemes involving two cases, *Marks* and *Peoples Bank*. The district court excluded expert testimony from two attorneys who would have testified that the two cases were decided correctly. The district court explained that an attorney could not speculate on the mental impressions of the Mississippi Supreme Court, which was better expressed in its written opinion. The Fifth Circuit agreed, concluding that the attorney's testimony was founded on unreliable methodology. Regarding the other attorney, the district court had excluded his testimony, in part, because it was based on suspicious methodology. The Fifth Circuit did not address these conclusions because the issue was waived on appeal.

- *Seaman v. Seacor Marine L. L. C.*, 2009 U. S. App. LEXIS 9202 (5th Cir. April 30, 2009). In this claim that the defendant's negligence caused the plaintiff's bladder cancer, the district court did not err in excluding the testimony of causation experts and granting summary judgment in favor of the defendant. The court reviewed the steps that must be proven in a toxic tort case. First, the plaintiff must show what quantity of the chemical is necessary to harm someone. Second, the plaintiff must prove exposure to such quantities. If the expert's opinion is “based on insufficient information, the analysis is unreliable.” Although the expert in this case cited various journals as the basis for his opinion, the expert never explained the studies.

- *IP Innovation L. L. C. v. Technology Licensing Corp.*, 705 F. Supp. 2d 687 (E. D. Tex. 2010). In this patent infringement suit, IP Innovation offered expert testimony about its reasonable royalty damages based on alleged infringement of its workplace switching feature, which is a small component of Red Hat's and Novell's Linux – based operating system. IP's expert based his royalty calculations on 100% of the operating system's revenue without accounting for the fact that it plays a small role in the overall product. Moreover, its expert did not take into account the fact that many users do not even enable or use the feature. Accordingly, the district court held that IP's expert could not testify absent a damages calculation based on accepted economic principles.

· *Williams v. Toyota Motor Corp.* , 2009 WL 305139 (E. D. Tex. Feb. 6, 2009). This personal injury lawsuit arose out of an auto accident in which the plaintiff's vehicle was rear – ended by a gravel truck. The defendant moved to limit the plaintiff's accident reconstruction expert's testimony because the expert's opinions were unreliable and unsupported by any testing. The trial court denied the motion after reviewing the evidence, explaining that the expert addressed at least two crash tests that were relevant to the issues in the case. On the other hand, the court granted the plaintiff's motion to strike the defendant's expert in metallurgical analysis on the basis that his opinions were unreliable under *Daubert.* The defendant's expert report consisted of subjective conclusions regarding the forces to which a driver's seat was subjected and was devoid of any discussion of methodology or scientific testing.

· *SEC v. Roszak*, 495 F. Supp. 2d 875 (N. D. Ill. 2007). The SEC brought a civil action alleging violations of the Securities Exchange Act of 1934 and Rule 10b – 5. One of the defendants moved to strike the SEC's expert's report on the ground that his methodology was not reliable. In concluding that the methodology used by the expert was reliable, the court found that "correlation coefficient analysis" had never been conducted in the manner in which the expert was using it in this case—but that it was a well – accepted methodology for evaluating between two variables, and had been used by courts in the securities fraud context and a variety of other circumstances. *Id.* at 881.

· *Dukes v. Wal – Mart, Inc.* , 509 F. 3d 1168 (9th Cir. 2007). In a class action suit involving sexual discrimination claims, the court of appeals upheld the district court's certification of the class, relying in part on statistical evidence presented by the plaintiffs' expert. The expert analyzed data on a regional level, running regression analyses for each region containing Wal – Mart stores. *Id.* at 1180. The expert came to the conclusion that there were significant statistical differences between men and women at Wal – Mart with regard to compensation and promotions, that the differences were similar across the different regions, and that the differences could only be explained by gender discrimination. *Id.* Wal – Mart challenged these findings, arguing that the expert's methodology was flawed in that he should have conducted research on a store – by – store basis, as opposed to a regional basis. *Id.* The court rejected this argument, stating whether the analysis of workforce statistics should be viewed on a "macro" or "micro" level depends on the "similarity of the employment practices and the interchange of employees at the various facilities". *Id.* Because the plaintiffs' expert provided a reasonable explanation for his research, the district court did not abuse its discretion in crediting the expert's analysis.

· *MicroStrategy Inc. v. Business Objects, S. A.* , 429 F. 3d 1344 (Fed. Cir. 2005). In this patent infringement case, the court affirmed the trial court's exclusion of plaintiff's damages expert because he used flawed methodology and did not accurately link the alleged damages to the torts. MicroStrategy suffered severe losses in the 1990's due to the dot – com bubble burst, which was exacerbated by an accounting error. MicroStrategy's expert did not consider these financial losses in his damages calculations but attributed all damages to the defendant's conduct in 2000 without explaining why the economic setbacks had no lingering effect in 2000 and thereafter. The expert ignored any significant non – tortious factor that might have attributed to MicroStrategy's damages, such as the introduction of new products by the defendant. The expert did not have to consider and rule out every possible factor, but he had the responsibility to consider other obvious factors.

· *Tunica Web Advertising, Inc. v. Barden Miss. Gaming, LLC*, 2007 WL 2768914 (N. D. Miss. Sept. 18, 2007) (slip op.); 2007 U. S. Dist. LEXIS 69132; 2007 – 2 Trade Cas. (CCH) P75, 871; 74 Fed. R. Evid. Serv. (Callaghan) 818. The plaintiff filed suit alleging various antitrust claims and claims for intentional interference with business and contractual relations. The defendant filed a motion to exclude the plaintiff's expert's testimony regarding the calculation of the hypothetical value of the plaintiff's business but for the alleged boycott by the defendant—and ascertaining the relevant market and public harm to competition caused by the alleged boycott. The defendant argued that "tunica. com" was not worth MYM1. 6M—nor the continued alleged profits of MYM10 990. 00 per month—because the plaintiff's expert's opinion was unreliable; his methodology was based on invalid or exaggerated assumptions; his opinions were based solely on his subjective opinion and experience—and not supported by objective, verifiable evidence; and that the irrelevant data did not "fit" his methodology in this case. The court observed that this former economics professor, President, CEO, and sole owner of DomainMart, Inc. had been continually engaged in real – life market experience, operating and brokering transactions for internet "domain names", and that he had been hired by over 1000 internet websites to prepare written reports appraising the market value of their websites and domain names. He held a Masters Degree in Economics from UC Berkley, and had been paid by major financial institutions to assist them in internet website valuations. The court also found the expert—though he hadn' t relied on other publications or considered other theories in reaching his valuation—was using *his same technique…used in everyday work*. This satisfied the *Daubert* gatekeeping requirement to ensure that the expert "employs ... the same level of intellectual rigor that characterizes the practice of an expert in the relevant field" —in this case, that of valuating and entering partnerships with domain names and their websites. *Id.* (quoting *Kumho*, 526 U. S. at 152).

· *Munoz v. Orr*, 200 F. 3d 291 (5th Cir. 2000). In this disparate impact employment claim under Title VII, the trial court did not err in excluding the statistical analysis of the plaintiff's expert because of a lack of reliability. First, the expert's reports contained a number of miscalculations. Additionally, Dr. Benz began his analysis with the assumption that Kelly's promotion system discriminated against Hispanic males, an indicator that he lacked the necessary objectivity to make his analyses credible. Dr. Benz also stated that discrimination was the "cause" of the disparities he had observed, a statement which he later recanted as "overzealous" since statistics can show only correlation and not causation.

In his depositions, he admitted to failing to consider other variables such as education and experience as explanations for any observed discrepancy between promotion rates and to not performing a multiple regression analysis. Finally, Dr. Benz relied on the plaintiffs' compilations of data, which gives rise to a "common – sense skepticism" regarding the expert's evaluation. *Id.* at 301 (citations omitted).

· In *Butler v. Union Carbide*, a mesothelioma case, a Georgia trial court rejected the theory that any exposure to asbestos will cause injury. The expert admitted that his any exposure of non – threshold theory was "not practically testable and has not been tested". 712 S. E. 2d 537 (Ga. App. 2010). The court went on to state that " [t] he claim that there is no known safe level of exposure does not mean that none exists; it simply means science today has not and cannot ... determine what that level of exposure is". Relying on David Faigman's book Modern Scientific Evidence: The Law and Science of Expert Testimony (West 2009 – 2010) ed.), the court held that the any exposure theory is "at most, scientifically – ground speculation". The court also observed that when the expert opinion is presented by "a 'quintessential expert for hire', then it seems well within a trial judge's discretion to apply the *Daubert* factors with greater rigor". *Id.* [quoting *Johnson v. Manitowoc Boom Trucks, Inc.*, 484 F. 3d 426, 435 (6th Cir. 2007)].

Texas Courts

· *Custom Transit, L. P. v. Flatrolled Steel, Inc.*, No. 14 – 10 – 00936 – CV (Tex. App. —Houston [14th Dist.] June 14, 2012, no pet. h.) also addressed whether a contention that the expert failed to rule out alternative causes of damage to the coils. The court observed, "there is room for discussion regarding the degree to which admissibility and sufficiency determinations depend on exclusion of proffered or alternative explanations for a particular event. While an expert should address evidence that contradicts his conclusion, [i] t is not required ... that an expert categorically exclude each and every possible alternative cause in order to render the proffered testimony admissible." In any event, the expert adequately addressed the other alternative sources of damage.

· *Harris Cnty. Appraisal Dist. v. Houston 8th Wonder Prop.*, *L. P.*, 01 – 10 – 00154 – CV, 2012 WL 1757591 (Tex. App. —Houston [1st Dist.] May 17, 2012, no. pet. h.) ("When a party asserts on appeal that an expert's testimony is insufficient because it is unreliable, a court will ordinarily consider both the *Robinson* reliability factors and the expert's experience.").

· *Dallas Cnty. v. Crestview Corners Car Wash*, 05 – 09 – 00623 – CV, 2012 WL 523920 (Tex. App. —Dallas Feb. 16, 2012, no pet.). The Dallas court of appeals affirmed the exclusion of testimony by a Dallas County appraisal expert in a case involving the value of land taken in an eminent domain proceeding. Because the expert – appraiser did not apply accepted appraisal methods to arrive at his valuation of the land before and after the taking, his testimony was properly excluded by the trial court.

· *Scott's Marina at Lake Grapevine Ltd. v. Brown*, 07 – 10 – 00277 – CV, 2012 WL 177970 (Tex. App. —Amarillo Jan. 23, 2012, no pet.). The court of appeals affirmed a jury award to an employee, overruling a legal sufficiency challenge. The employee was diagnosed with enteroviral meningitis and Lemierre's Syndrome after multiple workplace exposure to a spillage from a hub. He sued contending that the spillage was sewage containing human feces, and that this exposure caused his illnesses. Plaintiff's expert, a leading expert in the field of anaerobic infectious disease, opined that his workplace exposure proximately caused his illnesses. The court held that the causation opinion of the plaintiff's expert, a leading expert in the field of anaerobic infectious disease, was sufficiently reliable. First, the testing/testability *Robinson* factor was satisfied because medical literature and concessions by the defendant's medical established "some medical acceptance of a causal connection between exposure to human feces and Lemierre's Syndrome". *Id.* at *6. The court observed that the defendant's expert acknowledged that the primary cause of enteroviral infection is exposure to fecal matter. Second, the publication *Robinson* factor was satisfied. Third, and significantly, the expert ruled out other likely causes of the worker's illnesses based on evidence that the worker was not exposed to any of the other most common sources of his illnesses. "In the final analysis, [the plaintiff] was able to rule out the most likely other causes of [his] contracting the enteroviral infection. A medical causation expert need not disprove or discredit every possible cause other than the one he espouses." *Id.* at *8. Finally, the court rejected the marina's contention that the period between the worker's "exposure to the spillage and his development of symptoms does not correlate to the medically accepted incubation period for enterovirus". *Id.* The court found there was evidence of symptoms within the recognized incubation period.

- *DaimlerChrysler Motors Co., LLC v. Manuel*, 362 S. W. 3d 160 (Tex. App. —Fort Worth 2012, no pet.). The Fort Worth court of appeals declined to apply the *Robinson* factors for analyzing the reliability of a certified public accountant's opinion on lost profits and held that the trial court did not abuse its discretion in admitting the testimony. Instead, the court of appeals applied the "general reliability test" of *Gammill. Id.* (citing *Paschal v. Great W. Drilling, Ltd.*, 215 S. W. 3d 437, 448 (Tex. App. —Eastland 2006, pet. denied) (holding *Gammill* test appropriate for expert testimony of a certified public accountant regarding analysis of financial records for tracing of embezzled funds); *KMG Kanal – Muller – Gruppe Deutschland GmbH & Co. KG v. Davis*, 175 S. W. 3d 379, 391 (Tex. App. —Houston [1st Dist.] 2005, no pet.) (holding testimony on valuation of company based on projected lost profits by expert with doctorate in economics, who taught a university course in corporate evaluation and whose method of business valuation was not shown to have been rejected by any authority or opposing expert, was reliable under *Gammill* even though expert conceded that "corporate valuation necessarily entails a fundamental degree of speculation"). The court noted that the defense expert did not criticize the methodology used by the plaintiff's expert, nor did the defense expert identify another methodology or opine on a different amount of lost profits. Furthermore, "[t] here is no one proper method for determining lost profits as damages". One accepted methodology for new businesses is "the yardstick analysis" of "using a comparable established business that is also owned and operated by the plaintiff". The court therefore approved the expert's methodology but cautioned that a reliable methodology requires "one complete calculation". *Id.* quoting *Holt Atherton Indus., Inc. v. Heine*, 835 S. W. 2d 80, 85 (Tex. 1992).

· *U. S. Renal Care, Inc. v. Jaafar*, 345 S. W. 3d 600 (Tex. App. —San Antonio 2011, no pet.). Expert testimony on damages was unreliable in this breach of contract claim in which the sellers of a business claimed that the buyer wrongfully retained certain accounts receivable that were owed to the sellers under the terms of their sale agreement. To prove its damages, the sellers presented expert testimony from a valuation expert concerning the value of retained accounts receivable the buyer allegedly owed to the sellers. The buyer contended that the expert's valuation testimony was unreliable under the *Robinson* factors. The sellers argued that the *Robinson* factors were irrelevant, and the reliability of the expert's opinion is properly measured by the less rigorous "analytical gap" test. The court described *Whirlpool* as refusing to "focus on a fixed test" and instead applying "a more flexible approach" to the reliability of expert testimony. *Id.* at 608. Nevertheless, " [i] rrespective of the test applied, in its gate – keeping function, 'courts are to rigorously examine the validity of facts and assumptions on which the testimony is based, as well as the principles, research, and methodology underlying the expert's conclusions and the manner in which the principles and methodologies are applied by the expert to reach the conclusions'". *Id.* at 608. The court concluded that regardless of whether it applied *Gammill*'s analytical gap approach or the *Robinson* factors, the expert's opinion was unreliable. In addition to the fact that his analysis was developed solely for litigation purposes, his analysis "was subjective, his assumptions were unfounded, his opinion has not been subjected to peer review, and his technique has an unknown rate of error". The court specifically observed that there were "inequities resulting from" the expert's assumptions. He also failed to analyze much of the data that he was given.

· *Wilson v. Shanti*, 333 S. W. 3d 909, 913 (Tex. App. —Houston [1st Dist.] 2011, pet. denied). In this case, the court concluded that the plaintiff's expert never provided an explanation for the reliability of his opinion:

A court cannot simply accept expert testimony at face – value because unreliable expert testimony constitutes no evidence. The trial court should "undertake a rigorous examination" of the three components of the reliability inquiry—namely, the expert's methodology, foundational data, and whether too great an analytical gap exists as the expert connects the foundational data or methodology with the opinion. Each material part of an expert's theory must be reliable. Stated differently, "the expert's testimony must be reliable at each and every step or else it is inadmissible". There are limits to the trial court's rigorous examination. Courts may not second – guess the correctness of the expert's conclusions; they are only to examine whether the analysis used to reach those conclusions is reliable. A court's gate – keeping analysis is also not a substitute for cross – examination. A court is not permitted to determine reliability based on the weight of the evidence or the credibility of the witnesses.

Id. at 913.

· *Occidental Permian Ltd. v. Helen Jones Found.*, 333 S. W. 3d 392 (Tex. App. —Amarillo 2011, no pet.). In this claim by royalty interest owners seeking underpaid royalties, the court held that expert testimony on the market value of casing head gas was unreliable, and thus constituted no evidence to support their damage claim.

"Market value is generally determined by comparing the sale price to other sales 'comparable in time, quality, quantity, and availability of marketing outlets.' " A sale of gas of comparable quality involves gas with similar physical properties such as sweet, sour, or casing head gas. Proper expert testimony may make adjustments between sales of gas with differing physical properties so that the sales being compared truly are comparable.

Id. at 404 (citations omitted). The court identified a number of problems with the expert's evaluation including the lack of evidence on downstream prices.

- *Coble v. State*, 330 S. W. 3d 253 (Tex. Crim. App. 2010), *cert. denied*, 131 S. Ct. 3030, 180 L. Ed. 2d 846 (2011). A forensic psychiatrist's expert testimony concerning defendant's future dangerousness was unreliable.

- *Southland Lloyds Ins. Co.*, 2011 WL 1158244, at *2 (Tex. App. —San Antonio Mar. 30, 2011, no pet.). An independent insurance adjuster estimate of the cost of repairs to a home damaged in a hailstorm was sufficiently reliable. The expert adopted another expert's report as his estimate of the cost to repair the damage to the home that was caused by the hailstorm. He testified that "the manner in which the [other expert's] report was prepared was no different from any estimate he would have prepared for an insurance company" and that "if he had been asked .. to prepare the report, his investigation would have been the same". *Id.* Moreover, the software used to prepare the other expert's report is "accepted by most insurance companies". *Id.* He also explained that "the amount of work that must be done to repair damage to the house has nothing to do with the amount for which the house is insured". *Id.*

- *Valence Operating Co. v. Anadarko Petroleum Corp.*, 303 S. W. 3d 435 (Tex. App. —Texarkana 2010, no pet.). A certified professional landman with over 30 years of experience in the oil and gas industry and who had served as an instructor for the American Association of Professional Landmen was qualified to testify about the common understanding of the phrase "commence work on a proposed operation" in the oil and gas industry. The trial court also did not error in overruling a reliability challenge because his testimony "was not about science or scientific causation … but rather was about actual practice and the general understanding in the oil and gas industry as to what constitutes commencement of operations". *Id.* at 443.

- *TXI Transp. Co. v. Hughes*, 306 S. W. 3d 230 (Tex. 2010). In this wrongful death case, testimony from Dr. Kurt Marshek (an accident-reconstruction expert) was deemed reliable. The critical issue in the case was what caused the plaintiffs' Yukon—traveling westbound—to cross the center line into the eastbound lane and collide with TXI's eighteen-wheel tractor-trailer rig, which was heavily loaded with gravel. Marshek testified that the driver of the Yukon was forced to steer sharply into the eastbound lane to avoid the gravel track, which had veered into the westbound lane. TXI attacked Marshek's testimony as unreliable, contending that ①he assumed that a gouge mark in the road pinpointed the place where the Yukon collided with the gravel truck's second axle; ②he assumed the gouge mark indicated the angle of the gravel truck when the Yukon struck it; ③he miscalculated the gravel truck's position based on imprecise time estimates from witnesses, contrary to proper protocol; and ④he selectively relied on eyewitness line - of - sight testimony. The Court disagreed, concluding that Marshek's testimony was reliable because ①he explained the principles of physics supporting his theory; ②he did rule out alternate causes of the gouge mark, explaining how the physical evidence and physics supported his gouge - mark theory; ③his use of witness testimony did not violate proper protocol; and ④he did not base his conclusions on eyewitness line - of - sight testimony.

· *Enbridge Pipeline (East Texas) L. P. v. Avinger Timber, L. L. C.*, 326 S. W. 3d 390 (Tex. App. —Texarkana 2010, pet. filed). In this condemnation case, Pipeline challenged the expert testimony of Bolton regarding the fair market value of the real estate based on the willing seller - willing buyer test. In determining the fair market value, Bolton took into account unique improvements to the land that would make it more valuable to a natural gas pipeline company. The court held that Bolton properly calculated the effect that he improvements had on the market value of the land based on the best use of the land as a natural gas processing facility.

· *Lincoln v. Clark Freight Lines, Inc.*, 285 S. W. 3d 79 (Tex. App. —Houston [1st Dist.] 2009, no pet.). This personal injury lawsuit arose out of an intersection collision. The plaintiffs filed a *Daubert* motion to prevent a sheriff's deputy from testifying about the cause of the accident. The deputy had worked as an accident reconstructionist for 23 years, attended several schools for accident reconstruction starting in 1988, and had over 1000 hours in accident reconstruction training. The trial court allowed the deputy to testify that the plaintiff's father, who was driving a Ford Mustang caused the accident by running the red light.

Plaintiffs argued on appeal that there was too great an analytical gap between the data or observations and the deputy's conclusions because the deputy used a Camaro in his coefficient of friction test, rather than a Mustang; therefore, all of the opinions drawn from his calculations were flawed. More specifically, the defendant argued that the there was not substantial similarity between the experimental conditions and the accident conditions. The court disagreed, noting that the conditions do not need to be identical and a trial has discretion to determine whether the dissimilarities are substantial enough to warrant excluding the evidence.

The deputy had explained why the differences between a Camaro and a Mustang (e. g., one had a manual transmission while the other had an automatic transmission) have no effect on the coefficient of friction value. Accordingly, the court held that the trial court had not abused its discretion in admitting experiment data, explaining that a trial court does not abuse its discretion in admitting such testimony when any dissimilarities between the experiment and the relevant event are minor, can be made clear by explanation, or do not affect the result of the test.

· *Bechtel Corp. v. CITGO Prod. s Pipeline Co.*, 271 S. W. 3d 898, 924 (Tex. App. — Austin 2008, no pet.). In this legal sufficiency challenge to a future damages award, the court held that the expert's estimate of future environmental clean - up costs was sufficiently reliable as to constitute evidence and therefore overruled the no – evidence challenge. The expert used data points to create a circular area of contamination. His cost estimates detailed the costs for groundwater monitoring and reporting, laboratory costs, preparing site – specific discharge permits and remedial system design, capital equipment, and construction. Based on his "experience and the known data points, his testimony with respect to the initial cost estimate was reliable".

· *Mack Trucks, Inc. v. Tamez*, 206 S. W. 3d 572, 579 – 81 (Tex. 2006). The court identified a number of types of fire causation evidence were missing from the record: studies and tests, identification of a specific defect, inspect of the fire scene, observation of an exemplar product, and elimination of other causes. *Id.* at 580 – 81.

· *Cooper Tire & Rubber Co. v. Mendez*, 204 S. W. 3d 797 (Tex. 2006). In this products liability case, the Court reversed an MYM11 million verdict because there was no evidence of a manufacturing defect. Although the *Robinson* factors are not always useful in evaluating expert testimony in automobile accident cases, and although they do not provide a perfect template for evaluating the admissibility of an expert's testimony, the Court used them for guidance in finding unreliable an expert's opinion that a tire separated because of wax contamination. The expert's hypothesis was unsupported by any scientific testing, peer – reviewed studies or any support in the scientific community. It was nothing more than "subjective belief or unsupported speculation", and a naked hypothesis untested and unconfirmed by the methods of science and was legally insufficient to establish a manufacturing defect that caused the failure.

· *Thomas v. Uzoka*, 290 S. W. 3d 437 (Tex. App. —Houston [14th Dist.] 2009, no pet.). In this wrongful death case, the defendant argued that the trial court erred in admitting expert opinions from two police officers on the cause of the accident.

The first officer testified that the defendant caused the impact by swerving in front of the decedent's vehicle. The defendant argued that the officer failed to rule out other possible causes. The court found that the officer did not overlook an alternative cause; rather, the expert had ruled out other possible causes that were contradicted by the physical evidence at the accident scene.

The second officer, who was also an accident reconstructionist, testified that the defendant was driving 23 miles per hour over the speed limit. The defendant first argued that the measuring device used at the scene is less accurate than another measuring device. The court rejected that argument, finding that the device used did produce reliable measurements and the other device was only very modestly more accurate. The defendant also challenged the speed opinion that was based on a computer program called WinCrash. The court first rejected the argument that the results are unreliable unless the weight for the occupants and contents of the vehicle was added to the vehicle's weight. The court stated that accident reconstruction community uses estimates. The court also found that the computations were reliable notwithstanding several error messages reported by the program. The expert explained that the results are considered reliable within the accident reconstruction community when the error messages can be explained by the physical evidence. The software was peer reviewed and generally accepted within the accident reconstruction community.

· *Von Hohn v. Von Hohn*, 260 S. W. 3d 631 (Tex. App. —Tyler, 2008, no pet.). In this divorce case between a lawyer and his wife, the value of the husband's interest in his law was the primary issue at trial. The wife had an expert to testify about the value of the husband's interest in the law firm. Before trial, the husband filed a motion to exclude this testimony, arguing that the expert was unqualified and that his methodology was unreliable.

The court also rejected the husband's claim that the expert's methodology was unreliable. The court noted that this particular expert had valued this same law firm in a divorce case approximately five years earlier and had used the same methodology as in this case. He also stated that both he and the opposing expert in the previous divorce case had used the income approach to value the partnership interest in the firm. Since the husband's main complaint was the use of the income approach (as opposed to the asset approach) the court concluded that the trial court did not abuse its discretion in allowing the expert to testify regarding his valuation of the husband's interest in the law firm.

· *Goodyear Tire & Rubber Co. v. Rios*, 143 S. W. 3d 107 (Tex. App. —San Antonio 2004, pet. denied). In this tire products liability case, a research scientist at Georgia Tech was qualified to testify regarding general adhesion principles but not adhesion principles as they applied to the actual subject matter of defects in a tire.

· *Pena v. State*, 155 S. W. 3d 238 (Tex. App. —El Paso 2004, no pet.). A police officer's testimony of the Accident Investigation Measuring System ("AIMS") was not shown to be sufficiently reliable to establish the speed of the vehicle at the time of the accident. The expert conceded that he did not know whether the accuracy of the AIMS results could be validated and could not explain in detail the scientific principles involved in this type of measuring system. The officer stated that he used standard, widely – used formulas for capturing speed, but conceded he did not know who devised the formulas or the scientific principles underlying the formulas. Since the officer did not have any knowledge regarding the scientific principles for the equipment or the validity of the equipment, the trial court erred in admitting the evidence.

· *Hernandez v. State*, 127 S. W. 3d 206 (Tex. App. —Houston [1st Dist.] 2003, pet. ref'd). A psychiatrist's opinion about the defendant's state of mind at the time of the murder was not based on "hard science", so the opinion only had to meet the three – prong reliability test of *Nenno* instead of the *Daubert* factors. Unfortunately for the defendant, he argued only that *Daubert* applied, and then failed to meet that test. The appellate court concluded that the expert could not satisfy *Daubert* because he did not show a reliable basis to his opinion. The psychiatrist testified that he had based his opinion on "reasonable medical probability", "historical data", "mainstream psychiatry" and the "DSM – IV study" on disassociative disorders. However, "other than briefly mentioning that he had applied the DSM – IV, he did not explain on what other 'mainstream psychiatry' studies or techniques he relied, how he had applied those studies or techniques to [the defendant]. Likewise, the doctor did not identify the 'historical data' on which he based his opinion concerning [defendant's] mental state."

• *Martinez v. San Antonio*, 40 S. W. 3d 587 (Tex. App. —San Antonio 2001, pet. denied). In this personal injury case arising from exposure to lead contaminated soils during construction of the Alamodome, the trial court granted the defendants' no – evidence summary judgment motions after striking the testimony of the plaintiffs' causation experts. The appellate court held the trial court did not abuse its discretion by striking the expert witness testimony and upheld the summary judgment. *Id.* at 589 – 90. The case is a good demonstration that an expert who relies on a study to justify a methodology must demonstrate the applicability of the study to the case in question and that when one expert relies on data from a first expert as a foundation for his or her opinion, a flaw in the underlying expert's data will result in striking the second expert's opinion.

• *BNSF Ry. Co. v. Nichols*, No. 01 – 09 – 01141 – CV, 2012 WL 2344843 (Tex. App. —Fort Worth June 21, 2012). In this FELA claim by a former railroad switchman for "cumulative trauma injuries" leading to degenerative disc disease allegedly caused by mounting and dismounting moving equipment, the court rejected the defendant's argument that the switchman was "required to provide evidence of ①epidemiological studies showing that mounting and dismounting moving railway cars can cause degenerative disc disease and②the amount of force [the switchman] himself experienced when getting on and off moving railcars". *Id.* at *5. The switchman used a videotape to explain the mounting and dismounting from moving railroad cars, stated that he performed the task twenty times daily for over 25 years, and described the amount of force involved in the task based on a report by a railroad ergonomics manager. The treating an orthopedic surgeon testified about the treatment of "cumulative trauma injuries", which he stated—based on medical literature—is a recognized medical diagnosis that is common among workers whose jobs required repeated heavy lifting and manual labor and athletes. He further testified that mounting and dismounting at the speeds shown in the video would "cause force to a person's lumbar and cervical spine region", and that if a person performed that task twenty times a day, "over time he would suffer an injury in his lumbar and cervical spine".

The court noted that there was "nothing controversial" about a physician "determining causation of an injury through differential etiology". Nevertheless, its reliability as a methodology must be determined "on a case – by – case basis, focused on which potential causes should be 'ruled in' and which should be 'ruled out'. Calling something a 'differential diagnosis' or 'differential etiology' does not by itself answer the reliability question but prompts three more: ①Did the expert make an accurate diagnosis of the nature of the disease? ②Did the expert reliably rule in the possible causes of it? and③Did the expert reliably rule out the rejected causes? If the court answers 'no' to any of these questions, the court must exclude the ultimate conclusion reached". *Id.* at * 7. The court followed *Granfield v. CSX Transp.*, *Inc.*, 597 F. 3d 474, 485 (1st Cir. 2010) which held an that orthopedic surgeon's opinion on repetitive injury was reliable when the surgeon specialized in repetitive stress injuries, had treated the plaintiff, used differential diagnosis to determine causation, and had regularly diagnosed repetitive stress injuries. Like *Granfield*, the court in *Nichols* concluded that did the absence of any peer – reviewed studies was not necessary to determine possible causes of the switchman's injury. The surgeon also ruled out weight, genetics, age, other activity, and the switchman's general condition as causes. His "experience in his practice and the methodology he used to determine causation were sufficient to render his expert opinion testimony reliable and also sufficient to sustain [the plaintiff's] burden of proving causation under the standard applicable to FELA cases". *Id.* at *8.

E. Fifth Gate: Connective Reliability

In a part of the opinion that is often overlooked, the *Daubert* Court held that the reasoning underlying an expert's opinion *and the application of* the expert's methodology must be reliable. *Daubert*, 509 U. S. at 592 – 93. A precondition to the admission of evidence is that "a valid connection to the case must be shown". *Id.* at 592; *see also Kumho*, 119 S. Ct. at 1174 (expert's testimony may be based on the application of a theory to a particular case). *Daubert* does not leave this determination to the jury:

It is no longer the case that if the methodology is sound, the possible misapplication in a specific case becomes a question for the jury. *Daubert* provides that "*any* step that renders the analysis unreliable ... *renders the expert's testimony inadmissible. This is true whether the step completely changes a reliable methodology or merely misapplies that methodology*".

Daniel Capra, *The Daubert Puzzle*, 32 Georgia L. Rev. 699, 710 – 11 (1998) [quoting *In re Paoli*, 35 F. 3d 717, 745 (3d Cir. 1994)].

It is also true that an expert must be able to connect the foundational data to his conclusions. When the expert's logical analysis from premise to conclusion includes a leap of faith, the leap, if big enough, requires excluding the opinion as improper extrapolation. *Id.* at 715, 719.

For example, in *General Electric Co. v. Joiner*, an electrician who developed lung cancer claimed that his workplace exposure to highly toxic PCBs (polychlorinated biphenyls) from electrical transformers "promoted" or caused his cancer. 522 U. S. 136 (1997). Two experts supported his causation claim, based on①a study involving infant mice given high doses of PCB and②four epidemiological statistical studies of electrical workers. *Id.* at 144 – 46. The Court reasoned that the expert's reasoning connecting facts to conclusions (not the expert's methodology) was flawed. *Id.* at 149. The *Joiner* Court upheld the trial court's exclusion of opinion evidence from qualified experts because it was not supported by solid science.

Giving a trial court even more discretion than in *Daubert*, the Court indicated that the conclusions and methodology are not entirely distinct from one another; a trial court may consider the conclusions an expert reaches from data and studies. Although "experts commonly extrapolate from existing data", a court is not required "to admit opinion evidence that is connected to existing data only by the *ipse dixit* of the expert". *Id.* at 146. "A court may conclude that there is simply too great an analytical gap between the data and opinion proffered." *Id.* Thus, a trial court must review both the methodology used by an expert and the reasoning used by that expert in applying that methodology to his or her opinion. *Id.*

An expert must explain the "how" and the "why" behind his conclusions, including how he or she has extrapolated from certain data to conclusions. *Id.* at 144. The Court did not explain whether this application of the extrapolation test was based upon the relevance test or the reliability test. The district court in *Joiner* relied upon both the relevance and reliability tests for excluding the animal studies. *Id.* at 151 – 52 (Stevens, J., concurring in part and dissenting in part). The animal studies were not relevant because there was no connection between the amount of exposure and method of exposure for the mice and humans. *Id.* at 144. They also were not relevant because there was no connection between animal studies and humans. *Id.* Even if the animal studies were reliable, there was no showing that the expert's reasoning (that the animal studies supported their conclusions for humans) could be properly "applied to the facts in issue". *Daubert*, 509 U. S. at 593. "The studies were so dissimilar to the facts presented in this litigation that it was not an abuse of discretion for the District Court to have rejected the experts' reliance on them." *Joiner*, 522 U. S. at 144 – 45.

Kumho also examined the application of an appropriate methodology to the facts of the case. The Court observed that the application of an expert's methodology presents the specific question of the case to the court, rather than the general issue of the reliability of the methodology. *Kumho Tire*, 119 S. Ct. at 1177, 1178. The application of the methodology to the facts of the case evaluates an expert's ability "to draw conclusions" from the methodology.

An expert's reasoning must be explained or detailed in the record. *Mid – State Fertilizer v. Exchange Nat' l Bank*, 877 F. 2d 1333 (7th Cir. 1989) (holding that the expert must state both the foundation for the expert's opinion and the reasoning from that foundation). Unless an expert explains the correlation from the data to his conclusion or opinion, the opinion is inadmissible. *McMahon v. Bunn – O – Matic Corp.*, 150 F. 3d 651, 658 (7th Cir. 1998).

Havner noted that the expert had extrapolated from animal studies to humans but failed to offer any explanation for this leap of faith. *Merrell Dow Pharms., Inc. v. Havner*, 953 S. W. 2d 706, 729 (Tex. 1997). The *Havner* court also observed that "[a] flaw in the expert's reasoning from the data may render reliance upon a study unreasonable and render the inferences drawn therefrom dubious". *Id.* at 714. Although the court did not explicitly adopt a test evaluating the entire range of the expert's reasoning process, it did evaluate the expert's reasoning process from underlying data. *See id.*

The Texas Supreme Court in *Gammill*, following *Joiner*, also discussed whether "there is simply too great an analytical gap between the data and the opinion proffered". The Court held that the district court was not required to admit opinion evidence that is connected to existing data only by the *ipse dixit* of the expert. *Id.* at 1127, 1128 (quoting *Joiner*, 522 U. S. at 136, 118 S. Ct. at 519). The expert's methodology in *Gammill* was not challenged. Instead, the offering party failed to show that the data relied on by the expert lead to his conclusions:

[T]he "gap" in [the expert's] analysis was his failure to show how his observations, assuming they were valid, supported his conclusions that [the deceased] was wearing her seat belt or that it was defective ... [The expert] did not specify the gliding abrasions on [the deceased's] body, or his basis for attributing them to the seat belt. He made no attempt to explain why the markings on [the deceased's] shirt are distinctive or how they are typical of seat belt loading.

Id. at 1128. Therefore, the opinion was unreliable.

Since *Gammill*, Texas courts have repeatedly reiterated that expert testimony is unreliable if there is too great an analytical gap between the expert's data and the expert opinions. *See*, *e. g.* , *Ford Motor Co. v. Ledesma*; *Exxon Pipeline Co. v. Zwahr*, 88 SW. 3d 623, 628 - 29 (Tex. 2002); *Frias v. Atlantic Richfield Co.* , 104 S. W. 3d 925, 927 (Tex. App. —Houston [14th Dist.] 2003, no pet.); *Roise v. State*, 7 S. W. 3d 225 (Tex. App. —Austin 1999, pet. ref' d). Reliability "may be demonstrated by the connection of the expert's theory to the underlying fact and data in the case". *TXI Transp. Co. v. Hughes*, 306 S. W. 3d 230, 239 (Tex. 2010).

Analytical gaps frequently occur because an expert fails to explain adequately how data leads to the expert's conclusions. For example, in *Volkswagen of America, Inc. v. Ramirez*, the Texas Supreme Court repeatedly noted that the plaintiff's experts did "not explain" or offered an "insufficient explanation" for their conclusions. 159 S. W. 3d 897, 906 (Tex. 2004). The only evidence "to connect [the expert's] observations with his conclusions" was the expert's "so - say". *Id.* at 912 (Hecht, J. , concurring). The validity of the expert's conclusions could not be examined by objective tests, statistical correlations, or his literature, the validity could only be "measured by one thing, and one thing only: his personal credibility. *Id.* The "only bridge offered by the expert between [his] credentials, experience, and qualifications on one side, and [his] opinions on the other is [his] own veracity, which is not enough". *Id.* at 913.

In *Volkswagen*, the Court found the expert's opinion to be unsupported "by objective scientific analysis and ... based solely on subjective interpretation of the facts" in part because of the expert's failure to cite or conduct any supporting tests and failure to cite any studies. 159 S. W. 3d at 905 - 06. In *City of Pollock*, the studies relied upon by the plaintiffs' experts were in the record and demonstrated a "large gap" between the plaintiffs' claimed exposure levels and the exposure levels found in the literature to have caused the disease in question. *Id.* at 819. The plaintiffs' expert also argued that long - term exposure to a low level of toxin might cause the disease, but none of the literature in the record supported that assertion. *Id.* at 820. Because the studies did not support the expert's opinion, it was conclusory. Additionally, the opinions were conclusory for a second reason: all the epidemiological studies on the disease did not satisfy the *Havner* standards for causation evidence in a toxic tort case. These cases focus more on the "face of the record" rather than trying to squeeze the analysis into methodological or foundational reliability.

Similarly, in *Kerr - McGee v. Helton*, the expert "failed to sufficiently explain" why the differences between his predicted well and a well he used for comparison would not result in different production rates. 133 S. W. 3d 245, 258 (Tex. 2004). Quoting *Gammill*, the court stated that "the gap in [the expert's] analysis was 'his failure to show how his observations ... supported his conclusions'". *Id.* at 257; *see also Wal – mart Stores, Inc. v. Merrell*, 313 S. W. 3d at 839 (observing that an expert cannot neglect to account for inconsistencies raised by his theory and failed to explain why he ruled out another potential cause of the incident); *Cooper*, 204 S. W. 3d at 805 (stating that expert did not expert how defective tire could be used for 30 000 miles and suffer a nail puncture without failing); *Whirlpool*, 298 S. W. 3d at 631 (observing repeatedly that the expert did not explain how the data supported his opinion and that the expert's test "did not support all the various and critical aspects of his opinion").

Interesting or recent cases on Connective Reliability

Federal Courts

- *LeBlanc v. Chevron USA, Inc.*, 396 Fed. Appx. 94 (5th Cir. 2010). In this toxic tort case, Dr. Gardner testified that Malcom LeBlanc's exposure to benzene had caused his myelofibrosis with myeloid meaplasia. The Fifth Circuit concluded that this testimony lacked foundational reliability for four reasons: ①many of the studies he relied on did not contain statistically significant results; ②some of the studies did not establish causality because they only noted that subjects were exposed to a range of substances and then nonspecifically noted an increase in disease incidence; ③some of the studies expressly disclaimed any causal connection between benzene and myelofibrosis; and ④ some of the materials are not scientific evidence. Additionally, the court concluded that Dr. Gardner also did not have personal experience as a practitioner of causation. Thus, the trial court did not abuse its discretion in excluding Dr. Gardner's testimony.

- *Wal – mart Stores, Inc. v. Merrell*, 313 S. W. 3d 837 (Tex. 2010). In this product liability case, *Merrell's* family alleged that a defective halogen lamp sold by Wal – Mart caused his death. The trial court granted Wal – Mart's no – evidence and traditional motions for summary judgment. At issue on appeal was the summary judgment evidence of plaintiffs' expert, Dr. Beyler, that the halogen lamp caused the fire.

The court of appeals held that Wal – Mart's failure to object or make a *Robinson* challenge to Dr. Beyler's methodology, technique, or foundational data in the trial court meant that Wal – Mart had waived its right to attack Dr. Beyler's affidavit on these bases on appeal. Additionally, the court of appeals reasoned that there was no analytical gap in Dr. Beyler's opinion because he excluded other causes of the fire and based his opinion on his own expertise and his investigation of the facts in this case. The Texas Supreme Court disagreed.

The Court held that Dr. Beyler's testimony was legally insufficient to support causation because he did not eliminate another equally plausible theory of the fire (i. e., that lit smoking materials could have caused the fire) and he did not testify that the lamp in this case caused the fire, only that halogen lamps can generally cause fires. Even if Dr. Beyler was qualified in fire research, his testimony in this case was legally insufficient because it lacked objective, evidence – based support for his conclusions.

· *Interplan Architects, Inc. v. C. L. Thomas, Inc.*, No. 4: 08 - cv - 03181, 2010 U. S. Dist. LEXIS 107941 (S. D. Tex. Oct. 8, 2010). In this copyright infringement case, the defendants argued that an expert's opinion on defendants' gross revenues should be excluded because the expert had based his gross revenues calculation on faulty methodology and incorrect factual information. Regarding one of the defendants, the gross revenues calculation was problematic because the calculation was based on indirect profits — using the infringing stores to sell other products, including food, drink, and other merchandise that might have been sold irrespective of any infringement — rather than on direct profits. In considering whether the plaintiff had demonstrated a sufficient causal link between the infringement and a particular profit stream. Recognizing a split between the Fourth Circuit and the Ninth Circuit, the district court followed the Ninth Circuit and concluded that the gross revenues calculation must be based on evidence that the revenue was caused or in some way affected by the actual infringement. Thus, the district court held that the expert's opinion on gross revenues was inadmissible because the expert did not show that the infringement (i. e., the architectural design of the convenience store) increased the defendant's gross revenue.

Texas Courts

· *City of San Antonio v. Pollock*, 284 S. W. 2d 809 (Tex. 2009). The Texas Supreme Court held that there was no evidence that the Pollocks' daughter contracted acute lymphoblastic leukemia ("ALL") as a result of benzene exposure from a closed landfill near the Pollocks' home. The landfill had been closed and covered 20 before the Pollocks bought their home. The primary claim was that the City's negligence allowed benzene from the closed municipal waste disposal site to migrate through the soil to the Pollocks' home, reducing its value and causing their daughter to contract leukemia.

The City argued that the expert testimony was conclusory, and therefore legally insufficient to support the judgment. The City had made this objection repeatedly in the trial court, but did not object to the admission of the evidence and did not file a pre-trial *Daubert* challenge to the evidence. The Pollocks argued that the City was challenging the reliability, underlying data, and methodology of the expert's opinion, and not the legal sufficiency of the opinion. As such, the Pollocks argued that the City had waived any error in the admission of this testimony.

The Court held that the City's failure to object to the introduction of plaintiffs' expert evidence (and in failing to challenge its reliability under *Daubert*), did not waive their objection. Opinion testimony that is merely conclusory or speculative is not evidence. The Court then examined each expert's testimony in turn and concluded that there was no evidence to support the verdict.

The first expert, Dan Kraft, an engineer with experience in landfill management, testified that the Pollocks' daughter was exposed *in utero* to landfill gas at levels high enough to cause leukemia. Landfill gas had never been found on the Pollocks' property, but it had been found in other homes in the neighborhood. It was possible for landfill gas to have migrated to the Pollocks' property along underground utility lines or through the ground generally. The odors smelled by the Pollocks in their home and backyard might have been landfill gas and their backyard subsidence might have been due to the landfill. Using an EPA – approved gas model, Kraft extrapolated that in 1993 and 1994, gas in a well on the Pollocks' property would have been more than 50 percent methane with 160 parts per billion benzene by volume. Based on this analysis, Kraft concluded that the Pollocks were exposed to gas levels like that in the sealed well. The City did not challenge any part of Kraft's analysis other than his final conclusion. The City contended that none of the data supported this conclusion that the Pollocks were exposed to benzene at a level of 160 parts per billion in the air in their home and on their property.

Analyzing the data, the Supreme Court agreed, concluding that there was no evidence from which one can infer the concentration that the mother was exposed to in the ambient air of her home and yard, but even at the highest concentration possible, the methane could have been only a fraction of that in the sealed monitored well. Consequently, Kraft's opinion that she was chronically exposed to benzene concentrations of 160 parts per billion had no factual basis. In fact, the conclusion was directly contradicted by his own data. The court concluded the expert's opinion is the kind of naked conclusion that cannot support a judgment.

The Court next examined the causation testimony of Dr. Patel, a pediatric oncologist who had treated the child. The purpose of his testimony was to prove that Mrs. Pollock's exposure to benzene concentrations of 160 parts per billion (assuming Kraft to be correct) could cause the child's ALL *in utero*. The court examined the epidemiological studies that Patel relied on and concluded that none of the studies showed a relationship between the daughter's chromosomal anomalies and the exposure to benzene at the levels the Pollock's claimed. Given the large gap between the exposure levels in the studies that Dr. Patel relied on and the concentration that the Pollocks had allegedly been exposed to, the studies provided no basis for Dr. Patel's opinion that the Pollocks' claimed benzene exposure caused the daughter's ALL. Consequently, Dr. Patel's opinions were conclusory and provided no evidence that the daughter's ALL was caused by her mother's benzene exposure.

Justice Medina dissented, contending that the majority assumed the role of gatekeeper ex post facto by allowing the City to complain about analytical gaps for the first time on appeal. According to Justice Medina, the complaint about the expert testimony had been waived because the City did not object to the reliability of either expert witness in the trial court or complain about the analytical gaps it detailed on appeal. Noting that it is extremely important to distinguish between unreliable expert testimony and conclusory expert testimony, Justice Medina explained that an expert's testimony is conclusory if the expert merely gave an unexplained conclusion or simply asked the jury to take his word for it because of his status as an expert. However, if the expert purports to rely on something more than his credentials or reputation, then an objection is necessary.

- *Taber v. Roush*, 316 S. W. 3d 139 (Tex. App. —Houston [14th Dist.] 2010, no pet.). In this obstetrical malpractice case arising out of a birth after the baby suffered from shoulder dystocia, the causation dispute "centered on a battle of the experts". *Id.* at 148. The court rejected the plaintiff's contention that the trial court erred in overruling a reliability objection to testimony that maternal forces of labor may cause some forms of brachial plexus injury. Taber contended that "this opinion testimony is unreliable because ① the literature upon which it relies consists primarily of anecdotal case reports and speculative hypotheses; and ② there is an analytical gap between the nonspecific brachial plexus injuries discussed in the literature and the baby's severe brachial plexus injury known as an avulsion injury (a permanent injury which occurs when a brachial plexus nerve root is physically pulled out of the spinal cord)". *Id.* at 146 –47. The plaintiffs expert, in contrast, testified that natural forces of labor cannot cause such a severe injury, that there is no medical literature showing that in an unattended surgery, natural forces produced an avulsion, and that the cause of the avulsion was excessive stress, creating a strong enough stress on the nerve to rip the nerves from the spinal cord. *Id.* at 148 –49.

The court first observing that a court assessing reliability must examine all the evidence. *Id.* at 147 –48. Turning to the expert's reliance on retrospective studies rather than prospective studies, the court held that the "ascertainment bias" (the possibility of misreporting the number of shoulder dystocias in the data) inherent in such studies did not render the expert testimony unreliable. *Id.* at 152. These concerns went to the studies weight, rather than admissibility. *Id.* at 153. The court also observed that "[t] he death of prospective testing in support of the natural forces of labor theory is explained by ethical considerations that preclude a prospective study". *Id.* at 152.

Turning next to the plaintiff's argument that an analytical gap existed between the nonspecific brachial plexus injuries described in the literature and the particular avulsion injury suffered in this case, the court observed that it could not "weigh the relative persuasive power of competing medical articles in a vacuum" or "ask in the abstract whether an excessive lateral traction explanation for brachial plexus injuries has more medical merit than a natural forces of labor explanation" because "[c] ourts are not equipped to make medical judgments of this nature". *Id.* at 153 –54.

Fair and equitable application of the standards governing admissibility of expert testimony begins with fidelity to the record. The specific legal task this court is called upon to perform … must be accomplished in the context of specific testimony. This context encompasses not only the disputed expert testimony itself, but also [the plaintiff's] competing expert testimony and the testimony of fact witnesses.

Id. Although the defense experts "acknowledged that no medical literature attributes permanent avulsion injuries like the one [in question] to the natural forces of labor", both parties experts relied on a degree of interpretation "in applying the existing literature to opine about causation based upon specific circumstances" in question. *Id.* at 154 –56. The court stated that the 22 publications relied upon by the defense were sufficient to bridge the gap between the theory and the infant's specific avulsion injury even though the causation issue "unavoidably involves an element of speculation". *Id.* at 156.

Finally, the court held that although the natural forces of labor theory is a hypothesis, that label "is not dispositive because this characterization by itself does not answer the reliability question. If the 'hypothesis' is supported by reliable data and methodology, and proffered in conformity with existing standards governing admission of expert testimony, then it is admissible". *Id.* at 159.

The dissenting justice criticized the majority, in part, because the expert opinions of numerous medical doctors did not connect the foundational data to the particular type of injury (i. e. avulsion) in the case.

- *Escamilla v. State*, 334 S. W. 3d 263 (Tex. App. —San Antonio 2010, pet. denied). In this sexual assault case, Garza testified that her examination of the victim revealed indications of sexual abuse. Although Garza was qualified and able to explain her methodology with sufficient clarity, the court concluded that the trial court erred in allowed her to testify because her vague references to literature supporting her underlying scientific theory and technique (absent any evidence that they are accepted as valid by the scientific community) did not establish a foundation of reliability for her opinion.

- *Duncan – Hubert v. Mitchell*, 310 S. W. 3d 92 (Tex. App. —Dallas 2010, pet. denied). In this case involving an election contest pertaining to a special election, Duncan – Hubert responded to a no – evidence summary judgment motion filed by Mitchell by relying on the opinion of Daniel Powers, an assistant professor of sociology, that it was impossible, from a statistical analysis, to determine with any degree of reasonable accuracy whether the outcome of the election would have been different had the complained – of irregularities not occurred. The trial court granted the no – evidence summary judgment. The appellate court reversed, holding that Powers's opinions were neither mere speculation nor conclusory because Powers had testified about the facts supporting his opinion and explained how he reached that opinion.

- *Austin v. Kerr – McGee*, 25 S. W. 3d 280 (Tex. App. —Texarkana 2000, no pet.). If epidemiological studies are relied upon to show general causation, the proponent of the evidence must show that the plaintiff is similar to those in the studies. If the expert relies on studies of other types of leukemia to show an association between benzene exposure and the type of leukemia developed by the plaintiff, the expert must demonstrate a sufficient link between benzene exposure and CML specifically, and thus [the expert] must show further that all types of leukemia are related or interchangeable. *Id.* at 288.

F. Sixth Gate: Foundational Reliability

1. *The opinion must be based on sufficient facts or data*

"The opinion of an expert must be supported by an adequate foundation of relevant facts, data, or opinions." Graham, Handbook of Federal Evidence § 702. 1 at 614. In the absence of such a foundation, an expert's opinion as based on conjecture or speculation and should be excluded. *Id.* The sources or underlying data for the expert's opinion "must themselves be reliable". *Tex. Worker's Comp. Comm' n v. Garcia*, 862 S. W. 2d 61, 105 (Tex. App. —San Antonio 1993), *rev' d*, 893 S. W. 2d 504 (Tex. 1995); *see also Mitchell Energy Corp. v. Bart-*

lett, 958 S. W. 2d 430 (Tex. App. —Fort Worth 1997, no writ) (the expert's underlying foundation did not support his conclusions.). "If an expert relies upon unreliable foundational data, any opinion drawn from that data is ... inadmissible." *Helena Chem. Co. v. Wilkins*, 47 S. W. 3d 486, 499 (Tex. 2001); *see also Neal v. Dow Agroscis.*, 74 S. W. 3d 468 (Tex. App. —Dallas 2002, no pet.) (expert testimony must be based on a reliable foundation); *Union Carbide Corp. v. Mayfield*, 66 S. W. 3d 354, 362 (Tex. App. —Corpus Christi 2001, pet. denied).

Daubert recognized that expert testimony must rest "on a reliable foundation". 590 U. S. at 597. This means that the data underlying the expert's opinion must be reliable. *See* Brown, *Eight Gates*, 36 Hous. L. Rev. at 813; *see also Kumho Tire*, 119 S. Ct. at 1175 (recognizing that the "factual basis, data, [and] principles" must be reliable).

The Texas Supreme Court also observed that expert opinions must be based on a "reliable foundation". *Robinson*, 923 S. W. 2d at 556. evidence was unreliable and therefore "no evidence". The supreme court has emphasized that the underlying facts must be reliable; "an expert's bare opinion will not suffice". *Merrell Dow Pharms., Inc. v. Havner*, 953 S. W. 2d 706, 711 (Tex. 1997). "The substance of the testimony must be considered." *Id.* Thus, the expert opinion does not become admissible even if the expert testifies it is reliable or uses "magic language" that the opinion is based on "reasonable medical probability". *Id.* at 712. Instead, the underlying data needs to be independently evaluated to determine "if the opinion itself is reliable". *Id.* at 713.

The *Havner* court summarized all three components of its review of expert opinions. First, foundational reliability must be established: "[i]f the foundational data underlying opinion testimony are unreliable, an expert will not be permitted to base an opinion on that data because any opinion drawn from that data is likewise unreliable". *Id.* at 714. Second, methodological reliability must be shown: "an expert's testimony is unreliable even when the underlying data are sound if the expert draws conclusions from that data based on flawed methodology". *Id.* Third, connective reliability must be shown: "[a] flaw in the expert's reasoning from the data may render reliance on a study unreasonable and render the inferences drawn therefrom dubious". *Id.*

Courts will critically examine whether the expert's reliance upon underlying data is reasonable. *Id.* A trial court "is not bound to accept expert testimony based on questionable data simply because other experts use such data in the field". *United States v. Locascio*, 6 F. 3d 924, 938 (2d Cir. 1993). A trial court must perform its own, meaningful inquiry:

The view that courts should not look beyond an averment by the expert that the data underlying his or her opinion are the type of data on which experts reasonably rely has likewise been rejected by other courts. The underlying data should be independently evaluated in determining if the opinion itself is reliable.... "If the underlying data are so lacking in probative force and reliability that no reasonable expert could base an opinion on them, an opinion which rests entirely upon them must be excluded."

Havner, 953 S. W. 2d at 713 (quoting *In re Agent Orange Liab. Litig.* , 611 F. Supp. 1223, 1245 (E. D. N. Y. 1985), *aff' d*, 818 F. 2d 187 (2d Cir. 1987)); *see also In re Paoli R. R. Yard PCB Litig*, 35 F. 3d at 717, 747 - 48 (3d Cir. 1994).

Moreover, "an expert cannot dissect a study, picking and choosing data, or 'reanalyze' the data to derive a higher relative risk if this process does not comport with sound scientific methodology". *Havner*, 953 S. W. 2d at 720. The facts or data must be "sufficient." *Gen. Elec. Co. v. Joiner*, 522 U. S. 136, 118 S. Ct. 512 (1997) (" [I] t was within the District Court's discretion to conclude that the studies .... were not sufficient, whether individually or in combination, to support their conclusions. "); *see also* FRE 702 (the testimony must be "based upon sufficient facts or data"); TRE 705 (c) ("sufficient basis"); Graham, Handbook of Federal Evidence § 702. 1 at 614 ("adequate foundation").

Thus, a trial court must make a "quantitative" inquiry into whether the testimony is based upon sufficient facts or data. *Rudd v. Gen. Motors Corp.* , 127 F. Supp. 2d 1330, 1339 (M. D. Ala 2001); *see also Allstate Ins. Co. v. Hugh Cole Builder, Inc.* , 137 F. Supp. 2d 1283, 1285 -86 (M. D. Ala. 2001).

Finally, it may be permissible in some circumstances for one expert to rely on reliable data furnished or gathered by another party's expert. *See United Servs. Auto. Ass'n v. Gordon*, 103 S. W. 3d 436, 439 (Tex. App. —San Antonio 2002, no pet.); *United Servs. Auto. Ass'n v. Croft*, 175 S. W. 3d 457 (Tex. App. —Dallas 2005, no pet.).

2. *The foundation of experience*

Courts have struggled with determining the reliability of expert testimony based on experience. Historically a number of courts held that the *Robinson* factors were inapplicable to experienced - based opinions. *See, e. g.* , *Brandt v. Surber*, 194 S. W. 3d 108, 131 (Tex. App. —Corpus Christi 2006, pet. denied) ("Because the expert opinions are based on the experience of the experts, the *Robinson* factors are not applicable. "); *Olin Corp. v. Smith*, 990 S. W. 2d 789 (Tex. App. —Austin 1999, pet denied).

In cases involving scientific causation opinions by physicians based on their experience, many courts hold that experience is not a sufficient basis for the opinion. *See e. g.* , *Havner*, 953 S. W. 2d 706; *Minnesota Mining & Mfg. Co. v. Atterbury*, 978 S. W. 2d 183 (Tex. App. —Texarkana 1998, pet. denied). Other courts also treat opinions on topics that are technical in nature and therefore subject to testing (such as product liability cases) as requiring more than mere claims of experience. *See, e. g.* , *Watkins*, 121 F. 3d 984. In other cases, the courts have adopted a "more general rule of reliability" that permits expert testimony based on experience if it passes *Gammill*'s connective reliability test (the analytical gap test) by showing that a close connection exists between the expert's experience and the proffered opinions. *See, e. g.* , *JC Penney Life Ins. Co. v. Baker*, 33 S. W. 3d 417 (Tex. App. —Fort Worth 2000, no pet.); *In re D. S.* , 19 S. W. 3d 525 (Tex. App. —Fort Worth 2000, no pet.); *Ford Motor Co. v. Aguiniga*, 9 S. W. 3d 252 (Tex. App. —San Antonio 1999, pet. denied).

Two important cases for evaluating the reliability of experienced - based testimony are

Kumho Tire and *Gammill* in which both the United States Supreme Court and the Texas Supreme Court held that an expert's experience can form a reliable basis for an opinion. *Kumho Tire Co.* , *Ltd. v. Carmichael*, 526 U. S. 137, 119 S. Ct. 1167, 1175 (1999); *Gammill v. Jack Williams Chevrolet*, *Inc.* , 972 S. W. 2d 713 (Tex. 1998). An expert's opinions may be based on "specialized observations" or "specialized experience" that is "foreign in kind to [the jury's] own". *Kumho Tire*, 119 S. Ct. at 1174.

The assessment of the reliability of experienced – based expert testimony will vary in every case; no definitive test exists for every case. The *Daubert* factors "may or may not be pertinent in assessing reliability, depending on the nature of the issue, the expert's particular expertise, and the subject of his testimony". *Kumho Tire*, 119 S. Ct. at 1175. For experience – based expert testimony, some of the *Daubert* factors can be helpful in some cases. *Id.* at 1176. When experience is the basis for a methodology, many of the *Daubert* factors would apply. "In certain cases, it will be appropriate for the trial judge to ask, for example, how often an engineering expert's experience – based methodology has produced erroneous results, or whether such a method is generally accepted in the relevant engineering community. " *Id.* When experience qualifies an expert to review the facts of the case in a way that a jury is not qualified to do, it will be appropriate to determine if the expert's review is "of a kind that others in the field would recognize as acceptable". *Id.* The court announced an overriding objective under *Daubert* is to ensure that the expert "employs in the courtroom the same level of intellectual rigor that characterizes the practice of an expert in the relevant field".

In *Kumho Tire*, the plaintiff argued that the expert's methodology was supported by his "long experience". *Id.* at 1178. Applying its test of measuring a methodology based on experience by whether the method is generally accepted, the court observed that there was no evidence that other experts in the field used the method. *Id.* Similarly no literature validated the approach. Moreover, using the general test of comparable intellectual rigor in and out of the courtroom, the observed that "no one has argued that Carlson himself, were he still working for Michelin, would have concluded in a report to his employer that a similar tire was similarly defective on grounds identical to those upon which he rested his conclusion here". *Id.* at 1179. Although the expert claimed his method was accurate, the court did not have to accept "opinion evidence that is connected to existing data only by the ipse dixit of the expert". *Id.* [quoting *Gen. Elec. Co. v. Joiner*, 522 U. S. 136, 118 S. Ct. 512, 519 (1997)].

The Texas Supreme Court also determined that the requirement of *Daubert/Robinson* that scientific expert testimony must be reliable apply equally to experienced – based testimony in *Gammill.* The plaintiffs in *Gammill* conceded that the testimony of their mechanical engineer on seat belt design was scientific in nature. *Id.* at 721. It was not "other specialized knowledge" —the category under which most experienced – based testimony generally falls. *Gammill* rejected the argument that expert testimony based on the witness's skill, experience or training must meet the reliability requirements "in a fundamentally different way than scientific testimony". *Id.* at 722.

On the one hand, an exception for evidence based on a witness's skill and experience would easily swallow the rule. ⋯ If that were all Rule 702 required, merely establishing the witness's qualifications would show the relevance and reliability of the testimony every time. On the other hand, there are many instances when the relevance and reliability of an expert witness's testimony *are* shown by the witness's skill and experience. An experienced car mechanic's diagnosis of problems with a car's performance may well be reliable without resort to engineering principles.

Id. (emphasis in original.) The *Gammill* court noted that federal courts have struggled with the application of the Daubert general reliability requirements to experienced – based expert testimony "when the factors enumerated in *Daubert* to be considered in admitting scientific testimony do not fit". 972 S. W. 2d at 722. The court held that the *Daubert/Robinson* factors "cannot always" apply to expert testimony. Id. at 726.

But there must be some basis for the opinion offered to show its reliability. Experience alone may provide a sufficient basis for an expert's testimony in some cases, but it cannot do so in every case. A more experienced expert may offer unreliable opinion, and a lesser experience expert's opinions may have solid footing. The court in discharging its duty as gatekeeper must determine how the reliability of particular testimony is to be assessed. *Id.*

Gammill did not offer any criteria for admitting experienced – based testimony. But in explaining that a court must not blindly accept an expert's claim that his or her experience is a reliable basis for the opinion, the court made some statements that subsequent courts have interpreted as adopting a test for experience – based testimony. The court first quoted from *General Electric Co. v. Joiner*, 522 U. S. 136, 118 S. Ct. 512, 519 (1997) that a court should not accept expert testimony that is connected to the basis of the opinion "only by the ipse dixit of the expert" because there may be "too great an analytical gap between the data and the opinion proffered". *Gammill*, 972 S. W. 2d at 726. The *Gammill* court stated that the Joiner formulation is equally stated by the Havner rule that "it is not so simply because 'an expert says it is so'". *Id.* (quoting *Havner*, 953 S. W. 2d at 712). The point of the two quotes is not that the analytical gap test is the new criteria for experienced – based testimony, but that the court must critically examine claims that experience makes an opinion reliable.

This interpretation is buttressed by the court's approach to examining the reliability of the expert opinion in *Gammill.* It is true that the Texas Supreme Court used the analytical gap test. *Id.* at 727. But the court did not state that this test applied to experience – based expert testimony. Instead, it said the trial court's decision to utilize that test was not an abuse of discretion. *Id.* In reviewing the application of that test, *Gammill* did not look at whether there was an analytical gap between the expert's experience and the expert's opinions. Instead, the court examined whether there was a gap between the expert's observations of the vehicle and the decedent's body.

The interpretation that *Gammill* did not establish a definitive test for experienced – based expert testimony is also supported by a reading of *Joiner* itself. *Joiner* was a toxic tort case involving scientific causation. The analytical gap was between certain scientific articles and the facts in the case, not between the expert's experience and the opinion.

In *Minnesota Mining & Mfg. Co. v. Atterbury*, 978 S. W. 2d 183 (Tex. App. —Texarkana 1998, pet. denied), the court indicated treating physicians may consider their experience, along with other information, in reaching opinions on specific causation, but not in reaching opinions on general causation. A physician may testify regarding specific causation "if the expert based his opinion on an examination (or a review of medical records), his experience, and a broad reading of the literature". *Id.* at 193 (quoting *Kelley*, 957 F. Supp. at 883). A broad reading of the literature requires "the expert to point to specific passages in varied and different sources that are generally accepted as support for his conclusion". *Id.*

Even if these hurdles can be overcome, the treating physician's testimony on specific causation "will be insufficient in the absence of evidence of general causation". Pointing to several studies, rather than to a broad review of the literature, is insufficient.

Clearly, an expert's recitation that he has examined a patient and has done a history of the patient and has concluded that X caused the patient to suffer with Y would not be sufficient to support causation. If the physician explained the exact methodology that he used in arriving at the conclusion, including discussing the exact other causes that have been ruled out and the generally accepted literature that he relied upon in making that conclusion, the differential diagnosis evidence could be sufficient to prove specific causation. Even though some courts have held that differential diagnosis is a valid form of evidence to support general causation, it most likely is not sufficient under current standards promulgated by the Texas Supreme Court. This statement is made based upon what appears to be the court's total reliance on objective evidence and its disdain for any form of subjective analysis.

Id. at 199.

An expert's encounter with former patients constitutes "random experience" that, while perhaps supporting his qualifications, does not form a scientifically reliable basis for an opinion. *Id.* at 200.

Applying these factors, the court found that the testimony of a neurologist who examined the plaintiff and concluded that the silicone breast implants had caused an atypical multiple sclerosis ("MS") was inadmissible. First, that the temporal proximity of the implants with the MS symptoms was "some evidence of specific causation" but was "no evidence of general causation, in that it is an 'isolated case' and a 'random experience'". *Id.* at 200. The neurologist's reliance on an abstract did not support his opinion since he did not know its methodology, rate of error or "the effects of population variation". *Id.* His general experience with other patients was no evidence of causation because it is "random experience". *Id.* His reliance on animal studies was also insufficient since he did not name the studies or their results or provide any information about their methodologies.

A second neurologist who personally conducted and published a study on the rate of MS in 156 patients with implants also gave unreliable causation testimony. His study was "unstructured", was not based on formal epidemiological methods, and only stood for the proposition that further research was needed. He also did not testify concerning a rate of error or effect of population bias in his study. *Id.* at 201.

Finally, the *Atterbury* court found that a treating osteopathic rheumatologist's testimony was insufficient. The physician could not meet the *Daubert/Robinson* factors: he did not identify any testing, his opinion was entirely subjective, and he did not provide a rate of error. *Id.* at 202. The court was also troubled that the physician gave deposition testimony on causation that was contrary to his trial causation testimony. It is not clear whether, or how, this difficulty fits into the *Daubert/Robinson* analysis, but other courts have also found discrepancies between an expert's deposition and trial testimony to be an indicia of unreliability. The court further observed that the physician's opinion had never been published or subjected to peer review. Some would criticize an evaluation of this factor for treating physicians since many do not publish the results of their treatment of patients. If, however, the results are contrary to accepted medicine or support a controversial medical theory, the lack of publication is a factor indicating lack of reliability.

The court also noted that the treating physician's theory had not been generally accepted in the medical community. It appears that such an analysis is improper since *Daubert* and *Robinson* both caution courts to examine only the expert's methodology, not his conclusions. The methodology, as the court itself recognized later, was the "widely accepted" methodology used in the medical community of an examination and differential diagnosis. A more accurate way of stating the problem is that the generally accepted methodology (differential diagnosis) was not shown to be reliable for this particular condition. *See Kumho Tire*, 119 S. Ct. at 1177, 1178 (the application of an expert's methodology presents the specific question of the case to the court, rather than the general issue of the reliability of the methodology); *Black v. Food Lion, Inc.*, 171 F. 3d 308, 314 (5th Cir. 1999) (general methodologies such as differential diagnosis must "*be applied fact-specifically in each case*" and acceptance of a differential diagnosis to establish causation was based upon "a standard of meaninglessly high generality rather than boring in on the precise state of scientific knowledge in this case".).

The *Atterbury* court concluded:

"[W]ith regard to breast implants there is no generally accepted criteria by which doctors can link injuries and illness to implants. When his testimony is read in total, it is wholly devoid of any objective criteria by which a jury could reasonably conclude that breast implants cause any of the plaintiffs' injuries or illnesses in general. [The physician] relies upon subjective evidence such as uncontrolled case studies, unnamed articles and literature, nonspecific past experience, and differential diagnosis. These vague bases are insufficient."

Id. at 202.

In *Rehabilitative Care Sys. of Am. v. Davis*, 43 S. W. 3d 649 (Tex. App.—Texarkana 2001), *pet. denied*, 73 S. W. 3d 233 (Tex. 2002), a physician was permitted to testify that a plaintiff aggravated an existing injury in a subsequent accident based on the patient's history, the plaintiff's subjective description of the changes in the pain and differences between MRIs before and after the second accident. The defendant argued that the plaintiff failed to satisfy his burden to show that his current ailments were caused by the injury from the rehabilitation rather than from the underlying original injury. The court of appeals noted that the plaintiff must show a "reasonable probability of a causal connection between the allegedly negligent act and the present injury." *Id.* at 660. "An expert may appropriately testify concerning possible causes of a plaintiff's condition in order to assist the jury in evaluating other evidence of causation. However, a *possible* cause becomes *probable* only when in the absence of other reasonable causal explanations it becomes more likely than not that the injury was a result of its actions". *Id.* at 661. A jury can find causation when①general experience and common sense will enable a layperson to fairly determine the causal connection; ②expert testimony establishes a traceable chain of causation from the injuries back to the event; or③a probable cause nexus is shown by expert testimony. *Id.* at 661. If the expert testimony only establishes a possibility instead of a probability, "the evidence is not legally sufficient". *Id.* However, "reasonable medical probability" can be based on the evidence as a whole, and it is not absolutely necessary that an expert couch his or her opinion in terms of "reasonable medical probability". *Id.*

The appellate court accepted the testimony of the plaintiff's physician establishing causation even though he could not testify about the facts of the incident, noting that he was testifying as an expert and not as a fact witness. *Id.* at 663. The expert "did say that, to a reasonable medical probability, if the incident occurred as related to him by [the plaintiff], it could have caused the torn rotator cuff that he observed prior to and during the second surgery". *Id.* The doctor's acknowledgement that the injury may have existed before the second accident but was not picked up by an MRI went to the weight of the evidence rather than its admissibility.

In *JC Penney Life Ins. Co. v. Baker*, 33 S. W. 3d 417 (Tex. App. —Fort Worth 2000, no pet.), the court found that a physician's causation testimony was reliable based on his experience. The defendant argued that the plaintiff was not killed by an automobile accident, but rather was killed by a pre – existing cardiac problem. The medical examiner agreed that a cardiac problem was the cause of death, but was not certain whether the heart problem occurred before or after the accident. An internist testifying for the plaintiff said the heart problem did not cause the accident. The court held that his opinion was based largely on experience, and was admissible because there was no analytical gap in his analysis. *But see Purina Mills v. Odell*, 948 S. W. 2d 927, 939, (holding that veterinarian's personal experience from examining and diagnosis specific cows did not show reliability of causation opinion).

The Texas Supreme Court in *Mack Trucks v. Tamez*, 206 S. W. 3d 572 (Tex. 2006) makes it clear that it is an oversimplification to argue that the analytical gap test (or connective reliability test) applies in lieu of *Robinson* factors to experience – based testimony. The *Tamez* court stated that *Gammill* is not intended "to imply that a trial court should never consider the *Robinson* factors when evaluating the reliability of expert testimony that is based on knowledge, training or experience" We recognized that the criteria for assessing reliability must vary depending on the nature of the evidence. *Id.* at 579. But the court also reiterated that courts should use a flexible approach for evaluating expert testimony that examines "which factors and evaluation methodology are most appropriate to apply". *Id. See also Ford Motor Co. v. Ledesma*, 242 S. W. 3d 32, 24 (Tex. 2007).

The Court in *Whirlpool v. Camcho*, held that experience cannot serve as a trump card to insulate an expert's testimony from any reliability inquiry other than the analytical gap test lest an expert simply fill gaps in the testimony with almost any type of data or subjective opinions. 298 S. W. 3d at 639. Therefore, even when the testimony is based on the expert's experience, other reliability factors should also be considered. *Id.* In most cases, a court examining reliability should consider both the *Robinson* factors and the expert's experience. *Id.* at 638. "This is not one of the few cases in which appellate review of expert evidence should be limited to either an analysis focused solely on *Robinson* – like factors or solely on a an analytical gap test." *Id.* Experience cannot trump the other reliability criteria because it would otherwise insulate expert opinions from meaningful reliability review. *See Id. l*, at 639. Moreover, a reliability test that turns exclusively on qualifications conflates reliability and qualifications. Thus, an expert challenge may implicate both the *Robinson* – type factors and the analytical gap test. *Id.*

In *Goodyear Tire & Rubber Co. v. Rios*, 143 S. W. 3d 107 (Tex. App. —San Antonio 2004, pet. denied), a tire products liability case, the trial court erred in admitting the testimony of Robert Ochs that a manufacturing defect existed in a Goodyear tire. The court first noted that although experience may provide a sufficient basis for an expert's testimony in some cases, it does not do so in every case. Ochs methodology of using a visual/tactile inspection to conclude that a manufacturing defect was present was not shown to be used by any other experts in the field when there were steel wires in the tire with little to no rubber coverage. The expert's methodology did not demonstrate that a manufacturing defect existed as opposed to a defect caused by abuse of the tire. The expert did not refer to any article or publication that supported his methodology under these conditions.

3. *Supporting literature should be in the record*

For example, in *Minnesota Mining & Mfg. Co. v. Atterbury*, 978 S. W. 2d 183, 198 (Tex. App. —Texarkana 1998, pet. denied). The court held that the burden to show the reliability of epidemiological evidence requires the offering party to "identify the study, get it admitted into evidence, and explain how the methodology of the study is scientifically reliable". "An error in any of the preceding steps will likely result in the study not being considered by a reviewing court." *Id.* In addition to summarizing the factors that will make an epidemiological study unreliable, the court also summarized *Havner* as identifying other evidence that is also unreliable:

"Abstracts that reanalyze other epidemiological evidence and that do not state the methodologies used, specifically the significance level, the confidence level, and the choice of the control group, will not be considered.... [*I*] *n vivo* animal studies that have questionable dosage levels may not be considered. Further, *in vitro* animal studies may not be considered where the expert does not explain how he based his conclusions on humans from the animal study. The court seems unimpressed with animal studies altogether; thus, it would be fair to say that animal studies, standing alone, are not likely to support a finding of causation."

Id. at 199.

In *Green v. State*, 55 S. W. 3d 633, 640 (Tex. App. —Tyler 2001, pet. ref'd), the court of appeals held that the expert properly stuck an expert when the expert did not identify literature that supported opinion. Other courts have also noted an expert's failure to provide a source relied upon by the expert. On cross - examination, the expert identified three authorities but did not state that he relied upon those authorities. After the court's exclusion, the plaintiff offered pages from four textbooks, but did not identify the title or author of the textbook and did not provide evidence that his expert relied on these authorities. *See also In re Elamex, S. A. de C. V.*, No. 08 - 11 - 00110 - CV, 2012 WL 1529937 (Tex. App. —El Paso May 2, 2012, no pet. h.) (original proceeding). (A trial court ruling on a motion to dismiss could not rely on an expert's affidavit on the ownership of property because the affidavit contained unsupported assumptions; the expert's affidavit never stated that the expert reviewed and relied on specific documents that may have supported his conclusion, and the documents were not in evidence, and therefore there was no way to corroborate the expert's assertions;) *In re J. B.*, 93 S. W. 3d 609 (Tex. App. —Waco 2002, no pet. h.); *Frias v. Atlantic Richfield Co.*, 104 S. W. 3d 925 (Tex. App. —Houston [14th Dist.] 2003, pet. denied). In *Frias*, the employee claimed he was exposed to benzene which caused aplastic anemia. The court held that the plaintiff's expert did not show general causation because his affidavit referred to unspecified studies, did not indicate whether the studies had a certain time period for the exposure, did not address the confidence level of the studies and did not attach the studies. The affidavit because it used "abstract characterizations" regarding the level and length of exposure. The use of indefinite terms to describe the exposure was "subject to wide variance and thus largely open to speculation."

4. *The opinion must not be contrary to the undisputed facts*

The expert's opinion must not be contrary to the known, undisputed facts. *Brown, Eight Gates*, 36 Hous. L. Rev. at 871; *Whirlpool Corp. v. Camacho*, 298 S. W. 3d 631, 637 (Tex. 2009). "If an expert's opinion is based on certain assumptions about the facts, we cannot disregard evidence showing those facts are unfounded." *City of Keller v. Wilson*, 168 S. W. 3d 802, 813 (Tex. 2005). *See also Brinker v. Evans*, 07 - 11 - 0044 - CV, 2012 WL 1430367 (Tex. App. —Amarillo Apr. 25, 2012, no pet. h.). (Holding that the trial court did not abuse its discretion in excluding a soil engineer's testimony on the cause of an automobile leaving the roadway. The expert acknowledged that his opinion was based on a "number of assumptions" based on his interpretation of photographs because no soil studies were performed. He also conceded that his "findings cannot be conclusive unless detailed soil testing and slope stabilty analysis are done.") *Pilgrim's Pride Corp. v. Smoak*, 134 S. W. 3d 880, 899 - 900 (Tex. App. —Texarkana 2004, pet. denied) (holding that expert could rely on 6 - 7 weeks of post -

injury earnings to determine pre – injury earning capacity because proof of earning capacity is uncertain and left to jury and facts or assumptions relied on must be undisputedly wrong or erroneous in order to constitute no – evidence) ; *Gen. Motors Corp. v. Harper*, 61 S. W. 3d 118 (Tex. App. —Eastland 2001, pet denied) ; *Capital Metro. Transp. Auth. v. Cent. of Tenn. Ry. and Navigation Co. , Inc.* , 114 S. W. 3d 573 (Tex. App. —Austin 2003, pet. denied) (holding that party could challenge expert opinion in post – verdict motion based on unsupported assumption).

An expert's use of inferences from the factual record does not necessarily create an unreliable opinion. *See Harris v. Belue*, 974 S. W. 2d 386 (Tex. App. —Tyler 1998, pet. denied). The physician – expert in *Harris* did not rely on false assumptions regarding the events that occurred during the surgery in question. He used "simple deductive reasoning" to determine the events. *Id.* at 392. That reasoning process is not subject to a *Robinson* challenge. *Id.* Of course, if the expert builds inferences upon inferences, it is possible that the testimony could become unreliable.

5. *The sources relied upon must, in fact, support the opinion*

The sources relied upon by the expert must in fact support the opinion. Brown, *Eight Gates*, 36 Hous. L. Rev. at 812, 868 – 74. It is important to verify that the study or data actually says what the expert says it does. For example, in *Conde v. Velsicol Chemical Corp.* , the basis of the opinion did not in fact support the opinion. 24 F. 3d 809 (6th Cir. 1994). The plaintiffs offered the expert testimony of several non – medical doctors and a family practitioner to prove causation between the plaintiff's injuries and the use of a termiticide containing chlordane. The court found that the scientific literature relied upon by the doctors did not, however, support their conclusions. *Id.* at 813 – 14. "Their theories are inconsistent with the negative chlordane test results on the plaintiffs' tissue and the vast majority of the relevant, peer – reviewed scientific literature. " *Id.* at 814; *see also Burroughs Wellcome Co. v. Crye*, 907 S. W. 2d 497 (Tex. 1995) (concluding that the jury's causation finding was legally insufficient because the plaintiff's physician had relied on assumed facts, which were contrary to the undisputed facts in the record).

An expert must "answer why a study is reliable". *In re Allied Chem. Corp.* , 227 S. W. 3d 652, 656 (Tex. 2007). And in a toxic tort case, the expert must show "how the plaintiff's exposure is similar to that of the study's subjects". *Id.*

6. *The opinion must not be conclusory*

The expert opinion must not be conclusory; the expert must disclose the basis of the opinion, at least when the opinion is challenged. *See* Brown, *Eight Gates*, 36 Hous. L. Rev. at 823 – 26. "A jury verdict cannot rest solely on an expert's bottom line conclusion, without some underlying facts and reasons, or a logical inferential process to support the expert's opinion. " *Sullivan v. National Football League*, 34 F. 3d 1091, 1105 (1st Cir. 1994). Mere conclusions, without a "hint of an inferential process", are useless to the court. *Zamecnik v. Indian Prairie Sch. Dist. No.* 204, 636 F. 3d 874 (7th Cir. 2011).

· *Damian v. Bell Helicopter Textron Inc.* , No. 02 – 08 – 00210 – CV, 2011 WL 3836464 (Tex. App. —Fort Worth Aug. 31, 2011). In this products liability action, the court of appeals held that the expert's testimony regarding alternative safer helicopter windshield design was conclusory, speculative, and no evidence and therefore reversed the jury verdict.

Initially, although a trial court's ruling on the reliability of an expert's opinion testimony is generally reviewed for an abuse of discretion, a party may assert on appeal … that the unreliability of an expert's opinion makes it legally insufficient to support the verdict. This review "encompasses the entire record, including contrary evidence tending to show the expert opinion is incompetent or unreliable". *Id.* at *15. The court also noted that the defendant's pretrial motion to strike an expert's testimony preserved a reliability challenge to the testimony.

Turning to the merits, the court stated that the conclusory and speculative nature of the testimony was "illustrated by the testimony of other experts in the case and other parts of [the expert's] testimony". *Id.* at *18. The expert "did not evaluate the impact of his proposal for an alternate design on the rest of the [helicopter's] structural design". *Id.* at *19. Although the expert "testified that his opinions are based on basic engineering principles, he never explained how those principles or any tests or publications supported his opinion". *Id.* at *20. The court also relied on the absence of any testing by the expert. The plaintiffs argued, based on *General Motors Corp. v. Sanchez*, 997 S. W. 2d 584, 592 (Tex. 1999), that "there is no requirement that a plaintiff actually design or build or test the alternative". The court found *Sanchez* "distinguishable. The *Sanchez* Court's statement about testing related to a plaintiff's burden to show the existence of a safer alternative design and did not concern the *Robinson* factors or their application to the reliability of the expert's opinion testimony. " Indeed, G. M. failed in that case to preserve its challenge to the reliability of the expert's testimony. Unlike in *Sanchez* [the defendant here] preserved" its reliability challenge. *Id.* at *21.

· *Elizondo v. Krist*, 338 S. W. 3d 17 (Tex. App. —Houston [14th Dist.] 2010, pet. filed). In this legal malpractice action arising out of a settlement in the BP litigation, the trial court did not err by striking the affidavit of the plaintiff's expert witness on the value of a settlement. The expert testified that the plaintiff's underlying case was worth MYM2 to MYM3 million instead of the 50, 000 that the plaintiffs accepted. The expert listed specific criteria BP "focused on" when determining settlement values, but offered "no analysis to explain how these factors would be applied" to these plaintiffs. *Id.* at 21 – 22. He also did not link settlement amounts to specific injuries and circumstances, and provides no comparison of settlement amounts of similar claims. Therefore his affidavit contained "only conclusory and speculative opinions". *Id.* at 22.

· *Pink v. Goodyear Tire & Rubber Co.* , 324 S. W. 3d 290 (Tex. App. —Beaumont 2010, pet. filed). In this toxic tort lawsuit arising out of a plant workers' claim that benzene exposure caused his renal cell carcinoma, the trial court improperly granted summary judgment because an oncologist's causation opinion was not conclusory and the trial court did not rule on the reliability of the opinion. The expert stated that his opinion was based on his review of the plaintiff's medical records, the deposition testimony of four witnesses on the use of benzene in the plant, the deposition of another physician, and "scientific literature". The court concluded that the opinion was not conclusory.

Although the oncologist's affidavit does not itself disclose the specific scientific literature the oncologist consulted, and does not identify what the literature states, the implicit assertion is that the scientific literature reviewed supports his opinion.

Id. at 298. The court indicated that reliance on unspecified scientific literature was permissible under Rule 705 (a) in part because the trial court had not entered "any ruling requiring disclosure of the scientific literature or benzene exposure evidence on which the treating oncologist relied". Rule 705 (a) does not require the treating oncologist to introduce into evidence the underlying facts or data "unless the opposing party or the court insists". *Id.*

· *Paradigm Oil, Inc. v. Retamco Operating, Inc.*, 242 S. W. 3d 67, 72 (Tex. App.—San Antonio 2007, pet. denied). In this no-answer default judgment case, the court concluded that the landsman's testimony of over MYM5 million in damages was speculative and conclusory and therefore no evidence. The landman testified he was retained to review the 1984 purchase agreement, examine the leases sold under the agreement, ascertain if Retamco had been properly paid, and determine whether Retamco was entitled to further interests in wells pursuant to the agreement. His damages opinion was based on his own experience, his review of data relevant to the case, and his consultation with a petroleum engineer. He testified that he determined, but did not identify in court, the relevant leases for his calculations. *Id.* at 73. The court recognized that Rules of Evidence 704 and 705 permit an expert to give opinions without disclosing any underlying facts or data, but nevertheless found the testimony conclusory. *Id.* at 74.

The expert, did no more than identify the general types of information he reviewed and relied upon, give an incomplete summary of the procedure he followed to make his calculations, and render a conclusory opinion on the amount of damages. Although the evidence shows [the expert] examined facts and data that would be appropriate to consider in calculating damages, he failed to specifically identify any of the facts, failed to provide any of the data, failed to explain how the facts and data affected his calculations, and failed to show any of his calculations. *Id.* at 74-75.

· *Schronk v. City of Burleson*, No. 10-07-00399-CV, 2009 WL 2215081 (Tex. App.—Waco July 22, 2009, pet. filed). An expert's affidavit testimony that his opinions were "based upon information provided by the Plaintiff and my knowledge and expertise with medical devices, the medical industry, and FDA Rules and Regulations" was not, within its context conclusory. Although the statement "standing alone …probably would be insufficient", the reminder of his 15-page affidavit explained the basis for his opinion. *Id.* at *9.

7. *The expert's assumptions must be supported*

The assumptions of the expert must be assumptions the expert can vouch for or that are supported by the evidence. "If an expert's opinion is based on certain assumptions about the facts, we cannot disregard evidence showing those assumptions were unfounded." Brown, *Eight Gates*, 36 Hous. L. Rev. at 868 - 74. "If an expert's opinion is based on certain assumptions about the facts, we cannot disregard evidence showing those assumptions were unfounded." *City of Keller v. Wilson*, 168 S. W. 3d 802 (Tex. 2005). *See also Gen. Motors Corp. v. Harper*, 61 S. W. 3d 118, 130 (Tex. App. —Eastland 2001, pet. denied) (noting that expert's opinion "was based on an assumption that was rebutted by the evidence"); *Houston Mercantile Exch. Corp. v. Dailey Petroleum Corp.*, 930 S. W. 2d 242, 243 (Tex. App. —Houston [14th Dist.] 1996, no writ) "[a] n expert's opinion which is based on assumed facts that vary materially from the actual, undisputed facts is without probative value"); *Sipes v. Gen. Motors Corp.*, 946 S. W. 2d 143, 154 (Tex. App. —Texarkana 1997, writ denied) ("the expert's opinion must rely on the proven facts shown in the case on trial").

When an expert uses "simple deductive reasoning," and not assumptions, the expert is not subject to a *Robinson* challenge. *Harris v. Belue*, 974 S. W. 2d 386 (Tex. App. —Tyler 1998, pet. denied). In *Harris v. Belue*, the Tyler Court of Appeals held that the trial court abused its discretion in excluding expert testimony that the defendant surgeon fired an errant staple causing the obstruction of patient's small bowel. The expert applied his medical knowledge and experience in the use of a stapler in the same procedure and concluded, through simple deductive reasoning and not by relying on false assumptions, that there was no other way the staple could have got into patient's bowel wall without being fired into that location.

In contrast, when an expert relies solely on unsupported assumptions to reach his opinions, his opinions are inadmissible. *Rayon v. Energy Specialties, Inc.*, 121 S. W. 3d 7 (Tex. App. —Fort Worth 2002, no pet.). In *Rayon*, the plaintiffs' new home was damaged by a fire that originated in their fireplace. While fighting the fire, firefighters tore apart the wall surrounding the firebox, which caused insulation to scatter throughout the room, firebox, and house. The plaintiffs' expert found ashes on top of the firebox, but did not test them or take any steps to find out the type of material the ashes once were. He did not find any insulation on top of the firebox. Yet, he authored a report that "surmised" the insulation found around the firebox had been there when the fire started, instead of having fallen there after the fire started or when the firefighters and inspectors tore out the sheetrock, insulation, flue assembly, and chimney cap. The expert also concluded that, "that the ashes on top of the firebox were actually from insulation that 'someone' placed on top of the firebox at some point before the fire started; that the insulation on top of the firebox impeded the ventilation around the area where the flue connects to the top of the firebox; that the impeded airflow caused the area behind the firebox to become so heated that it caused the ventilation - blocking piece of insulation to catch fire; and that the ignited ventilation - blocking piece of insulation caused the wooden studs near the firebox to catch on fire". In his deposition, however, the expert conceded that he took no samples of the ashes on top of the firebox and did not know whether it was insulation. The trial court had granted Energy Specialties summary judgment. The appellate court agreed with that ruling, concluding that the expert's testimony was not more than a scintilla of evidence. In support of its ruling, the court pointed out that the expert's use of compound inferences was "insufficient to prove causation", and that the plaintiffs could not "establish a vital fact by piling one inference upon another".

In *Scott's Marina at Lake Grapevine Ltd. v. Brown*, 07 – 10 – 00277 – CV, 2012 WL 177970 (Tex. App. —Amarillo Jan. 23, 2012, no pet.), the assumption was supported by the record. A marina employee developed enteroviral meningitis and Lemierre's Syndrome after cleaning a substance from a hub drain at work. He asserted that the spillage was sewage containing human feces, and that this exposure caused his illnesses. Plaintiff's expert, a leading expert in the field of anaerobic infectious disease, opined that his workplace exposure proximately caused his illnesses. The marina challenged the expert's assumption that the employee was exposed to sewage containing human feces. The court of appeals held that "there was sufficient evidence" to support this assumption.

8. *Interesting or recent cases on Foundational Reliability*

Federal Courts

- *Clark v. Kellogg Brown & Root, L. L. C.*, 414 Fed. Appx. 623, 628 (5th Cir. 2011). In this Jones Act claim arising from benzene exposure that allegedly caused ACL, the court held that the evidence was sufficient to raise a fact issue on specific causation. The Fifth Circuit noted that the burden of proof in a Jones Act case is producing cause rather than proximate cause and is "featherweight". *Id.* at 626. General causation was established by "undisputed literature". *Id.* at 628. The court rejected KBR's contention that the plaintiff was "required to quantify precisely the dosage of benzene that is hazardous and the dosage of benzene to which [the plaintiff] was exposed. *Id.* at 629. The plaintiff satisfied his burden of proof by presenting evidence that he was exposed to *some* level of benzene high enough to cause AML". *Id.*; *LeBlanc ex rel. Estate of LeBlanc v. Chevron USA, Inc.*, 396 Fed. Appx. 94 (5th Cir. 2010). In this toxic tort claim, the court held that an hematologist's opinion that exposure to benzene caused myelofibrosis with myeloid metaplasia (MMM) was not sufficiently reliable. The hematologist relied on both epidemiological studies and his "clinical experience" to prove general causation, but the court found that neither was sufficient. *Id.* at 98. His reliance on the studies suffered "from common deficiencies", including the studies' lack of statistically significant results and studies express disclaimer of the causal connection claimed by the expert. *Id.*

The physician's clinical experience also did not provide reliable grounds for his opinion that benzene causes myelofibrosis in the absence of showing "some demonstrable and reliable basis in underlying facts" from that experience. *Id.* at 100. His clinical observations of myelofibrosis patients, "without more, give no basis for an expert opinion as to the general causal connection between myelofibrosis and benzene—it is not a question as to which clinical experience is likely to provide insight". *Id.* at 101. The question of whether benzene causes myelofibrosis "requires an epidemiological, scientific basis" and "is not a question as to which a clinician's firsthand observation of patients offers much insight". *Id.*

· *Norwood v. Raytheon Co.*, 2009 WL 677474 (W. D. Tex. Mar. 11, 2009). This product liability case arose from injuries that allegedly resulted from exposure to ionizing radiation from the defendant's HAWK weapons system. The trial court granted the defendant's motion to exclude plaintiffs' radiation dose expert who had reconstructed the plaintiffs' alleged potential radiation exposure. The expert's opinions were not based upon sufficient facts or data to justify his conclusions. In addition, the dose estimation methods were based on assumptions that were contradicted by the facts.

· *Galvan v. City of San Antonio*, 2008 U. S. Dist. LEXIS 26269, 2008 WL 5504697 (W. D. Tex. Sept. 17, 2008). In this wrongful death claim, the defendant sought to exclude an opinion from the plaintiff's expert, an economist, on the decedent's future earning capacity. The defendant contended that the opinion was not supported by sufficient factual data on the decedent's work history and past earnings. The trial court denied the defendant's motion explaining that even though some gaps existed in the documentation, the economist reviewed 12 years of employment records and the surviving widow's testimony concerning the decedent's earnings. The economist also utilized data from the U. S. Department of Labor and the Census Bureau relating to life expectancy and work life expectancy. Thus, the economist had sufficient facts on which to form his opinions on the decedent's earning capacity.

· *Lilley v. Home Depot U. S. A., Inc.*, 567 F. Supp. 2d 953 (S. D. Tex. 2008). In a personal injury case resulting from a plaintiff's claims that a boxed, hot water heater fell on him in a retail store, the defendant moved to exclude the plaintiff's testifying physician. The defendant specifically complained that the physician did not review all the plaintiff's medical records, relied solely on what the plaintiff told him, and thus lacked an adequate foundation to form an opinion on causation. The physician had not been provided with all the plaintiff's medical records until his deposition, but he remained resolute in his opinions despite being presented with additional medical records. The district court allowed the physician to testify. The court reasoned that the physician's lack of knowledge as to the plaintiff's history of previous injuries did not make his opinion about the causation of the plaintiff's back condition inadmissible.

· *Larson v. Matter*, 2008 U. S. Dist. LEXIS 63432 (N. D. Texas 2008). In this medical malpractice case against a cardiovascular surgeon for failure to recognize ill effects of using heparin as an anti – coagulant. The plaintiff offered a hematologist and a general surgeon to testify about causation. The defendant moved to exclude these opinions on the grounds that they were not supported by literature, articles, or other studies and didn't rule out the possibility that the plaintiff would have suffered the same injuries in the absence of the alleged negligence. The trial court held that both physicians would be allowed to testify regarding causation. The court specifically noted that the personal professional experience of both physicians constituted sufficiently reliable foundations for their expert opinions and the most appropriate way to attack those opinions would be through cross – examination.

· *24/7 Records, Inc. v. Sony Music Entm't, Inc.*, 514 F. Supp. 2d 571 (S. D. N. Y. 2007). A music producer brought suit against distributors alleging breach of record distribution contracts, tortious interference, and unfair competition. The defendant moved to exclude two experts on damages. The court concluded that the plaintiff's valuation experts relied only on instinct and a subjective "intrinsic value" analysis. The first of plaintiff's two experts was a CEO and owner of a management consulting firm specializing in startup music companies and had about 40 years in the music industry. He was not, however, licensed by any organization as a qualified appraiser, had no formal accounting or valuation training, and had never read any materials on valuation. The other expert was an attorney and consultant in the music industry, but was not licensed by any organization as a qualified appraiser, nor did he have any experience or training in business valuation. None of their opinion testimony about the value of the company had any supporting documentation or analysis of cash flow, and no explanation could be given as to their opinions about the "intrinsic value" of the company. Since these experts' assertions were without proof ("ipse dixit"), the court concluded that neither expert's testimony was admissible.

· *Curtis v. M&S Petroleum, Inc.*, 174 F. 3d 661 (5th Cir. 1999). In this toxic tort case, refinery workers sued various defendants for numerous health problems allegedly caused by exposure to benzene. The district court excluded the causation testimony of an industrial hygienist as unreliable because it failed to indicate with sufficient certainty the level of the plaintiff's benzene exposure. Additionally, the court excluded the evidence because the expert did not perform a differential diagnosis and thus, exclude other possible causes.

· *Watkins v. Telsmith*, 121 F. 3d 984, 992 (5th Cir. 1997), the Fifth Circuit demanded proof of specific instances of similar experiences and would not accept vague recollections by the expert. The court agreed that a lack of testing of the proposed alternatives is not determinative, but is a factor in assessing reliability. *Id. Watkins* looked at a number of other factors, many of which fit within the *Kumho Tire's* general reliability test of whether the expert follows the same standards of intellectual rigor as are used in the field for non – litigation purposes. *See id.* at 992 – 93 (discussing such factors as the lack of detail in the expert's testimony and the failure of the expert to make any drawings or perform calculations that would support his testimony). Thus, "just conceptualizing possibilities", as occurred in *Watkins*, would be insufficient. *See id.* at 992. Experience by itself could not demonstrate reliability; "it seems exactly backwards that experts who purport to rely on general engineering principles and practical experience might escape screening by the district court simply by stating that their conclusions were not reached by any particular method or technique. The moral of this approach would be, the less factual support for an expert's opinion, the better." Similarly, the failure of the expert in *Watkins* to investigate whether similar products use a safety device was contrary to good engineering practices. *See id.*

Texas Courts

· *Merck & Co., Inc. v. Garza*, 347 S. W. 3d 256 (Tex. 2011). In this wrongful death case against a pharmaceutical company by a 71 – year old man with a long – history of cardiac problems who suffered a myocardial infarction after using Vioxx for 25 days, the Court reiterated the necessity of satisfying *Havner*'s epidemiological requirements in order to provide scientifically reliable evidence of causation. The Court rejected the court of appeals' interpretation of Havner that relied on some arguably inconsistent language in Havner in concluding that *Havner* did not "establish such a bright – line test for causation" but mandated that the sufficiency of the evidence be determined from its totality.

First, the Court held that causation was not demonstrated based on data compiled in Merck – sponsored clinical trials of Vioxx. Although "the controlled, experimental, and prospective nature of clinical trials undoubtedly make them more reliable than" the retroactive, observational studies rejected in *Havner*, any study "must show a statistically significant doubling of the risk in order to be some evidence that a drug more likely than not caused a particular injury". *Id.* at 263.

The Court held that a two – prong inquiry applies for evaluating the scientific reliability of epidemiological evidence. The first requirement is that the plaintiff must present epidemiological evidence demonstrating "a statistically significant doubling of the risk". As part of this threshold inquiry, a plaintiff must show "that he or she is similar to [the subjects] in the studies" and that "other plausible causes of the injury or condition that could be negated [are excluded] with reasonable certainty". *Id.* at 265.

In addition to these threshold reliability requirements, sound methodology still necessitates that courts examine the design and execution of epidemiological studies using factors like the Bradford Hill criteria to reveal any biases that might have skewed the results of a study, and to ensure that the standards of reliability are met in at least two properly designed studies. Thus, a plaintiff must first pass the primary reliability inquiry by meeting *Havner*'s threshold requirements of general causation. Then, courts must conduct the secondary reliability inquiry that examines the soundness of a study's findings using the totality of the evidence test. *Id.* at 266.

The Court held that the plaintiffs could not meet these requirements. The first study did not meet the initial threshold requirement because it involved patients who used Vioxx for a longer period of time than the plaintiff and at double the dosage of that taken by the plaintiff. Therefore, its "finding of an increased risk does not necessarily mean that there is no increased risk at a lower dose and smaller duration". *Id.* A second study, a meta – analysis of the Merck clinical trials, also did not demonstrate causation. "[A]s meta – analysis, it combines the results of a number of different studies, with differing dosages, durations, and comparison drugs." *Id.* Another study might arguably have satisfied *Havner*, but it was insufficient because two studies are required. "Another study is still necessary, but lacking here." *Id.* at 267.

Finally, the court rejected the argument that the totality of the evidence can demonstrate causation in the absence of epidemiological evidence: "The totality of the evidence cannot prove general causation if it does not meet the standards for scientific reliability established by *Havner*. A plaintiff cannot prove causation by presenting different types of unreliable evidence." *Id.*

- *BIC Pen Corp. v. Carter*, 346 S. W. 3d 533, 543 (Tex. 2011). In this manufacturing defect case, a young child was severely burned as a result of her five year old brother igniting a child – resistant lighter. The lighter had five child – resistant designed features. During the manufacturing, two of the features had "small deviations" from the specifications. The court also observed that even if the lighter had met all five of the specifications, some young children could still operate the lighter. The plaintiff had to burden to show that the child "would not have operated the lighter but for the manufacturing defects". The Court rejected the plaintiff's contention that the doubling of the risk or "increased relative risk is evidence of causation based on *Havner*. The Court stated that this principle from *Havner* results from the practical difficulties in testing in toxic tort cases. But testing of lighters involved no unreasonable risk of injury to test subject. [T] he nature of the injury – causing activities and testing that would have to be done to show causation in this case are not similar to, nor do they pose the practical difficulties posed by, those we considered in *Havner*". *Id.* "Thus we decline to adopt a *Havner* – type analysis as to causation in this case where manufacturing defects are the basis for the liability claim." *Id.* The testing that was conducted "failed to demonstrate a causal link between lower sparkwheel force and an increased ability of children to operate the lighter."

- *Whirlpool Corp. v. Camacho*, 298 S. W. 3d 631 (Tex. 2009). In this products liability case, testimony from Judd Clayton, an electrical engineer, was the only evidence of a design defect in a clothes dryer's design that a jury found to have caused a fire. However, because the data that Clayton relied on did not support his opinions, the Texas Supreme Court described the opinions as "subjective, conclusory, and ... not entitled to probative weight". Thus, his testimony was no evidence of a design defect. Specifically, the Court noted that Clayton had not explain how testing data supported his theory that lint particles could have reached the clothes in the drum and ignited them. Moreover, the only test on which he did rely did not support his opinions. And the other *Robinson* factors do not help establish the reliability of his opinion—it was developed for litigation, was not subject to peer review, and had not been published. *Id.* at 643. Finally, the facts that the expert relied on were consistent with an entirely different theory as to the cause of the fire.

- *In re Global Santa Fe Corp.*, 275 S. W. 3d 477 (Tex. 2008). In this mandamus proceeding the court concluded that Chapter 90 of the Texas Civil Practices and Remedies Code governing certain silicone related cases is not preempted by the Jones Act. The Jones Act is not exempt from requirements that a plaintiff must prove through reliable medical evidence that he suffers from a silicone – related disease. Both state and federal law requires expert testimony to be grounded in principles of science. Although the Jones Act establishes a relaxed standard for proving causation, it does not exempt Jones Act cases from the general rules for admission of expert testimony

- *Taber v. Roush*, No. 14 – 08 – 00089 – CV, 2010 Tex. App. LEXIS 4508 (Tex. App. —Houston [14th Dist.] June 17, 2010, no pet.). In this health care liability case, Lauren Taber contended that the opinion testimony from the defendant's expert witnesses (three medical doctors) was inadmissible and unreliable because it was based on controversial medical literature, which claims that an avulsion injury to a newborn's brachial plexus can be caused by the maternal forces of labor, not by excessive traction by the delivering physician on the head and neck of the newborn. Taber's expert witness testified that in "the entire archives of medical literature", he was unaware of any article showing that the type of avulsion injury sustained by Taber's newborn child could have been caused by the natural forces of labor. The majority held that the trial court did not abuse its discretion in allowing defendant's experts to testify. But in a dissenting opinion, Justice Anderson argued that the opinion of defendants' expert witnesses was unreliable because①their opinion was not based on a broad reading of the medical literature and②they did not explain how their natural forces of labor hypothesis and the relevant avulsion injury.

· *DaimlerChrysler Motors Co., LLC v. Manuel*, 362 S. W. 3d 160 (Tex. App. —Fort Worth 2012, no pet.). The plaintiff's economist's estimate of lost profits for a car dealership was sufficiently reliable when the economist relied on the defendant's own sales forecasts. The defendant's challenge to the reliability of the foundational data used by the expert "merge [s] with a legal sufficiency type analysis for lost profits damages". Use of defendant's own forecasts was sufficiently reliable in part because "Chrysler's own national dealer placement manager responsible for placing, planning, and relocating dealerships, testified that planning potential is a common methodology prepared and used by automobile manufacturers". The court also rejected the defendant's contention that the expert's use of data from another dealership was unreliable; the other dealership was sufficiently comparable and that the time period selected did not render the opinion unreliable.

· *Royce Homes, L. P. v. Humphrey*, 244 *S. W.* 3*d* 570 (*T*ex. App. —Beaumont 2008, pet. denied). The plaintiff alleged that Royce Homes had wrongfully diverted surface waters onto the plaintiff's property, which caused flooding and damage. The plaintiff's expert calculated the home's diminished market value based on "flood stigma". Royce Homes objected to the testimony as unreliable because of an analytical gap.

The expert testified that, generally, even a single flood can diminish a home's market value. He based this opinion on his forty – year career in assessing flooded properties. The expert testified about all of the causes of so – called stigma damages and that he had dealt with over a hundred properties that had incurred such damages. He also testified that 23 years of handling housing foreclosures for a bank had provided him with a good working knowledge of what the market will pay for houses that have flooded.

The expert conceded that he did not use comparable homes that had been flooded in calculating the diminished value. Instead, he first determined the home's value as if it had not flooded and then estimated a percentage to deduct for the stigma attributed to the flood. Royce Homes's expert agreed that stigma damages lower a home's value, but asserted that the appropriate appraisal method is to compare sales of property involving the same or similar problem with sales of property that are otherwise similar but without the problem. Royce Homes argued that the plaintiff's expert testimony was unreliable because it was nothing more than speculation and supposition regarding the percentage to be deducted because of any stigma damage.

The appellate court—stating that expert opinions must rely on sufficient data and proper methodology—concluded that the trial court had abused its discretion in allowing the testimony and remanded the case back to the trial court because the plaintiff's expert did not include any data with his report to support the percentage deduction he applied to the home's value.

· *Abraham v. Union Pac. R. Co.*, 233 S. W. 3d 13 (Tex. App. —Houston [14th Dist.] 2007, pet. denied). This toxic tort suit filed under the Federal Employers Liability Act ("FELA") arose out of exposure to creosote used to treat railroad ties. The trial court set a "test plaintiff" for trial. The plaintiff, who had worked loading creosote – treated ties onto railcars, had died due to throat and lung cancer. The trial court struck the plaintiff's causation expert and granted summary judgment in the "trial plaintiff" case and, later, as to all remaining plaintiffs. On appeal, the court analyzed the expert medical evidence as it applied to all plaintiffs, not just the original "test plaintiff". The plaintiffs argued that FELA's relaxed causation burden allowed the trial court to withdraw the causation issue from the jury's consideration only if there was zero probability that any such negligence contributed to the injury of the employee.

The court held that the FELA causation standard and the standards for admission for expert testimony are distinct issues which do not affect each other. The proper focus in such situations was the reliability of the expert's opinion testimony because unreliable expert testimony amounted to "no evidence", and not even FELA's relaxed causation standard can transform "no evidence" into "some evidence".

The court then examined the scientific reliability and legal sufficiency of the plaintiffs' evidence. The plaintiffs' expert relied upon an EPA creosote study to provide descriptions of job categories and corresponding creosote exposure levels. He then used the EPA report to extrapolate the creosote exposures experienced by the plaintiffs in the suit. He did not include any specifics as to his extrapolation methods, and did not take any notes regarding the extrapolations when he performed them.

The expert's chart listed each plaintiff's purported exposure, but failed to include any job category information. Instead, he correlated each plaintiff's alleged creosote exposure to the length of employment at the facility. Because a plaintiff must prove his level of exposure using methods subject to scientific validation, the lack of evidence as to job categories meant the court could not determine whether any plaintiff had creosote exposure levels comparable to those in the EPA study.

The court held that scientific knowledge of the harmful levels of exposure to a chemical plus knowledge that the plaintiffs were exposed to such quantities were the minimum facts necessary to meet the plaintiffs' burden in a toxic tort case. While production of a mathematically precise table equating levels of harm with levels of exposure was not necessary, production of evidence from which a reasonable person could conclude that the exposure probably caused the injuries was necessary. Plaintiffs' lack of evidence of creosote exposures at levels equal to or greater than the exposures in the EPA study proved fatal to their case. The summary judgments were affirmed.

· *American Cas. Co. of Redding, PA v. Zachero*, No. 11 – 07 – 00183 – CV, 2008 WL 5205642 (Tex. App. —Eastland, Dec. 11, 2008, no pet.) (mem. op.). This workers' compensation case arose out of a fall at work. The question was whether her compensable injury included osteoarthritis and chondromalacia in the left knee. The insurer claimed that the employee's osteoarthritis was related to degenerative joint disease and was an ordinary condition of life. The court of appeals held that the employee's treating physician's opinions were reliable because they were based on his review of medical records, his physical examination, and other objective data showing the progression of osteoarthritis and chondromalacia. While the insurer offered the testimony of a physician that conflicted with that of the plaintiff's expert, this did not make those opinions unreliable.

· *Lincoln v. Clark Freight Lines, Inc.*, 285 S. W. 3d 79, (Tex. App. —Houston [1st Dist.] 2009, no pet.). This personal injury lawsuit arose out of an intersection collision. The plaintiffs filed a Daubert motion to prevent a sheriff's deputy from testifying about the cause of the accident. The deputy had worked as an accident reconstructionist for 23 years, attended several schools for accident reconstruction starting in 1988, and had over 1000 hours in accident reconstruction training. The trial court allowed the deputy to testify that the plaintiff's father, who was driving a Ford Mustang caused the accident by running the red light.

Plaintiffs argued that the coefficient of friction value that the deputy calculated was flawed because he did not use a Durometer to compare the Mustang's tires with those that he used on his tests. The deputy admitted that a Durometer would have measured the hardness of the tire's rubber but explained that he did not have one at the time of the accident reconstruction test. He determined the hardness of the tire rubber between the Mustang and the Camaro by eyeballing the tires. By observing the tires on both vehicles, he could tell that the tires were of a soft consistency. He testified that he has done testing previously involving similar tires that were involved in this crash, both on Mustangs and Camaros, and they would yield similar, if not the same, results. He concluded—on the basis of his experience in doing hundreds of tests with vehicles with soft rubber tires, regular passenger cars, and harder truck tires—that drag coefficient for the Camaro would be similar to, if not the same as, the drag coefficient for the Mustang. He chose the Camaro as a testing vehicle because it had soft rubber tires consistent with the wide, slick, soft rubber tires that were on the Mustang. Consequently, while he did not use a Durometer, the deputy was relying on his years of experience in testing the co – efficiency of friction with similar tires and which supplied evidence that the Camaro's drag coefficient would be similar to that of the Mustang. The court concluded the trial court did not err in finding that the expert's testimony was not based on merely subjective belief or unsupported speculation.

· *Arkoma Basin Exploration Co., Inc. v. FMF Assocs. 1990 – A, Ltd.*, 249 S. W. 3d 380 (Tex. 2008). Eight Virginia limited partnerships (the "partnerships") hired Arkoma Basin Exploration Company ("Arkoma") to estimate production from mineral properties in Oklahoma. When the properties failed to produce as predicted, the partnerships sued. Arkoma challenged the legal sufficiency of the damages evidence on appeal. The court concluded that the expert's testimony was legally sufficient. From the record, the court could not say that the expert's opinions were unreliable or speculative, nor were they conclusory as a matter of law. Although the court could not confirm the expert's damage calculations in the absence of foundational data in the record, the expert was not required to introduce such foundational data at trial unless the opposing party or the court insisted.

- *Abilene Ind. Sch. Dist. v. Marks*, 261 S. W. 3d 262 (Tex. App. —Eastland 2008, no pet.). In this workers' compensation case arising out of an injured knee, the employer challenged the trial court's decision to admit the testimony from the claimant's physician about the cause of the plaintiff's injured knee because the physician's causation opinion did not establish a causal link between the accident and the injured knee. *Id.* at 271. The appellate court held that a physician's expert testimony is not unreliable merely because the physician does not review all medical records; instead the scope of the review goes to the weight of the testimony. *Id.* at 272. The court of appeals further explained that the doctor's opinion regarding causation, while different from that of the employer's expert, had a reliable foundation because it was based on the physician's professional experience and review of sufficient medical evidence in the patient's file. *Id.*

- *Wooten v. State*, 267 S. W. 3d 289 (Tex. App. —Houston [14th Dist.] 2008, no pet). In an appeal from a conviction of intoxication manslaughter, the convicted defendant challenged the trial court's decision to admit expert testimony regarding blood testing, drug recognition, and accident reconstruction. The appellate court rejected these arguments and affirmed the conviction.

The appellate court determined the blood testing (which involved separating the blood serum and then performing an enzymatic reaction to detect toxins such as alcohol) was reliable and satisfied the three factors set forth in *Kelly v. State*, 824 S. W. 2d 568, 573 (Tex. Crim. App. 1992).

Regarding the drug recognition expert, the State elicited testimony from an officer trained to detect when an individual is under the influence of marijuana. The officer had taken several training courses (totaling over 152 hours of instruction) to be certified as a drug – recognition expert. Based on his experience and review of the hospital records, the officer testified that the records indicated that the appellant was likely under the influence of marijuana. The court held that the trial court had acted within its discretion in allowing the officer to testify regarding the factors and the likelihood of the defendant being under the influence and disallowing testimony that the defendant was actually under the influence of marijuana.

Finally, the appellate court found no harm in allowing the accident reconstruction expert to testify about the speed of the defendant's vehicle based on his reconstruction of the speed with a drag sled. The defendant argued that the drag sled was not the newest or most reliable instrument to calculate speed, but the appellate court held that the trial court had not erred in allowing the testimony because the officer had performed the test using acceptable methods.

· In *Moore v. Memorial Hermann Hosp. Sys, Inc.*, 140 S. W. 2d 870 (Tex. App. —Houston [14th Dist.] 2004, no pet.) a worker suffered a back injury while pushing a large food cart at a hospital. The plaintiff's workplace safety expert's opined that the hospital was negligent in its selection of patient food carts. But the expert had not personally observed the carts, did not know their size or weight, or how much weight they would carry. The court, therefore, excluded that opinion. The expert also opined that the hospital failed to train its employees on how to operate safely the patient food carts but he had no information concerning the training the injured worker or co – workers had received. Therefore, the court likewise excluded this opinion.

· *Wyndham Int., Inc. v. ACE Am. Ins. Co.*, 186 S. W. 3d 682 (Tex. App. —Dallas 2006, no pet.). Wyndham sued its insurance companies and broker for business income losses at its hotels resulting from the decline in business caused by the 9/11 terrorist attacks. The appellate court upheld the trial court ruling excluding the plaintiff's damages expert. *Id.* at 685. The defendants claimed the expert's testimony did not stand up to scrutiny for a number of reasons, including: ①the expert based his entire calculation on a comparison of monthly forecasts of hotel room revenue; ②the expert extrapolated from the original calculation that related to approximately 60% of the hotels to the remaining 40% of the hotels for which he did not have supporting data; and③he did not account for market factors affecting the hospitality industry in September and October of 2001 but instead concluded that the entire difference between Wyndham's forecast and actual results for the period analyzed was attributable to a covered loss. *Id.* at 686. The court concluded the opinions were based upon an unreliable foundation. The court specifically noted that Wyndham's forecasts "were not prepared pursuant to any company – wide 'hard and fast' rules". *Id.* at 689. Additionally, the court found the August 2001 forecasts used by the expert were flawed; fewer than 1/3 of the August 2001 forecasts for 101 properties were within Wyndham's own accuracy tolerance standard. *Id.* The court so included that the expert's extrapolation of revenue for a large number of properties were drawn from the forecasts and that extrapolated projections premised upon unreliable and flawed forecasts only served to compound the unreliability of the opinion. *Id.* Lastly, the court found the expert's failure to allow for rebookings or any other causes which could have affected Wyndham's profitability other than the terrorist attacks rendered the opinion "little more than speculation". *Id.*

· *Tex. Mut. Ins. Co. v. Lerma*, 143 S. W. 3d 172 (Tex. App. —San Antonio 2004, pet. denied). The family of a worker who died of tetanus in July 1999 claimed the worker contracted tetanus on the job two months earlier from a barbed wire puncture wound. At trial, the plaintiffs' expert testified that tetanus has an incubation period of fourteen days, and admitted he knew of no scientific literature indicating a person could get tetanus more than twenty – one days after being injured. Yet, he also testified that the worker's May injury caused his July death. The physician also admitted that the worker could have contracted tetanus from his "rotten tooth", his diabetes, or "[a] nywhere at all". Given this testimony, the court found that the physician failed to prove that, given within reasonable medical probability, the worker contracted tetanus in May. The expert's opinion was "just an inference of causation amounting to no more than conjecture or speculation".

· *Austin v. Kerr – McGee*, 25 S. W. 3d 280 (Tex. App. —Texarkana 2000, no pet.). In this wrongful death action against the maker of a product containing benzene, the court held that it was not an error to exclude the testimony of plaintiff's experts regarding the medical causation of chronic myelogenous leukemia (CML). The court concluded that the studies relied upon by the expert were insufficient to meet the requirements of *Havner* and *Robinson.*

Additionally, the plaintiff was unable to rule out exposure to radiation as a possible cause of the decedent's cancer.

" [Defendant] contends that [the expert's] conclusion is based on a reliable foundation only if the epidemiological evidence shows a relationship between benzene exposure and CML specifically. We disagree. [The expert's] conclusion may be reliable if it is supported by evidence that shows what [the expert] contends it shows, that there is an association between benzene exposure and the development of all types of leukemia generally. We believe, however, that there must be a sufficient link between benzene exposure and CML specifically, and thus that [the expert] must show further that all types of leukemia are related or interchangeable." *Id* at 288.

· *Hess v. McLean Feedyard, Inc.*, 59 S. W. 3d 679 (Tex. App. —Amarillo 2000, pet. denied). An engineer could not testify that runoff from a feedyard following a downpour caused the water supply on adjoining ranch land to be undrinkable. The expert had not tested the quality of the water before the spill and thus lacked evidence of an essential fact: that the water was potable before the heavy rains that caused the runoff.

· *TWCC v. Lopez*, 21 S. W. 3d 358 (Tex. App. —San Antonio 2000, pet. denied). In this occupational disease case, the court allowed the plaintiff's board – certified pulmonologist to testify that the plaintiff's chronic obstructive pulmonary disease (COPD) was caused by his 20 years of employment as a sandblaster. The court reasoned that the expert pulmonologist provided sufficient proof of general causation, i. e. that the disease, COPD, could be caused by his working conditions. The doctor's opinions were based on his own observations and examination of the plaintiff, his knowledge of the disease and its causes from medical literature, and the plaintiff's medical history. *Id.* at 364.

The court noted that the doctor's general causation opinions were based on two different studies. Both studies included testing and found a relationship between dust and COPD. The studies had confidence levels of 95% and therefore had a low rate of error. The court rejected the argument that a doubling of the risk is always necessary for statistical significance and distinguished *Havner. Id.* at 365. Finally, the court observed that the studies and opinions on the dangers of dust had been used for the non – judicial purpose of improving workers safety. The jury was not bound to accept the normal x – ray since even the defendant's expert conceded that COPD may be present with a normal x – ray.

The *Lopez* court further stated that the doctor's testimony on specific causation did not rely upon the subjective interpretation of the expert, even though the articles discussed gold miners as opposed to sandblasters because the article still stood for "the proposition that small particles (dust, sand, etc.) in a worker's lungs have harmful effects". *Id.* at 365. This extrapolation from gold miners to sandblasters, therefore, did not render the opinion unreliable. Specific causation was supported by evidence of exposure confirmed by numerous witnesses. *Minnesota Mining & Mfg. Co.* v. *Atterbury*, 987 S. W. 2d 183 (Tex. App. —Texarkana 1998, pet. denied). The court held that the burden to show the reliability of epidemiological evidence requires the offering party to "identify the study, get it admitted into evidence, and explain how the methodology of the study is scientifically reliable. An error in any of the preceding steps will likely result in the study not being considered by a reviewing court". *Id.* at 198. In addition to summarizing the factors that will make an epidemiological study unreliable, the court also summarized *Havner* as identifying other evidence that is also unreliable:

"Abstracts that reanalyze other epidemiological evidence and that do not state the methodologies used, specifically the significance level, the confidence level, and the choice of the control group, will not be considered.... [*I*] *n vivo* animal studies that have questionable dosage levels may not be considered. Further, *in vitro* animal studies may not be considered where the expert does not explain how he based his conclusions on humans from the animal study. The court seems unimpressed with animal studies altogether; thus, it would be fair to say that animal studies, standing alone, are not likely to support a finding of causation." *Id.* at 199.

G. The Seventh Gate: Underlying Inadmissible Evidence

Under Rule 703, an expert may give expert opinion based on facts or data not admissible in evidence if they are of a type reasonably relied upon by experts in the expert witness's field. A trial judge must determine ① whether other experts in the field rely upon the facts or data and ② whether such reliance is reasonable. *See* Brown, *Eight Gates*, 36 Hous. L. Rev. at 875 – 79. The reasonable reliance standard under the language of FRE 703 only applies to facts or data that are not admitted or are inadmissible at trial. *Claar v. Burlington Northern R. Co.*, 29 F. 3d 499, 501 (9th Cir. 1994); *Robinson*, 923 S. W. 2d at 563.

The expert's own statements may establish that the inadmissible facts or data are relied upon by other experts in the field. *St. Paul Med. Ctr. v. Cecil*, 842 S. W. 2d 808, 815 (Tex. App. —Dallas 1992, no writ); *Greenwood Utis. Comm'n v. Miss. Power Co.*, 751 F. 2d 1484, 1495 (5th Cir. 1985). Judicial notice may also be taken. *See*, *e. g.*, *Liptak v. Pensabene*, 736 S. W. 2d 953, 957 - 58 (Tex. App. —Tyler 1987, no writ). It is not necessary for the expert to testify specifically that the evidence is of a type relied upon by experts in the field; a trial court may infer this from other evidence in the case, including the expert's use and reliance on the evidence. *Welder v. Welder*, 794 S. W. 2d 420 (Tex. App. —Corpus Christi 1990, no writ.). *See also Moore v. Polis Power Inc.*, 720 S. W. 2d 183, 190 – 92 (Tex. App. —Dallas 1986, writ ref'd n. r. e.) (court reviewed record as a whole to conclude that the data, a test, was of the type reasonably relied upon by experts in the field instead of excluding testimony because the expert did not testify that it was reasonably relied upon in the field).

Courts will critically examine whether the expert's reliance on evidence is reasonable. A trial court "is not bound to accept expert testimony based on questionable data simply because other experts use such data in the field." *United States v. Locascio*, 6 F.3d 924, 938 (2d Cir. 1993) As explained in *Havner*:

The view that courts should not look beyond an averment by the expert that the data underlying his or her opinion are the type of data on which experts reasonably rely has likewise been rejected by other courts. The underlying data should be independently evaluated in determining if the opinion itself is reliable. "If the underlying data are so lacking in probative force and reliability that no reasonable expert could base an opinion on them, an opinion which rests entirely upon them must be excluded."

953 S. W. 2d at 713 [quoting *In Re Agent Orange Liab. Litig.*, 611 F. Supp. 1223, 1245 (E. D. N. Y. 1985), *aff' d*, 818 F. 2d 187 (2d Cir. 1987)] (internal citations omitted). But the examination does not end with a simple in – or – out decision:

If the court chooses to admit the underlying hearsay, the evidence is admissible "only for the limited purposes of identifying the bases of that opinion". Alternatively, the court may permit the expert to identify the type of evidence but preclude the witness from stating the specific inadmissible evidence.

Brown, *Eight Gates*, 36 Hous. L. Rev. at 876 (internal citations omitted).

TRE 705 codifies and clarifies these limitations on the use of an expert as a conduit for hearsay and other inadmissible evidence. TRE 705 (d) provides for a balancing test with limiting instructions:

When the underlying facts or data would be inadmissible in evidence, the court *shall exclude* the underlying facts or data *if* the danger that they will be used for a purpose other than as explanation or support for the expert's opinion outweighs their value as explanation or support or are unfairly prejudicial. If otherwise inadmissible facts or data are disclosed before the jury, a limiting instruction by the court shall be given upon request. Tex. R. Evid. 705 (d).

In *Linn v. Fossum*, 946 So. 2d 1032 (Fla. 2006), a medical malpractice case, a trial court erred in allowing an expert to testify on direct regarding consultations with her colleagues in forming an expert opinion. The Florida Supreme Court found this evidence inadmissible because it would allow experts to improperly bolster their opinions and allow experts to serve as conduits for opinions of others without safeguards.

New or Interesting Cases

- *Custom Transit, L. P. v. Flatrolled Steel, Inc.*, No. 14 – 10 – 00936 – CV (Tex. App. — Houston [14th Dist.] June 14, 2012, no pet. h.). An expert opinion is not unduly speculative because the expert only inspects a small sample of a large number of allegedly defective products. An expert may properly "rely on facts and data 'perceived by, reviewed by, or make known to him'. ... Under this standard, 'it is not necessary for a testifying expert to have personally inspected an object as a prerequisite to offering expert testimony regarding that object'". *Id.* (quoting *Schronk*; Tex. R. Evid. 703)

· *Nat'l Freight, Inc. v. Snyder*, 191 S. W. 3d 416 (Tex. App. —Eastland 2006, no pet.). A physician's experts' estimates of future medical care were not unreliable because he relied on a member of his staff to provide him with those costs. The testimony was admissible under the reasonable reliance requirement of rule 703. *Id.* at 422.

· *Schronk v. City of Burleson*, No. 10 - 07 - 00399 - CV, 2009 WL 2215081 (Tex. App. —Waco July 22, 2009, pet. filed). Under Rule 703, an expert may reasonably rely on the records of the manufacturer to evaluate whether the product in question is defective, and therefore, the admissibility of the underlying exhibits is irrelevant.

H. The Eighth Gate: Rule 403

The last gate the expert's testimony must pass is Rule 403. If testimony is of some marginal value to a jury, a court might exclude the evidence under Rule 403 on the grounds that undue delay, needless presentation of cumulative evidence, or even the misleading nature of the evidence substantially outweighs its probative value. "Expert evidence can be both powerful and quite misleading because of the difficulty in evaluating it. Because of this risk, the judge in weighing possible prejudice against probative force under R. 403 exercises more control over experts than over lay witnesses." *Daubert*, 509 U. S. at 595. *See also United States v. Posado*, 57 F. 3d 428, 435 (5th Cir. 1995) (Rule 403 may have an enhanced role for expert witnesses).

The importance of Rule 403 in Texas was highlighted in *Atterbury*. Indeed, *Atterbury* interprets *Robinson* as lowering the burden of proof of unfair prejudice for expert testimony.

[T] he burden [is] on the trial court to determine whether the probative value of the proffered testimony is outweighed by the danger of unfair prejudice.... This last burden is considerable because it requires a trial court to make a determination as to Rule 403 without a party making a timely and specific objection grounded on that rule. Further, the court lowers the burden from "substantially outweighed" to just "outweighed".

978 S. W. 2d at 188. Thus, *Atterbury* places significance on *Robinson*'s omission in its restatement of Rule 403 of the word "substantially". *Robinson* does not state that its paraphrase of Rule 403 was intended to change the substantive meaning of the rule and such a change would arguably be contrary to the plain meaning of that rule. *Daubert*, 509 U. S. at 595 (Rule 403 gives trial courts "more control over experts than over lay witnesses".); 3 Weinstein & Berger § 702. 05 [3] at 702 - 45 (2d ed. 1997) (*Daubert* may give Rule 403 "a more pivotal role than it plays in more prosaic cases."). Courts also hold that satisfying the *Daubert* reliability test does not necessarily mean the evidence satisfies Rule 403. *United States v. Hicks*, 103 F. 3d 837, 847 (9th Cir. 1996); *Guillory v. Domtar Indust., Inc.*, 95 F. 3d 1320, 1331 n. 11 (5th Cir. 1996). Despite these statements, expert evidence that passes all seven of the other gates will rarely violate the "unfairly prejudicial" or "confusing" prongs of Rule 403.

New or Interesting Cases

· *State v. Gaylor Inv. Trust P'ship*, 322 S. W. 3d 814 (Tex. App. —Houston [14th

Dist.] 2011, no pet.). The court held that the trial court had discretion to exclude multiple experts on a topic and did not abuse its discretion in excluding two rebuttal experts.

- *French v. Allstate Indem. Co.*, 673 F. 3d 571 (5th Cir. 2011). Insureds – plaintiffs argued that the district court erred in excluding expert testimony because it was relevant to①the scope and cost of damage to their homes and②the application of an extended limits endorsement and a particular version of a Louisiana statute. The Fifth Circuit upheld the district court, observing that①the insureds had presented other expert testimony on the scope and cost of their damages, rendering the excluded testimony "unhelpful and needlessly cumulative" and②the district court had resolved the endorsement and statutory application issues as a matter of law or based on undisputed facts.
- *U. S. v. Valencia*, 600 F. 3d 389, 424 – 29 (5th Cir. 2010). The Fifth Circuit noted that "[e] vidence of mere correlation, even a strong correlation, is often spurious and misleading when masqueraded as causal evidence, because it does not adequately account for other contributory variables", but the court held that the trial court did not err in admitting expert correlation evidence because evidence of correlation itself, independent of causation, was relevant to case.

III. PROCEDURAL MATTERS

A. The Level of Proof Needed To Show Reliability

1. *Federal courts*

Daubert held that the admissibility "should be established by a preponderance of proof". 509 U. S. at 592 n. 10. The court did not identify the party with the burden of proof, but courts have interpreted the opinion as placing the burden on the proponent to show the evidence is admissible by a preponderance of the evidence. *In re Paoli*, 35 F. 3d 717, 744 & n. 11; *Lust v. Merrell Dow Pharms., Inc.*, 89 F. 3d 594, 598 (9th Cir. 1996).

2. *Texas courts*

The party offering the expert testimony has the burden of demonstrating its admissibility by a preponderance of the evidence. *Robinson*, 923 S. W. 2d at 557. *See also Spivey v. James*, 1 S. W. 3d 380, 382 (Tex. App. —Texarkana 1999, pet. denied); Brown, *Procedural Issues*, 36 Hous. L. Rev. at 1135. Texas Rule of Evidence 104 (a) has been interpreted in Texas as requiring proof by preponderance of the evidence. 1 Steven Goode, et al., Guide to the Texas Rules of Evidence: Civil and Criminal § 104. 1 at 28 & n. 8 (Texas Practice 2d ed. 1993); Harvey Brown, *Procedural Issues Under Daubert*, 36 Hous. Law. Rev. 1133, 1135 – 36 & n. 9 (1999).

In addition, the party offering the expert testimony has the burden of demonstrating its admissibility with clarity. *Mack Trucks, Inc. v. Tamez*, 206 S. W. 3d 572 (Tex. 2006) (The offering party bears "the burden of presenting understandable evidence.... When an expert's processes or methodologies are obscured or concealed by testimony that is excessively internally contradictory, non – responsive or evasive," the trial court may strike the testimony.); *see also Blan v. Ali*, 7 S. W. 3d 741, 747 (Tex. App. —Houston [14th Dist.] 1999, no pet.)

(physician's affidavit did not explain how or why alleged negligent acts caused plaintiff's condition to deteriorate); *Hess* v. *McLean Feedyard, Inc.*, 59 S. W. 3d 679 (Tex. App. —Amarillo 2000, pet. denied) (affidavit failed to show expert ruled out other possible causes); *Hight v. Dublin Veterinary Clinic*, 22 S. w. 3d 614 (Tex. App. —Eastland 2000, pet. denied) (veterinarian did not demonstrate how he knew the applicable standard of care or cite any foundational facts to reach causation conclusion; it was impossible to determine reliability from the affidavit).

The proponent bears this burden "regardless of the quality or quantity of the opposing party's evidence on the issue and regardless of whether the opposing party attempts to conclusively prove the expert testimony is wrong". *Whirlpool Corp. v. Camacho*, 298 S. W. 2d 631, 639 (Tex. 2009). Part of the burden of proof is ensuring that the expert's testimony contains no internal inconsistencies and does not contradict testimony from other experts of the proponent of the testimony. *See Gen. Motors Corp. v. Iracheta*, 161 S. W. 3d 462, 470 – 72 (Tex. 2005).

Both plaintiffs and defendants are required to clear "gatekeeper" hurdles when offering expert testimony. "It would be an odd rule of evidence that insisted that some expert opinions be reliable but not others. *All* expert testimony should be shown to be reliable before it is admitted." *Gammill v. Jack Williams Chevrolet, Inc.*, 972 S. W. 2d 713, 726 (Tex. 1998) (emphasis added); *see also* Brown, *Procedural Issues*, 36 Hous. L. Rev. at 1136 ("The burden is not necessarily on the party with the ultimate burden of proof; it is on the party who offers the expert testimony."). In *Minnesota Mining & Mfg. Co. v. Atterbury*, 987 S. W. 2d 183 (Tex. App. —Texarkana 1998, pet. denied), the court held that the burden to show the reliability of epidemiological evidence requires the offering party to "identify the study, get it admitted into evidence, and explain how the methodology of the study is scientifically reliable. An error in any of the preceding steps will likely result in the study not being considered by a reviewing court".

In criminal cases a higher burden of proof must be satisfied for novel scientific evidence. *Kelly v. State*, 824 S. W. 2d 568 (Tex. Crim. App. 1992). The court held that the proponent of novel scientific evidence offered under then – Rule 702 of the Texas Rules of Criminal Procedure "must persuade the trial court, by *clear and convincing evidence*, that the evidence is reliable and therefore relevant". *Id.* at 573 (emphasis added). *Kelly* was subsequently followed in *Nations v. State*, 944 S. W. 2d 795 (Tex. App. —Austin 1997, pet. ref'd) regarding the admissibility of testimony on eyewitness identification. "The burden of persuasion is on the proponent of the novel scientific evidence to demonstrate by clear and convincing evidence, outside the presence of the jury, that such testimony is reliable and therefore relevant." *Id.* at 797. Appellate courts have recently allowed the clear and convincing standard to transmogrify into the standard for *all* scientific evidence, not just *novel* scientific evidence. *See, e. g.*, *Rodgers v. State*, 162 S. W. 3d 698, 706 (Tex. App. —Texarkana 2005), aff' d, 205 S. W. 3d 524 Tex. (Tex. Crim. App. 2006) ("The burden is on the proponent of the expert testimony to prove by clear and convincing evidence the [scientific] testimony is trustworthy. ").

3. *Evidence that may be reviewed to determine reliability*

In reviewing a trial court's ruling on expert challenges, appellate courts may consider the testimony of opposing experts. *Cooper v. Mendez*, 204. W. 3d 797 (Tex. 2006). Similarly, " [a] n appellate court considering a no – evidence review cannot consider only an expert's bare opinion, but must also consider contrary evidence showing it has no scientific basis." *City of Keller v. Wilson*, 168 S. W. 3d 802, 813 (Tex. 2005). In a no – evidence review, an appellate must also consider admissions by the expert on cross – examination. *Id.* at 827; *see also Cooper Tire & Rubber*, 204 S. W. 3d at 804 (stating that reliance on evidence that undermines [the expert's] hypothesis is another reason for concluding" that the testimony is unreliable.). Finally, courts should consider ① "undisputed evidence that allows only one logical inference", ②contrary evidence that "conclusively establishes" a fact, and③contrary evidence from an opposing expert "without some reasonable basis for doing so". *City of Keller*, 168 S. W. 3d at 814, 829. Thus, a party may in some circumstances lodge an objection to expert testimony "after the expert's testimony, *or even later*". *Gen. Motors Corp. v. Iracheta*, 161 S. W. 3d 462, 471 (Tex. 2005).

Inconsistencies in an expert's opinion may also cause it to be unreliable. As explained in *Mack Trucks Inc. v. Tamez*, 206 S. W. 3d 572, 578 (Tex. 2006), the offering party bears "the burden of presenting understandable evidence .... When an expert's processes or methodologies are obscured or concealed by testimony that is excessively internally contradictory, non – responsive or evasive", the trial court may strike the testimony. In *General Motors Corp. v. Iracheta*, 161 S. W. 3d 462 (Tex. 2005), the plaintiff alleged that a defective fuel system caused the vehicle to catch on fire. The Court held that the expert's opinion was inadmissible. First, after comparing pieces of trial testimony, the Court held that the expert's assertions "were irreconcilably self – conflicting". *Id.* at 471. Second, the Court rejected the plaintiff's attempt to "borrow from each of her experts pieces that seem to match, tie them together in an ill – fitting theory, discard the unwanted opinions ... and then argue there is some evidence ... Inconsistent theories cannot be manipulated in this way to form a hybrid for which no expert can offer support". *Id.* at 472. Finally, the Court cautioned that an expert should construct opinions in a transparent manner. *Id.*

Courts will also evaluate whether the studies or factual data cited by the expert actually support the expert's conclusion. *See City of San Antonio v. Pollock*, 284 S. W. 2d 809, (Tex. 2009); *Cooper*, 204 S. W. 3d 797; *Havner*, 953 S. W. 2d at 724 – 728; *Exxon Corp. v. Makofski*, 116 S. W. 3d 176 (Tex. App. —Houston [14th Dist.] 2003, pet. denied); *Austin v. Kerr – McGee Ref. Corp.*, 25 S. W. 3d 280, 288 – 90 (Tex. App. —Texarkana 2000, no pet.). For example, an expert who relies on the testimony of other witnesses must accurately describe the significant testimony. *Cooper*, 204 S. W. 3d at 799. Similarly, " [i] f an expert's opinion is based on certain assumptions about the facts, we cannot disregard evidence showing those facts are unfounded". *City of Keller v. Wilson*, 168 S. W. 3d 802, 813 (Tex.

2005). Additionally, an opinion is considered conclusory and unreliable if it has no factual support. *Romero v. KPH Consolidation, Inc.*, 166 S. W. 3d 212 (Tex. 2005).

In conclusion, as part of the transparency required by court, the expert should make plain the information that the expert considered, state how expert used the information, explain why the expert's use of the information leads to expert's conclusion, provide the court with copies of any supporting documents, and ensure that his opinion and analysis are internally consistent.

B. Object Before Trial, at Trial, or, Better Yet, at Both

1. *State court*

In the absence of an order requiring objections before trial, an objection can be made when the evidence is first presented at trial. *Guadalupe – Blanco River Auth. v. Kraft*, 77 S. W. 3d 805 (Tex. 2002). Indeed, the objection does not necessarily have to be made when the testimony is presented on direct examination; a motion to strike expert testimony "immediately after cross – examination when the basis for the objection becomes apparent is sufficient to preserve a no – evidence complaint on appeal". *Kerr – McGee v. Helton*, 133 S. W. 3d 245 (Tex. 2004); *see also Iracheta*, 161 S. W. 3d at 471.

While the Court in *Maritime Overseas v. Ellis* held that it is too late to object to the reliability of expert evidence after a verdict; it also indicated that it is, at least in some circumstances, sufficient to object before trial, as occurred in *Havner*. 971 S. W. 2d 402, 410 – 11 (Tex. 1998) ("To preserve a complaint that scientific evidence is unreliable and thus, no evidence, a party must object to the evidence before trial or when the evidence is offered."). The *Maritime Overseas* Court's use of the disjunctive "or" (that is, that one may object before trial *or* at trial) may indicate that it may not be necessary to object during the trial itself. Brown, *Procedural Issues*, 36 Hous. L. Rev. at 1160 – 62.

While a trial objection may be too late—for example, when a scheduling order sets a deadline for expert challenges, a pretrial objection will normally be sufficient to preserve error. *Marvelli v. Alston*, 100 S. W. 3d 460, 470 n. 3 (Tex. App. —Fort Worth 2003, pet. denied) (noting that a pretrial ruling is sufficient to preserve the error). The record must also reflect a ruling on the objection. *Pilgrim's Pride*, 134 S. W. 3d at 899 – 900. Pilgrim's Pride underscores the need to get ruling on every basis for an expert challenge. In that case, a pretrial motion to exclude was not implicitly overruled when the trial court allowed the expert to testify at trial. The at – trial objection incorporating all pretrial challenges did not preserve error on substantive challenges to expert testimony because the trial court's ruling indicated he was only ruling on issue of failure to supplement discovery.

A motion in limine does not preserve error in the admission of expert testimony but a motion to exclude does. *Huckaby v. A. G. Perry & Son, Inc.*, 20 S. W. 3d 194, 203 – 04 (Tex. App. —Texarkana 2000, pet. denied). The defendant in *Huckaby* argued that the plaintiff had waived error in the admission of opinion testimony of a police officer concerning an alternative cause of the accident. In that case, a police officer testified that ten to twenty similar accidents had occurred at the accident scene but did not explain the basis for his conclusion the other accidents were similar. The court found that the officer's opinion was conclusory, did not satisfy the offering party's burden to show similarity, and should have been excluded by the judge in his role as a gatekeeper. "The witness's opinion that the occurrences were similar must be based upon the legal requirements for similarity." The defendant argued that any error was waived because another police officer had testified without objection that there were similar accidents at the scene. Although the plaintiff was granted a running objection to the first officer's testifying regarding similar accidents, the running objection was not broad enough to cover all witnesses. "A properly framed running objection can extend to testimony by all witnesses pertaining to the same type of evidence, but such did not exist in this case."

The *Huckaby* court found, however, that a pretrial pleading entitled "Objections and Motion to Exclude Evidence" that addressed the similarity of the other accidents preserved the error. The court initially stated that this motion "amount [s] to a motion in limine, which does not preserve error". The court distinguished, however, a motion in limine from a pretrial ruling on admissibility. "The trial court has authority to make a pretrial ruling on the admissibility of evidence." Examining the motion and trial court ruling more closely, the court of appeals determined that it "did not use motion in limine language requiring the party to approach the bench before introducing such evidence". The trial judge's denial of the motion to exclude the evidence was, therefore, sufficient to preserve the error. *See also Greenberg Traurig of New York, P. C. v. Moody*, 161 S. W. 3d 56, 92 - 93 (Tex. App. —Houston [14th Dist.] 2004, no pet.) (rejecting argument that pretrial motions to strike testifying experts should be treated as motions in limine); *Doyle Wilson Homebuilder, Inc. v. Pickins*, 996 S. W. 2d 387 (Tex. App. —Austin 1999, pet. dism' d by agr.) (motion to strike preserved error).

Even if a motion to exclude is overruled before trial, a party still should object at trial because the expert's trial opinions may differ from the pre - trial opinions and the basis for the opinion may change. *Cf. Schindler Elevator Corp. v. Anderson*, 78 S. W. 3d 392, 404 (Tex. App. —Houston [14th Dist.] 2001, pet. granted, judgment vacated w. r. m.), (refusing to consider challenges to areas of expert testimony where trial objections were directed to other areas of the expert's testimony), *disapproved of on other grounds by Roberts v. Williamson*, 111 S. W. 3d 113 (Tex. 2003). Moreover, Texas appellate courts have concluded in other circumstances that expert challenges were made too early and therefore waived error. *Bushell v. Dean*, 803 S. W. 2d 711 (Tex. 1991) (objection to entirety of expert's testimony at outset did not preserve error where trial court asked counsel to reurge later); *Farm Servs., Inc. v. Gonzalez*, 756 S. W. 2d 747, 750 (Tex. App. —Corpus Christi 1988, writ denied) (objecting to expert before expert testified was premature).

Stated differently, a pre - trial objection to the reliability of expert testimony must encompass all of the expert challenges that are raised in the appeal; a trial court generally speaking (unless the evidence is no evidence) cannot be reversed for an evidentiary objection that was never presented or an objection for which no ruling was obtained. In *Nip v. Checkpoint Sys.*, 154 S. W. 3d 767 (Tex. App. —Houston [14th Dist.] 2004, no pet.), the appellant raised six separate challenges to the reliability of the expert's testimony. The appellee contended that the points were waived because they were not part of the basis for the challenge in the trial court. The court of appeal held that it first had to "determine whether appellants have preserved each of their six contentions" by raising them in their motion to strike the expert in the trial court. Finding that only one of the six arguments had been raised below, the court found the other five points were waived. The court also rejected the contention that the appellee adequately preserved error as to each of the contentions because these contentions were contained within an expert report that was attached to the motion to strike. The court observed that the report was one of many attachments and the motion did not reference the specific challenges that were part of the expert's report. We do not find it unreasonable for the trial court under such circumstances to assume that all legal grounds supporting the ruling sought by the movant are contained in the motion. *Id.* at 771 n. 1.

There are a number of cases outside the expert context that have required objecting at the time of a witness's testimony. These cases also suggest that it best practice to object at trial even if a pretrial motion was made. For example, a party must object to an undesignated witness testifying when the witness is actually called instead of relying on a pre – trial motion. *Clark v. Trailways, Inc.*, 774 S. W. 2d 644 (Tex. 1989) (finding Tex. R. App. P. 52 (b) inapplicable to pretrial objection). Similarly, an objection during a pretrial hearing in which the court and counsel engage in a premature interchange about peremptory challenges did not preserve error. *Tex. Commerce Bank Reagan v. Lebco Constructors, Inc.*, 865 S. W. 2d 68, 78 (Tex. App. —Corpus Christi 1993, writ denied). *See also Missouri Pac. R. R. v. Brown*, 862 S. W. 2d 636, 638 (Tex. App. —Tyler 1993, writ denied) (objecting when party indicates it will introduce evidence instead of when party actually offers evidence does not preserve error).

A trial court may order objections pretrial. Justice Gonzalez suggested this procedure in *Maritime Overseas*, 971 S. W. 2d at 412, 414 (Gonzalez, J., concurring); *see id.* at 423 (Hecht, J., dissenting) ("ordinarily the issue must be raised before the verdict"); *Park v. Larison*, 28 S. W. 3d 106, 112 (Tex. App. —Texarkana 2000, no pet.) (holding that trial court may set deadlines before trial and could sustain late objection when the scheduling order did not state that a failure to object would constitute waiver). A trial court may, however, grant a late reliability challenge. *State Farm & Cas. Co. v. Rodriguez*, 88 S. W. 3d 313 (Tex. App. —San Antonio 2002, pet. denied).

While in trial, a party may generally preserve error through running objections so long as the objection is specific and unambiguous. *Volkswagen of Am., Inc. v. Ramirez*, 159 S. W. 3d 897 (Tex. 2003) ("Because [the party's] initial objection to the evidence complied with TRAP 33. 1 (a) and its requested running objection clearly identified the source and specific subject matter of the expected objectionable evidence prior to its disclosure to the jury, recognition of the running objection for more than one witness was appropriate.").

Evidence from a pre – trial hearing probably may not be considered in a legal sufficiency review. *But see Exxon*, 116 S. W. 3d at 181 n. 13 (declining to decide issue); *Id.* at 193

(Seymore, J. , dissenting) ("A pretrial *Robinson* hearing is no different than one held during trial. "). Thus, a prudent practitioner will offer, at least as an exhibit for the court only, evidence from the pretrial hearing to support an expert opinion or that raises a reliability problem. Indeed, arguably it is necessary to introduce into evidence during the trial itself any evidence necessary to show the soundness (but not necessarily correctness) of expert testimony. One court of appeals has, however, considered evidence attached to a party's response to a motion to exclude expert testimony—but not admitted at trial—in conducting a legal sufficiency review on the basis that it was apparent from the trial judge's statements on the record that the trial judge had reconsidered the pretrial evidence in ruling on the objection at trial. *Gross v. Burt*, 149 S. W. 3d 213, 235 (Tex. App. —Fort Worth 2004, pet. denied) (noting that " [i] t is not clear whether an appellate court must take into account evidence pertinent to the issue of [expert] reliability that is reviewed by the trial court at the pretrial stage, but not lager admitted at trial, when determining the reliability of expert testimony for legal sufficiency purposes").

It is important to object not only to an expert's opinion but to exhibits that summarize or contain the expert's opinion because a failure to object could cause a party to waive error for the admission of expert testimony. *See Austin v. Weems*, 337 S. W. 3d 415, 422 (Tex. App. — Houston [1st Dist.] 2011, no pet.). *Mobil Oil Corp. v. Bailey*, 187 S. W. 3d 265 (Tex. App. —Beaumont 2006, pet denied). (Gaultney, J. dissenting). *But see Kerr – McGee* and *Flatrolled*, discussed supra.

Mid – Continent Group v. Goode, No. 07 – 09 – 0181 – CV, 2011 WL 3962502, at * 8 (Tex. App. —Amarillo Aug. 19, 2011, no pet.) demonstrates the need to be careful about exhibits containing expert opinions: The trial court denied the defendant's *Daubert* challenge to one of damages expert's exhibits. During the pre – trial hearing on the admissibility of exhibits, the parties agreed to the admissibility as to all other damages expert exhibits, including the plaintiff's "summary" of damages. The court of appeals treated the defendant's stipulation to admissibility as essentially a stipulation to the expert's damages calculations and held that the defendant could not contest the sufficiency of the evidence to support the jury's finding on damages (which was based on reasonableness of fees and necessity of medical treatments).

In *Austin v. Weems*, 337 S. W. 3d 415, 422 (Tex. App. —Houston [1st Dist.] 2011, no pet.), a wrongful death automobile – pedestrian accident case, the plaintiff's pretrial motion to exclude expert testimony by a deputy preserved error as to the deputy's oral testimony but did not preserve error as to three statements on the same subject contained in the officer's accident report. In the offense report the officer in five different statements offered the opinion on the point of impact. The plaintiff's motion to exclude only identified two of those statements, and therefore did not preserve error on the other three. "A motion to exclude, in effect, accomplishes the same thing as a running objection: it eliminates the need to repeat the objection each time evidence is admitted on a topic. A running objection reaches different types of evidence only if the objecting party specifically identifies the part of the evidence that is inadmissible and each source of that evidence. " *Id.* at 422 (citations omitted). When the three portions of the deputy's accident report on the point of impact were admitted into evidence without a specific objection, the plaintiff "allowed the same or similar opinion as [the deputy's] oral testimony to be admitted to the jury, making the objected – to evidence cumulative of the unobjected – to evidence. Any error as to the earlier objected – to evidence, therefore, was not preserved". *Id.* at 424.

In *Mobil Oil*, Justice Gaultney argued in his dissent, "when a learned treatise is offered as evidence, a party should object to its admission in evidence if the article is considered unreliable". Even if the article is not admitted but it contents are read to the jury, a reliability challenge should be made because "statements from a learned treatise may be considered by the jury as substantive evidence". In this lung cancer claim, a written objection filed before the expert's causation testimony preserved the issue for trial. The plaintiff claimed that his lung cancer was caused by asbestos but the defendant argued that the absence of asbestosis demonstrated that no reliable basis existed for the expert's causation opinion. The court reviewed three articles cited by the expert and determined that they did not demonstrate the methodology employed to reach the conclusion. The dissent argued that the three articles were admitted to the jury without any objection, except that the articles should not be permitted to go to the jury room. The dissent believed the absence of a reliability objection to the articles made them substantive evidence. "When a learned treatise is offered as evidence, a party should object to its admission in evidence if the article is considered unreliable. " *Id.* at 278. Moreover, even if the article is not admitted but it contents are read to the jury, a reliability challenge should be made because "statements from a learned treatise may be considered by the jury as substantive evidence". *Id.* at 279. Since an appellate court reviews all of the evidence, including any articles read to the jury, those statements are part of the record in determining whether there is no evidence to support a finding.

2. *Federal court*

In federal courts, a failure to object probably also waives any error. *Bradley v. Armstrong Rubber Co.*, 130 F.3d 168 (5th Cir. 1997). The Fifth Circuit found that the error was waived. In that case, the plaintiffs sought to recover for "market stigma" caused by a naphtha spill from the defendant's plant. The defendant did not object to the testimony at trial but argued on appeal that the testimony did not form an adequate basis for the jury's verdict. The Fifth Circuit found that the objections went to the admissibility of the testimony, and that the failure to object precluded the court from ignoring the evidence in determining whether a sufficient basis existed for the jury's decision. "Had the defendants objected to the admissibility of the evidence, their case would be strong. " *Id.* at 177. Nevertheless, the court determined that a jury verdict could not be based on erroneous evidence and remanded the case for further proceedings.

But a limine motion may preserve error in federal court. *Mukhtar v. California State University*, 299 F.3d 1053, 1064 (9th Cir. 2002), *amended on other grounds*, 319 F.3d 1073 (9th

Cir. 2003) (concluding that motion in limine preserved error); *Mathis v. Exxon Corp.*, 302 F. 3d 448 (5th Cir. 2002) (limine motion preserves error and overruling *Tanner*).

C. Is it Necessary to Object to Preserve Error?

1. *Conclusory Opinions*

The rules regarding preservation of error are simply stated but difficult to apply: when reliability objections are timely made, the admissibility of expert testimony overlaps with the sufficiency of expert testimony and the *Robinson* factors are considered by a court. *See Whirlpool Corp. v. Camacho*, 298 S. W. 3d 631, 638 (Tex. 2009). *See also Gen. Motors Corp. v. Sanchez*, 997 S. W. 2d 584, 590 (Tex. 1999) (the *Robinson* factors help "determine the reliability and competency of the expert's evidence"). And "a no – evidence review encompasses the entire record, including contrary evidence tending to show the expert opinion is incompetent or unreliable". *Whirlpool*, , 298 S. W. 3d at 638.

When a party fails to object at trial, the review is more limited and complicated. "Bare, baseless opinions will not support a judgment even if there is no objection to their admission in evidence." *City of San Antonio v. Pollock*, 284 S. W. 3d 809, 816 (Tex. 2009). Conclusory and speculative opinions are legally of no import; they are legally "no evidence" to support a judgment. Incompetent evidence admitted without objection carries no weight and is the equivalent of no evidence. *City of Keller v. Wilson*, 168 S. W. 3d 802, 812 (Tex. 2005).

But it is sometimes difficult to draw a line between challenges that are waived without objection and challenges that are not waived. "[S]ome objections will fall close to the line" between evidence that is conclusory and incompetent and evidence that is unreliable but not incompetent. *See Arkoma Basin Exploration Co. v. FMF Assocs.* 1990 - *A*, *Ltd.*, 249 S. W. 3d 380, 388 (Tex. 2008). Because of these uncertainties, the best rule of practice from an appellate standpoint is to object both before trial and during trial. The realities of trial, however, often make this difficult. Thus, the question arises whether a party may challenge testimony on appeal in the absence of a trial objection.

The short answer is, it depends. Texas courts have long allowed late challenges to incompetent and conclusory evidence. If the expert's testimony is "incompetent" or "conclusory", the objection may be raised for the first time on appeal as part of a challenge to the legal sufficiency of the evidence. "[A] party may assert on appeal that unreliable scientific evidence is not only inadmissible, but also that its unreliability makes it legally insufficient to support a verdict." *Whirlpool*, 298 S. W. 2d at 678.

The Texas Supreme Court has struggled, however, with trying to find a middle course that simultaneously allows no – evidence reviews but also prevents appeals on issues never raised before the trial court—that is, appeal by ambush. The struggle has largely focused on determining when an expert opinion is "bare" or "conclusory" and when it is incompetent.

To determine the contours of these simply stated preservation of error rules for expert challenges in the absence of an objection, it is important to understand the history of the development and application of these rules, including cases that are often overlooked in the expert testimony context, *Maritime Overseas* and *City of Keller*.

The preservation issue for challenges to the reliability of expert testimony begins with *Havner*. The Court there stated that an expert's "bare opinion" does not constitute evidence; to determine whether it qualifies as evidence "the substance of the testimony must be considered." *Id.* at 711. To begin with, an expert's "bald assurance of validity is not enough. . . . The underlying data should be independently evaluated in determining if the opinion itself is reliable. *Id.* at 712, 13. Additionally, an appellate court looks "at the testimony in its entirety", because to accept the expert's opinion as some evidence "simply because he used the magic words" would effectively remove the jurisdiction of the appellate courts to determine the legal sufficiency of the evidence in any case requiring expert testimony. *Id.* at 711 – 12.

It could be argued that looking beyond the testimony to determine the reliability of scientific evidence is incompatible with our no evidence standard of review. If a reviewing court is to consider the evidence in the light most favorable to the verdict, the argument runs, a court should not look beyond the expert's testimony to determine if it is reliable. But such an argument is too simplistic. It reduces the no evidence standard of review to a meaningless exercise of looking to see only what words appear in the transcript of the testimony, not whether there is in fact some evidence.

Id. at 712. Whether expert testimony "rises to the level of *evidence* is determined under our rules of evidence, including Rule 702, which . . . offers substantive guidelines in determining if the expert testimony is some evidence of probative value". *Id.*

The first case explicitly addressing the tension between requiring objections so a party may respond during trial and attempt to cure the defect and requiring jury verdicts to be based on reliable expert testimony was *Maritime Overseas Corp. v. Ellis*, 971 S. W. 2d 402 (Tex. 1998). In *Maritime Overseas*, the plaintiff won a jury verdict on his claim that he suffered from acute and long term effects from exposure to a chemical pesticide. The defendant contended that the standards "articulated in *Robinson* and *Havner* are the proper standards for reviewing the sufficiency of [the plaintiff's damages] evidence". *Id.* at 408. But the defendant did not challenge the admissibility of the testimony nor contend that there was no evidence of any damages. Rather, it argued that the evidence was not reliable for demonstrating the claimed long term damages and therefore "would be legally insufficient" if the court of appeals had applied the proper standard for a factual sufficiency review.

The Court held that "[t]o preserve a complaint that scientific evidence is unreliable and thus, no evidence, a party must object to the evidence before trial or when the evidence is offered". *Id.* at 409. This requirement gives the opposing party the opportunity to cure any defect in the evidence. *Id.* To hold otherwise would deprive the trial court of its role as "gatekeeper" of scientific evidence and would be "simply 'unfair'" to the party who relied on the admission of the evidence. *Id.* at 409, 411. The Court suggested that the failure to object to expert testimony waives error in all cases, *id.* at 409, and directly held that the appellant waives a factual insufficiency challenge based on the expert testimony when the appellant did not object at trial. *See* Brown, *Procedural Issues*, 36 Hous. L. Rev. at 1160 - 62; *see also Yarborough's Dirt Pit, Inc. v. Turner*, 65 S. W. 3d 210 (Tex. App. —Beaumont 2001, no pet.). To allow belated objections would also "usurp the orderly and efficient disposition of appeals, deprive the proffering party of an opportunity to cure any defects in its evidence that the objecting party might pose, and in some cases, place appellate courts in the undesirable position of making decisions about evidentiary reliability absent a fully developed record". *Id.* In response to the dissent, the Court observed that the appellant had not made a no - evidence challenge and therefore the case law on evidence that is not probative on its face was inapplicable. *Id.* at 412.

Justice Hecht dissented. He surveyed numerous cases in which the Texas Supreme Court had found that conclusory evidence was legally no - evidence. Among these cases, he relied heavily on *Havner. Havner* "held that the expert testimony, even that admitted without objection, was no evidence to support a judgment for *Havner* because the testimony showed that there was no basis for the experts' opinions". *Id.* at 420 (quoting *Havner*, 953 S. W. 2d at 711). *Havner* further explained:

If for some reason [patently unreliable expert] testimony were admitted in a trial without objection, would a reviewing court be obliged to accept it as some evidence? The answer is no. In concluding that this testimony is scientifically unreliable and therefore no evidence, however, a court necessarily looks beyond what the expert said. Whether [expert opinion testimony] rises to the level of *evidence* is determined under our rules of evidence, including Rule 702, which requires courts to determine if the opinion testimony will assist the jury in deciding a fact issue. While Rule 702 deals with the admissibility of evidence, it offers substantive guidelines in determining if the expert testimony is some evidence of probative value. " *Id.* (quoting *Havner*, 953 S. W. 2d at 712.)

The Texas Supreme Court in *General Motors Corp. v. Sanchez*, 997 S. W. 2d 584, 591 (Tex. 1999) continued to insist on specific *Robinson* challenges in the trial court and rejected an attempt to bypass that requirement through a speculation objection. The testimony was not speculative because the expert offered "more ... than [his] bald assertion that his design would be safer". Following *Maritime Overseas*, the Court refused to consider a reliability challenge raised for the first time on appeal. The expert described the product's operation "at length, and explained in some detail how his proposed design would make the transmission safer". The testimony was not speculative merely because the expert had not built and tested his design theory because it is unnecessary to "build and test [the alternative design] to prove a safer alternative design". *Id.* at 592.

Five years later, the Court distinguished *Maritime Overseas*, and adopted much of what Justice Hecht's dissent sought in that case, in *Coastal Transport Co. v Crown Cent. Petroleum Corp.*, 136 S. W. 3d 227 (Tex. 2004). An objection "is required only when a challenge to expert testimony questions the underlying methodology, technique, or foundational data used by the expert". *Id.* at 233. An objection is unnecessary when a party "simply argues that the testimony is non - probative on the face of the record". *Id.*

In *Coastal*, the plaintiff presented expert testimony that the defendant's conduct constituted gross negligence because it involved a high degree of risk that the defendant had "actual subjective awareness of the risk", and proceeded "with conscious indifference". The expert was not asked to explain the basis for his gross negligence opinion, although he had explained the basis for his opinion that the defendant was negligent. The defendant in its legal sufficiency appeal argued that the testimony "amounted to no more than a 'bare conclusion' that was 'factually unsubstantiated' and therefore constituted no evidence". The Court held that the conclusory testimony was "incompetent evidence", was "not relevant evidence", and did not support the judgment even without any objection. *See also Maritime Overseas Corp. v. Ellis*, 971 S. W. 2d 402, 412 (Tex. 1998) (no objection is necessary if the lack of reliability appears "on the face of the record".); *Offshore Pipelines, Inc. v. Schooley*, 984 S. W. 2d 654, 665 (Tex. App. —Houston [1st Dist.] 1998, no pet.) (no timely objection was asserted at trial regarding the reliability of expert testimony but also stating that "when on the face of the record the scientific evidence lacks probative value, no objection is needed to preserve a sufficiency of the evidence complainant").

Coastal relied on a long line of cases holding that an objection was not required to preserve a no – evidence objection. Indeed, of the seven cases relied upon by the court in *Coastal*, five were previously cited in Justice Hecht's dissent in *Maritime Overseas*. The *Coastal* court distinguished *Maritime Overseas* because the expert challenge there was a challenge to the expert's methodology, an analysis that should not "be undertaken for the first time on appeal". 136 S. W. 3d at 233. An objection to expert testimony is unnecessary when the testimony is conclusory or speculative and therefore is not probative on its face. The Court recognized a distinction between challenges to an expert's scientific methodology and "no evidence challenges where, on the face of the record, the evidence lacked probative value". When the expert's underlying methodology is challenged, the court "necessarily looks beyond what the expert said" to evaluate the reliability of the expert's opinion. When the testimony is challenged as conclusory or speculative and therefore non – probative on its face, however, there is no need to go beyond the face of the record to test its reliability. We therefore conclude that when a reliability challenge requires the court to evaluate the underlying methodology, technique, or foundational data used by the expert, an objection must be timely made so that the trial court has the opportunity to conduct this analysis. However, when the challenge is restricted to the face of the record—for example, when expert testimony is speculative or conclusory on its face—then a party may challenge the legal sufficiency of the evidence even in the absence of any objection to its admissibility. 136 S. W. 3d at 233.

As a result, a party can preserve error by filing post – trial challenges to the legal sufficiency of the evidence. *Id.* Applying this test to the facts of the case was relatively easy: the plaintiff's evidence on gross negligence consisted of only affirmative responses by the expert to three questions that largely tracked the statutory gross negligence definition without any explanation.

Coastal followed closely behind *Kerr – McGee Corp. v. Helton*, 133 S. W. 3d 245, 254 (Tex. 2004) where the Court earlier that year had rejected a contention that an objection to documents containing the expert's opinion was necessary to preserve a no – evidence challenge. The defendant there did not object to the expert's opinion testimony before trial or after taking the witness on voir dire; it objected after cross – examination. *Id.* at 251. The Court distinguished *Maritime Overseas* because the post – cross – examination objection—which was made "when the basis for the objection became apparent" — removed "trial or appeal by ambush". *Id.* at 252. Thus, the objection was timely.

Interestingly, Kerr – McGee had the expert's report and took his deposition before trial and there was no contention that the expert's opinion or the basis of his opinions changed from the report to the time of trial. Specifically, it was always true that the expert assumed the hypothetical well would produce at the same rate as two existing wells without explanation for differences between the wells that indicated that they would not produce at the same rate. Therefore, the Court apparently treated an objection to the basis for an expert's opinion as first becoming apparent when it first becomes apparent during the trial itself, not during the case. A party who has not previously objected should, therefore, consider asserting a *Daubert* objection after any cross – examination that raises reliability issues.

The Court also signaled more willingness to consider reliability challenges raised for the first time on appeal by overruling the plaintiff's contention that the defendant waived error when it failed to object to two documents that summarized the expert's opinion. The exhibits contained the same unreliable damages calculation as the testimony. The Court reasoned that if the opinion is unreliable, the exhibits were also unreliable and therefore no evidence. *Id.* at 252. The Court said the failure to object did not waive error because the defendant's challenge was a no – evidence challenge rather than a challenge to admissibility. The Court did not address why this same contention would not have supported a challenge to the expert's testimony as no – evidence rather than holding that an objection after cross – examination was timely. Such a holding is arguably consistent with the Court's subsequent holdings on error preservation, including in particular *Pollock*.

Coastal was expanded to examining not only the absence of evidence in the record, but also whether the foundational data relied upon by the expert supported the expert's opinion in *Volkswagen of America, Inc. v. Ramirez*, 159 S. W. 3d 897 (Tex. 2004). The Court applied *Coastal* to find that a failure to challenge the reliability of a metallurgist's testimony did not preclude an appellate challenge that his testimony was conclusory. *Id.* at 910. Because there was no reliability challenge, the Court limited its review to the face of the record—it would not consider the expert's methodology or foundational data. *Id.* at 911. The metallurgist testified that a defect existed in a metal bearing in the axle and also offered testimony that the wheel assembly broke before—and not after—a collision with a motorist. While his testimony was lengthy, the metallurgist did not identify any data, testing, or physical evidence (other than the grass in the wheel hub) supporting his causation opinion. *Id.* For example, the expert's testimony that a defect in the Passat's left rear wheel assembly would be consistent with "erratic vehicle behavior" was an "unsupported conclusion" because the expert did not identify any supporting data such as other testimony, tests, skids marks. The one piece of physical evidence that he relied on—the finding of grass in the wheel hub— was "just as consistent with the wheel coming off in the median after the Passat went out of control as it is with a wheel separation prior to entering the median". *Id.* Thus, he did not show a connection between the underlying data and the opinion. The Court noted that the plaintiff's expert did not "explain" or offered an "insufficient explanation" how the data supported the opinion. The Court concluded that the causation opinion was conclusory because of "fatal gaps in an expert's analysis... While juries are important to our legal system, they cannot credit as some evidence expert opinions that are not reliable or are conclusory on their face. These principles are consistent with a legal sufficiency review. *Id.* at 912.

Justice Hecht's concurrence detailed other gaps in the expert's analysis. While the expert performed a microscopic examination of the wheel bearing, he did not "connect [the metallurgist's] observations with his conclusions" except through his "so - say." *Id.* at 912 (Hecht, J., concurring). He did not present any "objective tests that actually associate microscopic conditions with producing causes, or by statistical correlations between such conditions and bearing failures, or by analyses in the professional literature of the science of metallurgy. *Id.* at 912 - 13. The validity of his opinions "can be measured by one thing, and one thing only: his personal credibility". *Id.* at 913.

Volkswagen is significant because it imports the "analytical gap" test into the analysis of whether expert testimony is conclusory and whether a trial objection is necessary. It also references a *Robinson* factor—the absence of testing—in support of its holding that the testimony was conclusory. The dissent, after quoting numerous portions of the expert's testimony, contrasted the expert's testimony with "the paltry testimony" in *Coastal*, and therefore argued that it could not disregard the expert's testimony in a no - evidence review. *Id.* at 917. Nevertheless, a cautious attorney might want to still object on the basis of an analytical gap (and an appellee might want to argue that an analytical gap challenge is not preserved absent an objection). *See Charter Oak Fire Ins. Co. v. Swanigan*, No. 02 - 11 - 00147 - CV, 2012 WL 1432559 (Tex. App. —Fort Worth Apr. 26, 2012, no pet. h.) ("Because Charter Oak did not object to Dr. Graybill's testimony, we hold that Charter Oak's analytical - gap complaint concerning Dr. Graybill's testimony is not preserved for our review.").

In *General Motors Corp. v. Iracheta*, 161 S. W. 3d 462 (Tex. 2005), the Court concluded that an expert's opinion "did not rise to the level of competent evidence". The Court explained:

Although expert opinion testimony often provides valuable evidence in a case, "it is the basis of the witness's opinion, and not the witness's qualifications or his bare opinions alone, that can settle an issue as a matter of law; a claim will not stand or fall on the mere ipse dixit of a credentialed witness". Opinion testimony that is conclusory or speculative is not relevant evidence, because it does not tend to make the existence of a material fact "more probable or less probable". This Court has labeled such testimony as "incompetent evidence", and has often held that such conclusory testimony cannot support a judgment. Furthermore, this Court has held that such conclusory statements cannot support a judgment even when no objection was made to the [testimony].

Id. at 470 – 71 [quoting *Burroughs Wellcome Co. v. Crye*, 907 S. W. 2d 497, 499 (Tex. 1995)] (concluding expert's testimony was no evidence of a causal connection between Polysporin spray and plaintiff's injury because there was less than a scintilla of evidence to support that causal connection). While the expert testified that he had eliminated other possible causes of the incident, he offered no basis for this statement except his say so. *Id.* at 470.

The next development in preservation of error occurred in *Romero v. KPH Consolidation, Inc.*, 166 S. W. 3d 212 (Tex. 2005) where the Court held that an opinion is considered conclusory and unreliable if it has no factual support. Unsupported opinions—opinions based on the mere *ipse dixit* of a credentialed witness—legally constitute no evidence. *Id.* at 223 – 24. The Court in *Romero* carefully combed through the evidence but found no factual basis for the expert's testimony. The Houston Court of Appeals had concluded earlier in that case that the expert's testimony that the hospital should not have allowed a physician with a drug addiction to operate "was vague" and the expert offered "no basis" for the opinion. *KPH Consolidation, Inc. v. Romero*, 102 S. W. 3d 135, 154 n. 12 (Tex. App. —Houston [14th Dist.] 2003), *aff' d*, 166 S. W. 3d 212 (Tex. 2005). In affirming the Supreme Court stated that the opinion had "no factual support" in the record and constituted the mere *ipse dixit* of the expert. *Id.* at 222. On one other occasion, the Court has similarly stated that "[e] xpert testimony lacking a proper foundation is incompetent". *TXI Transp. Co. v. Hughes*, 306 S. W. 3d 230, 239 (Tex. 2010). And if the opinion is incompetent—for whatever reason—no objection is necessary.

City of Keller summarized the existing law on no – evidence challenges involving expert testimony as follows:

When expert testimony is required, lay evidence supporting liability is legally insufficient. In such cases, a no – evidence review cannot disregard contrary evidence showing the witness was unqualified to give an opinion. And if an expert's opinion is based on certain assumptions about the facts, we cannot disregard evidence showing those assumptions were unfounded.

After we adopted gate – keeping standards for expert testimony, evidence that failed to meet reliability standards was rendered not only inadmissible but incompetent as well. Thus, an appellate court conducting a no – evidence review cannot consider only an expert's bare opinion, but must also consider contrary evidence showing it has no scientific basis. Similarly, review of an expert's damage estimates cannot disregard the expert's admission on cross – examination that none can be verified.

Thus, evidence that might be "some evidence" when considered in isolation is nevertheless rendered "no evidence" when contrary evidence shows it to be incompetent.

City of Keller v. Wilson, 168 S. W. 3d 802, 812 – 13 (Tex. 2005).

In *Cooper Tire & Rubber Co. v. Mendez*, 204 S. W. 3d 797, 804 (Tex. 2006), a products liability case, the Court indicated that the no – evidence standards and *Robinson* overlap. The Court reversed an MYM11 million verdict because there was no evidence of a manufacturing defect. The Court used the *Robinson* factors in finding an expert's opinion that a tire separated because of wax contamination constituted no evidence. The expert's hypothesis was unsupported by any scientific testing, peer – reviewed studies or any support in the scientific community. It was nothing more than "subjective belief or unsupported speculation", and a naked hypothesis untested and unconfirmed by the methods of science and was legally insufficient to establish a manufacturing defect that caused the failure. *Id.* at 805. Because the Court relied on the failure to satisfy the *Robinson* factors to support its conclusion that the testimony was speculative and an objection based on speculation does not normally need to be made to the trial court, *Cooper Tire* supports the proposition that the *Robinson* factors may be raised for the first time on appeal.

In *Arkoma Basin Exploration Co. v. FMF Assocs. 1990 – A, Ltd.*, 249 S. W. 3d 380 (Tex. 2008), the Court observed that it was "a closer question" whether Arkoma had to object to the damages evidence presented by the plaintiff during the trial. The Court observed that the categories drawn by *Coastal* for determining when a pretrial objection is necessary is not always clear because "some objections will fall close to the line between" the categories recognized in that case. *Id.* at 388. But the Court did not need to determine the proper category for the objection because the opinion here was legally sufficient. The Court rejected two contentions by the defendant for challenging the damage calculation.

First, the opinion was not conclusory. An opinion is conclusory when an expert simply states "a conclusion without any explanation, or ask [s] jurors to 'take my word for it'". *Id.* at 389 (citing Black's Law Dictionary that an opinion is conclusory when it expresses "a factual inference without stating the underlying facts on which the inference is based" and comparing conclusory testimony to *ipse dixit* testimony when an expert fails to "explain the basis of his statements to link his conclusions to the facts"). But an opinion is not conclusory merely because the underlying foundational data is not offered into evidence or the expert utilizes demonstrative exhibits that are not part of the appellate record. *Id.* The absence of the precise figures used by the expert to yield certain mathematical calculations from the record was not fatal because "expert are not required to introduce such foundational data at trial unless the opposing party or the court insists". *Id.* at 389 –90.

Second, the expert in *Arkoma* did not have to include in his damage calculations use an explicit discount rate because he did not use an income approach in determining the value of the wells in question. The expert had a basis that facially supported his damages conclusion—the expert used an 8 – year production valuation formula.

In *City of San Antonio v. Pollock*, 284 S. W. 3d 809, 818 (Tex. 2009), the Supreme

Court found no objection was necessary in the trial court and the opinion was conclusory because the cited tests and data did not support the expert's opinion. "[E]ven when some basis is offered for the opinion, if that basis does not, on its face, support the opinion, the opinion is still conclusory." *Id.* at 817. In other words, unreliable evidence admitted without objection is probative evidence only if a basis for the opinion is offered and the offered basis supports the opinion. *Id.* at 818. Otherwise, "the opinion is merely a conclusory statement and cannot be considered probative evidence". *Id.* The Court held that the expert evidence on the exposure levels in their homes was "directly contradicted by [the expert's] own data showing such concentrations present only in the well. [The expert's] opinion is the kind of naked conclusion that cannot support a judgment". *Id.* at 818 – 19. Additionally, a "large gap" existed between the exposure levels in the studies that the expert relied upon and the claimed exposure levels in this case, making all cited studies no basis for the expert's causation opinion. *Id.* at 819.

Later that same year, the Court held that an expert's failure to offer "an explanation of why" testing of the expert's opinion was not performed may, along with the absence of other *Robinson* factors, render that opinion conclusory and subjective. *Whirlpool*, 298 S. W. 3d at 643. The Court concluded that the expert's opinions that a fire started in a Whirlpool clothes dryer were conclusory. While the case does not address preservation of error issues—the defendant repeatedly objected to the reliability of expert testimony—the Court's statement that the expert testimony was conclusory based on an analysis of the *Robinson* factors, suggests that the *Robinson* factors may be raised for the first time on appeal as grounds for attacking the legal sufficiency of the evidence.

In *Wal – Mart Stores, Inc. v. Merrell*, 313 S. W. 3d 837 (Tex. 2010), the Texas Supreme Court summarized *Volkswagen* as holding that expert testimony that "failed to account for the sequence of events" was conclusory. While the expert in *Volkswagen* provided "some evidence" for his defect theory, he "neglected to account for inconsistencies raised by his theory, thereby nullifying the probative value of his testimony". In *Merrell*, the expert failed to explain how he had ruled out an alternative cause of the fire in question. "An expert's failure to explain or adequately disprove alternative theories of causation 'makes his, or her own theory speculative and conclusory." And the expert's specific causation theory was likewise speculative because evidence that a particular product "can cause fires generally .... does not establish that [it] caused *this* fire". *Id.* (emphasis in original) In conclusion, the expert's testimony "lacked objective, evidence – based support for its conclusions". *Merrell* reinforces that the analysis of whether an expert's opinion is conclusory includes an examination of the details, or lack thereof, offered by the expert to support the opinion and imports the analytical gap test into this analysis.

Volkswagen, *Pollock*, *Whirlpool* and *Merrill* raise the possibility that methodological and foundational challenges that are determinable on the face of the record may fall under both the *Maritime Overseas* and *Coastal* tests. For example, the court in *Whirlpool* relied on the absence of testing and evidence satisfying some of the other *Robinson* factors in holding that an expert's opinion was conclusory. While the case did not involve a preservation of error issue (there were objections at trial), the Court's holding applies to cases where there is no trial objection. And to do so is not far from agreeing with the appellant's original suggestion in *Maritime Overseas*, which the Court rejected, that that the standards "articulated in *Robinson* and *Havner* are the proper standards for reviewing the [legal] sufficiency" of expert testimony. 971 S. W. 2d at 408.

An expert's failure to explain was also the reason that the Court in *Jelinek v. Casas*, 328 S. W. 3d 526, 535 (Tex. 2010) held that an expert's testimony that "the Hospital's negligence 'in medical probability' caused [the patient] additional pain and suffering" was conclusory and no evidence. The expert based this opinion on the presence of an undetected intra – abdominal infection that could have been treated with certain antibiotics that the physicians prescribed to prevent certain intra – abdominal infections and that the hospital conceded it negligently failed to renew. There was circumstantial evidence of infection—primarily fever and increased heart rate—but there was no direct evidence of an infection. The expert conceded the circumstantial evidence supporting his infection opinion was equally consistent with two other infections the patient experienced—neither of which were treatable by the antibiotics in question. *Id.* The Court observed that an expert opinion is conclusory when the expert simply opines that the defendant's negligence caused the plaintiff's injury. *Id.* at 536. The expert must instead, explain, to a reasonable degree of medical probability, "how and why the negligence caused the injury". *Id.* The Court held that "[w] hen the only evidence of a vital fact is circumstantial, the expert cannot merely draw possible inferences from the evidence and state that 'in medical probability' the injury was caused by the defendant's negligence. Thus, when the facts support several possible conclusions, only some of which establish that the defendant's negligence caused the plaintiff's injury, the expert must explain to the fact finder why those conclusions are superior based on verifiable medical evidence, not simply the expert's opinion." *Id.* Applying the equal inference rule, the Court further explained that it was "equally plausible that the patient had an anaerobic infection or that she did not. [The expert] opined that she did, but he did not explain why that opinion was superior to the opposite view. Such evidence raises no more than a possibility of causation, which is insufficient." *Id.* at 537. The expert also relied on evidence of a foul smell, which is consistent with an anaerobic infection, to support his opinion that she suffered from an undetected anaerobic infection. *Id.* at 538. The hospital, however, offered other explanations for the smell. Thus, the evidence included "competing explanations for the smell" and "no more than circumstantial evidence". Quoting from *City of Keller*, 168 S. W. 3d at 814, the Court stated that "[b] ecause there is no direct evidence of the infection and the circumstantial evidence is meager, we must consider not just favorable but all the circumstantial evidence, and competing inferences as well". *Id.* That evidence "did not provide the jury a reasoned basis from which to infer the presence of a negligence—induced infection". *Id.* The Court summarized its holding as follows:

When circumstantial evidence is consistent with several possible medical conclusions, only one of which establishes that the defendant's negligence caused the plaintiff's injury, an expert witness must explain why, based on the particular facts of the case, that conclusion is medically superior to the others. If the expert fails to give any reason beyond an unsupported opinion, the expert's testimony is legally insufficient evidence of causation.

Id. at 529. *See Id.* at 539 – 40 (holding that expert report submitted in support of claim against one physician did not satisfy 4590i, stating that an expert's conclusion that "in medical probability" one event caused another differs little, without an explanation tying the conclusion to the facts, from "an *ipse dixit*" and requiring an expert go further and explain, to a reasonable degree, how and why the breach caused the injury based on the facts presented.); *also Bowie Meml Hosp. v. Wright*, 79 S. W. 3d 48, 52 (Tex. 2002) (holding medical expert report was deficient and stating that an expert "cannot merely state the expert's conclusions about" negligence and causation but rather must "explain the basis of his statements to link his conclusions to the facts").

Arkoma was applied to conclude that a fairly bare bones expert opinion was not conclusory in *Pink v. Goodyear Tire & Rubber Co.*, 324 S. W. 3d 290 (Tex. App. —Beaumont 2010, pet. dismissed). Although the defendant prevailed on its summary judgment motion, the court of appeals rejected its contention that a treating oncologist's affidavit was conclusory. The affidavit stated:

Based upon reasonable medical probability, the cause of Mr. Pink's renal cell carcinoma was exposure to chemicals, more than likely benzene. In rendering this opinion I have reviewed Mr. Pink's medical records, the deposition testimony of Mr. Pink and three of his co – workers, the deposition of Dr. Radelat, and scientific literature.

Id. at 296. The court observed that "[w] hile causal connection does not turn on the use of . . . any other particular phrase or term, [the oncologist] grounds his opinion under oath on reasonable medical probability". *Id.* at 298. The court in *Pink* observed that the affidavit references the materials the oncologist consulted. Although it does not identify the specific literature or what it says, the affidavit implicitly asserts that the literature supports the opinion. Under *Arkoma*, the affidavit does not need to provide the underlying foundational data. "A reasonable inference from his explanation is that his opinion concerning the cancer derives at least in part from first – hand knowledge and observations made during the treatment." *Id.* The Court did not discuss *Pollock's* corollary definition of conclusory as an opinion with a stated basis when basis does not, on its face, support the opinion. Arguably, the expert's statement that he reviewed the pertinent medical records, deposition testimony, and scientific literature does not support the expert's conclusion that chemical exposure caused the plaintiff's renal cell carcinoma; it merely shows *what* he reviewed without showing *how* that review supported the opinion. On petition for review, the Texas Supreme Court requested a response to the petition for review and full briefing on the merits before the petition was dismissed on the parties' motion.

The distinction between a challenge to an expert's methodology and a challenge that the expert testimony constitutes no evidence was recognized in *Graves v. Tomlinson*, 329 S. W. 3d 128, 141 (Tex. App. —Houston [14th Dist.] 2010, pet. denied). When a legal sufficiency challenge focuses in significant part on expert testimony, an appellate court must "consider the difference between①a challenge to an expert's methodology; and②a legal sufficiency challenge predicated on a contention that an experts testimony lacks probative value" because "[t] hese are distinct inquiries". *Id.* at 141. In this divorce proceeding, the wife, as part of her legal sufficiency challenge, argued that her former husband's valuation expert used an unreliable methodology to determine the value of a community property. Because the former wife did not object before or during trial to the expert's valuation methodology, she could not raise the issue on appeal.

The Houston Fourteenth Court of Appeals found an opinion was not conclusory in *Custom Transit, L. P. v. Flatrolled Steel, Inc.*, No. 14 – 10 – 00936 – CV (Tex. App. —Houston [14th Dist.] June 14, 2012, no pet. h.). After summarizing the expert's testimony and quoting *Pink*, the court stated that the expert there "sufficiently explained" the basis for his opinion. The court distinguished a challenge that an opinion is conclusory from a challenge that the opinion is speculative.

After *Maritime Overseas*, and before *Coastal Tankships*, many courts refused to entertain legal insufficiency challenges to expert testimony when *Robinson* – type "admissibility" objections were not made before or during trial. *See*, *e. g.*, *City of Dallas v. Redbird Dev. Corp.*, 143 S. W. 3d 375, 385 (Tex. App. —Dallas 2004, no pet.) (rejecting "the City's reliance on *Coastal Transport* as authority that it was not required to raise its legal sufficiency challenge in the trial court to preserve its complaint on appeal"); *Energen Resources MAQ, Inc. v. Dalbosco*, 23 S. W. 3d 551, 557 (Tex. App. —Houston [1st Dist.] 2000, pet. denied) (holding that party waived compliant that expert testimony was unreliable and speculative because of failure to object at trial); *Weidner v. Sanchez*, 14 S. W. 3d 353, 366 (Tex. App. —Houston [14th Dist.] 2000, no pet.) (rejecting sufficiency of evidence point when defendant failed to object "before trial, when the evidence was offered, or before the close of evidence"); *Reliance Ins. Co. v. Denton Cent. Appraisal Dist.*, 999 S. W. 2d 626, 630 (Tex. App. —Fort Worth 1999, no pet.) (holding that although the plaintiff artfully cross – examined the expert, it could not show any record references showing it had objected to the testimony as unreliable); *Gen. Motors Corp. v. Castaneda*, 980 S. W. 2d 777, 780 n. 2 (Tex. App. —San Antonio 1998, pet. denied) (refusing to consider challenge that expert testimony was not supported by the evidence and was speculative in the absence of an objection at trial); *Cass v. Stephens*, No. 08 – 97 – 00582, 2001 WL 28092 (Tex. App. —El Paso Jan. 11, 2001, pet. denied) (not designated for publication) (refusing to consider challenge to expert testimony on damages because of failure to object at trial), *cert. granted*, *judgment vacated*, 123 S. Ct. 2213 (2003); *Retzlaff v. Texas Dept. of Protective & Regulatory Servs.*, 1999 Tex. App. LEXIS 5547 (Tex. App. — Austin July 29, 1999, pet. denied) (not designated for publication) (finding waiver when the defendant did not object before or during trial to the state's expert on pedophilia tendencies even though the subject matter of his testimony was not disclosed before trial).

Other courts have not found a waiver when the challenge is not to the reliability of the expert's methodology, but instead presents a no – evidence challenge on appeal that contends that the opinions were conclusory or speculative or based on faulty assumptions. *See*, *eg. Twin City Fire Ins. Co. v. Vega – Garcia*, 223 S. W. 3d 762 (Tex. App. —Dallas 2007, pet denied) (no objection is necessary to speculative testimony to challenge the legal sufficiency of evidence even in the absence of an objection at trial); *Gabriel v. Lovewell*, 164 S. W. 3d 835 (Tex. App. —Texarkana 2005, no pet.) (stating that speculative and conclusory expert testimony is incompetent and will not support a verdict); *Capital Metro. Transp. Auth. v. Cent. of Tenn. Ry. & Nav. Co.*, 114 S. W. 3d 573 (Tex. App. —Austin 2003, pet. denied) (stating that an attack on an expert opinion on the basis that it is premised on unsupported assumptions, speculation, and surmise does not constitute an attack on the reliability of the methodology of the expert. Therefore, a *Robinson/Havner* challenge is not required.); *Gen. Motors Corp. v. Harper*, 61 S. W. 3d 118, 129 (Tex. App. —Eastland 2001, pet. denied) (holding that expert's testimony was based on a assumption that was rebutted); *Offshore Pipelines, Inc. v.* Schooley, 84 S. W. 2d 654, 665 (Tex. App. —Houston [1st Dist.] 1998, no pet.) (noting that although no timely objection was asserted at trial regarding the reliability of expert testimony, "when on the face of the record the scientific evidence lacks probative value, no objection is needed to preserve a sufficiency of the evidence complainant"); *see also McIntyre v. Ramirez*, 109 S. W. 3d 741 (Tex. 2003) (stating that an affidavit by a Maryland physician that a physician was entitled to bill for his services for delivery of a baby was a conclusion "with no supporting facts or rationale"); *Sparks v. Booth*, 232 S. W. 3d 853, 863 (Tex. App. —Dallas 2007, no pet.); *Gabriel v. Lovewell*, 164 S. W. 3d 835 (Tex. App. —Texarkana 2005, no pet.) (an expert opinion that has no facts to support is conclusory); *Rizkallah v. Conner*, 952 S. W. 2d 580, 587 (Tex. App. —Houston [1st Dist.] 1997, no writ) (conclusory opinions constitute "substantive" defects in summary judgment evidence, and no objection is necessary to preserve error).

2. *Speculative Testimony*

Although the issue of whether testimony is speculative may overlap to some degree with whether the testimony is conclusory, and the two "often are asserted in the same breadth and argued together", they are "distinct concepts". *Custom Transit, L. P. v. Flatrolled Steel, Inc.*, No. 14 – 10 – 00936 – CV (Tex. App. —Houston [14th Dist.] June 14, 2012, no pet. h.). In that case, the defendant challenged the testimony of the plaintiff corporation's owner on the value of damaged steel coils. The court held that his testimony was not speculative because he did not know the precise number of coils that he visually inspected. The owner – expert not only viewed and photographed a number of the coils but he also viewed invoices that included notations on damage to the coils and prices that reflect that the received coil was "less than prime".

In *Cooper Tire & Rubber Co. v. Mendez*, 204 S. W. 3d 797, 805 (Tex. 2006), the Court relied on the *Robinson* factors in holding that a tire expert's wax contamination theory constituted unsupported speculation and no evidence because " [h] is explanation for the tire failure was a naked hypothesis untested and unconfirmed by the methods of science".

It is well – established that speculative expert testimony is no evidence. *Coastal Transport*, 136 S. W. 3d at 233; *Burroughs Wellcome Co. v. Crye*, 907 S. W. 2d 497, 499 – 500 (Tex. 1995); *Schaefer v. Texas Emp's' Ins. Ass' n*, 612 S. W. 2d 199, 202 – 05 (Tex. 1980) *Marin Real Estate Partners, L. P.*, 2011 WL 5869520 (Tex. App. —San Antonio Nov. 23, 2011) (stating that an objection that expert testimony was pure speculation "is the type of challenge for which an objection is not required because the court need look no further than the face of the record to determine the reliability of the expert's opinion").

However, some post – *Maritime Overseas* courts have found that waiver occurs even when appellants assert that expert opinions are "speculative". *Energen Resources MAQ, Inc. v. Dalbosco*, 23 S. W. 3d 551, 557 (Tex. App. —Houston [1st Dist.] 2000, pet. denied); *Gen. Motors Corp. v. Castaneda*, 980 S. W. 2d 777, 780 n. 2 (Tex. App. —San Antonio 1998, pet. denied).

3. *Expert Opinions Based on Incorrect Assumptions*

An objection is not necessary when an expert's opinion is based on facts that are contrary to the undisputed evidence. *Arkoma Basin Exploration Co. v. FMF Assocs.* 1990 – *A, Ltd.*, 249 S. W. 3d 380, 383 (Tex. 2008) (stating that no objection is necessary when expert "assumed facts contrary to those on the face of the record"); *City of Keller v. Wilson*, 168 S. W. 3d 802, 813 (Tex. 2005) ("[I] f an expert's opinion is based on certain assumptions about the facts, we cannot disregard evidence showing those assumptions were unfounded".); *Burroughs Wellcome Co. v. Crye*, 907 S. W. 2d 497, 499 – 500 (Tex. 1995) (holding opinion that spray caused frostbite was legally insufficient as it assumed absence of redness when plaintiff admitted the contrary); *see also Price v. Divita*, 224 S. W. 3d 331 (Tex. App. —Houston [1st Dist.] 2006, pet. denied) (holding that expert presumed facts that were not supported by the record and therefore their testimony amounted to surmise, conjecture and speculation).

4. *An Expert's Qualifications*

A fairly undeveloped area of the law is whether an objection to an expert's qualifications is necessary at trial. If the lack of qualifications renders the testimony incompetent, no testimony is necessary. It is well – settled, however, that a trial court's ruling on a qualifications objection is reviewed by an abuse of discretion standard. *Broders v. Heise*, 924 S. W. 2d 148, 151 (Tex. 1996).

In *Gen. Motors Corp. v. Iracheta*, 161 S. W. 3d 462 (Tex. 2005) the Court concluded that there was no evidence that a defectively designed fuel system caused a second post – collision fire. The plaintiff's first expert was not qualified to offer his causation testimony. The Court did not, however, suggest that his lack of qualifications made his testimony incompetent; on the contrary, the Court reserved the incompetency label for the expert's failure to offer any basis for his opinion. *Id.* at 470 – 71.

City of Keller v. Wilson, 168 S. W. 3d 802 (Tex. 2005) indicates that unqualified expert testimony may be incompetent evidence and therefore no objection may be necessary. The Court first stated, "incompetent evidence is legally insufficient to support a judgment, even if admitted without objection". *Id.* at 812. *See also id.* ("evidence that might be 'some evidence' when considered in isolation is nevertheless rendered 'no evidence' when contrary evidence shows it to be incompetent"); *Henry v. Phillips*, 105 Tex. 459, 466, 151 S. W. 533, 538 (1912) ("incompetent testimony can never form the basis of a finding of facts in an appellate court, notwithstanding its presence in the record without objection"). The Court then applied this rule to unqualified opinion testimony by a lay witness: "When expert testimony is required, ... a no – evidence review cannot disregard contrary evidence showing the witness was unqualified to give an opinion." *Id.* While the Court's explanation is limited to unqualified testimony by a lay witness, the language is broad enough to hint that unqualified expert testimony may also be incompetent.

City of Keller relied on *Leitch v. Hornsby*, 935 S. W. 2d 114, 119 (Tex. 1996) where the Court announced that "[i] ncompetent opinion testimony is not evidence, and a finding supported only by such testimony cannot survive a no evidence challenge". *Leitch* did not involve an objection to an expert's qualifications. *Leitch* relied on Justice Calvert's famous article on legal and factual insufficiency, where Justice Calvert explained that whether the court is barred by rules of law or of evidence from giving weight to the only evidence offered to prove a vital fact is a legal question. *Id.* "The so – called evidence is present, and if it may be given probative force at all it will sustain a verdict and judgment. If, however, it must be discarded because it ... violates the parol evidence rule, or for some similar reason, there will be no evidence left on which the verdict and judgment may rest." Robert W. Calvert, "*No Evidence*" *and* "*Insufficient Evidence*" *Points of Error*, 38 Tex. L. Rev. 361, 363 (1960). *Leitch* also relied on *Missouri Pac. R. R. Co. v. Buenrostro*, 853 S. W. 2d 66, 77 (Tex. App. —San Antonio 1993, writ denied), a case that did involve an unqualified expert. "In order for an expert's testimony to be competent, it must be shown that he or she is trained in the science of which they testify, or have knowledge of the subject matter of the fact issue in question. Further, incompetent opinion testimony is not evidence, and a causation finding supported only by such testimony fails a 'no evidence' challenge. Moreover, the expert in stating his opinion must be restricted to his particular field." *Id.* (citations omitted)

In at least one other case, courts have treated a challenge to an expert's qualifications as a challenge to the competency of the evidence. *See Hous. Auth. of City of Galveston v. Henderson*, 267 S. W. 2d 843, 845 (Tex. Civ. App. —Galveston 1954, no writ) (reviewing whether expert's experience was so lacking as to render him incompetent to qualify). And the Dallas Court of Appeals has stated, in the summary judgment context, that "the failure of an affiant to establish her qualifications as an expert is a substantive objection that may be raised [for the first time] on appeal". *Strother v. City of Rockwall*, 358 S. W. 3d 462, 470 (Tex. App. —Dallas 2012, no pet.); *but see Duncan – Hubert v. Mitchell*, 310 S. W. 3d 92, 105 (Tex. App. —

Dallas 2010, pet. denied) (holding that defendant's objection that plaintiff's expert was "not adequately qualified to opine on the subject at issue is one as to form that must be raised in the trial court"). The intersection of the abuse of discretion standard used for reviewing a court's determination of the admissibility of expert testimony challenged on the basis of the expert's qualifications and a challenge that the evidence is incompetent and therefore no evidence as a matter of law is shown in *CHRISTUS Health Sys. v. Harlien*, No. 13 – 09 – 00446 – CV, 2011 WL 2394614 (Tex. App. —Corpus Christi June 9, 2011, pet. denied). The defendant argued that a physician was not qualified to testify on the standard of care for nurses and that his testimony constituted no evidence. The court evaluated the expert's qualifications under the abuse of discretion standard and separately as part of a no – evidence review of the competency of the expert's testimony. It concluded that the trial court did not abuse its discretion in admitting the physician's testimony. "And, for these same reasons", the expert's concessions during cross – examination did not demonstrate that his "testimony was incompetent as a matter of law. In so holding, we consider all of the evidence and find none that necessarily prevents [the physician] from being qualified as an expert on the nurses' standard of care in this case or from giving a competent opinion".

5. *Interesting or recent cases on Preserving Error*

· *Rodgers v. State*, 205 S. W. 3d 525 (Tex. Crim. App. 2006). The defendant's motion to strike a latent – print examiner's shoe comparison testimony served to preserve his complaint concerning the expert's tire comparison testimony as well. The examiner testified about his comparisons of the soles of the defendant's shoes and tire imprints from his van with impressions made from a shoe print and tire tracks found near the scene of the murder. The defendant cross – examined the expert on his qualifications on voir dire and objected that he was not an expert in either tire or shoe comparisons. The defendant later made a motion to strike the shoe – imprint – comparison testimony. The court held that this preserved the error because the record revealed that the trial judge and the prosecutor clearly understood that defendant objected that the examiner was not a qualified expert in *either* tire or shoe identification.

Because appellant's argument is precisely the same concerning both areas and because the trial judge and prosecutor clearly understood (and the trial judge rejected) appellant's same argument concerning both areas, the underlying purposes of Rule 103 (a) were served. In this particular scenario, then, appellant's motion to strike [the expert's] shoe comparison testimony served to preserve his complaint concerning [his] tire comparison testimony as well. *Id. at* 527 n. 2.

· *Harris Cnty. Appraisal Dist. v. Houston 8th Wonder Prop.*, *L. P.*, No. 01 – 10 – 00154 – CV, 2012 WL 1757591 (Tex. App. —Houston [1st Dist.] May 17, 2012, no. pet. h.) ("When a party asserts on appeal that an expert's testimony is insufficient because it is unreliable, a court will ordinarily consider both the *Robinson* reliability factors and the expert's experience.").

· *DaimlerChrysler Motors Co.*, *LLC v. Manuel*, 362 S. W. 3d 160 (Tex. App. —Fort

Worth 2012, no pet.) (when a party challenges the reliability of the foundational data used by the opposing expert, the admissibility issue "merge [s] with a legal sufficiency type analysis for lost profits damages").

- *Wells Fargo Bank Nw.*, *N. A. v. RPK Capital XVI*, *L. L. C.*, 360 S. W. 3d 691 (Tex. App.—Dallas 2012, no pet.) (the only evidence of lost profits, an expert's opinion, constituted no evidence when the expert's opinions were based on unsubstantiated assumed facts and verbally transmitted information; because the expert failed to provide objective evidence documenting his conclusions, the conclusions constituted no evidence of these damages).
- *Scott's Marina at Lake Grapevine Ltd. v. Brown*, No. 07 – 10 – 00277 – CV, 2012 WL 177970 (Tex. App.—Amarillo Jan. 23, 2012, no pet.). In this personal injury lawsuit claiming that workplace exposure to human feces caused the worker's illnesses, the Amarillo court of appeals stated that although the marina challenged the admissibility of the expert's opinion, its arguments challenged the sufficiency of the evidence to establish the reliability of the expert causation testimony. Therefore, the court's analysis of the sufficiency of the evidence supporting the reliability of the testimony "will determine our assessment of the admissibility of [that] testimony". *Id.* at * 5. In determining whether expert testimony is reliable, a reviewing court must employ "an almost *de novo* – like review and, like the trial court, look beyond the expert's bare testimony to determine the reliability of the theory underlying it". *Id.* The court applied the *Robinson* factors to determine the legal sufficiency of the expert evidence, and concluded that the evidence was sufficiently reliable.
- *Trinity River Estates*, *L. P. v. DiFonzo*, No. 02 – 08 – 393 – CV, 2009 Tex. App. LEXIS 4037 (Tex. App.—Fort Worth May 28, 2009, no pet.). To constitute competent evidence, "the testimony must provide an explanation linking the basis of the conclusion to the facts".

D. Appellate Standard of Review and Sufficiency v. Admissibility

The standard of review for an appellate court examining whether expert testimony was admissible is abuse of discretion. *Whirlpool*, 298 S. W. 3d at 638; *Cooper*, 204 S. W. 3d at 800. But the admission of expert testimony that is not reliable is in itself an abuse of discretion. *Cooper*, 204 S. W. 3d at 800.

For a legal sufficiency challenge, the court examines the entire record, including contrary evidence, to determine whether the expert evidence is reliable. *Whirlpool*, 298 S. W. 3d at 638, 643. This review is exacting. *See Walker v. Thomasson Lumber Co.*, 203 S. W. 3d 470, 475 (Tex. App.—Houston [14th Dist.] 2006, no pet.). In this context, Texas courts of appeals have applied a de novo standard of review. *Eg. Walker v. Thomasson Lumber Co.*, 203 S. W. 3d 470, 475 (Tex. App.—Houston [14th Dist.] 2006, no pet.); *Goodyear Tire & Rubber Co. v. Rios*, 143 S. W. 3d 107, 113 (Tex. App.—San Antonio 2004, pet. denied).

BIC Pen, a manufacturing defect case arising out of a fire caused by five – year – old's use of an allegedly defective lighter, is an example of a case where the Court examined all the data—not just the favorable data—and noted an expert's failure to explain other testimony in determining the legal sufficiency of the evidence. *BIC Pen*, 346 S. W. 3d at 542 – 43. BIC submitted five specifications for the lighter to the Consumer Product Safety Commission (CPSC) to establish compliance with the CPSC's child – resistance requirements. For the lighter in question, two post – accident measurements of the force necessary to operate the lighter—the sparkwheel force and the fork force—had small deviations from the approved specifications. The plaintiffs did not offer any "evidence that a lighter's failure to meet any particular one or more of the characteristics by some factor would negate the lighter's compliance with the CPSC requirements" nor any evidence "of which characteristic was the most or least important with regard to those requirements." *Id.* at 543. The plaintiffs relied on some data from BIC's certification test regarding use of the lighter by children when sparkwheel force was decreased. But the Court held that the data, on the whole, did not prove that noncompliance with the sparkwheel force specification caused "an increased ability of children to operate the lighter" because other portions of the test results "showed that the number of children who could successfully operate the ... lighters did not decrease as the sparkwheel force of the other surrogates increased". *Id.* at 543. (citing *Havner*, 953 S. W. 2d at 718 for the proposition that "studies showing an association between two matters or facts do not necessarily show a causal relationship between them"). Additionally, BIC's specifications "contemplate that some children less than five years old will be able to operate a lighter certified as child resistant". *Id.* at 544. "Because the lighter is designed so that when it is manufactured to specifications, it still can be operated by some children even younger than five years of age, [the plaintiff] had the burden to prove that [the child] probably would not have operated the lighter but for the manufacturing defects, regardless of his age and physical and mental condition". *Id.* While there was expert testimony that the five year old child "would have been functioning below his age level at the time of the accident", the expert "did not explain what that meant in terms of his physical ability to turn the sparkwheel and depress the fork". *Id.*

In *Exxon Corp. v. Makofski*, the court applied both the *Robinson/Havner* factors and the *Gammill* "analytical gap" test to decide a legal sufficiency challenge to the plaintiff's evidence that exposure to benezene caused a particular type of leukemia. 116 S. W. 3d 176, 180 (Tex. App. —Houston [14th Dist.] 2003, pet. denied). The *Makofski* court rejected the argument—made by the dissent—that Exxon waived its *Robinson* – based complaint by failing to obtain a record of the pretrial hearing on the admissibility of the expert testimony. *Makofski*, 116 S. W. 3d at 180. While the absence of a portion of the record normally is presumed to support the verdict, that rule applies to proceedings at the jury trial, "not by what happened before or after it". *Id.* at 181. Because Exxon challenged the sufficiency of the evidence to support causation and not the admissibility of expert testimony, the court did not need to review the record from the pretrial admissibility hearing. "Challenges to both the admissibility and legal sufficiency of expert testimony involve the same substantive guidelines for determining relevance and reliability... It is not our place to change this legal sufficiency point into something else, or dismiss it by reviewing a different decision ... according to a different standard of review."

Id. at 182; *see Kerr – McGee Corp. v. Helton*, 133 S. W. 3d 245 (Tex. 2004) (if an expert opinion is unreliable, it is no evidence and any demonstrative exhibits that reflect those opinions are also no evidence); *See generally Abraham v. Union Pac. R. Co.*, 233 S. W. 3d 13, 17 (Tex. App. —Houston [14th Dist.] 2007, pet. denied) ("In the context of a motion for summary judgment where, as here, expert evidence relied on by the nonmovant is objected to by the movant based on reliability, the evidence must be both admissible and legally sufficient to withstand the no evidence challenge."); *Frias v. Atlantic Richfield Co.*, 104 S. W. 3d 925, 928 n. 2 (Tex. App. —Houston [14th Dist.] 2003, no pet.) (declining to decide which standard of review applies to a no evidence motion for summary judgment when an challenge is made to expert evidence, because both standards of review—abuse of discretion and de novo—must ultimately be satisfied and "we cannot, as a practical matter, envision a situation in which expert testimony would be reliable enough to be admissible or legally sufficient, but not the other").

A number of courts have stated that while a challenge to the admissibility of expert evidence is subject to an abuse of discretion standard, the review of expert testimony for purposes of legal sufficiency is "almost de novo". *See Scott's Marina at Lake Grapevine Ltd. v. Brown*, 07 – 10 – 00277 – CV, 2012 WL 177970 at *5 (Tex. App. —Amarillo Jan. 23, 2012, no pet.) (stating that in determining whether expert testimony is reliable, a reviewing court must employ "an almost *de novo* – like review and, like the trial court, look beyond the expert's bare testimony to determine the reliability of the theory underlying it"); *Gen. Motors Corp. v. Burry*, 203 S. W. 3d 514, 526 (Tex. App. —Fort Worth 2006, pet. denied); *Gross v. Burt*, 149 S. W. 3d 213 (Tex. App. —Fort Worth 2004, pet. denied) (stating that the reliability of expert testimony is reviewed by an almost de novo like review); *Goodyear Tire & Rubber Co. v. Rios*, 143 S. W. 3d 107 (Tex. App. —San Antonio 2004, pet. denied) (stating that when a trial court admits expert testimony and an appellant challenges expert testimony as constituting no evidence, the appellate court considers "whether the expert testimony is reliable under a de novo standard of review"); *Frias v. Atlantic Richfield Co.*, 104 S. W. 3d 925, 927 (Tex. App. —Houston [14th Dist.] 2003, no pet. h.) (declining to decide which standard of review applies to a no evidence motion for summary judgment when an challenge is made to expert evidence, because both standards of review—abuse of discretion and de novo review— "must ultimately be satisfied and "we cannot, as a practical matter, envision a situation in which expert testimony would be reliable enough to be admissible or legally sufficient, but not the other"); *Austin v. Kerr – McGee*, 25 S. W. 3d 280, 285 (Tex. App. —Texarkana 2000, no pet.). In other words, in a legal sufficiency challenge, "[a] party may raise a properly preserved complaint ... that scientific evidence is unreliable and thus no evidence to support a judgment". *Volkswagen*, 159 S. W. 3d at 903. The reason is that unreliable expert evidence is not only inadmissible but is also incompetent. *City of Keller*, 168 S. W. 3d at 813.

According to *Minnesota Mining & Manufacturing Co. v. Atterbury*, 978 S. W. 2d 183 (Tex. App. —Texarkana 1998, pet. denied), the distinction between sufficiency and admissibility allows a defendant two bites at the apple. If the trial court excludes the expert's opinion, an appellate court will review that determination under a "lenient" abuse of discretion standard. If, on the other hand, the trial court admits the expert's opinion but the defendant argues on appellate that it was unreliable and constitutes no evidence, an appellate court will review the determination based on "an almost" de novo standard.

In *Austin v. Kerr – McGee*, 25 S. W. 3d 280 (Tex. App. —Texarkana 2000, no pet.), the court noted that although they overlap because they both involve reliability, admissibility and sufficiency of expert testimony are distinct questions. Expert evidence may be admissible but insufficient when "a party uses multiple experts or relies on other proof to establish an element of a claim". But when the expert evidence is only evidence of causation, a court uses the same test for admissibility and legal sufficiency of the expert's testimony.

The Court's use of *Robinson* factors—including the absence of testing—for determining whether the evidence was legally sufficient in *Whirlpool* demonstrates that the Court has blended the standard of review for legal sufficiency with the abuse of discretion standard for admissibility of expert testimony.

In *Custom Transit, L. P. v. Flatrolled Steel, Inc.*, No. 14 – 10 – 00936 – CV (Tex. App. —Houston [14th Dist.] June 14, 2012, no pet. h.), the court rejected a legal sufficiency challenge based on a challenge to the reliability of an expert's damages calculation. The defendant's challenge focused on three of the *Robinson* factors: testing, publication and error rate The court first noted that there is an "imperfect fit" between the *Robinson* factors and the expert testimony regarding certain technical issues. While the defendant challenged the statistical analysis performed by the expert, it did not offer any specifics regarding the statistical analysis that it contended should have been conducted. It also did not explain why the sample size used by the expert was "invalid". "We do not believe that these factors deprive [the expert's] testimony regarding cargo damage of all validity so as to make that testimony the equivalent of 'no evidence' or almost 'no evidence'". A wide analytical gap did not exist between the data and the expert's opinions and the expert explained the practical reasons that he did not inspect all the coils that he testified were damages.

The court in *Custom Transit* also addressed whether a contention that the expert failed to rule out alternative causes of damage to the coils. The court observed, "there is room for discussion regarding the degree to which admissibility and sufficiency determinations depend on exclusion of proffered or alternative explanations for a particular event. 'While an expert should address evidence that contradicts his conclusion, [i] t is not required ... that an expert categorically exclude each and every possible alternative cause in order to render the proffered testimony admissible.'"

E. Developments in the Standard of Review

Hernandez v. State, 116 S. W. 3d 26 (Tex. Crim. App. 2003), raised the issue of whether an appellate court should utilize a de novo standard of review to the reliability of an expert's theory or methodology but an abuse of discretion review to the trial court's application of the theory or methodology to the facts of the case. In *State v. Dahood*, 814 A. 2d 159, 161 - 62 (N. H. 2002), the court utilized a de novo review for determining the reliability of the horizontal gaze nystagmus test.

F. Use of Inadmissible Evidence

A trial court ruling on an expert challenge may consider inadmissible evidence. Tex. R. Evid. 104. For example, inadmissible evidence on an experts' qualifications could be considered by a trial court. *Magee v. Ulery*, 993 S. W. 2d 332, 333 (Tex. App. Houston [14th Dist.] 1999, no pet.).

G. Make a Specific Objection

How specific an objection must be by a party raising a reliability challenge is an open procedural question. Some parties make blanket reliability challenges to all of an expert's opinions, hoping to use the burden of proof placed on the offering party to obtain a preview of the full basis of the expert's opinions. Conversely, they hope for a failure to establish some link in the chain of proving reliability in order to exclude the testimony. In any event, it is important to object consistently. *Coastal Chem.*, *Inc. v. Brown*, 35 S. W. 3d 90 (Tex. App. —Houston [14th Dist.] 2000, no pet.) (no error in allowing the plaintiff's expert to testify since the testimony "was merely cumulative of" other evidence); *Cruz v. Hinojosa*, 12 S. W. 3d 545 (Tex. App. —San Antonio 1999, pet. denied) (trial court's refusal to permit the plaintiff to replay parts of the expert's videotaped deposition for rebuttal was not error since "the portions sought to be admitted had already come before the jury during the case - in - chief" and therefore was cumulative); *In re J. B.*, 93 S. W. 3d 609, 637 (Tex. App. —Waco 2002, pet. denied) ("the adequacy of an objection that the expert testimony is not sufficiently reliable should be questioned because there are multiple elements and ways to test reliability").

1. *State Court*

General rules on the need for specific objections suggest that a broad "unreliable" objection may not preserve error, particularly when the objection is made pretrial and is made to more than one witness. The party opposing admission of certain evidence has the burden of interposing timely and specific objections to evidence offered. *Wilkins v. Royal Indem. Co.*, 592 S. W. 2d 64 (Tex. Civ. App. —Tyler 1979, no writ); *s ee* Tex. R. Evid. 103.

Objections should be clear and specific so that they may be understood by the court and obviated by the opposing party, if they are capable of being removed by production of other evidence. *Campbell v. Paschall*, 121 S. W. 2d 539 (Tex. Comm. App. 1938, opinion adopted). A "specific objection" is one that enables the trial court to understand the precise question and to make an intelligent ruling, affording the offering party the opportunity to remedy the defect if possible. *De Los Angeles Garay v. TEIA*, 700 S. W. 2d 657 (Tex. App. —Corpus Christi 1985, no writ); *Texas Mun. Power Agency v. Berger*, 600 S. W. 2d 850 (Tex. Civ. App. —Houston [1st Dist.] 1980, no writ); *University of Texas System v. Haywood*, 546 S. W. 2d 147 (Tex. Civ. App. —Austin 1977, no writ).

Arguably *E. I. du Pont de Nemours & Co. v. Robinson*, 923 S. W. 2d 549, 557 (Tex.

1995) requires the party opposing the evidence to make a specific objection to a specific offer of expert evidence. In *Robinson*, the motion to exclude detailed the basis for the motion with specificity. *Id.* at 557. "At that point", the offering party bears the burden of proof. *Id.* The objection must be specific.

Subsequent courts have held that an objection that an expert fails to satisfy the requirements of Rule 702 is a general objection. *Gregory v. State*, 56 S. W. 3d 164 (Tex. App.—Houston [14th Dist.] 2001), *pet. granted in part*, 2002 Tex. App. LEXIS 61 (Tex. Crim. App. Mar. 20, 2002); *Hernandez v. State*, 53 S. W. 3d 742 (Tex. App.—Houston [1st Dist.] 2001, no pet.); *see also Scherl v. State*, 7 S. W. 3d 650, 652 (Tex. App.—Texarkana 1999, pet. ref'd) (objection that expert testimony inadmissible under Tex. R. Evid. 702 and *Daubert* insufficient); *Chisum v. State*, 988 S. W. 2d 244, 250 - 51 (Tex. App.—Texarkana 1998, pet. ref'd) (objection to expert opinions without specifying particular deficiency in qualifications or reliability waived error); *Gen. Motors Corp. v. Saenz*, 974 S. W. 2d 407, 408 n. 1 (Tex. App.—San Antonio 1998) (opinion and order on reh'g en banc) (Rickhoff, J., concurring), *rev'd on other grounds sub nom. Gen. Motors Corp. v. Sanchez*, 997 S. W. 2d 584 (Tex. 1999) (a specific objection is preferable, even if not mandatory, to preserve error).

An objection that an expert witness does not meet the standard for offering opinion testimony under *Daubert* and Rule 702 does not preserve error when the objection does not specify whether the defect is the expert's qualification, relevance or reliability. *GTE Mobilnet of S. Tex. Ltd. P'ship v. Pascouet*, 61 S. W. 3d 599, 613 (Tex. App.—Houston [14th Dist.] 2001, pet. denied). GTE objected to the Pascouets' expert's qualifications before trial. At trial, the Pascouets attempted to demonstrate their expert's qualifications. GTE then again objected to the expert's qualifications, and the Pascouets further examined the expert regarding his qualifications. GTE then told the court that the Pascouets had not "met the standard required under *Robinson* or *Daubert* or Rule 702".

GTE, however, did not specify the standard that it claimed had not been satisfied. For example, was GTE referring to the requirement that experts be qualified or that their testimony be relevant or that their testimony be reliable? Further, GTE made this general statement as an argument; rather than as an objection. GTE did not object on these grounds when [the expert] later testified as to his expert opinions.

The court then concluded that GTE had not preserved error regarding the reliability of the expert's testimony.

A speculation objection does not preserve a *Robinson* challenge. *Gen. Motors Corp. v. Sanchez*, 997 S. W. 2d584, 590 - 91 (Tex. 1999). Courts frequently treat objections that testimony is speculative and conclusory as interchangeable, and neither preserves a reliability challenge. For example, the Texas Supreme Court in *Sanchez* refused to consider a reliability challenge raised for the first time on appeal. *Id.* at 591. The Court did consider, but reject, a speculation objection because the expert offered "more ... than [his] bald assertion that his design would be safer".

The objection should also make it clear whether the party is objecting just on *Daubert/Robinson grounds or also on qualifications grounds*. A reliability objection does not preserve a qualifications objection. *Kroger Co. v. Betancourt*, 996 S. W. 2d 353, 360 - 61 (Tex. App. —Houston [14th Dist.] 1999, pet. denied) (holding that Kroger's objection that the expert's opinion was speculative and not reliable did not preserve any error based on lack of qualifications). And a qualifications objection does not preserve a reliability challenge. *Nissan Motor Co. Ltd. v. Armstrong*, 145 S. W. 3d 131, 143 – 44 (Tex. 2004) (pretrial motion to exclude the expert's opinions because of lack of qualifications did not preserve objection that his opinions were unreliable); *Schindler Elevator Corp. v. Anderson*, 78 S. W. 3d 392, 403 (Tex. App. —Houston [14th Dist.] (2001, pet. granted, judgment vacated w. r. m.) (holding that pretrial motion that focused on expert's qualifications did not preserve objection to reliability of testimony and stating that "objections to qualifications are thus distinct from objections about reliability"), *disapproved of on other grounds by Roberts v. Williamson*, 111 S. W. 3d 113 (Tex. 2003). *Cf. Guadalupe – Blanco River Auth. v. Kraft*, 77 S. W. 3d 805 (Tex. 2002) (finding error was preserved to expert testimony on market value of easement when the appellant objected that the expert's methodology did not meet the reliability standards articulated by *Gammill.* "This objection adequately informed the trial court to rule on the reliability of [the expert's] methodology and hence its admissibility").

In *Schindler Elevators*, the court held that a challenge to the reliability of an escalator designer's testimony in a motion in limine did not preserve error. The few reliability objections made during the trial did not preserve error because there was no running objection. Moreover, the occasional objections to reliability did not address the specific reliability objections raised on appeal. Objections to the expert's qualifications are distinct from objections about reliability.

An attorney should take care to ensure that any pretrial motion directed toward expert testimony does not include limine language. *Delane v. State*, No. 01 – 10 – 00698 – CR, 2012 WL 340234 (Tex. App. —Houston [1st Dist.] Feb. 2, 2012, no. pet. h.) (Brown, J. , dissenting). Defendant's motion in limine to suppress drug/medication evidence operated as a motion in limine, not a motion to suppress. *Id.* at 12. The pretrial motion was "ambiguously – titled" and was "most akin to a motion in limine". *Id.* at 13. The objecting party failed to satisfy its burden, "as the party charged with preserving error, to make clear the relief requested".

2. *Federal Court*

A general objection to evidence in federal court is also normally insufficient. Courts have noted on numerous occasions that general objections do not preserve error. *See*, *eg. United States – Limones*, 529 F. 2d 1183, 1190 (5th Cir. 1976) (relating that a nonspecific objection that "was too loosely formulated and imprecise to apprise the court of [the defendant's] complaint ... did not preserve error"). An objection must state its specific grounds. *Carona v. Pioneer Life Ins. Co.* , 357 F. 2d 477, 480 (5th Cir. 1966); *see also Goulah v. Ford Motor Co.* , 118 F. 3d 1997 (11th Cir. 1997) (holding that an objection on one ground does not preserve error for any other ground).

The federal courts have yet to explicitly address the burden on the movant seeking to strike expert testimony. *Kumho Tire Co. Ltd. v. Carmichael*, 526 U. S. 137, 149, 119 S. Ct. 1167, 1175, 1177 (1999) found that the objecting party had called the expert's testimony "sufficiently into question". The Fifth Circuit concluded that the issue was sufficiently raised "by providing conflicting medical literature and expert testimony". *Tanner v. Westbrook*, 174 F. 3d 542, 546 (5th Cir. 1999). *See also Rodriguez v. Riddell Sports, Inc.*, 242 F. 3d 567 (5th Cir. 2001) (challenge must sufficiently call into question expert's factual basis, data, principles, methods or their application); *Polypropylene Carpet Antitrust Lit.*, 2000 U. S. Dist. LEXIS 10322 (N. D. Ga. Apr. 27, 2000) (defendant "seems to acknowledge … that it must produce evidence").

In *Quiet Technology DC – 8 v. Hurel – Dubois UK Ltd.*, 326 F. 3d 1333 (11th Cir. 2003), the court noted that although qualifications, reliability and helpfulness objections may overlap to some degree, they "are distinct concepts that courts and litigants must take care not to conflate". *Id.* at 1341. An expert may be well qualified but still present unreliable testimony. Thus, a challenge to the methodology used by an expert cannot be used to attack the expert's credentials.

A specific objection does not, however, require presentation of opposing expert testimony. *Brooks v. Outboard Marine Corp.*, 234 F. 3d 89, 91 (2d Cir. 2000) ("Nowhere in either opinion [*Daubert* or *Kumho Tire*] is there any language suggesting that testimony could only be 'called sufficiently into question' by a rebuttal expert.").

3. *Conclusion*

Just as it is improper to make conclusory, no – evidence summary judgment motions without identifying the specific elements that are lacking evidence, Tex. R. Civ. P. 166a, cmt. (stating that the motion must be "specific" and forbidding motions that are "conclusory" or "general") it is improper to make conclusory reliability challenges without specifying the opinions that are challenged. *Id.* (permitting an award of sanctions for a conclusory motion and noting that the same remedy may be appropriate for an improper motion to exclude) Thus, there are strong arguments for suggesting that Texas requires specific objections to specific opinions. Tex. R. App. P. 33. 1 (a) (1) (A).

H. Differences between Pretrial Objections and Trial Objections

On appeal, it is important to rely only on evidence that was before the court at the time of the ruling. For this reason, it may be prudent to mark the record of any pretrial *Daubert* hearing as an exhibit during trial.

For example, in *Piro v. Sarofin*, 80 S. W. 3d 717 (Tex. App. —Houston [1st Dist.] 2002, no pet.), an objection was made to the trial court's denial of a pre – trial motion to exclude the expert. The appellate court refused to consider evidence from the trial that suggested deficiencies in the expert's opinion. A party cannot rely on trial testimony to demonstrate that the trial court erred in failing to strike in response to a pretrial objection to an expert witness. The review of an objection is based on evidence before the court at the time of the ruling, not trial evidence after the ruling. The court also held that a trial court has discretion in determining "whether, when, and how to hold a *Robinson* hearing".

In *Mack Trucks Inc. v. Tamez*, 206 S. W. 3d 572, 579 (Tex. 2006), the Supreme Court held that testimony from a bill of exceptions made at trial could not be considered in determining whether the trial court erred in sustaining a *Daubert* objection during the pre – trial proceedings.

In *Marvelli v. Alston*, 100 S. W. 3d 460 (Tex. App. —Fort Worth 2003, pet. denied), the pretrial objections and hearing raised each complaint regarding expert testimony that was presented at trial and therefore preserved the error. While the error was preserved in that case, it underscores the possibility that a pretrial objection may not reach a slight change or revision in the manner in which the opinion is articulated at trial, and certainly will not reach new opinions presented at trial.

Even if a pretrial *Daubert* hearing was conducted, it is generally wise to address the issue at trial. One reason is that the expert's opinions at trial may not be identical to the opinions given in discovery. If they differ and no objection is made to the new opinion, any error is waived (unless the opinion is considered conclusory or speculative or is apparent on the face of the record). There is a second reason to object at trial even if your pretrial objection was overruled: the judge, who now knows the case much better, may change his or her mind and rule in your favor. Finally, as noted above, it is not clear whether a reviewing court will consider pretrial evidence in considering the reliability of expert testimony when raised through a no – evidence challenge.

I. Object to Opinions, Not to the Witness

The motion to strike or the objection should be addressed to expert opinions, rather than to the expert testimony as a whole. The overruling of an objection to or motion to strike testimony as a whole is not error, when part of such testimony is admissible. *Dabney v. Keene*, 195 S. W. 2d 682 (Tex. Civ. App. —El Paso 1946, writ ref' d n. r. e.). Courts on numerous occasions have found that when evidence is admissible in part, an objection to the entire offer of proof does not preserve error. *See*, *eg. Speier v. Webster College*, 616 S. W. 2d 617 (Tex. 1981) (finding that error in admitting into evidence of a portion of a chart on damages which was filled in by plaintiff's attorney without any testimony supporting it is waived by the failure of the objector to object to a particular portion of the chart, and a general objection to the admission of the chart as a whole into evidence did not preserve error); *Killebrew v. State*, 746 S. W. 2d 245, 247 (Tex. App. —Texarkana 1987, pet. ref' d); *Ideal Mutual Ins. Co. v. Sullivan*, 678 S. W. 2d 98 (Tex. App. —El Paso 1984, writ dism' d) (concluding that where a party offers a voluminous document or several items as a unit and the opponent merely objects to the whole offer, if parts of the offer are admissible there is no error in overruling a general objection which does not specify specific part to which valid objection could be made); *Lade v. Keller*, 615 S. W. 2d 916 (Tex. Civ. App. —Tyler 1981, no writ) (stating that where the question propounded calls for an answer which is partly admissible and partly inadmissible, the objecting party must point out and distinguish the admissible from the inadmissible and direct objections specifically to that point which is inadmissible); *Hurtado v. TEIA*, 563 S. W. 2d 360 (Tex. Civ. App. —San Antonio), *rev' d on other grounds*, 574 S. W. 2d 536 (Tex. 1978) (holding that objection to voluminous medical records on grounds of hearsay, opinion and conclusory matters did not require objector to examine each of the 280 pages and segregate the inadmissible items from the admissible items).

In *Green v. Texas Workers Comp. Ins. Facility*, 993 S. W. 2d 839 (Tex. App. —Austin 1999, no pet.), the trial court struck a treating physician's causation testimony as unreliable under *Robinson*. The court of appeals found that the trial court's decision to strike his causation opinion ruling was "close" but within the trial court's discretion. The board - certified physician in environmental medicine concluded that the plaintiff's workplace exposure to trichlorethane caused him numerous physical ailments.

In language very similar to a reversed Fifth Circuit panel decision, *Moore v. Ashland Chem.*, *Inc.*, 126 F. 3d 679, 688 (5th Cir. 1997), *rev' d en banc*, 151 F. 3d 269 (5th Cir. 1998) (en banc), the court observed that "medicine is as much art as science, and clinical medicine necessarily evolves from a process of trial and error". *Id.* at 844. Therefore, "some leeway" is necessary for admitting clinical physician testimony on causation. "A physician may not always be able to isolate to a mathematical certainty *why* human beings react in certain ways or *why* certain ailments respond to certain cures. This does not necessarily render such diagnoses or treatment ineffective or unreliable." The court also recognized the importance of objective testing by a physician for reaching causation conclusions.

While the court's language is dicta, it is obviously true that the physician does not need to present evidence of mathematical certainty on the issue of causation. Science, including clinical medicine, can "produce very precise, accurate, and reliable information" without requiring mathematical certainty. Bert Black, *The Supreme Court's View of Science: Has Daubert Exorcised the Certainty Demon*, 15 Cardozo L. Rev. 2129 (1994).

Miscasting science in terms of certainty and then casting it aside in the courtroom is a form of know - nothing irrationality... The mistaken view that science somehow requires "absolute truth" reflects a fundamental misunderstanding that there exists a unitary and deterministic scientific method... Science is not, however, merely a matter of taste. Valid science is characterized by the systematic organization of information, by explanations of why observed phenomenon and events occur, and by empirical testing. Thus, the real question is not whether science requires too much certainty, but rather how scientists can reach conclusions at the level of certainty the law requires. *Id.* at 2130.

"Despite the elusiveness which forecloses an *absolute* determination of causality", a physician should follow a generally accepted protocol for rendering causation opinions for the specific condition instead of giving causation testimony based on speculation. *Black v. Food Lion*, *Inc.*, 171 F. 3d 308, 310, 313 - 14 (5th Cir. 1999). Future courts should not, therefore, read too much into *Green*'s discussion of the "leeway" given to clinical physicians.

The appellate court in *Green* concluded that the trial court had erred in excluding all of the expert's opinions. While some of the opinions may have been properly excluded, all of them were not.

J. Waiver by Presentation of Opposing Expert

One Texas appellate court has indicated that presenting an expert in response to objectionable opinions may waive any error. *Russell v. Ramirez*, 949 S. W. 2d 480, 488 (Tex. App. —Houston [14th Dist.] 1997, no writ). The court held that " [a] party on appeal should not be heard to complain of the admission of improper evidence offered by the other side, when he, himself, introduced the same evidence or evidence of a similar character". Thus, if a party presents a rebuttal expert, the party should make it clear on the record that it does so despite its objection to the opposing expert.

In one Nebraska case, a court held that if a plaintiff's expert critiques the defendant's expert, any error in the subsequent admission of the defense expert's testimony is waived. *Perry Lumber Co. v. Durable Servs.*, *Inc.*, 667 N. W. 2d 194 (Neb. 2003).

On the other hand, a party may not waive legal and factual insufficiency challenges to a damages award by introducing an affidavit from the supporting expert. *Custom Transit*, *L. P. v. Flatrolled Steel*, *Inc.*, No. 14 – 10 – 00936 – CV, 2012 WL 2154501 (Tex. App. —Houston [14th Dist.] June 14, 2012, no pet. h.). In that case, the defendant challenged the reliability of the plaintiff's damages expert before trial. The trial court granted in part and denied in part the motion. When the defendant offered into evidence the affidavit of the plaintiff's expert, the trial court then set aside its order granting part of the motion to exclude. The court of appeals held that the admission of the affidavit did not waive legal and factual sufficiency challenges. The court relied on *Kerr – McGee*, discussed earlier, where the Texas Supreme Court treated expert exhibits admitted without objection as "no evidence" based on a challenge to the reliability of the expert's analysis (i. e. the expert's assumption that one well would have had same production as another well in the area). The main procedural holding in *Kerr – McGee* was that the challenge to the expert testimony was timely raised by a post – cross objection, but the less – noticeable holding on the exhibits (if the testimony was no evidence, the exhibits were necessarily no evidence too) indicated that no objection was necessary to the exhibits.

K. Preserving Error for the Exclusion of Expert Testimony

If the trial court rejects expert testimony, it is necessary to make an offer of proof. A separate offer of proof is necessary for every excluded opinion. *Hernandez v. State*, 127 S. W. 3d 206 (Tex. App. —Houston [1st Dist.] 2003, no pet.). In this murder trial, the defendant preserved error for the exclusion for one part of his expert's testimony but not for a second opinion of the expert. The defendant sought to introduce testimony from a psychiatrist that ①he acted at the time of the murder in an excited emotional state and with sudden passion as a result of a multitude of factors and②that his lack of remorse after the murder was a result of disassociative mental disorders.

The defendant did obtain a ruling that the trial court was excluding his expert's testimony on his state of mind and thus preserved any error. Although the trial court twice referred to its ruling as a ruling on a motion in limine, the judge "repeatedly indicated that it was *presently* ruling that this line of testimony was prohibited. Accordingly, that ruling was not part of the trial court's general in limine ruling, and the court's ruling prohibiting testimony on appellant's mental state thus sufficed to preserve error".

However, the defendant did waive any error concerning a second opinion from the expert. The defendant never mentioned during the voir dire hearing that the psychiatrist would have testified about how the defendant's disassociative disorder accounted for appellant's behavior *after* the killing. An affidavit in a motion for new trial was insufficient to preserve error; "[w] aiting to make an offer of proof until filing his motion for new trial did not suffice". Therefore, the defendant waived any argument that the trial court erred in excluding such testimony.

L. Use a Court Reporter at Gatekeeper Hearings

It is unclear who bears burden of proof of obtaining a record from the *Daubert* hearing. *See Exxon Corp. v. Makofski*, 116 S. W. 3d 176 (Tex. App. —Houston [14th Dist.] 2003, pet. denied); *Coastal Tankships, U. S. A., Inc. v. Anderson*, 87 S. W. 3d 591 (Tex. App. — Houston [1st Dist.] 2002, pet. denied). But a court is required to provide a court reporter upon request by Texas Rule of Appellate Procedure 13. 1.

M. When to Hear a Daubert/Robinson Challenge

1. *There is no exclusive procedure for challenging the expert*

There are two fundamental options: require a pre – trial motion or permit the challenge to be made during trial by formal objection. It appears the Texas Supreme Court wants to give the trial courts an opportunity to experiment with different procedures before determining the best procedure. *Maritime Overseas*, 971 S. W. 2d at 425 (Hecht, J., dissenting).

The Texas Supreme Court does agree that such challenges should normally be made pre – trial. *Id.* at 412; at 414 (Gonzalez, J., concurring). *Id.* at 423 (Hecht, J., dissenting) ("ordinarily the issue must be raised before the verdict"). *See also Hose v. Chicago N. W. Transp. Co.*, 70 F. 3d 968, 973 n. 3 (8th Cir. 1995) (should challenge reliability pre – trial); *Robinson v. Missouri Pac. Railroad Co.*, 16 F. 3d 1083, 1089 (10th Cir. 1994) ("as gatekeeper, the district court should carefully and meticulously make an early pretrial evaluation of issues of admissibility").

The motion is typically called a "motion to strike" or "motion to exclude" if it is raised in advance of trial and a motion in limine if raised at the commencement of trial. There is some authority suggesting that a trial court may require through a pre – trial order that the challenge be raised in a pre – trial motion. In the absence of a court order, a Texas trial court would probably be unable to overrule an objection at trial due to lateness. *But see Bayliner Marine Corp. v. Elder*, 994 S. W. 3d 439 (Tex. App. —Beaumont 1999, pet. dism' d) (noting, without deciding whether it agreed, that the trial court held that an objection at trial to the reliability of the expert's testimony was waived by a failure to object pre - trial). The *Bayliner* court did agree that a trial court should be able to order expert challenges before trial. "The trial court must have the same kind of latitude in deciding ... whether or when special briefing or other proceedings are needed to investigate reliability, as it enjoys when it decides whether or not that expert's relevant testimony is reliable." *Id.* at 446.

2. *Trial courts are using a number of different procedures.*

Some courts require the challenge to be made long before the trial. Other courts require the motion to be heard no later than shortly before trial. Some courts hear the motion during a motion in limine. Some courts prefer to hear the motion in trial.

N. Combining No - Evidence Summary Judgment Motions with Expert Challenges

Rule 104 (a) permits a court to conduct a hearing on expert challenges. The difficulty is when a party files a motion for summary judgment to which the opposing party files a response that includes an affidavit from an expert, and the moving party then objects to the affidavit under *Robinson* and its progeny. In this situation, is either of the parties entitled to an evidentiary hearing on the admissibility of the expert testimony despite the prohibition in Rule 166a on oral testimony?

1. *Texas courts*

Many courts set both motions for the same time. These courts then hear the motion to strike the expert testimony first and conduct a full evidentiary hearing. During these hearings, some lawyers provide the court with live testimony from experts, while other attorneys rely solely on affidavits, reports, and depositions with attachments.

After ruling on the motion to strike, these courts then rule on the summary judgment motion. In most causation summary judgment motions, if the expert is struck there will be no evidence in opposition to the summary judgment motion and it will be granted. Fairness in some cases may require a continuance of the summary judgment hearing to allow the party whose expert is struck an opportunity to find a new expert. If the expert is not struck, the denial of the summary judgment is not reviewable on appeal. In this situation, the motion to strike will have to be revisited at trial to make the decision reviewable.

The Court in *Gammill* appears to have approved the procedure of reviewing the admissibility of the expert's opinions under Rule 104 (a) before ruling on the motion for summary judgment. *Gammill* was an appeal of a summary judgment for the defendants. In response to the motion, the plaintiffs contended that a fact issue was raised by the affidavits of their two engineers. In reply, the defendants moved to strike the testimony of the plaintiff's' experts. An evidentiary hearing, apparently under Rule 104 (a), was then conducted. The Court did not express any difficulty with the procedure, nor did it change the appellate standard for review of the trial court's determination both for qualifications and reliability: the standard remains abuse of discretion.

In *Praytor v. Ford Motor Co.*, 97 S. W. 3d 237, 246 (Tex. App. —Houston [14th Dist.] 2002, no pet.), the court concluded that a respondent to a no - evidence motion for summary judgment that involved the reliability of expert testimony could "request a continuance of the summary judgment proceeding in order to submit additional evidence. The non – movant [could] also request a *Robinson – Daubert* hearing in order to overcome the reliability challenge". If a hearing is held on the admissibility of the expert's testimony, the appellate court may not consider it if the record is not brought forward on appeal.

It should be noted that a trial court is not required to conduct a *Robinson – Daubert* hearing separate and apart from the summary judgment hearing to determine the admissibility of summary judgment evidence from an expert witness. *Rayon v. Energy Specialties, Inc.*, 121 S. W. 3d 7, 19 - 20 (Tex. App. —Fort Worth 2002, no pet.). In that case, the court observed that the standards for admissibility of expert testimony were the same in a summary judgment proceeding and in trial. Thus, a proponent of expert evidence presented in a summary judgment must demonstrate its reliability.

In making determinations of no – evidence challenges to expert testimony, a court's review should include contrary evidence. *City of Keller v. Wilson*, 168 S. W. 3d 802 (Tex. 2005) ("An appellate court considering a no – evidence review cannot consider only an expert's bare opinion, but must also consider contrary evidence showing it has no scientific basis."). This contrary evidence can be a wide array of things, including admissions by an expert on cross – examination as well as the testimony of opposing experts. *Id.* at 827; *Cooper Tire & Rubber Co. v. Mendez*, 204 S. W. 3d 797, 804 (Tex. 2006) ("Reliance on evidence that undermines [the expert's] hypothesis is another reason for concluding" that the testimony is unreliable.).

2. *Federal courts*

The federal courts have indicated that the trial court may consider a *Daubert* challenge before a summary judgment, and if the party prevails in striking an expert, grant a summary judgment. *Daubert*, 509 U. S. at 596 (the trial court should grant summary judgment in the event that the "scintilla of evidence supporting a position is insufficient to allow a reasonable juror to conclude that the position more likely than not is true"); *Barrett v. Atlantic Richfield Company*, 95 F. 3d 375, 383 (5th Cir. 1996) (affirming summary judgment because without the inadmissible and/or untimely expert testimony offered by plaintiffs, plaintiffs had "not produced any evidence demonstrating a causal link between their alleged damages and the chemicals at the disposal site"); *Cortes – Irizarry v. Corporacion Insula De Segurosr*, 111 F. 3d 184, 188 (1st Cir. 1997) ("If proffered expert testimony fails to cross *Daubert*'s threshold for admissibility, a district court may exclude that evidence from consideration when passing upon a motion for summary judgment" but cautioning that the proponent of the evidence must be afforded "adequate opportunity to defend its admissibility"); *Sheehan v. Daily Racing Form, Inc.*, 104 F. 3d 940, 942 (7th Cir. 1997) (Since the expert's statistical study "would not have been admissible at trial, it was entitled to zero weight in considering whether to grant or deny summary judgment".); *Hopkins v. NCR Corp.*, No. 93 – 188 – B – M2, 1994 U. S. Dist. LEXIS 17273 (M. D. La. Nov. 17, 1994) *aff' d*, 53 F. 3d 1281 (5th Cir. 1995) (the trial court must first determine if affidavits presented in opposition to a summary judgment are admissible. If the affidavit is from an expert, it must satisfy *Daubert*, and, if it does not, the court may grant a motion for summary judgment.).

The Fifth Circuit has recognized that there are separate standards for review of a trial court's decision to grant a summary judgment and a decision to exclude an expert witness. *Honeycutt v. Orr*, 200 F. 3d 291 (5th Cir. 2000); *Munoz v. Orr*, 200 F. 3d 291 (5th Cir. 2000); *Curtis v. M&S Petroleum, Inc.*, 174 F. 3d 661 (5th Cir. 1999). An expert witness exclusion is reviewed under the abuse of discretion standard, while a summary judgment is reviewed de novo. *Honeycutt*, 200 F. 3d at 300.

One Texas federal district court has stated that when determining the admissibility of expert testimony for purposes of a motion for summary judgment, the court "should be more careful about excluding testimony than including testimony". *Alcan Aluminum Corp. v. BASF Corp.*, 133 F. Supp. 482, 493 (N. D. Tex. 2001). The responding party must be given an adequate opportunity to defend its admissibility and therefore the court elected only to conduct a "preliminary review" of the admissibility of the expert's testimony. *Id.* "Courts need not, and perhaps often should not, apply *Daubert* at the summary judgment stage." *Id.* In this case, the court held there existed a genuine issue of material fact independent of the causation experts' testimony. Therefore, the court need not and did not reach the question of whether the experts' opinions could be considered for purposes of summary judgment.

O. Conclusory Affidavits Offered for Summary Judgment Purposes

Texas Rule of Civil Procedure 166a (f) requires that, in summary judgment proceedings, supporting and opposing affidavits "shall set forth such facts as would be admissible in evidence, and shall show affirmatively that the affiant is competent to testify to the matters stated therein". When a party relies on expert testimony as summary judgment evidence, the rule requires proof of the expert's qualifications and the reliability of the expert's conclusions. *Earle v. Ratliff*, 998 S. W. 2d 882 (Tex. 1999); *Hess v. McLean Feedyard, Inc.*, 59 S. W. 3d 679 (Tex. App. —Amarillo 2000, pet. denied). A trial court properly rejects the affidavit testimony of any expert witness whose qualifications are not established in the summary judgment record. *Boren v. Bullen*, 972 S. W. 2d 863, 865 (Tex. App. —Corpus Christi 1998, no pet.).

An affidavit by an expert that fails to outline facts upon which the opinion is based not only violates the duty to establish the reliability of opinions, pursuant to *Robinson* and its progeny, but also contravenes the rule that conclusory opinions in a summary judgment affidavit are not sufficient to raise an issue of fact. *Hess v. McLean Feedyard, Inc.*, 59 S. W. 3d 679 (Tex. App. —Amarillo 2000, pet. denied). For example, conclusory statements by a physician – expert in a medical negligence case do not raise an issue as to medical causation. *Blan v. Ali*, 7 S. W. 3d 741, 747 (Tex. App. —Houston [14th Dist.] 1999, no pet.). Moreover, an affidavit is conclusory when it does not contain a causation opinion that links the alleged cause to the result, as opposed to merely recognizing that the result could potentially be caused by the alleged cause. *Hight v. Dublin Veterinary Clinic*, 22 S. W. 3d 614, 621 – 22 (T. App. —Eastland 2000, pet. denied).

In *Hight*, the plaintiff appealed the granting of a no – evidence summary judgment when an expert's affidavit was stricken in a veterinary malpractice claim arising from the death of a goat following surgery to remove its horns. *Id.* at 621. The affidavit revealed that the expert had reviewed a lab report and various related documents and further stated that because of the risks involved with the use of anesthesia, a minimum standard of care would be to monitor the animal closely following surgery because of the potential side effects or adverse reactions." *Id.* Nevertheless, the court held that the affidavit was merely conclusory and did not "contain an opinion as to whether any of the *potential* side effects or adverse reactions *from the anesthesia* did in fact occur here". *Id.* at 622. The affidavit related the risks of anesthesia and the importance of monitoring an animal post – surgically, but contained no "foundational information" that the goat's death was in any way related to the anesthesia or the failure to monitor him. As the court pointed out:

Neither does the affidavit contain any foundational reliability for such an opinion. There is no indication of the potential success of any resuscitative treatments. The affidavit contains no foundational information that the goat's death was in any way related to the anesthesia or to the failure to monitor him. As the court stated in *Gammill*, "he has offered nothing to suggest that what he believes *could have* happened actually *did* happen". ... Here, although the affidavit does provide information that various records were reviewed and that certain general principles exist in connection with the use of anesthesia, there is no information as to the methodology and basis which underlie the opinion testimony and how those records and general principles relate to the opinions given. Without such information, it is impossible to determine the issue of reliability, as that concept has been defined in *Daubert*, *Gammill*, and *Robinson*. *Id.* at 622

P. Is a Hearing Required?

In *Pink v. Goodyear Tire & Rubber Co.*, 324 S. W. 3d 290 (Tex. App. —Beaumont 2010, pet. filed), the court held that a separate *Daubert* hearing was required before ruling on a summary judgment. In this toxic tort lawsuit arising out of a plant workers' claim that benzene exposure caused his renal cell carcinoma, the trial court improperly granted summary judgment because an oncologist's causation opinion was not conclusory and the trial court did not rule on the reliability of the opinion. Turning to the reliability challenge, the court held that the lack of a *Robinson* hearing record and the failure to obtain an explicit ruling was fatal to the challenge on appeal. A ruling sustaining the defendant's reliability "objections to the causation opinion is not implicit" in the trial court's granting of the motion for summary judgment because the trial court could have granted summary judgment on two other grounds urged in the trial court—no duty and no breach of a duty. *Id.* at 300. The court was also troubled about attempting to rule on reliability without a record of hearing because there two different standards of review implicated in the case: abuse of discretion for an evidentiary objection based on lack of reliability and legal sufficiency for a no – evidence summary judgment. If the abuse of discretion standard is applied to the evidentiary issue, this approach would reduce the summary judgment appellate review standard to an abuse of discretion standard whenever case – determinative *Robinson* objections, coupled with a no – evidence motion for summary judgment, are considered implicitly sustained by the granting of summary judgment. Whether or not the trial court abused its discretion in sustaining the *Robinson* objections would be determinative on appeal of whether the summary judgment must be reversed or affirmed. *Id.*

Another problem is that *Robinson* hearings can include live testimony but a summary judgment hearings cannot. *Id.*

Considered with notice and opportunity – to – be – heard principles, these differences require that the two proceedings be separate under the circumstances of this case, and that we not consider [the defendant's] reliability objections as implicitly sustained by the trial court. . . . By conducting a separate *Robinson* hearing before considering a no – evidence motion for summary judgment, the trial court applies the process applicable to each hearing, provides the parties notice and an opportunity to present the best available evidence, and provides the appellate court with a full record for review. That process is required here. . . . The process missing from this appellate record, and necessary in this case, is a *Robinson* hearing. If the trial court decides the affidavit must be stricken because of unreliable foundational data, methodology, or technique, or for some other reason, the trial court may then decide whether to grant the no – evidence summary judgment, or "order a continuance to permit affidavits to be obtained or depositions to be taken or discovery to be had or may make such other order as is just". Without an express ruling that the treating oncologist's causation opinion is unreliable, however, the treating oncologist's affidavit remains part of the summary judgment proof and provides some evidence to defeat the no – evidence motion for summary judgment on causation. *Id.* at 301 – 02. (citations omitted)

The Tenth Circuit Court of Appeals has recognized that although a trial court has discretion in *how* it conducts its gatekeeping function, it does not have discretion in performing its gatekeeping function. *Dodge v. Cotter*, 328 F. 3d 1212 (10th Cir. 2003). As part of the gatekeeping function, the court must ensure "the creation of 'a sufficiently developed record in order to allow a determination of whether the district court properly applied the relevant law' " and must make "specific findings on the record" to show it has performed its gatekeeping duty. *Id.* at 1223 – 24. The *Daubert* issues could not be reliably decided upon without a meaningful hearing, which of necessity depends upon the use of live witness testimony. The court of appeals held that the trial court abused its discretion by placing unreasonable limitations on counsel's ability to present information to the court when the expert testimony was crucial to the ultimate outcome, was vigorously challenged, and had several obvious areas of concern. The appellate court reasoned that it was unreasonable to limit so severely both the underlying documentation and the use of live witness testimony upon which the court might base a decision.

The Second Circuit Court of Appeals has similarly held that a trial court has discretion over the timing of a *Daubert* hearing. *United States v. Yousef*, 327 F. 3d 56 (2d Cir. 2003). In an appeal from judgments of conviction for conspiracy to bomb United States commercial airliners and the February 1993 bombing of the World Trade Center in New York City, the defendants argued that the district court committed reversible error by holding the *Daubert* hearing before trial, instead of during trial. Two months before the *Daubert* hearing was held, the district court informed counsel that it "may want to" call its expert during the *Daubert* hearing and the time to call the experts "is then". Although defendants asked for a "mini – *Daubert*" hearing to be held during trial, the Second Circuit held that the district court's refusal to postpone the *Daubert* hearing was well within its discretion, given that holding a *Daubert* hearing thereafter would have interrupted the trial and wasted the jurors' time. The court noted that a potential issue might have been whether the defendants were given adequate notice that they would be required to produce their experts at the hearing or be precluded from presenting them at trial, but since the defendants did not allege that they would have produced additional experts but for the lack of notice, the court did not rule on this issue.

Although the Ninth Circuit Court of Appeals has held that a trial court is not required to hold a *Daubert* hearing, but is required to make findings. *Mukhtar v. Cal. State Univ.*, 319 F. 3d 1073, 1074 (9th Cir. 2003), *amending* 299 F. 3d 1053, 1066 (9th Cir. 2002). It further noted that a post – verdict remand to determine the reliability of expert testimony runs the "undue risk of post – hoc rationalization". *Id.* at 1074. The court reasoned that "[t]his is hardly the gatekeeping role the Court envisioned in *Daubert* and its progeny". *Id* at 1074.

In criminal cases in Texas, a hearing outside the presence of the jury is required. *Jackson v. State*, 17 S. W. 3d 664, 670 (Tex. Crim. App. 2000); *Harris v. State*, 2004 Tex. App. LEXIS 1554, at *34 - 35 (Tex. App. —Texarkana Feb. 18, 2004, pet. denied). *See also Coble v. State*, 330 S. W. 3d 253, 273 (Tex. Crim. App. 2010) (in criminal cases, a trial court must conduct a gatekeeping hearing outside the presence of the jury, on request, to determine whether expert evidence is sufficiently reliable and relevant to help the jury). *See also Thompson v. State*, No. 01 – 10 – 00398 – CR, 2012 WL 668937 (Tex. App. —Houston [1st Dist.] Mar. 1, 2012, no pet.) ("a gatekeeping hearing is required before admitting the evidence, regardless of whether the expertise at issue is novel or well – established")

Q. Must the Supporting Evidence be Offered Before the Jury?

Neither *Robinson* nor *Havner* require that all the foundation necessary to establish reliability be in evidence before the jury to preserve an admissibility challenge. Because the admissibility determination is made under Rule 104 (a), a party may presumably offer evidence at the hearing but fail to present such evidence before the jury. Tex. R. Evid. 104 (a) (stating that in determining admissibility, the court is not bound by the Rules of Evidence). Indeed, some evidence on the reliability issue cannot be tendered to the jury because a Rule 104 (a) hearing is not conducted under the rules of evidence. Tex. R. Evid. 104 (a). If the expert's testimony is admitted after a Rule 104 (a) hearing, the evidence from the hearing will be available for consideration in determining both the admissibility and, indirectly, the sufficiency of the evidence, even if the evidence is not fully presented to the jury. But any evidence necessary to establish the reliability of a testifying expert's opinion should be offered at trial to ensure it will be available to defend the expert's opinion in a sufficiency of the evidence review.

R. Bench Trials

In a non - jury trial, a trial court may properly defer the expert challenges until trial and even until after trial. *Olin Corp. v. Smith*, 990 S. W. 2d 789 (Tex. App. —Austin 1999, writ denied); *s ee also Weingarten VOT Investors v. Harris Cnty. Appraisal Dist.* , 93 S. W. 3d 280 (Tex. App. —Houston [14th Dist.] 2002, no pet.) (noting that in this non - jury trial, the trial court carried the motion under advisement and that it was after the trial that the court granted the motion to exclude the expert's testimony); *Gibbs v. Gibbs*, 210 F. 3d 491 (5th Cir. 2000) (noting that most *Daubert* safeguards are unnecessary in a bench trial.). The defendant in *Olin* argued that the plaintiff's expert failed to present reliable testimony that a delay in the firing of a gun was caused by defective ammunition. The defendant attempted to exclude the expert testimony by a pretrial motion, but the trial court did not rule on this motion before trial. At trial, the defendant again raised the issue of its pending motion during the testimony of each of the plaintiff's expert witnesses and also objected to any testimony by those experts concerning hangfires. After the trial court rendered judgment for the plaintiffs, the defendant filed a motion seeking a ruling on its pretrial motion, which the trial court denied. The court of appeals found no error in the procedure used by the trial court nor any waiver by the defendant. The court acknowledged that "trial judges have a heightened responsibility to ensure that expert testimony show some indicia of reliability", but stated that " [t] hese concerns are somewhat reduced in a trial to the court. Here, the confluence of the gatekeeper and fact - finder functions in the trial court served to ventilate fully any *Robinson* issues". *Id.* at 796 n. 1; *but see Seaboard Lumber Co. v. U. S.* , 308 F. 3d 1283, 1295 (Fed. Cir. 2002) (stating that the *Daubert* standards of relevance and reliability for scientific evidence must be met in a bench trial); *National Western Reserve Life Ins. Co. v. Rowe*, 86 S. W. 3d 285 (Tex. App. —Austin 2002), *rev' d on other grounds*, 164 S. W. 3d 389 (Tex. 2005).

S. Expert Opinions in Public Records

Following federal authority applying a similar rule, a Texas court of appeals has held that a police officer's accident report—including opinions expressed in the report—is admissible as an official record under Rule 803 (8) so long as the opinions are "based on a factual investigation and satisf [y] the Rule's trustworthiness requirement". *McRae v. Echols*, 8 S. W. 3d 797, 800 (Tex. App. —Waco 2000, pet. denied) (in action by forklift driver against automobile driver, court admitted part of report containing officer's opinion as to contributing factors for accident; dissent argued that record was business record but reliability of expert opinion was not established under *Daubert*); *see also State v. Williams*, 932 S. W. 2d 546, 552 - 53 (Tex. App. —Tyler 1995), *writ denied*, 940 S. W. 2d 583 (Tex. 1996) (admitting police officer report without any evidence of the officer's qualifications or the basis for his opinions); *b ut see Mary Lee Found. v. Tex. Emp' t Comm' n*, 817 S. W. 2d 725, 728 (Tex. App. —Texarkana 1991, writ denied) (public records exception does not mean ex parte statements, hearsay, conclusions, and opinions contained within records are admissible). It is not entirely clear whether the burden of proof on the issue of the trustworthiness of expert opinions that are subject to a *Daubert* challenge should be on the proponent of the record or the party opposing admission of the record. For a fuller discussion, see Harvey Brown, *Daubert Objections to Public Records: Who Bears the Burden of Proof?* 39 Hous. L. Rev. 413 (2002); *cf. Ter – Vartanyan v. R & R. Freight, Inc.*, 111 S. W. 3d 779 (Tex. App. —Dallas 2003, pet. denied) (concluding that police officer's report was admissible because the officer's opinion satisfied *Robinson*, and the same arguments apply to both trustworthiness and reliability).

T. Experts on Lost Profits

Courts are critically reviewing expert testimony on lost profits. *Total Clean, LLC v. Cox Smith Matthews Inc.*, 330 S. W. 3d 657 (Tex. App. —San Antonio 2010, pet. denied); *Atlas Copco Tools, Inc. v Air Power Tool & Hoist, Inc.*, 131 S. W. 3d 203 (Tex. App. — Fort Worth 2004, pet. denied); *VingCard A. S. v. Merrimac Hospitality Sys., Inc.*, 59 S. W. 3d 847, 863 (Tex. App. —Fort Worth 2001, no pet.); *b ut see Meaux Surface Protection, Inc. v. Fogleman*, 607 F. 3d 161 (5th Cir. 2010) (holding that "[u] nless the issues concerning lost profits are 'highly technical', expert testimony is not required" and permitting CFO of plaintiff – corporation to testify regarding lost profits caused by departing former employees)

In *Capital Metropolitan Transportation Authority*, 114 S. W. 3d at 573, a breach of contract case, the court concluded that an expert's testimony on lost profits was legally insufficient to support the jury's award. The court found that the evidence did not support a number of assumptions made by the expert.

Likewise in *Total Clean*, 330 S. W. 3d at 657 the court concluded that the expert's lost profits testimony was unreliable. He expert's calculation on the lost profits of a start – up automated commercial truck wash company were based on projections that were not grounded in objective facts or data. Research conducted on the internet resulted in unverified data. The expert also made improper assumptions regarding a correlation between traffic volume and the number of trucks that would stop.

However, in *Toshiba Machine Co. v. SPM Flow Control, Inc.*, 180 S. W3d 761 (Tex. App. —Fort Worth 2002), *pet. granted, cause remanded* (March 31, 2006), an appellate court concluded that an expert's testimony on lost profits was reliable. In this breach of contract case stemming from SPM's purchase of machine tools from Toshiba, the court held that SPM's vice president of finance was qualified to opine on SPM's lost profits and that his testimony was sufficiently reliable to amount to more than a scintilla of evidence of lost profits. SPM purchased from Toshiba machine tools whose purpose was to internally contour blocks of solid steel into what is called the *fluid end* of heavy – duty oilfield pumps. The Toshiba machine tools were supposed to allow SPM to make the fluid ends in less time than the tools SPM had been using. There were performance issues with the machine tools and their software. SPM sued Toshiba for fraud, negligent misrepresentation, breach of contract, and breach of warranty. Toshiba countersued to the unpaid balance of the machine tools. The jury found for SPM on every issue, awarding, among other things, over MYM6 million in lost profits.

Ray Gilbert, SPM's vice president of finance, was SPM's lost profits expert at trial. Gilbert was a degreed accountant with nearly three decades of experience managing the accounting functions of companies engaged in the manufacture of various products. Gilbert had been with SPM for over five years when SPM purchased the Toshiba machine tools. Gilbert calculated three categories of lost profits caused by the problems with the Toshiba machine tools: ①the increased cost of producing fluid ends; ②lost fluid end sales; and③lost sales of flow control products associated with lost fluid end sales. Toshiba challenged Gilbert's qualifications, his reliance on hearsay, and the speculative nature of his lost profits testimony. The court concluded that Gilbert's education and experience gave him specialized knowledge that would assist the jury.

The court also concluded that Gilbert could rely inadmissible hearsay—the testimony of its customers—because an expert can rely on inadmissible facts if other experts in the field reasonably rely on those types of facts. Moreover, the court could not "think of a more appropriate method to determine why sales were lost than to ask the customer".

Toshiba also attacked Gilbert's lost sales testimony because Gilbert did not determine all of the details of the potential sales. For example, Gilbert did not know what price or delivery time would have induced SMP's customers to buy its fluid ends. Citing *Formosa Plastics Corp. USA v. Presidio Engineers & Contractors, Inc.*, 960 S. W. 2d 41, 50 (Tex. 1997), the court pointed out, however, that "[m] easuring lost profits is an inherently speculative undertaking". In *Formosa Plastics*, the Supreme Court of Texas had found a hypothetical bid for a construction project to be based solely on speculation. The *SPM* court distinguished *Formosa Plastics*, however, because the lost sales to which Gilbert testified were "the loss of sales of proven products to existing customers". As such, it was "not so speculative as to be legally insufficient".

In *Wells Fargo Bank Nw.*, *N. A. v. RPK Capital XVI, L. L. C.*, 360 S. W. 3d 691 (Tex. App. —Dallas 2012, no pet.), the Dallas court of appeals reversed an award of lost profits because the only evidence of the damages, an expert's opinion, constituted no evidence. The expert's opinions were based on unsubstantiated assumed facts and verbally transmitted information. Because the expert failed to provide objective evidence supporting his conclusions, the conclusions constituted no evidence of these damages.

In *DaimlerChrysler Motors Co.*, *LLC v. Manuel*, 362 S. W. 3d 160 (Tex. App. —Fort Worth 2012, no pet.), the plaintiff's economist's estimate of lost profits for a car dealership was sufficiently reliable when the economist relied on the defendant's own sales forecasts. Use of defendant's own forecasts was sufficiently reliable in part because "Chrysler's own national dealer placement manager responsible for placing, planning, and relocating dealerships, testified that planning potential is a common methodology prepared and used by automobile manufacturers". The court of appeals declined to apply the *Robinson* factors for analyzing the reliability of the certified public accountant's opinion on lost profits and held that the trial court did not abuse its discretion in admitting the testimony. Instead, the court of appeals applied the "general reliability test" of *Gammill. Id.* (citing *Paschal v. Great W. Drilling, Ltd.*, 215 S. W. 3d 437, 448 (Tex. App. —Eastland 2006, pet. denied) (holding *Gammill* test appropriate for expert testimony of a certified public accountant regarding analysis of financial records for tracing of embezzled funds); *KMG Kanal - Muller - Gruppe Deutschland GmbH & Co. KG v. Davis*, 175 S. W. 3d 379, 391 (Tex. App. —Houston [1st Dist.] 2005, no pet.) (holding testimony on valuation of company based on projected lost profits by expert with doctorate in economics, who taught a university course in corporate evaluation and whose method of business valuation was not shown to have been rejected by any authority or opposing expert, was reliable under *Gammill* even though expert conceded that "corporate valuation necessarily entails a fundamental degree of speculation"). The court noted that the defense expert did not criticize the methodology used by the plaintiff's expert, nor identify another methodology or opine on a different amount of lost profits. Furthermore, " [t] here is no one proper method for determining lost profits as damages". One accepted methodology for new businesses is "the yardstick analysis" of "using a comparable established business that is also owned and operated by the plaintiff". The court therefore approved the expert's methodology but cautioned that a reliable methodology requires " 'one complete calculation' ". *Id.* quoting *Holt Atherton Indus.*, *Inc. v. Heine*, 835 S. W. 2d 80, 85 (Tex. 1992).

In *Houston Mercantile Exch. Corp. v. Dailey Petroleum Corp.*, 930 S. W. 2d 242, 243 (Tex. App. —Houston [14th Dist.] 1996, no writ), a trade secrets and unfair competition case, the court concluded that an economist's opinion on lost profits was unreliable and no evidence. The economist multiplied the monthly number of Kenjer jars in operation by the plaintiff's "average monthly profit per jar to produce an amount of monthly lost profit for the period in question". *Id.* at 247. After observing that " [a] n expert's opinion which is based on assumed facts that vary materially from the actual, undisputed facts is without probative value", the court stated that there was no evidence to support his assumption that each Kenjer jar was rented every day of each month. *Id.* at 248. Second, he assumed—without evidentiary support—that every Kenjer drilling jar in operation represented lost profit to the plaintiff. *Id.*

One emerging theme in expert testimony on lost profits is the distinction between expert calculations that are unsound—and therefore no evidence—and those that are sound but not necessarily the optimal or exclusive means for calculating damages—and therefore subject to attack through cross - examination and counter evidence. For example, future profit testimony that wholly fails to take into account risks inherent in the relevant activity is unsound—and therefore no evidence. *See Ramco Oil & Gas Ltd. v. Anglo - Dutch (Tenge) L. L. C.*, 207 S. W. 3d 801, 822 (Tex. App. —Houston [14th Dist.] 2006, pet. denied) (holding that expert opinion on lost profits that failed to quantify risk that wells would not produce at early stage of development—as necessary to expert's damages model—was speculative). But future profit testimony that accounts for risk in one manner, generally accepted in the industry, may be some evidence of future profits even when another means for accounting for risk, also accepted in the industry, is arguably more accurate. *Cf. Arkoma Basin*, 249 S. W. 3d at 389 (rejecting argument that expert testimony on oil well reserves was unreliable due to expert's failure to discount estimates by a capitalization rate when expert's opinion was based on eight - year "payout" calculation that employed different manner of accounting for risk).

U. Necessity of Expert Testimony

In some situations, it is necessary to present expert testimony to get an issue before a jury. *Offshore Pipelines, Inc. v. Schooley*, 984 S. W. 2d 654, 665 (Tex. App. —Houston [1st Dist.] 1998, no pet.) (expert testimony needed when subject matter requires "scientific interpretation"); *Turbines, Inc. v. Dardis*, 1 S. W. 3d 726, 738 (Tex. App. —Amarillo 1999, pet. denied) (noting need for expert testimony on the performance of mechanical work on turbine aircraft engines). For example, expert testimony is ordinarily necessary to show that a medical condition is caused by an event. Lay opinion testimony is adequate to prove causation when general experience and common sense will enable a lay person to determine, with reasonable probability, the causal relationship between the event and the condition. *Morgan v. Compugraphic Corp.*, 675 S. W. 2d 729, 733 (Tex. 1984) (plaintiff could testify that chemical exposure caused her injuries).

In *FFE Transp. Servs.*, *Inc.* v. *Fulgham*, 154 S. W. 3d 84 (Tex. 2004) an appellate court had held in a negligence case that the inspection and detection of loose and rusty bolts connecting part of a tractor trailer is not a fact so peculiar to a specialized industry as to be beyond the experience of a layperson. The Supreme Court of Texas disagreed, holding that when the looseness or rust is sufficient to create a danger requires specialized knowledge that it not within the experience of the layman. The Court reasoned that "[f] ew people not involved in the trucking industry are familiar with refrigerated trailers, the mechanisms for connecting them to tractors, and the frequency and type of maintenance they require". As such, "the layman does not know what the standard of care is for inspection and maintenance of the upper coupler assembly, kingpin, and base rail of a refrigerated trailer".

In this products liability case, the Court reversed an MYM11 million verdict because there was no evidence of a manufacturing defect. Though expert had a degree in chemistry, he had no specialized expertise in tire chemistry, never worked for a tire company or published any articles on tire chemistry; he conceded that he does not consider himself an expert in tire design, does not consider himself a forensic tire examiner, and does not hold himself out as having any expertise in the field of tire manufacturing. Court found that he was not qualified to testify on the subject of wax migration and contamination in tires and their effect on tire adhesion without more specialized education, training, or experience in tire chemistry, noting that "chemistry is an exceedingly vast science divided into several branches and is far beyond the capacity of one person to master". *Id.* In *Goodyear Tire & Rubber Co. v. Rios*, 143 S. W. 3d 107 (Tex. App. — San Antonio 2004, pet. denied), a tire products liability case, the plaintiffs could not recover on their marketing theory in the absence of expert testimony. "A jury could not have determined, without the benefit of expert testimony, which among many warnings and instructions should be printed on a sidewall." Therefore, expert testimony was required.

Courts have observed that expert testimony is generally necessary to satisfy the statutory elements of a design defect case. *See*, *eg.*, *DeGrate v. Executive Imprints*, *Inc.*, 261 S. W. 3d

402, 410 (Tex. App. —Tyler 2008, no pet.) ("Generally, these requirements necessitate competent expert testimony and objective proof that a defect caused the injury."). In *BIC Pen*, 346 S. W. 3d at 543, the Texas Supreme Court observed that "expert testimony is generally required in manufacturing defect cases to prove that the specific defect caused the accident". Causation is not established merely by proving that a manufacturing defect existed, that an accident occurred, and that the accident involved the deficient parts. The alleged manufacturing defect in *BIC Pen* involved "small deviations" from two of five child – resistant designed features in a lighter. The Court held that the impact of those deviations on how a child would have used the lighter—and specifically whether those deviations made it easier for a child to use the lighter — "is not an issue within a lay juror's general experience and common understanding".

In legal malpractice actions over litigation, all indications are the plaintiff will need expert testimony. *Alexander v. Turtur & Assocs.*, 146 S. W. 3d 113 (Tex. 2004). For example, "[q]uestions regarding the reasonableness of a settlement in most personal injury cases are questions upon which the trier of fact must be guided solely by expert testimony". *Amerada Hess Corp. v. Wood Group Prod.*, 30 S. W. 3d 5, 11 (Tex. App. —Houston [14th Dist.] 2000, pet. denied).

In cases involving advice by an attorney on business matters (i. e. non – litigation), the plaintiff's testimony that she relied on her lawyer's advise can establish cause in fact. *Delp v. Douglas*, 948 S. W. 2d 483 (Tex. App. —Fort Worth 1997), *vacated in part, rev' d in part on other grounds*, 987 S. W. 2d 879 (Tex. 1999); *Streber v. Hunter*, 221 F. 3d 701 (5th Cir. 2000).

For personal injury practitioners, one of the most significant cases on the necessity of expert testimony is *Guevara v. Ferrer*, 247 S. W. 3d 662, 663 (Tex. 2007), which addressed "whether expert medical evidence is required to support a finding that an automobile accident caused medical expenses of over MYM1 million". The court concluded that expert medical testimony is "required to prove causation unless component evidence supports a finding that the conditions in question, the casual relationship between the conditions and the accident, and the necessity of the particular medical treatments are within the common knowledge and experience of lay persons". *Id.* The court also observed that temporal proximity is evidence of causation but is not sufficient in itself to demonstrate causation.

The standard of review for whether expert testimony is necessary is de novo and not abuse of discretion *FFE Transp. Servs., Inc. v. Fulgham*, 154 S. W. 3d 84 (2004).

Additionally, expert testimony is sometimes mandated by statute. For example, Texas's Civil Practice and Remedies Code requires claimants to file some type of expert testimony at the outset of health care liability litigation, certain suits relating to sports shooting ranges, and proceedings arising out of the provision of professional services provided by architects and engineers. *See* Tex. Civ. Prac. & Rem. Code Ann. § § 74. 351, 128. 053, 150. 002.

V. Disqualification of Experts

In order to disqualify an expert based on a prior relationship, moving party must establish that①the expert had an "objectively reasonable basis to believe that a confidential relationship existed between that party and the expert witness, ②confidential and privileged information was in fact provided to the expert by the moving party". *Formosa Plastics Corp. v. Kajima Int'l, Inc.*, 216 S. W. 3d 436 (Tex. App. —Corpus Christi—Edinburg 2006, pet. denied). In addition, the court held that it would apply other factors, such as "fundamental fairness" and "prejudice," in its analysis. *Id.* at 452 - 53.

In *Formosa*, the court stated that it was not an error to allow an expert to testify even though he worked for the same consulting firm as an expert retained by the opposing party and was copied on certain communications between the parties. *Id.* at 449 - 51. The court held that the movant had not demonstrated that any communication that the expert received was in fact privileged. *Id.* at 451 - 52. The court stated that it believed that experts should be permitted to pursue their trade, they parties permitted to select their own experts, and the one thing gained from this relationship outweighs the policy presenting conflicts under the particular circumstances present in the instant case.

New and Interesting Cases

- *Finger v. Ray*, 326 S. W. 3d 285 (Tex. App. —Houston [1st Dist.] 2010, no pet.). In this claim against an attorney for breach of fiduciary duty and DTPA violations arising out of the attorney's services in bankruptcy litigation, the court held that expert testimony on causation was necessary. The plaintiff argued that because she was not pursing a legal malpractice claim, she did not have to satisfy the "suit within a suit" causation requirement and did not need expert testimony. The court, however, held that her "claims require proof that the results she would have obtained without [the attorney's] representation would be better than she actually achieved with it". *Id.* at 292. Her claims necessarily "require [d] an evaluation of alternative litigation strategies and outcomes in the bankruptcy court. Such an evaluation is within the ambit of a legal professional, not a lay person". *Id.*

- *Goodner v. Hyundai Motor Co.*, 650 F. 3d 1034 (5th Cir. 2011). In this design defect case, a passenger was killed in a car accident that occurred as she was resting in the front passenger seat. Her family claimed that the front seat was defectively designed because it could recline more than 45 degrees, which allowed her to be ejected even though she was wearing a seat belt. The court observed that causation is "generally a question of fact for the jury". It held that the jury could make a reasonable inference—based on the expert's testimony that the seat recline cause her ejection and that ejection significantly increases the risk of injury and a comparison of her injuries and those of the driver—that the seat recline was a substantial factor in bringing about her injuries. The court rejected the defendant's contention that *BIC Pen* requires expert causation testimony in all cases. In this case the expert testified to "some of the causation elements" and the other reasonable inferences were sufficient to demonstrate causation.

W. Discovery of Privileged Documents Provided to an Expert

Privileged information provided to a retained expert loses its privilege. *In re Christus Spohn Hosp. Kleberg*, 222 S. W. 3d 434 (Tex. 2007). In that case, the Court held that work product material provided to expert was discoverable unless the expert is de – designated. The Supreme Court denied a writ of mandamus complaining about a trial court's denial of a hospital's request for documents to be returned under the "snap – back" provision of TRCP 193. 3 (d). The hospital in the case was a defendant in a medical malpractice action. While in the middle of litigation, certain privileged documents were sent to a testifying expert by a hospital system paralegal (this done outside the knowledge of defense counsel and the hospital system general counsel). When asked at her deposition, the expert presented all the documents provided to her, including the privileged documents. Immediately after this happened, defense counsel (and the hospital system general counsel) claimed privilege and filed a motion for the return of privileged documents under the "snap – back" provision of the TRCP. The trial court denied the motion, instead relying on TRCP 192. 3 (e) for the holding that all documents reviewed by a testifying expert are discoverable. The Texas Supreme Court upheld this decision, noting that expert witnesses play an important and powerful role in litigation today, and as such, the jury should be aware of documents and other tangible things provided to the expert that might have shaped the expert's opinion. However, the court allowed the hospital to de – designate the expert and thereby recover the privileged documents.

X. Spoliation and Experts

In *State Farm & Cas. Co. v. Rodriguez*, 88 S. W. 3d 313 (Tex. App. —San Antonio 2002, no pet. h.), a trial court did not abuse its discretion in striking a defendant's engineering expert's testimony when, despite repeated attempts by plaintiff to obtain a copy prior to trial, the defense failed to produce the expert's PowerPoint presentation before it was shown to the jury. It was within the trial court's discretion to disbelieve the attorney's explanation that the presentation was not available earlier.

Y. Judicial Notice of Expert's Reliability

In *Hernandez v. State*, 116 S. W. 3d 26 (Tex. Crim. App. 2003), the court held that the trial court abused its discretion in admitting evidence of ADx analyzer without proof of its reliability. The court rejected the trial court's attempt to take judicial notice of its earlier hearings and holdings in other cases, noting that judicial notice is improper without a sufficient number of adversarial *Daubert* hearings. Additionally, the court cannot take judicial notice of opinions from other courts as the sole source for support of its *Daubert* ruling; some Texas trial court must conduct a *Daubert* hearing so a record is presented for the Texas appellate courts. Finally, the Court of Criminal Appeals stated that if a trial court intends to rely on prior hearings conducted in its court on the same issue, the prior hearings must be in record.

Z. Can an appellate court consider literature outside the record?

The Texas Court of Criminal Appeals opinion in *Hernandez* v. *State*, 116 S. W. 3d 26 (Tex. Crim. App. 2003), raises the question of whether an appellate court can review literature that is not in the trial record. In *Exxon Corp. v. Makofski*, 116 S. W. 3d 176 (Tex. App. — Houston [14th Dist.] 2003, pet. denied) ; *Coastal Tankships, U. S. A, Inc. v. Anderson*, 87 S. W. 3d 591 (Tex. App. —Houston [1st Dist.] 2002, pet. denied) scientific literature was discussed at a *Daubert* hearing but was not in the trial record. The court of appeals ordered the parties to file the literature. In *Fuesting v. Zimmer, Inc.* , 421 F. 3d 528 (7th Cir. 2005) , the court struck references in appellate brief to medical literature that was not in the trial record.

AA. Can a party call an opponent's expert adversely?

Yes, provided the expert is properly designated. *Hooper v. Chittalura*, 222 S. W. 3d 103 (Tex. App. —Houston [14th Dist.] 2006, pet. denied) (stating that no reason exists for "why expert testimony should automatically be treated differently than any other evidence produced by opponents").

BB. Expert Testimony on Attorneys' Fees

"An attorney's testimony about the reasonableness of his or her own fees is not like other expert witness testimony. " *Garcia v. Gomez*, 319 S. W. 3d 638 (Tex. 2010). It is different because, at least in cases where the lawyer who performs the work testifies, the testimony is based not only on the lawyer's experience and expertise, but also on the lawyer's "personal knowledge an about the underlying work and its particular value to the client" . Moreover the opposing party's lawyer "likewise has some knowledge of the time and effort involved and if the matter is truly in dispute, may effectively question the attorney regarding the reasonableness of the fee" . Therefore, testimony on fees "is not objectionable as merely conclusory" even if it is extremely brief and lacks specifics.

CC. Hypothetical Questions

In *Allstate Tex. Lloyds v. Mason*, 123 S. W. 3d 690 (Tex. App. —Fort Worth 2003, no pet.), Allstate sought to exclude the Mason's foundation damage expert by demonstrating that he had not considered and ruled out other plausible causes of the damage to the Masons' home. While cross – examining the expert, Allstate suggested other plausible causes of the foundation damage. These questions, however, were based on hypothetical situations not supported by the record. "Without evidence to support the implications of Allstate's hypothetical, we cannot say that the trial court abused its discretion in not excluding the expert testimony, because Allstate came up with a hypothetical theory at the hearing that even Allstate could not show was provable until after trial began. " Although Allstate presented evidence at trial to support the hypothetical questions, it did not present that evidence to the court during the pretrial hearing. As such, the trial court could not be faulted for granting the motion to strike before trial based on the evidence before it. A motion to strike at trial would likely have cured this defect.

DD. Havner in Jury Instructions

In *Faust v. BNSF Ry. Co.* , 337 S. W. 3d 325, 330 (Tex. App. —Fort Worth 2011, pet. denied) , a toxic tort personal injury lawsuit, the use of a *Robinson – Havner* type of jury instruction was not error.

The jury charge instructed the jury not only on the PJC charge issues of negligence and proximate cause but also that the plaintiff had to "prove specific causation" for the plaintiff's stomach cancer resulting from exposure to the chemical in question and "must exclude, with reasonable certainty, other plausible causes of" her cancer, "such as her history of smoking cigarettes" and another disease. The plaintiffs objected that the charge improperly shifted the trial court's gatekeeper function to the jury. The court concluded that the charge did not misstate Texas law requiring specific causation in a toxic tort case because specific causation goes to both admissibility of the expert testimony and the sufficiency of the evidence. "Accordingly, although we agree with the [plaintiffs] that it is the role of only the trial court to determine whether an expert's testimony is reliable, we disagree with their argument that the burden to exclude other plausible causes of injury relates solely to the trial court's rule 702 reliability inquiry." *Id.* at 335. "The complained - of instruction is an accurate, albeit arguably incomplete, statement of the law, identifying" part of the plaintiff's burden of proof on causation. *Id.* And instructing the jury that other plausible causes had to be excluded with reasonable certainty assisted the jury by providing it with "the standard it was required by law to apply in making its finding on a hotly - contested issue—causation". *Id.* [quoting *Columbia Rio Grande Healthcare*, *L. P. v. Hawley*, 284 *S. W.* 3*d* 851, 855 (Tex. 2009)].

The court also held that the plaintiffs did not timely and plainly make the trial court aware that they were objecting on the grounds that the instruction improperly heightened their burden of proof and constituted an impermissible comment on the weight of the evidence.

EE. Property Owner Rule

Only a limited set of employees—those in certain managerial or comparable positions—of a business organization may qualify to testify about fair market value of organization's property under "Property Owner Rule". *Reid Rd. Mun. Util. Dist. No.* 2 *v. Speedy Stop Food Stores, Ltd.*, 337 S. W. 3d 846 (Tex. 2011). The managerial employee must have duties related to the property in question. *Id.* at 849. Other employees of the entity may also testify to value if they hold "substantially equivalent positions and duties". *Id.* The Court announced one limitation on the rule: "the Property Owner Rule falls within the ambit of Texas Rule of Evidence 701 and therefore does not relieve the owner of the requirement that a witness must be personally familiar with the property and its fair market value, but the Property Owner Rule creates a presumption as to both". *Id.*

This rule was applied in *Custom Transit*, *L. P. v. Flatrolled Steel*, *Inc.*, No. 14 - 10 - 00936 - CV (Tex. App. —Houston [14th Dist.] June 14, 2012, no pet. h.), to the testimony of a corporation's owner who was also the corporation's manager and corporate representative at trial. The first prong of Speedy Shop—testimony by a managerial employee with duties related to the property in question—was satisfied. The second prong—personal familiarity with the property and its fair market value— was also satisfied.

FF. Discovery

In *City of San Antonio v. Ash*, No. 04 - 09 - 00732 - CV, 2011 WL 446279 (Tex.

App. —San Antonio Feb. 9, 2011, op. withdrawn), the trial court did not abuse its discretion in striking the City's physician expert based on the City's failure to provide timely the disclosures required by Rule 194. 2 (f). Before his deposition, the City's discovery responses simply identified the expert, stated the subject matter of his testimony and the general substance of his opinion. The city did not produce his curriculum vita, provide the fact known to him that formed the basis for his opinion or identify or provide the documents provided to or reviewed by him.

In *PopCap Games, Inc. v. MumboJumbo, LLC*, 350 S. W. 3d 699 (Tex. App. —Dallas 2011, pet. filed), a trial court did not abuse its discretion by denying the plaintiff's motion for leave to supplement its expert disclosures by designating a new damages expert. Over three months before trial, the plaintiff requested leave for the late designation after the trial court had struck the original damages expert as unreliable, contending that the court's order striking the expert constituted good cause. The court first observed that the inadvertence of counsel and the uniqueness of the excluded evidence do not, standing alone, constitute good cause. *Id.* at 718. The court rejected the plaintiff's contention "that it needed new experts because of the incompetence of its original trial counsel and original expert. The trial judge reasonably concluded that the inadmissibility of the testimony of an expert witness on reliability grounds is not a difficult or impossible circumstance rising to the level of good cause". *Id.*

Expert Opinion as Evidence in Civil Cases Relating to Medical Errors [*]

Dr hab. Kinga Flaga – Gieruszyńska[**]

The main objective of this paper is to analyse the importance of expert opinion as key evidence in cases of medical errors. The Authors, on the example of Polish evidence law, show characteristics of an expert's opinion, its application scope and the complexity of the problem of the impact of expert's opinion on the adjudication manner in such cases. Due to the development of this area of evidence law Authors devote special attention to the typology of expert opinions in the field of medicine, taking into account collective opinions, pertaining to cases of error which bear potential multiple organ consequences (e. g. errors in the course of childbirth). The study highlights specific characteristics of expert opinion in the field of medicine, which in many cases needs to constitute not only the diagnosis of the current state of facts and evidence for its existence, but also the forecast for the impact of future events (such as for the development of the child). The paper also analyses the opinion of a research institute, as the one applied when there is a necessity for empirical research going beyond the analysis of medical records and examination of the patient's health. This study is the sum of Polish experience on evidence proceedings in cases of medical errors, relating not only to the proceedings issues, but also to collateral issues such as the expert's ethics (especially in the context of the common opinion of the "solidarity" of the medical community), or procedural protection of the rights of a patient as a person injured by a medical error.

1. *Introduction*

The Polish system of civil procedural law introduces an open catalogue of evidence, which is an important solution due to current scientific and technological developments, particularly in relation to the field of our special interest, i. e. medical sciences and related fields. These changes allow for the determination of facts of the case by means of increasingly sophisticated measures. This issue also applies to civil cases whose essence is to pursue claims of medical errors. Consequently, a whole palette of evidence is applicable in this category of cases – documentary evidence (in particular, evidence from medical records), evidence supplied by witnesses, evidence from parties' explanations and sometimes evidence by inspection. However,

---

* The introduction, part 2 and 3 as well as the summary were prepared by K. Flaga – Gieruszyńska, parts 4 and 5 were prepared by A. Klich.

** Professor of the University of Szczecin mgr Aleksandra Klich (M. A. L.), Lecturer Email: kingaflaga@ interia. eu.

due to the complexity of the issue of the state of health of the person injured by a medical error – more and more often of key importance is the opinion of an expert in the field of medicine. Depending on the complexity of the issues, diagnosing or interpreting of which is crucial to case adjudication, the court may use an expert's opinion (or an opinion of a group of experts – in complex, multi – dimensional cases) or, possibly, the opinion of a research institute (characteristics of the latter type of evidence will be the subject of further consideration).

In accordance with Art. 278 of the Act of 17 November 1964 – Code of Civil Procedure (Journal of Laws, No 43, item 296 as amended) (hereinafter CCP) in the cases requiring special information, the court, having heard the parties' claims as to the number of experts and the choice thereof, may allow for one or many experts in order to consult their opinions. Thus, expert opinion is only spoken of when a specialist of a given field conducts an analysis at the request of the court issued upon the motion of parties, and in some cases *ex officio* (e. g. in cases on incapacitation expert opinion is obligatory by the act of law). This is a clear demarcation line between expert opinion and private expertise, even if enclosed in the court case records.

The differentiation between an opinion prepared for the party's needs outside the proceedings and an opinion supplied under evidence proceedings before a civil court bears crucial importance for the evidential value of this opinion and its importance for court's further adjudication. Private expertise prepared on request of parties, either during the proceedings or before their initiation, needs to be treated – in the event of them gaining acceptance by the adjudicating court – as explanations constituting support for parties' positions with the inclusion of special information[1]. Such "expertise" constitutes solely a private document.[2] However, if – despite submitting private expertises by the parties – there is truly a need to explain the case's circumstances from the point of view requiring special information, the court should allow expert evidence. Thus, adjudication based on private expertises submitted in a different lawsuit is, above all, a violation of the provisions of the Code of civil procedure on the examination of evidence by experts[3].

In summary, an extra – judicial opinion – even one prepared by a permanent expert witness – does not constitute evidence within the meaning of Art. 278 et seq. of the CCP. However, if an expert appointed by the court challenges the extra – judicial opinion – it is critical for the court to consider arguments of both opinions[4]. Only the decision for the examination of evidence gives the expertise of the indicated expert therein the nature of expert evidence[5].

---

[1] SC [Supreme Court] Judgement of 11. 06. 1974, II CR 260/74, LEX No. 7517.

[2] SC Judgement of 08. 06. 200, I PKN 468/00, OSNP 2003, No 8, item 197.

[3] SC Judgement of 12. 04. 2002, I CKN 92/00, LEX No 53932.

[4] *A. Góra – Błaszczykowska*, *Opinia biegłych w postępowaniu cywilnym*, http: //www. edukacjaprawnicza. pl/artykuly/artykul/a/pokaz/c/artykul/art/opinia – bieglych – w – postepowaniu – cywilnym. html, 01. 05. 2013 and literature quoted there.

[5] SC Judgement of 20. 01. 1989, II CR 310/88, LEX No 8940.

Similarly, written opinion submitted for the files of a different case is not expert evidence by nature, as the court did not issue a decision on the admission of this evidence, nor did it appoint an expert or draw up the subject and limits within which he is to comment on[6] for the needs of the latter case in which it is to be used. This approach to aspects of subjective opinions of an expert is a clear demonstration of a strong relationship between the court and experts on the basis of a particular proceeding. The purpose of establishing these bonds is to ensure maximum standards of fairness and quality of work of an expert witness whose opinion may, in such cases as the assessment of the effects of medical errors, constitute evidence of breakthrough importance.

As M. Brulińska rightly points out, the meaning of these regulations leads to the conclusion that the purpose of the legislator was to facilitate the court in the discernment and understanding of the adjudicated issue, therefore, so that the expert acts as a kind of a court "assistant". It is not up to the expert, though, to adjudicate on legal issues (in the area of law the court is the "top expert"), but at the same time, this rule does not apply to rules of customary law, foreign law or the rules of life experience. The subject of evidence from expert opinion should not be the establishment of facts of the case, except when in order to make such decisions it is necessary to use a specialized research apparatus[7]. The latter comes into question particularly in the case of such advanced cases as those of medical errors, given that the real picture of the facts of the case in such situations can only be diagnosed on the basis of special information allowing to determine the patient's current and future state of health and the possible degree of disability.

As pointed out by J. Jaskiewicz, the specialisation of certain areas and the difficulty and complexity of the matter causes expert opinions to occupy a special place in the catalogue of evidence and the integrity and accountability of this group of assistant entities is reflected in the content of the decision of the court's application of law. The couplings occurring between an expert and procedural bodies are of informative and objective nature. The use of information provided depends on the fulfilment of procedural conditions on the validity of the appointment of an expert, and content (subjective) relationships are connected with the assessment of the adequacy and accuracy of response to the research task formulated by the court and then its proper use in the construction of the factual (and sometimes legal) basis for the final decision of court's application of the law[8]. In the context of such a perception of an expert's procedural status in civil cases it must be recognized that he is an essential personal source of knowledge in relation to medical errors and their civil and legal consequences, performing relevant competences to support court's actions within the limits outlined by this court, formulated as a cata-

---

[6] SC Judgement of 10. 12. 1998, I CKN 922/97, LEX No 50754.

[7] M. Brulińska, Biegły wświetle przepisów Kodeksu postępowania cywilnego i Kodeksu postępowania administracyjnego, http: //www. przasnysz. sr. gov. pl/docs/wyklad_ biegli - kpc_ i_ kpa. pdf, 01. 05. 2013.

[8] J. Jaśkiewicz, Podmioty pomocnicze [in:] Poznanie faktów w postępowaniu cywilnym, Warszawa 2013, LEX electronic collection.

logue of questions to the expert for the needs of the preparation of his opinion. As pointed out in the jurisdiction, the assessment of a health status requires examination of medical opinion evidence[9]. How efficiently will the assistant role of an expert be used by the court depends exclusively on the court itself, and especially on the relevance of the formulated theses of evidence proceedings which may grant the expert a key role for the content of future adjudication, or – through ill – considered determination of, for instance, too superficial questions to an expert – marginalize his importance. As for the cases relating to liability for medical errors the latter situation is unacceptable, since it is impossible to imagine a proper construction of the factual basis for adjudicating on these matters without special information in the area of medicine and related sciences.

2. *The significance of expert opinion in civil cases*

Of key importance for the determination of the essence of expert opinion is the term "special information". Special information – generally speaking – is particular specialized knowledge in a given area of arts, technology, culture, construction, industry, agriculture, transport, communications, IT, chemistry, etc., comprising information going beyond the scope of what the body of intelligent and generally – educated people have at their disposal[10]. Special information is thus knowledge exceeding general pool of information of people who have a certain store of general knowledge, even relatively large. In this scope, the judge's private store of knowledge (e. g. within his interest area) is not relevant. As stressed in the jurisdiction, by making Art. 278 § 1 of the CCP available, the legislator limited the court's jurisdiction independence by excluding from its competence the possibility of authoritative position taking on issues requiring special information. On the other hand, the established legal regulation clearly defines the framework for an expert's activity, whose duty is only to expose certain circumstances from the point of view of special information (i. e. information of technical, technological, medical nature etc.), rather than to resolve legal issues or also put forward theses pointing directly to the way of resolving the case[11]. As for the first aspect, which goes beyond the subject matter of this paper, there are exceptions as to these branches of law in which the court may not have adequate knowledge by principles of *iura novit curia.* As far as commenting on the relevance of a particular resolution, the prohibition is absolute.

Referring to the role of expert evidence in civil cases, it should be emphasized that the opinion of experts is to facilitate the court in a proper assessment of the case material gathered when it requires special information. It cannot, in itself, be the source of factual material of the case and, the more so, be a basis for establishing the circumstances that are the subject of expert assessment. Establishing facts of the case is in the hands of the ruling court, and experts should provide answers to specific questions tailored to the facts of the case, not excluding the

[9] For Example, Judgement of SAC [Supreme Administrative Court] in Wrocław of 25. 01. 1996, SA/Wr 830/95, LEX No 26592.

[10] SC Judgement of 18. 07. 1975, I CR 331/75, LEX No 7729.

[11] Judgement of the Court of Appeal in Białystok of 25. 09. 2012, I ACa 72/12, LEX No 1223152.

possible discussion of both versions resulting from the submitted documentation [12]. The task of an expert is not to establish facts of the case, but the exposure and explanation by the court of the circumstances from the point of view of the special information held by the expert, taking into account the case material gathered and made available to the expert [13]. Thus, expert opinion is not subject to verification as proof of the statement of facts on the basis of the truth and falsehood criterion. Parties' assessment not in competition to the proof as to the facts which are the subject of the opinion are not authoritative to the assessment of this proof [14]. Thus, the court – within the free evaluation of evidence – reviews the evidence gathered, including the opinion of an expert or experts, and on that basis establishes facts of the case forming grounds for the decision. In other words, the expert does not settle the case in place of the court, nor does he suggest ready – made solutions as to the facts of the case, since it is the court who is obliged to consider all the circumstances. The classic situation in this respect is the one in which an expert finds the occurrence of a medical error and determines its impact, but it's hardly a fraction of the facts of the case, which include, for example, informed consent of the patient, particular circumstances of the procedure, etc.

In this context, the undoubted problem – due to the secondary and not decisive nature of expert opinion – is a matter of the court's assessment of the relevance and accuracy of the opinion, where the court is not in possession of special information in the field of the science analysed. Therefore, a fundamental question concerns the criterion for the court's assessment of an expert's opinion. As the jurisdiction aptly points out, expert opinion is subject to evaluation according to Art. 233 § 1 of the CCP, however, based on the evaluation criteria specific to the evidence, which are: the level of the expert's knowledge, theoretical basis for the opinion, the manner of advocating the position formulated within and the degree of assertiveness of the expressed evaluations, as well as compliance with the rules of logic and general knowledge. The specificity of assessment of such evidence is expressed in the fact that the substantive sphere of the opinion is controlled by the court (who is not in possession of special information) in fact only in compliance with the principles of logical thinking and common knowledge [15]. Thus, expert evidence is examined properly when the opinion contains justification of final conclusions, formulated in a way that is intelligible and comprehensible for persons not in possession of special information [16]. It must therefore be concluded that the control of the court with respect to an expert's opinion is limited, dependent on the ability of the court as a non – specialist in a given field, therefore it is so important to choose as experts people who not only are in possession of real special information, but can also logically and accessibly present their analysis to the court, the parties and their attorneys. An opinion, even at a high level of expertise, drawn

---

〔12〕 SC Judgement of 19. 12. 2006, V CSK 360/06, LEX No 238973.

〔13〕 SC Judgement of 11. 07. 1969, I CR 140/69, OSNC 1970, No 5, Item 85.

〔14〕 Judgement of the Court of Appeal in Katowice of 01. 08. 2012, I ACa 40/11, LEX No 1217679.

〔15〕 Judgement of the Court of Appeal in Łódz of 11. 01. 2013, I ACa 1003/12, LEX No 1267339.

〔16〕 Judgement of the Court of Appeal in Warszawa of 14. 08. 2012, I ACa 372/12, LEX No 1220678.

in a hermetic language, presented in a non - understandable and chaotic way, will not constitute fully valuable evidence to the court, who must transpose the results for the needs of assessment of the establishment of facts which form the basis for the adjudication.

Due to the specific nature of expert evidence and that of a research institute, not all rules of evidence proceedings are applicable, and in particular Art. 217 § 1 of the CCP, according to which a party may - until the closing of the hearing - quote factual circumstances and evidence to justify their claims or to refute the conclusions and statements of the opposing party. Therefore, it cannot be assumed that the court is obliged to admit evidence of subsequent experts or the opinion of the institute in any case where the submitted opinion is unfavourable to the party. The court has a duty to admit evidence from a further opinion when such a need arises; that is, when the opinion at the court's disposal contains significant gaps because it does not address the evidential theses posed, it is unclear - inadequately justified or non - verifiable, i. e. when the analysis presented by an expert does not allow the adjudicating body to control his reasoning as to the correctness of his final conclusions [17]. Evidence hearing cannot be a duel between the parties using subsequent expert opinions until the moment when one of them gains advantage in the number of opinions favourable to them. Similarly, the court cannot manipulate expert opinion as a means only to confirm *a priori* accepted theses. Therefore, it is unacceptable and contrary to the essence of expert evidence, to the procedural principle of truth and to the principle of free evaluation of evidence, to direct actions of an expert in such a way which allows him, while preparing the opinion, to use one group of evidence while at the same time clearly prohibits basing the same issue on the opposing group of evidence relating to the same issue being the subject of the expert's examination [18]. The subject of the opinions of experts, as a principle, are phenomena, events and their effects, of measurable and verifiable character in the light of modern canons of science and technology, therefore each expert should reliably prepare his opinion based on the modern state of knowledge in a given field. At the same time, the court should use an expert's opinion (in particularly justified cases outlined above - a certain number of expert opinions) only to the extent that is necessary for the construction of a reliable factual basis for its decision.

It should be added that since an expert - as pointed out - performs supportive functions, then even if the court was in possession of special information, it still would be obliged to use expert evidence [19]. Expert evidence, in view of its component in the form of special information, is evidence of a type that cannot be replaced by another evidence activity, such as hearing a witness [20]. Expert evidence is unnecessary only if the court finds that it may perform the assessment on its own, as any intelligent person, and not as a man of specialised knowl-

---

[17] SC Decision of 19. 08. 2009, III CK 7/09, LEX No 533130.

[18] SC Judgement of 03. 06. 1974, II CR 273/74, LEX No 7510.

[19] SC Judgement of 03. 05. 1982, I KR 319/81, OSNPG 1982, No 11, item 149.

[20] SC Judgement of 24. 11. 1999, I CKN 223/98, Wokanda 2000, No 3, p. 7.

edge[21]. Expert witness is a person who has theoretical and practical special information as an authority in a given field, most commonly confirmed by an appropriate document[22]. Conditions to be met by a candidate for an expert witness, as well as the procedure for the appointment of an expert, are defined in the Regulation of the Minister of Justice of 24 January 2005 on expert witnesses (Journal of Laws, No 15, item 133). The expert is therefore an institution of judicial procedural law and may use the title of an expert witness only for the preparation of opinions for a particular circle of entities defined in the regulations. Therefore, using the title of an expert witness in other activities is unlawful and discredits the person sufficiently to conclude that he cannot offer adequate guarantee of proper performance of expert's duties[23]. This restriction emphasizes the special status of an expert, enclosed under civil procedural law, which is a manifestation of the trend for encasing bodies of the judiciary with supporting entities of the highly specialized nature.

In addition to the substantive issues, as already mentioned, a key role in assessing the significance of expert evidence in civil proceedings is played by ethical problems, in particular the postulate of impartiality of the expert. Hence, solutions of civil procedural law which are to secure the last issue safely are introduced. In accordance with the position of the Supreme Court, the institution of the exclusion of an expert aims to strengthen guarantees of objectivity of deciding on the case. According to Art. 281 of the CCP, until the completion of expert activities, a party may request his exclusion for the same reasons one may request the disqualification of a judge. The reason for the disqualification of a judge, and thus an expert, at the request of a party is the existence of such a circumstance that could give rise to a reasonable doubt as to his impartiality in a given case. Sufficient is any circumstance that may raise legitimate reason for doubt, even on the side of the party requesting the exclusion. Nonetheless, it regards giving rise to doubt that must be justified in the circumstances of the case[24]. Pursuant to the content of the regulation, excluding an expert after the commence of his activities may occur only at the request of a party (Article 281 of the CCP), also due to reasons justifying the disqualification of a judge by virtue of the same law (Article 48 of the CCP)[25]. There are views according to which, in the latter case, the court should also work *ex officio*, but the content of the provision in question does not authorize such a position.

It can therefore be concluded that a motion to disqualify a judge is a core procedural measure which can be used by the party that believes that expert opinion will, due to some circumstances, be charged with the lack of objectivity. Thus, one must conclude as accurate the position advocating that the quoted provision of Art. 281 of the CCP does not provide a legal basis

---

〔21〕 SC Judgement of 28. 06. 1932, II 4 K 448/32, http://www.amsik.pl/archiwum/1_2011/1_11m.pdf.

〔22〕 CT [Constitutional Tribunal] judgement of 2. 06. 2008, K 50/05, OTK - A 2008, No 5, item 79.

〔23〕 Judgement of SAC in Warszawa of 20. 08. 1998, II SA 992/98.

〔24〕 SC Judgement of 21. 06. 2012, III CSK 279/11, LEX No 1228591.

〔25〕 SC Judgement of 28. 11. 2000, II UKN 74/00, OSNP 2002, No 12, Item 293.

to challenge the opinion of an expert for whose exclusion a party filed a motion [26]. On the other hand, it needs to be remembered that the opinion of an expert who was excluded after having submitted his opinion, should be considered null and void on the model of evidence taken in the proceeding which was suppressed. Consequently, this opinion does not constitute any evidence in the case[27]. Polish legislature provides in this way adequate level of impartiality of experts in civil cases, although practice (including medical cases) shows that a serious problem, for which it is not always possible to find a remedy, is the opinion's substantive level and communicativeness of expert witnesses discussing their findings in the courtroom.

3. *Opinion of a research institute as a type of expert opinion*

An opinion of a research institute constituting a variation of expert opinion is only used when there are specific reasons for carrying it out instead of or alongside an individual expert's opinion. In accordance with Art. 290 § 1 of the CCP the court may request the opinion of a relevant research institute. In addition, the court may require further clarification from the institute, either written or oral, by a designated person; the court may also commission the submission of an additional opinion by the same or another institute. This seemingly simple provision in practice produces a lot of doubts of interpretation, especially in terms of its relationship to the expert's opinion and other evidence, such as documentary evidence or witness evidence.

The first issue relevant to the role of such evidence is its subjective aspects. In the past period of dominance of state organizational structures over private entities, it was pointed out that such a power lay in state research – and – development institutions. However, political and economic changes which included the sector of science and higher education have shown that such a narrow interpretation of the term "institute" is ineligible. As a result, now it must be assumed that such an opinion can be prepared by any research centre regardless of their organizational and legal form. Within the meaning of Art. 290 § 1 of the CCP a limited company may also be an institute. A basic criterion that allows the operator to be considered an institute, on the basis of the discussed provision, is its carrying out scientific research [28]. Thus, in practice, there is a move away from a subjective criterion for singling out eligible entities, towards an objective criterion, referring to the nature, scope and quality of conducted research in a given field of science or technology.

An opinion of a scientific institute is devised in a team and does not express positions of individual persons – although they should be indicated in the opinion under Art. 290 § 2 of the CCP – but of the institute itself. The conducted research should be examined in such a way that will allow for it to be presented to the court as the opinion of the research institution, also signed by the person(s) authorized to represent the institute [29]. Therefore, in the opinion of a research institute are only found the views represented inside it uniformly or for the most part;

[26] SC Judgement of 08. 07. 2008, II UK 344/07, LEX No 497701.

[27] SC Judgement of 27. 05. 1976, I PR 64/76, LEX No 7830.

[28] SC Decision of 19. 08. 2009, file reference number III CSK 7/09, LEX No 533130.

[29] Decision of the Court of Appeal in Rzeszów of 25. 01. 2013, I ACz 826/12, LEX No 1267392.

therefore the basis for decisions of the court examining this evidence cannot be personal sentiments of one of the authors of the opinion who gives explanations at the hearing on behalf of the institute[30]. Thus, the reliance by the adjudicating court in decisions (and, consequently, in the legal assessment) on the opinion of one of the institute's researchers, obtained with the breach of Art. 290 of the CCP disqualifying it as an opinion of the said research institute, while at the same time acknowledging it – due to it being issued by the research institute – as the basis for the rejection of the opinion in equal essence but presenting a completely different view is an infringement which could affect the outcome of the case (Article 398^3 § 1 point 2 of the CCP)[31]. In consequence, the institute's opinion constitutes a collective opinion which may not reflect personal views of individual researchers, but must reflect a common position of the research team or at least its majority, which predisposes the opinion of the institute for the use in more complex research tasks.

As for the merits of the application of an institute's opinion, it should be first and foremost pointed out that the quoted provision of the Code of Civil Procedure leaves the decision on whether or not there is a need to consult a research institute to the court examining evidence. Admission of evidence from such an institute is purposeful or necessary when there is a need to conduct complex research, there are diagnostic problems requiring specialized research or observation in a hospital environment, and also, when it is otherwise impossible to eliminate contradictions in the available opinions. However, the evaluation from the party dissatisfied with the expert's opinion does not justify the alleged breach of that provision[32]. Thus, the same rules apply to the opinion of a research institute as to an expert's opinion, but in this case one needs to be distinguish cases in which it is sufficient to apply only expert opinion, from those where special information of an institutionalized nature ought to be used.

In this case, one needs to consider as accurate a position acknowledging that allowing evidence from a research institute would be purposeful and justified in a situation where the court – assessed issue, due to its complexity, requires clarification by professionals with a particularly high level of theoretical background and, if necessary, the use of latest scientific research findings, as well as when it is otherwise impossible to eliminate contradictions arising in the available opinions. The higher rank of evidence from a research institute over expert evidence results *inter alia* from the fact, that as an opinion developed collectively in a research institute it enjoys the institute's research authority[33]. This position accurately reflects the relationship of both types of evidence relating to the use of special information as a tool for assessing facts of the case, indicating to first apply expert opinion as a less complicated and less costly measure.

However, it needs to be strongly emphasized that application of this opinion, as in the case of an expert's opinion, does not release the adjudicating court from establishing, in a de-

---

〔30〕 SC Judgement of 19. 07. 2001, II UKN 487/00, OSNP 2003, No 9, item 230.

〔31〕 SC Judgement of 10. 08. 2007, II CSK 228/07, LEX No 319623.

〔32〕 SC Judgement of 05. 05. 2009, I UK 1/09, LEX No 515412.

〔33〕 SC Judgement of 28. 08. 2008, III CSK 98/08, LEX No 450157.

fined procedural mode, the existence or non – existence of the circumstances put forward to justify the claims and allegations of the opposing party, and possibly other circumstances relevant to the proper resolution of the case. Proper assessment of the causes and consequences of a particular action or negligence, in the face of one event presented in divergent ways, is not possible in the light of the state of knowledge in a given area of science and professional experience, in a situation where there is no guarantee that the conclusions and information presented by the experts objectively reflect data and facts that took place in the past [34]. However, an opinion of an institute never settles a dispute as to the facts. It is not "super evidence" by which the adjudicating court is bound. It is assessed by the court, within the limits set out in Art. 233 of the CCP, like all other evidence [35]. Thus, the opinion of a research institute as an evidence measure needs to be referred to in all comments on the procedural importance of the expert opinion.

4. *Characteristics of the opinion of experts in cases of medical errors*

In lawsuits on cases concerning the so – called medical errors significant challenge is posed by evidence proceedings, which is mainly caused by complex medical terminology, the unpredictability of the human body, as well as a high level of difficulty of the examined matter. Attempts to prove to medical professionals a mistake committed by them, or on the contrary – demonstrating to the patient their lack of responsibility for the events which occurred during the diagnosis, treatment or hospitalization, to a large extent will me based on the opinions of other medical professionals appointed as expert witnesses. In many cases the complete medical records submitted by the party, containing the most accurate description of the treatment process does not constitute sufficient evidence which could form basis for adjudicating, because a mere submission of facts of the case together with the indication of the claim is not sufficient. It requires accurate and uncontested evidence to achieve a positive outcome and result of the case. A major problem is also the reliability and accuracy of keeping medical records by medical professionals, based on which opinions of medical experts are made. However, because of the breadth of the presented matters, the issue of the correctness of compiling and maintaining patient medical records will not be the subject of this study.

The burden of proving a medical error and circumstances justifying doctor's liability, in accordance with Art. 6 of the Law of 23. 04. 1964 – Civil Code (Journal of Laws of 1964 No. 16, item 93) rests on the patient. As noted by C. Gromadzki, the most difficult task incumbent on a person in the care of medical professionals, not having medical knowledge, is to demonstrate the fault of the person providing health services and the causation. Patients, apart from lacking expertise, often do not have the opportunity to observe the procedures or medical actions taken (usually such a situation occurs in connection with surgical procedures). The patient is naturally not in possession of medical knowledge, which, at the very beginning of the

[34] SC Judgement of 19. 12. 2006, V CSK 360/06, LEX No 238973.

[35] SC Judgement of 03. 10. 2000, I PKN 5/00, LEX No 1165859.

proceedings puts him in a non – equivalent position with respect to the medical professional.[36]

In support of this thesis is the position of the Supreme Court which stated that a sick person, lacking medical education, not having sufficient knowledge of the facts, is often deprived of information on the detailed results of the treatment[37]. In such situations, it is reasonable for the court to carry out examination of evidence, aimed at establishing thorough facts of the case and the reasons for the adverse effects of the treatment. It is also postulated that the end result of evidence proceedings should be the determination of the factor responsible for the damage caused to the patient. Due to the high degree of difficulty of medical terminology, it seems essential in this regard to be taking evidence from a medical expert. In medical trials, evidentiary proceedings are not limited to expert opinion. As already indicated, it is also possible to carry out documentary evidence (in medical lawsuits medical records are undoubtedly of essential importance), evidence from witness testimony, although in many cases it is the expert witness testimony that will bear essential significance.[38]

Expert evidence presented to the court during the examination of the case as evidence of a specific nature, based on knowledge of medicine, aims to provide a position based on both the specialist knowledge and professional practice of the medical professional. Expert opinion is formed on the basis of the evidence available to him, which in cases of the so – called medical errors will be made primarily on the basis of the above mentioned medical records accurately indicating the diagnostic process, the course of treatment, as well as prognosis with a detailed description of methods and means engaged in the treatment. The opinion of an expert, who in practice is usually a practising doctor or dentist, is to provide the court and the parties to the proceedings with a position with reference to the submitted allegations and circumstances of the case. The importance of expert opinion in the so – called medical lawsuits is even greater, because it facilitates the court (and the parties) in their understanding of medical terminology, which, for those without knowledge of medicine is often complicated and confusing.

Preceding the discussion of characteristics of expert evidence and admissibility of its preparation by authorized entities, I would like to draw attention to the diversity of terminology and interchangeable use in ordinary understanding of the terms: "medical diagnosis", "medical certificate" and "medical expert opinion". In accordance with Art. 2 § 1 of the Act of 5. 12. 1996 on the profession of a doctor and a dentist (Journal of Laws of 2005, No. 226, item 1943, as amended), issuing medical diagnoses falls within doctor's responsibility. They should not be unequivocally identified with the opinion of an expert witness, as they may be issued for the needs of various entities (e. g. insurers or employers) and their nature, purpose, or form can be heterogeneous and diverse. The fact that medical diagnoses are prepared for the so – called extra – medical entities does not preclude the submission, on court's orders, of state-

[36] C. Gromadzki, *Dowód: biegły. Jego rola w procesie lekarskim*, „Gazeta Sądowa" 2002, No. 5, p. 33.

[37] SC Judgement of 10. 10. 1954, OSN 1954, No 2, item. 50.

[38] C. Gromadzki, *Dowód: biegły* …, op. cit., p. 33.

ments included in the medical diagnosis in the course of civil proceedings. Then, statements of the medical professional appointed by the court as an expert will be treated as expert medical opinion.

Referring to the traditional classification of persons likely to be present in civil proceedings as experts (which will be discussed in detail later in this report), we can distinguish expert witnesses (those included in the list of expert witnesses) and the so called *ad hoc* experts (a non – expert witness, but appointed in that capacity because of being in possession of special information required for a particular case). It would be wrong to identify the function of a medical examiner with an expert witness, because, in the light of the Law of 1. 07. 2011 on medical examiners (Journal of Laws 2007, No. 123, item. 849), the competence of a medical examiner comprises issuing certificates proving the parties to the proceedings´illness – based ability or inability to attend on the summons or notice of the authorised body. There should be a clear distinction between certificates issued in this regard by a medical examiner employed by the district court, and expert opinion. The apparent similarity in terminology of a medical diagnosis or certificate and expert opinion carries the danger of misleading mutual identification of these terms and their interchangeable use. It is appropriate, therefore, to clearly differentiate between the meaning and scope of diagnoses, certificates and opinions issued by physicians. On the basis of Polish civil procedural law, in relation to the taking of evidence, both diagnoses and certificates may be regarded as documentary evidence and expert medical opinion prepared at the express request of the court will have the nature of direct evidence.

As indicated above, among expert witnesses one can distinguish permanent expert witnesses and *ad hoc* experts appointed to participate in particular cases. An expert witness is an individual appointed by the court for the period of five years to issue opinions within the scope of professional knowledge. Expert witnesses are appointed by a district court, whose president is obliged to maintain a list of expert witnesses prepared on the basis of precise and clear specialisations of experts. In cases of medical error it is relevant, because only doctors with an appropriate degree of specialization in a given field of medicine have sufficient professional qualifications and relevant experience also in the scope of cooperation with the courts. Organising the said list according to specialities of medical examiners makes it much easier for the court to appoint a suitable person as an expert witness on a case of a given type. It is not only important to have appropriate qualifications as a medical professional in order to participate in a case as an expert witness, but also for the court to choose appropriately for the sake of reliability of the justification of facts and circumstances presented by the party. The existence of the category of "permanent" expert witnesses does not preclude court's use of services of other people who, despite not being registered on the list of expert witnesses, may have qualifications comparable to those specified for expert witnesses [39]. In this case, he or she will acquire the status of an *ad hoc* expert.

---

[39] K. Piasecki, *System dowodów i postępowania dowodowe w sprawach cywilnych*, Warszawa 2012, pp. 240 – 241.

Under current law, an expert may be a person who enjoys full civil and civic rights, is over 25 years old, guarantees due performance of expert witness' duties and agrees to be appointed an expert. The most important formal requirement allowing a person to participate in civil proceedings as an expert is to have both theoretical and practical special information in a particular field (in the cases of medical law – in medicine), as well as other skills. The regulation on expert witnesses obliges the expert to supply documentation or other evidence proving that he demonstrates special information, and the assessment of their adequacy lies in the court's president.[40] The issue of defining "special information" was presented in greater depth in a different part of this study.

The requirement to have adequate resource of expertise almost automatically enables the perception of the person performing the medical profession as most suitable to act as an expert in cases of the so – called medical errors, because the right to practice medicine on the basis of the act on the medical profession is granted to a person who has a doctor's diploma awarded by a Polish school, or by another state recognized in the Republic of Poland as equivalent, confirming the completion of studies at the faculty of medicine. An expert in cases of medical errors may therefore be someone who has the expertise in the field of medicine, but it is not the only condition, as the person acting as an expert on the case should additionally demonstrate an appropriate level of knowledge in a particular field, which is confirmed by the achieved degree of specialization. In the subject literature it is pointed out that in this case the term "special information" should be equated with the specialisation demonstrated by the doctor or, alternatively, with certificates. Meeting this requirement is necessary for the reliability and correctness of the prepared opinion[41].

Preparing the opinion of a medical expert of a given specialization sometimes is not possible without the cooperation of another medical professional having additional knowledge, taking a complementary position to the expert witness' one. For this reason, the Polish legislator provides for the preparation of the so – called joint opinions. In accordance with Art. 285 of the CCP it is possible to provide a joint opinion, prepared by several experts concurrent in their views. In light of adjudicating, a joint opinion is not only an opinion drawn up by a number of experts in the same field of science, but also the opinion of several experts from different fields of science.[42] Referring these general provisions to the so – called medical errors, the possibility of producing a single, comprehensive opinion by doctors of various specializations needs to be indicated, as the court has the authority to appoint experts of several specialisations (e. g. an expert surgeon, anaesthetist and a psychologist) who can carry out research together,

---

[40] M. Rybarczyk, *Biegły w postępowaniu cywilnym: opina, odpowiedzialność, wynagrodzenie*, Warszawa 2001, p. 28 and further.

[41] R. Szozda, M. Procek, *Lekarz sądowy jako biegły*, „Nowiny Lekarskie" 2007, No 76/3, p. 261.

[42] T. Demendecki, *Komentarz do art.* 285 *k. p. c.* [in:] A. Jakubecki, *Kodeks Postępowania Cywilnego – Komentarz*, Warszawa 2012, pp. 369 ~ 370.

issuing a joint opinion or separate opinions.[43]

In the case of proceedings in medical cases it is so important that often the issue of doctor's liability for a mistake is complex, or the error's consequences for the patient's health are multi – organ and it is impossible to draw an accurate and reliable opinion by a doctor of one specialization. This regulation fully deserves approval, because its use increases in practice the likelihood of presenting an assessment of facts of the case as a whole, alongside the opportunity to minimize the risk of error of interpretation in the scope of adjudication on the liability of a medical professional.

According to § 4 of the Regulation of the Ministry of Justice on expert witnesses, before taking on the function, an expert is required to take an oath to the president of the court, in which he commits to perform tasks vested in him with diligence and impartiality, which is an important factor that prevents the bias of an expert in the course of issuing an opinion. The medical expert's opinion needs to be presented in such a way as to guarantee both accuracy and fairness of the judgement, as the gravity of expert evidence in most cases is of a decisive character to the outcome of the case, therefore, it is necessary for the medical expert to maintain impartiality in its preparation.[44] However, one must not forget about the subsidiary nature of expert evidence, which is part of the evidence gathered in the course of court proceedings. The court should not condition the outcome of the case entirely on the content of the opinion put forward by an expert physician. The degree of probability determined by an expert must not be mechanically transferred by the court to establish the fact and should not constitute the only basis for adjudicating, because an expert opinion constitutes one piece of evidence, subject to the rule of free evaluation by the court against the entire procedural material gathered. B. Janiszewska rightly notices that the position of an expert may be a starting point to further build on inference as to the circumstances presented. The court, assessing the contents of the opinion, may, while approving it, aim to further substantiate the rise of the liability by formulating an express request on the fact. It can also dismiss the action in the absence of a possibility to draw an unequivocal conclusion, the consequence of which may be failure to legally demonstrate the fact. The author rightly points out that the basis of proving claims may include not only the circumstances clearly, and, at the same time, positively proven, but also the conclusions drawn in the event of non – existence of occurrences.[45]

Referring to the content of the opinion and its consequences, one must not forget about the obligation imposed on the doctor, including an expert witness, in the act on the medical profession, which states that a doctor is required to maintain the confidentiality of information relating to the patient. The legislature prohibits the doctor form publicly disclosing information allowing

---

〔43〕 H. Wiśniewska – Śliwińska, J. T. Marcinkowski, *Biegły sądowy – tryb powoływania, wymagania, obowiązki*, „Orzecznictwo Lekarskie" 2011, No 8, p. 35.

〔44〕 T. Gleixner, *Dowód z biegłych lekarzy przed sądami ubezpieczeń społecznych*, „Nowe Prawo" 1965, No 12, p. 1442.

〔45〕 B. Janiszewska, *Dowodzenie w procesach lekarskich* (2), „Prawo i Medycyna" 2004, No 2, pp. 119 ~ 120.

for the identification of the patient without his consent. The whole opinion is covered under medical confidentiality, and disclosing it is limited exclusively to the parties to particular court proceedings.[46]

In the subject literature, there is no unambiguous classification of the typology of expert opinion in cases of medical errors. However, it seems legitimate to draw up their classification due to the nature of the most commonly occurring cases concerning the so – called medical errors. Therefore, we can distinguish types of medical expert opinions in the most common types of cases to be heard. Therefore, the following opinions are possible: opinions in cases brought by a patient against a medical professional for the payment of compensation for material damage (e. g. costs of treatment), in cases of non – pecuniary damage inflicted (such as pain), as well as in actions brought by a medical professional against a patient for the infringement of reputation. Admittedly, on the increase is public awareness of patients who exercise their rights in court proceedings, as well as of doctors who more and more daringly choose to fight in court for their good name (for example, in situations where patients manipulate facts, spreading information about the doctor's alleged errors).

5. *Form and content of a medical expert opinion*

The legislator provides for two possible forms of expert opinion. In the light of art. 278 § 3 of the CCP, the expert opinion may be prepared verbally or in writing. Selecting one of these forms is largely dependent on the complexity and structure of the issue that the medical expert is to face in the proceedings. In a situation where it is possible to issue an opinion immediately, and also when it does not require extensive explanations, the oral form of expert opinion is possible, recorded in the minutes of the court session. With respect to the proceedings in cases of medical errors it is rare to choose the verbal form of expert opinion, for it is not adequate to the intricate and complex nature of these cases. As a rule, opinions of experts in medical cases are issued in writing, after examining and analysing the medical records contained both in the case records and those in possession of the examined person[47].

Should the court choose the written form of an expert's opinion, it has a statutory authority to require an oral explanation of the opinion submitted in writing. At the same time, the court has the right to request an additional opinion from expert witnesses. The legitimacy of this right is confirmed by situations in which the content of a medical expert opinion is not sufficiently comprehensible due to medical terminology used, because, as M. Rybarczyk rightly observes, where the opinion is clear to the court, its verbal explanation is to confirm its content and to dispel any doubts or issues not wholly understood by the parties or other participants in the proceedings. An expert's written opinion should be submitted to the court alongside copies for the parties. This guarantees to provide the parties to proceedings an opportunity to review its content

---

[46] B. Gudowska, *Dowód z opinii lekarza biegłego*, „Przegląd ubezpieczeń społecznych i gospodarczych" 2001, No. 7, p. 10.

[47] T. Demendecki, *Komentarz do art.* 279 *k. p. c.* [in:] A. Jakubecki, *Kodeks*…, op. cit., p. 366.

and allows for making any reference it.[48] As noted by A. Zielinski, it became a custom, both in doctrine and in practice, to call to a session each time the expert who submitted a written opinion on the case, which is an implementation of one of the fundamental principles of civil procedure – the principle of immediacy. Such actions provide the parties with the opportunity to ask the expert questions directly related and referring to the opinion[49].

Under Article 40 of the Code of Medical Ethics[50], the doctor is obliged to issue certificates on the basis of an up – to – date examination or medical records. Those rules should be applied by analogy to medical – legal diagnoses issued, as well as expert opinion, because it expresses a general principle of the physician acting in accordance with the state of knowledge and on the basis of medical records, which is in accordance with the bioethics standards characterising the doctor's actions towards the injured person, that is the patient. A doctor undertaking the preparation of an opinion, which is an important item of evidence, should first of all review the contents of the provision of evidence, because an expert is required in his activities to comply carefully with the material scope, while at the same time to reference reliably to the thesis of evidence contained within. Accordingly, the opinion of an expert should address the questions posed in the thesis of evidence. It is not purposeful to make statements outside the scope determined by the court, and in some cases it may create a basis for recognizing expert's lack of objectivity.[51]

As already indicated, one must agree with A. Zielinski's position that the element which must be taken into account in the preparation of opinions in medical cases is medical records, as well as documents contained in the case files.[52] The issue of medical records, rules and modes of their preparation and storage are set out in the Act of 18. 05. 2011 on the type and scope as well as handling of medical records in health care institutions, created by the minister with competence over internal affairs (Journal of Laws of 2011, No. 125, item 712). For the purposes of this study it needs to be indicated that medical records are not limited solely to the coverage of subjective and objective examinations performed. These are also all annotations of the nature of interpretation, or qualifications, and these are also reports of procedures and exams, information cards (including hospitalization information sheets), referrals, certificates, diagnoses or plates and prints of image exams, etc. The above – mentioned catalogue of documents included in medical records is only an example, pointing to the variety and diversity (in the form, too) of sources which are the basis of evidence of an intermediate nature, which medical documentation undoubtedly constitutes.[53] By law, medical records are assigned a rank

---

[48] M. Rybarczyk, *Biegły w postępowaniu*…, op. cit., p. 11.

[49] A. Zieliński, *Teoretyczne i praktyczne aspekty dowodu opinii psychiatrycznej*, „Postępy Psychiatrii i Neurologi", 2000, No 9, p. 21.

[50] Kodeks Etyki Lekarskiej, przyjęty podczas Nadzwyczajnego II Krajowego Zjazdu Lekarzy z dnia 14 grudnia 1991 r.

[51] B. Gudowska, *Dowód z opinii*…, op. cit., p. 11.

[52] A. Zieliński, *Teoretyczne i praktyczne*…, op. cit., p. 22.

[53] R. Mądro, K. Wróblewski, G. Teresiński, *Informacja i uwagi na temat dokumentacji lekarskiej*, Lublin 1997, pp. 15 ~ 17.

of a document because they are a material object stating the occurred, in the right place and time, phenomenon, fact or human thought.[54]

If required by a particular factual situation, the expert doctor should carry out direct medical examination of the person concerned, while at the same time perform an interview. As noted by A. Zielinski, an important issue relating to matters of expert opinion is its categorical and alternative characteristics. The author draws attention to the fact that the most desirable are categorical opinions, because of their compelling character. Thanks to statements of a medical expert, presented to the extent possible in an unambiguous and concrete, yet convincing, way, the court is released from undertaking further evidentiary actions related to the content of the expert's opinion, which has a positive effect on the postulate for the pace of proceedings. Opinions of the alternative nature should not be, however, treated as defective, as in this case the expert presents a variety of possible causes of committing medical errors, leaving the final evaluation and choosing of the concrete situation among the possibilities presented by the expert to the court's consideration.[55]

Referring to the very structure of an expert's opinion, one should distinguish its descriptive part and the opinion itself. First, the expert should indicate whether he is the so called permanent exert witness or one appointed *ad hoc*, and also – what his specialization is in the field of medicine. This data serves to substantiate the validity of the preparation of an opinion by this doctor, as well as to confirm the special knowledge he is in possession of. The descriptive part should also reflect general information about the date and place of issue, together with the catalogue number of the files of the case to which it refers and the description of facts of the case. These elements may be attributed a technical character. Expert's indication of methods he used in the course of its preparation should constitute a summary of the descriptive part. The opinion itself will refer to the medical expert's conclusions that contain the answer to the question posed by the court in the thesis of evidence. The most important part of the opinion is its justification, because it facilitates the court in determining whether the expert's reasoning is consistent and adhering to the rules of logic. This justification is the most important part of a medical expert opinion, because in this part the interpretation of medical issues is performed, along with their translation into the language understood by a lawyer. The expert must also demonstrate here his knowledge of legal terminology, especially provisions of the law. It should be noted, however, that it is not the task of the expert to conduct an analysis and legal evaluation of the described facts of the case and reasons justifying or rejecting the claim of committing a medical error, as it remains in the exclusive competence of the court.

Summing up considerations in this regard, what needs to be highlighted is the repeatedly stressed expert evidence's subsidiary nature for the court, constituting auxiliary material for the

---

〔54〕 G. Teresiński, R. Mądro, *Rola dokumentacji medycznej w opiniowaniu sądowo – lekarskim*, „ Prokuratura i Prawo", 2012, No 11, pp. 23 ~24.

〔55〕 A. Zieliński, *Teoretyczne i praktyczne*…, op. cit. , p. 22.

court's substantive adjudicating on the case. The task of an expert is to answer the questions posed by the court in the thesis of evidence, while referring to facts of the case on the basis of his expert knowledge in the field of medicine. It is certainly not his task to adjudicate accurately on the examined case, as an expert cannot substitute the court in its jurisdiction capacities.

6. *Conclusions*

In summary, it needs to be stated that deliberations on the significance of evidence using special information for adjudicating in cases of medical errors constitute the court's and parties′ main instruments in the evaluation of medical events and responsibility for their negative effects. The practice of using this kind of opinion gives rise to many problems of interpretation relating to the role of an expert or of a research institute in the evaluation of elements of the facts of the case and the relationship of that evidence with other evidence used in the same proceeding.

As established in the course of these deliberations, an expert (institute) performs a supportive role towards the court. This means that his task is, for the court's needs, to explain aspects of the facts of the case which the court cannot properly interpret without specialist knowledge. But this subsidiarity means that the expert, by his participation in the case, does not relieve the court of the responsibility for the content of the issued decision, even if his opinion is the axis of evidence proceedings that led to that decision. It is the court that must assess the significance of expert opinion in conjunction with conclusions drawn from other types of examined evidence, and only after adding up all the results of evidence proceedings may the court construct the factual basis for the resolution.

In Polish practice, in respect to this type of evidence, there also arises a problem of reproducing it in a particular proceeding. There is no doubt that the court should commission repeating or completing the opinion by the same expert or other experts (or a research institute) when the initial opinion is incomplete, contains gaps, raises doubts as to its reliability, etc. However, the adjudicating court is not required to allow evidence from the opinion of an institute or from subsequent opinions of experts, in all instances where the submitted opinion is unfavourable to the party. Thus, the court is obliged to allow such evidence, where necessary, in particular, when conflicting opinions of experts were submitted[56]. In all instances the court must consider this necessity, because the multiplication of expert opinions can sometimes affect the opacity of the results of evidence proceedings, and certainly significantly influences the costs of civil proceedings.

The principal value of expert opinion (opinion of an institute) is the impartiality and objectivity of substantive conclusions contained in it. An opinion prepared without maintaining these standards rapidly looses on the suitability for the purposes of civil proceedings. Hence a very cautious approach of the legislature and judiciary to private expertise commissioned by parties, not by the court, in evidence proceedings, which – as pointed out – is treated as pri-

[56] SC Judgement of 09. 01. 2012, File Reference Number I UK 200/11, LEX No. 1162648.

vate documentary evidence. This is why so important is proper application of the statutory exclusion of an expert as a guarantee of adequate ethical level of the prepared expert opinions, independent of pressure and influences of either party.

All of these problems, especially in such a specific category of civil cases as those related to the civil and legal consequences of medical errors, are important for the accuracy of evidence proceedings, the results of which must be developed with the participation of special information. There is no doubt that the court's capabilities in the proper outlining of the framework of expert opinion (institute) and extraction out of it of information useful for developing a true picture of the facts of the case are of fundamental importance for the efficiency of this proceeding, and as a consequence – the relevance of the decision.

论书证优先原则

纪格非 *

一、书证优先原则与大陆法系国家的民事诉讼制度

书证优先原则是大陆法系某些国家在处理书证与其他证据的关系时奉行的原则。它是指法律规定对某些法律事实存在与否只能用书证证明，不允许当事人使用其他证据，比如证人证言代替书证。法国是采行书证优先原则的主要国家。但是在16世纪以前，在法国的诉讼制度中，证人证言是最重要的证据，当时奉行的是证言优先原则。在刑事诉讼中，被告人的口供甚至被赋予证据之王的优越地位。不过，证言优先原则随着1566年法兰西司法改革王令的颁布被书证优先原则取代了，该王令规定，凡是超过100里布尔金额或价额的交易，必须在公证人或证人面前缔结契约；没有缔结契约的合同纠纷，法院不得受理；契约以外所主张的合意事项发生的争议，如果只有证人的，法院将不接受该证据或认可该证据。立法上之所以产生这样的变化是基于以下原因：①由于合同纠纷不断增加，日益复杂化，书证比人证更能够准确反映案件事实，并且可以减少在实践中经常发生的收买证人作伪证的情况；②法国此时已形成了十分完善的公证制度，公证人的数量日益增多；③15世纪近代印刷技术的发明和迅速发展，为当事人提供书证造就了技术保证。[1] 此后，书证优先原则通过1667年的司法改革王令、1804年《法国民法典》和《法国民事诉讼法典》得到了进一步的确认，并成为法国证据规则中最重要的也是最具特色的部分。

书证优先原则虽然在提升书证在诉讼中的地位，倡导当事人用书面形式记载法律关系的发生、变更与消灭方面功不可没，但是该原则的负面效应也是显而易见的。不可否认，书证优先原则在某种程度上限制了当事人选择证据形式的自由。这就使该原则与当代商品经济社会通行的契约自由原则存在着某种程度的紧张关系。按照对契约自由精神的理解，当事人有权自主选择订立契约的对象、决定契约的内容以及契约的形式。但书证优先原则却使当事人对契约形式的选择权不能在诉讼中得到充分的体现，给契约自由原则在民事诉讼中的贯彻制造了障碍。

即便如此，书证优先原则还是对大陆法系的一些国家，比如意大利、奥地利，产生了重要影响。但是意大利充分考虑了该原则可能产生的负面影响，因此在借鉴这一制度时表现出了很大的灵活性。意大利诉讼法理论将书证的效力分为三种情况：①书证构成法律行为成立的要件，没有采取书面形式将导致法律行为无效，比如关于不动产变动或订立遗嘱的行为将因没有采取书面形式而无效；②书证虽不是法律行为成立的要件，但是却不允许当事人在诉讼中以证人证言或其他间接证据证明该法律行为是

---

* 纪格非，法学博士、中国政法大学副教授。

〔1〕 张卫平、陈刚：《法国民事诉讼法导论》，中国政法大学出版社1997年版，第84~86页。

否存在及其内容，比如保险合同或当事人的和解协议；③书证既不是法律行为成立的要件，法律也不硬性要求当事人必须以书证证明法律行为的内容，而是由法官来自由裁定是否排除证人证言的使用，比如当事人欲证明在合同签订后双方又订立了补充协议，一般而言，当事人必须用书面证据证明该补充协议的内容，但法官在考虑合同的性质及各种间接证据后可以采纳口头证据。〔2〕 由此可见，书证优先原则在意大利显然没有像在法国那样得到严格的贯彻，它给法官行使自由裁量权留下了一定范围的空间从而有利于避免由于贯彻该原则可能造成的形式主义危害。〔3〕

德国在20世纪民法典颁布前，也曾有严格限制证言使用范围的倾向，第二次世界大战后民事司法改革委员会在其1961年的报告中讨论过是否采取法国的书证优先主义的问题。但是委员会最终认为，书面合同并非德国的传统形式，排除或限制证言的规则可能导致不公正的判决，同时该委员会参照了1973年《海牙国际货物买卖统一规则》及《1980年联合国国际货物买卖合同公约》的规定，最终决定证人证言可以用来证明合同的内容。〔4〕 在德国现今的民诉法中，书证优先原则只在少数情况下适用，它们包括：①在证书诉讼与票据诉讼中只能使用书证方式，不允许采取其他方式（德国民诉法典第595条）；②诉讼代理人只能以书证方式证明代理权存在（德国民诉法典第80条）；③法庭程序是否得到遵循只能用记录证明，除非当事人举证证明记录是伪造的（德国民诉法第165条）。当事人的认诺、请求的舍弃、和解请求等也只能以记录证明（德国民诉法第160条）；④判决书记载的事实与法庭记录不符时以法庭记录为准（德国民诉法第314条）。

二、书证优先原则的性质及效力

大陆法系国家证据规则的一个显著特点是它分散规定在民事诉讼法和民事实体法中，例如，法国民法典第1341条规定，一切物体的金额或价值超过50法郎者，即使为自愿的寄存，均须在公证人前作成证书，或双方签名作成私证书。证书作成后，当事人不得就与证书内容不同或超出证书所记载的事项以证人证明，亦不得就证书作成之时、以前或以后所声明的事项以证人证明，如物件的金额或价值不足50法郎者，亦同。〔5〕 在实体法中规定书证优先原则容易使人产生书证优先原则属于实体规范的印象，其实不然，书证优先原则是一项证据规范，即法律关于某些法律行为的内容必须用书面形式予以证明的规定并不是这些法律行为成立或有效的要件，未采取法定的书面形式也不会使该法律行为无效。书证优先原则仅限制当事人在诉讼中证明某事实存在时必须使用书证这种证据形式，因此是一项诉讼规则而非实体规则。〔6〕

在前文所介绍的意大利诉讼法理论对书证效力划分的三种类型中，第一类规范属于实体规范，当然它对证据在诉讼中的使用也产生了影响，显然，在这种情况下，当

---

〔2〕 Mauro Cappelletti & Joseph M. Perillo, *Civil Procedure in Italy*, Martinus Nijhoff, 1965, pp. 198 ~ 199, pp. 217 ~ 219.

〔3〕 书证在民事法律关系发生、变更和消灭过程中的不同作用体现在《意大利民法典》第2721、2724、2725条中。参见费安玲、丁玫译：《意大利民法典》，中国政法大学出版社1997年版。

〔4〕 Hossein Safai, "The Probative Value of Testimony in Private Law", *Kluwer Law International*, 2005, pp. 116 ~ 117.

〔5〕 罗结珍译：《法国民法典》，北京大学出版社2010年版，第340页。

〔6〕 Peter Herzog, *Civil Procedure in France*, Martinus Nijhoff, 1967, p. 321.

事人只能以书面形式证明法律关系是否存在及其内容，其他种类的证据不能起到证明作用。第二类与第三类规范属于程序规范，其中第三类规则是关于证据力的规则。第二类规则是关于证据能力的规则，是书证优先原则的集中体现，此种情况下法律排除了在民事诉讼中其他证据特别是证人证言的可采性。与第一类规则相比，后两种规则更具有特色，它大大减少了由于合同形式不合法而导致合同无效的情况，维护了法律关系的稳定性，并且赋予了当事人更多的选择权，符合契约自由的基本原理。

在这里，有必要将大陆法系的书证优先原则同英美法系的最佳证据规则做一比较。书证优先原则和最佳证据规则都旨在促使当事人提交最易直接证明案件事实的、最不易被伪造的证据。但是二者的作用方式是不同的，书证优先原则通过排除书证以外的其他证据（主要指人证）的证据能力来保证证据的真实性，而最佳证据规则排除适用的主要是书证的复制品而非人证，它调整的是书证原件与复制品证据能力的问题。虽然大陆法系一些国家的立法中也有类似的规定，例如《法国民法典》第1334条规定："证书的原本存在时，其抄本仅为原本所裁内容的证明，并且得随时要求提交原本。"〔7〕但是这样的规定不属于书证优先原则的内容范围，因为它调整的并非书证与其他种类证据的关系而是书证原本与复制品的关系。

三、书证优先原则的限制

书证优先原则虽然有利于提高证明的准确性，有利于事实真相的发现，但由于其固有的形式主义特征难免会给诉讼证明带来一些潜在的危害。因为并非所有的口头证据都是不可靠的。同时，既然书面形式并不是法律关系的有效要件，但在诉讼中却坚持只能以书证证明该法律关系势必导致许多本应有效的法律行为无法通过诉讼得到确认，进而不利于保护法律关系的稳定和正常的交易秩序。书证优先原则的上述缺点已引起大陆法系国家的充分重视，德国民事诉讼法虽以法国民诉法为蓝本但却没有采用书证优先原则，在诉讼中某一事实应优先采用何种形式的证据由法官自由裁量之。意大利民诉法虽规定了书证的优越地位，但其民法典规定在下述情况下口头证言也是可采的：①如果当事人的主张依书面证据是可信的，但该当事人或其代理人提出了与书面证据记载内容相反的证言；②如果获得书证在道德上或实际上是不可能，比如证明家庭成员间的合同或协议可以不受书证优先原则限制；③由于非举证方的过失使书面证据遗失。〔8〕

即使在原来严格奉行书证优先原则的法国也对该原则的适用范围做出了限制，首先，根据《法国民法典》第1341条第2款规定，在商事案件的诉讼中不适用书证优先原则。其次，当事人可以协议不受书证优先原则的限制，书证优先原则的受益人也可以用明示或默示方式放弃该原则。再次，还存在所谓书证端绪例外，所谓书证端绪指某一书面材料虽然欠缺书证的必要条件（如缺少当事人签名的私文书或手续不正规的私文书），但是，在其他证据的佐证下却可以达到证明当事人主张的事实成立的效果的书证。法国的判例将书证端绪的范围扩大适用于草案、信件。〔9〕其新民诉法第198条

〔7〕罗结珍译：《法国民法典》，北京大学出版社2010年版，第338页。

〔8〕Mauro Cappelletti & Joseph M. Rerillo, *Civil Procedure in Italy*, Martinus Nijhoff, 1965, p. 199.

〔9〕沈达明：《比较民事诉讼法初论》（上），中信出版社1991年版，第318～319页。

规定法官对各方当事人的声明、对一方当事人不回答或拒绝回答问题之事实，得做出法律上的结论并且以书证端绪对待之。最后，《法国民法典》第1348条规定，债权人在不可能取得债权的书面证明时，不适用书证优先原则。不可能取得书证证明指：①因准契约、侵权行为或准侵权行为而发生的债务；②在火灾建筑物坍塌、骚乱或船只遇难时所作的必要寄存以及旅客留宿旅店时所作的寄存，此种情形应根据各人的身份及事实的情况而确定；③在不能预见的事故情况下所订立的债务而不能作成证书或④债权人因不可抗力而产生的意外事故而遗失其作为书证的证书者。[10] 正是由于上述种种例外的存在使某些学者甚至认为《法国民法典》第1314条的规定的主要目的并不是限制口头证据的使用，而是告诫当事人在订立书面合同时必须十分谨慎，因为在起草书面协议时，出现的错误和遗漏不能成为今后辩解的证据。[11]

总之，在当今的大陆法系各国，书证优先原则的适用也是灵活的，法律充分考虑了书证与人证的各自特点，没有一味地强调书证的可靠性而是倾向于由法官和当事人在各种证据方式中做出选择，从而使书证优先原则摆脱了形式主义的倾向。

四、书证优先原则与口头补证原则的区别

英美法系国家没有所谓的书证优先原则。相反，由于采用了陪审制而早期的陪审团的组成人员文化素质较低，有些人根本不识字，这就决定了通过诉讼程序对案件事实的揭示只能主要依靠证人证言。因此，在普通法中有口头证据优先的传统。但这不等于说书证在英美法系国家就处于不重要的位置。英国在历史上就经历过文书审阶段，在那时原告如果想在诉讼中获胜，就必须向法院提供一份由被告制作并签名的文书，以证实其权利的存在。英国学者边沁曾对口头证据与书面证据的关系加以详细的阐释。他将书证分为先前成立的书证（指双方当事人通过签字达成的协议），非正式书证（指信笺、便条或日记的摘录等）和书证式询问（指通过其他案件的审理而获得的证人证言或在书记官前所作的声明）三种。其中，后两种书证只有较低的证据力，它们应让位于证人亲自在法庭上提供的证言。但第一种书证，也就是先前成立的书证却具有较高的证据价值，当事人不能用口头证据推翻或代替它。[12] 现代英美法中的“口头补证原则”基本上采用了边沁的上述观点。这一原则对文书证据的效力产生了重要的影响。按照英美契约法的一般原则，口头证据的提出不发生增加、变更或抵触契约的效力。当双方形成书面契约时，对书面契约的解释必须以契约所载文字为准，对于任何书面契约成立前或同时的口头证据，或其他定约过程中的书面证据，凡与契约内容相抵触的均不得采用。也就是说，法律不允许以其他证据方式改变契约的内容。口头补证原则实际是上述原则的一个例外。当然，法律对何时允许用口头证据对书面契约加以完善、变更、解释作出了明确的限制性规定：首先，必须当事人已经订立的书面形式的契约的内容不足以成立完整的契约时，一方可以提出口头证据，补充其未完整的部分。其次，如果书面内容的契约含义不明，法院准许采用口头证据以解释其意义。最后，

---

〔10〕 罗结珍译：《法国民法典》，北京大学出版社2010年版。

〔11〕［法］勒内·达维：《英国法与法国法：一种实质性比较》，潘华仿、高鸿钧、贺卫方译，清华大学出版社2002年版，第142页。

〔12〕 Hssein Safai, “The Probative Value of Testimony in Private Law”, *Kluwer Law Internatinal*, 2005, pp. 180 ~ 181.

凡文字在字典上之意义与职业传统、社会习惯或术语之意义不相同时，为解释书面契约的真正含义，也可以采用口头证据。除此之外，如果书面契约因欺诈、胁迫或错误等无效或得撤销时，也允许当事人用口头证据证明存在导致契约无效的原因。[13]

显然，口头补证原则与书证优先原则具有不同的功能和性质。前者并不限制当事人在诉讼过程中用何种证据形式证明法律关系的状态，它仅要求当事人在对书面合同进行修改或补充时应同样采用书面形式，否则将不发生预期的法律效力。因此，口头补证原则主要是一项实体规则而非证据规则。

五、我国立法对书证优先原则的吸收与借鉴

我国《合同法》第10条规定，当事人订立合同，有书面形式、口头形式和其他形式。法律行政法规规定采用书面形式的，应当采用书面形式。当事人约定采用书面形式的，应当采用书面形式。理论界对于应当采用书面形式而没有采用的，应如何处理还有不同的理解，有人认为应认定合同无效，有人认为应认定合同没有成立。但是，无论将书面形式作为合同的成立要件还是有效要件，当事人享有的自由选择的权利都是有限的。从世界范围来看，合同形式自由已成为发展的趋势。《联合国国际货物销售合同公约》第11条规定："销售合同无须以书面订立或以书面证明，在形式方面也不受任何其他条件的限制。销售合同可以用包括人证在内的任何方法证明。"《国际商事合同通则》中也有同样的规定。尽管口头合同亦有便捷、灵活、成本低的优势。但是，用书面形式订立合同有发生纠纷时易于举证的优点。特别是记录重要的民事法律关系时，更有必要提倡采用书面形式。那么，应如何协调合同自由原则与法律对合同的法定形式的强制性规定之间的矛盾呢？大陆法系国家的书证优先原则为我们提供了一种解决问题的新思路。

事实上，书证优先原则在我国现有的法律规定中已经得到了部分的体现，例如，《合同法》第215条规定，租赁期限6个月以上的，应当采用书面形式。当事人未采用书面形式的，视为不定期租赁。也就是说，书面形式并不是租赁合同的有效要件，但是对于租期为6个月以上的租赁合同，当事人如果要证明租赁为定期租赁，则必须采用书证的证明方式，否则将被认定为不定期租赁。适当借鉴书证优先原则既有利于鼓励当事人用书面的形式订立合同，又有利于减少由于形式不合法而造成的合同无效的情况。

由于笔者在合同法领域没有作过深入研究，因此不敢贸然议论对哪些民事法律关系或法律事实的记载应采用书面形式，哪些应由当事人自己选择记录方式。但在此想要指出的是，我国合同法的不足之处在于没有像英美法系国家那样明确规定一些可以用其他证据弥补书面证据不足的例外情况，也没有像大陆法系国家中的意大利那样，将书面形式的作用区分为合同的效力要件与证据能力要件两种情况，实际上限制了当事人对合同形式的选择权。

因此，笔者建议，借鉴英美法系国家和意大利的作法，将合同的形式与效力的关系分为三种情况：

第一种情况是当事人可以自由选择合同的形式。这一情况适用于绝大多数合同。

---

〔13〕 杨桢：《英美契约法论》，北京大学出版社2007年版，第247页以下。

但是，如果当事人选择了以书面方式订立合同，就不允许采用其他与证据内容相抵触的证据，除非合同的内容不完整或当事人对合同的理解产生了分歧时，才允许使用其他证据对合同进行补充、解释。

第二种情况是法律规定必须以书面或其他特殊形式订立合同，没有采用法律要求的形式将导致合同无效。这类规定主要适用于诸如不动产买卖、变更、分割等重要的事项，欠缺特定的形式合同无效，而且在民事诉讼中当事人不得以法律规定的特定形式以外的其他任何证据形式证明合同的内容。

第三种情况是法律规定在民事诉讼中某类法律关系必须以书面形式证明，但是，如果当事人没有采用书面形式并不导致法律关系无效。双方当事人的法律关系在发生纠纷并诉至法院前处于有效状态。只是在发生纠纷时，原、被告只能以书面证据证明自己的主张，否则将承担败诉的后果。这一类规则实际上属于证据能力规范，它体现了诉讼法与实体法在某种程度上的分离与独立。

总之，笔者认为，在书证的证据能力问题上，应当采取有条件的书证优先原则。这既体现了保障合同自由原则与提高交易安全原则的有机结合，符合国际通行的惯例与做法，又顺应了书证优先原则在世界范围内的发展趋势。

关注底线：我国口供补强证据规则的适用反思与制度完善

——着眼于防止刑事冤假错案的实践维度

李　钢*

补强证据规则是指为了保护被告人的权利，防止案件事实的误认，对某些证明力显然薄弱的证据，要求有其他证据予以证实才可以作为定案根据的规则。[1] 与不少国家的法律或者实践中都有针对特定证据的补强规则或判例相比较，虽然我国刑事诉讼法早已确立了针对被告人口供的补强证据规则，但是对于口供补强证据规则的适用范围、补强证据应当符合何种条件及补强应达到的证明程度等方面，却未予明确界定与规范。认真反省当前已被确认的部分刑事冤假错案发生的原因，我们会为违法取证、刑讯逼供现象的存在，非法证据排除之难以实现有司法理念、体制方面的顽疾而愤慨，但冷静下来仔细分析：过度依赖口供，口供补强规则不够完善，且在实践中适用和把握不到位甚至“底线”失守也难辞其咎。为此，笔者着眼于防止刑事冤假错案的实践维度，以证据学理论为分析工具，从我国口供补强规则的制度功能入手，在阐述该规则的立法现状和司法适用情况的过程中，揭示和反思部分冤假错案在口供补强上存在的疑点和矛盾，借鉴域外法律和实践经验，对进一步完善我国的口供补强证据规则展开全面探讨，提出若干建设性意见，期望有利于刑事法治建设的科学发展。

一、关于口供补强规则的制度功能

从世界各国刑事证据法律实践来看，针对证明力运用立法区分严格等级的法定证据时代早已谢幕，司法文明开启着人类理性自我认知：尊重法官对证明的自由心证原则，极少的证明力规则意味着它被交由法官或陪审团加以自由判断，确立规则的重点则更多地集中在对公权力影响证据能力的高度关注上。即便如此，各国仍然立足人权保障的基本价值追求，在立法或实践中多以嫌犯供述为主设立例外情形，除英美法系对被告人审判当庭时自认犯罪可直接视为定案根据外，通常认为供述对认定案件事实不具有独立的和完全的证明力，尤其是被告人的有罪供述，要求必须有补强证据保证其内容的真实可靠。应当说，口供补强证据规则就是一项限定口供证明力的规则，要求对口供证据进行“补强”，否则不能进行直接定案。因此，口供补强证据规则不是一项可采性规则，而是证明力的判定规则。[2]

我国1979年《刑事诉讼法》第35条、1996年《刑事诉讼法》第46条，直到现行

---

* 李钢，辽宁省高级人民法院法官。Email：loveworldman@ sina. com。

〔1〕 刘善春、毕玉谦、郑旭：《诉讼证据规则研究》，中国法制出版社2000年版，第320页。

〔2〕 房保国：“只有口供能够定案吗？—论补强证据规则的适用”，载《第二届“证据科学与理论”国际研讨会论文集》2009年印行，第85页。

《刑事诉讼法》第53条的规定，这些条文像一条纵贯线始终不变地强调，在刑事诉讼中运用被告人供述确认犯罪时，必须有其他证据予以补强，否则不能认定犯罪要件事实。[3] 作为证明力判定规则，一方面，它明确禁止法官单纯依赖被告人供述定案，这是口供运用的“底线”，提出了采认口供必须有其他证据补强的硬性要求；另一方面，它断然否定了被告人供述在认定犯罪过程中的必要性，进而强调即使在只有其他证据的情况下，当证明状态达到确实、充分，仍可对被告人定罪和处刑。可见，该规则主旨即以法律形式对被告人供述的证明力予以削弱和限定，直接提示法官运用口供认定犯罪事实必须坚持的“底线”。我们会发现国家立法确立该规则的内在机理，是基于两个事实的担忧，体现两个价值追求：一是对被告人供述稳定性和真实性的担忧，致力于追求刑事定罪的公正准确；二是对我国封建司法刑讯遗毒之深的担忧，致力于保护犯罪嫌疑人、被告人的合法权利。以证据特征、司法理性、制度原理为指导，结合我国司法文化背景展开分析，我国口供补强规则被赋予以下两个制度功能：

（一）具有祛除司法任性以至防止裁判错误的功能

法官在刑事诉讼中的首要任务就是对案件事实的确认与判定。事实确认要依赖案件所涉证据的“再次构建”。不管由谁来做法官，他都天然喜欢会说话的证据，这是因为言词证据更容易成为直接证据，特别是被告人可能就是案件实施者，如果其自陈犯罪过程，不仅直接深入触及事实，而且全面具体达至细节。加之，侦查技术发展也经历了一个从粗浅到精细的过程。在国家侦查技术能力长期低下的漫长历史阶段内，世界大多数国家的司法都曾将口供视为“证据之王”，这种以口供为中心的判定事实模式至今仍难以完全摆脱。法官对被告人供述承认事实内容的行为，还会因一般人对自我叙述承责的习见而加深心理信度。然而，抛开来自侦查机关等外来干预不谈，刑事犯罪案件被告人面对被追诉甚至定罪的可能，从人性中本能自利的方面而言，其供述中掺杂选择性和虚假性内容是常见现象。受被告人性格、知识程度、理解能力等因素影响，供述内容主观性强较难稳定，与事实真相的差异也在所难免。客观地讲，在审查案件事实的过程中，过度依赖和夸大被告人供述的当然证明力，甚至突破口供不能独立定案的“底线”，这无疑体现了一种司法武断与任性，放纵则危害公正的实现。因此，遵循司法对被告人供述的理性认识，立法上不赋予其独立完整的证明价值，实质上是还原被告人供述的证据本来面目。确立和完善该项补强证据规则，将有利于纠正“口供中心主义”流弊，预防冤假错案的发生。

（二）具有引导公权力规范行使以至摒弃危害人权行为的功能

作为一部人权法，刑事诉讼法所要解决的核心问题是国家权力与公民权利的平衡问题。[4] 从诉讼结构关系上看，国家专门机关代表国家行使强大的侦查、追诉权，无论在庭前侦查阶段还是庭审对抗阶段，被追诉者作为可能的犯罪人不仅承受着正义的某种过程“荷载”，更处于客观的极为弱势的地位。司法实践中，处于强势的侦查机关对犯罪嫌疑人实施高压甚至刑讯手段，主要目的就是为了获取有罪供述。司法裁判的

---

〔3〕 各国立法规定主要指口供对直接定罪的影响，证明对象事实是前提要求。所以，笔者将其定位于犯罪要件事实。

〔4〕 陈瑞华：“法律程序构建的基本逻辑”，载《中国法学》2012年第1期，第65页。

口供中心主义，无疑是催生这种公权力严重践踏侵犯公民基本人权行为的内在动因。加之，中国古代长期崇尚严刑峻法，重刑主义思想久有溯源，以人犯口供为定案之本，戕害人命的刑讯逼供被合法化。这种迷信口供而动辄刑讯的封建司法伴生物，在近年来曝光的云南杜培武、河南赵作海等冤假错案中都能隐约可见其鬼魅再现。设立和完善口供补强规则，是刑诉法保障人权价值的体现，也是平衡国家权力与公民权利的需要。该规则以限制被告人口供证明力的方法，直接形成倒逼式的强化引导机制，客观上促使侦查机关转变重言词证据、轻客观证据的观念，围绕口供展开的单一侦查方式正逐步向多元获取客观证据的方向发展。新修订刑诉法着力强化的非法证据排除规则与之相辅相成，从证据能力角度，采取否认其证据资格的方法，着眼于取缔违法获取口供的“定案红利”。可见，口供补强规则与非法证据排除规则共同发挥着规范公权力正确行使，彻底摒弃危害人权行为的功能作用。

二、关于口供补强规则的适用范围

在英美法系，尽管制定法中很少规定补强规则，“但在美国的各司法区信奉这样一种要求，就是欲支持一项供认为基础的有罪认定，该供认必须为审理中提出的其他证据所佐证”。〔5〕从部分州通过的制定法或者判例法来看，补强规则适用范围包括经他人提出的、被告人在法庭审判外的自白，还有共犯的证言或一般陈述。对于叛国、伪证、妇女儿童犯风化罪案件的证明、儿童提供的不经宣誓的证言以及根据1960年道路交通法进行的证明也适用补强证据。〔6〕可见，这里补强的必要性体现为缺少某些证据，法官不得据以定罪的形态，还包括除非特定种类的证言得到补强，否则不能将案件提交陪审团的情形。〔7〕日本的刑事诉讼法认为，补强性的法理在于防止偏重自白的危险，补强规则仅仅适用于自白这一种证据，而不适用于一般证言真实性的担保。〔8〕在我国台湾地区“刑事诉讼法”中亦有类似日本的规则。根据我国现行刑事诉讼法规定，被指控者在不同的诉讼阶段有不同的称谓。只有当案件被提起公诉之后，被指控者才具备被告人的身份。据此，有学者认为，《刑事诉讼法》第53条中的被告人供述只能被理解为被告人在法庭上向法官所作的有罪供述。〔9〕这种观点脱离中国司法审判运行现状，对文义解释的运用过于僵化。应当讲，虽然在不同诉讼阶段称谓确实迥异，但是同案中被告人与犯罪嫌疑人还是同一人。检察机关举证的侦查机关对犯罪嫌疑人供述制作的讯问笔录，它反映的仍然是同一人对犯罪事实的全部承认或主要部分承认的陈述，由于判断和认定的场域已然定位于法院审理时段，对被告人在庭前阶段的供述显然没有再行区分称谓的必要。如果认为，被告人庭前的供述无需补强即可作为定罪的唯一证据，但被告人当庭作有罪供述尚尤需补强，以举重以明轻论，不仅明显有悖常理与逻辑，更是严重违反了第53条作为口供补强规则的立法本意。

---

〔5〕［美］约翰·W. 斯特龙主编：《麦考密克论证据》，汤维建等译，中国政法大学出版社2004年版，第274页。

〔6〕参见宋随军、姜涛、周富强、岳发泉主编：《刑事诉讼证据实证分析》，法律出版社2006年版，第89、90页。

〔7〕参见李训虎：“证明力规则检讨”，载《法学研究》2010年第2期。

〔8〕参见（台）陈朴生：《刑事证据法》，三民书局1979年版，第534~535页。

〔9〕参见徐美君：“口供补强法则的基础与构成”，载《中国法学》2003年第6期，第127页。

我国刑事司法实践中的庭前供述主要是指被告人在庭前阶段向侦查机关或者检察机关对犯罪事实的陈述。对于被告人在刑事诉讼中向非司法警察人员所作的陈述，或者在刑事诉讼前向其他人员所作的陈述，较庭审供述而言，这类由其他人员转述的证言无论是否经公安司法机关对其内容与形式加以固定，都属于典型的传来证据。[10] 就内容来讲，它们直接来源于被告人陈述，实质证明力也依赖于被告人陈述，还徒增了传闻的不稳定性。因此，它们既不能作为口供的补强证据，更不能用来独立确认被告人有罪。笔者认为，口供补强规则的适用范围应当包括被告人关于其对被指控犯罪事实的全部或主要部分承认的当庭供述、庭前供述，对其他人转述被告人承认案件事实而形成的证据也应比照适用。

三、关于口供补强证据的规格条件

补强证据的界定重在补强功能，而非该证据具有某种个性化“质”的规定性。只要其在一定程度上能够证明被告人供述内容的可靠性、真实性，发挥补充、加强其证明力的作用，且来源合法、内容客观，原则上在证据种类上是不受限的。另基于被告人供述的天然不稳定性，国家权力可能对被告人造成的影响，这种双重不信任叠加为对被告人供述证明力的“囚禁”，这是确立口供补强证据规则的前提。由此可见，应当要求该补强证据与被告人供述保持某种“疏离”，即具有相对独立性。一方面，通常要求补强证据与被告人供述的来源不能相同。实践中，较为常见的被告人在侦查阶段形成的自白书，亦属前文所述的适用口供补强规则的应予补强证据，系被告人供述的“另类”形态，不能纳入补强证据之列。至于被告人过去的日记、备忘录或信件，其中涉及了被告人所供述犯罪事实的记载内容，由于它们是被告人未进入司法程序前的历史性资料，虽制作人为被告人，但在无证据证明其系被告人预知侦查、审判而故意编造的情况下，经审查书证形成及内容原始可靠，可在个案综合裁量中将其作为补强证据。根据被告人或其他共犯供述所取得的被确认为凶器、赃物等物证，或者因被告人或其他共犯供认犯罪事实所提供的重要线索，从而找到的目击证人或知情人对案件嫌犯所做的辨认笔录和证言，因其独立于被告人及共犯供述本身，这些经有效转化的证据都可能具有印证和补强效力。对于被告人对同案非共同犯罪其他被告人犯罪事实的陈述，两人犯罪既无交叉，这种陈述显系其他被告人犯罪的证人证言，故可作为补强证据以资认定。对于能够准确印证被告人供述的犯罪现场技术复原证据或者勘查笔录，以及侦检部门对犯罪嫌疑人进行讯问时同步录音录像，均可以成为补强证据。[11]

另一方面，针对供述内容真实性的直接补强，还要求补强证据与案件犯罪事实具有相对独立的关联性。被告人供述可以是联接补强证据与案件犯罪事实的言词“索链”，但补强证据与犯罪事实的特定符合则必不可少。申言之，这种相对独立的关联性不是要反映被告人供述中所有的实质性细节，而是要体现与被告人有直接联系的那些

---

〔10〕 对于传来证据，学界认为是指不是直接来源于案件事实或原始出处，而是从间接的非第一来源获得的证据材料。参见樊崇义主编：《证据法学》，法律出版社2004年版，第220页。

〔11〕 胡嘉滨：“口供补强证据规则基本问题初探”，载《北京人民警察学院学报》2006年第1期，第36~37页。

特定细节的相对吻合。[12] 例如，被告人在侦查阶段供述被害人为其所杀，凶器系一把菜刀，公安机关在其家提取该把菜刀，但是经确认受害人死于窒息且无锐器伤。该案中，此菜刀显然不能作为被告人供述的补强证据，鉴于该菜刀与犯罪事实不相符合，可充分质疑被告人供述的真实性。

据此，我们反思河南赵作海杀人冤错案原判的定罪证据体系，会发现针对其当庭已推翻的侦查阶段供述而言，实际上原判决中采认的大多数证据与犯罪事实缺乏相对独立的关联性，比如家族间有仇、赵作海与赵振晌是情敌；赵振晌失踪当天，有人曾看到二人打斗等，这些证据无法对犯罪事实的发生构成特定符合性。而且，作为关键物证“被害人”尸体却因高度腐败，警方先后做了4次DNA都未确定死者身份，根本无法作为补强证据。唯一对原供述可能予以支持的证据即包裹赵振晌尸体的编织袋片，经赵作海的妻子和儿子辨认，是赵作海家的，但其特定符合性却因所包裹的尸体身份不明，难以与原供述形成可靠的“联接”，也难以发挥直接补强效力。可见，赵作海案的原判决在确认侦查阶段供述定案方面，即便从补强证据上分析也是极为薄弱且难以成立的。可见，补强证据是否适格、能否补强，直接关系到被告人供述的认定。只有严格把握补强证据规则条件，发现和暴露对供述的补强薄弱或不足的问题，才能为贯彻疑罪从无原则做好证据审查判断的基础工作。[13]

四、关于共犯供述“互补”问题批判

在实践中，广受争议的问题是共犯的供述之间能否互为补强。笔者认为，我国刑诉法第53条确立的口供补强规则，不仅适用于单个被告人供述，而且适用于同案共同犯罪被告人的供述。应当承认，共犯之间有时可以互为证人，比如共同犯罪的被告人互相检举揭发对方与自己无关的其他犯罪行为，但在关涉共同犯罪行为和责任分担方面，他们之间存在明显的利害冲突，[14] 基于推脱罪责或争取从宽处罚等需要，进行虚假供述的可能性极大。比较而言，同案非共同犯罪被告人的供述者与其他被告人犯罪事实相关联，其证明内容更为可信。另外，对于共同犯罪中另案处理被告人的供述，[15] 以及不予追究刑事责任的共同作案人的供述，司法实践中通常作为证人证言加以运用，但这两种证据系其对亲自实施行为的陈述，而非感知他人实施行为提供的证言，加之该两类人同样与案件审理难脱利害关系，具有主观不稳定性和易受外界影响的特点。因此，只要内容是关于自己和其他共同犯罪人的共同行为，并不会因为他被另案处理或不予追究刑事责任就能确证其言词真实可靠。申言之，这两种情形固然尚没有直接规定在现行规则之中，但着眼于口供证据的本质和防止冤假错案的发生，实践要谨慎把握：凡以此类证人证言为主要直接证据，必须由该证人出庭作证，以接受

---

〔12〕 在公检法司安共同制定的《关于办理死刑案件审查判断证据若干问题的规定》第34条明确规定，根据被告人的供述，指认提取到了隐蔽性很强的物证、书证，且与其他证明犯罪事实发生的证据互相印证，并排除串供、逼供、诱供等可能性，可以认定犯罪。

〔13〕 中央政法委新近出台的《关于防止冤错案的指导意见》强调，对于定罪证据不足的案件，应当坚持疑罪从无原则，依法宣告被告人无罪，不能降格作出“留有余地”的判决。

〔14〕 参见吴丹红：“论共犯口供的证明力”，载《中国刑事法杂志》2001年第5期。

〔15〕 在司法实践中，共犯由于部分在逃或者检察机关的诉讼策略需要，可能会分案处理。然而，这种异案仅仅是程序性异案，共犯罪行相关并不会因程序分离而改变。但是，实践中关于“线人”或者有些参与诱惑侦查的人，应系证人。

质证和询问。将来再逐步通过立法或司法解释将其纳入该规则适用范围。

英美法系国家崇尚个人主义哲学和正当程序理念，遵循和关注被告人的主体自觉性，[16] 他们原则上是允许以被告人当庭供述定罪的，而且构建了其独有的辩诉交易制度。尽管如此，他们对待共犯证言证明力的态度还是有所保留：根据某一共犯的证言对另一共犯定罪时，如果没有补强证据，依照惯例，法官应当向陪审团说明这样做的危险。如果法官未做上述提醒，对另一共犯的定罪是无效的。[17] 我国现有刑事司法秉承国家本位主义哲学，正在吸收的英美法系对抗制因素，并不能完全冲击和掩盖其固有的浓烈职权色彩，辩方自觉性理念和制度缺乏能够真正“落地生根”的土壤，侦查机关在履行追求事实真相、准确惩罚犯罪的义务过程中，对口供自愿性和真实性的保障程序还远不完备。因此，我们应当更加理性地看待共犯供述本身具有的证明力，即使相关共同犯罪被告人的供述一致，如果没有其他证据相互印证，以该供述作为其他被告人的定罪依据，或者以供述证实供述，显然个体证据评价“根基”不稳，难以保证支撑定罪事实的证据构架具有相当的客观性，最易出现“多米诺骨牌效应”，其结论始终呈现不确定性和可变动性。[18] 可见，共犯的供述尚需其他证据印证，相互之间“补而不强”，从内容上虽可对照审查，却不具备独立、实质性的证据补强能力。

2008 年《最高人民法院印发〈全国部分法院审理毒品犯罪案件工作座谈会纪要〉的通知》（以下简称《纪要》）指出：“有些毒品犯罪案件，往往由于毒品、毒资等证据已不存在，导致审查证据和认定事实困难。在处理这类案件时，只有被告人的口供与同案其他被告人供述吻合，并且完全排除诱供、逼供、串供等情形，被告人的口供与同案被告人的供述才可以作为定案的证据。仅有被告人口供与同案被告人供述作为定案证据的，对被告人判处死刑立即执行要特别慎重。”通常来讲，所谓“同案被告人”应包括同案共犯和同案非共犯的被告人两类。该纪要在表述中未对“同案被告人”加以具体区分，足见其系谨慎地允许在特定条件下仅以共犯口供定案。这种例外规则的存在体现着两种实务逻辑：①在正常情况共犯之间即使有机会串供，绝大多数情况是不承认犯罪或推翻原有侦查阶段的供述，所以在庭审上一致供认犯罪存有一定可信性；②在能够完全排除诱供、逼供、串供等情形的基础上，从严把握补强规则，可能会造成无原则放纵犯罪。

笔者认为，实务逻辑确属经验之谈，相信其中不少案件在事实上也是公正的，但是，这不足以支撑这种违反刑诉法第 53 条规定做法的合理性，因为共犯供述本身的不确定性，决定了其不能发挥独立补强功能以资定案。《纪要》所称同案被告人却未将共同犯罪的被告人区分出来，明显增加了仅以言词证据认定犯罪事实固有的风险，而且可能进一步诱导和强化侦查人员口供主义的破案方式，侵害犯罪嫌疑人的合法权利。在相当长时期内，中国司法体制和刑事法治正渐进式发展，能够有效保障被告人权利和共犯口供独立性的改革措施还无法一蹴而就，《纪要》中列举的所谓“完全排除诱

---

〔16〕 参见秦宗文：“论共同被告口供的性质及其证明力”，载《犯罪研究》2004 年第 1 期，第 42 页。

〔17〕 参见张建伟：《司法竞技主义——英美诉讼传统与中国庭审方式》，北京大学出版社 2005 年版，第 295 页。

〔18〕 参见沈德咏：“关于口供的几个理论问题”，载《诉讼法学新论》，中国法制出版社 2000 年版，第 327 页。

供、逼供、串供等情形”，在实践中确实很难把握。

当前，犯罪控制理念处于强势和案卷中心主义尚属常态，必须“勒紧”口供认定的缰绳，同案共犯定案导致错谬教训尤应汲取。以张辉、张高平强奸、杀人冤错案为例，该案始终就没有证明两被告人强奸杀人的客观性证据，间接证据也极不完整，缺乏对主要案件事实的同一证明力，没有形成有效的证据链。其实，原判据以定案的主要证据包括张辉、张高平的有罪供述等证据均系以非法方法获取。然而，直到“被害人”赵振裳的“死而复生”突然回家，再审法院才不得不依法排除相关违法取得的定罪口供。[19] 这难道还不足以说明，上述例外规则存在着被扩大运用的极大风险?![20] 所以，即便是重案且取证极为困难，也不能突破“底线”仅以同案共犯口供定案，为了防止冤假错案的发生，这种口供补强思维必须牢固树立和坚守。

五、关于口供补强程度的标准要求

国外理论上和司法实践中主要有绝对说和相对说之分，其区别主要在于是否要求补强证据能否单独证明，以及全案中是否所有犯罪构成要件都需要补强。我国在关于证据补强的程度上也有类似两种主张，一种是要求补强证据大体上能够独立证明犯罪事实的存在；另一种是要求达到与供述一致，并能够保证有罪供述的真实性。[21] 笔者认为，从补强规则的要求出发，补强证据运用的核心目的是为了保证据以定案口供的真实性。同时，口供的取得是否自愿不仅影响到对口供证据能力因素的评价，更关涉口供内容可信性的确认。所以，只有当口供的真实性和自愿性都得到补强之后，才属完成补强的目的。因此，我国的补强证据，宜以国外的相对说及国内的第二种主张标准为基础，对口供的内容及口供的作出同时进行补强。还要看到供述的补强程度与待证要件事实的证明标准密不可分，对客观要件事实应当要求供述和其他补强证据的证明作用之和达到排除合理怀疑的程度，而主观要件事实包括故意或者过失，以及特定犯罪目的、动机等，对于被告人在供述中陈明的心理认识和意志因素，通常无需其他证据加以补强，但个案中主观要件事实的法律确认，要以不违背具体客观行为事实能够直接体现或推定的行为人主观状态为限。

在司法实践中，法庭认定被告人关于犯罪事实的供述，特别是涉及重罪重刑案件，在不存在能够单独足以证实被告人犯罪事实的有效证据或者现有证据证明力相对单薄的情形下，需要多个证据印证或佐证被告人犯罪实质细节，补强证据数量不是重点，关键是形成支持心证的补强证据体系。在目前广受关注的王书金强奸、杀人案件中，虽然王书金自供其杀害了原聂树斌案中被害人康某，但现有证据不仅未能对其供述予以有力补强，而且表明在具体致死手段、工具等实质细节方面，王书金的供述与事实存在较大差异。所以，笔者认为，即便仅从口供补强规则和证据理论上分析，如果法院直接确认王书金杀害康某事实成立，显然也是不妥当的。至于聂树斌案究竟是否为冤案的问题，笔者则十分赞同何家弘教授的观点，即对王书金该笔自供事实不予认定并不等于聂树斌有罪。

---

〔19〕 参见“浙江警方跨省调人作伪证造两冤案 真凶漏网再杀人”，载《潇湘晨报》2013年3月27日。

〔20〕 事实上，最高人民法院新刑诉法解释也未规定同案犯口供互证可以定案的内容。

〔21〕 龙宗智：《相对合理主义》，中国政法大学出版社1999年版，第459页。

有人认为："在实务上，应当允许针对不同类型的案件，赋予其口供以不同的证明作用。在较为严重的犯罪中，如故意杀人、抢劫等，应严格限制犯罪嫌疑人、被告人口供的证明作用，要求具有比较完整的补强证据；而对于某些轻微的犯罪，则可以赋予口供以较大的证明力，仅要求一定程度的补强证据即可。"[22] 应当说，这种观点在一定程度上体现着法官面对重罪与轻罪案件，在定罪心证方面的压力差异。然而，现行刑事案件简易程序适用范围极大，只要被告人认罪，几乎超过半数属于基层法院管辖的刑事案件，无论是轻罪还是重罪，程序要求都可能被"松绑"，其重要附带条件之一就是"事实清楚、证据充分"。《刑事诉讼法》第53条第2款规定表明，"事实清楚、证据充分"既要求定罪量刑事实有证据证明，且定案证据经法定程序查证属实，又要求综合全案证据，对所认定事实已排除合理怀疑。在我国法治环境尚有待改善的条件下，如此之多的刑事案件被纳入程序简化的"犯罪确认流水线"，必然会带来相当大的事实认定风险。为确保司法公正，防止冤错案的发生，我们绝不能以效率和轻罪为由，无原则地降低或者放松对供述补强的力度和标准。笔者认为，现行刑诉法确立了当事人和解的公诉案件诉讼程序，这是具有中国特色的"刑事和解"制度。长期以来，我国探索"刑事和解"制度的实践表明，从尊重当事人自主决定权上讲，国家司法机关、当事人以及其他第三人在具体案件和解过程中，处于帮助、促使或者相互沟通、协商、交涉的地位，由此形成的和解协议不仅体现着受害人的自主决定权，而且被告人也发挥着对自我行为承认和担责的自愿性和能动性。所以，对于适用当事人和解的公诉案件诉讼程序且达成和解协议的案件，在庭审中双方对确认被告人犯罪无分歧的情况下，被告人供述显然可信度更高，如果犯罪人与被告人的同一性亦不存在疑点或反证，则通常确认对被告人供述具有相应支撑的有效补强证据，再结合自愿的有罪供述即可定案。但是，对于其他案件仍应坚持以下补强要求，即确认合法有效的补强证据体系至少要达到与供述相结合能够证明有罪供述的真实性和自愿性，且足以确认犯罪事实是被告人参与或者实施的。

结　语

笔者认为，完善口供补强证据规则仅仅是预防刑事冤假错案发生的一个环节，如上所述要与非法证据排除规则的构建完善相结合，进而应当形成一个相对完备的证据法规范体系才能至少在制度上有所支撑。在强烈期待当下中国能够有效改善和解决外部法治生态和司法体制内在性问题，支持和保障法官坚守规则"底线"，真正贯彻证据裁判、无罪推定等原则的同时，我们能否说证据法治建设是全面彻底防止冤假错案发生，实现依法治国和司法公正文明的一项重要的基础建设，答案已不言自明。让我们共同努力为之奋斗！

---

〔22〕 汪建成、孙远："刑事诉讼中口供规则体系论纲"，载《北京大学学报（哲学社会科学版）》2002年第2期，第80页。

证据合法性调查程序中的侦查人员出庭

张保生 * 张 伟 **

2012 年《刑事诉讼法》第 57 条第 2 款规定："现有证据材料不能证明证据收集的合法性的，人民检察院可以提请人民法院通知有关侦查人员或者其他人员出庭说明情况；人民法院可以通知有关侦查人员或者其他人员出庭说明情况。有关侦查人员或者其他人员也可以要求出庭说明情况。经人民法院通知，有关人员应当出庭。"该规定确立了我国刑事诉讼证据合法性调查程序中的侦查人员或者其他人员（以下简称侦查人员）出庭制度，对于保障人权、遏制非法取证行为具有重要意义。上述规定在审判实践中如何实施，仍存在一些需要深入讨论的理论和实践问题。

一、关于侦查人员出庭的启动程序

2012 年《刑事诉讼法》第 57 条第 2 款规定了侦查人员出庭的三种启动程序，即检察院提请的通知程序、法院通知程序、侦查人员要求程序。下面分别讨论一下这三种启动程序中的有关问题。

（一）检察院的启动权既是权利又是义务

从立法条文看，由检察院提请的通知程序分为两个步骤，即"人民检察院提请"和"人民法院通知"。就第一个步骤来说，由于提请程序与通知程序分属不同司法机关，且有先后顺序，可见检察院在侦查人员出庭问题上享有启动权。对此，最高人民检察院 2012 年《人民检察院刑事诉讼规则（试行）》第 446 条把"提请"解释为"申请"；第 449 条则把"提请"解释为"建议"，即"对于搜查、查封、扣押、冻结、勘验、检查、辨认、侦查实验等侦查活动中形成的笔录存在争议，需要负责侦查的人员……出庭陈述有关情况的，公诉人可以建议合议庭通知其出庭"。就第二个步骤来说，随后的法院通知程序应视为批准权。但是，启动权和批准权的性质不同。当代刑事诉讼程序与传统纠问制程序的一个重要区别在于：诉讼主体由控辩审三方组成，法官"在主审程序中指挥审判以及最后作出判决"，诉讼程序"赋予当事人双方同等权利"。[1] 法官的审判指挥权、自由裁量权属于权力（power）范畴，而检察院作为控诉方的提请、申请或建议权则属于权利（right）范畴。在我国司法实践中，可以预见，一旦检察院提请法院通知有关侦查人员出庭，法院一般不会不予批准。由此可见，尽管侦查人员是否出庭最终由法院通知决定，但该条款赋予了检察院提请通知权。

问题在于：检察院的提请通知程序仅仅是一种权利吗？或者，它同时也是一种义

---

* 张保生，中国政法大学证据科学教育部重点实验室教授。

** 张伟，中国政法大学博士研究生。

〔1〕 参见［德］拉德布鲁赫：《法学导论》，米健译，法律出版社 2012 年版，第 144 ~ 146 页。

务？澄清这种提请通知程序的性质，对于该规定的实施具有关键意义。

首先，从提请通知程序是一种权利来看，该权利的相对方应该是辩护方。根据控辩双方权利平等原则，法律在赋予控诉方提请法院通知侦查人员出庭启动权的同时，也应该赋予辩护方同样的权利。而且，2012 年《刑事诉讼法》第 56 条第 2 款规定："当事人及其辩护人、诉讼代理人有权申请人民法院对以非法方法收集的证据依法予以排除。申请排除以非法方法收集的证据的，应当提供相关线索或者材料"。根据上述规定，辩护方拥有向法院申请排除非法证据的权利和提供非法取证相关线索或材料的义务，该项权利和义务一旦行使，便会产生两个结果：一是将侦查人员取证合法性的证明责任转移给控诉方，"人民检察院应当对证据收集的合法性加以证明"，〔2〕需要对控方证据收集的合法性承担证明责任或义务；二是为了保证控辩双方权利的实现，辩护方将对侦查人员进行质证。因此，检察院一旦提请法院通知侦查人员出庭，出庭的侦查人员便不能一厢情愿地只来"说明情况"，说完情况就走，还将面临当事人面对面的质问。总之，关于检察院提请法院通知侦查人员出庭的程序需要强调两点，一是必须明确，检察院的这种启动权不是权力而是权利；二是必须维护控辩双方的权利平等。

其次，从提请通知程序是一种义务来看，控辩双方的责任或义务也应当是平等的。一旦辩护方提出排除非法证据的申请并提供了相关线索或材料，履行了存在非法取证的初步证明责任，检察院就不得不履行提请法院通知侦查人员出庭的义务。因此，在 2012 年《刑事诉讼法》第 56 条和第 57 条第 2 款中，"检察院可以提请人民法院通知"一语需作重大修改，即把"可以"改为"应当"。就是说，在"现有证据材料不能证明证据收集的合法性"的情况下，检察院别无选择，它必须提请法院通知侦查人员出庭，以履行"人民检察院应当对证据收集的合法性加以证明"的义务或责任。对于这个问题，陈光中教授和龙宗智教授都认为：我国检察院不仅是公诉机关，而且是法律监督机关，负有发现、纠正侦查机关违法行为的职责。〔3〕从检察院对侦查机关具有法律监督职能来看，可以把辩护方提出排除非法证据申请视为一种投诉行为，一旦有合法申请或投诉，检察院就应当自动履行提请法院通知侦查人员出庭的义务。在这个问题上，我国检察院可以借鉴英国 2004 年成立的"独立警方投诉委员会（IPCC）"，〔4〕负责调查监督警察不端行为的经验。

（二）法院通知程序是取证权的一种运用

2012 年《刑事诉讼法》第 57 条第 2 款规定了"人民法院可以通知有关侦查人员或者其他人员出庭说明情况。"这是法院取证权的一种运用。考虑到我国法院拥有一般的取证权，因而在证据合法性调查程序中通知侦查人员出庭是一件顺理成章的事情。在具体实施中，如果辩护方提出了排除非法证据的申请，"现有证据材料不能证明证据收集的合法性"，法院便可以通过主动取证和被动取证两种方式实施上述规定。

第一，从主动取证来看，法院可以根据《刑事诉讼法》第 57 条第 2 款的规定，依

---

〔2〕 2012 年《刑事诉讼法》第 57 条第 1 款。

〔3〕 参见陈光中："刑事证据制度改革若干理论与实践问题之探讨"，载《中国法学》2010 年第 6 期。另参见龙宗智："理性对待法律修改慎重使用新增权力"，载《国家检察官学院学报》2012 年 6 月。

〔4〕 See Petter Gottschalk, "Knowledge Management in Policing: The Case of Police Complaints and Police Crime", *The Police Journal*, 1st June 2010, PJ 83 2 (96).

职权通知侦查人员出庭。法院主动取证权启动的条件是，检察院应当提请法院通知侦查人员出庭却又拒绝履行其职责。在这种情况下，法院“可以通知”侦查人员出庭。

第二，从被动取证来看，法院可以应辩护方请求通知侦查人员出庭，这种做法更具有可操作性。例如，在职权主义传统最典型的德国刑诉法中有一个所谓“证据申请原则”：“此原则指检察院、辩护人有权，在特定前提下强迫法院采集证据。对于证据申请，法院只能在法定情况中才允许予以拒绝”。〔5〕从法院取证的被动性来看，德国《刑事诉讼法典》第245条第2款规定：“只有提出了查证申请，法院才负有义务将证据调查延伸到由被告人、检察院传唤并且到庭的证人、鉴定人以及其他所调取的证据之上。”〔6〕这种被动取证权的行使，由于具有被迫的特点，而更像是一种履行义务的行为，不会遭到滥用权力的质疑。因此，法院通知取证权的最佳运用，是以辩护方的请求为前提的被动取证。我国目前关于证据合法性调查程序的立法，虽尚未赋予辩护方申请法院通知侦查人员出庭的申请权，但法律并未禁止辩护方提出此种请求，所以，法院完全可以根据辩护方的请求被动行使取证权。这样做有两个好处：一是法院依申请而非依职权启动侦查人员出庭通知程序，维护了法官的消极中立地位，淡化了职权主义色彩；二是可避免陷入主动取证而造成侦查机关不配合而“法庭对此也无可奈何”的窘境。

当然，无论法院主动还是被动通知侦查人员出庭，都要以法院独立行使审判权为前提。目前，由于司法权受制于行政权的局面尚未改变，“在强制侦查人员出庭作证方面，中国法院还缺乏最起码的权威性和独立性”。〔7〕因此，证据合法性调查程序中的法院取证权，只有在确立法院真正拥有独立审判权的前提下才能实现。这是中国下一步司法改革面临的主要任务。

（三）侦查人员的自荐启动程序画蛇添足

“有关侦查人员或者其他人员也可以要求出庭说明情况”的规定，被称为侦查人员的自荐启动程序。该程序的设置存在两个问题：

第一，这种主动自荐程序的创设尽管愿望良好，但实际上却无法施行。究其原因，主要是侦查机关缺乏作为非法证据排除主体的内在动机。如何家弘教授所说，“侦查人员自然是不愿意出庭作证的，一方面，他们自己的任务已经完成，不愿意再花费时间去‘替别人干活儿’；另一方面，他们习惯于询问别人，不愿意站在法庭上成为别人的询问对象，那会‘有失身份’”。〔8〕

第二，立法上用“也可以要求”这类提倡或鼓励性的语言来规范侦查人员出庭的行为，违背了诉讼法的一般原理。从刑事诉讼构造控辩审三方主体的法律关系看，侦查机关及其侦查人员并不是独立于控诉方的诉讼主体，而“仅是检察院的一个‘辅助

〔5〕［德］约阿希姆·赫尔曼：“《德国刑事诉讼法典》中译本引言”，载李昌柯译：《德国刑事诉讼法典》，中国政法大学出版社1995年版，第16页。

〔6〕《德国刑事诉讼法典》，李昌柯译，中国政法大学出版社1995年版，第102页。

〔7〕陈瑞华：“论侦查人员的证人地位”，载《暨南学报》2010年第2期。

〔8〕何家弘：“对侦查人员出庭作证的实证研究”，载《人民检察》2010年第11期。

机构'”。[9] 所以，侦查人员不能不经检察院提请法院通知而自己主动出庭。在法治国家，警察权力包括主动作为的权力应受到严格限制。陈光中教授说：“我国非法证据排除规则的主体为法院和检察机关，侦查机关不宜作为排除主体。非法证据本身往往即产自侦查机关，侦查机关固然可以主动放弃使用非法证据，但这与排除规则所含的外部监督的意义不同，因此将侦查机关列为排除主体不符合非法证据排除规则的一般原理。”[10]

（四）关于侦查人员出庭启动程序的几点思考

第一，关于控辩双方的权利平等。以上三种启动权配置的主要问题，是控辩双方权利不平等。这种权利不平等，来源于传统职权主义诉讼模式的影响。从司法文明演进的过程来看，当代司法理念和司法制度的核心内容是权利平等。例如，德国刑事诉讼法的“手段同等原则”要求，“对于被告人，在原则上应当如同对刑事追究机关一样予以平等地对待”。[11] 然而，在我国刑事诉讼中，控辩双方的权利存在着天然的不平等。这表现在，一方面，“我国侦查人员的出庭作证几乎都是由检察机关安排的，没有经辩护方单方申请法院传唤侦查人员出庭作证的情况”；[12] 另一方面，“尽管越来越多的辩护律师都提出了排除非法证据的申请，并申请法庭通知侦查人员出庭作证，或者调取全案同步录像资料，但检察机关对此普遍予以拒绝，法庭对此也无可奈何”。[13] 总之，立法只赋予了检察院、法院甚至侦查人员在证据合法性调查程序中的“提请”、“通知”和“要求”侦查人员出庭的启动权，却偏偏没有赋予辩护方这种启动权，这是不合逻辑的，它违背了控辩双方权利平等的原则。

第二，关于检控方的证明义务与辩护方的主张权利。非法证据排除规则的实施以非法取证事实的准确认定为前提，因而涉及证明责任问题。首先，要明确检察院的证明责任。根据2012《刑事诉讼法》第57条第1款，“在对证据收集的合法性进行法庭调查的过程中，人民检察院应当对证据收集的合法性加以证明”。因此，检察院提请法院通知侦查人员出庭的启动权，与其说是一种权利，不如说是履行证明责任的一种义务。其次，要确立非法取证受害人的主张权。在证据合法性调查程序中，刑事诉讼辩护方是存在非法取证行为的主张方，按照“谁主张、谁举证”的一般原则，辩护方应当履行提请法院通知侦查人员出庭的责任或义务，这种提请通知权与其说是一种义务，不如说是一种权利，即对侦查人员进行质证的权利。

第三，关于检察院和法院的权力制约。2012年《刑事诉讼法》第7条规定，“人民法院、人民检察院和公安机关进行刑事诉讼，应当分工负责，互相配合，互相制约，以保证准确有效地执行法律”。这确立了我国公检法机关对侦查、起诉和审判工作既分工又配合的机制。然而，我国检察院“身兼多职”，既是公诉机关又是法律监督机关，

---

〔9〕［德］约阿希姆·赫尔曼：“《德国刑事诉讼法典》中译本引言”，载李昌柯译：《德国刑事诉讼法典》，中国政法大学出版社1995年版，第4页。

〔10〕陈光中：“论刑事诉讼中的证据裁判原则”，载《法学》2011年第9期。

〔11〕［德］约阿希姆·赫尔曼：“《德国刑事诉讼法典》中译本引言”，载李昌柯译：《德国刑事诉讼法典》，中国政法大学出版社1995年版，第12页。

〔12〕何家弘：“对侦查人员出庭作证的实证研究”，载《人民检察》2010年第11期。

〔13〕参见陈瑞华：“论侦查人员的证人地位”，载《暨南学报》2010年第2期。

还是职务犯罪等案件中的侦查机关，因而，当检察院在证据合法性调查程序中身陷“公诉利益”或“侦查利益”时，如何履行其审判监督职责就成为一个难题。例如，在“章国锡案”[14] 中，由于检察院身兼侦查机关和公诉机关两种职能，当法院通知侦查人员出庭时，侦查人员却拒绝出庭，检察院并未履行对侦查机关的法律监督职能。可见，要使证据合法性调查程序中侦查人员出庭的规定真正得到实施，就必须在下一步的司法改革中解决司法权的科学配置问题。

二、关于侦查人员出庭的身份

在证据合法性调查程序中，侦查人员究竟是以何种身份出庭“说明情况”，在法律条文上可谓语焉不详。从立法语言来看，规定侦查人员“出庭说明情况”而不是“出庭作证”，显然是受到公检法机关“平起平坐”的传统观念和部门利益关照的影响，暗示了侦查人员出庭拥有作“单向性说明”的特权。这使人联想到我国长期以来形成的“警察特权，让警察出庭与刑事被告人对簿公堂，被认为是降低了警察的身份”。[15] 然而，根据2012年《刑事诉讼法》第60条“凡是知道案件情况的人，都有作证的义务”的规定，警察或其他侦查人员作为案件知情人，显然负有一般证人的作证义务。这可从两个方面来进行分析。

第一，从证人的一般性规定来看，对案件事实有亲身知识的人都有作证义务，侦查人员也不例外。“英美法系国家普遍建立了警察作证制度，在一定程度上是出于对检警分立模式的缺陷的补救。当检察机关起诉时使用的证据受到质疑时，警察为支持公诉出庭作证就成为必然。”[16] 在美国，“进行侦查的警察必须以证人的身份出庭就侦查事项作证”。[17] 我国2012年《刑事诉讼法》第187条第2款也首次就“人民警察就其执行职务时目击的犯罪情况作为证人出庭作证”作了规定，尽管将其限于“目击的犯罪情况”，对作证范围的规定过于狭窄，但“警察特权”的城池显然已被打破一个缺口，警察将在这个范围内以普通证人的身份出现在法庭上，这是中国司法文明发展史上的一个进步。

第二，在证据合法性调查程序中，侦查人员是以程序性事实知情人的身份出庭作证的。从上述侦查人员出庭的三种启动程序来看，由检察院提请法院通知侦查人员出庭将是一种最常见的情况，也是检察院对证据收集的合法性进行证明的一种主要方式。因此，2012年《刑事诉讼法》第57条的“说明情况”，显然是指“证据收集的合法性”情况，即对讯问、勘验、检查、搜查、扣押、羁押等诉讼活动的合法性加以证明。侦查人员作为对程序性事实拥有亲身知识的人，对“程序性事实（如获取口供和提取物证的过程等情况），……如参与或目击抓捕嫌疑人和审讯嫌疑人的过程”[18] 等情况出庭作证，具有“程序证人”[19] 的身份。因此，关于证据收集合法性的法庭调查，需

---

〔14〕 参见《鄞州区人民法院判决书》（2011）甬鄞刑初字第320号，http://blog.sina.com.cn/s/blog_90de409601011yge.html，访问时间：2013年3月3日。

〔15〕 崔敏：“关于警察出庭作证的若干问题”，载《中国人民公安大学学报》2005年第5期。

〔16〕 何家弘：“论警察出庭作证的程序保障——以《波士顿警察局规则与程序规则320》”，载《犯罪研究》2010年第4期。

〔17〕 参见杨宇冠：《非法证据排除规则研究》，中国政法大学2002年博士学位论文。

〔18〕 何家弘：“对侦查人员出庭作证的实证研究”，载《人民检察》2010年第11期。

〔19〕 陈瑞华：“论侦查人员的证人地位”，载《暨南学报》2010年第2期。

要明确侦查人员是以证人身份出庭，其出庭“说明情况”的行为是出庭作证。

三、关于侦查人员出庭作证的方式

2012年《刑事诉讼法》第189条规定：“公诉人、当事人和辩护人、诉讼代理人经审判长许可，可以对证人、鉴定人发问”；“审判人员可以询问证人、鉴定人”。根据上述规定，侦查人员就“证据收集的合法性”出庭作证，可以采取“问—答”方式。另根据2012《刑事诉讼法》第59条关于“证人证言必须在法庭上经过公诉人、被害人和被告人、辩护人双方质证”的规定，证据合法性调查程序中的侦查人员出庭应采取直接询问、交叉询问和对质等方式，必要时可以聘请侦查活动“专家辅助人”出庭对其进行交叉询问。

（一）对侦查人员的直接询问

根据2012年最高人民法院《刑诉法解释》第212条的规定，在证据合法性调查程序中，对侦查人员的发问，“应当先由提请传唤的一方进行”，即由公诉人进行。在2012年《刑事诉讼法》第57条第2款规定的侦查人员出庭的三种启动程序中，因为检察院负有对证据收集的合法性进行证明的责任或义务，且侦查人员不是独立于控诉方的诉讼主体，所以，对侦查人员的直接询问均应由公诉人进行。直接询问是对己方证人的询问，其规则是不得提出可用“是”或“否”来回答的诱导性问题。

（二）对侦查人员的交叉询问

根据2012年最高人民法院《刑诉法解释》第212条的规定，在公诉人直接询问后，“经审判长准许，对方也可以发问”。对方对侦查人员的发问即交叉询问，是质证的一种形式，其基本规则是可以提出诱导性问题，并可以对侦查人员证言的可信性提出质疑。因此，对侦查人员的交叉询问无疑是辩护律师的权利。但目前我国刑事辩护律师在行使交叉询问的权利方面，存在着缺乏询问技巧和策略等方面的问题。在审判实践中，“辩护律师发问的技巧极为简单，一般直接提出‘你说没有刑讯逼供，那么被告人身上的伤是怎么形成的’之类的问题”[20]。有鉴于此，应当加强对律师进行交叉询问技巧和策略以及弹劾证人技术等方面的培训。

（三）当事人与侦查人员的对质

在证据收集的合法性调查程序中，当事人与侦查人员的对质是一种最佳质证方法。

第一，当事人与侦查人员对质是公民的一种诉讼权利。联合国《公民权利与政治权利国际公约》第14条也规定了被告人面对刑事指控享有与证人对质的权利。在证据合法性调查程序中，当侦查人员接受直接询问和交叉询问之后，被告人仍享有与其对质的权利，即有权对侦查人员非法取证的事实进行面对面的质问。在美国，联邦宪法第六修正案规定了被告人的对质权。针对警察不端行为往往缺少中立的目击证人从而导致被告人和警察对侦查行为是否违法各执一词的情况，美国第七巡回法院提出了被告人与警察单一对质的权利。[21] 虽然我国《宪法》和2012年《刑事诉讼法》都没有关于对质权的规定，2012年最高人民法院《关于适用〈中华人民共和国刑事诉讼法〉的解释》第199条只规定了“同案被告人等到庭对质”，却没有规定被告人与证人的对

---

〔20〕 参见牟绿叶：“侦查人员出庭作证的中国模式”，载《新疆警官高等专科学校学报》2012年第1期。

〔21〕 See Defense of a Police Misconduct Suit, 38 Am. Jur. Trials 493, Database Updated February 2013.

质权，但鉴于中国政府已正式签署联合国《公民权利与政治权利国际公约》，我国2004年《宪法》和2012年《刑事诉讼法》都明确规定了国家“尊重和保护人权”，因此，被告人在刑事诉讼中与证人对质的权利应作为一项基本人权得到尊重和保护，其中也包括被告人与侦查人员在证据合法性调查程序中的对质权。

第二，当事人与侦查人员对质权的启动应当体现控辩双方的权利平等。2012年《人民检察院刑事诉讼规则（试行）》第438条规定：“被告人、证人对同一事实的陈述存在矛盾需要对质的，公诉人可以建议法庭传唤有关被告人、证人同时到庭对质。”但这里所谓“对质权”只是公诉人的权利，这与被告人对质权的属性存在天壤之别。从性质上说，对质权本是被告人的一种宪法权利和基本人权，本应由被告人单方面启动，而上述第438条规定非但本末倒置地规定了对质程序的公诉人启动权，还无理地剥夺了被告人的对质程序启动权，这是一种侵犯被告人权利的表现。这也是司法改革应当解决的一个问题。

（四）探索建立证据合法性调查“专家辅助人”制度

在证据合法性调查程序中，由于侦查人员取证涉及大量的专门知识和技术问题，往往会给当事人对质或辩护律师质证带来一定困难。同时，警察为了避免所获的证据被法庭排除，有时候也会“作伪证”（police perjury）。[22] 因此，为了查明证据收集是否合法，可以借鉴国外建立侦查活动“专家辅助人”制度的经验。在美国，为了制约警察“越权行为”，有所谓“过度暴力专家”（excessive force expert）出庭作证的实践，这些专家受过正规的专业教育且具有丰富的经验，可为是否存在“警察不端行为”（police misconduct）提供专业意见。[23] 如克里斯·麦吉先生，至今已作为“安全专家证人”（security expert witness），在询证存录过程中作证400余次，出庭作证80余次。其作证范围涉及侦查人员疏于监管、不端行为、非法拘留、非法监禁和过度使用暴力等方面。他为控方和辩方充当顾问或专家证人的比例为45%和55%。[24] 根据我国2012年《刑事诉讼法》第192条第2款关于“公诉人、当事人和辩护人、诉讼代理人可以申请法庭通知有专门知识的人出庭，就鉴定人作出的鉴定意见提出意见”的规定，控辩双方均可申请法庭通知有专门侦查知识和经验的人出庭，对侦查人员出庭“说明情况”的证言提出专门意见，这有助于查清警察违法行为。

四、关于侦查人员拒不出庭的法律后果

2012年《刑事诉讼法》第57条第2款虽然规定了“经人民法院通知，有关人员应当出庭”，但对侦查人员拒不出庭的法律后果并未作出明确规定。这表明，我国刑事诉讼法还“没有确立强制侦查人员出庭作证的规则”。[25] 然而，如果“司法实践中侦查取证人员不愿意出庭，从而使得非法证据无法排除”，[26] 非法证据排除规则就会形同虚设。因此，在证据收集的合法性调查程序中，侦查人员拒不出庭应当承担的法律后果是“对有关证据应当予以排除”。其主要理由是：

---

〔22〕 See Charles M. Sevilla, “The Exclusionary Rule and Police Perjury”, 11 *San Diego L. Rev.* 839 (1973～1974).

〔23〕 See Defense of a Police Misconduct Suit, 38 Am. Jur. Trials 493, Database updated February 2013.

〔24〕 See http://www.crimedoctor.com/loss-prevention-expert.htm，访问日期：2013年5月19日.

〔25〕 陈瑞华：“论侦查人员的证人地位”，载《暨南学报》2010年第2期。

〔26〕 杨宇冠：“非法证据排除规则及其在中国确立问题研究”，载《比较法研究》2010年第3期。

第一，从取证合法性的证明标准来看，达不到确信无疑证明标准的有关证据应当予以排除。根据2012年《刑事诉讼法》第58条的规定，“对于经过法庭审理，确认或者不能排除存在本法第54条规定的以非法方法收集证据情形的，对有关证据应当予以排除。”这表明，在证据收集的合法性调查程序中，检控方对证据收集的合法性证明必须达到确信无疑的证明标准。就是说，在辩护方申请法院排除非法证据，并对取证的非法性达到优势证据标准即履行了提供非法取证相关线索或材料的义务之后，如果检察院拒不履行提请法院通知侦查人员出庭的义务，或者出现经法院通知但侦查人员拒不出庭的情况，就可以将其视为满足了“确认或者不能排除存在本法第54条规定的以非法方法收集证据情形的”要求，而将有关证据予以排除。因此，在司法实践中，法官可以参照2012年《刑事诉讼法》第187条第3款关于“经人民法院通知，鉴定人拒不出庭作证的，鉴定意见不得作为定案的根据”的规定，对拒不出庭作证的侦查人员获得的有关证据予以排除。

第二，从非法证据排除规则的立法宗旨和发展趋势来看，以侦查人员拒不出庭为由排除有关证据有助于遏制警察特权。非法证据排除规则的正当理由，在于维护公民的宪法权利和当事人的合法权益。以此为宗旨，它又体现为保障基本人权、维护司法纯洁、吓阻警察不法行为、彰显程序正义等多重价值取向。[27] 由于非法证据通常具有相关性，而且往往有较高的证明力，联合国《禁止酷刑和其他残忍、不人道或有辱人格的待遇或处罚公约》第15条和许多国家的非法证据排除规则一般仅严格禁止采纳非法口供，而对非法取得的物证、书证和“毒树之果”等证据大都由法官自由裁量是否予以排除，采用的是如美国《联邦证据规则》403的“危险性超过证明力”检验标准。这与我国2012年《刑事诉讼法》第54条关于“在侦查、审查起诉、审判”三个阶段全程排除非法证据，以及对口供、证人证言、被害人陈述、物证、书证和“毒树之果”等各种非法证据一概排除的做法明显不同。这就促使我们思考一个问题，在证据合法性程序中，是否应当把侦查人员拒绝出庭作为排除证据的一个重要考量因素，以便使其发挥遏制警察特权的作用？近年来，美国非法证据排除规则的适用出现了一个新动向，即非法证据排除“例外规则”的适用范围越来越宽。[28] 就是说，对非法证据不再是一概排除，而是要考虑是否有助于吓阻警察不法行为，“排除证据的同时一定要有助于对违法警察产生震慑作用”[29]。这也是章国锡案给我们的启示。所以，我国2012年《刑事诉讼法》第57条第2款的实施，如果能以侦查人员拒不出庭为由排除有关证据，会起到强制侦查人员出庭作证的作用。

结语：关于证据合法性调查程序及其实施的几点建议

第一，关于《刑事诉讼法》第57条第2款的修改建议：“现有证据材料不能证明证据收集的合法性的，人民检察院应当提请人民法院通知有关侦查人员或者其他人员出庭作证；当事人及其辩护人、诉讼代理人有权提请人民法院通知有关侦查人员或者

---

〔27〕 参见张保生主编：《证据法学》，中国政法大学出版社2009年版，第273～274页。

〔28〕 See Herring v. United States, 555 U. S. 135 (2009).

〔29〕 郑曦：“观往知来：美国第四修正案非法证据排除规则的新发展对中国的启示”，载《证据科学》2011年第5期。

其他人员出庭作证；人民法院可以通知有关侦查人员或者其他人员出庭作证。经人民法院通知，有关人员应当出庭作证。”上述修改建议，一是强调了侦查人员出庭的证人身份，二是补充规定了当事人和辩护人等提请法院通知侦查人员出庭的权利，三是删除了侦查人员的自荐启动程序。

第二，应当避免将证据合法性调查程序转变为行政诉讼程序。证据收集的合法性调查程序，以侦查人员的非法行为为调查对象，以检控方对证据合法性的证明达到确信无疑为证明标准，这些特征都很像“民告官”的行政诉讼，或陈瑞华教授所说的“诉中诉”〔30〕。“美国最高法院首席大法官伯格曾设想建立一种行政非法审判庭来代替排除规则。他认为这种行政审判庭的机制可以对警察非法行为的完全无辜的受害者提供补救，这是排除规则所不能达到的。”〔31〕然而，我们认为，刑事诉讼中的证据合法性调查程序应当尽量避免向行政诉讼转化。如果转化为行政诉讼，侦查人员出庭的身份就会成为被告，由此会带来一系列的问题，例如，按照我国《行政诉讼法》第48条关于被告无正当理由拒不到庭可以缺席判决的规定，尽管侦查人员放弃法庭答辩的权利要承担可能败诉的不利后果，但因其不能作为证人出庭就无法接受对方质证，所以不利于查明非法取证的事实真相。

第三，法官在证据合法性调查程序实施中应注意三个问题：首先，法官应当兼顾案件事实的查明和侦查人员非法取证事实的查明。刑事诉讼的庭审过程应当以查明案件事实为主要目的。对此，威格莫尔曾提出，“执行第四修正案的自然办法是对严重违法进行非法逮捕和搜查的警官作藐视宪法罪监禁30天，但肯定对罪犯的定罪”。〔32〕其次，法官应当知道证据法的宗旨是鼓励采纳证据，而非排除证据。因此，非法证据排除自由裁量权的行使，应当适用“危险性超过证明力”的检验标准。最后，我国2012年《刑事诉讼法》第57条第2款规定侦查人员出庭，主旨是遏制警察特权，因此，法官对非法证据的排除应当考虑其对强制侦查人员出庭作证能否发挥作用。

---

〔30〕 陈瑞华：“非法证据排除规则的中国模式”，载《中国法学》2010年第6期。

〔31〕 Bivens 403U. S. 388 (1971) (Burger, C. J. , dissenting)，转引自杨宇冠：《非法证据排除规则研究》，中国政法大学2002年博士学位论文。

〔32〕 参见杨宇冠：《非法证据排除规则研究》，中国政法大学2002年博士学位论文。

强制证人出庭作证除外条款研究

——兼论刑事诉讼中特定范围的近亲属拒绝出庭作证权

李佑标 *

新《刑事诉讼法》第188条第1款规定："经人民法院通知，证人没有正当理由不出庭作证的，人民法院可以强制其到庭，但是被告人的配偶、父母、子女除外。"为了研究和表述的方便，笔者将上述条文中的除外条款称之为"强制证人出庭作证除外条款"。这一规定，标志着我国刑事诉讼的文明与进步，不仅对于我国刑事诉讼具有重要的程序法治意义，而且对于我国民事诉讼和行政诉讼来说，都具有标志性的辐射作用。

一、强制证人出庭作证除外条款规定的称谓

强制证人出庭作证除外条款规定的称谓应当如何概括？论者见解不一，主要有以下四种表述：第一种表述为"近亲属拒绝作证权"；第二种表述为"亲属证人特免权"；第三种表述为"亲属拒绝作证权"；第四种表述为"免证权"。

笔者认为上述四种表述都是不太准确的，应当根据有关法律规定，并结合新《刑事诉讼法》第188条第1款的立法本意，对强制证人出庭作证除外条款规定的称谓作出较为准确的界定。

（一）从拒绝作证的主体范围来看，是指特定范围的近亲属

将拒绝作证的主体范围界定为"近亲属"和"亲属"的表述都是不准确的。从民法学的基本原理来看，亲属的范围要大于近亲属，而根据新《刑事诉讼法》第106条规定，"近亲属"是指夫、妻、父、母、子、女、同胞兄弟姊妹。据此，新《刑事诉讼法》第188条第1款的除外条款规定的拒绝作证主体要小于近亲属。同时，近亲属是亲属的子概念，新《刑事诉讼法》第188条第1款的除外条款规定的拒绝作证主体更要小于亲属。由此看来，拒绝作证的主体应当界定为特定范围的近亲属。

（二）从拒绝作证的诉讼阶段范围来看，只适用于刑事审判阶段

有论者认为，"'出庭指证'应该不单是在庭审阶段，而是从调查阶段就可拒绝指证。"[1] 对此，笔者不敢苟同。新《刑事诉讼法》第188条第1款的实际位置是在第三编"审判"之下，其法律用语是"被告人的配偶、父母、子女"。据此，笔者可以推论，立案、侦查、提起公诉阶段和执行阶段均不存在特定范围近亲属拒绝作证问题。在立案、侦查、提起公诉阶段，侦查或者公诉机关因为办理刑事案件的需要，也可以要求特定范围的近亲属到侦查或者公诉机关提供证言。同时，在执行阶段，由于刑事判决已经生效，不存在指证犯罪问题，因而不存在强制出庭作证问题，故也不存在拒

---

* 李佑标，武警学院边防系教授。Email：biaoyl@ sina. com。

〔1〕 刘栋："'不强制近亲属出庭指证'透出法治文明进步'大义灭亲'理念将被颠覆"，载《文汇报》2011年8月26日。

绝出庭作证问题。

（三）从拒绝作证的诉讼方式范围来看，只适用于审判阶段需要开庭审理的案件

新《刑事诉讼法》第188条第1款的具体内容是对强制证人出庭作证条款的除外规定。据此，对于不采取开庭方式审理的刑事案件，不存在特定范围的近亲属拒绝作证问题，特定范围的近亲属拒绝作证实际上应当是指特定范围的近亲属拒绝出庭作证。那么，特定范围的近亲属拒绝出庭作证适用于刑事诉讼审判阶段的哪些程序呢？

众所周知，刑事第一审程序的审理方式为开庭审理，因此，特定范围的近亲属拒绝出庭作证适用于刑事第一审程序不存在什么疑问。根据新《刑事诉讼法》第231条的规定，第二审人民法院审判上诉或者抗诉案件的程序，除本章已有规定的以外，参照第一审程序的规定进行。据此，笔者可以推论，特定范围的近亲属拒绝出庭作证也应当适用于刑事第二审程序。同时，新《刑事诉讼法》第223条还规定，第二审程序的审理方式既可以决定开庭审理，也可以决定不开庭审理。其中，第二审人民法院对于下列案件，应当组成合议庭，开庭审理：①被告人、自诉人及其法定代理人对第一审认定的事实、证据提出异议，可能影响定罪量刑的上诉案件；②被告人被判处死刑的上诉案件；③人民检察院抗诉的案件；④其他应当开庭审理的案件。因此，除上述刑事案件以外，第二审人民法院决定不开庭审理的，不存在特定范围的近亲属拒绝出庭作证问题。基于上述理由，对于适用审判监督程序审理的刑事案件，应当区分适用第一审或者第二审程序，且应当视审理的方式不同而判断特定范围的近亲属拒绝出庭作证是否适用问题。对于死刑复核程序，根据新《刑事诉讼法》第240条规定，最高人民法院复核死刑案件，应当讯问被告人，听取辩护人的意见。因此，不存在开庭审理问题，因而也就不存在特定范围的近亲属拒绝出庭作证问题。

基于以上分析，笔者认为应当将强制证人出庭作证除外条款的称谓确定为“特定范围的近亲属拒绝出庭作证权”。作为一种权利，也就意味着特定范围的近亲属出庭作证义务的免除。当然，这种权利只能严格限制在拒绝出庭作证权，而不是拒绝作证权，因此，并不意味着对被告人的配偶、父母、子女免除了作证的义务；同时，作为一种权利，也就意味着特定范围的近亲属可以放弃拒绝出庭作证的权利，并不排除其出于各种动机，例如因其证言对被告人有利而自愿出庭作证，或者在法庭上以书面证言、远程作证等其他方式作证。“但这与人们平时所讲的‘大义灭亲’不是一个概念，因为有些案件比如家庭暴力等，只要愿意，近亲属也是可以出庭指证的。”〔2〕

二、强制证人出庭作证除外条款的法理依据

强制证人出庭作证除外条款的法理依据是什么？论者见仁见智。有的认为是人格权；〔3〕

---

〔2〕 曹晓波：“刑诉法修改存四大期待”，载《法制周报》2011年8月30日。

〔3〕 作者认为，人权包括人格权，而近亲属拒绝作证权即是人格权的一种。参见胡勇：《刑诉法修正案确立近亲属拒绝作证权体现以人为本》，http://www.legaldaily.com.cn/rdlf/content/2011-08/24/content_2897945.htm?node=20948。

有的认为是隐私权;[4] 有的认为是相隐权。[5] 上述解释都有一定的道理。但是，笔者更倾向于用法律与道德的关系来加以诠释。

（一）强制证人出庭作证除外条款所确认的是家庭道德关系

道德是指依靠社会舆论、传统习惯、教育和人的信念的力量去调整人与人、个人与社会之间关系的一种特殊的行为规范。道德现象是人类社会独有的现象，它渗透于社会生活的每一个角落，因此，它的划分与社会生活的划分相一致。人类社会生活大致可以分为三种类型：即家庭生活、社会公共生活和职业生活。因此，道德也可以分为三种类型，即家庭道德、社会公德和职业道德。其中，家庭道德是指调整家庭成员之间关系的行为规范。家庭成员之间关系的核心关系是夫妻关系，由此发生上至父母下至子女及相应的一些亲属关系。新《刑事诉讼法》第 188 条第 1 款的除外条款所确认的正是家庭成员间关系中的夫妻、父母和子女之间在伦理与亲情方面的行为规范。[6] 诚如汪建成教授所言：“家庭是社会的基本细胞，家庭成员之间，尤其是配偶和近亲属之间的必要的伦理亲情，是支撑稳定的社会大厦一个不可或缺的支点。如果一个国家的法律制度总是在鼓励、甚至强迫配偶之间，近亲属之间相互揭发，指证犯罪，大义灭亲，则很难想象这个社会还有什么伦理亲情存在。”[7]

（二）强制证人出庭作证除外条款是对家庭道德的法律化

以法律的形式确认家庭道德只是问题的一个方面，问题的另一个方面是法律为什么要确认这种家庭道德，即为什么要将家庭道德法律化。[8]

1. 家庭道德法律化符合法理

从法理学角度来看，法律是最低限度的道德规则。法律是以道德为基础的，法律的源头是道德，真正的法律是符合道德的法律。“纵观人类文明史，道德法律化是人类规范世界的基本主题，换言之，将该社会至关重要的道德准则转化为法律，是每个时代道德建设和法制建设中的重大课题，于其社会的发展具有重要意义。同时，这无疑也是解决法与道德之冲突的重要途径。因为倘若人们在法律之外坚守着与现行法律相冲突的一系列道德规则，而这些道德规则于社会的发展又具有不可或缺的重要性（此为道德法律化的根本前提），那么，适时修改现行法律，并用‘招安’之法将某些适当的道德规则转化为法律，则既能消解法律与道德之间的冲突，亦能使法律体现出时代的伦理精神，进而使其赢得广泛的社会支持。”[9] 强制证人出庭作证除外条款所确认

---

〔4〕 论者认为，亲属特免权存在的基础之一便是保护基于家庭关系而产生的隐私权。参见何家弘主编：《证人制度研究》，人民法院出版社 2004 年版，第 243 页。

〔5〕 作者认为，相隐权是指相互隐瞒的权利，其产生的最大价值基础在于法律对伦理情感的尊重，它与拒绝作证权不同，后者是一种价值权衡的结果，是社会期望通过保守秘密来维护和促进某种重要的关系。参见雷钰：“现代刑事诉讼相隐权初探”，载《法制与经济》2012 年第 1 期。

〔6〕 2012 年 3 月 8 日，全国人民代表大会常务委员会副委员长王兆国在第十一届全国人民代表大会第五次会议上所作的《关于〈中华人民共和国刑事诉讼法修正案（草案）〉的说明》中有这样一段文字，即“考虑到强制配偶、父母、子女在法庭上对被告人进行指证，不利于家庭关系的维系，规定被告人的配偶、父母、子女除外”。在上述文字中有“家庭关系”的字样，并没有指明是家庭关系中的什么样关系。

〔7〕 汪建成：《理想与现实—刑事证据理论的新探索》，北京大学出版社 2006 年版，第 169 页。

〔8〕 从法理角度来看，家庭道德法律化应当是道德法律化的子概念，而道德法律化既是将人类的道德理想、原则、规范转化为法律的过程，也是善法由此而产生的过程。

〔9〕 徐显明：《法理学》，中国政法大学出版社 2007 年版，第 279 页。

的家庭道德的精髓也正在于此。

2. 家庭道德法律化利大于弊

从弊的角度来看，不利于揭露犯罪、追究犯罪和惩罚犯罪。但是，从利的角度来看，则有利于家庭伦理与亲情关系的维系。规定强制证人出庭作证除外条款，"主要是考虑证人作证可能会导致其家庭或者相关亲属不理解，因其作证行为导致家庭遭到破坏或者亲属关系受到影响。不能因为打击犯罪、惩罚犯罪而去影响社会最重要也是最基本的组织，也就是家庭，强迫家庭亲属成员之间相互指证犯罪，有违伦理亲情。从中国古代到国外的法律，都有类似于'亲亲相隐'这样的一种规定，体现了法律的人性化精神"。[10] 同时，我们"过去一直强调国家利益高于一切，于无形中漠视了公民的个人利益和对其权益的维护。这一次刑诉法的修改，把这样一条原则写进去，也许会影响到案件证据的收集和犯罪的追诉。但两害相权，我认为更重要的是维护了社会关系的稳定。没有了一种证据还可以有其他的证据。另外，公安司法机关办案，也不能建立在靠亲人之间相互检举揭发的基础上，这也可以使他们将来把办案重点转移到其他证据上"。[11] 因此，利弊权衡利大于弊。众所周知，家庭是社会的基本细胞，家庭的稳定是社会稳定的基础和前提，而揭露犯罪、追究犯罪和惩罚犯罪的目的是为了恢复被破坏的社会秩序，进而维护社会的稳定。"一旦强行要求亲属间提供不利于对方的证言，将导致'一人犯罪，一家遭罪'的尴尬局面。"[12] 故根据功利主义规则，两权相较取其重，两害相较取其轻，利弊皆有则取利大于弊。因此，当然应当选择强制证人出庭作证除外条款这一利大于弊的规定。

三、强制证人出庭作证除外条款的法理评析

（一）强制证人出庭作证除外条款的程序价值

强制证人出庭作证除外条款的程序价值主要体现在它蕴涵着一定的诉讼价值理念，在笔者看来，主要有以下三大诉讼价值理念：

1. 尊重和保障人权的理念

"尊重和保障人权"作为刑事诉讼法的一项任务被写入新《刑事诉讼法》第2条，这是对2004年宪法修正案中的"尊重和保障人权"原则的具体落实和体现，也是我国在基本法律中的首次规定。[13] 与其他任何法律不同，刑事诉讼法在尊重和保障人权方面的地位在所有法律中最为重要。因为刑事诉讼法的实施过程和实施后果涉及公民基本权利的限制与剥夺，而宪法则是关于公民基本权利的法律。因此，在学界，刑事诉讼法有"小宪法"之称。

在刑事诉讼中，对人权尊重和保障水平的衡量主要取决于对被追诉者权利的保护程度。因为任何人都是潜在的犯罪嫌疑人、被告人，任何人随时都有可能成为实际上的犯罪嫌疑人、被告人，只有犯罪嫌疑人、被告人的权利得到了切实地尊重和保障，

---

〔10〕 陈卫东："严禁刑讯逼供强迫自证其罪"，载《南方日报》2011年8月25日。

〔11〕 陈卫东："严禁刑讯逼供强迫自证其罪"，载《南方日报》2011年8月25日。

〔12〕 陈卫东：《模范刑事诉讼法典》，中国人民大学出版社2005年版，第249页。

〔13〕 陈光中教授认为，从"人权入宪"到"人权入法"是一重大突破，它明显提升了保障人权在《刑事诉讼法》中的价值。参见陈光中主编：《〈中华人民共和国刑事诉讼法〉修改条文释义与点评》，人民法院出版社2012年版，第15~16页。

犯罪嫌疑人、被告人以外的人的权利才能得到切实地尊重和保障。“各国法律及联合国有关文件之所以重视刑事程序中对犯罪嫌疑人和被告人的人权保障，首先是由于犯罪嫌疑人和被告人的人权保障，实质上也是对所有社会成员基本权利提供的保障。降低刑事程序中犯罪嫌疑人和被告人的人权保障，实际上是降低了所有社会成员基本权利的保障。”〔14〕

强制证人出庭除外条款是尊重和保障人权这一诉讼价值理念的具体制度设计的具体表现形式之一，它是对被告人的父母、配偶和子女作为证人时享有的出庭作证豁免权的确认，是被告一方对抗控诉方的一项重要权利。但是，在刑事诉讼中，作证是公民的一项法定义务，而对于特定范围的近亲属而言，出庭作证与否则是其一项权利。陈光中教授认为，“刑诉程序有它的独立价值，有时候为了程序的价值在一定程度上牺牲实体的价值也是允许的。比如这次修改，规定近亲属有拒绝出庭作证权，有限地改变了过去法律上的规定——公民都有作证的义务，但在侦查和审查起诉阶段，近亲属仍保留有接受调查询问的义务。在这个问题上一定程度地体现了程序的人性价值。”〔15〕换言之，强制证人出庭除外条款所体现的是尊重和保障人权的诉讼价值理念，而不是打击和惩罚犯罪的诉讼价值理念。

2. 有利被告的理念

有利被告作为一项原则是否同时适用于刑事实体法和刑事程序法，学界有不同意见。但是，对于有利被告原则适用于刑事程序法是不存在争议的。在刑事程序法中，有利被告在不同的语境中也有不同的解读。但是，概括起来主要有广义和狭义两种界定。狭义说认为有利被告是指与无罪推定原则相联系的一条原则，即在证据或者控诉有疑问时作有利于被告人的解释；而广义说认为有利被告是指一切有利于被告人的程序制度规定，例如，无罪推定、上诉不加刑、一事不再理等。

强制证人出庭作证除外条款所蕴涵的正是有利被告的诉讼价值理念，它意味着在被告人的父母、配偶和子女作为证人时，在指控被告人涉嫌犯罪的刑事案件开庭审理时享有拒绝出庭作证的权利，而控方证人则不享有此项权利。长期以来，人们对于有利被告往往只关注其事实存疑时的适用，而对于其他程序问题的适用则关注不够。在刑事诉讼中，与控诉方相比，被告方明显处于弱势。因此，在刑事诉讼中确立有限的拒绝出庭作证权，与其说是有利被告，倒不如说是赋予了被告方与控诉方相对抗的诉讼权利，以使控辩双方真正成为诉讼中的对立方。

3. 刑事诉讼谦抑性的理念

谦抑，顾名思义，就是指谦虚和抑制。谦抑性在不同的法学学科可能有不同的诠释。但是，上述基本含义是难以背离的，刑事诉讼法学也不例外。笔者认为，刑事诉讼法的谦抑性可以是指刑事诉讼法作为国家强制力的一种司法克制。“从立法谦抑看，并非任何一个问题，都可以诉诸法律主张立法，特别是不能把纯道德性问题（比如“常回家看看”）诉诸立法。法律对社会关系的调整，应当始终是保持一定的距离，而

---

〔14〕 宋英辉：《刑事诉讼原理导读》，法律出版社2003年版，第104页。

〔15〕 陈光中：“从单纯惩罚犯罪到保护人权”，载《新京报》2011年8月25日。

不能僭越自己的领地，试图规范人的内心灵魂。"[16]

就强制证人出庭作证除外条款而言，法律在要求证人出庭作证的同时限缩了公权力的强制性，使得强制手段不得适用于特定范围的近亲属证人。从刑事诉讼谦抑性角度来看，则意味着国家强制力在被告人的父母、配偶和子女作为证人出庭作证的后盾时的一种司法克制。也就是说，申言之，国家赋予专门的司法机关享有强制证人出庭作证的公权力。但是，这一公权力在适用到被告人的父母、配偶和子女作为证人出庭作证情形时，则通过权利（拒绝出庭作证权利）对抗权力（强制出庭作证权力）而保持着一定的司法克制。

（二）强制证人出庭作证除外条款的局限性

1. 除外条款本身的局限性

强制证人出庭作证除外条款只适用于特定的人员，即被告人的配偶、父母和子女；只适用于特定的诉讼阶段，即开庭审理阶段；只适用于特定的作证方式，即以直接言词的方式作证。因此，特定范围的近亲属作为证人作证的义务并没有免除。"在案件的侦查和起诉阶段，侦查机关和公诉机关仍可传唤被告人的近亲属作证，被告人近亲属非但不能拒绝还负有如实作证的义务，并且，该庭前书面证言笔录还可以在法庭上宣读。"[17] 正是在这个意义说，"新《刑事诉讼法》规定不得强迫被告人的配偶、父母和子女出庭作证，与证人拒绝作证特权不同"。[18]

2. 除外条款适用的局限性

强制证人出庭作证除外条款，对于人民法院来说是一项义务，对于特定范围的近亲属来说则是一项权利，如果人民法院不履行不得强制特定范围的近亲属出庭作证义务，即违背自愿原则，强制特定范围的近亲属出庭作证时，有没有相应的救济途径，对此，我国新《刑事诉讼法》没有规定相应的程序法律后果。同时，对于强制证人出庭作证除外条款有没有例外？例如，特定范围的近亲属如果是本案的关键证人时，是否意味着构成强制证人出庭作证除外条款的例外？我国新《刑事诉讼法》同样没有明确的规定。从理论角度来分析的话，如果答案是肯定的话，那么，特定范围近亲属享有的拒绝出庭作证权就有可能被变相剥夺；如果答案是否定的话，那么，人民法院就可能利用这一条款规避特定范围近亲属作为关键证人时出庭对质。[19] 因此，强制证人出庭作证除外条款的适用存在着不确定性。

---

〔16〕 王松苗："法治给力语境下的法律谦抑"，载《检察日报》2012年5月31日。

〔17〕 李轩："浅析强制证人出庭作证制度——兼评《刑事诉讼法修正案（草案）》的相关规定"，载《山西警官高等专科学校学报》2012年第2期。

〔18〕 陈光中：《〈中华人民共和国刑事诉讼法〉修改条文释义与点评》，人民法院出版社2012年版，第271页。

〔19〕 有学者认为，"证人证言如果对案件定罪量刑有重大影响，并且公诉人、当事人或者辩护人、诉讼代理人有异议，人民法院认为证人有必要出庭作证的，证人应当出庭。这里的证人证言，显然既包括普通的证人提供的证言，也包括被作为证人的被告人的近亲属提供的证言。这意味着，即使是被告人的近亲属，其如向检控方提供过证言，如果该证言对案件定罪量刑有重大影响，且辩护方也有异议，那么，法院在认为该证人有必要出庭作证的情况下，是应当通知其出庭作证的。只不过，出庭不出庭全凭被告人近亲属的自愿。在其拒绝出庭作证的情况下，法院既不能对其采取强制手段，也不能对其适用拘留措施。这在有些情况下可能会影响到被告人对质权的实现。"参见李奋飞："从'近亲属出庭作证豁免'说开去"，载《法制日报》2012年3月14日。

四、强制证人出庭作证除外条款的完善构想

新《刑事诉讼法》赋予特定范围的近亲属享有的拒绝出庭作证权属于有限的作证豁免权，为了将这一权利用足用好，享有司法解释权的主体应当作相应的扩大解释。

（一）扩大配偶、父母、子女的内涵范围

在民法亲属关系中，配偶又称夫妻，是指合法婚姻中的男女双方；父母和子女互为对称。但是，笔者认为，对享有拒绝出庭作证权的近亲属的内涵范围应当作扩大解释。其中，配偶应当既包括合法婚姻关系存续期间的配偶，也包括曾经具有合法婚姻关系的配偶；父母应当既包括婚生子女的父母、非婚生子女的父母，也包括没有血缘关系的有抚养教育义务的继子女关系的继父母；子女则应当既包括婚生子女、非婚生子女、养子女，也包括有抚养教育义务关系的继子女。当然，上述特定范围的近亲属应当局限于特定关系存续期间。换句话说，上述特定范围的近亲属与被告人只能对于上述特定关系存续期间所知道的案情享有拒绝出庭作证权。

（二）明确强制证人出庭除外条款的具体适用范围

特定范围的近亲属享有拒绝出庭作证权是否适用于所有的刑事案件，这在新《刑事诉讼法》中的规定是不清晰的。因为新《刑事诉讼法》第 188 条第 1 款的具体位置是第三篇“审判”之下的第二章“第一审程序”的第一节“公诉案件”，也就是说，特定范围的近亲属享有拒绝出庭作证权适用于公诉案件的第一审程序是确定的。但是，对于自诉案件和适用简易程序审理的自诉案件是否适用呢？笔者还不能得出一个明确的答案。因此，建议通过司法解释，明确强制证人出庭除外条款适用于开庭审理的所有刑事案件。

特定范围的近亲属享有拒绝出庭作证权是否适用于关键证人，这在新《刑事诉讼法》中的规定同样是不清晰的。所谓关键证人是指证人作证的内容对于案件的定罪量刑具有重大影响的人。“关键证人出庭作证是证人出庭作证的最低限度要求。”[20] 根据新《刑事诉讼法》第 187 条第 1 款的规定，公诉人、当事人或者辩护人、诉讼代理人对证人证言有异议，且该证人证言对案件定罪量刑有重大影响，人民法院认为证人有必要出庭作证的，证人应当出庭作证。那么，特定范围的近亲属如果符合上述条件，能否拒绝出庭作证呢？从法条的前后顺序来看，关键证人出庭作证条款在前，而强制证人出庭作证除外条款在后，因此，从逻辑顺序上可以推论，特定范围的近亲属如果作为关键证人也不应当被强制出庭作证。当然，上述逻辑推论同样应当由司法解释加以明确。

（三）明确保障强制证人出庭除外条款实施的程序

审判机关应当有义务保障特定范围的近亲属拒绝出庭作证权，因此，审判机关负有告知特定范围近亲属享有拒绝出庭作证的义务。从理论角度来看，告知的方式有口头与书面之分。笔者认为，为了保障特定范围近亲属享有的拒绝出庭作证权利得到真正实现，应当以书面通知为宜，不宜采取口头通知形式。同时，书面告知也应当采取直接送达的方式。特定范围近亲属作为证人时如果符合不被强制出庭作证的条件，那么应当向人民法院提出申请，并说明不被强制出庭作证的理由，同时应当提供相应证

---

〔20〕 何家弘：《证人制度研究》，人民法院出版社 2004 年版，第 123 页。

据。为了方便特定范围近亲属行使申请权，申请可以是口头的形式，也可以是书面的形式。人民法院对于特定范围的近亲属提出的不被强制出庭作证的申请，应当依法进行审查，对于符合不被强制出庭作证条件的，应当作出准许申请的决定，否则应当予以驳回。从司法实践来看，可以考虑建立申请复议制度。对于符合拒绝出庭作证法定条件的特定范围的近亲属应当赋予其不服强制作证决定申请复议一次的权利。

（四）规定违反强制证人出庭除外条款的法律后果

“众所周知，欲使某一法则真正发挥作用，具有足够的约束力，就必须明确规定违反该法则行为设置否定性的法律后果，否则，规则可能形同虚设。”[21] 如果审判机关强制享有拒绝出庭作证权的特定范围的近亲属出庭作证，那么，应当承担相应的法律后果。一方面，强制享有拒绝出庭作证权的特定范围的近亲属出庭作证属于程序违法，作证无效；另一方面，对于审判机关强制出庭作证的行为，享有拒绝出庭作证权的特定范围的近亲属有权提出控告。

〔21〕 房文翠、丁海湖：“关于证据排除规则的理性思考”，载《中国法学》2002 年第 4 期。

评中国新刑诉法证人出庭制度

——一种以限制证据证明力为核心的证据理念

万 毅*

证人出庭作证制度的建立，被誉为2012年刑事诉讼法修正案的“亮点”之一。的确，证人不出庭、书面证言滥用，已被公认为我国刑事诉讼制度的“痼疾”之一。本次刑诉法修改对症下药，在立法上明确了证人出庭的范围，加强了对证人的保护，这对于敦促证人出庭作证以及核实证据、查明案情、正确判决均具有重要意义。然而，由于立法者在立法思想上的相对保守以及立法能力和立法技术的明显欠缺，新刑诉法确立的证人出庭作证制度，在证人出庭的范围、强制证人出庭的手段以及证人不出庭的法律后果等关键环节，均遗留了一定的问题和缺憾。由于我国司法现实的相对复杂性，这些制度设计上的缺陷，很可能在实践中经由时间和空间的发酵，而形成一种制度“空转”效应，使得促使证人出庭作证的立法目的完全落空，甚至出现证人“依法不出庭”等制度“反转”效应。正基于此种忧思，本文拟从法解释学的角度，围绕证人出庭制度的若干基本问题，包括证人出庭的范围、强制证人出庭的手段以及证人不出庭的法律后果等展开初步探讨，以揭示现行法律规定的弊端，探讨完善证人出庭作证制度的方法和策略。

一、关于证人出庭作证的范围

从证据法理上讲，要求案件的所有证人都出庭作证，既不经济，亦无必要。因此，立法上构建证人出庭作证制度的目的，并非旨在让所有证人都出庭，而是敦促那些重要的、关键性证人出庭作证。对此，新《刑事诉讼法》第187条明确规定：“公诉人、当事人或者辩护人、诉讼代理人对证人证言有异议，且该证人证言对案件定罪量刑有重大影响，人民法院认为证人有必要出庭作证的，证人应当出庭作证”。根据该条规定，证人出庭作证，应当同时具备三个条件：①公诉人、当事人或者辩护人、诉讼代理人对证人证言有异议；②该证人证言对案件定罪量刑有重大影响；③人民法院认为证人有必要出庭作证的。具体而言：

第一，公诉人、当事人或者辩护人、诉讼代理人对证人证言有异议。这意味着法律授权控辩双方对证人证言的证据能力享有一定的程序处分权，即，只要控辩双方未对证人证言明确表示异议，则书面证言亦可使用。之所以将控辩双方同意（无异议）作为直接言词原则或传闻证据排除规则之例外，在控辩双方同意的前提下，允许传闻证据的使用，是因为“按传闻法则的重要理论依据，在于传闻证据未经当事人之反对

---

* 万毅，法学博士四川大学法学院教授、博士生导师，四川大学“985工程”——社会公正与公共危机控制研究创新基地研究人员。

询问予以核实，乃予排斥。惟若当事人已放弃对原供述之反对诘问权，于审判程序表明同意该等传闻证据可作为证据，基于证据资料愈丰富，愈有助于真实发现之理念，此时，法院自可承认该传闻证据之证据能力”。[1] 换言之，证人出庭作证制度之设立，旨在保障直接言词原则或传闻证据排除规则，而直接言词原则或传闻证据排除规则，又是为确保双方当事人的反对诘问权或曰对质权而设的。既然控辩双方[2]本身对使用书面证言并无异议，那么，可视为当事人已放弃了对该证人证言的对质权，则该书面证言自然可在法庭上使用。对此，即使明文采行直接言词原则或传闻证据排除规则的法治国家，在立法上也是予以认可的。例如，日本刑事诉讼法第326条规定，被告以外之人在审判外之陈述，经当事人于审判程序中同意作为证据的，法官可以承认该传闻证据的证据能力。这意味着，只要当事人无异议，证人可以不出庭，其书面证言可作为裁判定案的基础。

第二，该证人证言对案件定罪量刑有重大影响。换言之，只有对案件定罪量刑有重大影响的重要证人、关键证人，才需要出庭作证。但何谓“对案件定罪量刑有重大影响”？立法上语焉不详。新刑诉法出台后，立法机关曾经就此撰文解释道：“证人证言对‘定罪量刑有重大影响’包括直接目击案件的发生，是案件主要甚至唯一的证人，对于印证其他可能定案的证据具有重要意义等。既包括单独影响定罪、量刑，也包括既影响定罪，也影响量刑”。[3] 但这一解释仍然比较模糊，笔者认为，司法实务中在具体操作时可以借鉴相关司法解释的规定。2010年出台的《关于办理死刑案件审查判断证据若干问题的规定》（以下简称《规定》）曾经要求对于那些关系到死刑案件定罪量刑的重要事实、关键事实，必须达到“结论唯一”的证明标准，而在针对哪些事实属于死刑案件的重要事实、关键事实时，该《规定》第5条第2款明确指出：“办理死刑案件，对于以下事实的证明必须达到证据确实、充分：（一）被指控的犯罪事实的发生；（二）被告人实施了犯罪行为与被告人实施犯罪行为的时间、地点、手段、后果以及其他情节；（三）影响被告人定罪的身份情况；（四）被告人有刑事责任能力；（五）被告人的罪过；（六）是否共同犯罪及被告人在共同犯罪中的地位、作用；（七）对被告人从重处罚的事实”。显然，上述7项事实就属于关系到死刑案件定罪量刑的重要事实、关键事实。笔者认为，这7项事实不仅是关系到死刑案件定罪量刑的重要事实，也是关系到所有刑事案件定罪量刑的重要事实。因此，我们完全可以将上述7项事实视作判断证人证言是否“对案件定罪量刑有重大影响”的标准，即，凡是证人证言涉及上述7项事实的，都可视为对案件定罪量刑有重大影响，进而要求证人必须出庭作证。

第三，人民法院认为证人有必要出庭作证的。立法上设立证人出庭制度的目的，还在于确保法庭核实证据、查明案情，作出正确的判决。因此，在哪些证人应当出庭的问题上，承担审判职能的人民法院自当享有一定的裁量、酌处权。

---

〔1〕 林俊益：“传闻法则之研究”，载《刑事证据法则之新发展》，学林文化事业有限公司2003年版，第58页。

〔2〕 在域外，检察官虽然是司法官，但在诉讼角色上作为控方仍属于“当事人”范畴。然而，在我国，刑诉法明文规定的“当事人”范畴，并不包括检察机关在内。这里为避免误解，刻意使用了“控辩双方”这一用语。

〔3〕 郎胜主编：《中华人民共和国刑事诉讼法释义（最新修正版）》，法律出版社2012年版，第406页。

问题在于，所谓“人民法院认为证人有必要出庭作证的”，与前面两个条件之间究竟是并列关系，还是选择关系？根据全国人大法工委刑法室的解释：“根据本款规定，证人证言在同时符合三个条件的情况下，证人应当以出庭的方式作证。”[4] 据此，上述三项条件之间系并列关系而非选择关系，只有在同时符合三个条件的前提下，证人才应当出庭作证。

新刑诉法的这一规定，明显背离了之前司法解释的既有规定和《刑事诉讼法修正案（草案）》所确立的方案。2010 年出台的《关于办理死刑案件审查判断证据若干问题的规定》第 15 条第 1 款曾明确规定：“具有下列情形的证人，人民法院应当通知出庭作证；经依法通知不出庭作证证人的书面证言经质证无法确认的，不能作为定案的根据：（一）人民检察院、被告人及其辩护人对证人证言有异议，该证人证言对定罪量刑有重大影响的；（二）人民法院认为其他应当出庭作证的。”依据该条规定，所谓“人民法院认为其他应当出庭作证的”，与前一项规定即“人民检察院、被告人及其辩护人对证人证言有异议，该证人证言对定罪量刑有重大影响的”之间，是选择关系而非并列关系。换言之，即使人民检察院、被告人及其辩护人对证人证言无异议，只要人民法院认为有必要，仍然可以要求证人出庭作证。这一内容在 2011 年 8 月全国人大法工委公布的《刑事诉讼法修正案（草案）》（以下简称《草案》）中再次得到重申，该《草案》第 186 条第 1 款明确规定：“证人证言对案件定罪量刑有重大影响，并且公诉人、当事人或者辩护人、诉讼代理人有异议的，或者人民法院认为证人有必要出庭作证的，证人应当出庭作证”。该条款中的“或者”一词表明，前后两者之间是选择关系，只要人民法院认为证人有必要出庭作证，证人就应当出庭作证。但在 2012 年 3 月《刑事诉讼法修正案》正式通过后，我们突然发现，立法者对上述条款进行了文字调整，草案原本采用的选择式表述方式，在正式案中被改为了并列式表述方式。由此，人民法院丧失了要求证人出庭作证的裁量权，证人是否出庭作证，必须同时具备三项法定条件，即使人民法院认为证人有必要出庭作证，但若公诉人或被追诉方无异议，证人也无需出庭作证。

法理上该当如何评价这一立法调整和转向？对此，笔者持否定态度，这是因为，首先，从客观效果来看，立法上采取并列式表述，要求证人出庭须同时具备三个条件，客观上使得证人出庭的条件趋于严格，证人出庭的范围被进一步压缩，在司法实务中将导致证人出庭的比例降低。而这与本次刑诉法修改旨在敦促证人出庭作证的修法目标南辕北辙。更为重要的是，由于立法上严格了证人出庭条件，可能使得证人不出庭现象在新刑诉法下取得合法地位，证人不出庭，将不再是违法行为，而是合法行为，从而产生“证人依法不出庭”、“证人出庭违法”等令人啼笑皆非的司法悖论。

其次，这一立法调整和转向，在客观结果上对被告方是不利的。按照新刑诉法的规定，证人出庭须同时具备三个条件，只要被告方不表示异议，证人事实上就无需出庭作证。但问题在于，我国目前的刑事辩护率极低，绝大多数刑事案件并没有辩护律师的参与，而在辩护律师缺席的情况下，缺乏法律知识的被告人其实很难对证人证言

---

〔4〕 全国人大法工委刑法室编《关于修改中华人民共和国刑事诉讼法的决定：条文说明、立法理由及相关规定》，北京大学出版社 2012 年版，第 222 页。

表示出恰当的异议，如此一来，被告人很可能就会因此而丧失对该证人证言的对质诘问权。原本在被告人未对证人证言表示异议的情况下，人民法院仍可依职权通知证人出庭作证，从而在客观上使被告人的对质诘问权得到保障和实现。但在新《刑事诉讼法》第 187 条下，人民法院丧失了依职权通知证人出庭的权力，一旦被告人不明确表示异议，法庭就将依据书面证言定案，而这对于缺乏辩护律师帮助的被告人而言，显然是非常不利的。

再次，这一立法调整和转向，违背了法官依职权调查原则。在完全的当事人进行主义诉讼模式下，是当事人而非法官主导证据调查程序，通知哪些证人出庭作证，完全由控辩双方自行决定，法官既不介入证据调查过程，也不自行调查取证。然而，我国刑事诉讼法虽然在庭审阶段引进了部分对抗制因素，却并未完全采行当事人进行主义，而是维持了职权主义为主体的审判体制，尤其是保留了法官依职权调查取证的原则，允许法官在对证据有疑问的情况下，依职权启动证据调查程序，对证据进行调查、核实。对此，新《刑事诉讼法》第 191 条规定，法庭审理过程中，合议庭对证据有疑问的，可以宣布休庭，对证据进行调查核实。据此，如果法官在法庭审理过程中对证人证言存有疑问的，可以依职权对该证人证言进行调查核实，包括要求该证人出庭作证。然而，问题在于，依据同法第 187 条的规定，人民法院丧失了依职权通知证人出庭作证的权力，只要控辩双方对证人证言不表示异议，法院就无权要求证人出庭作证。如此一来，新《刑事诉讼法》第 187 条与第 191 条之间就产生了事实上的规范冲突，而严格执行新《刑事诉讼法》第 187 条确立的证人出庭条件，就将架空我国沿袭多年的法官依职权调查原则。

基于上述分析，笔者认为，新《刑事诉讼法》第 187 条是一条失败的立法，建议全国人大常委会通过立法解释的方式，对该条内容进行实质性修改，回到之前司法解释的既有规定和《刑事诉讼法修正案（草案）》所确立的方案，即改并列式表述为选择式表述。

二、关于强制证人出庭作证的手段和证人不出庭的后果

新《刑事诉讼法》第 188 条规定："经人民法院依法通知，证人应当出庭作证。证人没有正当理由不按人民法院通知出庭作证的，人民法院可以强制其到庭，但是被告人的配偶、父母、子女除外。"该条规定确立了强制证人出庭作证制度，据此，对于证人没有正当理由不按人民法院通知出庭作证的，人民法院有权强制其到庭。然而，从诉讼法理上分析，新刑诉法的该条规定，却存在颇多值得检讨之处。

首先，既然名为强制证人出庭，即意味着需要对证人的人身采取某种强制性手段，以迫使他到庭陈述。但问题在于，立法仅仅授权人民法院可以强制证人到庭，却并未明确规定人民法院强制证人到庭的具体手段。最高人民法院在于 2013 年 1 月 1 日起施行的《关于适用〈中华人民共和国刑事诉讼法〉的解释》第 208 条中也规定："强制证人出庭的，应当由院长签发强制证人出庭令。"但所谓"强制证人出庭令"，究竟如何执行尤其是通过何种强制性手段保证证人出庭，仍然不明确。从法理上讲，强制证人出庭的手段，因带有人身强制性，自然属于"强制措施"的范畴，但我国刑事诉讼法虽然明文规定了 5 种限制人身自由的强制措施：拘传、取保候审、监视居住、拘留、逮捕，然严格按照刑诉法的规定和我国理论界的通说，刑事诉讼中的强制措施，只能适用于犯罪嫌疑人和被告人，而不得适用于其他诉讼参与人。因此，强制证人出庭作证，是不能采用刑事诉讼法明文规定的5种强制措施的。但是，无论是从法理还是比较法的角度讲，强制证人出庭做证，实际就是强制证人到庭并保全其证言，类似于拘传被追诉人到场应讯，因而强制证人出庭作证最适当的手段就是拘传，这也是域外法治国家的普遍做法，例如，《日本刑事诉讼法》第152条规定："对于不接受传唤之证人，得再传唤或拘提（即拘传——笔者注）"。因此，笔者建议，通过全国人大常委会立法解释的形式，对拘传的适用对象和条件进行修改，明确规定："证人没有正当理由不按人民法院通知出庭作证的，人民法院可以拘传其到庭"。

其次，新《刑事诉讼法》第188条第2款规定："证人没有正当理由拒绝出庭或者出庭后拒绝作证的，予以训诫，情节严重的，经院长批准，处以10日以下的拘留。被处罚人对拘留决定不服的，可以向上一级人民法院申请复议。复议期间不停止执行"。据此，证人没有正当理由逃避出庭或者出庭后拒绝作证的，人民法院有权以训诫、拘留的方式进行处罚。《刑事诉讼法修正案（草案）》曾经直接规定，证人没有正当理由逃避出庭或者出庭后拒绝作证的，情节严重的，经院长批准，处以10日以下的拘留。笔者当时即认为，这一规定过于直接、严厉，不符合比例原则的要求。后《刑事诉讼法修正案》正式通过时，将之修改为"先训诫、后拘留"。笔者认为，所谓训诫，显然过轻，对拒不出庭的证人很难真正形成压力，进而敦促其出庭；而拘留又过重，关键是以拘留方式处罚证人，并不能真正达到强制证人出庭的目的，因为证人一旦被拘留，即"身陷囹圄"而不可能再作为证人出庭，这反倒会延宕庭审进行。因此，对证人的处罚，既要考虑比例原则，又要考虑通过处罚达到敦促证人出庭作证的目的。基于此，笔者建议，全国人大常委会通过立法解释的方式，在训诫和拘留中间增加"罚款"这一措施，即证人没有正当理由逃避出庭或者出庭后拒绝作证，予以训诫；经训诫仍不悔改的，处以罚款；罚款后仍拒不作证的，方可决定拘留。

再次，关于近亲属拒绝作证的问题。新《刑事诉讼法》第188条明文规定了被告人的配偶、父母、子女可以免于出庭作证的权利，遂引发学界及社会热议我国刑事诉讼法是否确立了近亲属拒绝作证权或曰作证豁免权的问题。但实际上，新《刑事诉讼法》第188条关于被告人的配偶、父母、子女可以免于出庭作证的规定，存在相当大的问题：

第一，立法上仅规定被告人的配偶、父母、子女在审判阶段享有出庭作证的豁免权，从而留下一个"盲点"，即在侦查阶段，侦查机关可否要求其作为证人接受询问。对于该条的立法目的，立法机关曾经指出："主要是考虑到强制配偶、父母、子女在法庭上对被告人进行指证，不利于家庭关系的维系和社会和谐的构建"。[5] 但从法理上讲，既然本条立法之目的在于尊重和维护"亲亲相隐不为罪"的文化传统以及家庭成员之间的人伦亲情，那么，被告人的近亲属不仅有权免于在审判中向法官作证，亦应当免于在侦查中接受警察调查，更不得将其询问笔录作为证据在法庭上出示。从域外立法例来看，被告人的近亲属既然享有作证豁免权，当然就有权在侦查阶段拒绝侦查机关的询问，如此方才可以称为"拒绝作证权或作证豁免权"。但新刑诉法出台后，立

〔5〕郎胜主编：《中华人民共和国刑事诉讼法释义（最新修正版）》，法律出版社2012年版，第409页。

法机关又撰文明确指出："这里的规定是免予强制出庭，不是拒证权。……本款规定并没有免除其作证的义务，只是规定在庭审阶段可以免予强制到庭"。[6] 笔者曾经在《刑事诉讼法修正案（草案）》出台后建议，将第188条中的"但是被告人的配偶、父母、子女除外"这一但书规定，移至第59条第1款，即"凡是知道案件情况的人，都有作证的义务。但是犯罪嫌疑人、被告人的配偶、父母、子女、兄弟姐妹除外"，由此构建起真正意义上的近亲属拒绝作证权。但立法者并未接受，这说明，立法者在立法思想上顾虑重重，既想革新传统的"大义灭亲"式作证条款、推动我国刑事诉讼制度的文明化进程，又想维护打击犯罪的实效性，折中之下，遂出现了既免予近亲属在庭审阶段强制出庭作证，又要求其在侦查阶段接受调查、询问，这种不伦不类的立法。

第二，如何保障被告人的对质诘问权。已经有学者指出，新《刑事诉讼法》第188条关于近亲属不得强制出庭作证的规定，妨碍了被告人面对并质询反对自己的证人的权利。该观点认为，由于亲属证言用于定罪，被告人应当享有面对和质询权，除非被告放弃这一权利，在具备出庭条件的情况下，应当让有争议的、提供了不利证言的证人出庭接受质询。而第188条的规定，将证人是否出庭的选择权赋予被告近亲属而不赋予受犯罪指控的被告人，亦有违程序公正的要求。因此，为实现程序公正的基本要求，保证法院的审判质量及被告人应享有的诉讼利益，应当赋予被告人一种权利，即如果其近亲属提供了不利证词，只有在被告人同意的情况下，其近亲属才能拒绝出庭作证。[7] 对此观点，笔者表示部分赞同，即赞同其提出的问题，但不同意其提出的改革方案，因为，如果按照该观点，要求在被告人同意的情况下，其近亲属才能拒绝出庭作证，这等于是将近亲属拒绝出庭作证的权利主体改造为了被告人，而这显然是于法无据的。笔者认为，更为妥当的做法是，近亲属如果提供了对被告人不利的证言，而又准备在审判期间拒绝出庭作证的，那么，在该案件的审前程序阶段（侦查或起诉），应当确保被告人有机会与该近亲属对质。如此，则既能确保被告人的对质诘问权，又不违反现行刑事诉讼法的规定。

最后，关于证人不出庭作证的法律后果问题。新《刑事诉讼法》第187条第3款规定："公诉人、当事人或者辩护人、诉讼代理人对鉴定意见有异议，人民法院认为鉴定人有必要出庭的，鉴定人应当出庭作证。经人民法院通知，鉴定人拒不出庭作证的，鉴定意见不得作为定案的根据"。但立法上并未明确规定，证人不出庭，其书面证言是否不得作为定案的根据。前已述及，证人出庭作证制度，本身并非目的，而是为了落实直接言词原则或传闻证据排除规则，确保当事人的反对询问权，因此，证人不出庭，即意味着当事人的反对询问权落空，该证人证言即应作为传闻证据予以排除，而不得作为定案根据，这是直接言词原则或传闻证据排除规则的题中应有之义。然而，我国新刑诉法一方面通过立法构建了证人出庭作证制度，甚至强制证人出庭作证，但另一方面却又不明文禁止书面证言的使用。这就使得司法实务中即使证人不出庭，书面证言仍可在法庭上使用，并且只要经过质证，可以确认其真实性的，即可作为定案的根据。对此，新刑诉法实际上再次重申了2010年"两高三部"在《关于办理死刑案件审

---

〔6〕 郎胜主编：《中华人民共和国刑事诉讼法释义（最新修正版）》，法律出版社2012年版，第409页。

〔7〕 龙宗智："进步及其局限——由证据制度调整的观察"，载《政法论坛》2012年第3期。

查判断证据若干问题的规定》第 15 条中确立的书面证言运用原则，即只有“经依法通知不出庭作证证人的书面证言经质证无法确认的，不能作为定案的根据”，换言之，即使证人经依法通知不出庭，但只要其书面证言经质证可以确认其真实性的，仍然可以作为定案的根据。这一做法，实际上将使得证人出庭作证制度因为缺乏法律后果上的保障而成为一种“空中楼阁”，而所谓新刑诉法确立了直接言词原则或传闻证据排除规则，更成为一个奢谈。

美国法中基于品性证据的证人弹劾

汪诸豪 樊传明 强 卉 *

一、引 言

司法审判被划分成事实认定和法律适用两部分，其中事实认定是法律适用的前提，因为“事实先于权利和义务而存在，并且决定了权利和义务。没有准确的事实认定，权利和义务就会失去意义”。[1] 在现代司法制度语境中，事实认定是通过对庭审证据的理性评价得出的，这是证据裁判原则[2]的要求。在对抗制模式下，或者在具有对抗制因素的诉讼模式中，对证据证明力的评价并不仅仅是事实认定者（法官或陪审团）的活动。司法程序也激励诉讼双方参与到证据评价的过程中，通过双方的举证、质证为事实认定者得出理性裁判提供保障。

对于证人证言这种言词证据而言，对抗制的作用尤其体现在证人弹劾制度上。诉讼中的任何一方，有权对对方提出的证人进行弹劾，攻击该证言的可信性。除此之外，如果己方证人在法庭上提供的证言对自己不利，即当自己的证人变成敌意证人时，该诉讼方也可以弹劾自己的证人。[3] 美国《联邦证据规则》607 规定：“任何一方，包括提出证据的一方，都可以攻击证人的可信性。”证人弹劾制度实际上给诉讼双方提供了一个质证的法律手段，有利于暴露证言中的错误风险，为在法庭上得出正确的事实认定结论提供了一个对抗制风格的程序保障。并且，证人弹劾制度实际上也是程序正义的要求，因为它体现了程序参与原则。[4] 因此，证人弹劾制度在司法证明程序中处于非常重要的位置。

本文研究美国证据法中以品性证据弹劾证人的规则。与影响证言可信性的各种因

---

* 汪诸豪，中国政法大学证据科学研究院讲师；樊传明，中国政法大学博士研究生；强卉，中国政法大学博士研究生。本文系教育部人文社会科学研究项目2013年青年基金项目“证人弹劾制度研究”的阶段性成果。项目编号：13YJC820073。

〔1〕［美］罗纳德·J. 艾伦：“证据法的理论基础和意义”，张保生、张月波译，载《证据科学》2010 年第 4 期。

〔2〕证据裁判原则有三个递进关系：“首先，裁判的形成必须以证据为依据；其次，裁判所依据的证据是具有证据能力（可采性）的证据；最后，据以作出裁判的证据必须达到法律规定的相应要求。”参见陈光中主编：《刑事证据法专家拟制稿（条文、释义与论证）》，中国政法大学出版社 2004 年版，第 127 页。

〔3〕美国《联邦证据规则》改变了禁止诉讼方弹劾己方证人的传统普通法规则。因为提出证人的一方无法保证证人值得信赖，如果不允许他弹劾己方证人，那么当他所提出的证人的当庭证词变得对其不利时，他就失去了防御手段。所以，《联邦证据规则》607 允许提出证人的一方弹劾证人。参见《美国联邦证据规则起草咨询委员会注释》英文原文索引：Fed. R. Evid. 607（b）advisory committee's note。

〔4〕参与原则要求，“受刑事裁判直接影响的人应当有充分的机会、富有意义地参与刑事裁判的制作过程。基本要求是，程序参与者应在裁判制作过程中始终在场，应有充分的机会提出本方证据、发表本方观点，应有充分机会反驳对方证据和观点，裁判结论应建立在各程序参与者提出的证据和观点之上。”参见陈光中主编：《刑事诉讼法》，北京大学出版社 2009 年版，第 94 页。

素相对应，存在着不同的弹劾方法，包括“错误”弹劾和“谎言”弹劾两大类。其中对于“谎言”弹劾，非常重要也非常复杂的方法是使用品性证据：指出该证人具有不诚实的一贯品格特性。然而，在英美法中，“品性证据不得用于证明特定情形下的行为一致性”是一条普遍的规则。所以以品性证据弹劾证人实际上是一项“例外”，需要重新设定这种情况下的品性证据可采性规则。作为英美成文证据法之典范的美国《联邦证据规则》详细界定了在弹劾证人时允许使用的证明品性的具体方法，概言之：允许使用名声和意见证言证明不诚实品性，但以具体行为或先前定罪记录证明不诚实品性要受到严格限制。本文通过对美国法中相关规则的介绍和分析，力求能够为中国的证据制度改革提供比较法上的参照。

二、证言品质与弹劾证人的方法

（一）证言品质：证言可信性的影响因素

弹劾证人实际上就是要暴露该证人所提供证言中存在的不可靠因素，从而对证言的可信性提出质疑，降低事实认定者（法官或陪审团）对证言证明力的评价。可见，对证人的弹劾取决于对证言可信性影响因素的前理解。有哪些因素影响到证言的可信性，从而可以作为弹劾的具体对象？或者说，影响证言品质（testimonial qualities）[5]的因素有哪些？

一份证言可以看作是一个关于案件事实的主张。证人形成该主张必须要有一定的依据，不外乎三类依据：第一种情况，证人以其感官感知（听、看、摸、嗅等）到了案件事实，即证人对于将要作证的事实具有亲身知识（personal knowledge）；[6] 第二种情况，证人并没有亲身感知案件事实，而是从别人那里听到相关的表述，即证人在转述他人的亲身知识，该证言是一项传闻（hearsay）；[7] 第三种情况，证人并没有亲身感知到其证言中所表述的案件事实，但他感知到了其他相关事实，并据此推测出其所要证明的事实，即证人根据其亲身知识进行推测，提供了意见证言（opinion）。[8] 根据英美证据法的一般规则，传闻和意见形式的证言原则上不可采；即使在例外可采的情况下，实际上也可以还原为基于亲身知识的证言，只不过是增加了进行转述或者形成意见的环节。因此，对于证言品质的研究，主要是针对基于亲身知识的证言性主张之形成过程。

亲身知识证言的形成要经过以下几个过程，每个过程都存在影响可靠性的因素：①在案件发生时，证人以其某种感官感知到了特定案件事实。但证人的感知能力是否良好？他是否存在某些感官（视觉、听觉、嗅觉等）上的缺陷或者具有误导性的心理认知倾向？并且，在案件发生的特定情境下，是否存在影响感知准确性的因素（例如

---

〔5〕 See Ronald J. Allen, Richard B. Kuhns, Eleanor Swift, and David S. Schwartz, *Evidence: Text, Problems, and Cases*, Aspen Publishers, p. 353 (5th ed. 2011).

〔6〕 对于除专家证人以外的普通证人而言，具有亲身知识是他具备证人资格的基本要求。美国《联邦证据规则》602 规定了证人的“亲身知识要求”。

〔7〕 什么样的证言才属于传闻？要符合以下三项要求：①传闻证据是一种陈述，其形式可以是口头的或书面的陈述。②传闻证据是在法庭上提出法庭外的人作出的意思表示，也就是说，原陈述者并没有出庭。③提出传闻证据的目的是为了证明其内容为真。参见张保生主编：《证据法学》，中国政法大学出版社 2009 年版，第 283 页。

〔8〕 关于证言主张形成根据的表述，参见特伦斯·安德森、戴维·舒姆和威廉·特文宁：《证据分析》，张保生等译，中国人民大学出版社 2012 年版，第 86 页。

光线、噪音等)？②证人在头脑中记忆其所感知的事实。但证人的记忆是否准确？间隔时间的长短、作证事项的细致程度等会影响记忆的准确性。③在法庭上给出证言前，证人必须决定是否如实说出他所信赖的事实版本。那么，证人是否会撒谎？在本案中是否存在引诱证人撒谎的因素（如特定的利益关系、偏见)？或者证人是否具有一贯不诚实的品格特征？④在法庭上，证人给出他的证言。他的表述是否精确？是否存在表达上的含混或者偏差？综上，证人品质的影响因素主要包括：①感知的准确性；②记忆的可靠性；③表达的精确性；④作证的诚实性。[9] 对证人的弹劾也主要集中于这几个方面。如果在这几个方面能够找到证言不可信之源，就可以有效地降低事实认定者对该证言证明力的评价。

（二）弹劾证人的方法与弹劾程序

弹劾证人就是对以上证言品质的攻击。根据所涉及的证言品质内容之不同，可以将这种攻击区分成两类主张。

第一，主张证人的感知、记忆或者表述存在错误（That's an error.)。这个或这些错误并非证人刻意为之——证人并未故意撒谎，而是归因于证人个体或者人类普遍的感知、记忆或表达能力缺憾；或者归因于客观物理环境的局限性。例如，主张证人是高度近视且在案件发生时未戴眼镜；或者主张案发现场光线非常昏暗，证人不可能隔那么远的距离辨认出被告人；或者主张从案件发生到现在时间间隔太长，证人很难记住一些细微的案情，因此证言可信性不强。对于这一类主张存在“错误”的弹劾，律师既可以通过交叉询问的方式直接进行弹劾，也可以通过独立地提出另外一个与该证言相冲突的证据进行弹劾。这类弹劾方法遵循一般的证据法规则或者程序规则，并不受特殊证据规则的约束。

第二，主张证人的证言是一个谎言（That's a lie.)。[10] 主张证人说谎要比主张证言中存在感知、记忆或表达错误更为复杂。具体而言，主张存在“谎言”的弹劾又包括两种不同的情况：第一种情况，不涉及证人的品格或行为习惯，而只是对当下证人所作证言的一个质疑——证人正在撒谎（You are lying.)；第二种情况，对证人是否诚实这一品格特性提出质疑——证人不诚实（You are a liar.)。我们将前者称为非品性弹劾（Non - character Impeachment)，将后者称为基于品性的弹劾（Character - Based Impeachment)。对于非品性弹劾而言，重要的是指出在当下案件中证人在说谎，但不涉及对证人的一般性评价。而基于品性的弹劾是以对证人的一个一般性评价（证人不诚实，具有说谎的一般倾向）为依据，从而指出在本案中证人的行为符合其说谎的品性，因而其证言不可信。

非品性弹劾的具体方法包括：提出相冲突的证据、提出该证人的先前不一致陈述、

---

〔9〕 在罗纳德·艾伦教授的《证据法》中，将这几个方面概括为“诚实作证的能力、准确叙述的能力、感知能力和记忆能力”，See Ronald J. Allen, Richard B. Kuhns, Eleanor Swift, and David S. Schwartz, *Evidence: Text, Problems, and Cases*, Aspen Publishers, p. 351 (5th ed. 2011). 在《证据分析》一书中，作者将影响证人可信性的因素概括为诚实性、客观性和观察灵敏度。参见特伦斯·安德森、戴维·舒姆和威廉·特文宁：《证据分析》，张保生等译，中国人民大学出版社 2012 年版，第 87 页。

〔10〕 对于 That's an error. 和 That's a lie. 这两种弹劾方式的分类，See George Fisher, *Evidence*, Foundation Press, p. 257 (3rd ed. 2013).

指出证人存在偏见。[11] 这些理由都支持证人在本案中说了谎这一主张，但与证人在品格上诚实与否无关，而当采用基于品性的弹劾这种方法时，是以更为间接的方式进行推论：首先，用证据表明，证人具有不诚实的一般品性；其次，论证在本案中，证人的行为符合他的不诚实品性，即证人在撒谎；最后，才是以证人撒谎为由弹劾证言的可信性。以不诚实品性弹劾证人，与品性证据排除规则存在关系。英美证据法的一般要求是，品性证据不得被用以证明行为人在特定情况下做出了与其品性相一致的行为。但是，当以不诚实品性弹劾证人时，改变了一般的品性证据不可采规则。另外，可以使用什么形式的品性证据（如意见证言、名声证言、具体行为事例或先前定罪）来弹劾证人，也是需要详细讨论的问题。

概括上文的描述，可以将证言品质与弹劾证人的方法图示如下：

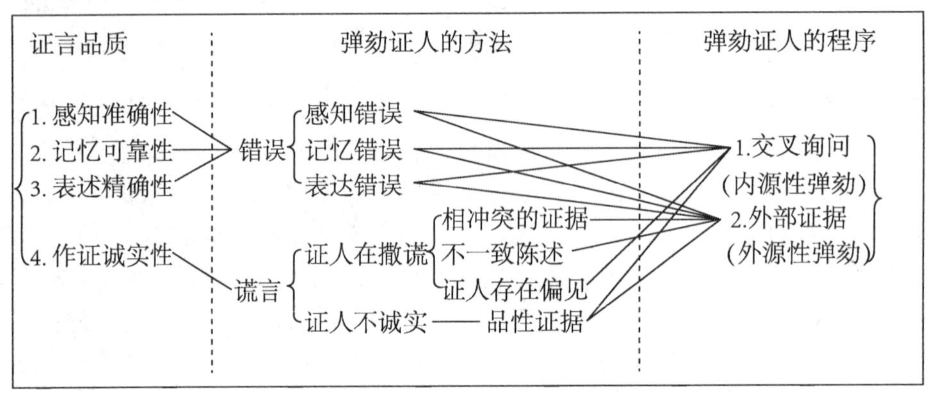

证言品质与证人弹劾的方法和程序图

其中，对证人进行弹劾包括两种程序或者说具体方式：内源性弹劾（intrinsic impeachment）和外源性弹劾（extrinsic impeachment）。[12] 内源性弹劾是通过对该证人的交叉盘问进行弹劾，交叉盘问“是我们曾经发明的揭示事实真相之最伟大的法律引擎”。[13] 通过交叉盘问可以指出证人在感知、记忆和表达上的错误，或者表明证人存在偏见。另外，在交叉盘问中也能够引出关于证人具有不诚实品性的主张。外源性弹劾是提出独立的外源证据（extrinsic evidence）与所要弹劾的证言相对抗。例如，提出另外一个证人或者物证、书证，证明所弹劾的证人证言中存在错误、该证人在本案中撒谎或者他具有一贯不诚实的品性。所有的弹劾方法都可以通过提出外源证据这种方式来进行。[14]

---

〔11〕 关于弹劾证据具体种类的更多叙述，See John Kaplan, Jon R. Waltz and Roger C. Park, *Evidence*, Harcourt Brace Legal and Professional Publications, pp. 186 ~ 202 （17th ed. 1998）。

〔12〕 有关内源性弹劾（intrinsic impeachment）和外源性弹劾（extrinsic impeachment）的定义，及其区别比较，See Ronald J. Allen, Richard B. Kuhns, Eleanor Swift, David S. Schwartz, and Michael S. Pardo, *Evidence: Text, Cases, and Problems*, p. 395 （5th ed. 2011）。

〔13〕 John Henry Wigmore, *A Treatise on the System of Evidence in Trials at Common Law*, 1904, p. 1697. 转引自张保生主编：《证据法学》，中国政法大学出版社 2009 年版，第 45 页。

〔14〕 弹劾证人的这两种不同程序，也被称为弹劾的两个阶段。第一个阶段是通过交叉盘问来弹劾，第二个阶段是通过提出外部证据（另外一位证人或者文书证据）来弹劾。见约翰·W. 斯特龙主编：《麦考密克论证据》，汤维建等译，中国政法大学出版社 2003 年版，第 67 页。

三、证人弹劾中品性证据的可采性原理

鉴于以不诚实品性弹劾证人这种方法改变了一般的品性证据排除规则，并且以何种证据形式来证明品性又受制于具体的可采性规则，因此，与其他方法相比，基于品性的弹劾在规则适用上更为复杂，需要给予特别的关注。

根据美国《联邦证据规则》404（“品性证据；犯罪或其他行为”），关于一个人品性的证据，原则上不得用以证明，在某个特定场合下该人做出了与其品性相一致的行为。例如，在一项故意伤害的指控中，针对被告人到底是否首先发起攻击这一争议事实，控方不能用被告人脾气暴躁且具有暴力倾向的证据来证明他在本案中是首先发起攻击者。再比如，在伪证罪的指控中，被告人在另外一个法庭上作为证人出席时是否说了谎是争议事实。但控方不能用表明被告人具有不诚实品性的证据来证明他提供了谎言证词。为什么英美证据法规定品性证据原则上不可采——不能用于证明特定场合下行为与品性的一致性？

当用品格证据证明特定行为时，实际上经过了这样的三段论推理过程：①大前提：人通常会按照与其品格特性相一致的方式做出行为；②小前提：证据显示某人甲具有某种品性 X；③结论：因此有理由相信，在该案的情境中，甲做出了与其品性 X 相一致的行为。按照普通的生活经验常识，这一推论往往是有效的。所以品性证据实际上在证明行为时具有经验和逻辑上的相关性。但是，“用于此目的的品格证据，虽然具有相关的些微价值，但常常带来危险的偏见、注意力的分散和时间的浪费”。[15] 所以，在证明特定行为时，品性证据的使用涉及两个方面：首先，品性证据在证明行为时，在生活经验上它是具有证明价值的。但证明价值比较微弱，因为没有更强的理由表明一个人在特定场合下一定会按照他的品性行事。其次，品性证据的使用具有危险性。它会导致不公正的偏见或者混淆本案的争点，例如，事实认定者（尤其是作为普通人的陪审团成员）可能过高地评估了品性与行为之间的相关程度，或者仅仅因为被告是个“坏人”而乐于惩罚他，而不管本案的证据情况。[16] 并且，对品性的调查会导致时间上的拖延。为了证明被告人具有某种品性，可能要引入意见形式的证言、关于其名声的证言、关于他之前特定行为的证据或他的先前定罪记录。对这些证据的调查将导致诉讼拖延，降低审判的效率。英美证据法对品性证据之证明价值和危险性权衡的结果就是，规定品性证据原则上不得用以证明特定行为，除非符合法律规定的例外情况。[17] 其中一项例外就是可以根据法律的要求，用品性证据弹劾证人。

当以弹劾证人为目的时，法律允许使用品性证据。但这里的品性指的是与证言可信性相关的品性，即证人是否诚实。具有相关性是所有证据可采的必备前提，而只有证人是否诚实的品性才与证言可信性相关，其他品性（如是否脾气暴躁、是否懒惰等）因不具有相关性而不可采。具体而言，以弹劾证人为目的提出品性证据，实际上是证明“不诚实”这一品性。证明“诚实”品性的证据，可以用于为证人“正誉”（Reha-

---

〔15〕 约翰·W. 斯特龙主编：《麦考密克论证据》，汤维建等译，中国政法大学出版社 2003 年版，第 367 页。

〔16〕 John Kaplan, Jon R. Waltz and Roger C. Park, *Evidence*, Harcourt Brace Legal and Professional Publications, p. 28 (17th ed. 1998).

〔17〕 关于品性证据排除规则的诸多例外，参见美国《联邦证据规则》404a（2）、（3）。

bilitation)[18] 的目的，但只有当证人的诚实品性被攻击之后才可采。[19] 当以不诚实的品性证据弹劾证人时，其推论过程与一般的以品性证明特定行为有何不同，从而导致了在这种情况下排除规则变成了可采规则？

在一般的情况下，法律假定以品性证明行为的危险性超过证明价值，但在证人弹劾的情况中有所不同。此时，不诚实的品性证据只是一项"附属证据"。如果一项证据通过一个推论链条与待证事实直接相关，那么它就是一项直接相关证据（directly relevant evidence）；但如果该证据本身并不与待证事实相关，它只是"对由一项直接相关证据建立起来的推理链条中的环节起着增强或削弱的作用"，那么它就是一项间接相关的或附属证据（indirectly relevant or ancillary evidence）。[20] 可见，在一般情况下，当以品性证据证明行为，而该行为是一项待证事实，那么，该品性证据是直接相关证据。但在证人弹劾中，不诚实的品性证据是为了证明证人的证言不可信，而该证言才是用于证明待证事实的直接相关证据。此时，不诚实的品性证据是间接相关（附属）证据。图示为：

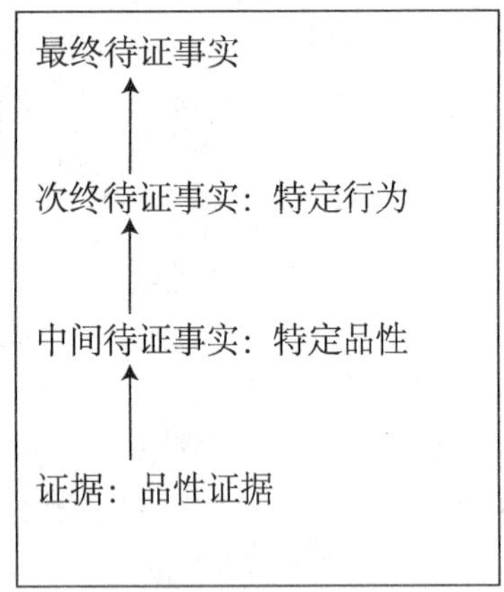

推论链条一：一般情况下，以品性证据证明行为

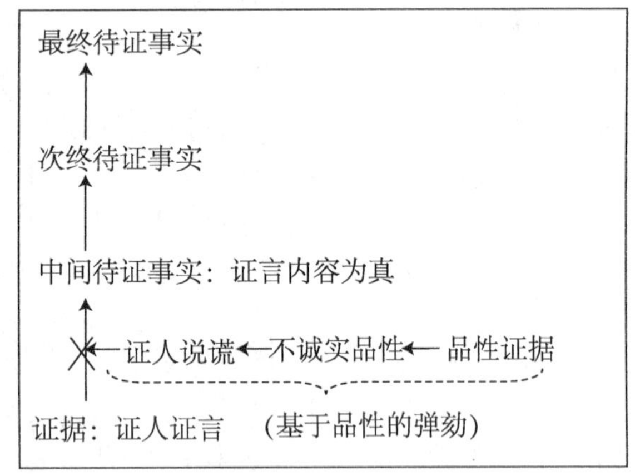

推论链条二：以品性证据弹劾证人

从两张图的比较可以看出，对于待证事实而言，当为弹劾证人目的使用品性证据时，该品性证据只是间接相关。由于与待证事实并不直接相关，因此它的误导性风险（引起不公正的偏见）就大大降低了，因为不会让事实认定直接形成关于待证事实的偏见。尤其是，对证人不诚实品性证据的提出，不会导致事实认定者形成对于被告的

---

〔18〕"当证人的诚实品性受到攻击时，反方当事人可随后通过引入关于该证人诚实品性的证据来为该证人正誉。正如提出弹劾证据意在证明证人在证人席上说谎，提出正誉证据是为了证明证人在证人席上是真诚的。"See Ronald J. Allen, Richard B. Kuhns, Eleanor Swift, and David S. Schwartz, *Evidence: Text, Problems, and Cases*, Aspen Publishers, p. 358 (5th ed. 2011).

〔19〕美国《联邦证据规则》608（a）："只有当证人的诚实品性被攻击之后，用于证明诚实品性的证据才可采。"

〔20〕直接相关证据和间接相关证据的分类，参见特伦斯·安德森、戴维·舒姆和威廉·特文宁：《证据分析》，张保生等译，中国人民大学出版社 2012 年版，第 83 页。这种分类不同于直接证据和间接证据（或者称为环境证据）的分类。

“坏人”偏见，因为该品性证据并不针对被告，而是针对证人。即使在被告作为证人提供证言时，由于法律要求只能以关于不诚实这一品性的证据进行弹劾，而不能提出关于其他品性的证据，这时引起坏人偏见的危险性也相对较小。而关于证人是否诚实的品性证据，对于其证言的可信性是相关的。所以，在“证明价值—危险性”的权衡中，法律选择认可其证明价值。这可以解释为什么在证人弹劾制度中，品性证据一般排除规则变成了（不诚实）品性证据一般可采规则。

四、基于品性之证人弹劾的证据形式

在证人弹劾中允许使用证人不诚实的品性，并不意味着在证明这种品性的具体证据形式上没有限制。恰恰相反，美国《联邦证据规则》通过规则608和609，对以何种品性证据形式弹劾证人作出了限定。总体而言，允许使用的证据形式包括：关于证人名声的证言，关于证人是否诚实的意见证言，证人的先前定罪记录，以及证人未被定罪的先前不良行为。但这几种证据的具体可采性受制于某些具体条件和诉讼程序。本部分将以美国《联邦证据规则》的立法文本，以及相关的立法史料、学理阐释为素材，分析这几种证据在用于基于品性之证人弹劾时的具体可采性。

（一）名声和意见证言

相区别于《联邦证据规则》404（a）禁止使用品性证据来证明与该品性一致的行为（要素性事实—“fact of consequence”〔21〕）之一般性禁止规定，608（a）允许为证人弹劾目的而采纳诚实与否的品性证据，并就该类证据的可用形式进行了具体限定：“可以用关于证人诚实与否之品性的名声（reputation）证言或者关于该品性的意见形式（opinion）的证言（testimony），来攻击或支持证人可信性。但是，只有在证人诚实品性受到攻击后，支持诚实品性的证据才具可采性。”〔22〕

根据上述规定，诉讼一方可以通过这样一种方式在法庭上攻击证人的诚实品性，即：通过传唤另一名证人（本文中称之为“品性证人”character witness）出庭作证，证明目标证人（target witness，也就是被弹劾对象）的不诚实品性。进一步而言，以弹劾目标证人为目的、出现在法庭上的品性证人可以提供两种形式的证言来向事实认定者展示目标证人的不诚实品性：第一种形式，就目标证人（被弹劾对象）在其生活的社区中有不诚实品性的坏名声进行作证；第二种形式，就该目标证人是否为一个具有不诚实品性的人而给出自己的负面意见观点。〔23〕

需要注意的是，《联邦证据规则》608（a）并不允许诉讼一方通过其传唤的品性证人在法庭上陈述目标证人在过去的具体不良行为实例（prior specific bad acts）来证明该目标证人具有不诚实品性。正如下文将会提到的，只有在交叉盘问程序中，根据《联邦证据规则》608（b），提问方才可以为弹劾目的而就某些特定类型的过去具体不

〔21〕 有关“要素性事实”（fact of consequence）的定义，参见［美］罗纳德·J. 艾伦、理查德·B. 库恩斯、埃莉诺·斯威夫特：《证据法——文本、问题和判例》，张保生、王进喜、赵滢译，高等教育出版社2006年版，第三章第一节“相关性基本概念”。See Ronald J. Allen, Richard B. Kuhns, Eleanor Swift, David S. Schwartz, and Michael S. Pardo, *Evidence: Text, Cases, and Problems*, p. 123 (5th ed. 2011).

〔22〕《联邦证据规则》608（a），英文原文索引：Fed. R. Evid. 608（a），其中文翻译参见王进喜：《美国〈联邦证据规则〉（2011年重塑版）条解》，中国法制出版社2012年版，第170页。

〔23〕 See Arthur Best, *Evidence*, Examples & Explanations, p. 161 (8th ed. 2012).

良行为实例向目标证人进行发问。但是《联邦证据规则》并不允许诉讼一方所传唤的品性证人在直接询问程序中陈述这些目标证人的先前不良行为。

此处还需要强调的是，用于弹劾证人的品性证据，无论是以名声还是意见形式出现，都必须要集中在与被弹劾方（目标证人）不诚实品性相关的品性证据上。有关被弹劾方（目标证人）诚实与否品性之外的其他品性证据，与其证言是否具有可信性之间缺乏相关性，证明力在实质上小于不公正偏见的危险性，因此在证人弹劾中不得使用。正如《美国联邦证据规则起草咨询委员会注释》中所述："根据大多数司法机关的意见，这种调查严格限制在诚实品性上，而不允许关于一般品性的证据提出。其效果是突出相关性，减少突袭、时间浪费和混淆。"[24]

在普通法上，对诉讼一方使用品性证据对目标证人的可信性进行提衬是受到禁止的，除非该证人的可信性受到了攻击。这是因为，如果证人的可信性还没有受到攻击，则对证人可信性的提衬活动就是在浪费时间。因此，传唤证人的诉讼一方通常只能在该证人可信性受到攻击之后，才可以提出有利于该证人可信性的证言来对证人进行"正誉"（rehabilitation）。[25]《联邦证据规则》沿袭了这一普通法原则。根据《联邦证据规则》608（a）的规定，关于证人具有良好诚实品性的名声和意见证言，只有在该证人的品性受到名声、意见证据或者其他证据的攻击后才能提出，获得法院的采纳。[26]

（二）证人的先前定罪记录

如上所述，根据《联邦证据规则》404（a），关于品性证据的基本原则是"品性不能证明行为"，因此事实认定者不能基于对象在法庭外的过去行为来做出判断对象在法庭上行为的结论。[27] 然而，根据《联邦证据规则》609（a）和（b），证人过去不尊重法律/违反法律的行为却可以被采纳用来证明该证人在法庭上作证时说谎。该规则背后的推论原理在于，如果证人过去曾被定罪，那么其被定罪的证据应当允许被法院采纳做出以下引申：①该证人曾经犯罪并被法院定罪量刑，这表明该证人表现出了对社会行为准则的不尊重；②该证人，尤其是曾犯有伪证罪或虚假陈述罪行的人，相比于遵纪守法的一般普通人，更具有说谎的品性倾向；③因为这种说谎的倾向，所以该证人在法庭证人席上作证时更有可能说假话。[28] ④并且，曾被定罪量刑的证人往往不敬畏法庭庄严的仪式，也不会认真对待在法庭上作证前的"宣誓说真话"（oath taking）环节。[29]

根据曾被定罪量刑所涉及罪名的不同，证人先前定罪记录的可采性问题可以区分

---

〔24〕 参见《美国联邦证据规则起草咨询委员会注释》，英文原文索引：Fed. R. Evid. 608 advisory committee's note。

〔25〕 有关"正誉"（rehabilitation）的定义参见：［美］罗纳德·J. 艾伦、理查德·B. 库恩斯、埃莉诺·斯威夫：《证据法：文本、问题和判例》，张保生、王进喜、赵滢译，高等教育出版社2006年版，第七章第一节"基本概念"。

〔26〕 参见王进喜：《美国〈联邦证据规则〉（2011年重塑版）条解》，中国法制出版社2012年版，第171页，条解［3］。

〔27〕 See Ronald J. Allen, Richard B. Kuhns, Eleanor Swift, David S. Schwartz, and Michael S. Pardo, *Evidence: Text, Cases, and Problems*, pp. 238 ~ 243 (5th ed. 2011).

〔28〕 See Arthur Best, *Evidence, Examples & Explanations*, pp. 153 ~ 154 (8th ed. 2012)。

〔29〕 See Barbri Review - Evidence - "Impeachment - Criminal Convictions Portion", Lectured by Professor Michael A. Simons, St. John's University School of Law.

为三种情况:

第一种情况，先前定罪的罪名涉及不诚实或虚假陈述。一个典型的例子就是证人曾经犯有伪证罪。此时，不管先前定罪的罪行是重罪（felony）还是轻罪（misdemeanor)[30]，该定罪记录都可以采纳，用来证明该证人的不诚实品性，进而弹劾证言可信性。根据《联邦证据规则》609（a）（2）的规定，这类涉及不诚实或虚假陈述的先前罪行可以被用来弹劾任何证人，且法院在证人弹劾程序中遇到诉讼方提出的这类证据时只能自动采纳，而没有排除该证据的自由裁量权。[31] 这也就是说，即便目标证人（被弹劾对象）是被告人本人的情况下，法院也无权对该种类型的先前罪行进行类似于《联邦证据规则》403 式的证明力与不公正偏见危险性的衡平比较。[32] 这种情况所涉及的唯一问题是：所提出的目标证人（被弹劾对象）先前罪行是否涉及“不诚实或虚假陈述”。有一些类型的犯罪，比如欺诈罪（fraud）或伪证罪（perjury），很显然涉及“不诚实或虚假陈述”。而其他类型的犯罪则并非如此清晰，比如抢劫罪。虽然一般普通人可能会认为抢劫是一种不诚实的获取金钱的方式，但是美国联邦证据规则起草咨询委员会却并不这么认为。[33] 事实上，起草咨询委员会在《联邦证据规则》609 语境下对“不诚实或虚假陈述范畴”的理解是比较具有限定性的，即：某种形式的欺诈必须是该种类型的犯罪行为不可分割的一部分，诸如“伪证或者教唆伪证、虚假陈述、刑事诈骗、贪污或者造假的因素或者欺诈”，且该目标证人（被弹劾对象）必须是曾有过某种形式的说谎。[34]

第二种情况，先前定罪的罪名不涉及不诚实或虚假陈述。这种情况下，作为具有可采性的前提条件，证人的先前定罪罪行必须是被判刑 1 年以上的重罪（felony），比如：谋杀罪（homicide）、强奸罪（rape）、银行抢劫罪（bank robbery）、销售毒品罪（drug selling），等等。根据《联邦证据规则》609（a）(1）的规定，这些目标证人（被弹劾对象）的上述定罪记录可由诉讼一方在对目标证人的弹劾中被提出来使用。此外，与《联邦证据规则》609（a）（2）所不同的是，审判法院对是否采纳该类不涉及“诚实性或虚假陈述”的重罪证据拥有自由裁量权。此外，审判法官会进行类似于《联邦证据规则》403 式的证明力与不公正偏见危险性的衡平比较。[35] 只有当这类重罪证据通过了衡平检验后，才能在证人弹劾程序中被法院采纳。

第三种情况，无论是上述涉及“不诚实或虚假陈述”的定罪记录，还是不涉及

---

〔30〕 在美国，被判一年有期徒刑或以上的被称为“重罪”（felony），被判一年以下有期徒刑的被称为“轻罪”（misdemeanor）。更为详细的定义解释，See Webster's New Dictionary of Synonyms 相关解释。

〔31〕 有关法官自由裁量权（discretion）的深入描述，See Ronald J. Allen, Richard B. Kuhns, Eleanor Swift, David S. Schwartz, and Michael S. Pardo, *Evidence: Text, Cases, and Problems*, pp. 157 ~ 159（5th ed. 2011）。

〔32〕 有关《联邦证据规则》403—证明力与危险性衡平比较的深入描述，参见：［美］罗纳德·J. 艾伦、理查德·B. 库恩斯、埃莉诺·斯威夫特：《证据法 ——文本、问题和判例》，张保生、王进喜、赵滢译，高等教育出版社 2006 年版，第三章第二节“证明价值与规则 403 危险”。

〔33〕 See Barbri Review – Evidence – “Impeachment – Criminal Convictions Portion”, Lectured by Professor Michael A. Simons, St. John's University School of Law.

〔34〕 参见《美国联邦证据规则起草咨询委员会注释》，英文原文索引：Fed. R. Evid. 609 advisory committee's note。另见王进喜：《美国〈联邦证据规则〉（2011 年重塑版）条解》，中国法制出版社 2012 年版，第 178 ~ 179 页，条解［5］。

〔35〕 参见《联邦证据规则》609（a）（1），英文原文索引：Fed. R. Evid. 609（a）（1）。

"诚实性或虚假陈述"的重罪定罪记录，如果自证人刑满释放之日起至在当前的弹劾程序中该定罪记录被作为弹劾证据提出来，之间的时间间隔超过10年期限的，一般来说该定罪记录将失去可采性。[36] 可以说，第三种情况是上述第一、二种情况的例外。其总体指导思想是：目标证人在10年之前被定罪的记录，由于在时间跨度上过于久远，因此无法指示他或她在当前状态下的可信性。

（三）证人未被定罪的不良行为

美国法允许在证人弹劾程序中采纳该证人的先前定罪记录以证明该证人不可信，其背后所假定的逻辑相关性同样适用于证人过去"未被定罪的不良行为"，即：一个严重不尊重法律的人（虽然他或她的行为未经审判定罪）在法庭上作为证人所作的证言，很有可能是不可信的。然而，相比于证明某人过去曾被法院判处了某项具体罪名（只需查询法院判决记录即可）而言，要证明某人过去曾经有过某项未被定罪的具体不法行为时，难度要大得多。[37]

《联邦证据规则》608（b）规定，在交叉盘问环节，提问方可以向目标证人（被弹劾方），以提问的方式，询问与诚实性相关的该证人的具体行为实例。[38] 根据《美国联邦证据规则起草咨询委员会注释》就规则608（b）的相关注解，[39] 这项证人弹劾方法的使用有四个限制：

1. 提问者必须是真诚地相信（good - faith belief），目标证人的确有该先前不良行为。如果连提问者本人都不相信目标证人有过该行为，则其不得故意进行相关提问。提问者在进行提问之前必须要已经掌握有相关信息，显示目标证人有该不良行为。[40]

2. 有关问题必须在交叉盘问环节中提出，而非在直接盘问环节（direct examination）中进行。[41]

3. 提问者仅能就目标证人（被弹劾方）在欺诈或说谎方面（deceit or lying）的过去未被定罪不良行为进行提问，而不能就其他与"证人可信性"无关的过去不良行为进行提问。

4. 提问者仅能对目标证人（被弹劾方）未被定罪的不良行为进行内源性提问（intrinsic questioning），而不能再提供任何外源性证据。[42] 当提问者向目标证人询问某项具体的过去未被定罪不良行为且该证人矢口否认后，提问者不得再另行传唤其他证人或出示书证、物证来进一步证明其主张。因此，通过提问过去未被定罪不良行为方式来弹劾目标证人是否能够成功，完全取决于该目标证人（被弹劾方）自己的回答，而

---

〔36〕 参见《联邦证据规则》609（b），英文原文索引：Fed. R. Evid. 609（b）。

〔37〕 See Arthur Best, *Evidence*, *Examples & Explanations*, p. 159（8th ed. 2012）。

〔38〕 参见《联邦证据规则》608（b），英文原文索引：Fed. R. Evid. 608（b）。

〔39〕 参见《美国联邦证据规则起草咨询委员会注释》英文原文索引：Fed. R. Evid. 608（b）advisory committee's note。

〔40〕 See Barbri Review - Evidence - "Impeachment - Prior Bad Acts", Lectured by Professor Michael A. Simons, St. John's University School of Law.

〔41〕 有关直接盘问和交叉盘问的定义及其区别比较分析，See Arthur Best, *Evidence*, *Examples & Explanations*, p. 149（8th ed. 2012）.

〔42〕 有关内源性弹劾（intrinsic impeachment）和外源性弹劾（extrinsic impeachment）的定义，及其区别比较，See Ronald J. Allen, Richard B. Kuhns, Eleanor Swift, David S. Schwartz, and Michael S. Pardo, *Evidence*: *Text*, *Cases*, *and Problems*, p. 395（5th ed. 2011）.

与其他因素无关。《联邦证据规则》608（b）仅允许对目标证人的过去未定罪不良行为进行内源性询问而不允许通过外源性证据证明之用意在于：目标证人究竟在过去是否有某项不良行为，对于当前审理的案件而言，仅仅是一个附属性问题（collateral matter），[43] 而非案件的待证事实，与案件的要件（essential element）[44] 之间不具有相关性。过度纠结于目标证人过去是否真正做过某件有关欺诈或说谎方面的不良行为，既费时费力，又容易把整个案件审理导向错误的方向，所谓“喧宾夺主”。[45]

五、结　语

综合本文的分析，对证人证言可信性的评价，取决于对证人感知、记忆、表达能力及诚实性的预先判断。弹劾制度实际上为事实认定者更理性地作出判断提供了程序上的保障。其中，基于品性的弹劾方法，激励对抗方提出质疑证人诚实性的证据，为事实认定者评估证言风险扩展了信息来源。但由于品性证据具有引发偏见和造成诉讼拖延的风险，因此以品性证据弹劾证人需要遵循严格且复杂的方法和程序。除了美国法，其他英美法系国家的证据法中也都规定了基于品性的证人弹劾规则。如澳大利亚《1995 年证据法》第 94 条和第 104 条分别对品性证据的排除与采纳进行了具体规定；加拿大《证据法》在第 9 条和第 12 条规定了证人弹劾规则。[46] 它们都采取了与美国《联邦证据规则》相类似的态度，允许在品性、声望、行为或者倾向成为争议事实时，或者在被告人提出证据证明自己在总体上或某一方面具有良好品性时，或者被告人提出证据来反驳控方证人的可信性时，对关于一个人品性、声望、行为及倾向的证据加以采纳，并且允许公诉人就仅仅与被告人的可信性有关的任何事项对被告人进行交叉询问。[47]

可见，在英美法系国家的证据法中，证人弹劾规则是一个非常重要的内容。但在法律全球化的背景下，证人弹劾制度的意义并不局限于英美法系。因为，不可否认的一个趋势是，传统上属于大陆法系国家的诉讼程序中，对抗制的因素在增加。大陆法系国家的民事诉讼程序已经呈现出明显的对抗制特征；即使在刑事诉讼领域，也已经不存在纯粹意义上的职权主义模式，而是或多或少地吸收了当事人主义因素，甚至出现了以日本、意大利为代表的所谓混合模式。有学者总结说，虽然职权主义与当事人主义在进行相互借鉴、吸收，但总的看来，职权主义对当事人主义因素的吸收明显强

---

〔43〕 有关“附属性问题”（collateral matter）的定义，See Arthur Best, *Evidence, Examples & Explanations*, pp. 164 ~ 165 (8th ed. 2012).

〔44〕 有关“要件”（essential element）的定义，参见：[美] 罗纳德·J. 艾伦、理查德·B. 库恩斯、埃莉诺·斯威夫特：《证据法：文本、问题和判例》，张保生、王进喜、赵滢译，高等教育出版社 2006 年版，第三章第一节“相关性基本概念”。

〔45〕 美国圣约翰大学法学院 Michael A. Simons 教授对笔者相应提问的回答。参见 Arthur Best：《证据法入门：美国证据法评释及实例解说》，蔡秋明、蔡兆诚、郭乃嘉译，元照出版公司 2002 年版，证人弹劾章节。See Ronald J. Allen, Richard B. Kuhns, and Eleanor Swift, *Evidence: Text, Cases, and Problems*, pp. 638 ~ 640 (2nd ed. 1997). 另见王进喜：《美国〈联邦证据规则〉（2011 年重塑版）条解》，中国法制出版社 2012 年版，第 171 ~ 172 页，条解 [5] 和 [6]。

〔46〕 See *Canada Evidence Act* (1985), Justice Law Website of Canada, http://laws-lois.justice.gc.ca/eng/acts/c-5/fulltext.html，访问时间：2013 年 6 月 12 日。

〔47〕 关于澳大利亚 1995 年《证据法》中涉及品性证据规则的内容，参见张保生主编：《〈人民法院统一证据规定〉司法解释建议稿及论证》，中国政法大学出版社 2008 年版，第 178 ~ 179 页。

势于相反的方向。[48] 对抗制的扩张会促动证人弹劾规则向英美法系外的法系扩张。因为按照本文的分析，证人弹劾是对抗制环境下诉讼双方协助事实认定者进行证据评价的一个程序保障。所以，对抗制构成了证人弹劾规则的适宜程序环境。在中国的司法制度背景下，鉴于当事人主义的引入（在民事诉讼中已经成为一个既有事实；在刑事诉讼中也构成了一个强势学术话语和改革方向），如何建立适合本土语境的证人弹劾规则也是一个值得研究的问题。本文希望能够通过对美国基于品性之证人弹劾规则的介绍，及对该制度背后基本原理的探究，为中国的证人弹劾制度构建提供一个比较法上的参照。当然，如何设计具体的能够契合中国诉讼制度的弹劾规则，是一个有待严谨论证的庞大课题。既需要对域外的证人弹劾制度及原理有全面的理解，也需要对中国本土法律制度和司法实践中的迫切需求有准确的把握。这将是本文作者继续深化研究的一个方向。

〔48〕 参见卞建林主编：《中国刑事司法改革探索》，中国人民公安大学出版社2007年版。

先前不一致陈述在弹劾证人过程中的运用

——以我国刑事诉讼为视角

强 卉*

为了保障被告人的质证权，交叉询问这种询问证人的制度被建立以及完善。在对抗制的庭审模式中，除了事实认定者要对证据的证明力进行评价，诉讼双方也通过举证和质证参与到证据评价的过程中，为事实认定者得出正确的裁判提供帮助。加之“当事人陈述……从应然的意义上来说，比任何其他证据形式都更能反映案件真实情况，具有更大的证明价值；但从实际情况来看，则不能忽视其虚假的一面，不可轻信之，以免被其误导、造成错判甚至冤枉无辜”，〔1〕从客观上来讲，由于证言又受到“客观和观察灵敏度”的影响，出现虚假和错误的可能性都较有形证据更大。〔2〕交叉询问尤其是反询问过程中对证人进行弹劾是发现真实的有力武器，主要通过“争辩在庭审上的证人陈述的证明力”〔3〕证明证人说谎以及证人的感知和记忆不可靠来实现。

所谓弹劾证人是“当证人作证时，当事人有权透过反诘问（cross examination)〔4〕提出其他使得证人显得较不可靠之证据的方式，来反制其证词。”〔5〕“根据上述定义，对证人进行弹劾的方法首先可以简单地划分为内在方法和外在方法。内在方法是指，在质证过程中从正在作证的证人或者被弹劾的证人的口中得出质疑证人可信性的事实。外在的方法或者说使用外来的证据进行弹劾是指，质疑证人可信性的事实是从其他途径，例如，文件或者其他证人，而不是从被弹劾的证人获得。”〔6〕弹劾证人的具体方法主要包括：①通过交叉询问或者运用与该证言相冲突的另一证据来证明证言是错误的，这种弹劾方式只需遵循一般的证据法规则及程序规则即可；②通过品性或非品性的方式来证明证人在说谎。〔7〕还有“一些攻击方式并没有被《联邦证据规则》或者修

* 强卉，中国政法大学博士研究生。Email：qianghui000@163.com。本文系北京市优秀博士学位论文指导教师人文社科项目“证据科学与司法文明”的阶段性成果。项目编号：20121005301。

〔1〕张保生主编：《证据法学》，中国政法大学出版社2009年版，第232页。

〔2〕关于有形证据和言词证据的证据属性，参见特伦斯·安德森、戴维·舒姆和威廉·特文宁：《证据分析》，张保生等译，中国人民大学出版社2012年版，第87页。

〔3〕［日］松尾浩也：《日本刑事诉讼法》（下卷），张凌译，中国人民大学出版社2005年版，第26页。

〔4〕多被翻译为“交叉询问”、“交互诘问”、“反询问”、“反对询问”，等等。

〔5〕［美］Arthur Best：《证据法入门》，蔡秋明、蔡兆诚、郭乃嘉译，元照出版有限公司2002年版，第186页。

〔6〕高忠智：《美国证据法新解——相关性证据及其排除规则》，法律出版社2004年版，第104页。

〔7〕对于“证明错误”和“证明”这两种弹劾方式的分类，参见George Fisher, *Evidence*, Foundation Press, p.257 (3rd ed. 2013).

订后的《统一证据规则》所规定，但是它们从这两个规则中获得授权。"[8] 本文则主要以如何运用内在方法以及非品性弹劾中的先前不一致陈述来弹劾证人为主要研究对象。

一、先前不一致陈述（prior inconsistent statement）

先前不一致陈述在法庭上不仅以弹劾证据的形式出现，还会以证明所主张案件事实的证据形式出现。根据传闻排除规则的观点，用以证明案件事实的庭外陈述包括先前陈述就是传闻，只有在符合传闻例外的规定时才能加以采纳。但在我国法律的态度中，部分先前陈述在符合一定条件的情况下可不被传闻规则所排除。最高人民法院、最高人民检察院、公安部、国家安全部和司法部联合制定，2010 年 7 月 1 日起实施的《关于办理死刑案件审查判断证据若干问题的规定》（以下简称《死刑案件证据规定》）第 22 条规定，在被告人庭前供述一致，庭审中翻供，但没有合理理由进行解释，且庭审供述与其他证据能够相互印证的，则可对其庭前供述进行采信。在该规定出台之前，司法实践中就有大量的被告人庭前不一致供述和证人证言被采纳证明主张事实的情况，本条则明确规定了采信的条件。[9] 本文所论述的仅指用作弹劾目的的先前不一致陈述。作为弹劾目的使用，无论前后哪种陈述是真实的，只要存在不一致，就可以用作证明证人具有撒谎或者感知、记忆不清的可能性，来影响事实认定者对证人证言证明力的判断。当证人被攻击伪造证言或者存在不适当的影响或动机时，则可利用先前一致陈述予以反驳从而恢复证人可信度。[10]

"先前"指庭审之前。与庭审中的证言相对，先前陈述是指庭审之前的陈述，形式不限，可以是书面或者口头。如我国刑事诉讼中侦查机关制作的询问笔录就是先前陈述。《联邦证据规则》并未对"不一致（inconsistent）"进行具体规定，但通常认为在所支持的事实主张上有区别就可认定为不一致。"无论是从被弹劾的证人处所取得的能够证明存在先前不一致陈述的证言，还是可证明先前不一致陈述存在的外部证据都属于弹劾证据。"[11]

"先前不一致的陈述，可以为弹劾证人的可信性之非传闻证据目的而被采纳。需要注意的是出于节约时间的考虑一般不允许引入外部证据。尤其是当证人已经承认存在先前不一致陈述且没有进行争辩意图使不一致最小化时，此外如果先前不一致陈述在符合联邦证据规则第 801 条（d）（1）A 的规定时则具有可采性。[12]《联邦证据规则》613（b）也对此有相应规定，通常情况下当事人不能提出先前不一致陈述的旁证，[13] 除非证人有机会解释或否认该陈述，并且对方律师有机会就该陈述对证人进行询问。虽然《联邦证据规则》613（b）在不一致陈述的旁证问题上放宽了普通法的基础铺垫

---

〔8〕［美］约翰·W. 斯特龙主编：《麦考密克论证据》，汤维建等译，中国政法大学出版社 2004 年版，第 66 页。

〔9〕陈意智：《论弹劾证据及其在刑事诉讼中的运用》，西南政法大学 2011 年硕士学位论文。

〔10〕Terry McCarthy, "A Guide to Impeachment in Federal and Alabama State Courts", 70 *Ala. Law.* 44 (2009), p. 50.

〔11〕陈意智：《论弹劾证据及其在刑事诉讼中的运用》，西南政法大学 2011 年硕士学位论文。

〔12〕［美］罗纳德·J. 艾伦、理查德·B. 库恩斯、埃莉诺·斯威夫特：《证据法：文本、问题和判例》，张保生、王进喜、赵滢译，高等教育出版社 2006 年版，第 454 页。

〔13〕"旁证（extrinsic evidence）"：非通过对证人的直接盘问或交叉询问而导出的任何证据。

要求，但如果弹劾方没有让证人注意到这一陈述，则一些联邦法院还是禁止使用旁证。"[14] 由此可知，外部证据只有符合该条要求才能具备可采性。

二、我国刑事诉讼中运用先前不一致陈述弹劾证人的现状

在我国，司法实务工作者对何为弹劾证据及相关理论知识还比较陌生，但在实际工作中却会对其进行运用以质疑证人的可信性。根据我国刑事诉讼法规定，证言的组成实际上包括证人证言、被告人供述、被害人陈述以及鉴定意见。[15] 但是，就其内容而言，都是针对诉讼各方主张的事实出庭作证，共性要远大于个性。

根据《人民检察院刑事诉讼规则（试行)》第 439 条第 2 款规定："被告人在庭审中的陈述与在侦查、审查起诉中的供述不一致，足以影响定罪量刑的，可以宣读被告人供述笔录，并针对笔录中被告人的供述内容对被告人进行讯问，或者提出其他证据进行证明。"检察机关取得了运用先前不一致陈述弹劾被告人可信性的权利。但是，《人民检察院刑事诉讼规则（试行)》中并没有对使用内部证据及旁证的顺序等具体程序进行明确规定。司法实践中也存在被告人出于各种原因而在庭上翻供的可能性，会部分否认甚至全盘否认其在先前阶段的供述，公诉人通常则会以其在侦查阶段由侦查机关制作的侦查讯问笔录来质疑甚至否定被告人庭上陈述的可信性。此时，侦查讯问笔录不仅是用来证明控诉方所主张的案件事实，还具有弹劾被告人的作用。此时，无论法官采纳了哪一份供述，都可以证明被告人有撒谎的倾向，或者出于主客观原因而记忆不清而对其陈述的证明力产生影响。这种影响还被多部司法解释所说明，如《死刑案件证据规定》第 22 条以及江苏省高级人民法院于 2008 年制定的《关于刑事案件若干证据问题的意见》第 33 条第 3 款[16] 都对此种情况如何审查判断被告人供述进行了具体的规定，也就是说，出现了先前不一致陈述有可能会对被告人陈述的证明力造成影响。"在我国刑事案件庭审过程中，运用先前不一致陈述的典型模式是：在法庭调查阶段，控方首先告知被告人存在先前不一致陈述，随后就会使用旁证对其进行弹劾。"[17]

根据《人民检察院刑事诉讼规则（试行)》第 442 条第 5 款、第 6 款、第 7 款规定："证人进行虚假陈述的，应当通过发问澄清事实，必要时还应当宣读证人在侦查、审查起诉阶段提供的证言笔录或者出示、宣读其他证据对证人进行询问。当事人和辩护人、诉讼代理人对证人发问后，公诉人可以根据证人回答的情况，经审判长许可，再次对证人发问。询问鉴定人、有专门知识的人参照上述规定进行。"在面对证人的当庭证言与先前陈述不一致的情况时，检察机关也被授权可运用证人先前不一致陈述来对证人的可信性进行弹劾。而且，在这部分内容中还对内部证据及旁证的使用顺序进行了明确的规定。也就是说，公诉人可以在证人当庭证言与先前陈述不一致时，提出侦查阶段制作的证人证言笔录来对证人的当庭陈述产生影响。江苏省《关于刑事案件若干证据问题的意见》第 44 条第 2 款也规定了在证人当庭证言与先前陈述出现矛盾

---

[14] [美] 罗纳德·J. 艾伦、理查德·B. 库恩斯、埃莉诺·斯威夫特：《证据法：文本、问题和判例》，张保生、王进喜、赵滢译，高等教育出版社 2006 年版，第 431 页。

[15] 参见《中华人民共和国刑事诉讼法》第 48 条。

[16] 《死刑案件证据规定》第 22 条以及江苏省高级人民法院于 2008 年制定的《关于刑事案件若干证据问题的意见》第 33 条第 3 款都是关于先前不一致陈述与庭上陈述审查判断方法的规定。

[17] 陈意智：《论弹劾证据及其在刑事诉讼中的运用》，西南政法大学 2011 年硕士学位论文。

时，控辩双方均可对其进行询问，甚至法官也可主动询问证人以确认其证言内容，并可要求其对矛盾的出现进行解释。同时，在本条还规定了对被害人陈述的认证适用证人证言的有关规定，因此，弹劾被害人的可信性参照弹劾证人证言可信性的相关规定。本条文比《死刑案件证据规定》第 15 条规定得更为详细。

以上叙及的都是对被弹劾的证据进行审查判断的相关司法解释。对于弹劾证据的审查判断并未详加规定。对于先前不一致陈述进行的审查判断规定也都是将其作为证明案件事实的证据进行审查，而非作为弹劾之用途进行审查。当然，这确是法律的不完善之处，但在司法实践中，如果提出弹劾证据旨在质疑或影响某一实质证据之证明力时，法官会对弹劾证据的可采性进行审查，如通过则继而对其证明力进行审查，即审查其对被弹劾证据的影响。在我国，这属于法官自由心证的范畴。也就是说，如果"辩护人对证人的可信性提出质疑，法官通常会对质疑证人可信性的证据进行自由心证，再将被弹劾的证人证言联系案件其他的证据看是否能形成证据链，从而决定是否采纳该证据"。〔18〕

三、我国刑事诉讼中运用先前不一致陈述弹劾证人过程中存在的问题

我国司法实践中虽然存在着对弹劾证据的使用，但弹劾的主要表现，即控辩双方对庭上证人进行询问或交叉询问及提出证据对其进行质疑并未完整地体现。我国法律中虽然存在一些实质上的弹劾规则，但相关的法律规定少而分散，加之在司法实践中，对证人和证言的考察出现严重分离，造成对证人可信性关注的缺乏。实际上不存在真正意义上的证人弹劾行为，弹劾证据的使用也存在问题。

首先，我国在理论和实践中并未对弹劾证据和实质证据进行明确的区分。《人民检察院刑事诉讼规则（试行）》第 336 条第 2 款、第 338 条第 5 款都只规定了允许先前证言或供述可为弹劾所用，但对于先前证言或供述是否可作为实质证据以及如何才能作为实质证据使用没有明确规定。2010 年公布施行的《死刑案件证据规定》规定在证人、被害人、被告人先前陈述与庭上证言不一致时，采"印证采信原则"。这说明先前陈述与庭上证言同样都具有可采性，只是将哪一个作为"定案的依据"有待审查判断。虽然有学者认为"在利用先前不一致陈述或者被告先前伪证罪进行弹劾时，期望陪审团在证据的弹劾使用和实质使用之间作出极其精细的区别是很荒谬的。"〔19〕但不区分就可能使本不应作为实质证据使用的证据成为定案的依据，影响事实认定的准确性。

其次，利用书面证言来弹劾书面证言，不仅有违程序正义，还不利于发现事实真相。"我国庭审过分倚重被告人的供述，证人出庭作证没有受到应有的重视，不少司法人员对证人不出庭作证从而减少的麻烦甘之如饴，证人也不愿意出庭作证接受盘诘，因此在我国，庭审之证人倒成了稀见之物。"〔20〕于是，对证人可信性和鉴定人的攻击与质疑也较多体现为书面证言之间的对质，而非交叉讯问中产生的证言，这种方式并非严格意义上的弹劾。《死刑案件证据规定》中规定的"印证采信原则"直接破坏了当

〔18〕陈意智：《论弹劾证据及其在刑事诉讼中的运用》，西南政法大学 2011 年硕士学位论文。

〔19〕［美］罗纳德·J. 艾伦、理查德·B. 库恩斯、埃莉诺·斯威夫特：《证据法：文本、问题和判例》，张保生、王进喜、赵滢译，高等教育出版社 2006 年版，第 451 页。

〔20〕张建伟："交叉询问制度的机理与应用"，载陈光中主编：《依法治国 司法公正——诉讼法理论与实践》，上海社会科学院出版社 2000 年版，第 207 页。

场质证原则，“针对不同种类的证据，质证的方式可能有所不同。针对证人证言、当事人陈述等言词证据来说，质证的基本方式是质问或交叉询问”。[21] 由于证人、被害人是否出庭对先前陈述能否得到印证没有影响，证人或者被害人出庭的积极性就进一步降低，被告人及其辩护人无法进行当面质证。这种所谓的“弹劾”方式就不利于发现事实真相。

最后，缺乏使用弹劾证据的详细规定及相关配套制度。①并未确立弹劾证人的前提，“即必须遵循所谓的善意要求（the good faith requirement）。一方当事人对证人进行弹劾必须是基于善意，这是一般的道德准则和公平观念的要求”。[22] ②法律对于弹劾及弹劾证据的使用没有直接规定。③美国证据法大师威格摩尔认为交叉询问制度乃人类为发现真实所发展出最伟大的法律引擎。[23] 但我国《刑事诉讼法》的相关司法解释和证据规定中提及证据必须当庭质证，但是如何在实质意义上质证并没有规定。④由于我国在开庭审理之前控辩双方并没有进行证据开示，庭审的争点也没有形成。因此在之后的庭审过程中，对证言的弹劾与对证人资格及证据可采性问题常常混为一谈。美国联邦最高法院在1963年的Brady v. Maryland案以及此后的一系列案件的判决中认为，根据联邦宪法的正当程序和公平审判条款，控方有义务应辩方要求向辩方开示可能影响定罪或判刑的一切有利于被告人的证据和有关的弹劾证据。[24] 因此，证据开示是弹劾规则能真正落实的必备举措。

四、完善的意义

“就弹劾规则本身而言，一方面它是经过长期的司法实践而发展起来的，对可能削弱证人证言可信性的因素进行了全面而细致地总结和归纳，能合理和有效地揭示不可靠的证人；另一方面它是一个方法性规则，与意识形态因素和经济因素联系较少，更突出的是技术性。”[25] 同样，关于如何利用先前不一致陈述来进行弹劾的相关规定对我国刑事诉讼具有重要意义。

首先，有助于查明案件事实真相。较之物证、书证、视听资料等证据形式，证人证言的一个突出特点就是受人的主观影响较大。证人在感知、记忆和陈述案件情况的过程中，充满着主客观的矛盾，真假难辨。[26] 在弹劾制度建立的情况下，事实认定者在听取主询问方对证人的询问后，能够再听取反询问方对证人和证言的质疑与攻击以及对虚假证言的揭露，那么，应该能在其更加审慎地判断证人可信性和证言证明力的前提下查明案件事实。

其次，有利于被告人质证权的实现。联合国《公民权利和政治权利国际公约》第14条第3款（戊）项规定受到任何刑事指控的任何人都有权“讯问或业已讯问对他不

---

〔21〕 何家弘、刘品新：《证据法学》，法律出版社2008年版，第238页。

〔22〕 ［美］托马斯·A. 马沃特，沃伦·D. 沃尔夫森：《审判证据》，中信出版社2003年版，第374页。

〔23〕 张保生主编：《证据法学》，中国政法大学出版社2009年版，第45页。

〔24〕 孙长永：“美国刑事诉讼中的证据开示”，载陈光中主编：《诉讼法论丛》（第3卷），法律出版社1999年版。

〔25〕 刘卓立：“弹劾规则研究”，载《海峡法学》2012年第1期，第115页。

〔26〕 陈卫东：“让证人走向法庭—— 事案件证人出庭作证制度研究”，载《山东警察学院学报》2007年第2期，第40页。

利的证人，并使对他有利的证人在与对他不利的证人相同的条件下出庭和受讯问”。[27]将被告人的质证权作为最低保障。

最后，符合实现程序正义的要求。刑事审判需要实现的最低限度程序正义包括六个方面。其中三个方面：程序的参与性、程序的对等性以及程序的合理性[28]都要求“那些其利益可能受到裁判结果直接影响的人充分而富有意义地参与到裁判结果的制作过程中来，从而对裁判结论的形成施加积极有效的影响”。[29]“裁判者在整个刑事审判过程中应给予各方参与者以平等的机会，对各方的证据、主张、意见予以同等的对待，对各方的利益予以同等的尊重和关注。”[30]以及“裁判者的结论必须以法庭调查中采纳的所有事实为根据，并顾及控辩双方提出的所有有效的证据、事实、主张和意见。”[31]

五、完善建议

我国司法实践和法律规定纵然有很多问题或者不足，但照搬国外的做法不仅会浪费资源，还会导致由于“水土不服”而使法律规定不能真正发挥作用。对证据的运用和证据规则实际上贯穿刑事诉讼过程的始终，尤其在审判阶段，进行事实认定的过程几乎完全是对证据进行审查判断的过程。交叉询问制度，作为弹劾规则发挥作用的基础，是在陪审团制度中发展完善的。由此弹劾规则及弹劾证据的引入在我国这种实际上的参审制的情况下遭到质疑，但“威格摩尔认为交叉询问是人们为探明事实所发明的最伟大的发动机，在制造假象方面也几乎是威力相当”。[32]加之我国现在只有“相互印证”这种方法来考察证言的可信性。弹劾证据的引入以及弹劾规则的建立甚至可以说是迫在眉睫。

本文研究的主要目的，是对先前不一致陈述这种证据种类及其运用方法进行阐述，进而谈到我国刑事立法及司法实践中存在的突出问题。在文章的最后，笔者想就某些方面的完善和改进提出一些自己的看法和建议，以期能达到抛砖引玉的目的。

（一）区分证据的使用目的并制定相应规则

首先，在建立弹劾规则之前必须要对弹劾证据进行定义，明确其相关性、可采性及表现形式，以区分于用以证明控辩双方事实主张的实质证据。其次，当具有不公平的偏见、争议事项的混淆、误导陪审员的危险或者不必要的诉讼拖延、时间浪费、不必要的重复等情况时，法官可对这些因素与该证据的证明力进行判断，并可以行使自由裁量权对具有相关性的弹劾证据予以排除。[33]“‘先前不一致的陈述’这类证据，出于不同的目的，既可以用作弹劾证据，也可以用作实质证据。”[34]由于弹劾证据的采

---

〔27〕赵建文：“《公民权利和政治权利国际公约》第14条关于公正审判权的规定”，载《法学研究》2005年第5期，第142页。

〔28〕陈瑞华：“程序正义论——从刑事审判角度的分析”，载《中外法学》1997年第2期，第37～74页。

〔29〕陈瑞华：“论程序正义价值的独立性”，载《法商研究》1998第2期，第27页。

〔30〕陈瑞华：“程序正义论——从刑事审判角度的分析”，载《中外法学》1997年第2期，第37～74页。

〔31〕陈瑞华：“程序正义论——从刑事审判角度的分析”，载《中外法学》1997年第2期，第37～74页。

〔32〕参见［美］达马斯卡：《漂移的证据法》，李学军等译，中国政法大学出版社2003年版，第109页。

〔33〕FRE403及关于其在此的运用，参见［美］罗纳德·J. 艾伦、理查德·B. 库恩斯、埃莉诺·斯威夫特：《证据法：文本、问题和判例》，张保生、王进喜、赵滢译，高等教育出版社2006年版，第428页。

〔34〕陈意智：《论弹劾证据及其在刑事诉讼中的运用》，西南政法大学2011年硕士学位论文。。

纳标准较实质证据来说比较低，因此，如何避免弹劾证据影响到事实认定者对案件的判断是区分证据使用目的的首要意义。将二者区分开来以后，进一步针对两种证据制定不同的采纳标准、明确弹劾证据的有限可采性及使用规则和评价方法则是完善这部分法律法规的重点内容。

就先前不一致陈述来说，尤其要区分这一陈述是作为弹劾证据还是实质证据使用。因为做出陈述是同一名被认为具有证人资格可以出庭作证的证人，当其先前不一致陈述被提出来是为了证明提出证人一方的事实主张，还是为了证明该证人的庭前证言有待进一步考证才能加以采纳并采信。这一问题不搞清楚就没法正确地运用先前不一致陈述以排除它的提出可能误导事实认定者的副作用。其次，先前不一致陈述从严格意义上来讲属于庭外陈述，也就是符合传闻证据的一般排除规则，在明确其用来弹劾证人时才能绕过传闻证据排除规则被允许在庭审中提出。所以，如果不明确其弹劾证据或是实质证据的身份为其放行，事实认定者在未明确其作用的情况下极有可能将其视作实质证据用于事实认定，那么，就会造成传闻证据排除规则的失效以及庭外陈述采纳标准的降低。

为了避免不必要拖延以及诉讼资源的浪费，只有在陈述人有机会对该陈述进行解释或者否认该陈述，并且对方律师也有机会就该陈述对证人进行询问的情况下，控辩双方才能提出先前不一致陈述的旁证。[35] 这样规定的目的就是给予被弹劾人正誉的机会以及避免不必要的浪费。当先前不一致的陈述涉及附属事实时，法官可以判断这种证据的较低证明力是否会导致事实认定的偏离并进行自由裁量。

（二）进一步落实交叉询问制度及完善相关配套制度

首先，作为英美对抗式审判核心的交叉询问制度，极大地体现了“公平竞争理论”和对个人主体性高度尊重的程序正义理念。[36] 交叉询问对某些物证之准确性进行判断的过程中也发挥重要作用。[37] “在证人接受主询问之后，对方当事人有权对该证人行反询问。反询问限于两个范围的询问：（1）证人主询问涉及的事项；（2）与证人可信度有关的事项。”[38] 根据最高人民法院《刑诉法解释》第 212 条规定，我国目前询问证人的顺序是：传唤方—对方—审判人员，这与英美法系的直接询问、交叉询问以及法官的裁量性询问基本相对应。[39] 弹劾证人是在交叉询问的过程中进行，这是弹劾证据得以正确并有效率使用的前提。“交叉询问者可以提出诱导性问题”，[40] 来揭示证人证言的不可信。

其次，弹劾存在的前提是证人必须出庭。保证证人出庭首先要确立传闻证据规则。“‘传闻’是指除陈述者在审理或听证作证时所作陈述外的陈述，行为人提供它旨在用

---

〔35〕 关于旁证在此的使用，参见［美］罗纳德·J. 艾伦、理查德·B. 库恩斯、埃莉诺·斯威夫特：《证据法：文本、问题和判例》，张保生、王进喜、赵滢译，高等教育出版社 2006 年版，第 424 ~430 页。

〔36〕 参见张月满：《刑事证人证言规则》，中国检察出版社 2004 年版，第 86 页。

〔37〕 参见特伦斯·安德森、戴维·舒姆和威廉·特文宁：《证据分析》，张保生等译，中国人民大学出版社 2012 年版，第 85 页。

〔38〕 王国忠：《刑事诉讼交叉询问之研究》，中国人民公安大学出版社 2007 年版，第 109 页。

〔39〕 张保生主编：《证据法学》，中国政法大学出版社 2009 年版，第 250 页。

〔40〕 张保生主编：《证据法学》，中国政法大学出版社 2009 年版，第 251 页。

作证据来证明所主张事实的真实性。"[41] "传闻证据是指被告人以外的人在庭审外作出的用以证明所主张事项之真实性的陈述。"[42] 根据美国《联邦证据规则》第802条以及澳大利亚《1995年证据法》第59条，传闻证据规则一般不允许采纳传闻证据禁止某些传闻证据，除非满足例外情况，证人应当出庭作证，宣誓并接受交叉询问。保证证人能够出庭还要建立较为完善的证人保护制度，例如"《美国联邦证据规则》规定证人享有不受强迫自证其罪、法庭保护证人不受折磨或者非难、获得经济补偿等权利"。[43] 通过以上这些措施使得证人出庭作证得到了保障，这是真正弹劾的前提。

最后，证据开示是指在案件开庭审理前双方当事人相互交换证据和获取有关案件信息的活动。控辩双方在法庭审理开始之前将各自掌握的证据互相展示给对方，交换有关案件事实的信息，是使得弹劾与正誉有效进行的保障。《联邦刑事诉讼规则》在第16条中规定了刑事案件中的证据开示，主要目的和功能是使双方当事人在庭前互相了解对方的案件情况，整理争点，固定证据，避免证据突袭，提高司法效率。[44] 控辩双方都能事先掌握不利于己的证据，充分准备问题或寻找外部证据以质疑证人的可信性，为弹劾与正誉做准备，更好地协助事实认定者发现案件真实情况。

六、结 语

证人弹劾制度在帮助事实认定者判断案件事实时具有不可替代的作用，笔者出于人类认识事物的本能以及司法实践活动经验的积累对此进行了分析，我国司法实践中利用先前不一致陈述来质疑被告人、被害人或者证人的现象时有发生，但由于缺乏有关具体规则和方法的法律依据，可能会出现适得其反的效果。加之弹劾还包括利用品性证据质疑证人的可信性或者通过旁证质疑证人的感知能力等方法，这些都有助于事实认定者进行有效的事实认定。如何使用这些方法或利用这些证据来发现事实，以及相应的配套措施如完善的律师制度等都是法律亟需解决的问题。

---

〔41〕［美］罗纳德·J. 艾伦、理查德·B. 库恩斯、埃莉诺·斯威夫特：《证据法：文本、问题和判例》，张保生、王进喜、赵滢译，高等教育出版社2006年版，第454页。

〔42〕张保生主编：《证据法学》，中国政法大学出版社2009年版，第283页。

〔43〕张保生主编：《证据法学》，中国政法大学出版社2009年版，第247页。

〔44〕张保生主编：《证据法学》，中国政法大学出版社2009年版，第162页。

美国证据法中的品格证据的正誉

郑 苒*

一、弹劾和正誉

当一名证人走入法庭，在证人席上宣誓并被直接询问时，他的可信性便成为了案件的一个争议点。当事人传唤证人作证，是想借助证人之口将证人所感知的对己方有利或对对方不利的事实展现给陪审团，从而帮助构建一个有利于己方的"故事"。从这种意义上来说，一方的友好证人往往就是另一方的敌意证人，因为没有人会明知证人的证言对己方不利或对对方有利而传唤这个证人出庭作证。

如果想要在另一方当事人的故事上打开一个缺口，似乎攻击证人的可信性是一个不得已的办法。一般有人会认为只有律师无法在交叉询问中对证人在直接询问中提到的事实问题做出有效的回应，又无法从这个证人口中得到任何有利于己方的事实时，才会攻击证人的可信性来尽量降低证人的证言对陪审团的影响。但是比起攻击证人证言的内容，攻击证人的可信性又是一个不用花费太多时间来思考和组织的方法。毕竟每个案件的事实问题千差万别，而攻击证人的可信性的那一套方法几乎可以适用于任何案件。

攻击证人的可信性又可以称作弹劾证人。所谓弹劾（impeachment），是指"在试图证明，证人也许对事件并非有意地作了不正确的叙述，也许是不诚实的（也就是在说谎），或者对证人作证所要证明的事件之感知是不正确的，或者忘记了某些或全部发生的事情。如果事实认定者相信对证据的弹劾，则事实认定者就应当得出这样的结论，若没有对证据的弹劾，证人所说的东西就可能更不准确"。[1] 弹劾证人所要达到的目的是证明证人的证言并不与事实相符。这种不相符有两个方面，一个是证人的主观方面，证人并没有诚实地讲述他的所见所闻，也就是故意说谎；另一个是客观的方面，证人认为他如实叙述了，但是其实与事实不符，也就是无意地说谎。弹劾证人有多种方法，比如证明证人具有不诚实的品性，或者证人与本案有利害关系，或者证明证人的感知能力存在缺陷，或者证人有先前不一致的陈述，或者证人的证言与其他证据存在矛盾等等。

如果证人的可信性在交叉询问中被弹劾了，那么传唤证人的一方当事人可以在再直接询问中恢复证人的名誉，这就是所谓的正誉（rehabilitation）。《布莱克法律词典》对"正誉"的解释就是"证人被弹劾之后对其可信性的恢复"[2]。传唤证人的当事人

---

* 郑苒，中国政法大学硕士研究生。Email：highobadiah@ qq. com。

〔1〕［美］罗纳德·J. 艾伦、理查德·B. 库恩斯、埃莉诺·斯威夫特：《证据法——文本、问题和案例》，张保生等译，高等教育出版社2006年版，第388页。

〔2〕*Black's Law Dictionary*, 9th ed., West Group, 2009, p. 1399.

可以用先前一致陈述来恢复证人的可信性，也可以用品性证据来证明证人拥有良好的品性。用品性证据正誉的过程大致如下："当事人——可能是原告——传唤1号证人来证明案件的事实。然后对方当事人可能会传唤2号证人——一名品性证人——来证明1号证人具有不诚实的声誉。为了恢复1号证人的可信性，当事人传唤3号证人——另一个品性证人出庭作证。3号证人与2号证人证明的内容发生矛盾：3号证人证明1号证人具有诚实的声誉。"〔3〕

正誉的存在有其自身的必要性。首先，品性有时会成为某些案件的事实构成要素，但是大多数案件中品性证据不会成为实质证据。对方当事人攻击证人品性的最终目的不仅仅是要在法庭上证明证人是一个不诚实的人，而是为了要向陪审团表明因为证人具有不诚实的品性，所以他对案件作证的证言可能是假的。弹劾证人的可信性就是在削弱证人证言的可信性，如果提出证人的当事人不及时对证人的可信性进行恢复，那么陪审团可能就会低估证人证言的证明力。其次，普通法中存在一种保证规则（voucher rule）。保证规则指传唤证人的当事人必须为证人的可信性担保，并且他自己不得弹劾证人的可信性。〔4〕这一规则的理论基础之一是"当事人在道义上有义务向法院提供真实的证据"〔5〕，对证人进行正誉和该道德上的义务是一致的，正誉就是在履行这一义务。

二、品性证据如何正誉

弹劾攻击的是证人的可信性，正誉所要达到的目的也是恢复证人的可信性。而正誉的方法基本上就是用品性证据来证明证人拥有诚实的品性。在弹劾证人的手段多样的对照下，用品性证据来正誉成为了少数能适用于几乎所有弹劾手段的正誉方法。

（一）品性、偏见和倾向

美国《联邦证据规则》没有对"品性"或"品性证据"作出界定。按照《布莱克法律词典》的解释，品性证据是指："有关某个人的值得赞许或应予谴责的一般个性特征或倾向的证据；关于一个人在社区中的道德立场的证据"。〔6〕美国学者认为"典型情况下，品格特性是一个人具有道德意味的（如诚实或不诚实）品质或方面，因此，内在地包含着偏见。"〔7〕也有人单纯认为品性是指人所具有的道德品质和是非感，去除了品性这个词在证据法意义上的倾向的含义。〔8〕

传统含义的"品性"都被描述为一种一般性的趋向或者倾向，当人们具有某种品性时，我们就可以认为他更有可能或者更不可能做某些事，更有人直接地说品性其实"内在地包含着偏见"。品性证据一般不能被采纳来证明某人在具体场合下的行为与其品性一致，但是可以用来攻击和恢复证人的可信性。所以品性和偏见是有区分的，在证明某人在具体场合下的行为时，品性证据是不可采的，但是偏见证据可采但是证明

---

〔3〕 Edward J Imwinkelried, *Evidentiary Foundations*, LexisNexis, 2008, p. 247.

〔4〕 王进喜：《美国〈联邦证据规则〉（2011年重塑版）条解》，中国法制出版社2012年版，第168页。

〔5〕 王进喜：《美国〈联邦证据规则〉（2011年重塑版）条解》，中国法制出版社2012年版，第168页。

〔6〕 *Black's Law Dictionary*, 9th ed., West Group, 2009, p. 636.

〔7〕 ［美］罗纳德·J. 艾伦、理查德·B. 库恩斯、埃莉诺·斯威夫特：《证据法——文本、问题和案例》，张保生等译，高等教育出版社2006年版，第270页。

〔8〕 参见张保生主编：《证据法学》，中国政法大学出版社2009年版，第299页。

力可以降低。另外，在原则上品性和偏见还是有区别的，“品性应该定义为主体所具有的一种长期的性格和普遍的道德本质。它是一种内部特征，通过考察主体的长期言行，能够进行外在的评估。而偏见则是主体的态度问题，在论证中通过他的表现来进行判断”。〔9〕

品性并不内在地包含偏见，但是品性内在涵盖了倾向。倾向是指“以一种特殊方式而行为的趋向性（tendency）或趋向（inlination）”。〔10〕如果从主体意义上来理解“品性”一词则更能清楚地反映出其内含倾向的特征。从主体的角度来看，“品性不仅仅是一种一般性的趋向或者倾向。它是一种与人际关系判断相联系的道德概念，在人际关系中，一个主体根据对其他主体的行为的观察和解释，对另一个主体作出有价值的判断”。〔11〕品性证人在庭外听到某人的言论或看到该人的行为时，他会选出一个对这些言论和行为的最佳解释，也就是对该人品性的最佳假说，然后通过将自身代入相同情景中来感受该人的思考和行为，在这种情况下“我”会怎么做，这么做的原因是什么。会怎么做就是一种倾向，思考为什么要这么做就可以验证解释或假说，从而得出确认解释或假说的真实性。所以“当我们把一个人描述为诚实的或具有一种诚实的品格特征时，我们是指，该人具有诚实行为的倾向……换句话说，包含在从品性到与品性一致的行为之推论中的归纳概括是，人们具有按其品格特征行事的倾向。”〔12〕

（二）具有正誉功能的品性证据

品性内在地包含倾向，证据法意义上的品性至少包括三种明确含义：“一是指某人在其生存的社区环境中所享有的声誉；二是指某人的为人处世的特定方式；三是指某人从前所发生的特定事件，如曾因犯罪行为而被判刑等”。〔13〕所以区分能够证明品性的倾向证据与品性证据的意义并不是很大，品性证据应该包括直接说明证人诚实与否的意见和声望证据，间接说明证人诚实与否的矛盾、不一致陈述、具体行为和成见，以及往往被归入倾向证据的先前定罪记录。

上面列出的所有证据类型都可以用来弹劾证人的可信性，但是不是每一种证据都能用来恢复证人的信誉。《联邦证据规则》608 规定了意见和声望证据可以用来恢复证人的名誉。从性质上来看，意见和声望证据具有两面的属性，它们既可以证明证人不诚实也可以证明证人具有诚实的品性，其他证据就没有正誉的功能，比如先前定罪记录。除了意见和声望证据，还有一种常用的正誉方法是证明先前一致陈述。“证据提出者证明在庭审时作证的证人对相同的事实作过有同一效果的庭前陈述。就像矛盾有弹劾的效果一样，一致性具有恢复的效果。”〔14〕但是先前一致陈述并不能对所有的弹劾

〔9〕［加］道格拉斯·沃尔顿：《品性证据——一种设证法理论》，张中译，中国人民大学出版社 2012 年版，第 47 页。

〔10〕［美］罗纳德·J. 艾伦、理查德·B. 库恩斯、埃莉诺·斯威夫特：《证据法——文本、问题和案例》，张保生等译，高等教育出版社 2006 年版，第 303 页。

〔11〕［加］道格拉斯·沃尔顿：《品性证据——一种设证法理论》，张中译，中国人民大学出版社 2012 年版，第 46 页。

〔12〕［美］罗纳德·J. 艾伦、理查德·B. 库恩斯、埃莉诺·斯威夫特：《证据法——文本、问题和案例》，张保生等译，高等教育出版社 2006 年版，第 303 页。

〔13〕参见张保生主编：《证据法学》，中国政法大学出版社 2009 年版，第 300 页。

〔14〕Edward J. Imwinkelried, *Evidentiary Foundations*, LexisNexis, 2008，第 244 页。

性的证据造成的影响进行恢复，而且还受到时间优先原则的限制。

（三）品性证据正誉的过程

《联邦证据规则》在第四章“相关性及其限制”中对品性证据作出了限制规定。规则401对相关性证据的标准的规定是具有使得对确定诉讼具有重要意义的事实更可能存在或者更不可能存在的任何趋向。因为品性证据内在的包含着倾向，品性证据对证明特定场合下的具体行为与品性一致是具有相关性的，但是规则404一般排除以这个目的而提出的品性证据。品性证据因为其虽然看似相关但是证明力低下，容易产生不公平的损害而被一般禁止，但是品性证据却可以采纳来弹劾和恢复证人的可信性。两者的区别在于目的不同，前者是为了证明具有某种品性的人在案件的特定场合下的行为与其品性一致，后者是为了证明拥有诚实品性的证人的证言是可信的，或不诚实的证人的证言是不可信的。

因为陪审员无法看到证人当时的行为再现，他们所能获得的判断品性的根据几乎都是以证词的形式出现，有时甚至只是“诚实的”一个词而已，所以他们对品性的理解就成了对言辞的理解。根据加达默尔的哲学诠释学理论，任何理解和诠释活动都离不开“前见”的作用，都是“视野融合”的结果。“我们总是被抛入到既定的状况之中，与我们照面的所有存在，以及我们自身，都要从状况中被认出。而且加达默尔将‘状况’称为‘地平’或‘视野’。成见[15]作为视野是使成见变成可能的地平。但是在另一方面，它又限定了成见的各种各样的可能性。成见是历史地形成的有限的地平。我们总是被抛入一定的地平，从而在这一地平上理解所有事物。”[16] 在同一历史时期内，在同一个区域，陪审团与证人具有相同的背景知识，这来源于他们之前的生活经验。当陪审团听到证人是“诚实的”这个描述后，要理解“诚实”这个词，他必须回到自身的经验生活中去判断，他的“前见”也就是他之前的生活经验会告诉他什么行为是诚实的而什么行为是不诚实的，再换位思考，如果“我”在处于证人的情况下“我”会怎么做，“前见”会判断这种倾向是诚实的还是不诚实的。当“前见”判断这种倾向是诚实的后，陪审团紧接着做出第二个推断，既然证人是诚实的，在法庭上证人如实陈述了证言更符合证人诚实品性的特征，而不是说谎。所以证人没有说谎，他在法庭上的陈述是如实的。

三、品性证据正誉的条件

2011年重塑后的《联邦证据规则》608（a）规定：“可以用关于证人诚实与否之品性的声望证言或者关于该品性的意见形式的证言，来攻击和支持证人可信性，但是，只有在证人诚实品性受到攻击后，关于诚实品性的证据才具可采性。”[17] 2011年的修改只是对先前版本的语顺上的调整，并未改变它的含义。先前版本的608（a）更为清楚地列出了用品性证据来恢复证人的名誉需要符合的两个条件：一是证人的名誉受到攻击，二是只有在证人名誉中的诚实与否这一点被攻击时才能用品性证据来恢复

〔15〕引文中的“成见”意同前见。

〔16〕转引自吴宏耀：《诉讼认识论纲——以司法裁判中的事实认定为中心》，北京大学出版社2008年版，第44页。

〔17〕王进喜：《美国〈联邦证据规则〉（2011年重塑版）条解》，中国法制出版社2012年版，第170页。

名誉。[18]

在先前版本的《联邦证据规则》608（a）中列举了证人的诚实品性会受到攻击的方式，即“以意见或名誉证据或者其他方法攻击”。[19] “其他方法”并没有在条文中明确其含义，但是在判例中对“其他证据”的范围也有一些界定，但未完全统一。判例中“其他证据”的范围主要包括矛盾、不一致陈述、具体行为和成见。

（一）正誉的主体

《联邦证据规则》607对弹劾证人的主体作了规定：“任何当事人，包括传唤证人的当事人，都可以攻击证人的可信性。”[20] 根据规则607，双方当事人都可以弹劾同一名证人，即使证人是己方的证人。当事人在交叉询问中弹劾对方证人是为了证明对方证人可信度低，当事人在直接询问时发现己方证人变成敌意证人时，可以申请对证人进行交叉询问来弹劾己方证人。但是允许传唤证人的一方当事人也有权弹劾证人会给证人带来一种潜在的强迫感，就是一旦作出了不利于己方的证言就有可能被己方弹劾，最后不管证人作出有利于哪一方的证言，他都有可能被另一方弹劾。“检察官让证人站在证人席上，他手中握有权力：如果证人为他说话就证明证人的证言是可信的，如果证人和他对着干就摧毁证人的可信性。当事人不应该被允许在不能获得有利的证言的情况下来弹劾自己的证人，并让陪审团推断已经发誓的证词的相反一面是真实的。就算没有被传唤证人的一方当事人威胁，具有不良品性的证人也已足够害怕对方当事人的弹劾。”[21]

对应的，当有利于自己的证人被弹劾时，当事人也可以对证人进行正誉，即使这个证人是对方当事人传唤的证人。所以任何当事人都可以对证人进行正誉。

（二）正誉的对象：证人的诚实性

《联邦证据规则》规定只有在证人诚实品性受到攻击后，关于诚实品性的证据才具可采性。弹劾的目标就是证明证人具有不诚实品性，正誉的目标也就是证明证人拥有诚实的品性。将弹劾和正誉的对象限制得如此狭窄主要是为了避免陪审团把过多的精力放在证明证人的品性上，这样会浪费诉讼时间。另外，如果允许当事人证明证人除诚实品性外的其他品格特征就可能会造成不公正的损害。

规则608先前的版本提到的是“信誉”，然而，2003年的修正案删除了“信誉”并且用“诚实与否的品性”替代。咨询委员会的注释称“信誉”这个词语“过于宽泛”。[22] 品性分为很多种类，有诚实与否的品性，暴虐与平和的品性，正直或虚伪的品性等等。而在对证人是否在法庭上说了真话这一点上说，提出证据证明证人是一个平和的人并没有关联。说真话往往和诚实有关，有时也可以说明一个人是正直的。但是正直并不是正誉所要恢复的对象。正直也是品性重要的种类之一，“正直有三个主要的决定性特征，首先……它是个人品性的一个固有属性。其次，它依赖于人们拥有的道德立场。再次，它要求人们所坚持的道德立场具有某种程度的一致性，尽管在某些

---

〔18〕 参见陈界融：《〈美国联邦证据规则（2004）〉译析》，中国人民大学出版社2005年版，第58页。

〔19〕 参见陈界融：《〈美国联邦证据规则（2004）〉译析》，中国人民大学出版社2005年版，第58页。

〔20〕 王进喜：《美国〈联邦证据规则〉（2011年重塑版）条解》，中国法制出版社2012年版，第167页。

〔21〕 People v. Minsky, 227 N. Y. 94, 124 N. E. 126 (N. Y. 1919).

〔22〕 Edward J Imwinkelried, *Evidentiary Foundations*, LexisNexis, 2008, p. 214.

情况下，作为权益之计，可以有所偏离”。[23] 诚实和正直有所交叉，说了谎话肯定是不诚实的，但不一定是不正直的，比如善意的谎言。正直的外延比诚实更大一些。加拿大学者沃尔顿认为正直具有整体性，整体是人的整个道德立场，正直处理的是如何坚持和遵守这种整体的问题。[24] 而诚实无法涵盖人所有的伦理道德问题。

（三）正誉的时间：证人的诚实品性受到攻击之后

1. 攻击证人品性

如果证人的诚实性没有受到攻击，那么就无从恢复证人的诚实性。在美国诉医疗科学公司[25]一案中，被告伯曼的上诉理由之一是政府方的证人拉塞尔的诚实品性并没有受到攻击，但是法院错误地允许政府提出品性证据来为其恢复名誉。

在上述案中，政府一方先提出了影响证人诚实品性的证据：证人的先前定罪记录和挪用资金的具体行为。根据规则607，政府作为传唤拉塞尔作证的当事人，法律也赋予他弹劾证人的权利，但是政府提出这样的证据性质并不是弹劾，也就是说这些证据并不是以弹劾的目的而提出的，按政府所说的，是为了“显示证人的背景”而提出的。纽约上诉法院认为“法律并不限制当事人向陪审团证明证人具有良好的品性，也不强迫当事人隐藏其证人的不良记录从而反被对方当事人在之后拿来利用。”[26] “政府有权在直接询问中引出可能损害证人可信性的信息，比如有罪的起诉，来防止对方制造误导性的影响，或者防止陪审团认为政府想要向陪审团保密些什么。”[27] 政府在对拉塞尔的直接询问中只是简单地问了证人的“背景”，仅仅显示证人的背景和把证人的诚实性作为案件的争点有很大的不同。上诉法院认为政府并没有想让证人的诚实性成为案件的争议点，“虽然我们认为在这种情况下审判法官对驳回品性证据的使用有自由裁量权，但是他也必须允许在直接询问中显示了证人的问题之后，对方当事人会用更具有攻击性的方式描绘证人，尤其像这里一样，不道德的行为涉及诚实性被提出和否认”。[28] 上诉法院同时认为伯曼在交叉询问中针对证人先前定罪记录的尖锐问题已经构成了对证人诚实性的攻击，尤其裁判的是以欺诈为特征的行为。“当这样的定罪记录以弹劾的目的在交叉询问中被使用时，我们认为恢复诚实性的证据之门已经打开。”[29]

传唤证人的一方当事人有权提出证人的不良记录，这样做的目的不是弹劾，可能是一种诉讼策略：与其让对方当事人提出来攻击证人的品性，不如由己方首先提出来尽量降低之后对方的弹劾对陪审团的影响，这样也可以给陪审团留下一个坦白的印象，也避免了让陪审团认为是在故意隐藏这些信息。“即使在当事人不会弹劾己方证人的司法辖区，先前定罪记录也会以非弹劾的目的在直接询问中被提出。”[30] 界定什么行为

---

〔23〕［加］道格拉斯·沃尔顿：《品性证据——一种设证法理论》，张中译，中国人民大学出版社2012年版，第91页。

〔24〕［加］道格拉斯·沃尔顿：《品性证据——一种设证法理论》，张中译，中国人民大学出版社2012年版，第93页。

〔25〕United States v. Medical Therapy Science, Inc., 583 F. 2d 36 (1978 U. S.).

〔26〕People v. Minsky, 227 N. Y. 94, 124 N. E. 126 (N. Y. 1919).

〔27〕United States v. Rothman, 463 F. 2d 488 (C. A. 2, 1972).

〔28〕United States v. Medical Therapy Science, Inc., 583 F. 2d 36 (1978 U. S.).

〔29〕United States v. Medical Therapy Science, Inc., 583 F. 2d 36 (1978 U. S.).

〔30〕United States v. Medical Therapy Science, Inc., 583 F. 2d 36 (1978 U. S.).

是在攻击证人就是要考察提出这个证据的目的是不是要弹劾证人的诚实性。

2. 可以用品性证据进行补救的攻击

对证人的攻击可以在三个不同的层次上进行，一是偏见或成见，二是先前不一致的陈述，三是犯罪前科和劣迹。[31] 在这些攻击之中，先前不一致陈述一般用证明先前一致陈述的方法来进行正誉。“例如反对方用先前不一致陈述来弹劾证人，许多司法辖区按照时间优先原则确定，只有当一致陈述先于被诉的不一致陈述，证据提出者才可以用先前一致陈述来进行恢复。”[32] 所以可以用品性证据来正誉的攻击方法有意见和声望证据、矛盾、先前定罪记录、具体行为和成见。

（1）意见和声望证据。当事人可以直接证明证人具有不诚实的品性的特征。如果证人具有不诚实的品性特征，这种品性特征就增加了证人说谎的可能性——他很可能在法庭上说谎。

为了弹劾证人，反对方传唤一名或多名品性证人来证明该证人具有不诚实的品性特点。品性证人通过两种方式来证明该证人的品性，一是品性证人描述证人在社区中拥有不诚实的声誉，这种证据又叫声望证据；二是品性证人可以对该证人的诚实性表达自己意见，这种证据就是意见证据。

（2）矛盾。《加利福尼亚证据法典》第 780 条规定当事人可以通过证明“所证述事实之存在与否”来弹劾证人。[33] 这个弹劾技巧通常叫作矛盾法或特定矛盾法。1 号证人证明事实 A，然后对方律师传唤 2 号证人证明事实非 A。2 号证人的证言的弹劾效果不是直接的，是据推论得出的：如果 2 号证人是正确的，1 号证人肯定错误或说谎。[34]

（3）先前定罪记录。先前定罪记录有助于弹劾证人的可信性。一个普遍的推论是，证人有时会违反社会规则，曾被定罪的证人现在也可能在违背另外的规则并且说谎。如果违法行为是包含欺骗或欺诈因素在内的伪证罪或贪污罪这样的犯罪，定罪就有更大的证明价值。[35] 能够对证人的诚实性进行攻击的犯罪要求具有不诚实的要素。所谓不诚实的要素，联邦证据规则的会议报告说：“伪证、教唆伪证、不实陈述、刑事欺诈、贪污挪用、虚假伪装或其他任何具有虚假性质的犯罪，这些犯罪涉及诸如欺骗、不诚实、作假的要素，并且与被告不会如实作证的倾向有关”。[36]

（4）具体行为。对方当事人可以用证人曾经的涉及不诚实因素的行为来弹劾证人，即使这些行为并没有导致证人被定罪。其中的理论很简单：如果证人在过去曾有过不诚实的行为，他很有可能在证人席上撒谎。当然，行为必须具有不诚实的因素，也就是只限于那些反面印证了证人的诚实性的行为。

（5）成见。如果证人具有对某一方当事人的成见，就可能在法庭上夸大不利于那

---

〔31〕 参见［美］乔恩·R. 华尔兹：《刑事证据大全》，何家弘等译，中国人民公安大学出版社 2004 年版，第 161 页。

〔32〕 Edward J Imwinkelried, *Evidentiary Foundations*, LexisNexis, 2008, p. 244.

〔33〕 参见［美］艾伦·辛德、安东尼·巴契诺、大卫·索纳辛：《加州证据法与异议实务》，蔡秋明等译，商周出版 2005 年版，第 146 页。

〔34〕 Edward J Imwinkelried, *Evidentiary Foundations*, LexisNexis, 2008, p. 224.

〔35〕 Edward J Imwinkelried, *Evidentiary Foundations*, LexisNexis, 2008, p. 235.

〔36〕 United States v. Dixon, 547 F. 2d 1079 (C. A. Cal 1976).

方当事人的证言，这与证人的诚实性也是相关的。但是成见并不全部被认为是对证人诚实性的攻击。“某些类型的成见，例如因与当事人存在某种关系而产生的成见，并不必然涉及证人道德品性方面的任何问题，只能表明该证人的证言可能会因为与不诚实之一般倾向无关的原因而无意地出现偏倚。如果这样的话，品性证据在回应这种攻击方面不具有相关性。另一方面，如果通过贿赂证人等行为而寻求证明，那么基于敌意或自私的偏见则可能会具有更大的影响。”[37]

四、品性证据正誉的方法

当事人传唤品性证人来证明对方证人不诚实的品性特征，这就是对证人品性的明示攻击。如果当事人提出证人涉及不诚实因素的具体行为或先前定罪纪录的证据，这就是对证人品性的默示攻击。在这样的案件中，法官会允许当事人通过证明己方证人诚实的品性特征来正誉。在让品性证人说出“该证人具有诚实的品性或声誉”之前，当事人必须要奠定基础（lay the foundation）。“最重要的诉讼规则就是证据的提出者在正式出示证据之前通常要奠定基础。”[38] 基础通常由数个与证据证明力相关的要素组成，当事人按照一定的逻辑顺序通过提问将这些要素展示给法官，法官将判断这些要素从而作出是否采纳这个证据的决定。

“用于证明某人品性的意见或名声证据之证明力，将在一定程度上取决于证人提供的用于证明其人品性的证据，已经形成（意见）或知晓（名声）了多长时间、多么充分及其情境条件。”[39] 在用意见和声望证据来正誉时，品性证人应该具有给出意见和描述声望的基础，通常情况下品性证人应该熟知该证人或与其生活在同一社区，并且持续了很长一段时间。还有值得注意的一点是法官可能会要求正誉一方的当事人提出的用来正誉的证据必须是与对方相同的证据种类，并且两者在大致相同的时间和地点产生。“如果对方使用名誉证据，法官就不会允许证据提出者使用意见证据。法官可以对证据提出者的品性证据作出限制：要与对方的品性证据的时间段和社区大致相同。如果反对方提出证人过去5年在底特律的声誉这样的品性证据，法官可以排除证据提出者提供的证人10年前在拉斯维加斯的声誉这样的品性证据。”[40]

（一）奠定声望证据的基础

信誉证据基础包括以下要素：

1. 品性证人和被弹劾的证人是同一个社区（居民区或社会）的成员。在现代，任何大型的社会团体都可以作为社区。比如，一个教堂里的会众或者一所学校里的学生都可以构成社区，在同一个地点工作的同事也能构成社区。但是也有法院采纳非同一社区成员提供的声望证据。在美国诉奥格罗[41]一案中，品性证人没有和被弹劾的证人住在同一个社区，或和他在同一个地方工作，使他作出确信的声望证据的依据是与和

---

〔37〕［美］罗纳德·J. 艾伦、理查德·B. 库恩斯、埃莉诺·斯威夫特：《证据法——文本、问题和案例》，张保生等译，高等教育出版社2006年版，第396页。

〔38〕 Edward J Imwinkelried, *Evidentiary Foundations*, LexisNexis, 2008, p. 3.

〔39〕［美］罗纳德·J. 艾伦、理查德·B. 库恩斯、埃莉诺·斯威夫特：《证据法——文本、问题和案例》，张保生等译，高等教育出版社2006年版，第275页。

〔40〕 Edward J Imwinkelried, *Evidentiary Foundations*, LexisNexis, 2008, p. 247.

〔41〕 United States v. Augello, 452 F. 2d 1135 (C. A. 2, 1971).

弹劾证人在同一社区的12名成员的关于被弹劾证人声望的会谈。法院采纳了这个品性证人作出的声望证据，上诉法院认为“虽然社区里的声望证据必须由这个社区的成员之一来作证，但在此案中这个要件的缺失没有显示任何明确的损害”。[42]

2. 品性证人定居于此已有相当长的一段时间。长时间的定居意味着品性证人熟悉社区里的情况和信息，弹劾证人在这个社区里的声誉也属于信息之一。同时，长时间的定居也更有机会获知弹劾证人声望的发展变化，虽然声望是一种客观存在，但是决不排除它会发生变化。

3. 被弹劾的证人在这个社区中有着不诚实的声望。“一个人的声誉他所生活的社区认识他的人对他的一般看法。”[43] 一个人的声望并不是由自己决定的，而是由他人决定的，所以具有一定的客观性和稳定性。这个声望同时要被整个社区或者大多数成员所知晓，不能只是被小范围的传播。

4. 品性证人知道被弹劾的证人有不诚实的声望。品性证人可以没有与弹劾证人发生直接的接触而获知他的声望。比如在上述案件中，非同一社区成员的品性证人与和弹劾证人住在同一社区的12名成员进行了会面。与这些成员的会谈中涉及了弹劾证人在社区中的声望和这些成员与之交往时的声望，品性证人因此在法庭上提供了声望证据。[44]

5. 一些司法辖区允许品性证人根据被弹劾的证人的声望来补充，品性证人相信发过誓的证人。[45] 进行正誉的当事人可能会这么问：“考虑到被弹劾证人的声誉，你会相信发过誓的他吗?”品性证人会回答：“我相信。”

（二）奠定意见证据的基础

意见证据基础包括以下要素：

1. 品性证人自己熟悉被弹劾的证人。“对于弹劾证人的诚实品性之意见证言，规则608并没有要求品性证人在做出弹劾证人具有诚实与否的品性之前必须认识弹劾证人很长一段时间或者获知其近期的信息。”[46] 所以时间并不是必须要被证明的对象，相反，证明认识时间的长短有助于使陪审员理解证人之间的熟悉程度。虽然严格上来说熟悉程度并不和认识时间的长短成正比，但我们一般会得出这样的结论。

2. 品性证人足够熟悉被弹劾的证人以至于能对其诚实性形成意见。一方面，一般情况下品性证人会描述自己对该证人的熟知程度。另一方面，品性证人可以说明自己认识该证人有多少年了或者每周见到该证人的次数来证明他们的熟悉程度。

3. 品性证人对该证人诚实与否形成了意见。形成意见必须是基于自己的亲身感受，就是品性证人看到的弹劾证人的所作所为，听到的亲口叙述等等由自身的感官所感知的事实。也就是说意见证据必须基于第一手资料而产生，他人转述等二手资料不能成为形成意见证据的基础。除此之外，有公信力的公文也可以成为品性证人做出意见依

---

〔42〕 United States v. Augello, 452 F. 2d 1135 (C. A. 2, 1971).

〔43〕 ［加］道格拉斯·沃尔顿：《品性证据——一种设证法理论》，张中译，中国人民大学出版社2012年版，第27页。

〔44〕 United States v. Augello, 452 F. 2d 1135 (C. A. 2, 1971).

〔45〕 Edward J. Imwinkelried, *Evidentiary Foundations*, LexisNexis, 2008, p. 215.

〔46〕 United States v. Thomas, 768 F. 2d 611 (1985 U. S.).

据的基础，比如宣告弹劾证人无罪的判决。

4. 品性证人认为该证人是一个不诚实的人。品性证人根据自己的所见所闻做出判断，有可能是目睹了弹劾证人某一具体行为，但是即使是在陈述自身意见的基础的情况下，品性证人也不能够描述该证人这些具体行为。《联邦证据规则》咨询委员会对规则 405 的注释指出，使用意见证言证明品性不应当演变成关于意见所立足的具体行为的诉讼。“具体事例方面的证言，在对普通意见证人涉及品性的直接盘问中一般是不允许的。……在这些情况下，直接盘问中的意见证言一般而言应该与所提供的名声证言相符，即被限制在作为意见之基础的观察和熟识程度的性质与范围之内。”[47]

5. 允许品性证人根据意见证据来表示自己是否会相信该发过誓的证人。[48] 进行正誉的当事人可能会这么问：“根据这个意见，你会相信发过誓的他吗？”品性证人会回答：“我相信。”

结　语

正誉依存于弹劾，如果证人的诚实品性没有被攻击，也就没有理由和必要恢复证人的名誉。正誉体现了一种公平对待证人的精神，也是一种保护证人的方法。弹劾证人是当事人削弱、摧毁对方案件事实的重要武器，弹劾一方往往对证人穷追猛打，尽可能地破坏证人的可信性，极易导致证人对作证的不安、恐惧情绪。正誉不仅是对证人可信性的救济，也能够起到安抚证人情绪的作用。正誉立足于直接言词原则，证人必须出庭接受直接询问和交叉询问。然而，我国的证据规则倾向于对证言内容的考察，而较少涉及证人可信性的判断。另外新修订的《刑事诉讼法》虽然规定了有必要出庭作证的证人应当出庭，但是没有涉及品性证人的问题，对品性作证的证人相对于对案件事实作证的证人而言恐怕不能成为“有必要”出庭的证人。对证人的弹劾和正誉是当事人质证权的重要组成部分，是实现程序正义的需要，也能促进案件事实的发现，从而实现实体正义。

---

〔47〕［美］罗纳德·J. 艾伦、理查德·B. 库恩斯、埃莉诺·斯威夫特：《证据法——文本、问题和案例》，张保生等译，高等教育出版社 2006 年版，第 277 页。

〔48〕 Edward J Imwinkelried, *Evidentiary Foundations*, LexisNexis, 2008, p. 216.

Forensic Metrology: The New Honesty about the Uncertainty of Measurements in Scientific Analysis

Edward Imwinkelried *

"It would be unreasonable to conclude that the subject of scientific testimony must be 'known' to a certainty; arguably, there are no certainties in science." –Justice Blackmun, *Daubert v. Merrell Dow Pharmaceuticals, Inc.* [1]

In many cases, forensic scientists rely on measurements as a basis for their opinions. Toxicologists measure the concentration of the toxic drug found in human bodies to determine whether the level of toxin was high enough to have caused the person's death.[2] Accident reconstruction experts measure the length of skid marks[3] and yaw marks[4] to determine the velocity of a vehicle. In speeding cases, prosecutors rely on radar measurements of the velocity of the vehicle driven by the defendant.[5] Drug analysts measure the weight of seized contraband drugs to determine whether the weight was large enough to violate criminal statutes.[6] Measurements have long been critical in drunk driving prosecutions. Many jurisdictions have statutes that erect a presumption of intoxication when the measured blood alcohol concentration exceeds a prescribed threshold.[7] Moreover, many countries and states have gone farther and adopted *per se* statutes proscribing the operation of a vehicle by a person with a specified blood alcohol concentration.[8] Under these statutes, the prosecution need not show that the operator was impaired or intoxication; proofing that the driver had a certain blood alcohol concentration such as 0.08% is sufficient. In some jurisdictions, the driver is subject to an en-

* Professor at University of California, Davis. Email: ejimwinkelried@ucdavis.edu.

[1] 590 U. S. 579, 590 (1993).

[2] 2 Paul C. Giannelli & Edward J. Imwinkelried, Scientific Evidence § 20.05 [d], at 260 (4th ed. 2007).

[3] Id. at § 27.06 [a].

[4] Id. at § 27.06 [b].

[5] John Jendzurski & Nicholas G. Paulter, Calibration of Speed Enforcement Down–the–Road Radars, 114 Journal of *Research of the National Institute of Standards and Technology*, 137 (2009).

[6] SWGDRUG, *Measurement Uncertainty for Weight Determinations in Seized Drug Analysis* (2010).

[7] 2 Paul C. Giannelli & Edward J. Imwinkelried, *Scientific Evidence* § 22.01, 2007, 4th ed., p. 359.

[8] Id. at § 22.01, at 361–62.

hanced sentence if the blood alcohol concentration exceeds an elevated level such as 0.15%.[9] In all these cases, the testimony about the forensic scientist's measurement is usually the most important evidence in the case.

In the past, forensic scientists testifying about such measurements have often presented the court with a single point value.[10] When the expert does so, there is a distinct possibility that the trier of fact will treat the testimony as an exact value.[11] In the words of Washington State Commissioner Paul Moon: "It has been this court's experience since 1983 that juries it has presided over place heavy emphasis on the numerical value of blood alcohol tests. If an expert testifies that a particular blood alcohol content measurement is value A, without stating a confidence interval, it is this court's opinion that the evidence is being represented as an exact value to the trier of fact."[12]

The problem is that metrology, the science of measurement, tells that there is an unavoidable, inherent element of uncertainty in every measurement.[13] If the expert does not give the trier of fact some sense of that uncertainty, the statement of the single point value - a number[14] — is incomplete[15] and therefore potentially misleading.[16] The trier could place undue trust[17] in the testimony about the numerical value. That mistake might affect the trier's ultimate decision,[18] prompting the trier to either convict an innocent person or exonerate a guilty person.

However, metrology has not only demonstrated the inherent uncertainty of measurements. It has also developed several methods of quantifying a measurement's margin of error or

---

[9] Ted Vosk, *Measurement Uncertainty: Forensic Metrology and Result Interpretation*, Part Two: Legal Analysis, in Understanding DUI Scientific Evidence 255, 2011, p. 323.

[10] Ted Vosk, *Measurement Uncertainty: Forensic Metrology and Result Interpretation*, Part One: Measurement Results and Interpretation, in Understanding DUI Scientific Evidence 159, 2011, p. 220.

[11] State of Washington v. Weimer, #7036A - 09D (Snohomish Cty. Dist. Ct., Wash. Mar. 23, 2010); Ted Vosk, *Measurement Uncertainty: Forensic Metrology and Result Interpretation.* Part Two: Legal Analysis, in Understanding DUI Scientific Evidence 255, 2011, p. 311.

[12] State of Washington v. Weimer, #7036A - 09D (Snohomish Cty. Dist. Ct., Wash. Mar. 23, 2010).

[13] See Raghu Kacker, Klaus - Dieter Sommer & Rudiger Kessel, Evolution of Modern Approaches to Express Uncertainty in Measurement, 44 Metrologia 513 (2007); Jesper Kristiansen & Henning Willads Peterson, An Uncertainty Budget for the Measurement of Ethanol in Blood by Headspace Gas Chromatography, 28 *Journal of Analytical Toxicology* 456 (2004).

[14] Ted Vosk, *Measurement Uncertainty: Forensic Metrology and Result Interpretation*, Part One: Measurement Results and Interpretation, in Understanding DUI Scientific Evidence 159, 190, 225 (2011 ed.).

[15] Id. at 191; Ted Vosk, *Measurement Uncertainty: Forensic Metrology and Result Interpretation*, Part Two: Legal Analysis, in id. at 255, 230.

[16] Id.; State of Washington v. Weimer, #7036A - 09D (Snohomish Ct. Dist. Ct., Wash. Mar. 23, 2010); State of Washington v. Fausto and Ballow, #C076949 and 9Y6231062 (King Cty. Dist. Ct., Wash. Sep. 21, 2010).

[17] Raghu Kacker, Klaus - Dieter Sommer & Rudiger Kessel, "Evolution of Modern Approaches to Express Uncertainty in Measurement", 44 *Metrologia* 513, 518 (2007).

[18] State of Washington v. Fausto and Ballow, #C076949 and 9Y6231062 (King Cty. Dist. Ct., Wash. Sep. 21, 2010).

uncertainty.[19] By using these methods, the testifying expert can put the trier in a much better position to determine the appropriate evidentiary weight of the measurement.[20] As we shall see in Part IV, there are multiple approaches to quantifying the degree of error or uncertainty of a measurement. The expert can draw on these approaches in order to prevent the jury from ascribing inordinate weight to the testimony about the point value.

The purpose of this paper is to document the evolution of the law's treatment of the problem of uncertainty in forensic science and in particular uncertainty in measurements by forensic scientists. Part I of this paper demonstrates that at first, many courts insisted that the expert vouch for his or her opinion as a scientific or medical certainty. Part II points out that later, as the courts began to realize the foolishness of such insistence, they permitted experts to testify without opining that the point value was certainly exact. Part Ⅲ shows that the evolution of the law on this topic continues. Influenced by critiques from several prestigious scientific organizations, a large number of courts now forbid the expert from couching his or her opinion as a certainty. Finally, Part IV will describe an incipient judicial trend to require that in some way, the expert quantity the degree of error or uncertainty in the expert's measurement testimony. This part discusses a number of recent cases as well as important developments in the field of metrology. The paper concludes that this trend holds out the promise for more honest and open cooperation between law and science.

I. THE FIRST STAGE: THE ORIGINAL JUDICIAL INSISTENCE THAT EXPERTS VOUCH FOR THEIR OPINIONS AS SCIENTIFIC OR MEDICAL CERTAINTIES

In 1979, the International Association for Identification (I. A. I.) passed a resolution making it professional misconduct for a member latent print examiner to provide courtroom testimony describing an identification as "possible, probable, or likely" rather than "certain."[21] It became a widespread practice at American trials for the expert's proponent to invite the expert to testify that the expert's opinion was a scientific or medical "certainty". Eventually, many courts elevated the practice to the status of a legal requirement.[22] In some jurisdictions,

---

〔19〕 Raghu Kacker, Klaus – Dieter Sommer & Rudiger Kessel, "Evolution of Modern Approaches to Express Uncertainty in Measurement", 44 *Metrologia* 513 (2007).

〔20〕 Ted Vosk, *Measurement Uncertainty: Forensic Metrology and Result Interpretation.* Part One: Measurement Results and Interpretation, in Understanding DUI Scientific Evidence 159, 218 (2011 ed.).

〔21〕 Nat' l Inst. Standards & Tech., Latent Print Examination and Human Factors: Improving the Practice through a Systems Approach 350 (2012), citing I. A. I. Resolution VII. Identification News 29 (Aug. 1979). See also Note, *Daubert* Rises: The (Re) applicability of the Daubert Factors to the Scope of Forensics Testimony, 96 Minn. L. Rev. 1581, 1597 (2012) ("Most forensic examiners are trained to either testify with absolute certainty or not at all. A firearm – and – toolmark examiner testified that . . . 'if two cartridge cases share the same magazine mark, then one could say with one hundred percent certainty that the two cartridge cases had been cycled through the same magazine'. [A] forensic shoe print analyst 'offered a potential error rate of zero for the method . . . . '").

〔22〕 State v. Holt, 246 N. E. 2d 365 (Ohio 1969); Bert Black, The Supreme Court's View of Science: Has *Daubert* Exorcised the Certainty Demon?, 15 Cardozo *Law Review* 2129 (1994); Gregory Joseph, Less Than "Certain" Medical Testimony, 1979 *Medical Trial Technique Quarterly* 10 (1979); Gregory Joseph, Less Certain Medical Testimony, 14 Trial, Jan. 1978, at 51; Medical Evidence – Sufficiency of Expert's Opinion, 17 *Defense Law Journal* 181 (1968).

it was not merely that less certain testimony was legally insufficient to sustain a judgment in the proponent's favor; rather, if the expert refused to characterize his or her opinion in those terms, the opinion was inadmissible as a matter of law.

That legal requirement reflected an idealized [23] view of the physical world, which was very widespread and shared by many, including judges and attorneys. According to this view, the universe is orderly; and its phenomena are governed by invariable, determinist [24] natural laws. Those laws are not only mechanical and inexorable, but also discoverable by the scientific method. [25] A scientist could learn those natural laws by carefully applying the classic Newtonian method of hypothesis formulation and empirical testing.

Newton had refined the scientific experimental technique in the late 17th and early 18th centuries. [26] The Age of Enlightenment began soon after. [27] The supporters of the Enlightenment were sanguine about the power of the human mind. One of the key events triggering the Enlightenment was a translation of Newton's *Prinicipia* into French with a preface by Voltaire. [28]

"The Age of Reason" promoted the notion that armed with Newton's systematic methodology, the human intellect[29] could identify and master the laws governing natural phenomena. Science appeared to offer a "vision of total control"[30]. Adherents of this view believed that proof of scientific propositions was capable of attaining certainty and that scientific propositions could be conclusively validated. [31] In this simplistic universe, complete truth is attainable. [32] In such a universe, it is justifiable that the courts require that expert witnesses vouch for their opinions as certainties.

II. THE SECOND STAGE: THE COURTS' ABANDONMENT OF THE REQUIREMENT THAT EXPERTS VOUCH FOR THEIR OPINIONS AS CERTAINTIES

As Part I explained, the courts' original insistence that experts vouch for their opinions as certainties reflected a particular, simplified view of the physical world. Eventually, new scien-

---

[23] Brief Amici Curiae of Physicians, Scientists, and Historians of Science in Support of Petitioners at 11, Daubert v. Merrell Dow Pharmaceuticals, Inc. (U. S. No. 92 – 102).

[24] Margaret G. Farrell, Daubert v. Merrell Dow Pharmaceuticals, Inc. : Epistemology and Legal Process, 15 Cardozo *Law Review* 2183, 2194 (1994).

[25] Anthony Z. Roisman, Conflict Resolution in the Courts: The Role of Science, 15 *Cardozo Law Review* 1945, 1950 (1994).

[26] 5 The Encyclopedia of Philosophy 489 (Paul Edwards ed. 1967).

[27] Will Durant, The Story of Philosophy 199 (1961)

[28] 2 The Encyclopedia of Philosophy 519 (Paul Edwards ed. 1967).

[29] Id.

[30] Michael Crichton, Jurassic Park 313 (1990).

[31] Brief Amici Curiae of Physicians, Scientists, and Historians of Science in Support of Petitioners at 8, Daubert v. Merrell Dow Pharmaceuticals, Inc. (U. S. NO. 92 – 102).

[32] Bert Black, "The Supreme Court' View of Science: Has *Daubert* Exorcised the Certainty Demon?", 15 *Cardozo Law Review* 2129, 2129 – 30 (1994).

tific discoveries shattered that view.[33] Those discoveries prompted the scientific community to abandon the assumption that the universe is entirely orderly. Quite to the contrary, they have confronted the reality that the universe is at least partially chaotic and indeterminate. In 1927, Heisenberg discovered "that electrons could not be assigned a position in time and space simultaneously, nor their future predicted by their present". His discovery led to the formulation of the principle of uncertainty. That principle undermined the conception of an "orderly world in which [a] perfect understanding of cause and effect" is possible. [S] cience is now reconciled to the fact that some natural phenomena occur erratically.[34]

Science not only reassessed its macrocosm view of the orderliness of the universe; it also rethought the microcosm of the validation of individual scientific hypotheses. In some instances, experts rely on deductive reasoning. If one assigns certain definitions to "two" and "four", one can reason with inexorable deductive logic that two plus two equals four. However, in investigational science exploring phenomena in the physical world, experts typically resort to another mode of analysis, that is, inductive reasoning. Having observed specific instances of a phenomenon, the scientist formulates a general hypothesis about the phenomenon and then engages in controlled laboratory experimentation or systematic field observation to falsify or validate the hypothesis.[35] If the outcomes of numerous empirical tests of the hypothesis all confirm the hypothesis, we can have increasing confidence in the validity of the hypothesis.[36] However, we cannot regard as the hypothesis as "definitively confirmed because it is always

---

[33] Bert Black, "A Unified Theory of Scientific Evidence", 56 *Fordham L. Rev.* 595, 616 (1988) ("Around the turn of the twentieth century, ... advances in physiology and psychology and the advent of the quantum and relativity theories in physics destroyed simple, mechanistic certainty. Quantum theory tells us that certainty is a physical impossibility, relativity that time is not absolute, and psychology that preconceptions color supposedly objective accounts of the natural world."); Richard G. Halpern, Opening a New Door to Negotiation Strategy, 35 Trial, June 1999, at 22, 24 ("physicist Henri Poincare noticed that the orbits of certain planets did not follow the paths predicted by the application of Newtonian physics. Poincare discovered that for certain astronomical systems, typically those involving interactions among three or more heavenly bodies, even the tiniest imprecisions in the measurement of a starting point would lead to huge variations in the final result - so huge that the measured prediction based on the principles of Newtonian, or linear, physics would be no more accurate than a random position picked out of a hat. He had discovered dynamical instability or chaos").

[34] Edward J. Imwinkelried, "Evidence Law Visits Jurassic Park: The Far-Reaching Implication of the *Daubert* Court's Recognition of the Uncertainty of the Scientific Enterprise", 81 *Iowa Law Review* 55, 60 (1995), citing Bert Black, "The Supreme Court's View of Science: Has *Daubert* Exorcised the Certainty Demon?", 15 *Cardozo Law Review* 2129 (1994), Margaret G. Farrell, Daubert v. Merrell Dow Pharmaceuticals, Inc.: Epistemology and Legal Process, 15 *Cardozo Law Review* 2183 (1994), and Brief Amici Curiae of Physicians, Scientists, and Historians of Science in Support of Petitioners, Daubert v. Merrell Dow Pharmaceuticals, Inc. (U. S. No. 92-102). See also Richard G. Halpern, Opening a New Door to Negotiation Strategy, 35 Trial, June 1999, at 22, 25 ("First stated by physicist Werner Heisenberg in 1927, the Heisenberg uncertainty principle was ... a major revelation .... The principle has three parts: The act of observation changes any observed system irrevocably; precise measurement of any system requires observation; because observation changes the system, accurate measurement is impossible.").

[35] Bert Black, Francisco J. Ayala & Carol Saffran-Brinks, "Science and the Law in the Wake of *Daubert*: A New Search for Scientific Knowledge", 72 *Texas Law Review* 715, 755 (1994).

[36] Brief of the American Medical Association, American Medical Association/Specialty Society Medical Liability Project as Amici Curiae in Support of Respondent at 11, Daubert v. Merrell Dow Pharmaceuticals, Inc. (U. S. No. 92-102).

possible that an empirical test will some day demonstrate the theory to be incorrect"[37]. Another empirical test is always conceivable; and so long as that is true, a theoretical possibility of falsification or disproof remains.[38] In short, "[n]o amount of testing can establish that a scientific theory is 'true' in every conceivable circumstance"[39]. When an expert relies inductive reasoning to investigate the truth of an hypothesis, at most the hypothesis can be accepted contingently[40] or provisionally.[41] Given the imperfect,[42] incomplete[43] state of our knowledge, the investigation can never validate the hypothesis as a certainty.[44] As of July 2010, the International Association for Identification changed its policy and expressly allowed members to testify to qualified, uncertain opinions when such opinions are statistically defensible.[45]

The changed views of the scientific community eventually had an impact on the legal community. The courts gradually began relaxing the requirement that the expert affirm that he or she could testify to their opinion as a scientific or medical certainty. In some jurisdictions, the initial relaxation was selective. For example, although the court might insist that the expert vouch for opinions about diagnosis[46] or causation[47] as a certainty, the courts accepted prognosis[48] opinions lacking that degree of certitude. Prognoses are futuristic predictions, and in these jurisdictions it struck the courts as unrealistic to demand the same definiteness as in opinions about past causation or present diagnosis.[49] Other courts generally abandoned the requirement.[50] These courts reason that the indefiniteness of an opinion couched as a possibility or

---

〔37〕 Id.

〔38〕 Bert Black, Francisco J. Ayala & Carol Saffran – Brinks, "Science and the Law in the Wake of *Daubert*: A New Search for Scientific Knowledge", 72 *Texas Law Review* 715, 764 (1994).

〔39〕 Clifton T. Hutchinson & Danny S. Ashby, Daubert v. Merrell Dow Pharmaceuticals, "Inc.: Redefining the Bases for Admissibility of Expert Scientific Testimony", 15 *Cardozo Law Review* 1875, 1885 (1994).

〔40〕 Bert Black, Francisco J. Ayala & Carol Saffran – Brinks, "Science and the Law in the Wake of *Daubert*: A New Search for Scientific Knowledge", 72 *Texas Law Review* 715, Bruce S. Koukoutchos, "Solomon Meets Galileo (And Isn' t Quite Sure What To Do With Him)", 15 *Cardozo Law Review* 2237, 2253 (1994).

〔41〕 Brief Amici Curiae of Nicolas Bloembergen et al., at 9 n. 8, Daubert v. Merrell Dow Pharmaceuticals, Inc. (U. S. No 92 – 102).

〔42〕 Brief of the Carnegie Commission on Science, Technology, and Government as Amicus Curiae in Supprt of Neither Party at 22, Daubert v. Merrell Dow Phamaceuticals, Inc. (U. S. No. 92 – 102).

〔43〕 Bruce S. Koukoutchos, "Solomon Meets Galileo (And Isn' t Quite Sure What To Do With Him)", 15 *Cardozo Law Review* 2237, 2253 (1994).

〔44〕 Vern R. Walker, "The Siren Songs of Science: Toward a Taxonomy of Scientific Uncertainty for Decisionmakers", 23 *Connecticut Law Review* 567 (1991).

〔45〕 Nat' l Inst. Standards & Tech., Latent Print Examination and Human Factors: Improving the Practice through a Systems Approach 73 (2010), citing I. A. I. Resolution 2010 – 18, dated July 16, 2010.

〔46〕 Gregory Joseph, Less Than Certain Medical Testimony, 14 Trial, Jan. 1978, at 51 – 52.

〔47〕 Id. at 51.

〔48〕 Id. at 51 – 52.

〔49〕 Id. at 52.

〔50〕 United States v. Oaxaca, 569 F. 2d 518, 526 (9th Cir.), cert. denied, 439 U. S. 926 (1978); United States v. Spencer, 439 F. 2d 1047, 1049 (2d Cir. 1971); Burke v. Town of Walpole, 405 F. 2d 66 (1st Cir. 2005); United States v. Glynn, 578 F. Supp. 2d 567 (S. D. N. Y. 2008), cert. denied, 131 S. Ct. 2960, 180 L. Ed. 2d 250 (2011); Huck v. State, 881 So. 2d 1137, 1150 (Fla. Dist. Ct. App. 2004); State v. Boyer, 406 So. 2d 143, 148 (La. 1981).

probability reduces the weight of the testimony[51] and renders the opinion more vulnerable to discretionary exclusion,[52] but they no longer enforce a rigid requirement automatically excluding any opinion that is not phrased as a certainty.

The Supreme Court itself recognized this insight. In *Daubert*, a large number of scientists and scientific organizations submitted amicus curiae briefs.[53] Many of those briefs attempted to educate the members of the Court about the modern understanding of the limitations of the scientific method. Drawing on several of those briefs,[54] Justice Blackmun wrote: "It would be unreasonable to conclude that the subject of scientific testimony must be 'known' to a certainty; arguably there are no certainties in science."[55] That frank recognition by the Court has prompted other courts to be more receptive to uncertain testimony such as statistical evidence. In the final analysis, statistical testimony is overtly uncertain expert testimony.[56] By way of example, the expert concedes that she does not know the true value of a certain parameter of the universe, but she has sampled the universe and computed a statistic that is an estimator of the parameter. Several of the amicus briefs filed in the *Daubert* predicted that if the Court embraced a more realistic view of the limits of the scientific method, the Court's adoption of that view would pave the way for the more liberal admissibility of a particular type of statistical testimony, that is, testimony about the confidence intervals for point estimates.[57] In the past, the courts were often squeamish about explicitly acknowledging the uncertainty of testimony such as scientific evidence.[58] Some feared that doing so would undermine the public's faith in the legal system and their acceptance of the system's outcomes as legitimate.[59] However, once the Supreme Court itself forthrightly conceded the inevitable uncertainty in scientific testimony, the lower courts, both federal and state, were less reluctant to make the same concession. Once they had done so, it became clear that it was wrong – minded for the courts to continue to de-

---

〔51〕 In re Swine Flu Immunization Prods. Liability Litrigation, 533 F. Supp. 567, 578 (D. Colo. 1980).

〔52〕 Fed. R. Evid. 403, 28 U. S. C. A.

〔53〕 Daubert v. Merrell Dow Pharmaceuticals, Inc., 509 U. S. 579, 581 – 82 * (1993) (listing the amicus briefs).

〔54〕 Id. at 590.

〔55〕 Id.

〔56〕 Edward J. Imwinkelried, "Evidence Law Visits Jurassic Park: The Far – Reaching Implication of the *Daubert* Court's Recognition of the Uncertainty of the Scientific Enterprise", 81 *Iowa Law Review* 55, 65 (1995).

〔57〕 Id. at 67 n. 131, citing Brief Amicus Curiae of Professor Alan R. Feinstein in Support of Respondent at 3, 16, Daubert v. Merrell Dow Pharmaceuticals, Inc. (U. S. No. 92 – 102), Brief Amici Curiae of Professors Kenneth Rothman et al. in Support of Petitioners at 7, Daubert v. Merrell Dow Pharmaceuticals, Inc. (U. S. No. 92 – 102), and Brief of the United States as Amicus Curiae Supporting Respondent at 6, Daubert v. Merrell Dow Pharmaceuticals, Inc. (U. S. 92 – 102).

〔58〕 Daniel Shaviro, "Statistical – Probability and the Appearance of Justice", 103 *Harvard Law Review* 530, 534, 538, 547 (1989).

〔59〕 See generally Laurence H. Tribe, "Trial by Mathematics: Precision and Ritual in the Legal Process", 84 *Harvard Law Review* 1329 (1971); Charles Nesson, "The Evidence or the Event? On Judicial Proof and the Acceptability of Verdicts", 98 *Harvard Law Review* 1357 (1985).

mand that experts always vouch for their opinions as certainties. It was generally[60] permissible for the expert to testify that the opinion he or she was asserting amounted to only a probability or possibility.[61]

Ⅲ. THE THIRD STAGE: THE COURTS' PROHIBITION OF OPINIONS STATED AS CERTAINTIES

As Part II explained, the concession of the inevitable uncertainty of investigational science led to the courts' abandonment of the traditional rule that experts had to vouch for their opinions as scientific or medical certainties. However, the logic of the concession leads beyond the rejection of the traditional rule. If investigational science relying on inductive reasoning cannot attain certainty, the courts should not only permit expressly uncertain expert testimony; they also ought to forbid experts from testifying to purportedly certain opinions – such opinions are unwarranted as a matter of logic.

Within the past five years, two reports on forensic science, both coauthored by scientific and legal authorities, drew this conclusion. Both reports attacked overstated expert opinions. In 2009, the National Research Council of the National Academies released *Strengthening Forensic Science in the United States: A Path Forward.*[62] The drafting committee included such members as Judge Harry Edwards of the United States Court of Appeals for the District of Columbia Circuit and Professor Constantine Gatsonsis, the Director of the Center for Statistical Sciences at Brown University as well as two medical examiners and professors of biology, chemistry, engineering, law, and physics. The report was highly critical of claims that "the error rate for fingerprint comparison [is] 'essentially zero'".[63] The report stated flatly that the claim is "not scientifically plausible".[64] The report not only opposed the admission of expert opinions couched as certainties; the report also went to the length of urging that "all results for every forensic science method ... indicate the uncertainty in the measurements that are made."[65] The report formally recommended "the development of quantifiable measures of uncertainty in the conclusions of forensic analyses".[66] The report stated that "as a general matter, laboratory reports ... should identify ... the sources of uncertainty in the ... conclusions

---

[60] There are two caveats. The limited nature of the opinion might make the opinion vulnerable to discretion exclusion under a statute such as Federal Rule of Evidence 403, and without more an opinion worded as a mere possibility is legally insufficient to sustain the proponent's initial burden of production. Fed. R. Civ. P. 56, 28 U. S. C. A. . See Daubert v. Merrell Dow Pharmaceuticals, Inc. , 509 U. S. 579, 595 –96 (1993).

[61] Nat' l Inst. Standards & Tech. , Latent Print Examination and Human Factors: Improving the Practice through a Systems Approach 118 (2012) ["courts do not normally demand absolute certainty from scientists (or any other experts) ... "].

[62] Nat' l Research Council, Strengthening Forensic Science in the United States: A Path Forward (2009).

[63] Id. at 103. See Sandy Zabel, "Fingerprint Evidence", 13 *Journal of Law and Policy* 143, 177 (2005) ("examiners have made assertions that fingerprints are 'infallible', that an identification is '100 percent positive', and that the 'methodological error rate' for parts of the process is zero").

[64] National Research Council, supra note 62, at 142. See also Sandy Zabel, Fingerprint Evidence, 12 *Journal of Law and Policy* 177 (2005) ("no scientific basis").

[65] National Research Council, supra note 62, at 184.

[66] Id. at 190.

along with estimates of their scale. "[67] In particular, the report took the position that any measurement of a subject's blood alcohol concentration "needs to be reported, along with a confidence interval" indicating the uncertainty of the measurement.[68]

The second report was published in 2012. In that year, the National Institute of Standards and Technology's Expert Working Group on Human Factors in Latent Print Analysis published *Latent Print Examination and Human Factors: Improving the Practice through a Systems Approach.*[69] Like the National Research Council committee, the working group had a diverse membership, including fingerprint examiners, computer scientists, cognitive researchers, law professors, and statisticians. Like the National Research Council report, the N. I. S. T. report faults experts' overstated claims that they could certainly attribute an impression to a single person "to the exclusion of all others in the world".[70] The report urged research into the development of a probabilistic model for fingerprint testimony, similar to the model used in DNA cases.[71] The report observed that a "number of courts have curtailed the certainty with which a judgment of individualization of toolmarks may be expressed".[72]

In part inspired by critiques such as these two reports, there is now a definite judicial trend to forbid experts from testifying to purportedly certain opinions. If, as Justice Blackmun declared in *Daubert*,[73] it is impossible to attain certainty in investigational science, an opinion couched as a certainty cannot qualify as reliable "scientific ... knowledge" under Federal Rule of Evidence 702; the available empirical data cannot support that knowledge claim. That message has not been lost on the lower courts. As the N. I. S. T. report pointed out, several courts have already forbidden purportedly certain opinions by toolmark experts.[74] Similarly, in a 2010 opinion,[75] a federal court prohibited a fingerprint examiner from testifying to such an opinion. Furthermore, as we shall see in Part IV, in the same year a number of state courts have

---

[67] Id. at 186.

[68] Id. at 117.

[69] Nat'l Inst. Standards & Tech., Latent Print Examination and Human Factors: Improving the Practice through a Systems Approach (2012).

[70] Id. at 72.

[71] Id. at 85 – 86.

[72] Id. at 120 n. 382, citing United States v. Willock, 696 F. Supp. 2d 536 (D. Md. 2010), cert. denied sub nom. Smith v. United States, 132 S. Ct. 430, 181 L. Ed. 2d 279 (2011); United States v. Taylor, 663 F. Supp. 2d 1170, 1180 (D. N. M. 2009), and Commonwealth v. Pytou Heang, 458 Mass. 827, 942 N. E. 2d 927 (2011).

[73] Daubert v. Merrell Dow Pharmaceuticals, Inc., 509 U. S. 579, 590 (1993).

[74] Note 69, supra.

[75] United States v. Zajac, 748 F. Supp. 2d 1327 (D. Utah 2010). See Paul Giannelli, Fingerprints: Misidentifications, 20 Criminal Justice, Spr. 2005, at 50 (it is "astounding" that experts still sometimes attempt to testify "that there is a 'zero error' rate in fingerprint examination"); Tamara F. Lawson, Can Fingerprints Lie?: Re – weighing Fingerprint Evidence in Criminal Jury Trials, 31 *American Journal of Criminal Law* 1, 7 (2003) (it is "[in] appropriate to allow latent fingerprint expert witnesses to testify regarding their findings which are purported to conclusively link an accused to a crime"); Note, Recognizing and Responding to a Problem with the Admissibility of Fingerprint Evidence Under *Daubert*, 45 Jurimetrics Journal 41, 57 (2004) (the expert should not "testify that a match conclusively ties a defendant to a print found at the crime scene"; the state of the empirical research does not support "an absolutist claim").

ruled that a toxicologist may not describe a single point value for a subject's blood alcohol concentration as a certainty.[76]

IV. THE FOURTH STAGE: THE INCIPIENT JUDICIAL TREND TO INSIST THAT THE EXPERT ACKNOWLEDGE AND PROVIDE A MEANINGFUL QUANTITATIVE MEASURE OF THE UNCERTAINTY OF THE MEASUREMENT

Measures of Error or Uncertainty That the Courts Have Already Approved

This paper began by reviewing the early judicial view that the expert must vouch for his or her opinion as a scientific or medical certainty. Part Ⅲ pointed out that today many courts not only do not mandate such opinions; quite to the contrary, they forbid them. These courts understandably preclude the expert from expressly misleading the trier of fact by claiming that the expert's conclusion is certainly correct. However, other courts have gone farther. Knowing that a single measurement is inherently uncertain and that metrology recognizes several quantitative measures of the margin of error or uncertainty, these courts demand that the expert clarify the probative value of the measurement by proffering such a quantitative measure to accompanying the testimony about the single point value. To date, these judicial demands have taken two forms.

The Safety Margin or Band Gap Approach. The early cases opted for the safety margin or band gap approach.[77] In the 1940s the Swedish Supreme Court declared that in all drunk driving prosecutions, the error or uncertainty of the blood alcohol concentration measurement must be specified.[78] Several American jurisdictions have followed suit. In evaluating the legal sufficiency of the government's evidence to sustain a conviction,[79] courts in these states demand that the inherent margin of error be deducted from the single point value. Suppose, for example, that in a given jurisdiction, the law criminalizes operating a motor vehicle when the driver has a blood alcohol concentration of 0.08% or more. Assume that in the instant case, the measurement testimony is that the intoxilyzer reading indicated that the driver had a concentration of 0.081%. However, suppose further that based on expert testimony, the court concludes that inherent margin of error of the intoxilyzer is plus or minus 0.002%. On that set of assump-

[76] State of Washington v. Fausto and Ballow, Case No. C076949 and 9Y6231062 (King Cty. Dist. Ct., Wash. Sep. 21, 2010); State of Washington v. Weimer, #7036A-09D (Snohomish Cty. Dist. Ct., Wash. Mar. 23, 2010).

[77] Ted Vosk, Measurement Uncertainty: Forensic Metrology and Result Interpretation. Part One: Measurement Results and Interpretation, in Understanding DUI Scientific Evidence 159, 206-07 (2011 ed.). See also State v. Finch, 291 Kan. 665, 244 P. 3d 673 (2011) (despite the margin of error, the trial judge should not have granted the accused's motion for acquittal; however, the testimony about the error margin was a permissible factor for the jury to consider during deliberation); State v. McGinley, 229 N. J. Super. 191, 550 A. 2d 1305 (1988) (since the breathalyzer has a substantial error margin, the blood alcohol measurement must be adjusted), overruled on other grounds, State v. Downie, 117 N. J. 450, 569 A. 2d 242 (1990).

[78] Ted Vosk, Measurement Uncertainty: Forensic Metrology and Result Interpretation, Part One: Measurement Results and Interpretation, in Understanding DUI Scientific Evidence 159, 214 (2011 ed.).

[79] Ted Vosk, Measurement Uncertainty: Forensic Metrology and Result Interpretation, Part Two: Legal Analysis, in id. at 255, 266.

tions, the driver's true concentration could be as low as 0.079% – falling below the 0.08% standard. After considering all the evidence, the court would find the accused not guilty; the government's testimony is legally insufficient to support a finding that the accused's blood alcohol concentration was 0.08% or higher.

For its part, the intermediate appellate court in Hawaii has found that the inherent margin of error for such blood alcohol readings is 0.0165%.[80] The court stressed that as a matter of interpretation, the trigger for the criminal prohibition is an actual blood alcohol concentration, not a mere instrumental reading. The court reasoned that in order to present a legally sufficient case, the government had to account for the margin of error in measurement.[81] The court elaborated:

"In both of the cases at bar, the State has failed to establish a critical fact. The State merely demonstrated that the reading of the breathalyzer machine was 0.10% for Defendant Boehmer and 0.11% for Defendant Gogos. The inherent margin of error could put both defendants' actual blood alcohol level below the level necessary for the presumption to arise. The failure of the prosecution to establish beyond a reasonable doubt that the actual weight of alcohol in defendants' blood was at least 0.10% required the trial judge to ignore [any presumption based on the test result]."[82]

The Nebraska Supreme Court has reached a similar result.[83] The court has stopped short of announcing that the blood alcohol concentration measurement must always be adjusted for a fixed margin of error.[84] The need for an adjustment "is dependent upon the credible evidence in each case".[85] However, the court has reiterated that when the credible evidence establishes "the margin of error", that figure must be "deducted" from the reading to "reduce the test result . . . ."[86]

Unlike the Nebraska and Hawaii courts, the Iowa Supreme Court refused to require that the trial judge deduct the figure representing the inherent margin of error from the single point value for the blood alcohol concentration in determining whether the government has met its burden of going forward.[87] While the Iowa court rejected the argument that the margin of error should be subtracted, the Iowa legislature found the argument persuasive. That legislature then amended its statute to read:

The results of a chemical test may not be used as the basis for a revocation of a person's driver license or nonresident operating privilege if the alcohol or drug concentration indicated by the chemical test minus the established margin of error inherent in the device or method

[80] State v. Boehmer, 1 Haw. App. 44, 613 P.2d 916 (1980).

[81] Id. at 918 – 19.

[82] Id. at 918.

[83] State v. Bjornsen, 201 Neb. 709, 271 N.W.2d 839 (1978).

[84] State v. Babcock, 227 Neb. 649, 419 N.W.2d 527, 530 (1988).

[85] Id. at 530.

[86] Id.

[87] Nugent v. Dept. of Transportation, 390 N.W.2d 125 (Iowa 1986).

used to conduct the chemical test is not equal to or in excess of the level prohibited.[88]

In reporting its results, the Virginia Department of Forensic Science has adopted the same practice.[89]

The confidence interval approach. While Hawaii, Iowa, and Nebraska have used the safety margin approach to compensate for the uncertainty of measurements, Washington has taken another approach. In Washington, the authorities administer two tests to each drunk driving suspect and present testimony about the arithmetic mean or average of the two measurements at trial.[90] Two state courts have ruled that in order to convey a sense of the uncertainty of the measurements to the trier, the prosecution expert must accompany that testimony with an explanation of the confidence interval for the mean.

In March 2010 in *State v. Weimer*,[91] Commissioner Paul Moon stated that testimony about a single point value is misleadingly complete unless it is accompanied by evidence of the confidence interval for the value. The commissioner cited the state version of Federal Rule of Evidence 403 which empowers a trial judge to exclude an item of evidence if, in his or her discretion, the judge believes that the probative dangers attending the evidence substantially outweigh its probative value. As the commissioner explained, one of the recognized dangers under Rule 403 is that the trier of fact will overvalue the item. Drawing on his previous experience presiding over drunk driving trials, the commissioner concluded that if the trier does not have the benefit of a quantified measure of the measurement's uncertainty such as a confidence interval, there is an intolerable risk that the jury will treat the point value as "exact" and attach undue weight to the value. Near the end of his opinion, Commissioner Moon tersely asserted that "to allow the test value into evidence without stating a confidence level violates" Rules 403.

In September of the same year, a three – judge panel handed down its decision in *State v. Fausto and Ballow.*[92] The panel asserted that standing alone, the testimony about the mean measurement paints a "false picture". In the panel's view, without an indication of the uncertainty of the mean, the jury is likely to misinterpret the single point value. The panel bluntly stated that "given the inherent variability of measurement, a statement of a measurement result is incomplete (perhaps even meaningless) without an accompanying statement of the estimated uncertainty of measurement". The panel acknowledged that there are numerous ways of calcu-

---

〔88〕 Iowa C. A. § 321J. 12 (6). See also State v. Schuck, 22 Ohio St. 3d 296, 490 N. E. 2d 596, 598 (1986); State v. Prestier, 7 Ohio Misc. 2d 36, 455 N. E. 2d 24, 38 – 39 (Mun. Ct. 1982).

〔89〕 Ted Vosk, Measurement Uncertainty: Forensic Metrology and Result Interpretation. Part One: Measurement Results and Interpretation, in Understanding DUI Scientific Evidence 159, 209 (2011 ed.).

〔90〕 State of Washington v. Fausto and Ballow, Case No. C076949 and 9Y6231062 (King Cty. Dist. Ct. Sep. 21, 2010); Ted Vosk, Measurement Uncertainty: Forensic Metrology and Result Interpretation. Part Two: Legal Analysis, in Understanding DUI Scientific Evidence 255, 312 (2011 ed.). Taking two measurements enables the analyst to determine whether the subject was in the absorption or elimination phase at the time of the initial test. 2 Paul C. Giannelli & Edward J. Imwinkelried, Scientific Evidence § 22. 04, at 398 – 99 (4th ed. 2007).

〔91〕 State of Washington v. Weimer, #7036A – 09D (Snohomish Cty. Dist. Ct., Wash. Mar. 23, 2010).

〔92〕 Case No. C076949 and 9Y6231062 (King Cty. Dist. Ct. Sep. 21, 2010).

lating uncertainty. Indeed, the court expressly cited the Hawaii and Nebraska decisions adopting the safety net approach requiring testimony about the inherent margin of error. However, in the instant case the panel decided to require the presentation of testimony about a bias – corrected mean [93] and a confidence interval for the mean. On the one hand, the panel did not make a sweeping ruling that the prosecution must always present testimony about the confidence interval. On the other hand, the panel mandated that the government laboratory provide the defense with the confidence interval to enable the defense to present that testimony to the jury:

Absent a confidence interval, a "final" breath – alcohol measurement is only a "best estimate" of a person's breath – alcohol level. Given . . . the discovery rules and E[vidence] R[ule] 702, the State must provide Defendants with a confidence interval for each Defendant's breath – alcohol measurement. Absent this information, a defendant's breath – alcohol measurement will be suppressed.

In all the Washington decisions, the court selected a confidence interval as the most appropriate measure of the point value's uncertainty. Before turning to the future of forensic metrology in the next section, it is important to clarify the notion of a confidence interval. A confidence interval gives the statistician a sense of the dispersion of the values. [94]

· The initial step in computing a confidence interval is identifying the sample statistic to construct the interval around. [95]

· The next step is determining the standard error or deviation for the statistic. In effect, the standard deviation measures the average deviation from the average [96] or mean:

The statistician takes the difference between each value and the mean (the average) and then squares the differences, adds these squares, and divides by N (or N – 1). Squaring the value is critical. If the statistician simply took the differences and added them, the sum would be zero; there would be some values higher than the mean and others lower. The zero would give no insight into the dispersion, squaring the difference yields a positive number. The standard deviation incorporates all the elements of the set in its computation, and its magnitude is directly related to the amount of variation in the data. [97]

· The third step is the choice of a confidence coefficient:

---

[93] In this context, a bias – corrected mean is the mean adjusted for systematic error. Systematic errors are those that consistently result in the under or overestimation of the true value. Ted Vosk, Measurement Uncertainty: Forensic Metrology and Result Interpretation, in *Understanding DUI Scientific Evidence* 159, 168 (2011). Such errors remain constant or vary in a predictable manner. Id. They can be caused by such factors as a calibration mistake or environmental conditions. Id. A researcher can determine the bias by comparing the measurements against a reference standard. Id. at 168 – 69. Having determined the bias, the researchers corrects the point value to that extent. Id. at 169 – 70.

[94] 1 Paul C. Giannelli & Edward J. Imwinkelried, Scientific Evidence § 15. 02

[95] See generally Donald P. Land & Edward J. Imwinkelried, Confidence Intervals: How Much Confidence Should the Courts Have in Testimony About a Sample Statistic?, 44 *Criminal Law Bulletin* 257 (Mar. – Apr. 2008); Edward J. Imwinkelried, Expert Witness: A Look at Intervals, *National Law Journal*, May 19, 2008, at 13.

[96] David H. Kaye & David A. Friedman, Reference Guide on Statistics, in *Reference Manual on Scientific Evidence* 211, 298 (3d ed. 2011).

[97] 1 Paul C. Giannelli & Edward J. Imwinkelried, *Scientific Evidence* § 15. 02 [b], at 770 – 71 (4th ed. 2007).

The coefficient equals one minus the significance level for the test. Thus, suppose the expert wanted a significance level of .05, at which an outcome has a probability of occurring by chance 5% of the time or less. He or she would choose a coefficient of .95. Researchers commonly use one of three coefficients - .68, .95, or .99. [W] hen the values are normally distributed, 68.26% should fall within one standard error of the sample statistic, 95.44% within two standard errors, and 99.73% within three standard errors.[98]

At this point, the statistician is ready to compute the confidence interval. There are numerous formulae for computing the interval. As a generalization, though, the formula incorporates the sample statistic, the sample size, the standard error, and the coefficient.[99] There are various ways of expressing the interval. For instance, the expert might note: 95% CONF (67; 62, 72).

In this notation, 67 is the sample statistic, perhaps a mean. The remaining entries indicate that with 95% confidence, the interval runs from a lower boundary of 62 to an upper boundary of 72. It is important to appreciate both what a confidence interval means and what it does not mean. By way of example, it does not mean that the interval certainly includes the true value of the population parameter or even that there is a certain probability that the interval includes the true value.[100] What then does the interval denote? The interval represents the proportion of similarly constructed intervals that should capture the true value:

It is not so much that we have confidence in the particular interval computed from the initial sample. Rather, we can have a degree of confidence in the formula, method, or process. Suppose, for instance, that the expert employed a .95 confidence coefficient. In the long run on average, 95% of the confidence intervals based on similarly sized, similarly drawn samples from the same population will capture or cover the true value of the population parameter.[101]

If the interval is narrow with a high confidence coefficient, it is justifiable to attach great weight to the interval.[102]

The Future

As we have seen, several American jurisdictions have already mandated the use of quantitative measures of error or uncertainty by forensic experts to ensure that testimony about a point value does not mislead the trier of fact. To date, the courts have approved the use of margins of error and confidence intervals. However, those figures do not exhaust the possibilities. As the Washington court noted in *Fausto*,[103] there are several quantitative measures of error or uncer-

---

[98] Donald P. Land & Edward J. Imwinkelried, "Confidence Intervals: How Much Confidence Should the Courts Have in Testimony About a Sample Statistic?", 44 *Criminal Law Bulletin* 257, 263 (Mar. - Apr. 2008).

[99] Edward J. Imwinkelried, "Expert Witness: A Look at Intervals", *National Law Journal*, May 29, 2008, at 13.

[100] Donald P. Land & Edward J. Imwinkelried, "Confidence Intervals: How Much Confidence Should the Courts Have in Testimony About a Sample Statistic?", 44 *Criminal Law Bulletin* 257, 270 - 71 (Mar. - Apr. 2008).

[101] Id. at 267 - 68.

[102] Id. at 270.

[103] State of Washington v. Fausto and Bellow, Case No. C076949 and 9Y6231062 (King Cty. Dist. Ct., Wash. Sep. 21, 2010).

tainty.

The safety margin and confidence interval approaches illustrate the classical approach.[104] In evaluating the point value, the challenge is identifying and accounting for all the sources of error or uncertainty. There are two types of problems: systematic errors (bias) and random errors.[105] Systematic errors consistently cause the point value to under or overestimate the true value.[106] If an instrument is improperly calibrated, it might underestimate each measurement; or the temperature in a controlled environment could result in consistent overestimations.[107] In contrast, random errors such as operator mistakes occur in an unpredictable fashion.[108] The analyst approaches the two types of error in different manners:

(1) The analyst attempts to identify and eliminate all systematic errors.[109] It is virtually impossible to know whether one has identified all the sources of systematic error.[110] Often the best approach is to compare the measurements in question against measurements with a reference material.[111] Based on that comparison, the analyst can compute a bias - corrected statistic.[112] Otherwise, after making his or her best efforts to remove the sources of bias, the analyst has to assume that all systematic error has been eliminated.[113]

(2) The random error, though, is calculable.[114] The analyst makes a large number of replicate measurements to determine how they vary in an unpredictable manner.[115] Given that set of measurements, the analyst can compute a standard error or deviation[116] (which, in turn, can be employed to calculate a confidence interval).

However, there is no generally accepted method of combining systematic and random errors into an overall error.[117] Thus, under classical approach, the witness would testify to both a

---

[104] Charles Erlich, Rene Dybkaer & Wolfgang Woger, "Evolution of Philosophy and Description of Measurement (Preliminary Rationale for VIM3)", 12 *Accreditation and Quality Assurance* 201 (2007).

[105] Raghu Kacker, Klaus - Dieter Sommer & Rudiger Kessel, Evolution of Modern Approaches to Express Uncertainty in Measurement, 44 Metrologia 513, 515 (2007).

[106] Ted Vosk, "Measurement Uncertainty: Forensic Metrology and Result Interpretation. Part One: Measurement Results and Interpretation", in *Understanding DUI Scientific Evidence* 159, 168 (2011 ed.).

[107] Id.

[108] Id. at 170.

[109] Charles Erlich, Rene Dybkaer & Wolfgang Woger, "Evolution of Philosophy and Description of Measurement (Preliminary Rationale for VIM3)", 12 *Accreditation Quality Assurance* 201, 203 - 05 (2007).

[110] Id. at 206.

[111] Ted Vosk, Measurement Uncertainty: Forensic Metrology and Results Interpretation. Part One: Measurement Results and Interpretation, in *Understanding DUI Scientific Evidence* 159, 168 - 69 (2011 ed.).

[112] Id. at 169 - 70, 185.

[113] Id. at 175, 179.

[114] Charles Erlich, Rene Dybkaer & Wolfgang Woger, "Evolution of Philosophy and Description of Measurement (Preliminary Rationale for VIM3)", 12 *Accreditation and Quality Assurance* 201, 206.

[115] Id. at 207; Ted Vosk, "Measurement Uncertainty: Forensic Metrology and Results Interpretation. Part One: Measurement Results and Interpretation", in *Understanding DUI Scientific Evidence* 159, 170 - 71, 174, 176 (2011 ed.).

[116] Id. at 171.

[117] Id. at 179; Charles Erlich, Rene Dybkaer & Wolfgang Woger, "Evolution of Philosophy and Description of Measurement (Preliminary Rationale for VIMS)", 12 *Accreditation and Quality Assurance* 201, 206 (2007).

bias – corrected statistic (to compensate for systematic error) and a separate confidence interval (reflecting random error).

Yet, modern metrology is moving away from the classical approach.[118] Uncertainty analysis is replacing error analysis.[119] Today one of the foundations for uncertainty analysis is the 1995 *Guide to the Expression of Uncertainty in Measurement* (*GUM*).[120] The International Committee for Weights and Measures (CIPM), the International Bureau of Weights and Measures (BIPM), and several national metrology institutes collaborated to develop the recommendations forming the core of the *GUM* approach.[121] The essence of the approach is combining systematic and random effects[122] to generate a coverage interval that includes the true value of the measurand to a certain probability.[123] Just as the classical approach attempts to identify systematic and random errors, the *GUM* approach considers two types of uncertainty. The two types differ in the manner in which their numerical values are estimated:[124]

(1) Type A uncertainty can be determined by the statistical analysis of a series of replicate measurements or observation.[125] The analyst can use several statistical techniques such as the calculation of a standard deviation to quantify the random effects.[126]

(2) Type B uncertainty is determined "by means other than the statistical analysis of series of observations".[127] The analyst exercises judgment based on such considerations as his or her personal experience with the limits of the measurement technique employed.[128]

Type A evaluations are sometimes called "objective" since they rest on direct analysis of measurement results while Type B evaluations are termed "subjective" because they rely on "researcher judgment and other information".[129] However, it cannot be assumed that Type A

---

〔118〕 Id. at 206; Appendix, *Understanding DUI Scientific Evidence* 459, 514 – 18 (2011 ed.).

〔119〕 Ted Vosk, Measurement Uncertainty: Forensic Metrology and Results Interpretation, Part One: Measurement Results and Interpretation, in *Understanding DUI Scientific Evidence* 159, 180 (2011 ed.).

〔120〕 Raghu Kacker, Klaus – Dieter Sommer & Rudiger Kessel, Evolution of Modern Approaches to Express Uncertainty in Measurement, 44 Metrologia 513, 513 (2007).

〔121〕 Id.

〔122〕 Id. at 520; Charles Erlich, Rene Dydkaer & Wolfgang Woger, Evolution of Philosophy and Description of Measurement (Preliminary Rationale for VIM3), 12 *Accreditation and Quality Assurance* 201, 209, 211 (2007).

〔123〕 Id. at 210 – 12.

〔124〕 Id. at 181.

〔125〕 Id. at 211; Ted Vosk, "Measurement Uncertainty: Forensic Metrology and Result Interpretation. Part One: Measurement Results and Interpretation", in *Understanding DUI Scientific Evidence* 159, 211 (2011 ed.).

〔126〕 Id. at 194.

〔127〕 Id.

〔128〕 Id. at 194 – 95 ("It relies on scientific knowledge, experience, and judgment in the context of all available information to create *a priori* probability density functions based on the degree of belief about effects that are not characterized, at least not completely, through measurement itself. The information relied on may include: [q] uantity values from authoritative publications and handbooks, [q] uantity values from reference material certifications, [c] alibration certificates, [m] anufacturer specifications, [a] ccuracy classifications of a verified measuring instrument, [l] imits deduced through personal experience, [and e] xperience with, or general knowledge of the behavior and property of relevant materials, methods, and instruments.").

〔129〕 Id. at 196.

evaluations are necessarily more reliable; while a Type A evaluation might be based on a small number of measurements, a Type B evaluation could be informed by extensive experience.[130]

In any event, after conducting both evaluations, the analyst treats the Type A and Type B standard uncertainties alike[131] and uses Bayesian techniques[132] to combine[133] the two evaluations. The purpose of the combination is to describe the true state of knowledge about the overall uncertainty of the point value.[134] What is the degree of belief about the accuracy of the point value?[135] The analyst can use an uncertainty budget, listing all the types of Type A and Type B uncertainties and their magnitudes.[136] The end result is a combined standard uncertainty and coverage or credible interval.[137] With a specified level of confidence,[138] this "coverage"[139]

---

[130] Id.

[131] Id. at 198.

[132] Charles Erlich, Rene Dybkaer & Wolfgang Woger, "Evolution of Philosophy and Description of Measurement (Preliminary Rationale for VIM3)", 12 *Accreditation and Quality Assurance* 201, 212 (2007); Ted Vosk, Measurement Uncertainty: Forensic Metrology and Result Interpretation, Part One: Measurement Results and Interpretation, in *Understanding DUI Scientific Evidence* 159, 181 (2011). The theorem, devised by the Reverend Thomas Bayes, permits the combination of probabilities, namely, the use of a new input to revise a prior probability to yield a posterior probability. 1 Paul C. Giannelli & Edward J. Imwinkelried, Scientific Evidence § 15.07 [a], at 840 – 42 (4th ed. 2007), citing Thomas Bayes, An Essay Toward Solving a Problem in the Doctrine of Chances, 53 Phil. Transactions Royal Society 370 (1963).

[133] Ted Vosk, Measurement Uncertainty: Forensic Metrology and Result Interpretation, Part One Measurement Results and Interpretation, in *Understanding DUI Scientific Evidence* 180, 182, 198 (2011 ed.) ("Regardless of whether Type A or Type B analysis is engaged in, both are based on probability distributions, and the uncertainty so determined is quantified as either a variance of standard deviation. When expressed as a standard deviation, each quantified source constitutes a standard uncertainty. 'The combined standard uncertainty of a measurement result ... is taken to represent the estimated standard deviation of the result.'"); Charles Erlich, Rene Dybkaer & Wolkgang Woger, Evolution of Philosophy and Description of Measurement (Preliminary Rationale VIM3), 12 *Accreditation and Quality Assurance* 201, 209, 211 (2011 ed.).

[134] Id. at 212; Raghu Kacker, Klaus – Dieter Sommer & Rudiger Kessel, Evolution of Modern Approaches to Express Uncertainty in Measurement, 44 Metrologia 513, 517 (2007); Ted Vosk, Measurement Uncertainty: Forensic Metrology and Result Interpretation, Part One: Measurement Results and Interpretation, in *Understanding DUI Scientific Evidence* 159, 183, 186 (2011 ed.).

[135] Id. at 181.

[136] Id. at 197; Raghu Kacker, Klaus – Dieter Sommer & Rudiger Kessel, Evolution of Modern Approaches to Express Uncertainty in Measurement, 44 Metrologia 513, 521 (2007); Jesper Kristiansen & Henning Willads Petersen, "An Uncertainty Budget for the Measurement of Ethanol in Blood by Headspace Gas Chromatography", 28 *Journal of Analytical Toxicology* 456 (Sep. 2004).

[137] Charles Erlich, Rene Dybkaer & Wolfgang Woger, "Evolution of Philosophy and Description of Measurement (Preliminary Rationale for VIM3)", 12 *Accreditation and Quality Assurance* 201, 211 (2007); Raghu Kacker, Klaus – Dieter Sommer & Rudiger Kessel, Evolution of Modern Approaches to Express Uncertainty in Measurement, 44 Metrologia 513, 519 (2007).

[138] Ted Vosk, Measurement Uncertainty: Forensic Metrology and Result Interpretation, Part One: Measurement Results and Interpretation, in *Understanding DUI Scientific Evidence* 159, 203 (2011 ed.).

[139] Id.; Charles Erlich, Rene Dybkaer & Wolfgang Woger, "Evolution of Philosophy and Description of Measurement (Preliminary Rationale for VIM3)", 12 *Accreditation and Quality Assurance* 201, 211 – 12 (2007); Ted Vosk, Measurement Uncertainty: Forensic Metrology and Result Interpretation, Part One: Measurement Results and Interpretation, in *Understanding DUI Scientific Evidence* 159, 188, 203 – 04, 224 (2011 ed.).

or "credible"[140] interval includes the true value. Thus, unlike a confidence interval,[141] this coverage interval includes the true value with a stated probability.[142] Together, the best estimate and the coverage interval completely characterize our knowledge of the quantity value sought.[143]

The *GUM* approach is not the only alternative to classical error analysis.[144] For instance, there is a hybrid approach, sometimes called the Conventional Value Hybrid Approach.[145] This is a two – step procedure. First, the analyst calibrates a measurement standard by using a "high – level" measuring system. Second, the analyst performs a second measurement on the calibrated measurement standard by using a "lower – level" procedure. "An example of the CHVA is the use of a standard weight to verify the performance of a balance. The weight is the (calibrated) measurement standard, and the balance is the lower – level measuring instrument used to obtain the measured quantity value .... The knowable measurement error is the difference between the indication and the conventional quantity value of the weight that is placed on the balance."[146] The International Electrotechnical Commission has developed still another approach.[147] The pragmatic IEC approach concentrates on the compatibility of measurement results rather than any true value.[148] The focus is on the question of whether the measurements are sufficiently compatible for operational purposes.[149] For operational purposes, it is often unnecessary to know the true value.[150]

V. CONCLUSION

As Part I noted, at one time many courts subscribed to the silly view that an expert opinion was admissible only if the expert was prepared to vouch that the opinion was certainly true. In a series of steps, the courts have retreated from that view. Initially, as Part II explained, the courts took the small step of ruling that it was permissible for an expert to testify to

---

〔140〕 Raghu Kacher, Klaus – Dieter Sommer & Rudriger Kessel, Evolution of Modern Approaches to Express Unceraint y in Measurement, 44 Metrologia 513, 516 (2007); E – mail communication from Professor David H. Kaye (Nov. 12, 2012).

〔141〕 Ted Vosk, Measurement Uncertainty: Forensic Metrology and Result Interpretation, Part One: Measurement Results and Interpretation, in *Understanding DUI Scientific Evidence* 159, 204 (2011 ed.).

〔142〕 Id.; Charles Erlich, Rene Dybkaer & Wolfgang Woger, "Evolution of Philosophy and Description of Measurement (Preliminary Rationale for VIM3)", 12 *Accreditation and Quality Assurance* 201, 211 – 12 (2007).

〔143〕 Ted Vosk, Measurement Uncertainty: Forensic Metrology and Result Interpretation, Part One: Measurement Results and Interpretation, in *Understanding DUI Scientific Evidence* 159, 186 (2011 ed.).

〔144〕 Jack Wallace, Ten Methods for Calculating the Uncertainty of Measurement, 50 *Science and Justice* 182 (2010). The American Society of Crime Laboratory Directors "does not prescribe a specific formula" or "a specific approach to estimating uncertainty of measurement". Ted Vosk, "Measurement Uncertainty: Forensic Metrology and Result Interpretation. Part One: Measurement Results and Interpretation", in *Understanding DUI Scientific Evidence* 159, 213 (2011 ed.).

〔145〕 Charles Erlich, Rene Dybkaer & Wolfgang Woger, "Evolution of Philosophy and Description of Measurement (Preliminary Rationale for VIM3)", 12 *Accreditation and Quality Assurance* 201, 215 – 17 (2007).

〔146〕 Id. at 216 – 17.

〔147〕 Id. at 213.

〔148〕 Id.

〔149〕 Id.

〔150〕 Id.

an opinion couched as a mere probability or possibility. The courts began to realize that especially in investigational science when experts rely on inductive reasoning, in principle an expert can never validate any hypothesis as a certainty. Of course, as Step III demonstrated, the logic of that realization led farther; the logic dictated that the courts forbid overstated opinions phrased as certainties. Steps IV documents the denouement of this new line of authority: judicial mandates that whenever practical, the expert give the trier of fact a quantitative measure of the error or uncertainty of the measurements underlying his or her opinion.

That denouement represents progress in two important respects. First, this incipient trend promotes honesty in the courtroom. It is axiomatic that measurements are inherently uncertain. As the Washington cases emphasize, it is misleading to present the trier of fact with only a single point value. There is a grave risk that without the benefit of qualifying testimony, the trier will mistakenly treat the point value as exact and ascribe undue weight to the evidence. The antidote—the necessary qualification—is a quantitative measure of the margin of error or uncertainty. Second, this trend should foster a more cooperative relationship between law and science. Scientists often complain that the law forces them to use artificial standards and pressures them to testify in terms that make them uncomfortable. Psychiatrists frequently assert that the law compels them to use definitions of insanity that have no counterpart in their professional discipline.[151] Likewise, experts who know that their measurements are uncertain are ill at ease opining that their opinion is a scientific or medical certainty.[152] Like any other witness, the expert takes an oath to tell "the whole truth"[153]; and an expert with any familiarity with metrology knows that his or her testimony about the single point value is far from "the whole truth". The law should permit and encourage experts to "employ in the courtroom the same level of intellectual rigor that characterizes the practice of an expert in the relevant field"[154]. In *Daubert*, Justice Blackmun acknowledged that "there are important differences between the quest for truth in the courtroom and the quest for truth in the laboratory"[155]. However, there is one point on which judges, attorneys, and lawyer ought to agree: No expert should be permitted to

---

〔151〕 T. L. Clanon, Lois Shawer & Douglas Kurdys, Less Insanity in the Courts, 68 American Bar Association Journal 824, 824 (July 1982) (in court, psychiatrists and psychologists "are asked to testify on issues that have no scientific definitions..."; psychiatrists and psychologists are "dissatis [fied]" because the law relies on "an obsolete concept... of the relationship between mental illness and crime"; the disconnect is so extreme that "[m] any [scrupulous] psychiatrists and psychologists refuse to participate in criminal trials...").

〔152〕 Rod Gullberg, "Professional and Ethical Considerations in Forensic Breath Alcohol Testing Programs", 5 *Journal of the Alcohol Testing Alliance* 22 (2006).

〔153〕 State of Washington v. Fausto and Ballow, No. CO76949 and 9Y6231062 (King. Cty. Dist. Ct., Wash. Sep. 21, 2012); Ted Vosk, Measurement Uncertainty: Forensic Metrology and Result Interpretation, Part Two: Legal Analysis, in *Understanding DUI Scientific Evidence* 255, 312 (2011 ed.).

〔154〕 Kumho Tire Co., Ltd. v. Carmichael, 526 U. S. 137, 152 (1999).

〔155〕 Daubert v. Merrell Dow Pharmaceuticals, Inc., 509 U. S. 579, 596-97 (1993).

mislead the trier of fact.[156] There is an unavoidable uncertainty in every measurement underpinning an expert opinion, and it is intellectually dishonest for the expert to pretend otherwise in court.

[156] In the words of Federal Rule of Evidence 702 (a), misleading testimony does not "help the trier of fact to understand the evidence or to determine a fact in issue ... " Furthermore, Federal Rule 403 recognizes that the risk of "misleading the jury" can justify the exclusion of relevant, otherwise admissible evidence.

刑事证明标准的理解与适用

卞建林* 张 璐**

刑事证明标准不仅是中国的问题，也是一个世界性的问题，不同的国家在不同的时期对刑事证明标准的研究与讨论的角度和重点也有所不同。如在英美法系国家，刑事证明标准问题研究的是如何对“排除合理怀疑”进行解释和运用。而在我国，刑事证明标准的认识论基础与具体表述等问题曾经引发了热烈争论且一直延续至今。近期的立法修改对刑事证明标准进行了一定程度的完善，是我国证据制度改革的重要方面。此时，探讨对刑事证明标准的理解与适用，具有重大的理论与实践意义。

一、证明标准相关概念之辨析

探讨证明标准的概念首先离不开对“证明”的理解。《现代汉语词典》中对“证明”的解释为：“用可靠的材料来表明或断定人或事物的真实性。”〔1〕《布莱克法律词典》中的定义为：“运用证据以确认某一事实是否成立的活动……”〔2〕据此，证明标准就是指按照法律规定认定案件所要达到的程度或标准，故也可称为证明要求或法定证明程度等。在刑事诉讼中，证明标准则是指认定犯罪嫌疑人、被告人犯罪所要达到的程度。〔3〕

刑事证明标准的确立受到诸如历史传统、宗教信仰、哲学思维与政治制度等多种因素的影响。当代刑事诉讼中作出有罪裁判的证明标准主要表述有大陆法系国家的“内心确信”与英美法系国家的“排除合理怀疑”；而我国则在1979年《刑事诉讼法》中确立了“事实清楚，证据确实、充分”的证明标准并沿用至今。一般认为“内心确信”、“排除合理怀疑”均是提出证据证明要使法官达到的一定程度的主观心理状态，属于主观证明标准，二者是从积极与消极两方面作出的相通的表述。而我国的“事实清楚，证据确实、充分”则是提出证据证明所要达到的事实与证据的状况，属于客观标准。对我国刑事证明标准的主要批判在于其规定的客观性，在司法实践中难以掌握与适用。故学者多提出引入西方国家“内心确信”或“排除合理怀疑”的表述以对我国的刑事证明标准进行重塑。

案件是客观存在的，但人们对其的认识是主观的，对案件事实的认定离不开裁判者的主观判断。“无论采用何种证明标准，对于是否符合此一标准之证明程度之判断无

* 卞建林，法学博士，中国政法大学诉讼法学研究院院长，教授、博士生导师。

** 张璐，法学博士，中国政法大学诉讼法学研究院教师。

〔1〕《现代汉语词典》，商务印书馆2012年版，第1663页。

〔2〕“The establishment or refutation of an alleged fact by evidence……”, *Black's Law Dictionary* (8th ed.), Thomson West, p. 1251.

〔3〕参见陈光中主编：《刑事诉讼法》，北京大学出版社、高等教育出版社2013年版，第178页。

法求诸客观的数量化……对证明程度所为之判断，不外为法院主观之符合度判断。"[4]"法官所确定的（承认或确认）那个东西，应当符合于真实。但是为了做到这一点，就必须使法官本人确信案件情况的真实。法官在研究案件情况的时候，要得出对于事件的盖然性或确实性的程度的一种看法；这样法官才能认定这个情况是真实的（法官确信其真实），或是不真实的（法官确信其不真实）或是半信半疑的（法官怀疑）。"[5]"把审判员主观主义与证据的客观主义对立起来，是不正确的，因为证据的客观属性只是借助审判员的主观领会，才可能认识。"[6] 刑事诉讼中的证明活动不仅仅是对过去发生事情的认识过程，更是司法人员的主观判断活动。可以说，刑事证明标准实质上是法律规定的对事实裁判者做出判断或认定时主观认识的要求。

事实上，我国刑事证明标准本身也是带有主观性的。因为尽管"事实清楚，证据确实、充分"是从客观方面设定的证明所要达到的程度，但在司法实践中，"清楚"、"确实"、"充分"都是主观对客观的一种判断。对证明标准既可以从客观方面进行设定，也可以从主观方面进行设定。客观方面设定的证明标准与主观上的相信程度是可以相对应的，如"事实清楚，证据确实、充分"在主观上即可以与"确定无疑"相对应。因此，应当对我国刑事证明标准做出准确的理解，即我国刑事诉讼法所规定的"犯罪事实清楚，证据确实、充分"是主客观相结合的证明标准。首先，案件"事实清楚"，是指认定事实的司法人员对与定罪量刑有关的事实和情节已经认识清楚，是主观状态。其次，"证据确实、充分"是对证据质与量的综合要求，是实现对案件事实认识清楚的客观依据，"确实"要求每个证据都必须是客观真实的，并具有关联性，"充分"要求一切与定罪量刑有关的事实都有证据加以证明，且证据数量足以确定性地认定案件事实。[7]

我国"事实清楚，证据确实、充分"的刑事证明标准是历史的产物与司法经验的总结。我国古代立法就强调定罪要做到"无疑"、"明白"；新民主主义革命时期相关法律规定中就要求在证据"确实"、"充分"的基础上作出裁判，明确达不到"确属真实"证明标准时应按疑罪从无作出处理；新中国成立后的相关文件中继续强调要"取得确凿的证据"、"查明确实与客观事实相符"等。可见，我国刑事证明标准的确立经历了漫长自我发展过程，符合我国语言表达习惯和诉讼文化背景，具有其存在的合理依据。[8] 但是，证明标准应当是明确、具体、可操作的标准，不能仅仅规定客观方面的确定性和真实程度，还需要着眼于司法人员对待证事实可信度的描述。必须承认，"事实清楚，证据确实、充分"确实存在过于偏重客观层面的表述而忽略了裁判者主观方面的确信程度的问题。且这一客观表述方式容易造成对其进行任意解读，反而给司法人员以很大的自由裁量权。正如近年来出现的冤假错案中，明明事实不清、证据不足，

---

〔4〕 蔡敦铭：《刑事证据法论》，五南图书出版公司1997年版，第360、363页。

〔5〕［苏］安·扬·维辛斯基：《苏维埃法律上的诉讼证据理论》，王之相译，法律出版社1957年版，第171页。

〔6〕［苏］安·扬·维辛斯基：《苏维埃法律上的诉讼证据理论》，王之相译，法律出版社1957年版，第253页。

〔7〕 参见陈光中主编：《刑事诉讼法》，北京大学出版社、高等教育出版社2013年版，第179页。

〔8〕 参见陈光中、郑曦："论刑事诉讼中的证据裁判原则——兼谈《刑事诉讼法》修改中的若干问题"，载《法学》2011年第9期。

而法院有罪判决书都有“事实清楚，证据确实、充分”的表述。鉴于上述问题，2012年《刑事诉讼法》修改对证明标准相关规定进行了完善，明确了“证据确实、充分”的必要条件，认可了主观判断在事实认定中的地位，增加了“排除合理怀疑”这一主观方面判断标准的表述作为对“证据确实、充分”的解释，符合证明标准的确立应坚持主客观相结合的原则，一定程度上体现了我国刑事证明标准由客观向主客观相结合的发展动向。

二、新刑诉法与相关司法解释规定之理解

确立证明标准的目的在于指导办案，故证明标准应具有现实的可操作性。我国“事实清楚，证据确实、充分”受到最大的诟病在于其较为模糊而缺乏可操作性，在司法实践中难以把握从而导致适用混乱。为解释此原则标准以便实践中掌握，中国政法大学严端教授总结为：“（1）每一定案的证据都应当查证属实；（2）每一认定的事实、情节都应当有证据加以证明；（3）证据与证据之间、证据与案件事实之间不存在矛盾或者矛盾得以合理排除；（4）有证据得出的结论是唯一的，排除其他可能性”。这四项具体标准一度成为学界共识并得到实务部门的认可与应用。[9] 此后，理论界与实务界在进行理论研究和实践运作时陆续提出了不同观点或新的观点。如在20世纪80年代“严打”运动中，为从重从快地惩罚犯罪，“事实清楚，证据确实、充分”的证明标准被解释为“基本事实清楚，基本证据确实、充分”的“两个基本”论。2006年11月7日，时任最高人民法院院长肖扬在第五次全国刑事审判工作会议上的讲话明确指出：“如果认为犯罪的事实不清、证据不足，特别是影响定罪的关键证据存在疑问，不排除合理怀疑得出唯一结论的，就应当坚决按照事实清楚，证据确实、充分的裁判标准，果断作出证据不足、指控的犯罪不能成立的无罪判决”。为规范司法实践中的证据运用，特别是在办理死刑案件时严格掌握证明标准，2010年最高人民法院、最高人民检察院、公安部、国家安全部、司法部联合制定《关于办理死刑案件审查判断证据若干问题的规定》（以下简称《死刑案件证据规定》），对死刑案件证明标准作了阐释与细化。2012年刑事诉讼法修改以及随后最高人民法院颁布的适用刑事诉讼法的解释，对刑事证明标准作了进一步完善和明确。对此，梳理分析如下：

（一）“证据确实、充分”的条件

《死刑案件证据规定》第5条将“证据确实、充分”细化为五项内容：①定罪量刑的事实都有证据证明；②每一个定案的证据均已经法定程序查证属实；③证据与证据之间、证据与案件事实之间不存在矛盾或者矛盾得以合理排除；④共同犯罪中，被告人的地位、作用均已查清；⑤根据证据认定案件事实的过程符合逻辑和经验规则，由证据得出的结论为唯一结论。2012年《刑事诉讼法》修改，增加第53条第2款规定“证据确实、充分”应当符合以下条件：①定罪量刑的事实都有证据证明；②据以定案的证据均经法定程序查证属实；③综合全案证据，对所认定事实已排除合理怀疑。”总体看来，二者对“证据确实、充分”的规定涵盖了对证据的量与质的要求以及综合审查判断证据的内容。

1. 对证据量的要求。《刑事诉讼法》与《死刑案件证据规定》均规定“定罪量刑

---

〔9〕 参见张建伟：《证据法要义》，北京大学出版社2009年版，第382页。

的事实都有证据证明”。“定罪量刑的事实”是认定被告人是否犯罪、犯何种罪，决定是否对其判处刑罚及判处何种刑罚所依据的事实。《死刑案件证据规定》第5条第3款规定办理死刑案件，对于以下事实的证明必须达到证据确实、充分：①被指控的犯罪事实的发生；②被告人实施了犯罪行为与被告人实施犯罪行为的时间、地点、手段、后果以及其他情节；③影响被告人定罪的身份情况；④被告人有刑事责任能力；⑤被告人的罪过；⑥是否共同犯罪及被告人在共同犯罪中的地位、作用；⑦对被告人从重处罚的事实。而根据最高人民法院《关于适用〈中华人民共和国刑法〉的解释》（以下简称《解释》）第64条规定，认定被告人有罪和对被告人从重处罚，应当适用“证据确实、充分”的标准，而该部分事实则主要包括：①被告人、被害人的身份；②被指控的犯罪是否存在；③被指控的犯罪是否为被告人所实施；④被告人有无刑事责任能力，有无罪过，实施犯罪的动机、目的；⑤实施犯罪的时间、地点、手段、后果以及案件起因等；⑥被告人在共同犯罪中的地位、作用；⑦被告人有无从重处从轻、减轻、免除罚情节；⑧有关附带民事诉讼、涉案财物处理的事实；⑨有关管辖、回避、延期审理等的程序事实；⑩与定罪量刑有关的其他事实。

“定罪量刑的事实都有证据证明”以证明对象为参照标准，确定了证据量的规定性。只有与定罪量刑有关的全部证明对象都有证据加以证明才能达到“证据确实、充分”的标准。根据法律规定，对构成犯罪要件的事实和影响量刑的各种情节都要有经法定程序收集的证据证明，即，为证明被告人犯罪，检察机关需要提出证据证明犯罪事实已经发生、被告人实施了犯罪行为以及犯罪行为的具体情节、被告人的身份与刑事责任能力、被告人的罪过以及共同犯罪中被告人的地位和作用等。如果未能提出相应证据，就是未能达到“有证据证明”的要求，即未达到证明标准。

2. 对证据质的要求。法律要求“据以定案的证据均经过法定程序查证属实”。这是提交庭审的证据转化为定案根据的要求。“经法定程序”是对证据能力的要求，“查证属实”指证据要满足客观性的要求。该条规定确定了证据质的规定性，对证据“确实”提出了具体要求，要求对证据应从其来源、表现形式、收集程序等方面审查其是否具有合法性，排除非法证据；还要审查其是否具有真实性，鉴别虚假证据，既强调了用以定案的证据是查证属实的结果，又强调了对各种证据查证属实的过程。在司法实践中应注意，只有经法定程序查证属实的，才能作为据以定案的证据。而在具体适用中，尤其应注意严格遵守2012年刑事诉讼法增加的关于排除非法证据的相关规定，对证据进行审查并作出相应处理。

3. 对全案证据综合判断。刑事诉讼法要求“综合全案证据，对所认定事实已排除合理怀疑”，就是要求在对每一个证据进行查证属实的基础上对全案证据进行综合审查，对被告人犯罪的事实不存在任何有合理依据的怀疑，即产生内心确信。而《死刑案件证据规定》中的表述为“由证据得出的结论为唯一结论”，即根据证据所得出的事实结论为唯一结论、排除其他可能性，要求检察机关对被告人犯罪事实的证明达到排除其他可能性的程度。理论上“唯一性”的要求比“排除合理怀疑”更为严格，但在法官形成内心确信方面，二者是可以相通的。同时《死刑案件证据规定》第5条第3项还明确要求在综合全案证据中，应做到“证据与证据之间、证据与案件事实之间不存在矛盾或者矛盾得以合理排除”。在司法实践中即是要求对全案证据进行综合审查，审查单个证据内容是否前后一致，如证人证言、被告人供述等；审查证据与证据之间，证据与案件事实之间是否一致。如果存在矛盾或不一致之处，需要通过合理的解释或说明予以排除。如存在不可排除的矛盾，则为未达到证明标准。

对全案证据的综合判断确定了证据的综合运用法则，要求全案证据应相互印证，用以定案的证据之间不能存在矛盾，如有矛盾应得到合理排除，对案件事实的认定应根据经验和逻辑法则得出唯一结论或者排除其他可能性。

（二）对“排除合理怀疑”的理解

将“排除合理怀疑”写入刑事诉讼法作为对“证据确实、充分”证明标准的解释，是对英美证据法理论与制度的借鉴。排除合理怀疑是人类认识活动规律在刑事诉讼中的体现，很好地反映了现代社会的价值选择，能够实现“疑罪从无”的人权保障观念，确保事实认定者作出正确的决定，同时也有利于减少错判的风险。〔10〕但是“排除合理怀疑”自身就是一个较为复杂的问题，需要在借鉴域外经验的基础上，结合我国实际加以理解与运用。

作为其发源地的英美法系国家对“排除合理怀疑”的证明标准在立法中并没有作出明确的解释，有人认为是指每个陪审员必须95%或99%相信被告人有罪，也有人认为是指若没有其他对证据的解释是合理的，则起诉方已经完成了证明被告人有罪的举证责任。〔11〕日本刑事诉讼法中对刑事证明标准没有明确规定，而是通过判例和法理确认了排除合理怀疑的证明标准，但实践中也存在“任何人对真实性都确信无疑”、“高度的盖然性”等表述。一般认为“高度盖然性”标准是双重肯定的评价方法，“无合理怀疑”是排除否定的评价方法，二者是同一判断的表里关系，在达到不允许相反事实可能存在的程度上，二者在程度上无很大差异。〔12〕而在我国，全国人大常委会法制工作委员会刑法室对“排除合理怀疑”的解释是“对于事实的认定，已没有符合常理的、有根据的怀疑，实际上达到确信的程度”。〔13〕因此，在中国法语境下，对“排除合理怀疑”应作如下理解：首先，关键在排除“合理”的怀疑，即具有正当理由而非任意妄想的怀疑。其次，我国传统证据理论一般从逻辑学的角度将“事实清楚，证据确实、充分”的标准解释为“唯一性”、“排他性”，从理论上来说，其标准是高于“排除合理怀疑”的。但根据上述解释，“排除合理怀疑”的实质是要求法官确信指控的犯罪事实的存在，在这一点上，与“唯一性”是相通而可以互换的。因此，在理解和运用“事实清楚，证据确实、充分”标准时，是可以借助“排除合理怀疑”的说法的，因为毕竟只有排除了合理怀疑，才能达到唯一性、排他性。

与此同时，正确理解“排除合理怀疑”还应当对其定位进行明确的认知。对于将“排除合理怀疑”写入刑事诉讼法，立法机关的解释为：“‘证据确实、充分’具有较

〔10〕参见樊崇义、张中：“排除合理怀疑：刑事证明的新标准”，载《检察日报》2012年5月16日，第3版。

〔11〕参见［美］爱伦·豪切斯泰勒·丝黛丽、南希·弗兰克：《美国刑事法院诉讼程序》，陈卫东、徐美君译，中国人民大学出版社2002年版，第72页。

〔12〕参见［日］田口守一：《刑事诉讼法》，刘迪、张凌、穆津译，法律出版社2000年版，第223页。

〔13〕全国人大法制工作委员会刑法室：《关于修改中华人民共和国刑事诉讼法的决定：条文说明、立法理由及相关规定》，北京大学出版社2012年版，第53页。

强的客观性，但司法实践中，这一标准是否达到，还是要通过侦查人员、检察人员、审判人员的主观判断，以达到主客观相统一。只有对案件已经不存在合理的怀疑，形成内心确信，才能认定案件‘证据确实、充分’。这里使用‘排除合理怀疑’这一提法，并不是修改了我国刑事诉讼的证明标准，而是从主观方面的角度进一步明确了‘证据确实、充分’的含义，便于办案人员把握”。[14] 立法机关认识到对案件事实的认定必然包含着裁判者的主观判断，故不能仅从客观的角度界定证明标准，而“排除合理怀疑”作为“证据确实、充分”在人的主观方面要求达到的标准，不仅符合人的认识规律，而且更具可操作性。根据上述解释，“排除合理怀疑”定位是“证据确实、充分”标准的判断依据，是对“证据确实、充分”的解释。“排除合理怀疑”是“证据确实、充分”的必要条件，而非充分条件，将“排除合理怀疑”写入刑事诉讼法，只是为在司法实践中如何判断“证据确实、充分”增加了一个容易掌握的主观性标准，而非对长期坚持的“排他性”、“唯一性”标准的动摇。[15]

此外，还需认识到，《死刑案件证据规定》、2012 年《刑事诉讼法》及相关司法解释虽然对证明标准问题作出了重大完善，但仍遗留有一定问题，有待进一步完善。首先，证明标准的实质是承担证明责任的主体需要将案件事实证明到何种程度才能让法官接受或确认本方所主张的事实作为裁判基础，而侦查、起诉阶段对案件事实的认识不具有终局意义，严格意义上属于查明而非证明活动。但我国刑事诉讼法规定的相关标准均为“案件事实清楚，证据确实、充分”。这一统一标准规定固然有利于查明案件事实真相、保障无罪的人不受刑事追究，但实践中也极易造成冤假错案，且成为相关部门拒绝纠正错误的借口。其次，对被告人承担证明责任的情形以及程序性事实的证明，法律与司法解释尚未明确证明标准。此外，对适用简易程序、刑事和解案件的证明标准也没有相应规定。法律不确立具体标准，将会造成司法证明机制混乱，甚至导致法官自由裁量权滥用。[16]

三、从错案看刑事证明标准的适用

新刑诉法与相关司法解释已开始施行，在司法实践中如何保障刑事证明标准的正确适用成为第一要务。对此可以通过总结刑事错案的反面经验教训获得一定的启示。冤假错案发生的原因众多，如技术发展水平与人类认识能力的局限性、程序或制度的疏漏等等，而错误适用或者不严格适用刑事证明标准亦是其中的重要方面。从杜培武案、佘祥林案、赵作海案到最近的浙江张氏叔侄案、河南李怀亮杀人案，近年来发生的冤假错案似乎有着一套固定的模式，即在案件侦查中采取违法手段获得犯罪嫌疑人供述，在鉴定、辨认、勘验、检查等环节出现错误，而法院审判中发现案件事实不清、证据不足，在定罪问题上存在疑虑，但仍勉强作出有罪判决。因此，正确、严格适用证明标准成为保障无辜、防止错案、维护司法公正的重要环节。

---

〔14〕 全国人大法制工作委员会刑法室：《关于修改中华人民共和国刑事诉讼法的决定：条文说明、立法理由及相关规定》，北京大学出版社 2012 年版，第 53 页。

〔15〕 参见陈光中主编：《〈中华人民共和国刑事诉讼法〉修改条文释义与点评》，人民法院出版社 2012 年版，第 68 页。

〔16〕 参见陈瑞华：“刑事诉讼中的证明标准”，载《苏州大学学报》2013 年第 3 期，第 83 页。

（一）严格遵守有关证据量与证据类型的规定

刑事诉讼法规定的“证据确实、充分”的具体条件包括“定罪量刑的事实都有证据证明”，这是对证据量的要求。在司法实践中正确适用刑事证明标准，首先要确保涉及定罪量刑的证明对象达到证明标准的要求。证明对象及相关证据范围的确定应以实体法的相关规定为根据——如《刑法》关于某类犯罪构成要件的规定，同时还应根据具体个案的特殊情况。如果没有相关证据加以证明，则未达到证明标准，不能作出被告人有罪的判定。更重要的是，对某些案件，尤其是死刑案件，仅有被告人供述而无其他证据的，不得作出有罪认定，这是对证据类型的要求。《刑事诉讼法》第53条第1款规定：“对一切案件的判处都要重证据，重调查研究，不轻信口供。只有被告人口供，没有其他证据的，不能认定被告人有罪和处以刑罚；没有被告人供述，证据确实、充分的，可以认定被告人有罪和处以刑罚。”《死刑案件证据规定》第34条规定：“根据被告人的供述、指认提取到了隐蔽性很强的物证、书证，且与其他证明犯罪事实发生的证据互相印证，并排除串供、逼供、诱供等可能性的，可以认定有罪。”最高人民法院《关于适用〈中华人民共和国刑事诉讼法〉的解释》第106条亦作出了相同规定。

错案的出现，有时往往并非因为没有证据，而是证据量的要求未得到满足。浙江张氏叔侄案中，被告人张辉、张高平被指控强奸并杀害同乡少女王东，定案的主要证据是被告人的有罪供述及同室关押的犯人袁连芳关于被告人张辉被关押期间告知其不小心将受害人掐死的证言，而尸体上找不到被告人的精斑、被告人供述称在驾驶座上实施强奸而未找到相关物证，而本案唯一的物证——侦查机关提取的被害人指甲中的DNA则是被害人与另一名男性DNA混合而并不能作为判定被告人有罪的证据。[17]法院仅依据被告人供述及所谓的“证人证言”而作出有罪判定，明显有悖于法律规定，导致了错案发生。

因此，司法实践中，应严格遵守法定证明标准有关证据量与证据类型的规定，尤其是死刑案件中，必须坚持只有被告人口供而没有其他证据的不得认定被告人有罪和判处刑罚。

（二）综合全案证据，排除合理怀疑

在最近引发热议的“死刑保证书”案件即河南李怀亮杀人案中，被告人共作出10次供述，其中第3到第8次作有罪供述，其后翻供，但一审庭审中法庭并未采纳其翻供供述，而作出了有罪判决。但本案最终因供述不稳定，有罪供述前后矛盾等原因作出事实不清，证据不足而宣判无罪的判决。[18]《死刑案件证据规定》第22条规定：“对被告人供述和辩解的审查，应当结合控辩双方提供的所有证据以及被告人本人的全部供述和辩解进行。被告人庭前供述一致，庭审中翻供，但被告人不能合理说明翻供理由或者其辩解与全案证据相矛盾，而庭前供述与其他证据能够相互印证的，可以采信被告人庭前供述。被告人庭前供述和辩解出现反复，但庭审中供认的，且庭审中的供述与其他证据能够印证的，可以采信庭审中的供述；被告人庭前供述和辩解出现反

〔17〕有关张氏叔侄案的资料来源：《南方周末》，http：//www.infzm.com/content/89144，最后访问时间：2013年6月20日。

〔18〕有关李怀亮案件的资料来源：搜狐新闻，http：news.sohu.com/20130503/n374690436.shtml，最后访问时间：2013年6月20日。

复，庭审中不供认，且无其他证据与庭前供述印证的，不能采信庭前供述。”刑事诉讼法中要求认定案件事实，应综合全案证据，排除合理怀疑。《死刑案件证据规定》要求证据与证据之间、证据与案件事实之间不存在矛盾或者矛盾得以合理排除，根据证据认定案件事实的过程符合逻辑和经验规则，由证据得出的结论为唯一结论。据此，对案件事实的认定，应综合全案证据，排除证据与证据之间、证据与案件事实之间的矛盾，最终排除合理怀疑而获得唯一结论。

刑事错案的发生往往存在证据相互矛盾、合理疑点未能引起重视的问题。在张氏叔侄案中，被告人张高平、张辉的供述在关键作案细节上严重地不吻合，如前往作案现场的行车路线说法不一、作案现场的车辆行驶停放情况不一：如张辉供称到达现场是先将卡车掉头，然后实施了强奸行为，张高平却说是在作案后将车掉头再抛尸；抛尸的细节叙述也不一致：侄子说是叔叔从车上递下来的尸体，他一人扛着扔进了水沟；叔叔却说，是侄子抬上身，他抬脚，一起将尸体抛至水沟。同案被告人的有罪供述之间存在矛盾未能排除，显然未能达到“证据确实、充分”的证明标准。而对被害人指甲中的DNA为被害人与另一男性混合的鉴定结论这一关键疑点也被忽视，浙江省高级人民法院的判决认为：“本案中的DNA鉴定结论与本案犯罪事实并无关联，不能作为排除两被告人作案的反证。”事实上，根据该证据完全可能得出犯罪为第三人所为之结论，属于不能排除合理怀疑，根据现行刑事诉讼法的规定，则无法达到法定证明标准，不得作出有罪判决。

（三）坚持疑罪从无原则，摒弃“留有余地”的裁判方式

疑案是指在刑事诉讼中因事实不清、证据不足，没有达到证明标准而难以决断的案件。司法实践中，由于各种主客观条件的限制，疑案的出现是不可避免的。对疑案的处理，我国古代实行的是“疑罪从有”的方法，如唐律中就有疑罪以赎论的规定。我国自1996年《刑事诉讼法》确立疑罪从无原则，现行《刑事诉讼法》第195条第3项规定，“证据不足，不能认定被告人有罪的，应当作出证据不足、指控的犯罪不能成立的无罪判决。”最高人民法院《关于适用〈中华人民共和国刑事诉讼法〉的解释》第241条进一步明确，“证据不足，不能认定被告人有罪的，应当以证据不足、指控的犯罪不能成立，判决宣告被告人无罪”；“案件部分事实清楚，证据确实、充分的，应当作出有罪或者无罪的判决；对事实不清、证据不足部分，不予认定”。但司法实践中，由于有罪推定观念的影响，事实上实行的是一套“疑罪从有”的做法。近年来出现的典型错案的共同特征就包括，法院对被告人是否犯罪的问题存在疑问，但仍选择疑罪从有，对事实不清、证据不足，未达到法定证明标准的案件作出有罪判决，但在同时，为避免错杀而在量刑上选择从轻，即对依法应判处死刑立即执行的改判死缓或无期徒刑，即“疑罪从轻”。这就是我国司法裁判中特有的“疑罪从轻”、“留有余地”的判决方式。如浙江张氏叔侄案，2004年2月杭州市中级人民法院一审分别判处无期徒刑与死刑；10月，浙江省高级人民法院二审改判张辉死缓，张高平有期徒刑15年，判决书中对此一笔带过：“鉴于本案的具体情况，张辉尚不属必须立即执行死刑的罪犯”。

对“留有余地”的判决方式，2007年6月，时任最高人民法院院长肖扬在广东法院考察调研，谈及死刑案件审判时曾对此作出说明：“必须始终贯彻证据裁判这条线。

要做到事实清楚，证据确实、充分。如果定罪的关键证据存在疑问，不能排除合理怀疑的，应当作出证据不足、指控的犯罪不能成立的无罪判决。如果定罪证据达到了确实、充分的裁判标准，但影响量刑的事实、证据存在疑问的，则应当留有余地，尤其是死刑案件，必须做到杀者不疑，疑者不杀”。[19] 在当时语境下，“留有余地”仅适用于定罪证据确实、充分，但影响量刑的事实、证据存在疑问的情况，其主要目的在于要求法院在判处死刑立即执行时应采取极为慎重的态度。但到司法实践中，“留有余地”的判决方式却演化为对某些存在疑点、证据不足的案件但却是严重危害社会治安的重大案件作出妥协性判决。刑事诉讼中不可避免会出现定罪证据不足，而对无罪又难以下定论的情况，此时就形成了“疑案”。对疑案的处理存在判决有罪可能冤枉无辜，判决无罪又有可能放纵罪犯的两难困境。此时，选择“疑罪从轻”、“留有余地”的判决，实质上是有罪推定思想作祟，违反了无罪推定原则，不仅无法获得所预想的公正与和谐共赢的局面，反而造成社会舆论的质疑，被害人、被告人同时不服判决而进行申诉、上访，对法院形象与司法权威造成恶劣影响。

因此，刑事诉讼中应当严格依据“事实清楚，证据确实、充分”的定罪量刑标准，坚持疑罪从无原则，本着宁纵勿枉的精神，对定罪事实不清、证据不足而未达到法定证明标准的案件依法作出无罪判决，而不得疑罪从有，搞“留有余地”的判决。在定罪证据确实、充分，而影响量刑的证据存在疑点，对被告人是否适用死刑有争议的，法院应采取极为慎重的态度，作出有利于被告人的解释，尽量不适用死刑，以避免误判，防止死刑滥用。

---

〔19〕 参见“死刑案件必须做到杀者不疑，疑者不杀”，载《人民日报》2007年6月9日，第4版。

论刑事证明标准的经济学分析

张 卿 *

一、问题的提出：我国传统法学对证明标准理论分析的不足

一般认为，证明标准是指法律规定的完成证明任务及认定案件事实所需证明应达到的程度或标准。[1]它既是衡量当事人举证达到何种程度才能满足举证要求的标准，又是法官据以认定案件事实以及评判法官对事实认定是否妥当的尺度。[2]英美法系国家对刑事诉讼和民事诉讼采用不同的证明标准。[3]对刑事诉讼通常采用“排除合理怀疑”标准（英文为“beyond a reasonable doubt”），一般指刑事诉讼公诉人的证明必须达到使一个理性的人对该案被告人有罪这一认定不再有合理怀疑的程度。[4]而在民事诉讼上通常采用“盖然性占优”标准（英文为“preponderance of the evidence”），指民事诉讼的证明应达到使事实判定者认为该被证明的有争议事实存在的可能性超过不存在可能性的程度，[5]或使其认为该被证明的有争议事实存在的可能性超过50%。“盖然性占优”标准也意味着：如双方提供的不同证据及其证明使得原告对事实的主张更为可信，则采信原告的事实主张；反之，则采信被告的事实主张。[6]因此，“盖然性占优”标准所代表的确定性一般低于“排除合理怀疑”标准。

从我国的情况看，法学理论界和实务界在此前相当长的一段时期里采纳证明标准的“客观真实说”。[7]这种观点认为，无论是民事诉讼还是刑事诉讼，都要求查明案件客观真实。当事人对案件事实的证明和法院认定案件事实时，要达到“事实清楚，证据确实充分”的程度。[8]这种证明标准要求司法人员主观认识所认定的定罪事实必须

---

* 张卿，中国政法大学法与经济学研究中心副教授。本文系中国政法大学法和经济青年创新团队资助项目的阶段性成果。

〔1〕 参见张保生主编：《证据法学》，中国政法大学出版社2009年版，第317页；刘金友主编：《证明标准研究》，中国政法大学出版社2009年版，第6页；江伟主编：《证据法学》，法律出版社1999年版，第121页；樊崇义等：《刑事证据法原理与适用》，中国人民公安大学出版社2003年版，第215页；姜明安主编：《行政法与行政诉讼法》，北京大学出版社2007年版，第536页。

〔2〕 姜明安：《行政法与行政诉讼法》，北京大学出版社、高等教育出版社2011年版，第536页。

〔3〕 Kevin Clermont & Emily Sherwin, “A Comparative View of Standards of Proof”, *American Journal of Comparative Law*, Vol. 50 (2002), p. 251.

〔4〕 参见维基百科 Wikipedia 对“排除合理怀疑”标准的定义，http://en.wikipedia.org/wiki/Beyond_a_reasonable_doubt，访问时间：2012年2月16日。

〔5〕 Steven Grifis, *Law Dictionary*, New York: Barron's Educational Series Inc., 1975, p. 159.

〔6〕 Robert Cooter & Thomas Ulen, *Law & Economics*, New Jersey: Pearson Education, Inc., 2008, p. 67.

〔7〕 张卫平：“证明标准建构的乌托邦”，载《法学研究》2003年第4期；沈德咏、江显和：“对我国刑事证明标准的再探讨”，载《人民司法》2009年第5期。

〔8〕 张卫平：“证明标准建构的乌托邦”，载《法学研究》2003年第4期。

完全符合案件的客观事实，达到绝对的、确定无疑的程度。[9]此外，这一证明标准也被长期适用于民事和行政诉讼，因此也称为“一元化”证明标准。[10]但目前，“客观真实说”的必要性和可行性已遭到各方的质疑。[11]作为一种特殊的社会认识活动，诉讼认识受到人的有限认知能力、案件已发生无法亲眼目睹、诉讼程序和伦理要求等主客观诸多因素的制约，从而导致了运用证据认定案件事实在大多数情况下只能达到相对真实，而不可能是绝对真实。[12]

或许是认识到“客观真实说”的不足，我国法律和司法解释现已经在一定程度上采用“排除合理怀疑”和“盖然性占优”标准”。我国最新修改颁布的《中华人民共和国刑事诉讼法》第53条规定：[13]“证据确实、充分，应当符合以下条件：（一）定罪量刑的事实都有证据证明；（二）据以定案的证据均经法定程序查证属实；（三）综合全案证据，对所认定事实已排除合理怀疑。”而在民事诉讼中，《最高人民法院关于民事诉讼证据的若干规定》第73条规定：“双方当事人对同一事实分别举出相反的证据，但都没有足够的依据否定对方证据的，人民法院应当结合案件情况，判断一方提供证据的证明力是否明显大于另一方提供证据的证明力，并对证明力较大的证据予以确认。”[14]

尽管我国新《刑事诉讼法》作出了上述规定，但我国有的学者仍然反对使用“排除合理怀疑”标准。[15]更值得注意的是，我国法学界对刑事证明标准如何设定仍存在较大争论。[16]有较多学者认为：刑事诉讼也坚持证明标准的多元化，应从同一案件的不同诉讼阶段、不同证明对象等方面进行区分。[17]但我国立法至今仍规定在移送起诉，提起公诉，进行审判这三个不同诉讼阶段使用同一的证明标准，[18] 且支持证明标准多元化的学者尚未对其观点给出进一步的有说服力的分析。还有许多学者提出：刑事证明标准应当根据不同案件所涉利益的重要程度加以设置；在刑事诉讼中，作为可能剥夺

---

〔9〕 沈德咏、江显和：“对我国刑事证明标准的再探讨”，载《人民司法》2009年第5期。

〔10〕 刘金友主编：《证明标准研究》，中国政法大学出版社2009年版，第262～267页。

〔11〕 批评文章可参见如樊崇义：“客观真实管见——兼论刑事诉讼证明标准”，载《中国法学》2000年第1期；裴苍龄：“论证明标准”，载《法学研究》2010年第3期。沈德咏、江显和：“对我国刑事证明标准的再探讨” 载《人民司法》2009年第5期。

〔12〕 沈德咏、江显和：“对我国刑事证明标准的再探讨”，载《人民司法》2009年第5期。

〔13〕 2012年3月14日第十一届全国人民代表大会第五次会议通过《关于修改〈中华人民共和国刑事诉讼法〉的决定》。

〔14〕 《最高人民法院关于民事诉讼证据的若干规定》已于2001年12月6日由最高人民法院审判委员会第1201次会议通过，自2002年4月1日起施行。

〔15〕 李玉华：“刑事证明标准的新发展——评刑事诉讼法修正案（草案）第52条及相关规定”，载《中国人民公安大学学报（社会科学版）》2012年第1期。

〔16〕 关于如何理解刑诉法对证明标准的最新修改，可参阅《检察日报》对陈光中先生的采访。具体可见谢文英：“‘排除合理怀疑’包括‘唯一性、排他性’”，载《检察日报》2012年5月14日。

〔17〕 参见熊秋红：“对刑事证明标准的思考——以刑事证明中的可能性和确定性为视角”，载《法商研究》2003年第1期；李学宽、汪海燕、张晓玲：“论刑事证明标准及其层次性”，载《中国法学》2001年第5期，第125～130页；聂立泽、苑民丽：“主客观相统一原则与刑事证明标准的层次性研究”，载《法学评论》2011年第2期，第41～42页；陈光中：“构建层次性的刑事证明标准”，载《诉讼法论丛》2002年第7卷。

〔18〕 《中华人民共和国刑事诉讼法》第160条、第172条、第195条。

被告人生命权的死刑案件，理应享有比一般刑事案件更高的证明标准。[19]但也有较多的学者对此持不同意见。[20]此外，我国学者还对是否将审判程序分为定罪和量刑两个阶段，以及定罪阶段的证明标准是否应低于量刑阶段的证明标准上存在争议。[21]本文认为：上述学者之所以仍存在较多争议且一方往往无法说服争议另一方，其根本原因在于这些观点和论证只是简单地提出了可能影响刑事证明标准高低的因素，但对为何以这些因素作为决定证明标准高低的尺度，我国学界尚没有进一步的解释和系统分析。从整体来看，我国既有的相关文献尚未较为全面、系统和准确地分析影响刑事证明标准设定的因素，因而在解释力和说服力上存在不足。

相比较，本文的以下分析将说明：法经济学的理论框架不仅能较为全面和科学地揭示影响证明标准高低程度的因素，而且能使用统一的评价目标和分析框架来系统地解释和论证刑事诉讼中的证明标准设定的相关问题，因而在分析上述争议问题时具有较强的说明力。本文的第二部分提出：从法律经济学的角度出发，在可获的信息量确定不变的条件下，刑事证明标准的设定应考虑如何平衡第一类错误成本和第二类错误成本，前者是指对无辜者错误定罪的成本，后者是指对有罪者错误释放的成本。在本文中，错误成本是指采用某一证明标准后仍存在的司法决定的错误所带来的社会成本。现实中法官往往没有充分的正确信息，这会导致他们在适用实体法时的错误。当正确信息进一步增加，法官的错误决定就会减少。本文所讨论的刑事证明标准实际上是对法官或陪审团认定被告人有罪所依据正确信息量的最低要求。在一个给定的刑事案子中，法官或陪审团必须根据既有证据所展示的确定信息量和法定的证明标准，作出被告人是否有罪的决定。由于刑事案件的公诉人制度和“疑罪从无”的原则要求，在可获的信息量确定不变的条件下，证明标准的提高会导致第一类成本的减少同时带来第二类错误成本的提高。因而证明标准的设定应充分考虑如何平衡第一类错误成本和第二类错误成本。本文的第三部分进一步论证：在可获信息量能够发生变化的情况下，刑事证明标准的设定应使该标准使用时仍存在的错误成本与为达到该证明标准而付出的行政成本之和最小化。在本文中，行政成本指参与该案件审理的所有诉讼参与人为了遵守某一证明标准而付出的所有的人力、物力和时间上的成本。从动态的角度来看，一个案件中证明标准的提高往往会促使该案件或以后类似案件的公诉人向法官提供更多的真实信息，这将会减少法院判决带来的第一类和第二类错误成本；但为了满足提高后证明标准的要求，公诉人和其他诉讼参与人往往必须付出更高的行政成本来取得证据。在此基础上，本文的第四部分讨论了在刑事诉讼的不同阶段是否应采用不同的

---

〔19〕 何家弘：“刑事证据的采纳标准和采信标准”，载《人民检察》2001年第10期，第12页；参见赵秉志、邱兴隆主编：《死刑正当程序之探讨》，中国人民公安大学出版社2004年版，第661页；

〔20〕 如陈虎：“提高死刑案件证明标准一个似是而非的命题”，载《中外法学》2010年第3期，第459页；杨宇冠：“论死刑案件证明标准之完善——新刑事诉讼法实施问题思考”，载《清华法学》2012年第3期，第68页。

〔21〕 支持定罪阶段的证明标准应低于量刑阶段的证明标准的观点可见，陈卫东、李训虎：“分而治之：一种完善死刑案件证明标准的思路”，载《人民检察》2007年第8期；陈卫东：“刑事诉讼法证据制度修改的宏观思考”，载《法学家》2007年第4期；反对意见如樊崇义：“量刑程序与证据”，载《南都学坛》2009年第4期；陈瑞华：“论量刑程序的独立性——一种以量刑控制为中心的程序理论”，载《中国法学》2009年第1期，第178页；陈虎：“提高死刑案件证明标准一个似是而非的命题”，载《中外法学》2010年第3期，第456页。

证明标准、死刑案件的证明标准是否应高于一般的刑事案件、死刑案件是否应将审判程序分为定罪阶段和量刑阶段并在后一阶段采用更高的证明标准这三个争议问题。本文的第五部分则分析适用较高证明标准的具体方法。最后，在第六部分，本文提出了结论。

二、可获信息量确定不变时设定证明标准需平衡两类错误成本

从经济学角度来看，在可获正确信息量确定不变时，证明标准的设定应平衡下列两类错误成本：[22]第一类错误成本通常是指司法决定让本不应该承担责任或损失的人承担责任和损失（包括多承担责任和损失的情形）带来的成本；在刑事诉讼中主要是指法院对无辜的被告人作出有罪的判决、采取强制措施及让其多承担责任带来的成本和损失。第二类错误成本是指司法决定让本应该承担责任和损失的人免除承担责任和损失（包括少承担责任和损失的情形）而带来的成本。在刑事诉讼中主要是指法院宣告实际有罪或应承担责任的被告人无罪、不承担或少承担责任而带来的成本。充分信息条件下的司法决定和实际中的司法决定之间的差异，反映司法决定的错误程度。但司法决定的错误程度不等于其带来的错误成本。计算错误成本首先必须计算原诉讼参与人、法院或其他司法机关为执行错误的司法决定而花费的成本，还必须包括原诉讼参与人、法院或其他司法、监督机关因司法决定的错误进行再审（或其他监督行为）所付出的人力、物力和时间上的成本。此外，更重要的是，错误成本的计算还必须包括错误的司法决定给社会带来的其他所有直接或间接成本。如在刑事诉讼中法院对一个无罪的被告人做出的死刑判决将不仅仅给该无辜的被告人施加无可挽回的自由损失和肉体消灭的损失，而且会给该被告人的亲朋好友乃至其他社会成员施加一种较大的精神损失或不安全感，即他们同样有可能被冤枉而判处死刑。当社会大众都存在这种不安全感时，这种错误成本就相当高了。

还值得注意的是，错误更多并不一定意味着错误成本更高。错误成本往往跟该错误所导致的权益损失大小直接相关。而对这些权益损失大小的判断又往往是基于我们现有的社会规范等价值判断。[23]例如，下文我们所提到的刑事诉讼的第一类错误成本的大小往往跟该案所涉及错误对相关权益的影响大小有关。一般认为，对无辜被告人适用十年有期徒刑的判决所带来的错误成本远远超过对其适用罚金两万元的判决所产生的错误成本。对无辜被告人判处死刑带来的错误成本将远大于适用其他刑罚的判决带来的错误成本。而西方的法律格言——“宁可让十个有罪的人逃脱，也不愿让一个无辜的人受罚”[24] 也表明人们对自由的格外珍惜，因而判决无辜的人有罪所带来的错误

---

〔22〕 Larry Laudan, “Is Reasonable Doubt Reasonable?”, 9 *Legal Theory* (2003), p. 325; Erik Lillquist, “Recasting Reasonable Doubt: Decision Theory and The Virtues of Variability”, 36 *U. C. Davis Law Review* (2002), pp. 148 ~ 149; Daniel Rubinfeld and David Sappington, “Efficient Awards and Standards of Proof in Judicial Proceedings”, 18 *The RAND Journal of Economics* (1987), pp. 308 ~ 315.

〔23〕 Erik Lillquist, “Recasting Reasonable Doubt: Decision Theory and The Virtues of Variability”, *U. C. Davis Law Review*, Vol. 36 (2002), pp. 102 ~ 107.

〔24〕 William. Blackstone, *Commentaries on the Laws of England* (1765 ~ 1769), Chicago: University of Chicago Press, 1979, p. 358.

成本要远远高于判决有罪的人无罪所产生的错误成本。[25] 在实际中，计算错误成本通常有许多困难，法官往往不愿意承认可能存在的错误成本，也可能缺乏足够信息作为预估错误成本的基础。此外，对计算错误判决导致无辜的人被判死刑或有期徒刑所带来的成本，法官们也面临巨大的困难。虽然存在一些方法，如使用支付意愿的计算方法，[26] 但是对于许多经济学家来说，人身损害和死亡所导致损失的量化仍然不是一件容易的事。[27]

在刑事诉讼中，法官或陪审团在作出被告人是否有罪判决时，通常面临两个选项，宣告该被告人无罪或者对该被告人作出有罪判决。现有的证据能证明该被告人有罪的可能性为P；而理性的法官或陪审团之所以作出有罪判决，其原因用经济学的语言来表述即为，宣告该被告人无罪给社会带来的社会成本将高于对该被告人作出有罪判决带来的社会成本。我们可以使用一个不等式来表述上述条件成立，即 $P \times Cag > (1 - P) \times Cci$，[28] 其中 Cci 系第一类错误成本，在此是指将无罪的被告人作出有罪判决而给社会带来的成本，而 Cag 系第二类错误成本，在此是指将有罪的被告人宣告为无罪给社会带来的成本。将该不等式进行整理，可以得出 $P > 1/(1 + Cag/Cci)$，即只有在现有证据证明该被告人有超过 $1/(1 + Cag/Cci)$ 的可能性为有罪的情况下，理性的法官才应定被告人为有罪。

如果该法官认为：将无罪的被告人作出有罪判决而给社会带来的成本远远大于将有罪的被告人宣告为无罪给社会带来的成本，如同西方的法律格言所说的“宁可让十个有罪的人逃脱，也不愿让一个无辜的人受罚”；[29] 那么我们在此可以假设在一般的刑事案件中 $Cci = 10Cag$，代入不等式 $P > 1/(1 + Cag/Cci)$，即可得到 $P > 0.90909$，四舍五入后，我们得到 $P > 0.91$。在此情况下，只有在现有证据能证明该被告人有罪的可能性超过91%的条件下，理性的法官才应作出有罪判决。这就是该一般刑事案件中法官应采用的证明标准，即我们通常所说的刑事案件中的“排除合理怀疑”标准。在不同刑事案件中，由于 Cag、Cci 发生变化导致 Cag 和 Cci 之间的比率发生变化，即 Cag/Cci 的值发生变化，这些案件的证明标准也会相应发生变化，因而上述的“排除合理怀疑标准”也应根据不同案件进行调整。

上述不等式也可以用于解释民事诉讼的证明标准。在民事诉讼中，法官同样面临着是否根据原告提供的证据来认定由被告来承担责任的问题。如果原告的证据能证明该被告应承担责任的可能性为P；理性的法官或陪审团之所以作出让被告承担责任的判

---

〔25〕 Frederick Schauer and Richard Zeckhauser, “On the Degree of Confidence for Adverse Decisions”, *Journal of Legal Studies*, Vol. 25 (1996), p. 27.

〔26〕 使用支付意愿的方法来计算人身损害和死亡所导致损失主要是通过观察和测算消费者为那些能减少人身损害和死亡发生概率的安全措施及设备而支付的花费数额，并根据上述概率的减少值折算得出。详见 Mark A. Geistfeld, “Placing a Price on Pain and Suffering: A Method for Helping Juries Determine Tort Damages for Nonmonetary Injuries”, *California Law Review*, Vol. 83, (1995), pp. 773 ~ 843.

〔27〕 James Hammitt, “ QLAYs Versus WTP”, *Risk Analysis*, Vol. 22 (2002), pp. 985 ~ 1001.

〔28〕 John Kaplan, “Decision Theory and the Fact - finding Process”, 20 *Stanford Law Review* (1968), pp. 1071 ~ 1072.

〔29〕 William. Blackstone, *Commentaries on the Laws of England* (1765 ~ 1769), Chicago: University of Chicago Press, 1979, p. 358.

决，其原因也可以用经济学表述为，认定该被告不承担责任给社会带来的社会成本将高于认定该被告应承担责任带来的社会成本，即不等式 P > 1/（1 + Cag/Cci）应能够成立。其中 Cci 系第一类错误成本，是指将本不应承担责任的被告认定为应承担责任而给社会带来的成本，而 Cag 系第二类错误成本，是指将应承担责任的被告认定为不应承担责任而给社会带来的成本。在多数民事案件中，由于责任应在原被告方之间分配，法官犯的第一类错误往往也是第二类错误，如将本不应承担责任的被告认定为应承担责任也就意味着将本应承担责任的原告认定为不承担责任。再加上原被告方地位和权益平等，这就可能导致在许多情况下，犯第一类错误带来的成本等于犯第二类错误带来的成本，即 Cci = Cag。此时，不等式 P > 1/（1 + Cag/Cci）可得到 P > 0.5。[30] 在此情况下，只要现有原告的证据能证明该被告应承担责任的可能性超过百分之五十，理性的法官应作出对原告有利的判决，即被告应承担责任。这就是该一般民事案件中法官采用的证明标准，即“盖然性占优”的标准。

上述分析说明，证明标准的高低首先应取决于第一类错误成本与第二类错误成本之间的比值。在多数情况下，基于上述“宁可让十个有罪的人逃脱，也不愿让一个无辜的人受罚”的法律理念，前述案件中的第一类错误成本 Cag 会高于第二类错误成本 Cci。但在一些特殊情况下，某些社会当局也可能认为第一类错误成本会低于第二类错误成本，即判决无辜的被告人有罪带来的错误成本要远远小于让某些犯有某种特殊罪行的被告人“逃脱法网”所带来的错误成本。例如，在 1927 年，汪精卫曾代表国民党当局要求相关机构在逮捕和处死共产党人时，“宁可错杀一千，不可放过一人”。[31] 当前社会也存在着第二类错误成本较大的情况。如一个被指控犯有恐怖主义罪行的被告人是一名极端宗教分子且掌握良好军事技能，他被释放后就极可能继续制造恐怖事件给社会带来的巨大损失。这一类恐怖主义犯罪从整体上看，审理案件的第二类错误成本较大，第一类错误成本与第二类错误成本之间的比值较小，那么 Cag/Cci 的值相应较大，则 P 值相对较小，证明标准就应相对较低。除了上述组织、领导、参加恐怖组织罪外，被告人如犯有叛国罪却被错误释放也可能造成较高的第二类错误成本，因而对叛国罪这类案件的审理也应适用较低的证明标准。

进一步的结论是，根据刑罚严厉程度等直接影响犯罪嫌疑人和被告人权益的因素来决定刑事证明标准高低的观点可能不够科学，因为其只考虑第一类错误成本，完全忽视了第二类错误成本，即未考虑将那些真正有罪的人无罪释放可能给社会带来的成本。按照该观点进行制度设计无法准确反映法官等决策者在设定刑事证明标准高低时应考量的因素，也不符合效率原则要求的社会总成本最小化的目标。相比较，根据案件的具体类型等能直接影响 Cag/Cci 值的因素来决定证明标准高低，这一制度安排可能更为科学且符合效率原则。

三、可获信息量能变化时设定证明标准需平衡错误成本和行政成本

从动态的角度看，在法院可获信息量可因举证责任人的努力不同而变化的情况下，

---

〔30〕 John Kaplan, “Decision Theory and the Fact - finding Process”, 20 *Stanford Law Review* (1968), p. 1072.

〔31〕 参见“百度知道”，http：//zhidao. baidu. com/question/184463457. html。

证明标准还被认为是影响举证责任人取得信息的数量和对其激励的一个重要的工具。[32]在此情况下，法院可以通过提高证明标准来促使负有举证责任的公诉人提供更多的信息，并通过使用这些更多的信息进一步减少判决的第一类和第二类错误成本。反之，如法院降低证明标准，这将可能促使负有举证责任的公诉人提供较少的信息，进而导致判决的错误成本提高。

当证明标准提高时，为达到这一较高的证明标准，公诉人往往要付出较高的行政成本。如前所述，行政成本指参与该案件审理的所有诉讼参与人为了遵守某一证明标准而付出的所有的人力、物力和时间上的成本。它主要包括侦查机关、公诉机关为达到该证明标准而付出的在收集、保存和调查证据、分析证据、举证、认证、质证等环节付出的成本，也包括被告人及其代理人针对侦查机关、公诉人上述行为而在收集证据和举证等类似环节上付出的相应成本。当然，上述行政成本还包括法院为了安排诉讼参与人举证、认证、质证等行为以及自行调查举证和分析证据而付出的人力、物力和时间上的成本。上述行政成本不仅包括直接的成本，如诉讼参与人花费的人力、物力和时间成本，还包括间接成本，如在公安机关或公诉人为了达到该证明标准而收集更多证据期间，因犯罪嫌疑人、被告人是否有罪尚不确定的状态会给嫌疑人、被告人带来的拖延成本。一个典型的例子就是，某一公司因涉嫌走私罪被公安机关立案调查并移送给检察院审查起诉，检察院为了达到刑诉法规定的证明标准又退回公安机关补充侦查。在补充侦查期间，该公司往往无法正常如期开展业务，其顾客或债权人的合法权益也会因此受到较大影响。从理论上说，这些顾客或债权人的权益损失最终往往会向该公司追偿而体现在该公司的成本中。总之，随着证明标准的提高，定案所需的信息量越大，诉讼参与人整体付出的行政成本也越高。因此，即使在具体案件中我们真能满足“客观真实”的证明标准，这也意味着诉讼参与人将付出巨大的行政成本。此外，还值得注意的是，提供更多信息所需的成本通常由公诉机关等负有举证责任的诉讼参与人承担，法院往往无需承担这部分增加的成本。而当证明标准降低时，负举证义务的诉讼参与人虽然能节省在提供信息方面的成本，但却可能导致法院判决产生更多的错误成本。在后一种情况下，法院和另一方诉讼参与人可能要为增加的错误承担成本。

如前所述，在证明标准能被法院用来影响举证责任人取得信息数量和对其激励的一个工具时，其在经济学上的目标应该是使采用该标准所带来的错误成本和行政成本之和最小化。[33]决策者应根据错误成本和行政成本的不同决定不同证明标准。如图 1 所示，水平轴表示由法官决定的证明标准的高低程度。纵轴表示适用证明标准后司法决定给社会带来的成本。图 1 的曲线 C 向下倾斜，意味着随着证明标准的提高，相应的错误成本越小。但是，证明标准的提高也带来行政成本的升高。这反应在曲线 B 的稳定上升上。可以看出，行政成本和错误成本是此消彼长的关系。进一步地讲，司法决定带来的社会总成本是可以用司法决定的错误成本和行政成本相加而得到。因此，将

〔32〕 Matthew C. Stephenson, “Evidentiary Standards and Information Acquisition in Public Law”, *American Law and Economics Review*, Vol. 10 (2008), p. 351.

〔33〕 Richard Posner, “An Economic Approach to Legal Procedure and Judicial Administration”, 2 *Journal of Legal Studies*, p. 399.

曲线 C 的值及曲线 B 垂直相加，即可获得社会总成本曲线。社会成本曲线是 U 型曲线，由 A 表示。在曲线 A 的最底部，M 点对应横轴的值为 X。X 的值是证明标准的最优水平，此时错误成本和行政成本之和最小化，即社会总成本最小化。更高的证明标准将增加司法决定的行政成本。在这里，其增加量是边际成本，即每提高一个单位的证明标准带来的行政成本的增量。同时，它可以降低司法决定的错误成本，其减少量是边际收益，即每提高一个单位的证明标准带来的错误成本的减少量。在 M 点，边际成本等于边际收益。该表也可说明，证明标准通常无需提高到“绝对确定的事实”的程度，其原因就在于达到这一程度所需的边际成本（即最后一个单位的行政成本的增加）已超过边际收益（即最后一个单位的错误成本的减少）。

图 1：

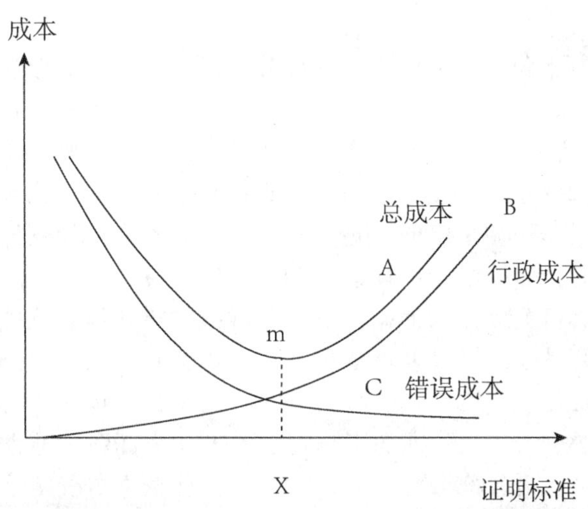

四、刑事诉讼不同阶段所用证明标准的层次性之争议分析

我国有较多学者提出，对应于我国司法程序中的立案、移送审查、提起公诉、有罪判决四个阶段，当前的刑事证明标准应该是一个由低到高的走向和模式。[34] 但是，我国刑事诉讼法规定的上述四个阶段的证明标准却没有一个由低到高的递进关系。具体而言，除了立案的证明标准表述为“人民法院、人民检察院或者公安机关……认为有犯罪事实需要追究刑事责任的时候，应当立案”外，[35] 侦查机关侦移送起诉，检察机关提起公诉，人民法院做出有罪判决的证明标准均表述为“犯罪事实清楚、证据确实、充分”。[36] 持“证明标准应分阶段逐步提高”观点的学者主要有以下理由：其一，诉讼

---

〔34〕 熊秋红：“对刑事证明标准的思考——以刑事证明中的可能性和确定性为视角”，载《法商研究》2003 年第 1 期，第 83 页；李学宽：“论刑事证明标准及其层次性”，载《中国法学》2001 年第 5 期，第 127～130 页；聂立泽、苑明丽：“主客观相统一原则与刑事证明标准及其层次性研究”，载《法学评论》2011 年第 2 期，第 41～42 页。

〔35〕《中华人民共和国刑事诉讼法》第 110 条。

〔36〕《中华人民共和国刑事诉讼法》第 160 条、第 172 条、第 195 条。我国最高人民法院的有些法官却对此存在不同意见。他们认为：我国侦查、起诉阶段不存在证明问题，亦无所谓证明标准在不同诉讼阶段的层次性问题，中国刑事证明及证明标准问题只存在于法庭审判阶段。参见最高人民法院刑事审判第三庭：《刑事证据规则理解与适用》，法律出版社 2010 年版，第 79 页。

三阶段证明标准同一的规定过于强调标准的“绝对的确定性”，忽视了司法人员对案件认识的“渐进性”和其对案件事实的主观判断，未能将认识论中的“可能性”范畴纳入考虑的因素。[37] 如果法律要求在审判前的程序中就达到最高程度的证明标准，这就存在逻辑上的矛盾。因为如果在侦查程序、起诉程序达到最高程度的证明标准，那么为何还需要审判程序呢？[38] 其二，不同的机关在不同的诉讼阶段作出相应的决定对犯罪嫌疑人和被告人产生不同的影响程度，故有必要适用不同的证明标准。[39] 如侦查机关在侦查过程中采取有关的强制性措施仅有暂时性和预防性，因此无须过高的标准。相比较，享有审判权的法院可以对被告人进行定罪量刑，对其权益产生重大的实质性的影响，因而审判阶段的证明标准要求必须很高。[40] 而公诉机关的起诉权仅仅是一种司法请求权，仍不具有对案件进行实体性处分的性质。故其证明标准应介于侦查行为与审判定罪证明标准之间。

本文认为：相较于我国刑事证明标准应分阶段逐步提高的做法，我国刑事诉讼法作出关于移送起诉，提起公诉，作出有罪判决诉讼三阶段证明标准同一的规定可能更具有正当性。理由如下：其一，前述司法人员对案件认识的“渐进性”现象和认识论中的“可能性”限制并不能作为诉讼三阶段的证明标准必须由低到高加以设定的充分理由。因为证明标准只是一种法定的“把关”要求，并不要求侦查机关、检察机关在每一个移送起诉或提起公诉的案子中均能达到；相反，我国刑事诉讼法的设计本身就要求审判机关核查公诉机关提供的证据、要求公诉机关核查侦查机关提供的证据，而不是要求审判机关去帮助公诉机关采集更多证据，在实践中也很少由公诉机关来帮助侦查机关来补充采集证据。[41] 其二，根据“不同的机关在不同的诉讼阶段做出相应的决定对犯罪嫌疑人和被告人产生不同的影响程度”而认为证明标准也应不同的前述论证也缺乏说服力。本文在第二部分已论证，在可获正确信息量确定不变的情况下，影响证明标准变化的主要因素在于第一类错误成本与第二类错误成本之间的比值，并非前述的“对犯罪嫌疑人和被告人产生不同的影响程度”。其三，根据上述的法经济学分析框架，三阶段证明标准同一的规定可以较大程度地减少刑事诉讼中第一类错误成本。如果能得到严格执行，三阶段证明标准同一的规定将使侦查机关和公诉机关对那些未满足“犯罪事实清楚、证据确实、充分”标准的无辜犯罪嫌疑人或被告人（以下简称“无辜被告人”）及时作出“不移送起诉”或“ 不提起公诉”的决定，从而终结刑事诉讼程序。而在我国刑事证明标准应分阶段逐步提高的制度安排下，那些未满足“犯

---

〔37〕 熊秋红：“对刑事证明标准的思考——以刑事证明中的可能性和确定性为视角”，载《法商研究》2003年第1期，第83页。

〔38〕 熊秋红：“对刑事证明标准的思考——以刑事证明中的可能性和确定性为视角”，载《法商研究》2003年第1期，第83页。

〔39〕 聂立泽、苑明丽：“主客观相统一原则与刑事证明标准及其层次性研究”，载《法学评论》2011年第2期，第41~42页。

〔40〕 聂立泽、苑明丽：“主客观相统一原则与刑事证明标准及其层次性研究”，载《法学评论》2011年第2期，第41~42页。

〔41〕《中华人民共和国刑事诉讼法》第49条规定：公诉案件中被告人有罪的举证责任由人民检察院承担。从司法实践看，“当检察机关遇到需要补充侦查的情况时，往往将案件退回公安机关补充侦查，很少自行补充侦查，出现退回补充侦查比率高的情况。”参见黄烨：“论补充侦查制度”，载《中国刑事法杂志》2005年第4期，第64页。

罪事实清楚、证据确实、充分”标准的无辜被告人往往可能直到进入审判程序后才可能被法院确认为无罪从而终结刑事诉讼程序。由于我国绝大多数刑事案件的犯罪嫌疑人或被告人在侦查立案后就已经被采取拘留或者逮捕此类强制措施，早日终结上述刑事诉讼程序意味着那些无辜的犯罪嫌疑人或被告人能早日获得人身自由，这将在很大程度上减少第一类错误成本。除了早日获得人身自由外，早日终结上述刑事诉讼程序也意味着无辜被告人能早日恢复正常的生活和经营，减少经济和名誉上的损失。[42] 此外，早日终结上述刑事诉讼程序也会降低法院、检察、侦查机关及其他司法机关为执行刑事诉讼程序而付出的人力、物力和时间上的成本，如关押该无辜犯被告人所付出的成本。最后，早日终结上述刑事诉讼程序还会减少对该无辜被告人的亲朋好友乃至其他社会成员施加的精神损失或不安全感。

相较于刑事证明标准应分阶段逐步提高的做法，上述我国刑事诉讼法三阶段证明标准同一的规定可能会增加刑事诉讼中第二类错误成本。具体而言，根据三阶段证明标准同一的规定，那些实际有罪的犯罪嫌疑人或被告人（以下简称“有罪被告人”）可能会因为侦查机关和检察机关未满足“犯罪事实清楚、证据确实、充分”标准而不被移送起诉或不被提起公诉，并进一步被释放。理论上，这些有罪被告人有可能会在社会上从事新的犯罪行为，给社会造成新的损失。但实践中，这些有罪被告人也可能考虑到自己已经被有关机关怀疑而不愿意再轻易冒险犯罪，这可以在一定程度上降低上述的第二类错误成本。为取得进一步准确的结论，我们必须比较上述我国刑事诉讼法三阶段证明标准同一的规定可能导致的第二类错误成本的增加量和该制度带来的第一类错误成本的减少量。如前所述，在大多数案件中，第一类错误成本通常会比第二类错误成本更大。三阶段证明标准同一的规定能减少无辜的犯罪嫌疑人或被告人陷于“牢狱之灾”的可能性，这能使第一类错误成本大量减少，再加上司法机关还可采取派人监视被释放但仍可能有罪的犯罪嫌疑人的方法来减少该规定可能带来第二类错误成本的增加量，因此，采用三阶段证明标准同一的规定似乎比证明标准分阶段逐步提高的制度设计更符合效率原则。

五、提高死刑证明标准之争议分析[43]

最高人民法院副院长熊选国在2009年刑事诉讼法学年会上曾指出：“对于死刑案件必须采用绝对标准，必须高于、严于其他刑事案件，坚持最高的标准和最严的要求，既要注重查明定罪事实，也要非常注重查明影响量刑的重要事实和证据。”[44] 在学术界也一直有学者认为死刑案件的证明标准应当高于普通案件。如“在适用普通程序的刑事案件中，证明标准是‘排除合理怀疑的证明’，…… 在适用死刑的刑事案件中，证明标准则应该是更高的‘排除一切怀疑的证明’。”[45] 支持上述观点的一个重要依据就是

---

〔42〕 例如，银行的贷款合同通常规定：一旦借款人涉嫌犯罪，贷款银行将提前收回贷款；这往往影响作为借款人的无辜犯罪嫌疑人的正常生产经营，并可能进一步造成较大的经济损失。

〔43〕 尽管学术界存在争议，我国刑事诉讼法并未要求死刑案件的证明标准必须提高，而是规定所有刑事案件均适用“排除合理怀疑标准”，参见我国最新修改颁布的《中华人民共和国刑事诉讼法》第53条。

〔44〕 唐亚南、闫继勇：“熊选国：严把证据关确保把死刑案件办成铁案”，载《人民法院报》2009年11月3日，http://www.stcourts.gov.cn/nin.asp? ty=1&page=18&cxid=6595［EB/OL］，http://www.chinacourt.org/html/article/200911/03/379561.shtml，访问日期：2009年11月11日。

〔45〕 何家弘：“刑事证据的采纳标准和采信标准”，载《人民检察》2001年第10期，第12页。

国外证明标准应随案件性质不同而变化，如英美国家根据罪行轻重，适用不同的证明标准的原因主要是从保障人权的机理考虑。[46]上述依据更准确的表述也许应是，证明标准的设置应当与诉讼涉及利益的重要程度成正比，重要性越大，证明标准就应越高。[47]

而反对死刑案件适用更高证明标准的学者则认为：其一，就定罪的证明标准而言，判处死刑立即执行案件和普通案件的定罪标准应当是相同的。因为死刑案件关系一个人的生命，普通案件关系一个人的自由，这两者对一个人来说都是非常重要的，剥夺一个人的生命和自由同样需要严格的程序和标准。[48]其二，最推崇程序保障的美国，实际上也没有在死刑案件中采用更高的证明标准。[49]其三，在死刑案件中适用更高的证明标准如排除一切怀疑标准，要么面临被实践架空和降格适用的危险，要么导致在绝大部分案件中无法完成证明任务的尴尬境地，故不具有可行性。[50]其四，提高死刑证明标准带来的一个最大的问题就是放纵犯罪、增加错误宣判无罪的风险，导致更多真正有罪的被告人被无罪释放。[51]

本文的上述分析已论证：在可获的正确信息量确定不变的情况下，影响证明标准变化的主要因素在于上述不等式 $P > 1/(1 + Cag/Cci)$ 中 Cag/Cci 的值，即第一类错误成本与第二类错误成本之间的比值，并非前述的“诉讼涉及利益的重要程度”。为进一步准确地分析，下文将利用该不等式进行实例分析。我们假设，在一个一般刑事案件中，第一类错误成本是第二类错误成本的10倍，即Cci的值为100，Cag的值为10，$Cci = 10Cag$，C代入不等式 $P > 1/(1 + Cag/Cci)$，我们得到 $P > 0.91$。而在死刑案件中，由于死刑的可能适用，第一类错误成本要远比其他可能判处有期徒刑或罚金刑案件中的第一类错误成本要高。我们可以假设死刑案件的第一类错误成本为1000，即 $Cci = 1000$，如果在该死刑案件中的第二类错误成本同其他一般刑事案件相同的话，即 $Cag = 10$，那么代入不等式 $P > 1/(1 + Cag/Cci)$，我们得到 $P > 0.99$。然而，上述对死刑案件的第一类错误成本和第二类错误成本的假设可能会与实际不符。具体有以下两点：其一，相当多的死刑案件的被告人最终都未被执行，这会导致上述对死刑案件的第一类错误成本的高额假设与实际不符。如在实际中，被判处死刑缓期执行的被告人绝大部分最终都被改判为无期徒刑。在缺少死刑实际执行的情况下，死刑案件的第一类错误成本可能不一定会比其他普通的判处有期徒刑的案件高出许多。其二，一些死刑案件中的被告人往往可能罪大恶极且对社会有极大的破坏性，因而如将这些实际有罪的被告人宣告无罪并释放可能导致比其他一般刑事案件更高的第二类错误成本。例如，同其他普通刑事案件相比，在一些涉嫌组织、领导、参加恐怖组织罪的案件中，实际

〔46〕 陈卫东、李训虎：“分而治之：一种完善死刑案件证明标准的思路”，载《人民检察》2007年第8期，第53页；汪海燕、范培根：“刑事证明标准层次性”，载《政法论坛》2001年第5期。

〔47〕 陈虎：“提高死刑案件证明标准一个似是而非的命题”，载《中外法学》2010年第3期，第458页。

〔48〕 李玉华：“刑事证明标准的新发展——评刑事诉讼法修正案（草案）第52条及相关规定”，载《中国人民公安大学学报（社会科学版）》2012年第1期，第11页。

〔49〕 陈卫东、李训虎：“分而治之：一种完善死刑案件证明标准的思路”，载《人民检察》2007年第8期，第54页。

〔50〕 陈虎：“提高死刑案件证明标准一个似是而非的命题”，载《中外法学》2010年第3期，第462页。

〔51〕 陈卫东、李训虎：“分而治之：一种完善死刑案件证明标准的思路”，载《人民检察》2007年第8期，第53页。

有罪的被告人往往受狂热思想、极端宗教教义或理念的指引，显然具备更大的人身危险性。[52] 他们一旦被释放，往往又会不顾一切地参加恐怖活动。这些恐怖活动犯罪不仅可能直接对他人的人身、财产等权益造成损害，更在社会上制造长久、持续的恐怖气氛。考虑到以上两点，我们很难通过上述不等式来证明死刑案件的证明标准会高于其他普通的刑事案件。而是，我们必须根据具体案件情况，比较案件中第一类错误成本和第二类错误成本的变化情况，来判断该案的证明标准是否应该提高。

六、定罪量刑分而治之并在量刑阶段适用更高证明标准之争议分析

我国学者大多都认为应当采取定罪量刑分而治之模式，所争议的问题在于量刑阶段的证明标准是否应高于定罪阶段的证明标准。认为量刑阶段应采用更低的证明标准的学者大多主张在量刑阶段使用“高度盖然性’的证明标准，具体有以下理由：其一，无罪推定原则和严格证明方法在量刑阶段都不再适用，因而，对一般量刑情节而言，较高的量刑证明标准设置是没有必要的。[53] 其二，量刑阶段的证明对象并非单纯的事实判断，且措辞模糊，因而无法适用超过定罪标准的“绝对确定”标准。[54] 如量刑程序中酌定情节的适用与判断需要一定的弹性，且“对社会的危害程度”进行评定也较为抽象，无法用相对具体的证明标准加以评价。所以，在量刑程序中确立高度盖然性证明标准正好满足了酌定情节和“社会危害程度”评定的弹性需求。其三，从诉讼经济的角度出发，对量刑程序中犯罪前的表现、犯罪后的态度和表现这些问题的证明无需达到很高的证明标准，只要法官对客观情况的认识能够形成心证即可，无需花费更高的诉讼成本达到确定无疑的证明程度。[55] 其四，从涉及利益的重要性程度来看，如何防止对无辜者错误定罪要比防止对其错误量刑重要得多，量刑证明标准不能超过定罪证明标准。[56]

相比较，认为量刑阶段应采用更高的证明标准的学者主要针对死刑案件。其主要理由如下：其一，量刑阶段适用“排除一切怀疑”这一更高的证明标准符合我国长期以来坚持的对待死刑的有关刑事政策。即“ 少杀、慎杀”的死刑政策。[57] 其二，在量刑阶段采用更高的证明标准不会导致放纵犯罪的可能。[58] 因为在先前的定罪阶段被告人已经被确定有罪，不管被告人在量刑阶段被判处何种刑罚，都不会逃脱法律的制裁。[59]

本文认为：上述支持量刑阶段证明标准降低的理由缺乏说服力。其一，在量刑阶段无需采用无罪推定原则是因为被告人是否有罪已由定罪阶段确定，但这不意味着在量刑阶段一切严格证明方法都不采用，更不意味着较高的证明标准没有必要；其二，在量刑阶段，一些事实如加重情节的认定可能直接关系到死刑是否真正适用，这就可能要求适用更高的证明标准。前述“犯罪前的表现、犯罪后的态度和表现这些问题”

---

〔52〕 赵秉志、杜邈：“中国惩治恐怖主义犯罪的刑事司法对策”，载《北京师范大学学报》（社会科学版）2008 年第 5 期。

〔53〕 陈虎：“提高死刑案件证明标准一个似是而非的命题”，载《中外法学》2010 年第 3 期，第 462 页；

〔54〕 樊崇义：“量刑程序与证据”，载《南都学坛》2009 年第 4 期。

〔55〕 樊崇义：“量刑程序与证据”，《南都学坛》2009 年第 4 期。

〔56〕 陈虎：“提高死刑案件证明标准一个似是而非的命题”，载《中外法学》2010 年第 3 期。

〔57〕 樊崇义：“量刑程序与证据”，载《南都学坛》2009 年第 4 期。

〔58〕 陈卫东、李训虎：“分而治之：一种完善死刑案件证明标准的思路”，载《人民检察》2007 年第 8 期。

〔59〕 陈卫东、李训虎：“分而治之：一种完善死刑案件证明标准的思路”，载《人民检察》2007 年第 8 期。

在特定案件上也可能直接影响死刑的适用，如自首和立功情节能否认定就可能导致适用死刑还是死刑缓期执行这两种截然不同的判决。其三，认为“防止对无辜者错误定罪要比防止对其错误量刑重要得多”的观点本身就难以成立，如在错误量刑可能导致适用死刑的情况下。其四，在对酌定情节和“社会危害程度”评定时给法官的弹性空间恰恰要求法官对其自由裁量权的行使作出更为明确的解释。特别是对这些情节或程度的错误评定可能导致较大的第一类错误成本的情形下，更高的量刑阶段证明标准就更有必要了。

下面我们进一步适用前述不等式来具体分析定罪量刑分而治之模式下量刑证明标准是否应高于定罪证明标准的问题。我们先考虑定罪量刑合一模式，用其来做比较。还有我们仍以死刑案件为例。假设死刑案件的审判程序仍只定为一个阶段，第一类错误成本（即将无罪的人错误定罪并执行死刑的成本）Cci 的值为 1000，第二类错误成本（即将有罪并应被判处死刑的被告人宣告无罪并释放带来的错误成本）Cag 的值为 20。我们将上述假设代入不等式 $P>1/(1+Cag/Cci)$，那么此时的证明标准 P 为 0.98。如果我们将死刑案件的审判程序分为二个阶段，那么在定罪阶段第一类错误成本可能会变小。因为即使被告人在定罪阶段被定为有罪，其在量刑阶段却往往不会被执行死刑，故其被确定执行死刑的可能性会大幅减少。在此我们可以假设定罪阶段第一类错误成本 Cci 的值为 500。在定罪阶段的第二类错误成本可能保持不变，因为在此阶段有罪的被告人可能仍被宣告无罪并释放，故假设其第二类错误成本 Cag 的值为 20。在量刑（判处死刑）阶段，第一类错误成本可能保持不变，因为无罪的被告人可能仍会被判处死刑，故我们假设第一类错误成本 Cci 的值为 1000；而第二类错误成本可能会变小，因为在量刑阶段，那些本应判处死刑的被告人虽然可能逃脱被执行死刑的命运，但其仍可能被判处有期徒刑，故我们假设在此第二类错误成本为 10。我们将上述假设代入不等式 $P>1/(1+Cag/Cci)$，可以得出在定罪阶段，证明标准 P 应大于 0.96；而在量刑阶段，证明标准 P 应大于 0.99。虽然这些证明标准的差距很小，但他们确实表明在定罪量刑分而治之模式下，量刑阶段的证明标准应比定罪阶段要高；且分立模式下定罪阶段还可以使用一个比现行定罪量刑合一模式更低的证明标准。这样的安排会使得在分立模式下定罪阶段的有罪认定比现行制度设计下的有罪认定更为容易。[60] 当死刑案件的被告人更多地必须依靠量刑阶段更高的证明标准来避免第一类错误成本时，我们就必须警惕那些被告人可能会承受更多的第一类错误成本。因为同分立模式下一些无辜被告人直到量刑阶段才被确定不适用死刑相比，在定罪量刑合一模式下，这些被告人可能早已被释放。[61]

七、适用更高刑事证明标准的具体方法

假设立法要求我国死刑案件的证明标准必须提高，那么就存在如何满足这一要求的问题，即法院如何适用更高的证明标准和各诉讼主体如何满足该更高的证明标准？

有美国学者艾瑞克·李尔奎斯特（Erik Lillquist）认为：要在死刑案件中适用比现

---

〔60〕 Erik Lillquist, “Absolute Certainty and The Death Penalty”, *American Criminal Law Review*, Vol. 42 (2005), p. 50.

〔61〕 Erik Lillquist, “Absolute Certainty and The Death Penalty”, *American Criminal Law Review*, Vol. 42 (2005), p. 50.

行更高的证明标准，需要取消现行制度中关于死刑案件陪审员资格限制和改变向陪审员指示证明标准的方法。[62]美国有实证研究表明：由于死刑案件陪审员资格限制制度的存在，那些有死刑案件陪审员资格的陪审员比其他无此资格的陪审员更容易认定被告有罪，即基于对同样证据材料的评估，有死刑案件陪审员资格的陪审员比其他无此资格的陪审员更可能投票认定被告有罪。[63] 这表明有死刑案件陪审员资格的陪审员比其他无此资格的陪审员采用更低的证明标准。因此，艾瑞克·李尔奎斯特提出，取消死刑案件陪审员资格限制将使得其他无此资格的陪审员也能参与对死刑案件证据的评估，从而在实际中导致更高的证明标准的适用。其次，艾瑞克·李尔奎斯特还认为改变现行的向陪审员指示证明标准的方法也可能会在实践中导致更高证明标准的适用。[64]他认为：现行的向陪审员指示证明标准的方法使得陪审员可能既没有认真听取该指示，也不理解该指示，更没有适用该指示要求的证明标准；而改变向陪审员指示证明标准的方法则可能会在实践中导致更高证明标准的适用。这些方法包括如要在庭审开始时而非庭审结束时指示陪审员如何适用证明标准，要采用书面指示以及明确对证明标准的定量比较。[65]本文认为，上述改变向陪审员指示证明标准的方法仅仅是帮助陪审员理解和掌握证明标准的高低以及如何适用证明标准，并不能保证陪审员会真正适用更高的证明标准。而取消死刑案件陪审员资格限制的做法是否能真正导致证明标准的提高，则不仅要求美国上述实证研究结果必须真实地反映当时的整体实际情况，而且还需满足另一个重要条件，即这些没有死刑案件陪审员资格的陪审员在参与死刑案件审理时仍然会保持其适用更高证明标准的一贯做法。如果上述条件无法满足，则艾瑞克·李尔奎斯特提出的做法就无法达到适用更高证明标准的目的。

我国学者认为：不需要通过证据种类和证据数量提高证明标准，而通过刑事程序的设置，如增加死刑案件的证明次数和判断人数；要求最高法院院长对死刑案件进行审查和签发执行命令等来提高证明标准。[66]其理由在于：增加死刑案件的证明次数和判断的人数，这样的多次证明和向多人证明的方法可以提高事实判断的准确性。[67]本文认为该观点有失偏颇。增加死刑案件的判断人数只是增加达成一致意见的难度或成本，并不一定导致更高证明标准的适用。在这些行使判断权的人中，如果持较低证明标准的人有较强的说服力来说服其他持较高证明标准的人，则较低的证明标准将得到适用。而增加证明的次数，尽管是在严格执行上诉不加刑和复核不加刑的前提下，也不一定导致更高证明标准的适用。比如，在初审法院判处被告人死刑的上诉审中，二审法院

---

〔62〕 Erik Lillquist, "Absolute Certainty and The Death Penalty", *American Criminal Law Review*, Vol. 42 (2005), pp. 45 ~46.

〔63〕 Samuel Gross, "The Risks of Death: Why Erroneous Convictions Are Common in Capital Cases", 44 *Buffalo Law Review* (1996), pp. 469 ~494.

〔64〕 Erik Lillquist, "Absolute Certainty and The Death Penalty", 42 *American Criminal Law Review* (2005), pp. 45 ~46.

〔65〕 Erik Lillquist, "Absolute Certainty and The Death Penalty", 42 *American Criminal Law Review* (2005), pp. 45 ~46.

〔66〕 杨宇冠："论死刑案件证明标准之完善——新刑事诉讼法实施问题思考"，载《清华法学》2012 年第 3 期，第 72 ~74 页。

〔67〕 杨宇冠："论死刑案件证明标准之完善——新刑事诉讼法实施问题思考"，载《清华法学》2012 年第 3 期，第 73 页。

仍然可以采用相对于初审法院较低的证明标准，作出维持原判的决定。

在我国现实情况下，适用更高证明标准的一个前提条件是法院必须能够区分证明标准高低的情况以及掌握与其相对应的在证据上的不同要求。进一步地，法院还可以通过对具体案件作出有罪判决所必需的定案证据在种类和数量上的更高要求来引导公诉机关提高所提交证据的证明力，从而满足更高证明标准的要求。当然必须注意，公诉机关无法在所有案件中都满足该更高证明标准的要求，而我们只是要求公诉机关朝着这个方向努力而已。尽管学术界存在批评，但实务界中法官仍然推崇并实施证明力规则。[68]在现实情况下，法官可以依据司法实践中所采用的证明力规则，通过对定案证据在种类和数量的更高要求来引导公诉机关提高所提交证据的证明力并进而满足更高证明标准的要求。比如，在最近引起轰动的“浙江叔侄冤案”中，原审法院对该叔侄定罪依据的主要证据是两人的有罪供述等间接证据。[69]无疑，对该案的错判能说明原审法院原本适用的证明标准过低。假设原审法院能够适用更高的“排除合理怀疑”的定罪证明标准，通过要求公诉机关提供除了口供以外的更多、更强证明力并相互印证的证据（如DNA证据或监控摄像等）才能定罪，那么该叔侄有可能不会被定罪而形成冤案。然而，要取得DNA证据或监控摄像证据，往往意味着公诉机关或其他有举证责任的主体必须付出更高的行政成本。如从事DNA证据的采集和分析，要求有关部门在更多的犯罪易发地安装摄像头，均要求相关部门付出更高的行政成本；在特殊情况下，还可采用极端昂贵但有可能十分精确的做法，即调用案发当时的各国卫星对当地地面拍摄的卫星图片。至于是否通过要求公诉机关提供上述具有更强证明力的证据来适用更高证明标准，应权衡相关错误成本的减少量和行政成本增加量后作出决定。

在采用证明力规则的前提下，有学者担心提高证明标准会造成刑讯逼供和侦查人员伪造证据几率的增加。[70]本文认为，如果设计得当并严格实施，证明标准的提高会降低刑讯逼供和伪造证据的可能性。如上述，提高证明标准是通过对定案证据在种类和数量的更高要求来引导公诉机关提高所提交证据的证明力来实现的。提高对物证而非言辞证据的要求，实则是降低侦查人员刑讯逼供的激励，因为，随着言辞证据证明力的削弱，侦查人员为了结案会更加努力寻找物证，而非仅仅寄希望于言词证据结案。进一步而言，对收集证据的程序正当性的要求，必然会增加侦查人员伪造证据的成本；再加上非法证据排除等相关制度的适用，即使证据得以成功伪造后，在后续的刑事程序中证据的证明力也会降低甚至为零，因而侦查人员将缺乏激励去从事刑讯逼供及伪造证据的行为。故提高证明标准并不会一定增加侦查人员刑讯逼供和伪造证据的几率。

八、结 论

本文采用法经济学的分析框架，较为全面、系统地阐述了刑事证明标准设定应考虑的相关因素，即在可获的信息量确定不变的条件下，刑事证明标准的设定应考虑如何平衡第一类错误成本和第二类错误成本，即对无辜者错误定罪的成本及对有罪者错误释放的成本；在可获信息量能够发生变化的情况下，刑事证明标准的设定应使该标

---

〔68〕 李训虎：“证明力规则检讨”，载《法学研究》2010年第2期，第156～157页。

〔69〕 参见“浙江省高级人民法院新闻发言人就张辉、张高平一案答记者问”，载扬子晚报网，http：//www.yangtse.com/system/2013/03/28/016712827.shtml，访问日期：2013年6月9日。

〔70〕 陈虎：“死刑案件证明标准改革之理论误区”，载《法学论坛》2010年第2期，第99页。

准使用时仍存在的错误成本和为达到该证明标准而付出的行政成本之和最小化。在此基础上，本文对刑事证明标准的层次性、死刑的证明标准及定罪量刑分而治之并在后一阶段适用较高证明标准等争议问题进行了分析。除了上述关于刑事证明标准设定影响因素的分析框架以外，本文主要还有下列新结论：

第一，根据刑罚严厉程度等直接影响犯罪嫌疑人和被告人权益的因素来决定刑事证明标准高低的传统观点可能无法准确反映法官等决策者在设定刑事证明标准时必须考量的因素；根据该观点进行制度设计很可能因忽视证明标准设定对第二类错误成本的影响而未能实现社会总成本最小化的目标。相比较，根据案件的具体类型或其他能直接影响第二类错误成本和第一类错误成本比值的因素来设定证明标准的高低，这一制度安排可以更为科学、准确地体现客观实际的要求并符合效率原则。

第二，根据上述法律经济学的分析框架，我国刑事诉讼法关于移送起诉，提起公诉，作出有罪判决诉讼三阶段证明标准同一的规定可能较逐步提高的规定更具有正当性；而死刑案件的证明标准并不必然要高于其他普通的刑事案件；且我们还应对定罪量刑分而治之并在量刑阶段适用更高证明标准。

第三，通过如增加死刑案件的证明次数和判断人数等刑事程序的设置变更无法达到适用更高证明标准的目标；在现实条件下，我国法院可以通过对具体案件定案证据在种类和数量上的更高要求来引导公诉机关提高所提交证据的证明力，从而满足更高证明标准的要求。

Presumptions in Dutch Private Law (1838 – 1988) within a European Context

C. H. van Rhee *

Introduction

The topic of presumptions has caused many difficulties and differences of opinion since its first comprehensive scholarly study by Jacopo Menochio (1532 ~ 1607) in the early – modern period.[1] The German author Hugo Burckhard (1838 ~ 1918), who wrote an interesting study on the subject in the Pandektist tradition of the 19th century, states that this is already the case when one consults "die älteren, diesen Gegenstand behandelnden Schriftsteller, die ihr Werk beginnen oder endigen mit einem Klagelied über die Schwierigkeit der Materie, mit Anrufung des gättlichen Beistandes in Erkenntniss der menschlichen Schwäche gegenüber der Unermesslichkeit dieses Gebiets" ("the older authors dealing with this subject, who start or finish their work with a lamentation regarding the complicated nature of the matter, invoking God's assistance while recognizing human frailty in respect of the infinity of this matter"). According to Burckhard, some of the older authors were even of the opinion that a study of the topic should be qualified as "ein unglückliches und nutzloses Unternehmen" ("an unfortunate and pointless enterprise").[2] Even though one may not agree with these authors, one will often think about these words during research into the topic in Dutch civil procedure. It appears that many of the problems that were discussed in earlier centuries still remained unresolved in later centuries. In fact, often the old problems continued to play a role. Even today, when presumptions are not mentioned as a separate, abstractly defined category any more in the Dutch Codes (they were removed as a separate category in 1988),[3] legal literature contains references to specific presumptions and the role they (should) play.[4] In addition, examples of specific

* Professor at Maastricht University. Email: remco. vanrhee@ maastrichtuniversity. nl.

〔1〕 J. Menochius, De praesumptionibus, coniecturis, signis et indiciis commentaria (first edition in two volumes, Venice 1587 ~ 1590).

〔2〕 H. Burckhard, Die civilistischen Präsumtionen, Weimar: Landes – Industrie – Comptoir, 1866, 1 – 2.

〔3〕 Law of 3 December 1987, Official Journal Nr. 590.

〔4〕 Some random examples: I. Giesen, Bewijs en aansprakelijkheid. Een rechtsvergelijkend onderzoek naar de bewijslast, de bewijsvoeringslast, het bewijsrisico en de bewijsrisico – omkering in het aansprakelijkheidsrecht, Ph. D. thesis Tilburg, The Hague: BJu, 2001, 64ff; A. J. Akkermans, De 'omkeringsregel' bij het bewijs van causaal verband, inaugural lecture, The Hague: BJu, 2002, 9ff; C. Bosse, Bewijslastverdeling in het Nederlandse en Belgische arbeidsrecht, Ph. D. thesis Tilburg, Deventer: Kluwer, 2003, 36ff.

presumptions can be found at various places in the Codes, for example in Article 7: 610a of the present Dutch Civil Code (presumption as to the existence of a labour contract).

The central theme of my paper is the 19th and 20th century discussion on presumptions in the Netherlands. It will concentrate on two questions: ①What is a presumption in Dutch private law?, and②What types of presumptions can be distinguished? In answering these questions, the Articles 1903, 1952 – 1953 and 1958 – 1959 of the former Dutch Civil Code of 1838 (abrogated in 1992) will be discussed. Article 1903 lists various means of proof that are recognized by this Code, including presumptions.[5] Article 1952 contains a definition of presumptions. It makes a distinction between presumptions that are specifically regulated by statute (these will also be called "legal presumptions"), and presumptions where this is not the case (these will also be called "judicial presumptions"). Article 1953 further defines presumptions regulated by statute and lists four examples.[6] Article 1958 continues with general rules on presumptions regulated by statute, whereas the final Article 1959 contains rules on presumptions that are not regulated by statute. Articles 1952 ~ 1953 and 1958 ~ 1959 are to a certain extent based on the French Civil Code of 1804 (Articles 1349, 1350, 1352 and 1353 respectively).

1. What is a presumption in Dutch law?

As stated above, a definition of presumptions is provided by Article 1952 of the former, 1838 Dutch Civil Code. Translating this Article into English without at the same time interpreting the Article (at least slightly) is impossible. My translation of the first part of the Article runs as follows:

"Presumptions are conclusions of the legislature or the judge as regards an unknown 'matter' ('daadzaak') based on a known 'matter' ('daadzaak')."[7]

Traditionally, presumptions are dealt with under the heading of evidence. The usual explanation is as follows. He who submits a claim to the court needs to prove the facts on which his claim is grounded, at least, as far as these facts are denied by his opponent.[8] In some cases, however, it is not necessary for the claimant to prove the very facts that are being denied. This occurs when the facts on which the claim is based can be presumed on the basis of other facts that can be established or proven by the claimant.[9] In this case presumptions are

---

[5] Although Art. 1903 may give the impression that it contains an exhaustive list of all the available means of proof, most authors and case law recognized means of proof that were not included in this list. E. g. R. van Boneval Faure, Het Nederlandsche burgerlijk procesrecht, Vol. IV. 1, Leiden: Brill, 1896, 32.

[6] Specific rules regarding one of these examples, i. e. the existence of a judgment having the force of *res iudicata*, are to be found in Arts. 1954 ~ 1957 (see below).

[7] "Vermoedens zijn gevolgtrekkingen, welke de wet of de regter uit eene bekende tot eene onbekende daadzaak afleidt. (…)."

[8] Of course, presumptions may also be at work where the defendant is required to prove certain matters.

[9] E. g. R. van Boneval Faure, Het Nederlandsche burgerlijk procesrecht, Vol. IV. 2, Leiden: Brill, 1897, 186. A. Grünebaum, "De verhouding tusschen wettelijke vermoedens en de verdeeling van den bewijslast", Rechtsgeleerd Magazijn 1905, 77 ~ 104 (89).

at work. Since, according to the traditional explanation, presumptions allow the claimant to prove other facts than the very facts on which his claim is based, they are often classified as mediate proof,[10] or artificial proof.[11]

Even though on the basis of the above one might think that presumptions do not pose many difficulties, it appears that this is not at all true: the subject has caused many problems. It has taken a long time to solve even the more obvious questions. This is due to the fact that the 1838 Civil Code is far from clear on this topic.

A first problematic issue is whether or not presumptions can be classified as a means of proof. The conclusion depends, of course, on how one defines means of proof. One definition is that the means of proof are *potentially* all those facts which are perceived by the judge during the legal action. However, due to the fact that in the greater part of the period discussed in this paper – just as in the preceding period – the law contained many restrictions as regards the manner in which evidentiary facts could be perceived by the judge, these facts are only *potentially* means of proof. They become real means of proof when they are perceived in a certain manner, e. g. by way of witness depositions or specific documents.[12] It has become practice to identify the facts that are perceived in this certain manner with the manner of perceiving these facts. Consequently, the usual approach is to refer to the various authorized manners of perceiving facts as means of proof. As a result, witness depositions may, for example, be classified as a means of proof.

For modern observers, it seems clear that presumptions are not a means of proof. After all, presumptions may determine that a party is *exempted* from proving certain facts; they are not a means of perceiving these facts in a certain manner. This does, however, not mean that the burden of proof is shifted, because the party who wants to have certain facts established by way of presumptions needs to adduce and, when necessary, prove other facts.[13] As regards these other facts, the majority of authors held that these needed to be proven by way of the usual means of proof. The most that can be said about presumptions is that they may alleviate the burden of proof since they allow parties to prove facts other than the ones that are to be presumed. Consequently, the *onus probandi* is not shifted.

In some countries, such as Belgium, even in the 21st century it was still subject to debate

---

〔10〕 E. g. A. Anema, Mr C. Asser's Handleiding tot de beoefening van het Nederlandsch burgerlijk recht (Vol. 5: Van bewijs), 4th ed., Zwolle: Tjeenk Willink, 1940, 287: "Voor de beoordeling of een bepaalde bewijsvoering tot de vermoedens behoort, stelle men zich enkel de vraag, of het bedoelde bewijs onmiddellijke zekerheid verschaft over *het gestelde feit zelf*, dan wel over *een feit, dat niet is gesteld*, maar alleen met de gestelde feiten in meer of minder eng verband staat." See also J. Eggens, Verklaring van het Burgerlijk Wetboek door Mr N. K. F. Land (Vol. 6: Boek IV, Titel I – VI), 2nd ed., Haarlem: De Erven F. Bohn N. V., 1933, 28.

〔11〕 E. g. J. Eggens, o. c., 202; A. Anema, o. c., 284.

〔12〕 Cf. J. Eggens, o. c., 26 ~ 27.

〔13〕 Consequently, Art. 1352 of the 1804 French *Code civil* is mistaken when it states that a (legal) presumption "dispense de toute preuve celui au profit duquel elle existe". See also A. Anema, o. c., 296.

whether (judicial) presumptions should or should not be classified as a means of proof.[14] In the Netherlands, the issue was only decisively solved by the legislature in 1988:[15] they could not be classified as such. One of the sources of confusion may have been Article 1316 of the 1804 French Civil Code, an Article that has remained in force in Belgium until today and that was replaced in the Netherlands by Article 1903 of the 1838 Dutch Civil Code. It reads as follows:

"Les régles qui concernent la preuve littérale, la preuve testimoniale, les présomptions, l' aveu de la partie et le serment, sont expliquées dans les sections suivantes."

Although the French Article is superfluous since it is only an introduction to what follows, it may give the impression that it is more, i. e. that it contains a list of some or all of the means of proof that are allowed by the Code. The Dutch legislature of 1838 must have thought that in this respect an improvement could be introduced and, consequently, did not copy Article 1316. It introduced Article 1903 in the 1838 Code which makes it clear that what is meant is indeed a list of the means of proof.[16] Unfortunately, the Dutch legislature forgot to remove presumptions from this list, even though the definition of presumptions in Article 1952 indicates that they should not be classified as such. It is significant in this respect that the confusion regarding the classification of presumptions only ended in the Netherlands in 1988, since it was in this year that the Dutch law of civil evidence was modernised and transferred from the former 1838 Civil Code to the Code of Civil Procedure. As stated above, from 1988 presumptions are not mentioned as a separate, abstractly defined category any more in Dutch legislation; Article 1903 was struck from the statute book.

Let us have a closer look at the authors who, before 1988, positively held that presumptions should *not* be classified as a means of proof.[17] Authors who embraced this idea stated that Article 1952 of the 1838 Civil Code proved that a *judicial* presumption was merely the *re-*

---

[14] C. Bosse, o. c., 36. The question whether or not presumptions should be regarded as a means of proof was a point of debate in various European countries. For 19th century Germany, see H. Burckhard, o. c., 3 ~ 4.

[15] See however, before World War II, already A. Anema, o. c., 285: "De oude leer der vermoedens als afzonderlijk bewijsmiddel heeft vrijwel afgedaan."

[16] Art. 1903 Dutch Civil Code (1838): "De bewijsmiddelen bestaan in: het schriftelijk bewijs, het bewijs door getuigen, de vermoedens, de bekentenis, den eed. Alles met inachtneming der regelen bij de volgende titels voorgeschreven."

[17] Examples of such authors are E. M. Meijers, "Bijdrage tot de leer van het middellijk bewijs", in: Verzamelde privaatrechtelijke opstellen, Vol. II, Leiden: Universitaire Pers, 1955, 223; J. Eggens, o. c., 28; A. Anema, o. c., 287 ~ 288: "Hieruit blijkt tevens, hoe onjuist de wet doet, door de vermoedens tot een afzonderlijk bewijsmiddel te maken. Vermoedens vloeien voort uit de gewone middelen, waarmee ook het onmiddellijk bewijs wordt geleverd (...)." Also A. Anema, o. c., 285, where it is stated that presumptions are not classified as a means of proof in Germany and Austria. It is interesting to observe that in an early draft of the Dutch Civil Code from 1820, presumptions were not listed as a means of proof (Art. 3311 of the 1820 Draft; see Ontwerp van het Burgerlijk Wetboek voor het Koningrijk der Nederlanden aan de Staten – Generaal aangeboden den 22sten November 1820, 2nd edition, Leiden: J. W. van Leeuwen, 1864; see, however, R. van Boneval Faure IV. 2, o. c., 136). The Dutch Minister of Justice doubted whether presumptions should be classified as a means of proof, at least in 1824 ~ 25, when the draft Civil Code was discussed in Parliament [J. J. F. Noordziek, Geschiedenis der beraadslagingen gevoerd in de Tweede Kamer der Staten – Generaal over het ontwerp van Burgerlijk Wetboek (zittingjaar 1824 ~ 1825, Vol. II, Bijlagen, bladz. I – XIV, 1 ~ 946), The Hague: Martinus Nijhoff, 1878, 636].

sult of a *mental activity* of the judge based on one of the "real" means of proof, for example witness depositions. The fact that Article 1903 expressly classified presumptions themselves as means of proof could not change this situation. The authors emphasized the soundness of their approach by pointing out that the 1838 Dutch legislature had introduced restrictions to the ways in which parties could prove their case by listing the means of proof that were allowed and by laying down specific rules as regards these means of proof. These restrictions were based on the fact that the legislature did not want to leave it completely to the judge's "intimate conviction" to decide whether or not a case was proven, but wanted him to reach his conclusion only on the basis of specific means of proof (here, the 1838 Dutch legislature was, of course, influenced by the system of legal proof of the *Ancien Régime*).[18] The authors held that if presumptions would have to be classified as separate means of proof, this would allow litigants to prove their case in a way that the legislature had most likely deemed to be unacceptable.[19] For instance, this would allow a party to prove his case by way of a single witness deposition, since this deposition might give rise to a presumption even though Article 1942 of the 1838 Dutch Civil Code specifically stated that a single witness deposition itself was insufficient.[20] If this approach was chosen, the only restriction that would apply could be found in Article 1959 of the 1838 Civil Code, i. e. that presumptions were forbidden in most cases where proof by witnesses was not allowed (for example, where a sum of money of more than 300 guilders was at stake). However, if presumptions would not be classified as a means of proof, but as conclusions based on the "real" means of proof, to which certain restrictions applied, this problem would not exist.

A prominent Dutch legal author, J. Eggens (1891 – 1964), claimed that it would, nevertheless, not be a bad idea to classify judicial presumptions as a separate means of proof.[21] In his opinion, such presumptions should be viewed as a manner to escape from the strict rules on evidence regulating the other means of proof, allowing the judge to freely evaluate this evidence. Part of Eggens' explanation was that examples could be found, where presumptions were not based on facts proven by one of the "real" (in his opinion "other") means of proof, for example, where a presumption was based on a party's refusal to follow the judge's orders. That such examples existed was, in Eggens' opinion, not a surprise since Article 1952 of the 1838 Code did not require that the facts on which presumptions were based should be facts proven by one of these means of proof. As has been noted, the Article only stated that a presumption is a conclusion based on a "known" matter and not on a "proven" matter. In Eggens' opinion, this was a possible explanation for the fact that presumptions were often regarded

---

[18] On presumptions and the system of legal proof, see e. g. H. Burckhard, o. c.

[19] E. g. E. M. Meijers, o. c., 221 ff. R. van Boneval Faure IV. 2, o. c., 190, who positively classified presumptions as a means of proof, did not see this as a problem where it concerned, e. g., the introduction of *de auditu* witness depositions by way of a presumption.

[20] Art. 1942 of the 1838 Dutch Civil Code was abolished in 1988 with the modernization of the law of civil evidence.

[21] J. Eggens, o. c., 34, 201.

as a "weak" type of proof.[22] This was not so because presumptions would always result in a situation where some doubt might exist regarding the veracity of what was established on their basis. The contrary could indeed be true, for example in the traditional textbook example of presumptions, where the absence of a person from the place where a deed was signed at the very moment this occurred would prove that this person's signature was false.[23] However, they could be regarded as a weak type of proof due to the fact that they were *in abstracto* "distrusted" by the legislature because they were not necessarily based on a proven matter.[24] Consequently, according to Eggens, the legislature did not prescribe their probative value beforehand, but gave the judge freedom in what conclusion to reach on their basis.[25] This was different for the other means of proof. Originally, as regards these means of proof the 1838 legislature had strictly defined their probative value. Only as regards witness depositions this had been different. Eggens' conclusion, therefore, was that presumptions formed a separate category of means of proof, i. e. those means of proof which were not given a separate name by the legislature and whose probative value was left to the judge's discretion. This also led to the conclusion that witness depositions, whose probative value was not determined by the Code either, could, strictly speaking, also be considered as presumptions, but due to the fact that the legislature had regulated these means of proof separately and given them a separate name, they did, according to Eggens, not belong to presumptions in the strict sense (they did, however, belong to this category in the wider sense).[26]

Related to the classification of presumptions as a separate means of proof, was the question how judicial presumptions could be distinguished from the other means of proof. We have seen that Article 1952 defines judicial presumptions as "conclusions" of the judge as regards an unknown matter based on a known matter. According to some authors, this very definition did not set presumptions apart as a separate category, since the definition was also valid for means of proof other than the ones that would usually be classified as presumptions. In actual practice, proving a case always means bringing about conclusions of the judge on the basis of known matters resulting in knowledge about something that was not known before.[27] If witnesses, for example, state that at a certain moment in time they were present when the parties to an action uttered phrases which may be interpreted as the parties concluding a contract (and this is the only thing witnesses can declare; they cannot declare that they have seen the parties conclude a contract because they cannot be sure that the parties were *ad idem*), it is in the end the judge who, on the basis of a process of interpretation of these circumstances or matters, decides whether a contract has come into being and, consequently, whether the existence of a

[22] J. Eggens, o. c., 33. For a different explanation, see A. Anema, o. c., 286 ~ 287.

[23] Also E. M. Meijers, o. c., 211 ~ 212.

[24] See also R. van Boneval Faure IV. 2, o. c., 187.

[25] J. Eggens, o. c., 33, 202. Also E. M. Meijers, o. c., 229.

[26] J. Eggens, o. c., 33 ~ 34.

[27] See, e. g., E. M. Meijers, o. c., 226 ~ 228. Also R. van Boneval Faure IV. 2, o. c., 138.

contract between the parties has been proven.[28] One could hold that also in this case an unknown matter (the existence of a contract) has been proven on the basis of the judge's conclusions based on a known or proven matter (the parties uttering certain phrases). However, this way of proving a case is not referred to as proving by way of presumptions. Nevertheless, this case does not differ at all from the standard textbook example of proving a case by way of presumptions, i. e. establishing that the signature at the bottom of a deed is false by way of proving the presence of the person whose signature is at stake at a place different from the one where the deed was signed at the very moment of signing this deed, for example on the basis of witness depositions.[29] Again, it is the judge's conclusion that counts. To phrase it differently, the judge is in both cases doing the same: he is giving "legal significance" to the "matters" that he bases his decision on, in both cases witness depositions. The legal significance the judge attaches to the presence of a certain person at a certain place is that the signature must be false, just as the legal significance the judge attaches to the parties uttering certain phrases is that a contract has come into existence. Of course, the usual explanation of the difference between the two cases is that what is proven in the former case is the absence of the person from the place where the deed was signed and only indirectly that the signature is false, whereas it is held that in the latter case the existence of a contract is directly proven. However, on second thoughts the difference is hard to see. In fact, if one approaches the issue of proof from the perspective of giving legal significance to facts, the difference evaporates. In each case the question then is: what legal significance should be given to the facts in question? It can be said that in both cases, one is dealing with mediate proof by way of presumptions since in both cases the proof is based on deductions. A possible way to distinguish these situations is that presumptions are *in abstracto* ultimately (only) based on what usually happens in similar types of cases,[30] whereas the degree of certainty reached by way of the other means of proof may be higher, at least *in abstracto*.

Apart from these issues of classification, differences of opinion existed throughout the 19th and 20th centuries as regards the correct interpretation of Article 1952. According to the influential Leiden law professor R. van Boneval Faure (1826 – 1909), Article 1952 should be interpreted in the following manner:

"a presumption is the conclusion that a fact that cannot be proven immediately is true, on the basis of a deduction based on another, proven fact. This deduction should be justified by

---

[28] J. Eggens, o. c., 30 ~ 31.

[29] It should be noted that some authors questioned this standard textbook example. They felt that this was not a presumption at all. See, e. g. R. van Boneval Faure IV. 2, o. c., 139.

[30] Cf. R. van Boneval Faure IV. 2, o. c., 138, who refers to R. – J. Pothier, Traité des obligations (various editions), Nr. 840: "Ces conséquences sont fondées sur ce qui arrive communément et ordinairement." E. M. Meijers, o. c., 226 ~ 228, tried to save the distinction between presumptions and the 'real' or other means of proof by stating: "Het eigenaardige van het directe bewijs is dan ook niet hierin gelegen, dat men zijn bewijs niet op een gegeven feit opbouwt, maar *dat dit gegeven feit een mondelinge of schriftelijke verklaring van een persoon is en men uit deze verklaring tot de juistheid van het verklaarde besluit.*"

the circumstance that as a result of the existence of the proven fact, the fact that cannot be proven immediately can or must be considered to have taken place. "[31]

This definition has "translated" the rather vague expression of "matter" in Article 1952 of the 1838 Civil Code into "fact", whereas it states positively that the "known matter/fact" on which the presumption is based should be a proven matter/fact. Additionally, some information is given as regards the relationship between the "known matter/fact" and the "unknown matter/fact" ("can or must be considered to have taken place"). Consequently, information has been supplied that is missing in the Article. After all, neither in the Code nor in the Article is anything said on the meaning of "matter" ("daadzaak") or on the necessity of proving the "known matter", whereas information on the closeness of the relationship between the matter/fact that is known and the matter/fact that is to be presumed (in other words, the degree of certainty or probability that is needed as regards the truth of the knowledge acquired on the basis of the known matter/fact) is absent too [this is not changed by the very cryptic Article 1959 of the Code, which admonishes the judge only to take into consideration presumptions (*lege*: facts)[32] that are sufficiently grave, defined and in accordance with each other].[33]

The lack of clarity in Article 1952 was especially problematic as regards judicial presumptions, since these presumptions were left to the discretion of the judge, who, consequently, could not use statute as a guideline.

As regards the meaning of the word "matter", the discussion focussed on the question whether the unknown matter that was to be presumed on the basis of a known matter could be a subjective right. This question was linked to the more general discussion on how the existence of a right could be established. Was it necessary to prove the facts which had given rise to the creation of this right – an approach that was popular in Germany at the end of the 19th century and the beginning of the 20th century – or could the existence of such a right also be proven in a different manner, for example by way of facts which could *not* have given rise to the creation of such a right but which could nevertheless give rise to the presumption that such a right existed? Only in the latter case could presumptions be used to directly establish the existence of a right and, in that case, the words "unknown matter" in Article 1952 should not be interpreted as "unknown fact" only, but should also include "unknown right".[34]

The authors who were of the opinion that rights could be established directly on the basis of presumptions, referred to Articles in the Code which in their opinion could be classified as legal presumptions and which directly resulted in the establishment of a right. An example was

---

[31] R. van Boneval Faure IV. 2, o. c. , 134: "Een vermoeden is een besluit tot de waarheid van een niet onmiddellijk bewijsbaar feit, bij gevolgtrekking uit een bewezen feit, welke gevolgtrekking wordt gerechtvaardigd doordien, om het bestaan van het bewezen feit, het niet onmiddellijk bewijsbare kan of moet worden aangenomen te hebben plaatsgehad. "

[32] Ibid. , 136 ~ 137.

[33] The phrase "in accordance with each other" in Art. 1959 of the 1838 Civil Code should *not* be understood in the sense that it requires several presumptions to coincide. See J. Eggens, o. c. , 198 ~ 199; R. van Boneval Faure IV. 2, o. c. , 136 ~ 137, 186, 189.

[34] E. M. Meijers, o. c. , 213ff; J. Eggens, o. c. , 31 ~ 33.

Article 681 of the 1838 Civil Code, in which the known matter that a wall separated two properties was taken as giving rise to the presumption of the joint ownership of the wall by the owners of those two properties.[35] In addition, one author approached the issue by looking at the history of Article 1952.[36] Since the preparatory works of the 1838 Dutch Civil Code did not contain relevant information, he turned to Article 1349 of the 1804 French Civil Code, on which the Article in the Dutch Code was based. Article 1349 gave the following definition of presumptions:

"Les présomptions sont des conséquences que la loi ou le magistrat tire d' un fait connu ǎ un *fait* inconnu." (italics supplied, CHvR)

Evidently, this Article uses the word "fact" ("fait") where the 1838 Dutch Civil Code uses the word "matter" ("daadzaak") and, therefore, one could come to the conclusion that establishing the existence of a *right* by way of a presumption was not what the legislature had intended. However, according to this author, one should not attach too much significance to the use of the word "fact". He referred to a draft of Article 1349, which reads:

"La présomption est un jugement, que la loi ou le magistrate porte sur la vérité d' une *chose*, par une conséquence tirée de faits et circonstances et qui est fondée sur ce qui arrive communément et plus ordinairement."

This draft is based on a definition of R. - J. Pothier (1699 - 1772), who stated that a presumption should be defined as "un jugement que la loi ou l'homme porte sur la vérité d' une chose, par une conséquence tirée d'une autre chose", adding that "[c] es conséquences sont fondées sur ce qui arrive communément et ordinairement".[37] Later, however, a definition was chosen for Article 1349, which to a certain extent followed J. Domat (1625 - 1696), who stated that presumptions are "des conséquences qu' on tire d' un fait connu, pour servir ǎ faire conno? tre la vérité d'un fait incertain, dont on cherche la preuve".[38] The replacement of the word "chose" by "fait" in Article 1349 does not appear to have been a deliberate choice and, consequently, it was held that "fait" could be read as "chose". Consequently, the wording of Article 1349 did not prevent the establishment of a right directly on the basis of a presumption.

The second problematic issue of the above interpretation of Article 1952 was whether indeed presumptions could only be based on *proven* matters. This question is tightly linked to the question whether or not presumptions are a separate means of proof. If the answer would be "no", and if this would mean that in the case of presumptions only the means of proof that were specifically allowed by the Code could be used, situations could be avoided in which mat-

---

[35] Other authors, however, stated that in this case there was no presumption in the sense of Art. 1952. This case was, according to them, an example where the *onus probandi* was shifted, not where an unknown matter was proven on the basis of a known matter. E. g. R. van Boneval Faure IV. 2, o. c., 150.

[36] J. Eggens, o. c., 178ff.

[37] R. - J. Pothier, o. c., Nr. 840.

[38] J. Domat, Les loix civiles dans leur ordre naturel (various editions), III. VI. IV. 1.

ters could be established by way of presumptions in a manner that most likely was considered to be unacceptable by the legislature. As was noted above, the question whether or not presumptions were a separate means of proof, and, consequently, the question whether or not they should be based on proven facts, was subject to debate.[39]

As we have seen, the interpretation of R. van Boneval Faure also contains some information on the relation between the known matter/fact, and the unknown matter/fact. This issue is especially relevant for judicial presumptions, since these are to a large extent left to the discretion of the judge. The author states that the deduction that is made in the case of presumptions "should be justified by the circumstance that as a result of the existence of the proven fact, the fact that cannot be proven immediately can or must be considered to have taken place". Of course, this interpretation does not offer much guidance. The author himself refers to Pothier to clarify his point of view.[40] As we have seen above, Pothier stated that the deduction should be based on what usually happens, or, in the terminology of Cujacius (1522 ~ 1590), to whom Pothier refers, "id quod plerumque fit". Again one may ask how much guidance is offered by this approach. The legislature must have realized that it was difficult (and maybe impossible) to abstractly describe the relation between the known and the unknown matter and, therefore, the Code only admonishes the judge to be careful where presumptions are at stake (Article 1959).

3. Which types of presumption can be distinguished in Dutch law?

In Section 1, an attempt has been made to establish how presumptions were characterised in Dutch civil procedure in the 19th and 20th centuries. It has been shown that differences of opinion existed regarding various important issues. In the present section, the different types of presumptions that were distinguished will be discussed. Again, many differences of opinion as well as ambiguities may be observed.

In the introduction, it was stated that Article 1952 of the 1838 Civil Code makes a distinction between presumptions that are specifically regulated by statute, and presumptions where this is not the case.[41] In Article 1952, the former type of presumptions are referred to as "legal presumptions" ("wettelijke vermoedens") and the latter type as "non – legal presumptions" ("vermoedens welke niet op de wet zelve gegrond zijn"). In the present paper, the latter presumptions are referred to also as "judicial presumptions".

Judicial presumptions are not specifically defined in a separate Article in the Code. This was possibly not found to be necessary, since they are sufficiently covered by the general Article 1952 which makes it clear that these presumptions are to be defined as "conclusions of the judge as regards an unknown matter on the basis of a known matter". From Article 1959 it ap-

---

[39] An author who held that presumptions were not necessarily based on proven facts is A. Grünebaum, o. c., 90.

[40] R. van Boneval Faure IV. 2, o. c., 138ff; R. – J. Pothier, o. c., Nr. 840.

[41] Art. 1952: "(…) Zij (i. e. presumptions) zijn van tweederlei aard: wettelijke, en de zoodanige welke niet op de wet zelve zijn gegrond."

pears that these presumptions are left to the judge's discretion.[42] Nevertheless, certain restrictions apply. As we have seen, they could, for example, not be used in cases where proof by way of witnesses was forbidden.[43] In Section 1 of this paper, many of the issues concerning judicial presumptions have been discussed. What has not been discussed in this section are the different names under which judicial presumptions were known in legal literature. In fact, often authors used the terminology from the *ius commune* and referred to these presumptions as *praesumptiones hominis*[44] or *praesumptiones facti*.[45] The name *praesumptiones simplices* was not as popular in the Netherlands as in France, where Pothier had introduced the French translation of the latter term ("présomptions simples").[46] Sometimes the traditional terminology was criticised. J. Eggens, for example, stated that the terminology *praesumptiones facti* was inadequate since it gave the impression that the unknown matter that was to be presumed could only be a fact and not a right. It is not a surprise that Eggens was critical as regards this terminology, since it was this author who claimed that rights could also be established by way of presumptions. Eggens was of the opinion that the name *praesumptiones facti* could only be justified if one focussed on the activity of the judge giving rise to a judicial presumption, the starting point of which was indeed a (known) fact.[47] However, as stated, the end – result could in his opinion be that a right was held to be established on the basis of this fact.

Let us now turn to legal presumptions. These presumptions were also referred to by their names from the period of the *ius commune*: either *praesumptiones iuris*,[48] or *praesumptiones legis*[49] or, in French, "présomptions légales".[50] Although Article 1952 of the 1838 Dutch Code contains a definition of both judicial and legal presumptions, a further definition of legal presumptions is given by Article 1953 of the Code. There we find that they are presumptions,

---

[42] Art. 1959: "Vermoedens welke niet op de wet zelve gegrond zijn worden overgelaten aan het oordeel en aan de voorzigtigheid van den regter, die echter op geene andere letten mag dan op die welke gewigtig, naauwkeurig, bepaald en met elkander in overeenstemming zijn. Zoodanige vermoedens kunnen alleenlijk in aanmerking komen in de gevallen waarin de wet het bewijs door getuigen toelaat, en ook bijaldien, uit hoofde van kwade trouw of bedrog, tegen eene handeling of akte wordt opgekomen." Cf. Art. 1353 French *Code civil* (1804): "Les présomptions qui ne sont point établies par la loi, sont abandonées aux lumière et à la prudence du magistrat, qui ne doit admettre que des présomptions graves, précises et concordantes, et dans les cas seulement où la loi admet les preuves testimoniales, à moins que l' acte ne soit attaqué pour cause de fraude ou de dol."

[43] Art. 1933 Dutch Civil Code (1838).

[44] J. Voetius, Commentarius ad Pandectas, XXII. 3. 14.

[45] H. Burckhard, o. c., 4.

[46] R. – J. Pothier, o. c., Nr. 849. From Pothier's description of "présomptions simples" it may, however, be deduced that only a particular type of judicial presumptions could be classified as "présomptions simples".

[47] J. Eggens, o. c., 204 ~ 205.

[48] J. Voetius, Commentarius ad Pandectas, XXII. 3. 15.

[49] H. Burckhard, o. c., 4.

[50] E. g. Art. 1350 French *Code Civil* (1804).

"which by virtue of a specific legal provision, are linked to certain acts or certain matters".[51] This definition is not very clear, but from legal literature it appears that these presumptions could best be described as presumptions based on legal provisions that prescribe the particular conclusion the judge must reach when certain facts are established. The conclusion itself is not drawn by the judge, but has been drawn by the legislature.[52] Consequently, the judge does not have any discretion in this respect.[53] His only task is to determine whether the facts on which the presumption is based are sufficiently established. Therefore, legal presumptions can best be viewed as legal rules regulating the probative force of a known matter.[54] Their result is that the person in whose favour the legal presumption exists is freed from the obligation to introduce further proof (*not* freed from introducing any proof, as the 1804 French *Code civil* states, since the facts giving rise to the legal presumption need to be established or proven).[55]

A legal presumption that is not mentioned in legislation does not exist. Therefore, it is important that it is clear when a particular legal provision contains a legal presumption. The 19th century legislature, however, did not choose a uniform way of making this clear. At times it seems that no effort at all was made to demonstrate that a legal presumption was at stake, as in the case of Article 1475 of the 1838 Civil Code. This Article states that where a creditor has voluntarily returned the document in which a debt is recorded to the debtor, this "proves" that the debtor is liberated from the debt.[56] Nevertheless, most authors were of the opinion that this was an example of a legal presumption. As a result of this lack of clarity, part of the discussion of 19th and 20th century authors consisted of an evaluation of which provisions of the various codes dealt with presumptions and which did not. Some help was offered by Article 1953 of the 1838 Dutch Civil Code, which contains a list of examples where legal presumptions are at work.

The examples given in Article 1953 are:

(1) Acts that are declared to be void by the law because on the basis of their character it must be presumed that they are performed in order to circumvent the law;

(2) Cases in which the law states that (the right of) ownership or the liberation of a debt must be deduced from certain specific circumstances;

(3) The significance the law attaches to a judgment having the force of *res iudicata*;

---

[51] Art. 1953: "Wettelijke vermoedens zijn de zoodanige welke, uit krachte eener bijzondere wetsbepaling, met zekere handelingen of met zekere daadzaken verbonden zijn. (…)." Cf. Art. 1350 French *Code civil* (1804): "La présomption légale est celle qui est attachée par une loi spéciale à certains actes ou à certains faits. (…)."

[52] J. Eggens, o. c., 196 ~ 197.

[53] R. van Boneval Faure IV. 2, o. c., 174; A. Grünebaum, o. c., 98 ~ 99.

[54] J. Eggens, o. c., 194.

[55] Art. 1958 Dutch Civil Code (1838): "Een wettelijk vermoeden ontslaat dengenen, in wiens voordeel hetzelve bestaat, van alle verdere bewijzen." Cf. Art. 1352 Cc: "La présomption légale dispense de toute preuve celui au profit duquel elle existe." See R. van Boneval Faure IV. 2, o. c., 170.

[56] The Dutch word "kwijtschelding" in Article 1475 of the 1838 Code should be interpreted as 'liberation' according to, e. g., R. van Boneval Faure IV. 2, o. c., 151 ~ 155.

(4) The force the law attaches to a confession or an oath of a party.[57]

Example (1) concerns wills and donations in which the apparent beneficiaries are presumed to be a front for persons who are not allowed to benefit. An example is where, for reasons of safeguarding the rights of children from an earlier marriage, a donation by the husband to a close relative of his wife or by the wife to a close relative of her husband was void because it was presumed to be a forbidden donation of a husband to his wife or vice versa.[58]

As regards the first type of cases mentioned under two, the authors found it difficult to give examples. They referred to Article 214 of the 1838 Civil Code concerning the purchase of immovables and stocks during the marriage of spouses who had opted for a specific marital property regime, the so-called "gemeenschap van winst en verlies" ("community of profits and losses"); in that case there was a rebuttable legal presumption that the purchased immovables and stocks were to be classified as profits and therefore belonged to the community at the moment the community was terminated.[59] An example of the second type is where the creditor has voluntarily returned the document in which a debt is recorded mentioned above.[60] Example (3) and (4) were deemed to be useless by most authors, since they were said to concern matters other than legal presumptions. According to these authors, example three is mentioned not because a presumption is at stake, but most likely because the drafters of the Code copied Pothier, who in his *Traité des obligations* discussed *res iudicata* directly after the presumptions and who needed some kind of introduction to his discussion of this topic.[61] Example four was generally held not to be concerned with presumptions, but with two separate means of proof that should not be classified as presumptions.[62]

Apart from the fact that the legislature was not very successful in giving examples of legal presumptions or referring to legal presumptions in a uniform way, further difficulties were caused by the fact that various provisions of the Code, due to the terminology used, gave the

---

[57] Art. 1953: " (...) Van dien aard zijn onder andere:

De handelingen welke de wet nietig verklaart, omdat zij, door haren aard en hare hoedanigheid alleen, vermoed worden gepleegd te zijn om eene wetsbepaling te ontduiken;

De gevallen waarin de wet verklaart dat de eigendom, of de bevrijding van schuld uit zekere bepaalde omstandigheden wordt afgeleid;

Het gezag hetwelk de wet aan een regterlijk gewijsde toekent;

De kracht welke de wet aan de bekentenis van eene der partijen of aan derzelver eed toekent."

Art. 1350 French *Code civil* (1804): " (...) tels sont:

Les actes que la loi déclare nuls, comme présumés faits en fraude de ses dispositions, d'après leur seule qualité;

Les cas dans lesquels la loi déclare la propriété ou la libération résulter de certaines circonstances déterminées;

De l'autorité que la loi attribue à la chose jugée;

La force que la loi attache à l'aveu de la partie ou à son serment."

[58] Art. 239 Dutch Civil Code (1838); R. van Boneval Faure IV. 2, o. c., 146 ~ 147.

[59] Ibid., 148 ~ 151.

[60] Art. 1475 Dutch Civil Code (1838); R. van Boneval Faure IV. 2, o. c., 151 ~ 155.

[61] Ibid., 145 ~ 146. See also R. van Boneval Faure, Het Nederlandsche burgerlijk procesrecht, Vol. II, Leiden: Brill, 1900, 309ff, and A. Anema, o. c., 293.

[62] R. van Boneval Faure IV. 2, o. c., 158 ~ 161, and A. Anema, o. c., 295.

impression that they were dealing with legal presumptions where, on close inspection, this was not the case. A provision the authors referred to was Article 627 of the 1838 Civil Code, which provides that "(the right of) ownership is presumed to be unburdened". However, this is not a presumption in the sense of Article 1952/1953. After all, the question could be asked from which known matter the legislature could have deduced the unknown matter of the right of ownership not being burdened. It is unlikely that the right of ownership itself could have functioned as such a known matter.[63]

Another example of a provision that gives the impression that it is dealing with legal presumptions in the sense of Articles 1952/1953, where on close inspection this appears not to be the case, is according to various authors Article 589 of the 1838 Civil Code. In this Article it is stated that "the good faith of a possessor will always be presumed".[64] In Article 2002 of the same Code, one reads that generally "good faith is to be presumed". In these two cases, again, we are not dealing with presumptions in the sense of Articles 1952 and 1953, since a known matter on which the unknown matter (good faith) can be presumed is absent. This known matter can definitely not be someone's possession, whereas other candidates for being the "known matter" cannot be found.[65]

Generally speaking, the group of cases to which the above two examples belong concerns provisions shifting the *onus probandi* from the person stating a fact to the opposing party; not proving an unknown matter on the basis of a known matter.[66]

In addition to the problems that arose in the determination of the legal presumptions acknowledged in Dutch law, further problems were caused by the traditional distinction between rebuttable and irrebuttable legal presumptions in Article 1958 of the 1838 Civil Code[67] (in the terminology of the *ius commune*: "praesumptiones iuris tantum" and "praesumptiones iuris et de iure" respectively). Rebuttable legal presumptions allow the opposing party to prove that what is presumed on their basis is wrong. An example of a rebuttable legal presumption can be found in Article 1430 of the 1838 Dutch Civil Code: the payment of three consecutive instalments of a debt leads to the presumption that the previous instalments have also been paid, at least if the requirements of Article 1430 are met.[68]

Irrebuttable presumptions, on the other hand, do not allow the opposing party to prove

---

[63] R. van Boneval Faure IV. 2, o. c., 140 ~ 141.

[64] Cf. Art. 3: 118 (3) of the present Dutch Civil Code and I. Giesen, o. c., 67.

[65] R. van Boneval Faure IV. 2, o. c., 141, 164 ~ 166.

[66] e. g. R. van Boneval Faure IV. 2, o. c., 141; J. H. Polenaar, Mr. B. J. Polenaar's Schets van het Nederlandsche Burgerlijk Procesrecht, 6th ed., Haarlem: Tjeenk Willink & Zoon, 1925, 179.

[67] Art. 1958: "(...) Geen bewijs wordt tegen een wettelijk vermoeden toegelaten, in geval de wet, op grond van dit vermoeden, zekere bepaalde handelingen nietig verklaard [sic], of den regtsingang weigert; ten zij de wet zelve het tegenbewijs mogt hebben vrijgelaten, en onverminderd hetgeen omtrent den geregtelijken eed en de geregtelijke bekentenis vastgesteld is." See also Art. 1352 French *Code civil* (1804): "(...) Nulle preuve n'est admise contre la présomption de la loi, lorsque, sur le fondement de cette présomption, elle annulle certains actes ou dénie l'action en justice, à moins qu' elle n'ait réservé la preuve contraire, et sauf ce qui sera dit sur le serment et l'aveu judiciaires."

[68] A. Anema, o. c., 296.

that what is presumed on their basis is wrong. According to various authors, these presumptions should, nevertheless, be distinguished from fictions. The difference between fictions and irrebuttable legal presumptions is that in the case of fictions, certain facts are held to exist even though other, known facts do not necessarily make it likely that this is indeed the case. In the case of irrebuttable legal presumptions, however, the known facts make the existence of the unknown matter likely.[69]

According to Article 1958, a presumption should be classified as irrebuttable where, on the basis of this presumption, statute determines that a legal act is void[70] or where it "refuses a legal action", unless counter proof is specifically allowed (if counter proof is allowed, the presumption should, accordingly, be classified as rebuttable).[71] The phrase "where statute refuses a legal action" should, according to the authors, not be taken too literally, but referred to cases where a peremptory exception could successfully be introduced against the claim.[72] In actual practice, it appeared to be very difficult to establish whether or not a legal presumption could be classified as irrebuttable.[73]

Most authors held that irrebuttable presumptions are in actual fact mandatory statutory rules which have nothing to do with presumptions or proof.[74] An example of a legal presumption that was classified as irrebuttable was where statute declared – for reasons of safeguarding the rights of children from an earlier marriage – a donation by the husband to a close relative of his wife or by the wife to a close relative of her husband illegal because it was presumed to be a be a forbidden donation of a husband to his wife or vice versa.[75] In the opinion of most authors, the legislature had unjustly disguised this mandatory statutory rule as a presumption; in their opinion, the legislature should have stated positively that donations of a husband or of a wife to certain relatives of the wife or the husband respectively are illegal: exit presumptions.

---

〔69〕 A. Grünebaum, o. c. , 102: "Noodig is echter, dat de *mogelijkheid* van de juistheid der gevolgtrekking bestaat, anders betreedt men het terrein van de *fictie*"; C. Bosse, o. c. , 40, defines *fictions* as "vaststellingen die menselijkerwijs niet waar kunnen zijn", whereas P. Scholten, Mr. C. Asser's Handleiding tot de beoefening van het Nederlands burgerlijk recht (Algemeen deel), Zwolle: Tjeenk Willink, 1974, 51, states that they result in "iets bewust in strijd met de waarheid als feitelijke toestand [aannemen]". See also A. Anema, o. c. , 290, and H. Burckhard, o. c. , 28, who states that according to Alciatus the "Unterschied zwischen Fiction und Präsumtion, [···] darin gefunden wird, dass diese in veritate fundatur, die Fiction aber legis adversus vertitatem dispositio ist".

〔70〕 According to R. van Boneval Faure IV. 2, o. c. , 176 ~ 177, Art. 1958 should be read in conjunction with Art. 1953 (1): the act is void because it is presumed to be executed in order to evade the law.

〔71〕 According to most authors, examples where statute allowed counter proof in cases where, on the basis of a presumption, a legal act was held to be void or a legal action was refused could not be found in the original 1838 Civil Code. See R. van Boneval Faure IV. 2, o. c. , 179.

〔72〕 Ibid. , 177 ~ 178; A. Anema, o. c. , 296 ~ 297.

〔73〕 R. van Boneval Faure IV. 2, o. c. , 176.

〔74〕 E. g. A. Anema, o. c. , 288 ~ 289; R. van Boneval Faure IV. 2, o. c. , 142; A. Grünebaum, o. c. , 104; E. M. Meijers, o. c. , 209 ~ 210; J. H. Polenaar, o. c. , 179: "*wettelijke vermoedens* (...), die echter zoo min vermoedens zijn als bewijsmiddelen, maar bepaalde wettelijke voorschriften van *materieel recht*, of wel regelen, omtrent de *verdeeling van den bewijslast.*"

〔75〕 Art. 239 Dutch Civil Code (1838). A. Anema, o. c. , 294 ~ 295.

Conclusion

The present contribution has shown that presumptions were a phenomenon in the law of civil procedure that posed considerable problems, both from the perspective of classification and conceptually. It was not clear how presumptions had to be classified, even if irrebuttable legal presumptions, which according to the majority of authors had nothing to do with presumptions proper, were left apart. Were presumptions to be classified as means of proof, or should they only be seen as conclusions based on means of proof? In addition, there was a conceptual problem since the Dutch Civil Code did not define presumptions very clearly. This became apparent where, for example, the question was asked whether or not a presumption should be based on a proven matter. Also, the meaning of "matter" itself was subject to debate, especially where it concerned the "unknown matter". Did "matter" mean fact, or could the unknown matter also be a right? In other words, was it possible to establish the existence of a right on the basis of a presumption? And, as regards legal presumptions: they could only exist if they were regulated as such by statute. However, it appeared not to be an easy task to determine whether indeed a legal provision aimed at creating a legal presumption. It was, therefore, not a bad idea of the Dutch legislature to remove presumptions as an abstract category from the statute book in 1988 since the legal rules were defective in many ways. This did, however, not mean that presumptions themselves disappeared from the Dutch legal landscape, as has been shown in this article. Nevertheless, it does not seem that in actual practice the disappearance of the abstract rules regulating presumptions has caused many difficulties in the Netherlands, even though this change in the law means that the judge is left without any statutory guidance in solving the questions that may arise as regards presumptions.

循证刑事证明研究

刘立霞* 杨 雪**

一、根据个人经验进行证明的危害

刑事证明是指在刑事诉讼过程中，公安机关、人民检察、当事人及其代理人、辩护人等证明主体在证明责任的作用和机制下，依照法定的程序，调查、收集、提供证据，对待证事实进行求证的诉讼活动。[1] 刑事证明的目的就是运用推理等方法查明案件事实，决定犯罪嫌疑人、被告人有罪或无罪，是否受处罚、如何处罚和程序问题。刑事证明是一种追本溯源的复杂过程，但是，其证明对象是具有不可回溯性的，任何一个犯罪事件都是独一无二的，想象的或模糊的重建都几乎无法确切地复原案件事实。实践中，刑事证明的常用方法就是刑事推定，即在认定刑事案件事实的过程中，司法人员在不得已的情况下，根据法律规定或经验法则，在没有相反证据反驳推翻的情况下，从已知的基础事实推导出另一未知事实（推定事实）存在的一种证明方法。对于案件事实的复原需要推定，推定是要以司法人员的个人经验为基础的，但是司法人员的个人经验是具有局限性的，容易受到人格、工作能力、法律经验、审判标准、政治经验、经验积累程度、地域、“错误经验”、法律价值取向、理论高度及其自身纪律约束等诸多因素影响的。而且由于工作地区、机关级别、机关性质的差异，也会导致司法人员的素质参差不齐。刑事诉讼证明过程的重点就是证明主体根据个人经验运用搜集到的证据证明案件事实的过程，人的主观能动性在其中起着重大作用。

在司法实践中因犯罪事实难以认定或认定错误而导致一系列冤错案件的情况屡见不鲜，不仅使一些罪犯逃避了法律制裁，更是给受害者及其家属带来极大的创伤；不仅导致刑事案件的改判率、发回重审率居高不下，浪费了司法资源，还损害法律权威，威胁法律信仰，降低法律公信力。最高人民法院常务副院长沈德咏大法官明确指出：“当前部分群众对司法的不信任感正在逐渐泛化成普遍社会心理，这是一种极其可怕的现象。”沈德咏2013年5月6日在《人民法院报》发表题为《我们应当如何防范冤假错案》的署名文章。文章称，“思想上要进一步强化防范冤假错案的意识，要像防范洪水猛兽一样来防范冤假错案，宁可错放，也不可错判。错放一个真正的罪犯，天塌不下来，错判一个无辜的公民，特别是错杀了一个人，天就塌下来了”。在刑事证明中起到重要作用的是司法工作者的经验，无论是寻找证据还是证明案件事实，个人经验在其中起着举足轻重的作用，如果个人经验得不到合理的修正，那么对刑事证明工作将产生决定性的重大影响。实践中根据司法者个人经验导致的冤假错案屡见不鲜。例如

---

* 刘立霞，河北省秦皇岛市燕山大学教授。Email：liulixia@126.com。

** 杨雪，燕山大学文法学院硕士研究生。

〔1〕 郭志远：《证明标准研究——以刑事诉讼为视角》，中国人民公安大学出版社2010年版，第9页。

轰动一时的张高平、张辉叔侄强奸案，明明案件存在诸多疑点，办案者却一开始便本着“有罪推定”来证明案件，凭着所谓的经验来演绎，没有证据，便硬性推出“证据”。在这起冤案中，叔侄两人被错误羁押10年之久，给被冤者及其家属造成巨大的物质损失和精神创伤，而且由于当时张高平、张辉叔侄被“绳之以法”，真正的犯罪者继续逍遥法外，在2004年10月19日，张氏叔侄案在浙江高院终审判决之后，不到3个月，真正的罪犯勾海峰又在相同的地点以相同的手法继续犯下命案。根据当年从死者身上提取的DNA混合物比对结果令人瞠目结舌：可能的真凶，已于2005年因涉及另一起具有相似事实的命案，被枪决。仔细思考这起案件疑点太多：一是全案定罪仅有口供，而无任何物证，而两人供述的作案细节多处不同；二是受害人指甲里检出的DNA混合谱带根本就没有张辉、张高平的DNA。如果对案件的这些疑点进行考虑，那么叔侄两人的嫌疑在侦查阶段就可以被排除，但是，办案人员坚定地认为叔侄二人是真凶，并且沿着这个方向去侦查和证明。这起冤案的制造者之一，是一个所谓神探，是一个意气风发的被褒以“无懈可击”的女神探聂海芬。经过调查，在这起案件的侦查审讯过程中，并没有掺杂其他不法程序，侦查者“很认真”地将这一起冤案进行证明并且达到“事实清楚，证据充分”的要求。但是他们为了达到破案的目的，刻意忽略影响案件的证据，单纯地考虑有利于案件迅速破获的证据，甚至创造证据来支撑案件的成立。但是正是因为作为神探的聂海芬根据以往的个人经验办案，受到各方的关注和好评，所以她很自信地继续着自己的法律观念和一些侦查、证明手段，这样看似正确的经验反而成了造成冤假错案的真凶。司法实践中，不止一个聂海芬，我相信还有很多聂海芬的存在，他们认真工作，但是就是因为长期单纯依靠个人经验判断，造成一些疑点重重的案件被定案。因为司法者的错误的证明经验和法律价值取向，不仅造成一起冤假错案，而且助长了犯罪者的嚣张气焰，很可能导致下一个刑事案件的发生。显而易见，在刑事证明中修正办案人员的个人经验和法律观念，是司法工作的重中之重。

二、循证刑事证明产生背景及思想来源

“大数据时代的来临使人类第一次有机会和条件，在非常多的领域和非常深入的层次获得和使用全面数据、完整数据和系统数据，深入探索现实世界的规律，获取过去不可能获取的知识，得到过去无法企及的商机。”[2] “大数据时代的经济学、政治学、社会学和许多科学门类都会发生巨大甚至本质上的变化和发展，进而影响人类的价值体系、知识体系和生活方式。”[3] 全球知名咨询公司麦肯锡，麦肯锡公司称：“数据，已经渗透到当今每一个行业和业务职能领域，成为重要的生产因素。”大数据的核心就是预测，将为人类的生活创造前所未有的可量化的维度。大数据已经成为了新发明和新服务的源泉，而更多的改变正蓄势待发。循证实践就是大数据时代最好的展现方式之一。将循证与刑事证明相结合，就是对大数据的最好应用之一。在刑事证明领域，我们可以立足于大数据时代的背景，将循证实践引入刑事证明，利用相关性的海量数

---

〔2〕［英］维克托·迈尔-舍恩伯格、［英］肯尼思·库克耶：《大数据时代》，盛杨燕、周涛译，浙江人民出版社2012年版，第5页。

〔3〕［英］维克托·迈尔-舍恩伯格，［英］肯尼思·库克耶：《大数据时代》，盛杨燕、周涛译，浙江人民出版社2012年版，第5页。

据来进行更精准的证明工作。

循证刑事证明的思想主要来源于循证医学，所谓循证医学就是“将最好的研究证据与临床技能与病人的价值观三者结合起来（进行治疗决策）”。[4] 首先，研究者中至少有一部分人密切关注医学实践，提供解决临床实践问题的证据；其次，医生从诊断、治疗、评估到预后均应参考相应的治疗指南或研究证据；最后，病人的价值观、主观意愿得到了重视，医生不再主宰治疗进程，病人亦可基于证据参与治疗决策，选择自己喜欢的治疗方案，积极主动地参与到治疗的过程中。[5] 其参与临床决策的因素可用图进行说明：见图1。

在大数据时代背景和循证理论视角下，司法者的个人经验不再是主宰整个案件事实证明工作的唯一标准，而是将刑事案件事实的证明导入庞大的法律数据库体系中，综合考虑学者理论研究、司法判例、取得的客观证据、他人证明方法和思维方式、犯罪嫌疑人或被告人的犯罪前的情况等各方面的因素。循证刑事证明的出现，降低了证明者个人经验的地位，大大提高了证明结果的准确性。例如张高平、张辉叔侄强奸案，司法者如果从数据库中搜索到一个或多个类似案件的证明经验，发现并且认知到DNA在整个案件事实中的决定性作用，也许就不会导致恶果。循证刑事证明要考虑的因素可图示：见图2。

图1 循证医学影响因素

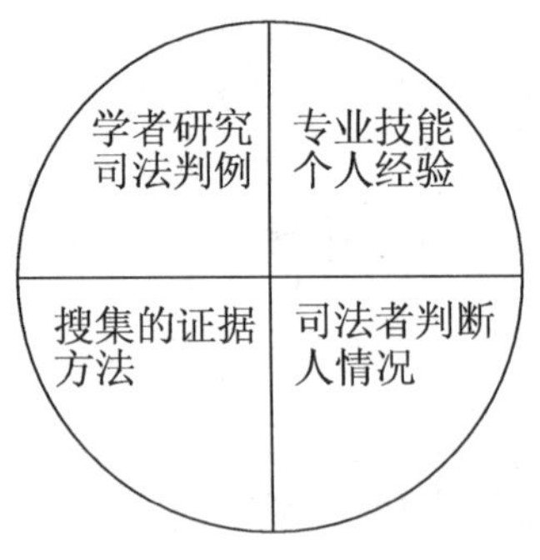

图2 循证刑事证明影响因素

循证刑事证的思想来源主要是循证医学，但是并不是完全套用循证医学的固有模式，二者是存在差异的。循证医学强调的是医生和病人之间的互动，需要病人的配合。而循证刑事证明活动的对象是案件事实，达到证明案件事实真相的目的就终止。一方面，循证刑事证明的互动过程体现在待证案件事实与理论研究、司法判例之间的互动，根据待证事实搜索所需法律资源，将引用的法律资源的使用效果进行反馈；另一方面，循证刑事证明的互动过程体现在一种隐形的知识框架的互动，比如各级司法机关通过循证手段，将不同的证明经验输入到同一数据库中，便于相互学习和交流。

---

〔4〕 Sackett, D. L. Straus, S. E. Richardson, *W. S. Evidence – based Medicine: How to Practice and Teach EBM*, London: Churchill Livingstone (2000).

〔5〕 杨文登：《循证心理治疗》，商务印书馆2012年版，第49页。

三、循证刑事证明的理论基础

（一）实证主义理论

实证主义思想方法和认识方法的一般特点是：研究“确实存在”的东西，追求“确实存在”的知识。实证主义的基本理论观：①任何概念和理论都必须以可观察的事实为基础，只有那些能够从我们自己的经验或观察中找到证据的东西才能称作为知识；②认为任何一般观念都必须有客观所指，而且这个“客观所指”与“事物”必须是我们能够通过实验或观察找到证据的，必须是一种对应的关系；③坚信科学方法的统一性，意味着实证主义者只接受一种探索世界、为知识提供证据的方法。[6] 这几条基本的实证主义理论观点对循证刑事证明产生了重要影响。循证刑事证明是一个独特的、综合的实践体系，它的数据基础包罗万象，来自各个学派的理论研究，来自各个法院的实务工作资料，进行循证证明实践的司法者也受到不同价值体系的影响。而只有那些可以客观、中立观察的内容才会得到关注。循证刑事证明所遵循的定案根据更多是严格的实证的资源，能为经验或从经验合乎逻辑的引申物所证实。

首先，实证主义强调感觉经验，认为人类对世间万物的了解不是生而有之，是不断地透过直接或间接的感觉或体验，从不同的情境中获得的。循证刑事证明中，案例库中的司法案例不是凭空产生的，是来源于各个不同实务部门的，是经实践检验并且证明可行的。科学研究的目的是为了发现自然法则，以便人们预测事件的发生、控制物质和社会环境。就循证来说，人们可系统地探讨影响案件证明的种种因素，用法学理论研究指导证明实践，从实践中获取验证理论，然后再指导实践。循证刑事证明是一个对证明经验的不断探索、应用、检验、指导的一个无止境的循环过程。

其次，实证主义强调客观性原则，而且社会现实稳定有序，原本就存在模式和规律。循证中，相同或相似案件的证明就存在内在的一种模式和规律，虽然不会存在完全相同的两种证明模式，但是模式的主体部分保持一致的可能性还是有的。循证就是要在司法群体中建立一套系统的证明规范，促使证明者的证明技术逐渐成熟。而且，刑事证明的过程中，要将客观的案件事实和证明者个人的情感、态度、价值观等区分开，用他人的经验去修正个人经验的不足之处，相对客观地看待每一个案件的证明程序。司法者站在一个更高的高度，将个人经验和他人成功经验相结合，运用结合后的经验进行证明活动，有利于证明者厘清思路，有利于更客观地揭开案件事实真相。在这里强调修正的结果只能是更接近客观，由于人的因素和复原案件事实的难度，不可能达到百分百的客观。

最后，实践是检验真理的标准，科学的解释必须经受得住客观事实的检验。此外，解释必须经得起重复。任何研究者都可重复他人的研究，这给创造知识的过程提供了一个监控的机制。法律研究的理论只有在实践中接受检验，才能确定是否符合社会发展规律。司法判例只有经得起重复质疑和监督，才能证明其准确性。在循证中，那些被反复引用的案例必然是引用率高的案例，那么对实践的指导意义更强，说明其证明经验更准确更实用。在原始案例和引用案例之间形成一个体系，并引入科学的管理要素。例如，一个案件的证明经验被引用100次，有99次的结果反馈都是成功的，那么

---

〔6〕 何雪松：《社会工作理论》，上海人民出版社2007年版，第17页。

其成功率就是99%，这些反馈由计算机系统自动生成。这个成功率99%的被引用案例经验的理论价值和实践价值是十分重要的，可以作为经典案例指导。而那些被引用率低或应用效果不好的案例，更是需要对其证明工作提出质疑，有助于发现冤假错案，当然对于几乎零引用的案例可以定时地进行清理。法学研究者在研究理论的同时，到法律数据库中寻找相关的司法判例，根据经典案例进行研究，观察理论与实践的差别，更接近于现实，有利于达到理论与实践的统一。法律理论和法律案例都得经得起实践的检验，才有利于法律的发展。

（二）建构主义理论

杨龙立在《建构主义教学的检讨》一文中，从三个方面概括了建构主义的基本主张：①人们知识的形成是主动建构产生的，而非被动接受产生；②人们的知识并非说明世界的真理而是个人经验的合理化；③人们的知识有其发展性、演化性，并非一成不变。他认为，首先，建构主义强调认知主体的主动性与重要性，认为非经主体的主动建构，知识不可能由外人传递给认知主体，认知主体也不会对他人传送的知识照单全收。所谓主动意味着认知主体对各种出现的知识现象会依据自己先前的知识、经验来衡量并赋予意义，从而以自己的观点诠释他人提供的知识。其次，建构主义认为，当我们只依据自己有限的知识、经验来诠释意义时，我们实际上无法确定建构出的知识是否是对世界的终极写照，所以建构主义回避真理的问题，并强调建构出的知识只是个体经验的合理化及实用化而已。最后，建构主义认为，由于知识由个人主动建构起来，而非终极真理，所以知识是不断发生变化的。

社会建构论属于建构主义中比较激进的一个分支。作为对后现代主义的超越，社会建构主义主要由三个方面所构成：①反本质主义，主张从本质主义转向建构主义，强调知识的建构性；②在"个体—社会"向度上，具有典型的社会取向性特点，主张从个体主义转向群体主义，强调知识建构的社会性；③关注社会实践与互动，主张从决定论转向互动论，强调知识"共建"的辩证性。任何知识都不是个人的产物，而是"集体智慧的结晶"。[7] 建构主义者承认并且尊重社会经验和个人经验的多样性，因历史、地域、情境、个人因素的不同而有所不同。知识既不单纯来自主体，也不单纯来自客体，而是来自主客体之间的相互作用。就实际的研究活动来说，研究者与被研究者之间是一个互为主体的关系，研究结果是由不同主体通过互动而达成的共识。知识既是人和世界建构的产物，又是人和人建构的产物。循证刑事证明恰到好处地体现了社会建构主义，证明者不再单纯依靠自身的经验进行证明，而是依靠诸多力量完成证明过程。不仅司法者自身要通过数据库学习他人的经验，也要将自身好的经验输入到数据库中去，供他人学习使用，这是一种司法者之间的变相互动方式。循证刑事证明促使刑事证明从个体的思维活动向吸收他人的思维活动的转变，考虑因素更多，结果就更加严谨，单个个体不再是不相关的，而是一个存在隐形关系的大群体。例如，最高人民法院的法官和基层人民法院法官的经验交流是较少的，但是通过对法律数据库的使用，基层法院的法官可以接触和学习到高层次的法官的断案经验，这样看似相关性不大的两个个体就联系起来，形成一种隐性的交流。循证刑事证明中，研究者和实

〔7〕 杨莉萍：《社会建构论心理学》，上海教育出版社2006年版，第30页。

践者的法律价值观也是处在一个互动的过程。理论研究者从数据库中寻找实实在在的司法案例，从实务中寻找研究方向。大多数司法者对前沿理论研究了解得不多，但是通过法律数据库的应用，司法者或多或少地学习到先进的前沿理论研究。这样，很多有价值的思想集中到一起，使每一个案件尤其是疑难案件不再是个人证明的结果，而是集体智慧的结晶。

四、循证刑事证明的意义

（一）有利于经验法则的运用

经验法则具有盖然性、无限性、抽象性、主观性等基本特征，这些特征决定刑事证明活动本身就具有较高的难度。司法者必须根据不同案件具体的复杂多变的情况，决定是否适用和如何适用经验法则，这是需要充分发挥个人的主观认知能力和专业知识技能才能完成的任务，并不是一项可以简单重复或机械套用的认知活动。经验法则的运用具有双刃剑的效应：一方面，它可以为认定某些难以证明的案件事实提供捷径；另一方面，它也可能使事实认定落入陷阱或步入歧途。[8] 为了防止后一种情况的出现，或者将其出现的可能性压缩到最小，法官在运用经验法则时必须坚持严格的原则。在这种情况下，循证的应用，不仅增强经验法则运用的可靠性、可信性、精确性，而且能够有效避免落入陷阱。经验法则不仅是不完全归纳的产物，而且还会受到一定的价值观念和社会政策的影响。虽然法律的基本价值内涵是公正的，但是选择经验法则的价值取向并非绝对公正，而是会有一定的倾向性，即优先或侧重考虑某种价值的需求。价值观念和社会政策会随着社会的发展而变化，不同的历史时期会有不同的价值观念和社会政策。在循证刑事证明中，司法者自身的法律价值观随着时代的发展可能出现这样或者那样的偏差。循证刑事证明的法律数据库中的海量信息都是处在不断更新的动态变化之中的，司法者在运用数据库的过程中与时俱进，不断纠正自身错误的、陈旧的法律价值观念。通过循证刑事证明，经验法则不仅运用难度降低了，提高了其可靠性，更加有利于复原案件事实，而且有助于纠正司法者的法律价值观，更有助于减少冤假错案，从而准确地认定案件事实。

“案件事实实际上是参与案件活动的司法人员、当事人、相关证人等各类人员对实际发生的案件进行逐步认知并经记忆、提取等心理活动的结果，案件事实的形成过程实际上是以人的认知活动为核心的内在的建构过程。”[9] 既然是以人为核心的活动，那么如何提高人的判断的准确性，就是至关重要的。循证就为证明者进行证明活动提供海量的可靠信息和丰富的断案经验，形成一种案例指导制。证明者在证明中无形地充实了自己的个人能力，通过吸取理论研究、司法判例、他人证明经验、思维方式等，逐渐突破司法认知的局限性，或者这种局限性的力度逐渐变弱，通过严谨的证明，尽可能地复原案件事实。

（二）有利于填补法律漏洞

法律规范的缺陷进一步增加了同案同判的难度。就法律漏洞来说，由于立法能力的有限性，法律规范从制定之时起就有可能落后于社会现实的发展。固定的法律规范

---

〔8〕 张亚东：《经验法则——自由心证尺度》，北京大学出版社2012年版，第112页。

〔9〕 陈增宝、李安：《裁判的形成：法官断案的心理机制》，法律出版社2007年版，第30页。

与动态的社会情况之间的“距离”不断增大，将来必然会通过司法案件反映在法律领域之中，此时就有可能出现需要对法律的漏洞进行补充的情形。如果面对丰富的案件事实仍然固守静态的、封闭的、狭隘的个人经验，很可能使得法律所追求的正义诉求无法完成，甚至损害个案正义的实现。由研究者和司法者协同合作建立法律数据库，研究者负责建立专家库，司法者负责建立案例库，逐渐改善法学理论研究、法律法规、实务工作的脱节现象。司法工作者根据判例库的相关案例抽象出法学理论来指导实践，从而弥补法律的滞后性，解决司法实践中的新情况、新问题。

（三）真正体现“公平 、公正、公开”原则

循证刑事证明所建设的法律数据库具有开放性和共享性，各方利用数据库搜索法律信息。循证刑事证明提供了一种科学的证明机制，能真正体现“公平、公正、公开”的原则。

法律数据库不仅能帮助司法者准确地、严谨地分析案件，证明犯罪事实，而且能被辩护方所用，使本来处于弱势的辩护方享受平等的法律数据库使用权，平衡控辩双方实力。循证刑事证明有利于保障犯罪嫌疑人、被告人的合法权利。循证刑事证明目的不仅仅是定罪量刑惩罚犯罪，而且包括保护犯罪嫌疑人、被告人人权。在刑事案件中，控诉机关不再处于绝对强势的地位，犯罪嫌疑人、被告人及其辩护人可以有资格使用法律数据库，从中找到与自己犯罪情况相关的法律资源。例如，案件相关的法律法规、理论研究或与自己犯罪情况相似的司法判例。之所以允许辩护方也具有使用法律数据库的资格，是因为不是只有司法者素质参差不齐，律师的素质也是高低不等的。律师在帮助犯罪嫌疑人、被告人辩护的过程中，律师能力的提升，有利于平衡控辩双方的能力。更重要的一点是，由于我国法律法规的普及不到位，绝大部分的犯罪者是无法预计到自己的危害行为将会受到怎样的法律惩罚，犯罪嫌疑人或者被告人可以根据此套系统预先知道自己所犯罪行可能受到的惩罚。有利于这些人对自己的罪行、相关的法律和案件进行了解，不仅便于保护自己的合法权利，而且具有普法教育意义。

另外，循证刑事证明有利于加强司法监督。对外，主要是有利于检察机关的监督工作，循证刑事证明需要海量的数据资源，这些资源中司法判例占有绝大部分，以往的案件资料都是以纸质的形式储存在“鲜为人知”的档案袋之中，通过循证刑事证明机制，将司法判例资料作为一种法律资源传入法律数据库中，便于检察机关监督案件，增强了司法工作的透明度，提高“公平、公正”的可能性。对内，由于判决的透明度提高了，对法院审判工作的要求也随之提高，审判人员的警觉性将会提高，达到一种“从被监督到自我监督”的意识转变。在循证刑事证明中，司法者正处于一种不断变化却日趋精密的被监视之中，事实上，他们的一举一动都能在某个数据库中找到线索。对司法工作的监督增强了，法律的“公平、公正”原则自然得到保障。

五、循证刑事证明的特征及实施步骤

（一）循证刑事证明的特征

循证刑事证明的五个特征：①科学与真实。循证刑事证明以学者的前瞻性研究和各地区的司法判例、司法者技能和经验为基础，以计算机技术为依托，用科学的方式进行数据化的管理，更加注重科学的思维方式和实务工作。更值得注意的是，循证刑事证明的案例来源于真实的法律实务工作，不是凭空产生的，更加贴近真实的社会现

状。②系统与量化。通过对各方面法律信息的收集，将散乱的理论和司法判例纳入到一个统一体系的大数据库中去，并将多元化的资源进行量化管理，既符合大数据时代的特征和循证理论基础，也是法律领域跟上时代步伐的大好时机。③动态与更新。在大数据时代的背景下，数据不同于静止不动的书本知识，无论是理论研究还是司法判例的更新都是非常迅速的，计算机技术的应用使法律的数据库随时处于动态与更新之中，不断有新的理论研究和新的案例被输入到数据库中去，更是有利于司法人员随时跟进最新的法律发展状况。④共享与实用。知识是无界限的，在传统证明中，个人经验具有私有性和封闭性的特点。现代的技术手段使大量的理论研究和司法判例可以通过网络传入法律大数据库中，以数据的形式进行存储和传播。这个数据库是开放式的，库里的资源具有可获取性，不同地域、不同部门、不同岗位的司法人员都可以共享其中的资源，根据获得的法律资源进行实践工作，提高其实用价值。⑤分类与分级。首先，法律数据库中的案件根据犯罪类型、罪行的轻重、主观方面、证明程度难易进行分类分级处理，便于清晰明了地查找相关性强的法律资源。另外，对案例指导可以按照提供案例机关的级别进行分级处理。其次，对于其中数据资源的引用率也进行分级处理，分为高级、中级和低级，分别是引用率70%以上、50%～40%和40%以下。最后，对于反馈的引用效果进行分级处理，分为经典案例（成功率80%）、一般案（40%～80%）、少引案例（40%以下）。

循证刑事证明是理性证明，传统证明是个人经验证明为主，二者的差别主要体现在以下五个方面：①证明来源。传统证明的根据多数来源于控诉者或法官个人的经验积累，而前者的证明来源在传统证明的基础上还包括学者研究、司法判例、他人的思维方式和经验，证明的影响要素更多、范围更广、结果更准确。②拿到证据后评价。传统证明并没有要求司法人员对自己的证明过程和证据的运用进行评价和反思，往往是证明活动一旦结束就彻底告一段落，直到发现新的证据或者多年后被作为冤假错案指出。前者则要求对获得的法律资源进行严格评价和反思，反思自己进行证明活动中有没有漏洞，有哪些好的经验，有哪些需要修正的，并且有一套严格的规定办法和反馈系统。③判效指标。传统证明更多地注重证据服务于案件结果，遵循因果关系。一个案件证明结束就是结束，没有判效指标。而前者更加注重相关性要素的运用，以相关性、相似性强的数据为基础，搜索对证明案件有帮助的相关性资源来证明犯罪事实。对于被引用的经验的效果进行适合或不适合的判断。④证明模式。对于传统证明，证明者往往以个人经验为中心，其证明范式多是几个处理案件的人在一起商量讨论，就结束证明活动，较少有人到网络中去查找相似案件的情况。而前者以个人经验和他人经验的综合应用为核心，司法者到数据库中寻找相似案例，既避免了在网络上盲目搜索的弊端，又有利于准确复原案件事实，构建一个符合刑事证明活动的认知框架和证明模式。

（二）循证刑事证明实施步骤

循证实践不只提供了一个全面的理论体系，还利用最新的科学方法与统计手段，以计算机网络信息技术为依托，为研究与实践的整合提供了一个现实的、具体可行的实践框架。建设法律数据库：罪犯思想变化的瞬时性和行为转变的反复性，要求各种信息的交流和矫治力量的整合与运用要具有及时性，决定了“循证刑事证明”模式的构建必须要以“高速化”的信息平台建设为依托，扩大信息交流容量。实现信息的快速交流，最新资料的快速更新，只有实践者能够快速地获得和提供最准确的实务信息，并能快速地参与到经验与信息的交流与互动中去，实现循证的互补与参考。建立科学证据获得方法体系，建立专家库、案例库和标准库，其中专家库主要是在刑事领域最前沿的专家学者的理论研究和对实证的评论，案例库主要是司法实务部门海量的司法案例，标准库主要是经被引用证明其经验具有可靠性的经典法律资源。让实践者更加方便、快捷、准确地检索所需要的研究信息，证明活动关键点所需要的资料，为证明活动实践奠定坚实的基础。循证刑事证明的实施步骤如下：

第一步，提出待证明的法律问题。证明者要详细考察搜集的案件的合法客观证据，根据案件的客观情况，通过相关的客观证据、犯罪嫌疑人供述、被害人陈述方面应尽可能全面地收集有关案件事实的信息。司法人员只有在充分了解这些信息的基础上，才能提出合适的、便于检索的问题。例如，金融诈骗罪中“非法占有目的”如何认定这个问题，司法人员要在全面搜集诈骗者虚构的事实、诈骗的具体手段、事后的补偿行为等客观情形的基础上，提出待证关键点“非法占有目的”的认定问题。

第二步，基于问题检索根据。在第一步证明主体准确地找到待证问题，将这个问题导入法律数据库中，从专家库、案例库、标准库或者选择一个需要的库对待证问题进行检索，找出相关的或者类似案件的解决方案，如果初步检索没有找到最佳的类似案件解决方法，则应将第一步的待证事实转化成可以进行检索的目标问题，选择适当的关键词，到相应的数据库中进行再次检索。

第三步，对获得的根据进行评价批判，选择最佳的、可供使用的法律资源。如果在第二步没有找到有关的系统综述或分析，则应输入关键词，根据科学标准判定此根据可信度的级别，将可信度高的根据纳入评价范围。然后，再对纳入的所有资料进行批判评价，找出最佳的研究依据或司法判例。评价检索到的信息的有用性，从中找出能够解决问题的最佳信息。

第四步，决定最佳资源是否能迁移到真实的案例情景中。必须在同时考虑研究证据的效果的基础上，才能决定它是否可以迁移到待证事实的证明活动中。例如，要综合考虑案件的客观证据采集情况和质量、犯罪者的个人情况、犯罪行为和后果的相似度，迁移的案例要求的相似度、可靠性和适用性等。例如，搜集到的学者的前瞻性研究要符合现行法律和法律发展趋势，要顺应时代潮流，不能与国家法律条文相违背。

第五步，证明和判断。在证明过程中，控诉机关要时刻紧盯所要解决待证的问题，如实记录证明过程中的每一个步骤，并根据证明不同性质案件的难易程度和效果进行实时反馈，随时调整证明计划和方法。

第六步，总结、评估。司法人员要反思整个运用法律资源证明案件的过程中涉及的客观证据、证明方法、证明经验等，针对证明问题的解决程度，总结经验资料并传入数据库，供其他人参考，完成整个循证刑事证明程序。

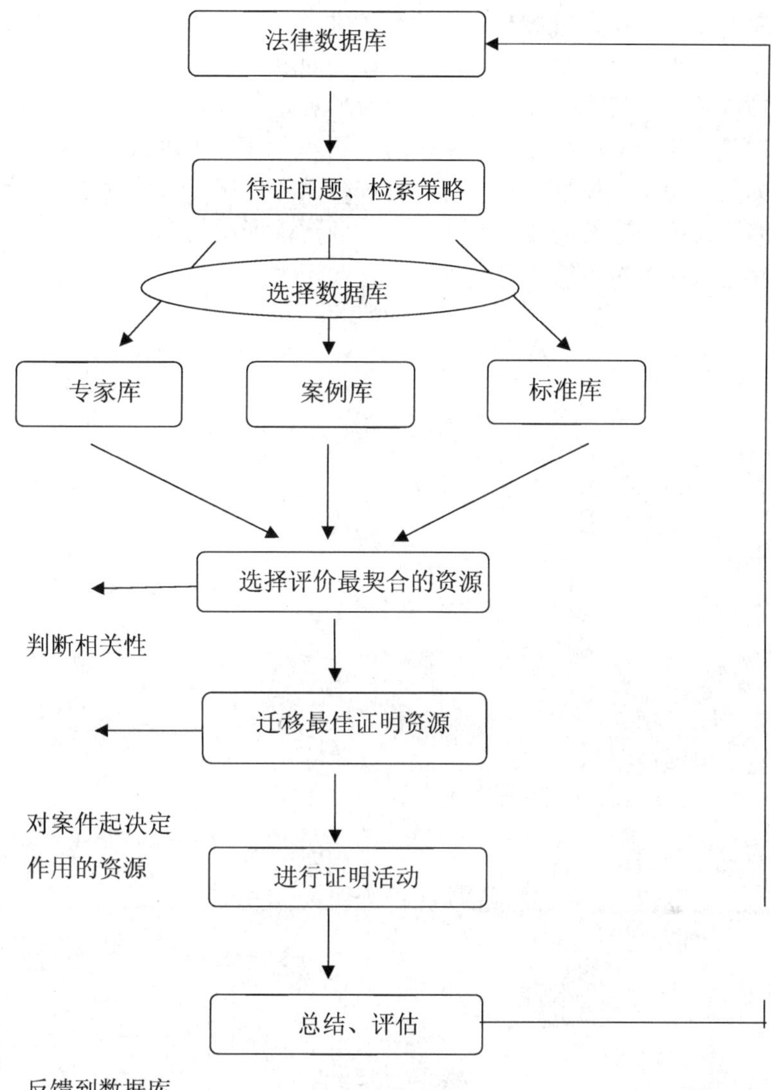

循证刑事证明的实施步骤图

六、循证刑事证明的前景及面临的重要问题

综上所述，循证实践在医学领域取得重大成果，为刑事证明与循证的结合提供丰富的实践经验，有实证主义和建构主义两个坚实的理论基础作为支撑，更重要的是将对刑事证明产生重大的有利影响。循证刑事证明的前景是十分广阔的，可以说揭开了刑事证明领域的新篇章，为刑事证明工作的继续开展注入了新的血液。经过初步研究，我们发现循证刑事证明是一个值得肯定的发展方向，但是继续深入研究将面临一些重点问题：①法律数据库的建立问题，即法律数据库中的各种资源如何系统地整合到一起。②循证意识的树立，司法者在证明工作中发挥重要的决策作用，循证意识的灌输十分重要。即使建立了健全的循证刑事证明模式，如果司法者没有循证意识也是不行的，循证刑事证明工作的开展，需要司法者和法学学者的配合，例如，由什么级别的

机关承担向数据库中输入法律案例的任务，法律研究者是否配合司法工作，将先进理论输入数据库等。③司法者如何判断什么是最佳的定案根据。利用循证的方法找到相关案例后，司法者能否判断出影响案件证明的影响因素，如何确定最佳的定案根据及判效指标等都是需要进一步研究的。④应用问题。先进的法律数据库以计算机技术为依托，对于如何应用搜索技术，要对司法者进行学习培训。这些问题是需要进一步深入研究，在未来需要解决的问题，本文是对循证刑事证明的初步研究，要掀起一场证明领域的变革需要继续付出艰辛的努力。

司法证明的理据

李昌盛 *

提供理据，简单说，就是讲出所以然。理性认知不仅知其然，而且知其所以然。只有知其所以然，才叫理解。一个正确的答案，如果我们不知道它为什么正确，不知它的由来之路，那对于我们来说，它和错误的答案有什么区别呢？[1]

——陈嘉映

一、从所谓“直接证据”谈起

在我国证据学理论中，证据分类是其重要组成部分。证据分类是根据不同标准把证据划分为二元对立、相互排斥的不同类型。其中，直接证据和间接证据是得到理论界和实务界普遍认同的一组证据类型。根据证据与案件主要事实的关系，“凡能直接证明案件主要事实的证据，叫做直接证据”；“凡需与其他证据相结合才能证明案件主要事实的证据，叫做间接证据”。[2] 概言之，直接证据与案件主要事实的关系，是无需进行推理的直接证明关系。例如，张三作证说：“4 月 12 日下午，我看见王五拿刀砍死了李四”。由于该证言能够无需推理，直接证明“王五拿刀砍死了李四”的犯罪事实，所以它是直接证据。

每当我在课堂上向学生讲授直接证据的概念时，学生们总是感到迷惑不解，学生们总是会提出如下问题：如果张三说谎，那么如何得出“王五拿刀砍死了李四”的结论呢？此时，根据传统的证据学理论，我只能向学生解释：证据是否是真实的，属于证据的审查判断问题，与是否能够直接证明案件主要事实不是一回事。但是，即使如此向学生解释，很多学生在考试时还是会做错，没有把目击证人的证言等证据作为直接证据。问其原因，他们的回答还是一样：凭什么认为证人说的就是实情？

学生的质疑，是直接证据概念违背一般论证规则的“直接证据”，也戳中了直接证据概念的软肋。

当一个完全陌生的人走到你的面前，告诉你：“4 月 12 日会有地震”。你是否会得出“4 月 12 日会有地震”的结论，并作出相应的决定（如离开本地，4 月 12 日跑到开阔的室外）呢？至少对于一个理性的人，可能不会遽然得出那个结论。当你面对一个陌生人时，你没有较为有效的信息，判断陌生人所提供信息的可信性，即使你当时或许有点儿不安，可能随后就把它当作“疯人疯语”给忘了。但是，当你在地震局工作的挚友告诉你“4 月 12 日会有地震”。我想你更有可能接受“4 月 12 日会有地震”的结论，并据此作出相应的决定和安排。为什么对于提供相同信息的不同人员，一个基

---

* 李昌盛，法学博士、西南政法大学副教授。Email：lichangsheng77@gmail.com。

〔1〕 陈嘉映：《说理》，华夏出版社2011 版，第 193 页。

〔2〕 巫宇甦：《证据学》，群众出版社 1983 年版，第 108 页。

本上不接受，另一个基本上接受？事实上，我们对两个信息来源进行分析时，采用了不同的生活“常识”。针对前者，该常识是“一个陌生人关于地震发生时间的预测通常是不可信的”；针对后者，该常识是“一个在地震局工作的挚友告诉我们有关地震的信息通常是可信的”。由此可见，作为信息来源的证据和从证据中得出的结论并不是一回事，两者在逻辑结构上只是小前提和结论的关系，从证据来源中能否得出特定的结论及结论的可信度，必须要有一个依据，即推理出特定结论的大前提。在日常生活和司法证明中，该依据通常是经验、常识、一般性知识等存储在我们大脑中的“知识库”。

直接证据概念存在的最大问题就是混淆了证据材料和推理结论的关系，它是建立在这样一个错误的概括之上：“所有直接证据中蕴含的信息都是真实的”。就张三的证言而言，我们能够从“张三作证说：‘4 月 12 日下午，我看见王五拿刀砍死了李四’”得出“王五拿刀砍死了李四”的结论，只能建立在如下概括之上：张三的证言绝对是真实的。但是由于没有任何其他信息（如张三的人品、职业、与当事人的关系、目击犯罪时的客观条件、精神状态等）帮助我们判断张三言词的可信性，肯定“张三的证言绝对是真实的”没有任何正当理由。当然，各国立法都把证人证言规定为一种合法的证据材料，其潜在的假设，认可了证人证言能够为我们认定案件事实提供可信的信息，因此相反的概括（“张三的证言绝对是虚假的”）也是错误的。[3] 一般来说，当证人作证时，我们使用的常识是“证人所说的话通常/一般/多数情况下是真实的”。我相信这才是符合我们经验的概括。因此，从证明实践来看，几乎不可能存在所谓的“直接证据”。

二、证明结构

（一）证据材料和推论

之所以说不存在所谓的“直接证据”，不仅因为从任何证据材料中得出的事实认定结论都是盖然性的（“通常/一般/多数情况下/有时候”），不是完全确定的，更因为世界上不存在不经过推论即可证明案件主要事实的“直接”证据。在司法证明领域，我们所说的“证据”通常是指证据材料，如证人证言、子弹、信札等。它们通过威格摩尔所称的“实感为真”过程（autoptic proference），[4] 进入事实认定者的头脑。纵使对证据材料的感知可能存在缺陷，但是证据材料客观存在的事实，在认知上是无法否认的。否则，人类的实践认知，包括司法活动中的事实认定，将无法进行。

任何证据材料，都包含某种具体的肯定性内容，通过实际感知而确认为真。例如，张三就王五杀人的事实所提供的证言，该证据材料的肯定性内容是“张三作证说‘4 月 12 日下午，他看见王五拿刀砍死了李四’”。当我们听到“张三作证说‘4 月 12 日下午，他看见王五拿刀砍死了李四’”，命题“张三作证说‘4 月 12 日下午，他看见王五拿刀砍死了李四’”的真实性通常是无需给出理由的。但是，证据材料中的肯定性内

---

〔3〕 贝克斯等人指出：“法律也会向我们指明常用的推理模式：例如，在荷兰的法律中，证人证言是法律明确规定可以作为法官判决基础的一种证据。因此，认为立法者默认有关证人证言的概括是错误的概括，是极其荒唐的。” See Floris Bex and Bart Verheij, *Solving a Murder Case by Asking Critical Questions: An Approach to Fact - Finding in Terms of Argumentation and Story Schemes*, Argumentation, 2012, p. 337.

〔4〕 J. H. Wigmore, *The Principles of Judicial Proof or the Process of Proof as Given by Logic, Psychology, and General Experience, and Illustrated in Judicial Trials, Little*, Brown and Company, 1931, p. 10.

容并不能将其自身转化为证据。[5] 换句话说，就证人证言而言，我们能够绝对肯定的只能是“证人甲说了事件 E”，而不是“事件 E”。要确定事件 E 是否发生了，司法证明必须以证人证言或者其他证据材料为客观基础，依靠推理论证来解决。[6] 因此，没有所谓的“直接证据”，从证据材料得出一个事件 E 至少包含一个步骤的推论。

（二）司法证明的基本构造

推论的过程就是证明的过程，即从已知证据材料中推理出待证事实的过程。为了使人信服，从已知的信息中推论出新的事实，必须要给出充分的理由。该理由不可能从证据材料本身中找到，因为它自己只能证明自身的存在。即使法官听到“张三作证说‘4 月 12 日下午，他看见王五拿刀砍死了李四’”，而且其他证据表明张三与诉讼结果、当事人没有利害关系，还不足以成为“王五拿刀砍死了李四”事实认定结论的根据。为了得出该结论，法官需要一个概括：通常情况下，与当事人没有利害关系的证人所说的话是真实可信的。否则，根据张三的证言认定“王五拿刀砍死了李四”，就是没有正当性的。从任何证据材料中得出特定的结论，都必须要经历类似的“证明”过程。

当通过证据材料证明案件事实时，其步骤一般为：我们通过实际观察，能够接受的只能是证据材料本身在事实上是存在的，运用该材料进一步进行推理，要求我们进行论证，以便从证据材料中得出某个结论，把证据材料和结论连接起来，并为论证提供了正当性根据的，是一个与特定证据材料有关的概括。因此，司法证明的一般结构，是由作为前提的证据材料、证明结论和为从前提推理出特定结论提供正当性根据的概括所组成的。与特定证据材料有关的概括，可以看作是把证据和结论粘贴在一起的“胶水”（glue）。借用图尔敏的话，概括是司法证明的“理据”（warrant）。[7] 沃尔顿则把作为论证根据的概括称为“论证模型”（argumentation schemes）。[8]

概括通常源自日常生活经验、常识等得到一定程度普遍认同的一般性知识。因此，概括的本质是“归纳性的”。通过对大量案件中证人作证可信性的归纳总结，我们获得了如下知识：与当事人没有利害关系的证人所说的话通常是真实可信的。由归纳获得的概括在司法证明中实际发挥了论证大前提的作用，使我们得以结合证据材料，推论特定的事实。[9] 因此，司法证明是一种以归纳法为基础的准演绎过程。没有与案件有关的特定概括，裁判者不仅无法从证据材料推理出特定的事实，甚至无法确定证据材料中的肯定性内容。[10]

---

〔5〕 Alex Stein, *Foundations of Evidence Law*, Oxford University Press, 2005, p. 93.

〔6〕 Terence Anderson, David Schum, William Twining, *Analysis of Evidence*, Cambridge University Press, 2005, p. 60.

〔7〕 Stephen E. Toulmin, *The Uses of Argument*, Cambridge University Press, 2003, pp. 91 ~92.

〔8〕 Douglas N. Walton, *Legal Argumentation and Evidence*, Pennsylvania State University Press, 2002.

〔9〕 Terence J. Anderson, On Generalizations I: A Preliminary Exploration, 40 *S. Tex. L. Rev.* 455 (1999), p. 455.

〔10〕 我们在前文中提到，证据材料中的肯定性内容可以通过我们的感知器官直接获得，看起来是“不证自明的”。例如，当我们听到“证人甲说了事件 E”，往往可以直接得出“证人甲说了事件 E”的结论，无须再经过推论。但是，这是建立在对我们的感知器官的信任之上的。换句话说，它是建立在“眼见为实”的概括之上的。由于在实践推理中，对此概括也加以审查，既没有必要性，也使认知成本和负担过重，所以在此情形下进行的推论一般都是“前提——结论”的缺省（大前提）推理。但是，它背后所依赖的概括是无法否认的。

三、概括的类型

概括，是指把有关事物的共同特点归结在一起，从而形成事物普遍性认识的过程和结果。所有的知识都建立在概括之上。司法证明作为人类的实践认知活动，没有基于概括之上的知识是不可能完成的。因此，在法律领域，没有所谓的“神童”。[11] 儿童即使具有超越常人的“智力”，但是却不具备认识社会现象及其一般规律的“经验”。由概括获得的知识为司法证明提供了正当性理据，使事实推论得以完成。从概括的来源而言，概括可能源自科学知识、生活经验、教育、阅读，有时候甚至来自成语故事、寓言、童话、传闻等。[12] 从概括的普遍性而言，概括可能是抽象的原理，如能量守恒定理，也可能是某个具体案件的具体知识，如像被告人这种人一般会歧视女性。从概括的可靠性而言，有可能是得到科学验证或普遍认可的科学知识、一般性知识，也可能是源自个人经历的偏见。从概括的共享性而言，概括可能是长时间内人类社会所普遍认可的知识，也可能只是一时一地特定社会所认可的知识。由于概括的来源、普遍性、可靠性和共享性存在差异，而司法证明又必须要依靠各种各样的概括，所以为了正确运用概括，我们必须首先要认识概括的类型。司法证明中的概括通常包括：科学知识和专家意见、普遍接受的知识、经验性知识、综合直觉概括和与案件证据材料有关的具体概括。

（一）科学知识和专家意见

科学知识是指已经得到科学方法验证或者尚未证伪的事物运作规律。科学知识一般源自科学发现和实验，具有普遍性，较为可靠且为科学界群体所公认。例如，万有引力定理。但是，科学概括也并非都是完全确定的知识。有的科学概括可能是建立在不扎实的研究之上的（如测谎实验或者吸烟与肺癌之间的关系）。通常情况下，由于科学概括涉及专业技术知识，所以科学知识在诉讼中的应用需要得到专家的帮助。当专家利用他们的科学知识就案件中的某个问题提供专业意见时，其意见通常必须要依赖于相关的科学概括。但是有关专家意见的概括和科学概括并不是一回事。科学概括是专家意见的基础，往往直接通过司法认知的方式确认它的真实性。但是，专家意见的概括一般为：

专家 e 是一个领域 d 内的一个专家。
e 声称，命题 a 是真实的（虚假的）。
a 属于 d。
因此，a 可以合理地视为是真实的（虚假的）。[13]

---

〔11〕 正如新加坡国立大学法学院教授 H. L. Ho 所言：“如果我们期望事实发现者理性行事，我们就必须保证他们有‘能力’理性行事。理性行事的基本条件是具备认识能力，它包括相互联系的两个方面。一方面，事实发现者必须具有理性思考的正常智力并能够运用一般的推理原则。智障者不具备这个能力；另一方面，事实发现者必须要具备丰富的社会阅历和社会常识。儿童无法达到这个标准。” H. L. Ho, *A Philosophy of Evidence Law: Justice in the Search for Truth*, Oxford University Press, 2008, p. 37.

〔12〕 William Twining, “Narrative and Generalizations in Argumentation About Question of Fact”, 40 *S. Tex. L. Rev.* 351 (1999), pp. 265 ~ 266.

〔13〕 D. Walton, C. Reed and F. Macagno, *Argumentation Schemes*, Cambridge University Press, 2008, p. 244.

由于专家意见概括不同于科学知识，所以专家意见必须接受审查，才能作为可靠的概括适用于案件中，它不具有预定的可靠性。针对专家意见概括，我们至少可以从以下六个方面审查它的可靠性：

（1）专业知识问题：e是专家吗？
（2）领域问题：e是d领域内的一个专家吗？
（3）意见问题：e断言的东西是a吗？
（4）诚实性问题：e本人作为证据来源是可靠的吗？
（5）一致性问题：a与其他专家所断言的内容是一致的吗？
（6）支撑性证据问题：a的内容是建立在证据之上吗？

对上述六个问题的任何一个方面的否定性回答，都可能削弱或者否定专家意见概括在特定案件中的适用力。

（二）普遍接受的知识

普遍接受的知识，是在特定时空下特定共同体所确立的得到普遍接受的概括。例如，北京是中国的首都；在重庆，夏天非常炎热。普遍接受的概括，在特定共同体内是被广泛知晓的，它们可能源自教育、生活经验或者科学知识。在诉讼中诉诸普遍接受的概括，其可靠性一般是较高的，通常直接以司法认知或者经验法则的方式被接受。但是在特定时间特定社会被认为是普遍接受的知识，后来可能是不真实的。例如，在以前，一般认为太阳是绕着地球转的，但现在的科学研究已经证明相反的看法才是正确的。因此，普遍接受知识的可靠性会受到时间、地域甚至接受群体的限制。

（三）经验性知识

在社会生活中，大多数用来指导我们行为的知识主要源自经验。某些基于经验的概括，可能是特定共同体内广泛体验的经历。例如，雨水落在身上，衣服会湿。此时，它事实上就是普遍接受的知识。但是，有时候个人经验性知识可能来自不具有普遍性的个人经历。例如，某开发商老板被当地政府官员索贿，他就可能得出如下概括：所有或者大多数政府官员都存在腐败行为。像这种概括显然根据不足，可以看作是没有可靠性依据的信念或者偏见。如果根据它们进行事实推论，极有可能导致错误结论。

（四）综合直觉概括

有些概括，表面上看起来好像是“常识”，但是人们并不知道概括源自何人的经验，也不知道概括是何人总结，更不知道概括的认识基础是什么。[14] 因此，更像是一个直觉。安德森认为“逃离犯罪现场是有罪的证据”就属于此种概括。[15] 我们从直觉上好像接受“实施犯罪的人通常从犯罪现场逃走”的概括。但是，反过来认为“没有实施犯罪的人，为了避免嫌疑，会迅速离开犯罪现场”也是可以接受的概括。因此，逃离犯罪现场的概括只是一个源自我们的综合直觉的概括，没有什么清楚的来源。它

〔14〕［意］米歇尔·塔鲁夫（Michele Taruffo）：“关于经验法则的思考”，孙维萍译，载《证据科学》2009年第2期。

〔15〕吴奇、申寻兵、傅小兰：“微表情研究及其应用”，载《心理科学进展》2010年第9期；傅小兰：“转瞬即逝的微表情成为自动‘测谎仪’”，载《民主与法制时报》2011年3月28日。

更为准确的版本可能是“有时，从犯罪现场逃离的人是罪犯”。但该概括明显是缺乏可靠性的。

（五）与案件证据材料有关的具体概括

上面所说的4种概括都是“抽象”的概括，并没有与案件的具体情况结合起来。在司法证明的具体活动中，通常情形下，每一个概括都会与案件的特定证据材料和待证事实联系在一起。因此，抽象的概括就可能转为一种更为具体的与特定证据材料相关的概括。例如，刚才所谈到的逃离犯罪现场的概括，可能会在某个具体的案件中转化为：某个人在下午4：50神色慌张地离开另一个人的家，而另一个人在4：30左右被人杀死，因此该人有可能是凶手。一般来说，适用于案件的概括越具体，就使我们更有可能发现其中存在的可疑之处，从而为纠正错误推论创造条件，保障事实认定的准确性。

四、概括的危险性

（一）盖然性

概括的第一个风险源自它的盖然性。所谓盖然性，就是没有达到确定程度的可能性。如果确定状态为1，那么盖然性则是介于0至1之间的某种状态。一般来说，人类的知识达到完全确定状态的，几乎没有。即使是科学知识，也是如此。例如，随着DNA技术的不断发展，DNA比对已经成为同一认定的重要科学方法。如果遗留在犯罪现场的毛发DNA图谱与犯罪嫌疑人张三的DNA图谱是一致的，由此推论犯罪现场的毛发绝对为张三的毛发，则是不准确的。因为DNA比对的准确率，目前只有99.9999999%，尚未达到完全确定的程度。不过，在诉讼活动中，我们追求的不是完全确定的客观事实，而是“排除合理怀疑”[16]的事实或者“盖然性占优势”[17]的事实，证明标准本身已经蕴含着盖然性的要求，适度的误差只要在可容忍的范围之内，并不能阻碍我们从特定的概括中作出推论。但是，以科学知识、专家意见作为推理判断前提的事实认定，在诉讼中并非常态，科学证据不仅只能适用于一部分案件，而且还只能证明一部分事实。现代诉讼制度，还是离不开各种各样的无法精确判断其盖然性程度的经验概括。其中，典型表现就是针对各种言词证据的概括。例如，证人证言。单就从证人举止来判断证言的可信性程度来看，经验概括盖然性判断的复杂性，也可见一斑：

举止不仅仅是举止，而是一套复杂的变量。证人出汗或者肌肉抽搐了吗？如果这样，是出于无辜地紧张、撒谎的压力、身体问题或者仅仅是在令人遗憾的童年当中形成的不雅习惯？身体语言是在暗示诚实还是逃避；作证时的慵散是证明了其在撒谎还是在轻松地讲述坦率的故事？证人是在直视询问者的眼睛吗？如果这样，这说明其品性值得称赞还是表明这是善于交际的万灵油推销员的一种自信？声音变调表明的是正

[16]《刑事诉讼法》第53条规定：“证据确实、充分，应当符合以下条件：（一）定罪量刑的事实都有证据证明；（二）据以定案的证据均经法定程序查证属实；（三）综合全案证据，对所认定事实已排除合理怀疑。”

[17]《关于民事诉讼证据的若干规定》第73条规定：“双方当事人对同一事实分别举出相反的证据，但都没有足够的依据否定对方证据的，人民法院应当结合案件情况，判断一方提供证据的证明力是否明显大于另一方提供证据的证明力，并对证明力较大的证据予以确认。因证据的证明力无法判断导致争议事实难以认定的，人民法院应当依据举证责任分配的规则作出裁判。”

直人的端正品性还是紧张，紧张的声音表明的是捏造还是在关心案件的结果？等等。[18]

正是由于诉讼中的经验概括具有如此大的复杂性，而司法证明通常又不得不依靠源自经验的概括，这就要求我们选择可适用的概括时，必须要谨慎，防止把盖然性过低的概括甚至没有根据的信念、偏见作为司法证明的理据。

（二）临时性

概括的第二个风险源自它的临时性。一般来说，司法证明所依赖的概括通常不是抽象的概括，而是依赖于特定证据材料的具体情况概括。例如，张三作证说："4月12日下午，我看见王五拿刀砍死了李四"。假设现在没有其他证据帮助我们判断张三证言的可信性，我们以此证据材料为基础所进行的推论，只能诉诸抽象的概括："证人说p，那么通常是p"。但是，依据该概括作出的推论，极有可能随后就被推翻，因为我们并没有多少额外的信息帮助我们判断张三所陈述的事实到底可不可信。假设我们现在有证据表明，张三是一个与案件当事人及处理结果没有任何利害关系的人，相关的经验概括可以特定化为："一个中立的证人说p，那么通常是p"。假设我们还有证据表明，张三在案发时就在现场，相关的经验概括可以进一步特定化为："一个在犯罪现场目睹了犯罪经过的中立的证人说p，那么基本上是p"。这比抽象的概括要稳定得多。

但是，司法证明始终受困于诉讼的时间压力和资源供给，加上证据材料本身的有限性，我们不可能收集到所有能够证明证人可信性的信息。[19] 依赖于证据材料本身的概括，始终可能会受到新信息带来的新概括的挑战和质疑。例如，假设后来有证据表明张三在4月12日下午不在犯罪现场附近，而是在距离现场100米之外透过自己家的窗户看到犯罪经过的。此时，相关的概括可能就会变为："一个事实上距离犯罪现场100米之外，透过自己家窗户看到犯罪经过的人，却声称自己在犯罪现场看到了犯罪经过，那么他的证言基本上是不可信的"。其背后的抽象概括是："一个不诚实的人说p，通常是非p。"因此，建立在特定证据材料之上的概括都只能是"临时性的"，而不是确定性的。临时性与盖然性不同，临时性所带来的认知风险是无法控制的，不规则的，而盖然性所带来的认知风险一般是能够认识到的，也是可以估量的。即使我们无法精确地计算出中立的证人所提供的证言可信性有多大（例如90%、80%或75%等），我们认为通常是可信的，当然承认例外存在。但是，对于不确定的未来信息，我们无法预测，它到底是会提高还是会降低证人的可信性。

（三）隐蔽性

概括的第三个风险源自它的隐蔽性。所谓隐蔽性，是指概括在推动我们从特定证据材料中得出某个结论时，隐含在我们的推论过程之中，而我们自己却浑然不知或者认为理所当然。前文已经论述，所有的论证都有一个与其相关的概括起作用。但是，人类是认知的吝啬鬼。很多情形下，除非迫使我们给出特定结论的理由，否则我们不会思考推论的理据何在。尤其是在较为复杂的案件当中，当同样的概括反复出现，我们通常也不会明确反思自己诉诸的概括。司法证明中基于证据材料的论证经常依赖于

---

〔18〕［美］罗纳德·J. 艾伦："论司法证明的性质"，王进喜等译，载《证据科学》2011年第6期。

〔19〕［美］David A. Schum："关于证据科学的思考"，王进喜译，载《证据科学》2009年第1期。

诸如这样的隐含前提："每个人都是接受那个论述；因此此处并不受质疑。"[20] 例如，在福尔摩斯的经典故事"白额马案"中，福尔摩斯的论证就是一个略去了相关概括的"缺省论证"：

一只狗关在马厩里，然而，有人已经潜入马厩并偷走了马，狗并没有叫醒阁楼里的两位女士。显而易见，午夜中的入访者是那只狗熟悉的某个人。

福尔摩斯的论证就是一个没有明确表达相关概括的隐蔽性论证。事实上，他的论证是建立在如下经验概括之上的："除非一只狗对午夜入访者熟悉，否则当那个人进入一个封闭的马厩时，那只狗通常会叫"。即使没有明确表述经验概括，我们也基本上认同福尔摩斯的论证，原因就在于我们默认了那个概括。但是，由于缺省论证中的隐含概括通常诉诸各种常识，如果不将其挖掘出来，不仅无法揭示它的可靠性和力度，而且也无法对它进行批判性审查，极容易导致无效推论。

五、降低风险的路径

一个完整的证明是由证据材料、证明结论和相关的概括所组成的。诉诸概括既是必要的，也是危险的。如何合理运用概括并同时降低它的风险，是一个亟待思考的问题。概括的风险主要源自三个方面：盖然性、临时性和隐蔽性。其中，某些风险源自人类认知活动的本质局限性，如盖然性和临时性，因此只能最大限度地降低由此导致的风险；而隐蔽性风险通常与人类认知活动的慵懒特征和惯性思维有关，只要在诉讼中给予相对方足够的质疑机会，要求裁判者保持谨慎细致的推理精神，在个案中是可能消除的。不过，从整体上而言，概括的风险只能得到最大限度的减少，而无法完全清除。

判断一个概括的盖然性大小，首先取决于确定特定的概括。假如概括本身都处于不确定的变化状态，我们不仅无法确定它是否是普遍的概括，还是一个受到范围限制（通常/有时/或许）的概括，而且也无法检查概括的来源到底是源自科学规律、一般经验、常识、推测还是偏见。但是，我们也认识到，诉讼中的概括由于只能建立在不完全的证据材料之上，只是临时性的，随时可能被新的证据推翻。因此，从理论上而言，完全确定的概括是得不到的。使问题进一步加剧的是，裁判者还要受到审判期限的限制。他们必须要在法定的期限内作出裁判，不能因为信息尚未完全而拒绝作出裁判。可见，盖然性和临时性风险本质上源自司法证明的不确定性，它是比概括的隐蔽性更难以化解的风险。因此，一般来说，不存在事实论证中使用的概括类型的争论，唯一的争论就是一个特定的概括是否可以适用于特定的案件。

（一）信息最大化原则

想要降低司法证明所依赖的概括的不确定性，首要的一步是必须要尽可能最大限度地实现证据材料的最大化，保证裁判者接受并审查所有与案件有关的具体证据。我们可以称之为"信息最大化原则"。当裁判者所获得的信息越是充分，就越是能够把概

---

〔20〕 Fabrizio Macagno and Douglas Walton, "Common Knowledge in Legal Reasoning About Evidence", *International Commentary on Evidence*, 2005, Vol. 3, No. 1, p. 17.

括建立在相对稳定的材料之上，同时也能够使建立在特定证据材料之上的概括更加特定化。

当概括建立在相对稳定的证据材料之上，它的临时性风险就能够得到降低，使其获得相当程度的确定性。例如，就证人证言而言，如果我们了解到某个证人感知案件事实时的身体条件、观察条件，也了解到他的记忆能力、个人品格，还了解到他作证时的行为举止，那么相对于只是知道他是一个了解案件事实的证人而言，更能够为我们提供一个相对稳固的概括。而当概括相对稳定之后，也就为我们评价它的盖然性创造了条件。

当建立在特定证据材料之上的概括越是特定化，我们就越是能够检查出概括的可适用性，防止把盖然性太低的概括或者无关的概括运用到司法证明当中。例如，当裁判者面对一份书面证言，没有其他信息辅助判断证言的可信性。那么他通常只能诉诸抽象的概括：证人所说的话通常是可信的。但是，如果他进一步了解到，该证言是在警察威胁下取得的，那么相关的概括可能就变为：警察威胁证人所取得的证言，通常是不真实的。〔21〕这就防止了错误概括在当前案件中的适用。司法审判活动信息最大化原则的实现，必须要依靠具体的法律原则和规则予以保障才能实现。

一方面，鉴于裁判者取证的被动性和滞后性，法律制度必须要把实现信息最大化的主要任务放在双方当事人身上：一是法律必须要充分保障当事人双方具有对等的取证机会；二是法律必须要通过适当的激励机制促使当事人尽最大限度地收集证据。例如，就取证机会而言，刑事诉讼当事人之间存在国家和个人之间实力悬殊的问题，尤其是个人（包括律师）没有直接以强制力获取证据的机会，因此除了要保证辩方独立合法取证的权利外，还必须要充分保障被告人借助国家权力的申请取证权。就激励机制而言，刑事诉讼要求控方承担证明责任，且必须要达到排除合理怀疑的最高标准，从而促使本来具有取证便利和条件的一方尽可能地收集并提供充分的证据。

另一方面，鉴于与特定证据有关的概括误用的危害过大，法律可以通过制定相应的规则，要求提交特定证据的一方，必须提交辅助证据，来验证概括的可靠性，从而引导双方当事人收集更多的证据，扩大裁判者的信息库。例如，在一般情形下，一个理性的犯罪嫌疑人没有明显的动机作出虚假供述，因为供述意味着承认犯罪，不仅可能无法得到什么利益，反而可能因“撒谎”而失去自由等利益。因此，在对供述进行真实性判断时，供认犯罪通常会被评价为可信的，因为此时被告人缺乏欺骗他人的动机。口供有关的概括就变为：通常情况下，被告人供认了自己的罪行，他就是罪犯。由于口供的证明力极高，该概括一旦误用，可能导致被告人被错误定罪，其危害性太大，所以口供证据的采信必须要有独立的证据予以补强。〔22〕补强证据的作用在于，让我们能够通过其他证据，审查有关口供的概括是否能够适用于特定的案件，防止概括

---

〔21〕当然，此处的概括也可以根据证据排除规则来表达：警察威胁证人所取得的证言，不得作为定案的根据。由于本文重点探讨的是司法证明的认知机理，所以我们暂时不考虑司法证明的价值/道德方面。但是，这并不是说后者并不重要。事实上，论证中的概括也涉及不同价值的选择问题。See Alex Stein, “The Refoundation of Evidence Law”, 9 *Can. J. L. & Juris.* 279 (1996).

〔22〕Richard A. Leo, Steven A. Drizin, Peter J. Neufeld, Bradley R. Hall & Amy Vatner, “Bring Reliability Back in: False Confessions and Legal Safeguards in the Twenty – First Century”, 2006 *Wis. L. Rev.* 479, pp. 520 ~ 522.

的错误运用。通过要求收集其他证据印证口供，口供补强规则可以激励控方寻找口供以外的其他证据，从而增加审判中的证据量。

（二）相对方最大限度质疑原则

想要降低司法证明所依赖的概括其所蕴含的风险，还必须要确保证据论证的相对方有最大限度的机会，质疑、挑战对其不利论证背后所依赖的概括。我们可以称之为“相对方最大限度质疑原则”。该原则要求，每一个基于证据材料的论证及其所依据的概括，必须以实际可行的方式（如交叉询问、辨认、鉴定等）交付审查，保证相对方能够检验有关概括的准确性、盖然性和可适用性。例如，以张三的证言为例。如果当前可以得到的证据，没有显示出张三具有什么不值得信任的特征，同时其可信性也经受住了相对方的交叉询问，那么对于裁判者而言，此时他就具有认知上的正当根据，认定张三确实没有什么值得怀疑的地方。据此，裁判者就可以适用与证人张三直接相关的概括：可信的证人所陈述的内容，基本上是真实的。以该概括为基础，裁判者就有“理据”接受张三证言中所提供的信息。

一个基于证据材料之上的论证及概括，只要经受住了相对方最大限度的质疑和挑战，那么就是可接受的。裁判者就可以信赖那个论证。当结合第一个信息最大化原则，案件中当前可以得到的证据材料都接受了批判性的审查，裁判者就有权力宣布当前的信息已经处于“闭合”状态，并据此作出相应的裁判，从而在某种程度上结束概括的不确定性状态，增强了裁判的整体安定性。

相对方最大限度质疑原则也可以降低概括的盖然性风险。每个特定的论证都具有某种程度上的自身的力度或证明力。所谓论证力度，是指我们确信某个论证的确证程度。证据材料本身的存在是无法否认的，所以这种材料具有最高程度的力度。如果用一种数字化的概率来表示，证据材料存在的概率是1。但是，一份证据支持某个结论的程度，取决于连接证据和结论的推论的力度。该推论的力度转而又取决于为推论提供正当性根据的概括的信任程度。此时，确定盖然性程度所遇到的难题之一就是通常不易于以数字进行表达。例如，如果我们说，宣誓证人通常说真话，我们是指在75%的时刻相信他会说真话呢？还是85%的时刻呢？

由于该难题的存在，通常表达概括力度的最简单的方式，就是进行相互比较，即概括的力度是以一种相对值来表达的，我们并不提及概括的确切力度，而是认为某个概括是否优先于其他的概括。[23] 例如，“由于张三戴眼镜，而李四没戴眼镜”，所以我们认为，“建立在李四的证言基础之上的论证比建立在张三提供的证言基础之上的论证，更具有可靠性”。因为有关李四证人证言的概括（即，如果李四说“p”，那么“p”）比有关张三证人证言的概括更为有力，因此，建基于“李四的概括”的论证比建基于“张三的概括”的论证更为强大有力。通过给予相对方最大限度质疑不利于他的论证和概括，概括的盖然性就可以通过相互比较的方式得到评估和确定，从而不仅可以避免使用盖然性过低的概括，而且可以为判断盖然性程度提供路径。

相对方最大限度质疑原则还可以降低概括的隐蔽性风险。概括的隐蔽性是人类日常实践推理的常态。例如，针对言词证据问题，在日常交流过程中，人们对他人所陈

〔23〕 Floris J. Bex, Arguments, *Stories and Criminal Evidence: A Formal Hybrid Theory*, Springer, 2011, p. 43.

述信息的评价，通常是不会质疑其真实性的。其背后的原理是，人类在生活交往中，一般会自发地受到诚实性道德准则的约束，不会去欺骗对方，只有当存在欺骗的动机时，才会故意说假话。由于人们在绝大多数情况下都是根据该原理行事，所以人们也同样相信其他人也会如此行事。因此，通常我们在与他人交流时，在对方没有欺骗的动机存在时，都会默认对方给出的信息是真实的。默认真实的倾向性既是人类有效交流的需要，也是人类思维的惰性所致。同信任相比，不相信他人所陈述的信息需要更为积极的能动思维，倾向于信任交流中的对方是普遍存在的现象。[24] 因此，一般来说，除非受到其他人的质疑和挑战，我们通常很少反思自己推论的依据何在。有时候，在被质疑后，我们甚至找不出推理的依据是什么。通过赋予相对方最大限度质疑不利于他的论证的权利，论证背后隐藏的概括就可能被揭露出来。例如，“如果两个证人作证说 p，那么 p”，可能至少还隐藏这么一个条件：证人之间没有商谈。因为经过商谈的证人，可能会改变他们的证言，以使相互之间的证言是一致的。我们可以通过改变概括形式，让其变得明确：“如果两个证人作证说 p，且证人之间没有商谈，那么 p”。因此，赋予相对方审查质疑的机会，可以揭露论证中隐藏的条件，让概括中可能存在的例外情形明确化。如此一来，概括将变得越来越详细，直到裁判者相信，概括中存在的最重要的例外情形已经明确。这不仅有利于防止错误的概括运用到论证当中，降低概括的隐蔽性风险，而且可以使概括建立在一个更为扎实的概括之上，降低了概括的不确定性风险。

同信息最大化原则一样，相对方最大限度质疑原则也必须通过具体的法律原则和规则予以保障才能得以实现。任何不利于诉讼一方的论证必须要给予该方充分的机会挑战、质疑其背后所依据的概括。转化成诉讼制度，就是必须要尽力保障当事人所享有的质证权；转化为证据制度，就是无法对其背后概括进行有效检验的证据，不得作为定案的根据。例如，刑事诉讼中辩方所享有的同不利证人进行对质诘问的权利就是最大限度质疑原则的体现，而排除真实性无从检验的二手证据，例如，原始证据规则、传闻证据规则等，则属于实现最大限度质疑原则的证据规则。

（三）阐明理由原则

对于诉讼中证据和事实的认定，我们向来强调所谓的“自由心证”，要求裁判者秉持自己的良心、理性和经验“自由”认定证据的价值。但是，自由心证只是赋予了裁判者认知过程的自由，并没有免除他为判决提供正当理由的义务。“证据的证明力问题极难驾驭，因此绝不能唯立法者的马首是瞻；而且其非常复杂，所以绝不能用一套法律分类标准一网打尽”，但是“审判法官需要以书面意见的方式说明其认定事实的理由”。[25] 因此，为事实认定结论进行说理，既是对自由心证的限制，也是它的正当化路径。否则，判决就很难得到接受。

正如德国著名刑事诉讼法学者洛克信（Roxin）所言：“仅以主观的确信，尚不足

---

〔24〕 Timothy R. Levine, Rachel K. Kim & J. Pete Blair, “(In) accuracy at Detecting True and False Confessions and Denials: An Initial Test of a Projected Motive Model of Veracity Judgments”, *Human Communication Research* 36 (2010), pp. 86 ~ 88.

〔25〕［美］米尔建·R. 达马斯卡：《漂移的证据法》，李学军等译，中国政法大学出版社 2003 年版，第 30 页。

以由所调查之证据，合理地推论出客观的结果。由于必须保护被告，免受法官于形成心证之际，恣意认定事实之所害，法官形成判决之过程，必须达到其他法官追证（复验）可能之程度。"[26] 所谓"追证可能"，就是指法官不能仅仅在主观上达到内心确信状态，而且在客观上必须达到"其他法官"也能够予以认同的程度，经受住外部的质疑和指摘。因此，《德国刑事诉讼法典》第267条规定："被告人被有罪判决的时候，判决理由必须写明已经查明的、具有犯罪行为法定特征的事实。证据如果是根据其他事实推断出来的时候，也要写明这些事实"。在司法实务中，对于有争议的事实，判决都应包含证据评价的内容，否则将会以"心证瑕疵"为由予以撤销。[27]

裁判者的认知过程无法通过法律进行直接的控制，但是最终的认识结果必须要能够展现推论的依据。否则，信息最大化原则和相对方最大程度质疑原则降低风险的作用，就可能被弱化甚至消失。毕竟，裁判者在认定案件事实的时候，也会诉诸他们自己的概括，其中有的概括可能是较为确定的常识，而有的则可能是不太确定的纯属个人的经验甚至偏见，有时候他们可能自觉地认识到自己所运用到的概括，有时候可能是隐藏在他们的推论之中的。如果没有强制说理的机制，裁判者就没有外在的动力"反思"他们所诉诸的概括，也可能意识不到其中存在着诸多错误风险。

在中国引起极大社会影响的"南京彭宇案"中，其中引发较大社会争议的就是法官所使用的概括：一是见义勇为的人通常不仅要扶持被撞倒的人，而且要抓住撞人之人；二是做好事的人在被撞倒之人的家属赶到后，通常应当自行离开，而不是陪同家属到医院救治被撞倒之人。[28] 我们认为，就经验来看，其中第一个概括虽然不是没有可能性，但是盖然性确实较低，如果用数字表示，应当低于0.5；而第二个概括的盖然性则是较高的，应当高于0.5。不管该判决引起的道德谴责有多大，我们认为，该案中的法官有一点是值得学习的，即进行事实认定的"说理"活动。我们可以假设，如果该案中的法官所撰写的判决书，只是在罗列证据后，直接以"综合以上证据，本庭认定的事实如下"的形式下判，我们就难以审查法官判决背后所依赖的概括，也难以检验概括的可靠性和盖然性。

阐明理由原则也应当通过具体的法律制度予以保障才能实现。一方面，对于当事人双方有争议的事实，法官必须要通过明确的书面说理，阐明采信其中一方或者自己认定的事实的根据；另一方面，没有达到上述要求的，必须要给予程序性的制裁，上级法院应当直接以事实不清为由撤销判决。

六、结　论

司法证明是对无法直接观察的历史事件的重塑过程，它只能依赖留存在当前的证据材料推论待证事实发生的可能性。当确定通过证据材料推论案件事实是否存在时，

---

〔26〕 Roxin, Claus/Kern, Eduard, Strafverfahrensrecht: Ein Studienbuch, 16, Aufl. S. 71. 转引自雷万来：《民事证据法论》，瑞兴图书股份有限责任公司1997年版，第93页。

〔27〕［德］克劳思·罗科信：《刑事诉讼法》，吴丽琪译，法律出版社2003年版，第465页。

〔28〕 判决书的原文为："如果被告是见义勇为做好事，更符合实际的做法应是抓住撞倒原告的人，而不仅仅是好心相扶；如果被告是做好事，根据社会情理，在原告的家人到达后，其完全可以在言明事实经过并让原告的家人将原告送往医院，然后自行离开，但被告未作此等选择，其行为显然与情理相悖。"参见南京市鼓楼区人民法院民事判决书（2007）鼓民一初字第212号。

我们必须借助于一个与特定证据材料有关的概括，才能有正当根据地完成一个或者多个步骤的证明。诸如此类的概括是人类通过各种途径积累起来的“知识库”。它们可能是已经得到科学方法验证或者尚未证伪的科学知识，可能是得到广泛认可的专家意见，可能是源自生活经验的常识，可能是源自个人经历的偏见，甚至可能是说不清道不明的直觉。虽然依靠概括进行证明是必要的，但同时也是存在风险的。概括通常都不是绝对确定的，这就需要我们注意不同概括的盖然性问题；概括还可能受到新信息的冲击，这就需要我们注意概括的临时性或者稳定性问题；概括还可能自动适用于我们的推论过程，这就需要我们注意概括的隐蔽性问题。为了降低运用概括进行证明所产生的风险，至少需要从以下三个方面着手：一是实现司法证明信息的最大化，二是保障相对方最大限度的质疑挑战机会，三是把司法证明说理落到实处。为此，我们也需要重新检视我们的法律规范，并通过制度设计将降低风险的原则转化为相应的法律制度。

Evaluation of the System of Direct Taking of Evidence in the European Union—a Change in Paradigm or a Solid Step forward Made under the Pressure of Checks and Limits?

Dr. habil. Harsági Viktória PhD *

The direct taking of evidence, in principle, means a simpler method for the judges of the trial court, nevertheless, it has not become a well – established method: it is rather seldom applied in practice. On the other hand, it may be pointed out that the creation of the possibility of the direct taking of evidence in the European Judicial Area has undoubtedly meant a significant step forward. This legal institution *has broken through the traditional frames of state sovereignty* by opening up the possibility for the courts to perform certain procedural acts beyond the borders of the state. However, this *breakthrough is restricted in extent* as it concerns only a small subfield of the exercise of judicial power and even in this area a whole range of restrictive rules (lack of coercive measures, conditions defined by the central body and grounds for refusal) are built into the Regulation as "checks" in the interests of protecting retained state sovereignty.

In the case of cross – border disputes it may constitute a problem for the courts to obtain evidence that could well be conclusive if the means of evidence is located or resides abroad (for example, if the witness lives abroad; the scene to be inspected is located in another state, or documentary evidence is kept outside the territory of the state where the trial court is situated). In the European Judicial Area it had become obvious by the millennium that the traditional system of legal assistance known from international civil procedure law no longer offered an adequate answer – corresponding to the degree of integration – to solve the problem of taking of evidence abroad. The effective improvement of cooperation in the field of taking of evidence may be achieved only *at the Community level.* The coming into effect of Regulation (EC) No. 1206/2001[1] has, for the first time, enabled the courts in all states of the European Judicial Area to proceed based on *uniform rules* during their cooperation in the taking of evidence abroad – in civil and commercial matters.

---

* Associate Professor, Head of Department, Pázmány Péter Catholic University (Budapest), Department of Civil Procedure Law. E – mail: harsagi. viktoria@ jak. pkke. hu.

[1] Council Regulation (EC) No. 1206/2001 of 28 May 2001 on cooperation between the courts of the Member States in the taking of evidence in civil or commercial matters. OJ L 174, 27. 6. 2001, pp. 1 ~24.

As regards the nature of Regulation (EC) No. 1206/2001, it constitutes a technical rule basically. It has not resulted in the genuine unification of the laws relating to the taking of evidence abroad, it merely simplifies the process, unifies its technical aspects and accelerates it Europe – wide.[2] It does not directly regulate the method of carrying out the actual taking of evidence abroad [cf. Article 1 (1)]. These questions are governed by the provisions of international treaties and the domestic laws of the Member States or they fall within the court's discretion.[3] The taking of evidence itself follows the principle of *lex fori* regardless of whether it is carried out by the trial court or the requested court. In *Heβ*' s opinion, this step may be considered only a temporary intermediate solution, as even in the present European Judicial Area parties may still be subject to the collision of numerous procedural laws. In the medium run, therefore, it would be absolutely necessary to elaborate a more generally applicable system of rules relating to the *European law of evidence.*[4]

1. "Breaking through" sovereignty by ensuring the possibility of the direct taking of evidence

The principle of immediacy requires that taking of evidence are carried out by the trial court as a general rule. Within country borders it is usually possible to make an exception for the reason of the effective conduct of lawsuits. On an international scale, such acts of the trial court are limited by the territorial sovereignty of other states. Because judicial power forms part of state power, it may be exercised basically within the territory of the given state. Without the approval of the state concerned it is not possible to perform the taking of evidence or oblige persons residing in the territory of the state to participate in the proceedings.[5] Therefore, state sovereignty functions as a limit to the *extraterritorial taking of evidence*. The possibility to take evidence directly means an important step forward compared to the earlier situation, since this constitutes such an act carried out in the territory of a foreign state which would not be permitted in a classical international legal sense. Heβ considers that these *limits stemming from sovereignty* may no longer play a role in the relations between the states of the European Judicial Area.[6]

In the traditional system based on conventions on legal assistance there are basically three possible ways for obtaining evidence located abroad: taking of evidence performed by the for-

---

[2] Berger, Christian: Die EG – Verordnung über die Zusammenarbeit der Gerichte auf dem Gebiet der Beweisaufnahme in Zivil – und Handelssachen (EuBVO). *Praxis des Internationalen Privat – und Verfahrensrecht*, 2001, pp. 524 ~ 527.

[3] Schulze, Götz: Dialogische Beweisaufnahmen im internationalen Rechtshilfeverkehr. *Praxis des Internationalen Privat – und Verfahrensrecht*, 2001, p. 528.

[4] Heβ, Burkhard: Die Integrationsfunktion des Europäischen Zivilverfahrensrecht. *Praxis des Internationalen Privat – und Verfahrensrecht*, 2001, p. 393. Heβ, Burkhard – Müller, Achim: Die Verordnung 1206/01/EG zur Beweisaufnahme im Ausland. *Zeitschrift für Zivilprozess International* (Jahrbuch des Internationalen Zivilprozessrechts), 2001, p. 150; Hess, Burkhard: *Europäisches Zivilprozessrecht.* C. F. Müller, Heidelberg, 2010, p. 462.

[5] Nagel, Heinrich – Gottwald, Peter: *Internationales Zivilprozessrecht.* Münster – Köln, 2002, Aschendorff Rechtsverlag – Verlag Dr. Otto Schmidt, p. 414.

[6] Heβ, Burkhard: Aktuelle Perspektiven der Europäischen Prozessrechtsangleichung. *Juristenzeitung*, 2001, pp. 579 ~ 580.

eign court *upon the request* of the trial court, taking of evidence *directly by the consul* and (where it is permitted by the domestic law of the state of the trial court) the domestic use of a *means of evidence "imported"* from abroad by the party.[7]

As a result of the coming into effect of the Regulation on the taking of evidence, one has been able to observe a shift from the traditional system of cross – border legal assistance toward a *new model of cooperation* in the European Union, where the direct taking of evidence in the national territory of another Member State has also become possible within the frames set by the Regulation. By this partial relinquishment of the exercise of judicial power, the Member States have *given up a small segment of state sovereignty*, which means an essential change compared to the rules contained in either the Hague Convention of 1954[8] or that of 1970[9].[10]

Regulation (EC) No. 1206/2001 distinguishes between *two essentially different ways* of obtaining evidence located abroad. The *request*, well – known from the traditional model of co-operation, has been supplemented with the possibility of the *direct taking of evidence* by the court of the requesting state. The two methods of solution (active and passive legal assistance) constitute alternatives of equal rank;[11] where there is no need for the application of coercive measures in order to render the taking of evidence feasible, the requesting court (trial court) has the right of choice between the two alternatives. When *deciding which method to choose*, the traditional request or the direct taking of evidence, the *trial court* must have regard to *expedience*. In general, it may be considered an argument for the direct taking of evidence that the trial court knows more about the case and it is subject to its own domestic law during this part of the procedure as well. Thus, one unified procedural law is applied throughout the whole procedure. It is also an advantage of this solution that the principle of immediacy is implemented better. On the other hand, this way of taking of evidence is usually more costly.

2. Voluntary cooperation as a pre – condition

Direct taking of evidence may only take place in the other Member State if it can be performed on a voluntary basis *without the need for coercive measures* [Article 17 (2) first sentence]. With regard to the hearing of persons it means that the witness or expert is willing to make a statement or provide an expert opinion. If the taking of evidence concerns physical evi-

---

[7] As a fourth type, one could also mention the taking of evidence by a special representative (commissioner) – appointed by the trial court – known from the common law system. Geimer, Reinhold: *Internationales Zivilprozeβrecht.* Verlag Dr. Otto Schmidt, Köln, 2001, p. 183. This type of taking of evidence can also be interpreted in a sense as a transitory stage leading to the *direct* taking of evidence by the trial court. However, some authors do not attribute great practical significance to this solution, since its application depends on the approval of the state concerned, which approval may not be granted by the state generally, but only with regard to a specific case. Leipold, Dieter: Neue Wege im Recht der internationalen Beweiserhebung – einige Bemerkungen zur Europäischen Beweisaufnahmeverordnung. In von Schwenzer, Ingeborg – Hager, Günter (eds.): *Festschrift für Peter Schlechtriem zum 70. Geburtstag*, Tübingen, 2003, Mohr, p. 99.

[8] Hague Convention of 1 March 1954 on Civil Procedure

[9] Hague Convention of 18 March 1970 on the Taking of Evidence Abroad in Civil or Commercial Matters

[10] For more detail on this topic, see Nagel, Heinrich: *Nationale und internationale Rechtshilfe im Zivilprozeβ; das europ? ische Modell.* Baden – Baden, 1971, Nomos, p. 78; Nagel – Gottwald: op. cit. (see note 4), p. 449, pp. 456 ~457.

[11] Heβ – Müller: op. cit. (see note 4), p. 159.

dence (documents or objects to be inspected), the holder of the document or object should voluntarily permit the requesting court to examine the above physical evidence.

If it is necessary to *hear a witness* residing abroad, the court may choose either alternative offered by the Regulation if the witness is prepared to give evidence without the application of coercive measures. The disadvantage of the request to examine the witness lies in the fact that the court has no opportunity to *get direct impression* by questioning the witness.[12] This way the advantages of this particular means of evidence (interactivity) cannot prevail. As a matter of course, Article 17 also enables the requesting court to take evidence directly in the Member State of the residence of the witness *on a voluntary basis*. However, if the witness appearing voluntarily during the direct taking of evidence gives testimony, the question of his criminal liability for breaching his *duty to tell the truth* is not clear. Without the clarification of this issue, the mentioned legal institution cannot fully perform its function.[13]

Moreover, the European Court of Justice did answer another unclarified question when it held in Case C170/11 Lippens, Mittler, Votron v Kortekaas[14] that Articles 1 (1) (b) and 17 of the Regulation (EC) No. 1206/2001 must be interpreted as meaning that the court of one Member State, which wishes the task of taking of evidence entrusted to an expert to be carried out in another Member State, is not necessarily required to use the method of taking of evidence laid down by those provisions to be able to order the taking of that evidence.

A foreign expert may be used in the case of either of the two methods of taking of evidence. Consequently, a request may be directed at obtaining an expert opinion from abroad, but in case of the voluntary participation of a foreign expert, it is also possible for the requesting court to examine that expert directly in the Member State of his residence. In one of its latest judgments passed this year (in case C332/11, ProRail BV v Xpedys NV, 21 February 2013), the European Court of Justice deals with the possibility of proof by expert opinion as reflected in the rules applicable to the direct taking of evidence. In so far as the expert designated by a court of a Member State must go to another Member State in order to carry out the investigation which has been entrusted to him, that might, in certain circumstances, affect the powers of the Member State in which it takes place, in particular where it is an investigation carried out in places connected to the exercise of such powers or in places to which access or other action is, under the law of the Member State in which the investigation is carried out, prohibited or restricted to certain persons.[15] "In order to complete his task, the expert needs to have access to objects, information or places which are not public, he must obtain the assistance of the authorities of the other Member State. In that case, in which there is an exercise of judicial power with exter-

[12] Hess op. cit. (see note 4) p. 472.

[13] Berger: op. cit. (see note 2), p. 526, Cf: Müller, Achim: Grenzüberschreitende Beweisaufnahme im Europäischen Justizraum. Mohr Siebeck, Tübingen, 2004, pp. 114 ~ 116.

[14] European Court Reports 2012 Page 00000, see Besso, Chiara: Cooperation in the taking of evidence: the European Attitude. International Journal of Procedural Law, Vol 2 (2012) No. 1, p. 84.

[15] Case ProRail BV v Xpedys NV, C332/11, Nr. 47.

nal effect, namely effect in the territory of another Member State, the procedure for the direct taking of evidence laid down in Article 17 of Regulation No. 1206/2001 must be applied in order to obtain assistance in the requested Member State and to be entitled to all the attributes of the corresponding power. "[16] In such circumstances, unless the court wishing to order cross – border expert investigation foregoes the taking of that evidence, and in the absence of an agreement or arrangement between Member States within the meaning of Article 21 (2) of Regulation No 1206/2001, the method of taking of evidence laid down in Articles 1 (1) (b) and 17 thereof is the only means to enable the court of a Member State to carry out an expert investigation directly in another Member State. It is clear from the foregoing that a national court wishing to order an expert investigation which must be carried out in another Member State is not necessarily required to have recourse to the method of taking of evidence laid down in Articles 1 (1) (b) and 17 of Regulation No. 1206/2001.[17]

Where the direct taking of evidence implies that *a person shall be heard*, the requesting court shall inform that person that the performance shall take place on a voluntary basis [Article 17 (2) second sentence]. However, the Regulation prescribes no specific time when this information should be supplied. Neither does it lay down an obligation for the requesting court to conduct preliminary enquiries in order to ascertain that the person to be heard really intends to give testimony. In spite of this, it would be reasonable for the court to obtain such information in advance prior to the request.

When choosing the most reasonable method of obtaining and examining *objects to be inspected that are located abroad*, the requesting court must have regard to numerous circumstances. First of all, it shall consider the nature of the object to be examined, in particular, whether the object in question *can be transported or presented* before the court without substantial difficulty. In the case of immovable property or objects that are difficult to move, the only possibility is on – the – spot inspection by the requested court. Where the holder of the object to be inspected is willing to cooperate, the requesting court may also perform the *on – the – spot inspection* directly in accordance with the provisions of Article 17. In some case it may be reasonable to assign an expert to the task of carrying out the direct taking of evidence.

In the case of minor movable property, again both solutions are possible, as a matter of course, there is no need to carry out the inspection on the spot. With regard to such movable objects the question of the *import of evidence* also arises, which is neither regulated, nor precluded by the Regulation. During the taking of evidence before the requested court there is no obstacle to using a web camera, which enables the requesting court to receive a more direct impression.[18]

---

〔16〕 Opinion of Advocate General Jääskinen delivered on 6 September 2012, Case C332/11, Nr. 59.

〔17〕 Case ProRail BV v Xpedys NV, C332/11, Nr. 48 ~49.

〔18〕 von Hein, Jan: Verordnung (EG) Nr 1206/2001 des Rates vom 28. 5. 2001 über die Zusammenarbeit zwischen den Gerichten der Mitgliedstaaten auf dem Gebiet der Beweisaufnahme in Zivil – und Handelssachen (EG – BewVO). In Rauscher, Thomas (ed.): *Europäisches Zivilprozeßrecht. Kommentar.* Sellier, München, 2004, p. 879.

Another aspect to be considered by the requesting court when choosing between a request and the direct taking of evidence is the intention or lack of intention to cooperate on the part of the holder of the object to be inspected. In the absence of voluntary cooperation the direct taking of evidence is not possible. Naturally, concerning the inspection, a situation may arise where no such obstacle presents itself regarding the object to be inspected, because it is situated in a public place for example (for instance, the scene of the traffic accident in an action for compensation etc.). In this latter case there is practically no need to examine the precondition contained in Article 17 (2). In case of the *lack of cooperation* it is also significant whether the object is in the possession of the party or a third person, since the requesting court usually has more limited coercive measures at its disposal if the object is in the possession of the party. In the latter situation, however, preventing the examination of the object to be inspected may lead to other procedural consequences.

In the lack of voluntariness, the court of the other Member State cannot effect coercive measures against the *person holding the document in his possession abroad*, this in any case presupposes the involvement of a foreign court, moreover, in the form of classical legal assistance: on the basis of a request addressed to a foreign court to carry out acts of taking of evidence.

Even in the European Judicial Area coercive measures may be applied against citizens only by their state of residence.[19] In the lack of voluntary cooperation - within the frames of the Regulation - the trial court has no other possibility at its disposal to obtain the required evidence than a request for the taking of evidence. This is explained by the fact that the requesting court *cannot request* the courts of the requested state for legal assistance *in the interests of applying coercive measures* necessary for taking of evidence in the other Member State - for example, in the form known from arbitration procedures, neither is the requesting court entitled to apply such measures itself in the foreign state.

3. Initiation of the direct taking of evidence

Where a court requests to take evidence directly in another Member State, it shall submit a request to the *central body* or the competent authority in that State, using *form I in the Annex* [Article 17 (1)], which body or authority shall decide about the granting of the request and define the conditions for its execution. The request and all documents accompanying the request shall be exempted from authentication or any equivalent formality (for example, from the authentication clause: "apostille" known from the Hague Convention of 1961[20]) [Article 4 (2)]. The contents of the request are governed by the provisions of Article 4. In accordance with this, the request *shall necessarily contain* the following details regardless of the type of means of evidence the examination of which is sought by the request: *a*) in the case of a request for the direct taking of evidence: the requesting court; *b*) the names and addresses of the parties to the proceedings and their representatives; *c*) the nature and subject matter of the

---

〔19〕 Berger: op. cit. (see note 2), p. 526.

〔20〕 Hague Convention of 5 October 1961 Abolishing the Requirement of Legalisation for Foreign Public Documents

case and a brief statement of the facts; *d*) a description of the taking of evidence to be performed [Article 4 (1) points *a*) - *d*)].

The legal consequence of submitting a request that does not contain all the necessary information concerning the direct taking of evidence may be a *refusal* by the central body or competent authority *of the direct taking of evidence* [see Article 17 (5) point *b*)].

The Member States shall indicate which means they regard acceptable for the transmission of requests and communications. Within the frames of these means, printed forms must be forwarded in the most expeditious way. Under the Regulation, forwarding may take place by any suitable means. Only one restriction is specified concerning the *means of communication*: it must be ensured that the *integrity of content* of the document *is not injured* by the given means, in other words: "the document received accurately reflects the content of the document forwarded" and the Regulation also prescribes the requirement that information must be legible (Article 6). In practice, these criteria may be met by the electronic transmission of the request, in other words, its forwarding either *by fax* or *e – mail*, unless the state of the requested court has precluded the use of such means.[21] The individual Member States shall also inform the Commission about the possible means of transmission. These data are also recorded in the Manual, which may be downloaded from the internet.[22]

4. Radical transformation of the role of the central body

In traditional conventions on legal assistance, the central body was assigned the role of an intermediary between the requesting and requested courts. As opposed to this, in accordance with Regulation (EC) No. 1206/2001, the central body *primarily plays a coordinating, advisory and supportive role* in the "request model". However, the possibility of the direct taking of evidence has also imposed new tasks on central bodies: *to take decisions on requests for the direct taking of evidence.*

Within 30 days of receiving the request, the central body or the competent authority of the requested Member State shall inform the requesting court if the request is accepted and, if necessary, under what conditions according to the law of its Member State such performance is to be carried out. The Regulation also mentions one of the possible conditions specifically. The central body or the competent authority may assign a court of its Member State to take part in the performance of the taking of evidence in order to ensure the proper application of the Regulation and the fulfilment of the conditions that have been set out [Article 17 (4)]. A further requirement could be constituted by the involvement of an attorney – at – law (if this is still not possible under the law of the state of the requesting court) and, maybe, of an interpreter

---

[21] Klauser, Alexander: *Europäisches Zivilprozessrecht.* Wien, 2002, Manz, p. 427; Schlosser, Peter: *EU – Zivilprozessrecht. Kommentar.* München, 2009, Beck, p. 493.

[22] The Manual may be downloaded from the Internet from the official website of the European Union at the following address: http://ec.europa.eu/justice_home/judicialatlascivil/html/index_en.htm. On the website there is a search system called "*European Judicial Atlas*" built on the data of the Manual, which facilitates access to the data of the trial court.

etc.[23]

The central body must be *designated* by the given Member State. In most Member States the function of central body is performed by the Ministry of Justice of that state, while in other cases by some other ministry or possibly by a court appointed to this role etc.[24]

5. Grounds for refusal

Refusal of the direct taking of evidence *may take place only within a narrow scope defined by the Regulation.* The central body or the competent authority may refuse direct taking of evidence only if *a*) the request does not fall within the scope of this Regulation, *b*) the request does not contain all of the necessary information pursuant to the Regulation, or *c*) the direct taking of evidence requested is contrary to fundamental principles of law in the Member State [Article 17 (5)].

(1) Ad a)

The scope of the Regulation is defined by Article 1. Pursuant to this, the Regulation shall apply in *court proceedings* – *commenced or contemplated* – concerning the resolution of *civil or commercial matters.* The scope of the Regulation does not extend to the taking of evidence that is not intended for use in judicial proceedings [Article 1 (1) – (2)]. In the lack of a provision for their exclusion non – litigious proceedings may also fall within this range.[25] With regard to the interpretation of the *notion of "civil and commercial matters"*, the explanation attached to Article 1 (1) of the Brussels I Regulation and the relating case – law must serve as a basis while having regard to the difference that the Regulation on the taking of evidence *does not contain the exceptions mentioned in Article* 1 (2) *Brussels I Regulation.* This latter fact leads to the conclusion "*a contrario*" that these areas – if they are of a civil or commercial nature and fall within the jurisdiction of courts – are covered by the scope of the Regulation on the taking of evidence.[26] It is without doubt that, similarly to the Brussels I Regulation, tax, customs or administrative matters cannot be regarded as civil or commercial matters. It is not possible to question the civil law nature of procedures relating to the personal status of natural persons, their capacity to have rights and obligations as well as their capacity to act, procedures connected with laws regulating matrimonial property, wills and succession, bankruptcy proceedings, forced settlements and similar procedures. On the other hand, applicability in matters relating to social security mentioned in Article 1 (2) point *c*) of the Brussels I Regulation seems problematic. Just like in the case of the Brussels I Regulation, classification as a civil or commercial matter *is not determined by the type of the court*, but by the substantive law character of the matter. The notion of civil and commercial matters must be *interpreted autonomously*. This means that this question is not governed by the laws of the Member States, but Community law and in the final analysis, by the future case – law of the European Court of Justice to

---

〔23〕 Berger: op. cit. (see note 2), p. 526.

〔24〕 See http: //ec. europa. eu/justice_ home/judicialatlascivil/html/index_ en. htm.

〔25〕 Leipold: op. cit. (see note 7), p. 93.

〔26〕 Berger: op. cit. (see note 2), p. 112.

be developed having in view the purpose and meaning of the Regulation.[27] The scope of the Regulation does not extend to *arbitration proceedings*. As a matter of fact, this is not regulated directly in the Regulation, but Article 1 (2) speaks about the taking of evidence by the court (of the Member State).[28]

Schlosser is of the opinion that the notion of taking of evidence must be interpreted expansively so as to include all judicial measures aimed at the obtaining of information,[29] including the common law "*discovery*" as well, which takes place at the pre – trial stage of the legal action. The *notion of taking of evidence* – be it carried out either upon request or directly – must be *interpreted autonomously*, just like the notion of civil and commercial matters. In other words, it should not be interpreted proceeding from the laws of the individual Member States (concerned), but independently of them, with a pan – European character.[30] With regard to the means of evidence actually concerned by the taking of evidence, there is no general restriction. Article 4 (1) of Regulation (EC) No. 1206/2001 mentions requests for the hearing and examination of persons in the first place, since such requests are expected to be the most common, however, point *f*) also deals with the possibility of taking other type of evidence, by which one is to understand the presentation of documents and inspection.

(2) Ad b)

In the procedure for the granting of the request for the direct taking of evidence there is no possibility for supplying the missing information. The rejection of the incomplete application, however, does not preclude the possibility to file a repeated request.[31]

(3) Ad c)

The direct taking of evidence may be refused on the ground that it is contrary to the fundamental principles of law in the Member State. By this, as a matter of fact, Member States were permitted to retain a part of their sovereignty. *Schmidt* refers to this as the maintenance of a specific procedural ordre public.[32] Others speak about a restricted public policy clause.[33] In any case, here one should think only of injuries that actually result from the taking of evidence itself. The fact alone that a means or method of evidence does not exist or is not recognized by the system of evidence of the given state (for example, the institution of oath or discovery) does not necessarily result in the refusal of the request with reference to public policy. At the

---

[27] von Hein: op. cit. (see note 18), p. 867.

[28] Schmidt, Uwe: *Europ? isches Zivilprozessrecht in der Praxis*. München, 2004, Beck, p. 112.

[29] Similarly to the Hague Convention of 1970, the Regulation also includes *discovery measures*. As opposed to Article 23 of the Hague Convention, *in this case* Member States *cannot avoid* the performance of such requests. Schlosser: op. cit. (see note 21), pp. 490. However, Jan von Hein revises the statements made in academic literature, in his interpretation only standard disclosure may be unambiguously considered as falling within the scope of the Regulation. von Hein: op. cit. (see note 18), p. 891.

[30] von Hein: op. cit. (see note 18), pp. 872 ~ 873.

[31] Huber, Stefan: Europäische Beweisaufnahmeverordnung (EuBVO) In Gebauer, Martin – Wiedmann, Thomas (Hrsg.): *Zivilrecht unter europäischem Einfluss*. Stuttgart 2010, Boorberg, p. 1818.

[32] Schmidt: op. cit. (see note 28), p. 115.

[33] Heβ – Müller: op. cit. (see note 4), p. 161.

same time, the question arises as to what practical importance such reservations may have in the case of voluntary cooperation.[34]

6. The taking of evidence

The taking of evidence is performed by the requesting court, one of the designated judicial representatives or some other person - for example, an expert - based on the procedural law of the state of the forum delegating him or of the trial court (lex fori). The central body or the competent authority shall encourage the use of communications technology, such as videoconferences and teleconferences [Article 17]. The Regulation does not expressly provide for the supply of technical means other than those mentioned above or for ensuring a recorder of minutes, but there is such a possibility.

While performing the direct taking of evidence abroad and proceeding based on the law of its own Member State, the trial court may also use such methods of taking of evidence that do not exist in or differ essentially from the law of the Member State where the taking of evidence is carried out (such as, for example, cross - examination). The reference to the principle of lex fori also applies to the language used, which serves to avoid possible losses or distortions of information. A further *advantage* of the direct taking of evidence is that the domestic and foreign stages of the proceeding are performed based on the same procedural rules.[35] However, *a disadvantage* of this solution is that it is typically more costly and that the successful performance of the taking of evidence may be prevented by the lack of voluntary cooperation on the part of the witness, expert or holder of the object or document to be inspected.

Conclusion

On the one hand, the direct taking of evidence, in principle, means a simpler method for the judges of the trial court, nevertheless, it has not become a well - established method: it is rather seldom applied in practice.[36] On the other hand, it may be pointed out that the creation of the possibility of the direct taking of evidence in the European Judicial Area has undoubtedly meant a significant step forward. This legal institution *has broken through the traditional frames of state sovereignty* by opening up the possibility for the courts to perform certain procedural acts beyond the borders of the state. However, this *breakthrough is restricted in extent* as it concerns only a small subfield of the exercise of judicial power and even in this area a whole range of restrictive rules (lack of coercive measures, conditions defined by the central body and grounds for refusal) are built into the Regulation as "checks" in the interests of protecting retained state sovereignty.

---

[34] Schlosser: op. cit. (see note 21), p. 496.

[35] Besso: op. cit. (see note 14), p. 77.; Müller: op. cit. (see note 13) p. 112., cf.: Report from the Commission to the Council, the European Parliament and the European Economic and Social Committee on the application of the Council Regulation (EC) 1206/2001 of 28 May 2001 on cooperation between the courts of the Member States in the taking of evidence in civil or commercial matters, COM (2007) 769 final, p. 14.

[36] Klötgen, Paul: Bewährungsprobe für den Europäischen Justizraum: Grenzüberschreitende Zustellung und Beweisaufnahme. In: Rechberger, Walter H. / Kengyel, Miklós (eds.): Europäisches Zivilverfahrensrecht. Bestandsaufnahme und Zukunftsperspektiven nach EU - Erweiterung. Neuer Wissenschaftlicher Verlag, Wien - Graz, 2007, p. 103.

试论被诉具体行政行为“认定事实错误”

高家伟 *

准确认定事实是从证据确凿充分的客观事实此岸达到案件事实清楚的主观真实彼岸的中介与桥梁。这里所说的事实认定是指行政机关在行政程序中针对特定的公民、法人或者其他组织作出具有法律效果的处理决定之前，根据证据材料的采信结果和相关实体法律规定而对全案事实进行综合分析与判断的认识行为。在进入行政审判程序后，法院对被诉具体行政行为的合法性审查分为法律审和事实审两个层面，学界对事实审的研究薄弱，现有的法律法规和司法解释对此规定甚少，而张保生教授主持的《人民法院统一证据规定》和张军先生主持的《统一诉讼证据规定》〔1〕也未对此给以足够的重视。这是本文的缘由。

引言：意义和问题

《行政诉讼法》第54条第1款将“主要证据确凿”作为事实审方面的维持理由，相应地于第54条第2款第1项将“主要证据不足”作为事实审方面的撤销理由。关于何谓“主要证据不足”，《行诉法意见》、《行诉法解释》、《行诉证据规定》未对此作任何扩张解释。〔2〕至少从规范的层面上来说，“认定事实错误”、“案件事实清楚”等都没有被纳入到被诉具体行政行为的事实审查标准之中。不过，第61条在规定对一审判决的上诉审查标准时明确地使用了“认定事实清楚”、“认定事实不清”等术语。相比较之下，可以发现这并非立法者的无意疏忽，而是基于行政执法与行政审判的区别而有意确立不同的事实认定标准：对被诉行政行为在事实认定方面的要求比较低，只需“主要证据确凿”即可——甚至连“充分”一词都去掉了；对一审判决在事实认定方面的要求比较高，要在“主要证据确凿”的基础上，进而达到“认定案件事实清楚”的程度。

但是，《行政复议法》第28条第1款第3项第1目将“主要事实不清、证据不足”

---

* 高家伟，中国政法大学诉讼法学研究院教授、博士生导师，中国政法大学、吉林大学、武汉大学司法文明协同创新中心签约研究员。Email：gaojiawei@263.net。本文系教育部人文社科重点研究基地中国政法大学诉讼法学研究院自设项目“行政执法决定中的证据问题研究”的最终成果之一。

〔1〕张保生主编：《人民法院统一证据规定：司法解释建议稿及论证》，中国政法大学出版社2008年版；关于张军先生主持的《统一诉讼证据规定（建议稿及论证）》，见最高人民法院应用法学研究所与中国政法大学证据科学研究院于2012年6月30日在京联合举办的“诉讼证据规定研究论证会”材料。

〔2〕《行诉法意见》：最高人民法院《关于贯彻执行〈中华人民共和国行政诉讼法〉若干问题的意见（试行）》，1991年5月29日通过；《行诉法解释》：最高人民法院《关于执行〈中华人民共和国行政诉讼法〉若干问题的解释》，1999年11月24日经最高人民法院审判委员会第1088次会议讨论通过；《行诉证据规定》：最高人民法院《关于行政诉讼证据若干问题的规定》，2002年7月24日公布，2002年10月1日起施行。

规定为被诉行政行为合法性审查的一个撤销理由，《行政复议法实施条例》第43条将“认定事实清楚”作为复议决定的维持理由，第47条第2项将“认定事实不清，证据不足”作为复议决定的变更理由。有鉴于行政复议与行政审判之间的连贯关系，这实际上意味着，在证据充分确凿之外，事实认定准确清楚已经成为一个单独存在的事实审标准。相关案例也证明了这一点。[3]

将前述有关的法律法规和司法解释的规定结合起来，可以认为，事实认定是否正确已经成为审判实践中实际采用的事实审标准。接下来值得研究的问题是具体的标准是什么。本文尝试从“认定事实错误”的角度对此展开思考。

一、范围：相关性规则的拓展

准确认定案件事实的首要一环是搞清楚哪些事实应当纳入本案事实认定的范围，哪些事实应当排除在考虑之外。应当考虑的事实而没有考虑的，构成事实的遗漏；不应当考虑的事实而考虑的，构成事实的多余。这就是在范围把握方面可能出现的两种事实认定错误。对此，可以从如下方面把握：

（一）标　准

亦即认定某一项事实是否与本案相关以及在哪方面相关从而应予考虑的相关性标准。申言之：

1. 规范标准。具体可分为：

（1）规范要件标准。如果相关的法律法规、规章或者司法解释对规范要件事实有明确的规定，则无论在实质认定上作何种考虑，都应当认为相应的案件事实具有相关性。

（2）规范目的标准。如果没有相关规定或者相关规定不明确，那么，应当从立法目的——亦即规范保护目的——的角度进行考虑。

2. 权益标准。凡是与被诉行政行为所处理或者直接影响的公民（法人或者其他组织的）权益有关的要件事实，无论是否发生了争议，都应当认定与本案相关，必须纳入本案事实认定的考虑范围。具体可分为：

（1）当事人权益标准。亦即与被诉行政行为直接针对的公民权益有关的要件事实。

（2）利害关系人权益标准。这方面最为典型的例子是涉及相邻权的建筑许可行为。无论相邻人是否提出争议，建设主管部门在颁发建设许可证之前都必须将相邻人的权益（要件）事实纳入本案建筑许可决定的事实认定范围之内；否则，即构成实质性的案件事实遗漏。

3. 意义标准。如果某一项事实对本案事实的全面、客观、一致的认识具有意义，则无论该意义是正向支持性的，还是反向否定性的，都应当纳入本案考虑的范围。

4. 争议标准。只要一项事实在本案中被当事人或者利害关系人合理地引起了争议，那么，即应当认为与本案相关。请注意：这里所说的“合理”是指具有证据材料支持或者科学论据、法律规范等方面的正当理由支持，并且不会因争议的提出而造成

---

〔3〕“泸州工商局处罚决定认定事实错误被撤销”，载 http：//www.chinacourt.org/article/detail/2006/05/id/206928.shtml，访问时间：2013年5月13日（行为定性错误：将未获得《医疗广告许可》而发布广告的行为视为未经审查批准而发布广告的行为）。

案件处理程序的过分迟延，或者造成不合乎比例的社会、道德、经济等方面的成本。作为拖延战术、烟幕战术、心理战术、抹黑战术、宣传战术等而提出的争议，即使具有表面正当理由的支持，也因具有内在不正当的目的而丧失其合理性。

行政机关在对本案事实进行总体性的分析判断时对前述四类事实没有纳入本案考虑，无论采取的是明示拒绝、暗示疏漏的方式还是无意疏忽的方式，都构成“认定事实错误”，导致“案件事实不清”。

（二）分　类

为了进一步准确把握案件事实的认定范围，可以从立法性事实、政策性事实、预测性事实、社会背景事实、情节事实、要件事实、证据事实、显而易见的事实和众所周知的事实这一分类的角度进行认识。

证据事实、情节事实、要件事实是刑事、民事、行政三大诉讼学理共同采取的有关案件事实的基础分类。证据事实是在经采信的证据材料中记载的、用来证明某一法律主张或者事实主张的事实，情节事实是有关案件事实具体发生过程的事实，要件事实是在案件事实之中蕴含的、为适用特定法律规范而必须具备的基本事实。

除了前述三类事实之外，在必要的情况下，显见事实和周知事实也会以司法认知的方式进入案件事实的认定过程中。

行政案件事实的范围具有其特殊性，表现在：除了前述五类事实之外，在被诉具体行政行为的事实认定还可能涉及如下四类特殊的事实：一是立法性事实，二是政策性事实，三是预测性事实，四是社会背景事实。

立法性事实是指作为立法机关在制定相关法律规范时所考虑的事实，例如，有关社会立法需求和推动力的事实、有关法律实施条件的事实、有关立法成本收益分析的事实等。与法律的规范性特征一致，这些事实也具有概括性、抽象性、普遍性、预测性等特征。行政执法机关为了准确地理解和适用相关的法律规范，通常要考虑这方面的事实因素。

政策性事实的考虑因素在被诉行政行为的事实认定中更为突出，因为所有的行政行为虽然是针对特定的公民、法人或者其他组织的具体事件作出，但无一不包含政府在特定时期内的政策取向因素，无一不包含带有特定政治价值权衡的因素。法院在审查被诉行政行为时，如果不了解政策性事实，也就难以把握行政机关作出被诉行政行为的动机。政策性事实可能外在地表现为作为政策载体的红头文件（行政规范性文件）中所声称的目的、目标、根据、措施等之中，也可能内在表现为蕴含在被诉行政行为之后的价值偏好或者利益平衡方面的政策动机之中。

所谓预测性事实是指根据现有的知识和信息，按照科学的方法进行分析预测而认定的对未来可能发生的事实。其中最为典型的是所谓的风险评估事实。这一点在大型投资或者建设项目的许可中最为突出。另外，绝大多数的行政规划行为也都是根据预测性事实作出的，这种预测事实可能表现为对经济、社会和科技发展的趋势的预测，或者表现为对未来产业发展、城市发展的远景规划等。

所谓社会背景事实，是指作为案件事实发生的社会背景的事实，例如，特定时期的政治、经济和社会的发展状况，地方居民的风俗习惯，国民的日益增长的物质和精神需要等。同样的法律规范和政策因社会背景不同，其适用的具体方式也就不同。

有鉴于行政执法的专业化发展趋势，政策事实与背景事实往往不是证据法上所说的显而易见、众所周知的事实。显而易见是相对于一般民众的生活经验而言的，众所周知是相对于业内人士的一般知识水平而言的。

上述分类是不全面的，其意义在于说明：行政案件事实是多层面、多位方面的事实交织互动的产物，法官要理解被诉行政行为认定的要件事实（亦即裁判事实），不仅需要了解案件事实的具体发生过程（亦即情节事实），而且要了解行政机关在作出被诉具体行政行为时所考虑的立法性事实、政策性事实或者预测性事实，必要时还要了解相关的社会背景事实。这就是说，只有将具体个案中的事实放在宏观的社会生活背景和政府的相关政策考量因素中，才可能把握行政机关作出被诉具体行政行为的"事实真相"。

（三）错误的界定

如果法院经审查发现被诉具体行政行为，

（1）除了要件事实、情节事实、证据事实、周知事实和显见事实之外；

（2）在调查收集阶段，举证、质证和认证阶段，或者在全案事实认定阶段；

（3）没有以适当的方式考虑相关的立法性事实、政策性事实、预测性事实或者社会背景事实；

（4）对案件事实的准确认定产生了实质性的影响。

即构成事实认定错误。

二、方法：科学主义宗旨的贯彻

与其他部门法相比较，我国证据法在发展路径上的一个鲜明特征在于它是在哲学的理论基石上建立起来的一座科学大厦。承蒙以张文显教授、樊崇义教授为代表的部门法哲理化思潮的推动，[4] 哲学在我国证据法的前期奠基阶段起到了应有的先导作用，为我国证据法体系的建构奠定了一个高起点、宽容量的理论基础。继此之后，科学证据的力量日渐突起，将在以后的发展过程中起主导的作用。笔者认为，应当将科学主义确立为我国建构统一诉讼证据规则的核心指导思想。

前文分类从一个角度揭示了行政案件事实的特殊复杂性。从方法论的角度来看，行政案件事实的正确认定既要遵循一般证据科学的方法，也要针对特有的事实类型而采取不同的认定方法。

（一）一般方法

体现科学主义宗旨的一般证据认定方法有：

1. 科学定律。当特定的案件事实需要遵循特定的科学定律才能获得正确的认识时，那么，对科学定律的违反即构成认识事实的错误。

2. 经验法则。当某种生活现象经长期的生活实践检验而上升到普遍经验的层面时，即构成一种公众的生活常识。这种常识可能成为判断日常生活中的显而易见事实的标准。

除了以上两点之外，随着科学证据的发展，如下两个方面的作用日渐凸显：

---

〔4〕 樊崇义：《刑事诉讼法哲理思维》，中国人民公安大学出版社2010年版，第1～33页、第257～283页；高家伟："部门法学的哲理化走向"，载《人民法院报》2005年1月26日"理论与实践周刊"。

3. 思维方法。亦即不同的案件事实需要不同的思维方法。当特定的案件事实类型只有通过特定思维方法才能得到正确的认识时，不采用特定思维方法认定相应案件事实的，即构成思维方法的错误。

4. 操作规程。不同的科学证据类型在调取、保管、鉴定、认定等各环节都具有特殊的技术操作规程。违反操作规程可能造成调取或者保管的证据材料失去证据资格，致使相应的案件事实得不到认定。

（二）特殊方法

就行政执法中的正确事实认定而言，比较突出的特色是：

1. 思维方法方面：整体思维、大局思维和未来思维的应用。如前文所述，行政案件的事实类型之所以如此复杂多样，一个很重要的原因在于政府职能的积极、能动和创造的属性。这种面向未来进行积极能动的筹划与发展的职能属性引导行政机关在作出行政决策时，往往要从全局和长远的角度来看待一个具体、微观的事件。对相关的法律规范的适用而言，某个特定的具体事件中所蕴含的要件事实是简单明了的。但是，从全局和长远的角度来看，则会发现具体事件的中所蕴含的许多关联点，很有可能产生“牵一发而动全身”的所谓“蝴蝶效应”。对站在社会矛盾的焦点前线的行政机关来说，许多案件事实不仅是法律上的事实，而且是社会上的事实，甚至是历史上的事实。这种事实维度的多元复杂性导致了行政案件事实认定必须采取一种多向度一体化整合的、能动积极创造性的全局发展型的思维方法。

将这一点与司法职能比较，会更易理解。现代的司法职能日渐走向积极和能动，法官的司法造法职能、公共政策拟定职能、社会引导和塑造职能等受到学界越来越多的肯定，笔者就是其中之一。但是，即使将能动的司法职能与消极的行政职能相比较，也会发现司法的事后性、审查性、助成性的特征，仍然与行政职能的事前性、开创性、生成性的特征形成鲜明的对照。

由此可见，行政案件事实维度远远复杂于民刑事案件，准确而又全面地认定涉及政治、经济、文化、科技、法律等多方面的因素，需要采用政治学、伦理学、社会学、经济学等多学科的知识，采用多学科的分析方法。这正是现代大科学区别于古典科学的之处所在。古典科学的突出特征是讲求方法的实证性、直观性、相对性、精确性，现代大科学在方法论上的突出特征是在此基础上进而力求方法的综合性。之所以如此，是因为任何一种科学方法都具有的局限性，只有不同学科知识综合协同，才能有效地相互避免各自的局限性，从而降低错误的风险概率。就此而言，“事实认定错误”是指因思维方法的片面性而增加了错误发生的可能性（概率）。

2. 认知心理层面：事实判断、价值判断、规范判断与情感判断的分离与协调。高度的专业性是行政案件事实认定区别于刑民事案件的另一个显著特征。在任何部门行政执法案件的事实认定中，除了高度专业化的科学判断（事实层面）之外，还蕴含着政策判断、规范判断和价值判断。即使不采取弗洛伊德的心理分析方法，而仅仅根据一般的生活经验常识，人们也不难发现在其中还存在一个可能起更大的作用的判断机制，那就是所谓的情感判断。一个正确的、清楚的案件事实认定必须力求这几个方面判断在各行其道、各安其位基础上的协调统一。如果行政执法人员不能妥善地协调好这几类判断之间的关系，那么，案件事实难以判断正确，更难以认定清楚。

要在如此复杂的认知结构中而不至于陷入迷途，对行政执法人员来说，首先必须将前述认知心理层面的各种判断方式在对象、内容、方式、后果等方面区分开来，使其各自遵循不同的判断法则。事实判断遵循的是科学的法则。要搞清楚事实，必须首先将情感判断、价值判断和规范判断等都排除在事实认定的心理过程之外。

如果说情感是尚可擦拭干净的灰尘，那么，在个人的潜意识中隐藏的个人价值偏好则是永不磨灭的有色眼镜，它不仅框定了人的认知范围，而且对人所认识的一切都蒙上某种意识形态的色彩。因此，如果行政执法人员将个人的情感判断与价值判断因素加入到案件事实的判断过程中，即构成“事实认定错误”。

规范判断的方法用于法律上权利义务的分析，不能直接地用于证据法上事实真假判断，因此两者必须分离开来；但证据法上的事实判断是最终服务于规范判断的，因此，两者在裁判阶段最终要走向合一。为此，事实审与法律审不仅要在（法庭）审理的时空阶段上相对地分离开来，而且要在目的、内容、方法、程序等方面也分离开来。就执法人员个人的思维过程而言，事实判断与规范判断在前理解阶段是模糊地混合在一起，在调查和审理阶段逐渐走向分离，到了法律论证阶段又走向完全理性的合一：裁判事实与裁判规范的合一。如果行政执法人员不能正确地处理规范判断与事实判断之间的关系，在目的、方法、程序等方面出现的混淆，那么，就可能构成事实认定的错误。

至于事实判断与价值判断之间的关系，是一个纠结的难题。证据法位于事实判断与价值判断之间的激烈碰撞地带，两者之间的冲突及协调将永远伴随证据法的兴衰沉浮。就整个证据法体系的建构而言，符合科学方法论意义上的中庸之道〔5〕是在尊重两者各自界限的基础上力求将两者结合起来，采取一种二元平行论的结构：〔6〕一方面，确保科学的态度与方法在事实发现方面的主导地位，以科学性为核心确立有关的证据规则，例如相关性规则、意见证据规则等；另一方面，注重人文价值的关怀，使科学的探究朝着人类福祉的方向迈进而不突破人类伦理道德的底线，确立以伦理性为宗旨的证据规则，例如，非法证据排除规则、特权证据规则等。借此使自然科学方法与人文社会科学方法在证据法领域中相辅相成地良性互动起来，唯有此才能使事实的发现过程与真实的追求过程达成圆满的统一。

就行政案件的事实认定这一环节而言，行政执法人员要力求客观上的“准确”与主观上的“清楚”之间的统一，力求事实的客观发现与多元价值诉求平衡之间的良性互动。

（三）错误的界定

将前述两个方面的论述总结起来，可以归纳如下：

如果行政机关在认定事实时，

---

〔5〕［法］笛卡尔：《谈谈方法》，王太庆译，商务印书馆2000年版，第19~20页（合乎中道作为科学方法论的原则之一）。

〔6〕［德］H. 赖欣巴哈：《科学哲学的兴起》修订第2版，伯尼译，商务印书馆1983年版，第43~61页。（第4章“道德指导的寻求与伦理——认识平行论”），尤其是第45页（“自然和数学的规律首先得被认为是规律、是把认知力加于我们身上、不容有任何例外的关系，然后才能被认为是伦理规条的平行物。‘规律’这个字的双重意义，道德命令和自然或理性规律这两种意义，可以证明这种平行论的结构”）。

（1）未将情感判断从事实判断中清除；或者

（2）将事实判断与价值判断、规范判断混淆；或者

（3）没有采用正确的思维方法而导致事实认定在知识或者方法上存在着明显的片面性缺陷；

（4）致使事实判断、价值判断、规范判断和情感判断之间出现明显的失衡状况。

即构成在事实认定在方法科学性方面的错误。

三、过程：心证自由的开放与透明

对行政执法人员而言，无论是对案件事实的范围和种类的准确把握，还是在协调事实判断、价值判断与情感判断的基础上动用多学科的知识与方法，在完成了对个别证据材料的认证和采信之后而进入对全案事实进行综合全面的认定阶段时，都要将自己的主观认识过程上升为一种直觉的判断。这种直觉判断的功能在于将在各个证明环节所获得的分散、点滴的经验作为一个完整的心证过程而融贯起来。

（一）心证自由的一般属性

就这种直觉的判断作为心证自由的内核而言，行政执法人员与司法人员是一致的，表现在：

1. 独立性。在对案件事实的主观认知自由方面，行政执法人员与法官、检察官享有完全相同的独立性。这种独立性不仅表现为执法人员作为认知主体的人格独立性，而且表现为执法人员思维过程的独立性。尽管在思维方法的选择和语言表达等方面，执法人员受到思维科学规范和法律语言规范的限制，但是在思维内容的具体展开这一主观心理认知的层面，执法人员是完全独立的。这种主观认知层面的独立性归根结底在于人的意志自由，亦即摆脱了一切外在干扰的绝对的心灵自由。

2. 综合性。心证之所以要自由的，不仅是因为它需要摆脱一切外在干扰因素的蒙蔽或者束缚，而且是因为它是一种综合性的认知心理水平。只有绝对的意志自由和心灵自由才能将执法人员的认知心理过程提升到综合性认知的高度。这种综合性不是认知片段的简单拼凑，而是认知要素的重现构造。在这个过程中，不仅思想适应着事实，事实也适应着思想，主观的思想与客观的事实之间在互动交融之中走向真实的彼岸。

3. 直觉性。心证自由是一种直接指向案件事实本质的直觉认识。任何一个案件事实作为一种生活现象都具有其内在的本质。要认识案件事实的真相，除了搞清楚其外在的表现——过程、原因和结果——之外，更主要的是获得对其本质属性的认识——对人性的深刻洞察，对自然和社会规律的清晰把握。只有获得了对这种本质属性的认识，才能对案件事实作出准确的定性。

就制度设计而言，独立性的保障是关键所在。只有充分地保障执法人员在事实认定主体方面的独立性地位，他的认识才有可能进入本质的直觉性与结构的综合性这一更高的认知水平上。在独立性不能得到保障的情况下，执法人员只有可能获得对案件事实的表面认识，亦即只可能认识到现象意义上的案件事实，而不可能认识到本质意义上的案件事实。

（二）行政执法人员心证的特殊性

证据法上的心证自由在行政法中则被视为行政机关的事实裁量权，所设定的约束措施主要是程序的正当性（正当法律程序）。从心证自由的角度来看，行政程序的正当

性表现在：

1. 知识来源上的开放性。案件事实类型结构的复杂性需要多学科知识与方法的综合协同整合，正确的事实认定过程越来越依赖于多学科知识的交融过程。只有使知识来源尽可能地开放，行政机关才可能获得知识优势，对外赢得民众的公信力，对内获得对案件事实的正确认识。

之所以如此，是因为行政执法的过程不仅是一个面向过去的事实还原和再现的过程，而且是一个听取意见、凝聚各方智识以群策群力，面向未来（可能发生的事实）而进行积极能动筹划的事实型构过程。这是行政执法在目的定位、职能运作等方面区别于以名分止争、恢复秩序为主旨的民事审判，尤其是区别于以矫正正义、惩罚正义为旨趣的刑事审判的根本所在。

这就意味着，行政机关在作出具体行政行为时，如果没有通过一个广泛参与、深度论证的程序来确保与当事人、利害关系展开实质性的意见交换与知识交流，尤其是在相关的专业知识上没有获得应有的优势时，即构成事实认定过程上的知识封闭性错误。

2. 思辨过程的透明性。政府公信力的危机在很大程度上是科学主义危机的一种表现，其实质是知识与道德的分离。在这种知识与道德二分的纯科学主义模式下，知识来源的开放性有助于在一定程度上提高知识的正确性而不一定能保持道德伦理上的正当性。甚至恰恰相反，对康德所说的“理性魔鬼”而言，知识越多，道德反而更有可能走向堕落。

就案件事实认定的心证自由而言，这种知识与道德二元分立的结构可能造成的问题首先是行政执法人员专业知识水平的提升与职业道德素质下降之间的强烈反差以及因此而产生的在事实认定方面的“准确”与“清楚”之间的戏剧性悖论。在这种悖论式的认知逻辑中，案件事实在科学的层面被认定得越是“准确”，就越是可能被因此而激发出来的各种利益诉求、情感冲动和价值偏好而纠缠得“不清楚”。要想在事实认定之上吹去各方利益和情感的尘封，冲淡各种价值偏好的遮蔽，一个有效的办法是增强司法过程的透明性，在本文的语境中，也就是提高执法人员认定案件事实的认知过程的透明性。在古典主义的证据法模式下，案件事实的认定过程作为执法人员（法官）的心证自由在很大程度上保持某种神秘的色彩。具体的心理认知过程似乎一直是法官个人的隐私，当事人在裁判文书中只知道证据采信和事实认定的结果及其简单的（表面的）理由，至于在法官的内心之中进行的深层次的心理认知过程，迄今为止一直是神秘的。这种主观心理认知的神秘性，因其中可能蕴含的司法专横主义倾向，在当今科学、民主与法治的时代下，显得越来越不能接受了。一言以蔽之，心证过程的完全彻底的透明既是确保案件事实认定“清楚”的一项有效措施，也是建设开放透明的法治型政府的一项有效措施。

（三）错误的界定

用规范化的语言可以将前述理论分析框架中的事实认定错误总结如下：

行政机关在认定被诉行政行为的要件事实时，如果

（1）没有通过听取意见、协商、辩论等组成的开放型程序来确保当事人、利害关系人和其他方面相关人士的有效参与，从而形成利益方面的广泛代表性和智识方面的

综合优势；或者

（2）没有通过诸如充分说明理由等的方式将事实认定的过程全方位地公开，以确保行政执法人员主观认知过程的透明性；

（3）不能有效地排除事实认定的片面性狭隘或者神秘性专横时。

即构成事实认定在过程正当性方面的错误。

结语：从准确到清楚

除了前述范围、方法和过程中可能出现的三大类错误之外，行政执法机关在事实认定中还可能出现的是定性错误和命名错误。这两类错误互为表里，位于事实审与法律审的交叉地带。

造成定性错误的原因既可能事实方面的，例如，案件事实的调查范围不全面；也可能是法律方面的，例如，对法律规范的错误选择或者解释。对事实认定来说，定性错误是根本性的、全局性的错误，它表明行政执法人员对案件事实的认识没有达到应有高度，因此不能对案件事实进行完整的、与本质一致的把握。执法人员可能在案件事实的细节上或者某方面是“清楚”的，但在整体结构、属性及其法律后果的把握方面却是糊涂的。

除了修辞学方面的原因外，命名错误通常是定性错误的直接后果。行政执法人员之所以没有使用正确的法律术语，主要是因为对案件事实性质的认识不正确。

如果行政机关既排除了范围、方法、程序三个方面的局部错误，进而又避免了定性和命名两个方面的整体性错误，那么，它的事实认定，至少可以在相对真理的意义上被认为，从“正确”的事实此岸迈向了清楚的真实彼岸。

至于到了真实的彼岸之后，人们又会遇到什么？证据法回答不了这个问题。在上帝给予人类以确切的回答之前，人们恐怕要在科学与宗教之间徘徊。

亲子关系推定的许可与禁止

——对最高人民法院《婚姻法司法解释（三）》第二条的评论

叶自强 *

一、《婚姻法司法解释（三）》第二条创立的亲子关系推定及其后果

2011年8月13日，最高人民法院颁布并实施了《关于适用〈中华人民共和国婚姻法〉若干问题的解释（三）》（以下简称《婚姻法司法解释（三）》）。其中第2条规定："夫妻一方向人民法院起诉请求确认亲子关系不存在，并已提供必要证据予以证明，另一方没有相反证据又拒绝做亲子鉴定的，人民法院可以推定请求确认亲子关系不存在一方的主张成立。当事人一方起诉请求确认亲子关系，并已提供必要证据予以证明，另一方没有相反证据又拒绝做亲子鉴定的，人民法院可以推定请求确认亲子关系一方的主张成立。"可见，该条款以司法解释的形式确立了一种新型的推定——亲子关系推定（经过精确分析之后，它其实可细分为两种推定，即亲子关系存在的推定和亲子关系不存在的推定）。从该司法解释实施以来至今已经一年多了。在亲子关系诉讼领域，如果说在《婚姻法司法解释（三）》颁布之前某些法官还只是十分勉强地使用推定的话，那么，现在他们终于可以持这把"尚方宝剑"扬眉吐气地、公开地使用推定了，而不用担心受到公众的责难。

然而，适用《婚姻法司法解释（三）》第2条进行亲子关系推定的实际效果又如何呢？大致分为三种情况：一是许多人感到强烈不安和忧虑，甚至痛苦和责骂；[1] 二是担

---

* 叶自强，中国社会科学院法学研究所研究员。Email：yeziqiang@ hotmail. com。

〔1〕 有人写道："当我看到新婚姻法的时候，我第一反应是气愤，第二反应是觉得悲哀，第三反应是狂笑中国竟然有本事倒退到1000年前。""在欧美等发达国家，都非常重视妇女权利的保障，像这些国家的离婚成本是非常之高的。离婚后，男方不单要支付巨额离婚费，还要每个月付给前妻赡养费和小孩抚养费。像日本，男方的工资都是直接打到女方所开银行卡号上的，如果离婚，房产和孩子都是归女方所有。每个有良知的国家都在竭力为保护妇女权利而不断完善法律。因为所有发达国家都信奉一点，对妇女权利的充分保障是一个民族强大和优秀的基础和根源，因为孩子的第一个教师就是母亲。因为他们知道，妇女在社会生存环境的安定程度，可以影响甚至决定下一代的总体发展。""不管你承认不承认，信不信，妇女相对而言还是社会的弱势群体。一个国家连弱势群体都不能好好保护，甚至还把这个群体往绝路上逼，只能说它堕落到无药可救了。就算是战争，就算是杀红了眼的残酷军队，他们都知道一点，不要把炮弹往有女人和孩子的地方打。"《婚姻法司法解释（三）》对女性的保护已经不复存在（见"新婚姻法伤透了女人心?"，载中国宁波网2011年8月18日，来源：新浪博客）。上述观点是针对《婚姻法司法解释（三）》整体而言的，自然也包括了对第2条的强烈批评，可以说它一针见血地击中了亲子关系推定的要害，需引起国家高层和全社会的足够重视。

心后果严重，要求法院“慎用推定”;[2]三是促进了商业味浓厚的亲子鉴定市场的“火爆”。其中，第三种情况是《婚姻法司法解释（三)》第2条施行以来造成的最主要局面。[3]其实，这种局面的形成还暗示了以下问题：法院受理亲子关系纠纷案件有了明显增加；亲子关系鉴定机构的业务有了明显增长。两者之间是相互促进的。但是我们应该冷静地想一想，这是一种正常的现象吗？对于社会上相当一部分人的忧虑和痛恨，以及另一部人的谨慎立场，可以漠然视之吗？鉴于亲子关系推定是一个相当生僻的、许多人感到陌生的专业领域，本文打算抛开情感好恶立场，着重从证据法（推定和亲子关系推定均是其中的研究对象之一）专业的角度，科学地探讨亲子关系推定的利与弊，以及我们应该做出何种正确的政策选择，这对于巩固婚姻家庭关系，保护妇女和未成年子女的合法权益，对于政府所倡导的“和谐社会”建设，无疑有着重要的现实意义。

二、《婚姻法司法解释（三)》实施前后亲子关系推定的依据

（一）《婚姻法司法解释（三)》实施之前推定亲子关系不存在的依据

《婚姻法司法解释（三)》实施之前，在亲子关系诉讼中进行亲子推定的法律依据是《证据规定》第75条。《证据规定》第75条规定：“有证据证明一方当事人持有证据无正当理由不提供，如果对方当事人主张该证据的内容不利于证据持有人，可以推定该主张成立。”鉴于我国最高人民法院改革开放以来长期承担着很大一部分立法职能的实际情况，应该将该规定视为一个法律推定，而不是事实推定。在2001年到2011年这10年间，据考察，该规定在民事诉讼（不仅仅是亲子关系诉讼一种）中被广泛引用，容易导致说服责任和举证责任的转移，从而造成错判。让我们结合如下案件作出分析。

2000年底，李明与妻子刘梅领了结婚证，当时他们已交往了5年。6个月后，刘梅生下女儿。孩子生下后，李明越看越不像自己，并开始与妻子闹起别扭。一个坚持要带孩子去做亲子鉴定，一个坚决不让。从2006年六七月份起，李明正式与妻子刘梅

〔2〕 南京红十字血液中心司法鉴定所的专家指出，亲子鉴定表面上看是一项医学鉴定技术，实际上却涵盖了法律、伦理和家庭等多方问题、操作上如有失误，几个字的鉴定结果就有可能摧毁一个家庭甚至导致法律纠纷。从科学层面看，目前DNA亲子鉴定的结果准确率可以达到99.99%，但即使差错率只有万分之一，对于一个具体的家庭来说，都是100%的致命打击。（见《新婚姻法推热亲子鉴定 无资质民间机构泛滥》，滨州传媒网2011年10月02日，来源：中国娱乐资讯网。）在审判实践中，也有个别法院在实践中确能严格掌握标准，拒绝许可亲子鉴定和拒绝亲子关系推定。例如，江苏省沭阳县人民法院2011年受理了一起诉讼，丈夫在没有任何依据的情况，要求做亲子鉴定，结果没有得到法院的支持。（见人民网海南视窗2011年08月22日。）然而，客观地说，《婚姻法司法解释（三)》实施之后，这些所谓“慎用推定”的声音已明显减少了。

〔3〕 据中国之声《央广新闻》报道，《婚姻法司法解释（三)》出台后，人们对亲子鉴定的关注度高了，需求多了。亲子鉴定市场就像一块“肥肉”，除了具有合格资质的司法鉴定机构参与之外，还引来了许多缺乏资质的民间机构来染指这个行业。据江苏省人民医院司法鉴定所法医物证室主任周惠英说，该机构于2001年开展亲子鉴定，起初是和司法部门联合，并不对外开放，一年仅做几十例。2002年下半年向社会开放后，来做鉴定的人明显增多（当时双亲和子女三方必须全部到场）。推出更为先进的单亲鉴定以后（只需带上身份证和户口本就可以了)，人数更是激增。这10年下来，江苏省人民医院已经做了6000余例亲子鉴定。尤其是近两年，每年都以15%的速度递增，2010年一年更是超过了1000例。（见人民网海南视窗2011年08月22日。）另据北京市西城区人民法院的调查，《婚姻法司法解释（三)》施行仅半年，申请亲子鉴定、接受亲子鉴定的当事人均明显增多。西城法院已受理涉及亲子鉴定案件23件，比去年同期增长43.7%。（汪丹、郭威：《新婚姻法促亲子鉴定增4成，慎用“推定”规则》，2012年03月06日，新华网。）

分居。当年年底，李明一纸离婚诉状递至南京市秦淮区人民法院，法院认为，李明与刘梅感情基础应该是牢固的，况且还有个5岁的女儿要抚养，不能证明双方感情破裂。法院判决不准双方离婚。[4] 2007年，李明再次将离婚诉状递至法院。李明主张女儿不是自己亲生的，要求进行DNA亲子鉴定。但遭到刘梅一口拒绝。刘梅既不同意女儿与丈夫李明进行DNA亲子鉴定，又没有提供其他的证据来证明女儿确实是她与李明所生，一审法院经审理推定：女儿不是李明亲生。据此，2008年7月，法院判决准许李明与妻子刘梅离婚。[5]

从表面上看，该推定的根据是：被告依法应承担举证不能的后果，因为原告要求做亲子鉴定，被告明确拒绝。被告对此不能作出合理解释，对原告主张的事实又没有提供证据予以反驳。实际上，该推定的根据是《证据规定》第75条的规定，即“有证据证明一方当事人持有证据无正当理由不提供，如果对方当事人主张该证据的内容不利于证据持有人，可以推定该主张成立。”仔细分析该规定，可以发现基础事实和推定事实。基础事实有二：①原告有证据证明被告持有（关于孩子身世的）证据无正当理由不提供；②原告主张该证据的内容不利于证据持有人（被告）。推定事实是：该（关于孩子身世的）证据，其内容不利于证据持有人（被告）。暗示这孩子是被告与原告之外的其他男人所生。可见，《证据规定》第75条确立了一个事实推定。据初步考察，该规定在民事诉讼中被广泛引用，造成了不小的混乱。让我们结合本案继续作出分析。

该规定最突出的问题是，它容易导致举证责任和说服责任的转移，造成错判。在本案中，原告请求与被告离婚，解除与小孩之间的父女关系，由被告单独负担孩子的抚养费。为了实现自己的请求，原告应该承担本案的举证责任（因为本案属于普通民事诉讼）。原告必须提出确实的证据，以证明孩子不是原告与被告婚姻期间的亲生女儿。

原告提出了两项证据，一是夫妻领结婚证6个月后，刘梅即生下女儿，且被告对此不能作出合理的解释；二是请求去做亲子鉴定，但被告拒绝做亲子鉴定。在这两个证据中，后一个证据并非真正的有力的证据，因为依据最高人民法院当时关于亲子鉴定的批复，亲子鉴定必须当事人自愿，任何人都不得强迫。据此，本案被告拒绝做亲子鉴定，完全合法；不能把被告拒绝做亲子鉴定看做一项不利于她本人（而利于原告）的证据。

令人惊讶的是，受案法院却反其道而行之，违反最高人民法院关于亲子鉴定必须自愿，不得强迫的有关规定，把被告拒绝做亲子鉴定看做一项不利于她本人（而利于原告）的证据。据此作出了小孩非原告亲生女儿的事实推定。接下来，法院作出了显然不利于被告的一审判决：原告李某与被告刘某离婚。

从举证责任的技术层面上说，该事实推定帮助原告摆脱了其理应承担的说服责任和举证责任。否则，仅仅依据原告所提出的证据（看起来是两项，其实只有一项），是根本无法完成其举证责任的。

从上面可以看到，受案法院撇开其他规定不管，单纯依据《证据规定》第75条的司法解释，作出了孩子“非原告亲生女儿”的事实推定。该推定除了违反婚姻法和具

〔4〕 秦少冒群：“结婚6个月当上爹 法院推定孩子非男方亲生”，载《南京晨报》2009年2月4日。

〔5〕 秦少冒群：“结婚6个月当上爹 法院推定孩子非男方亲生”，载《南京晨报》2009年2月4日。

有落后性之外，[6]还违反了举证责任的基本原则，将说服责任和举证责任转移到被告一方。

这个案例基本能说明《证据规定》第75在亲子关系诉讼中所起到的消极作用。

据考察，《婚姻法司法解释（三）》实施以前的几年中，我国离婚案件和亲子关系纠纷案件频发。在这些案件中，如果单纯适用《证据规定》第75条，则往往流于简单化，因为在这些案件中不仅涉及法律技术的应用，更需要法官们精通相关的法律政策，需要正确处理推定与政策的关系，否则，如果单纯适用《证据规定》第75条，则容易导致说服责任和举证责任的转移。其结果是造成举证责任的分担不公平，判决的社会影响也很不好。既然如此，在没有找到正确处理推定与政策的关系的良策之前，建议废弃该条款。实际上，更准确地说，在推定领域，很难总结出用以指导司法实践的一般性规则，例外的情况很多。拿推定与政策的关系来说，某一项推定总是出自某一项具体的政策（它是特定的而不是抽象的、泛泛的）。假如存在许多这样的具体的政策，那么，这些政策之间难免出现矛盾。与此相应的是，在这些政策之下所形成的具体的推定之间，也会出现矛盾。因此，在法律上或司法解释中，关于推定条款的规定，应当是具体的、有条件使用的，并规定严格的限制范围。

（二）《婚姻法司法解释（三）》实施以来推定亲子关系不存在的依据

2011年8月13日《婚姻法司法解释（三）》被宣布实施。从此，我国各级法院在亲子关系推定中均适用该司法解释第2条的规定。据最高人民法院有关部门的说明，第2条规定正是基于《证据规定》第75条而制定的，是《证据规定》第75条的具体化。可以理解为这是最高人民法院从事司法精确化的一种积极尝试。但遗憾的是，由于立法者并没有认识到《证据规定》第75条的弊端，更谈不上及时予以纠正，故这些弊端自然被带入《婚姻法司法解释（三）》第2条中。具体来说，第2条规定存在如下严重的问题：

第一，转移了举证责任，违反了举证责任的基本原则。在我国，亲子关系诉讼包括两种类型，即亲子关系的确认（即亲子关系存在）诉讼和亲子关系的否认（即亲子关系不存在）诉讼。它们都属于普通民事诉讼。在这种诉讼中，举证责任完全由原告方承担，被告不需要承担举证责任。但是，根据《婚姻法司法解释（三）》第2条规定，本由原告承担的举证责任却转移给了被告，从而违反了举证责任的一般原则，违反了举证责任的基本性质——确定性或不可转移性。

为什么说举证责任发生了转移呢？例如，按照第2条第1款规定，一边是，要求"起诉请求确认亲子关系不存在"的原告方提供"必要证据"，另一边则是要求被告不得拒绝做亲子鉴定，否则就败诉。表面上看，这样的安排对双方是平等的，也符合常理。但仔细分析就会发现，双方在举证方面是非常不平等的。对被告来说，必须提供相反证据，且不得拒绝做亲子鉴定，这要求被告提供实实在在的证据，且必须提供，具有强制性。而对于原告来说，只需要提供含糊其辞的所谓"必要证据"。然而，何谓必要证据？一年多过去了，司法解释的制定者至今也给不出一个确切的答案，以致许

---

〔6〕 参见叶自强："论推定的根据"，载《河北法学》2009年第11期。

多法官对什么是“必要证据”仍感到惘然无措。[7]这说明了立法的准备工作何其不足，何等粗陋。所谓粗，即缺乏精细的研究。但愿不要把应该明确界定的“必要证据”偷换成“莫须有证据”。因为在该司法解释颁布之前的亲子关系诉讼中，有的法官用的就是“莫须有证据”偏袒原告。

第二，由于将举证责任转移给被告承担，暴露了立法者的另一项企图，即把亲子关系诉讼的“普通民事诉讼”形态转变为一种特殊民事诉讼形态，使诉讼形态发生根本的改变。这就超越了最高人民法院自身的权限，是一种不该发生的轻率行为。哪些属于普通民事诉讼，哪些属于特殊民事诉讼，这个事项只能由全国人民代表大会在《民事诉讼法》中予以界定。此外，其他任何机构和个人都无权作出规定。从本条的后果可以看出，我国最高人民法院作为立法者的权力何等巨大，又多么可怕。

第三，转移举证责任的手法是什么？是推定。采用推定的方式转移举证责任，违反了举世公认的“推定不得转移举证责任”的基本原则，是不能够被允许的。为什么第2条要用“推定”这个工具转换举证责任？因为这样做具有很深的隐蔽性，没有接受先进证据法学训练的人通常是无法轻易地察觉其致命缺陷的，而且这种转移符合所谓常理（即符合普通人通常的思维模式），容易被普通人所接受。另外，如果有人明目张胆地宣称要转换举证责任，一定会遭受一些人反对。因为十多年来，通过反复的宣传，不少法律界人士已经接受了“举证责任不能转换”的观点。然而，不管怎样，推定这种工具是不能随意采用的。具有必要的证据法科学知识的人都应该懂得，“推定不得转移举证责任”是证据法科学准则之一，必须得到遵守。

第四，具有明显的强迫性。《婚姻法司法解释（三）》第2条第1款规定：“夫妻一方向人民法院起诉请求确认亲子关系不存在，并已提供必要证据予以证明，另一方没有相反证据又拒绝做亲子鉴定的，人民法院可以推定请求确认亲子关系不存在一方的主张成立。”这种“如果……就”式的条件句结构明确表达了立法者的强迫意志，即强迫被告做亲子鉴定，否则就会立即做出不利于被告的决定。这条规定改变了过去亲子鉴定由当事人自愿的做法，对被告是不公平的。

综上所述，鉴于《婚姻法司法解释（三）》第2条存在以上多种严重缺陷，笔者建议有关部门应重新加以检讨，予以适当修改。

三、“必要证据”与亲子关系推定的关系

在这一部分我们必须首先考察“必要证据”，为什么呢？因为根据第2条的规定，亲子关系推定与“必要证据”之间具有密切的联系，必要证据”是作出亲子关系推定的前提条件。具体言之，在确认亲子关系不存在的诉讼中，如果原告方（男）提供了“必要证据”，被告方（女）没有相反证据又拒绝做亲子鉴定的，人民法院可以推定请求原告方（确认亲子关系不存在一方）的主张成立。在确认亲子关系存在的诉讼中，如果原告方（女或其子女）提供了“必要证据”，被告方（男）没有相反证据又拒绝做亲子鉴定的，人民法院可以推定请求原告方（确认亲子关系存在一方）的主张成立。

然而，在《婚姻法司法解释（三）》第2条中，所谓“必要证据”却是一个抽象的、模糊的概念，不存在明确的标准。这也是到目前为止法院内部广泛存在的一种认

---

〔7〕 汪丹、郭威：“新婚姻法促亲子鉴定增4成，慎用‘推定’规则”，2012年03月06日。

识。在北京，《婚姻法司法解释（三）》施行半年以后，西城区人民法院已受理涉及亲子鉴定案件23件，比去年同期增长43.7%。根据《婚姻法司法解释（三）》第2条的规定，原告在起诉时可提供“必要证据”，以获得法院推定其主张成立。但由于“必要证据”的具体标准模糊，故应当对“必要证据”能达到的程度和标准进行具体界定。对缺席审理的案件，为保障原有的亲缘关系稳定，应要求申请鉴定方提供血型不合等直接证据，才能使用“推定”规则。另外，鉴于亲子鉴定是确认亲子关系的直接证据，更能令当事人服判息诉，法院应在使用“推定”规则前，向拒绝鉴定方释明其可能承担的不利后果并询问是否仍拒绝鉴定，再作出判决。〔8〕2012年10月12日，上海律协民事业务研究委员会主办了《婚姻法司法解释（三）》实施一周年热点问题研究与实务研讨会。来自上海市的法官、专家、学者和律师同聚一堂，就《婚姻法司法解释（三）》的适用与热点问题进行了研讨。关于第2条规定的亲子鉴定的推定原则，其中提到了一方当事人要提供必要证据。但何为“必要证据”现在是法院审理工作的难点。吴薇法官客观地指出，目前对于何为必要证据法院没有标准可以参照，并且要平衡孩子的生父母以及孩子本身的权益所以较难适用。但是目前所能达成的共识是，在涉及未成年子女权益的情况下，推定尤其是推定子女与父母关系不存在的，应当非常谨慎地适用。〔9〕

与立法上“必要证据”之模糊性和不明确性形成鲜明对照的是，审判实践中的“必要证据”是明确的、毫不含糊的。从一些案例可以看出，所谓“必要证据”是指亲子鉴定报告。在某些案例中，亲子鉴定报告甚至是原告所提供的唯一证据，此外并没有其他证据。那么，这个“必要证据”是通过什么方式得到的呢？在原告（男）要求确认亲子关系不存在的诉讼中，在“赵先生诉张女士离婚纠纷案”中，原告赵某听信流言蜚语，“不由得生起疑心病，想到最近在妻子手机上看到的暧昧信息，疑心更重。为了搞清楚事实，他瞒着妻子，偷偷地抽取了小女儿的血样”，带到了上海某鉴定中心进行了鉴定。在“夏某与胡某离婚纠纷案”中，夏某在没有告知胡某的情况下，自行委托湖南省天衡司法鉴定所，对自己与夏某皓之间有无亲生血缘关系进行了鉴定。在“阿勇诉小萍离婚纠纷案”中，在没有经过妻子同意和法院许可的情况下，阿勇的亲戚委托了杭州的一家司法鉴定所，对阿勇与芳芳做了亲子鉴定。可见，在诉讼前的亲子关系鉴定的整个过程中，只有作为原告的男人知道，妻子始终被瞒着。亲子鉴定的整个过程始终笼罩着一股神秘的气氛。

从上述案例中，我们无法确切得知原告（丈夫）起诉时是如何得到亲子鉴定报告的，就是说，亲子鉴定报告是由什么单位作出的，它们有没有合法的从业资质？它们是通过何种程序作出的？亲子鉴定报告的科学性、客观性有多大？这些问题无法获得答案。但是我们通过更加细致的考察之后发现，这个过程十分令人忧虑，十分不可靠。

首先，受理亲子鉴定的机构有许多缺乏应有的资质。它们是通过虚假宣传而获得不明真相的人的认可。上海市司法局司法鉴定管理处处长李柏勤指出，一些亲子鉴定

---

〔8〕 汪丹、郭威：“新婚姻法促亲子鉴定增4成，慎用‘推定’规则”，2012年3月6日。

〔9〕 上海律协民事业务委员会：《上海律协婚姻法司法解释三实施一周年热点问题》，上海市律师协会2012年10月23日。

机构说它们是由司法部认可的。这是明显的虚假宣传。根据国家规定，现在司法鉴定的审核批准都是在各省（市），因此在上海的亲子鉴定机构其许可证都是由上海市司法局颁发的，不可能由司法部认可，对方的说法存在明显的常识性差错。[10]

其次，送件材料的传递过程十分随意，缺乏严格的监控，因此存在检验材料被污染的可能性。亲子鉴定是一件严肃的事情，按照规定，不但鉴定机构要有司法鉴定许可证，而且从事鉴定的人员必须持有执业证书。亲子鉴定的采样也有严格的规定，如果是司法鉴定就必须确认双方当事人身份后才能采样鉴定。即使是非司法鉴定，也要填写申请书等表格，一般情况不上门采集，除非是瘫痪在床等特殊情况。[11]但是在亲子鉴定市场上，却存在随意采样的现象。一位记者曾经就此问题采访深圳某鉴定机构工作人员。后者回答："就是那种带有毛囊的头发就可以，竖直拔起来，头发的根部会有一个白色的小点。拔起3到4根，放到白纸上，晾干几分钟，然后再把它包起来。样本可以邮寄。口腔试纸的话，在口腔腮部刮5下，然后需要5个棉签。取了之后，放在常温下自然干燥之后，再用纸把它包好。"[12] 如此简单的取样，能保证最后结果的准确吗？记者就此专门采访了省人民医院医学遗传研究所所长廖世秀。廖所长说："这个很容易误差，我取个头发或者唾液斑，理论上讲绝对可以，但是这个取得过程中一定要严格注意，不要被污染了。比方说头发，你取别人的三根头发，那自己说话的时候唾液细胞喷到头发上了，这个唾液细胞，DNA鉴定特别灵敏，所以说你用这些标本的时候，最关键的就是一定要注意，要不就容易导致这个结果的误差，那就做错了。"[13]据了解，目前很多的所谓鉴定机构其实根本没有相关资质，甚至没有专业实验室和设备，也没有技术人员，有的就干脆开在居民区里。更有甚者，样本拿到手后，根本不进行鉴定，直接在报告上填写"样本一致"的结果，就送到委托人手里。[14]南京东南司法鉴定中心主任沈晓林说："从技术本身来看，我们认为它有被污染的可能性，同时这样的传递过程，也有可能在传递过程中发生，不仅仅是污染，有一些样本的交错、损失，还有一个搞错掉丢失。"沈晓林介绍，正规机构开展亲子鉴定，一种是通过机构委托，由公检法等部门出具委托书，当事人带身份证前来检测；另一种则是家庭内部协商同意，夫妻双方及孩子带上身份证、出生证到现场进行样本采集，管理要求都十分严格。[15]

实践一再证明，那些无证机构的鉴定结论往往是错误的。例如，王亮（化名）是一家公司老板。2007年9月，因为遗产分割问题，他决定与儿子做一个亲子鉴定，并坚持要找一家匿名的鉴定机构。通过百度搜索，王亮找到该亲子鉴定中心，发现公司宣传其鉴定的准确率高达99.9999%，并提供上门采集血样、匿名鉴定等便利服务。该中心宣称获得了国家权威部门认可，实验室为国际一流水平，并在网页上出示了众多权威部门的证书。王亮与对方联系后，一拍即合，当即支付了2000元鉴定费。9月上

〔10〕《亲子鉴定竟然搞促销 无证鉴定作出错误报告》，中国经济网财经频道2007年10月11日。

〔11〕《亲子鉴定竟然搞促销 无证鉴定作出错误报告》，中国经济网财经频道2007年10月11日。

〔12〕《亲子鉴定热的冷思考》，映象网－新闻广播2012年09月11日。

〔13〕《亲子鉴定热的冷思考》，映象网－新闻广播2012年09月11日。

〔14〕《亲子鉴定热的冷思考》，映象网－新闻广播2012年09月11日。

〔15〕吴新生：《亲子鉴定鱼龙混杂　个人隐私不容儿戏》，CNC中国电视网2011年10月13日。

旬，王亮对上小学的儿子谎称要为他做体检，需要抽点血进行化验，随后就请亲子鉴定中心的工作人员到他指定的地方为他们采集了血样。一个星期后，公司电话通知王亮："儿子是你亲生的"。王亮觉得亲子鉴定是件非常严肃的事，怎么连书面鉴定报告都没有呢？该中心解释说，由于他申请的是非司法鉴定，所以没有书面报告，仅口头通知。经过再三交涉，对方终于拿出一份书面报告，可在上面找了半天也没一个公章。通过向上海司法局咨询后，王亮才知道该亲子鉴定中心是一家未经认可的机构。此后，王亮决定在权威机构鉴定，最终发现无证机构的鉴定结论是错误的。〔16〕

从上面的叙述可以看出，原告在起诉时所提供的亲子鉴定报告，在证据的科学性、客观性方面存在明显的疑点，具有非法证据的嫌疑。有不少是应当通过法庭严格排除的。根据民事诉讼的举证责任分配原则，原告在离婚纠纷案或亲子纠纷案中应当承担举证责任。如果原告仅凭借这类存在疑点的不可靠的证据就能起诉的话，他们不但不可能获得胜诉的判决，还要受到提供伪证的处罚。可是在审判实践中，这类存在疑点的不可靠的证据已经通过或者正在源源不断地通过法庭的审查，并证明原告已经完成其举证责任，这是何等令人悲哀的事实啊！这些事实说明一些审判机关对"必要证据"的具体要求是不清晰的，因此缺乏严格的审查措施，放纵了一些不合格的亲子鉴定报告，需要大力改进。

由于对"必要证据"的要求标准过低，使得不合格的亲子鉴定报告蒙混过关，实际上减轻了原告方的举证责任，却反过来加重了被告方的举证责任，这对被告显失公平。我认为，这种涉及婚姻家庭、亲子关系的诉讼必须非常严格地对待。对起诉初期原告单方所提出的亲子鉴定报告，必须进行开庭审查，要求鉴定人到场回答法官和对方当事人的问题。允许被告进行反驳。如果原告不能完成举证责任，即应当驳回起诉，同时保护了妇女和未成年人的合法权益。

以上我们考察了"必要证据"与亲子关系推定之间的因果关系，以及它的立法形态和司法形态，懂得了在亲子关系推定中，"必要证据"所担负的关键角色。首先，如果"必要证据"并不可靠和确实（不科学、失真），而亲子关系推定也硬要做下去（对被告不利），那么被告就会蒙冤受屈。为了避免出现这种情况，我们必须就所谓"必要证据"的具体标准进行仔细完善。其次，《婚姻法司法解释（三）》第2条中的"一手硬"与"一手软"问题。一方面，对"必要证据"要求不严（规定得十分模糊）；另一方面，实行强制亲子关系推定（规定得十分明确），人为地制造了诉讼的不公平。这应当立即予以纠正。建议尽快出台新的关于"必要证据"的司法解释，消除一手硬与一手软的弊端，以维护诉讼公平。

四、许可什么？禁止什么？

最后让我们对以上讨论作一个基本总结：

首先，可以肯定的是，我国目前亲子关系诉讼可分为两种形态：一种是以争取抚养费为目的的亲子关系确认诉讼，另一种是以离婚和解脱抚养义务为目的的否认亲子关系的诉讼。与此相对应的是，存在两种推定，即亲子关系存在的推定和亲子关系不存在的推定。

---

〔16〕《亲子鉴定竟然搞促销 无证鉴定作出错误报告》，中国经济网财经频道2007年10月11日。

其次，上述推定，不论是哪一种，它们都违反了举证责任基本原则，使本该由原告承担的举证责任转换到被告身上；同时它们也违反了“推定不能转移举证责任的”原则，造成了不利于被告的不公平的局面。因此，从尊重证据科学这个原则出发，在亲子关系的诉讼中，是不能进行推定的。

最后，从前文所述的一些判例来看，上述两种推定所产生的社会效果是很不相同的。在以争取抚养费为目的的亲子关系确认诉讼中，确立亲子关系存在的推定，有利于保护未成年人的利益，有利于保护孩子的母亲，使其减轻经济负担。相反，在以离婚和解脱抚养义务为目的的否认亲子关系的诉讼中，确立亲子关系不存在的推定，则很不利于保护未成年人的利益，不利于保护孩子的母亲，反倒会造成加重其经济负担等严重后果。在这种情况下，我们能不能采取简单化的做法，笼统地搞“一刀切”，把这两种推定都予以禁止呢？这需要具体分析，不能一概而论。

当一种推定（亲子关系不存在的推定）在违反法律原则的情况下确立（即构成违法推定）并实施之后，产生了不良的社会效果，这种推定不但没有存在的根据，也失去了存在的意义。但是，当一种推定（亲子关系存在的推定）在违反法律原则的情况下确立并实施之后，却产生了良好社会效果，这种推定显然有存在的意义，虽然它并没有存在的合法依据。那么，我们可否设想在保留其积极意义的前提下，通过正确的法律技术手段，使其具有合法性呢？通俗地说，就是在某一个既违反法律原则又有良好社会效果的推定规则中，如何消除这两者的冲突？

也许有人提出指责说，这不就是实用主义的做法吗？不是的。客观地说，由于我们目前对推定的知识比较欠缺，依法科学地创制推定规则还具有很高的难度。这一方面给我们提出了进一步努力学习的艰巨任务，同时也很难避免“摸着石头过河”的现象（笔者一直坚持科学立法，并不提倡和鼓励立法和司法解释中的“摸着石头过河”的现象）。这一次《婚姻法司法解释（三)》第 2 条的规定无疑欠缺立法的严格科学依据，然而我们从中却意外发现了在以争取抚养费为目的的亲子关系确认诉讼中，确立亲子关系存在的推定，有利于保护未成年人的利益，有利于保护孩子的母亲。这是经过科学的批判分析之后所做出的意外发现。如果我们在法律技术上对它做出适当处理，对发展正确的推定规则、对保护妇女和未成年人的进步事业是能够做出有益贡献的，舍弃实在可惜。

必须申明的是，对于请求确认亲子关系存在的诉讼，应当适用亲子关系推定，这不是无条件的，否则就无法消除亲子关系推定违反举证责任基本原则和“推定不能转移举证责任的”原则的严重问题。如何消除该推定之潜在违法性呢？我建议在《证据规定》第 4 条增加第 9 款，把“请求确认亲子关系存在的诉讼”作为一种特殊的民事诉讼。只有这样，才能避免亲子关系推定与举证责任基本原则之间的冲突，避免发生亲子关系推定转移举证责任的现象，同时也能产生良好的社会效果。

最后，是做出抉择的时候了。笔者认为，对于《婚姻法司法解释（三)》第 2 条的亲子关系推定，不应笼统使用，应部分禁止。具体是，对于请求确认亲子关系不存在的诉讼，要禁止适用亲子关系不存在的推定；同时对于请求确认亲子关系存在的诉讼，应当适用亲子关系存在的推定，但要运用适当的法律技术做出修改，以消除其与举证责任规则的冲突。

新民事诉讼法举证时限制度的完善

刘金华*

从广义上讲，举证时限制度包含举证期限的确定、逾期举证的法律后果和新的证据等内容。2012年8月31日第十一届全国人民代表大会常务委员会第28次会议通过的，2013年1月1日施行的《中华人民共和国民事诉讼法》第65条规定：当事人对自己提出的主张应当及时提供证据。人民法院根据当事人的主张和案件审理情况，确定当事人应当提供的证据及其期限。当事人在该期限内提供证据确有困难的，可以向人民法院申请延长期限，人民法院根据当事人的申请适当延长。当事人逾期提供证据的，人民法院应当责令其说明理由；拒不说明理由或者理由不成立的，人民法院根据不同情形可以不予采纳该证据，或者采纳该证据但予以训诫、罚款。上述法律规定，对举证期限的确定及当事人逾期举证应当承担的法律后果作出了明确的规定，应当说是立法的一大进步，有利于督促当事人及时提供证据，也有利于法院及时审结案件。但是，法律规定的缺陷也比较明显，包括举证期限确定的职权化，证据失权的宽松化，强制措施的行政化等。本文着重从举证期限的确定、逾期举证的法律后果和新证据的界定几个方面对其进行梳理，提出相应的立法建议，以期进一步完善法律。

一、举证期限的确定

举证时限制度，是指负有举证责任的当事人应当在法律规定或法院指定的期限内提出证明其主张的相应证据，逾期不举证则承担证据失权法律后果的一项民事诉讼期间制度。[1] 我国1991年《民事诉讼法》没有规定举证时限制度，实行“证据随时提出主义”，即当事人可以在一审、二审甚至再审程序中提出证据。这种制度设置带来了如下问题：①影响法院办案效率。举证无时限造成部分当事人拖延举证，使法院迟迟不能下判，而法院办案又有审限的要求，举证无期限与办案有审限的矛盾变得相当突出。②诉讼中出现“证据突袭”。诉讼中，一些当事人或诉讼代理人为了对对方实施意外打击，收到出奇制胜的效果，将关键性的证据藏而不露，等到开庭审理时作为杀手锏，突然抛出，使对方当事人措手不及，无法进行有效的质证。③增加司法成本，浪费司法资源。在诉讼中，一方当事人突然提出证据，另一方当事人往往要求给予必要的准备时间，认真审查对方提出的证据，或者收集相反的证据进行反驳。法院也需要时间审核新提出的证据。因此，法官往往不得不将正在进行的审理活动停下来，择日再开庭。多次开庭势必增加当事人和法院的诉讼成本。④有损生效裁判的稳定性。个别当事人故意在一审中不提供证据，而将证据在二审中提交，二审法院只能依据当事人提出的新证据将一审判决撤销，发回重审或改判。如果当事人在再审中提交关键性

* 刘金华，法学博士、中国政法大学民商经济法学院民事诉讼法研究所副教授、硕士生导师。

〔1〕 叶自强：《民事证据研究》，法律出版社1999年版，第136页。

的证据，已经发生法律效力的判决就会被推翻，使得法院判决的稳定性受到了相当大的威胁。[2] 针对上述存在的问题，2001 年 12 月 21 日最高人民法院颁布的《关于民事诉讼证据的若干规定》（以下简称《证据规定》），对当事人行使举证权的期限，以及举证期限届满后提出证据的效力问题作出了详细的规定，标志着我国从“证据随时提出主义”向“证据适时提出主义”的转变。但是，《证据规定》毕竟是司法解释，存在效力问题，同时制度设置也存在诸多不完善之处。新修改的《民事诉讼法》第一次以立法的形式规定了举证时限制度，可以说是立法的一大进步。

举证时限制度的法定化，对于解决“证据随时提出主义”产生的问题，必将起到一定的积极作用。但是，该项法律制度在司法实践运用中将要产生的问题，也不得不引起我们的注意，主要体现在以下两个方面：

（1）没有明确规定确定的举证期限的时间。根据新修改的《民事诉讼法》第 65 条规定，举证期限由人民法院根据当事人的主张和案件审理情况确定。从现在法院案件审理程序设置看，主要包括立案阶段、审前准备阶段、法庭审理阶段。立案法官与庭审法官分别设置，在诉讼过程中，在哪个阶段确定举证期限，是立案阶段，还是法庭审理阶段？新修改的民事诉讼法规定，根据“当事人的主张”、“案件审理情况”确定，可以理解为立案阶段和庭审阶段，法官都可以根据当事人的主张和案件审理情况确定举证时限，然而，在庭审过程中再确定举证期限显然有违诉讼效率原则。

（2）举证期限确定职权化，即没有赋予当事人协商确定举证期限的权利。从举证时限制度的发展历程看，《证据规定》第 33 条不仅规定了法院指定举证期限，而且规定了当事人协商确定举证期限。新修改的民事诉讼法，仅规定了法院指定举证期限，没有赋予当事人协商确定举证期限的权利，应当说是一种退步，忽视了当事人诉讼主体的地位，体现出较强的法院职权主义色彩。[3]

针对上述存在的问题，本文相应地提出以下两项建议：

（1）立法应当明确规定举证期限的时间和终点。举证期限终点问题，直接关系到当事人诉讼权利的行使，关系到举证时限制度的价值实现。目前关于举证期限的终点问题，我国理论界主要存在两种观点：一种观点认为，应当将举证期限确定为一审法庭辩论终结时；[4] 另一种观点则主张，将举证期限确定为法庭开庭审理之日。[5] 本文认为，随着我国民事诉讼法的修改，以“证据交换，明确争点”为核心的审前准备程序的设置，应当将举证期限的终点明确规定在审前准备程序终结前，并且由负责审前准备的法官确定。因为在立案阶段，法官对案件情况不甚了解，确定举证期限存在一定的困难。在庭审阶段确定举证期限，会影响庭审的顺利进行，拖延诉讼进程，而在案件审前准备阶段，随着法官对案件情况的进一步了解，可以根据案件的具体情况，确定合理的举证期限，既可以为庭审做好准备，通过证据交换确定无争议的证据，排除与案件无关联的证据，又可以保证庭审工作的顺利进行。

---

〔2〕 参见江伟主编：《民事诉讼法》（第二版），高等教育出版社 2005 年版，第 190～191 页。

〔3〕《证据规定》第 33 条第 2 款、第 3 款规定：举证期限可以由当事人协商一致，并经人民法院认可。由人民法院指定举证期限的，指定的期限不得少于 30 天，自当事人收到案件受理通知书和应诉通知书的次日起计算。

〔4〕 参见李浩：《民事举证责任研究》，中国政法大学出版社 1993 年版，第 93 页。

〔5〕 参见陈桂明、张锋：“民事举证时限制度初探”，载《政法论坛》1998 年第 3 期。

（2）赋予当事人协商确定举证期限的权利。在民事诉讼中，当事人是案件的当事者，是举证主体，对证据获得的难易程度了如指掌，因此由双方当事人通过协商的方式确定举证期限，最科学合理。赋予当事人双方协商确定举证期限，可能会产生这样的异议，即当事人在诉讼中是存在利益冲突的双方主体，由其自己协商确定举证期限不可能，利益冲突的双方当事人之间不可能找到共同点。[6] 本文认为，案件情况是错综复杂的，司法实践中，双方当事人之间确实存在利益冲突，但是，利益冲突的双方主体之间并不是不能找到利益共同点，例如，诉讼中的调解协议，就是双方当事人互谅互让达成一致的结果。随着社会经济的发展进步，公民法律意识的提高，诉讼主体的诉讼行为越来越理智，到法院诉讼主要是为了解决矛盾和纠纷，为了节省诉讼时间和费用，双方当事人存在共同协商的可能性。法院是案件的事后裁判者，诉讼是双方当事人的事情，当事人是自身利益的最好维护者，因此法律应当赋予当事人更多的自主选择权，使当事人享有协商确定举证期限的权利，只有在当事人协商不成的情况下，才由法院依法确定举证期限，而且为了防止法院随意行使指定权，损害当事人的合法权益，法律应当确定法院指定举证期限的原则，即法院指定举证期限不得少于30天。关于法院指定举证期限时间的限制，《证据规定》中已经有规定，建议将司法解释的内容纳入法律规定。

二、逾期举证的法律后果

设定逾期举证的法律后果，是为了使当事人遵守已经确定的举证期限，如果不规定逾期举证的法律后果，举证期限将变得毫无约束力。我国新修改的《民事诉讼法》规定，当事人逾期提供证据的，人民法院应当责令其说明理由；拒不说明理由或者理由不成立的，人民法院根据不同情形可以不予采纳该证据，或者采纳该证据但予以训诫、罚款。从上述法律规定可以看出，法律规定逾期举证的法律后果有两个，一是证据失权，即当事人逾期提供证据，拒不说明理由或者理由不成立的，人民法院根据不同情形可以不予采纳该证据；二是证据不失权，但要对逾期提供证据者采取强制措施，即采纳该证据，但对逾期提供证据的当事人予以训诫、罚款。

法律条文内容的规定主要存在以下问题：

（1）证据失权情形的放宽，可能会导致举证时限制度难以落实。从条文规定的内容看，当事人逾期举证，拒不说明理由或者理由不成立的，人民法院根据不同情形可以不予采纳该证据，或者采纳该证据但予以训诫、罚款。但是，此项法律规定“分号”前，还有一项规定，即当事人逾期提供证据的，人民法院应当责令其说明理由。根据这项法律规定，如果当事人逾期提供证据，并且说明了理由，是否适用证据失权，是否适用采纳证据，对当事人训诫、罚款的规定。如果立法本意是当事人逾期提供证据，只要说明理由，理由成立，法院就可以采纳该项证据，那么逾期举证法律后果的规定就过于宽松，对当事人行为制约的举证时限制度将无法落实。同时，逾期举证的理由成立不成立，法律规定的较原则，一方面，法官与当事人对理由成立与否可能会出现

〔6〕 全国人大常委会法制工作委员会民法室编写的相关著作中也认为，从我国司法实践的情况看，当事人协商确定举证期限的方式操作性很差，双方当事人很难达成一致意见。参见全国人大常委会法制工作委员会民法室著：《〈中华人民共和国民事诉讼法〉释解与适用》，人民法院出版社2012年版，第103页。

理解不一致的情形，导致当事人与法官矛盾激化；另一方面，司法实践中法官的自由裁量权过大，容易滋生司法腐败。

（2）人民法院采取的强制措施行政化。罚款是一种重要的行政处罚手段，是行政执法单位对违反行政法规的个人和单位给予的行政处罚，不需要经人民法院裁决，只要行政执法单位依据行政法规的规定，作出处罚决定即可执行。行政机关在依法履行法定职责时，经常适用该项行政处罚手段依法行政。在民事诉讼中，训诫、罚款属于对实施了妨碍民事诉讼行为的人采取的强制措施，如果当事人不提供证据支持自己的诉讼主张，可以判决该当事人败诉，使其承担举证不能的法律后果，而不宜适用训诫、罚款等强制措施。从证据提供角度看，公权力不应当过度介入私权领域，当事人提供证据不是公法义务，因此对怠于行使举证权利的当事人，法律不应当规定采取训诫、罚款的强制措施。否则，可能会诱发法官滥用该项权利借罚款之名违法敛财等不法行为。

针对上述存在的问题，本文提出以下完善建议：

（1）严格实行证据失权制度。法律规定证据失权制度，主要是为了提高诉讼效率，保证举证期限制度的贯彻落实。如果只规定举证期限制度，没有证据失权制度与之相配套，举证期限制度形同虚设。〔7〕最高人民法院的《证据规定》中已经规定了证据失权制度，在司法实践施行中产生了较大的负面效应，导致出现较多的反对声音。〔8〕新修改的民事诉讼法放宽了对证据失权制度的要求，规定当事人逾期举证，如果能够说明理由，证据可以被采纳。本文认为，《证据规定》中规定的证据失权制度在司法实践中贯彻落实失败，属制度设置不完善所至，新修改的民事诉讼法放宽该项制度的适用，不够慎重，可能又会变相地重走"证据随时提出主义"的老路。因此在完善相关法律制度的同时，应当继续坚持严格的证据失权制度。〔9〕

根据《证据规定》的规定，由人民法院指定的举证期限不得少于30天，证据交换之日举证期限届满。除重大、疑难和案情特别复杂的案件外，证据交换一般不超过2次。〔10〕上述法律规定存在的问题是，立法没有合理地协调举证期限与证据交换的关系，

〔7〕从外国法律规定看，大多数国家实行较为严格的证据失权制度。例如，美国《联邦民事诉讼规则》第16条第3款第15项规定：法院可以在审前会议的事项中，确定允许提出证据的合理时间限制；在法官作出的最终审前命令中，主要就双方当事人将在法庭审理时所需证据开列证据目录，未列入审前命令中的证据不允许在开庭时提出；若当事人违反审前命令提出新证据，法官可拒绝审理或者限制当事人的证明活动。德国《民事诉讼法》第296条也规定：在作为判决基础的言辞辩论结束后，不能再提出攻击和防御方法。参见宋朝武：《民事证据法学》，高等教育出版社2003年版，第55页。

〔8〕《证据规定》第34条规定："当事人应当在举证期限内向人民法院提交证据材料，当事人在举证期限内不提交的，视为放弃举证权利。对于当事人逾期提交的证据材料，人民法院审理时不组织质证。但对方当事人同意质证的除外。当事人增加、变更诉讼请求或者提起反诉的，应当在举证期限届满前提出。"

〔9〕按照新修订的《民事诉讼法》的规定，当事人逾期提交证据的理由不成立，法院仍然采纳该证据，其结果必然是退回到《证据规定》出台前的老路上，证据随时提出的做法将再度泛滥成灾，即使存在训诫、罚款等配套措施，仍然难以有效防止实行证据随时提出主义带来的诉讼弊端，因为人们的意识中自觉或者不自觉地会形成这样一种认识，即逾期提交证据没关系，挨骂或者花钱就能摆平。

〔10〕《证据规定》第33条第3款规定：由人民法院指定举证期限的，指定的期限不得少于30日，自当事人受到案件受理通知书和应诉通知书的次日起计算。第38条第2款规定：人民法院组织证据交换的，交换证据之日举证期限届满。当事人申请延期举证经人民法院准许的，证据交换日相应顺延。第40条第2款规定：证据交换一般不超过2次。但重大、疑难和案情特别复杂的案件，人民法院认为确有必要再次进行证据交换的除外。

将证据交换作为举证期限届满的最后期限，并且限制证据交换的次数，导致当事人在举证期限内，不知道该提交何种证据，证据交换之时，发现还有证据需要收集、提交，但是举证期限已经届满，再收集、提供的证据不被采纳，合法权益得不到维护，对法律规定提出质疑。况且，在司法实践中，还存在有些案件不进行证据交换的情形。[11]实际上，在诉讼进行中，当事人之间通过证据交换，了解对方证据提交的情形，经过法官的释明，有时方能知晓自己应当或者需要向法院提交何种证据支持自己的诉讼主张，反驳对方的诉讼主张。而根据《证据规定》的规定，证据交换之日举证期限届满，恰恰堵死了当事人相互了解的渠道，导致证据交换之时，再想提交对自己有利的证据为时已晚。[12]

解决上述问题的具体方法是，将举证时限确定在审前准备阶段，延长审前准备时间，形成在举证期限内多次进行证据交换的“交换证据，整理证据—提交证据—再交换证据，整理证据—提交证据”的循环过程。首先由双方当事人协商确定举证期限，当事人协商不成的，由法院指定举证期限。根据案情需要，在举证期限内，法院可以多次组织双方当事人进行证据交换。多次进行证据交换的目的主要有两个，一是督促当事人尽快地提交证据；二是通过证据交换、整理证据，使双方当事人互相了解案件情况，法官向当事人释明需要收集、提交哪些未出示的证据，利于当事人在举证期限内收集，并向法院提交。上述整个运行过程可以循环往复进行，直至双方当事人将所有能够向法院提交的证据穷尽为止。为了防止诉讼拖延，法院可以依职权对整个运行过程进行控制。可以说，该项法律制度的确立，既有利于督促当事人及时、有针对性、全面地举证；也有利于保证法院案件审理的公正性，提高诉讼效率。同时，通过证据制度的设定，在知己知彼的情况下，还可以促进当事人达成和解协议，减轻庭审负担，充分发挥审前准备的作用。

（2）取消罚款强制措施的适用。从司法实际情况看，当事人逾期举证主要存在以下两种情形：一是当事人逾期向法院提交的证据对自己有利；二是当事人逾期向法院

---

〔11〕《证据规定》第38条第2款规定：人民法院对于证据较多或者复杂疑难的案件，应当组织当事人在答辩期届满后、开庭审理前交换证据。可见，根据上述法律规定，并不是所有案件的审理都需要进行证据交换，只有涉及“证据较多”或者“复杂疑难”的案件，才需要进行证据交换。司法实践中，证据交换的落实也存在较大的障碍。根据一些调研数据表明，一审证据交换的案件不到40%，并且绝大部分是在中级人民法院进行。许多基层法院的法官认为，基层法院审理的案件百分之八九十都是适用简易程序，一般一次开庭审理即可解决纠纷，没有必要在简易程序中引入证据交换。参见厦门市中级人民法院、厦门大学法学院联合课题组：“新民事诉讼证据司法解释的执行与完善——厦门市两级法院执行〈关于民事诉讼证据的若干规定〉情况的调研报告”，载《法律适用》2003年第4期。

〔12〕在我国，无论是《证据规定》还是新修改《民事诉讼法》中规定的证据交换，目的都是为了明确和固定争点，而在美国，审前准备程序包括证据开示和审前会议两个阶段，证据开示是多样化地获取证据和信息的手段和方法，审前会议在证据开示的基础上固定争议的争点。证据开示可以多次、反复地进行，当事人可以边保存证据边收集证据，因为对方当事人披露的信息可能会是发现新证据的线索，这样在客观上要求证据交换的重复进行，也就是每当有新的证据出现，证据开示就有必要进行，双方当事人在一个互动的过程中，尽可能地发现更多的证据。我国《证据规定》确立的证据交换制度与审前会议实质上合二为一，一方面，证据交换的手段其实只有一种，即通过申请人民法院组织交换；另一方面，又规定证据交换的次数一般不超过两次，这样的限制使证据交换仅仅成为整理争点的一道工序，而不是收集证据的方式。同时，当事人收集证据是封闭进行的，直到证据开示那一天，双方才互相了解对方的实力和“武器”，从本质上说，我国并没有确立严格意义上的证据开示制度。参见韩象乾主编：《民事证据理论新探》，中国人民公安大学出版社2006年版，第9～10页。

提交的证据对自己不利。当事人逾期向法院提交对自己有利的证据，法律应当规定严格实行证据失权制度，因为根据本文上述对举证期限制度与证据交换制度的完善，已经给予当事人充分的举证时间，除非属于新证据，当事人再逾期举证，已经没有任何理由，证据失权当事人也无话可说。如果此时还规定可以采纳该项证据，诉讼一审、二审、再审将无休止地进行，既对对方当事人不公平，也会影响诉讼效率，浪费国家的司法资源。从追求司法公正的价值目标与我国目前当事人举证能力较差、律师制度不发达的角度考虑，可以作出法定的有限制的例外规定，赋予法官有限的自由裁量权，即法律明确规定：如果当事人逾期提出的证据涉及“妨碍判决实体公正”，当事人逾期提出无过失，并且不至于延迟诉讼终结的，可以由法庭自由裁量是否将其纳入质证程序。〔13〕 司法实践中，当事人往往不愿意将对自己不利的证据向法院提交。但是，如果对方当事人主张该证据的内容不利于证据持有人，并且有证据证明证据持有人持有证据，无正当理由拒不提供的，人民法院可以责令证据持有人提交证据，逾期提交的，可以对证据持有人进行训诫；拒不提交的，人民法院可以推定该项主张成立。如果因为当事人无正当理由拒不提交证据的行为，导致诉讼拖延，给对方当事人造成损失的，对方当事人可以要求赔偿。我国新修订的《民事诉讼法》规定逾期举证强制措施的适用范围广泛，适用条件原则，司法实践中适用不宜掌握，容易被滥用，需要立法进一步完善，予以取消。

三、“新的证据”的界定

根据1991年《民事诉讼法》的规定，我国实行的是证据随时提出主义，允许当事人在诉讼程序进行的任何阶段提出证据。《证据规定》初步实现了证据随时提出主义向证据适时提出主义的转变，即当事人应当在举证期限内提出证据，否则需承担由此导致的不利后果。2012年新修改的《民事诉讼法》以立法的形式对举证时限制度作出了规定，应当说是立法的一大进步，该项法律制度的确立，对克服证据随时提出主义产生的弊端必将产生较大的作用。但是，需要注意的是，一方面，举证时限制度的设置还不完善，存在本文上述的诸多弊端；另一方面，实践中各类案件的情况非常复杂，如果绝对不允许当事人在举证期限届满后提交证据未免过于严苛。因此，作为举证期限制度的例外，应当对举证期限届满后当事人可以提交“新的证据”作出专门的规定。纵观世界各国，诸多国家法律都对“新的证据”提交有例外规定，因为举证时限制度

〔13〕 在以美国、英国为代表的英美法系，以严格的正当程序理念支撑的诉讼模式中，法律规定了严格的举证时限，以防止诉讼进程被恶意拖延。在审前程序通过证据交换制度，裁定证据的范围，避免诉讼进程中的证据突袭，维护当事人的平等权与辩论权等，但是对于“妨碍判决实体公正”的证据，由法庭自由裁量是否将其纳入质证程序。参见肖建华：《民事诉讼立法研讨与理论探索》，法律出版社2008年版，第176页。以德国、日本为代表的大陆法系，也有相关的法律规定。例如，德国《民事诉讼法》第356条规定：因为有不定期的障碍致不能调查取证，法院应规定一定的期间，如在期间内仍不能调查，那么，只有在法院依其自由心证，认为不致拖延诉讼程序时，才可以在期满后使用该证据方法。此项期间可以不经言辞辩论定之。根据上述规定，德国的民事诉讼中证据失权需要符合以下条件：①法官实施了审前准备，为当事人提交证据提供了足够的时间和机会；②逾期举证将导致诉讼被延迟；③当事人逾期举证有重大过失。日本《民事诉讼法》第356条也规定：在准备性口头辩论终了之后，当事人提出的攻击和防御方法，如果对方当事人要求，则应向其说明在准备性口头辩论终了之前未能提出的理由，即迟延提出证据的理由是否正当、法院是否采纳、证据是否失权，由法官自由裁量。见前引注释7。上述国家的法律规定说明，在当事人逾期举证时，各国法律都赋予法官一定的自由裁量权，来动态地衡量实体公正与程序公正之间的价值，最终作出决定。具体的法律规定，成功的经验，可供我国完善举证时限制度时作为参考。

与“新的证据”本来就是一对天生的矛盾。举证时限制度体现了程序的不可逆性，而允许“新的证据”的提出必然引起程序的反复性和不安定性，弱化了举证时限制度对程序的固定作用。为了实现案件审理的公正性，立法需要平衡这一矛盾。

我国《证据规定》第41条、第44条对1991年《民事诉讼法》第125条、第179条关于“新的证据”的规定作了限制性解释，以限制“新的证据”出现的情形，并通过第46条规定，由于“新的证据”的提出，给对方当事人造成损失应承担相应法律责任，对当事人施加压力，以督促当事人遵守举证期限的规定。[14] 但是，关于“新的证据”的规定，在性质上应当也只能是举证时限制度的例外情形，而这种例外在实际效果上形成了对举证期限制度的限制。因此，《证据规定》所确立的举证期限制度实质上是一种相对化的举证期限制度。[15]

我国新修订的《民事诉讼法》没有对“新的证据”的范围作出明确规定。从现行法律规定看，有关“新的证据”规定存在的主要问题是：法律对“新的证据”认定标准规定得过于原则，且一审、二审在“开庭前或者开庭审理时”都可以提出“新的证据”。这样规定的结果，会使某些当事人搞“证据突袭”仍然有机可乘，将所谓“新的证据”不在庭前提交，而选择在开庭审理时向法庭提交。有些案件当事人提交的“新的证据”不止一份，信息量很大，涉及范围较广，使对方当事人措手不及，难以当庭对证据的真伪提出有针对性的意见，导致在诉讼中处于被动地位。同时，法官对这些“新的证据”在短时间内，也往往很难判断是否属于新发现的证据，是否决定组织对“新的证据”进行质证，直接影响了庭审的质量和效果。

针对上述存在的问题，本文提出以下完善建议：

（1）明确“新的证据”的认定标准。“新的证据”认定标准的确立，直接影响对“新的证据”的认定。我国《证据规定》对“新的证据”规定的认定标准是“新发现的证据”，但是，何谓“新发现”？是主观标准还是客观标准？法律并没有作出明确的规定。[16] 新修订的《民事诉讼法》对此问题也未涉及，导致司法实践中具体判断的随意性。为了切实保障当事人诉讼权利的充分行使，维护当事人的合法权益，保障人民法院充分高效地行使审判权，考虑到随着案件审理中新情况、新问题的出现，一些地方对《证据规定》中个别条款规定理解的不统一，2008年最高人民法院发布了《最高人民法院关于适用〈关于民事诉讼证据的若干规定〉中有关举证时限规定的通知》

---

〔14〕《证据规定》第41条规定：1991年《民事诉讼法》第125条第1款规定的“新的证据”，是指以下情形：（一）一审程序中的新的证据包括：当事人在一审举证期限届满后新发现的证据；当事人确因客观原因无法在举证期限内提供，经人民法院准许，在延长的期限内仍无法提供的证据。（二）二审程序中的新的证据包括：一审庭审结束后新发现的证据；当事人在一审举证期限届满前申请人民法院调查取证未获准许，二审法院经审查认为应当准许并依当事人申请调取的证据。第42条规定：当事人在一审程序中提供新的证据的，应当在一审开庭前或者开庭审理时提出。当事人在二审程序中提供新的证据的，应当在二审开庭前或者开庭审理时提出；二审不需要开庭审理的，应当在人民法院指定的期限内提出。第46条规定：由于当事人的原因未能在指定期限内举证，致使案件在二审或者再审期间因提出新的证据被人民法院发回重审或者改判的，原审裁判不属于错误裁判案件。一方当事人请求提出新的证据的另一方当事人负担由此增加的差旅、误工、证人出庭作证、诉讼等合理费用以及由此扩大的直接损失，人民法院应予支持。1991年《民事诉讼法》第125条、第179条关于“新的证据”的规定，在新修改的民事诉讼法中没有改变，只是第125条变为第139条，第179条变为第200条。

〔15〕孙辙：“新的证据和相对化的举证时限制度”，载《人民司法》2002年第5期。

〔16〕参见韩波：“论举证时限的裁量空间”，载《证据科学》2010年第6期。

（以下简称《举证时限通知》），其中第10条对“新的证据”的认定作出了规定。根据《举证时限通知》的规定，人民法院对于“新的证据”，应当依照《证据规定》第41条、第42条、第43条、第44条的规定，结合以下因素综合认定：一是证据是否在举证期限或者《证据规定》第41条、第44条规定的其他期限内已经客观存在；二是当事人未在举证期限或者司法解释规定的其他期限内提供证据，是否存在故意或者重大过失的情形。上述规定对“新的证据”的认定标准从主观、客观两个方面进一步进行了明确，应当说是一大进步。

但是，本文认为，在“新的证据”的界定上，将“新发现”的认定标准囊括主观原因和客观原因似有不妥。根据《证据规定》的规定，无论出于什么原因，只要是在一审举证期限届满后新发现的，或者是在一审庭审结束后新发现的证据，就可以分别作为一审、二审的“新的证据”。这样的法律规定，是不能鼓励当事人积极收集、调查取证的，是与举证时限制度设立的目的背道而驰的，是对举证时限制度的突破。因此，对“新发现”的认定，应当排除当事人的主观原因，即因当事人的主观原因逾期提供的证据，不能作为“新的证据”，对“新发现的证据”的认定标准应当确定为，在一审举证期限内或者在一审程序中，当事人不知道的或者在其后才产生的证据。由此建议，将“新的证据”的认定标准确定为：一是该证据在法院指定或者当事人协商确定的举证期限内没有出现过；二是虽然当事人意识到该证据有可能存在，但当事人并不知道该证据已经存在；三是当事人对该证据并不持有，也不知道他人持有。对于再审程序中“新的证据”的提出，《证据规定》第44条规定，再审程序中“新的证据”，是指原审庭审结束后新发现的证据。由于我国在审级制度上实行的是二审终审制，允许以“新的证据”启动再审程序，会损害程序的安定性，也会遏制举证时限制度功能的发挥，因此本文认为，从维护法院裁判的稳定性和权威性出发，不应当将“新的证据”作为发动再审程序的理由。[17]

（2）赋予对方当事人异议权并设置完善的责任赔偿制度。严格地讲，有关案件的全部证据都应当在举证期限内提供，举证期限届满后提供“新的证据”仅仅是例外。人民法院送达当事人的《举证通知》已经把举证不能的后果及诉讼风险告知了当事人。如果可以轻而易举地提供“新的证据”，就不能达到庭前固定证据、整理争议焦点的目的。因此，对当事人提出的“新的证据”必须严格把握，对不属于“新的证据”的情形，应当不予质证。建议法律修改时增加以下两项规定：

第一，赋予对方当事人异议权。一方当事人提出“新的证据”，对方当事人可以提出异议，要求当事人说明“新的证据”的来源和种类。因为通常情况下，在提供这些证据时，仅仅是提供方当事人认为是“新的证据”，法官和对方当事人则未必这样认为。对于这些证据法官必须尽到释明义务，对方当事人对该证据同意质证的，法官可以组织质证。对方当事人对新证据有异议的，提供证据的一方当事人应当对该证据是否属于“新的证据”说明理由，并提供相应证据予以证明。法官根据当事人提供的证据和陈述的理由，及时决定是否属于“新的证据”，是否准予质证。

---

〔17〕 法国、德国、日本的民事诉讼法均否认当事人以“新的证据”为由提起再审之诉。参见田淑霞：“浅议‘新的证据’”，载《法制与经济》2012年第8期。

第二，设置完善的责任赔偿制度。在很多情况下，“新的证据”起着扭转被动局面的作用，决定着诉讼的成功与失败，直接关系当事人的合法权益，同时也涉及法律的公平和正义。司法实践中，当事人提出“新的证据”通常涉及两种情形，一是确实属于“新发现的证据”；二是该项证据本不属于“新的证据”，而是当事人为了拖延诉讼，或者某些当事人为了搞“证据突袭”，以达到胜诉的目的，将所谓“新的证据”不在庭前提交，而选择在开庭审理时向法庭提交。不论是哪一种情形，“新的证据”的出现，都会增加对方当事人的诉讼成本。为了兼顾双方当事人合法权益的维护，彰显诉讼制度设置的公正性，我国《证据规定》第46条规定：由于当事人的原因未能在指定期限内举证，致使案件在二审或者再审期间因提出新的证据被人民法院发回重审或者改判的，原审裁判不属于错误裁判案件。一方当事人请求提出新的证据的另一方当事人负担由此增加的差旅、误工、证人出庭作证、诉讼等合理费用以及由此扩大的直接损失，人民法院应予支持。根据上述法律规定，本文提出以下两点完善立法的建议：一是将上述司法解释的规定纳入法律，以增强法律适用的效力性；二是对于前述当事人提出“新的证据”涉及的第二种情形，建议纳入恶意诉讼的范畴，在这种情况下，对方当事人额外付出了较多的人力、物力、财力和精力，法律除规定其有权要求赔偿额外参加诉讼支付的合理费用外，还有权提出惩罚性赔偿，要求恶意诉讼的当事人额外支付相应的费用，具体数额由法院根据当事人受损害的程度确定，主要目的是对恶意诉讼的当事人进行惩处，以防止此类恶意诉讼的发生。

需要注意的是，根据法律规定，在二审程序中，还存在“视为新的证据”的情形，即当事人经人民法院准许延期举证，但因客观原因未能在准许的期限内提供，且不审理该证据可能导致裁判明显不公的，其提供的证据可视为新的证据。对此等新证据，几乎可以说完全要靠法官裁量，因为是否导致裁判明显不公，只能由法官来把握。〔18〕因此，在法律对“新的证据”作出限制性规定外，法官的自由裁量权也是不容忽略的。本文认为，为了保证案件审理的公正性，法律应当对“新的证据”作出例外规定，明确“新的证据”的认定标准，赋予对方当事人异议权，设置完善的责任赔偿制度，并赋予法官一定的自由裁量权。

总之，为了保证诉讼公正与效率最大限度的实现，维护当事人的合法权益，法律应当对举证时限制度进一步进行完善，赋予当事人双方协商确定举证期限的权利，严格逾期举证的证据失权制度，在审前准备阶段，确定举证期限，并且在举证期限内多

---

〔18〕《证据规定》第41条规定：“1991年《民事诉讼法》第125条第1款规定的“新的证据”，是指以下情形：（一）一审程序中的新的证据包括：当事人在一审举证期限届满后新发现的证据；当事人确因客观原因无法在举证期限内提供，经人民法院准许，在延长的期限内仍无法提供的证据。（二）二审程序中的新的证据包括：一审庭审结束后新发现的证据；当事人在一审举证期限届满前申请人民法院调查取证未获准许，二审法院经审查认为应当准许并依当事人申请调取的证据。”第42条规定：“当事人在一审程序中提供新的证据的，应当在一审开庭前或者开庭审理时提出。当事人在二审程序中提供新的证据的，应当在二审开庭前或者开庭审理时提出；二审不需要开庭审理的，应当在人民法院指定的期限内提出。”第46条规定：“由于当事人的原因未能在指定期限内举证，致使案件在二审或者再审期间因提出新的证据被人民法院发回重审或者改判的，原审裁判不属于错误裁判案件。一方当事人请求提出新的证据的另一方当事人负担由此增加的差旅、误工、证人出庭作证、诉讼等合理费用以及由此扩大的直接损失，人民法院应予支持。”1991年《民事诉讼法》第125条、第179条关于“新的证据”的规定，在新修订的《民事诉讼法》中没有改变，只是第125条变为第139条，第179条变为第200条。

次进行证据交换，督促、协助当事人在举证期限内及时、全面地向法院提交证据。对于有利于证据提交一方当事人的证据，在举证期限内当事人不提交或者不能提交的，除属于法定的“新的证据”范畴，或者该证据“妨碍判决实体公正”，当事人逾期提出无过失，并且不至于延迟诉讼终结的，可以由法庭自由裁量是否将其纳入质证程序，其余逾期提交的证据严格适用证据失权制度。同时，取消罚款强制措施的适用，如果有证据证明一方当事人持有证据无正当理由拒不提供，对方当事人主张该证据的内容不利于证据持有人，人民法院可以责令证据持有人提交证据，证据持有人拒不提交的，法院可以推定该项主张成立，由此导致诉讼拖延，使当事人遭受损失的，当事人可以要求赔偿。此外，为了保证案件审理的公正性，法律应当对“新的证据”的认定标准作出明确的规定，赋予当事人对“新的证据”的异议权，设置完善的责任赔偿制度，以防止恶意诉讼的发生，保证案件审理的公正性。

检察机关矛盾言辞证据之审查判断：案例样本分析

张 弘*

刑事诉讼中的言辞证据包括被害人陈述、犯罪嫌疑人和被告人供述与辩解、证人证言、自诉人陈述、刑事附带民事当事人陈述。言辞证据具有直接性，细节性、信息量大等优势，同时伴随复杂性、虚伪性、反复性等缺陷，主客观并存。矛盾言辞证据往往把判断者带入扑朔迷离的认识迷宫。检察机关在逮捕与公诉审查时，需要秉持中立和理性的心态，如果主要案件事实由言辞证据构建，无论表面看起来多么可信，实则隐藏着高风险和高隐患。检察官需要运用规则判断证据而不是混沌的感觉作出逮捕与公诉决定，否则等到开庭时，一旦言辞证据者在庭审中反言，公诉人必将面对证据体系坍塌，孤证悬案的结局。而到庭审阶段，涉案人已经被羁押多时，面对我国公检法配合大于制约的现实，勉强起诉和勉强判决的被动司法时有发生，缠讼上访在所难免。

本文以被害人陈述、犯罪嫌疑人和被告人供述与辩解、证人证言三类矛盾言辞证据为研究目标，所选择的案例样本具有下述两个特征：其一，案件证据以言辞证据为主，其他证据种类匮乏、没有或证明力很低；其二，言辞证据呈现一对一矛盾或组群矛盾，呈现出两个主要案件事实相反的故事版本。

案例样本

（一）被害人陈述与犯罪嫌疑人矛盾言辞判断：孙某涉嫌强奸、抢劫案

本案自命被害人赵某（女，27岁，西安人，大专文化程度）于2013年3月20日前来报案，称被其前男友孙某（男，29岁，山东人，小学文化）强奸、抢劫。赵某称，2013年3月18日，其前男友孙某将其从工作单位强行拉到其出租屋内，要求继续交往并要求女方和他回山东，赵某拒绝遭到孙某殴打。孙某用烟头烫伤其右肩，用棍子打她，用针在她臀部刺字，强行脱掉其衣服，用手机拍裸照威胁，用胶带纸捆绑其手脚，又强行与其发生性关系（第一次陈述未提发生性关系）。随后强迫她在附近的ATM机上取钱，后因只取出有300元不够，孙某又强迫她到宿舍拿工资卡再取钱。到宿舍后，赵某乘孙某买啤酒之机，拦出租车逃离。其随身携带的小包，内有三星手机一部被孙某抢走。赵某提交了医院验伤证明，诊断为一般皮外伤，未构成轻伤。

孙某遂被抓获，承认对赵某有轻微打骂、刺字、捆绑等细节，但辩解说烟头烫伤赵某肩头为不小心，刺字是女方为示爱愿意的，用胶带纸捆绑赵某双手是赵某自己提出的，因为其间有男性持续发来短信和电话，赵某要求绑住双手以示她不会乘孙某下

---

* 张弘，西安交通大学法学院副教授、西安市碑林区人民检察院副检察长。

楼之机回短信。他返回后即松解，前后只有十几分钟时间。拍裸照是想证明他与赵某是恋爱关系。孙某否认发生性关系，称其二人一直断续同居，经济未分开。钱是赵某自己在ATM机上取款后给了他200元。到宿舍取钱是因为要去找发短信的男同学钱不够想多拿点。手包是赵某让他拿着的。

民警在其出租屋内查获赵某手包，内有三星手机一部。侦查机关以涉嫌抢劫罪刑拘赵某，一个月后报请检察院批捕。

（二）被告人与同案犯矛盾言辞审查：张某、钱某、李某强奸案

以下分别以被告一、被告二、被告三替代张某、钱某、李某，其中，被告一、二为同事，被告一、三为朋友，被告二、三初识，被害人与被告三初识。

被害人于某（女，21岁）于2009年9月2日前往派出所报案，称被三名男子强奸。于某陈述：2009年8月28日晚，其与朋友在街上候车时，被告一、被告二开车向其问路，并捎带她回家，路上被告一出示一份军官证给她看，二人互留手机号。之后几天，被告一几次电话邀请她吃饭，她未应允。9月2日晚，被告一再次邀请她一同唱歌，于是她与被告一、二、三聚合。凌晨2点他们离开歌厅，乘坐被告二开的车送被害人回家。被告三坐副驾驶。被告一与被害人坐在后排。被告一要求与被害人发生关系被拒，遂拳击被害人头部和身体，被害人欲跳车，车门被锁，被告一搂住其脖子，被告三也拉了被害人一把。被告一强奸了被害人。之后，被告一要另两人到后排与被害人发生关系，由被告一开车。车一直往城外方向行驶。被害人坐在二人之间，被告二将被害人抱至腿上强行发生性关系，期间由于被拒，打了被害人一拳。被告二强奸后将被害人交给被告三。被告三小声说，做个样子，二人未发生关系，被告三手淫。后被告一再次与被告二、三换回原先位置，再次强奸被害人。过程中，被告二提醒到了被害人家附近，遂将被害人放下车，还其包物，逃离。

被害人于案发三天后9月5日报案，称其次日还遭到被告一威胁不许报案。

三被告人供述情况：三被告在公安机关的前二次供述中认罪，供述情况与被害人陈述基本印证，但第三次开始，被告一、二翻供。被告一称被害人是酒托，骗他们当晚酒水消费4600元，他有打骂被害人，但未强奸。反控被害人诬告陷害，称被害人事后打电话索要钱未果报复，否则为何被害人案发数日后才报案？这期间就是敲诈他钱。被告二称被害人自愿坐到他腿上与其发生性关系。二被告翻供理由是被逼供。被告三始终未翻供，且指证被告一、二强奸，但被告二质疑被告三，称其与被告一之间有债务纠纷。

被害人送检的案发时穿的内衣裤和连衣裙保留，但鉴定结果为：只见被害人自身组织痕迹，未发现三被告人DNA；作案车辆，被告二已于被转捕数月前卖给他人。

（三）非中立证人证言审查：林某篮球伤害案

2012年7月22日下午，被害人王某（男，24岁，学生）和同学在西大球场与犯罪嫌疑人林某及其球友一起打篮球，双方原本不认识。打球分三组，每组4人，输队下场，轮换上场。林某与被害人王某相互打盯防，二人在打球过程中互有身体接触碰撞。在一次攻防中，林某右手肘击打到王某下颌部，王某倒地，嘴部流血不止。王某给家长打电话，林某见状上前抓住其衣领问：是不是喊人？之后双方散去，王某与一名同学去医院看伤，另两名同学杨某、白某前往派出所报案，称王某被打。

王某数次就诊，经法医鉴定为下颌骨骨折，构成轻伤害，住院医院开刀治疗，有轻微后遗症。王母常常守候在案发球场，2个月后在球场发现林某，遂报警。

犯罪嫌疑人林某在首次讯问中承认因为连续输球，与王某的盯防中有身体磕碰，心中急躁"心中有气"，动作幅度大了点伤到对方；第二次讯问否认上述说法，称打球过程中，磕磕碰碰难免，对王某没有怨气，不小心撞到对方下巴。被害人王某则认为，其受伤倒地后，对方冲过来两人，其中一人踢其背部一脚，该行为难以解释，认为王某蓄意伤害，原因是打球中二人身体数次碰撞而起报复之心。

被害方证人杨某和白某系被害人同学，二人的证言与被害人控诉一致，指出被告人方有一左肩部有圆形印记的人踢了王某背部一脚；犯罪嫌疑人方证人黄某和李某，当时与林某为同一组打球，陈述事实与林某相似，均否认有人踢王某一脚。

二、言辞证据的本质：存在的反映

言辞证据描述的事实非存在本身，而是存在的反映。言辞证据本身是否能够成为事实，取决于其反映的内容是否具有真实性。裴苍玲教授认为："证言、陈述、供述和辩解都是人做出的证明，证言笔录、陈述笔录、供述和辩解笔录就是由被害人、被告人和民事当事人取得的证明……这些资料本身都不是证据，而是证据的反映。证据材料同证据之间有着不可分割的联系。但是，又有本质的区别。"[1] 证据不可替代、证明材料却可以补充、修改、重做或废弃。证据是客观存在的，证明材料却具有主观性。人证有三个特点：其一，言辞证据反映的事实已经消失。人证中的事实不是现实的存在。所谓"存在"是指事实发生时，人是可以感知的。人证中的证据一般是已经发生过的事实，而非现实的存在，它的形象已经消失了，不能再被人感知了。而陈述者的描述具有主观随意性的可能。[2] 其二，言辞证据本身是证明对象。言辞证据所描述的事实是否发生过，该事实是否符合陈述者描述的事实，这些本身都需要求证。言辞证据因而具有极大的复杂性。物证和书证都可以被探查者亲自验证，因为他们有形有物有记载，载体上记载的内容所反映的事实，可以被感知、被研究。而言辞证据隔开了探查者与客观事实，办案人员不能直接亲身感知事实，只能依赖人证言辞去分析判断，这其中主客观纠结。真实、部分真实、虚假伪证都可能单独或综合存在。其三，人证有两种效力，陈述的性质是证明，事实的性质是证据。而物证书证则与此不同，书证的存在是一种事实，书证的记载又是一种事实。物证的存在蕴含了大量可以被鉴定的案件信息，客观性强。物证和书证都存在于案件实体过程中，不是在诉讼发生后获得的。而人的言辞陈述是两个分开的过程。消失的事实处于实体过程，言辞陈述处于程序过程。[3]

言辞证据不具有物质性、有形性，而且除中立证人证言外，被害人、犯罪嫌疑人和被告人以及非中立证人，都容易渗入个人的主观情感和恩怨：不诚实、偏袒、推诿、夸大、缩小、抵赖等等诸多主观因素，与物证、书证相比，复杂程度很高。此外，言辞陈述者本身的客观状况也有待考察：记忆力、表述力、理解力、感官力、知识结构、

---

〔1〕 裴仓龄：《裴仓龄文集》第一卷，法律出版社2011年版，第9页。
〔2〕 裴仓龄：《裴仓龄文集》第一卷，法律出版社2011年版，第196页。
〔3〕 裴仓龄："论人证"，载《现代法学》1996年第2期。

有无生理缺陷等等，这些因素与反映的事实的准确性密切相关。

既然言辞证据非证据本身，而是证据资料，是事实存在的反映，其中，曲直真伪并存，那么对主要由言辞证据构建的案件事实，尤其是矛盾言辞构建的事实判断，就具有相当的难度，应当遵循有如下三个规则：孤证不定案、同案犯证言谨慎采用、非中立证言补强。

三、“一比一”矛盾言辞词，孤证不定案

案例一样本分析：

被害人与犯罪嫌疑人分别给出的言辞证据能够相互印证的事实是：被害人被打、骂、刺字、捆手、取钱、拍裸照等，这些事实相当程度上补证了被害人的描述，使被害人陈述相比犯罪嫌疑人孙某而言更具有可信性。依常理，被害人为年轻女性，在暴力犯罪中属于易受侵害的弱势个体，尤其案发在夜间和封闭的空间里。被害人关于受害的案情描述在很多细节上得到孙某承认，手包、手机也在男住处被查扣。而孙某对上述行为种种行为解释显得牵强和不合常理。审查批捕检察官综合间接证据，从案发的时间（深夜）、地点（封闭的出租屋）、过程（打骂、威胁、拍裸照、捆双手、刺字、烟头烫）综合分析，依据经验与逻辑，倾向于采信被害人陈述，认为在特定情绪与环境里，作为打骂等伤害行为的延续，强行发生性关系与迫使被害人去取钱都很可能发生，且刺字拍裸照等行为恶劣，不容放纵。

依据新修订的《刑事诉讼法》第 79 条之规定，逮捕的证据条件为有证据证明有犯罪事实。两高的司法解释对逮捕证据明确规定为四条：有证据证明有犯罪事实发生、证据指向该犯罪嫌疑人、证据应当查证属实、数犯罪行为中只要有一项犯罪证据落实即可。在仅有双方矛盾的言辞证据来判断是否推进程序时，有两点值得注意：其一，可以立案侦查。被害人的报案表明可能确有犯罪发生，至于报案内容是否属实，需要立案后采取侦查行为进一步调查。但逮捕涉及严厉的限制人身自由，通常附随后续移送起诉的后果，对证据要求提升，需要有证据证明确有犯罪发生且犯罪证据指向犯罪嫌疑人，这是最基本的，社会危险性考虑则更符合人权保障精神。如果没有确实的确罪证据，则不能逮捕；其二，全面权衡矛盾言辞证据的证明力，以中立而不是有罪推定心态来审查证据，预防错诉错判。事实上，本案中，由于被害人与被告人彼此之间纠缠不清的复杂情感关系，被害人报案事实可能为真，也不排除虚假，因为被害人也存在报复并借机摆脱孙某的动机。如果以中立心态审视双方言辞，也会发现犯罪嫌疑人的解释也有可信之处。首先，孙某承认了诸多对其不利的侵害细节，没有抵赖和推诿，而他本可以全部否认。如果全盘否认的话，侦查人员心证的基础将大大下降，其被追诉的风险也随之下降。也许，嫌疑人认为自己叙述了一个事实，谎必要撒谎。其次，二人之间为同居男女朋友关系，即便发生性关系也没必要隐瞒。至于钱，二人经济不分，与抢无关。那么孙某有没有可能避重就轻，采用选择性撒谎，承认无关紧要的细节，否认关键的犯罪情节以换取如实交待的评价呢？也有可能，但前提条件是，他应该足够狡猾且精通法律，他需要懂得哪些承认不会带来麻烦，而哪些承认会自陷于罪。但小学文化程度的孙某在没有准备的情况下，能够挑拣出强奸罪和抢劫罪的犯罪构成要件，以决定承认什么，否认什么，显然概率极低。

由于案外人无法直接感知已经发生过的事实，在一比一矛盾言辞陈述情况下，任何一方的陈述都是没有印证的证明，逝去的事实，如果仅凭言辞确定，无论采信哪一方都可能错误，误断风险极高。故此，所谓“一比一”言辞证据终究可以归属于零证据。

戏剧化逆转的事实活脱脱验证了“孤证”不定案的规则。就在检察官倾向于批捕孙某时，被害人前往公安机关要求撤案，称孙某并没有强奸与逼迫她取钱。所以报假案是出于对孙某当晚打骂的报复并希望借此摆脱孙某纠缠。关于被捆绑双手、刺字、取钱，被害人称均为自愿，手包也是她让男拿着的。一切都印证了孙某的辩解。检察官错愕之余，首先想到的是被害人是否遭受了威胁、求情或其他因素，迫使其撤案？被害人称没有受到任何外界干扰，愿意承担报涉嫌触犯“诬告陷害罪”的法律后果。

四、同案犯口供分情形选择审慎采用

刑事案件中的同案犯供述有时具有较高的证明价值，唯其彼此有刑法上的利害关系，或常常相互推诿，或存在案前案后串供危险，虚假性大，偏复杂，所以历来被立法和学界防范。在仅有被告人供述和同案犯供述的情形中，同案犯口供证据归属种类很关键。如果同属于被告人供述，则必须补强，如果属于证人证言性质，属于两种独立证据种类，可以定案。

对于证言之考察，一般从两方面进行，一是证人名声和品行，以判断其诚实可靠性。西方传统理论一般认为，具有前科犯罪记录之人，破坏法律，道德水平不值得信任。同案犯为涉罪之人，诚实性遭受怀疑；二是实体利害关系。同案犯惨入虚伪陈述动因很大，难以信任。这正是大陆法系国家普遍要求证人为中立第三人的重要原因。关于同案犯口供的证据价值和证据地位，法律上并没有明确规定，学界对此有争议。司法实践中有三种意见。一种认为，同案被告人之间可以互为证人；第二种认为，即使同案被告人之间供述一致，也只能说明案情趋于可靠，但如无其他旁证印证，依然不能定案；第三种意见认为可以谨慎采纳。[4]

笔者认为，依据共同犯罪处罚体系，共同被告人之间常常区分为首犯、主犯、从犯、胁从犯、教唆犯、帮助犯等，量刑差异较大。如果赋予同案犯口供以独立证据地位，则被告人被定罪风险加大。我国修订后的《刑事诉讼法》第53条规定（1996年《刑事诉讼法》第46条），只有被告人供述，没有其他证据的，不能对被告人定罪处刑。其他证据，是指除被告人供述之外的其他7个证据种类中的任何证据。如果同案犯供述属于被告人供述，则仅有被告人有罪供述和同案犯指控的，只有被告人供述一种证据，不能对被告人定罪。如果同案犯供述具有证人证言地位，则仅有被告人有罪供述和同案犯指控，就可以依法对被告人定罪量刑。对于前者，如果给予同案犯法定独立证据的地位，一旦警方刑讯逼供或指供，冤假错案将难以避免。可以预测，在警方破案压力持续上升的情况下，在“命案必破”的思维下，被告人的命运堪忧。由于蕴含极大的风险，所以一般需要口供补强。但一概排除同案犯口供也有以偏概全之嫌。在有些隐蔽犯罪，证据收集很困难的案件类型中，一味排斥同案犯口供，不利于打击犯罪。同案犯口供的证据地位，应当依据同案犯之间的关系予以甄别，区别对待，不宜一概否定。

---

〔4〕 李剑、陈轶群：“论同案人口供价值的程序保障”，载《魅力中国》2011年7月。

最高人民法院法院就此秉承了谨慎采信同案犯供述的精神。2000 年 4 月，为打击日益猖獗、取证困难的毒品犯罪，最高人民法院在《全国法院审理毒品犯罪案件工作座谈会纪要》中指出：在处理毒品、毒资等证据已不存在或被告人翻供等毒品案件时，当被告人的口供与同案其他被告人供述吻合，并且完全排斥诱供、逼供、串供等情形，被告人的口供与同案被告人的供述才可以作为定案的证据。但此情形在判处死刑立即执行时要特别慎重。由此可见，最高人民法院并未一概排除同案犯口供的证据能力和证明力，而是在确保来源合法的情形下，仅有被告人供述和同案犯口供印证的话，对被告人可以定罪量刑，此时，同案犯口供被作为证人证言采用。

案例二分析：

从定罪证据分析，在前两次讯问中，三被告均认罪，被害人与被告人言辞证据之间、被告人供述彼此之间达到相互印证，事实清楚。但被告一、被告二翻供后，证据链条被打断，只有被害人陈述与被告三供述能够印证和构建案件事实。如果不能排除刑讯逼供，也不考虑被告三的同案犯口供可以成为单独的证据，那么仅有被害人陈述一种证据，对三被告显然不能定罪，被告人一、二属于孤证不能定罪，被告三未实施强奸，不够罪。但如果被告三的供述可以作为独立证据的话，被害人指控加上被告三指控，成为两种独立证据，加之被告一和被告二之前的有罪供述与被害人陈述相一致，对于被告一、被告二可以定罪。

对于被告人的庭前供述反复和翻供的情况，最高人民法院的司法解释 84 条第 7 款规定，被告人必须对此有合理说明，如果其辩解与全案证据矛盾，但庭前供述与其他证据相互印证的，可以采信其庭前供述。对被告人的翻供结合其他证据予以审定。

五、非中立证人矛盾言辞证据补强

我国三大诉讼法均规定，证人为了解案情的中立第三人，之所以将证人证言与当事人言辞证据分别规定为不同的证据种类，正是因为他们与案件的处理结果有本质的差异。证人为案外人，案件处理结果与其无关，其与被害人、被告人双方也没有任何利益和情感纠葛，做虚伪陈述的动因远远低于后者，如果排除贿买、胁迫等人为因素影响，在双方当事人各执一词时，证人证言值得更多信赖。

但很多案件中，当事人以外的证人并非是完全中立第三人，而是属于被害人或被告人各自方的亲友，或本身就是冲突参与人。比如群体纠纷中，双方均为三人以上，其中二人发生冲突，被害人被打伤，打群架最为典型。此类案件证据常常表现为被害人、被告人双方言辞矛盾，各方的证人证言矛盾，各自偏向自己，指控对方。

案例三样本分析：

犯罪人的主观心态是证明难题。主观故意、过失或是意外，都需要通过外部关系和行为进行分析。本案伤害发生在高危风险体育运动中。众所周知，运动过程中的冲突和身体碰撞在所难免，每一个参与运动的人对此都应该有心理预知并积极防御，减少运动伤害。但是否运动中的伤害都可归结为意外或风险？是否存在借运动风险之机故意伤害情形？答案是肯定的，而且情形日益严重。在百度输入词条“竞技运动中的故意伤害”，搜索结果为 539 000 条，网刊“广州恒大足球队与日本浦和红宝石亚冠比赛过程中，恒大球员黄博文遭对方报复飞踢，痛苦倒地。”日方球员的行为在一片声讨中被指为故意伤害。由于运动本身蕴含的高风险，在运动中即使故意伤害，其主观故意也很难证明。像泰森那样当众撕咬对手耳朵的明显故意伤害很少见，多数报复性运动伤害都是隐性的，以意外解释，通常以行政处罚或民事侵权解决。

本案中，是故意伤害还是意外伤害，当事人双方争执难解。如果被告方同伴没有踢被害人一脚的情节，被害方很难坚持刑事诉讼。被害人方两名证人与被害人是同学，被告方两名证人与被告为球友，经常在一起打球。当天下午两组人已经作为对手打球2小时左右，这期间有共同的情绪交流，易于形成情感共同体。因此，关于踢人情节，双方所陈述事实相反并各自有利于双方也在意料中。从报案时间看，被害方证人在案发后立即报案，双方就踢人事实的细节描述彼此印证。犯罪嫌疑人方证人证言于2个月后做出，时间间隔长，而且涉及刑事责任，踢人还可能涉及证人，他们有避重就轻的本能心理。尽管被害人方证言更加符合情理，但即便踢人事实可以固定，如果不能证明彼此间有恶意串通，也难以证明被告人的主观故意，但却可以向被害人解释，消除其疑问防止缠讼。

关于非中立证人证言，最高人民法院《关于适用〈中华人民共和国刑事诉讼法〉的解释》第109条第2款规定：与被告人有亲属关系或者其他密切关系的证人所作的有利被告人的证言，或者与被告人有利害冲突的证人所作的不利被告人的证言，应当审慎使用，要有其他证据印证时，方予以采信。2002年，最高人民法院颁布的《民事诉讼证据规则》第77条也有类似规定。非中立证人证言证明力小于中立证人，需要补强，判断证人证言时要注意证人与当事人之间关系。

六、结　语

矛盾言辞的判断审查需要考虑三个方面：其一，孤证不定案。仅有被害人与被告人矛盾言辞证据时，即便一方的陈述更合乎情理，但相反的情况总有可能存在，孤证定案风险甚高，远远不符合证据要求。即便被告人认罪，也需要特别慎重，如果没有其他证据，一旦被告人翻供，则形成孤证，难以定罪，因此应当有补强证据；其二，案件主要证据为被告人及其同案犯供述时，需要仔细审视被告人与同案犯之间的关系、他们在犯罪中的地位，通常实体共犯比牵连共犯（如销赃、窝藏等）证言在证言评估上更需谨慎。同案犯之间供述在满足排除非法取证、三人以上一致、细节可信的状态下可以采纳；其三，证人地位审查，非中立证人证言证明力低，如果没有补强，不宜认定。

刑事法官庭外调查活动的初步研究

褚福民 *

一、问题的提出

刑事法官的证据调查活动包括庭审中的证据调查和庭外证据调查两类。[1] 其中，法官庭外调查活动对证明责任的分配、诉讼构造的转变等问题具有显著影响，因此备受学界和立法、司法实务界的关注。目前，学界对于法官进行庭外调查活动的正当性存在较大争议，部分学者对此持否定态度。[2] 然而，我国立法中对法官的庭外调查活动作出了授权性规范，2012 年《刑事诉讼法》第 191 条延续了 1996 年《刑事诉讼法》中对庭外调查权的规定，“法庭审理过程中，合议庭对证据有疑问的，可以宣布休庭，对证据进行调查核实。人民法院调查核实证据，可以进行勘验、检查、查封、扣押、鉴定和查询、冻结。”[3] 司法实践中，虽然法官对于庭外调查活动的讨论不多，但是实际运用并不少见。如此看来，学界的观点与立法、司法实务界的观点存在很大的差异。那么，法官的庭外调查活动在我国呈现为何种形态，法官进行庭外调查活动的原因何在，应当如何进行理论解读，其未来前景如何？针对这些问题，本文拟展开描述、解释和分析。

首先，我们来分析一个司法实践中的案例。

1997 年 3 月 18 日，湖南省永州中院公开审理王永东故意杀人案。在庭审前，主审法官审查案卷后发现，王永东在公安预审阶段就开始翻供，称其未犯罪，原来所作的三次有罪供述都是在刑侦人员对其刑讯逼供、诱供的情况下作出的。为慎重起见，主审法官组织案发当天与唐勇（同案犯，在侦查阶段已自杀）打过照面的村民胡某对王永东进行混合辨认。胡某指认王永东就是案发当天下午与唐勇一起到过九江村的那个男青年。庭审中，王永东推翻了自己之前的有罪供述，提出自己过去的交待都是在刑讯逼供、诱供的情况下作出的，起诉书中的证据均是建立在刑讯逼供基础之上的。但是，经合议庭评议，法庭当庭宣判王永东犯故意杀人罪，判处死刑、缓期二年执行，剥夺政治权利终身。王永东不服一审判决，以“没有作案，过去所作的供述是公安人员刑讯逼供所致”为由，向湖南省高级人民法院提起上诉。

案件移送到湖南省高院后，主审法官发现一审法院认定王永东作案的主要证据有

---

* 褚福民，法学博士，2011 司法文明协同创新中心、证据科学教育部重点实验室（中国政法大学）副教授。
本文为中国政法大学证据法学青年教师学术创新团队的阶段性成果。

〔1〕 本文讨论的对象是刑事法官的庭外调查活动。为行文的方便，后文不再一一标明刑事法官的庭外调查活动，而代之以法官的庭外调查活动或者庭外调查活动。

〔2〕 参见黄文：“法官庭外调查权的合理性质疑”，载《当代法学》2004 年第 2 期。

〔3〕 与 1996 年的规定相比，该规定仅增加了“查封”这一种庭外调查的方式，除此之外没有变化。

三个：一是村民胡某的辨认笔录，二是同案人唐勇的供述，三是王永东自己的供述。唐、王二人的口供与现场勘验结果几乎如出一辙，且相互印证。因此，如果口供的取得是合法的，那么王永东当然构成犯罪。但是，主审法官在审查案卷时发现，唐勇自缢身亡后，公安、检察机关的尸检报告记载：唐双侧前线至背部、双上骨、双下肢有分布不均、大小不等呈块状或条状或中空性的皮下瘀血区。用通俗的话说，唐死前可谓是遍体鳞伤，而唐在留置室是单独关押的。据此推论，唐受到过刑讯逼供。另外，王永东无论是在一审时，还是在上诉时，均称被办案人员用手铐铐着双手吊在树上，进行逼供、诱供、指名问供；其二审辩护人还向高院提交了王的同监人犯所书的证实王进看守所时伤势严重，经过一个多月的治疗才痊愈的证言。为慎重起见，主审法官提审了王永东。他发现王的右眉弓、左手掌、双手腕及腿上均有明显的伤痕。随后，主审法官又调查了看守所医务人员及王的同监人犯，得以证实公安机关在审讯时对唐勇、王永东、江元胜有过刑讯逼供行为。更为关键的是，主审法官发现唐勇、王永东口供中存在明显漏洞。从这些漏洞可以看出，唐、王的有些口供是在诱供的前提下作出的，已经查证唐勇作了假供的地方，王永东也“作”了同样的供述。另外，主审法官对于胡某的辨认也提出了重大质疑。鉴于这种情况，本案二审合议庭形成一致意见，在与公安机关、检察机关进行沟通后，以“事实不清，证据不足”发回永州中院重审，后该案以永州市人民检察院决定撤回起诉终结。[4]

这是一起法官进行庭外调查的典型案例，从中我们能够大体了解法官开展庭外调查活动的实践做法。关于庭外调查活动的对象，本案中法官的庭外调查活动是针对刑讯逼供这一程序性争议，一、二审法官为了查明侦查人员是否对被告人实施过刑讯逼供，进行了庭外调查活动。当然，法官针对刑讯逼供问题进行庭外调查活动，最终是要查明被告人的口供是否真实，从而确保准确认定案件事实，防止出现冤假错案。

在适用条件方面，本案的一、二审法官均是在经过阅卷认为可能存在刑讯逼供，对被告人口供的真实性存在疑问时，进行庭外调查活动。例如，一审法官发现，“王永东在公安预审阶段时就开始翻供，称其未犯罪，原来所作的三次有罪供述都是在刑侦人员对其刑讯逼供、诱供的情况下作出的”，法官据此对被告人供述是否真实进行调查。二审法官认为，同案被告人的尸检报告显示其受到过刑讯逼供，王永东本人多次提出受到逼供、诱供，且有同监舍犯人的证言，在对刑讯逼供存在重大疑问的情况下，法官开展庭外调查活动。可见，该案中启动庭外调查活动的条件与立法中的要求基本一致，均是在“合议庭对证据有疑问时”进行庭外调查活动。

为确定被告人是否曾经受到过刑讯逼供，其口供是否真实，本案中一审法官安排目击证人进行辨认，通过目击证人的辨认活动，证明被告人在案发当天曾经在九江村出现，以此推翻被告人否认实施犯罪行为的辩解。在二审中，主审法官为了查明是否存在刑讯逼供，采取了讯问、调查等方式，提审了被告人，并调查看守所的医务人员及王永东同监舍犯人，通过他们的证言查明被告人是否受到过刑讯逼供。可见，本案中法官进行庭外调查活动时，采取了辨认、讯问被告人、调查证人等方式。根据1996年《刑事诉讼法》规定，庭外调查活动只能采取勘验、检查、扣押、鉴定和查询、冻

---

〔4〕 参见文裴：“刑讯逼供的惨痛代价”，载《南方周末》1998年11月27日。

结这6种方式，除此之外的其他方式均是违法的。显然，该案中法官采取的调查方式已经超出了法律规定范围。

在调查程序方面，该案中一审、二审法官均是在阅卷后自行启动庭外调查活动，虽然被告人提出自己受到了刑讯逼供，但是报道中并未提及被告人提出进行庭外调查活动的申请；而且，该案中的两审法官均是在开庭审理之前即进行庭外调查活动，在对刑讯逼供问题进行庭外调查之后，一审法官开庭审理，二审法官直接作出裁定。从报道来看，本案中一、二审法官应当是单独进行庭外调查活动，控辩双方并未参与其中；在实施庭外调查活动时，无论是辨认，还是讯问被告人、询问证人，均是法官亲自实施，由此可以推断出，相关的证据也是由法官亲自提取。关于庭外调查所得证据的使用，根据报道中二审法官对一审判决认定证据的分析，一审法官庭外调查所得的辨认证据被认定为定案根据，但其是否经过庭审质证，报道中没有介绍；二审法官庭外调查所得的证据同样成为其作出裁定的依据，在二审不开庭的情况下，控辩双方应该没有机会进行质证。

从法官庭外调查活动的运行来说，该案例能够大体反映司法实践中的运作现状。当然，这仅是法官进行庭外调查的部分情况。例如，从调查对象的角度来说，法官的庭外调查活动还可能针对定罪问题和量刑问题，刑事诉讼法中对此没有限制，而且针对量刑问题的庭外调查活动还有法律解释中的明确授权。[5] 司法实践中，当涉及罪与非罪的关键证据存在疑问时，或者对于被告人量刑问题的证据存在争议时，法官在特定情况下也会进行庭外调查活动。即使在由最高人民法院复核死刑的案件中，当影响定罪量刑的关键证据出现疑问时，法官为了确保复核死刑裁判的准确性，也会进行庭外调查活动。[6]

另外，该案例只是体现了案件审理时的庭外调查活动规则，近些年来关于该问题又有了最新进展。例如，在1996年最高人民法院《关于执行〈中华人民共和国刑事诉讼法〉若干问题的解释》中规定，“证据必须经过当庭出示、辨认、质证等法庭调查程序查证属实，否则不能作为定案的根据”，但是对庭外调查所得证据的使用问题并无专门规范，本案中二审法官未经质证即将庭外调查所得证据作为定案根据。2010年，最高人民法院等共同出台的《关于办理死刑案件审查判断证据若干问题的规定》中对该问题作出了明确规范。“人民检察院、辩护人补充的和法庭庭外调查核实取得的证据，法庭可以庭外征求出庭检察人员、辩护人的意见。双方意见不一致，有一方要求人民法院开庭进行调查的，人民法院应当开庭。”可见，对于庭外调查所得证据的使用，该法律解释确立了两步式的审查方式：其一，在庭外征求控辩双方的意见；其二，如果控辩双方无意见，可以将该证据直接作为定案的根据；如果控辩一方或者双方有异议，要求法院开庭调查的，法院应当开庭审查、质证。这意味着，控辩双方的态度决定了法官庭外调查证据的审查和采信，这对于庭外调查活动具有一定的约束作用。

---

〔5〕 最高人民法院、最高人民检察院、公安部、国家安全部、司法部颁布的《关于规范量刑程序若干问题的意见（试行）》第12条，对量刑问题的庭外调查活动做出了明确规定，“在法庭审理过程中，审判人员对量刑证据有疑问的，可以宣布休庭，对证据进行调查核实，必要时也可以要求人民检察院补充调查核实。……”

〔6〕 关于死刑复核程序中的庭外调查活动，参见陈虹伟、焦红艳：“死刑复核：对生命的慎重无止境”，载《法制日报》2007年3月18日。

对于法官庭外调查活动中证据的提取问题，2012 年最高人民法院发布的《关于适用〈中华人民共和国刑事诉讼法〉的解释》中进行了调整，“人民法院调查核实证据时，发现对定罪量刑有重大影响的新的证据材料的，应当告知检察人员、辩护人、自诉人及其法定代理人。必要时，也可以直接提取，并及时通知检察人员、辩护人、自诉人及其法定代理人查阅、摘抄、复制”。这就对法官自行提取的证据范围进行了规范，如果仅核实了证据，或者发现对于定罪量刑影响不大的新证据材料，法官可以自行提取；如果发现对定罪量刑有重大影响的新证据材料，原则上应当告知控辩双方进行提取。该规定实际上对法官提取新证据的权力进行了限制，当庭外调查中发现重要的新证据时，一般应当由控辩中的一方进行提取，以保障法官的中立地位。当然，“必要时”的存在还是为法官自由裁量权的行使提供了较大的空间。

综合以上分析，笔者认为我国刑事法官进行庭外调查活动拥有较大的自由裁量权，体现在多个方面。例如，在法官庭外调查活动的启动方面，虽然法律中规定了法院依职权启动和依当事人申请启动两种方式，但是当事人启动庭外调查活动的申请是否能够发挥作用，最终要取决于法官的裁量，因为法律中只是赋予当事人启动庭外调查活动的申请权，对法官没有约束力。对于法官进行庭外调查活动时的控辩双方在场问题，最高人民法院在 1996 年《关于执行〈中华人民共和国刑事诉讼法〉若干问题的解释》第 54 条规定，“必要时，可以通知检察人员、辩护人到场。”此后的规则基本没有变化，这就将法官进行庭外调查时控辩双方能否在场的决定权赋予了法官，只有在法官通知时，控辩双方才可能到场。在上述案例中，法官进行庭外调查活动中均无控辩双方在场，这反映出司法实践中的通常做法，法官基本上不会通知辩方到场，在特定情况下或许会通知检察机关参与庭外调查，这完全取决于法官的自由判断。[7] 再如，对于法官庭外调查活动中证据的提取，虽然 2012 年最高法院的司法解释中对其进行了规制，但是其中“对定罪量刑有重大影响”、“必要时”等表述较为模糊，实际上仍然将决定权交由法院行使。

尽管法律中授予法官很大自由裁量权，对法官的约束性规则不多，但是法律中仅有的约束规则还会经常被违反。例如，对于法官庭外调查的方式，法律中以列举的方式作出了明确的规定，但是在上述案例中，一审法官采用辨认的方式进行庭外调查，二审法官使用了讯问被告人、询问证人等方式，明显超出了法律规定的 6 种庭外调查方式。对于法官开展庭外调查活动的时间，1996 年《刑事诉讼法》中明确废除了开庭前的庭外调查活动，然而在上述案例中，一、二审法官实施的庭外调查活动均是在庭审前，这显然违反了法律的规定。

另外还要明确，庭外调查所得的证据对法官的裁判影响较大，甚至在某种程度上对于法官心证的形成起到决定性作用。正如上述案例分析所展示的，法官在司法实践中会根据审判的需要主动开展庭外调查活动，甚至违反法律规定进行庭外调查，这显示出法官对庭外调查活动的重视；在所得证据的使用方面，法官庭外调查的证据往往会作为定案的根据，甚至在与案件现有证据发生矛盾时，法官会更加相信自己调查所

---

〔7〕 笔者在对法官进行培训的课堂上，对该问题进行调查，多数法官认为或者自己单独调查，或者与检察官一起进行庭外调查，基本不会通知律师到场。

得的证据，它们对于法官形成心证具有至关重要的作用。例如，在上述案例中，无论是一审法官组织的辨认，还是二审法官进行的调查证人活动，均成为法官裁判的基础，它们对于解决控辩双方关于刑讯逼供的争议提供了证据基础；尽管在二审中，侦查人员、公诉人坚持其控诉主张，并针对案件中的疑点进行过补充侦查，但是二审法官经过庭外调查活动已经对刑讯逼供问题形成心证，控诉方提供的后续证据无法动摇法官的内心确信。〔8〕

二、法官为何进行庭外调查活动?

通过以上分析可以发现，在法官对庭外调查活动拥有自由裁量权的情况下，其对开展庭外调查活动持比较积极的态度，甚至会违反法律规定的各种限制进行庭外调查活动，其原因何在？笔者认为需从以下三方面进行解释。

第一，我国法官积极开展庭外调查活动，是法官自身定位的内在要求。

纵观世界各国的刑事诉讼理论和制度设计，对于法官的定位各不相同。在英美法系国家，法官主要依据证据规则，通过对诉讼律师的证明活动设立限制而控制审判过程，以实现结果的合理性、社会和道德价值及其效率，〔9〕法官被定位为维护审判秩序的消极中立裁判者；而在大陆法系国家，刑事审判法官不仅是裁判者，还常常被赋予事实发现者的角色和地位，因此他们在刑事诉讼中会进行积极的事实发现活动，其审理和裁判的范围也会超出控辩双方的争论范围。〔10〕在这种背景下，法官的庭外调查活动具有不同的存在空间。在英美法系国家，法官几乎不会进行庭外调查活动〔11〕；而大陆法系的法官担负着查明事实真相的责任，因此往往具有较大的庭外调查空间。〔12〕

再来看我国的规定。在 1996 年《刑事诉讼法》修改之前，我国的刑事诉讼制度被划归为职权主义的诉讼模式，法官在诉讼过程中处于积极调查者的地位，其庭外调查活动受到的限制很少；1996 年《刑事诉讼法》修改之后，我国的刑事审判方式从职权主义向当事人主义诉讼模式转变，法律赋予控辩双方在庭审中更多的程序性权利，同时限制法官在庭审中的审判职权，意图将法官从积极的事实调查者向消极的中立裁判者转变，这种背景下的法官庭外调查活动必然会受到限制。

然而，仅仅立法调整无法转变法官的身份定位，审判方式改革并未触及一些深层次的问题。其中，实体真实探知主义的刑事司法传统仍然是确定法官在刑事诉讼中实

〔8〕 参见文裴："刑讯逼供的惨痛代价"，载《南方周末》1998 年 11 月 27 日。

〔9〕 参见［美］罗纳德·J. 艾伦、理查德·B. 库恩斯、埃莉诺·斯威夫特：《证据法：文本、问题和案例》（第三版），张保生、王进喜、赵滢译，高等教育出版社 2006 年版，第 101 页。

〔10〕 如有的研究者分析了调查原则或者澄清义务，其法理基础在于发现实体真实。参见林钰雄：《刑事诉讼法》（上册），中国人民大学出版社 2005 年版，第 50 页。

〔11〕 参见陈如超：《刑事法官的证据调查权研究》，中国人民公安大学出版社 2011 年版，第 78 页。

〔12〕 例如，德国刑事诉讼法中有多个法条规定了法官的庭外调查活动。第 165 条规定：在延误就有危险的时候，如果不能与检察官取得联系，法官也可以无检察院申请实施必要的调查行为。第 166 条（一）规定：被法官讯问时，被指控人申请收集对他有利的一定证据，如果证据有丧失之虞，或者收集证据能使被指控人得以释放的，法官应当收集他认为重要的证据。第 173 条（三）规定：为了作准备裁判，法院可以命令调查并且嘱托一名受托或者受命法官进行调查。第 244 条（二）规定：为了调查事实真相，法院应当依职权将证据调查延伸到所有的对于裁判具有意义的事实、证据上。参见李昌珂译：《德国刑事诉讼法典》，中国政法大学出版社 1995 年版，第 83、87、101 页。

质身份定位的主导因素。[13] 在这种诉讼传统中，发现事实真相是刑事诉讼活动的最终归宿，实事求是、有错必纠是该传统的基本要求，它们成为诉讼主体开展活动的主要目标，体现在刑事诉讼的各个方面。例如，在我国刑事诉讼中，审判人员、检察人员、侦查人员必须依照法定程序，收集能够证实犯罪嫌疑人、被告人有罪或者无罪、犯罪情节轻重的各种证据，必须保证一切与案件有关或者了解案情的公民，有提供证据的条件；在审查起诉和审判过程中，如果案件事实不清、证据不足，侦查机关、检察机关可以进行补充侦查。在这种背景下，法官在法庭审判中有权进行庭外调查活动，即使在死刑复核程序中，法官为查明事实真相仍然有权开展庭外调查活动。

除了实体真实探知主义司法传统的影响，我国一直以来对于法官积极调查者的身份定位，也是法官积极开展庭外调查活动的重要原因。从历史发展来看，新中国成立之前的刑事诉讼制度采职权主义诉讼模式，强调法官在刑事诉讼中的积极调查者身份。在新中国的刑事诉讼发展史中，也一直强调法官的积极调查者角色，对于马锡五审判方式的重视和推广是最典型的表现。该审判方式强调法官必须深入群众，进行调查研究；查明案件的基本事实后，法官到案件发生地进行开庭审判；审判过程应尽量简化诉讼手续，方便人民群众。直到今日，该审判方式依然被最高人民法院所强调，[14] 由此可见我国对于法官定位的历史传统一直没有变化。在这种法官的身份定位中，明确要求法官深入调查研究，而法官积极进行庭外调查活动是其必然表现。

实体真实探知主义的刑事司法传统，要求法官使用包括庭外调查活动在内的各种方式发现事实真相，防止错误认定案件事实；而我国法官一直以来所具有的积极介入诉讼、调查案件事实的定位，则为法官积极进行庭外调查活动奠定了前提。在这种法官身份定位的背景下，立法为法官庭外调查活动提供广阔的自由裁量空间，司法实践中法官任意开展庭外调查活动，就具有了合理的解释。

第二，我国法官积极开展庭外调查活动，是为了避免可能受到的追究而作出的“趋利避害”式选择。

实体真实探知主义的刑事司法传统，积极主动调查事实的身份定位，为法官进行庭外调查活动提供了制度前提，在这种背景下法官有可能进行庭外调查活动。然而，需要进一步讨论的问题是，法官为何必然要进行庭外调查活动？众所周知，目前法院审判案件的压力非常大，特别是在一些案件量大的地区，一名法官每年审判几百件案件的情况并不少见。在办案压力如此巨大的情况下，法官为何仍然要拿出时间、精力进行庭外调查活动呢？

笔者认为，法官可能受到的外部追究，是其进行庭外调查活动的重要推动力。其中，法官考评机制中的错案追究制度，对法官积极进行庭外调查活动具有最为直接的

---

〔13〕 关于实体真实探知主义的详细论述，参加陈瑞华：“中国刑事司法的三个传统”，载《社会科学战线》2007年第4期。

〔14〕 例如，“案结事了”等要求不断在法院系统内被提出，参见陈光中、陈学权：“中国语境下的刑事证明责任理论”，载《法制与社会发展》2010年第2期。

影响,[15] 这种对法官错误认定案件事实的惩戒机制，将法官推到了必须进行庭外调查，以避免错案、避免受到责任追究的境地。尽管学界和司法实务界对于错案本身的理解有很多质疑，但是如果法官错误认定案件事实，例如，将无罪之人认定为有罪的罪犯，或者遗漏了被告人的立功情节而错误核准死刑，或者将刑讯逼供得来的虚假口供作为定案的根据，最终错误认定案件事实，或者在案件事实不清、证据不足的情况直接作出有罪裁判，事后被发现确实出现了“错案”，则极有可能受到追究。

一旦法官审理的案件被认定为“错案”，法院内部的考核机制往往带来“一票否决制”的后果。所谓“一票否决制”，是指发生“错案”后，法院即对法官的全部工作予以否定。各地法院往往将错案责任与法官的工资、职务、升迁直接挂钩，有的法院规定只要发生错案，就要扣发有关人员当月、当季或当年的奖金，有的法院甚至规定，错案带来一票否决，不得评先评优。[16] 更为严重的是，错案还会带来“连带责任制”。“连带责任制”是指个人发生的“错”，将导致对其部门工作的否定评价，部门发生的“错”将导致对其单位工作的否定评价。[17] 可想而知，这种将“错案”与法官、审判组织、法院的利益直接挂钩的业绩考评机制，迫使法官不敢在事实不清的情况下贸然作出裁判。而法官为了避免受到责任追究，必然要在作出裁判前尽可能地核实证据、查清案件事实，积极进行庭外调查活动也就成为了一种重要的选择。

在更为重大的案件中，如果由于证据问题被认定为“错案”，导致无罪的人被错误认定有罪，对于审理案件的法官可能带来更为严重的惩罚。例如，在前几年备受关注的赵作海案件中，当“被害人”赵振裳重新出现后，河南省高级人民法院迅速启动再审程序，宣告赵作海无罪。随后，当年审理赵作海案件的三名法官均被停职接受调查。[18] 该案中，赵作海在侦查阶段曾经受到过刑讯逼供，其在庭审过程中也提出自己受到刑讯逼供，但并未受到法官的重视，导致错案的发生。按照法官考核制度的逻辑，假设法官当年能够进行必要的庭外调查，核实清楚是否存在刑讯逼供，则该起错案可能被避免，法官也不会因此受到制裁。与此相对应，在前文分析的案例中，二审法官通过庭外调查活动查清了案件中是否存在刑讯逼供的证据疑问，并最终促使检察机关撤回起诉。从相关报道中可以推测，案件的主审法官进行庭外调查活动，在避免错案的同时，也避免了个人可能受到的不利追究。由此可以看出，司法实践中对于法官的不利追究，是促使法官进行庭外调查活动的重要原因。

第三，我国法官积极开展庭外调查活动，是控辩双方在诉讼中无法提供必要证据，以及控辩双方力量悬殊的无奈选择。

从证明案件事实的角度来说，如果诉讼中的控辩双方或者一方能够提供确实、充

---

〔15〕 虽然错案追究制本身的概念非常模糊，受到很多非议，但是该制度对于法官进行庭外调查活动的影响是客观存在的。本文不再详细分析错案追究制度的内涵，而是在最为狭义的角度理解该概念，即法官错误地认定案件事实，由此带来的不利后果。

〔16〕 参见黄欣:《中国法院绩效考核制度及其对刑事诉讼之影响》，上海交通大学 2010 年硕士学位论文，第 8 页；管丽琴:《现行法官考核制度的理性考量》，苏州大学 2008 年硕士学位论文，第 14 页。

〔17〕 参见黄欣:《中国法院绩效考核制度及其对刑事诉讼之影响》，上海交通大学 2010 年硕士学位论文，第 8 页。

〔18〕 参见“审理‘赵作海案’的三名法官被停职”，http://news.xinhuanet.com/legal/2010-05/14/c_12102215.htm，最后访问日期：2013 年 1 月 20 日。

分的证据证明案件事实，法官没有必要进行庭外调查活动。然而，我国司法实践中控辩双方均存在无法提供确实、充分证据的问题，这导致法官不得不开展庭外调查活动。也就是说，法官进行庭外调查活动的一个重要前提，是控辩双方或者一方没有提供处理定罪、量刑或者程序性争议的必要证据。

从控方角度来说，在我国司法实践中，公诉人对于定罪证据往往比较关注，相关的证据材料也比较充足。然而，由于检察官无法参加侦查活动，他们对于侦查机关搜集证据的活动缺乏足够的制约手段。虽然按照刑事诉讼法的规定，侦查机关搜集的证据达不到确实、充分的标准，检察机关可以将案件退回补充侦查；侦查机关补充所得的证据达不到公诉标准，检察机关可以作出不起诉的决定。但是，在一些重大、特殊的案件中，在媒体关注、被害人申诉上访、政法委协调等外部压力下，即使案件证据不足还是有可能被检察机关起诉到法院，[19] 这种情况下法官要想准确认定案件事实、避免错判风险，往往也会选择进行庭外调查。

虽然提交到法官面前的定罪证据会出现不确实、不充分的问题，但是与涉及量刑、程序性争议事项的证据相比，定罪证据通常还是比较完备的，至少从公诉人的角度来说是比较重视的。关于量刑证据，在 2010 年颁布《关于规范量刑程序若干问题的意见（试行）》之前，公诉机关对其往往不太关注，因为能够成功定罪是公诉机关最关心的问题，而量刑证据的收集往往没有受到足够的重视；在该意见中，对侦查机关、公诉机关搜集、移送量刑证据等问题作出了规范，这有利于量刑程序中法官对于证据的审查。尽管如此，与定罪证据相比，量刑证据的受重视程度仍然会低一些，特别是对于被告人有利的从轻量刑证据，要求处于控方的侦查人员、检察人员收集、提供，可以预见会存在很大的障碍。在这种情况下，量刑程序中的证据很可能要由法官进行庭外调查。例如，在前文提到的死刑复核案件中，即使已经到了死刑复核阶段，仍然存在关于量刑问题的不同意见，而相关证据在案卷中并不完备，最高人民法院的法官为了准确作出死刑复核裁判，只能选择到案发现场进行庭外调查。

对于程序性争议，诉讼中往往以诉讼一方提出异议为审查前提，因此法官通常不会提前关注，相关证据的搜集情况很可能不充分。当庭审中控辩双方对于程序性事项发生争议时，经常会面临证据不足的问题，而控辩双方能否提供解决争议的必要证据，往往也存在疑问，最终调查证据的责任很可能落到法官身上。例如，对于刑讯逼供这种程序性争议，虽然刑事诉讼法中规定了录音录像等保全证据的规则，以及警察出庭作证的制度，但是其在庭审中能否发挥作用，受到很多质疑，法官进行庭外调查活动还会是其重要选择。

从辩护方的角度来说，在庭审中可能针对定罪、量刑、程序性事项提出自己的主张，但是其搜集证据的能力不足。在我国刑事司法实践中，被告人在审判前往往处于被羁押状态，根本无法搜集证据，相反其口供往往成为指控证据。作为辩护的主体，辩护人是提出辩护意见、搜集辩方证据的主要人员。然而，辩护人在刑事诉讼中搜集证据的活动受到各种限制，其中最致命的是控诉方的任意追诉，《刑法》第 306 条的规

---

〔19〕 关于法官审判中面临的外部压力，可以参见沈德咏："我们应当如何防范冤假错案"，载《人民法院报》2013 年 5 月 6 日，第 2 版。

定导致律师不敢调查取证。为规避风险，辩护律师往往在庭审中申请法院调取侦查机关、检察机关已经取得的、对辩护有利的证据，或者申请法院调取新证据，这就把调查取证的“球”又踢给了法院，而法院在必要时只能选择庭外调查。

另外，控辩双方在调查取证能力上的悬殊差异，也是法官进行庭外调查的重要原因。按照刑事诉讼的基本要求，控辩双方在诉讼过程中的对抗应当以“平等武装”为前提，只有在控辩双方具有平等对抗能力的前提下进行审判活动，才被视为公正审判。而在我国刑事诉讼中，控辩双方搜集证据的能力差距巨大。侦查机关利用国家行政机关的权力和资源开展刑事追诉活动，在搜集证据的能力上具有各种保障措施；而被告人即使再富有、辩护人即使再专业，与国家追诉机关相比仍然具有较大的差距，更不用说法律中对辩护律师的取证活动设置了各种限制条件，侦检部门在司法实践中任意追诉辩护律师的取证活动。这就对法官的庭外调查活动提出了要求，他应该通过自己的庭外调查弥补辩护方调查取证能力的不足，为实现控辩双方的平等对抗提供保障。

三、解读庭外调查活动的三个理论问题

从以上分析可知，法官的庭外调查在我国立法中被明文规定，在司法实践中得到运用；法官的身份定位、可能受到的追责压力，以及控辩双方无法提供必要证据的现实，使得法官进行庭外调查活动成为一种必然。与之相对，刑事诉讼法学界对法官进行庭外调查活动的正当性争议较大。有的研究者明确主张应废除法官的庭外调查制度，因为法官庭外调查活动的存在，混淆了侦查与审判的职能、侵害了被告人的合法权益、不利于查明案件的事实真相、有损法官的中立形象、违反了刑事诉讼中的举证责任规则、使法庭审理流于形式。[20] 而有些学者则支持该制度，认为法官进行庭外调查活动并不必然违背程序正义、控审分离、法官中立等原则。事实上，在一定条件下赋予法官受一定程序规制的庭外调查权，还是实现程序正义的特殊要求或实现法官实质中立的必要途径，[21] 法官的庭外调查活动与证明责任分配规则并不冲突。

那么，面对理论与实践中的矛盾与冲突，我们应当如何解读法官的庭外调查活动？其中有哪些理论问题值得反思？笔者认为，在解读该制度的存在逻辑时，需要分析三大理论问题。法官开展庭外调查活动是否为承担证明责任？开展庭外调查活动与维护被告人利益的关系应如何协调？法官庭外调查程序应如何设计？

第一，证明责任，还是查明活动？

支持抑或反对法官庭外调查活动的学者，一个核心争议点在于其性质，即法官进行庭外调查活动是否为承担证明责任的体现？有些研究者认为法官在刑事诉讼中进行庭外调查活动是承担证明责任的体现，[22] 而更多的研究者则主张法官并不承担证明责任。[23] 如何定位法官庭外调查活动的性质，如何分析其与证明责任的关系，是解读该制度和相关实践时绕不开的问题。

根据证据法的基本原理，证明责任与四方面问题紧密相连：特定的诉讼主张、举

---

〔20〕 参见黄文：“法官庭外调查权的合理性质疑”，载《当代法学》2004 年第 2 期。

〔21〕 参见卫跃宁、孙锐：“对法官庭外调查权取消论的质疑”，载《扬州大学学报（人文社会科学版）》2008 年第 4 期。

〔22〕 参见陈光中、陈学权：“中国语境下的刑事证明责任理论”，载《法制与社会发展》2010 年第 2 期。

〔23〕 参见陈如超：《刑事法官的证据调查权研究》，中国人民公安大学出版社 2011 年版，第 55 页。

证义务、论证待证事实的义务、败诉风险。[24] 具体来说，承担证明责任的主体应当提出一定的诉讼主张，为了证明该诉讼主张应提供证据、进行论证，如果其举证不能达到法定标准，需承担主张不能成立的败诉风险，只有符合上述条件的行为才是承担证明责任的行为。如果诉讼主体仅提供一些证据，但没有特定的诉讼主张，并不承担论证义务，更不负担败诉风险，那么该主体的活动不能被界定为承担证明责任的活动。

法官的庭外调查活动即是如此。虽然法官在刑事诉讼中进行庭外调查活动，可能会调取特定的证据供诉讼中使用，但是法官本身在诉讼中并无主张，作为裁判者的法官没有、也不会在诉讼中提出主张；如果法官庭外调查所得的证据无法证明特定案件事实，根本不存在承担证明不能的败诉风险。需要明确的是，法官没有实现庭外调查活动的目的，可能因错误认定案件事实受到法院内部考核等追究，这种不利后果与承担证明责任的败诉风险是两回事，不能混同。

既然法官进行庭外调查活动并非承担证明责任，那么对该行为应当如何定位呢？有学者已对此问题进行了深入的研究，并提出了具有解释力的理论：对法官在法庭上进行的证据调查活动，我们应将其解读为一种对司法证明过程的积极验证活动，而对于法官在法庭之外进行的调查核实证据活动，我们可以不将其视为司法证明活动，带有对司法证明的补充和替代性质。也就是说，法官所进行的调查核实活动，是在法庭上的司法证明活动无法进行下去的情况下进行的，这种真相探知活动本身并不是司法证明活动，而属于法官主动发现事实真相的查明活动。[25] 也有学者将此称为法官审判权以及审判权中所包含的事实查证权的一种表现。[26]

要区分承担证明责任与开展查明活动，应当首先明确证明和查明的差异。在刑事诉讼中，证明活动中的命题是已知的，其目的是对已知事实或者主张的真实性加以验证，因此带有回溯性；而查明的对象往往是未知的，是对未知事实和主张的积极发现活动，带有探知性。查明活动可以被界定为一种认识活动，而证明活动则是一种验证活动。[27] 在审判活动中，一般的审理活动应当被界定为证明活动，因为法官的工作是验证控辩双方对于诉讼主张的论证是否成立，这种证明活动中的证据已经被控辩双方提出，论证方式是一种回溯式的当庭验证；而法官在审判过程中的庭外调查活动，则是在控辩双方未提出必要证据，或者所提证据存在疑问的情况下，针对特定问题展开的搜集证据、探知事实的查明活动。例如，在前面的案例中，法官对被告人是否受到刑讯逼供存在疑问，而案卷中的材料无法提供必要的证据，一、二审法官因此在庭外进行辨认、询问证人等活动，是对未知事实的发现活动，属于查明活动的范畴。

第二，有利控方与有利辩方的庭外调查活动。

从行为性质来说，笔者认为法官进行庭外调查活动，是其实施的积极的事实发现活动，属于查明的范畴，并非承担证明责任。因此，对于法官庭外调查活动的理论解读，既不能以法官承担证明责任为由加以否定，也不能以承担证明责任是司法机关的责任为由论证其正当性。那么，如何评价法官的庭外调查活动？我们认为，是否影响

---

〔24〕 参见陈瑞华：《刑事证据法学》，北京大学出版社 2012 年版，第 223 页。

〔25〕 参见陈瑞华：《刑事证据法学》，北京大学出版社 2012 年版，第 242 页。

〔26〕 参见龙宗智：《刑事庭审制度研究》，中国政法大学出版社 2001 年版，第 383 页。

〔27〕 参见陈瑞华：《刑事证据法学》，北京大学出版社 2012 年版，第 203 页。

法官地位的中立性，如何维护程序正义，是法官庭外调查活动的争议焦点，也是重要的分析工具和标准。从诉讼原理来说，作为裁判者的法官进行庭外调查活动，必然会带来程序正当性的质疑。然而，法官地位的中立性与维护程序正义是否应有适用的范围？对此，笔者认为需要进行更细致的分析，由于庭外调查活动所涉诉讼主体的力量差异，对法官庭外调查活动的解读也应有所差异。

有些研究者提出，法官进行庭外调查活动，所得的证据应当对诉讼一方有利，因此法官进行庭外调查活动后无法在控辩双方之间保持中立，进而影响裁判的公正性和可接受性，庭外调查活动不具有正当性。笔者认为这是一种形式上的解读，其假设前提是控辩双方的实力是对等的。然而，如果控辩双方在诉讼中的实力不对等，法官通过庭外调查的方式为实力较弱的一方提供帮助，这实际上可以促进控辩双方的实质平等，那么法官的庭外调查活动是否具有了正当性呢？换个角度来说，在控辩双方的力量严重失衡的情况下，形式上的对等、法官完全中立裁判真的是司法公正的要求吗？

在我国，控辩双方在诉讼中的力量悬殊问题非常突出。正如前文所分析的，作为控诉一方的侦查机关、检察机关拥有国家的各种资源作为保障，即使被告人具有雄厚的经济实力，辩护律师具有丰富的职业经验和技巧，但是在庞大的国家机器面前仍然是微不足道的。在这种力量对比非常鲜明的现实情况下，如果一味地强调控辩双方的形式对等，只能带来对辩护一方明显不利的实质不对等。那么，国家的审判活动将毫无公正性可言，只能沦为弱肉强食的游戏。

在这种背景下，法官的庭外调查活动应当成为推动控辩双方实质对等的制度工具。具体来说，在诉讼过程中出现证据疑问时，如果该证据是有利于控诉方而不利于辩护方的，即能够证明被告人有罪或者罪重的证据，应当由控诉方承担证明责任、进行调查，这是无罪推定原则的基本要求，法官不应在庭外对此类证据进行调查。如果对被告人有利的证据存在疑问，能够证明被告人无罪或者罪轻的证据需要调查核实的，在特定情况下法院应当启动庭外调查活动进行取证。

例如，当被告人提出正当防卫等积极抗辩事由，或者提出量刑从轻的辩护意见，或者提出对自己有利的程序性主张时，法官在进行初步审核后，如果认为辩护方的主张有其合理性，即使没有达到法定的证明标准，法官也可以对待证事实进行必要的调查核实活动，而不应轻易以证明责任未达到法定标准为由，拒绝辩护方的诉讼请求。这种情况下，法官不应简单地坚持中立立场，而应秉持“平等武装”和“天平倾向弱者”的理念，对于被告方的证明活动实施积极的协助和干预，这也就是进行庭外调查活动的正当性空间。[28]

可见，为了实现诉讼中控辩双方的实质对等，法官的庭外调查活动在有利于被告人的情况下具有某种程度的正当性，而对于不利于被告人的证据，法官不应进行庭外调查。在前文所举的案例中，法官对刑讯逼供问题进行庭外调查，如果能够调取证据证明存在刑讯逼供，那么侦查阶段的被告人口供笔录要被排除，被告人是否构成犯罪需要重新审查，这对被告人而言是有利的。该案二审中，法官经过庭外调查最终没有排除存在刑讯逼供的可能性，将案件撤销原判、发回重审，该结果对于被告人来说非

〔28〕 参见陈瑞华：《刑事证据法学》，北京大学出版社2012年版，第242页。

常有利，那么此种庭外调查活动就具有了正当性。

然而，需要说明的是，本文所引用的案例表明法官的庭外调查活动对被告人有利，但是这并不代表司法实践中的情况都是这样。与此相反，我们认为司法实践中的普遍情况并不乐观。有学者总结，实践中，凡有利于证明犯罪、追诉犯罪的事项，法官的补充调查、补充举证就显得较为积极、主动；而凡是有利于辩护，尤其是涉及辩护方提出的某一程序性辩护的事项，法官的补充调查、补充举证就极为消极、被动。[29] 这种情况下，从诉讼主体力量差异的角度解读法官的庭外调查活动，对于进一步的规制将具有重要的指引意义。

第三，法官庭外调查活动的程序设计。

将法官的庭外调查活动定位为查明，为其存在奠定了理论基础；对于有利控方、有利辩方的庭外调查活动进行区分，能够为其正当性论证及未来的制度构建提供进一步的论据。那么，在分析法官庭外调查活动的基本理论后，庭外调查活动的程序应如何设计，是随之而来的问题，这对庭外调查活动的正当运作同样具有重大影响。

需要明确的是，前一部分从所涉利益主体的角度分析法官的庭外调查活动，提出所涉不同利益主体的法官庭外调查活动，在正当性方面存在区分；而本部分分析法官庭外调查活动的程序设计，对其正当运作同样具有影响，但两者是不同层面的问题。即使在对被告人有利的情况下，法官的庭外调查活动也必须遵守特定的程序规则，否则将难以保障其正当运作。正如前文分析的案例，法官对刑讯逼供是否存在问题进行庭外调查，这是对被告人有利的情况，因此从庭外调查活动类型的角度来说具有正当性。然而，上述报道中没有提到法官进行庭外调查时通知控辩双方到场，所得证据在二审程序中没有经过质证即作为定案根据，这显然违反了相关程序规则，影响了庭外调查活动的正当性。

那么，法官庭外调查活动的程序规则应当如何设计？我国立法中的相关规则是否完善？根据前文的分析，我国立法中对法官庭外调查活动的程序规则主要包括两方面内容：一是调查程序，二是所得证据的使用程序。在调查程序中，法律中对程序启动[30]、在场制度和证据提取问题作出了规范。法官可以依职权启动，或者根据当事人的申请启动庭外调查活动；在调查过程中，检察人员、辩护人在必要时可以在场；对于庭外调查所得新证据的调取，法律中规定了控辩双方调取和法官调取两种方式。在所得证据的使用程序中，法律规定了两步式的审查要求：庭外征求意见与当庭质证。

对于法官庭外调查活动程序规则的完善，控辩双方参与调查活动的“庭外质证式”改造方案，得到了学界和司法实务界的支持，[31] 这一点也大体获得了立法的认可。然而，对于维护法官庭外调查活动的正当性而言，笔者认为有两个核心问题亟需完善。

---

〔29〕 参见陈瑞华：《问题与主义之间》，中国人民大学出版社2003年版，第444页。

〔30〕 最高人民法院《关于执行〈中华人民共和国刑事诉讼法〉若干问题的解释》第158条中规定，“人民法院向人民检察院调取需要调查核实的证据材料，或者根据辩护人、被告人的申请，向人民检察院调取在侦查、审查起诉中收集的有关被告人无罪和罪轻的证据材料，应当通知人民检察院在收到调取证据材料决定书后3日内移交。”虽然该条款没有明确说明是针对庭外调查问题，但从中可以解读出法官庭外调查活动启动的两种方式：一是由法院主动调查，二是根据诉讼当事人的申请调查。

〔31〕 参见张军、姜伟、田文昌：《刑事诉讼：控辩审三人谈》，法律出版社2001年版，第325页；黄文：“法官庭外调查权的合理性质疑”，载《当代法学》2004年第2期。

第一，法官自由裁量权的制约。前文分析立法规定时曾经提出，有关法官庭外调查的规则赋予法官太大的自由裁量权，导致法官可以任意进行选择。例如，法官庭外调查活动的在场制度中，“必要时”的表述实际上授权法官决定控辩双方能否在场；在证据调取时，法官有权决定调取的主体，当事人在此过程中完全处于被动状态；对于所得证据的使用，法律中授权法官“可以”庭外征求意见，这种模糊的表述为自由裁量权的行使提供了空间。可见，对于庭外调查活动的程序问题，立法中授予法官极大的自由裁量权，控辩双方根本无法有效约束，由此会带来程序的正当性质疑。如何有效限制法官的自由裁量权，将是程序设计中必须解决的一个课题。

第二，权利受到侵犯的救济问题。我国立法中对于庭外调查活动的程序规范，采取了正面表述的方式，而对于控辩双方的权利受到侵犯后如何救济的问题，法律中没有规定。例如，控辩双方在诉讼过程中申请法官庭外调查证据，如果法官没有进行调查，对其申请没有回应，法律中是否应当有救济措施？在法官独自进行庭外调查的情况下，控辩双方事后认为自己应当在场，但未接到法官的通知，如此情况下的救济措施也没有规定。对于庭外调查所得的证据，法官没有在庭外征询控辩双方的意见，也没有经过庭审质证即作为定案根据，控辩双方依然缺乏救济途径。可见，控辩双方的权利救济问题没有得到法律规定，这是庭外调查活动程序规则中的重大缺陷。

综合以上分析，在法官庭外调查活动的程序设计方面，立法中应当重点关注两大理论问题：法官自由裁量权的制约、权利受到侵犯的救济。在具体制度设计方面，通过加强控辩双方的权利制约法官的自由裁量权，通过完善程序性制裁手段和裁判机制保障控辩双方的权利，尤其是辩方的权利，将是基本的完善路径。

四、法官庭外调查活动的未来

以上对法官庭外调查活动的存在原因和理论解读进行了分析。展望未来，笔者认为上述原因分析与理论解读对于法官庭外调查活动的发展将具有决定性的影响。

首先，法官庭外调查活动的性质界定是决定其未来发展的基础性问题。通过前文论述，笔者认为法官庭外调查活动的性质，应当界定为查明活动，是积极进行事实发现活动的一种表现形式。在现代刑事司法理论中，在无罪推定原则的约束下，法官不承担证明责任，只有控辩双方才是承担证明责任的主体，这一点已经成为多数人的共识。在这种理论体系中，法官的庭外调查活动如果被界定为承担证明责任的活动，将与现代刑事司法的基本理念相悖，没有可以讨论的空间；如果界定为积极的查明活动，与承担证明责任没有关系，对于法官庭外调查活动的各种讨论和分析才可能具有正当性的基础，这是决定法官庭外调查未来发展的基础性命题。

其次，所涉利益主体与程序设计决定着庭外调查活动的未来发展空间。法官的庭外调查活动不是承担证明责任，而是一种查明活动，这种性质定位为庭外调查活动提供了空间，但这并不意味着所有的庭外调查活动均具有正当性。无论如何理解法官的庭外调查活动，其最终的结果是法官通过调查取得了证据，而作为刑事诉讼中使用的证据，其必定会有利于诉讼一方。按照控辩对等、平等武装的基本要求，以及我国司法实践中控辩力量失衡的现状，诉讼制度的设计应当有利于保障控辩双方的实质对等。在这种背景下，法官通过庭外调查所得的证据应当有利于辩护一方，以推进控辩实力的平衡。如果法官进行庭外调查是为控诉方提供武器，其结果只能是使本已失衡的实力天平进一步向控方倾斜，公正审判无从谈起。基于以上分析，法官庭外调查活动的适用范围在未来发展中应当从利益主体角度加以限制，只有在有利于辩护一方的证据存在疑问时，即为了辩护方的利益需要，法官才能进行庭外调查活动；为了公诉需要的法官庭外调查活动应当原则上被禁止。

法官庭外调查活动的程序设计，决定了该制度在司法实践中能否正当运作。即使被定位为查明活动，即使是符合正当性要求的法官庭外调查活动的类型，如果没有正当程序作为保障，所有的庭外调查活动都将面临正当性质疑。因此，构建维护法官庭外调查活动正当运作的程序，也是决定法官庭外调查活动未来发展空间的重要因素。根据前文的分析，我国在构建法官庭外调查活动程序时，需要重点解决两方面问题：法官自由裁量权的制约和权利受到侵犯的救济。那么，在未来的制度构建中，如果立法中能够赋予控辩双方对于庭外调查活动更多的参与权，由控辩双方、而不是法官更多地控制庭外调查活动的程序事项，控辩双方的权利受到法官侵犯时拥有有效的救济途径，庭外调查活动的正当运作将得到更多的保障。反之，法官庭外调查活动的发展空间必将受到消极影响。

最后，法官自身定位、可能受到的追究、控辩双方取得证据的能力，将决定着法官庭外调查活动的未来发展趋势。前面分析的主要是影响法官庭外调查活动的正当性要素，包括如何解读庭外调查活动的性质，何种庭外调查活动具有正当性保障，它们对于法官庭外调查活动的未来制度构建发挥着重要影响。然而，法律制度在司法实践中的运行状况受到各种实践因素的影响，正如前文分析的法官进行庭外调查活动的原因。法官积极调查者的身份定位，实体真实探知主义的司法传统，使得法官具有开展庭外调查活动的内在动力；法院内部的考评机制，特别是因错误认定案件事实而追究法官责任的错案追究制，成为法官开展庭外调查活动的外在压力；控辩双方在诉讼过程中取证能力的不足，迫使法官不得不采取庭外调查活动。

从法官庭外调查活动的未来发展来说，这些因素不仅将继续发挥作用，而且这些因素的变化，将在某种程度上决定法官庭外调查活动的发展趋势。例如，法官的身份定位变化将影响庭外调查活动的运行。我国 1979 年《刑事诉讼法》中采职权主义的诉讼模式，而在 1996 年《刑事诉讼法》中向当事人主义模式转变。随着诉讼模式的变化，法官的身份定位也在调整，从积极行使证据调查权的职权角色向消极中立裁判者的角色转变，其庭外调查活动也随之发生转变，例如，调查范围受到限制、调查程序逐步规范等。尽管法官的角色定位会受到多种因素的影响，但可以预见的是，随着法官角色定位的转变，庭外调查活动的立法设计和司法实践也将随之变动。

再来看法官可能受到的各种追究。在目前的法官考核体制中，刑事裁判中认定案件事实的准确性是对法官的基本要求之一，如果错误认定案件会对法官进行制裁。然而，如何理解认定案件事实的准确性，如何定位法官在认定案件事实准确性中的作用和责任，目前存在很多争议。可以想见，未来在法官认定案件事实的责任考核方面必然会有变化，而这些外部的压力将成为法官是否开展、如何开展庭外调查活动的指挥棒。

控辩双方取得证据的能力，与法官是否进行庭外调查活动紧密相关。目前，控辩双方的取证能力受到多方面因素的影响，包括技术手段、法律规则、证据资料来源的保障等，而这些因素正在发生重大的变化，并将影响法官庭外调查活动的开展。具体来说，随着法庭科学技术的不断发展，日益完善的技术手段能够为审判提供更为丰富和准确的证据资料；对于辩护方调查取证活动的不合理限制，例如《刑法》第306条对辩护律师调查取证活动的威慑，或许会随着相关法律的完善而取消，辩护方的取证能力将得到加强；法律制度的完善，还能够提供更多的证据资料来源保障，例如，讯问犯罪嫌疑人、被告人录音录像制度的真正实施，能够为讯问活动合法性的证明提供证据。这些影响控辩双方取证能力因素的变化，能够为法庭审判带来更为丰富的证据资料，不断压缩需要法官进行庭外调查的空间，这也注定会影响法官庭外调查活动的未来发展。

论比例原则在警察侦查取证程序中的适用

樊传明 *

一、比例原则及其在公法领域的扩张

起源于德国法的比例原则，在现代公法领域具有明显的扩张趋势。比例原则在德国法中的确立，始于1794年《普鲁士一般邦法》。在“警察国家”[1] 的背景下，为限制庞大的警察权，该法第10章第17条规定：“警察机关为了维护公共安宁、安全与秩序，必须为必要之处置。”[2] 由此要求警察权不得超出“必要”的程度来干预人民的权利。[3] 这一规定的内容在普鲁士高级行政法院审查警察自由裁量权的实践中进一步丰富。后来，德国著名行政法学家奥托·麦耶在讨论行政法基本原则时，对该原则进行了阐述和总结：“行政权追求公益应有凌越私益的优越性，但行政权力对人民的侵权必须符合目的性，并采用最小侵害之方法”。[4] 由此，产生于警察法的比例原则，成为行政法的基本原则，要求行政机关为达成行政目的要选择适当的、对人民权利侵害最小的手段，且手段与目的之间符合比例关系。

按照作为通说的“三阶理论”，比例原则的内涵包括三项子原则，即适当性原则、必要性原则和比例性原则。适当性原则要求一个公权力措施的手段可达到目的，即手段与目的之间具有对应关系；必要性原则要求在所有能够达成目的的方式中，必须选择对公民权利侵害最小的方法；比例性原则又称狭义的比例原则，指“一个措施虽为达成目的所必要，但是，不可予以人民过度之负担。……即衡量目的与人民权利损失两者有无成比例。”[5]

比例原则并未停留在行政法基本原则的层面。20世纪50年代以后，德国联邦宪法法院大量援用该原则进行违宪审查，由此开启了比例原则宪法化的时代。在宪法层级上，比例原则主要限制立法者：立法机关在制定限制公民权利的法律规范时必须考虑其对人民权利的限制是否有必要，是否成比例。尽管对于将比例原则提升至宪法效力

---

* 樊传明，中国政法大学证据法学专业博士研究生。Email：fanchuanming123@163.com。本文系北京市优秀博士学位论文指导教师人文社科项目“证据科学与司法文明”（项目编号20121005301）的阶段性成果之一。

〔1〕 18世纪前，德国的警察事务涵盖外交、国防、财政、司法以外的所有国家行政范围，因此当时德国被称为“警察国家”。自18世纪初期，警察权逐渐有所收缩，仅限于管理国家的内部行政事务，警察权的意义等同于所有国家内政。

〔2〕 朱武献：《言论自由之宪法保障》，参见辅仁大学丛书编辑委员会：《公法专题研究（二）》，1992年版，第38页。

〔3〕 陈新民：《德国公法学基础理论（下）》，山东人民出版社2001年版，第76页。

〔4〕 奥托·麦耶在其《德国行政法学》一书中分章讨论行政法的基本原则时，提出了该“比例原则”。参见陈新民：“德国行政法的先驱者——谈德国19世纪行政法学的发展”，载《行政法学研究》1998年第1期；叶俊荣：“论比例原则与行政裁量”，载《宪政时代》1986年第3期。

〔5〕 陈新民：《德国公法学基础理论（上）》山东人民出版社2001年版，第417页。

位阶存在着反对声音，如“其增大了司法控制立法的危险，有使司法权凌驾于立法权之上的嫌疑，从而导致对立法形成自由权的过当干涉，导致对人民的保护不利”。[6] 但比例原则的宪法化在德国早已成为不可否认的事实。经由宪法位阶的提升，比例原则进而向整个公法领域扩张。不仅学界越来越倾向于认可它是公法领域的普遍原则，如认为“‘比例原则’如同民法之‘诚信原则’一般，以帝王条款的姿态，君临公法学界，成为公法学上最重要的原则之一。”[7] 而且，这一趋势也体现在大陆法系的立法和判例上。[8]

起源于德国的比例原则也被逐渐引入其他国家。不仅欧洲大陆国家的法律中明显可见比例原则的内容[9]，而且英美法系国家的立法和判例也深受其影响。在传统英美法中，承担着与比例原则相似功能、用以规范行政权的是“温斯伯里合理性原则”[10]。但从1998年开始，受欧共体法和《欧洲人权公约》的影响，英国法院在对行政决定进行审查时，不仅仅局限于传统的合理性原则，已经出现了适用比例原则的案例。在英国的国内法中引入比例原则的呼声也越来越高。[11] 也有学者认为，在英美法系引入比例原则，不太可能取代合理性原则成为另一个独立标准，但会“进一步丰富合理性原则的内涵，构成不合理的一个特别的表征，更加精细化原来的范围或界限。换句话说，就是想利用大陆法比例原则所具有的客观性、可操作性之长处来弥补普通法上合理性原则过于抽象性之短处。”[12]

比例原则早已不仅是行政法的基本原则，而且已经扩张成为整个公法领域对公权力运行的一项普遍要求，并且成为跨法域甚至法系进行移植和借鉴的对象。其扩张力源于这样一个事实：在现代社会，约束国家公权力以防止对私人权益的不当侵犯是各国法律（尤其是公法）的一个核心关注，而比例原则能够通过权衡手段和目的，为公

---

〔6〕 关于这一争论的详细内容，参见姜昕：《比例原则研究：一个宪政的视角法律》，法律出版社2008年版，第59页。

〔7〕 阮文泉：“比例原则与量刑”，载《法律评论》（台湾地区）1991年第9期。陈新民教授也认为，比例原则堪称“公法里的‘帝王条款’，其重要性比起诚信原则之在民法内，有过之而无不及。”参见陈新民：《德国公法学基础理论（下）》，山东人民出版社2001年版，第380页。我国大陆学者张绍彦称“比例原则”是公法领域对剥夺公民自由的“黄金条款”的三大原则之一，其他两项原则是法定原则和必要性原则。参见张绍彦：“法治、人权是现代国家必须遵循的基本原则”，载《人大复印资料刑事法学》2001年第10期。

〔8〕 比例原则在整个公法领域的扩张的一个例子，就是刑事诉讼法对该原则的吸收。关于德国、法国及我国台湾地区刑事诉讼立法和判例中体现比例原则的论述，详见秦策博士论文：《刑事诉讼比例原则研究》，藏于《中国政法大学博士学位论文库》。

〔9〕 德国法深深影响了大陆法系其他国家的立法。有些国家的立法虽然没有对“比例原则”的明确表述，但许多规定实质上在贯彻比例原则。如荷兰1994年的《行政法通则》第3章第3条规定：“①在某个法律未作限制性规定时，行政机关制作命令仍然应当考虑直接相关的利益。②某个命令对一个或更多的利害关系人产生不利后果，这个不利后果需与命令的目的适当。”葡萄牙1996年《行政程序法典》规定：“行政当局的决定与私人权利或受法律保护的利益有冲突时，仅可在对拟达致的目标系属适当及适度的情况下，损害这些权利或利益”。参见王名扬、冯俊波：“论比例原则”，载《时代法学》2005年第4期。

〔10〕 在英国法院审查行政行为时，传统上遵守的是确立于1947年的“温斯伯里不合理性原则”，只有在“某一行政决定是如此的不合理，以至于任何一个有理性的机构都不会作出”的情形下，法院干预行政决定才是正当的。这为行政决定划定了一个巨大的免受司法审查的保护圈。详见何海波：《司法审查的合法性基础——英国话题》，中国政法大学出版社2007年版。

〔11〕 参见何海波：《司法审查的合法性基础——英国话题》，中国政法大学出版社2007年版。

〔12〕 余凌云：“论行政法上的比例原则”，载《法学家》2002年第2期。

权机关的自由裁量施加具有操作性的衡量标准和制裁后果。涉及公权力运行的法律领域中，如果存在公权力的自由裁量空间并且需要以限制私人权益为手段来追求公共利益，那么就应当确立某些原则作为权衡标准和规制手段。比例原则提供了这样一个备选项。本文将关注中国法律语境中的警察侦查取证程序。在这一程序中，存在警察滥用裁量权的危险，对“尊重和保障人权”的刑事诉讼立法任务构成潜在威胁。中国当前的刑事诉讼立法尚未、但有必要引入比例原则，规制警察侦查取证裁量权。

二、警察取证程序的利益关涉与裁量权规制：适用比例原则的必要性

（一）警察侦查取证程序的利益关涉

侦查是刑事诉讼程序中的重要阶段，一方面，通过收集证据认定犯罪事实；另一方面，采取必要措施（主要是强制措施）保证犯罪嫌疑人在案待审。〔13〕收集证据是侦查程序中非常核心、必不可少的任务，各种侦查行为的目的主要在于获取证据。而只有根据案件情况确有必要时，才可以采取强制性措施控制犯罪嫌疑人。并且，控制犯罪嫌疑人的目的之一也是为了获取口供。因此，有学者认为侦查程序应当“定位为一种诉前调查取证程序”〔14〕。在以公诉为原则的现代刑事诉讼制度背景下，警察是主要的控方取证主体。警察的侦查取证行为尽管是刑事诉讼程序的一部分，但侦查取证权从权力属性来看实际上是一种行政权〔15〕，通过行政手段搜集证据为实现国家追诉职能提供条件。而规制行政裁量权正是比例原则的核心适用领域。

警察的侦查取证行为具有公共利益属性。与早期社会弹劾式诉讼模式下的私人控告相比，现代刑事公诉制度假定：刑事诉讼并非私人事务，而是关涉公共利益。这取决于对犯罪性质的理解：“任何侵害某一‘个人’的犯罪，同时也会侵害到‘整体社会’的共同生活秩序。”〔16〕所以，刑事诉讼作为对犯罪的追究程序必然是保护“整体社会”的手段。警察取证获得的证据具有证明价值，能够促进对案件事实的认定，进而得出适用刑法的事实小前提。所以，警察取证具有促进公共利益的属性，应当赋予警察强大的取证权，有效率地收集证据。与此同时，警察取证也涉及私人利益，这表现在具有强制性的取证手段上〔17〕。侦查取证是为了获取证据资料，但证据资料的持有人可能并不具有交出该资料的意愿。因此，法律会授权警察在具备法定情形时强制获取。所谓“强制”，意味着对诉讼参与人或其他人权利的处分：一种情况是限制人身自由，例如，通过拘传、逮捕等措施强制到案接受讯问；另一种情况是限制财产权，例如，扣押物证、书证，冻结存款；除此之外还可能涉及对隐私权、通信自由等权利的

〔13〕即侦查程序的两项基本任务是查清犯罪事实、查获犯罪嫌疑人。对这项任务的表述，可见于中国刑事诉讼法第113条：“公安机关对已经立案的刑事案件，应当进行侦查，收集、调取犯罪嫌疑人有罪或者无罪、罪轻或者罪重的证据材料。对现行犯或者重大嫌疑分子可以依法先行拘留，对符合逮捕条件的犯罪嫌疑人，应当依法逮捕。”

〔14〕樊崇义、吴光升：“刑事诉讼法再修改背景下侦查程序的改革方向”，载《铁道警官高等专科学校学报》2009年第1期。

〔15〕司法权是一种“判断权”，是对纠纷的居中裁判。但作为侦查机关的公安警察在机构设置上属于行政机关，而且侦查行为更像是行政行为，具有“行政机关—相对人”的双向结构，而非司法裁判的三方结构。

〔16〕林山田：《刑法通论（上册）》，北京大学出版社2012年版，第2页。

〔17〕侦查程序中的取证措施按照是否限制、侵犯公民权利可以分为一般取证措施和强制性取证措施，后者为了获取证据材料而必须采取对公民权利强制处分的方式。这里的“强制性取证”与我国《刑事诉讼法》规定的“强制措施”含义不同，但强制措施往往是实现强制性取证的方式。

限制，例如，监听、截取通信等措施。[18]

因此，警察取证行为必然涉及两种利益：通过有效率地获取证据来促进公共利益；采用强制性手段而限制私人权益。前者是目的，后者是手段。公共利益和私人权益之间存在竞争关系，需要通过比例原则权衡："除必须是能达到公益目的的手段外，还要选择对公民权利造成损害或限制最小的手段，而且这种造成损害的手段要与目的的达成后，所获得的利益处于均衡的状态。"[19]。警察取证程序具有适用比例原则的二元利益竞合关系。

（二）对警察取证裁量权的规制

以上从侦查权运行所涉利益关系的角度看，存在对警察取证程序适用比例原则的法律关系结构。另外，从当前中国立法对警察取证权的规制现状看，也存在适用比例原则的必要性。

目前我国对警察取证行为的规制主要体现在"程序法定原则"上。法律预先规定各种程序条件和实施步骤，参与刑事诉讼的专门机关必须严格按照这些法律要求。[20]例如，我国《刑事诉讼法》规定，警察为讯问而传唤犯罪嫌疑人，持续的时间一般不得超过 12 个小时；讯问被羁押的犯罪嫌疑人，应当在看守所内进行；进行搜查，需事先取得并在执行时出示搜查证；扣押邮件、电报，应当经公安机关负责人批准；等等。[21]按照程序法定原则，除非有法律规定的授权并且遵循法定程序，警察在取证时不能采用限制公民权利的方式。如果违反法律规定，将会导致特定的制裁后果，最为典型的是排除非法证据。

确立程序法定原则，并且在立法中明确规定各类侦查手段的适用条件和程序，是规制警察取证权力的必要条件。然而，这对于保障私权利来说是否充分？举例来说，法律要求警察传唤犯罪嫌疑人持续的时间一般不得超过 12 个小时。如果警察传唤犯罪嫌疑人在讯问了 3 小时后，事实已经查清，没有必要继续讯问。但仍继续控制犯罪嫌疑人不允许其离开，直到临近 12 个小时才将其放出。该行为是否适当？又如，法律规定侦查机关按照法定程序（出示搜查证等）可以对相关诉讼参与人的住处进行强制搜查。那么，如果警察明知犯罪嫌疑人住宅中可能藏有的证据对认定案件事实不起关键作用，且该证据在短期内不会灭失。但警察却选择在午夜强制搜查住宅，并邀请邻居到场见证。即使警察依法办理了搜查证，这一严重扰乱犯罪嫌疑人生活安宁的取证手段是否恰当？

以上两例中，警察的取证行为在形式上遵循了相关法律规定，不违反程序法定原则。但过多地限制了犯罪嫌疑人或者其他诉讼参与人的权利，而该手段对于达成刑事诉讼目的而言并不必要或收效甚微。遵守法定程序只是警察侦查取证的一个最低法律

---

〔18〕 在这些限制私权利的取证措施中，有些是直接的取证手段，例如强制搜查就是为了获得可能藏匿在某处的证据资料；也有一些是间接的取证手段，例如，拘留、逮捕本身是控制犯罪嫌疑人的强制措施，但拘留、逮捕后羁押间接地、部分地也是为了通过讯问获取口供。

〔19〕 姜昕：《比例原则研究：一个宪政的视角法律》，法律出版社 2008 年版，第 16 页。

〔20〕 关于程序法定原则的详细论述，参见宋英辉主编：《刑事诉讼原理》，法律出版社 2003 年版，第 66～74 页。

〔21〕 以上规定可见于我国修改后的《刑事诉讼法》第 116～117、136 和 141 条。

要求，它对于保障相关诉讼参与人的私权利来说是必要而不充分条件。因为法律规定必然存在自由裁量空间。尤其是，基于侦查程序的紧迫性，法律通常赋予侦查机关足够的裁量权以提高侦查效率。但有自由裁量就有滥用裁量，滥用裁量权虽具有“遵守法律规定”的外表却从根本上违背了法律的精神。仅有法定程序原则不足以防止警察对私人权益的不当侵犯。因此需要在严守程序法定要求的前提下，确立某些有约束力的法律原则作为衡量标准并辅之以制裁后果，规制警察取证裁量权。但反观中国刑事诉讼立法，尚未确立这样有约束力且具有可操作性的原则。[22] 因此，引入比例原则确有必要。

三、在警察取证程序中适用比例原则的具体要求

比例原则主要针对公权力的自由裁量，防止因滥用裁量权而侵犯私人利益。比例原则适用的前提是，公权力行为符合合法性原则。如果公权力行为不合法，应直接依据法律规定否定其效力，无需援引比例原则。具体到警察侦查取证程序，对取证权的规制首先是程序法定原则。公安机关必须在法律有明确授权的情况下按照法定程序才能采用限制公民权利的调查取证方法，即强制取证措施。如果违背了法律有关取证程序的规定，将引起特定的制裁后果，其中最为典型的就是非法证据排除规则。这种规制警察强制取证行为的机制可简单表示为：

程序法定原则——→具体的程序规定——→发现程序违法——→对程序违法进行制裁

如果警察取证程序违法，将按照以上逻辑顺序施加法律制裁，这时并无比例原则的适用余地。只有警察取证遵循了法定程序，在此前提下针对个案尚存在自由裁量空间，且该取证措施涉及对私人权益的限制时，才有适用比例原则的问题。表示为：

符合法定程序——→存在自由裁量——→要求符合比例原则——→对违反行为进行制裁

因此，在适用顺序上，比例原则相对于合法性原则而言是第二位的。针对警察取证，首位的要求是程序法定原则，次位的要求是比例原则，它们构成了双层的法律规制。按照通说的“三阶理论”,[23] 比例原则包括适当性原则、必要性原则和比例性原则这三项具体要求，它们在警察侦查取证程序中都应得到遵守。需要说明的是，比例原则在警察取证领域的适用，可以分成两个层面：首先，要求相关刑事诉讼法律规范的设定符合比例原则。这实际上是宪法层面的问题，意在约束刑事诉讼立法权。其次，要求警察在进行侦查裁量的时候符合比例原则。这是在刑事诉讼法层面对比例原则的适用。本文的讨论仅针对后者。

---

〔22〕 中国《刑事诉讼法》明确规定的原则包括：侦查权、检察权、审判权由专门机关依法行使；人民法院、人民检察院依法独立行使职权；依靠群众；以事实为根据，以法律为准绳；对一切公民在适用法律上一律平等；分工负责、互相配合、互相制约；人民检察院依法对刑事诉讼实行法律监督；各民族公民有权使用本民族语言文字进行诉讼；犯罪嫌疑人、被告人有权获得辩护；审判公开；未经人民法院依法判决，不得确定有罪；保障诉讼参与人的诉讼权利；依照法定情形不予追究刑事责任；追究外国人犯罪适用我国刑事诉讼法。这些原则无法有效规制警察在侦查程序中的裁量权。

〔23〕 对于比例原则的具体内涵，存在“三阶理论”和“二阶理论”。“三阶理论”认为该原则具体包括适当性、必要性和比例性三项子原则，而“二阶理论”认为包括必要性和比例性两项子原则。目前，“三阶理论”为更多的学者所接受。

（一）对强制取证行为的适当性要求

适当性原则要求公权力机关在执行职务时，仅得选择能够达到所追求目的的方法。[24] 它要求在手段与目的之间必须具有对应关系，特定权力行为要有助于目的之达成。警察侦查取证的直接目的在于获取潜在的证据材料，因此，能否获得证据材料是判断取证措施是否符合适当性原则的依据。只有可能存在需要获取的证据，其对于认定案件事实有证明价值时，才能够采取特定侦查取证行为。这一要求可见于《德国刑事诉讼法典》第 103 规定："对其他人员（指非嫌疑人），只有在为了破获被指控人、追踪犯罪行为线索或者扣押一定的物品，并且只能在依据事实可以推测所寻找的人员、线索或者物品就在应予搜查的房间里的时候，才准许予以搜查。"根据这一规定，只有"依据事实可以推测"犯罪嫌疑人或者证据在房间里的时候，即存在获取证据可能性时，才能实施搜查。

但判断一项侦查取证措施能否获取证据，不应要求过严，因为在采取取证措施之前，往往无法确切地知道证据的存在情况。因此，如果同时符合以下两个条件就满足了适当性原则的要求：

首先，存在取证的可能性。在当时的条件下，侦查机关认为采取某取证措施可能收集到有助于认定案件事实的证据。只要存在获取证据的可能性即可，不应强求最终一定要取得证据；

其次，具有合理根据。作出以上判断需合理，即根据当时所掌握的线索能够合理地认为具有获得证据的可能性。这一可能性是有初步证据支持的、具体的经验意义上的可能性，而非抽象的哲学意义上的可能性。

因此，判断是否满足适当性主要是进行经验判断的过程。根据适当性原则，警察在决定是否搜查私人场所时，必须合理地认为该场所中可能存在实物证据或有义务提供证据的人，搜查的范围限于有证据藏匿可能性的范围；在进行扣押物证、书证或冻结存款、汇款前，应有根据地认为所涉物品具有证据意义，是侦查取证的对象。明知与案件无关的物品，不在扣押、冻结之列，除非具有其他的理由（如扣押违禁品或进行财产保全，但这并非本文讨论的取证措施）。

（二）对强制取证行为的必要性要求

必要性原则又称为"最小侵害原则"，指当存在几种可以选择的方法时，应当选择对私权利侵害最小的方法为之。警察获取证据的方法可能有多种，这时必须选择尽可能减少对私人权益限制的方式。

首先，这种选择发生在任意侦查和强制侦查措施之间。强制侦查是指"不受受侦查人意思的约束而进行的强制处分"[25]，而任意侦查不涉及对受侦查人权利的处分或者经过其同意才进行处分。如果为了获取某项潜在的证据材料，通过任意侦查和强制侦查都能够达到目的，则应当选择任意侦查的方式。只有当任意侦查无法实现取证目的的情况下，才能采取限制诉讼参与人人身、财产权利的强制侦查取证措施。所以，在考虑是否适用搜查、冻结、拘传、强制采样、监听等具有强制性的取证措施时，应

[24] 参见城仲模：《行政法上之基础理论》，三民书局 1980 年版，第 40 页。

[25] 宋英辉主编：《刑事诉讼原理》，法律出版社 2007 年版，第 280 页。

当遵循谦抑、克制的原则，优先采用不涉及限制权利的一般取证方法。

其次，即使在确有必要采取强制侦查取证手段时，也应作出进一步的选择，因为可能存在多种可用的强制侦查措施。在这些措施里面，要选择对私权利侵害最小的方式。至于如何判断对私权利的侵害最小，取决于两个要素：①该强制取证措施所限制的权利在整个权利体系中所处的位阶。虽然我们无法给每项权利的重要性赋予数值并进行精确计算，但通常可以比较不同权利的位阶高低。例如，一般情况下，逮捕羁押所限制的人身自由权要比监听所限制的隐私权更重要，而后者又比扣押物证、书证所限制的财产权重要。②该强制取证措施对权利的限制程度。一次性的强行搜查对住宅安宁权的侵犯，相对于长期监听对隐私权的侵犯而言，在限制权利的程度上明显较轻；短期的拘留讯问相比于长期的羁押待审，在限制人身自由的程度上要轻。所以，比较不同种类强制性取证措施对私权利的侵害程度，要同时考察所限制权利的种类、程度两个要素。除非确有必要采取更严厉的方法，否则应综合判断取其轻。

最后，对于同一种强制取证措施，其强制的程度也要受到必要性原则的限制。一个比较法上的例子是英国1984年《警察与刑事证据法》以及该法的实施细则之一《警察官行使拦截和搜查的成文法权力行为准则》。它们对警察的搜查作了细致的分类：公开场合的搜查必须限于外部衣服的表层检查，但如果存在进一步搜查的合理根据，可以在附近的警察行李车内或者警察分局进行较深入的搜查。留置人或车辆的时间仅限于进行这种搜查所必要的合理时间。搜查须受到怀疑的性质的限制，因此，警察如果怀疑某人外衣口袋内藏有枪支，他只能搜查那个外衣口袋。[26] 据此，在公开场合的人身搜查仅限于对外衣的表层检查；只有存在进一步搜查的合理根据，才能进行“较深入的搜查”；但搜查的范围限于所怀疑的范围。这种具有层次性的关于搜查方式的规定，正是贯彻了必要性原则。即使法律没有对每种取证手段都进行如此详细的规定，也应当恪守比例原则的要求将强制程度限制在必要性的范围内。

（三）对强制取证行为的比例性要求

比例性原则（也被认为是狭义的比例原则）要求“对所牵涉的相关价值法益作轻重的权衡”[27]：“权力的行使，虽是达成目的所必要的，但是不可给予人民超过目的之价值的侵害。”[28] 所以，比例性原则是对公共利益和个人利益的权衡，以保护私人利益为取向。即使警察侦查取证符合了适当性和必要性的要求，仍然要权衡它所促进的公共利益（目的）和侵害的私人利益（手段），不能使对私人利益的侵犯超过所追求的公共利益。根据德国学者约阿希姆·赫尔曼的表述，“刑事追究措施，特别是侵犯基本权利的措施在其种类、轻重上，必须要与所追究的行为大小相适应。”[29]

警察侦查取证所追求的公共利益表现在：可能获取的证据材料具有证明价值，能够促进对案件事实的认定。因此，判断一项取证行为所促进的公共利益，要考虑三个因素：①该取证措施可能获取到证据的概率。越有可能获取到证据，说明采取该措施

---

〔26〕 参见孙长永：《侦查程序与人权》，中国方正出版社2000年版，第24页。

〔27〕 姜昕：《比例原则研究：一个宪政的视角法律》，法律出版社2008年版，第17页。

〔28〕 参见陈新民：《行政法学总论》，三民书局1995年版，第62页。

〔29〕［德］约阿希姆·赫尔曼：《德国刑事诉讼法典》，李昌珂译，中国政法大学出版社1995年版，第13页。

越有必要；②该取证措施可能获取到的证据的证明价值。一方面，证明价值取决于该证据的特征；属性，另一方面，证明价值也取决于整个证据体系的情况。如果对待证事实已经具有足够证据来证明，则再收集累积证据的必要性就降低了；③所追诉的犯罪行为本身的危害性程度。一般而言，犯罪的危害性程度越高，我们制裁该犯罪的动力就越大。所以，某特定取证措施可能收集到证据的概率越大、该证据可能具有的证明价值越高、追究该犯罪的必要性越大，则这一取证措施能够促进的公共利益就越大。

取证措施对私人利益的侵犯表现为对权利的限制，其程度取决于上文所说的权利位阶和侵犯程度两个要素。比例性原则要求不能为追求公共利益而过度侵犯私人利益，所以必须权衡这两个因素。如果对私人权利的侵犯程度超过了对公共利益的促进程度，则即使符合法律程序规则，也不应当采取该措施；一旦不恰当地采取了该措施，就应该伴随制裁后果——否定该行为的法律效果。可见，比例性原则要求权衡公共利益和私人权益，但以保护私人权益为价值导向，内含有否定公权行为法效果的效力。

四、在侦查取证程序中适用比例原则的保障机制：令状主义

在侦查程序中适用比例原则，为警察行使取证裁量权确立了较为具体而又富有弹性的规范标准。然而，要使比例原则真正发挥实效还必须确立必要的保障机制。比例原则在警察取证程序中的运行特别有赖于一项配套制度：作为外在制约机制的令状主义。

比例原则的适用与司法审查制度有着密不可分的联系。比例原则意在规制公权力，为裁量权的行使确立标准。但公权力存在天然的扩张性，不具有保护私人利益的动因，因此也就不具有恪守比例原则的动因。倘若将是否符合比例原则的判断权完全交给作出公权力行为的机关自身而不存在外在制约，将无法保障该原则的适用。并且，这违背了古老的正当程序要求——“任何人不得作自己案件的法官”。〔30〕因此，应当由独立的司法机关对行政机关（包括刑事警察）的自由裁量行为进行审查，判断是否符合比例原则并据此施以法律上的制裁。其实，从比例原则的发展历史也可以看出，它与司法审查有着难以割舍的联系。比例原则在德国最早确立于当时普鲁士高级行政法院在行政诉讼中审查警察权的行使是否超出“必要”的程度；〔31〕比例原则引入英国，也起因于法院对行政决定的审查，意图在合理性原则之外确立更严格的审查标准。〔32〕可见，一方面，司法审查为比例原则的有效贯彻提供了程序上的保障；另一方面，比例原则也为法院审查行政决定提供了超越合法性、合理性标准的更高标准。“比例原则当作司法审查的标准，可表现在其限制立法权力及行政权力两大范畴。易言之，可以比例原则对立法裁量及行政裁量之限制。”〔33〕

在警察侦查取证程序中适用比例原则，也同样须确立某种形式的司法审查制度。这意味着，在刑事诉讼中法院不应只参与审判阶段，在审前阶段的侦查程序中也要行使审查职能。这种司法审查表现为令状规则。令状规则（也称令状主义）最早确立于英国的刑事侦查法律规范，但到现在已经成为两大法系通行的规则，是指“在进行强

---

〔30〕 参见［美］约翰·V. 奥尔特：《正当法律程序简史》，杨明成、陈霜玲译，商务印书馆2006年版，第12页。

〔31〕 陈新民：《德国公法学基础理论（下）》山东人民出版社2001年版，第76页。

〔32〕 参见何海波：《司法审查的合法性基础——英国话题》，中国政法大学出版社2007年版，第85～90页。

〔33〕 陈新民：《德国公法学基础理论（上）》，法律出版社2010年版，第431页。

制性措施时，关于该强制性措施是否合法，必须由法院或法官予以判断并签署令状；当执行强制性措施时，原则上必须向被处分人出示该令状。”〔34〕令状规则不仅要求法院或法官对强制性措施进行事先批准，还授权法官在签发令状并经侦查机关执行后，审查判断是否有必要继续进行该强制性措施。令状规则能够使警察的强制性取证手段受到法院监督，保障比例原则的贯彻：

首先，法院在审查侦查机关依法提出的强制取证申请时，在判断合法性之后，应进而审查是否符合比例原则，将此作为是否签发令状的依据。这是一种事先的规制，把满足比例原则作为采取强制取证措施的前置要求。

其次，在事后审查是否有继续进行强制性取证的必要，或者在审理犯罪嫌疑人一方针对强制性措施的申诉时，将是否满足比例原则作为裁决标准。这是一种事后救济，将违反比例原则作为提供司法救济的条件。

可见，令状规则能够为比例原则适用于警察取证程序提供司法保障。但是，在设定令状规则时必须考虑自由裁量与司法审查之间的紧张关系。自由裁量有利于促进效率目标，这对于经常具有紧迫性的侦查行为而言尤为重要。并且，面对不能为僵硬的法律规则所涵盖的无限丰富多样的生活事实，公权力机关也必须要有发挥裁量权的空间。而令状规则以人权保障为目标，意味着通过司法机关的审查将警察裁量权置于监督之下，缩小自由裁量的空间。因此，一方面，缺乏外在司法制约的警察权会导致人权受到威胁；另一方面，过于严苛的司法审查势必降低打击犯罪的效率。刑事诉讼立法必须在两者之间做出权衡，确立宽严得当的令状规则。考虑到中国的司法现状和改革趋势，笔者认为进行以下设置是合理的：首先，对于那些可能严重侵犯公民权利的侦查取证措施，如监听、逮捕后羁押等，必须设定令状规则，将启动该类措施的批准权交给法院，并且法院可随时审查继续该措施的必要性。其次，与此同时，考虑到某些紧急情况下侦查机关无法及时提请法院批准，可将这些特殊情况下法院的事先批准转为事后审查。例如，在执行其他侦查任务的过程中发现有罪证可能藏匿于犯罪嫌疑人住宅，若不及时取证将导致该证据灭失，则执行侦查的警察可径行强制搜查，但事后要将该措施报告给法院并接受审查。最后，对于并不直接限制公民权利或者限制程度较轻的取证措施，可以不自动适用令状规则，但应当赋予诉讼参与人向法院申请救济的权利。如果参与人对侵犯自己权利的取证行为提出控告并启动法院审查程序，法院需要将是否满足比例原则作为审查内容的一部分。

然而，反观我国现有刑事诉讼立法，尚未在侦查程序中建立起能够保障比例原则适用的令状规则。根据我国刑事诉讼法，侦查机关进行的绝大多数包括取证措施在内的强制性侦查行为，例如，搜查、扣押、拘留等，无需经外在的司法机关事先批准，而只要本部门或机关负责人批准即可。只有公安机关在实施逮捕这种最严厉的强制措施时要经过检察院批准，但这也并非真正意义上的令状规则，充其量只是“准司法审查”〔35〕。因为，尽管在我国检察院被归入广义上的司法机关范畴，但它在刑事诉讼中承担公诉职能和部分侦查职能，具有强烈的追诉倾向。它并非中立的司法机关，也就

---

〔34〕 宋英辉主编：《刑事诉讼原理（第二版）》，法律出版社2007年版，第277页。

〔35〕 龙宗智：“强制侦查司法审查制度的完善”，载《中国法学》2011年第6期。

不是批准令状的适格主体。法院在我国的刑事审判前程序尤其是侦查程序中的缺位，使警察侦查取证权缺乏有效制约。正如有学者所分析的："由于侦查机关为完成其任务，不可避免地从侦查效益与便宜性考虑，最大限度地利用强制侦查措施，对强制侦查如无外部节制，对公民与组织权益的不当侵犯将不可避免。"〔36〕因此，即使在我国立法上明确规定比例原则，也将因缺少令状主义这一保障机制而无法真正贯彻。我国刑事诉讼法今后的改革，应当在考虑确立比例原则的同时建立宽严合理的令状规则，将法院的司法审查权逐步引入刑事诉讼审前程序。

五、结 语

继2004年"人权"入宪后，2012年中国《刑事诉讼法》修改将"尊重和保障人权"列为该法的基本任务之一。〔37〕这一难得的立法共识是当代中国刑事司法改革中多种力量角力的结果，对于巩固既有法制建设成果、确立进一步改革目标具有重要意义。但任何宏伟立法目标都要借助具体的制度构建才能得以实现。本文的分析已经显示，在中国刑事诉讼侦查程序中警察取证裁量权尚缺乏有效规制，这对于诉讼参与人尤其是被追诉人的人权是一个潜在而现实的威胁。作为解决这一问题的备选方案，本文认为应该在我国的刑事诉讼（尤其是侦查程序）中确立内涵丰富的比例原则，以此规制警察取证裁量权的运作，为公民权益提供基于程序法定原则而又超越于此的保障。虽然现行刑事诉讼法尚无关于比例原则的表述，但已有学界呼声，如陈光中教授主编的《中华人民共和国刑事诉讼法再修改专家建议稿与论证》将确立比例原则作为立法建议："人民法院、人民检察院和公安机关实施强制性诉讼行为，应当严格限制在必要的范围内，并与所追究罪行的严重性、犯罪嫌疑人、被告人的社会危险性相适应。"〔38〕这一立法建议将比例原则进一步拔高，不仅仅针对侦查程序中的警察行为，还规制所有的公、检、法强制性诉讼行为，使比例原则具有刑事诉讼基本原则的位阶。但本文的分析仅针对警察取证权。实际上，在中国的刑事司法实践中，人权遭侵犯的频发领域正是警察侦查取证程序，包括获取口供和实物证据。因此，警察侦查取证程序是最迫切地需要通过比例原则来规制的刑事诉讼环节。而且，为了使比例原则的要求能真正落实，必须确立作为外在的保障机制的令状规则，将中立的司法机关——法院的审查引入审前阶段的侦查程序。

---

〔36〕 龙宗智："强制侦查司法审查制度的完善"，载《中国法学》2011年第6期。

〔37〕 参见《中华人民共和国刑事诉讼法》第2条："中华人民共和国刑事诉讼法的任务，是保证准确、及时地查明犯罪事实，正确应用法律，惩罚犯罪分子，保障无罪的人不受刑事追究，教育公民自觉遵守法律，积极同犯罪行为作斗争，维护社会主义法制，尊重和保障人权，保护公民的人身权利、财产权利、民主权利和其他权利，保障社会主义建设事业的顺利进行。"

〔38〕 见陈光中主编：《中华人民共和国刑事诉讼法再修改专家建议稿与论证》，中国法制出版社2006年版，第258页。

论检察机关二审主动提交证据的司法控制

郭文利 *

刑事司法实践中，若法院未采信一审检察机关证据，否定其相关公诉意见，则在二审程序中，检察机关往往会在一审证据的基础上主动向法院提交其他证据。例如，在被告人M受贿案中，一审法院根据辩方提出非法取证的线索，要求检察机关提供同步审讯录像等证据被拒绝后排除了被告人M的有罪供述，而在二审阶段，检察机关又向法院主动提交了相关同步录音录像。对于是否准许出示此类证据，支持者从有利于查明事实，正确适用法律的角度，认为在充分保证辩方质证权的基础上应当允许出示。反对者认为，一审法院根据控方已有证据作出判决后，准许出示这些证据既不符合司法经济原则，又损害一审法院权威。况且，一旦二审法院采信此类证据并改变一审判决，则会剥夺被告人的上诉权。面对检察机关在二审中主动提交的证据，法院应如何处置才符合公平正义呢？

一、检察机关二审主动提交证据的规范分析

分析刑事诉讼法〔1〕及其司法解释关于检察机关在二审中主动提交证据的规定是解决该问题的重要前提。分析发现，仅在例外情形下允许检察机关在二审中主动提交新证据。

（一）检察机关在二审中一般不得主动提交证据

刑事诉讼法及其司法解释要求检察机关在提起公诉时必须向人民法院移交全部证据。《刑事诉讼法》第172条规定，人民检察院向人民法院提起公诉时，应将案卷材料、证据移送人民法院。《人民检察院刑事诉讼规则（试行)》（以下简称“高检规则”）也规定人民检察院提起公诉的案件，应当向人民法院移送起诉书、案卷材料和证据。通过新旧高检规则的不同表述可以明确，此处的证据既包括主要证据、又包括次要证据。例如，旧高检规则第282条第1款规定，人民检察院提起公诉的案件，应当向人民法院移送的是主要证据复印件或者照片，而新高检规则第394条第1款则直接表述为证据，删除了“主要”措辞的限定，表明移送的证据不限于主要证据，非主要证据也要移送。根据最高人民检察院的观点，人民检察院在提起公诉时应将全部证据材料移送人民法院。〔2〕刑事诉讼法虽未明确规定检察机关的举证期限，但检察机关不属于当事人范畴，而系公权机关，法无授权不可为，检察机关在提起公诉时需要向人民法院移交全部证据的规定，实际将检察机关提交证据的期限限于提起公诉时。因此，检

---

* 郭文利，法学博士、浙江省湖州市中级人民法院法官。Email：guowenlihz@163.com。

〔1〕指修改后的刑事诉讼法，下同。

〔2〕参见孙谦主编：《〈人民检察院刑事诉讼规则（试行)〉理解与适用》，中国检察出版社2012年版，第294页。

察机关在二审中一般不得主动提交证据。

（二）允许检察机关在二审中主动提交证据属于例外

仅允许检察机关在提起公诉时主动提交证据是刑事诉讼法的一般规定，但检察机关在二审中可以通过补充侦查的例外授权主动提交证据。根据《刑事诉讼法》第198条及其司法解释的规定，在法庭审判过程中检察人员有补充侦查的权力，授予了公诉机关通过补充侦查主动提交证据的权力。第二审人民法院审理上诉或抗诉案件，除刑事诉讼法二审程序已有规定的外，参照第一审程序的规定进行，而刑事诉讼法二审程序的规定中并不存在关于检察机关主动提交证据的内容，应当参照一审程序的规定进行。因此，检察机关在二审中同样具有通过补充侦查主动提交证据的权力。

同时，根据《最高人民法院关于适用〈中华人民共和国刑事诉讼法〉的解释》（以下简称"高法解释"）第221条第1款、第2款的规定，在辩护方同意的前提下，检察机关可以出示开庭前未移送人民法院的证据；[3] 而在辩护方提出异议的情况下，若检察机关申请出示开庭前未移送人民法院的证据，则不仅需要说明理由，而且还必须满足两个条件：说明的理由成立，且确有出示此类证据的必要。事实上，这些规定对应的也是立法中关于补充侦查的内容，在解释刑事诉讼法时，最高人民法院与最高人民检察院针对诉讼的不同阶段以及各自的职责分别进行了解释，互为补充，在各自解释出台之前，也会征求彼此的意见，以尽量避免重复解释带来的法律适用分歧。高法解释中在一定条件下允许检察机关出示开庭前未移送人民法院的证据，它衔接的是高检规则中关于检察机关向人民法院出示这些证据的规定。而在法庭审理阶段，检察机关仅能通过补充侦查的形式向人民法院提交证据，因此，高法解释中允许检察机关在满足一定条件下出示开庭前未移送人民法院的证据实质对应的仍然是关于补充侦查的授权规定。

综上，允许检察机关在二审中通过补充侦查主动提交证据属于例外。

（三）例外情形下仅允许检察机关在二审中主动提交新证据

虽然在例外情形下允许检察机关在二审中主动提交证据，但并非允许其主动提交所有类型的证据，它仅限于新证据。[4]

补充侦查不等于补充提交，按照字义解释规则，检察机关在二审中通过补充侦查主动提交证据的类型限于新的证据。众所周知，字义在解释上既可以作为方向标，又可以作为划定解释的界限。[5] 在《现代汉语大词典》中，"补充"的含义为因不足或损失而加以添补或者在主要事物之外另行追加的，[6] 前者属于动词，后者属于形容词，在"补充侦查"中补充为形容词，因此，"补充"的含义应为"在主要事物之外另行

---

〔3〕 此处内容系根据该解释原有内容的推论得出。

〔4〕 2007年6月22日公布的《人民检察院办理死刑二审案件工作规程》（试行）也规定可以提交的为新证据，例如，该规程第10条规定，办案人员应当客观全面地审查原审案卷材料，并重点审查抗诉、上诉中是否提出或者第一审判决后是否出现了可能影响定罪量刑的新事实、新证据；第13条规定，讯问在押被告人应当核查是否有新证据、是否有自首和立功等情节以及其他需要核实的问题；第31条规定，对于新收集的与定罪量刑有关的证据，应当当庭举证。该规程虽不属于司法解释范畴，但其中"新证据"的措辞能够印证刑事诉讼法在例外情形下仅赋予检察机关主动提交新证据的权力。

〔5〕 参见［德］卡尔·拉伦茨：《法学方法论》，陈爱娥译，商务印书馆2003年版，第204页。

〔6〕 《现代汉语大词典》（下），上海辞书出版社2009年版，第2807页。

追加的”。对于“补充侦查”中“侦查”的字义，《刑事诉讼法》第106条规定，“侦查”是指公安机关、人民检察院在办理案件过程中，依照法律进行的专门调查工作和有关的强制性措施。因此，“补充侦查”可解释为公安机关、人民检察院在办理案件过程中，在原有侦查基础上依照法律再次进行的专门调查工作和有关的强制性措施。以此方式提交的证据属于新的证据，而不是在补充侦查之前即已收集在案的证据。

新高检规则相关条文证明了这个结论，新高检规则第397条规定，对提起公诉后，在人民法院宣告判决前补充收集的证据材料，人民检察院应当及时移送人民法院，它的措辞为“补充收集”，指在原有基础上再进一步收集证据。除此以外，提起补充侦查的法律要件也充分证实以上观点，根据新高检规则第455条的规定，犯罪事实不清、证据不足、遗漏罪行、遗漏同案犯罪嫌疑人以及其他类似的情形是补充侦查的法律要件。依照法律规定，庭审前公诉机关应当已将所有证据移送人民法院，在犯罪事实不清、证据不足时进行补充侦查，指的只能是重新调查、收集证据而不是其他。而在遗漏罪行、遗漏同案犯罪嫌疑人情形下，“遗漏”表明之前并未关注，也不可能收集相关证据，因此，此时的补充侦查也一定是重新调查、收集相关证据。

高法解释允许检察机关在二审中通过补充侦查主动提出的证据限于新的证据。高法解释第221条规定，公诉人在满足一定条件时可以出示开庭前未移送人民法院的证据，辩护方提出需要对新的证据[7]作辩护准备的，法庭可以宣布休庭，并确定准备辩护的时间。结合上下文的解释规则，该条款“辩护方提出需要对新的证据作辩护准备的”条文中“新的证据”措辞表明，公诉人可以提交的开庭前未移送人民法院的证据可概括为新证据。同时，高法解释关于抗诉程序的规定进一步明确了此处提出的证据类型应仅限于新证据。例如，该解释规定，抗诉案件应着重审查抗诉是否提出新的证据；第二审期间，人民法院应当及时通知对方查阅、摘抄或者复制人民检察院提交的新证据；开庭审理抗诉案件，法庭调查应当重点围绕对第一审判决提出异议的事实、证据以及提交的新的证据等进行。

因此，在例外情形下，仅允许检察机关在二审中通过补充侦查形式主动提交新的证据。

二、刑事二审新证据标准的界定

新提交的证据未必是新证据，如果检察机关在二审中通过补充侦查主动提交的证据属于新证据，则法庭应当准许出示。[8] 反之，法庭应当拒绝出示此类证据。对于公诉机关主动提交证据的方式是否属于补充侦查以及补充侦查是否符合刑事诉讼法及其司法解释的规定，法庭审查判断比较容易，关键在于这些证据是否属于新证据。因而，需要对检察机关在二审中主动提交的证据从形式要件和内容类型两方面进行界定。

（一）形式要件

在刑事诉讼中，2012年1月1日施行的最高人民法院《关于审理人民检察院按照

---

[7] 斜体加粗系本文表示强调所为，下同。

[8] 高法解释第221条规定，公诉人申请出示开庭前未移送人民法院的证据，辩护方提出异议的，审判长应当要求公诉人说明理由；理由成立并确有出示必要的，应当准许。在辩护方提出异议时，公诉机关说明的理由主要集中于两个方面：其一，这些证据系通过补充侦查方式收集并提供，补充侦查次数未超过两次，每次均未超过一个月。而且，在补充侦查影响庭审进行时，已经建议法庭延期审理并获得准许。其二，这些证据属于新证据，且有出示的必要性。

审判监督程序提出的刑事抗诉案件若干问题的规定》（以下简称《审监规定》）认为，审判监督程序中新证据的形式要件需要指向原起诉事实并可能改变原判决、裁定。该解释制定者也认为，“新证据在内涵上必须符合以下两个特征：其一，新证据应具有相当强的证明力，必须达到可能改变原生效裁判据以定罪量刑的事实的程度；其二，新证据与原审起诉事实具有不可分性，如果新的证据不是指向原审起诉事实，应另行起诉”。〔9〕可能改变原生效裁判据以定罪量刑的事实以及原审起诉事实均系诉讼中的重要事实，因而，审监规定中新证据的形式要件为与诉讼中的重要事实具有相关性，且对该事实具有较强的证明力。而民事诉讼以及行政诉讼中均未对新证据设定形式要件。此种差异，虽可以刑事诉讼对证据要求更为严格加以解释，但尚不充分。在界定刑事二审新证据时是否需要设置此种形式要件必须作进一步的分析。

审监规定中“与诉讼中的重要事实具有相关性，且对该事实具有较强的证明力”的形式要件是对证据相关性的表达。此种综合论的相关性界定源于重塑后美国《联邦证据规则》的表达模式，根据后者，如果一项证据具有使确定诉讼具有重要意义的事实更可能存在或更不可能存在的任何趋向，则该证据具有相关性。〔10〕而在证据法中，相关性是可采性的前提，不具备相关性的证据是不可采的。“在可采性问题出现之处，相关性问题都出现两次：与要件事实的相关性以及与可信性的相关性”。〔11〕前者可称之为事实相关性，后者可称之为法律相关性。民事诉讼以及行政诉讼中对新证据相关性要求的不足，最大善意推测可能是将证据相关性标准仅理解为事实相关性，而司法实践中，在举证期限内法官对于当事人提交的证据〔12〕形式并不拥有裁量权，一般是当事人将所有证据在法庭出示，经过举证、认证程序，由法官判断这些证据是否有相关性，是否具有证明力，该二者甚至并无严格的步骤区分，很可能混同进行。在修改后刑事诉讼法背景下，能够准许二审提交新证据已属例外，理应遵循更为严格的标准，对刑事二审新证据设定比一般相关性标准更为严格的条件，既关注事实相关性、又关注法律相关性。同时，允许二审提交新证据本身即是在综合考虑司法成本与司法效益后进行的折中选择，若再不设置准入门槛对证据进行初步的筛选，则可能导致“泥沙俱下”的局面，加剧程序的不安定性以及对诉讼程序的延拓和诉讼资源的浪费。也正缘于此，高法解释规定，人民法院在辩护方提出异议的情况下，对公诉人申请出示开庭前未移送人民法院的证据需要进行必要性判断，此举蕴含了对证据事实相关性和法律相关性的要求。因此，在界定刑事二审新证据时，应当设置准入门槛，提出综合性的证据相关性要求，要求必须与诉讼重要事实相关，且对该事实具有较强的证明力。

（二）内容类型

综合考察我国三大诉讼程序中关于新证据内容的规定，一定期限后新发现的证据

---

〔9〕 官鸣、黄永维、聂洪勇、仇晓敏：“《关于审理人民检察院按照审判监督程序提出的刑事抗诉案件若干问题的规定》的理解与适用”，载《人民司法应用》2011年第23期。

〔10〕 参见王进喜：《美国〈联邦证据规则〉(2011年重塑版) 条解》，中国法制出版社2012年版，第56页。

〔11〕［美］特伦斯·安德森、戴维·舒姆、［英］威廉·特文宁：《证据分析》（第二版），张保生、朱婷、张月波等译，中国人民大学出版社2012年版，第389页。

〔12〕 此处的“证据”并非指采信意义上的证据，仅指形式意义的证据，基本等于证据材料。

以及虽已发现，但因客观原因未经法庭斟酌的证据均属于新证据，[13] 被改变或否定的证据仅在刑事诉讼审判监督程序和民事诉讼审判监督程序中属于新证据。将一审程序结束后新发现的证据以及虽已发现，但因客观原因未经法庭斟酌的证据纳入刑事二审新证据范畴并无太大争议。对于被改变或否定的证据而言，无论新发现的证据、还是因客观原因未经法庭斟酌的证据均可涵盖此类证据类型，在刑事二审新证据中不需要单独作为一种类型规定，此种模式得到民事诉讼和行政诉讼关于二审新证据规定的支持。界定刑事二审新证据内容类型时的关键问题是，在刑事二审程序中为何检察机关主动提交的“虽已发现，但因主观原因未经法庭斟酌的证据”以及改变了的证人证言不属于二审新证据。

1. 虽已发现，但因主观原因未经法庭斟酌的证据不属于二审新证据。司法公信力的存在是维系社会稳定的基石，社会公众对司法的信任是司法服从文化的源泉。在刑事诉讼中追求真相的高贵目的并不能正当化所有手段，[14] 一审程序中，因检察机关主观原因，特别是故意，未能充分举证，在二审程序中又以追求客观真实的高贵目的将相关证据呈交于法院，二审法院接受此类证据无疑是以高贵目的的旗号来破坏正当程序，会蚕食社会公众对司法的信任，长此以往，司法判决会存在合法性危机，社会的稳定性也将堪忧。此类个案的所谓“胜利”恰恰可能是法治城邦的失守，必须警惕。

司法公信力还体现为对法官的尊重，特别是对法官依法履职结果的尊重，不尊重法官的社会将无任何稳定可言。虽然我国二审审理兼具事实审理和法律审理的功能，但上下级法院分工不同、各有侧重却是不容回避的事实。既然如此，则上级法院应当尽可能地认可下级法院的职能所在，在下级法院已要求检察机关补充证据，而其主观上予以拒绝时，下级法院严格依据证据规则作出了裁判，上级法院更应当承认一审法院的履职结果，以确保司法权威的培育。虽然美国的法院系统和我国存在诸多不同，但其上下级法院之间存在分工这一事实则是和我们相同的，它们的上级法院如何处理与下级法院的关系对我国同样具有启示意义，即尊重上下级法院的分工，维护下级法院的判决，“通常情况下，上诉法院只有在陪审团的事实判断与任何理性人的认知完全相悖，或者初审法官的事实判断不仅存在错误，而且非常明显时，才会推翻初审法院认定的事实”。[15] 一审法院法官基于检察机关提交的“所有”证据，经审查后，在建立裁判事实基础上适用法律，作出了判决。而二审程序中检察机关又像魔法师一样的提交其他证据，若二审法院接受此类证据并据以改变一审法官认定的事实，乃至法律适用结果，是对一审法官依法履职结果的公然践踏，必将极大地损害司法权威。

在一审检察机关怠于举证情形下，接受这些证据，违背了司法经济原则。本来如果检察机关在一审阶段积极举证，则相关事宜均可在一审阶段获得解决，而如今检察

---

〔13〕 这些内容主要体现于最高人民法院《关于审理人民检察院按照审判监督程序提出的刑事抗诉案件若干问题的规定》、《关于民事诉讼证据的若干规定》、《关于适用〈中华人民共和国民事诉讼法〉审判监督程序若干问题的解释》、《关于适用〈关于民事诉讼证据的若干规定〉中有关举证时限规定的通知》以及《关于行政诉讼证据若干问题的规定》中。

〔14〕 参见［美］亚伦·德肖维茨：《合理的怀疑——从辛普森案批判美国的司法体系》，（台）高忠义、侯荷婷译，法律出版社2010年版，第31页。

〔15〕［美］斯蒂芬·布雷耶：《法官能为民主做什么》，何帆译，法律出版社2012年版，第181页。

机关又在二审阶段主动提出相关证据，重新要求举证、质证、认定事实，适用法律，将本应在一审阶段解决的问题延沓至二审阶段，二审法院如果采纳这些证据，不仅针对本次审判会投入原本不必要的司法资源，而且，由于判决的示范效应，该举动形成的预期将会鼓励检察机关采取类似行动，从更广泛的层面进一步导致对司法资源的浪费。

综上，在二审程序之前虽已发现，但因检察机关主观原因未经法庭斟酌的证据不属于二审新证据。

2. 证人改变或者否定其之前陈述的证言不属于二审新证据。在证人一审证言属于庭外陈述时，因其陈述属于传闻证据，根据传闻证据规则，一般不可采纳。其理论基础在于证人的陈述不仅会随着记忆发生变化，而且容易受到不当干扰。在证人表达一项内容时，证人的语言表达能力，记录者的理解与证人表达的契合度，当庭转述证人的陈述者的表达及理解能力均可能导致证据内容失真。证人的庭外陈述作为传闻证据仅在例外情形下被法庭接受，此时控方除了需要证明陈述者不能出庭的原因外，还必须证明他们提供陈述的可信性具备充分保障。[16] 我国修改后刑事诉讼立法及其司法解释采取的即是此种例外适用情形——未确立直接言辞证据原则，而是强调通过审查证人庭外证言取得形式等要件确保庭外陈述的可信性。而二审中证人改变或者否定其之前的陈述，无疑表明其之前陈述的真实性未获得保障，恰恰是与传闻证据例外适用相违背的。在证人一审证言属于当庭陈述时，证人前后不一的陈述本身即是用来弹劾证人的重要手段，既然前一次陈述被证人自认为不真实，法庭又凭什么相信证人此次的陈述是真实的呢?

无论一审证言属于庭外陈述，还是当庭证言，按照禁止反言原则，“如果一个人作为当事人或者利害关系人曾做出先前行为或者陈述，则禁止该人事后证明存在与该行为或者陈述所表明的事态不同的事态”。[17] 证人改变或者否定其之前证言违背了禁止反言原则。同时，为确保证人证言的真实性不受其他不当影响，对证人一般均采取隔离措施，而一审程序经过后，证人接受到案件信息的概率提高，受不当影响的程度随之加深。况且，按照记忆的一般规律，距离事发越近的证言其记忆越清楚，也相应更真实，二审中改变或否定的证人证言真实性较差。

综上，证人改变或者否定其之前陈述的证言不属于二审新证据。

三、刑事二审新证据标准的审查

形式要件与内容类型是判断刑事二审新证据的标准。司法实践中，面对检察机关在二审程序中提出的所谓新证据，法官需要对它们进行初步的审查，以决定是否允许检察机关出示此类证据。

（一）新证据“相关性”标准审查

刑事二审新证据设置相关性形式要件后，法官需要对检察机关新提交的证据进行相关性审查。而“为了具有相关性，证据必须使一个次终待证事实更有可能或更无可

---

〔16〕 参见［美］约翰·W. 斯特龙主编：《麦考密克论证据》（第五版），汤维建等译，中国政法大学出版社2004年版，第497页。

〔17〕［英］克里斯托弗·艾伦：《英国证据法实务指南》（第四版），王进喜译，中国法制出版社2012年版，第362页。

能（或者必须与证人的可信性或案件中提供的其他证据相关)”。[18] 因此，在对证据相关性进行判断时，首先需要判断证据与重要诉讼事实的关系。其次需要判断证据对证实该事实存在或者不存在的证明价值。

为了满足新证据的第一项要求，检察机关新提交的证据“必须是实质性的、必要的证据。它的影响必须是关键性的或者至少是重要的”。[19] 例如，我国台湾地区司法实践认为，新证据必须具有确实性，如果证据从形式上显然具有足以改变原确定性判决的则证据满足确实性要求。[20] 又如，在数额型犯罪中，关于犯罪数额的证据就具有实质性，若刑事一审已经存在犯罪金额的鉴定结论，而二审中检察机关又提出新的关于犯罪金额的鉴定结论，则审理法院将会作为新证据采纳。[21]

为了满足新证据的第二项要求，需要审查检察机关新提交证据的证明价值，它包括绝对意义上的价值和相对意义上的价值。前者指的是证据证明关键事实存在与否的倾向性程度，后者指的是接受该证据的收益与损害之间是否符合比例原则。如果新提出的证据绝对证明价值很小则不属于新证据。同时，法官应衡量接受此类证据对司法公正的影响，[22] 若会损害司法公正，则不应当认定其为新证据。因此，检察机关新提出的相对价值较小的证据不应被接受为二审新证据。

（二）新证据中“新发现”与“客观原因”标准审查

界定二审新证据后，法院需要审查新证据中的“新发现”与“客观原因”标准。

1. “新发现”标准的审查。新发现证据中的“新发现”标准在适用中存在模糊认识，“就像被扔在烟雾缭绕房间内烫手的山芋。烟雾代表的就是对处理新证据清晰标准的匮乏”，[23] 需要我们尽可能驱散烟雾，令其面目清晰起来。关于新发现的证据，审监解释对之前因过错未发现，随后又发现的证据认定为新证据，但同时需要对因此遭受损失的被申请方进行赔偿。[24] 而举证通知中，将未发现证据的过错限定为故意或者重大过失。在界定刑事二审新证据时，应当时刻关注其与民事诉讼的区别，它不存在类似于审监解释中的过错赔偿机制，不可能将之前有过错而未发现的证据统统纳入新证据范畴。而检察机关在证据的调查、搜集上又存在巨大优势，它“雇有职业调查人

[18] ［美］特伦斯·安德森、戴维·舒姆、［英］威廉·特文宁：《证据分析》（第二版），张保生、朱婷、张月波等译，中国人民大学出版社 2012 年版，第 82 页。

[19] Major Michael R. Stahlman, “A Verdict Worthy of Confidence? Petitioning for a New Trial before Authentication Based on New Evidence”, *Military Law Review*, June, 2001, pp. 10 ~ 11.

[20] 参见高点法学编辑委员会：《发现确实之新证据的认定标准为何？——“最高法院”99 年度台抗字第 984 号裁定》，《判解集》，高点文化事业有限公司 2011 年版。

[21] 参见刘军华、唐震、巩一鸣：“二审新证据的审查及销售假冒注册商标的商品罪中销售金额的认定”，载《人民司法·案例》2011 年第 12 期。

[22] Major Michael R. Stahlman, “A Verdict Worthy of Confidence? Petitioning for a New Trial before Authentication Based on New Evidence”, *Military Law Review*, June, 2001, pp. 10 ~ 11.

[23] Major Michael R. Stahlman, *A Verdict Worthy of Confidence? Petitioning for a New Trial before Authentication Based on New Evidence*, Military Law Review, June, 2001, pp. 10 ~ 11.

[24] 审监解释第 39 条第 2 款规定，申请再审人或者申请抗诉的当事人提出新的证据致使再审改判，被申请人等当事人因申请再审人或者申请抗诉的当事人的过错未能在原审程序中及时举证，请求补偿其增加的差旅、误工等诉讼费用的，人民法院应当支持；请求赔偿其由此扩大的直接损失，可以另行提起诉讼解决。

员来侦查犯罪，收集证据；它有着大多数被告所得不到的科学资源，以及进行细致、漫长调查的人力。它有法律咨询人员来使指控与证据相适应”。[25] 故而，未能在规定期限内提出证据，不能存在过错。[26] 只要新发现的证据系因之前存在过错而未发现，则不应成为新发现的证据。此解释能够得到行政诉讼司法实践的印证，在行政诉讼中，若作为被告的行政机关在一审中举证存在过错，而在二审期间又提交相应证据的，则不属于新发现的证据。[27]

未发现不仅不能存在过错，而且必须尽了合理努力。前南国际刑庭认为，只有在案件结束之前，检控方尽了合理努力仍然不能拥有的证据才属于新发现的证据。只有在证据是尽了合理努力仍旧不能获得的情况下，法庭才会行使裁量权判断它的证明价值以及接受后对被告的公正性。[28] 合理努力的标准既能督促检察机关积极调查、收集、提交证据，又能在其取得证据的客观可能性与举证要求之间取得平衡，应当予以肯定。

关于何谓合理努力，按照一般理性人的判断标准，对于摆在面前的证据而不能意识到它的重要性当然是不应当被接受的。[29] 它要求检察机关在调查、收集证据时以真诚、善意的态度，积极作为，不得延误、更不得采取欺诈、伪造等手段策略性地谋求诉讼利益。对检察机关而言，源于其在证据调查、搜集方面的优势地位，法官通常应秉持高于一般理性人的审查标准。

2. “客观原因”标准的审查。司法实践中对因客观原因导致未经法庭斟酌的证据中的“客观原因”内涵争议不大，例如，不可抗力、证人不在国内等均属于此处的客观原因。但需要提醒的是，此处的客观原因不仅需要审查原因的类型，还需要审查在客观原因出现前，检察机关是否已积极行为，在客观原因出现之前，检察机关不仅不能存在主观过错，而且应当尽了合理努力，以真诚、善意的态度作为，不得延误。例如，就证人不在国内导致的无法取证而言，如果检察机关发现该证人后未能立即对该证人进行调查询问，而是因对证据重要性认识不足等原因在一段时间后才开始此项工作，但证人已于检察机关取证前一天出国，则因其怠于取证，不能认定为因客观原因取证不能，二审中检察机关提交的新取得的该证人证言当然不属于新证据。

四、结 语

法院仅在例外情形下允许出示检察机关在二审中通过补充侦查形式主动提交的新证据。这些证据必须满足相关性要求，仅限于和重要诉讼事实相关、具有证明价值的在一审程序结束后新发现的证据以及因客观原因未经一审法庭斟酌的证据，但证人自

---

〔25〕［英］克里斯托弗·艾伦：《英国证据法实务指南》（第四版），王进喜译，中国法制出版社2012年版，第136页。

〔26〕参见李浩：“民事诉讼法典修改后的‘新证据’——《审监解释》对‘新证据’界定的可能意义”，载《中国法学》2009年第3期。

〔27〕参见人民司法研究组：“被告在二审期间提供的证据能否作为判决的依据?”，载《人民司法》1992年第7期。

〔28〕See Prosecutor V Zejnil Delali, Zdravko Muci (aka" Pavo"), Hazim Deli and Esad, in the appeals chamber, para. 280 ~ 293.

〔29〕Major Michael R. Stahlman, “A Verdict Worthy of Confidence? Petitioning for a New Trial before Authentication Based on New Evidence”, *Military Law Review*, June, 2001, pp. 10 ~ 11.

我改变或否定的证言除外。对新发现的证据以及因客观原因未经一审法庭斟酌的证据，检察机关之前不得存在过错，且应尽了合理努力进行调查、收集、提交，否则法院也不允许出示。[30]

---

〔30〕 对于可能导致被告人无罪、罪轻以及与被告人立功、自首、坦白相关的证据，虽然二审阶段检察机关不能主动提出，但并不会损害被告人合法权益。对这些证据，人民法院完全可以依据职权调取，这也是人民法院调查取证的范围所在——人民法院依职权调查的权力，不应越俎代庖，不应查证、收集本应属于检察机关负有举证责任的证据。对此问题，我国台湾地区已经有了明确的态度，认为法院依职权调查的证据限于对被告有利事项，对被告不利事项应晓喻检察官举证，作出这样规定的基础在于，依据台湾现行刑事诉讼法，检察官负责举证被告犯罪事实，此举可以落实检察官举证，符合无罪推定原则。具体内容参见月旦法学教室编辑部："刑事诉讼法官依职权调查证据限有利被告事项"，载《月旦法学教室》2012 年第 114 期。而根据我国《刑事诉讼法》第 49 条的规定，公诉案件中被告人有罪的举证责任由人民检察院承担，若检察机关举证不能，自当承担对其不利后果。因此，证实被告人有罪的证据，人民法院不可以依职权调查，而对于除此之外的对被告人有利的证据，在必要时人民法院可以依职权调查。该观点也能够得到高法解释相关规定的印证，例如，高法解释第 110 条规定，对被告人及其辩护人提出有自首、坦白、立功的事实和理由，有关机关未予认定，或者有关机关提出被告人有自首、坦白、立功表现，但证据材料不全的，人民法院应当要求有关机关提供证明材料，或者要求相关人员作证，并结合其他证据作出认定；该解释第 184 条规定，在召开庭前会议时，审判人员可以就是否申请调取在侦查、审查起诉期间公安机关、人民检察院收集但未随案移送的证明被告人无罪或者罪轻的证据材料向控辩双方了解情况，听取意见；该解释第 224、226 条还规定，人民法院根据被告人、辩护人的申请，向人民检察院调取在侦查、审查起诉期间收集的有关被告人无罪或者罪轻的证据材料，应当通知人民检察院在收到调取证据材料决定书后三日内移交；审判期间，合议庭发现被告人可能有自首、坦白、立功等法定量刑情节，而人民检察院移送的案卷中没有相关证据材料的，应当通知人民检察院移送。

存疑不起诉案件证据适用问题研究

宋　鹏[*]

存疑不起诉作为检察机关公诉权的一项重要内容，其适用的基本条件是案件“事实不清，证据不足”。存疑不起诉的关键在于如何正确地认识和把握证据，这是司法实践中分歧较大的问题，也是目前迫切需要解决的问题。鉴于此，笔者将所在检察院近五年的存疑不起诉案件的处理作为基本的研究素材，并结合我国新《刑事诉讼法》的规定，就存疑不起诉案件中证据不足问题进行探讨。

一、司法实践中存疑不起诉案件证据不足的具体表现

根据新《刑事诉讼法》的规定，定罪起诉的基本条件是证据确实、充分，而存疑不起诉的实质条件是证据不足，这里的证据不足应该指两方面内容：一是证据不确实；二是证据不充分。笔者将通过以下几组数据对存疑不起诉案件的证据情况进行分析。

（一）存疑不起诉案件的特点

根据表1可以发现，2007年至2011年，我区检察院存疑不起诉案件占全部不起诉案件的34.8%。其中牵涉的罪名达18个之多，基本上涵盖了刑法分则每一章的内容，包括强奸、故意伤害等侵犯人身权利的犯罪，合同诈骗、非法经营等破坏社会主义市场经济秩序的犯罪，盗窃、诈骗等侵犯公民财产权利的犯罪等。虽然存疑不起诉案件罪名达18个，但是主要集中在强奸、诈骗、盗窃罪中。根据调查，上述三种犯罪共计23件46人，占存疑不起诉案件的49.8%。

表1

年份	不起诉	存疑不起诉	证据不足具体表现					
			危害行为	因果关系	犯罪手段	犯罪主体	犯罪故意	犯罪目的
2007	29件41人	10件16人	2件5人	2件4人	2件3人	1件1人	3件3人	
2008	15件20人	5件6人	3件4人				1件1人	1件1人
2009	24件24人	9件9人	5件5人				3件3人	1件1人
2010	29件37人	11件19人	6件13人	1件2人	3件3人		1件1人	
2011	38件52人	12件16人	4件6人	1件2人	3件3人	1件2人	1件1人	2件2人
合计	135件174人	47件66人	20件33人	4件8人	8件9人	2件3人	9件9人	4件4人

* 宋鹏，北京市顺义区人民检察院检委会秘书、助理检察员。Email：whosuwho110@sina.cn。

表2

罪名	强奸	诈骗	盗窃	职务侵占	故意伤害	寻衅滋事	挪用资金	抢劫	合同诈骗	交通肇事	猥亵儿童	滥发林木	非法经营	非法采矿	以危险方法危害公共安全	掩饰隐瞒犯罪所得	敲诈勒索
数量	10	9	4	3	3	3	2	2	2	1	1	1	1	1	1	1	1

（二）存疑不起诉案件证据不足的具体表现

《人民检察院刑事诉讼规则》第286条其中第2项“犯罪构成要件事实缺乏必要的证据予以证明”是存疑不起诉的关键。所谓的“犯罪构成要件事实”是指犯罪的主观方面、客观方面、主体、客体四个要件。四个要件中又具体包含不同的内容，笔者结合案例予以具体阐明。

1. 证明行为人危害行为的证据不足。根据调查，证明危害行为的证据不足的案件多达20件33人，主要集中在故意伤害、诈骗等案件中。主要表现为：证明是犯罪嫌疑人实施犯罪行为的证据不足。第一种情形为只有被害人的陈述没有其他证据相互佐证。如赵某某涉嫌故意伤害案中，只有被害人张某一人在陈述中指控赵某某用铁锹将其打成重伤，并且鉴定结论中写明被害人的伤系钝器所致重伤。但是现场既没有提取到作案工具，也没有其他证人证言能够证实赵某某实施了伤害被害人的行为，并且赵某某也始终否认被害人的伤是其所致。第二种情形是侦查机关取证违反法定程序导致证据无法采信。如周某某寻衅滋事罪中，公安机关找到被害人并让其辨认，但是在辨认之前办案人员将系统中周某某的户籍材料给被害人过目，户籍材料中有周某某的照片，这导致后来的辨认无法作为证据予以采信。而有没有其他证据来证实周某某实施了寻衅滋事的行为，最后只能存疑不起诉。

2. 证明行为人有犯罪故意的证据不足。根据调查，因无法证实行为人有犯罪故意而存疑的案件有9件9人，主要集中在强奸罪中。主要表现为：证明行为人是否“明知”的证据不足。如张某涉嫌强奸案中，行为人张某与被害人王某某多次发生性关系，虽未采用暴力、威胁手段强行与被害人发生性关系，但是被害人王某某系幼女，根据相关司法解释的规定，行为人张某是否“明知”王某某是幼女就成为本案的关键。而现有证据只能证明张某知道被害人的出生月份和日期，但不知道具体的出生年份。再如王某涉嫌强奸案中，对于行为是否“明知”被害人周某是精神病患者的证据不足，故对王某作存疑不起诉处理。

3. 证明行为人实施了某种犯罪手段的证据不足。犯罪手段是刑法规定的某些特殊犯罪的构成必备要件，如抢劫罪。以孟某某、殷某某抢劫案为例，嫌疑人孟某某伙同殷某某深夜潜入被害人李某家中意图盗窃财物，不料被李某发现两嫌疑人之一持刀刺伤了被害人。由于本案是转化型抢劫，必须要求行为人当场实施了暴力的行为，但是现有证据只有嫌疑人孟某某和殷某某相互指证对方实施了持刀伤人行为并否认自己实施了持刀刺伤被害人的行为，而又没有其他证据来佐证。由于当时是深夜，被害人也无法辨认究竟是谁刺伤了他，更为困难的是，侦查机关没有及时提取作案工具，导致有效的物证灭失，最终不得不对二人作存疑不起诉处理。

4. 证明危害行为和危害结果之间有因果关系的证据不足。按照《刑法》的规定，行为人对某种行为负刑事责任的必要条件是其实施的危害行为和危害结果之间存在刑法上的因果关系。根据调查，该类案件主要集中在故意伤害、重大责任事故等案件中。如李某故意伤害案中，犯罪嫌疑人李某确实实施了殴打被害人张某的行为。后被害人张某坠楼死亡，根据法医检验，张某颅骨骨折致颅内大出血死亡并且腿部受轻微伤。现有证据虽能证实嫌疑人李某实施了殴打张某的行为，但是证人证言、鉴定结论以及犯罪嫌疑人供述等证据不能证实李某殴打张某致使其从高处坠下，不能排除张某在被李某殴打后由于自己想不开而自杀，危害行为和危害结果之间不具有唯一的因果关系。

5. 证明行为人有某种特定的犯罪目的的证据不足。刑法中有一些行为必须要有特定的犯罪目的才能构成犯罪，这也是刑法上的“目的犯”，例如，诈骗罪、合同诈骗罪中以非法占有为目的，出售出入境证件罪以营利为目的等。如姜某某诈骗案中，姜某某系飞轮公司的总经理，法定代表人为张某。姜某某与被害人李某某合作建了三座加油站，但是姜某某在李某某不知情的情况下将其中三座加油站变卖给中国石油，并将所得款项用于偿还新时代公司的贷款。虽然嫌疑人姜某某采取了隐瞒事实的手段变卖了加油站，但是其并不是将所得款项据为已有，而是用于偿还其所担任职务的公司的贷款和利息，也没有证据证明新时代公司的贷款是姜某某所贷。由于证实姜某某非法占有的目的证据不足，只能对其作存疑不起诉处理。

6. 证明犯罪主体的证据不足。这里主要包括两种情形：一是证明嫌疑人是否达到刑事责任年龄的证据不足。如谢某交通肇事案中，根据嫌疑人谢某自己的供述，其已经满16周岁，但是嫌疑人的父母却提出其不满16周岁，身份证上所记载的日期应为农历而不是公历，其老家有把农历作为出生日期的传统。现有证据无法证实谢某的真实出生年月，进而无法确定其是否达到刑事责任年龄，故只能作存疑处理。二是证明嫌疑人系特殊主体的证据不足。如汪某某挪用资金一案中，由于挪用资金罪的主体要求是特殊主体，但是嫌疑人洪某某案发当时的身份就是某村一普通村民，没有证据证实其是受村主任贾某某的指派或者默许，代表村委会去北京青苹果公司收取土地尾款，故其不能成为挪用资金罪的犯罪主体。

二、存疑不起诉案件中证据存在的问题

根据对47件存疑不起诉案件的调查情况来看，在证据的认定中主要存在以下问题：

（一）侦查机关取证不及时、不全面、违法取证现象普遍

1. 取证不及时。一起犯罪行为的实施，从犯罪的预备到实施犯罪行为以及犯罪结果的出现，都会留下一系列的“痕迹”，这些“痕迹”经过侦查人员的依法收集就会成为证明案件事实的证据。[1] 但是在实践中，侦查机关不及时进行取证导致认定案件的关键证据灭失，使犯罪嫌疑人逍遥法外的现象时有发生。如不及时提取现场指纹导致无法确定嫌疑人，不及时对现场的物证、书证等进行搜集导致证据灭失等。如王某

〔1〕 刘福谦：“排除四对矛盾可有效减少错案发生”，载《检察日报》2006年8月15日。

某故意伤害案中，被害人报案后，侦查机关虽然及时到场并控制了犯罪嫌疑人，但是由于侦查机关没有及时勘查现场并及时提取犯罪嫌疑人的作案工具并进行指纹检测，导致最终难以认定被害人所受重伤是嫌疑人所为，故只能对其作存疑不起诉处理。

在张某某强奸一案中，由于没有及时提取被害人的内衣，致使内衣被被害人清洗并丢弃，导致无法做精液 DNA 鉴定，在嫌疑人否认自己作案的情况下，又没有其他证据证明是嫌疑人实施强奸行为，导致无法认定本案为张某某所为，检察机关只能对其作存疑不起诉处理。

2. 取证不全面。证据必须形成有效的链条才具有较强的证明力，如果证据比较单一，就难以形成有效的证据链条来证明案件的事实。根据新《刑事诉讼法》的规定，定罪、量刑的证据都必须要有，不能只注重收集定罪的证据而忽略量刑的证据。但是实践中一些侦查人员只注重犯罪嫌疑人口供的突破，而忽视其他相关证据尤其是物证、书证的发现与收集。[2] 如周某某盗窃案中，侦查机关只注重口供的取证，在现场勘查没有提取有效的物证如足迹、指纹等，导致嫌疑人在后来翻供而又没有其他证据来证实其到过现场，最后只能作存疑不起诉处理。

在栗某某故意伤害案中，栗某某因琐事同被害人发生争吵，栗某某往被害人头上打了一拳，被害人被打后十分气恼，跑回家一个人喝闷酒，而后不久在家中死亡。侦查机关对嫌疑人进行了讯问，栗某某也承认殴打了栗某某。但是侦查机关并未对被害人的死因进行法医鉴定，由于缺少这一关键证据，导致无法仅凭口供进行定案。后检察机关要求公安机关对被害人尸体解剖鉴定被害人死亡的原因。经法医鉴定死亡原因是脑蛛网膜出血，并分析引发脑蛛网膜出血的诱因有喝酒过度激动、头部受到外力打击等多种因素。那么，根据法医鉴定这一证据得出的结论就有多种可能性，因而怀疑被害人死亡不一定是栗某某伤害所致，而可能是喝酒所致，因此检察机关只能对栗某某作存疑不起诉处理。

3. 取证违反法定程序。根据《刑事诉讼法》的规定，审判人员、检察人员、侦查人员必须依照法定程序，收集能够证实犯罪嫌疑人、被告人、有罪或者无罪、犯罪情节轻重的各种证据。在实践中存在着多种形式的非法取证行为，如刑讯逼供、诱供、骗供；侦查人员以暗示性的语言或者动作提示，或对辨认对象作标记等取得辨认笔录；鉴定对象或者送检材料不合格的鉴定结论；以违反法定程序的方法取得实物证据等等。如新《刑事诉讼法》明确要求侦查机关讯问未成年人必须要法定代理人在场，讯问女性未成年人必须要求有女工作人员在场，而实践中，由于侦查机关对新法的不了解，导致嫌疑人的口供或者无法采用，或者退回侦查机关补正。如苑某某寻衅滋事案中，在侦查机关组织对嫌疑人的辨认中，由于辨认的照片数量没有达到法定的数量，导致辨认无效。

（二）检察机关审查、固定证据能力不足

1. 批捕部门审查证据不严。根据新刑诉法的规定，只有对那些有证据证明有犯罪事实，可能判处有期徒刑以上刑罚的犯罪嫌疑人、被告人，采取取保候审尚不足以发生危险的才应当予以逮捕。实践中，批捕部门由于审查逮捕的期限有限，再加上为了

---

〔2〕 向少良："珠海市检察机关存疑不起诉案件分析"，载《检察官学院学报》2008 年第 6 期。

保障侦查机关的进一步侦查而放松了对证据的把关导致捕后有些证据难以补充，最后不得不作存疑处理。如赵某某妨害公务案，由于此案在当地的影响较大，为了配合侦查机关进一步取证，批捕部门作了批准逮捕的决定，在羁押了数月之后，侦查机关没能获取有力的证据，导致案件只能作存疑处理，并且嫌疑人还向检察机关提起了国家赔偿。

2. 证据审查不全面、固定证据能力欠缺。审查证据的目的是要判断所收集的证据能否确实、充分地证明案件的真实情况，包括对单个证据的审查判断和对全案证据的审查判断。在单个证据审查方面，主要是审查证据的“三性”，即客观性、关联性、合法性，但实践中存在顾此失彼的情况，在全案证据审查方面，主要是从质和量两个方面综合审查案件证据是否达到确实、充分，而实践中存在对证据的审查不够全面、过分重视口供和证人证言而忽视对其他证据的审查。[3] 另外，检察机关在提讯犯罪嫌疑人时有时会出现每次提讯的询问笔录都不一致，嫌疑人每次的供述都不一致，尤其是在自侦案件中，不少贪污、贿赂案件，被告人翻供后，使原先收集的证据的证明力弱化，达不到起诉标准，只得作存疑不诉。

如文某某等人拐卖妇女一案。侦查机关指控文某某伙同沈某某、龙某某、刘某某、魏某某以介绍到国内打工为名，先后拐卖 4 名妇女到某县，造成严重后果和恶劣的社会影响。后经检察机关审查提起公诉，法院经审理后认为，从主观方面看，被告人沈某某、刘某某、龙某某的供述中均没提到与被告人文某某预谋商量拐卖被害人，文某某供述中更未谈及拐卖的故意。沈某某曾对文某某说，这些女孩已在国内自愿嫁人，当时文某某还劝沈某某说她们不愿意就不要强迫，由此看来，文对沈此前的行为是不知情的，不具有拐卖妇女的主观故意。从客观方面看，文某某只是述称被害人三人曾到其家要求其帮忙找工作，其打电话与被告人刘某某联系，让刘替被害人联系工作，然后刘某某将其带的这三位姑娘交给被告人沈某某，其不久就回家了。还辩称沈某某返回后交给其的 500 元，是当作三位姑娘在其家里的伙食费用。三位被害人的证言亦没有讲到文某某骗她们，只是称文某某介绍她们认识刘某某，过后刘某某、沈某某带她们去，文某某没有去。综上，文某某的供述与沈某某、刘某某的供述及三被害人的陈述能相互印证，证实文某某主观上没有拐卖妇女的共同犯意，客观上没有参与拐卖的行为，其行为不构成犯罪。检察机关没有对证据进行进一步的审查，导致案件只能撤回。

（三）检察机关、审判机关对证据的认识标准不一致

由于司法职能、刑法适用立场及法律解释方法的不同导致检法在法律适用上差异的存在，尤其是对证据认识的不一致导致对法律的权威、审判的权威造成负面的影响。办案人员对法律的理解及对案件把握程度的不同，对同一案件的证据条件是否达到确实充分和对案件证据的采信上有时会存在比较大分歧。

如已经经过庭审的李某某盗窃案，现有证据有被害人的陈述、从被告处起获的被盗物品以及其他物证、书证等证据，唯一缺少的是犯罪嫌疑人的供述，嫌疑人始终辩解说被盗物品是从别处购买而来的，但是经检察机关进一步的查证，嫌疑人的辩解基

---

〔3〕 陈金石等：“存疑不起诉的规范适用”，载《西部法学评论》2008 年第 3 期。

本上都不是事实。因此检察机关认为，现有证据虽然都是间接证据，但是现有的间接证据已经形成链条，可以定罪。法院则认为，现有的证据都是间接证据，没有证据证据能够证明李某某到过案发现场并承认自己盗窃了被害人的物品，因此对于此案只能认定为无罪，建议检察机关撤案作存疑不起诉处理。

三、如何正确把握存疑不起诉案件中的证据

审查起诉工作中，存在存疑不起诉案件是正常的，也有利于保护犯罪嫌疑人的合法权益。但是，从惩罚犯罪的职责出发，对于那些因不能正确把握证据而导致的存疑不起诉案件则实属不应该。针对实践中，存疑不起诉案件中证据把握存在的问题，结合新的刑诉法规定的证据标准，笔者认为应从以下三个方面来进一步提高把握证据的能力：

（一）严格遵守新刑诉法规定的证据标准

新的刑事诉讼法对证据标准做了重大修改，在原有的“事实清楚、证据确实充分”的基础上，对“证据确实充分”进行了界定，并明确了“排除合理怀疑”和非法证据排除规则。

（1）正确把握“合理怀疑“的界限。对于“合理怀疑”应从两个方面理解：首先，“合理怀疑”是基于一定的证据产生的，而不是凭空的想象。主要表现在两点：一是据以定罪的证据之间的矛盾不能合理排除。二是根据证据得出的结论具有其他可能性。其次，合理怀疑必须具有一定的现实可能性，它合乎常理而不能违背常理。在司法实践中，某一怀疑是否合乎常理，具有一定的现实可能性，也因案而异，具体如何判断，需要司法人员吃透案情，感受证据，正确运用逻辑思维，以人们日常生活常识为依据，对事物存在和发展的常态作出判断，使自己的怀疑疑之有据，疑之有理，而不是匪夷所思，这样才能准确地把握疑罪。

如谢某交通肇事案中，现有证据不能确定谢某已年满16周岁，也没有证据能够确定其已满16周岁，这样的证据就不能排除谢某未满16周岁的“合理怀疑”。再如汪某某故意伤害案，现有证据不能排除被害人所受的重伤是由其他人所致，也就是结论不具有唯一性。

（2）严格排除“非法证据”。存疑不起诉案件的证据中有一部分证据是违法取证获得的，对于该部分证据必须严格予以排除。非法证据包括非法的言词证据和非法的实物证据。在实践中，主要有以下几种情形：一是辨认程序违法，如辨认之前辨认人获得侦查机关的暗示、辨认照片的数量不符合法定要求等，如刘某某涉嫌寻衅滋事案中，被害人钟某在辨认时得到侦查人员的暗示，导致辨认结论不能采用。二是鉴定机构不具有鉴定资质，如贾某某涉嫌重大责任事故一案中，两家鉴定结构出具的火灾损失的鉴定结论由于两家机构不具鉴定资质而被排除。三是采用诱骗、威胁方法取得的言辞证据。如赵某某涉嫌妨害公务案中，嫌疑人在审查起诉阶段翻供，其供述在侦查阶段侦查人员对其实施了诱供，其在侦查机关所作的供述不是真实的。

（二）严格把握证据不足的范围和标准

对证据不足而作出的存疑不起诉案件，审查起诉机关必须明确证据不足的范围和标准。

（1）明确证据不足的范围。根据新刑诉法的规定，所谓的“证据不足”并不是指案件所有的证据都不确实、充分，而是指定罪量刑的证据不充分。证据不足并不是对证据数量和种类的简单描述，而是指案件的现有证据不足以使司法人员确信犯罪嫌疑人或被告人实施了被指控犯罪或者具备被指控的犯罪情节。[4] 因此，在对存疑不起诉案件的证据进行把握时，必须要明确证据不足是指现有证据不能使承办人自己排除合理的怀疑并达到内心确信。

（2）明确证据不足的标准。《人民检察院刑事诉讼规则》第286条对证据不足列出了四个标准，在笔者看来，四个标准之间多有交叉，实践中难以正确把握。如定罪证据存在疑问，无法查证属实的情况，必然导致定罪事实缺乏必要证据；再如证据存在矛盾不能合理排除的情况，必然导致得出的结论不唯一。[5] 从实践来看，存疑不起诉案件的证据不足的标准只有一个：现有证据不足以排除对已认定案件事实的“合理怀疑”，不能达到司法人员对案件定罪量刑的内心确信。实践中，对存疑不起诉案件的证据审查不能只揪住无关大局的枝节证据，要从全局着眼。只要现有证据能够认定案件的基本事实就达到起诉的标准，避免将疑难案件、有疑点的案件与存疑案件混为一谈，避免“伪存疑案件”的出现。

（三）正确运用证据矛盾排除方法

检察机关在审查起诉阶段对证据的判断和分析对于适用存疑不起诉至关重要。证据的判断分析过程本质上也就是排除矛盾证据的过程。在矛盾的证据中寻求真相是每一个公诉人必备的能力。有学者指出应对证据矛盾的方式和方法主要包括有效的排除、合理的解释、充分的证明以及适当的容忍这四个方面。[6] 这种解决证据矛盾的方法对于司法实践有极大的借鉴意义。下面笔者结合实践谈谈证据矛盾排除方法。①直接排除矛盾。如果矛盾证据一方符合客观性、关联性和合法性这三个基本特征，则与此矛盾的证据可以排除。②通过调查方式排除矛盾。在审查案件中，通过对证据进行比对，发现矛盾后，通过调查来核实证据的真实性。如证人证言前后存在矛盾，可以对其继续调查，查明其前后矛盾的原因，矛盾的原因是否能够合理的解释，能否与其他证据进行印证，使其矛盾得到解决。③运用比较、鉴别、分析的方法，合理解释矛盾。有些案件无法继续侦查，或者经过侦查仍不能消除证据矛盾，可以通过合理解释来消除矛盾，即合理解释矛盾形成原因及矛盾信息本身的内容与意义。[7] 办案人员要客观细致地分析证据之间的矛盾点以及产生矛盾的原因，如受害人作出有利于被告人的证据，显然有悖于常理，如果已经查明受害人与被告人之间私下达成协议，则其与其他有罪证据相矛盾的原因得到了一定的解释，减弱证据矛盾对事实认定的损害。[8] ④通过补强证据排除矛盾。运用前三种方法无法排除矛盾的情况下，可以通过补充其他证据充分证明案件事实。如在盗窃罪转化抢劫罪案件中，犯罪嫌疑人与同案人关于谁采用暴力的证据“一对一”，形成证据矛盾。可以通过收集其他目击证人、犯罪工具、提取作案工具上的指纹等证据来印证抢劫事实。当无法通过上述方式合理排除证据矛盾时，

---

〔4〕 段启俊：“疑罪的认定与处理”，载《人民检察》2006年第7期（上）。

〔5〕 何柏松：“存疑不起诉若干问题辨析”，载《中国检察官》2009年第3期。

〔6〕 龙宗智：“试论证据矛盾及矛盾分析法”，载《中国法学》2007年第4期。

〔7〕 龙宗智：“试论证据矛盾及矛盾分析法”，载《中国法学》2007年第4期。

〔8〕 龙宗智：“试论证据矛盾及矛盾分析法”，载《中国法学》2007年第4期。

仍然有肯定有罪的证据，又有否定有罪的证据，不能得出唯一的结论，即可视为证据不足。

（四）加强司法机关的沟通、协调

公、检、法三机关目前在证据采信标准上存在分歧，应在坚持法律原则的同时，加强相互之间的沟通、协调。在检、法之间，要针对司法实践中存在的对证据认识的分歧，努力探索并建立检察院与法院之间的沟通协调工作平台和机制，并使之规范化、科学化，使双方能够形成“庭上就个案各司其职，庭外就证据标准和尺度共同研究”的良性互动关系，既确保“分工负责，相互制约”原则的落实，又能在“互相配合”中推动法律在实践中不断完善和进步。

司法精神病学在西方发展历史的回顾 *

陈立成 庞春红 *

由于罹病后大多缺乏自知力和自制力，精神障碍者比其他医学专业领域的疾病患者具有更多的特殊性，精神科医师同样也承担着一种更高度专业的受托义务，从而就造成了比其他医学专业更大的权力不对称的人际关系和更广泛的伦理问题。[1] 而作为一类表现特殊的社会现象，精神活动——无论是“正常”的还是“异常”的抑或是“病态”的——都一直被认为属于一类社会文化现象，精神障碍也一直被当作是社会文明的产物，文化的差异和政治的力量对精神障碍者的“病理性”体验以及对治疗的影响都是非常大的。[2] 因此，精神卫生问题遭遇到了更多的社会学方面的问题和伦理学方面的问题，使用精神医学的理论、概念、知识和技术，也就更有可能会做出违反人道主义和侵犯人权的事情。

在这方面，西方社会一直都是处于“遥遥领先”的位置的，这与中国社会的发展历史中，对待异常精神活动和精神障碍者的态度一直比较开明和宽容是明显不同的。

在这方面众所周知的一些基本事实包括：发生在20世纪上半叶的两次世界大战，特别是第二次世界大战，给世界各国人民都造成了极大的苦难，可以说是人类历史上空前的浩劫。其中，尤其是纳粹德国滥用精神医学知识和技术，对精神障碍者施以医疗暴行。[3] 据统计，[4][5] 从1939年到1945年，有近18万“被纳粹认为是没有生存价值”的精神障碍者，被以“安乐死”的名义杀害。

其实在这方面，美国并不比纳粹“落后”，甚至反而是更具有“超前”意识。因为早在纳粹之前，美国就早已经就开始进行“优化人种”的工作。20世纪20年代至30年代，[6] 美国有20个州都以立法的形式，对罹患精神障碍者和有智力缺陷者实施

---

* 本文为国家社科基金后期资助项目（10FFX005）的部分成果。

* 中央司法警官学院，E-mail：chenlicheng2005@163.com。

〔1〕 李亚琼、谢侃侃、李艳等：“从《夏威夷宣言》到《马德里宣言》”，载《临床精神医学杂志》2011年第21卷第5期，第356~357页。

〔2〕 李洁：《文化与精神医学》，华夏出版社2011年版，第3~4页。

〔3〕 [英] Bridget Giles：《变态心理学》，潘华译，黑龙江科学技术出版社2007年版，第182页。

〔4〕 李亚琼、谢侃侃、李艳等：“从《夏威夷宣言》到《马德里宣言》”，载《临床精神医学杂志》2011年第21卷第5期，第356~357页。

〔5〕 [美] Paul Roland：《超级谋杀者的心理画像》，翁里、徐镇强等译，中国人民公安大学出版社2008年版，第25~53页。

〔6〕 [美] Malcolm Potts，Roger Short：《自亚当和夏娃以来——人类性行为的进化》，张敦福译，商务印书馆2006年版，第338~339页。

强制性的阉割手术，尤其是当他们涉嫌性犯罪时。而在更早的1851年，[7]曾经被路易斯安那医学委员会（这个委员会是专门调查在美国的非洲裔奴隶身上所表现出来的"奇怪"行为的）任命为委员长的塞缪尔·卡特莱特（Samuel Cartwright），就在一本医学杂志上发表了一篇题为《黑人的疾病和身体特征》的研究报告。这份报告以"无可争议的科学证据"证明，在黑人身上确实存在着一种特有的、被称为"类躁狂"的"精神疾病"，这类"精神疾病"的主要特征就是寻求自由，具体表现就是黑人奴隶从他们的奴隶主那里设法逃走。因此，该报告的结论认为，出于"高尚"和"人道"的目的，奴隶主就应该将这些逃跑的奴隶抓回来，以便对其进行"治疗"，从而消除其追求自由的"类躁狂"症状。该报告的另一个重大的"科学"发现是：黑人都罹患有"感觉疾病"，这种疾病使得他们在"受惩罚时对于疼痛"不敏感。所以，在对黑人进行"治疗"时是不需要吝惜使用皮鞭的。进而，这份报告中的"科学证据"充分证明了奴隶制的做法是正当的。

20世纪70年代初期，[8][9]苏联、罗马尼亚、南非等国家也曾滥用精神医学。据说在苏联，[10]当时是由克格勃主持召开精神病学委员会会议，"由2~4名克格勃官员和1~2名未必是医生的'医生'组成一个小组"，将反对现行制度的人和持不同政见者诊断为"潜隐型精神分裂症"，然后再将其无限期监禁于专门对付"政治患者"的特种病院中进行"治疗"。这些远离人烟的特种病院大都隶属于克格勃，并由武装哨兵进行"保护"。

正是由于在西方历史上，长期存在着这类对精神病学（psychiatry）的误用（misuse）和滥用（abuse），20世纪极富挑战性和反叛性，并曾经罹患过"忧郁症"的法国哲学家和思想家米歇尔·福柯（Michel Foucault），才对精神病院以及精神病学的政治应用（他称之为"精神病学政治"或"政治精神病学"）提出了严厉的批评和指责。米歇尔·福柯（Michel Foucault）认为，精神病学从一开始就具有维护社会秩序的镇压功能，[11]因为"疯癫不是一种自然现象，而是文明的产物。"[12]精神病院实际上是具有医学外表的软禁之所，"禁止发疯如同禁止发言"。他还认为，在精神病的发展、诊治过程中，表面上看是知识、科学的作用，实则透出权力的魅影。事实上，真正的危险不在于精神病人数的增长，而是没有一个稳定可靠的机制去区分病人还是正常人。所以，精神疾病并不可怕，可怕的是对精神病患者的误解，以及对精神病管制的矫枉过正。[13]

---

〔7〕［美］Richard J. Gerrig, Philip G. Zimbardo：《心理学与生活（第16版）》，王垒、王甦等译，人民邮电出版社2003年版，第419页。

〔8〕Helmchen H, *Okasha A. From the Hawaii Declaration to the Declaratin of Madrid*, Acta Psychiatry Scand, 2000, 101, pp. 20~23.

〔9〕［美］Richard J. Gerrig, Philip G. Zimbardo：《心理学与生活（第16版）》，王垒、王甦等译，人民邮电出版社2003年版，第419页。

〔10〕余凤高：《天才就是疯子》，湖南人民出版社2002年版，第162~168页。

〔11〕何恬："试论司法精神病学中'偏执性精神病'的诊断地位"，载《法律与医学杂志》2007年第4期，第S6~S8。

〔12〕郭志媛："刑事诉讼中精神病鉴定的程序保障实证调研报告"，《证据科学》2012年第6期，第721~736页。

〔13〕［英］Bridget Giles：《变态心理学》，潘华译，黑龙江科学技术出版社2007年版，第182页。

由此也不难看出，精神医学专业比其他医学专业具有更大的权力不对称的人际关系，涉及了更为广泛的伦理学问题和法律问题。也正因为如此，作为为法学和法律服务的司法精神病学，在其起步和发展的整个历程中，也一直是走在一条蜿蜒曲折、甚至是不断折返的道路上，迄今仍然在饱受社会各界的争议乃至非议。系统地回顾这一历史发展过程，对于司法精神病学学科的健康发展，具有极为重要的现实意义。

一、相关理念的早期萌芽

西方有关精神障碍的法律条文最早见于奴隶制时代。公元前 18 世纪的古巴比伦国王汉谟拉比（Hammurabi）颁布的《汉谟拉比法典》（*The Code of Hammurabi*）中就明确地规定：买来的奴隶不满一个月就患癫痫或精神障碍者，可以退还给卖主，并收回付款。因该法典被刻在石柱上，所以后人亦称其为《石柱法》。公元前 5 世纪中叶，罗马共和国颁布的《十二铜表法》（*Law of The Twelve Tables*）中提出：患精神障碍或痴呆者丧失处理财产、买卖、婚姻和订立遗嘱的能力，并应对其进行监护。据说这是目前发现的对精神障碍者行为能力和监护措施的最早立法。

被誉为欧洲医学之父的古希腊医生希波克拉底（Hippocrates）（公元前 460 年～公元前 377 年）也曾经描述过精神障碍者的一些表现。与之同时代的著名哲学家柏拉图（公元前 427～公元前 347 年）在其《理想国》一书中提出，精神障碍者应该得到家属很好的照顾，不应让其流浪在外；如果家属没有做到，就必须处以罚金。柏拉图还认为，精神障碍者造成危害后果的，除应该赔偿由其所造成的经济损失外，不应受到其他惩罚。这是最早提出的保护精神障碍者的立法主张，可以被视为是现代司法精神病学基本概念的萌芽。在罗马帝国时代，法律还规定将精神障碍作为丧失权利和免除刑罚的一种依据。古罗马皇帝马可·奥勒留（Marcus Aurelius）也曾经热心地劝说人们应该同情精神障碍者，并发出手谕对一名因罹患精神障碍而杀死自己母亲的当事人免除了刑罚。西塞罗（Cicero）（公元前 106 年～公元前 43 年）主张，兴奋躁动的精神障碍者如果触犯了刑法不应承担法律责任。

可见，当时的社会及其统治者对待肇事肇祸精神障碍者的态度，大多是比较宽容的，反映出古代西方社会对精神障碍及患者的认识已经具有了朴素唯物主义的萌芽。

二、宗教统治的中世纪

罗马帝国瓦解后的中世纪（公元 476 年～公元 17 世纪），随着西方人认识问题角度的变化，教会与神权统治了整个欧洲，宗教信仰的重点——世界是上帝与魔鬼之间的战场的观点——自然而然地导致了精神障碍存在着超自然基础的观点。这种观点认为，人们之所以会出现异常的精神活动，是因为他们的心智已经被魔鬼或者邪恶的灵魂所控制。精神障碍被认为属于“原罪”，精神障碍者被认为是魔鬼的化身，是妖魔作祟，是被上帝惩罚的人。为了“拯救”这些可怜的人，人们倾向于用魔法和巫术解决精神障碍的问题。当时采用了很多种“治疗”方法，被现代人看起来比较人道的方法如牧师的祈祷，或者是让高洁的圣者举行驱魔仪式以驱赶魔鬼，或者是使用所谓“圣水”、“圣药之类的物质。而更多被现代人认为是“愚昧”、“无知”、“野蛮”、“迷信”和不人道的方法如：用烙铁烧炙患者的皮肤、长针穿舌头、火焚、活埋、带上镣铐终身监禁，有的甚至是在患者的头骨上打洞等，或者用铁链将患者锁起来关在岩洞中挨饿，以便将其体内的魔鬼驱除出来，甚至是直接消灭其肉体等。

当时的教会还出版了很多专门的“科普”书籍来研究魔鬼的类型、性质及其与异常精神活动之间的关系。其中有一本由教皇指定编辑的手册，名叫《魔鬼的锤子》（*Malleus Maleficorum*），为拷问、审讯、发现、驱赶和消灭“魔鬼”并“治愈”精神障碍，提供了很多具体方法。[14][15] 被认为非常博学的英格兰国王詹姆斯一世（James I）甚至还撰写出了一本名为《对魔鬼的研究》（*Study on the Devil*）的书，列出了如何识别女巫的标准。[16][17] 在当时情况下，就连声援精神障碍者的正义呼声也往往被宣判为异端邪说，这些人也被当作社会上的危害分子而遭受与精神障碍者同等的待遇。对精神障碍者的肇事肇祸行为，更是采取了“以眼还眼，以牙还牙”的摩西复仇法则，不仅严刑拷打，甚至经常采用火焚、活埋等消灭肉体的方法将精神障碍者置于死地。

即使是在这个时期，也有一些开明人士提出了不同的意见。1265 年，英国首席法官亨利·布雷克顿（Henry Bracton）就针对精神障碍者的危害行为，提出了著名的“野兽条例”（The Wild Beast Test）：“因为精神错乱的行为类同一头野兽，所以应该免于治罪。”“除非行为人具有伤害的意图，否则不应被判处有罪。”1556 年，菲茨·赫伯特（Fitz Herbert）则提出了比较具有可操作性的标准：[18]“当一个人不能数清 29 个便士，或者不能讲出自己的父母是谁，或者不知道自己几岁时，应免除罪责”。

1724 年，罹患偏执性精神障碍的爱德华·阿诺德（Edward Arnold）认为昂斯洛（Onslow）勋爵对自己施以了魔法，进入自己体内进行折磨，并因此而企图刺杀昂斯洛勋爵。英格兰的大法官特雷西（Tracy）对该案件的判决就遵循了“野兽条例”，而最终判决结果却仍认为爱德华·阿诺德有罪，并将绞刑改为终身监禁。[19][20] 1326 年，爱德华二世（Edward II）统治时期也制定了有关的法律条例，提出被告若精神失常（Madness，后来又被称做“精神错乱”Insanity）可以免除其刑事责任。[21]

三、文艺复兴后的快速发展

随着科学技术的发展和社会历史的进步，人们开始逐渐以更加客观、理性的态度来看待异常精神活动和精神障碍者。欧洲文艺复兴运动时期及以后，科学逐渐摆脱了宗教的束缚，得到了较快的发展。对于精神活动和精神障碍的研究和关心逐渐显现，过去对精神障碍者那些残忍的“治疗”行为等也逐渐得到纠正，迷信的思考方式开始消退，有关感知、情绪、联想等心理学观念也逐步得到发展。

16 世纪的法官 E. 科克（E. Coke）把各种不同类型的精神障碍归纳起来统称为

---

〔14〕 沈渔邨主编：《精神病学》，人民卫生出版社 1998 年版，第 4 页。

〔15〕 据说当时用来审讯“女巫”的某些方法在西方某些国家一直沿用至今，甚至被写入了美国中情局的《库巴克审讯手册》（KUBARK Interrogation Manual，1963）中，并用于最近几年对恐怖分子的审讯。参见［英］Dominic Streatfeild：《洗脑术——思想控制的荒唐史》，张孝铎译，中国青年出版社 2011 年版，第 363 ~ 400 页。

〔16〕 ［美］Malcolm Potts，Roger Short：《自亚当和夏娃以来——人类性行为的进化》，张敦福译，商务印书馆 2006 年版，第 182 页。

〔17〕 见百度百科：“詹姆斯一世”，http：//baike. baidu. com/view/675823. htm？ pid = baike. box#sub7560603，访问时间：2012 年 11 月 1 日。

〔18〕 徐一峰主编：《社会精神医学》，上海科技教育出版社 2010 年版，第 126 页。

〔19〕 刘白驹：《精神障碍与犯罪》，社会科学文献出版社 2000 年版，第 728 ~ 729 页。

〔20〕 张伟：“精神障碍与法律问题”，载孙学礼主编：《精神病学》，高等教育出版社 2008 年版，第 132 页。

〔21〕 于靖涛、田祖恩：“英美法系对精神病患者刑事责任能力的评定标准”，载《中华精神科杂志》2000 年第 33 卷第 4 期，第 249 ~ 251 页。

“精神不健全”，认为这类患者都是缺乏理解力的人而需要法律予以特殊保护。12 世纪产生的“犯罪意图”（Mens Rea）学说已被法学界广泛接受，认为犯罪意图与“犯罪行为”（Actus Reus）是有区别的。精神障碍者由于丧失了“理解力和判断力”（Ratio Et Dis Eretioneum），是“心神不健全”者，且其主观上没有犯罪的意图，故“不构成犯罪”。并将犯罪意图作为判定精神障碍者法定能力的基础。

（一）精神错乱者法

1800 年在英国发生了一件社会影响很大的刺杀事件影响了相关立法。[22][23][24][25]詹姆斯·哈德菲尔德（James Hadfield）是一名在英法战争中头部受伤的士兵，之后因罹患现代所说的脑器质性精神障碍（颅脑损伤所致精神障碍）而退役。病后的詹姆斯·哈德菲尔德出现了妄想等病理性心理体验，他认为上帝即将毁灭整个世界，而拯救全人类的唯一方法就是牺牲自己的生命，只有自己死去，世界才能幸免于难。但是，作为一名虔诚的宗教徒，詹姆斯·哈德菲尔德又不能自杀，因为教义中规定自杀是一种严重的道德犯罪。因此，詹姆斯·哈德菲尔德就采取了间接的方式，认为行刺皇帝肯定就会被处以极刑，从而达到牺牲自己、拯救英国、拯救人类的“高尚”目的。[26]

詹姆斯·哈德菲尔德在采取行动刺杀英皇乔治（George Ⅲ）被捕之后，后来被任命为大法官的英格兰律师托马斯·厄斯金（Thomas Erskine）使用“野兽条例”为其进行了成功的辩护。托马斯·厄斯金指出，可以成为辩护理由的精神错乱，并不意味着患者必须不知道自己的名字，不知道自己的处境，也不知道自己与别人的关系，在这个世界上从来就没有这样的疯狂存在。“他的犯罪是在精神错乱的影响下实施的”，托马斯·厄斯金据此说服陪审团认可了詹姆斯·哈德菲尔德是一名精神障碍者，具有妄想的事实，并以妄想作为精神障碍者无罪的评定标准（此标准被称为妄想标准 delusion test），因而免除了詹姆斯·哈德菲尔德应该承担的法律罪责，但却判决将其无限期的羁押以避免其再次危害社会和公众。

詹姆斯·哈德菲尔德的案件直接促进了《精神错乱者法》（*The Lunatics Act*，1800 年）的颁布，该法允许以精神错乱作为叛国罪、谋杀罪和重罪的辩护理由。该法同时也规定，在宣告无罪裁决后，法院必须命令将被告人严加看管。该法也为后来的有关立法奠定了基础，后续有关的立法准许对精神障碍犯罪人执行预防性拘留和不定期拘留。

（二）麦克·纳顿条例

1843 年，在英国伦敦又发生了一件轰动全社会的刺杀事件。丹尼尔·麦克·纳顿

---

〔22〕 何恬：“英美两国对精神病人刑事责任能力评判的演变”，载《证据科学》2008 年第 16 卷第 1 期，第 99 ~ 110 页。

〔23〕 刘白驹：《精神障碍与犯罪》，社会科学文献出版社 2000 年版，第 728 ~ 729 页。

〔24〕 张钦廷、汤涛：“从经典判例之行为人处置看强制监护治疗制度”，载《第十一届全国司法精神病学学术会议论文集》，2009 年 5 月印行，第 334 ~ 336 页。

〔25〕 ［英］Ronald Blackburn：《犯罪行为心理学理论、研究和实践》，吴宗宪、刘邦惠等译，中国轻工业出版社 2000 年版，第 215 页。

〔26〕 这种自杀方式目前被称为“曲线式自杀”或是“间接自杀”，即：自杀者并不是采取直接的方式自愿结束自己的生命，而是通过杀死其他人，继而使自己获得极刑的方式，来达到使自己死亡的目的。

(Daniel MacNaughten)[27] 原本是英格兰的一名木匠，平素郁闷，沉默寡言，不爱交际，却不幸罹患了一种相当于现在被称为“偏执型精神分裂症”的精神障碍。自案发前两年，麦克·纳顿就开始不断向周围人抱怨说，自己正被警察及为天主教和保守党（英国当时的执政党）工作的间谍跟踪、监视与迫害，伦敦的报纸也在败坏自己的名誉。为此，麦克·纳顿曾一度逃亡到法国寻求“避难”，但在“避难”时他仍然强烈地感觉到迫害并未中断。感到走投无路的麦克·纳顿遂决定采取“主动自卫”的方式以消除并反击保守党对自己的迫害。于是逃亡一年多的他又带着绝望的心情返回伦敦，于1843年1月20日误将首相（也是保守党的党魁）罗伯特·皮尔（Robert Peer）爵士的秘书爱德华·德拉蒙德（Edward Drummond）当做首相而射杀。

在伦敦中央刑事法庭（the Old Bailey）接受审判时，精神错乱辩护第一次被提了出来[28]。法官C. J. 廷代尔（C. J. Tindal）在按“政治谋杀案”进行审理的过程中认为，麦克·纳顿是一个精神障碍者，其在实施杀人的过程中，不知道对错（right and wrong）的区别，不知道自己行为的性质和后果（the nature and consequence of his act），因此法庭判决麦克·纳顿因“精神错乱”而无罪（not guilty by reason of insanity, NGRI）。

这一判决立即引起了英国社会的强烈反应和公众的愤怒，因为当时的社会舆论都认为这应该属于一起政治谋杀案。曾经有过三次未遂暗杀经历[29]（其中一次暗杀的刺客就是因为罹患精神障碍而得以豁免）的英国维多利亚女王也十分关注此案。女王表示，自己既不理解国家首相为什么要去迫害一个身为木匠的普通公民，也不相信一个企图杀害保守党首相的人会有精神障碍。最后，女王在听取了有关专家的意见和陈述后，认可了麦克·纳顿罹患精神障碍的事实，并发出谕旨免除了麦克·纳顿的死刑。

之后，为了平息舆论，英国上议院要求法官对公众提出的一系列问题作出解答。英国法院遂会同有关医学专家，对社会舆论的一系列质疑以条例的形式作出了解答，从而形成了历史上著名的“MacNaughten Rules”（或称“MacNaughten Act”，即《麦克·纳顿条例》）。“MacNaughten Rules”的中心内容是：每一个人都应该假定为是精神健全的和有足够的理智对自己的行为负责的，除非有相反的证据。如果被告人以精神错乱作为辩护理由时，必须能清楚地证明其在实施危害社会的行为时，由于罹患精神病（disease of mind）而缺乏理智，以致其不能了解（know）自己行为的性质（nature）和特性（quality）；或者虽然了解，但他不知道自己的行为是错误的（wrong），则不能

〔27〕不同资料中对该名字的拼写形式不是很一致的，比较多见的拼写形式有：McNaghten，McNaghton，M' Naghten，M' Naughten，M' Naghton，Macnaughton，McNaughton，Mac Naghten，MacNaughten，Macnaughten，MacNaughten，McNaughtan 等。本书采用 MacNaughten 一词的根据是《牛津精神病学教科书（中文版）》（Shorter Oxford Textbook of Psychiatry），第914页。该书由 Michael Gelder，Richard Mayou，Philip Cowen 编著，刘协和、袁德基主译，四川大学出版社2004年版。

〔28〕［英］Michael Gelder，Paul Harrison，Philip Cowen：《牛津精神病学教科书（第五版·中文版）》，刘协和、李涛主译，四川大学出版社2010年版，第859页。

〔29〕据说，在位63年零7个月的维多利亚女王，曾先后7次幸免于刺杀事件，而第一次向维多利亚（Victoria）女王开枪的刺客就是一名精神障碍者，该精神障碍者刺杀女王的目的仅仅是为了出名。参见“英女王40年间七次遇刺，精神病人打响第一枪”，转引自：《环球日报》2010年12月16日，http：//history. huanqiu. com/world/2010－12/1346673. html，访问时间：2011年8月9日。

认定被告负有刑事责任。

在 MacNaughten Rules 中，另一个足以为患者辩护的有力理由是存在妄想。由于这些妄想确实存在，且患者是由于妄想的缘故才引起了犯罪的行为。因此，《MacNaughten Rules》有时又被称为是“正误法则”（right and wrong tests）或“精神错乱的认知标准”（cognitive test of insanity）。[30]

MacNaughten Rules 的诞生，被认为是司法精神病学史上具有划时代意义的里程碑，并成为了英、美等国对违法精神障碍者刑事责任能力认定的主要判例依据。同时，这一条例的基本思想，也被世界上绝大多数国家所接受和肯定，并在后来的刑事立法方面加以借鉴。美国几乎是未作任何修改就直接接受了该标准。[31]

但 MacNaughten Rules 并不是很完善，因为它只片面强调了以被告人在行为当时的智力或认识性理解能力的缺失作为判断法律性精神错乱（legal insanity）的唯一根据。即只强调了“认知”成分（知道行为的本质和特性的能力）的损害，没有考虑到“意志”（控制自己行为的能力）的损害，因而受到了后来者的不断批评和修正。

（三）无法抗拒的冲动准则

1922 年，英格兰的法学家重新审核了 MacNaughten Rules，并建议使用“不可抗拒的冲动”这一观点来补充刑事案件中“精神错乱”的概念。

“无法抗拒的冲动”观点来源于 1840 年。当时英国 18 岁的男招待奥克斯福德（Oxford）向维多利亚（Victoria）女王和孔韦尔（Consert）王子开了 2 枪。被捕后的奥克斯福德因精神错乱辩护而无罪。当时的登曼（Denman）法官在向陪审团论证时提出了“无法抗拒的冲动准则”（Irresistible Impulse Rules，Lord Denman's Ruling of 1840）。登曼法官陈述道：某人可以对违法行为不负责任，如果有一类疾病是他行为的真正动力，他就不可能抗拒，那么他将不负责任。

到 1844 年，美国有 19 个州法院采用了这一准则，并作出了更进一步的解释：[32]“假使有证据使陪审团确信，被告人在精神上有病和不健全，需要澄清：①这种精神病是否达到使当时被告丧失理智、意识和判断力的严重程度？②被告在杀人时是否受到一种不可抗拒的冲动而达到自己无法控制的程度？如果确证如此，那么被告人的行为不是有意图的，而是无意识的，缺乏思想上的共同支配。”

英格兰的法学家在审核 MacNaughten Rules 时主张：“如果被告是在冲动情况下实施犯罪行为的，而被告因罹患精神疾病不能抗拒这一冲动，并在该冲动的支配下产生犯罪行为，那么，被告对其犯罪行为不负刑事责任。”法庭将这一条例解释为“警察在侧条例”（The Policeman – At – The – Elbow Law）。

“警察在侧”的意思是指，即使警察当时就在犯罪现场，行为人是否仍然会采取危害行为。如是，则认为其控制能力削弱或丧失，否则就认为其有控制能力。法庭认为，

---

〔30〕［美］Lawrence S. Wrightsman：《司法心理学》，吴宗宪、林遐等译，中国轻工业出版社 2004 年版，第 211 页。

〔31〕胡纪念：“美国精神错乱辩护标准的启示”，载《第十届全国司法精神病学学术会议论文集》2007 年 11 月印行，第 114 ~ 116 页。

〔32〕徐一峰主编：《社会精神医学》，上海科技教育出版社 2010 年版，第 132 页。

只有在这种丧失控制能力的情况下，行为人冲动的产生才是不可抗拒的[33][34]。但这显然是一个缺乏可操作性的原则，事实上某些案例中的行为人在实施危害行为时，会有意识地主动与警察公开对峙、对抗或是直接袭击警察，但在鉴定时并不能证明他们对自己的行为丧失了控制能力。[35]

四、近现代的理念及立法

1920～1940年，德国、日本、美国等国家的专家，在判定精神障碍者的法定能力方面一般是以医学标准（即单纯的医学诊断结论）为主要依据的，[36]当事人在被确定为精神分裂症之后，通常的做法是不考虑法律规定的情况而直接判定其为无责任能力。这种情况被称为“有病无罪”论。不分情况的一律按照有病即无罪去操作这种做法，显然不能客观地反映精神障碍者责任能力的实际情况，因此，随着法学与精神医学的发展与进步，随着对精神障碍与刑事责任能力丧失之间相互关系的认识逐渐深化，专业人员进而逐渐倾向于认为：应根据不同病情，酌情判定精神障碍者应承担的相应责任，并逐渐调整、规范和完善了一些法律法规。在这方面的发展和演变情况，尤以美国和英国的情况比较具有代表性。

（一）英国的立法情况

虽然世界上第一部正式的精神卫生法诞生在1938年的法国，但英国却是国际上最早进行精神卫生相关立法的国家之一，[37]英国的精神卫生立法可以追溯到18世纪的流浪者法律——允许关押“狂怒的疯子和危险者”以及管理私有的疯人院（madhouse）的法律。[38]

早在18世纪末，英国就开始对精神卫生领域进行综合性立法，并在詹姆斯·哈德菲尔德刺杀英皇乔治三世的案件判决之后颁布了《精神错乱者法》（The Lunatics Act，1800年），1890年将其更名为《精神错乱法》（The Lunacy Act），强调要保护精神障碍者的权益和财产，不得非法拘禁精神障碍者。这是世界上第一次以法律制度来保障精神障碍者的权益。

1808～1891年，英国议会就通过了20部法律，专门调整在公立或私立机构中对精神障碍者的治疗问题。在《精神错乱法》的基础上，经过陆续的修订和完善，于1959年形成了《精神卫生法》（The Mental Health Act），并于1983年进行了修订和更新。1983年的《精神卫生法》规定，医生有权强制住院精神障碍者进行各种检查和治疗。自20世纪90年代中期以来，在英国又展开了对精神卫生法的修订和讨论，并于1998

---

〔33〕于靖涛、田祖恩：“英美法系对精神病患者刑事责任能力的评定标准”，载《中华精神科杂志》2000年第33卷第4期，第249～251页。

〔34〕何恬：“英美两国对精神病人刑事责任能力评判的演变”，载《证据科学》2008年第16卷第1期，第99～110页。

〔35〕纪术茂、高北陵、张小宁主编：《中国精神障碍者刑事责任能力评定案例集》，法律出版社2011年版，第6页。

〔36〕李植荣、高镇松：“不同年代精神分裂症违法者责任能力评定比较”，载《临床心身疾病杂志》2005年第11卷第1期，第50～51页。

〔37〕戴庆康：“英国精神卫生法修订评介”，载《法律与医学杂志》2002年第9卷第3期，第179～182页。

〔38〕［英］David Semple，Roger Smyth，Jonathan Burns：《牛津临床精神病学手册》，唐宏宇、郭延庆主译，人民卫生出版社2006年版，第667页。

年10月由英国卫生部吸收精神卫生领域的医学专家和法律专家参加，组织成立了精神卫生法修订调研委员会。

（二）美国的立法情况

在美国，曾经任何人都可以强行将自己的某个亲属直接送入精神病院。1860年，一名女患者帕卡德（Packard）从精神病院逃了出来，并到美国各地宣传游说，声称自己没有精神病，是自己的父亲硬将自己强行关进精神病院长达三年之久。她还呼吁公众密切注意精神健康法规的制定。

就在这一年，美国立法当局制定了一个司法精神病学规则，并沿用至今。规则要求：任何人被送进精神病院住院时，必须通过一定的法律程序；精神障碍者的住院问题，不仅是其家属和精神科医生的事情，同时也是在法律界参与的情况下才能进行的事宜。

在美国的刑事判例法中，最有争议的问题就是精神错乱辩护。在精神错乱辩护案件中，回顾性地评估被告在犯罪时的精神状态，对于鉴定人而言也是最具挑战性的工作之一。虽然“如何从法律的角度来定义精神疾病是非常重要的”，〔39〕但是，因为在“法律上不存在一个被普遍接受的精神错乱的定义。多年来，精神错乱测验标准受到很大争议，被不断修改和完善。因此，精神错乱辩护标准在美国有多个变异形式，这取决于不同州或法律辖区内适用的法律”。〔40〕

1.《德赫姆准则》（Durham Test）。〔41〕〔42〕MacNaughten Rules之后，一些批评者认为，仅仅是根据罪犯有无判断对错的能力来决定判决，太过简单化了，应该采用更适当的标准。因为精神障碍不仅会影响患者的认知功能，同时也影响患者的情绪反应。精神卫生机构认为，在决定一个人是否应该对自己的行为负责时，应该综合考虑其精神状况的所用方面。

1954年，美国哥伦比亚特区联邦巡回上诉法院审理的德赫姆案中，裁决驳回了一审判决。虽然23岁的蒙特·德赫姆（Monte Durham）坚持以罹患精神障碍为理由，一直在为自己进行无罪辩护，但法院仍然坚持于1951年7月13日，将具有长期犯罪史和精神病史的德赫姆以盗窃罪判刑。上诉法院裁决驳回的理由就被称为《德赫姆准则》（Durham Test），又称为“结果规则”：“……将‘是和非’作为唯一标准是不恰当的，因为它没有充分考虑到精神病的实质和科学常识，而只是根据个别的症状，因此不能有效地应用到所有的情况上。我们认为‘无法抗拒的冲动’标准也不恰当，因为它没有认识到有深思和反省特征的精神病，……我们决定采用更广泛的检测：被告人之所以不负刑事责任，简单地说来，只是由于他的违法行为是精神病或智能不足的结果。”

也就是说，《德赫姆准则》将精神障碍者是否应对自己的危害行为负责的标准，从

---

〔39〕［美］David H. Barlow，V. Mark Durand：《异常心理学（第四版）》，杨霞等译，中国轻工业出版社2006年版，第615页。

〔40〕［美］Robert E. Hales，M. D.，M. B. A.；Stuart C. Yudofsky，M. D.；Glen O. Gabbard，M. D. 主编：《精神病学教科书（第五版）》，张明园、肖泽萍主译，人民卫生出版社2010年版，第1084页。

〔41〕［美］David H. Barlow，V. Mark Durand：《异常心理学（第四版）》，杨霞等译，中国轻工业出版社2006年版，第620页。

〔42〕徐一峰主编：《社会精神医学》，上海科技教育出版社2010年版，第133页。

是否存在判断对错的能力改为了是否存在“精神疾病或者智能缺陷”。这条原则一出台，就受到了精神卫生工作者的一致欢迎，因为他们终于可以完整地向法官或者陪审团陈述患者的病情了。这也被认为是“法律对现代精神病学的正式认可”，并因而成为了一个里程碑式的法律事件。[43]

但很不幸的是，人们很快就发现，精神卫生工作者没有办法精确地评估一个人的精神疾病是否是导致其犯罪的原因。因此，判决也就不再被认为是建立在科学基础之上的，而是基于非科学的个人意见。[44]

虽然《德赫姆准则》很快就不再被使用了，但对《德赫姆准则》的批评，却促使人们对用于精神错乱辩护的标准开始进行重新审视。

2. ALI 条例。在美国制定的很多地方性法规或联邦法规中，最著名并在美国近代具有广泛影响的，是 1962 年美国法律研究所（American Law Institution，简称 ALI）制定的《标准刑法典》（又译作《模范刑法典》Model Penal Code Rule，简称 MPC Rule 或 ALI 条例）。其中有关“精神错乱辩护”（Insanity Defense）的内容主要有两条：“①如果一个人发生了违法行为，而这种行为是由于精神疾病或精神缺陷造成的结果，并且精神疾病或精神缺陷使他缺乏实质性辨认能力，从而不能正确认识其行为的违法性或错误性，或者不能使其行为符合法律要求，那么，他就不能对自己的违法行为负责。②本条使用的精神疾病或精神缺陷术语，不包括那些只有屡次犯罪或其他反社会行为的异常表现。”第 2 条强调的是，“屡次犯罪或其他反社会行为的异常表现”本身不能被视为是精神疾病或精神缺陷，目的是将反社会人格障碍或其他人格障碍划入应承担刑事责任的范畴。

ALI 条例的特点，是将认知（Cognitive，主要涉及行为人的辨认能力）和意志（Volitional，主要涉及行为人的控制能力）两种成分结合起来考虑。在约翰 · W · 欣克利（John W. Hinckley. Jr）刺杀美国总统罗纳德 · 威尔逊 · 里根（Ronald Wilson Reagan）的案件中，法庭成功引用了 ALI 条例，于 1982 年宣判在约翰欣克利因罹患精神障碍而不负刑事责任。[45][46][47]

3. 欣克利事件的后续影响。对欣克利的判决，当即在全美国的法律界乃至公众中，都引起了极为强烈的反应和轩然大波，被认为是一个“不得人心的裁决”，[48] 再加上媒体在对类似案件进行的渲染性报道时，精神障碍者往往被描述为是具有极端暴力行为的人。这就使得公众对于精神障碍者的保护条例产生了极其不良的印象，公众

---

〔43〕［英］Bridget Giles：《变态心理学》，潘华译，黑龙江科学技术出版社 2007 年版，第 210～211 页。

〔44〕［美］David H. Barlow，V. Mark Durand：《异常心理学（第四版）》，杨霞等译，中国轻工业出版社 2006 年版，第 620 页。

〔45〕［美］Robert G. Meyer：《变态行为案例故事（第七版）》，张黎黎、高隽译，世界图书出版公司 2007 年版，第 362～365 页。

〔46〕［英］Bridget Giles：《变态心理学》，潘华译，黑龙江科学技术出版社 2007 年版，第 211～213 页。

〔47〕［美］David H. Barlow，V. Mark Durand：《异常心理学（第四版）》，杨霞等译，中国轻工业出版社 2006 年版，第 622 页。

〔48〕［美］Lawrence S. Wrightsman：《司法心理学》，吴宗宪、林遐等译，中国轻工业出版社 2004 年版，第 214 页。

尤其担心会出现“精神错乱的滥用和犯罪的‘精神病学化’(psychiatrisation)”[49]的糟糕情况。

根据当时的调查,[50]美国公民中有91%的人认为“法官与陪审团很难分辨被告是否真的是精神错乱,以及因此而确定的有罪或无罪”,近90%左右的美国人认为“精神错乱辩护所造成的漏洞让许多有罪人得以逃脱”,近90%的人认为“《精神病患者保护条例》被过多地引用,过多的人靠着证明自己患有精神疾病来逃过惩罚”。

因此,80%以上的美国公民强烈要求废弃或修改精神错乱无罪辩护(Not Guilty by Reason of Insanity, NGRI)。

但是,专业人员的研究认为,舆论和公众的这种骚动掩盖了这样一个基本事实,即:事实上很少有被告是因为有精神病而被判无罪。[51]也就是说,公众实际上是过高地估计了这种免刑取得成功和个体被判NGRI而释放的案例,[52]因为事实上,个体被判NGRI进入医院接受治疗的时间,要超出其因被判犯罪而遭受监禁的时间。

虽然多项调查明确显示,[53][54][55][56][57][58]精神障碍者实际上并没有因被判NGRI而经常逃过“惩罚”。但这种巨大的社会压力引起了司法系统对此类案件广泛而深入的探索,复燃了美国法律界长期存在的关于废除或修改NGRI的要求,最终使得全美国范围内“因精神错乱而无罪”的辩护法律条例也随之得到了修改。国会则是在欣克利案件判决的3天后,就组建了一个特别委员会以加强对有关法律的研究。[59]几周之内,就有多达26项不同的法案被引入来修正联邦法案中关于精神失常辩护的规定。[60]

鉴于上述这些复杂的情况,美国精神病学协会(American Psychiatric Association, APA)在综合考虑了各方面的意见后,于1982年年底郑重发表声明,明确反对取消NGRI,强调应以某种形式保留NGRI以维护刑事法律的基本原理和人道主义的完整性。

---

〔49〕[英] Ronald Blackburn:《犯罪行为心理学·理论、研究和实践》,吴宗宪、刘邦惠等译,中国轻工业出版社2000年版,第218页。

〔50〕[美] David H. Barlow, V. Mark Durand:《异常心理学(第四版)》,杨霞等译,中国轻工业出版社2006年版,第622页。

〔51〕[美] Lauren B. Alloy, John H. Riskind, Margaret J. Manos:《变态心理学(第9版)》,汤震宇、邱鹤飞、杨茜译,上海社会科学院出版社2005年版,第781页。

〔52〕[英] Ronald Blackburn:《犯罪行为心理学理论、研究和实践》,吴宗宪、刘邦惠等译,中国轻工业出版社2000年版,第219页。

〔53〕[美] David H. Barlow, V. Mark Durand:《异常心理学(第四版)》,杨霞等译,中国轻工业出版社2006年版,第623页。

〔54〕[美] Robert E. Hales, M. D., M. B. A.; Stuart C. Yudofsky, M. D.; Glen O. Gabbard, M. D. 主编:《精神病学教科书(第五版)》,张明园、肖泽萍主译,人民卫生出版社2010年版,第1084页。

〔55〕[英] Bridget Giles:《变态心理学》,潘华译,黑龙江科学技术出版社2007年版,第209~210页。

〔56〕纪术茂、高北陵、张小宁主编:《中国精神障碍者刑事责任能力评定案例集》,法律出版社2011年版,第6页。

〔57〕[英] Ronald Blackburn:《犯罪行为心理学·理论、研究和实践》,吴宗宪、刘邦惠等译,中国轻工业出版社2000年版,第218页。

〔58〕[美] Richard J. Gerrig, Philip G. Zimbardo:《心理学与生活(第16版)》,王垒、王甦等译,人民邮电出版社2003年版,第425页。

〔59〕[英] Bridget Giles:《变态心理学》,潘华译,黑龙江科学技术出版社2007年版,第212页。

〔60〕[美] Richard J. Gerrig, Philip G. Zimbardo:《心理学与生活(第16版)》,王垒、王甦等译,人民邮电出版社2003年版,第364页。

APA 同时建议严格精神错乱的法学定义，对于可能导致无罪判决的精神障碍，应该在严重程度方面等同于精神病学家诊断为“精神病”（psychosis）的情况。[61][62]

APA 的立场与国内司法精神病学界的大多数专家的观点基本上是一致的。[63]

欣克利事件还直接促成美国联邦法院于 1984 年颁布了《精神错乱辩护改革法》（Federal Insanity Defense Reform Act of 1984，以下简称《改革法》）。《改革法》对 ALI 标准进行了修改，更严格地限制了精神障碍者启动无罪辩护程序的范围，对启动精神障碍犯罪辩护（insanity defense）司法程序的主体作了新的规定，严格限制了专家证人判定被告或嫌犯刑事责任能力的权力。

《改革法》规定的对精神错乱无罪辩护的标准是：在实施违法行为时，如果被告因患严重精神疾病或缺陷，不能辨认其行为的本质和特性或其行为的错误性，则不负刑事责任；而只有精神疾病或缺陷并不能作为无罪辩护的理由。

这一标准强调的是认知成分，而排除了意志或不可抗拒的冲动成分，也废弃了被告不能使其行为符合法律要求的条款，并把举证责任转移给被告。

但是，在美国各州实施的法律和法规不尽相同，至今采用的精神错乱无罪辩护的标准颇不一致。但许多州对精神障碍者触犯刑律的法律所做改进的总的结果是：法律的天平更多地向着公众利益倾斜。少数州甚至完全取消了精神障碍者的无罪辩护，仍保留精神障碍者无罪辩护的大多数州，则大幅度地提高了门槛，几乎所有州的法庭都让被告方承担证明自己精神错乱的举证责任。[64] 具体表现在：①有犯意的精神障碍者触犯刑律被认作犯罪；②将开始的举证责任转移至被控方，公诉方仅承担最终的举证责任；③法律要求被控方提供的精神障碍的证据，必须是“清楚而令人信服的证据”（clear and convincing evidence），此标准严于过去的“优势证据”（preponderance of the evidence）。即被告首先被假定为是精神活动是正常的，除非他能够使法官和陪审团相信他确实精神失常。

在美国，另一个改革精神错乱免刑的尝试，是将 NGRI 的判决替换为“有罪但有精神病”（Guilty but mental ill，简称 GBMI）。[65] 这种替代判决的“法律效果与判决被告有罪没有什么不同”。[66] 因为从理论上讲，被判决 NGRI 者不会被监禁，但要接受评估，并被送往精神病医疗机构，直到其被裁定可以释放时为止，而一旦被裁定精神障碍痊愈就必须释放。而且，“经常缺乏针对犯人的适当精神科治疗增加了这一判决的虚

---

〔61〕贾谊诚、纪述茂：“美国精神病学协会（APA）关于‘精神错乱辩护’的声明（上）（1982 年 12 月）”，载《上海精神医学》1987 年第 1 卷第 2 期，第 88 ~ 92 页。

〔62〕贾谊诚、纪述茂：“美国精神病学协会（APA）关于‘精神错乱辩护’的声明（下）（1982 年 12 月）”，载《上海精神医学》1987 年第 1 卷第 4 期，第 163 ~ 167 期。

〔63〕纪术茂、高北陵、张小宁主编：《中国精神障碍者刑事责任能力评定案例集》，法律出版社 2011 年版，第 6 页。

〔64〕［美］Lawrence S. Wrightsman：《司法心理学》，吴宗宪、林遐等译，中国轻工业出版社 2004 年版，第 214 页。

〔65〕［美］David H. Barlow，V. Mark Durand：《异常心理学（第四版）》，杨霞等译，中国轻工业出版社 2006 年版，第 623 页。

〔66〕［美］Robert E. Hales，M. D.，M. B. A.；Stuart C. Yudofsky，M. D.；Glen O. Gabbard，M. D. 主编：《精神病学教科书（第五版）》，张明园、肖泽萍主译，人民卫生出版社 2010 年版，第 1085 页。

伪性”。[67] 相比之下，GBMI 的判决在理论上允许法律既对其进行治疗又对其进行惩罚，至于是被监禁在医院还是在监狱，则由法院裁定。即使是监禁在医院中并在刑满之前达到了康复的程度，也将会被送往监狱完成余刑至期满。或者，被裁定为 GBMI 者将直接被监禁在监狱，并由监狱在许可的情况下提供精神卫生服务。[68]

在美国的另一些州，被判处 GBMI 的人比申请精神错乱免刑的人更多地被监禁，并被判处更长的刑期，同时，被判处 GBMI 的人比其他罹患精神障碍的囚犯得到的治疗更少。

很显然，GBMI 有可能会引起更多的道义、法律、精神病学等诸多方面的问题。[69]

不难看出，欣克利案导致的全美范围内有关 NGRI 法律条例的修改，总的趋势是法律的天秤由过去对精神障碍者的宽容，开始向公众利益倾斜，各州都更严格地限制、减少乃至取消了精神错乱无罪辩护，其中半数以上的州修改了辩护的法律，3 个州取消了精神错乱辩护。[70][71][72][73]

如此做法的一个直接结果是：虽然美国总人口数已经由 1955 年的 1.66 亿增加到了 2000 年的 2.7 亿，但在州立医院接受治疗的精神障碍者数量，却由当初的 56 万人（1955 年）骤减到不足 5.5 万人（2000 年）。相差的 80 余万精神障碍者中，将近 30 万人被关在各级监狱中，另 50 万人则正在执行法院判处的缓刑，其中有不少人流浪和露宿街头。而每年美国的刑事司法系统要处理的精神障碍者多达 100 万人。因此，目前“在美国，最大的公共精神卫生设施不是精神病院，而是洛杉矶县监狱。”[74][75]

由于已经认识到，“美国‘疯狂’的精神卫生体制及相关立法和司法的缺失，已经给无数的家庭造成灾难性的后果”，美国目前又开始了新的一轮精神卫生改革。

从上述现象中不难发现，西方社会对精神卫生工作的认识和对精神障碍者的态度，似乎一直是处于左右摇摆的窘境，迄今仍然没有找到一个相对稳定的利益平衡点。而作为为法学和法律服务的司法精神病学及其相关理念，就是在这种摇摆不定的状态下，于 20 世纪 30 年代在英美国家起步，并于 70 年代中期逐渐建立起来。[76][77]

---

〔67〕 同注〔66〕。

〔68〕 ［美］Lawrence S. Wrightsman：《司法心理学》，吴宗宪、林遐等译，中国轻工业出版社 2004 年版，第 213 页。

〔69〕 纪术茂、高北陵、张小宁主编：《中国精神障碍者刑事责任能力评定案例集》，法律出版社 2011 年版，第 6 页。

〔70〕 何恬：“英美两国对精神病人刑事责任能力评判的演变”，载《证据科学》2008 年第 16 卷第 1 期，第 99 ~ 110 页。

〔71〕 高北陵，Li SQ：“从美国刑事法律沿革思考我国司法精神病学鉴定模式的转变”，载《中华精神科杂志》2009 年第 42 卷第 1 期，第 47 ~ 49 页。

〔72〕 徐声汉：“美国司法精神鉴定的状况”，载《精神卫生通讯》2009 年 2 月 1 日。

〔73〕 纪术茂、高北陵、张小宁主编：《中国精神障碍者刑事责任能力评定案例集》，法律出版社 2011 年版，第 6 页。

〔74〕 Pete Earley：《疯狂——美国精神病患者的遭遇》，钟广昌、卢姗译，新世界出版社 2011 年版，第 2 页。

〔75〕 汪有芬：“前言”，载 Pete Earley：《疯狂——美国精神病患者的遭遇》，钟广昌、卢姗译，新世界出版社 2011 年版。

〔76〕 纪术茂、高北陵、张小宁主编：《中国精神障碍者刑事责任能力评定案例集》，法律出版社 2011 年版，第 3 页。

〔77〕 刘协和主编：《法医精神病学》，人民卫生出版社 2004 年版，第 4 页。

一例医疗纠纷诉讼的鉴定和出庭

狄胜利*

一、简要案情

被鉴定人吕×（女，1943年出生），因双膝疼痛活动受限10年、加重1年就诊，门诊以“双膝关节类风湿性关节炎”收入院，期间行“双侧人工膝关节置换术”。被鉴定人认为医院对其所行手术存在过错导致目前行走困难为由起诉至法院。法院委托我所进行法医学鉴定，委托鉴定目的“医院的医疗行为是否存在过错；如有过错与被鉴定人目前的不良后果有无因果关系”。

接受鉴定委托后，我所组织双方当事人进行听证以了解相关情况，对送检材料进行了文证审查，对被鉴定人进行身体检查，并最终经过鉴定人认真分析、讨论，形成鉴定致意见。

在诉讼过程中，由医院提出申请，经法官同意，鉴定人出庭接受质询。

二、法医学鉴定

（一）病历摘要

法院送检鉴定资料包括医院住院病历，门诊病历，影像学片共16张。上述资料均在委托鉴定前经双方当事人认可。确认鉴定资料是鉴定的前提，鉴定人是通过对资料的审查来了解医疗过程。

1. 住院病历摘录

主诉：双膝疼痛，活动受限10年，加重1年。现病史：10年前，患者无明显诱因双膝疼痛，活动时加重，休息可缓解，经关节镜治疗，症状无明显改善，近1年来疼痛加重，步行不超过500米。

骨科检查：步态跛行，膝关节被动活动度：屈：左90°，右90°；伸：左-10°，右-10°；大腿周径（髌上10cm）：左43cm，右43cm；小腿周径（髌下10cm）：左33cm，右33cm，双侧髌研试验（+），双侧浮髌试验（±），内翻应力试验（+），外翻应力试验（+），过伸试验（+），过屈试验（+）。

辅助检查：双膝X线片示“双膝关节骨性关节炎”。

入院诊断：双膝关节骨性关节炎。

诊疗计划：行人工全膝置换术（双）。

手术记录：麻醉完成后，患者仰位，常规消毒，铺巾单。上空气止血带，压力为400mmHg。膝关节正中切口切开皮肤皮下。髌旁内侧入路切开关节囊。切除部分髌骨上下脂肪垫，适当松解内侧侧副韧带，切除膝关节前后交叉韧带及内外侧半月板。术

* 狄胜利，中国政法大学证据科学教育部重点实验室副教授。Email：dishengli1967@sina.com。

中所见膝关节内侧室及髌骨软骨消失，露出软骨下骨。①股骨采用髓内定位，外翻6度，远端切骨量9mm。股骨假体测量后使用7号股骨假体，截除前后、上下斜面以及髁间窝。②向前脱位胫骨，使用髓外定位进行胫骨平台垂直切骨，胫骨平台切骨量为10mm，后倾3度。③假体复位确认膝关节活动度良好，膝关节周围软组织平衡后，大量抗生素盐水脉冲冲洗伤口，纱布予以干燥后，用含抗生素骨水泥分别固定7号的股骨假体与7号的胫骨假体。④12mm的试模垫片复位后，伸直膝关，清除多余的骨水泥。待骨水泥聚合后，清除假体周缘的骨水泥。⑤向前脱位胫骨，安置12mm的聚乙烯垫片。⑥左侧术式与右侧相同……

2. 门诊复查摘录

双膝置换术后4个月，左膝疼痛，查：左膝外翻，侧方应力试验（-）。

双膝关节置换术5月，X线片，左膝关节外翻16度，右膝外翻7度。

（二）鉴定过程

1. 听证记录

听证环节，是为双方当事人提供陈述自己观点的机会；便于鉴定人了解争议的焦点，利于以后的鉴定工作方向和重点。

本例听证情况摘录

患方认为：医方类风湿性关节炎的诊断为误诊；缺乏全膝关节置换手术适应症；手术不当造成下肢承重力线改变，加重下肢功能障碍。

医方认为：类风湿性关节炎诊断明确，且为类风湿性关节炎疾病发展晚期，人工全膝关节置换术是治疗晚期类风湿性关节炎的一种比较肯定的治疗。术前对患者进行了充分准备，进行了明确的告知，手术顺利，术后体检，血沉及CRP正常，无关节感染迹象，术后拍片患者膝关节假体位置良好，无松动，右膝无肿胀，查体患者膝关节屈伸功能基本正常。目前患者踝关节肿痛，关节变形等症状为类风湿性关节炎疾病发展的结果。

2. 检查记录

鉴定人根据鉴定的需要对被鉴定人进行躯体检查，对被鉴定人功能状况进行评价。目前被鉴定主要功能障碍表现为左膝关节外翻畸形。

检查记录摘要

被鉴定人自诉：站立、行走不利，双足肿胀。

检查：一般情况可。左膝明显外翻畸形，站立位双膝并拢时，双内踝距离约10cm。双踝肿胀明显，指压陷凹征（+）。膝关节活动度检查，屈曲：左90°、右120°；伸直：左0°、右0°。双下肢长度（髂前上棘至内踝）：左94cm，右96cm。（见后附照片1）

3. 阅片意见

影像学资料是对被鉴定人不同时期影像学表现的即时、直接的反映，鉴定人通过对影像学资料的审查可以直接了解当时的情况，尤其在涉及骨科医疗纠纷鉴定中意义重大。本例对负重位下双下肢全长X片的相关测量可以客观反映手术的效果。

本例阅片意见

手术前膝关节X片示：双膝骨质疏松，骨质增生，关节间隙变窄。（见后附照片

2）

鉴定时复查负重位下双下肢全长 X 片示：双膝髋人工关节置换术后，双膝间隙对称，植入关节稳定无滑脱；左膝外翻明显，下肢机械轴外翻角度约 10°。（见后附照片 3）

（三）鉴定意见

1. 对医院医疗行为的评价

对医院医疗行为的评价依据法律、法规、规范、行业共识、习惯等所反映的注意义务。对医疗行为的分析方法通常情况下有二，一是按照诊疗过程逐一判断医疗行为合理性；二是根据医疗行为后果反推医疗行为的合理性。前者对病历资料的全面、真实性要求高，如果鉴定资料存在缺陷，往往对评价结果的客观性有不利影响；后者以已知不良后果为出发点分析其发生的原因，如果存在多种可能性的情况下要进行必要的鉴别。综合使用两种方法可以提高评价的准确性。

（1）关于诊断。病史了解、临床检查、辅助检查，是明确诊断的基础。通过对病历资料相关内容的审查，医院对被鉴定人"双膝类风湿性关节炎"的诊断正确。

（2）关于手术。手术方式选择无误，具备双侧全膝关节置换手术的适应症，同时未见手术禁忌症；术前准备充分；手术记录，记述手术操作过程无误；术后处理相关无误；手术后临床、放射检查确证被鉴定人左膝明显外翻畸形。说明未能实现保证下肢生理力线以获得良好的髌股关系、改善关节功能之全膝关节置换手术的目的，反推手术操作存在不当。

2. 被鉴定人不良后果的评价

不当医疗行为通常对被鉴定人所造成的不良后果，可简单归纳为两类：一是结果加重，包括：由于不当医疗行为直接可间接引起的人体组织器官的损害，以及功能障碍；二是结果无加重、而过程改变，医疗过失行为导致被鉴定人原发疾患的正常转归过程发生改变，如病程的迁延、死亡的加速、治疗条件恶化。

目前被鉴定人站立、行走明显不利，左膝外翻明显，双膝并拢时两内踝相距约 10 厘米，复查双下肢负重位 X 线片示，右下肢机械轴接近 0°，左下肢机械轴翻角度达 10°。

本例被鉴定人目前不良后果为左膝外翻，未能达到手术治疗效。如果被鉴定人经过二次手术翻修，左下肢力线恢复、关节稳定达到手术治疗效果，被鉴定人不良后果即表现为过程改变。

3. 不当医疗行为与被鉴定人不良后果之间的因果关系分析

本例被鉴定人手术后出现不良后果是左膝外翻明显，左下肢机械轴外翻角度约 10°，应与膝关节置换手术有关节。文字资料反映手术操作步骤符合规范，不能分析出不良后果的原因；根据检查结果及影像学资料所见，考虑左膝关节外翻原因应为人工关节置入位置不当所致。

被鉴定人目前左膝外翻明显，致使下肢负重、行走困难及左膝屈伸活动受限，与医院所行全膝关节置换手术未能对其左膝建立良好的髌股关系有关。综合考虑医院医疗行为的不当与被鉴定人目前不良后果中的参与度考虑为 E 级（理论系数 75%）。

三、鉴定人出庭

鉴定结论作为一种法定证据，同其他形式的证据一样，必须经过查证属实方可成为定案的依据，这是证据法的基本要求。我国《刑事诉讼法》第82条、154条、156条、157条，《民事诉讼法》第124条、第125条，《行政诉讼法》第47条对鉴定人出庭作了原则性规定；《最高人民法院关于民事诉讼证据若干规定》和《最高人民法院关于行政诉讼证据若干问题规定》中对鉴定人出庭作了具体规定。

（一）出庭前准备

鉴定人出庭是法定义务，收到法院出庭通知后，应当积极准备。

首先，应熟习案情，从鉴定完成到出庭间隔时间往往较长，出庭前熟习案情十分必要，医疗过程中重要的时间节点及内容要烂熟于胸。在全面了解案情的同时，应当对出庭时可能提出的问题进行重点准备。必要时向法官索要当事人质询问题内容，以便有针对性地进行准备。本例鉴定核心问题是膝关节置换手术，那么围绕手术及手术效果评价是重中之重。

其次，要出庭推演，鉴定人可以分配不同庭审中的角色，模拟出庭情况进行预演，熟习出庭过程，把握出庭节奏，感受出庭气氛。本例是由医院提出鉴定人出庭申请，模拟出庭时应当就鉴定中的医疗专业技术环节充分准备。本例在出庭推演过程中发现，医院证明医疗行为无过错的依据事实是既往医疗事故鉴定中测量被鉴定人左侧股胫机械角165°，其提交的文献认为股胫机械角大于165°是安全范围。对此我们从新对被鉴定人手术后复查双下肢负重位X线片测量股胫机械角度；并对相关文献及著作进行复习。

最后，资料准备，包括鉴定意见得出所涉及的理论依据，以及为增加说服力的资料和图表。本例我们资料准备的是《膝关节外科的基础和临床》（人民卫生出版社，1999年第1版，王亦璁主编）；对被鉴定人手术后复查双下肢负重位X线片进行翻拍、标记（见后附照片3）后打印多份，并准备量角器一个。

（二）出庭接受质询

鉴定人在庭审中的作用好比是桥梁，横跨法律与医学，把专业性医疗专业问题通过鉴定人用浅显易懂的方式、方法阐述清楚，利于法官作出客观公正的判断。用直白通俗的语言来清晰阐释专业性问题最能体现鉴定人的能力。

出庭时，鉴定人往往处于相对被动的地位，难免受到当事人无理的攻击和刁难，鉴定人可以适时向法庭提出合理的建议，避免当事人毫无意义的纠缠。平静的心态和确凿的证据是鉴定人可以凭借的有力武器。

本例，医院作为主要质询方提问直奔主题，“被鉴定人股胫机械角为165°，而有关文献认为股胫机械角大于165°是膝关节外科手术的安全范围”。

鉴定人首先从理论层面回复，专业权威著作的理论价值优于非专业的著述；人工膝关节置换术后功能评价方法包括临床评价和放射学评价，被鉴定人临床表现完全能够说明人工膝关节置换术未能达到治疗的要求；关于放射学评价庭审现场就可以验证。鉴定人向法官提出现场测量被鉴定人左侧股胫机械角度的请求，并争得法官同意，将事前准备的被鉴定人手术后复查双下肢负重位X线片进行翻拍并标记的资料发放给法官及当事人，在说明测量方法后现场进行测量，被鉴定人股胫机械角为160°。此结果从事实层面对医院所持观点给予了有力的驳斥。

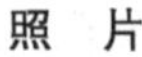

照　片

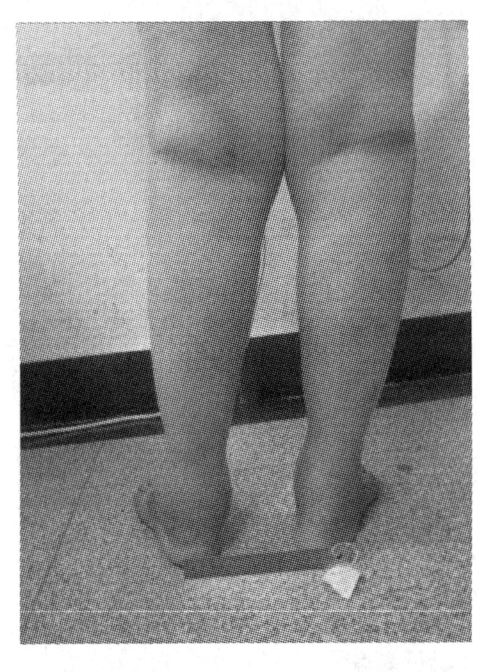

照片 1 −1 检查时站立位正面观

照片 2 −2 站立位背面观

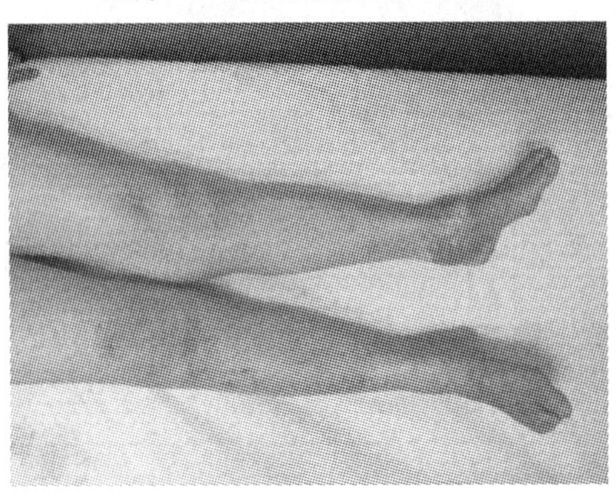

照片 1 −3 平卧位

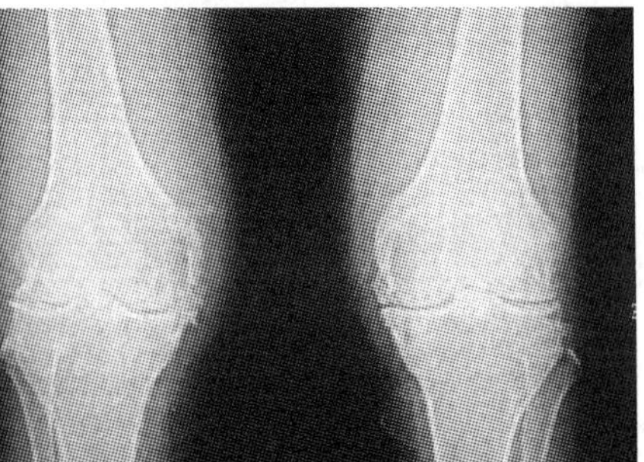

照片 2 −1

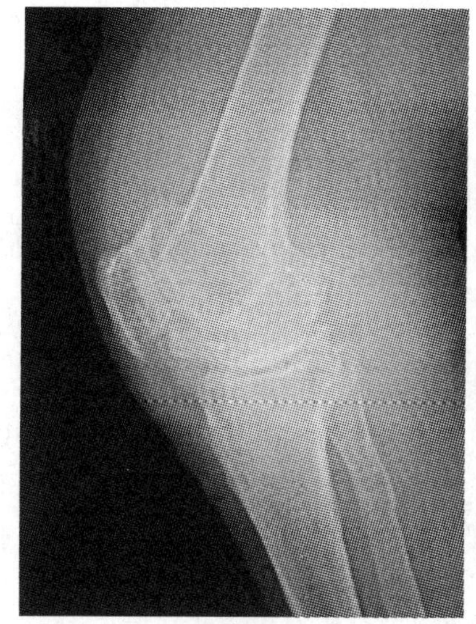

照片2-2

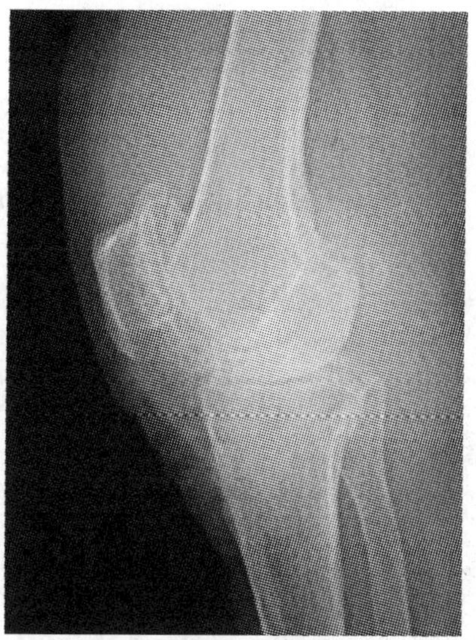

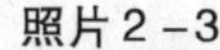

照片2-3

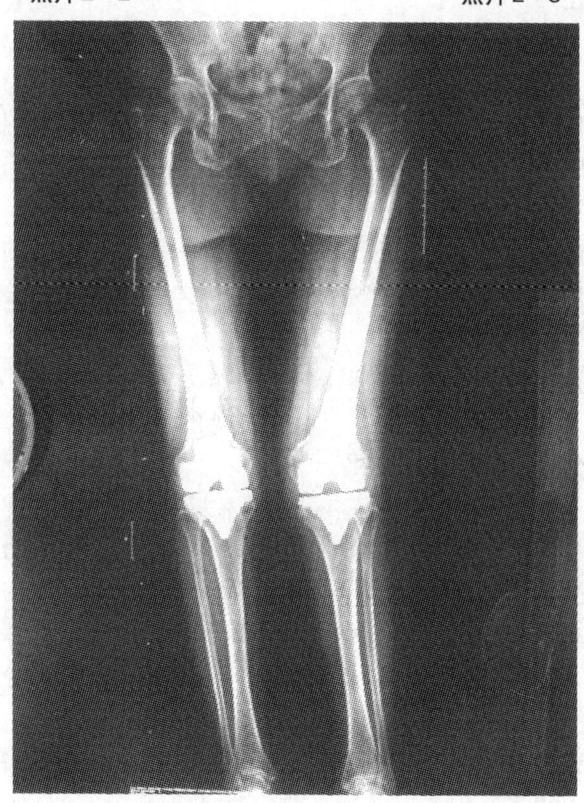

照片3

61例产科医疗损害鉴定回顾性分析

傅 博*

近几年，随着我国社会经济的快速增长，人们对医疗服务质量的要求不断增高，同时法律观念的全面普及，人们的法律维权意识不断增高，越来越多的人带着维权的思想对自身接受的医疗服务进行审度。加之产科的工作性质是患者多、周转快、病情复杂、变化快，患者及家属期望值高，并且妊娠分娩的特殊性、复杂性和现代医学的局限性，妊娠分娩存在一定风险，关系到母婴的生命安全，存在一定的并发症和不良妊娠结局的可能性，因此，产科就更容易发生医疗纠纷。

一、材料与方法

（一）取样

2006~2011年，由我所受理的全部医疗过失鉴定案例中筛选出产科案例61例。每一案例均有完整的原始资料，包括鉴定委托书、相应的病历和医患双方的陈述意见，按统一格式逐一登记。

（二）产科医疗过失行为的表现形式

将《侵权责任法》中认定医疗技术责任的标准——“与当时的医疗水平相应的诊疗义务”转化为临床诊疗过程的医疗过失评价指标体系，按照经验法则，并借鉴国外关于医疗过错的分类，[1]产科医疗过失的表现形式为：①产前检查不规范或因产前检查不到位未能适时终止妊娠；②漏诊、误诊；③手术适应症掌握不当；④术前准备不充分；⑤手术操作不当；⑥用药瑕疵；⑦ 其他可避免的治疗延误；⑧术后病情监测不力；⑨告知与说明不充分；⑩管理体系不足。

注：知情同意作为医学伦理学的基本原则，在《侵权责任法》中体现为“病情及医疗措施的说明义务，特别是手术治疗、特殊检查治疗的医疗风险、替代方案的说明义务”，其过失评价指标：告知与说明不充分；医疗行为的管理体系作为医方提供医疗服务的组成部分，在《侵权责任法》中体现为病历资料的填写、保管等义务，其过失评价指标：管理体系不足。[2]

（三）损害后果的评定

目前产科的损害后果分为产妇和新生儿的损害。新生儿的损害后果表现为：新生儿窒息、死亡、出生缺陷及损伤。产妇的损害后果表现为：死亡、残疾或功能障碍、一过性损害或未遗留明显不良后果。要求评定伤残等级的，以《劳动能力鉴定 职工工伤与职业病致残程度鉴定》标准（GB/T16180－1996）和北京市普通人身损害案件适用标准《人体损伤致残程度鉴定标准（试行）》进行评定。

* 傅博，中国政法大学法庭科学技术鉴定研究所鉴定人助理。Email：81555358@qq.com。

（四）医疗过失参与度标准确定

表 1　医疗过失参与度对照表

划分等级	损伤后果	责任程度	理论系数值	参与度参考值
A	完全由疾病造成	无责任	0%	0%
B	绝大部分由疾病造成	轻微责任	10%	1% ~20%
C	主要由疾病造成	次要责任	25%	20% ~40%
D	由损害后果与疾病共同作用	同等责任	50%	40% ~60%
E	主要由损害后果造成	主要责任	75%	60% ~90%
F	全部由损害后果造成	全部责任	100%	90% ~100%

二、结　果

（一）委托方情况

因考虑到单方不能提供完整的病历材料，且有可能因为患方不认可病历等因素，所以本所不接受除法院以外的任何委托的医疗纠纷鉴定。

（二）案件的年度分布

2006 年共有医疗损害案件 5 例，2007 年共有医疗损害案件 13 例，2008 年共有医疗损害案件 13 例，2009 年共有医疗损害案件 9 例，2010 年共有医疗损害案件 11 例，2011 年共有医疗损害案件 10 例，共 61 例。

（三）案件中不同级别医院分布情况

61 例医疗损害案件中，涉及三级医院 28 例，二级医院 29 例，乡镇卫生院 7 例，其中三例中涉及两家被告医院，两例中第一医院为 2 级医院，第二医院为 3 级医院，第三例中第一医院为乡镇卫生院，第二医院 2 级医院，共 64 家医院。

（四）产科医疗过失行为的表现形式分布

本组资料中，50 例（81.97%）存在不同程度的医疗过失行为。

表 2　产科医疗过失行为的表现分布

产前检查不当或未能适时终止妊娠	漏诊误诊	手术适应症掌握不当	术前准备不充分	手术操作不当	用药瑕疵	其他可避免的治疗延误	病情监测不利	告知与说明不充分	管理体系问题
12	6	3	2	9	8	6	6	2	10
19.67%	9.84%	4.92%	3.28%	14.75%	13.11%	9.84%	9.84%	3.28%	16.39%

(五) 损害后果分布

表3 产科医疗纠纷损害后果分布

受害人	损害后果	例 数	比 例
新生儿	新生儿窒息	12	19.67%
	出生缺陷及损伤	19	31.15%
	死亡	14	22.95%
产妇	残疾或功能障碍	6	9.84%
	一过性损害	4	6.55%
	死亡	6	9.84%

(六) 医疗过失参与度分布

本组资料中，同时存在医疗过失行为和相应损害后果共计47例，其中7例有过失，与损害后果有关系，但无明确参与度。其中1例涉及两家医院均有过失，与损害后果有关系（表4、表5）。

表4 不同医院医疗过失的因果关系及参与度分布［例（%）］

医疗机构	A	B	C	D	E	F	无明确参与度
三级医院	4（20.00）	4（20.00）	6（30.00）	3（15.00）	1（5.00）	0（0.00）	2（10.00）
二级医院	3（15.00）	2（10.00）	8（40.00）	1（5.00）	2（10.00）	0（0.00）	4（20.00）
乡镇卫生院	1（14.29）	1（14.29）	1（14.29）	2（28.57）	1（14.29）	0（0.00）	1（14.29）
合计	9（19.15）	7（14.89）	15（31.94）	6（12.77）	3（6.38）	0（0.00）	6（14.89）

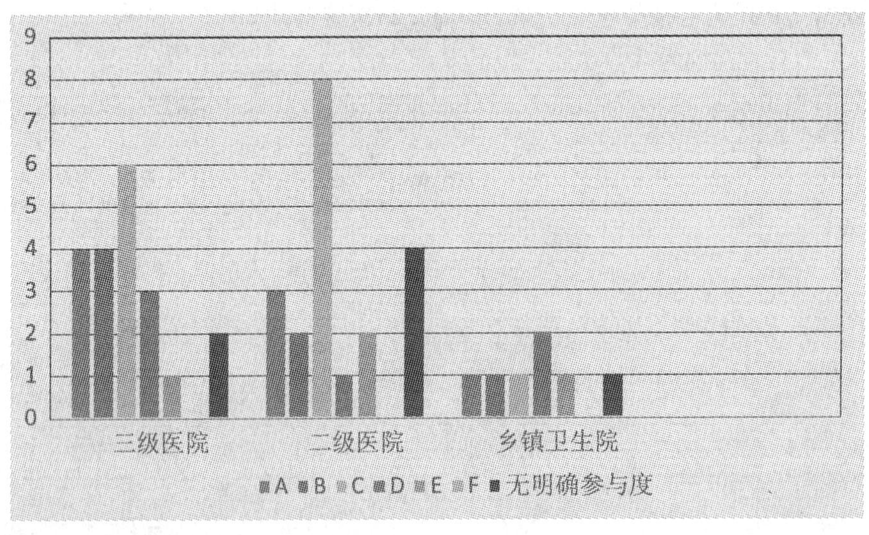

表5　过失行为与不同损害后果的因果关系及参与度分布　[例（%）]

损害后果	A	B	C	D	E	F	无明确参与度
新生儿窒息	4(30.76)	0(0.00)	4(30.76)	1(7.69)	0(0.00)	0(0.00)	4(30.76)
新生儿臂丛神经伤	0(0.00)	1(20.00)	4(80.00)	0(0.00)	0(0.00)	0(0.00)	0(0.00)
新生儿骨折	1(100.00)	0(0.00)	0(0.00)	0(0.00)	0(0.00)	0(0.00)	0(0.00)
新生儿先天疾病	3(60.00)	1(20.00)	0(0.00)	0(0.00)	0(0.00)	0(0.00)	1(20.00)
新生儿头皮瘢痕	0(0.00)	0(0.00)	0(0.00)	0(0.00)	0(0.00)	0(0.00)	1(100.00)
新生儿死亡	1(0.91)	1(0.91)	4(36.36)	2(18.18)	3(27.27)	0(0.00)	0(0.00)
孕妇子宫、输卵管切除	1(20.00)	2(40.00)	0(0.00)	1(20.00)	0(0.00)	0(0.00)	1(20.00)
人工剥离胎盘造成大出血	0(0.00)	0(0.00)	0(0.00)	1(100.00)	0(0.00)	0(0.00)	0(0.00)
孕妇肢体功能障碍	0(0.00)	1(100.00)	0(0.00)	0(0.00)	0(0.00)	0(0.00)	0(0.00)
孕妇死亡	1(25.00)	1(25.00)	1(25.00)	1(25.00)	0(0.00)	0(0.00)	0(0.00)
合计	11(23.40)	7(14.89)	13(27.66)	6(12.76)	3(6.38)	0(0.00)	7(14.89)

三、讨论

（一）产科本身是导致医疗纠纷高发的主要原因

产科工作十分繁忙及快节奏，病情变化快，意外情况多，在工作中稍有疏忽就会出现问题。现代医学对某些特殊情况在产前无法做出预测和明确诊断，而且分娩过程复杂、多变、病理情况随时都可能发生，而家属或产妇根本不了解其特殊性，[3]长期以来人们对正常分娩、胎儿健康寄予厚望，一旦出现问题，就造成了纠纷的高发。

（二）产科医疗过失的表现形式及可能原因

本组资料显示，产科医疗过失行为的常见表现形式为：产前检查不当或未能适时终止妊娠占19.67%；漏诊误诊占9.84%；手术适应症掌握不当占4.92%；术前准备不充分占3.28%；手术操作不当占14.75%；用药瑕疵占13.11%；其他可避免的治疗延误占9.84%；病情监测不力占9.84%；告知与说明不充分占3.28%；管理体系不足占16.39%。上述医疗过失产生的原因，其重要依据就是在为病人提供服务的过程中是否尽到了注意义务。注意义务分为具体注意义务和抽象注意义务。具体注意义务系指是否违反医疗卫生法规和诊疗规范：如诊断过程中的注意义务，治疗过程中的注意义务，手术过程中的注意义务等。抽象注意义务又分为知情告知义务、预见义务、回避义务和转医义务等。[4]

（三）损害后果分析

医疗损害鉴定所称的“损害后果”系指患者遗留的较稳定的不良后果，包括但不限于医疗过失行为造成的损害以及患者本身所具有的伤病。本组资料显示，新生儿的损害后果表现为：新生儿窒息占19.67%、死亡占22.95%、出生缺陷及损伤占31.15%。产妇的损害后果表现为：死亡占9.84%、残疾或功能障碍占9.84%、一过性损害或未遗留明显不良后果占6.96%。出生缺陷是指婴儿在出生前，在母亲的子宫内发生的发育异常，而在产前检查时未能发现；损伤是指新生儿骨折、神经损伤等，多由于临床对胎儿大小估计不足或胎位检查错误，导致难产，引起新生儿的损伤。[5]多发巨大儿、难产儿，在生产过程中，需要用到产钳等辅助工具而引起损伤，占新生儿损害后果比例较大；其次为新生儿死亡，最后为新生儿窒息引起的缺血缺氧性脑病，多为胎心监护不规范、催产素使用不规范、产程过长等因素引起。产妇的损害主要表现在产后大出血、术中或术后发现器官损伤、未能及时采取相应措施补救，产妇轻则切除子宫、输卵管，造成残疾或功能障碍，重则死亡。

（四）过失行为与不同损害后果的因果关系及参与度

1. 不同等级医院的过失行为

从表6的数据分析，三级医院中医疗过错参与度为同等及以上的比例明显低于其他两组，以乡镇卫生院比例最高，反之三级医院轻微关系及无关系比例则明显偏高，二级及乡镇卫生院比例最低。由此可以看出，医疗单位的硬件设施、医务人员的医疗知识、技术水平、临床经验等是造成过错的主要原因。在二级及乡镇卫生院中，对危重病例的发生、发展及其后果缺乏认识，或者遇到不能处理的病人未及时转诊从而导致不良后果等。二级及乡镇卫生院的医疗过失以违反抽象注意义务为主，在知情告知义务、预见义务及回避义务上发生率高。这可能与在一些危重、特殊病例的诊疗上，二级及乡镇卫生院医务工作者的平均医疗水平通常比三级医院相对为低等因素有关。

2. 过失行为的因果关系及参与度

在医疗损害赔偿案件中，法院常要求鉴定机构对医疗过失行为在患者损害后果构成中的原因力大小及参与度进行划分，以作为赔偿额度的参考。进行参与度划分，应围绕患者的损害后果，根据诊疗机构的医疗过失行为，结合疾病的特点和医院的等级及相应诊疗水平综合分析以给出公平合理的责任度划分。

从产科发生的特点来看，孕妇病情变化快，在分娩过程中，母亲和胎儿状况随时都在变化，有时医务人员难以预料，虽经积极抢救但可能造成损伤或死亡，[6]医务人员在诊疗构成中虽存在过失行为，但并不是直接导致孕妇或婴儿损害或死亡的因素，因此要充分考虑到患者自身情况和转归对损害后果的影响，并将其作为参与度划分的权衡因素之一，从医院的水平来看，在级别相对高的医院，其诊疗水平相对高，一旦发生明显过错行为造成不良后果，其承担的责任度可能要大，因此，医院的层次和诊疗水平也是参与度划分必须要考虑的因素。

（五）纠纷产生原因

1. 医务人员方面的因素：①服务态度缺乏；②与病人及家属沟通不够；③医疗知识和技术的缺乏；④法律意识淡薄。

2. 医院管理方面的因素：科室管理缺乏，例如，①思想工作不到位，有消极因素存在；②医疗管理制度不安全，业务技术培训欠缺，设备管理不善等都会给患者造成不安全；③如医疗文书书写不规范，欠缺完整的医疗护理记录过程且记录缺乏真实性等。病历作为原始资料是医生对病人病情发展及诊治过程的真实记录，它不仅是医疗事故鉴定中的重要文书，也是医疗诉讼中的重要依据；[5]④各种规章制度措施实施不到位，没有很好执行，如三级医院查房制度，三级以上手术制度等；⑤没有严格按医疗法律法规办事，导致医疗护理纠纷发生。如产钳使用时，不能很好地把握每一种情形，一旦发生并发症（如臂丛神经损伤、产后大出血），从而导致医疗纠纷的发生。[7]

3. 患者及家属方面的因素：①期望过高；②医疗知识的缺乏；③法律知识的淡薄。

（六）预防措施

1. 医务人员方面

全面提高医务人员素质是预防和控制纠纷的关键。提高医务人员的素质，主要从医德修养和业务能力培训两方面着手。提高医务人员的业务能力，关键在于不断学习业务和练好基本功。医德方面，要求医务人员以提高认真负责的态度去对待工作，严格遵守医疗制度和操作规章，全心全意为病人服务，克服对病员漠不关心、马马虎虎的工作态度，使医务人员懂得亲切、耐心、体贴、关怀、救死扶伤的重要性，还要懂得病人的心理，在同情和做好解释工作的基础上，接受病人某些合理的意见和要求，不仅可以提高医疗效果而且还可以避免事故和纠纷的发生。[8]

2. 规范产科医疗管理与提高医疗质量

必须健全各种规章制度，使医疗活动有法可依，有据可查，并严格遵守各项规章制度，如三级医师查房制度、交接班制度、查对制度、安全管理制度等。依据《病历书写基本规范》要求，确保病历质量；认真执行医护操作规程，避免医疗技术风险；加强医患沟通，落实医患谈话和告知制度；加强科室内部管理，合理安排工作人员，加强各科室之间的配合，避免科室配合不力或意见不一致而导致的医疗纠纷。

3. 开展产科医疗卫生教育和知识宣传

要求广大医务人员增强法律意识，在诊疗护理中严格依照操作规程，同时，对产科医疗上，如正常和异常妊娠分娩、一些常见的并发症等情况进行普及宣传，从而使产妇及家属对医患之间相互理解，有效防范医疗纠纷的发生。

参考文献

[1] Oyebode F.，“Clical Errors and Medical Negligence”，*Advances in Psychiatric Treatment*，2006，12：221～227.

[2] 胡晓翔、孔蓬、邹效波等：《侵权责任法》系列讲座：“医疗损害责任的举证责任配置与鉴定”，载《临床误诊误治》2011 年第 3 期，第 11～13 页。

[3] 郑玉平：“产科医疗纠纷的特点及防范”，载《中国误诊学杂志》2002 年第 7 期，第 l066 页。

[4] 徐代化、胡玲、熊先伟：“医疗纠纷司法鉴定 40 例分析”，载《法医学杂志》2009 年第 8 期，第 297～281 页。

[5] 王枫华、娄继权、顾桂国等：“妇产科医疗纠纷和事故的常见原因分析与防范”，载《中国卫生事业管理》2010 年第 4 期，第 234～237 页。

[6] 郑玉平：“产科医疗纠纷的特点及防范”，载《中国误诊学杂志》2002 年第 2 期，第 1066 页。

[7] 朱慧娟：“我院 91 例产科医疗纠纷案例原因分析及对策”，载《当代医学》2011 年第 17 期，第 104～105 页。

[8] 王传益：《最新医疗事故防范与处理实用全书》，警官教育出版社 1998 年版，第 11 页。

9 例重症手足口病致死病例尸体解剖法医病理学形态特点分析

蒋剑英 刘 牧 郭忠辉 赵铁钢 刘建军 *

手足口病（hand，foot and mouth disease，简称 HFMD）是一种急性肠道传染病，多由肠道病毒 CoxA16 和 EV71 等引起，主要通过消化道、呼吸道或密切接触等途径传播。[1]易感人群多为儿童，尤其是 5 岁以下儿童。成人也可以感染，但绝大多数为隐性感染。手足口病的主要临床症状为手、足、口及臀等部位出现疱疹、斑疹，伴疼痛，伴或不伴发热。绝大多数患儿愈后良好，少数患儿伴发脑脊膜炎、脑炎、脑干脑炎，并伴发脑水肿，颅内压增高等症状；极个别患儿会因脑疝形成和/或呼吸、循环衰竭而死亡。

2008 年 1 月至 2012 年 12 月，研究人员对 9 例重症手足口病致死病例进行了尸体解剖。复查临床资料，大体标本检查记录及病理组织学变化等文字材料，结合文献资料，将这些病例的临床特点和病理学特点分析总结如下。

一、资料与方法

2008 年 1 月至 2012 年 12 月，研究人员对 9 例重症手足口病致死的尸体进行了解剖，收集、复查临床资料，根据病理组织学变化，结合文献资料进行分析。9 例患儿的临床特征符合手足口病的诊断标准:[2]手、足、口和臀部疱疹或斑丘疹，均伴有发热，有嗜睡、昏迷及抽搐等中枢神经系统受累的症状，有呼吸系统受累的症状，如呼吸困难、咳嗽、咳痰、肺部可闻及湿罗音等。9 例患儿均为男性，年龄 6 个月 ~4 岁，平均年龄为 2.3 岁。

二、结 果

1. 一般特征。死亡时间：5 月份 3 例，6 月份 4 例，8 月份 2 例。9 例患儿中 4 例居住农村，1 例居住牧区，3 例居住城乡结合部，1 例居住县城。最初就诊机构：8 例于个体诊所，1 例于县妇幼保健所。病情加重后，8 例转入旗县医院或市内医院，1 例死于个体诊所。最初诊断：5 例为流行性感冒，2 例为不明原因发烧，1 例为急性扁桃体炎，1 例为肺炎。

2. 临床症状。9 例手、足、口及臀部均有典型的疱疹或斑丘疹。体温持续 >39℃。9 例均有中枢神经系统症状：精神萎靡，嗜睡，7 例肢体抖动，5 例颈部抵抗，频繁抽搐，1 例呕吐。呼吸系统症状：8 例呼吸困难，咳嗽，6 例咳白色、粉红色或血性泡沫样痰。9 例肺部可闻及湿罗音或痰鸣音。消化系统及泌尿系统无明显症状。

3. 实验室检查。9 例患儿中，8 例于正规医院进行了血常规、心电图等检测。1 例

* 蒋剑英，包头医学院病理教研室；刘牧，包头市公安局；郭忠辉，包头市公安局东河分局；赵铁钢，包头市公安局青山分局。Email：lium5630bl@sina.com。

死于个体诊所，未进行实验室检查。4例患儿进行了腰穿、脑脊液生化检查。7例末稍血白细胞升高（11.5～24）$\times 10^9$/L。2例进行了EV71相关抗体检测，结果为阳性。

4. 尸表检查。9例患儿手、足、口及臀部均有疱疹或斑丘疹，大部分已结痂，部分疱疹内有淡黄色液体。口唇及四肢末端发绀7例。5例患儿眼睑结膜有出血点。

5. 尸体解剖脏器肉眼检查。脑水肿、脑脊液混浊9例，肺被膜出血点及出血斑8例，肺切面暗红色，可见暗红色液体流出，胸腺出血点及出血斑7例，肾脏被膜出血点2例，胃黏膜出血点1例，肠系膜淋巴结肿大7例。

6. 病理组织学检查记录。中枢神经系统病理变化：9例患儿的病变部位主要位于脑桥、中脑、延髓、脊髓及小脑，均见神经元尼氏小体消失，部分神经元核消失，可见红色神经元及典型或不典型的淋巴细胞血管套形成，并见嗜神经元现象，伴少量淋巴细胞浸润，2例可见中性粒细胞浸润。脑膜及蛛网膜血管扩张、瘀血，淋巴细胞、单核细胞散在浸润。蛛网膜下腔脑脊液增多，见少量淋巴细胞及单核细胞。呼吸系统病理变化：9例肺泡间隔毛细血管扩张、瘀血，大部分肺泡腔内充满蛋白水肿液，部分肺泡间隔断裂，肺泡腔扩张，融合形成代偿性肺气肿。4例肺泡间隔明显增宽，其间较多量淋巴细胞及单核细胞浸润，并见典型或不典型的病毒包涵体形成。6例肺间质及肺泡间隔点状或灶状出血。消化道：肠系膜淋巴结免疫母细胞、中心母淋巴细胞、小淋巴细胞增生，形成淋巴滤泡。胃肠黏膜固有层少量淋巴细胞、单核细胞浸润。心脏：1例心肌间质少量淋巴细胞浸润，心肌细胞水肿。肾脏、肾上腺、脾脏及肝脏病理组织学变化均为血管扩张、瘀血。

三、讨　论

手足口病是由EV71、CoxA等病毒感染所致，大多数患儿病情轻，预后良好，少数患儿发生嗜睡、抽搐、昏迷等中枢神经系统受累的症状。极少数患儿会发生死亡。

本组9例重症手足口病患儿死亡时间均于春、夏季节。9例重症手足口病患儿均有手、足、口及臀部丘疹及斑丘疹，均有高烧，体温高于39℃，均有嗜睡、昏迷等中枢神经系统受累的症状，均有咳嗽、咳痰等呼吸道症状，7例外周血白细胞数目增高。临床症状与报道的重症患儿临床症状相符。[3]由于重症患儿呼吸系统症状明显，易被误诊为呼吸系统疾病。本组检验误诊率为100%，误诊为呼吸系统疾病者为6例，占75%。本组病例提示当患儿出现皮疹，持续高热，体温高于39℃，嗜睡、呼吸困难等症状时，临床医生应高度怀疑重症手足口病。

9例患儿病理学检查：神经系统多部位脑炎，以脑干、脊髓为明显，这与Chang等报道相符。[4]本组病例肺部有明显的肺水肿、部分有肺出血，其中，4例泡间隔中有明显的淋巴细胞、单核细胞浸润，并见典型或不典型的病毒包涵体形成。此4例肺部病变与报道不符。以往报道重症患儿一般肺部表现为肺瘀血、出血、肺水肿，无明显的炎细胞浸润，认为是EV71等感染后，重症患儿病程极短，一般不会继发肺部感染。[5]本组病例的肺部出现间质性肺炎，我们认为一种可能是患儿在患间质性肺炎的基础上，又继发EV71等所致；另一种可能是EV71等病毒通过呼吸道传播，直接引发肺部间质性炎症，因本组部分病例肺泡间隔中可见病毒包涵体形成，表现为病毒性肺炎的特征性变化。循环系统，仅一例心肌间质轻度炎细胞浸润，无明显损伤。消化系统肠系膜淋巴结反应性增生，肠黏膜固有层正常或仅有少量的淋巴细胞、单核细胞浸润。泌尿系统、内分泌系统均表现为瘀血、水肿，未见明显异常。

而 EV71 等致手足口病病毒如何在短时间内通过消化道、呼吸道进入中枢神经系统机制需要进一步去研究、阐明。

参考文献

[1] Schmidt NJ, Lennette EH, HoHH. An apparently new enterovirus isolated from patients with diseases of the central nervous system [J]. J Infect Dis, 1974, 129: 304 – 309.

[2] 中华人民共和国卫生部《手足口病诊疗指南》2008 年。

[3] 陆国平、李兴旺、吕勇："危重症手足口病（EV71 感染）诊治体会"，载《中国小儿急救医学》2008 年第 5 期。

[4] Chang LY, Lee CY, Kao CL, et al Hand, foot and mouth disease complicated with central nervous system involvement in Taiwan in 1980 – 1981 [J]. J Formos Med Assoc, 2007, 106 (2): 173 – 176.

[5] 高子芬、陆敏："肠道病毒 EV71 感染重症儿童的病理学特点"，载《临床与实验病理学杂志》2008 年第 5 期。

食尸性蝇类表皮碳氢化合物在法医学应用的研究进展

罗 浩 周伟光 徐 宏 谢良兴 朱光辉*

尸食性昆虫在死亡时间（post - mortem interval，PMI）推断上有重要的价值。人死后，在适宜的环境下，尸食性蝇类能在较短时间内抵达尸体并产卵。蝇卵在尸体上发育，并可随发育进程发生一系列规律性变化，因此可用于PMI的推断。几乎所有的昆虫表皮都覆盖着一层菲薄的蜡质层，用以维持昆虫正常的生理活动。一方面，是为了维持昆虫体内水代谢的平衡，起到水屏障的作用；另一方面，在昆虫与外界环境进行信息沟通时作为信息素存在。蜡质层在昆虫生长发育过程中也是随着年龄的增长而变化。已有的研究结果表明，尸食性蝇类表皮碳氢化合物对PMI的推断具有很大的应用潜力。本文对昆虫表皮碳氢化合物组成及其在PMI推断的研究进展上进行系统阐述。

一、表皮碳氢化合物的组成

昆虫表皮含有丰富的碳氢化合物，其成分主要是C20 - C37的直链烷烃、单甲基烷烃、二甲基烷烃、三甲基烷烃和烯烃。表皮碳氢化合物存在于昆虫的各个发育阶段，是昆虫基因型的表现，受各种因素的调节，如生殖状态[1]、发育阶段[2]、饮食[3]或温度[4-6]等。因此，昆虫表皮碳氢化合物的组成随环境、种群、虫龄之间的不同而有显著的差异。

直链烷烃是昆虫表皮碳氢化合物的主要组成成分，存在于所有昆虫中，链长一般为C21 ~ C38。奇数碳直链烷烃通常比偶数碳直链烷烃含量更丰富，其性质也比相邻的偶数碳烷烃性质相对稳定。这可能是昆虫表皮碳氢化合物中，奇数碳直链烷烃含量相对较多的缘故。Faurot - Bouchet等对7种介壳虫的研究表明，其表皮碳氢化合物全为C15 ~ C35的直链烷烃，其中以奇数碳直链烷烃为主。[7]

单甲基烷的碳链长度介于C20 ~ C41之间，其中多数支链位于奇数碳原子上。具内部支链的二甲基烷具有类异戊二烯的结构，但并非来自类异戊二烯单体。最常见的异构体有9，13 - 二甲基、11，15 - 二甲基、13，17 - 二甲基、15，19 - 二甲基和17，21 - 二甲基烷。越来越多的研究表明，甲基可位于主链的任何位置。但甲基位于奇数位碳原子的异构体比位于偶数位碳原子的异构体更加普遍。

三甲基烷的种类较为稀少，迄今在昆虫表皮中得到鉴定的三甲基烷仅十余种，其中除5，9，15 - 和5，9，17 - 三甲基烷外，其余三甲基烷均具有类异戊二烯间隔的甲基支链。因为在碳氢化合物中，支链越多，其分子间的距离越大，色散力越小，其性质

* 杭州市公安局拱墅区分局，浙江杭州，310000；汕头大学医学院法医学教研室，广东汕头，515031。E - mail：ghzhu@126. com。

越不稳定，因而在昆虫表皮碳氢化合物中的种类和含量相对较少。

烯烃的主链长度通常为C20～C39，其中主链长度为奇数的占多数，双键可处于任何位置。根据双键的位置，烯烃可以有不同的功能，家蝇（*Musca domestica*）的性信息素是（Z9）-C23：1，其主链上第9位是双键；黑腹果蝇（D. *melanogaster*）中，性信息素是（Z7）-C23：1，双键位于第7位，诱导其在求偶时产生剂量依赖性抑制。[8]因此，对于烯类，确定其双键的位置是至关重要的。烯烃类的化合物中，以单烯较多，二烯较少，三烯最少。双键数目越多，烯烃的性质越不稳定，而反式双键结构要比顺式双键结构更加稳定。

二、法医昆虫种属和地理种群差异鉴别

国内外研究表明，表皮碳氢化合物主要由昆虫自身合成，可作为一类有效的生化分类特征。[9,10]同时，昆虫表皮碳氢化合物的组成和含量在种类之间存在差异，即使在近缘种之间也有显著区别。[11]此外，昆虫表皮碳氢化合物的组成具有一定的地理种群特异性，自洛基（Lockey，1976）首先比较了5种蝗虫的表皮碳氢化合物组成以来，表皮碳氢化合物在昆虫分类学中，已得到越来越多的研究和应用。[10,12,13]主要集中在：①用于形态相似、难以或根本不能根据形态特征区分的近缘种（幼期昆虫或成虫）的鉴别及其关系的研究；②用于地理种群的鉴别及其关系的研究。叶恭银等[14]从6种食尸性蝇类的蛹壳中提取出碳氢化合物，运用气相色谱和气-质联用仪对提取物进行分析并对所有色谱峰进行判别分析后，可将6种不同蝇类的所有蛹壳彼此分离，从而很好地证实了这一点。

有些种类昆虫的表皮碳氢化合物组成在不同地理种群间差异很大，而在另一些昆虫中则无显著差异。[15,16]因此，根据尸体上昆虫所属的种群是否为本地种群，可以确定尸体是否被移动过。同时，也可以通过遗留的蛹壳或是昆虫幼虫，发现第一案发现场，这对命案的侦破可起到关键作用。亚历克西斯（Alexis et al.，1995）对来自美国 *Tucannon River* 和 *Lyle Grove*，Washington 和 Rensselaer，Indiana 三个地理种群的伏蝇 *Phormia regina*（Meigen）表皮碳氢化合物组成的研究表明，根据地点和性别，应用判别分析可以将三个地理种群分开。

三、PMI推断和影响因素

（一）应用表皮碳氢化合物进行PMI推断

昆虫表皮碳氢化合物在PMI推断方面主要有以下两方面的作用：①蝇类幼虫或者蛹的表皮碳氢化合物组成随发育的增长发生显著的变化，[14,17-19]在幼虫或蛹的年龄推断方面有很大的价值；②尸食性蝇类蛹壳表皮碳氢化合物的组成随着风化时间的延长有着规律性变化，因此可通过蛹壳风化时间对腐败尸体的PMI进行推断。

绯颜裸金蝇幼虫表皮碳氢化合物随发育产生时序性变化，离食期幼虫中尤其显著。其中低分子量烷烃的百分含量随着日龄的增长逐渐降低，正二十九烷相对含量与日龄呈指数函数或幂函数关系增加。[20]罗克斯等（Roux et al.，2008）对反吐丽蝇（*Calliphora vomitoria*）、红头丽蝇（C. *Vicina*）和新陆原伏蝇（*Protophormia terraenovae*）的研究，进一步证实了表皮碳氢化合物在蝇类幼虫日龄的推断上具有较大的应用潜力。

大头金蝇蛹壳表皮碳氢化合物的组成在0～80 d内，可发生有规律性变化。随着风化时间的延长，所有支链烷烃的百分含量降低，偶数碳直链烷烃的百分含量呈线性增加。因此，蛹壳表皮碳氢化合物风化规律在推断腐败尸体的PMI上有很大的应用前景。

（二）尸食性蝇类表皮碳氢化合物组成的影响因素

1. 温度。在适宜温度内，昆虫发育速率随温度呈S型非线性增加。温度是昆虫的生长发育最主要的影响因素之一，对其研究主要包括对各虫态发育速率和对各日龄指标的影响。[21]同时，温度还可影响昆虫表皮碳氢化合物的组成种类和含量。如埃及伊蚊（*Aedes aegypti*）雌成虫全虫和足中，一些表皮碳氢化合物含量随日龄发生显著变化，并受温度的显著影响。[16,22]朱光辉（2003）研究了在四种温度下巨尾阿丽蝇幼虫表皮碳氢化合物组成的时间特征，筛选出各温度下百分含量变化趋势一致的色谱峰，建立可用于各种温度下巨尾阿丽蝇幼虫日龄推断的数学模型。[23]

2. 湿度。昆虫表皮蜡质对于维持昆虫体内的水分平衡有关键作用。托尔逊（Toolson）将果蝇（*Drosophila pseudoobscura*）成虫表皮的脂质除去以后，其表皮对水的通透性增加13倍。[4]对水分保持要求越高的昆虫，其表皮脂类物质的含量也越高。一些鳞翅昆虫的滞育蛹在土中度过的时间达8个月，这些滞育蛹的脂质层比非滞育蛹的脂质层更厚。家蝇雌雄成虫在环境湿度为90%相对湿度（RH）下，总表皮碳氢化合物的含量比20% RH和50% RH下显著较高。[24]

3. 食物种类。食物可直接影响到昆虫表皮碳氢化合物的组成，不同食物饲养幼虫所得蛹壳表皮碳氢化合物组成也有区别。[25]同时，不同食物饲养的昆虫生长周期及其个体发育存在差别。[26-28]在法医昆虫学研究中，由于伦理和来源等方面原因，很少用人尸体来进行相关试验，而用其他动物尸体代替。因此，应用其他动物尸体进行相关试验前，应阐明食物种类对蛹壳表皮碳氢化合物组成的影响。此外，还应注意一些中毒死亡尸体中所含毒物对于尸食性蝇类蛹壳表皮碳氢化合物的影响。

4. 昆虫种属。昆虫种属对于蛹壳表皮碳氢化合物组成的影响也应引起相应的重视。不同种类的昆虫，其表皮碳氢化合物的组成不同，因此针对不同种昆虫蛹壳所建立的风化时间推断模型也不尽相同；未风化蛹壳表皮碳氢化合物的组成受温度、湿度等环境因素影响的程度在不同种昆虫间可能存在显著差异；[29,30]不同昆虫种属之间存在种间竞争，这也使得化蛹时间和蛹壳大小的变化很大。[27]因此，多种尸食性蝇类同时存在时应选择表皮碳氢化合物组成受影响较小的蝇类用于PMI推断。

5. 其他。地理种群对昆虫表皮碳氢化合物的组成有显著影响。[31,32]伯恩（Byrne）等研究发现，伏蝇（*Phormia regina*）成虫表皮碳氢化合物的组成受地理种群的显著影响。[25]此外，野外自然条件下蛹壳表皮碳氢化合物的风化程度和风化速度受紫外线、降水、土壤微生物等因素的影响，值得进一步深入研究。

四、展　望

表皮碳氢化合物是食尸性昆虫表皮腊层中的主要成分。表皮碳氢化合物在法医昆虫学中具有很大的应用潜力。由于幼虫、蛹壳表皮碳氢化合物的组成变化受诸多环境因素的影响，因此，要通过相关的因素研究而建立切实可行的数学模型来推断蝇类幼虫的日龄和蛹壳风化时间。

参考文献

[1] Monnin T., “Chemical Recognition of Reproductive Status in Social Insects”, *Ann Zool Fennici*,

2006, 43, pp. 515 ~ 530.

[2] Martin C, Salvy M, Provost E, et al., "Variations in Chemical Mimicry by the Ectoparasitic Mite Varroa jacobsoni According to the Developmental Stage of the Host Honey – bee *Apis mellifera*", *Insect Biochem Molec*, 2001, 31, pp. 365 ~ 379.

[3] Buczkowski G, Kumar R, Suib S L, et al., "Diet – related Modification of Cuticular Hydrocarbon Profiles of the Argentine Ant, *Linepithema humile*, Diminishes Intercolony Aggression", *J Chem Ecol*, 2005, 31 (4), pp. 829 ~ 843.

[4] Toolson E C., "Effects of Rearing Temperature on Cuticle Permeability and Epicuticular Lipid Composition in *Drosophila Pseudoobscura*", *J Exp Zool*, 1982, 222 (3), pp. 249 ~ 253.

[5] Savarit F, Ferveur J – F, "Temperature Affects the Ontogeny of Sexually Dimorphic Cuticular Hydrocarbons in *Drosophila Melanogaster*", *J Exp Biol*, 2002, 205, pp. 3241 ~ 3249.

[6] Rouault J – D, Marican C, Wicker – Thomas C, et al., "Relations between Cuticular Hydrocarbons (CH) Polymorphism Resistance Against Desiccation and Breeding Temperature; A Model for CH Evolution in D. Melanogaster and D. Stimulans", *Genetica.*, 2004, 120, pp. 195 ~ 212.

[7] Faurot – Boucher E, Michel G. Ibid., 1964, 41, p. 418.

[8] Scott D., "Sexual Mimicry Regulates the Attractiveness of Mated Drosophila melanogaster Females", *Proc Natl Acad Sci USA.*, 1986, 83 (21), pp. 8429 ~ 8433.

[9] Blomquist G J, Dillwith J W. Cuticular lipids, In: Kerkut GA and Gilbert LI (Eds), *Comprehensive Insect Physiology Biochenistry and Pharmacology*, Oxford: Pergamon Press, 1985, 3, pp. 117 ~ 154.

[10] Lockty K H., "Insect Cuticular Lipids", *Comp Bilchem Physiol*, 1988, 89B, pp. 595 ~ 645.

[11] Pennanech M., "Insect hydrocarbon: Analysis, Structure and Function", *Eppc Bulletin*, 1995, 25, pp. 343 ~ 348.

[12] 高明媛："昆虫表皮中碳氢化合物在昆虫分类中的应用"，载《昆虫学报》2001, 44 (1), pp. 119 ~ 120.

[13] 朱光辉、叶恭银、胡萃："表皮碳氢化合物在城市昆虫某些类群分类中的应用"，载《全国第六届城市昆虫学术讨论会论文集》2001 年版。

[14] Ye G Y, Li K, Zhu J Y, et al., "Cuticular Hydrocarbon Composition in Pupal Exuviae for Taxonomic Differentiation of Six Necrophagous Flies", *J Med Entomol*, 2007, 44, pp. 450 ~ 456.

[15] Roux O, Gers C, Legal L., "Ontogenetic Study of Three Calliphoridae of Forensic Importance through Cuticular Hydrocarbon Analysis", *Med Vet Entomol*, 2008, 22, pp. 309 ~ 317.

[16] Desena M L, Clark J M, Edman J D, et al., "Potential for Aging Female *Aedes Aegypti* (Diptera: Culicidae) by Gas Chromatographic Analysis of Cuticular Hydrocarbons including a Field Evaluation", *J Med Entomol*, 1999, 36, pp. 811 ~ 823.

[17] Zhu G H, Ye G Y, Hu C, et al., "Development Changes of Cuticular Hydrocarbons in *Chrysomya Rufifacies* Larvae: Potential for Determining Larval Age", *Med Vet Entomol*, 2006, 20, pp. 438 ~ 444.

[18] Zhu G H, Xu X H, Yu X J, et al., "Puparial Case Hydrocarbons of *Chrysomya Megacephala* as an Indicator of the Postmortem Interval", *Forensic Sci Int*, 2007, 169, pp. 1 ~ 5.

[19] Roux O, Gers C, Legal L., "Ontogenetic Study of Three Calliphoridae of Forensic Importance Through Cuticular Hydrocarbon Analysis", *Med Vet Entomol*, 2008, 22, pp. 309 ~ 317.

[20] Millar J G. Liquid chromatography. In, Millar J G, Haynes K F (eds), *Methods in Chemical Ecology*, Kluwer, Dordrecht, 1998, pp. 85 ~ 126.

[21] Higley L G, Haskell N H., "Insect Development and Forensic Entomology, Byrd J H, Castner J L", *Forensic Entomology: the Utility of Arthropods in Legal Investigation*, Boca Raton: CRC Press.

[22] Desena M L, Edman J D, Clark J M, et al. , "*Aedes Aegypti* (Diptera: Culicidae) Age Determination by Cuticular Hydrocarbon Analysis of Female Legs", *J Med Entomol*, 1999, 36, pp. 824 ~ 830.

[23] 朱光辉:《尸食性蝇类的生物化学特征用于死后间隔时间推断的基础研究》, 浙江大学 2003 年博士学位论文。

[24] Noorman N, Cornelis J. Den Otter. , "Effects of Relative Humidity, Temperature, and Population Density on Production of Cuticular Hydrocarbons in Housefly *Musca Domestice* L. ", *J Chem Ecol*, 2002, 9 (28), pp. 1819 ~ 1829.

[25] Liang D, Silverman J. "You Are What You Eat: Diet Modifies Cuticular Hydrocarbons and Nestmate Recognition in the Argentine ant, Linepithema Humile", *Naturwissenschaften*, 2000, 87, pp. 412 ~ 416.

[26] Dos Reis S F, Von Zuben C J, Godoy W A C. , "Larval Aggregation and Competition for Food in Experimental Populations of *Chrysomya Putoria* (Wied.) and *Cochliomyia macellaria* (F.) (Dipt. , Calliphoridae)", *J Appl Ent*, 1999, 123 (8), pp. 374 ~ 378.

[27] Kaneshrajah G, Turner B. , "*Calliphora Vicina* Larvae Grow at Different Rates on Different Body Tissues", *Int J Legal Med*, 2004, 118, pp. 242 ~ 244.

[28] Ireland S, Truner B. , "The Effects of Larval Crowding and Food Type on the Size and Development of the Blowfly, *Calliphora vomitoria*", *Forensic Sci Int*, 2006, 159, pp. 175 ~ 181.

[29] Grassberger M, Reiter C. , "Effect of Temperature on Development of the Forensically Important Holarctic blow Fly *Protophormia Terraenovae* (Robineau – Desvoidy) (Diptera: Calliphoridae)", *Forensci Sci Int.* , 2002, 18 (3), pp. 177 ~ 182.

[30] Grassberger M, Reiter C. , "Effect of Temperature on *Lucilia Sericata* (Diptera: Calliphoridae) Development with Special Reference to the Isomegalen – and Isomorphen – diagram", *Forensic Sci Int*, 2001, 120 (1 ~ 2), pp. 32 ~ 36.

[31] Ratchadawan N – K, Kittikhun M, Tunwadee K – K, et al. , "Do climatic and Physical Factors Affect Populations of the blow Fly *Chrysomya Megacephala* and House Fly *Musca domestica*?", *Parasitol Res*, 2011, 109, pp. 1279 ~ 1292.

[32] Jessica D, François J. Verheggen, et al. , "Carrion Beetles Visiting Pig Carcasses during Early Spring in Urban, Forest and Agricultural Biotopes of Western Europe", *J Insect Sci*, 2011, 11, pp. 1 ~ 13.

6 个 X－STR 基因座的连锁不平衡和单倍型分析

唐剑频 于 昕 蒋丰慧 *

X 染色体具有遗传变异度低、有效群体小的特点，是群体遗传学研究的重要遗传标记之一。X 染色体遗传标记具有特殊的遗传特点，使其成为法医学亲权鉴定的重要辅助遗传标记，[1,2] 尤其祖母—孙女等亲权关系的鉴定。X 染色体短串联重复序列（short tandem repeat，STR）构成几个连锁群，应用于法医学时，不仅要考虑 X－STR 间的连锁关系，也要考虑不同 X－STR 等位基因间是否存在连锁不平衡。本研究分析 Xq21、26 区域 6 个 X－STR（DXS10101、HPRTB、DXS10103、DXS6799、DXS6789、DXS6801）的连锁不平衡状态及其单倍型分布，为法医学应用提供基础。

一、材料与方法

1. 样本。按照知情同意权原则，采集 160 名广东地区汉族无关健康男性血液样本。

2. DNA 提取。用 Chelex－100 法提取样本的基因组 DNA。

3. PCR 扩增及分型。6 个 X－STR 基因座的引物来自 X－STR 数据库（www. chrx－str. org），其中一条引物 5 端用荧光染料 FAM 修饰。PCR 产物用 ABI3130 进行分型，分型标准物由各等位基因 PCR 产物混合而成。等位基因经测序后，按照国际法医遗传学会的命名原则对各基因座的等位基因进行命名。[3]

4. 数据分析。用 BLAT[4] 检索工具确定各基因座的物理位置。用直接计数法计算等位基因和单倍型频率。应用 Arlequin3. 5 软件分析连锁不平衡（linkage disequilibrium，LD）、男性样本个人识别率（power of discrimination in males，PD_m）、单倍型变异度（haplotype diversity，HD），比较不同群体的单倍型分布。

二、结 果

1. 等位基因频率分析结果。160 名男性样本中，DXS10101、HPRTB、DXS10103、DXS6799、DXS6789、DXS6801 分别观察到 14、6、7、7、9、5 个等位基因。DXS10101、HPRTB、DXS10103、DXS6799、DXS6789、DXS6801 的 PD_m 值分别为 0. 771、0. 698、0. 791、0. 653、0. 748、0. 570。等位基因频率分布见表 1。

* 广东医学院法医学教研室，桂林市公安局刑侦支队，广东医学院门诊部。Email：tangjianpin@ hotmail. com。

表 1　男性样本的 5 个 X－STR 基因座的等位基因频率

DXS10101		HPRTB		DXS10103		DXS6799		DXS6789		DXS6801	
等位基因	等位频率	等位基因	等位频率	等位基因	等位频率	等位基因	等位频率	等位基因	等位频率	等位基因	等位频率
28	0. 025	11	0. 038	15	0. 025	8	0. 006	14	0. 006	7	0. 019
28. 2	0. 013	12	0. 312	16	0. 307	9	0. 063	16	0. 131	10	0. 181
29	0. 131	13	0. 412	17	0. 181	10	0. 244	17	0. 444	11	0. 612
29. 2	0. 063	14	0. 175	18	0. 150	10. 2	0. 006	18	0. 069	12	0. 144
29. 3	0. 006	15	0. 050	19	0. 206	11	0. 512	20	0. 044	13	0. 044
30	0. 131	16	0. 013	20	0. 125	12	0. 144	21	0. 125	—	—
30. 2	0. 056	—	—	22	0. 006	13	0. 025	22	0. 125	—	—
31	0. 424	—	—	—	—	—	—	23	0. 050	—	—
31. 1	0. 013	—	—	—	—	—	—	24	0. 006	—	—
31. 2	0. 025	—	—	—	—	—	—	—	—	—	—
32	0. 075	—	—	—	—	—	—	—	—	—	—
32. 2	0. 019	—	—	—	—	—	—	—	—	—	—
33	0. 013	—	—	—	—	—	—	—	—	—	—
35	0. 006	—	—	—	—	—	—	—	—	—	—

2. 连锁不平衡及单倍型的分析结果。DXS10101－HPRTB－DXS10103 同属于一个连锁群，共观察到 87 种单倍型，其中 55 种单倍型观察到一名男性样本；单倍型变异度为 0. 987。DXS6799－DXS6789－DXS6801 同属于一个连锁群，共观察到 60 种单倍型，33 种单倍型观察到一名男性样本；单倍型变异度为 0. 968。比较 XS10101－HPRTB－DXS10103 构成的单倍型在不同群体间分布差异，广东汉族群体与韩国群体[5]有 46 种单倍型相同，与德国群体[6]有 19 种单倍型相同；广东汉族群体与德国[5]、韩国群体[6]的群体间遗传距离 *Fst* 值分别为 0. 02324、0. 0377，群体间差异检验 *P* 值均少于 0. 05。

表2 DXS10101 – HPRTB – DXS10103 和 DXS6799 – DXS6789 – DXS6801 单倍型分布

DXS10101 – HPRTB – DXS10103										DXS6799 – DXS6789 – DXS6801				
编号	DXS 10101	HPRTB	DXS 10103	数量	编号	DXS 10101	HPRTB	DXS 10103	数量	编号	DXS 6799	DXS 6789	DXS 6801	数量
H1	28	12	16	1	H61	31	14	20	2	H1	8	21	10	1
H2	28	12	19	1	H62	31	14	22	1	H2	9	16	11	1
H3	28	13	17	1	H63	31	15	16	3	H3	9	17	10	2
H4	28	14	18	1	H64	31	15	17	1	H4	9	17	11	2
H5	28. 2	13	15	1	H65	31	15	20	1	H5	9	17	12	1
H6	28. 2	13	18	1	H66	31	16	19	1	H6	9	18	10	1
H7	29	12	16	2	H67	31. 1	12	16	1	H7	9	20	10	1
H8	29	12	17	1	H68	31. 1	16	19	1	H8	9	22	11	2
H9	29	12	18	1	H69	31. 2	12	17	1	H9	10	14	11	1
H10	29	12	20	2	H70	31. 2	13	17	1	H10	10	16	10	1
H11	29	13	15	2	H71	31. 2	13	18	1	H11	10	16	11	1
H12	29	13	16	2	H72	31. 2	15	19	1	H12	10	16	12	1
H13	29	13	17	1	H73	32	11	16	1	H13	10	17	7	1
H14	29	13	18	2	H74	32	11	19	1	H14	10	17	10	7
H15	29	13	19	2	H75	32	12	17	1	H15	10	17	11	7
H16	29	13	20	1	H76	32	12	19	1	H16	10	17	12	4
H17	29	14	16	3	H77	32	12	20	1	H17	10	18	11	2
H18	29	14	19	1	H78	32	13	18	1	H18	10	20	11	1
H19	29	15	18	1	H79	32	13	19	1	H19	10	21	11	4
H20	29. 2	11	19	1	H80	32	14	16	2	H20	10	21	12	1
H21	29. 2	12	16	1	H81	32	14	19	2	H21	10	22	10	1
H22	29. 2	12	18	1	H82	32	14	20	1	H22	10	22	11	4
H23	29. 2	12	20	1	H83	32. 2	13	17	2	H23	10	23	10	1
H24	29. 2	13	16	2	H84	32. 2	14	18	1	H24	10	23	11	2
H25	29. 2	13	18	1	H85	33	12	20	1	H25	10. 2	20	11	1
H26	29. 2	13	19	1	H86	33	14	16	1	H26	11	16	10	2
H27	29. 2	14	18	1	H87	35	15	17	1	H27	11	16	11	10
H28	29. 2	14	19	1	—	—	—	—	—	H28	11	16	12	1
H29	29. 3	14	16	1	—	—	—	—	—	H29	11	16	13	1
H30	30	12	16	6	—	—	—	—	—	H30	11	17	7	2
H31	30	12	17	1	—	—	—	—	—	H31	11	17	10	6
H32	30	12	18	1	—	—	—	—	—	H32	11	17	11	18
H33	30	13	16	4	—	—	—	—	—	H33	11	17	12	6
H34	30	13	17	4	—	—	—	—	—	H34	11	17	13	1
H35	30	13	18	2	—	—	—	—	—	H35	11	18	11	3
H36	30	13	19	1	—	—	—	—	—	H36	11	18	13	2
H37	30	13	20	1	—	—	—	—	—	H37	11	20	11	2

续表

DXS10101－HPRTB－DXS10103										DXS6799－DXS6789－DXS6801				
编号	DXS 10101	HPRTB	DXS 10103	数量	编号	DXS 10101	HPRTB	DXS 10103	数量	编号	DXS 6799	DXS 6789	DXS 6801	数量
H38	30	14	16	1	—	—	—	—	—	H38	11	21	10	3
H39	30. 2	12	19	2	—	—	—	—	—	H39	11	21	11	8
H40	30. 2	12	20	1	—	—	—	—	—	H40	11	21	12	1
H41	30. 2	13	16	2	—	—	—	—	—	H41	11	21	13	1
H42	30. 2	13	18	1	—	—	—	—	—	H42	11	22	10	2
H43	30. 2	13	19	2	—	—	—	—	—	H43	11	22	11	9
H44	30. 2	14	16	1	—	—	—	—	—	H44	11	23	11	3
H45	31	11	16	2	—	—	—	—	—	H45	11	23	12	1
H46	31	11	19	1	—	—	—	—	—	H46	12	16	11	2
H47	31	12	16	4	—	—	—	—	—	H47	12	17	11	8
H48	31	12	17	5	—	—	—	—	—	H48	12	17	12	5
H49	31	12	18	4	—	—	—	—	—	H49	12	18	10	1
H50	31	12	19	3	—	—	—	—	—	H50	12	18	11	1
H51	31	12	20	6	—	—	—	—	—	H51	12	18	12	1
H52	31	13	15	1	—	—	—	—	—	H52	12	20	11	1
H53	31	13	16	5	—	—	—	—	—	H53	12	21	11	1
H54	31	13	17	6	—	—	—	—	—	H54	12	22	11	1
H55	31	13	18	4	—	—	—	—	—	H55	12	23	13	1
H56	31	13	19	8	—	—	—	—	—	H56	12	24	13	1
H57	31	13	20	2	—	—	—	—	—	H57	13	16	12	1
H58	31	14	16	4	—	—	—	—	—	H58	13	17	11	1
H59	31	14	17	3	—	—	—	—	—	H59	13	20	11	1
H60	31	14	19	1	—	—	—	—	—	H60	13	22	11	1

3. 连锁不平衡分析结果。DXS10101、HPRTB、DXS10103 位于 Xq26.2 的 133654471－133419091bp 区域，DXS6799、DXS6789、DXS6801 位于 Xq21.3 的 97378914－92511298bp 区域。为了解 6 个 X－STR 基因座的连锁不平衡状态，通过对这些基因座的两两间连锁不平衡分析，各基因座间的连锁不平衡分析 P 值见表 3。

表3 6个基因座连锁不平衡分析结果

配对基因座	P值
DXS10101 - HPRTB	0.3401
DXS10101 - DXS10103	0.4291
DXS10101 - DXS6799	0.0621
DXS10101 - DXS6789	0.1755
DXS10101 - DXS6801	0.5099
HPRTB - DXS10103	0.1660
HPRTB - DXS6799	0.0843
HPRTB - DXS6789	0.1976
HPRTB - DXS6801	0.5034
DXS10103 - DXS6799	0.4054
DXS10103 - DXS6789	0.5426
DXS10103 - DXS6801	0.5537
DXS6799 - DXS6789	0.3308
DXS6799 - DXS6801	0.3095
DXS6789 - DXS6801	0.2717

三、讨 论

群体遗传学调查结果表明，所分析的男性样本中，DXS10101 基因座观察到的等位基因最多，DXS6801 基因座观察到的等位基因数最少；DXS10103 的 PD_m 值较好，DXS6801 的 PD_m 值最低；分析结果说明广东汉族群体中 DXS10103 男性样本中鉴别效能较好，DXS6801 的鉴别效能最差。

通过对6个X-STR基因座的连锁不平衡分析，所分析的群体中，6个X-STR基因座两两间没有观察到显著连锁不平衡。由于连锁不平衡分析是分析不同基因座的等位基因间关系，并不能说明基因座间的连锁关系；而 DXS10101 - HPRTB - DXS10103、DXS6799 - DXS6789 - DXS6801 分别位于 Xq26.2、Xq21.3 区域同一连锁群内，物理距离较近；虽然不同基因的等位基因间没有观察到显著连锁不平衡状态，但是同一连锁群内的X-STR应用于法医学时，应该用单倍型频率代替等为基因频率分析法医物证学鉴定结果。

通过对 DXS10101 - HPRTB - DXS10103、DXS6799 - DXS6789 - DXS6801 构成的单倍型分析，这2个连锁群构成的单倍型种类较多、鉴别能力较强，可成为常染色体 STR 的补充遗传标记。分析结果说明广东汉族群体与德国[6]、韩国群体[5]的 DXS10101 - HPRTB - DXS10103 单倍型分布存在显著差异，不同群体的X-STR单倍型分布不同，X-STR单倍型具有群体特性。

参考文献

［1］刘秋玲、吕德坚、张建苗等："X－STR 体系在特殊亲子鉴定案中的应用 1 例"，载《中国法医学杂志》2011 年第 2 期，第 147～148 页。

［2］王新杰、许欣、吴洪浦等："潍坊汉族男性 27 个 X—STR 基因座遗传多态性"，载《法医学杂志》2010 年第 4 期，第 301～303 页。

［3］Bär W，Brinkmann B，Budowle B，*et al.*，"DNA Recommendations. Further Report of the DNA Commission of the ISFG Regarding the Use of Short Tandem Repeat Systems"，*Forensic Sci Int.*，1997，87（3），pp. 179～184.

［4］http：//genome. ucsc. edu/cgi－bin/.

［5］Sim JE，Lee HY，Yang WI，*et al.*，"Population Genetic Study of Four Closely－linked X－STR Trios in Koreans"，*Mol Biol Rep*，2010，37（1），pp. 333～337.

［6］Rodig H，Kloep F，Weissbach L，*et al.*，"Evaluation of Seven X－chromosomal Short Tandem Repeat Loci Located within the Xq26 Region"，*Forensic Sci Int Genet*，2010，4（3），pp. 194～199.

视敏度与微视野检测的相关性*

王 旭 刘 会 项 剑 郑 拓 于丽丽**

视觉功能作为一种主观的、躯体特殊感觉功能，其客观评定疑难而复杂，长期以来，视觉功能的客观评定一直是法医临床学的研究重点，其中，以视敏度的客观评定最重要；目前，此方面的研究主要集中在视觉电生理（如 VEP、ERG 等）的手段上，其他方面的研究罕见报道。本文旨在探讨固视性质检查在客观评估视敏度方面的可行性，以寻找视觉电生理以外的方法客观评估视功能，以利于法医临床学应用。

本文应用 MP-1 型微视野计，对 85 眼别（75 眼别为不同程度的眼底损伤者、10 眼别为正常者）进行固视性质检查，应用 SPSS 17.0 软件进行统计学处理。

一、对象与方法

（一）测试对象

本实验选取北京某三甲医院眼科就诊的眼底损伤者，需满足下列条件：①检查配合，智力水平可；②不涉及诉讼，视敏度真实可靠；③受检者除眼底损伤外，不存在屈光间质混浊；④年龄在 20~55 岁之间、性别不限；⑤损伤距检查时间超过 3 个月，视网膜新鲜出血、挫伤已愈合（遗留视网膜瘢痕）。

本文另设正常对照组：均为眼底正常者，矫正视力 1.0，除眼底病变外，其余条件同上。

（二）测试方法

1. 视敏度检查

应用国际标准对数视力表，按照《标准对数视力表 GB11533》对受试者进行视敏度检测，矫正其屈光不正，记录矫正对数视力。

2. 微视野检测

应用 MP-1 微视野仪行微视野检测，具体涵盖两项内容。

A. 评估固视状态检测：嘱受检者在确切注视固视目标后接键应答，重复 30~50 次（可增加），仪器记录下每次按键时固视光标在眼底的确切投射位置，并与眼底图重叠显示，计算 2 度范围固视率，用以评估固视状态。

B. 视网膜光敏感度检测：检查黄斑 20°范围视网膜光敏感度阈值，计算平均值。

---

* 基金项目：十二五科技支撑计划项目 2012BAK16B03；国家自然科学基金项目 81172912；上海市法医学重点实验室开放基金 KF1108。

** 王旭，女，辽宁省兴城市人，教授，主任法医师，主要从事法医临床学鉴定及研究工作。Email：xuw01@cupl. edu. cn。

【通讯作者】同上。1. 司法文明协同创新中心，2. 中国政法大学证据科学教育部重点实验室 北京 100088。Email：xuw01@cupl. edu. cn。刘会，主检法医师；项剑，主检法医师；郑拓，中国政法大学研究生；于丽丽，法医师。

（三）分组

根据微视野黄斑中心 2°直径范围内的固视百分率分组：A 组（中心固视组）：需 80%以上固视点落在黄斑中心 2°直径范围内；B 组（不确定组）：即 20% ~80% 固视点落在黄斑中心 2°直径范围内；C 组（偏心固视组）：即小于 20% 固视点在黄斑中心 2°直径范围内。

（四）统计学分析

所有数据经 SPSS 17.0 软件包处理：①对 3 组被检者视敏度行均值、标准差计算，F 检验；②以被检者视敏度与视网膜平均光敏感度值分别行 Pearson 相关、回归分析，以 $P<0.05$ 为差异具有统计学意义。

二、结　果

（一）一般情况

本实验共获得符合条件的受检者 75 例（均单眼受损），其中左眼 40 例，右眼 35 例。年龄在 28 ~56 岁不等（其中 28 ~38 岁者 42 例，38 ~48 岁者 22 例，48 ~56 岁者 11 例）；性别：男性 54 例，女性 21 例；均为各种原因所致的视网膜损伤（不包含玻璃体积血致屈光间质混浊者）。正常对照组 10 例（10 眼别），男女各 5 人，左、右眼各 5 例。

（二）不同固视性质组视敏度的统计分析

1. 不同固视性质的微视野图示（详见图 1 ~3）。

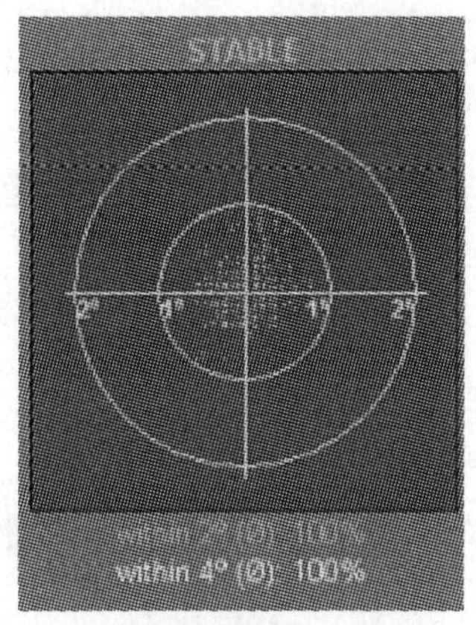

图 1　固视稳定，视力 1.0

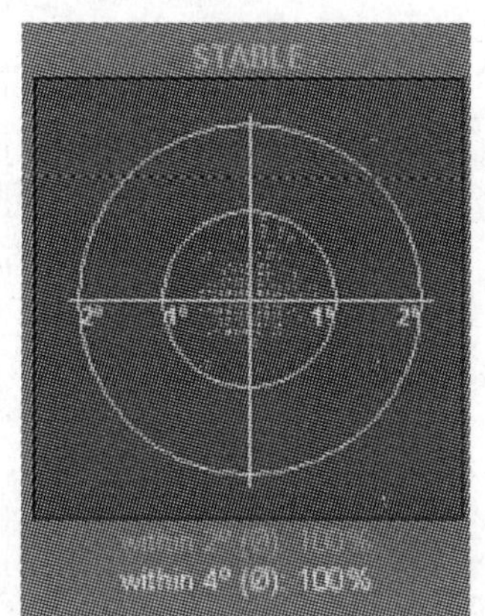

图 2 固视相对不稳定，视力 0.2

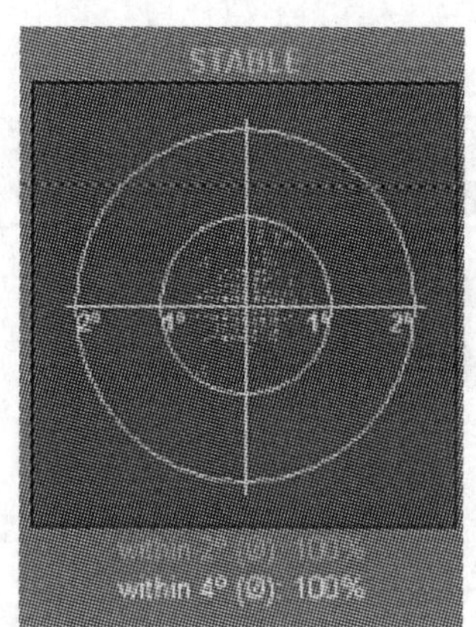

图 3 固视不稳定，视力 0.02

2. 上述眼别对应的微视野敏感度地形图（详见图 4 ~6）

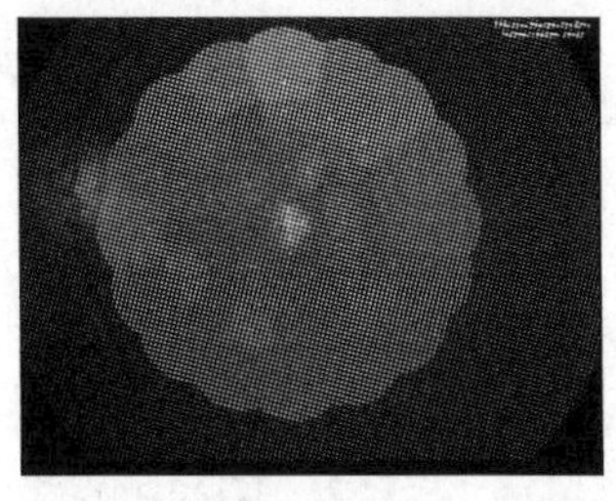

图 4

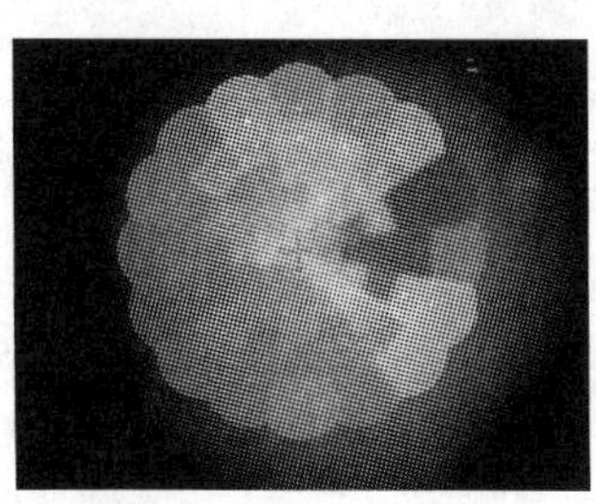

图 5

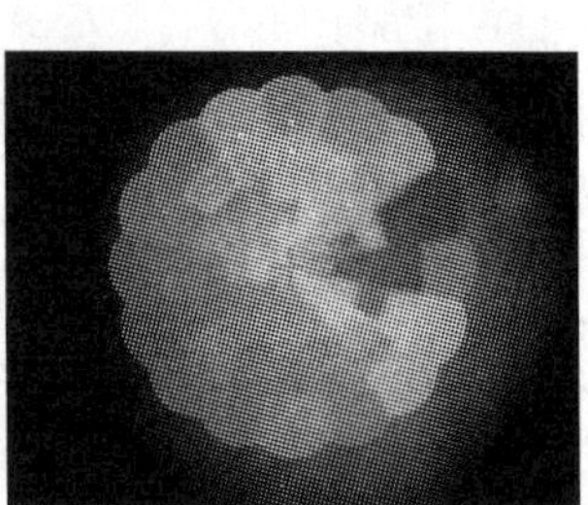

图 6

3. 受检者视敏度分布：光感至1.0（即对数视力为1.0至5.0）不等（详见表1）

表1　不同固视性质组的视敏度水平统计（ ±s）

固视性质分组	例数（N）	视敏度均值	视敏度标准差	变异系数CV
中心固视组（A组）	31	4.8	0.16	0.03
不确定组（B组）	27	4.2	0.45	0.11
偏心固视组（C组）	17	3.4	0.57	0.17
正常对照组	10	5.0	—	—
合计	85	—	—	—

表1显示：三种固视性质组的描述性统计结果：其视敏度的均数±标准差，分别为4.8±0.16，4.2±0.45，3.4±0.57。行单因素方差分析，$P = 0.000 < 0.05$，提示三组间的视力水平存在统计学上的显著性差异。

计算显示：A组的变异系数小（CV=0.03），提示数据不离散，可以用于视敏度的评估；其余两组变异系数偏大（均>0.1），提示数据过于离散，不能用于视敏度的评估。

统计结果显示：A组的最差对数视力为4.6（即小数视力0.4），C组的最好对数视力为4.4（小数视力0.2）。

（三）对数视力与2o范围固视百分率的相关、回归分析

85例受检者，其对数矫正视力与2o范围固视百分率的相关分析，Pearson相关系数为0.724（散点图详见图7），单尾显著性检验 $p = 0.000 < 0.05$。说明视敏度与2o范围固视百分率存在统计学意义上正相关。

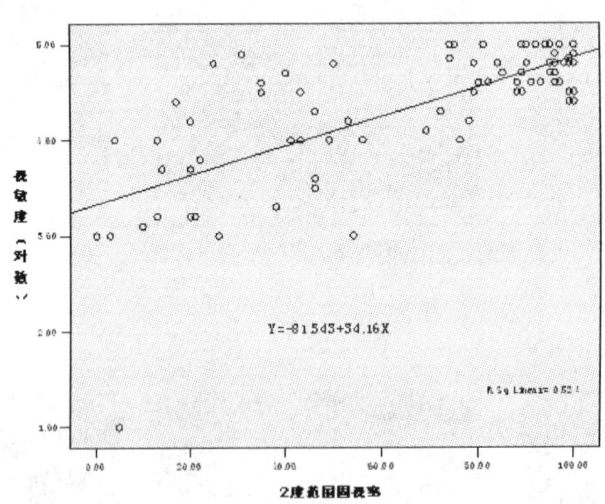

图7　对数视力与2o范围固视百分率的相关分析散点图

模型的方差分析结果 $P = 0.000 < 0.05$，说明因变量视敏度与自变量2o范围固视百分率之间有线性关系。推导一元线性回归方程：$Y = -81.543 + 34.16X_1$。其中Y为对数视力，X_1 为2o范围固视百分率。

（四）对数视力与微视野视网膜平均敏感度的相关、回归分析

共85例受检者，其对数矫正视力与视网膜平均光敏感度的相关分析，Pearson 相关系数为0.707，（散点图详见图8），单尾显著性检验 p = 0.000 <0.05。说明视敏度与视网膜平均光敏感度之间存在统计学意义上正相关。

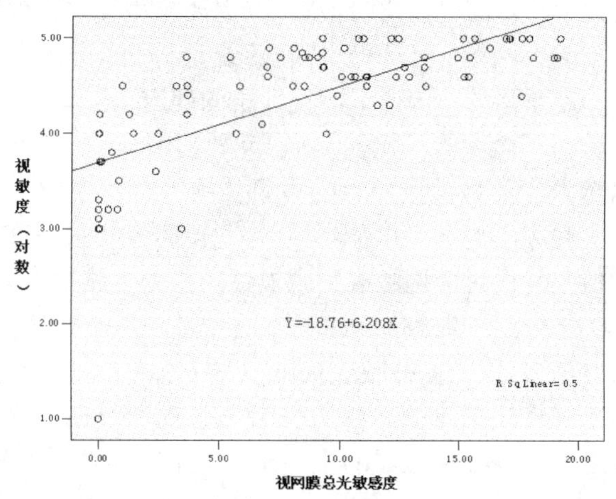

图8　对数视力与视网膜平均光敏感度的相关、回归分析散点图

模型的方差分析结果 P = 0.000 < 0.05，说明因变量视敏度与视网膜平均敏感度之间存在线性关系，推导一元线性回归方程：$Y = -18.76 + 6.208X_2$。其中 Y 为对数视力，X 为视网膜平均敏感度。

三、讨　论

（一）固视理论与微视野检测

固视理论[1]认为：视网膜黄斑中心凹处的视敏度最佳（为1.0，即对数视力5.0），中心凹以外，视敏度迅速降低，距中心凹2°的视敏度为0.4，5°的视敏度为0.1，10°时降至1/15（如图2）。上述理论的生理学基础：视敏度的好坏取决于视网膜上的光感受器 - 视锥细胞分布的多寡，视网膜视锥细胞主要分布于黄斑中心凹处，至周边部越来越少，视锥细胞的分布特点决定了黄斑中心凹处的视敏度最好。由此可见，黄斑中心凹是正视眼（即视力正常者）所用的固视点，如果黄斑功能受损，视力便明显下降，此时患眼会将在黄斑中心凹外的视网膜作建立新的固视点，[2]固视的性质也由中心固视变成偏心固视。

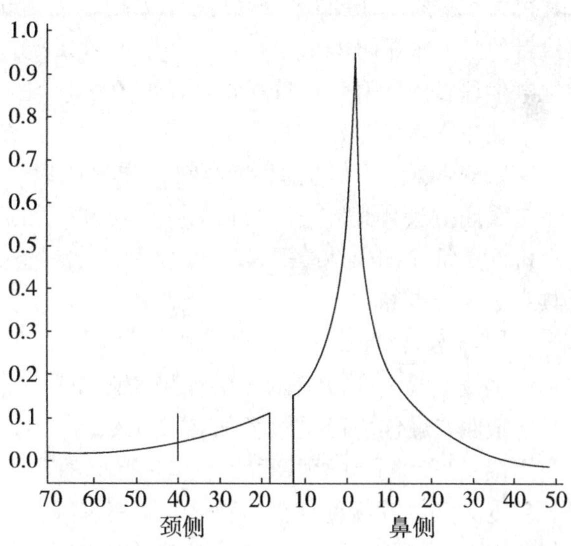

基于固视理论，我们可以这样理解：每个视网膜点均有其相应的视敏度值（即微

视力），当损伤或疾病使黄斑中心凹的视功能丧失时，人眼所建立的中心外固视（即偏心固视）的视敏度水平，取决于该偏心固视点的微视力值；而基于视觉生理学上，视锥细胞的分布特点及规律，通过检查其固视性质，理论上，可以在一定程度上推测其偏心视力的大小，此点具有法医临床学意义。

在既往的眼科实践中，对固视性质的检查，[3] 主要应用直接检眼镜的固视度数测量来完成，其方法简单、结果粗略，不利于精确的统计分析。同时，人眼的固视度数，在正常情况下也是有一定漂移的；因此，固视性质的确定，需要精密检测仪器来完成。

微视野检测（又称黄斑微视野检测）是近年来应用于国内、外眼科检查的一种高端检测设备，它可以较为精确测量受检者的黄斑功能及固视情况，为固视性质的研究提供了检测手段。本实验应用 MP－1 型微视野计，行固视相关检查，以确证固视性质理论的法医学应用价值，并探讨应用微视野固视性质检查推测视敏度的可行性。

（二）固视理论的法医学应用价值探讨

国内外的学者研究认为：[3~5] 各种眼底病变（包括外伤与疾病），最终都会导致固视性质的变化，按照固视性质的不同，视力分为中心视力及偏心视力，中心视力者的视力水平一般在 0.1 之上，偏心视力者的视力水平多在 0.4 以下，而 0.1～0.4，为两种视力的交叉。

本研究显示：A 组，即中心固视组中的 31 例被检者，其最差对数视力为 4.6（小数视力 0.4）；而 C 组即偏心固视组中的 17 例被检者，其最好对数视力为 4.4（小数视力 0.2），印证了上述“中心固视理论”中关于视力界限的评价。此理论的印证，无疑对法医学“客观评估视敏度”具有应用价值。

当被检者的微视野/眼底检查，结果证实其视力性质为中心固视时，我们可以断定其视力水平应高于 4.0（小数视力 0.1）；若确证其视力性质为偏心固视时，那么，被检者的视力水平可能低于 4.6（小数视力 0.4）。此理论为法医学眼损伤鉴定提供了视觉电生理以外的客观评价视觉功能的方法学。

在法医临床学鉴定实际中，多数的伪装者属“夸大伤情”而非“完全地伪装成无光感”，故此，多数的伪盲者存在“光感”以上的主观视力。固视检查中无论是微视野还是眼底镜法，其检查手段均为光觉刺激，因此，被检者出于“证明自己无伪装”的动机，常常在固视性质的检查时给予充分的配合，所以，固视性质检查在实际工作中具有一定的可靠性。

（三）微视野检测客观评定视敏度的价值探讨

栗改云等[8] 研究显示：微视野的固视稳定性与最佳矫正视力呈正相关：固视 2°、4°稳定性与最佳矫正视敏度的相关系数分为 0.456、0.434（$P<0.05$）；故此，认为：应用微视野计测得的固视稳定性具有预估视敏度的潜在功能。

本文对“视敏度与视网膜平均光敏感度”行相关、回归分析。结果显示：视敏度与微视野视网膜平均光敏感度之间存在统计学意义上的正相关（Pearson 相关系数为 0.707，$P<0.05$）。该结果与栗改云[7] 的统计结果基本一致，因统计内容不同，数据有所差异。

本实验模型的方差分析结果 P 值小于 0.05，说明因变量“视敏度”与自变量“视网膜平均敏感度”之间有线性关系，推导一元线性回归方程：$Y = -18.76 + 6.208X2$

（其中 Y 为视敏度，X 为视网膜平均敏感度），$R^2=0.5$。

当然，需要指出的是：从司法鉴定应用的角度讲：上述 R^2 值偏低，故此回归方程的实用性仍受到很大的限制。

参考文献

［1］［日］松崎浩：《新实际眼科学》，东京：金原出版株式会社 1990 年版，第 45 页。

［2］Shih Y F, Ho T C, Hsiao C K, et al. ,“Visual Outcomes for High Myopic Patients with or Without Myopic Maculopathy：A 10 Year Follow up Study”, *Br J Ophthalmol*, 2006, 90（5）, pp. 546 ~550.

［3］刘会、项剑、王旭等：“固视（视力）性质理论在视力客观评估中的法医学价值”，载《中国法医学杂志》2012 年第 5 期，第 386 ~389 页。

［4］夏德昭：“视神经、黄斑病须行视敏度分析，再谈树立中心视力和中心外视敏度两种视敏度观的必要”，载《中国实用眼科杂志》2004 年第 8 期，第 575 ~581 页。

［5］Wolf S, Lappas A, Weinberger AW, Kirchhof B. Macular,“Translocation for Surgical Management of Subfoveal Choroidal Neovascularizations in Patients with AMD：First Results. Graefes Arch Clin Exp Ophthalmol”, 1999, 237, pp. 51 ~57.

［6］张蕴达、贾亚丁：“病理性近视继发中心凹视网膜劈裂的固视特点”，载《中华眼底病杂志》2011 年第 3 期，第 259 ~262 页。

［7］栗改云、贾亚丁：“黄斑区视网膜光敏感度与视敏度的相关性分析”，载《中国实用眼科杂志》2005 年第 12 期，第 1281 ~1283 页。

《国际功能、残疾和健康分类》分类架构与编码系统*

杨天潼 王 旭**

世界卫生组织（World Health Organization，简称 WHO）于 2001 年将原有残障分类系统修订为《国际功能、残疾和健康分类》（ International Classification of Functioning ，Disability and Health，简称 ICF），中文简称为《国际功能分类》，[1] 并敦促会员国结合本国的具体情况并特别考虑到今后可能作出的修订，在研究、监测和报告中酌情使用 ICF。同时，要求总干事根据会员国提出的要求在使用 ICF 方面向它们提供支持。它标志着经过多年由多国专家共同努力完成的 ICF 正式在全球使用。中文版作为 WHO 正式发布的 6 种语种之一与其他 5 种版本同时发布。[2]

WHO 认为，身心障碍并非个人问题，而是一种人权与政治问题。ICF 完全放弃使用疾病名称描述身心障碍的模式，[3] 采用对健康状态进行说明的方式，将残障解释为“每个人都可能有面对身体与环境互动时发生障碍”的普遍模式。[4] 因此，促进“处于障碍情境”的公民，平等地参与社会生活，成为社会核心价值。所以，ICF 最有意义的改变，就是重新看待什么是“身心障碍”，正视环境因素与疾病或损伤后果之间的联系，将评定重点定位于“障碍情境”，而不是“障碍者”本身，体现了人文价值的关怀。

一、ICF 分类架构及其编码

从 ICF 的发展史来看，ICF 已经从“疾病的转归”分类转变为一种“健康的成分”的分类 。“疾病的转归”着重于疾病的影响或由此可能产生的其他健康状况；而“健康的成分”确定了由什么构成健康。根据 ICF 的模式，某种“健康状况”或“功能状态”的产生并非单纯由一种损伤或疾病引起，它是由包括环境因素、个人因素、活动

* 证据科学教育部重点实验室（中国政法大学）中国政法大学青年教师学术创新团队资助项目；教育部人文社会科学规划项目“人身伤害赔偿中的伤残标准研究”（10YJA820105）。

** 杨天潼，讲师，通讯作者。Email：yangtiantong@ 126. com；王旭，教授。

〔1〕 The text represents a revision of the International Classification of Impairments, Disabilities, and Handicaps (ICIDH), which was first published by the World Health Organization for trial purposes in 1980. Developed after systematic field trials and international consultation over the past five years, it was endorsed by the Fifty – fourth World Health Assembly for international use on 22 May 2001 (resolution WHA54. 21).

〔2〕 World Health Organization. ICF: International Classification of Functioning, Disability and Health. Geneva: Author. 2001.

〔3〕 World Health Organization, ICD – 10, “International Statistical Classification of Diseases and Related Health Problems (10th rev.)”, Geneva: Author, 1992.

〔4〕 “International Statistical Classification of Diseases and Related Health Problems”, *Tenth Revision*, Vols. 1 ~ 3, Geneva, World Health Organization, 1992 ~ 1994.

参与等在内的所有因素决定的，同时它对ICF的其他方面也有影响。[5]

部分和成份：ICF分类架构的总体分为两个部分，“功能和残疾”，以及“背景因素”。这两个部分分别由不同的成分组成。“功能和残疾”的组成要素为身体功能、身体结构、活动和参与；“背景因素”的组成要素有环境因素和个人因素（图1）。[6]

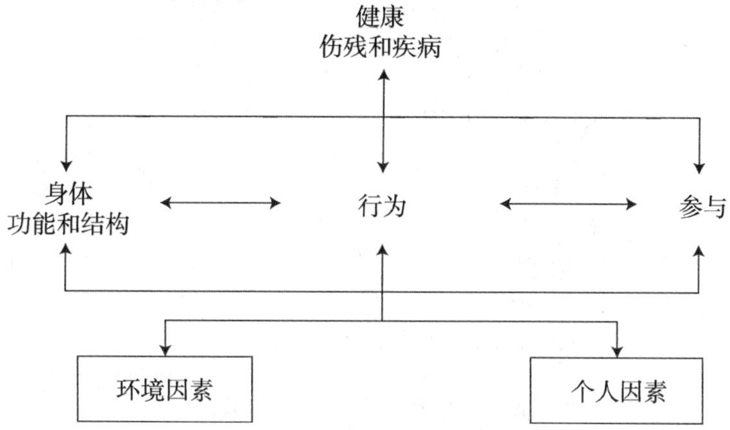

图1　ICF各成分之间的交互式关系

类目：类目是在一种成分中的分类，分为不同级别。不同的成分，身体功能（Body functions）、身体结构（Body structures）、活动和参与（Activities and Paticipation）、环境因素（Environmental factors），分别以b、s、d/a/p和e进行编码。每个一成分由不同的章节构成，分别对该成分进行具体细化，以章节数和分类码进行编码。如，在成分“身体功能”中，共有8个章节，其中第7章涉及全部的神经肌肉骨骼和运动功能（Neuromuscloskeletal and movement - related functions），编码为b7。我们可将b7及其他编码，s1、d2或e3等，称为“一级水平分类”（One - level classification），由定义成分的英文字母与定义章节一位数字表示。[7] 为ICF第一层次分类。由于个人社会、文化背景过于复杂，ICF并没有对个人因素进行具体分类（表1）。[8]

---

〔5〕 ICF differs substantially from the 1980 version of ICIDH in the depiction of the interrelations between functioning and disability. It should be noted that any diagram is likely to be incomplete and prone to misrepresentation because of the complexity of interactions in a multidimensional model. The model is drawn to illustrate multiple interactions. Other depictions indicating other important foci in the process are certainly possible. Interpretations of interactions between different components and constructs may also vary (for example, the impact of environmental factors on body functions certainly differs from their impact on participation).

〔6〕 These terms, which replace the formerly used terms “impairment”, “disability” and “handicap”, extend the scope of the classification to allow positive experiences to be described. The new terms are further defined in this Introduction and are detailed within the classification. It should be noted that these terms are used with specific meanings that may differ from their everyday usage.

〔7〕 邱卓英、张爱民：“《国际功能、残疾和健康分类》应用指导”，载《中国康复理论与实践》2003年第9期。

〔8〕 杨天潼、王旭：“《国际功能、残疾和健康分类》评述及其法医临床学应用价值”，载《证据科学》2012年第5期。

表 1　ICF 一级分类（1 级水平分类）

	1 级水平分类
b 身体功能 (Body functions)	b1 心理功能（Mental functions） b2 感觉功能和疼痛（Sensory functions and pain） b3 发声和言语功能（Voice and speech functions） b4 心血管、血液、免疫和呼吸系统功能（Functions of the cardiovascular, haematological, immunological and respiratory systems） b5 消化、代谢和内分泌系统功能（Functions of the digestive, metabolic and endocrine systems） b6 泌尿和生殖系统功能（Genitourinary and reproductive functions） b7 神经肌肉骨骼和运动相关功能（Neuromusculoskeletal and movement - related functions） b8 皮肤及附属器机构功能（Functions of the skin and related structures）
s 身体结构 (Body structures)	s1 神经系统结构（Structures of the nervous system） s2 眼、耳相关结构（The eye, ear and related structures） s3 发声和言语相关结构（The eye, ear and related structures） s4 心血管、免疫和呼吸系统结构（Structures of the cardiovascular, immunological and respiratory systems） s5 消化、代谢和内分泌系统结构（Structures related to the digestive, metabolic and endocrine systems） s6 泌尿和生殖系统结构（Structures related to the genitourinary and reproductive systems） s7 运动相关结构（Structures related to movement） s8 皮肤及附属器结构（Skin and related structures）
d/a/p 活动和参与 (Activities and Paticipation)	d1 学习和知识应用（Learning and applying knowledge） d2 一般任务与要求（General tasks and demands） d3 交流（Communication） d4 活动（Mobility） d5 自理（Self - care） d6 家庭生活（Domestic life） d7 人际交往和联系（Interpersonal interactions and relationships） d8 主要生活领域（Major life areas） d9 社区、社会和公民生活（Community, social and civic life）

续表

	1 级水平分类
e 环境因素 (Environmental factors)	e1 用品和技术（Products and technology） e2 自然环境和对环境的人为改变（Natural environment and human - made changes to environment） e3 支持和相互联系（Support and relationships） e4 态度（Attitudes） e5 服务、体制和政策（Services, systems and policies）
个人因素 (Personal factors)	未分类

ICF 定义的“二级分类”（Two - level classification）是对一级分类更为具体的细化，分为两个级别的具体分类。如在 b7 神经肌肉骨骼和运动功能的一级分类水平下，又具体细化为“关节和骨骼的功能”（Functions of the joints and bones）、“肌肉功能”(Muscle functions)、“运动功能”（Movement functions），分别编码为（b710 - b729）、(b730 - b749）和（b750 - b789）。上述分类被称为二级水平分类，由定义要素的英文字母与 3 位数字表示的，为 ICF 的第二层次分类（表 2）。

表 2　ICF 结构二级分类（2 级水平分类，以 b7 神经肌肉骨骼和运动功能为例）

	2 级水平分类	
b7 神经肌肉骨骼和运动功能（Neuromusculoskeletal and movement - related functions）	b710 - b729 关节和骨骼功能（Functions of the joints and bones）	b710 关节活动功能（Mobility of joint functions）
		b715 关节稳定功能（Stability of joint functions）
		b720 骨骼活动功能（Mobility of bone functions）
		b729 其他特指或未特指的关节和骨骼功能（Functions of the joints and bones, other specified and unspecified）
	b730 - b749 肌肉功能（Muscle functions）	b730 肌肉力量功能（Muscle power functions）
		b735 肌张力功能（Muscle tone functions）
		b740 肌肉耐力功能（Muscle endurance functions），0
		b749 其他特指或未特指的肌肉功能（Muscle functions, other specified and unspecified）

续表

	2 级水平分类	
	b750 - b789 运动功能（Movement functions）	b750 运动反射功能（Motor reflex functions）
		b755 不随意运动反应功能（Involuntary movement reaction functions）
		b760 随意运动控制功能（Control of voluntary movement functions）
		b765 不随意运动功能（Involuntary movement functions）
		b770 步态功能（Gait pattern functions）
		b780 与肌肉和运动功能有关的感觉（Sensations related to muscles and movement functions）
		b789 其他特指或为特指的运动功能（Movement functions, other specified and unspecified）
		b798 其他特指的神经肌肉骨骼和运动有关的功能（Neuromusculoskeletal and movement - related functions, other specified）
		b799 神经肌肉骨骼和运动有关的功能，未特指（Neuromusculoskeletal and movement - related functions, unspecified）

ICF 还包括“分类细化定义”（Detailed classification with definitions）主要包括两方面内容：限定值和定义。其中，“定义”是对健康和与健康有关的类目的操作性说明，描述了每一领域的基本特性（如性质、构成和关系），并且包含了每一类目下包括和不包括内容的信息。如对二级水平分类 b710“关节活动功能”的定义为，关节活动的幅度和灵活性的功能。同时使用“包括”和“不包括”术语，进行进一步的精确定义，如 b710“关节活动功能”定义包括“单个或多个关节的活动、椎、肩、肘、腕、髋、膝、踝、手及足部小关节的功能；全身关节活动能力；如关节过度活动、冻关节、冻肩、关节炎的损伤”，但不包括“关节稳定功能（b715）；随意运动控制功能（b760）”。

除了对二级水平分类进行定义外，“分类细化定义”还对二级水平分类进行了再次的细化分类。如对 b710“关节活动功能”再次进行分类，分为 b7100 单关节活动（Mobility of single joint）、b7101 多关节活动（Mobility of several joint）、b7102 关节整体活动（Mobility of joint generalized）、b7108 关节活动功能，其他特指（Mobility of joint, other specified）和 b7109 关节活动功能，未特指（Mobility of joint, unspecified）。上述分类被称为三级水平分类，由定义要素的英文字母与 4 位数字表示，为 ICF 的第三层次分类（表 3）。

表 3　ICF 分类细化定义（3 级水平分类，以 b710 关节活动功能为例）

2 级水平分类	3 级水平分类
b710 关节活动功能（Mobility of joint functions）	b7100 单关节活动（Mobility of single joint）
	b7101 多关节活动（Mobility of several joint）
	b7102 关节整体活动（Mobility of joint generalized）
	b7108 关节活动功能，其他特指（Mobility of joint，other specified）
	b7109 关节活动功能，未特指（Mobility of joint，unspecified）

“分类细化定义”还对一些三级水平分类进行了更进一步的细化分类。如将三级水平分类 b2100 视敏度功能（Visual aculty functions）进一步分类为 b21000 双眼远距离视敏度（Binocular acuity of distant vision）、b21001 单眼远距离视敏度（Monocular acuity of distant vision）、b21002 双眼近距离视敏度（Binocular acuity of near vision）、b21003 单眼近距离视敏度（Monocular acuity of near vision）、b21008 视敏度功能，其他特指（Visual acuity functions，other specified）和 b21009 视敏度功能，未特指（Visual acuity functions，unspecified）。上述分类被称为四级水平分类，由定义要素的英文字母与 5 位数字表示，为 ICF 的第四层次分类（表 4）。

表 4　ICF 分类细化定义（4 级水平分类，以 b2100 视敏度功能为例）

2 级水平分类	3 级水平分类
b2100 视敏度功能（Visual aculty functions)）	b21000 双眼远距离视敏度（Binocular acuity of distant vision）
	b21001 单眼远距离视敏度（Monocular acuity of distant vision）
	b21002 双眼近距离视敏度（Binocular acuity of near vision）
	b21003 单眼近距离视敏度（Monocular acuity of near vision）
	b21008 视敏度功能，其他特指（Visual acuity functions，other specified）
	b21009 视敏度功能，未特指（Visual acuity functions，unspecified）

ICF 的四层分类，赋予了 ICF 极大的交互式编码形式。在一级分类水平，最大编码数可达 34 个；在二级分类水平，最大编码数可达 362 个；在更为细致的分类水平上，最大编码数则可达 1424 个。ICF 的使用说明中明确指出，在实践应用过程中，两个层次（三位数）的一组 3 至 18 个编码就足够描述个体的健康状态了。而最为详细的四层次编码则是用于专业服务的。现以身体功能（b）为例，说明 ICF 的四层分类结构：（图 2）

b2　感觉功能与疼痛　第一层次分类（类目）

b210　视觉功能　第二层次分类（类目）

b2102　视觉质量　第三层次分类（类目）

b21022　对比感觉　　第四层次分类（类目）

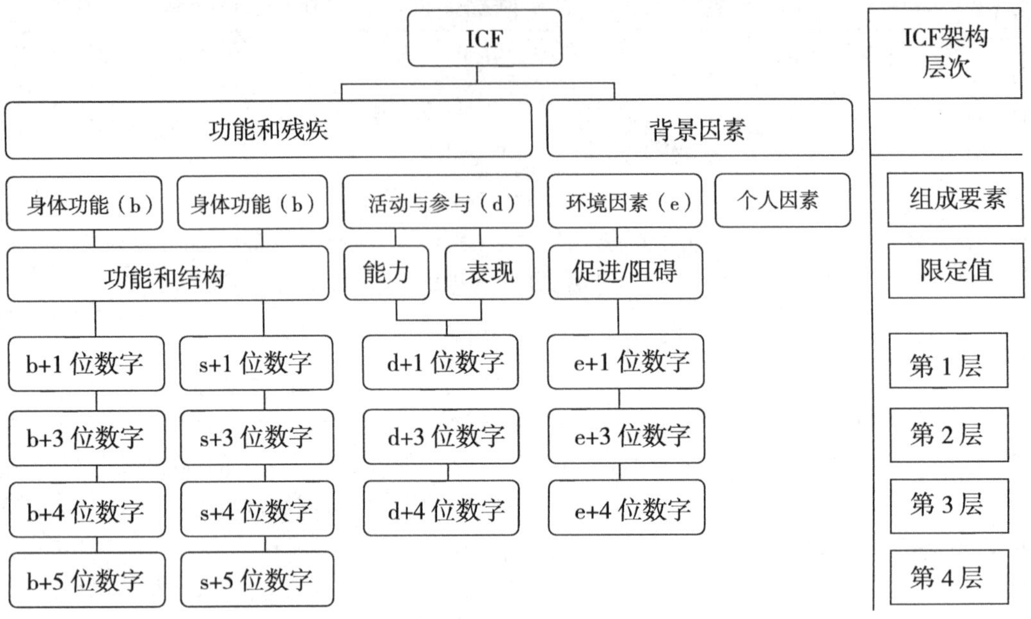

图 2 ICF 分类系统与层次

二、ICF 编码限定值

ICF 在“分类细化定义”中，设置了一个或多个具有特定含义的限定值，限定值常列在分类编码的小数点后面，用以显示健康水平的程度或出现问题的严重程度。限定值为数字，在一级分类“身体功能”和“活动和参与”中，只有一类限定值，分别编码为 0、1、2、3、4、8、9（表 5、表 6）。

表 5 b 身体功能（Body functions）限定值

b. 身体功能（Body functions）	xxx. 0 没有损伤（无，缺乏，微不足道……）	0% ~4%
	xxx. 1 轻度损伤（略有一点，很低……）	5% ~24%
	xxx. 2 中度损伤（中等程度，一般……）	25% ~49%
	xxx. 3 重度损伤（很高，非常……）	50% ~95%
	xxx. 4 完全损伤（全部……）	96% ~100%
	xxx. 8 未特指	
	xxx. 9 不适用	

如 b2100. 2，b2100 代表视觉功能，限定值 2 则代表中度损伤（损伤程度）。还可以对身体功能丧失程度或损伤程度进行一定程度的量化。如当“没有损伤”或“完全损伤”时，编码具有 5% 的误差范围，当“中度损伤”时，编码的误差范围可以是完全损伤者的一半程度。不同领域中的百分率，需要参照相应的人口百分比率标准，进行校正。

表 6　d 活动和参与（Activities and Paticipation）限定值

d 活动和参与 (Activities and Paticipation)	xxx. 0 没有困难（无，缺乏，微不足道……）	0% ~4%
	xxx. 1 轻度困难（略有一点，很低……）	5% ~24%
	xxx. 2 中度困难（中等程度，一般……）	25% ~49%
	xxx. 3 重度困难（很高，非常……）	50% ~95%
	xxx. 4 完全困难（全部……）	96% ~100%
	xxx. 8 未特指	
	xxx. 9 不适用	

如 d166. 3，d166 代表阅读能力，限定值 3 则说明阅读存在重度困难。

而在“身体结构”中，则有三类限定值，分别为第一限定值（First qualifier）、第二限定值（Second qualifier）和第三限定值（Third qualifier），其中第三限定值为建议使用。第一限定值编码为 0、1、2、3、4、8、9，第二限定值编码为 0 ~9，第三限定值编码为 0 ~9（表 7）。

表 7　s 身体结构（Body structures）限定值

s. 身体结构 (Body structures)	第一限定值 (First qualifier)	xxx. 0 没有损伤（无，缺乏，微不足道……）	0% ~4%
		xxx. 1 轻度损伤（略有一点，很低……）	5% ~24%
		xxx. 2 中度损伤（中等程度，一般……）	25% ~49%
		xxx. 3 重度损伤（很高，非常……）	50% ~95%
		xxx. 4 完全损伤（全部……）	96% ~100%
		xxx. 8 未特指	
		xxx. 9 不适用	
	第二限定值 (Second qualifier)	0 结构无改变	
		1 全部缺失	
		2 部分缺失	
		3 增生或增加部分	
		4 异常尺寸	
		5 断裂	
		6 异常体位	
		7 器质性结构改变，包含体液堆积	
		8 未特指	
		9 不适用	

续表

s. 身体结构（Body structures）	第三限定值（Third qualifier）	0 多于一个区域
		1 右侧
		2 左侧
		3 双侧
		4 前面
		5 后面
		6 近端
		7 远端
		8 未特指
		9 不适用

如 s2203. 221，s2203 代表视网膜，限定值 2、2 和 1 分别说明中度损伤（损伤程度）、部分缺失（损伤性质）和右侧（损伤位置）。

在“环境因素”有两类限定值，第一限定值为 0、1、2、3、4、8、9，并可在限定值前加“ + ”，以表示促进作用，第二限定值仍在开发中（表 8）。

如 e1251. 1，e1251 代表沟通、使用辅助产品与科技的能力，限定值 1 说明该项能力轻度障碍；如果表述为 e1251. +1，则表示轻度促进。

任何 ICF 编码都应给予限定值，没有限定值，不能明确该分类的健康水平程度和出现问题的严重程度，没有限定值的编码没有意义。

表 8 e 环境因素（Environmental factors）限定值

e 环境因素（Environmental factors）	第一限定值（First qualifier）	xxx. 0 没有阻碍（无，缺乏，微不足道……）	0% ~4%
		xxx. 1 轻度阻碍（略有一点，很低……）	5% ~24%
		xxx. 2 中度阻碍（中等程度，一般……）	25% ~49%
		xxx. 3 重度阻碍（很高，非常……）	50% ~95%
		xxx. 4 完全阻碍（全部……）	96% ~100%
		xxx. 8 未特指	
		xxx. 9 不适用	
		xxx +0 没有促进	
		xxx +1 轻度促进	
		xxx +2 中度促进	
		xxx +3 重度促进	
		xxx +4 完全促进	
		xxx +8 不特定促进	
		xxx. 9 不适用	
	第二限定值（Second qualifier）	开发中	

三、ICF 编码系统的应用

ICF 是 WHO 用来收集健康功能状态的统计分析工具[9]。从最初英国皇家医学会组建雏形，直至现在全球推广使用，WHO 的健康统计、社会医疗、经济保障、社会安全和劳动政策等诸多领域的专业人士进行了大量的讨论、修订和测试工作。[10] WHO 为推动测量健康功能状态而制定 ICF，最初目的是为了应对未来社会逐渐增减的老龄化人口，也为了从预防疾病角度，介入治疗障碍状态而衍生的一套健康状态评估工具。实际上，ICF 就是一套复杂、但已经结构化的编码系统。[11]

目前，德国政府已将 ICF 纳入社会保险制度的给付架构，日本政府应用 ICF 作为评估长期看护给付的依据，澳大利亚政府依据 ICF 编码系统，重新评估残障人口数量，意大利政府将 ICF 整合到国家基层医疗与保健机构中，各个政府应用 ICF 的事实证明，ICF 是一套极有应用价值的工具（表 9）。

表 9 ICF 编码系统应用领域

<table>
<tr><td rowspan="5">社会共同政策</td><td>残障人口统计</td></tr>
<tr><td>伤残评定</td></tr>
<tr><td>伤残赔偿需求评估</td></tr>
<tr><td>伤残人员权益保护立法</td></tr>
<tr><td>公民健康保障政策制定</td></tr>
<tr><td colspan="2">伤残人员自主生活计划</td></tr>
<tr><td colspan="2">伤残人员生活品质评估</td></tr>
<tr><td colspan="2">医疗服务品质评估</td></tr>
</table>

ICF 引入我国时间不长，主要应用集中在康复医学领域，在司法鉴定领域，尤其是法医临床学伤残评定方面，仍鲜见报道。就 ICF 本身来说，虽然我们认为它是一项新生事物，但是，这个工具已经经过了近六十多个国家的实际资料收集，并已由这些国家的专科医师临床应用，在它背后凝集了丰富、可观的实践经验。在我国司法鉴定领域应用 ICF，可使我国的伤残评定与国际接轨，成为推动 ICF 全球化的重要环节。以往展开国际研究，常因统计工具的差异，而造成样本间无从比较，但在应用 ICF 之后，我们也就可以应用 ICF 的编码语言，进行国际交流合作，并将我国的健康、残疾等数据与国际进行比较研究。学习与应用 ICF 对于完善伤残评定，参与国际标准化进程具有十分重要的理论与实践意义。

---

〔9〕 Bickenbach JE, Chatterji S, Badley EM, üstün TB. Models of disablement, universalism and the ICIDH, Social Science and Medicine, 1999, 48: 1173~1187.

〔10〕 Institute of Medicine, *The future of Disability in America*. Washington, DC: Author. 2007.

〔11〕 The Standard Rules on the Equalization of Opportunities for Persons with Disabilities. Adopted by the United Nations General Assembly at its 48th session on 20 December 1993 (resolution 48/96). New York, NY, United Nations Department of Public Information, 1994.

SEP检查对弥漫性轴索损伤法医鉴定的价值探讨*

杨英恺 王 旭**

在法医临床学鉴定中，颅脑损伤导致肢体功能障碍者屡见不鲜，其中局灶性脑损伤的诊断及后果评价较为明确，但对于弥漫性脑损伤，无论是临床诊断还是后遗肢体功能障碍程度的客观评价，目前仍存在困难。那么如何利用科学的检测手段，最大限度地客观评价肢体功能障碍的存在与否及严重程度，成为此类损伤中法医临床学研究的关键。

体感诱发电位（somatosensory evoked potential，简称SEP）是适当的电刺激作用于感觉系统而在特定部位检出与刺激有固定关系的电位反应，是一种躯体神经功能评定的客观检查方法，其法医学应用价值一直备受关注。而该检查手段对弥漫性脑损伤后果评价的应用及研究，在法医临床领域尚未深入展开。本文选取上述两类颅脑损伤的法学临床学鉴定案例，分别进行SEP检查，并对肢体功能障碍与SEP结果进行相关性分析，针对性地探讨SEP检查对弥漫性轴索损伤法医临床学鉴定中的应用价值。

一、对象与方法

（一）检查对象

本文从2007年~2012年中国政法大学法庭科学技术鉴定研究所受理的涉及颅脑损伤的法医临床学鉴定案件中选取部分有价值的案例共42例，受检者中男性29例，女性13例，年龄在21岁~65岁不等，均为临床治疗终结，且伤情恢复相对稳定。42例颅脑损伤均有影像学结果支持，并排除周围神经病变及其他中枢神经病变。

（二）检查方法

1. 资料信息收集

对受检者伤后病历材料进行审查，记录伤者一般情况、损伤方式、伤后昏迷史、临床诊断以及治疗、康复等情况；审阅受检者伤后、术后以及近期复查的影像学资料，明确颅脑损伤的原始伤情及遗留病灶等情况。

2. 分 组

本文收集2007年~2012年我所受理的涉及弥漫性轴索损伤的案例17例，纳入弥

---

* 基金项目：十二五国家科技支撑计划课题（2012BAK16B03），国家自然科学基金面上项目（81172912）。

** 杨英恺，女，法医师，主要从事法医临床学鉴定技术及辅助工作。Email：yyk_ 810820@ sina. com。联系电话：010－68642359。通讯地址：北京市石景山区鲁谷路116号（100040）。

【通讯作者】王旭，教授，主任法医师，主要从事法医临床学鉴定及研究工作。Email：xuw01@ cupl. edu. cn。联系电话：010－68622921。通讯地址：北京市石景山区鲁谷路116号（100040）（1. 司法文明协同创新中心，2. 中国政法大学证据科学教育部重点实验室 北京 100088），Email：yyk_ 810820@ sina. com。

漫性脑损伤组，另选取同期鉴定中局灶性脑损伤案例 25 例，归入局灶性脑损伤组。

弥漫性脑损伤的诊断依据为：[1] ①明确外伤史；②伤后昏迷史；③头颅 CT 片有弥漫性脑肿胀表现和（或）蛛网膜下腔出血，MRI 示胼胝体、脑干、基底节区、脑室等中线结构及皮髓质交界区散在点片状小出血灶或非出血性损伤，一般不伴占位损害。④常有临床症状严重程度与影像学表现不符的情况等。

局灶性脑损伤的诊断依据为：头部外伤史明确，经头颅 CT 证实有局部表层脑挫裂伤、硬膜下及硬膜外血肿或脑内血肿等，即浅表型脑损伤。

3. 神经系统查体

对两组受检者进行颅神经检查、四肢肌力、肌张力、肌容积、生理反射、病理反射、深、浅感觉以及共济/平衡功能（如闭目难立征、双手轮替试验、指鼻试验）等神经系统查体，根据临床诊断及查体情况确定 SEP 检查的部位，同时判断是否需要进一步进行精神智能检查。

4. SEP 检查方法

应用美国尼高力公司生产的 Viking Quest 多功能电生理检测仪对全部受检者进行 SEP 检查。电极安置及实验室条件参照相关国内国际标准。[2] 下肢 SEP 刺激踝部胫后神经，记录电极位于顶正中，以 P40 的潜伏期及波幅为主要观测指标。上肢 SEP 刺激腕部正中神经，记录电极位于 Erb 点、颈 7、顶部功能区，分别以 N9、N11、N20 的潜伏期及波幅为主要观测指标。刺激电量以所刺激神经的支配肌出现轻微收缩为准，刺激率为 5C/S，分析时间 100ms，叠加次数不低于 250 次，重复检测不低于 2 次。

5. SEP 结果判断标准

我所 SEP 正常值设定以国内相关 SEP 正常值权威报告为基准，[2] 对所应用仪器经正常人检测验证后使用。鉴于 SEP 受身高等因素影响，以及波幅个体差异较大的特点。我们对单侧病变者以自身健侧为对照辅助判断，潜伏期较正常侧延长（上肢延长 2ms，下肢延长 3ms）判断为异常；波幅以正常侧对照，降低或增加 50% 判断为异常；对于双侧病变者及波形分化不佳的受检者，我们采取多次重复检查的方法，最终确定潜伏期和波幅与正常值的差异。

（三）统计学分析

应用平行效度（又称标准关联效度 criterion - related validity）的统计学分析方法，分别对两组的 SEP 结果和肢体功能情况，以及弥漫性脑损伤组 SEP 结果和智能检查结果进行数据统计，分别计算相关系数 R，分析 SEP 结果与肢体功能以及智能障碍之间是否存在相关性。

二、结果

（一）一般情况

本文选取的 17 例弥漫性脑损伤案例均为交通事故伤所致的闭合性颅脑损伤，该组伤者中有伤后昏迷史的 16 例（94%）；另 25 例局灶性脑损伤的损伤方式包括有交通事故伤、坠落伤和打击伤，多为开放性或内开放性颅脑损伤，该组伤者中有伤后昏迷史的 10 例（40%）。

（二）神经系统检查结果（详见表 1）

表 1 弥漫性脑损伤与局灶性脑损伤神经系统检查结果对比

损伤类型	运动功能（肌力、感觉功能肌张力）				生理反射		病理反射		共济/平衡功能	
	正常	异常	正常	异常	正常	异常	阴性	阳性	阴性	阳性
弥漫性脑损伤例数（%）	16（94%）	1（6%）	15（88%）	2（12%）	9（53%）	8（47%）	10（59%）	7（41%）	3（18%）	14（82%）
局灶性脑损伤例数（%）	3（12%）	22（88%）	13（52%）	12（48%）	2（8%）	23（92%）	10（40%）	15（60%）	—	6＊

＊局灶性脑损伤组中 14 例进行了共济/平衡功能检查，11 例因肢体瘫较重未行该项检查。

（三）SEP 检查结果（详见表 2）

表 2 弥漫性脑损伤与局灶性脑损伤 SEP 结果对比

损伤类型	SEP 结果正常		SEP 结果异常图形分类		
	正常	异常	潜伏期、波幅异常	波形分化差	波形消失
弥漫性脑损伤例数（%）	4（24%）	13（76%）	4（23%）	8（47%）	1（6%）
局灶性脑损伤例数（%）	13（52%）	12（48%）	9（36%）	1（4%）	2（8%）

（四）统计学分析

1. 弥漫性脑损伤 SEP 结果与肢体功能的对应情况详见表 3，该组 SEP 结果异常与共济/平衡功能障碍之间存在正相关（$R=0.84$，$P<0.01$）。

表 3 弥漫性脑损伤组 SEP 结果与肢体功能的对应情况（$n=17$）

共济/平衡试验	SEP 结果		合计
	异常	正常	
阳性（例）	13	1	14
阴性（例）	3	0	3
合计	13	4	17

2. 局灶性脑损伤 SEP 结果与肢体功能的对应情况详见表 4，该组 SEP 结果与肢体瘫之间无明显一致性（$R=0.36$，$P>0.05$），两者相关性缺乏统计学意义。

表 4 局灶性脑损伤组 SEP 结果与肢体功能的对应情况（n=25）

肢体瘫	SEP 结果		合计
	异常	正常	
阳性（例）	12	10	22
阴性（例）	3	0	3
合计	12	13	25

3. 弥漫性脑损伤组 SEP 结果与智能障碍的对应情况详见表 5，该组 SEP 结果异常与智能障碍之间存在正相关（$R=0.86$，$P<0.01$）。

表 5 弥漫性脑损伤组 SEP 结果与智能障碍的对应情况（n=17）

智能障碍	SEP 结果		合计
	异常	正常	
阳性（例）	12	0	12
阴性（例）	5	1	4
合计	13	4	17

三、讨论

1. 弥漫性轴索损伤的诊断和愈后特点

弥漫性轴索损伤（Diffuse Axonal Injury，简称 DAI）亦称弥漫性脑损伤，系指头部在特殊外力（主要是旋转暴力）作用下，脑组织间发生剪切、伸展和压缩应力，造成以脑深部神经轴索肿胀、断裂为特征的脑损伤类型。多数在交通事故中形成。[3] 昏迷、意识障碍是弥漫性轴索损伤典型的临床表现。重型弥漫性轴索损伤，数小时可死亡，或呈植物生存状态。轻者可造成皮质神经元短暂的功能障碍，临床上脑震荡被认为是一种程度最轻的弥漫性轴索损伤。[4] 此外，脑干损伤与 DAI 之间有非常密切的关系，原发脑干损伤很少单独发生，在对该病的死亡患者进行尸检时发现，脑干、胼胝体和白质内存在广泛的 DAI 改变。因此，许多学者建议将其并入中重型 DAI 诊断中，能更准确地反映脑损伤的本来面目和实际范围。鉴于以往分类存在与原发脑损伤相互交叉、相互伴存的情况，目前多数学者主张将脑损伤分为局限性和弥漫性损伤两大类更为实用。

弥漫性轴索损伤的临床诊断较为困难，80% 的 DAI 为非出血性病灶，因此 CT 检查对弥漫性轴索损伤的诊断具有局限性。[5] 而 MRI 检查较 CT 检查灵敏度相对较高，能更清晰地显示脑干和胼胝体等结构的小局灶性病变，尤其对非出血性弥漫性轴索损伤存在一定诊断价值。但目前临床上对弥漫性轴索损伤尚无统一的诊断标准，主要通过临床表现及影像检查进行推断性诊断，最终必须依靠病理组织学检查才能确诊。[6]

弥漫性轴索损伤预后的影响因素依次为昏迷程度、昏迷时间、影像学表现、瞳孔变化、脑挫伤程度、年龄大小。[7] 昏迷程度与昏迷时间作为影响弥漫性轴索损伤的首要因素，严重影响着弥漫性轴索伤者的愈后，原发昏迷时间的长短和程度与中线区轴索损伤的程度和范围有关。[8] 因此，在鉴定工作中应仔细审查病历资料，通过了解其伤后昏迷史等病情，为分析后遗功能障碍程度寻找客观依据。

2. SEP 检查原理及应用

体感诱发电位系对躯体感觉系统（包括感觉纤维或感觉径路）中的任何一点给予适当电刺激，在短时间内在该系统特定的通路上的某一部位能检出与刺激有固定关系的电位反应。目前常用的是短潜伏期 SEP，主要反映感觉神经中粗感觉纤维传入冲动上行至皮层记录到的相应的电活动，可借此了解相应部位的功能状态。[1,9] 按检测部分可分为上肢 SEP 和下肢 SEP，临床上常用刺激上肢正中神经和下肢胫神经来获得的 SEP 反应波形。

体感诱发电位可以反映感觉传导通路直至皮层的功能状态，理论上任何影响该通路的损伤均可引起 SEP 的变化。因此，SEP 对感觉神经系统损伤的评价理论上是全面和有效的。同时由于感觉、运动神经纤维相伴行，损伤常常同时累及感觉及运动神经纤维，因此，可以通过对感觉系统的评价来间接评判运动系统的功能。从理论上讲，SEP 有助于解决法医临床学把关于神经系统损伤的两大难题：①感觉系统功能障碍客观评判上的困难；②运动系统上位神经元损伤的客观的辅助检测的证据。[10]

3. SEP 检查在弥漫性轴索损伤的法医学鉴定中的应用价值

在法医临床学鉴定中，对于弥漫性脑损伤后遗肢体功能障碍程度的评定，目前主要依靠神经系统查体、病史及影像材料支持等方法，而此类伤者一般不遗留明显肢体瘫痪症状，多表现为共济运动障碍等。因此，对损害后果的确定缺少一个相对客观的评价指标，也成为伤残及损伤程度评定时的难点问题。目前，临床上已有学者研究 SEP 等神经电生理检查对弥漫性轴索损伤患者的脑功能状态评估的应用价值。[11] 施瓦茨（Schwarz）等的研究表明，SEP 正常与否与昏迷患者的预后密切相关。[12]

本文实验结果显示：弥漫性脑损伤组 SEP 的异常率为 76%，且 SEP 结果异常与共济/平衡功能障碍之间正相关（R = 0.84），虽检查例数有限，研究结果可能存在一定局限性，但已高度提示 SEP 检查对弥漫性轴索损伤后遗非肢体瘫性功能障碍存在较高的敏感性。同时，弥漫性脑损伤组 SEP 结果异常与智能障碍之间存在明显一致性（R = 0.86），因此，在鉴定中可通过受检者的智能缺损情况反推其肢体功能状态，从而为伤害后果的评价提供依据。对于局灶性脑损伤组，实验中 SEP 检查结果的异常率为 48%，且 SEP 结果与肢体瘫之间无明确一致性（R = 0.36），因此，SEP 检查结果尚不能完全反应此类颅脑损伤的肢体功能情况。

分析上述结果的理论基础：DAI 是以脑内神经轴索断裂为特征的病理生理变化，使大脑皮质与脑干网状结构的联络中断，而 SEP 是脑干及大脑皮质传入通路功能状态的反应，因此一旦脑内神经轴索传导功能障碍，必然会影响其 SEP 波形的正常诱出，从而也解释了此类损伤以波形分化差为主要异常表现的特征。而局灶性脑损伤的结局，是以局部脑组织发生变性坏死，且发生部位多浅表。考虑皮层的中枢放大作用导致异常率降低的可能，有时甚至出现患侧波幅异常增高的现象。因此，SEP 检查对局灶性颅脑损伤功能障碍程度的客观评价价值相对有限。

四、小　结

上述研究结果表明，SEP 检查可作为弥漫性轴索损伤后，非肢体瘫性功能障碍的较为敏感而准确的神经电生理检查方法，可作为此类法医临床学鉴定工作中的客观检查手段。弥漫性轴索损伤的损害后果评价，应做到主、客观检查相结合、肢体障碍与智能缺损相互支持，从而体现法医临床学鉴定的科学与公正。

参考文献

[1] 潘国南、吕凌：“ 112 例脑弥漫性损伤分析”，载《法医学杂志》2009 年第 5 期，第 370 ~ 372 页。

[2] 卢祖能、曾庆杏、李承晏等主编：《实用肌电图学（第一版）》，人民卫生出版社 2000 年版，第 636 ~ 680 页。

[3] 季卫阳、鲁晓杰：“弥漫性轴索损伤 48 例临床分析”，载《中国交通医学杂》2005 年第 6 期，第 628 页。

[4] 马超、麦明泉、许俭兴等：“脑梗死急性期下肢运动功能与体感诱发电位变化的关系”，载《中国康复理论与实践》2004 年第 2 期，第 88 ~ 89 页。

[5] 杨佳勇、杨振九、冯承宣等：“ 169 例脑弥漫性轴索损伤的诊断和预后分析”，载《中华神经医学杂志》2005 年第 8 期，第 835 ~ 836 页。

[6] 蓝威：“脑弥漫性轴索损伤 46 例的 MRI 诊断价值”，载《浙江创伤外科》2010 年第 4 期，第 540 ~ 541 页。

[7] 王少锦、齐岚平：“中西医结合疗法干预脑弥漫性轴索损伤预后 30 例临床观察”，载《中医杂志》2004 年第 12 期，第 921 ~ 922 页。

[8] 刘旭、李红梅：“弥漫性轴索损伤愈后相关因素临床评价”，载《中国伤残医学》2011 年第 8 期，第 92 ~ 93 页。

[9] 汤晓芙主编：《 临床肌电图学（第一版）》，北京医科大学出版社 1995 年版，第 131 ~ 145 页。

[10] 王旭、卞晶晶：“ SEP 检查在法医学鉴定中的应用探讨——附 60 例检查分析”，载《中国法医学最新科研与实践（二）——全国第一次法医学术交流会论文精选》2004。

[11] 张福生、闫长祥、张文彬等：“应用神经电生理检测评估弥漫性轴索损伤患者脑功能状态及其预后”，载《中国临床康复》2004 年第 7 期，第 1222 ~ 1223 页。

[12] Schwarz S, Schwab S, Aschoff A, et al. , “Favorable Recovery from Bilateral Loss of Somatosensory Evoked Potentials”, *Crit Care Med*, 1999, 27 (1), pp. 182 ~ 187.

Haplotype Diversity of 17 Y – STR Loci in a Chinese She Ethnic Group Population Sample from Fujian Province, Southern China

Bai Rufeng, Jiang Lizhe, Liang Quanzeng, Zhang Zhong, Shi Meisen *

1. *Population*

Blood samples were obtained from 152 unrelated healthy male individuals of the Chinese She ethnic group from Fujian province, Southern China. (see Fig. S1) All participants signed the informed consent and provided the information about birthplace, parents and grandparents at the same time. Their ancestors had lived in the region for at least three generations. The She ethnic minority, with a population of 709 592 (year of 2000). They are the largest minority in Fujian province. They are also present in the provinces of Zhejiang, Anhui, Jiangxi and Guangdong. Some descendants of the She also exist amongst the Hakka minority in Taiwan. The She language is very close to the Hakka dialect of the Hans, and most Shes speak Chinese instead of their ethnic tongue; a few Guangdong Shes speak a language similar to the Miao.

2. *DNA Extraction*

Genomic DNA was extracted using the Chelex – 100 method as described by Walsh et al.. [1]

3. *Amplification*

17 Y – STR marker (DYS19, DYS389I, DYS389II, DYS390, DYS391, DYS392, DYS393, DYS385a/b, DYS438, DYS439, DYS437, DYS448, DYS458, DYS456, DYS635, and Y – GATA – H4) were co – amplified using an AmpFLSTR Y – filer kit (Applied Biosystems, USA). [2] PCR amplification reactions were carried out using a GeneAmp PCR system 9700 (Applied Biosystems, USA) following the protocol provided by the manufacturer.

4. *Electrophoresis and typing*

The amplified products were separated by capillary electrophoresis on ABI Prism1 3130 Genetic Analyzer (Applied Biosystems, USA) using GeneScanTM – 500 LIZ internal size standard. The sample run data were analyzed together with an allelic ladder and positive and negative controls using GeneMapper ID Software Version 3.2 (Applied Biosystems, USA).

* Key Laboratory of Evidence Science (China University of Political Science and Law), Ministry of Education, 25 Xitucheng Road, Beijing 100088, PR China. Email: brf1000cn@ aliyun. com.

The updated recommendations of the DNA Commission of the International Society of Forensic Genetics for analysis of Y - STR systems were followed. [3]

5. *Analysis of data*

Allelic frequencies were estimated by direct gene - counting. Gene and haplotype diversities were calculated according to the formula by Nei. [4] The discrimination capacity was calculated as the proportion of different haplotypes in the sample. Pairwise values of Rst were calculated to measure the genetic distance corresponding to complete 17 - marker haplotypes (DYS19, DYS389I, DYS389II, DYS390, DYS391, DYS392, DYS393, DYS385a, DYS385b, DYS437, DYS438, DYS439, DYS448, DYS456, DYS458, DYS635, Y - GATA - H4) of She sample and compared with 15 other published data or data from neighbouring countries submitted to Y - STR haplotype database (YHRD), using ARLEQUIN software Version 3. 1. [5] Chromosomes carrying null alleles or duplicated loci were excluded from the haplotype calculation at the 17 Y - STR loci level. To illustrate the relationship between populations based on pairwise Rst, multidimensional scaling (MDS) plot and unrooted neighbor joining (NJ) dendrogram were built utilizing the PHYLIP v3. 6 program. [6]

6. *Quality control*

Our laboratory has participated in the Y - STR haplotype reference database (YHRD) quality assurance exercise in 2009 typing the YHRD core loci as well as additional loci DYS437, DYS448, DYS456, DYS458, DYS635 and Y - GATA - H4. The Y - STR haplotype data were contributed to the Y Chromosome STR Haplotype Reference Database (http: // www. yhrd. org), with the accession number YA003747.

7. *Results*

Table 1 summarizes the allele frequencies of 17 Y - STR loci, whilst Table 2 lists the haplotypes of 152 unrelated Chinese She ethnic individuals from Fujian Province. The Rst values calculated to measure genetic distances between 17 Y - STR haplotypes of 15 neighbour populations (n = 4, 261) with the statistical significance were calculated in Table 3. Phylogenetic relationships between She sample and referenced populations were assessed using NJ (Fig. 1) and MDS (Fig. 2) analyses.

8. *Other remarks*

As shown in Table 1, The gene diversity values for the Y - STRs loci a minimum 0. 4037 for DYS391 locus to a maximum 0. 9725 for DYS385a/b loci in the She sample. 98 alleles and 50 phenotypes (DYS385a/b) were detected, with the allele frequencies ranging from 0. 0066 to 0. 7500 (Table S1). Duplications were observed in three She ethnic individuals at locus DYS19 (alleles 16, 18), DYS390 (alleles 25, 26), and DYS385a/b (alleles 12 - 13, 17), respectively. All duplications were confirmed by repeating the amplification process.

A total of 144 different haplotypes were identified from 152 unrelated male individuals, of which 138 (95. 83%) were unique to a single individual. The overall haplotype diversity was calculated as 0. 9990 with a discrimination capacity of 0. 9474. We also compared our 17 Y - STR haplotype data with YHRD database, Release 41, which currently includes 46, 450 haplotypes over 303 populations. 132 (91.67%) haplotypes detected in the Chinese She sample are in zero matches in YHRD with AmpFlSTR Yfiler database. Ht79 is found to match most frequently in YHRD's AmpFlSTR Yfiler database with a hit of 10 with East Asian Metapopulation.

For having extensive illustration of the genetic relation, the studied data were compared via AMOVA on the same 17 Y – STR loci set with data from 15 reference populations (published and referenced in the YHRD). Namely 119 Han Chinese individuals residing in South China,[7] 203 Han Chinese individuals from Zhejiang,[8] 207 Han Chinese individuals from Beijing (YHRD, Accession # YA003470), 222 Han Chinese individuals from Shanxi,[9] 200 Han Chinese individuals from Taiwan,[10] 200 Chinese Manchu ethnic individuals from Liaoning (YHRD, Accession # YA003590), 100 Chinese Yao ethnic individuals from Guangxi,[11] 105 Chinese Yi ethnic individuals from Guangxi,[11] 103 Chinese Jing ethnic individuals from Guangxi,[11] 107 Chinese Zhuang ethnic individuals from Guangxi,[11] 143 Chinese Hui ethnic individuals from Ningxia,[12] 133 Chinese Salar ethnic individuals from Qinghai,[13] 167 Chinese Tibetan ethnic individuals from Qinghai,[14] 1079 Japanese individuals,[15] and 1021 Korean Individuals from South Korea.[16] With the statistical significance determined by a permutation test (10, 000 replicates,).

AMOVA analysis showed that 91.37% of the variation was found within populations, whereas 8.63% was among populations (fixation index FST = 0.08626, P = 0.00000). Pairwise analysis showed no significant differences (P > 0.05) in the comparison of She sample and Zhejiang Han (Rst = 0.00559), indicating little genetic difference. With other Chinese Han populations from Beijing, Taiwan, South China, and Shanxi, although significant, low Rst values were obtained (0.00846, 0.01231, 0.01855, and 0.01879, respectively). In comparison to the remaining Chinese minority ethnic groups and two Asian populations, highly significant distances were observed (P = 0.00000). The NJ tree and MDS plot built from the Rst distance matrices were generated (Fig. 1, Fig. 2), where She ethnic sample stands far apart of the reference populations and has much closer relationships between some south China Han populations. The reason might be historical in accordance with their ancestry migration process, and then they settled down and could get married to Han populations. While Populations from Chinese minority group (Yao, Yi, Salar and Tibetan) demonstrated significant population heterogeneity, in this case attributable to the differentiation of China, presumably because of differences in ancestral components. As demonstrated in the NJ tree and MDS plot, Japanese and South Korean individuals from population had a close genetic relationship (Rst = 0.03140). This reflects that culture trait may be related to migration and marriage.

In conclusion, these data in Chinese She ethnic group could be potentially useful for the regional specific and prerequisite reference to the forensic, genealogical, and evolutionary purposes. These regional differences indicate that more subpopulations need to be typed to obtain reliable population data for Y – chromosome markers.

This study was followed the guidelines for publication of population data requested by the journal and the DNA Commission of the International Society of Forensic Genetics.[17, 18]

Table 1. Allele frequencies data of Y – STR haplotypes from 152 unrelated Chinese She ethnic males

Allele	DYS 19	DYS 389I	DYS 389II	DYS 390	DYS 391	DYS 392	DYS 393	DYS 437	DYS 438	DYS 439	DYS 448	DYS 456	DYSS 458	DY 635	Y-GATA -H4	Allelic Class	DYS 385
7																7-12	0.0066
8						0.0066			0.0329							8-13	0.0066
9					0.0461				0.0461	0.0131						9-9	0.0132
10					0.7500	0.0526			0.7434	0.0592					0.0131	9-10	0.0066
11		0.0066			0.1842	0.0987			0.1711	0.4868					0.2895	9-12	0.0066
12	0.0066	0.5987			0.0197	0.1316	0.5000		0.0066	0.3289					0.6184	9-13	0.0066
13	0.0197	0.3026				0.3158	0.3289			0.0921		0.0131	0.0131		0.0789	9-14	0.0066
14	0.1316	0.0921				0.3092	0.0987	0.6118		0.0131		0.0855	0.0263			10-13	0.0132
15	0.5329					0.0197	0.0658	0.3684		0.0066		0.4737	0.1974			10-14	0.0132
16	0.2303					0.0395	0.0066	0.0197			0.0789	0.1842	0.1184			10-15	0.0066
17	0.0724					0.0131					0.0263	0.2303	0.1382			10-19	0.0066
18						0.0131					0.2500	0.0131	0.2171	0.0066		10-20	0.0066
16, 18	0.0066															10-21	0.0066
19											0.2829		0.2434	0.1645		11-11	0.0197
20				0.0066							0.2237		0.0395	0.1513		11-12	0.0329
21				0.0066							0.0724		0.0066	0.2566		11-16	0.0132
22				0.0658							0.0461			0.2303		11-17	0.0066
23				0.4211							0.0131			0.0921		11-18	0.0066
24			0.0263	0.3158							0.0066			0.0658		11-19	0.0263
25				0.1776										0.0263		11-20	0.0132
26			0.0131											0.0066		12-13	0.0329
25, 26				0.0066												12-13-17	0.0066
27			0.0921													12-14	0.0263
28			0.3487													12-15	0.0066
29			0.2566													12-16	0.0395
30			0.1711													12-17	0.0395
31			0.0592													12-18	0.0395
32			0.0131													12-19	0.0263
33			0.0197													12-20	0.0592
34																12-21	0.0329
																13-13	0.0526
																13-14	0.0789
																13-15	0.0132
																13-17	0.0263
																13-18	0.0460
																13-19	0.0329
																13-20	0.0263

Table 2: Haplotypes for the 17 Y-STR loci observed in 152 unrelated Chinese She ethnic males from Fujian Province, Southern China

Haplotype	n	DYS19	DYS389I	DYS389II	DYS390	DYS391	DYS392	DYS393	DYS385a/b	DYS438	DYS439	DYS437	DYS448	DYS456	DYS458	DYS635	Y-GATA-H4
H001	1	15	12	28	25	9	13	12	14,17	10	12	14	19	13	20	23	13
H002	1	16	14	30	24	11	13	14	13,18	10	11	14	18	13	18	24	12
H003	1	17	12	28	24	10	13	12	12,20	10	11	15	20	15	19	23	12
H004	1	16	12	28	24	10	13	12	13,21	10	11	15	20	15	19	22	11
H005	1	16	12	28	24	10	18	12	13,21	10	11	15	20	15	19	22	11
H006	1	15	12	28	25	10	12	12	12,17	10	12	15	19	17	19	19	12
H007	2	16	12	27	23	11	14	13	13,14	10	12	14	18	16	14	21	13
H008	1	15	12	28	22	10	13	12	12,19	10	13	14	19	14	17	20	12
H009	1	17	12	28	24	10	13	12	12,20	10	11	15	20	15	19	24	12
H010	2	15	13	29	23	11	14	13	11,12	10	10	14	18	14	18	21	11
H011	1	16	12	28	24	10	11	12	13,22	10	11	15	20	15	19	22	11
H012	1	15	13	29	23	10	10	14	12,16	10	12	14	18	15	16	20	12
H013	4	15	12	28	25	10	12	12	12,13	10	12	15	19	17	19	19	12
H014	1	15	12	30	23	11	13	12	12,16	10	11	14	20	14	16	21	11
H015	1	17	12	28	24	10	13	12	12,20	10	11	15	20	16	14	22	12
H016	1	15	12	28	23	10	14	12	13,19	11	13	14	20	17	17	20	12
H017	1	16	12	24	24	10	12	12	13,13	10	11	15	20	15	19	22	11
H018	1	13	14	28	23	10	13	15	12,18	11	11	14	20	15	15	23	12
H019	1	15	14	31	23	10	11	15	11,19	10	11	14	21	15	15	23	12
H020	1	17	12	28	24	10	16	12	12,20	10	11	15	20	15	19	23	12
H021	1	15	12	29	23	10	14	13	13,18	10	11	15	18	17	16	20	11
H022	1	15	12	31	23	10	12	12	11,16	10	12	15	19	15	18	19	12
H023	1	17	12	28	24	11	14	12	12,20	10	11	15	19	15	19	24	12
H024	1	16	12	27	23	10	14	13	13,14	11	11	15	16	17	18	21	12
H025	1	16	12	27	23	10	14	13	13,15	10	11	14	16	17	18	21	12
H026	1	14	12	27	24	10	14	12	18,20	11	13	15	19	15	16	18	12
H027	1	15	13	29	24	10	13	12	13,22	10	12	15	19	15	17	21	11
H028	1	15	12	28	24	10	14	12	14,20	11	14	15	20	15	19	20	11
H029	1	16	12	28	24	10	13	12	12,21	10	11	15	20	15	19	22	12
H030	1	17	12	28	24	10	13	12	12,17	10	12	15	21	15	16	21	11
H031	2	15	12	28	24	9	13	12	12,17	10	12	14	19	14	18	21	13
H032	1	14	12	30	25	9	12	12	16,20	11	9	14	22	14	18	24	13
H033	1	15	12	31	25	10	13	12	13,18	11	12	15	19	17	19	19	12
H034	1	16	12	28	25	10	12	12	13,22	10	11	15	20	15	18	23	13
H035	1	15	12	28	25	10	15	12	12,14	10	12	15	19	17	19	19	12
H036	1	15	12	28	25	10	16	12	12,14	10	12	15	19	17	19	19	12
H037	1	15	13	28	25	10	18	12	12,14	10	12	15	19	17	19	19	12
H038	1	14	12	28	25	11	14	12	14,20	11	12	16	20	15	17	21	12
H039	1	14	12	29	25	10	14	12	13,18	11	13	15	21	14	17	20	12
H040	1	16	12	29	25	9	13	12	12,20	10	11	14	19	15	15	22	12
H041	1	16,18	12	28	24	10	13	12	13,20	10	11	15	20	15	19	21	11
H042	1	14	13	29	22	10	14	12	13,19	11	11	14	20	16	18	20	12
H043	1	15	12	28	25	10	13	12	12,16	10	12	15	19	17	19	19	12
H044	1	15	12	30	25	10	13	12	14,19	10	12	15	19	17	19	19	12
H045	1	15	12	28	23	10	11	12	11,19	10	9	15	20	17	19	26	12
H046	1	17	13	29	23	10	11	15	11,16	10	12	14	21	15	13	21	11
H047	1	16	13	29	23	10	15	14	13,13	10	11	14	18	15	16	21	12
H048	1	15	13	30	24	11	11	15	12,17	10	11	14	21	17	17	22	11
H049	1	17	12	28	24	10	15	12	7,12	10	11	15	20	16	20	23	12
H050	1	14	13	28	23	10	14	12	14,19	11	11	14	20	15	18	20	11
H051	1	15	13	30	25,26	10	11	15	11,18	10	11	14	21	15	15	22	11
H052	1	15	13	32	23	10	12	14	12,19	10	11	14	19	14	18	21	11
H053	1	15	13	28	24	9	14	13	11,12	11	13	14	18	15	15	21	12
H054	1	16	13	29	24	10	14	13	13,14	10	12	14	18	15	16	19	11
H055	1	15	13	29	24	10	13	12	12,21	10	12	15	19	15	17	22	13
H056	1	15	13	30	24	10	13	12	13,21	10	11	15	20	17	18	22	12
H057	1	15	13	29	24	10	14	15	13,17	10	11	14	18	15	19	24	10

Haplotype	n	DYS19	DYS389I	DYS389II	DYS390	DYS391	DYS392	DYS393	DYS385a/b	DYS438	DYS439	DYS437	DYS448	DYS456	DYS458	DYS635	Y-GATA-H4
H058	1	15	13	29	24	10	13	12	14,21	10	13	15	19	15	20	21	11
H059	1	15	13	29	24	10	13	12	13,22	10	11	15	20	15	19	22	12
H060	1	15	13	30	25	10	13	14	12,16	10	11	14	19	15	15	21	12
H061	1	15	13	30	24	12	11	15	11,19	10	11	14	22	15	16	21	11
H062	1	14	13	30	24	11	13	12	14,21	10	11	14	17	15	17	25	12
H063	1	16	13	30	24	10	13	12	12,15	10	11	15	19	15	16	21	12
H064	1	17	13	30	24	10	13	12	12,19	10	12	14	20	15	17	22	11
H065	1	17	13	30	24	10	13	12	12,21	10	12	14	20	15	17	23	11
H066	2	16	12	27	23	10	14	13	13,14	10	11	14	16	17	18	21	12
H067	1	14	12	28	22	10	16	12	13,19	10	11	15	23	15	19	25	12
H068	1	15	12	27	23	10	14	13	13,14	10	11	14	16	17	19	22	12
H069	1	15	14	30	24	10	13	14	12,16	10	12	14	18	15	16	21	11
H070	1	12	14	30	24	10	13	13	11,20	10	11	14	20	15	17	20	11
H071	1	15	14	32	24	10	13	13	12,20	10	11	14	19	15	17	21	11
H072	1	16	14	27	20	10	14	14	12,18	11	10	14	19	15	18	25	12
H073	1	15	12	28	23	10	14	13	12,18	9	12	14	18	16	15	20	13
H074	1	15	12	28	23	10	12	13	14,16	10	11	14	16	17	18	21	12
H075	1	15	12	27	23	10	12	13	12,20	10	11	14	16	17	18	21	12
H076	1	15	12	27	23	10	12	13	13,14	10	11	14	16	17	18	21	12
H077	1	14	12	29	24	10	10	12	10,20	10	11	15	20	15	18	23	12
H078	1	15	12	30	23	10	14	13	16,20	10	11	14	16	17	18	21	12
H079	1	15	12	29	23	11	14	13	13,13	10	11	14	18	16	15	19	12
H080	1	16	12	27	23	10	13	13	13,14	10	11	14	16	17	18	21	12
H081	1	15	14	33	23	10	13	13	13,20	11	11	14	18	17	16	21	10
H082	1	16	14	30	23	10	13	13	15,15	10	11	14	18	15	16	24	12
H083	1	15	13	29	24	11	13	14	13,19	10	12	14	18	15	18	24	11
H084	1	15	12	28	24	10	11	13	15,16	11	13	15	19	14	15	19	12
H085	1	15	12	33	22	10	11	13	9,12	8	11	14	22	16	15	22	12
H086	1	15	12	28	24	10	14	12	14,20	11	12	16	20	15	21	20	12

Haplotype	n	DYS19	DYS389I	DYS389II	DYS390	DYS391	DYS392	DYS393	DYS385a/b	DYS438	DYS439	DYS437	DYS448	DYS456	DYS458	DYS635	Y-GATA-H4
H087	1	15	12	28	21	10	11	12	11,17	10	11	14	20	15	18	24	12
H088	2	16	13	30	25	10	13	12	13,20	11	10	15	19	18	19	21	12
H089	1	14	13	29	24	10	13	12	13,17	10	12	14	18	16	18	21	11
H090	1	14	13	29	23	10	13	12	12,13	10	13	14	18	15	17	21	11
H091	1	15	12	28	23	11	11	13	9,10	8	10	14	22	17	15	23	12
H092	1	15	12	29	24	11	14	17	13,14	10	11	14	18	17	15	19	12
H093	1	16	12	27	23	10	14	13	13,13	10	12	14	18	17	15	20	12
H094	1	16	12	33	23	10	10	13	13,13	11	12	14	18	15	16	20	12
H095	1	16	13	30	24	11	13	14	14,18	10	13	14	17	15	16	22	11
H096	1	15	12	29	23	11	14	13	10,15	10	11	14	18	17	15	19	12
H097	1	15	12	28	23	10	14	12	14,20	11	13	16	20	15	20	20	12
H098	1	13	14	31	24	9	14	13	16,21	12	11	14	19	15	16	22	12
H099	1	16	13	29	22	11	13	12	12,21	10	12	14	19	16	16	22	11
H100	1	15	14	31	23	10	14	13	11,11	11	11	14	19	15	15	25	11
H101	1	17	13	29	25	11	13	14	13,18	9	12	14	18	15	17	22	11
H102	1	15	12	28	23	11	11	13	9,9	9	15	14	21	17	15	24	12
H103	1	15	12	28	23	11	14	13	10,14	10	11	14	18	17	15	19	12
H104	1	15	13	29	24	10	10	12	8,13	10	13	15	19	15	19	22	11
H105	1	15	13	29	23	11	8	15	11,11	10	11	14	21	15	17	22	12
H106	1	16	12	27	23	10	10	13	13,14	10	11	14	21	16	19	21	12
H107	1	15	13	31	25	11	14	13	13,18	10	10	14	18	14	17	22	11
H108	1	15	14	31	24	10	11	13	13,14	10	12	14	21	15	15	22	12
H109	1	13	12	28	25	10	14	12	13,13	11	13	15	20	15	19	20	12
H110	1	15	13	29	23	10	17	13	11,12	10	10	14	18	15	18	20	11
H111	1	16	12	31	23	10	10	13	14,18	10	11	14	18	16	15	21	12
H112	1	15	14	30	25	10	10	14	11,11	11	11	14	19	15	17	23	12
H113	1	14	13	29	25	10	10	15	13,18	10	12	14	18	15	19	21	11
H114	1	14	13	29	24	10	13	12	13,21	10	12	15	19	15	17	21	11
H115	1	15	13	31	23	10	12	14	12,19	10	11	14	17	15	16	22	13

Haplotype	n	DYS19	DYS389I	DYS389II	DYS390	DYS391	DYS392	DYS393	DYS385a/b	DYS438	DYS439	DYS437	DYS448	DYS456	DYS458	DYS635	Y-GATA-H4
H116	1	16	14	26	23	11	13	14	10,13	8	11	14	23	15	18	20	11
H117	1	15	13	24	22	10	16	12	9,14	9	11	14	16	16	19	22	12
H118	1	16	12	29	23	10	14	13	13,19	10	11	14	22	17	15	20	12
H119	1	14	12	30	22	10	16	12	10,19	10	11	15	16	15	18	19	12
H120	1	14	12	30	23	10	12	12	10,21	9	11	15	22	16	15	23	12
H121	1	14	12	30	23	10	11	12	9,13	9	12	15	24	15	19	19	12
H122	1	15	13	29	23	10	14	13	13,13	10	11	14	18	17	15	19	12
H123	1	15	12	24	22	10	11	13	9,9	8	11	14	22	15	15	21	12
H124	1	15	13	24	22	12	16	14	10,14	8	12	14	20	15	17	20	11
H125	1	16	12	29	23	10	14	13	13,13	10	11	14	18	15	15	19	12
H126	1	14	13	30	23	12	14	13	11,12	11	13	14	19	15	15	22	12
H127	1	16	13	29	24	10	13	12	12,21	10	12	14	19	14	18	22	11
H128	1	16	12	28	25	10	13	12	12,20	10	13	14	19	14	20	21	12
H129	1	14	12	29	25	10	14	12	13,17	11	12	15	20	15	19	21	12
H130	1	15	12	26	24	10	14	13	12,13,17	11	12	15	20	16	18	21	12
H131	1	16	12	30	22	11	12	14	12,14	10	12	14	17	16	14	23	12
H132	1	16	13	29	23	10	17	15	11,19	10	11	15	21	15	13	21	11
H133	1	15	12	28	23	10	14	13	12,16	9	12	14	18	16	15	20	12
H134	1	15	12	28	23	10	14	13	13,15	10	11	14	18	16	15	20	11
H135	1	14	12	28	23	11	12	12	12,18	10	12	15	19	16	17	20	13
H136	1	15	12	28	23	10	12	12	13,17	10	12	14	19	16	17	19	13
H137	1	14	12	28	23	11	12	12	14,20	10	14	15	19	16	18	21	11
H138	1	15	12	28	23	10	13	12	14,19	10	12	14	19	16	18	19	12
H139	1	15	12	28	23	10	13	12	12,18	10	12	15	20	16	19	22	12
H140	1	15	12	28	23	10	12	12	12,17	10	11	15	18	16	20	19	12
H141	1	15	11	29	23	10	14	13	10,13	10	10	14	18	16	15	19	12
H142	1	15	12	29	23	10	14	13	15,21	10	12	14	18	16	15	19	12
H143	1	15	12	29	23	11	14	13	12,18	10	11	14	18	16	15	19	12
H144	1	15	12	29	23	11	14	13	11,20	10	11	14	18	16	16	22	11

Table 3: Pairwise Φst values (below diagonal) and P values (above diagonal) calculated for the Chinese She ethnic and 15 reference populations

Population	the Chinese She Ethinc	South, China[Han]	Zhejiang, China [Han]	Beijing, China [Han]	Shanxi, China [Han]	Taiwan[Han Chinese]	the Chinese Manchu Ethnic	the Chinese Yao Ethnic
the Chinese She Ethinc	0.00000	+	−	+	+	+	+	+
South, China[Han]	0.01855	0.00000	+	+	+	+	+	+
Zhejiang, China [Han]	0.00559	0.01115	0.00000	−	+	−	+	+
Beijing, China [Han]	0.00846	0.01065	0.00270	0.00000	−	+	−	+
Shanxi, China [Han]	0.01879	0.01381	0.01561	0.00375	0.00000	+	+	+
Taiwan[Han Chinese]	0.01231	0.01526	0.00335	0.01927	0.03137	0.00000	+	+
the Chinese Manchu Ethnic	0.01217	0.02154	0.00694	0.00175	0.00750	0.02193	0.00000	+
the Chinese Yao Ethnic	0.11786	0.13341	0.16179	0.13561	0.09193	0.18449	0.14191	0.00000
the Chinese Yi Ethnic	0.16166	0.20376	0.19987	0.19821	0.13566	0.18587	0.19407	0.28065
the Chinese Jing Ethnic	0.06875	0.03330	0.07192	0.06003	0.04336	0.08242	0.06791	0.09190
the Chinese Zhuang Ethnic	0.04422	0.02851	0.04997	0.04735	0.03517	0.04423	0.05904	0.13269
the Chinese Hui Ethnic	0.05826	0.07861	0.06376	0.06339	0.04993	0.06241	0.05691	0.19686
the Chinese Salar Ethnic	0.08670	0.11176	0.10274	0.10077	0.07132	0.10076	0.08570	0.19725
the Chinese Tibet Ethnic	0.23998	0.28539	0.26242	0.26871	0.23303	0.26009	0.25847	0.38184
Japan Individuals	0.10841	0.09950	0.09712	0.09227	0.10187	0.12186	0.08177	0.18979
Korean Individuals	0.06272	0.06390	0.05414	0.04145	0.05460	0.08425	0.03995	0.15438

"+": $P<0.05$; "−": $P>0.05$

Population	the Chinese Yi Ethnic	the Chinese Jing Eth	the Chinese Zhuang Et	the Chinese Hui Ethn	the Chinese Salar Eth	the Chinese Tibet Ethn	Japan Individuals	Korean Individuals
the Chinese She Ethinc	+	+	+	+	+	+	+	+
South, China[Han]	+	+	+	+	+	+	+	+
Zhejiang, China [Han]	+	+	+	+	+	+	+	+
Beijing, China [Han]	+	+	+	+	+	+	+	+
Shanxi, China [Han]	+	+	+	+	+	+	+	+
Taiwan[Han Chinese]	+	+	+	+	+	+	+	+
the Chinese Manchu Ethnic	+	+	+	+	+	+	+	+
the Chinese Yao Ethnic	+	+	+	+	+	+	+	+
the Chinese Yi Ethnic	0.00000	+	+	+	+	+	+	+
the Chinese Jing Ethnic	0.22005	0.00000	+	+	+	+	+	+
the Chinese Zhuang Ethnic	0.13543	0.03999	0.00000	+	+	+	+	+
the Chinese Hui Ethnic	0.11452	0.14427	0.09406	0.00000	+	+	+	+
the Chinese Salar Ethnic	0.08760	0.15813	0.10812	0.00994	0.00000	+	+	+
the Chinese Tibet Ethnic	0.20248	0.33374	0.28849	0.11162	0.11703	0.00000	+	+
Japan Individuals	0.26700	0.09739	0.14274	0.16048	0.17012	0.31899	0.00000	+
Korean Individuals	0.25909	0.08970	0.10860	0.13620	0.16074	0.32882	0.03140	0.00000

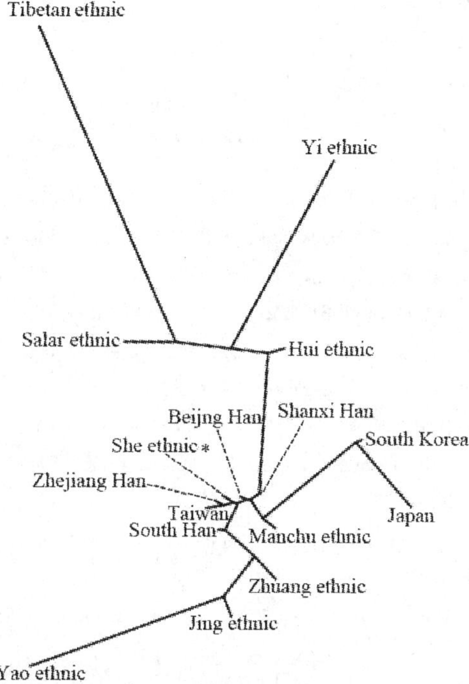

Fig. 1 Unrooted NJ tree based on pairwise Rst genetic distances using 17 Y - STR haplotype data for She ethnic and 15 reference populations

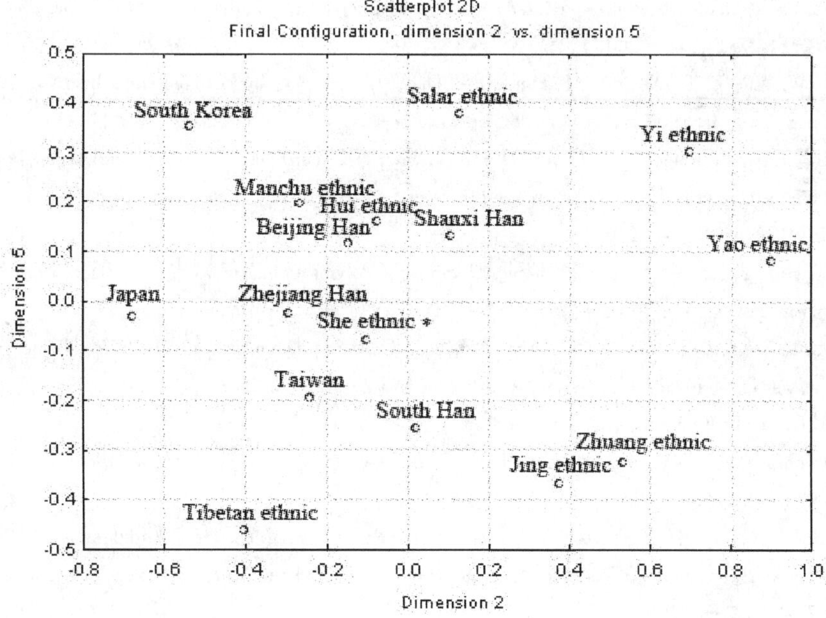

Fig. 2 Multi - dimensional scaling (MDS) plot of She ethnic and 15 reference populations, from pairwise Rst values. Stress value = 0. 002.

Acknowledgements

We thank all sample donors for their contributions to this work and all those who helped with sample collection. This study was supported by The National Natural Science Foundation of China (NSFC. No.

81172902), and The Program for New Century Excellent Talents in University (No. NCET - 10 - 0773), and the New - Star Program of Science and Technology of Beijing Metropolis (2010B073), and the Program for Young Innovative Research Team in China University of Political Science and Law.

References

[1] P. S. Walsh, D. A. Metzger, R. Higuchi, "Chelex 100 as a Medium for Simple Extraction of DNA for PCR - Based from Forensic Material", *Biotechniques*, 10 (1991), pp. 506 ~ 513.

[2] J. J. Mulero, C. W. Chang, L. M. Calandro, R. L. Green, Y. Li, C. L. Johnson, L. K. Hennessy, "Development and Validation of the AmpFlSTRYfiler PCR Amplification kit: A Male Specific, Single Amplification 17 Y - STR Multiplex System", *J. Forensic Sci.*, 51, (2006), pp. 64 ~ 75.

[3] L. Gusma ~ o, J. M. Butler, A. Carracedo, P. Gill, M. Kayser, W. R. Mayr, N. Morling, M. Prinz, L. Roewer, C. Tyler - Smith, P. M. Schneider, "DNA Commission of the International Society of Forensic Genetics (ISFG): An Update of the Recommendations on the Use of Y - STRs in Forensic Analysis", *Forensic Sci. Int.*, 157 (2006), pp. 187 ~ 197.

[4] M. Nei, *Molecular Evolutionary Genetics*, Columbia University Press, New York, 1987, pp. 176 ~ 179.

[5] http: // cmpg. unibe. eh//software//arlequin3. Arlequin Ver3. 1: An integrated software package for population genetics.

[6] J . Felsentein, *Phylogeny Inference Package* (*Phylip*), version 3. 6a3. Department of Genetics, University of Washington, Seattle, distributed by author.

[7] Y. K. Chen, Q. Li, D. C. Li, Z. H. Deng, "Study on the genentic polymorphism of 17 Y - chromosome specific STR loci of non - related male individuals in southern Chinese Han population", *Experimental&Lab Med.*, 26 (2008), pp. 351 ~ 354, 386.

[8] W. W. Wu, X. T. Zheng, L. P. Pan, H. L. Hao, T. Fu, "A study of polymorphisms of 16 Y - STR loci in Han population in Zhejiang", *Forensic Sci and Tech* (*China*), 5 (2005), pp. 11 ~ 17.

[9] R. F. Bai, Z. Zhang, Q. Z. Liang, D. Lu, L. Yuan, X. Yang, M. S. Shi, "Haplotype diversity of 17 Y - STR loci in a Chinese Han population sample from Shanxi Province, Northern China", *Forensic Sci Int Genet.*, 7 (2013), pp. 214 ~ 216.

[10] T. Huang, Y. Hsu, J. Li, J. Chung, C. Shun, "Polymorphism of 17 Y - STR loci in Taiwan Population", *Forensic Sci Int.*, 174 (2007), pp. 249 ~ 254.

[11] D. L. Feng, C. H. Liu, Z. R. Liang, C. Liu, "Genetic polymorphism of 17 Y - STR loci in Four Minority Populations in Guangxi of China", *Hereditas* (*Beijing*), 31 (2009), pp. 921 ~ 935.

[12] H. Guo, J. W. Jiang, Z. P. Jiao, H. Tang, Q. X, Zhang, L. Zhao, N, Hu, H. F. Li, Y. C. Liu, Genetic Polymorphisms for 17 Y - Chromosomal STRs Haplotypes in Chinese Hui Population, *Legal Med* (*Tokyo*), 10 (2008), pp. 163 ~ 169.

[13] B. F. Zhu, C, M. Shen, X. Xun, J. W. Yan, Y. J. Deng, "J. Zhu, Population genetic polymorphisms for 17 Y - Chromosomal STRs Haplotypes of Chinese Salar Ethnic Minority Group", *Legal Med* (*Tokyo*), 9 (2007), pp. 203 ~ 209.

[14] B. F. Zhu, Y. M. Wu, C, M. Shen, T. H. Yang, Y. J. Deng, X. Xun, Y. F. Tian, J. C. Yan, T. Li, "Genetic analysis of 17 Y - Chromosomal STRs Haplotypes of Chinese Tibetan Ethnic Group Residing in Qinghai Province of China", *Forensic Sci Int*, 175 (2008), pp. 238 ~ 243.

[15] M. Hashiyada, K. Umetsu, I. Yuasa, A. Tamura, A. Matsusue, K. Suzuki, S. Kashimura, M. Funayama, "Population Genetics of 17 Y - Chromosomal STR loci in Japanese", *Forensic Sci Int Genet.*,

2 (2008), pp. e69 ~ e70.

[16] K. M. Seong, S. Y. Yoo, J. H. Hwang, S. H. Kim, K. W. Chung, N. S. Cho. "Population Genetic Polymorphisms of 17 Y - Chromosomal STR Loci in South Koreans", *Forensic Sci Int Genet.*, 5 (2011), pp. e122 ~ e123.

[17] A. Carracedo, J. M. Butler, L. Gusmao, W. Parson, L. Roewer, P. M. Schneider, "Publication of Population Data for Forensic Purposes", *Forensic Sci Int Genet.*, 4 (2010), pp. 145 ~ 147.

[18] L. Gusmao, J. M. Butler, A. Carracedo, P. Gill, M. Kayser, W. R. Mayr, N. Morling, M. Prinz, L. Roewer, C. Tyler - Smith, P. M. Schneider, "DNA Commission of the International Society of Forensic Science Genetics (ISFG): An Update of the Recommendations on the Use of Y - STRs in Forensic Analysis", *Forensic Sci Int.*, 157 (2006), pp. 187 ~ 197.

Profiling of RNA Degradation in Deseased Rat's Adipose Tissue for Determination of Postmortem Interval

Lv Yehui[1], Ma Kaijun[2], Pan Hui[1], Chen Long[1] *

For more than 100 years, many methods have been investigated to accurately and systematically determine the postmortem interval (PMI), or exact time of death, in autopsy cases. The estimation of PMI is mostly based on the evaluation of livor mortis, rigor mortis, and cooling of the body after death. [1] In addition, these postmortem phenomena can't change continuously in the long term of PMI. [2, 3] For example, body temperature approaches ambient temperature approximately 30 h after death and thus cannot be used to assess longer term PMI. [1] Therefore, reliable and reproducible methods to determine the time since death for the extended postmortem interval are still required. Numerous methods have been proposed in the recent years for the determination of the time since death by chemical means and biological means. [4-8] However, these methods estimate PMI using only a few or even just one specific parameter and have limitations in forensic practice.

An accurate estimation of the PMI requires the evaluation of parameters that change constantly with time after death. This definition seems to fit well in post mortem degradation of nucleic acids. [9, 10] With the advances of molecular biology, especially the invention of real-time quantitative PCR, [11] the analysis of time-dependent degradation of RNA became a focus of attention in clinical medicine as well as in forensic science. The estimation of the PMI by studying the RNA decay may be within reach since RNA degradation or loss of RNA transcripts after death seems to be rapid and time-dependent. Housekeeping mRNAs were commonly used for analysis and comparison of gene expression levels as standardized control, but also can be used as opportune indicators of the PMI due to degradation of RNA with PMI. [12] It is extremely important to carefully validate the normalization strategy, an ideal endogenous reference gene for estimating PMI should show relatively stable expression after death. [13] MicroRNA (miR) was considered to be less susceptible against degradation affected by environmental conditions owing to their tiny size of about 22bp. U6 was also as included in this research because it was frequently chosen as endogenous control markers in miRNA studies. Therefore, this study aims

* 1. Department of Forensic Medicine, Shanghai Medical School of Fudan University, Shanghai, 20032;

2. Forensic lab, Criminal Science and Technology Institute, Shanghai City Public Security Bureau, Shanghai, 200032.

Email: chenlong@ shmu. edu. cn.

to define a panel of RNA transcripts in adipose tissue, by which postmortem degradation may be used to significantly correlate with PMI. Subsequently, the combined quantification of the previously defined transcripts was used to develop a mathematical model for PMI estimation, which provides a serious advantage to currently available methodology that can be used as a co-adjuvant approach to increase the accuracy of PMI estimation

1 *Materials and methods*

1.1 Tissue samples

120 adult Sprague – Dawley rats (body weight: 240 ±20g), healthy and male, were sacrificed by cervical amputation and randomly divided into 2 group. 60 of them were kept at 15 ± 2°C in a controlled environment chamber, while another sixty were kept at 25 ±2°C. These rats were used to develop models for estimating PMI. The adipose samples were taken from corpses at PMI of 0h, 3h, 6h, 12h, 24h, 36h, 48h, 60h, 72h and 96h (n = 6 at each time point) then immediately transferred to RNAlater (Ambion, USA). Moreover, 10 same rats were sacrificed by the same way and randomly divided into 2 groups for validation of the models. 5 of them were kept at 15 ±2°C and another 5 were kept at 4 ±2°C. Adipose samples were taken at PMI of 10h, 20h, 30h, 50h and 80h then stored at −80℃ until extraction of RNA. All of the animal experiments in the present study were performed in accordance with the principles for the Care and Use of Laboratory Animal Committee of Fudan University Shanghai Medical College.

1.2 Endogenous molecular biological markers

7 endogenous molecular biological markers were chosen in present study. Glyceraldehyde −3 − phosphate dehydrogenase (GAPDH), β − actin (ACTB) and hypoxanthine Hypoxanthine phosphoribosyl transferase − 1 (HPRT1) were housekeeping genes used as endogenous control genes commonly. [14, 15] Considered to be relatively stable, microRNAs were included in this research due to its short length. After compared with miRBase, [16] miR − 143 and miR − 10b are adipose − enriched and have recently been recognized to function as important modulators of gene regulation in adipose development and function. [17, 18] Meanwhile, 18S ribosomal RNA (18S rRNA) and U6 small nuclear RNA (U6) were also selected as RNA markers in this research, which were frequently chosen as endogenous control markers in miRNAs study. [19] The primers were used to span at least one exon/exon boundary to insure amplification and detection of cDNA only. Details are given in Table 1.

Table 1 Primers of endogenous molecular biological markers for RT – qPCR

Primer name	Forward sequence (5' -3')	Reverse sequence (5' -3')
GAPDH	CTGGTGCTGCCAAGGCTGTG	TTCTCCAGGCGGCACGTCAG
ACTB	GTGACGTTGACATCCGTAAAGA	GCCGGACTCATCGTACTCC
HPRT1	CCTAAGATGAGCGCAAGTTGAA	CCACAGGACTAGAACACCTGCTAA
18S	GTAACCCGTTGAACCCCATT	CCATCCAATCGGTAGTAGCG
U6	TGACACGCAAATTCGTGAAGCGTTC	CCAGTCTCAGGGTCCGAGGTATTC
miR – 143	TGAGATGAAGCACTGTAGCTCA	CCAGTCTCAGGGTCCGAGGTATTC
miR – 10b	CCCTGTAGAACCGAATTTGTGT	CCAGTCTCAGGGTCCGAGGTATTC

1.3 Extraction of total RNA

All materials and bench surfaces were treated with RNase Away prior to handling the samples to minimize the risk of RNA degradation by RNase during the experimental process. 20 – 50mg adipose tissue is homogenized with 1ml Trizol solvent (Invitrogen, USA) and 0.2ml chloroform, supernatant is decanted and mixed with 0.5 ml iso – propanol, then placed at – 20°C for 1hour to be precipitated. The mixture is then centrifuged at 12000r/min at 4°C for 10min and then total RNA is dissolved in 100μL nuclease free water finally. Concentration and purity of RNA were assessed by NanoDrop 1000 (Erlangen, Germany).

1.4 Reverse transcription quantitative real time PCR (RT – qPCR)

Before RT – qRCR, 5μg total RNA was incubated for 10 minutes at 37°C with 5U RQ1 RNase – Free DNase (Promega, USA) to remove genomic DNA then heated at 65°C for 10minutes to inactivate DNase. RT – qPCR was performed using a two – step protocol. Complementary DNA (cDNA) was generated from 1μg total RNA. Firstly, total RNA was added polyA using polyA polymerase according to the manufacturer's protocol, and then using MMLV Reverse Transcriptase 1st – Strand cDNA Synthesis Kit (Promega, USA) to generate cDNA with reverse primer miRdT – RT, whose sequence is 5' – CGACTCGATCCAGTCTCAGGGTCCGAGGTATTCAGTCGCACTTTTTTTTTTT TT – 3'. Secondly, the cDNA product was diluted by 1:10 for further use. Real – time PCR was performed by fluorescence quantitative PCR instrument (ABI 7500, USA). Amplification mixture was made using SYBR Premix Ex Taq™ kit (TaKaRa, Japan) according to the manufacturer's protocol. The reactions were performed in a total volume of 20μl containing 2μl cDNA, 10μl SYBR premix 0.4μl Dye, 0.4μl forward primers, 0.4μl reverse primers and 6.8μl RNase – free water. Cycling parameters was 30s at 95°C, 40 cycles (5s at 95°C, 34s at 64°C). Reactions were prepared in duplicates for each sample and each of the 3 assays. Copies of the particular endogenous genes were quantified and presented as average cycle threshold (Ct) value.

1.5 Statistical analysis

Statistical analysis was conducted by evaluating the mean value of Ct values, the experimental replicates were averaged and the mean values + standard deviation (SD) were calculated for each time point (six replicates at 15°C or 25°C) by GraphPad v5.0 (GraphPad software Inc, USA). In attempts to find the least unstable control molecular biological marker, the geNorm [20] software for processing RT – qPCR data was used and specific operation was completed according to specifications of genorm^{PLUS} (Biogazelle, Belgium). Delta Ct meant the differences of Ct values between the most stable control marker and the other RNA markers. Curve estimation analysis between delta Ct values and PMI were performed for getting the best mathematical model function. 6 mathematical model functions were explored (linear, quadratic, cubic, reciprocal, exponential and logarithmic). Curves with the highest coefficient of determination (R2) were considered to be the best mathematical models. The rest 10 rats were used for verification. After taking the delta Ct values into each mathematical model, mean and SD values of estimated PMI were surmised at both 15°C and 25°C.

2 *Results*

2.1 RNA yield and RT – qPCR

Total RNA was successfully extracted from all 130 samples. The 260/280 ratio of all samples ranged from 1.8 ~ 2.2 after purification. The mean RNA yield of group 15°C was obtained from adipose tissue (mean 323 ng/mg of tissue, range 212 - 458 ng/mg) compared to group 25°C (mean 353 ng/mg of tissue, range 257 - 504 ng/mg), that was quite close ($P > 0.05$). Moreover, correlations between total RNA yield and PMI after death were not observed ($r < 0.15$) (data not shown). Amplification were successful in all adipose tissues. Replicate samples were processed in this study to correct run – to – run variations, the average Ct values and standard errors were calculated. The Ct values and thus the copy number of template molecules varied among the postmortem intervals, showed in Table 2. In general, the SD values of each RNA markers were higher at 25°C than at 15°C. Moreover, the SD values of GAPDH and ACTB were significantly larger than other RNA markers at both 15°C and 25°C.

Table 2 Primers of endogenous molecular biological markers for RT – qPCR

Gene symbol	Ct value of 15°C (n = 60)				Ct value of 25°C (n = 60)			
	Max	Min	Mean	SD	Max	Min	Mean	SD
GAPDH	23.43	16.52	19.16	1.59	27.83	16.19	22.15	2.65
ACTB	26.30	18.11	21.70	1.95	30.83	17.69	24.43	3.15
HPRT	26.54	21.04	23.47	1.35	20.83	31.08	25.66	2.35
18S	17.16	12.36	14.21	1.29	18.19	12.07	14.72	1.49
U6	16.14	13.61	14.91	0.66	18.96	13.88	16.28	1.20
miR – 143	17.34	13.16	15.37	0.80	19.31	13.57	16.41	1.14
miR – 10b	18.63	13.81	15.83	1.02	19.28	14.02	17.03	1.05

2. 2 Evaluation of expression stability of candidate control molecular

Control molecular biological markers ranked in order of their expression stability from high to low at 15°C was miR - 143/U6 > miR - 10b > 18S > HPRT1 > GAPDH > ACTB (Fig. 1a). Pairwise variation V2/3 value was below 0. 15 (Fig. 1b), thus 3 markers can be used as endogenous reference markers (miR - 143, U6 and miR - 10b) at 15°C within PMI of 96h. The expression stability from high to low at 25°C was miR - 10b/miR - 143 > U6 > 18S > HPRT1 > ACTB > GAPDH (Fig. 1c). However, none reference markers were selected within PMI of 96h since none V values were below 0. 15 (Fig. 1d). Then we grouped all the samples into 2 separate time spans (0h ~ 36h, 36h ~ 96h) and re - examined these reference genes in the exclusive and defined conditions by geNorm software. At 25°C, miR - 10b, 18S, U6 and miR - 143 had the appropriate stability when 0h ≤ PMI ≤ 36h, while U6, miR - 143, miR - 10b and HPRT1 were considered to be the stable markers when 36h ≤ PMI ≤ 96h (Fig. 1c, d). Since miR - 143, miR - 10b and U6 always occupied the first three positions following the geNorm results of all investigated groups, these three markers were selected to be endogenous reference at both 15°Cand 25°C. On the contrary, ACTB and GAPDH always showed particularly high M values in three tissues, so these two markers were selected as target markers to estimate PMI for their susceptibility against degradation affected by postmortem interval.

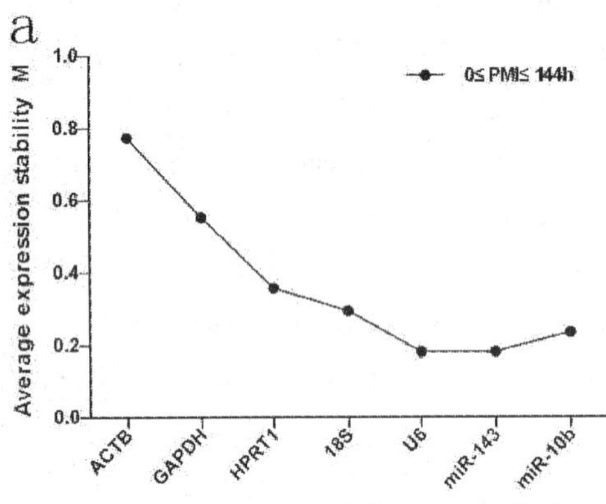

Average expression stability meassure M of reference genes in postmortem adipose tissue at 15°C

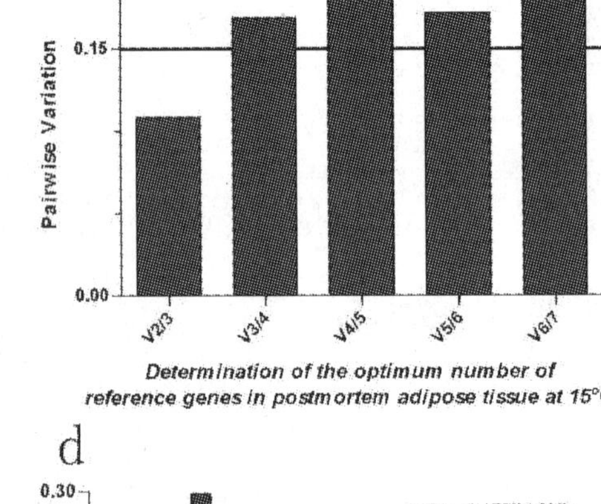

Determination of the optimum number of reference genes in postmortem adipose tissue at 15°C

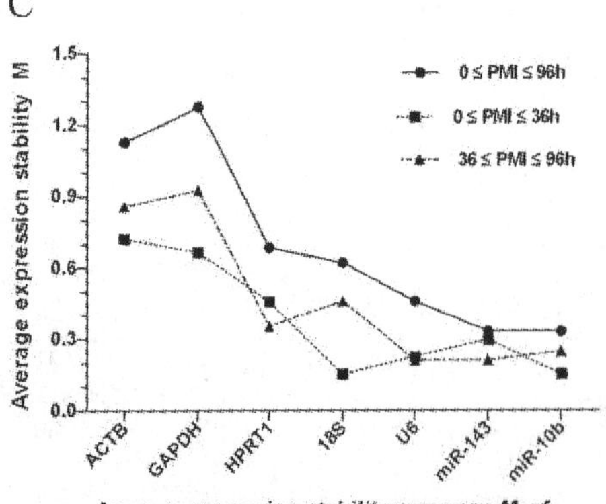

Average expression stability meassure M of reference genes in postmortem adipose tissue at 25°C

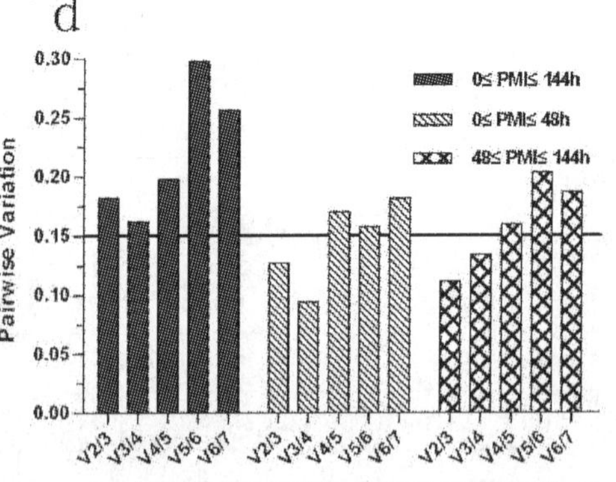

Determination of the optimum number of reference genes in postmortem adipose tissue at 25°C

Fig 1 Average expression stability of seven refernece genes and determianation of the minimal number of control genes required for data normalization at 15°C (a, b) and at 25°C

2.3 Relationship between PMI and delta Ct values of candidate genes

Delta Ct values represents the differences between the Ct values of target markers (ACTB and GAPDH) and the geometrical mean Ct values of stable markers (miR – 143, miR – 10b and U6). Curve estimation analysis between delta Ct values and PMI were performed by 6 mathematical model functions (linear, quadratic, cubic, reciprocal, exponential and logarithmic). The cubic model function showed a better correlation than the other models ($p < 0.05$) (data not shown). The relations between delta Ct values and PMI were presented in Fig. 2a (GAPDH) and Fig. 2b (ACTB) and corresponding mathematical equations with R^2 were given in Table 3, respectively. Both ACTB and GAPDH showed a close relationship with postmortem intervals, and the increments of delta Ct values were significantly affected by temperatures, which increased faster at 25°C than at 15°C.

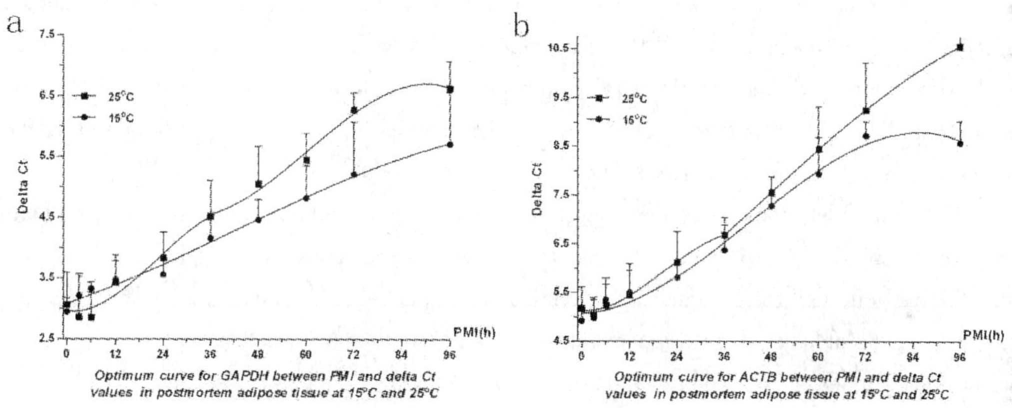

Fig 2 Optimum curves of GAPDH (a) and ACTB (b) between PMI and Delta – Ct values

Table 3 Best mathematical model functions used to describe the time courses of delta Ct values for GAPDH and ACTB in postmortem adipose tissue

T (°C)	RNA marker	PMI (h)	Optimum curve equation	R^2
15	GAPDH	[0, 96]	$Y = 3.083 + 0.023x + 1.973 * 10^{-4}x^2 - 1.589 * 10^{-6}x^3$	0.793
25	GAPDH	[0, 36]	$Y = 2.960 - 0.009x + 0.003x^2 - 4.806 * 10^{-5}x^3$	0.685
25	GAPDH	[36, 96]	$Y = 6.913 - 0.176x + 0.004x^2 - 2.11 * 10^{-5}x^3$	0.843
15	ACTB	[0, 96]	$Y = 5.071 + 0.004x + 0.001x^2 - 1.137 * 10^{-5}x^3$	0.902
25	ACTB	[0, 36]	$Y = 5.134 - 0.008 + 0.003x^2 - 5.546 * 10^{-5}x^3$	0.713
25	ACTB	[36, 96]	$Y = 4.381 + 0.049 + 5.619 * 10^{-4}x^2 - 4.196 * 10^{-6}x^3$	0.831

2. 4 Validation of mathematical models

We decided to challenge our system by sampling adipose tissues from intact rat corpses at 10, 20, 30, 50 and 80h after death at both t 15°C and 25°C. The PMI was calculated using the equation shown in Table 3 by taking delta Ct values for both GAPDH and ACTB. Remarkably, the medium PMI values obtained were 12. 1 ±0. 9, 17. 6 ±1. 6, 32. 5 ±6. 1, 57. 3 ±4. 2 and 92. 1 ±4. 9 at 15°C and 11. 9 ±2. 3, 19. 5 ±1. 4, 36. 0 ±0. 7, 43. 0 ±4. 5 and 83. 5 ±6. 3 at 25°C, respectively. It seemed to be surmised PMIs at 15°C were not as accurate as at 25°C.

3 *Discussion*

Postmortem interval is defined as the time interval between death and the examination of the deceased. Current methods of PMI estimation are often rough and not repeatability, so reliable and reproducible methods to determine the time since death for the extended postmortem interval are still required. With the development of molecular biology, recently, RT – qPCR has been used widely in the research of PMI. This method, characterized by sensitivity and specificity, is a powerful tool of quantifying gene expression level with great efficiency in signal detection. It was reported that some organs like brain, heart and skeletal muscle showed great stability up to 96h postmortem, [21, 22] but these organs were not suitable to estimate early PMI. Nevertheless, the enzymatic activity activated immediately after body death and RNA degraded rapidly due to abundant nuclease in adipose. It's helpful to accurately estimate early PMI by figuring out how and when RNA degradate.

An ideal endogenous reference marker is extremely important for estimating PMI; it should show relatively stable expression after death. Therefore, the study of correct normalization of quantitative gene expression data is a crucial point to get reliable results. [15, 23] With the help of geNorm, it's able to identify the endogenous markers with the most stable amount of transcript among a set of 7 candidate reference genes. We considered that the primary task was to find the special makers which were not or less influenced by PMI. Within all PMIs, miR – 10b, miR – 143 and U6 showed the most stable RNA expression at 15°C. However, none reliable normalization gene was found due to long PMIs at 25°C but when using a 0. 15 cut – off of pairwise variation. Then we sequenced all the samples by the PMI and re – examined these reference by geNorm software. According to the cut – off value as 0. 15, miR – 143 and miR – 10b always occupied the first three positions of most stable markers at 25°C. Prerna Sethi [24] found some specific miRs showed relatively short half – life and a limited stability of early PMI. The results confirmed our hypothesis, which microRNA was less susceptible against degradation affected by PMI and by environmental conditions since its tiny length of only 21 –25 bp. U6 snRNA is belong to small nuclear RNA family which is also involved with protein complex, called small nuclear ribonucleoprotein particle (Sn RNP), and only exist in the eukaryotic nuclear. [19, 25] Short hairpin structure it has and no nuclease found in the nuclear may endow U6 the perfect stability.

Many housekeeping mRNA genes were studied for postmortem interval estimation, including ACTB, GAPDH, CyA, TBP, HPRT1 and so on. [14, 15, 20, 26] These genes were frequently used endogenous reference genes in RT – qPCR data analysis in general molecular biology experiment, but they showed a close relationship with PMI, it's unsuitable to be used as endogenous reference markers. In present study, ACTB and GAPDH always showed particularly high M values, which indicated that these two markers were highly correlated with PMI. Bauer [10] had pointed out that the degradation of target gene fraction located near the 5' – end of mRNA is faster than fragment located towards the 3' – end of mRNA, and therefore, it is better to choose the target gene sequence located at the 5' – end of mRNAs when using mRNAs to estimate PMI. Based on this theory, we chose ACTB and GAPDH gene sequences located near the 5′– end of corresponding mRNAs to eliminate the variance due to the location along the transcripts. Since RNA degradation was only related with PMI at each temperature group, ACTB and GAPDH were selected as target markers to determine PMI in present study for their high susceptibility against degradation. In a sense, the main goal of PMI – related studies was to develop mathematical model to describe the behavior of gene transcripts decay over PMI, no exception of this study. After curve estimation, optimum mathematical models for both ACTB and GAPDH were also significantly correlated PMI. In addition, the process of mRNA degradation probably is significantly slowed down at lower temperature, [10, 26] thus the increment of delta Ct values at each time point were generally higher at 25°C than at 15°C. Nevertheless, under higher ambient temperatures, the specific pattern of mRNA degradation appeared earlier, thus helpful to estimate PMI more accurate in the early PMI.

The results of this study impelled us to develop a mathematical model to describe the behavior of the identified gene transcripts decay over PMI as a valuable tool for forensic pathologists. In order to validate our mathematical model, we applied it using adipose specimens recovered from rat corpses kept 10, 20, 30, 50 and 80 hours at 15°C and 25°C, without any control on environmental or microbiological conditions. After validation, the results demonstrate the reliability of this mathematical model, which represents a new progress to increase the accuracy of PMI estimation and even becomes a practical tool for forensic experts. Though the method of RT – qPCR was very reliable and accurate for analysis of RNA level in the specimens from autopsy samples, the influences of such as temperature, age, sex, cause of death, pathological state and other external factors have to be taken into account, so practical application to estimate PMI is much more complicated than the experimental condition. In the future, brain injury, massive hemorrhage and mechanical asphyxia model of animals will be made with more groups of diverse ambient temperatures and more different organs. We have been trying to collect the human body sample for PMI estimation all the time. And more importantly, we will do our efforts to include of human samples and transfer the mathematical functions of animal models to human field study by this RT – qPCR method.

4 *Conclusion*

Currently, we devote ourselves to screen new molecular biological markers from our well designed animal model. With the assistance of geNorm, a quantitative analysis of seven RNA transcripts allowed the identification of GAPDH and ACTB that were found to significantly correlate with PMI in postmortem adipose tissues. Meanwhile, miR – 143, miR – 10b and U6 were found to be appropriate control markers, which were less affected by PMI and temperature. These results allowed us to develop mathematical functions to estimate PMI and fitted formulas for estimating PMI had been given (Table 3). After validation, the relatively low error of estimated PMI confirmed that this method may represent a new paradigm to estimate PMI and become a complementary tool for traditional methods, with the ultimate goal to increase the accuracy of the PMI estimation. Furthermore, the suitability of these strategies for postmortem human autopsy material as well as the influence of the various parameters (eg. age, sex, cause of death and storage conditions of the body) will be addressed in future studies.

References

[1] Chandra J, Sabharwal K. Determination of time since death from a study of various postmortem changes, *J Indian Med Assoc*, 1968, 51 (7), pp. 336 ~41.

[2] Henssge C, Althaus L, Bolt J, Freislederer A, Haffner HT, Henssge CA, et al. Experiences with a Compound Method for Estimating the Time Since Death. I. Rectal Temperature Nomogram for Time Since Death, *Int J Legal Med*, 2000, 113 (6), pp. 303 ~ 19.

[3] Henssge C, Althaus L, Bolt J, Freislederer A, Haffner HT, Henssge CA, et al. Experiences with a Compound Method for Estimating the Time Since Death. II. Integration of Non – Temperature – Based Methods, *Int J Legal Med*, 2000, 113 (6), pp. 320 ~31.

[4] Mel'Nikov I, Postmortem changes in the liver as a criterion for the establishment of the time of death (experimental study), *Sud Med Ekspert*, 1969, 12 (4), pp. 20 ~3.

[5] Dmitrienko I, Kononenko VI, Lakiza BS. Postmortem Changes in Bone Marrow Tissue as a Criterion of Time of Death, *Sud Med Ekspert*, 1983, 26 (4), pp. 19 ~21.

[6] Bocaz – Beneventi G, Tagliaro F, Bortolotti F, Manetto G, Havel J. Capillary Zone Electrophoresis and Artificial Neural Networks for Estimation of the Post – Mortem Interval (PMI) Using Electrolytes Measurements in Human Vitreous Humour, *Int J Legal Med*, 2002, 116 (1), pp. 5 ~11.

[7] Poloz YO, O'Day DH. Determining Time of Death: Temperature – Dependent Postmortem Changes in Calcineurin A, MARCKS, CaMKII, and Protein Phosphatase 2A in Mouse, *Int J Legal Med*, 2009, 123 (4), pp. 305 ~14.

[8] Matuszewski S. Estimating the Preappearance Interval from Temperature in Creophilus Maxillosus L. (Coleoptera: Staphylinidae), *J Forensic Sci*, 2012, 57 (1), pp. 136 ~45.

[9] Kang S, Kassam N, Gauthier ML, O'Day DH. Post – Mortem Changes in Calmodulin Binding Proteins in Muscle and Lung, *Forensic Sci Int*, 2003, 131 (2 ~3), pp. 140 ~7.

[10] Bauer M, Gramlich I, Polzin S, Patzelt D. Quantification of mRNA Degradation as Possible Indicator of Postmortem Interval—a Pilot Study, *Leg Med (Tokyo)*, 2003, 5 (4), pp. 220 ~7.

[11] Bustin SA, Benes V, Garson JA, Hellemans J, Huggett J, Kubista M, et al. The MIQE Guidelines: Minimum Information for Publication of Quantitative Real – Time PCR Experiments, *Clin Chem*, 2009, 55 (4), pp. 611 ~22.

[12] Vennemann M, Koppelkamm A. Postmortem mRNA profiling II: Practical Considerations, *Forensic Sci Int*, 2010, 203 (1 ~3), pp. 76 ~82.

[13] Elesha SO, Adepoju FB, Banjo AA. Rising Incidence of Cerebral Malaria in Lagos, Nigeria: a Postmoterm Study, *East Afr Med J*, 1993, 70 (5), pp. 302 ~6.

[14] Koppelkamm A, Vennemann B, Fracasso T, Lutz - Bonengel S, Schmidt U, Heinrich M. Validation of Adequate Endogenous Reference Genes for the Normalisation of qPCR Gene Expression Data in Human Post Mortem Tissue, *Int J Legal Med*, 2010, 124 (5), pp. 371 ~ 80.

[15] Romanowski T, Markiewicz A, Bednarz N, Bielawski KP. Housekeeping Genes as a Reference in Quantitative Real - Time RT - PCR, *Postepy Hig Med Dosw* (*Online*), 2007, 61, pp. 500 ~ 10.

[16] Griffiths - Jones S, Grocock RJ, van Dongen S, Bateman A, Enright AJ. miRBase: microRNA Sequences, Targets and Gene Nomenclature, *Nucleic Acids Res*, 2006, 34 (Database issue), pp. D140 ~ 4.

[17] Civelek M, Hagopian R, Pan C, Che N, Yang WP, Kayne PS, et al. Genetic Regulation of Human Adipose microRNA Expression and Its Consequences for Metabolic Traits, *Hum Mol Genet*, 2013.

[18] Li G, Li Y, Li X, Ning X, Li M, Yang G. MicroRNA Identity and Abundance in Developing Swine Adipose Tissue as Determined by Solexa Sequencing, *J Cell Biochem*, 2011, 112 (5), pp. 1318 ~ 28.

[19] Chen PS, Su JL, Cha ST, Tarn WY, Wang MY, Hsu HC, et al. MiR - 107 Promotes Tumor Progression by Targeting the Let - 7 microRNA in Mice and Humans, *J Clin Invest*, 2011, 121 (9), pp. 3442 ~ 55.

[20] Vandesompele J, De Preter K, Pattyn F, Poppe B, Van Roy N, De Paepe A, et al. Accurate Normalization of Real - Time Quantitative RT - PCR Data by Geometric Averaging of Multiple Internal Control Genes, *Genome Biol*, 2002, 3 (7), p. H34.

[21] Trotter SA, Brill LN, Bennett JJ. Stability of Gene Expression in Postmortem Brain Revealed by cDNA Gene Array Analysis, *Brain Res*, 2002, 942 (1 ~ 2), pp. 120 ~ 3.

[22] Yasojima K, McGeer EG, McGeer PL. High Stability of mRNAs Postmortem and Protocols for Their Assessment by RT - PCR, *Brain Res Brain Res Protoc*, 2001, 8 (3), pp. 212 ~ 8.

[23] Mehta R, Birerdinc A, Hossain N, Afendy A, Chandhoke V, Younossi Z, et al. Validation of Endogenous Reference Genes for RT - qPCR Analysis of Human Visceral Adipose Samples, *BMC Mol Biol*, 2010, 11, p. 39.

[24] Sethi P, Lukiw WJ. Micro - RNA Abundance and Stability in Human Brain: Specific Alterations in Alzheimer's Disease Temporal Lobe Neocortex, *Neurosci Lett*, 2009, 459 (2), pp. 100 ~ 4.

[25] Burke JE, Sashital DG, Zuo X, Wang YX, Butcher SE. Structure of the Yeast U2/U6 snRNA Complex, Rna, 2012, 18 (4), pp. 673 ~ 83.

[26] Henssge C, Althaus L, Bolt J, Freislederer A, Haffner HT, Henssge CA, et al. Experiences with a Compound Method for Estimating the Time since Death. I. Rectal Temperature Nomogram for Time Since Death, *Int J Legal Med*, 2000, 113 (6), pp. 303 ~ 19.

Genetic Analysis of 17 Y - chromosomal STRs Haplotypes of Chinese Manchu Ethnic Group Residing in Liaoning Province, Northern China

Shi Meisen, Jiang Lizhe, Zhang Zhong, Ma Shuhua, Bai Rufeng *

Population: A total of 261 unrelated, healthy male individuals of Chinese Manchu ethnic group, living in Shenyang, Liaoning province of China and the male children of 65 among these, confirmed by autosomal STR analysis using AmpFLSTR Identifiler Plus PCR amplification kit (Applied Biosystems), with paternity probability >99.9%, were studied. The sample collection was permitted by the Ethical Committee of Medical Faculty of Shantou University Medical College in this study and all participants signed the informed consent and provided the information about birthplace, parents and grandparents at the same time. Their ancestors had lived in the region for at least three generations. The Manchu ethnic minority, with a population of 10 682 263 (year of 2000), about 46.2 percent of the total live in Liaoning province of north China. The Manchu language is part of the Tungus - Manchu group, a branch of Altaic phylum. As the Manchu people have come into extensive contact with the country's Han Chinese majority over the centuries, they learned and adopted the Chinese language of the dominant Han.

DNA extraction: Genomic DNA was extracted from bloodstains using the Chelex - 100 protocol as described by Walsh et al.. [1]

PCR amplification: Amplification was carried out in GeneAmp PCR system 9700 (Applied Biosystems, Foster City, CA), using AmpFlSTRYfiler™ PCR Amplification kit, according to the manufacturer's recommendation.

Electrophoresis and typing: The amplified products were separated by capillary electrophoresis on ABI Prism1 3130 Genetic Analyzer (Applied Biosystems, USA) using GeneScan™ -500 LIZ internal size standard. The sample run data were analyzed together with an allelic ladder and positive and negative controls using GeneMapper ID Software Version 3.2 (Applied Biosystems, USA). The updated recommendations of the DNA Commission of the International Society of Forensic Genetics for analysis of Y - STR systems were followed. [3]

* Key Laboratory of Evidence Science (China University of Political Science and Law), Ministry of Education, 25 Xitucheng Road, Beijing 100088, PR China. Email: shimeisen2000@yahoo.com.cn.

Quality control: Our laboratory has participated in the Y - STR haplotype reference database (YHRD) quality assurance exercise in 2009 typing the YHRD core loci as well as additional loci DYS437, DYS448, DYS456, DYS458, DYS635 and Y - GATA - H4. The Y - STR haplotype data were contributed to the Y Chromosome STR Haplotype Reference Database (http: //www. yhrd. org), with the accession number YA003590.

Analysis of Data: Allelic frequencies were estimated by direct gene - counting. Gene and haplotype diversities were calculated according to the formula by Nei. [4] The discrimination capacity was calculated as the proportion of different haplotypes in the sample. Pairwise values of Rst were calculated to measure the genetic distance corresponding to SWGDAM haplotypes (DYS19, DYS389I, DYS389II, DYS390, DYS391, DYS392, DYS393, DYS385a, DYS385b, DYS438, DYS439) of Manchu sample and compared with 23 other published data[5-27] (Table S1), using ARLEQUIN software Version 3. 1. [28] To illustrate the relationship between populations based on pairwise Rst, a multidimensional scaling (MDS) plot was built utilizing the PHYLIP v3. 6 program. [29] In population comparisons, the haplotype 116 was not considered.

Results: Supplementary Table 1 summarizes the allele frequencies of 17 Y - STR loci, whilst Supplementary Table 2 lists the haplotypes of 261 unrelated Chinese Manchu ethnic individuals. The Rst values calculated to measure genetic distances between 11 Y - STR haplotypes of 23 neighbour populations ($n = 4, 920$) with the statistical significance were calculated in supplementary Table 3. Phylogenetic relationships between Manchu sample and referenced populations was assessed using MDS (Fig. 1) analyses.

Other remarks: Among the 17 Y - STR loci analyzed, DYS385a/b and DYS391 were calculated to be the highest (0. 9711) and lowest (0. 4792) values for gene diversity, respectively. Ninety - seven alleles and fifty - three phenotypes (DYS385a/b) were detected, with the allele frequencies ranging from 0. 0038 to 0. 6858 (Table S2). In the 65 father/son pairs with full profiles, 4 mutations were observed with the 17 Y - STR loci. Three of the mutations in DYS456 loci between father and son resulted in the gain of a repeat in the son while 1 mutations resulted in the loss of a repeat in DYS439. One sample (Ht116) observed a duplication (alleles 19 and 20) at DYS448 loci in both the father and son which demonstrates that these allele patterns can be inherited.

A total of 237 haplotypes were identified in the set of Y - STR loci, of which 224 (94. 51%) were unique. 9, 1, 1 and 2 haplotypes were shared by 2, 3, 4 and 5 individuals, respectively. The overall haplotype diversity for the set of Y - STRs loci was 0. 9988, and the discrimination capacity was 0. 9080. Our haplotype data were also compared against the data available at the Y Chromosome Haplotype Reference Database (YHRD, Release 43, currently including 83 350 haplotypes in 603 populations worldwide for SWGDAM haplotypes data set and 53 577 haplotypes in 382 populations worldwide for AmpFlSTR Yfiler haplotype data set. 165 (69. 62%) haplotypes detected in the Manchu population found zero matches in YHRD when SWGDAM haplotypes data were compared, and 215 (90. 72%) haplotypes were not previously observed when AmpFlSTR Yfiler haplotype were compared. The haplotypes which found matches in YHRD matched only to those detected in Asian populations. The haplotype #11 seen most frequently in Manchu population also found matches most frequently in YHRD (16 hits in the AmpFlSTR Yfiler haplotype database).

A total of 23 reference populations from the published literature were included for comparison across SWGDAM haplotypes (DYS19, DYS389I, DYS389II, DYS390, DYS391, DYS392, DYS393, DYS385a, DYS385b, DYS438 and DYS439), since the data for the remaining loci typed in this study were not reported for all reference collections. AMOVA analysis showed that 90. 15% of the variation was found within populations, whereas 9. 85% was among populations (fixation index FST = 0. 09124, P = 0. 00000). Pairwise analysis showed no significant differences ($P > 0.05$) in the comparison of the Manchu population with Han populations from Northeast, Sichuan, and Yunnan (0. 00206, 0. 00387, and 0. 00579, respectively). With typical south part of China Han populations from Minnan, HongKong, Taiwan and Singapore, although significant, low Rst values were obtained (0. 02105, 0. 01255, 0. 02452, and 0. 01327, respectively). In the comparison with the remaining Chinese minority ethnic groups, highly significant distances were observed (P = 0. 0000), with the corresponding Rst value ranging from 0. 02757 to 0. 32167. The significant difference between the two Chinese Manchu samples (Rst = 0. 03879; P = 0. 0000) may be due to sampling variations, and so these cannot be summed up and used as an overall Chinese Manchu ethnic database.

The Singapore Chinese population has affinities with populations from HongKong, Taiwan and Chaoshan. This may be explained by the large migration (many Chinese emigrated from Guangdong and Fujian to Singapore) of China to Southeast Asia between the end of 19th century and the beginning of 20th century, which results in the smaller differences in whole genetic structure among those regions.

Fig. 1 shows a multi – dimensional scaling plot built from the Rst distance matrices where 24 populations have been included. Two Chinese Manchu populations are closer with the China Han origin populations compared with other Chinese minority ethnic groups. This is probably their ancestors mixed more with Han Chinese, Mongolian and Koreans in their early settlement. They governed and greatly influenced China history for more than 300 years during Qing Dynasty.

These results demonstrated significant population heterogeneity, in this case attributable to the differentiation of China, presumably because of differences in ancestral components. In conclusion, these data in Chinese Manchu population could be potentially useful for the regional specific and prerequisite reference to the forensic, genealogical, and evolutionary purposes.

This paper strictly followed the guidelines for publication data requested by the journal and the ISFG recommendations.[30, 31]

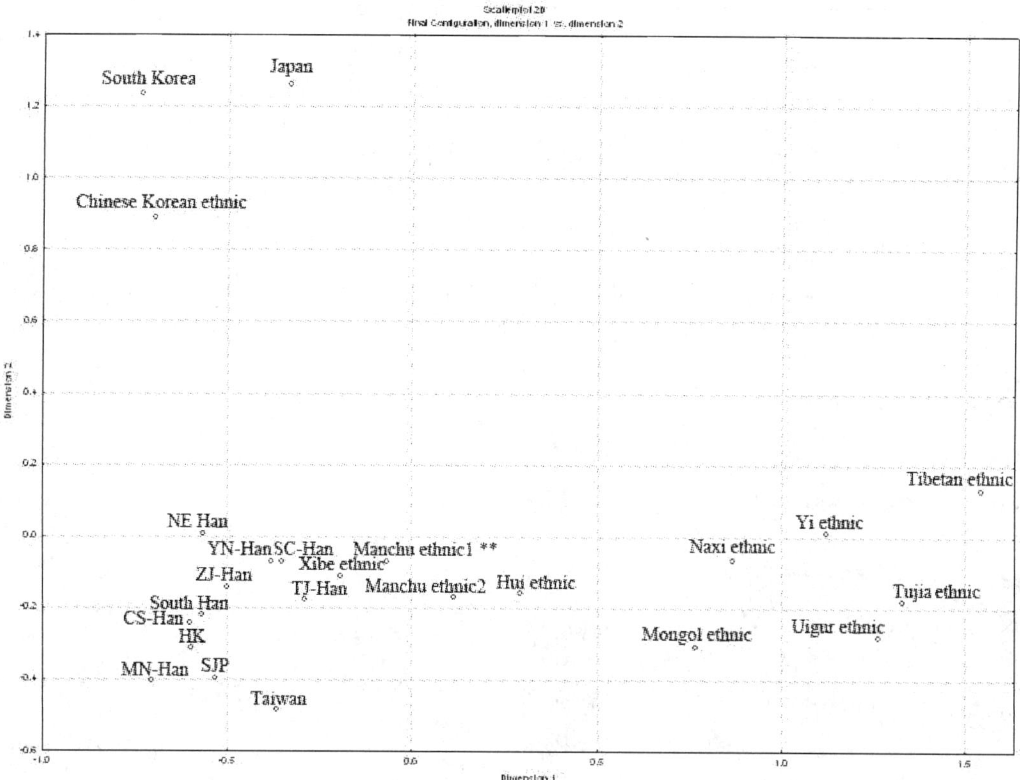

Fig 1 Multi – dimensional scaling plot based on pairwise *Rst* genetic distances using YHRD'11 Y – STR haplotypes' data for Manchu ethnic and 23 previously published populations

Table 1 Allele frequencies data of Y – STR haplotypes from 261 unrelated Chinese Manchu ethnic males

Allele	DYS 19	DYS 389I	DYS 389II	DYS 390	DYS 391	DYS 392	DYS 393	DYS 437	DYS 438	DYS 439	DYS 448	DYS 456	DYS 458	DYS 635	Y – GATA – H4	Allelic Class	DYS 385
7						0.0038										10 – 12	0.0038
8															0.0038	10 – 14	0.0038
9					0.0498				0.0192	0.0192						10 – 15	0.0038
10					0.6858	0.0153	0.0077	0.0077	0.5364	0.0728					0.0690	10 – 17	0.0115
11		0.0038			0.2184	0.1609	0.0153		0.2759	0.3525					0.2452	10 – 18	0.0077
12		0.4598			0.0460	0.1341	0.4330		0.1418	0.4253					0.5517	10 – 19	0.0038
13	0.0383	0.3640				0.3142	0.3870	0.0153	0.0268	0.0996		0.0307			0.1303	10 – 20	0.0115
14	0.3103	0.1379				0.2835	0.1494	0.6054		0.0307		0.1111	0.0038			10 – 21	0.0038
15	0.3218	0.0345				0.0728	0.0077	0.3410				0.4521	0.1303			11 – 12	0.0038
16	0.2299					0.0153		0.0268				0.2414	0.2146			11 – 13	0.0268
17	0.0958							0.0038			0.0038	0.1188	0.2797			11 – 14	0.0230

续表

Allele	DYS 19	DYS 389I	DYS 389II	DYS 390	DYS 391	DYS 392	DYS 393	DYS 437	DYS 438	DYS 439	DYS 448	DYS 456	DYS 458	DYS 635	Y-GATA-H4	Allelic Class	DYS 385
18	0.0038										0.1494	0.0421	0.2452			11-15	0.0115
19				0.0038							0.3065	0.0038	0.0996	0.0843		11-16	0.0077
20				0.0038							0.4138		0.0268	0.2567		11-17	0.0421
19,20											0.0038					11-18	0.0268
21				0.0077							0.0843			0.2682		11-19	0.0115
22				0.0192							0.0230			0.2375		11-20	0.0077
23				0.4061							0.0153			0.1226		11-24	0.0038
24			0.0038	0.4061										0.0268		12-12	0.0383
25			0.0077	0.1456										0.0038		12-13	0.0498
26			0.0077	0.0077												12-14	0.0268
27			0.0805													12-15	0.0268
28			0.2452													12-16	0.0536
29			0.3065													12-17	0.0536
30			0.2720													12-18	0.0498
31			0.0536													12-19	0.0268
32			0.0230													12-20	0.0153
33																12-21	0.0153
34																13-13	0.0383
																13-14	0.0038
																13-16	0.0077
																13-17	0.0268
																13-18	0.0345
																13-19	0.0536
																13-20	0.0460
																13-21	0.0115
																13-22	0.0038
																14-16	0.0077
																14-17	0.0115
																14-18	0.0536
																14-19	0.0192
																14-20	0.0153
																14-21	0.0038
																15-15	0.0153
																15-17	0.0077
																15-18	0.0077
																15-19	0.0192
																15-20	0.0115
																15-21	0.0077
																16-18	0.0038
																16-19	0.0077
																16-20	0.0077
																16-23	0.0038
GD*	0.7395	0.6383	0.7649	0.6509	0.4792	0.7742	0.6425	0.5182	0.6173	0.6809	0.7073	0.7109	0.7910	0.7859	0.6161		0.9711

GD * = Gene diversity

Table 2 List of Y - chromosome haplotypes detected in 261 unrelated males in Chinese Manchu ethnic population

Ht	n	DYS 19	DYS 389I	DYS 389II	DYS 390	DYS 391	DYS 392	DYS 393	DYS 385 a/b	DYS 438	DYS 439	DYS 437	DYS 448	DYS 456	DYS 458	DYS 635	Y - GATA - H4
Ht1	1	17	13	29	25	10	11	13	12, 12	10	10	14	21	15	19	21	11
Ht2	1	16	13	30	23	10	13	12	12, 17	10	11	14	19	14	18	21	12
Ht3	1	16	15	30	23	10	13	13	10, 17	13	12	14	18	15	18	21	11
Ht4	4	14	12	30	24	10	11	13	15, 15	11	11	15	19	14	16	19	12
Ht5	1	15	12	30	23	10	14	13	13, 13	10	11	14	18	16	15	19	12
Ht6	3	14	12	28	23	10	14	12	13, 19	11	11	14	20	15	17	20	12
Ht7	2	16	12	28	25	10	13	12	12, 20	10	13	14	19	16	19	22	12
Ht8	1	13	14	30	24	10	14	13	15, 20	12	11	14	19	16	17	22	10
Ht9	1	15	13	30	24	10	14	13	12, 14	11	12	14	22	16	16	21	11
Ht10	2	17	12	27	25	10	13	12	14, 18	10	11	14	20	13	19	22	12
Ht11	5	16	13	29	24	10	11	13	12, 12	10	11	14	20	15	17	23	10
Ht12	1	17	12	29	24	10	13	12	12, 19	9	12	15	20	15	18	22	11
Ht13	1	15	12	27	24	10	13	12	12, 17	11	11	15	20	15	15	21	12
Ht14	1	14	14	29	23	11	16	15	11, 13	11	10	14	19	14	17	21	12
Ht15	1	14	12	28	24	10	15	12	14, 18	10	11	16	20	15	16	20	12
Ht16	1	14	12	28	24	10	14	12	15, 19	11	13	15	20	15	19	22	13
Ht17	1	16	15	30	22	10	13	13	10, 18	13	12	14	18	15	18	21	11
Ht18	1	15	12	28	24	10	12	12	12, 18	10	12	15	19	15	18	20	12
Ht19	1	14	13	28	24	10	14	12	13, 17	11	13	15	20	15	17	20	11
Ht20	1	16	13	30	23	10	11	14	11, 20	10	12	14	20	16	14	21	12
Ht21	1	16	12	29	25	10	13	12	12, 18	11	11	15	19	15	17	21	12
Ht22	1	14	12	28	23	10	14	12	13, 17	11	12	14	21	15	17	20	12
Ht23	1	14	12	27	24	10	14	12	13, 19	11	11	15	20	15	17	21	12
Ht24	1	15	13	29	24	10	13	14	12, 16	10	12	15	19	14	18	22	12
Ht25	1	16	13	31	24	11	13	12	12, 19	12	11	14	20	13	17	21	13
Ht26	1	14	12	29	23	10	11	14	12, 18	10	12	14	20	13	18	20	13
Ht27	1	15	13	30	23	10	13	14	12, 17	11	13	14	18	16	18	21	12
Ht28	1	15	13	30	23	10	13	12	11, 17	10	11	15	20	16	15	19	12
Ht29	1	15	12	29	24	10	13	13	12, 18	11	11	14	20	15	16	22	12
Ht30	1	15	11	30	24	11	13	13	12, 17	10	11	15	19	14	18	23	11
Ht31	1	17	14	31	25	11	11	13	11, 16	11	11	14	20	15	15	23	12
Ht32	1	15	13	28	21	9	11	13	11, 13	10	11	14	20	16	17	21	11
Ht33	1	16	12	29	21	10	12	13	12, 21	10	12	13	22	15	16	20	12
Ht34	2	17	12	28	23	10	11	14	11, 17	10	12	15	23	16	17	21	11
Ht35	1	16	13	29	25	10	11	13	12, 13	10	10	14	22	15	18	21	11
Ht36	1	14	12	28	23	10	13	13	12, 17	10	12	15	19	16	17	21	11

续表

Ht	n	DYS 19	DYS 389I	DYS 389II	DYS 390	DYS 391	DYS 392	DYS 393	DYS 385 a/b	DYS 438	DYS 439	DYS 437	DYS 448	DYS 456	DYS 458	DYS 635	Y-GATA-H4
Ht37	1	14	13	28	23	11	15	13	11, 13	10	10	14	19	15	16	22	13
Ht38	1	14	12	28	23	10	14	12	13, 18	11	12	14	20	15	17	20	11
Ht39	1	14	14	30	23	10	14	13	11, 12	10	10	13	18	13	16	20	11
Ht40	1	14	12	30	24	10	14	13	10, 12	10	10	14	22	15	16	23	12
Ht41	1	14	12	27	23	11	14	12	13, 19	11	12	15	20	17	18	20	12
Ht42	1	16	12	29	23	11	12	12	12, 16	10	14	15	20	16	18	20	12
Ht43	1	13	14	30	24	9	14	13	15, 21	12	11	14	19	15	18	22	10
Ht44	1	15	15	30	23	10	12	13	12, 20	10	12	14	19	15	18	22	12
Ht45	1	16	12	28	25	10	13	12	14, 17	10	13	13	20	14	17	22	13
Ht46	1	14	13	29	25	10	12	13	12, 14	12	11	14	18	15	18	22	12
Ht47	1	13	15	31	24	9	14	14	14, 21	11	11	14	19	16	16	22	10
Ht48	1	15	12	28	24	10	11	14	12, 18	10	12	14	18	16	19	21	11
Ht49	1	17	12	30	25	10	13	12	14, 17	10	12	14	19	14	19	22	13
Ht50	1	16	12	29	24	9	13	12	11, 19	10	10	15	17	15	16	21	12
Ht51	1	14	12	27	24	10	14	12	13, 17	11	11	17	20	15	16	20	12
Ht52	1	14	12	27	23	11	15	12	13, 19	11	12	15	20	17	18	21	12
Ht53	1	15	13	30	23	10	13	12	13, 20	10	11	15	20	14	16	21	12
Ht54	1	17	12	28	25	11	12	14	11, 14	12	12	15	17	15	16	23	12
Ht55	1	16	14	28	23	10	13	13	10, 21	13	12	14	18	15	17	21	11
Ht56	1	13	15	30	24	10	14	12	10, 15	10	12	14	18	16	16	22	12
Ht57	1	16	15	28	25	11	15	14	13, 13	10	12	14	19	15	18	22	11
Ht58	1	17	13	30	24	11	14	14	12, 15	11	13	15	18	16	19	20	12
Ht59	1	15	12	27	23	10	12	12	12, 14	10	12	15	20	15	19	21	11
Ht60	1	15	12	29	24	10	12	12	13, 17	10	11	14	19	16	17	21	12
Ht61	1	14	14	30	23	11	15	13	12, 13	10	11	14	23	16	18	21	12
Ht62	1	15	12	29	23	11	12	12	13, 17	10	12	14	19	16	17	19	12
Ht63	1	15	12	28	23	10	13	12	12, 16	10	12	15	19	15	18	20	13
Ht64	1	15	13	27	23	10	13	13	10, 18	13	13	14	18	15	17	20	13
Ht65	1	17	12	28	23	10	11	14	11, 17	10	12	15	23	16	17	21	11
Ht66	2	15	13	32	23	10	14	12	13, 18	11	12	14	20	15	17	21	12
Ht67	1	14	14	30	23	10	16	14	11, 13	12	10	14	19	14	17	23	12
Ht68	1	14	13	29	23	10	15	12	13, 19	11	12	15	20	18	18	20	12
Ht69	1	16	12	24	24	10	13	12	12, 17	10	12	15	19	15	17	21	11
Ht70	2	14	12	28	23	10	14	12	13, 19	11	12	14	20	15	18	20	12
Ht71	1	14	13	30	24	11	13	13	11, 14	12	12	14	18	16	18	22	13
Ht72	2	15	14	30	24	12	10	13	14, 20	11	11	16	19	15	17	24	12
Ht73	1	14	13	25	24	11	13	13	12, 14	12	11	14	20	16	19	23	11
Ht74	1	16	12	28	25	10	13	12	14, 19	10	12	14	20	14	17	23	12
Ht75	1	15	13	29	24	10	12	13	13, 20	9	12	15	20	16	18	22	12

续表

Ht	n	DYS 19	DYS 389I	DYS 389II	DYS 390	DYS 391	DYS 392	DYS 393	DYS 385 a/b	DYS 438	DYS 439	DYS 437	DYS 448	DYS 456	DYS 458	DYS 635	Y - GATA - H4
Ht76	1	15	14	32	23	10	11	14	11, 18	10	11	14	20	15	15	22	12
Ht77	1	16	14	30	22	10	12	14	12, 16	10	12	14	20	15	16	22	13
Ht78	1	15	12	28	24	12	14	13	13, 13	10	11	14	18	17	15	19	12
Ht79	1	15	12	27	24	10	13	13	14, 18	10	12	15	19	15	17	21	12
Ht80	1	17	12	28	25	12	13	13	12, 15	10	12	15	18	16	18	21	12
Ht81	1	16	14	29	23	10	12	14	10, 20	10	9	14	20	15	17	21	12
Ht82	1	14	13	30	24	11	13	13	12, 21	12	12	14	18	15	18	20	12
Ht83	1	17	13	31	25	10	11	12	16, 19	10	12	15	20	16	15	20	12
Ht84	1	14	13	29	24	11	13	14	11, 18	12	12	15	19	17	18	22	12
Ht85	1	15	12	29	23	10	13	12	12, 16	9	11	14	19	16	15	22	12
Ht86	1	16	13	29	24	10	11	12	11, 17	10	11	14	21	15	16	22	11
Ht87	1	14	12	27	24	10	15	10	13, 19	11	12	15	20	15	18	20	13
Ht88	1	14	13	27	24	10	16	10	14, 19	11	13	15	20	15	17	20	13
Ht89	1	16	12	27	25	10	13	12	14, 18	10	11	14	20	13	19	23	12
Ht90	1	15	14	30	25	11	13	11	11, 13	11	9	14	19	14	15	23	12
Ht91	1	17	13	29	25	10	13	12	14, 18	9	11	14	20	14	18	22	12
Ht92	1	15	13	29	23	10	12	12	12, 16	10	12	15	19	15	20	20	12
Ht93	1	17	12	29	25	10	13	12	12, 17	10	12	15	19	15	17	22	12
Ht94	1	15	14	30	24	12	10	13	14, 20	11	11	16	19	15	17	24	12
Ht95	1	16	12	27	24	10	13	12	15, 17	11	12	14	20	14	18	23	11
Ht96	1	16	13	27	25	11	12	12	15, 19	11	11	15	20	15	17	23	12
Ht97	1	15	13	31	24	10	11	13	13, 20	11	12	14	20	15	15	23	11
Ht98	1	15	12	29	24	10	13	12	13, 20	10	10	15	20	14	15	21	13
Ht99	1	17	13	25	24	11	13	13	15, 19	12	11	14	19	16	17	22	12
Ht100	1	15	13	28	23	10	13	14	12, 17	11	13	14	18	16	15	21	12
Ht101	1	15	14	30	24	10	12	12	12, 16	10	11	15	19	16	15	20	11
Ht102	1	17	12	29	24	10	13	12	12, 18	9	12	14	20	15	17	22	11
Ht103	1	15	12	29	23	10	12	12	12, 16	10	11	15	19	15	19	21	12
Ht104	1	16	13	29	23	10	12	11	12, 17	10	13	15	20	15	20	19	13
Ht105	1	16	13	29	23	10	14	13	13, 14	10	12	15	18	14	15	20	11
Ht106	1	17	13	30	25	11	13	12	13, 18	12	12	14	18	15	17	20	12
Ht107	1	14	13	26	23	10	13	13	11, 18	12	13	15	18	14	16	23	11
Ht108	1	15	13	29	24	10	12	12	12, 17	10	13	15	20	15	18	21	12
Ht109	1	16	15	31	24	10	13	13	12, 17	10	11	14	20	15	16	22	13
Ht110	1	15	12	26	23	10	12	12	12, 12	10	12	14	19	15	17	19	12
Ht111	1	15	13	30	24	11	13	14	11, 19	12	12	15	21	17	20	20	11
Ht112	1	14	12	30	24	10	14	11	13, 18	11	12	14	20	16	19	20	12
Ht113	1	18	12	30	23	10	11	13	15, 17	10	12	15	19	16	20	23	12
Ht114	3	15	12	29	23	12	14	13	13, 13	10	11	14	19	17	15	19	12

续表

Ht	n	DYS 19	DYS 389I	DYS 389II	DYS 390	DYS 391	DYS 392	DYS 393	DYS 385 a/b	DYS 438	DYS 439	DYS 437	DYS 448	DYS 456	DYS 458	DYS 635	Y-GATA-H4
Ht115	1	14	12	28	23	10	12	12	12, 18	10	13	15	19	15	17	19	12
Ht116	1	15	12	28	25	10	13	13	14, 18	10	11	14	19, 20	15	17	23	10
Ht117	1	14	13	29	23	11	15	13	12, 13	10	12	14	19	15	16	21	12
Ht118	1	15	13	29	23	11	12	12	14, 18	10	11	14	19	16	17	21	12
Ht119	1	16	12	28	24	11	15	13	12, 16	12	12	14	20	16	16	22	10
Ht120	1	17	15	30	24	12	12	13	15, 19	10	12	15	19	17	18	21	11
Ht121	1	14	13	29	24	11	13	13	12, 14	12	11	14	22	17	15	20	10
Ht122	1	15	12	31	26	12	14	14	16, 20	11	12	14	20	18	15	20	11
Ht123	1	17	13	30	25	10	14	14	11, 18	10	12	14	20	15	18	21	12
Ht124	1	16	12	31	23	10	11	13	12, 12	10	12	14	18	17	20	20	12
Ht125	1	15	13	30	23	10	14	12	12, 21	10	11	14	19	15	19	22	11
Ht126	1	15	13	29	23	10	7	14	14, 17	10	11	14	20	17	16	23	12
Ht127	1	17	12	30	24	10	13	12	12, 19	10	12	14	19	14	17	22	11
Ht128	1	14	12	28	24	10	12	12	13, 20	11	9	15	20	15	17	19	12
Ht129	5	14	13	29	23	10	15	13	12, 13	10	11	14	19	15	16	21	12
Ht130	1	14	12	30	24	11	14	12	13, 19	11	12	15	20	16	17	20	12
Ht131	1	13	13	29	24	11	15	12	14, 18	12	11	14	19	16	17	22	10
Ht132	1	16	13	28	23	11	12	14	12, 19	10	12	14	20	15	18	24	10
Ht133	1	15	13	29	23	11	13	13	15, 20	12	13	15	20	16	18	23	13
Ht134	1	16	12	28	24	10	14	12	13, 20	10	12	15	20	15	19	21	11
Ht135	1	14	12	28	23	10	14	12	13, 20	11	11	14	20	15	17	20	12
Ht136	1	13	12	28	23	10	14	12	15, 19	11	12	15	20	15	17	20	12
Ht137	1	15	12	29	24	11	14	12	13, 21	10	12	15	21	18	16	19	12
Ht138	1	16	12	29	23	10	12	13	12, 19	10	11	15	19	17	18	20	13
Ht139	1	14	13	29	23	10	15	13	12, 13	10	11	14	19	15	17	22	12
Ht140	1	14	13	30	24	11	13	13	11, 14	12	12	14	20	16	16	22	13
Ht141	1	15	14	30	25	11	13	13	12, 18	10	10	15	18	14	15	22	10
Ht142	1	15	15	28	23	10	13	13	13, 20	10	12	14	22	16	16	21	13
Ht143	1	16	12	27	23	10	11	13	12, 17	10	12	16	21	17	19	23	12
Ht144	1	16	12	27	24	11	13	13	12, 15	13	11	15	20	15	18	20	11
Ht145	1	14	13	29	24	11	13	14	11, 14	12	12	15	20	15	18	22	13
Ht146	1	15	12	28	23	10	12	12	12, 15	10	14	15	19	16	17	19	12
Ht147	1	13	14	30	24	9	14	14	16, 23	12	12	14	19	16	18	22	10
Ht148	1	16	13	31	24	10	11	14	11, 17	10	12	14	21	15	15	21	11
Ht149	1	15	13	29	23	10	12	12	12, 16	10	13	15	19	15	18	20	12
Ht150	1	15	13	29	23	10	11	14	11, 18	10	12	14	21	15	15	22	11
Ht151	1	15	12	30	23	11	14	12	12, 13	10	13	15	19	15	18	19	12
Ht152	1	16	13	30	24	10	12	14	10, 17	10	10	14	21	15	16	21	11
Ht153	1	17	12	29	25	9	13	14	10, 20	12	11	14	18	14	16	23	12

续表

Ht	n	DYS 19	DYS 389I	DYS 389II	DYS 390	DYS 391	DYS 392	DYS 393	DYS 385 a/b	DYS 438	DYS 439	DYS 437	DYS 448	DYS 456	DYS 458	DYS 635	Y-GATA-H4
Ht154	1	15	13	29	23	11	13	13	11, 14	12	13	14	19	15	18	22	13
Ht155	1	16	12	31	23	10	14	13	11, 20	10	10	14	20	14	17	22	12
Ht156	1	16	14	30	23	10	13	13	10, 20	13	11	14	18	16	16	20	11
Ht157	2	15	12	28	23	10	14	13	12, 13	10	12	14	19	15	16	20	12
Ht158	1	15	12	28	24	10	14	12	14, 18	11	12	15	20	15	17	20	12
Ht159	1	14	12	28	24	10	15	12	13, 17	11	11	16	20	16	17	20	13
Ht160	1	16	12	27	26	10	13	12	14, 18	10	11	14	20	13	20	22	12
Ht161	1	15	12	28	23	11	14	13	13, 13	10	11	14	18	18	15	19	13
Ht162	2	13	13	28	24	10	14	12	11, 17	12	11	14	18	17	16	22	12
Ht163	1	14	14	30	19	11	13	13	13, 13	10	13	15	19	15	16	24	11
Ht164	1	16	12	29	23	10	12	13	12, 18	10	11	10	20	19	18	22	13
Ht165	1	16	13	31	23	11	11	14	10, 17	10	11	14	21	15	16	22	11
Ht166	1	15	13	29	23	10	10	14	15, 18	10	11	14	21	16	19	21	12
Ht167	1	15	14	32	23	11	13	14	12, 17	10	12	14	18	15	16	22	13
Ht168	1	15	12	29	24	11	14	12	13, 21	10	12	15	20	16	18	20	12
Ht169	1	14	12	27	24	10	14	12	13, 20	11	11	15	20	16	17	20	12
Ht170	1	14	14	30	23	10	13	13	11, 15	12	13	15	18	17	18	20	12
Ht171	1	13	12	27	23	10	12	12	12, 16	10	12	15	19	15	18	19	12
Ht172	1	14	14	30	24	11	13	13	11, 15	12	11	14	19	16	15	20	12
Ht173	1	15	12	29	23	10	14	13	13, 13	10	11	14	19	17	15	20	12
Ht174	1	14	13	30	24	11	13	13	11, 17	12	11	14	20	17	16	22	11
Ht175	1	15	13	29	24	10	13	13	12, 16	10	10	14	18	16	15	21	12
Ht176	1	17	14	29	23	10	11	13	12, 12	10	12	14	18	17	15	20	12
Ht177	1	15	12	30	24	10	13	12	11, 17	11	10	14	20	16	15	22	12
Ht178	1	16	14	28	25	10	14	13	14, 16	10	12	15	20	16	19	20	13
Ht179	1	15	13	29	24	11	13	13	13, 18	10	12	10	18	17	16	23	12
Ht180	1	15	14	32	23	10	11	12	13, 16	11	12	13	21	15	17	20	11
Ht181	1	15	14	29	23	10	14	13	13, 19	10	12	14	21	15	18	20	11
Ht182	1	16	14	30	23	11	13	12	12, 19	10	14	15	21	14	17	23	11
Ht183	2	14	12	28	24	10	14	12	13, 18	11	12	15	20	15	16	21	13
Ht184	1	14	13	32	25	10	14	12	11, 19	11	9	14	20	17	17	20	13
Ht185	1	14	12	29	23	10	14	12	14, 19	11	9	15	18	15	16	20	13
Ht186	1	14	13	30	23	10	13	13	11, 14	12	13	15	21	14	17	21	12
Ht187	1	14	13	29	25	11	14	13	12, 12	13	14	14	21	15	17	22	13
Ht188	1	16	12	30	23	11	14	13	13, 13	10	12	14	18	16	15	19	12
Ht189	1	14	14	30	24	10	13	13	12, 15	12	11	14	18	17	16	21	13
Ht190	1	14	12	28	24	10	14	12	13, 18	11	14	15	20	15	17	20	11
Ht191	1	14	14	30	22	9	11	13	12, 17	10	12	16	21	16	19	22	12
Ht192	1	14	12	30	23	10	14	12	13, 16	11	12	14	20	15	17	20	12

续表

Ht	n	DYS 19	DYS 389I	DYS 389II	DYS 390	DYS 391	DYS 392	DYS 393	DYS 385 a/b	DYS 438	DYS 439	DYS 437	DYS 448	DYS 456	DYS 458	DYS 635	Y-GATA-H4
Ht193	1	14	14	30	24	10	12	12	12, 18	11	14	14	20	17	18	21	12
Ht194	1	15	12	28	25	10	14	11	12, 16	12	13	15	20	15	18	21	11
Ht195	1	16	14	31	24	11	14	12	13, 19	11	12	14	18	15	19	21	10
Ht196	1	14	12	31	25	10	13	13	12, 14	12	12	15	18	17	17	23	8
Ht197	1	15	13	28	24	10	15	13	12, 15	10	10	14	20	18	16	25	11
Ht198	1	14	12	30	24	12	14	12	14, 18	11	11	15	19	16	16	24	12
Ht199	1	15	12	28	24	10	11	14	11, 13	10	11	14	20	18	15	24	12
Ht200	1	15	12	29	23	10	14	12	13, 20	10	12	14	18	16	16	20	11
Ht201	1	16	14	30	24	11	13	12	12, 16	11	14	15	19	16	18	21	11
Ht202	1	14	13	29	24	11	13	13	12, 14	12	11	14	20	17	15	20	10
Ht203	1	15	12	31	24	12	14	12	16, 18	11	12	14	20	18	15	20	12
Ht204	1	15	13	30	25	10	14	14	14, 18	10	12	14	20	16	18	21	12
Ht205	1	16	12	29	23	10	11	13	12, 15	10	12	14	18	17	20	20	12
Ht206	1	14	13	30	23	10	14	12	12, 18	10	11	14	20	18	19	22	11
Ht207	1	15	13	29	23	10	12	14	14, 19	10	11	14	20	17	18	23	12
Ht208	1	16	12	28	24	10	13	12	12, 19	10	12	14	19	15	18	22	11
Ht209	1	15	12	28	24	10	12	12	15, 18	11	10	14	20	16	17	19	12
Ht210	1	15	13	30	23	10	14	13	12, 13	10	12	14	20	18	16	21	12
Ht211	1	14	13	30	24	11	14	12	13, 19	11	12	14	19	16	17	20	12
Ht212	1	15	13	30	24	11	15	12	14, 18	12	11	14	19	17	18	22	10
Ht213	1	16	12	28	23	10	12	12	16, 19	10	12	14	20	17	18	22	11
Ht214	1	15	13	29	23	11	13	13	15, 20	12	13	15	20	16	18	23	12
Ht215	1	14	12	28	24	10	14	12	13, 20	10	12	14	20	15	19	21	11
Ht216	1	14	14	30	24	9	14	14	16, 20	12	11	14	19	15	19	22	11
Ht217	1	16	13	29	23	10	11	15	13, 17	10	11	14	21	16	16	21	13
Ht218	1	15	13	29	24	11	11	13	10, 14	11	14	14	20	18	18	21	11
Ht219	1	16	12	28	25	10	13	12	12, 20	10	12	14	19	14	18	22	11
Ht220	1	15	12	29	24	10	13	12	12, 18	11	10	15	20	15	17	21	12
Ht221	1	14	13	29	24	11	13	12	11, 16	12	12	15	19	14	16	23	12
Ht222	1	17	13	28	24	10	12	13	12, 18	10	12	15	19	15	19	21	12
Ht223	1	14	13	30	23	10	11	12	11, 17	10	10	14	20	16	18	21	11
Ht224	1	14	13	30	25	10	16	12	14, 19	11	12	15	20	17	18	20	12
Ht225	1	15	13	30	22	10	13	12	11, 13	10	13	15	19	15	17	20	11
Ht226	1	16	13	29	24	10	13	13	14, 20	10	13	14	21	13	18	22	12
Ht227	1	16	13	29	20	10	11	14	11, 18	10	11	14	21	15	15	22	11
Ht228	1	16	14	30	25	11	11	12	11, 15	11	12	14	20	15	17	23	12
Ht229	1	15	13	28	25	10	11	13	11, 18	11	10	14	20	15	18	23	12
Ht230	1	17	12	28	24	10	13	12	12, 21	10	11	14	18	14	18	22	13
Ht231	1	15	14	29	22	10	11	14	10, 19	10	12	14	21	18	17	21	10

续表

Ht	n	DYS 19	DYS 389I	DYS 389II	DYS 390	DYS 391	DYS 392	DYS 393	DYS 385 a/b	DYS 438	DYS 439	DYS 437	DYS 448	DYS 456	DYS 458	DYS 635	Y-GA TA - H4
Ht232	1	14	12	28	23	10	14	12	13, 21	11	13	15	20	15	16	20	11
Ht233	1	14	12	29	24	10	14	12	13, 22	11	12	15	20	16	19	21	12
Ht234	1	16	12	28	23	10	11	14	11, 24	10	12	14	21	14	15	21	11
Ht235	1	14	12	28	25	10	14	12	13, 20	11	12	15	19	15	17	20	12
Ht236	1	14	12	27	23	10	14	12	15, 21	11	12	14	20	15	18	20	11
Ht237	1	16	12	29	25	10	13	12	14, 16	10	12	14	19	16	16	22	12

Acknowledgements

We thank all sample donors for their contributions to this work and all those who helped with sample collection. This study was supported by The National Natural Science Foundation of China (NSFC. No. 81172902), and The Program for New Century Excellent Talents in University (No. NCET - 10 - 0773), and the New - Star Program of Science and Technology of Beijing Metropolis (2010B073), and the Program for Young Innovative Research Team in China University of Political Science and Law.

References

[1] P. S. Walsh, D. A. Metzger, R. Higuchi, Chelex 100 as a Medium for Simple Extraction of DNA for PCR - Based from Forensic Material, *Biotechniques*, 10 (1991), pp. 506 ~ 513.

[2] J. J. Mulero, C. W. Chang, L. M. Calandro, R. L. Green, Y. Li, C. L. Johnson, L. K. Hennessy, Development and Validation of the AmpFlSTRYfiler PCR Amplification Kit: a Male Specific, Single Amplification 17 Y - STR Multiplex System, *J. Forensic Sci.*, 51 (2006), pp. 64 ~ 75.

[3] L. Gusma ~ o, J. M. Butler, A. Carracedo, P. Gill, M. Kayser, W. R. Mayr, N. Morling, M. Prinz, L. Roewer, C. Tyler - Smith, P. M. Schneider, DNA Commission of the International Society of Forensic Genetics (ISFG): An Update of the Recommendations on the Use of Y - STRs in Forensic Analysis, *Forensic Sci. Int.*, 157 (2006), pp. 187 ~ 197.

[4] M. Nei, *Molecular Evolutionary Genetics*, Columbia University Press, New York, 1987, pp. 176 ~ 179.

[5] B. Q. Yang, M. B. Gu, G. Wang, X. P. Li, Y. C. Liu, W. S. Yang, Population Data for 11 Y - Chromosome STRs in Northeast China Han, *Forensic Sci. Int.*, 164 (2006), pp. 65 ~ 71.

[6] J. Z. Kuang, T. G. Nie, Y. Liu, M. N. Liu, Y. J. Wang, Polymophisms of 12 Y - STR Loci in Han Population in Tianjin, *Forensic Sci. Technol.* (China), 1 (2005), pp. 19 ~ 26.

[7] Y. J. Zhang, H. J. Zhang, Y. Cui, H. Cui, Q. S. Xu, S. Sun, L. P. Sun, J. B. Lee, Population Genetics for Y - Chromosomal STRs Haplotypes of Chinese Korean Ethnic Group in Northeastern China, *Forensic Sci Int.*, 173 (2007), pp. 197 ~ 203.

[8] R. F. Bai, M. S. Shi, X. J. Yu, J. S. Zhang, L. Bai, Y - Chromosomal STRs Haplotypes in Chinese Manchu Ethnic Group, *Forensic Sci Int Genet.*, 3 (2008), pp. e13 ~ e15.

[9] M. S. Shi, R. F. Bai, , L. Bai, X. J. Yu, Population Genetics for Y - Chromosomal STRs Haplotypes of Chinese Xibe Ethnic Group, *Forensic Sci Int Genet.*, 5 (2011), pp. e119 ~ e121.

[10] R. F. Bai, M. S. Shi, X. J. Yu, L. Chang, Y - Chromosomal STRs Haplotypes in Chinese Hui Eth-

nic Group, *Forensic Sci Int Genet.*, 3 (2008), pp. e17 ~ e19.

[11] B. F. Zhu, Z. Y. Wang, C. H. Yang, X. S. Li, J. Zhu, G. Yang, P. Huang, Y. Liu, Y – chromosomal STR Haplotypes in Chinese Uigur Ethnic Group, *Int. J. Legal Med.*, 119 (2005), pp. 306 ~ 309.

[12] B. F. Zhu, X. S. Li, Z. Y. Wang, H. Y. Wu, Y. F. He, J. Zhao, Y. Liu, Y – STRs Haplotypes of Chinese Mongol Ethnic Group Using Y – PLEXTM12, *Forensic Sci. Int.*, 153 (2005), pp. 260 ~ 263.

[13] Y. K. Chen, Q. Li, D. C. Li, Z. H. Deng, Study on the Genentic Polymorphism of 17 Y – Chromosome Specific STR Loci of Non – Related Male Individuals in Southern Chinese Han Population, *Experimental&Lab Med.*, 26 (2008), pp. 351 ~ 354, 386.

[14] S. P. Hu, Polymorphism of Y – Chromosomal STR Haplotypes in the Chaoshan Han Chinese in South China, *Forensic Sci Int.*, 158 (2006), pp. 80 ~ 85.

[15] S. P. Hu, Genetic polymorphism of 12 Y – Chromosomal STR Loci in the Minnan Han Chinese in Southeast China, *Forensic Sci Int.*, 159 (2006), pp. 77 ~ 82.

[16] W. W. Wu, X. T. Zheng, L. P. Pan, H. L. Hao, T. Fu, A Study of Polymorphisms of 16 Y – STR Loci in Han Population in Zhejiang, *Forensic Science and Technology* (*China*), 5 (2005), pp. 11 ~ 17.

[17] S. M. Yeung, L. M. Wong, B. K. K. Cheung, K. Y. To, Allele Frequencies and Haplotypes of 12 Y – STR Loci for the Local Chinese Population in HongKong, *Forensic Sci. Int.*, 162 (2006), pp. 55 ~ 63.

[18] T. Huang, Y. Hsu, J. Li, J. Chung, C. Shun. Polymorphism of 17 Y – STR Loci in Taiwan Population, *Forensic Sci Int.*, 174 (2007), pp. 249 ~ 254.

[19] H. J. Zhang, L. B. Yun, Y. B. Li, J. Zhang, J. Wu, J. Yan, Y. P. Hou, Haplotype of 12 Y – STR Loci of the PowerPlex Y – System in Sichuan Han Ethnic Group in West China, *Forensic Sci Int.*, 175 (2008), pp. 244 ~ 249.

[20] X. H. Zhang, W. W. Wu, J. X. Tang, G. L. Qiang, X. M. Zhang, Polymorphisms of Eleven Y – Chromosome STR Loci and Forensic Application in Yunnan Han Population, *J. Forensic Med.*, 22 (2006), pp. 291 ~ 294.

[21] M. S. Shi, R. F. Bai, , L. H. Wan, X. J. Yu, L. Chang, Population Genetics for Y – Chromosomal STRs Haplotypes of Chinese Tujia Ethnic Group, *Forensic Sci Int Genet.*, 2 (2008), pp. e65 ~ e68.

[22] B. F. Zhu, S. Z. Liu, D. Ci, J. F. Huang, Y. C. Wang, L. P. Chen, J. Zhu, Y. C. Xu, Q. Z. Zhao, S. B. Li, Y. Liu, Population Genetics for Y – Chromosomal STRs Haplotypes of Chinese Tibetan Ethnic Minority Group in Tibet, *Forensic Sci Int.*, 161 (2006), pp. 78 ~ 83.

[23] B. F. Zhu, C. M. Shen, G. L. Qian, R. Y. Shi, Y. H. Dang, J. Zhu, P. Huang, Y. C. Xu, Q. Z. Zhao, J. Ma, Y. Liu, Genetic Polymorphisms for Eleven Y – STRs Haplotypes of Chinese Yi Ethnic Minority Group, *Forensic Sci. Int.*, 158 (2006), pp. 229 ~ 233.

[24] N. Xin, T. Chen, B. Yu, S. B. Li, 12 Y – STRs Haplotypes in Chinese Naxi Ethnic Minority Group, *Forensic Sci Int.*, 174 (2008), pp. 244 ~ 248.

[25] J. S. Tang, H. Y. Wong, C. K. Syn, W. F. Tan – Siew, S. T. Chow, B. Budowle, Population Study of 11 Y – Chromosomal STR Loci in Singapore Chinese, *Forensic Sci. Int.*, 158 (2006), pp. 65 ~ 71.

[26] M. Hashiyada, T. Nagashima, Y. Itakura, J. Sakai, Y. Kanawaku, J. Kanetake, M. Nata, M. Funayama, 12 Y – Chromosomal STR Haplotypes in Japanese, *Forensic Sci. Int.*, 158 (2006), pp. 204 ~ 212.

[27] B. W. Chun, S. C. Shin, Y. J. Kim, K. S. Kim, D. H. Choi, K. H. Kim, J. Y. Kim, H. S. Kang, Allele Frequencies and Haplotypes of the STR Loci of the PowerPlex Y – System in Southern Populations from Korea, *Forensic Sci Int.*, 148 (2005), pp. 225 ~ 231.

[28] http: // cmpg. unibe. eh//software//arlequin3. Arlequin Ver3. 1: An integrated software package

for population genetics.

[29] J . Felsentein, Phylogeny Inference Package (PHYLIP), version 3. 6a3. Department of Genetics, University of Washington, Seattle, distributed by author.

[30] L. Gusmao, J. M. Butler, A. Carracedo, P. Gill, M. Kayser, W. R. Mayr, N. Morling, M. Prinz, L. Roewer, C. Tyler - Smith, P. M. Schneider, DNA Commission of the International Society of Forensic Science Genetics (ISFG): An Update of the Recommendations on the Use of Y - STRs in Forensic Analysis, *Forensic Sci Int.* , 157 (2006), pp. 187 ~ 197.

[31] New Guidelines for the Publication of Genetic Population Data Forensic Science International: Genetics, 7 (2013), pp. 217 ~ 220.

中文签名笔迹检验研究

白晓峰 *

一、中文签名检验的现状

名虽然以不同的形式在我国流传了几千年，但是按传统的习惯，盖章则更加显得庄严、正规，人们对印章的信任度远远高于签名。即使是在现代，我国的金融系统对于支票而言也只是预留法人和法人代表人的公章和名章，很少见有个人的签名。直到距今17年前，《中华人民共和国票据法》（1996年1月1日）的颁布实施，才将签名以法定的形式表达出来，结束了只认盖章不认签名的历史。《票据法》中规定："票据上的签章，为签名、盖章或者签名加盖章。"法律同时还规定："在票据上的签名，应当为该当事人的本名。"所谓的本名，是指本人户籍和身份证上的姓名，即不能是其他形式的别名、化名、假名。所以，在经济往来和较为正规的场合中的签名都要求签写与其身份证一致的姓名。

在民事诉讼、行政诉讼、刑事诉讼的各类案件中，鉴定签名真伪的目的在于证明签名文件的真伪，或者证明签名人与案件之间的关系。可见，需要对签名进行鉴定的检材有各种票据、合同、契约、协议、证明、担保书、公证书、委托书、遗嘱，以及其他证件和公文等。随着社会的政治、经济的发展，法制的不断完善，签名笔迹检验的案件在我国的笔迹检验总的工作量中占据了近80%。如我学院的物证鉴定中心2011至2012这两年间共受理笔迹检验案件108件，其中刑事案件33件，约占总数的30%；民事案件75件，占总数的70%；涉及签名笔迹检验的案件74件，约占总数的78%。

二、中文签名的表现形式

西方严格区分签名与写名，并认为写名不能与签名相比较。[1]而我们没有这种意识，几乎所有的人，包括笔迹鉴定人在内不将写名与签名相区分。其根本的原因在于中外政治、经济、文化上存在的差异。西方很多人的签名为符号式的签名，类似于我们的花体签名，很多签名分不清是由哪些字母组成。这类签名书写速度较快，笔画线条流畅，很难被他人仿写，所以他们认为这种签名是真实可靠的，而用单个字母组合成的慢写名字，则很容易被他人仿造形成。实际上，由于汉字的所包含的笔画、构字部件，以及它们的时空顺序和位置安排错综复杂，所以中文签名不论是行书还是楷书，不论是快写还是慢写，不论是连接笔画还是单个笔画都存在可供进行观察和检验的特征点。中文签名常见的形式有楷书体、行草体、组合式（花体）、反向式和符号式5种。

---

* 白晓峰，中国刑事警察学院、文件检验技术系副教授。Email：zgxjxybxf@ sina. com。

〔1〕 贾玉文："'世纪争产案'签名鉴定和出庭作证"，载《第五届全国文检学理论与实践研讨会论文集》2006年印行，第8页。

（一）楷书体签名

楷书体签名，即一笔一画书写出来的正体字签名，单字内部的笔画之间不连贯。使用这种书体书写的名字与印刷字体相类似，是一种工整庄重的签名，就是我们常说的写名。这种签名由于书写速度较慢，结构清晰，与其他类型的签名相比较，确实是一种较为容易被他人仿造的一种类型（见图1 楷书体签名）。

（二）行草体签名

行草体签名，是为加快书写速度，加强了笔画之间的连接，以行书或草书体形式书写的名字。汉字的行书和草书在独体字、合体字的部件在结体上有着特殊的表现形式和标准，不是笔画间的随意连接（见图2 行草体签名）。

图1 楷书体签名

图2 行草体签名

图3 组合式签名

（三）组合式签名

组合式签名，亦称花体签名，在写法上突破了文字的书写规范与规则，是经过特殊设计，多在签名单字的结构上进行简化和重组而成，具有特殊的外部轮廓特点。这种签名难以辨读，具有很强的防伪性（见图3 组合式签名）。

（四）翻转式签名

翻转式签名，亦称反向签名，是经过自行设计书写的反字签名。这种签名多以行草体和花体签名为基础，从纸张的背面透光观察或从平面镜的映像中可以进行辨读（见图4 翻转式签名）。

（五）符号式签名

符号式的签名，是使用字母或自行设计、含有特殊意义的符号来代替本名的签名。这种签名他人无法辨读，一般情况下不能作为正规的签名使用，多为自己使用的一种标记性的签名（见图5 符号式签名）。

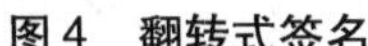

图4 翻转式签名

图5 符号式签名

三、中文签名的造假方式

签名的造假多见于伪造他人的签名，也有一小部分是自己恶意书写假名或伪装书写自己的签名。伪造他人签名常见的方法有直接代写、摹仿书写、使用印刷的方法进行复制等。

（一）直接代写

直接代写常见于邮件、工资、汇款等被冒领，或盗取他人信用卡进行消费的案件当中。这种方式书写的姓名一般表现的是作案人的书写技能和书写习惯，同其本人亲笔签名比较会发现存在很大的区别。

（二）摹仿书写

主要是利用临摹、套摹、描摹或经过大量练习后的忆摹这四种手段完成。前三种在书写的过程中有一个共同的特点，就是书写动作的缓慢性。由于摹仿的目的就是要做到形似，摹仿者的书写动作必须小心翼翼，边看边写，由此造成了形快实慢、运笔迟疑、笔力平缓、中途停顿、笔画抖动等反常的迹象。而经过大量练习后的忆摹，可以大大提高书写的速度，书写速度的提高就可以减少上述的反常迹象，甚至使这些反常的迹象消失。

（三）印制形成

随着印刷技术的发展，复制他人签名的方法也出现了新的变化。目前常见的伪造签名主要利用转印、复印、扫描打印、制章等方式进行造假。转印伪造签名，是采取物理、化学的方法对真签名进行脱色、再把真签名笔画的色料转印到伪造的文件上。复印伪造签名，是利用复印件将真签名复印到伪造的文件上。打印伪造签名，是利用扫描仪对真签名进行扫描，再经过图像处理后打印出来。制章伪造签名，是利用各种制章技术把真签名制成印章图文，再把签名印文盖印到伪造的文件上。

（四）自我伪装签名

在签名上进行伪装的目的在于事后不认账或要摆脱自己应负的责任。要进行伪装但又不能出大格，伪装过于严重会引起他人的注意，所以多采用降低书写速度，运笔变得拘谨、呆板；或者改变倾斜方向；或者改变书体，如将平时签写的行草体改变为楷书体；或者改变某个字的习惯写法；或者在起笔处附加动作，在收笔时故意环绕或加长。〔2〕

四、中文笔迹检验策略

签名作为一种较为特殊的笔迹，对它的检验除了要遵循笔迹检验的一般的原理和方法外，还要根据这种笔迹的特点和发案的具体情况，而采取以下检验策略。

（一）创造良好的检验条件

签名字迹属于少量字笔迹检验范畴，有字数少、特征少、抗干扰能力若、易于被伪造等特点，也是笔迹检验难点之一，很多的错案就发生在这里。所以，鉴定人鉴定签名笔迹时首先就应当为自己的检验工作创造一个良好的检验条件。主要包括：全面了解案情；坚持检验签名原件；选取可比性强的样本。

全面了解案情，就是要知晓本案签名争议的由来；签名形成的时间、地点、环境、姿势、纸张及笔的来源；签名人的年龄、文化、职业、身心状况；争议双方确认或否认的依据；其他物证、人证的看法等等。可以向办案人询问，也可一调阅卷宗，或亲自询问当事人并制成询问笔录。详细、客观了解案件的情况，有利于鉴定人扩展思路，有利于客观分析签名笔迹的某些具体现象，有利于对比较的结果进行科学的综合评断。

〔2〕 贾玉文：《笔迹检验》，警官教育出版社2004年版，第406页。

判断一个签名是正常笔迹，还是存在反常迹象，以及分析这个签名书写人的细小动作特点都需要对签名的原件进行放大观察。另外，我国的民诉法和刑诉法对“笔迹鉴定中的检材需要使用的是原件”都有所规定，而复印和打印等本身就是签名造假的一种手段，所以，原则上我们就不应该使用检材的复制件进行签名笔迹的检验。

一个人的签名常常会有多种写法、字体或式样，而且它们之间的笔画形态和签名的结构也相差甚远。即使是同种字体、同种式样的签名，由于书写用笔、书写场合、书写的年代、书写人的身心状态不同，也会存在特征上的差异。所以，选取形成条件一致、形成时间相近、式样相同这些可比性强的签名样本进行比较，有助于防止鉴定人过多的主观臆断，有助于鉴定人更加客观、全面地进行比对检验。

（二）准确判断签名的形成方法

签名笔迹检验的第一步，就是要判断检材签名笔迹是否为通过书写活动、使用笔直接书写形成。采用的主要方法是显微放大观察。观察构成笔画的色料是否为常见书写工具所使用的油墨或墨水；笔画在纸张上是否产生了向下的凹痕。符合这两个现象，则应为直接书写形成，否则很有可能存在造假。此时，需要进一步通过笔画的墨痕、色料的形态或成分去判断造假的具体方式和手段。如果是直接书写形成，则按照操作的程序继续检验；如果不是直接书写形成，则可以终止进行比对检验，在检验意见中直接表述出签名形成的方法。如我国公安系统内部的 CCPUIFS 02 - 01 - 01 - 2008、CCPUIFS 02 - 01 - 02 - 2008、CCPUIFS 02 - 01 - 03 - 2008 等检验方法和操作手册中对此都有严格的规定。

（三）正确识别摹仿笔迹

签名笔迹检验的最终目的是判断检材签名与样本签名是否为同一人所写。在比较检验中主要会出现两种情况，即“像”或“不像”，此时就需要鉴定人在下一步的检验中要有一个清晰的思路。“不像”，则需要考虑是否为他人代签、本人伪装，或者是否所使用的样本签名不够全面、有局限性。“像”，则存在是本人亲笔签写、他人摹仿签写、自我仿写（实际很少出现）这三种可能。思路清晰，很快就会找到答案。但是，检验实践中遇到的难点在于是否能够准确地判断出检材签名是否为摹仿形成。其中主要的困难则是摹仿与伪装、摹仿与条件变化都会出现相同的反常迹象和特点。检材签名这些反常迹象出现得越少，就越是难以进行判断。由此，正确识别摹仿笔迹，必须做到以下三个环节：一是注意发现检材签名上是否存在摹仿笔迹固有的反常特点和反常迹象；二是通过与样本签名的比较进一步发现二者间存在的不同，这些不同点应该是细节特征上的不同；三是要客观、有机地结合案情进行分析。

（四）全面掌握本人签名发生变化的原因

检材签名同样本签名比较存在“大同小异”的现象，而且这个“小异”主要为细节特征上的差异，往往是作为判断摹仿书写的一个依据。相反，这些细节特征相符，则是作为同一认定的主要依据。所以，细节特征的运用在签名笔迹检验当中尤为重要。签名笔迹检验和一般笔迹检验一样，在得出最终的鉴定结论之前，都要经过一个全面、科学、客观的综合评断过程。包括细节特征在内，检材签名和样本签名笔迹间符合点再多，如果二者间存在着一些差异，就需要对这些差异点的性质进行一个客观的判断，即判断其是属于本质性的差异（不同人之间的差异）还是非本质性的差异（同一人自身的差异)，否则就不能给出明确的认定意见。这就需要我们弄清不同人之间，尤其是本人笔迹发生变化的原因和表现。

我们说一个人的书写运动是一种机体运动，而不是机械的精密重复，一个人在不同的时间和地点签写的姓名不可能完全一样。书写人本人签名笔迹现象发生变化的原因主要有：

本人签名本身存在多样性而样本没有表现出来；签写时书写人生理或心理发生了变化，如酒后笔迹、手部受伤或病变（关节炎)、身体生病而体质虚弱、极度的恐慌或兴奋、认真仔细或敷衍了事；签写时书写环境和书写条件的影响；本人签写时的故意伪装。一个原因就会导致一种结果，即每一种原因所导致的笔迹发生相应的变化，这就要求鉴定人全面、准确掌握各种类型笔迹的变化规律。

4.5 综合运用科学的检验方法

笔迹检验应当是对笔迹现象进行全面、科学、客观的分析，但是这期间又离不开鉴定人的主观判断。所以，我们不应该否认笔迹检验是包含鉴定人主观经验成分的一项技术。为了尽可能减少由于主观偏差和经验不足带来的失误，鉴定人就应该运用科学的检验方法进行鉴定。

签名笔迹检验主要是应用特征比对的方法，能否进行科学、客观比对的前提是能否全面认识笔迹的特征，选取笔迹特征至关重要。不论是笔迹现象的静态特征还是笔迹的动态特征，我们可以参考陈明春教授提出的“全、深、细、特”选取笔迹特征四字法。四字虽然不多，但是要想真正掌握每一个字，都需要付出很多的努力。近年来，国内很多研究者尝试使用西方的画线测量的方法，也取得了一定的进展。还有很多人正在研制和尝试使用计算机专家系统进行鉴定，但是由于研制者的设计角度和采取的算法不同，都不同程度的存在着弊端。可见，正确的检验方法应该是传统与现代相结合。坚持传统的检验方法，参考较为成熟的现代技术手段，经过科学的思维、推理及论证得出正确的鉴定意见。

笔迹样本存在的问题及对策

高学林*，杨国锋[2]，方洪远[3]，刘连山[1]，鲁爱军[3]，刘树桂[3]，
陈志强[3]，陈玉辉[3]，章景林[3]，刘 超[3]，周永贺[4]**

笔迹检验中，检材笔迹是无法改变的，要及时、准确地得出鉴定意见，主要依赖送检嫌疑人的笔迹样本。笔者从事文件检验二十多年，深感在送检的笔迹样本方面存在着案前笔迹样本不足、提取越来越困难，案后样本不符合鉴定要求等诸多问题。现结合实践体会，参考有关文献，就笔迹样本存在的问题、原因及对策谈些粗浅的看法。

一、笔迹样本存在的问题

（一）案后样本多，案前样本、同期样本少

送检的笔迹样本大多是案后样本，主要是办案人员让嫌疑人当场、当庭、送检时一次性现写的样本占绝大多数，此类笔迹变化大，稳定性特征不易把握。发案前的样本多是在鉴定人再三要求下才送交，且与检材同期、书写条件相同或接近的仍不多。

（二）笔迹样本重“量”不重“质”，[1]缺乏可比性

笔迹样本数量不少，与检材笔迹书证相同的字迹却寥寥无几，“量、质”相差悬殊，特别是其他部门送检的案件，此类现象尤为突出。2011 年 12 月份，我们检验的一起匿名信案件，检材为两个信封，十几个字迹；样本数量很多，有 100 多页，但与检材相同字迹寥寥无几，且两者书写速度相差甚远，自然以无法做出明确意见告终。

（三）笔迹样本与检材形成条件相差悬殊，缺乏针对性

提取笔迹样本就事论事，如涉及签名书写纠纷，就让当事人一次性书写一页几个与检材字迹相同的签名了事，且书写工具、承受载体（纸张的规格、薄厚、印刷格式）与检材明显不同，甚至字形、字体、书体也不一样；有的形成时间相差十几年的并不鲜见。2012 年 7 月，我们检验的一起放火案，检材为火灾现场提取的留言条 3 张，用纸为报刊里页 2 张及挂历纸 1 张，字迹较大，笔画较粗，分析为记号笔书写。嫌疑人样本为中性笔书写在 A4 纸上，字迹较小。对此，我们提出让嫌疑人用与检材相同的书写工具——记号笔书写大字样本的建议，提取的实验样本与检材之间反映较好，为同一认定提供了依据。

（四）多人笔迹样本混淆，张冠李戴，缺乏真实性

笔迹样本中有的掺杂与案件无关人的笔迹，有的甚至与笔迹书证混淆在一起。轻

---

* 高学林（1966～），男，现任河北省唐山市丰南区人民检察院检察技术科科长、文件检验高级工程师、四级高级检察官、河北省唐山市人民检察院司法鉴定中心文件检验检测项目授权签字人。研究方向：文件检验、职务犯罪侦查。Email：gaoxuelin_ 2004@163. com。

** 1. 河北省唐山市丰南区人民检察院，河北唐山，063300；2. 唐山物证司法鉴定中心，河北唐山，063000；3. 河北省唐山市人民检察院司法鉴定中心，河北唐山，063000；4. 唐山公安局国保支队，河北唐山，063000。Email：gaoxuelin_ 2004@163. com。

则导致需重新收集样本或核实样本，影响案件侦破、审理，重则导致鉴定意见出现偏差，造成严重后果。

(五) 笔迹样本单一，[2]难以反映演变规律

能否提取到反映书写人笔迹演变规律的样本，对于正常书写的检材并不十分重要，但在伪装、变化案件检验时，则必不可少。由于历时样本由于能够反映书写人书写习惯的演变过程及规律，现实的伪装变化只能以固有的书写技能与习惯为基础，现实的伪装变化很可能就是历史上书写特征的“翻版”或“再现”。2012 年 9 月，我们检验的一起协议签名书写纠纷案。协议标称时间为 1991 年 1 月，样本为送交鉴定后 2012 年 9 月书写的，由于相隔 21 年，两者在相同签名字迹的笔画组成、形态方面存在明显差异，直接影响到鉴定意见的做出。

(六) 笔迹样本书写方式异常，[3]导致笔迹变化

书写方式异常的表现主要是隔着栅栏、以座椅扶手为依托、戴手铐以及高位执笔、触笔书写等，这些非正常的书写方式导致书写水平下降，笔迹特征相应发生改变。2011 年 4 月，我们检验的一起签名书写纠纷案。贾某某在书写签名样本时，采取站立高位执笔的方式书写，经鉴定人再三工作，才勉强坐下但仍高位执笔书写。高位执笔书写的样本笔迹不仅字形变大，且将“祥”字“羊”部的两点笔写成对号状，与检材形成明显差异。

(七) 提取方法不当，导致笔迹样本变化甚至引起其他后果

方法不当的表现主要是照抄检材笔迹、照抄办案人书写的字迹，照抄报纸、期刊以及打印的文稿等。特别是照抄检材后果是最为严重的，轻者导致笔迹样本失真，需要重新提取样本，重则失去检材笔迹书证，造成难以挽回的损失。1993 年 4 月，我院立案侦查了一起以伪造病历为手段诬告陷害他人的案件。办案人员提取笔迹样本时，直接将“可疑病历”原件交给嫌疑人之一方某某照抄。不仅笔迹样本伪装严重，而且“可疑病历”中的“主任查房”记录丢失。破案后方某某交待：在抄写时，趁办案人员不备，将自己亲笔伪造的“主任查房记录”偷偷撕下销毁。案件虽最终告破，但作为直接证据的部分书证已不复存在。这一教训非常值得一线办案人员引以为戒。[4]

二、笔迹样本出现问题的原因

笔迹样本之所以出现上述情况，其原因主要有以下两方面：

(一) 笔迹样本书写人 (嫌疑人或被鉴定人) 方面

1. 书写人的主观方面

书写人对提交、书写笔迹样本的态度，影响笔迹样本的数量和质量。有的为逃避责任不愿意提供真实正常的笔迹样本；有的案件当事人以患病为由拒绝书写笔迹样本。特别是诉讼时当事人已经死亡的，有的家属为了弄清真相，千方百计寻找其生前笔迹样本；有的为了回避责任，则以生前没有留下笔迹或虽有但已随遗物烧掉为由拒绝提供。对此，我们要广辟样本来源，特别要充分利用对方当事人或其他有关联人提供的线索，以取得符合鉴定要求的样本。2003 年 5 月，检验王某某诉田某某民间借贷一案。检材为“王怀某”签名的借款条，王某某称：借款条的内容及签名均为田某某丈夫王怀某亲笔书写。由于王怀某因交通肇事死亡，故起诉其妻田某某。同时提供，2003 年 1 月，王怀某因被指控涉嫌犯罪，曾被唐山市公安局路南分局文北派出所留置。田某某

则否认此笔债务，并称家中已无任何王生前留下的字迹，亦否认王曾被文北派出所留置。于是我们通过文北派出所证实了原告王某某提供的情况，并借得案卷中有“王怀某”签名及相关字迹的继续盘问（留置）审批表和讯问笔录。与检材比对检验，做出了同一认定。

2. 书写人客观方面

书写人书写水平较低、没有书写能力（如文盲）或从事纯体力劳务活动，不经常书写字迹或没有书写字迹的事务及条件，因此，难以提取到平时样本。[5]

（二）笔迹样本提取人（侦查、检察、审判人员、执法、执纪人员以及律师等办案人员）方面

办案人员对笔迹样本应具备的条件、提取笔迹样本的方法、技巧是否了然于胸，是关系笔迹样本质量的决定性因素。如果不具备这方面的知识，提取的样本很难符合鉴定要求。

1. 办案人员文检技术缺乏了解

对笔迹鉴定的原理、笔迹样本应具备的条件、提取笔迹样本的方法、技巧知之甚少，想当然地认为只要有嫌疑人的笔迹样本就能鉴定。因此，送检的笔迹样本往往只是让嫌疑人随意现写的几个字迹。

2. 办案人员责任心方面

有的办案人员责任心不强，敷衍塞责，有的出于某种不可告人的目的，故意将不真实的样本提供给鉴定人。1997 年 11 月间，某市某中学校园内连续三夜发现 29 条张贴的煽动性标语。通过分析，文检人员认为嫌疑人为男性且应为该校学生。经提取全校 1800 余名学生的作业笔迹样本进行排查，没有发现作案人。后侦查人员通过蹲点守候，将再次作案的犯罪嫌疑人安某（男，14 岁，该校初三学生）抓获。破案后证实，在提取样本时，安某没有到校上课，也没有交作业，而这一情况侦查人员没有及时反馈给技术人员。[6]

3. 办案人对档案中的笔迹样本提取重视不够

理想的笔迹样本是嫌疑人的历时样本特别是同期样本，此类样本一般需要在档案资料中提取。对于档案样本要注意与现实样本进行甄别，以防止将他人代写笔迹当成嫌疑人书写而造成的鉴定失误。在民事案件中，送检的笔迹样本大多数是诉讼后书写的，可比性较差，因此，应加大对档案笔迹样本的提取，以满足鉴定的需要。2012 年 6 月，我们检验的一起不服法院判决的申诉案。涉及标称日期为 2005 年 1 月的模板租赁协议签名，当事人陈某某否认书写，样本为 2012 年 5 月一次性书写的 2 页签名，与检材签名之间在相同字迹的写法、书写速度等方面明显不同。对此，我们没有急于出具鉴定意见，而是建议提取案前特别是同期签名样本。陈某某没有提供，后经技术人员与办案人员通过银行提取到陈某某 2011 年 9 月在存款凭条上的签名（依据身份证号码确认）。经比对检验做出了同一认定，陈某某没有提出异议。

（三）期刊、网络等媒体中对错误提取笔迹样本方法报道的影响

一些期刊、网络对笔迹样本提取方法的不当宣传，也产生了不良的影响。2008 年 10 月，某新闻网以“欠账不还想逃避，笔迹鉴定还公道”为题报道：“债务人否认欠条中的签名系本人所写，并在随后的笔迹鉴定提交样本过程中故意放慢书写速度，降

低书写水平，企图以此逃避还款。经笔迹鉴定，法院终还债主公道。”“为减少当事人故意改变书写习惯导致鉴定结论不准的弊病，承办法官在提取用以对照的文字样本时，刻意将样本（应为‘检材’）文字打乱分步（应为‘布’）在长篇文字中让其抄写。经某司法鉴定所鉴定，样本文字有故意放慢书写速度、降低书写水平的迹象，但字迹在书写水平、基本布局及风貌、运笔、笔画搭配、字迹的倾斜度等特征与欠条记载符合点多，价值高，认定是同一人所写。”[7]该文作者的本意是当事人虽然书写时对样本故意进行了改变，但仍然没能逃避过笔迹鉴定。殊不知导致笔迹样本发生变化的原因，恰恰是法官让当事人照抄编有欠条内容的文稿造成的（根据检材内容编写文稿是正确的，除非当事人没有独立书写能力，或难以写成与检材相同书写模式的字迹，否则绝不能让其照抄）。试想如果看过这篇新闻的办案人员都效仿文中法官的做法，势必会造成更多案件的笔迹样本失真。因此，法官错误地让当事人照抄文稿的提取样本方法、外行作者的宣传报道，给提取笔迹样本工作带来的负面影响是不言而喻的。

三、提高笔迹样本质量的对策

如何提高笔迹样本的质量，主要是通过学历教育、岗位培训等，使每一个办案人员达到了解笔迹样本的种类及其在检验中的作用，明确笔迹样本应具备的条件，掌握提取笔迹样本的方法、技巧。做好送检及提取笔迹样本前的准备工作，紧紧围绕嫌疑人的个性信息，全方位提取符合鉴定要求的笔迹样本，从而为笔迹鉴定做出准确鉴定意见奠定坚实基础。

（一）提高认识，加大教育培训力度

如果说让所有的办案人员（包括侦查、检察、审判、执法执纪以及律师等）都精通文检技术，显然不切合实际，也是不可能的。但通过培训使办案人员具备提取笔迹样本、印文样本、指印样本的能力并非遥不可及。关键是让他们在思想上重视起来，认识到提取各类物证、书证及样本的能力，是本人办案能力的重要组成部分，克服依赖和等靠思想。因为，提取各类样本是办案人员特别是侦查人员随时都会遇到的，技术人员毕竟有限，不可能随时随地配合侦查人员提取相关样本。在法律类基础学历教育中，应将物证技术、司法鉴定引入必修课程。在上岗培训、岗位培训中将物证技术、司法鉴定中的物证、书证及相关样本的提取纳入必训内容。通过互联网、局域网发布物证、书证及相关样本的提取方法、技巧方面的资料。使笔迹样本具备字迹清晰、真实可靠、充分、具有可比性的条件，提取方法、技巧真正入脑入心，应用时才能得心应手。

（二）做好送检及提取笔迹样本前的准备工作

首先通过聘请文检技术人员对检材进行分析和讯（询）问书写嫌疑人、当事人，全面了解检材笔迹的形成时间、地点，书写姿势、环境、衬垫物，承受载体（纸张）、书写工具的来源，执笔人，在场的证明人，检材笔迹的原始状态，争议的字迹、内容、签名、不同栏目字迹的相应书写人以及书写人书写时的状况，是否酒后书写（如是酒后书写，还应了解数量多少、状态如何）等细节，并以笔录的形式加以固定，嫌疑人、当事人签名确认。在送检时，移交鉴定人，以便鉴定人有针对性的分析检验，亦可防止鉴定意见做出后当事人再信口雌黄。其次，通过嫌疑人及其所在单位，了解其年龄，出生地，政治面目，文化程度，书写技能，从事职业，个人经历，学识修养，生活环

境，业余爱好，健康状况以及获得奖励、荣誉以及受过党纪、政纪处分、行政、刑事处罚等情况。这些情况与形成笔迹的自身条件以及笔迹样本的来源密切相关，既有利于分析嫌疑人的书写能力，更有利于拓宽提取笔迹样本的渠道。如果缺失则会妨碍鉴定人对笔迹特征的分析判定，严重时可能造成鉴定意见失误。对于检材字迹较多的要从中找出主要特征字迹拟好文稿，文稿与检材笔迹要有所区别，不能出现反动、歧视、侮辱诽谤、涉及国家、商业秘密、个人隐私的内容。同时，准备好与检材相同的书写工具，大小、薄厚、印刷格式基本一致的纸张10～20张。如一起借条书写纠纷案，与被告周某某案前及案后样本比对检验，发现两者之间相同字迹的符合点较多，但也存在一些规律性差异。经鉴定人亲自提取样本，上述差异点仍难以解释。进一步了解，周某某提出自己为孪生妹妹还债曾给原告写过借条，但没有写过此笔60万元的。周某某与妹妹两人性格接近，一起上学、辍学（初中二年级），书写的笔迹也十分相近，在一起经商时妹妹经常摹仿她的笔迹签署文件，有时自己也难以分清。因此，怀疑借条是其妹妹摹仿自己的笔迹写的。提取其妹笔迹样本，比对检验，两者的书写特征完全一致。[8]

（三）全方位提取笔迹样本

针对检材笔迹的形成条件，围绕书写嫌疑人日常工作、学习、生活、职业、职务、个人经历以及社会交往等方面细致工作。通过嫌疑人所在单位以及社会管理、执法执纪、公共服务、金融机构等相关部门，力争取得符合鉴定要求的案前（同期、历时样本）、案后平时笔迹样本。如果案前、案后的现成样本不足，则需提取现写样本。[9]首先，让嫌疑人亲笔书写检材笔迹的形成过程以及其他与案件有关的情况；其次，提取听写样本，听写样本是办案人员（或文检技术人员）诵读拟定文稿，要求嫌疑人用与检材笔迹相同的书写工具、相同或相近规格、薄厚、印刷格式的承受载体（纸张等），按照嫌疑人供述、认可以及分析判定的检材形成条件（衬垫物、环境、书写姿势等），与检材笔迹一致的字体听写。诵读时要注意语速，快、中、慢相间，在嫌疑人书写过程中，还要适时讯（询）问与案件有关或无关的问题，以干扰、打乱其可能伪装的企图，听写5～10遍后，再让其以不同的速度背书，并以物证笔迹的书写速度为依据，要求其逐渐慢写或快写。同时密切注意书写人的神态表情，记录在卷，以为检验工作提供笔迹特征之外的信息。2002年1月，我们检验了签名"王某某"的借条书写纠纷一案，被告王某某否认借条是自己所写，原告周某某则提供了王某某向她借款时书写借条的圆珠笔和笔记本，并称王是趴在写字台上写的。王某某虽然否认向原告借款，但为了表示自己没有说谎，也不得不按照我们的要求配合书写笔迹样本。在法院提供以及王某某自己提交样本的基础上，我们特别要求王某某按照原告周某某所说的书写姿势，使用原告提供的圆珠笔，在与借条大小接近的纸张上，用不同的书写速度听写与借条内容一致的笔迹样本。在王某某书写时，我们还适时询问有关问题，让其边书写边回答问题。虽然王某某的案后样本不同程度存在故意放慢书写速度现象，但固有的稳定性书写特征仍有流露，特别是圆珠笔的笔痕特征更是难以改变。[10]

（四）侦技密切配合提高提取笔迹样本的质量

要做好笔迹样本的提取工作，确保笔迹样本可靠、充分、具有可比性，办案人员与文检技术人员要密切配合，以达到事半功倍的效果。办案人员应事先就如何提取笔迹样本向文检技术人员进行咨询，文检技术人员应耐心指导，直至亲自参与提取。鉴于当前社会关系复杂，对于提取难度较大、技术性较强的听写样本、涉及摹仿的对照样本及实验样本，文检技术人员最好亲自参与，以确保笔迹样本符合鉴定要求。笔者身在基层，有接近案件涉嫌人员的便利条件，因此对重大、疑难案件始终坚持在认真听取送检单位介绍案情的基础上，亲自查阅案卷核实，有针对性地接触嫌疑人，提取其笔迹样本及相关材料，而后与送检单位提供的样本互相甄别使用，在少量字、摹仿及添加等案件的检验中取得了比较明显的效果。[11] 2012 年 5 月，我们检验的窦某某涉嫌贪污案的支款凭单签名，侦查人员提供的样本是窦某某在 A4 复印纸上书写的“吕某某”签名，与检材之间在字形、书写速度方面相差较大，虽然窦某某承认书写，但两者之间差异点的存在显然无法做出同一认定。对此我们采取让窦某某用与检材相同格式的支款凭单、书写工具，按其承认的书写姿势、作案时使用的字体书写了实验样本，与检材之间的同一性反映较好，顺利做出了鉴定意见。

（五）逐步建立健全笔迹档案以适应办案需要

同刑事案件的犯罪嫌疑人、治安管理重点人员一样，在目前指印留档的基础上，将笔迹留档落到实处。天津市公安局物证鉴定中心文检室在这方面进行了专题立项研究并通过了验收，很有借鉴推广价值。内蒙古自治区已于 2012 年在高考报名中，开始采集本人笔迹，以杜绝替考等作弊行为。[12] 从 2013 年开始，新启用的第二代身份证已经加入了指纹信息，为此，笔者建议由公安部门联合教育、人力资源和社会保障部门、鉴定机构以及用人单位、基层村居委会等部门，特别是与指印信息加入身份证工作相结合，建立全员笔迹档案并非难事，只是与指纹相比由于笔迹会随着时间的推移发生演变，需要相隔几年（如 3 ~ 5 年）进行补录。

参考文献

[1] 李鹏、李德营、王孔宝：《浅谈笔迹样本收集中存在的问题，文件检验的理论与实务》，人民法院出版社 2005 年版，第 76 ~ 79 页。

[2] 沈臻懿、沈洁：“刑事案件笔迹鉴定样本收集规范探析”，载《湖南警察学院学报》2011 年第 2 期，第 141 ~ 144 页。

[3] 赫平、郭江：“海关文件检验工作特点及对策”，载《第四届全国文检学理论与实践研讨会论文集》，中国公共安全出版社 2003 年版，第 63 ~ 64、72 页。

[4] 高学林、刘连山、李桂兰等：“笔迹检验感悟”，载《刑警与科技》2009 年第 3）期，第 101 ~ 103 页。

[5] 李光：“当前经济案件中笔迹样本的收集与运用”，载《第六届全国文检学理论与实践研讨会论文集》，中国人民公安大学出版社、群众出版社 2010 年版，第 271 ~ 276 页。

[6] 李晓明：“特定范围内排查大量嫌疑人笔迹可行性初探”，载《文件检验的理论与实务》人民法院出版社 2005 年版，第 178 ~ 181 页。

[7] 张鑫：“欠账不还想逃避笔迹鉴定还公道”，http：//lhnews. zjol. com. cn/lhnews/system/2008/10/27/010724732. shtml，访问日期：2008 年 10 月 27 日。

[8] 邵连华、刘安民：“一起孪生妹摹仿姐笔迹的检验”，载《法制与社会》2010 年第 30 期，第 78 页。

[9] 李福奎、王伟、李洁：“论民事诉讼案件笔迹样本”，载《第六届全国文检学理论与实践研讨会论文集》，中国人民公安大学出版社、群众出版社 2010 年版，第537 ~ 540 页。

［10］高学林、刘连山、陈志强等："借条真伪检验分析一例"，载《刑警与科技》2009 年第 3 期，第 90 ~ 91 页。

［11］高学林："笔迹样本及提取技巧"，载《中国司法鉴定》2004 年第 3 期，第 16 ~ 18 页。

［12］贾立君："内蒙古 2012 年高考报名将首次采集本人笔迹"，http：//www. gaokao. com/e/0111117/24ec4e 3a84129c. shtm，访问时间：2011 年 11 月 17 日。

借收据笔迹的检验

高学林*，杨国锋[2]，方洪远[3]，刘连山[1]，鲁爱军[3]，刘树桂[3]，
陈志强[3]，陈玉辉[3]，章景林[3]，刘 超[3]，周永贺[4**]

《现代汉语词典》中，“借据”的解释是：借用别人的钱或物品时所立的字据，由出借的人保存；“收据”的解释是：收到钱或东西后写给对方的字据。“借据”、“收据”通称为“借条”、“收条”。借收据是人们在日常工作、生活中应用广泛的一种应用文体。市场经济下，单位之间、单位与个人之间、个人之间的借贷行为经常发生。由于借收据与经济利益密不可分，加之书写的随意性。因此，容易引发纠纷和违法犯罪。如何全方位发掘借收据信息，以确定书写人，判明形成的时间以及有无添、改变造，为诉讼活动和纠纷处理提供科学依据，成为当前文件检验的一项迫切任务。笔者从事文件检验工作20多年，实战检验了大量借、收据案件，现就此类案件的表现形式、特点、特征、检验对策方面谈几点粗浅的认识。

一、借收据案件的表现形式

文检实践中，借收据案件主要有两种形式：

（一）印制的借收据

印制的借收据，主要有印刷、刻写油印、打印的等。一般有固定的格式，用时填写相应栏目即可。

（二）书写的借收据

书写的借收据，虽然有约定俗成的格式要求，但由于规范的宽容性以及受书写时的条件限制，一般会在书写格式上表现出各自的特点。

二、借收据案件的特点

（一）案件当事人明确

借收据书写纠纷案件的当事人，双方一般比较熟悉，有经济、业务往来。涉案人范围较小，当事人明确，大多非此即彼，这对于检验工作来说是一个非常有利的因素。

（二）形成条件复杂

形成条件复杂主要是书写环境光线的明暗、气温的冷暖，书写位置的宽窄，衬垫物的软硬，如以手、膝盖或手包、墙壁等为依托书写，书写姿势如坐、立、蹲、躺、卧、侧身、俯身等。

* 高学林，现任河北省唐山市丰南区人民检察院检察技术科科长、文件检验高级工程师、四级高级检察官、河北省唐山市人民检察院司法鉴定中心文件检验检测项目授权签字人。电子邮箱：gaoxuelin_ 2004@163. com。

** 1. 河北省唐山市丰南区人民检察院，河北唐山，063300；2. 唐山物证司法鉴定中心，河北唐山，063000；3. 河北省唐山市人民检察院司法鉴定中心，河北唐山，063000；4. 唐山公安局国保支队，河北唐山，063000。Email：gaoxuelin_ 2004@163. com。

（三）书写工具、纸张随意性大

限于发生事务时的条件，书写工具、纸张多就地取材，没有过多的讲究。2005 年 5 月，我们检验一起借条书写纠纷案，用纸为整条香烟外包装的纸片。

（四）易添改变造

借收据案件中，有的内容与签名非同一人书写，因此内容中的字迹、数字易被添改变造，或使用物理或化学方法消退原书写字迹再添加内容。此外，利用占有或窃取的盖有、写有对方单位、当事人真实印文、签名的纸张，添加内容变造借收据的案件已屡见不鲜。此类案件中，仅仅要求鉴定印文、签名真伪是不够的，印文、签名真，借收据未必真。此外，还存在复制伪造印文、签名变造借收据以及在打印文件的空白处，利用同台微机打印添加的。因此，只有全方位研究借、收据中的诸多信息，系统鉴定，才能透过现象揭示其本质。2004 年 12 月，我们检验的唐某某、邢某某借款协议真伪纠纷案，检验结果借款协议是唐某某利用邢某某签名的收条消退原内容字迹添加变造而成。

（五）易摹仿

借、收据中的书写字迹数量较少，一般十几个、二十几个字，属于少量字案件。字数少的仅涉及 2 ~3 个字签名，因此易被摹仿。

（六）多有指印和印文

如果借、收据中有指印及单位印文，则增加了可资利用的信息，对于充实笔迹鉴定意见提供了有利条件，在检验时，要注意研究指印及印文是否存在转印、打印、复印以及其他高仿真手法伪造的可能。

三、借收据的特征

特征是事物特性的表现，是事物间相互区别的标志，借收据案件除了字迹书写特征之外，还表现出一些独有的特征，主要有：

（一）借收据的书写格式特征

借收据（条）一般由标题、正文、署名、日期四部分组成。其格式特征主要包括标题安排、分段缩头、署名、日期位置方面。由于印制借收据均有固定的格式，因此其格式特征主要表现在书写的借收据中。书写格式特征同书写动作、文字布局特征一样，是书写人通过书写活动表现借收据式样安排形式的特点。2003 年 7 月，我们受理的一起收条签名书写纠纷案。被告张某某提供了一张“李某某”签名的收条（内容及日期字迹为张某某书写），原告李某某否认签名及收款。检验发现，两者签名、日期的书写格式特征明显不同，检材签名书写在日期的下方。而五张收（欠）条样本，其中 4 张为李某某收张某某酒款的收条，但无论是张某某书写内容由李某某签名的，还是李某某既书写内容又签名的收条，上面均没有书写日期；而另一张李某某签名的欠条，日期书写在签名右下方。检材、样本签名虽在字的基本写法、字间组合、明显的搭配、比例、笔顺、起笔位置、收笔方向特征上有共同反映，但在整个签名的熟练程度、相同字迹的起笔形态、行笔弧度、连接环绕、转折角度、照应关系、笔力分布等细节特征上存在本质差异。结合检材签名与正文内容字迹在整体风貌以及相同偏旁、笔画圆珠笔笔痕特征上的共同反映，综合评断，确定检材签名系张某某练习摹仿李某某签名伪造而成。在鉴定面前，张不得不放弃自己的主张。

(二) 借收据的文字布局特征

借、收据中文字布局特征是指字迹书写在借、收据上的安排形式及分布特点。文字布局主要有字行的形态、字间与行间的间隔、字间组合、字行与格线的关系、字行与页边的关系、字位的偏正等方面特征。文字布局特征同书写动作、格式特征一样，具有较强的稳定性、特殊性、自身同一性。在一般情况下，作案人利用借、收据进行作案时，往往只注意对字迹、笔画进行有意识的伪装造作，而忽视或根本意识不到对布局特征的改变，特别是添加变造借收据，往往在文字布局方面露出破绽。因此，充分运用文字布局特征，对于认定书写人、识别添加具有重要意义。2001 年 5 月，我们检验的签名“刘某某”借款条案。检验发现：借款条内容字迹，字形、大小不一，第 1 行字迹竖向高为 1.6cm ~ 0.4cm 间，第 2 行为 1.55cm ~ 0.7cm 间，第 3 行为 1.3cm ~ 0.65cm 间，第 4 行为 0.65cm ~ 0.25cm 间。第 1 行字迹距上边缘 0.8cm，第 2 行与第 3 行字迹相隔 3.85cm，而第 1、2 行字迹及间隔共 3.6cm，第 3 行“经手人”字迹距下边缘 0.6cm，“刘某某”签名距下边缘 0.3cm、右边缘 3.55cm，第 4 行日期字迹则书写在签名右侧纸张的下边缘上、距右边缘仅 0.55cm，且字迹突然变小，显得紧凑、拥挤。陈某某的样本借款条书写亦无标题，与检材比较，两者第 1、2 行字迹的大小、书写格式、文字布局基本一致，但第 3、4 行字迹的位置安排、第 4 行日期字迹的大小、文字布局明显不同。检材借款条中经手人及日期字迹的书写，明显受“刘某某”签名字迹的限制。结合纸张印刷、断离痕迹以及文字书写压痕等方面的信息，确定签名“刘某某”的借款条是利用“刘某某”签名添加内容变造而成。在鉴定面前，陈某某承认了骗取刘某某签名，添加内容、日期字迹变造借款条的过程，并承担了相应的责任。

(三) 借收据的物质材料特征

物质材料主要是书写工具和纸张。

1. 借收据的书写工具特征

常用的书写工具主要有中性笔、圆珠笔、钢笔等，对借收据中书写字迹笔痕的研究，有助于笔迹鉴定意见的做出。有时仅检验签名真伪是不够的，因为签名真，借收据的内容未必真，应全方位检验借收据中的诸多信息综合分析判定其真伪。2003 年 3 月，我们受理的一起要求确定收款条内容有无添加的案件。检验发现，收款条中蓝色圆珠笔字迹颜色不同，第 1 行的阿拉伯数字“1”与第 2 行“壹万捌仟元正”相对于其他字迹颜色略浅。细致研究“1”、“壹万捌仟元正”与同一人书写的其他正文内容字迹相同笔画的圆珠笔笔痕特征反映不一致。此外，我们还使用 Docucenter3000 文检仪在 ex = docuba = 645nm 条件下检验：“1”和“壹万捌仟元正”与“今收到冰款 8000 元正”、“毕某某、2002 年 8 月 8 日”字迹间在荧光效应上存在明显差异。仪器的运用既印证了笔痕检验的结果，又使鉴定依据更加充分。

2. 借收据的纸张特征

对借、收据所用纸张以及纸张与书写字迹之间的关系进行分析检验，有时会起到事半功倍的效果。2011 年 6 月，我们检验的签名“李某某”借条一案，鉴定要求是借条正文内容字迹与地址姓名字迹的书写先后顺序。检验发现，借条全篇字迹均用黑色签字笔书写在一张黑色横格纸上。字迹墨迹颜色基本一致，正文内容和地址姓名、日期两部分相同字迹、偏旁的书写细节特征明显不同，可以确定为两个人书写。上述检验结果并不能满足鉴定要求，进一步研究，发现纸张上发现4处折叠印痕迹。其中纵向折叠痕1处。正文内容部分字迹与姓名地址部分字迹均被该纵向折痕贯穿。比对折痕处的书写字迹，发现正文内容字迹与姓名、地址字迹特征反映不同。正文内容字迹笔画在折痕交叉处纸张纤维翘起、笔画运笔“受阻”、运笔不流畅。而姓名地址被折叠交叉处的字迹笔画运笔流畅，书写正常。3处横向折叠痕，均在正文内容之中。在相应折痕处书写的字迹笔画不流畅，出现白点和横向白条状痕；且伴有纸张纤维“毛刺”、墨点堆积、洇散以及不规则的笔画变细、变粗、断笔等现象。上述特征反映出正文内容字迹是在该纸张被折叠后书写形成的特点。这一纸张中的折痕与书写字迹间时序信息的解读，使得检验工作柳暗花明。

（四）借收据的数字笔迹特征

借收据的数字笔迹特征主要指阿拉伯数字的书写特征。阿拉伯数字虽然笔画少，结构简单，但我们仍不能忽视对它的研究运用。作案人在伪造借、收据时往往只注意对汉字进行伪装，而在数字的书写上暴露其固有特征。因此，应从数字间的组合、连写形式以及单个数字的写法、起笔、收笔、笔力、笔顺、搭配、比例等细节形态特征上进行全方位分析研究。1999年12月，我们检验的一起借款条书写纠纷案，摹仿嫌疑人姜某某书写水平很高，其通过精心练习与透视套摹组合伪造的借款条在字迹上下了很大功夫，有些字迹、笔画摹仿的惟妙惟肖甚至相应重合，但在阿拉伯数字“9、6、2”字的回转、收笔、行笔弧度等细节形态特征上与被摹仿笔迹表现出本质差异。

（五）标点及其他符号特征

标点及其他符号是指在书写表示停顿、物品数量单位或金额中的标点、小数点、分节号等符号时的安排位置、写法、大小、起、行、收笔形态、笔顺、搭配、比例等特征。研究运用借收据中出现的标点及符号特征，对于扩大利用特征范围，充实鉴定意见的根据具有重要作用。如上述3.4案例中，姜某某不仅在阿拉伯数字方面，在逗号、句号等的写法方面也表现出与被摹仿人的不同而与自身同一，为否定、同一认定提供了重要依据。实践中，我们还发现有的人习惯在年月日、数字、签名以及一组或一行字迹的结尾处点一点笔。其形态、大小、位置安排、用笔力度等亦能反映书写人的固有书写特征，且不易自身察觉伪装和他人摹仿。

四、检验对策

借收据笔迹字迹数量少，相同字迹、偏旁重复出现的机会亦少，少的只涉及2~3个字的签名或单独的姓或名，甚至只有单个偏旁或笔画。字迹少，则规律性书写特征不易把握。因此，应从以下几个方面进行检验：

（一）详细了解收据的形成过程

详细了解检材笔迹的形成过程，是进行笔迹检验的必经程序。对于借、收据类书写纠纷案件尤为重要，应向双方当事人特别是借收据的持有人了解有关借收据形成的详细过程，如书写的时间、地点、环境、书写人的书写姿势、衬垫物、书写工具、纸张的来源，有无在场人证明等情况。这项工作最好由鉴定人与审判人员共同完成，并以笔录的形式固定，当事人签名确认，这样既利于检验时有针对性地分析，同时有效避免鉴定结论做出后不利方当事人再信口雌黄。询问最好在双方当事人都到场的情况下分别进行，一是利于及时印证双方的说法，二是防止冒名顶替，造成案情失实、笔迹样本失真。2002 年 1 月，我们检验的一起借条书写纠纷案。为了解案情，我们通知双方到场说明情况同时，还告知了是否持有与书写借条有关的纸张、书写工具及对方笔迹样本等与检验工作有关的问题。因此，原告周某某提供了笔记本和圆珠笔，被告王某某则提供了事先写好的笔迹样本。而审判人员送检时并没有提到原告还保存着被告书写借条时所用的笔记本和圆珠笔。我们根据原告所说的王俯身在写字台上书写的借条的姿势。要求王某某按照原告周某某所说的书写姿势，使用原告提供的圆珠笔，在与借条大小接近的纸张上，用不同的书写速度听写与借条内容一致的笔迹样本。王某某虽然否认向原告借款，但为了表示自己没有说谎，也不得不按照我们的要求配合书写。在王某某书写时，我们还适时询问有关问题，让其边写边回答问题。虽然王某某的案后样本不同程度存在故意放慢书写速度现象，但固有的稳定性书写特征仍有流露，特别是圆珠笔的笔痕特征更是难以改变。此案中笔记本中的撕痕确定了检材借条纸张的来源，样本与检材中圆珠笔笔痕的符合，无疑为笔迹同一认定提供了更为可靠的依据。

（二）提取符合鉴定要求的同期样本

对借、收据案件应尽量提取与检材借、收据格式相同或相近的样本，在形成时间、字的形体、书写速度、工具、姿势、衬垫物也要尽量一致或相近。提取符合鉴定条件的高质量笔迹样本，有助于我们通过充分研究样本笔迹，发挥逆向思维优势，印证特征价值。如上述 2003 年 3 月受理的一起要求确定取款条内容有无添加的案例，我们通过询问原告毕某某得知：收款条是由被告方的合伙人书写，圆珠笔也是被告方当事人的，纸张是从自己孩子上学用的数学本上撕的。根据毕某某介绍的纸张来源情况，我们认为有必要到其家中寻找与检材相关的纸张，遂与法院审判人员一同到其家中，虽时隔 8 个月，还是比较理想地找到了与检材纸张、时间一致，金额数（为 8000 元）不同的 3 张收款条草稿（实为写废的收款条与笔迹物证连续性的同期样本）。而我们询问时，毕某某并没有说起曾写废过收款条的情况。上述同年同月同日样本的提取，为确定添加提供了重要依据。

（三）要注意借收据中印文的研究运用

对收据中出现的印文进行检验，对于认定书写人、确定借收据形成时间、真伪有一定的辅助作用。在检验时要力争提取同期及历时印文样本，此类样本的提取应从印章开始启用之日至争议发生之时，以争议和怀疑时间盖印的印文样本为主，多多益善，以便于我们把握该印章印文印迹的变化规律，为鉴定意见提供可靠依据。1989 年 7 月，我们检验的一起涉嫌贪污案。检材系三张复印的收据，字迹书写有故意降低熟练程度现象，且由于复印原因造成一些字迹笔画残缺、间断，但这三张收据上印文的安排位置、倾斜方向基本一致。在检验嫌疑人吴某某填写的收据样本时，发现检材、样本收据的印刷格式虽略有不同，但“秦皇岛市商业街建设领导小组办公室”印文在收据中的布局特征两者反映一致。笔迹特征结合印文细节特征、印文布局特征的共同反映，综合评断做出了认定意见。据此，吴被依法逮捕提起公诉。在法院开庭审理的前一天，吴某某自感抵赖不过，供述了犯罪事实。

（四）坚持综合分析系统鉴定

对于借、收据笔迹案件，既要分析文字的概貌特征，又要研究文件格式、文字、印文布局特征，既要运用阿拉伯数字、符号特征，又要精细比对单字个性、签名的细节及笔痕特征。同时，还要注意分析借、收据记载的内容，结合现代科学仪器，对纸张上出现的折叠、拼接、断离、剪切、擦刮、消退、复写、复印、文字书写压痕等相关信息也要进行全方位发掘解读，不放过任何蛛丝马迹，使鉴定意见建立在坚实的物质基础之上。

印迹分子吗啡与功能单体相互作用的紫外光谱研究 *

曾 玲[1]，李红旭[1]，周 红[2]，郝红霞[1**]

引 言

我国毒品犯罪日趋猖獗，吸毒人员逐年增加，对社会的安定产生极大的危害。毒品检验作为药物分析的一个发展学科，已经日益凸显其重要性。而我国目前毒物毒品检验还没有现场快速定量手段，检验的水平和现状不容乐观。吗啡是最常见、使用最为普遍的一类毒品，其危害也尤为严重。众所周知，吗啡虽然可以作为临床药物减轻患者的痛苦，但是当被过度使用或者长期使用时，它就成为了一种毒品，因此检验活体体液和尸体生物检材中的吗啡浓度便成为法庭毒物分析的一项重要任务。近年来，现场快速检测毒品的研究工作受到国内外的广泛关注。目前针对吗啡的检验方法主要有高效液相色谱法，[1] 气相色谱与质谱串联法，[2] 毛细管电泳法，[3][4] 比色法和荧光法，[5][6] 电化学分析，[7] 放射免疫测定法，[8][9] 酶联免疫吸附[10] 等。然而这些传统的实验室检验方法都在一定程度上存在局限性，如操作步骤繁杂，鉴定周期较长，需要昂贵的设备，缺乏生物试剂的选择性以及稳定性差等问题，已经不能满足实际办案的需要。因此，毒物分析要发展，就必须重视新仪器、新技术、新方法的研究和开发，以缩短与世界先进水平的差距。为此，我们把分子印迹技术（MIT）应用到法庭毒物分析中，充分将 MIT 技术的选择性高、识别性能好、灵敏度高等优点发挥出来，探讨其在毒品检验中的应用。并通过一系列实验，对吗啡分子印迹膜的制备条件进行了优化，从而提高印迹效率。

分子印迹技术（Molecularly Imprinting Technique，MIT）是一门新型的多学科交叉技术，起源于 1894 年 Fischer's[11] 提出的“锁匙理论”。分子印迹技术（MIT）也叫分子模板技术，是制备空间结构和结合位点与模板分子完全匹配的聚合物，即分子印迹聚合物（Molecularly Imprinting Polymer，MIPs）的实验技术。[12] 分子印迹聚合物（MIPs）对某一特定目标分子具有选择性。[13] 分子印迹技术的基本原理是将模板分子与功能单体在交联剂的作用下进行聚合反应，待反应完成后，再通过理化方法去除模板分子，这

* 资助项目：国家自然科学基金（No. 81001348），教育部长江学者和创新团队发展计划资助项目“证据科学研究与应用”（IRT0956），中国政法大学青年教师学术创新团队资助项目（1000－10814344），中国政法大学省部级合作项目（23212052）。

** 1. 证据科学教育部重点实验室（中国政法大学），北京 100088；2. 公安部物证鉴定中心，北京 100038。Email：haohx@ 126. com。

样原模板分子所在位置就留下了一系列结合位点，而这些结合位点对与模板分子同种的分子具有专一识别性，从而识别出某一类特殊的分子。根据印迹分子与功能单体相互作用的化学键的不同，分子印迹技术主要分为共价法（预组织法），非共价法（自组织法）和共价—非共价复合法。[14]分子印迹聚合物的制备方法目前主要有：本体聚合、悬浮聚合、扩散聚合、乳液聚合、原位聚合、电聚合、沉淀聚合、溶胶－凝胶技术、多步溶胀聚合、表面印迹、膜制备技术、种子溶胀法、硅胶接枝以及组合化学等方法，其中原位聚合、表面印迹法、沉淀聚合、溶胶—凝胶技术是近年来发展的新型、实用性强的制备方法。综合利用各种分析技术、各种光谱质谱分析手段和化学分析手段来解决法庭科学领域的问题已经成为时代发展的必然趋势。本文利用分子印迹技术探讨了毒品吗啡与功能单体相互作用的情况，是为了解决如何快速、灵敏、准确地检测到吗啡的问题，并期望在吗啡检测的基础上，找到一种能够为法庭科学毒物分析服务的新型分析方法。

一、实验部分

（一）实验仪器

Varian 公司的 Cary－50 型号的紫外光谱仪

（二）实验用品

盐酸吗啡（MO），公安部物证中心提供；

甲基丙烯酸（MAA），分析纯，国药集团上海总公司；

去离子水，

甲醇，分析纯，国药集团上海总公司

（三）实验步骤

1. 印迹分子 MO 与功能单体相互作用方式和强弱的研究

首先配制 0.1mmol/L 的 MO 溶液。用 25ml 移液管准确量取 25ml 浓度为 0.2mmol/L 的 MO 溶液至 50ml 容量瓶中，用甲醇稀释至刻度线，即配制成 50ml 浓度为 0.1mmol/L 的 MO 溶液（超声 5min）。然后按以下步骤进行研究：

（1）以纯甲醇作为参比溶液，分别将 0.1mmol/L 的 MO 溶液和 0.4mmol/L 的 MAA 溶液进行紫外－可见吸收光谱扫描，扫描波长为 200nm～400nm，得到纯 MO 和纯 MAA 的紫外吸收光谱谱图。

（2）现场配制 MO（0.1mmol/L）与 MAA（0.4mmol/L）混合溶液。用 10mL 移液管量取 10mL 浓度为 0.1mmol/L 的 MO 溶液至 10mL 容量瓶中，用 0.5μL 微量进样器向其中加入 0.34μL 的 MAA，混合均匀后静置三分钟。然后以纯甲醇作为参比，进行光谱扫描，找到最大吸收峰波长的大概位置，在该波长处按时间扫描 MO（0.1mmol/L）与 MAA（0.4mmol/L）预聚合溶液的紫外吸收光谱 4h。

（3）待最大吸收峰值随时间不再变化时，对 MO（0.1mmol/L）与 MAA（0.4mmol/L）混合溶液进行紫外－可见吸收光谱扫描。比较 MO 与 MAA 在甲醇中混合前后紫外光谱的变化情况。

2. 印迹分子 MO 与功能单体 MAA 形成的主客体配合物的结合常数 K 的求算

取 13 个 10mL 容量瓶，每次用 5mL 移液管准确量取浓度为 0.2mmol/L 的 MO 溶液 5ml 至每个容量瓶中，用甲醇溶剂稀释至相应刻度即可得到一系列浓度为 0.1mmol/L 的

MO 溶液。利用微量进样器向每个容量瓶中加入不同量的 MAA，渐增功能单体 MAA 的量，配制一系列预聚合体系，混合均匀后静置 4h。再取 13 个 10mL 容量瓶，配制成相应的 MAA 纯溶液。以相应的纯 MAA 溶液作为参比，如表 1 所示。用紫外－可见吸收光谱对上述一系列不同量比的预聚合溶液进行分析，扣除溶剂和 MAA 的背景吸收后，得到 MO 的紫外吸收光谱图。

表 1 实验中所用的试剂量及比例

预聚合溶液编号	比例	MO（0.1mmol/L）	MAA	参比溶液编号
(1)	1：0	10mL	0μL	(14)
(2)	1：1	10mL	0.08μL	(15)
(3)	1：2	10mL	0.17μL	(16)
(4)	1：3	10mL	0.25μL	(17)
(5)	1：4	10mL	0.34μL	(18)
(6)	1：6	10mL	0.51μL	(19)
(7)	1：8	10mL	0.64μL	(20)
(8)	1：10	10mL	0.85μL	(21)
(9)	1：18	10mL	1.53μL	(22)
(10)	1：25	10mL	2.12μL	(23)
(11)	1：36	10mL	3.05μL	(24)
(12)	1：42	10mL	3.56μL	(25)
(13)	1：56	10mL	4.75μL	(26)

3. 探究温度对 MO 与 MAA 形成的复合物的影响

现场配制三组 MO（0.01mmol/L）与 MAA（0.04 mmol/L）混合溶液。按照 2.1 中的方法先配置好 0.1mmol/L 的 MO 溶液，再用 10ml 移液管量取 1ml 浓度为 0.1mmol/L 的 MO 溶液至 10ml 容量瓶中，然后向其中加入甲醇溶液直至容量瓶刻度线，最后用 0.1μL 微量进样器向其中加入 0.034μL 的 MAA，即得 MO（0.01mmol/L）与 MAA（0.04 mmol/L）混合溶液。混合均匀静止 4h 后，再将这三组混合溶液分别在 30℃、40℃、50℃的恒温水浴加热 10 分钟。加热完成后，迅速将这三组混合溶液进行紫外－可见吸收光谱扫描，扫描波长为 200nm～400nm，比较它们的紫外吸收光谱图。

二、结果与讨论

（一）印迹分子 MO 与功能单体 MAA 相互作用方式和强弱的研究

分子印迹聚合物识别机理的研究对解释聚合物印迹和识别的现象是非常重要的。在分子印迹聚合物合成之前，均有模板分子与功能单体预聚合的过程，此时尚未添加交联剂和引发剂，模板分子与功能单体在振荡器中充分摇匀，使两者之间自行调整空间取向以产生最佳效果的非共价相互作用，形成稳定的主客体配合物，这个过程也称之为自组装。分子印迹的基本原理就在于将预聚合反应混合溶液中自组装形成的超分子结构尽可能地移入聚合形成的固体高分子聚合物中。模板分子与功能单体的作用的强弱直接影响着分子印迹聚合物的选择性和亲和性。如果预聚合反应时功能单体与模板分子没有很好地定向自组装，功能基团的分布是任意的，这样就会形成大量非选择性的结合位点，使印迹聚合物的选择性降低。相反，如果功能单体与模板分子的配合能力强，那么就能形成拥有许多高选择性的识别位点的聚合物，使聚合物的识别能力大大提高。因此，研究聚合反应前混合物溶液中模板分子与功能单体的相互作用以及主客体配合物的形成条件，有利于从分子水平上了解分子印迹聚合物的识别机理，提高分子印迹聚合物的选择性结合能力以及研究模板分子的结构对印迹效应的影响。

本实验通过紫外吸收光谱法研究了以甲醇作为溶剂时模板分子 MO 与功能单体 MAA 在甲醇溶剂中相互作用情况。以甲醇作为溶剂的各组分紫外光谱图，见图 1。

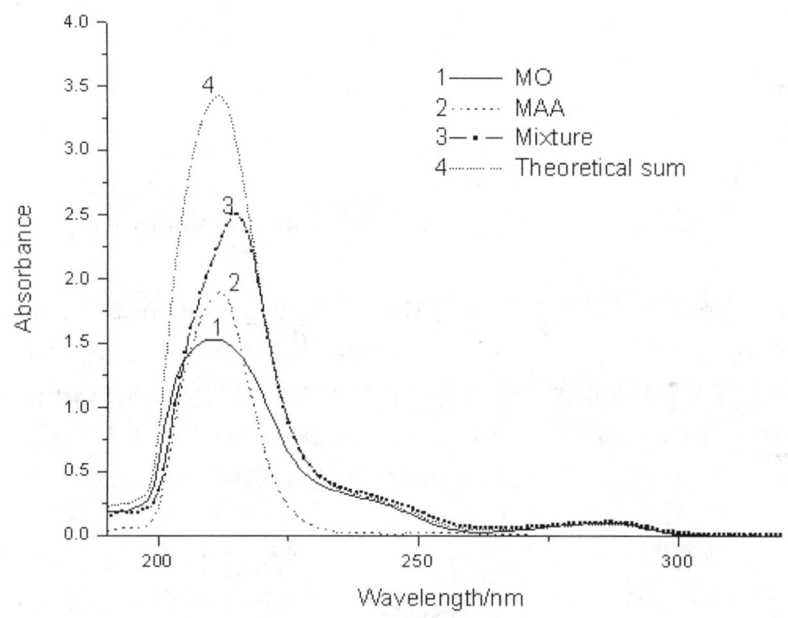

图 1 MO 与 MAA 在甲醇中紫外吸收光谱图

1—MO 的甲醇溶液（0.1mmol/L），2—MAA 的甲醇溶液（0.4 mmol/L），3—MO + MAA，4—曲线 1 和 2 的理论加和值。

在图 1 中，MO 在 211nm 和 287nm 附近有两个特征吸收峰（曲线 1）；功能单体 MAA 的最大吸收峰 $\lambda_{max}=212nm$，与 MO 的最大吸收峰非常接近，但是它只有一个特征吸收峰（曲线 2），且谱图形状与曲线 1 不同。将 MO 溶液与 MAA 混合后扫描，得到曲线 3，它就是 MO 与 MAA 混合后所得到的溶液的实际光谱图。该曲线的 $\lambda_{max}=214nm$，与 211nm 相比发生了红移，同时在 287nm 处仍然有一个吸收峰，该峰的外形几乎没有发生变化。将曲线 1 和曲线 2 进行图像处理，叠加成曲线 4，即曲线 4 反应的是 MO 没有与功能单体 MAA 接触，与之没有发生任何作用情况下的 MO 与 MAA 两种组分叠加的理论紫外吸收谱图。比较曲线 3、4 可知，$\lambda_{4max}=211nm\neq\lambda_{3max}$，虽然二者的 $\Delta\lambda$ 较小，但是 MO + MAA 体系在甲醇溶剂中确实发生了红移；此外，$A_4 > A_3$，二者的 ΔA 相差较大，这就表明两种溶液混合后，体系表现出来的吸光度值不是两者的简单叠加，而是二者自组装作用以后形成新物质的吸收光谱。由于曲线 3 和曲线 4 两条谱线的最大吸收峰值相差较明显，说明在甲醇溶剂中 MAA 与 MO 相互作用较强，即模板分子与功能单体之间预组织性较强，这预示着合成出的分子印迹聚合物薄膜对模板分子 MO 的特异选择性可能就会较好。

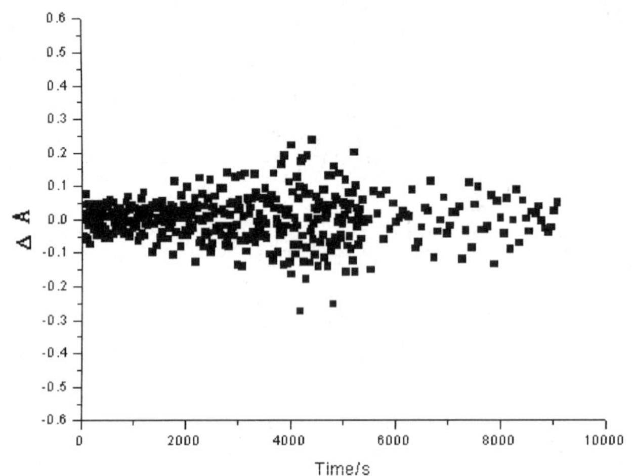

图2 MO 与 MAA 混合溶液在 214nm 处吸光度随时间的变化

本实验中我们还具体研究了 MAA 与 MO 摩尔比为 1：4 时在甲醇溶剂中相互作用情况。我们对 MO 与 MAA 混合溶液在 214nm 处的吸光度随时间的变化进行了考察，如图 2 所示。MAA 与 MO 混合溶液在 214nm 处的吸光度随时间的变化在不断地发生变化，在将 MAA 加入到 MO 的溶液中，开始时混合溶液在 214nm 处的吸光度随着时间的变化逐渐增强，大约在 1.5h 左右达到最大，之后又随着时间的变化逐渐降低，大约在 3h 左右混合溶液在 214nm 处的吸光度到达稳定，不再随时间的变化而变化。这说明 MO 与 MAA 自组装体系需要在二者混合 4h 后才能达到稳定的状态。

（二）印迹分子 MO 与功能单体 MAA 形成的主客体配合物的结合常数 K 的求算

为了更进一步了解功能单体 MAA 与模板分子 MO 在预聚合溶液中相互作用力的具体情况，作者在实验中固定 MO 的用量，改变 MAA 的用量，采用差示紫外吸收光谱，扣除溶剂和 MAA 的背景吸收后，得到 MO 的紫外吸收光谱图，如图 3 所示。根据图 2，我们可以得到 MAA 对 MO 紫外吸收光谱图影响的大小（图 4），由此可确定 MAA 与 MO 相互作用的强弱。

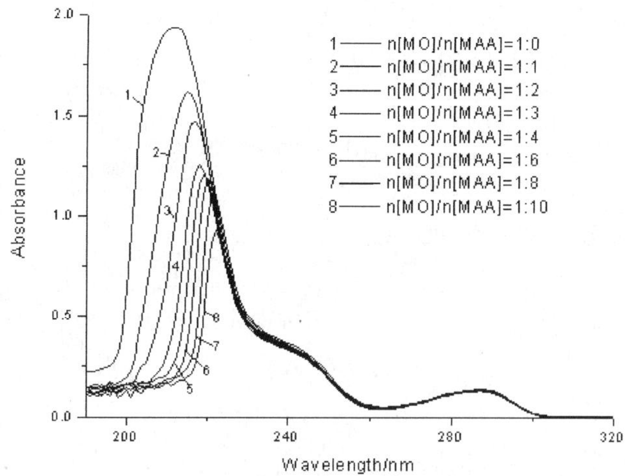

图 3 MO – MAA 不同量比溶液的紫外吸收光谱图

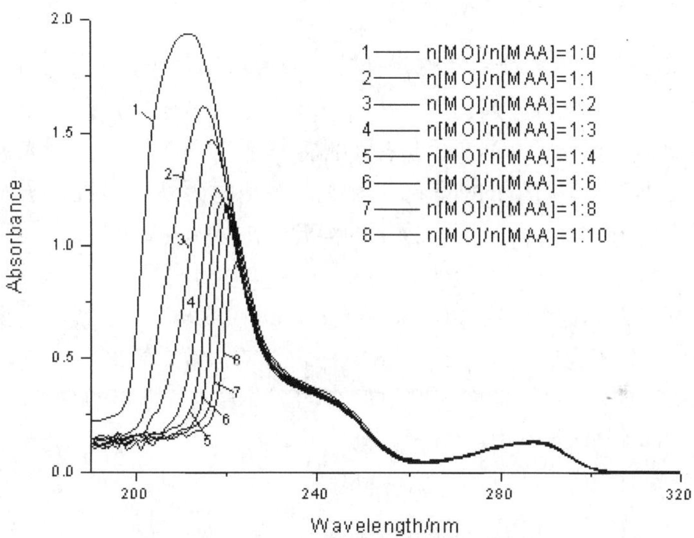

图 4 MAA 对 MO 的 λ_{max} 和 A_{max} 的影响

在分子印迹技术中，我们可以通过紫外 - 可见吸收光谱法研究预聚合体系中模板分子与功能单体相互作用力的强弱，采用差示紫外吸收光谱在功能单体大大过量的情况下求算模板分子与功能单体形成的主客体配合物的结合常数和化学配位比。设印迹分子 A 与功能单体 B 之间自组装发生的反应为：

$$A + nB = C \qquad \text{(公式 1)}$$

则此反应的平衡常数，即主客体配合物 C 的稳定性常数 K 为：

$$K = \frac{[C]}{[A][B]^n} \qquad \text{(公式 2)}$$

如印迹分子 A 的总浓度为 a_0，加入的功能单体的总浓度为 b_0，根据物料平衡方程有：

$$[A] + [C] = a_0 \qquad \text{(公式 3)}$$

$$[B] + n[C] = b_0 \qquad \text{(公式 4)}$$

式中 $[A]$ 、$[B]$ 和 $[C]$ 分别为印迹分子 A、功能单体 B 和主客体配合物 C 的平衡浓度，当 $b_0 \leqslant a_0$ ，式（4）中的 $[C]$ 可以忽略，即：

$$[B] = b_0 \qquad \text{（公式 5）}$$

将式（4）和式（5）代入式（2）中，整理后得：

$$[C] = \frac{Kb_0 * a_0}{1 + Kb_0^n} \qquad \text{（公式 6）}$$

若溶液中 A、B、C 三种物质在测量波长下都有吸收，则预聚合体系的吸光度为：

$$A = \varepsilon_A l[A] + \varepsilon_B l[B] + \varepsilon_C l[C] = \varepsilon_A la_0 + \varepsilon_B lb_0 + (\varepsilon_C - \varepsilon_A - n\varepsilon_B)l[C] \qquad \text{（公式 7）}$$

令 $A_A^0 = \varepsilon_A la_0$, $B_B^0 = \varepsilon_B lb_0$ ，即以溶剂为参比时纯 A 和 B 的吸光度，则：

$$\Delta A = A - A_A^0 - A_B^0 = (\varepsilon_C - \varepsilon_A - n\varepsilon_B)l[C] = \Delta\varepsilon \times l \times [C] \qquad \text{（公式 8）}$$

将式（9）代入式（7），整理得：

$$\frac{\Delta A}{b_0^n} = -K\Delta A + K \times \Delta\varepsilon \times l \times a_0 \qquad \text{（公式 9）}$$

式中 n 为主客体配合物的化学配位比，取 $n = 1$，2，…，分别求算 $\Delta A/b_0^n$，并以求得的 $\Delta A/b_0^n$ 对 ΔA 作图为一条直线，由此求得预聚合体系中印迹分子与功能单体的结合常数 K 以及化学配位比 n。本文所选择的测定波长为吗啡分子的最大吸收波长之特征波长（217nm，反应前模板分子的吸光度为 A_0，反应时因消耗模板分子而形成主客体配合物，所对应的吸光度为 A，因模板分子的消耗，故 $A < A_0$ ，所以，它们的差值为 ΔA（ $\Delta A = A - A_0$ 为负值）。如图 5 所示，当 $n = 1$ 和 3 时为曲线，当 $n = 2$ 时为一条良好的直线，其回归方程为 $y = -6.83448 - 4.16932x (R = 0.99639)$ ，说明在此条件下 MO 和 MAA 形成了 1：2 的配合物，由直线的斜率可求得结合常数 K 为 $4.169 \times 10^6 mol^{-2}/L^{-2}$ ，这个结果表明吗啡能和 MAA 形成主客体配合物，并具有一定的稳定性，$n = 2$ 表明了一个吗啡分子能和两个 MAA 结合。

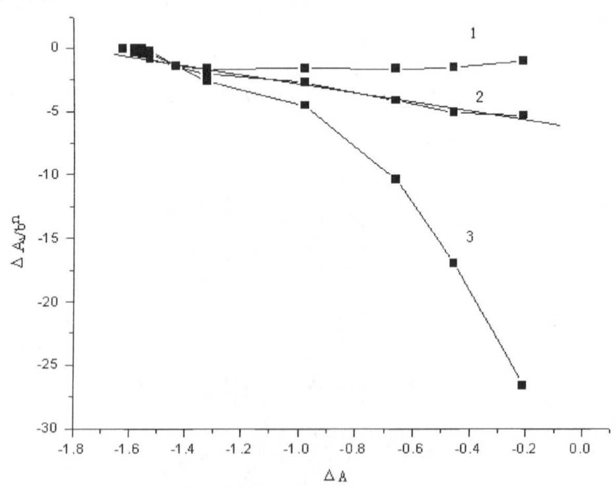

图 5　MO 和 MAA 在甲醇中的结合常数图

（三）探究温度对 MO 与 MAA 形成的复合物的影响

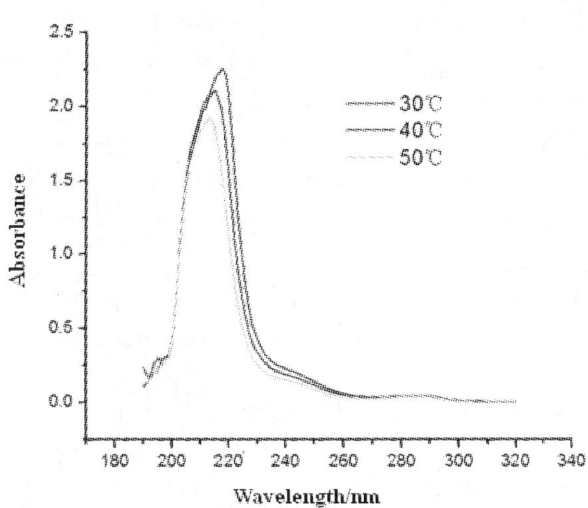

图 6　相同浓度的 MO 和 MAA 随温度的改变在甲醇中的紫外吸收光谱

由前述及图 1 可知 MO 和 MAA 溶液混合后，体系表现出来的吸光度值不是两者的简单叠加，而是二者通过氢键发生自组装作用以后形成新复合物的吸收光谱。为了进一步证实氢键在形成这种复合物中的重要性，我们通过加热的方式使得氢键断裂，并用紫外光谱来印证这一假设，所得紫外图谱如图 6 所示。通过比较不同温度下 MO 和 MAA 形成的复合物的紫外吸收光谱，我们发现该复合物的最大吸收峰随着温度的升高发生了蓝移。这种结果归因于氢键在较高温度下的断裂。结果显示 MO 与 MAA 的相互作用受温度的影响。

三、结　论

本文利用分子印迹技术，制备了 MO 与 MAA 的印迹聚合物，并采用紫外光谱对分子印迹合成的机理进行表征，探究了 MO 与 MAA 相互作用方式、强弱以及温度对聚合物形成的影响。实验结果表明在甲醇溶剂中 MAA 与 MO 相互作用较强，即模板分子与功能单体之间预组织性较强，这预示着合成出的分子印迹聚合物薄膜对模板分子 MO 的特异选择性较好。MO 和 MAA 以氢键能形成主客体配合物，并具有很好的稳定性，分子印迹技术可以应用到吗啡的检测中。在此基础上，我们会探讨分子印迹聚合物传感器的研制与表征，这将实现吗啡传感芯片的快速定量检测。

参考文献

[1] S. O. Mashayekhi, M. Ghandforoush – Sattari, and R. D. W. Hain, "Rapid and sensitive quantitation of morphine using HPLC with electrochemical detection", *J. Clin. Pharm. Ther.*, 2008, 33 (4), pp. 419 ~ 427.

[2] Khosrou Abdi, Abbas Shafiee, Mohsen Amini, Mahmood Ghazi – Khansari, and Omid Sabzevari, "Detection of morphine in opioid abusers hair by gc/ms", Daru, 2004, 12 (2), pp. 71 ~ 75.

[3] N. W. Barnett, B. J. Hindson, and S. W. Lewis, "Determination of morphine, oripavine and pseud-

omorphine using capillary electrophoresis with acidic potassium permanganate chemiluminescence detection", *Analyst*, 1999, 125 (1), pp. 91 ~95.

[4] A. O. Alnajjar, "Capillary electrophoresis with fluorescence detection for sensitive analysis of morphine and 6 – acetylmorphine in human urine", *Acta Chromatographica*, 2008, 20 (2), pp. 227 ~238.

[5] H. C. Hsu, L. C. Chen, and K. C. Ho, "Colorimetric detection of morphine in a molecularly imprinted polymer using an aqueous mixture of fe3 + and fe (cn) (6) (3 –)", *Anal. Chim. Acta*, 2004, 504 (1), pp. 141 ~147.

[6] Hannu S. Valimaki, Timo Pulli, and Kirsi Tappura, "Applying total internal reflection excitation and super critical angle fluorescence detection to a morphine assay", *Journal of Fluorescence*, 2010, 20 (5), pp. 1003 ~1008.

[7] Aso Navaee, Abdollah Salimi, and Hazhir Teymourian, "Graphene nanosheets modified glassy carbon electrode for simultaneous detection of heroine, morphine and noscapine", *Biosens. Bioelectron.*, 2012, 31 (1), pp. 20 ~211.

[8] T. B. Yang, Y. H. Yuan, P. Zhong, L. N. Qu, B. Yang, Y. H. Li, and G. Ju., "Group – selective immunoassay for the detection of morphine in urine", *Hybridoma and Hybridomics*, 2004, 23 (1), pp. 69 ~72.

[9] A. S. Yuan, F. M. Rubio, and S. E. Wagner, "A dual radioimmunoassay for the detection of morphine and cocaine in urine", *Clin. Chem.*, 1988, 34 (6), pp. 1161 ~1161.

[10] S. Stanley, A. Jeganathan, T. Wood, P. Henry, S. Turner, W. E. Woods, M. Green, H. H. Tai, D. Watt, J. Blake, and T. Tobin, "Morphine and etorphine. 14. Detection by elisa in equine urine", *J. Anal. Toxicol.*, 1991, 15 (6), pp. 305 ~310.

[11] Fischer E, "Synthese derm annose und lavulose", *Ber dtsch Chen Ges*, 1890 (23), pp. 799 ~805.

[12] 王艳荣、王培龙、王静、王锡昌、钟耀广："分子印迹技术的研究的新进展及应用"，载《现代科学仪器》2008 年第 1 期，第 11 页。

[13] 才华：《左旋沙丁胺醇印迹聚合物的合成及性能表征》，北京理工大学 2007 年硕士学位论文。

[14] 赖家平、何锡文、郭洪声："分子印迹技术的回顾，现状与展望"，载《分析化学研究报告》2001 年第 7 期，第 836 ~844 页。

建立笔迹样本数据库的可行性初探

黄 旭 刘建伟 *

笔迹检验是司法鉴定领域中依赖鉴定人主观能动性比较强的一门鉴定技术，不同于法庭科学其他学科，如DNA检验、微量物证检验等有着较为系统的生物、化学等自然科学技术知识做支撑，笔迹检验主要依靠鉴定人的知识和经验对文字进行识别与判断，通过比对检材和样本中的笔迹特征来进行同一认定。因此，笔迹检验的科学性一直以来都受到国际上的质疑，而目前能使笔迹检验的准确性得到充分体现在很大程度上依赖于样本收集的真实性、可靠性、充足性以及可比性。笔迹检验是通过检材笔迹与样本笔迹之间的特征比较进行的，而提取满足一定要求的样本笔迹是进行比较检验的基础。笔迹样本的真实性及对书写人书写习惯反映的可靠性，是鉴定意见正确与否的关键。提供可靠、充足的样本笔迹能够更好地帮助鉴定人做出正确的鉴定意见，相反，就难以做出鉴定意见，甚至做出错误的判断。在现实办案中，笔迹样本的数量与质量往往对鉴定结论起到至关重要的作用。着眼于部分地区试点实行、并逐步扩大覆盖范围，建立一个全国范围内的笔迹样本数据库不失为解决日常办案中样本数量不充足、质量不过关等问题的一个有效途径。笔者试从以下几个方面简单谈谈对建立笔迹样本数据库的粗浅认识。

一、国内外研究现状

（一）国内现状

目前，我国已逐步建立起各种法庭科学数据库，如DNA数据库、指纹库，随着时间的推移和技术的发展，人像数据库等新型数据库还要逐步建立。但是，对于需要充足样本的笔迹检验领域，还未有多少声音或技术力量提出建立笔迹检验的样本库。昆明市公安局曾经致力于建立一个包含人体8种特征的数据库系统，包括DNA、指纹、人像、声纹等，其中也包含笔迹样本数据库，但由于各种原因，笔迹样本库最终未能成功建立起来。近两年，为了打击法轮功邪教组织的活动，建立重点人员管控机制，昆明市公安局建立了邪教组织和有害气功人员的笔迹档案库，这是我国实务中建立有关笔迹数据库的一个为数不多的范例。但总体来说，我国国内笔迹样本数据库的发展过程比较缓慢。

（二）国外现状

在国外，计算机化和自动化正不断蔓延到法庭科学各个领域，大多数检验手段和检验过程已离不开计算机的帮助。数据库、文件归档、过程记录、数据采集、几乎每

* 黄旭，中国政法大学硕士研究生；刘建伟，博士，中国政法大学副教授。Email：huang1122334054@126.com。

一环节都与计算机操作息息相关，就连最需要鉴定人主观经验的文件检验也不例外。在过去的30年中，国外的笔迹检验专家们正致力将计算机辅助系统引入笔迹检验过程中，力争使笔迹检验也变得自动化并得到数据支持，进而提高笔迹检验专家的检验水平，增强笔迹鉴定的科学性。许多研究致力于研发一种图案识别技术以提取检材和样本文字中稳定的书写动力定型特征，以帮助检验人进行特征的筛选和比对，因此，国外研究机构开发了许多类似的软件系统，如1993年由德国专家开发出来的“FISH system”就是这类软件的代表之一。这类特征自动比对系统既采集样本与检材的概貌特征，如基本书写水平特征与布局特征，还采集细节特征，即个人具体的用字特征。但是，软件只是辅助鉴定人进行比对的工具，并不能代替“人工”比对分析。虽然国外有很多笔迹自动比对系统，这类系统也同样注重样本的收集提取。但到目前为止，还没有将计算机化和自动化的优势用于样本的保存和建库，也没有人提出关于采集单一样本与建立独立样本库的方案。因此，对于笔迹样本数据库的建立，国内外目前均未有人系统研究，这一领域仍属空白。

二、存在问题

（一）理论界和实务界对建立笔迹样本数据库的重要性未给予充分的关注

一直以来，行业内外对笔迹样本库用途的认识仅局限在刑事案件中。随着电子信息时代的到来，尤其是计算机的迅猛发展，快速和便捷的键盘打字在一点一点地侵蚀着传统笔迹的生存空间。随着科技知识普及面的扩大，人们的防范意识和反侦查意识也越来越高，就像作案要戴手套以免留下自己的指纹一样，犯罪嫌疑人在犯罪现场留下自己笔迹的情况也越来越少。这是理论界和实务界没有对建立笔迹样本数据库的重要性给予充分关注的一个重要原因。但是，随着人们经济往来的增多，法律意识的逐渐增强，民事纠纷也越来越多，很多民事案件如民商事合同，个人借款欠条等都涉及笔迹鉴定问题。甚至毫不夸张地说，目前笔迹鉴定在民事诉讼活动中应用的广泛程度，已超过刑事案件的侦查阶段。现在的社会已经不是原始的熟人社会，很多有经济往来的双方当事人对彼此都不是很了解，一方当事人要求对一份写有对方当事人笔迹的文件进行鉴定，却又提供不出对方当事人的平时样本；而对方当事人提供的所谓的平时样本的真实性又会受到质疑，如果要收集实验样本，它的鉴定价值又大大缩减，此时笔迹样本数据库的用途就凸显出来了。因此，社会各界对笔迹样本数据库重要性的忽视，是影响目前建立笔迹样本库的一个意识问题，需要重申并探讨，给予足够关注。

（二）目前笔迹样本数据库的建立只针对部分区域和特定人群，有一定局限性

正如前文国内现状中提到，目前国内鲜有文章提出建立笔迹样本数据库并对此进行系统研究。仅有个别地方的公安部门，针对特定人群，为稳定不安全因素，建立了一些笔迹档案库。但这种数据库有很大的局限性，一是地理范围上只能适用于当地地区，二是仅能针对那些不安定人群，三是数据库只能应用于刑事案件。这样远远没有发挥出笔迹样本库应有的功能，无法满足现实案件量的需要。

（三）建立笔迹样本数据库是一个浩大的工程，面临诸多难题

任何一个数据库的建立都不可能是一蹴而就的，需要做好前期考察并进行系统性的研究。在有扎实的理论研究并做好充分准备的基础上，才能付诸实践，由点到面、从小到大，渐渐形成规模。一些地方曾经努力尝试建立笔迹样本库，但中途夭折，最

终没有成功。可见，建立笔迹样本数据库的艰难性比想象中还要大，建库过程需要耗费大量的人力、物力、财力。除此之外，如果要完成这些工作还需要解决以下问题：①这些工作谁来牵头、谁来支持、谁来配合；②大范围地收集公民的笔迹样本需要公开，能否得到公民认可，是否侵犯人权，是否符合法律规范；③样本数据库的覆盖率能有多少，能多大限度地满足案件需求，如果数据库建成，收获与付出是否正相关；④样本的实际采集情况，如何操作；⑤笔迹鉴定原则上要使用原件，扫描入库的笔迹在一定程度上丧失了一些笔迹特征，怎样看待这个问题。

三、建立笔迹样本数据库的初步设想

一个人的书写活动在最初的学习和训练中是随意性的，这一时期的书写动作主要依靠人的意识支配来完成。随着书写训练的进行，渐渐会形成书写技能，书写技能逐渐成熟并形成书写习惯之后，他的书写活动才有可能摆脱意识的支配，由随意性的运动转化为自动化的运动。书写技能的提高依靠练习来完成，练习的进步表现在书写技能上的规律则是先快后慢，一个人的书写技能的提高与发展从高中后期就开始呈缓慢态势，进入中年后几乎看不到明显的变化。[1]因此，收集过小年龄的笔迹样本对办案来说没有实际意义，再结合现在刑事案件犯罪嫌疑人年龄的大致波动范围，初步设想可将中考考试试卷作为一个人第一次的笔迹样本扫描收集入库。因为我国实行九年义务教育，受教育既是公民的权利也是公民的义务，中考覆盖率相对较大，这样能尽可能大范围地收集到更多人的笔迹样本。同理，高考考试试卷可作为第二次样本扫描收集。早在几年前，我国很多地方就已经开始将试卷扫描进计算机后网上阅卷，这也相对减少了扫描收集样本入库所须花费的人力资源。其余的样本收集工作可落实在公共机关保存档案的过程中，如公安局户籍登记、出入境申请管理、各单位人事处登记备案等，这些材料中既有签名笔迹，也会有大量的阿拉伯数字、标点符号和其他字迹，包含笔迹种类较多。

四、研究建立笔迹样本数据库可行性的理论及现实意义

（一）在笔迹鉴定中保障样本的真实性

保障样本的真实性是笔迹鉴定的前提。笔迹样本是否可靠、充分、具有可比性，直接关系到鉴定结论准确与否。中考考试试卷、高考考试试卷、公安局户籍管理、出入境记录管理，各单位人事处登记档案等，都是公共机关保存的档案文件。学生在考试时全神贯注于考试试题，书写时奋笔疾书，留下的笔迹能很好地反映出他当时的书写习惯；被收集人在填写公共机关登记材料时，也不会预料到自己以后是否会涉及诉讼，留下的笔迹对自己在诉讼中是能起到积极作用还是消极作用。所以，没有人会在这些登记的材料中伪装笔迹。一般来说，发案时期及案前样本应用价值最大，能全面、真实反映书写人固有的书写习惯特征，而上述可以作为样本库采样对象的文字恰恰属于发案时期样本或案前样本，如果能将这些材料扫描录入计算机制成个人笔迹样本库，既能够保证收集到的笔迹确系被收集人亲笔所写，又能够充分地反映出他的书写习惯特征，排除伪装。

（二）弥补因样本不足而无法出具鉴定意见的遗憾

样本收集是否充足在笔迹鉴定中十分重要，有时甚至可以说具有决定性意义。现在的实践中经常出现这样的情况，一方当事人要求对一份文字材料上的笔迹进行鉴定，原告提供的样本被告不认可，而被告提供的样本原告又不认可，只能去第三方诸如银行、工商局、保险公司等机构提取样本，而当事人在这些机构留下的往往只是些签名，日期等文字信息，对于要求鉴定全文的申请无法满足样本在数量上的需求。刑事案件中，要对现场留下的笔迹进行大范围的排查，能否搜集到大量充足的笔迹样本是个关键。研究笔迹样本库建立的可行性，可以为上述问题提供一个解决机制，探讨能否从根本上找到一种措施，如何操作，如何落实，才能让样本的收集不再是一个难题。笔迹样本数据库中收集的笔迹应当是一个人在不同时期书写，并存储录入计算机系统的，如果这样的数据库具有建立的可行性，不单单从横向的数量上保障了样本的充足性，在纵向上也能提供涉案人在历史上各个时期的笔迹样本，这也为刑事案件中寻找发案时期嫌疑人样本提供了便利。

（三）对文件检验学科特别是笔迹检验领域具有研究价值

排除样本库中的笔迹作为司法鉴定中样本的需要，大量的笔迹本身就是可供文件检验学科研究的宝贵资源。本文拟探讨的样本库中会包含大量不同历史时期扫描入库的样本，随着时间的推移，能覆盖一个自然人从小到大再到老的历时性笔迹样本，这就为文检鉴定人研究历时性笔迹特征的变化打下基础。同时，样本库中采集的笔迹样本，来自不同时期，不同环境，不同书写条件，所用的书写工具也不会全部相同，这样也为文检鉴定人研究不同条件下形成的笔迹提供了很充分的参考样本。文件检验是一门实践型学科，在注重一个学科实践应用的同时，学科自身的研究发展也是不容忽视的。研究笔迹样本库建立的可行性对文件检验的学科建设有促进意义。

（四）各种数据库的建立和完善是一个不可阻挡的发展趋势

如今，在世界范围内，DNA 和指纹数据库已经具备一定规模。随着信息化的高速发展和数据库的建立、完善，案件的侦破速度有了前所未有的提升。各种信息通过计算机系统互通有无，既增加了各地办案机关获取资料的便利性，也在很大程度上节约了人力、物力和财力。法庭科学各个学科数据库的建立和完善是将来的一个发展趋势。研究笔迹样本库建立的可行性，进而为建立笔迹样本数据库提供一个可行性方案，对法庭科学的系统完善有着重要意义。当需要某人的笔迹样本时，可以直接从样本库中提取，免去样本一案一收集的重复工作，例如在北京发现了一个案子需要进行笔迹鉴定，而嫌疑人却在新疆，如果能够建立起一个笔迹样本数据库，就可以直接从数据库中提取离他作案时期最近时间的样本笔迹，而不用再特意跑去新疆收集嫌疑人样本，这样既能节约时间，提高办案效率，同时又能节约大量司法资源。此外，从自然科学角度出发，研究逐步建立一个大范围的笔迹样本库可促进文件检验学科的发展和完善；从另一个角度看它还具有多重价值，将一个人的重要信息资料登记录入计算机数据库工作本身，就是对一个人的档案进行归档保存，是对他重要信息的一个妥善保管程序，当他的某一信息丢失或参与诉讼，样本库中的内容又可以作为较好的依据或证据使用。

五、建库过程中可能产生的疑惑

（一）大范围的收集公民的笔迹样本需要公开，能否得到公民认可，是否侵犯人权

DNA、指纹数据库的入库对象一般限制为已决犯或犯罪嫌疑人，有特定指向性，而本文探讨的笔迹样本数据库的入库对象是普通群众，具有普遍性。有些人可能会认为，公开收集普通公民的笔迹样本，是将他们看做潜在的罪犯或犯罪嫌疑人，侵犯了

公民的一般人格权；笔迹样本数据库中的个人基本信息如果保管或使用不当，如被保险机构、招聘机构非法获取，还可能会侵犯到他们的隐私权。尊重和保障人权是近几年法学界和社会上讨论较多的热门话题，2004 年引入宪法，2012 年又写入新刑事诉讼法。社会民众的人权观念也越来越强，公开收集公民笔迹样本触及人权问题，如果处理不当，容易引起不必要的麻烦。

笔者认为，笔迹样本库不同于 DNA 和指纹数据库，它的适用范围不仅仅局限于刑事领域，在民事案件的审判中也大有用途。笔迹样本库在将来的司法审判中对被收集人是否有利，要取决于他在案件中所处的“角色”：如果被收集人在日常生活中造假、涉嫌欺诈，诚信缺失，那么当他涉诉时笔迹样本库中的样本对他来说是不利的；相反，如果被收集人在民商事交往中以诚待人，当他涉入民事或商事纠纷时，笔迹样本库中的样本恰恰成为揭示事实真相，保护其正当利益的证明材料。再如，遗嘱纠纷中，当一份遗嘱的真实性受到质疑，同时又收集不到立遗嘱人生前样本时，笔迹样本库中的样本就可作为有效样本用于鉴定，从而保障被收集人的真实意思表示。从这个角度上看，样本库可以被看作是“诚信者的保护伞，造假者的曝光器”。因此，公开收集公民的笔迹样本，并没有侵害被收集人的人格平等、人格独立、人格自由或人格尊严，不会侵犯公民的一般人格权。

另外，对于样本库能否侵犯到公民隐私权的问题，应当慎重考虑。样本库中保存有公民大量的基本信息，对样本库的保管部门以及样本调取部门应做严格的限制。尤其是样本调取部门，首先它必须是公权力机关，任何个人、团体、企事业单位都无权接触或调取。原则上，法院应为调取样本的合法机关。对于刑事案件，还可赋予侦查机关适当调取样本的权力。同时，在立法上，应严惩通过非法手段从样本库中获得公民笔迹样本的行为，从源头充分保护被收集人的个人隐私。

（二）笔迹鉴定原则上要使用原件，扫描入库的笔迹样本能否视为原件

用于笔迹鉴定的样本材料，原则上要求应为原件。倘若建立起笔迹样本数据库，库中的样本都是扫描件，这些“扫描”样本能否被视作原件，是否符合笔迹鉴定的规定方法？笔者认为，之所以规定笔迹鉴定原则上要使用原件，最主要的目的是要保障样本的真实性，规定中的“原件”针对的主要是复印件，防止张冠李戴。从笔迹特征角度看，样本扫描件除了在一定程度上丧失了少量笔迹特征（如笔痕）之外，与原件的差别并不大，样本的扫描件上仍旧能保留大量的笔迹特征，同样能反映出书写人固有的书写习惯。如今文件检验的工作中，鉴定人采用手工仿形描绘法制作特征比对表的已经不多了，普遍做法是将检材或样本原件进行扫描后，利用软件对扫描件进行裁剪并粘贴。由此可见，利用笔迹样本数据库中的样本扫描件进行笔迹鉴定，不影响结论的可靠性，其价值近似于原件。

（三）如何看待因替考而影响样本真实性的问题

对于数据库中样本的真实性，前文提到，大多数情况下是有保证的。但是，一些个别的情况也不能忽视。近年来，大型考试作弊的情况越来越多，替考也永禁不止。笔者实习的鉴定所一年内就接到了数件对考卷笔迹进行同一认定的案子，从研究生入学考试到同等学力人员申请硕士学位全国统一考试，都存在替考情况。虽然中考和高考的监督和管理相对更加严格，但也未必能够完全杜绝替考情况发生，即使存在的比

率极低，其真实性还是容易受到质疑。因此，笔者认为，在调取试卷样本时应更加谨慎，为避免上述情况发生，最好再调取一到两份其他时期的样本进行辅助比对，以确保样本的真实性。

参考文献

[1] 贾玉文、邹明理：《中国刑事科学技术大全文件检验》，中国人民公安大学出版社2002年版。

[2] 高学林："笔迹样本及提取技巧"，载《中国司法鉴定》2004年第3期，第8页。

[3] 胡立海、裴雷："笔迹样本中的五种假象不容忽视"，载《中国司法鉴定》2002年第3期，第3页。

交通事故中汽车信号灯丝痕迹研究 *

贾常明**

在交通事故处理工作中，往往需要对汽车信号灯丝进行检验，判断有关车辆在事故发生时是否给信号。对于汽车信号灯泡破碎了的情况，如果当时灯泡点亮，灯丝处于热的状态，进入空气后将发生高温氧化，产生新的氧化物，或灯丝有被烧断痕迹。但是也有灯泡没有破碎的情况，如何判断灯丝是点亮时振动断裂还是没点亮振动断裂？灯丝的新旧将对灯丝的变形或断口形态产生怎样影响？这是本文重点研究的问题。

一、灯丝的结构与性质

汽车信号灯丝与室内照明灯丝有所不同，一是电流强度大，一般是“12”，二是机械强度大，国家对汽车用灯丝有振动标准。所以在加工制作上就有差异。

物理性质：灯丝是由钨及掺杂物质组成，由钨棒经拉丝加工而成，在表面上留有拉丝模痕迹。钨为74号元素，钨原子最外层电子数目为2，呈金属性，具有导电、导热、可塑性和金属光泽。钨的熔点为3410±20℃，熔化热为2.55×10^5J/kg。

钨的抗拉强度与加工变形程度有关，直径为0.127mm的钨丝抗拉强度为3150MPa。

对于汽车信号灯丝，一般要掺杂Al_2O_3，SiO_2，K_2O，Fe_2O_3等，用以增强抗震性能。

化学性质：钨的化合价从-2到+6。钨与氧气的作用，在通常条件下，钨是很稳定的金属，但在空气中加热时，加热到400℃时，钨开始氧化，在表面生成蓝褐色氧化钨薄膜层；随着加热温度升高而氧化加剧，在更高的温度下，钨氧化成黄色的三氧化钨。

二、金属材料断裂类型

根据断裂前是否存在明显的宏观塑性变形，可将断裂分为脆性断裂和塑性断裂。

脆性断裂：断裂时没有明显的塑性变形，断口形貌光亮结晶状。

塑性断裂：断裂时有塑性变形，断口形貌暗灰色纤维状。

金属多晶体的断裂，依其断裂路径的走向，可分为晶间断裂和穿晶断裂。

晶间断裂：裂纹沿晶界扩展，断口表面上有许多闪闪发光的亮面，每一个亮面都是一个晶粒的界面。

穿晶断裂：裂纹穿过晶粒内部，又可分为解理断裂和剪切断裂。

解理断裂：为脆性，断口特征为：宏观断口十分平坦，微观断口由一系列小断面构成，即存在解理台阶。

---

* 获国家自然科学基金项目资助（批准号61071057）。

** 贾常明，吉林农安人，中国刑警学院刑技系副教授，从事交通事故方面教学研究工作。Email：jcm12367@126.com。

剪切断裂：在切应力作用下，沿滑移面滑移造成的断裂。断口特征为：宏观断口呈纤维状，微观断口呈蜂窝状。

疲劳断裂：金属材料在交变载荷下产生的断裂。

冲击断裂：金属材料在冲击力作用下一次快速断裂。

热疲劳是零件在循环热应力作用下发生的疲劳破坏。从宏观上，零件的热疲劳破坏以表面出现特有的龟裂裂纹为其特征。

钨为体心立方晶格金属，脆塑转变温度在室温之上，所以在室温下呈现为脆性断裂。对于汽车灯丝属于掺杂钨丝，既有热的作用，也有机械振动或冲击作用。

三、检验方法

主要工具是光学显微镜和扫描电子显微镜或透射电子显微镜．扫描电子显微镜景深好，放大倍数高，即可看宏观断口，也可看微观断口，也能做元素分析，但缺少对颜色和光泽的观察。一般分析有断口的宏观分析和微观分析，宏观分析是对断口的整体形貌进行观察分析，用以分析载荷条件，需要有经验；微观分析是对断口局域点进行分析，用以分析断裂机理，如是解理还是空洞聚集。

四、实验研究

对于汽车转向灯丝的检验，首先分为灯泡碎裂和没碎两种情况；也考虑灯丝的新旧情况：新灯丝表面光滑发亮、有一定塑性，如图 1 所示；老化灯丝表面有老化迹象、呈脆性，如图 2 所示。

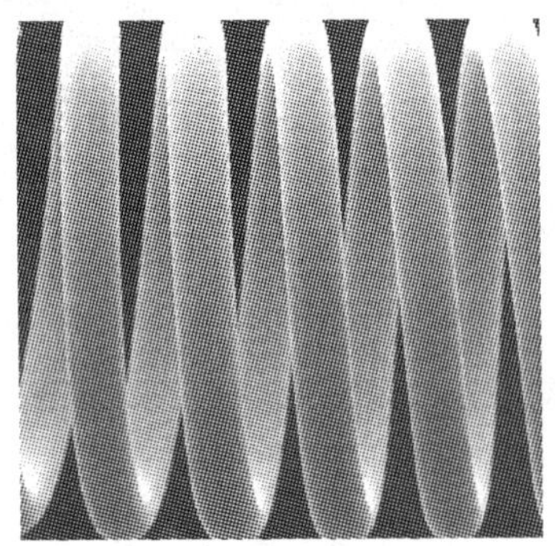
图 1　新灯丝表

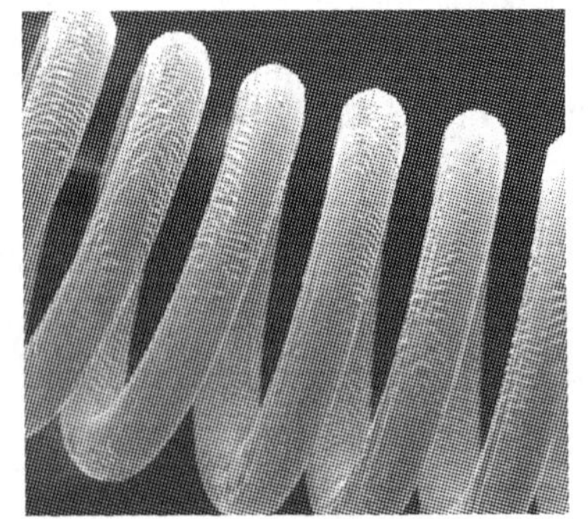
图 2　热疲劳灯丝表面

（一）灯泡碎裂情况

在通电情况下灯泡破碎进入空气，灯丝可能烧断、没断或撞断。

烧断：灯丝表面有氧化迹象（灯丝表面呈黑褐色），烧断处变细，有热作用痕迹，灯丝固定部位有黄绿结晶毛，如图 3 所示，来自实验室。烧断时间需要几秒钟。

没断：灯泡破碎后立刻断电或灯泡断电后立刻破碎灯泡，灯丝表面有颜色变化，呈蓝紫色，或黑褐色；如图 4 所示，来自实验室。

撞断：如图 5 所示，来自实验室。该样品是在灯泡断电瞬间外力冲击下，不但灯泡破碎，灯丝也被撞断。灯丝表面呈黑褐色，断口没有显著塑性变形和热熔痕迹 呈纤维状。

未通电情况下灯泡破碎灯丝被拉断情况，如图 6 所示，来自实验室。灯丝表面光亮，断口呈脆断，该样品有解理条纹。

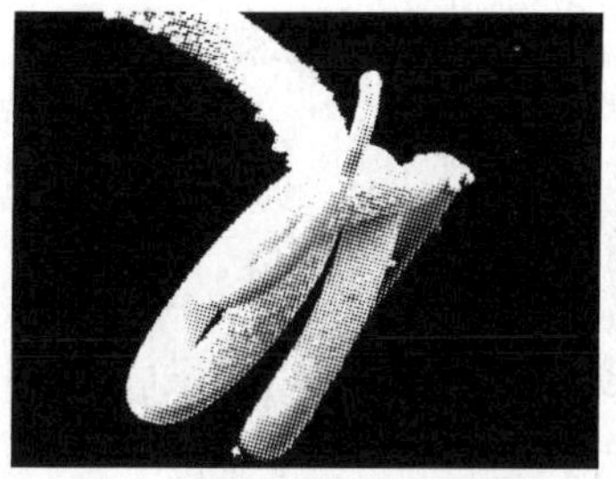

图 3 通电烧断情况

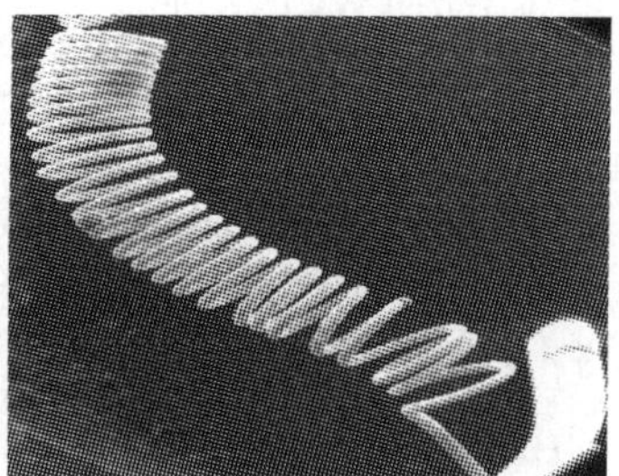

图 4 通电没断情况

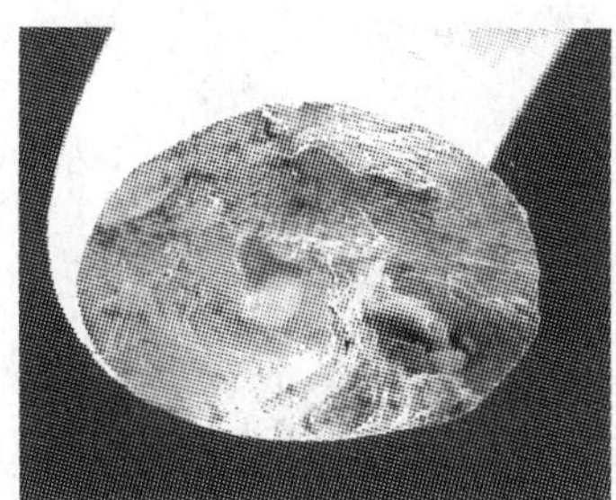

图 5 通电撞断情况断口

图 6 未通电机械拉断断口

（二）灯泡没碎裂情况

在通电情况下，灯丝振动会使灯丝变形或“断裂”。

灯丝变形：如图 7 所示，来自事故车辆；可反应冲击方向，一个是前后方向，一个是左右方向。

灯丝振动断裂：如图 8 所示，来自事故车辆。断口有熔断痕，灯丝有热变形。

灯丝高压熔断：如图 9 所示，来自实验室，断口有熔断痕迹。

在未通电情况下振动断裂：如图 10 所示，来自事故车辆，断口没有热作用痕迹，属于机械断裂痕迹。

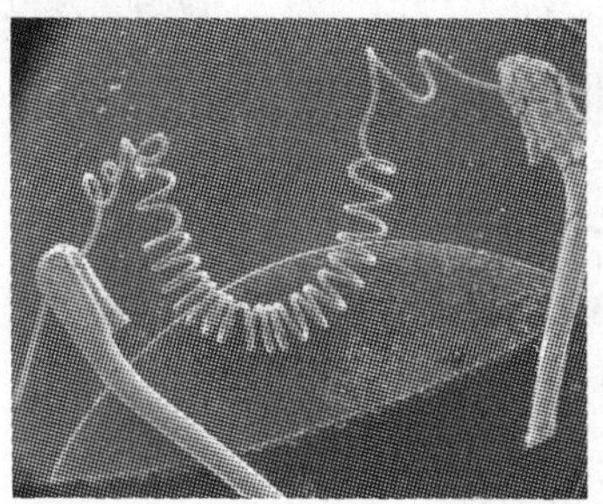

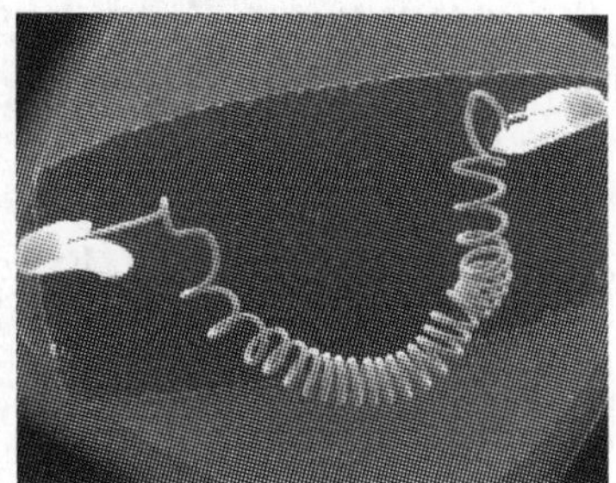

图 7　通电灯丝变形

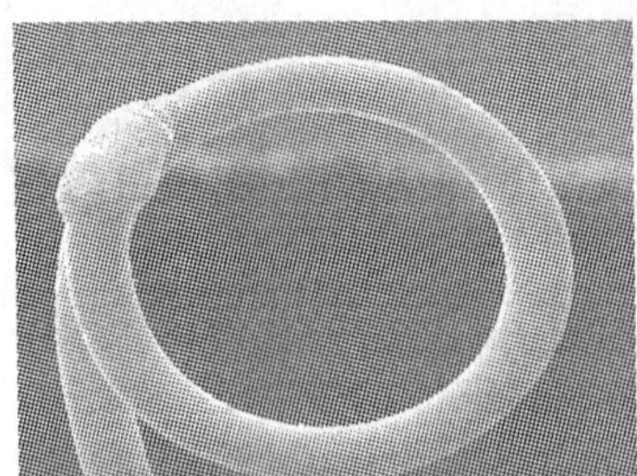

图 8 通电振动断口

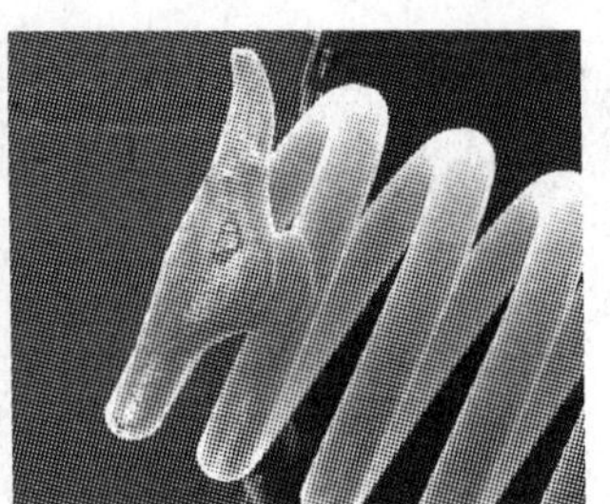

图 9 高压熔断断口

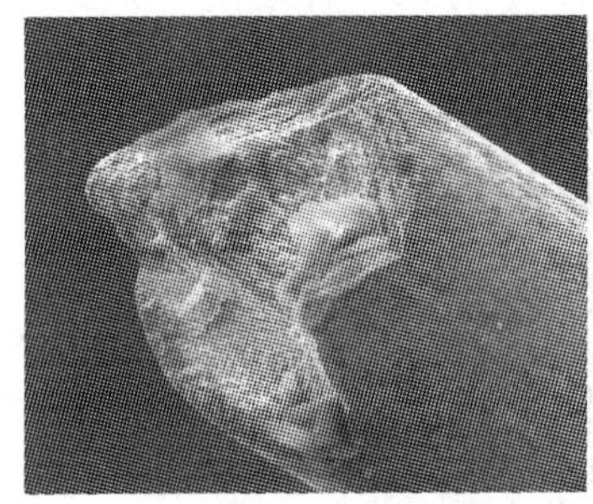

图 10 未通电振动断裂

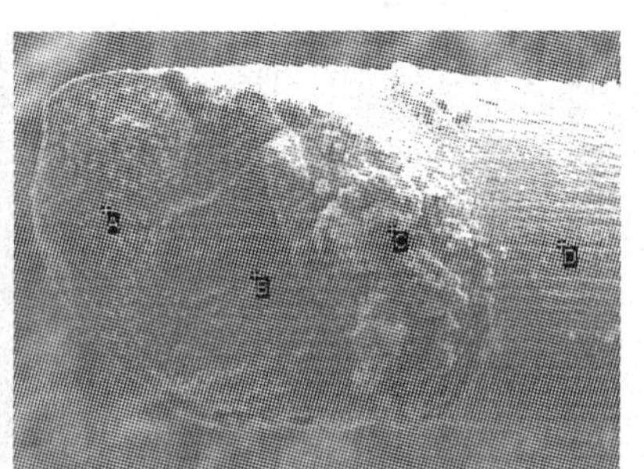

图 11 要求鉴定的案例

五、讨论与结论

通过以上的实例研究，注意烧断、熔断和机械断裂的差别，注意汽车信号灯丝的一亮一灭状态的影响。得出以下几条结论：

1. 观察检验部位，有灯丝表面状态，断口形态和灯丝固定部位。灯丝表面比较光亮，或有疲劳痕迹或电弧痕迹，或经空气氧化变黑褐色；

2. 对于灯泡破碎情况，通电与否的最典型特征是灯丝表面颜色的变化；

3. 对于灯泡未破碎情况，通电与否的最典型特征是灯丝的变形，断口有短路热熔痕迹。由于振动造成灯丝短路，在断口产生热熔痕迹。

以上断裂研究都是较新灯丝，对于热疲劳灯丝可能有其他情况，如图 11 所示，来自事故车辆，断口既有热作用痕迹，也有机械断裂痕迹。

参考文献

[1] 印协世：《钨丝生产原理、工艺及性能》，冶金工业出版社 1998 年版，第 319 ~ 324 页。

[2] [美] 查利 · R. 布鲁克斯等：《工程材料的失效分析》，谢雯娟等译，机械工业出版社 2003 年版。

傅立叶变换红外光谱法检验润唇膏的研究

姜 红* 陈元章 阎子龙 王 晨 李晓白 金 玥 杜 岩**

引 言

在各类刑事案件现场中经常能提取到各类化妆品物证，化妆品物证的分析检验是法庭科学研究的重要内容之一。唇部护理的化妆产品主要有两大类，[1]一类是针对女性的口红和唇彩系列，一类是针对男士的无色润唇膏系列，有些女性也会用无色润唇膏打底，配以口红，保持口红鲜艳亮丽。对口红和唇彩的检验已建立了一些分析方法，主要有薄层色谱法[2][3][4][5][6][7]、高效液相色谱法[8][9]、紫外/可见光谱法[10]、红外光谱法[11][12][13][14]以及扫描电镜/能谱法[15][16][17]等，但利用傅立叶变换红外光谱法对无色润唇膏的检验研究尚未见报道。本文利用傅立叶变换红外光谱仪，采用 Smart Performer 采样器对不同厂家、不同品牌和同一品牌不同系列的 50 个无色润唇膏样本进行了分析检验。实验中用优选出的制样方法对润唇膏样本进行了反射分析，依据红外光谱图中峰位、峰形和相对峰高比的不同，对润唇膏样本进行区别，并对该方法的重现性进行了考查，为公安实战部门检验润唇膏物证提供了一种方法。

一、实验仪器、试剂及实验样本

（一）实验仪器及条件

Nicolet - 6700 傅立叶变换红外光谱仪（美国赛默飞世尔），Smart Performer 采样器，小压片机（天津）。

测定参数：扫描次数 32；分辨率 4cm^{-1}；波数范围 4000cm^{-1} ~ 400cm^{-1}；Y 轴格式 A（吸光度）；增益 1。

（二）试剂

无水乙醇（分析纯）、溴化钾（光谱纯）。

（三）样本

不同产地、不同品牌、同一品牌不同系列的润唇膏样本 50 个（见表 1）。

表 1 润唇膏样本表

编 号	品 牌	系 列	产 地
1	屈臣氏	保湿清凉	香港
2	雅芳	Man daily performance	广州

* 姜红，女，辽宁沈阳人，中国人民公安大学刑科技系副教授，13641067746。Email：jiangh2001@163. com。
** 中国人民公安大学，北京 100038。Email：jiangh2001@163. com。

续表

编　号	品　牌	系　列	产　地
3	雅芳	Green tea	广州
4	雅芳	Fruit shine	广州
5	雅芳	Moisture therapy	广州
6	雅芳	Green tea	广州
7	Korea	男士润唇	韩国
8	蕾琪	男士	广东
9	蕾琪	深层补水	广东
10	蕾琪	Run lipstick	广东
11	蕾琪	Metrosexual double	广东
12	曼秀雷敦	Men Cool	广东
13	曼秀雷敦	Lip balm sunscreen	广东
14	曼秀雷敦	Lip pure natural	广东
15	曼秀雷敦	Medicated lipbalm	广东
16	曼秀雷敦	Natural treatment	广东
17	曼秀雷敦	Men lip balm cool aqua	广东
18	曼秀雷敦	Organic raspberry	广东
19	曼秀雷敦	Water in lip	广东
20	曼秀雷敦	专为男士设计	广东
21	曼秀雷敦	For man	广东
22	曼秀雷敦	Men extreme	广东
23	曼秀雷敦	Cool aqua	广东
24	曼秀雷敦	水凝	广东
25	妮维雅	Lip care essential	上海
26	妮维雅	Care essential	上海
27	妮维雅	Soft rose	上海
28	妮维雅	粉色润唇	上海
29	妮维雅	Med protection	上海
30	妮维雅	Pinkish boost	上海
31	妮维雅	Lip care	上海
32	妮维雅	Active care	上海
33	冰之恋	香蕉果晶	上海
34	冰之恋	小小苹果	上海
35	采诗	柠檬润唇	广州

续表

编 号	品 牌	系 列	产 地
36	唇点	韩宅保养	韩国
37	恒芳	维他命圣典 VE	深圳
38	诗晶	草本花香	浙江
39	雅邦	深层补湿	汕头
40	隆力奇	Men lip	江苏
41	美德普诺	Cool wise men	上海
42	丁家宜	水亮润唇	苏州
43	欧莱雅	男士	苏州
44	欧莱雅	劲能极润	苏州
45	H2O	8 杯水	韩国
46	美宝莲	Smooth extra	苏州
47	The body shop	Lip protector	苏州
48	娇兰	Super moisturizing	法国
49	Chapstick	High power water	美国
50	Baviphat	水蜜桃	韩国

二、实验内容

（一）样本检验方法的选择

选取 12（曼秀雷敦 Men Cool）润唇膏样本，分别采用透射法、反射法进行检验。

1. 透射法检验

（1）将样本均匀涂抹在白色涤纶布上，然后放在载物片上采集谱图，再与白色涤纶布的红外谱图做差谱。

（2）将样本直接涂抹在空白的 KBr 压片上，[18]然后放入载物片上采集谱图。

2. 反射法进行检验

将样本直涂抹在 Performer 采样器上，采集谱图。

（二）润唇膏的红外光谱分析

在上述实验条件下，采用 Performer 采样器分别对 50 个润唇膏样本进行反射分析测定。

对同一品牌、不同系列的样本进行比较研究，选取“曼秀雷敦”（12 ~ 24）13 个润唇膏样本进行比较研究。

（三）重现性实验

选取 2 样品（雅芳 Man daily performance）重复测定 5 次。

三、结果与讨论

（一）红外光谱分析润唇膏的理论依据

润唇膏的基本成分是凡士林和蜡质，此外还含有维生素 A 和维生素 E 等抗氧化成分以及 SPF 具有防晒性能的物质，有些产品还会选择性地添加含天然香料的物质。此外，还有些辅助成分，比如薄荷、樟脑、羊毛脂和芦荟等，不同的生产厂家添加的辅助成分也会不同。即使是同一厂家，也会研发适合不同性别、不同年龄、不同人群的产品。因此，同一厂家生产的润唇膏，所用的原料可能相同，但配比不一定相同。另外，不同厂家生产的同一种原料，尽管其分子结构式、化学成分相同，但由于各厂家使用的中间体质量、合成工艺路线、生产设备以及商品化的助剂等诸多因素存在差异，其成分、色光与其性能等也会有所不同，这些差异均会使红外光谱图中特征峰的数目、峰位、峰高比不同，这就是我们利用红外光谱法分析鉴别润唇膏的理论依据。

（二）润唇膏的红外光谱分析

1. 制样方法的比较

直接将涂抹在白色涤纶布上的样本放在载物片上进行谱图的采集，谱图的信噪比较小，因为红外吸收受到涤纶纤维的干扰，在指纹区的吸收峰受到的干扰较大，谱图价值不是很大。

将样本涂抹在空白的 KBr 压片上，放在载物片上采集谱图，谱图的信噪比较大，由于 KBr 在红外没有吸收，指纹区的吸收峰较明显，有利于润唇膏样本的检验，谱图效果较好。

采用 Smart Performer 采样器进行采样，实验过程中没有受到外界因素的干扰，谱图的信噪比较大，谱图效果好。

表 2 制样方法的比较

操作方法	操作过程	信噪比	谱图效果
透射法（白涤纶布制样）	耗时短，操作简便，无损	小	*
透射法（压片法制样）	耗时长，操作复杂，有损	大	* *
Smart Performer 采样器	耗时短，操作简便，无损	大	* * *

注：* 一般，* * 较好，* * * 好。

2. 润唇膏样本的分类

通过对 50 个润唇膏样本的红外谱图的分析，可以看出润唇膏样本具有下列一些共同特征：在 $2965cm^{-1}$ 附近存在着由于 CH_3 反对称伸缩振动形成的特征峰，在 $2920cm^{-1}$ 处存在着由于烷烃 CH_2 反对称收缩形成的特征峰，在 $2851cm^{-1}$ 处存在着由于烷烃 CH_2 对称伸缩形成的特征峰，在 $1745cm^{-1}$ 处存在着由于饱和脂肪酸脂 $C=O$ 伸缩振动形成的特征峰，在 $1462cm^{-1}$ 处存在着由于 CH_3 不对称变角振动和烷烃 CH_2 变角振动形成的特征峰，在 $1376cm^{-1}$ 处存在着由于 CH_3 对称变角振动形成的特征峰，从这些吸收峰可以推断出润唇膏的基本成分是脂肪酸类、脂类和烷烃类化合物。

分析润唇膏样本在 $1300cm^{-1}$ 以下指纹区的吸收峰，可以根据其在 $1250cm^{-1}$ 附近是否存在吸收峰为依据，将 50 个样本分成两大类，一类存在该特征峰，共有 16 个样品；另一类不存在该吸收峰，共有 34 个样品。对第一类样本又可以根据其在 $1060cm^{-1}$ 附近，有无吸收峰将其分为两类，a 类有吸收峰的样品有 8 个（见图 1）；b 类没有吸收峰的样品有 8 个（见图 2）。对第二类样本也可根据在 1110cm^{-1}附近有无吸收峰，将其分为两类，c 类在 1110cm^{-1}附近有吸收峰（见图 3），共有 16 个样本；d 类没有吸收峰（见图 4），共有 18 个样本。

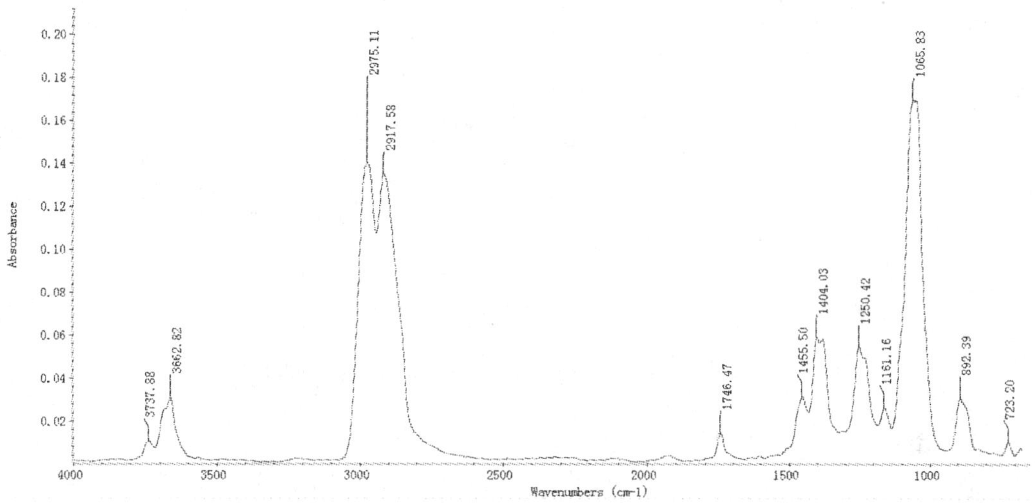

图 1　第一类（a）2 样本 雅芳 Man daily performance 的红外光谱图

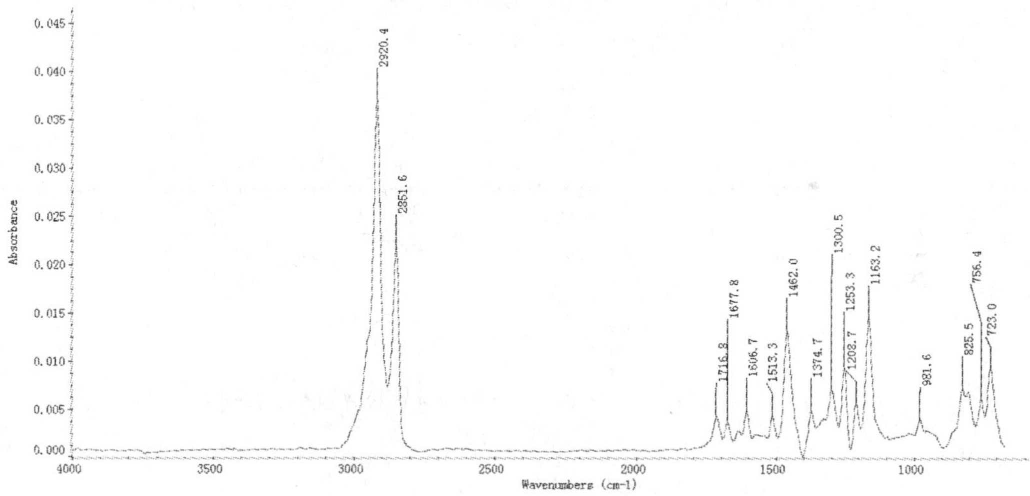

图 2　第一类（b）13 样本曼秀雷敦 Lip balm sunscreen 的红外光谱图

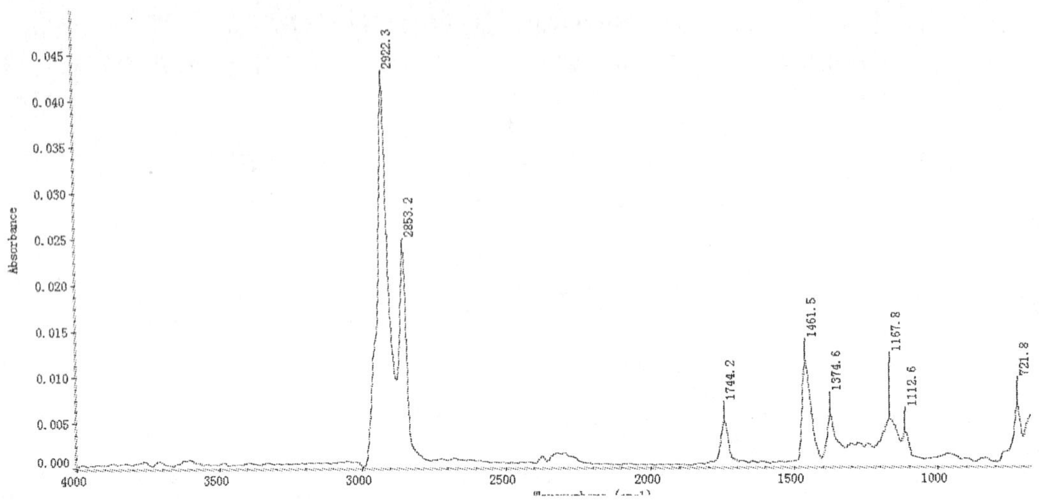

图3 第二类（c）35 样本采诗柠檬润唇膏的红外光谱图

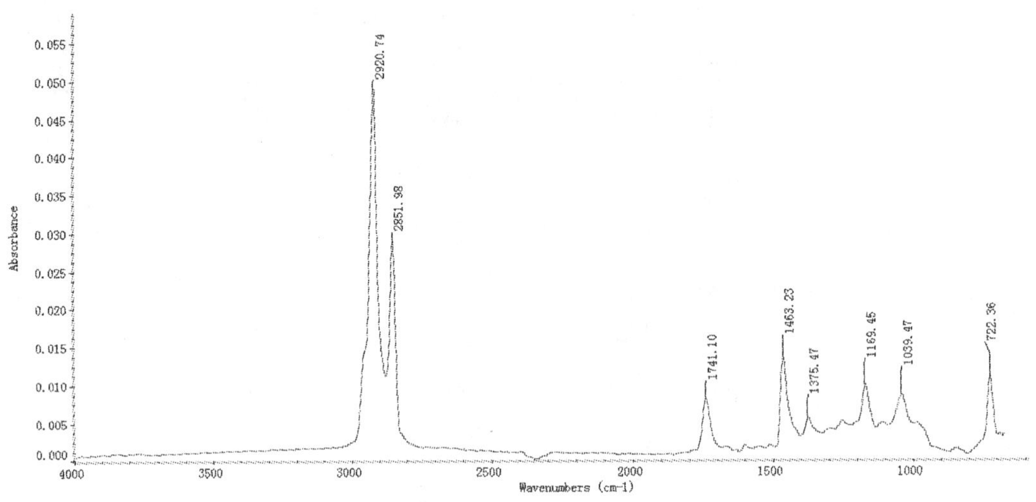

图4 第二类（d）27 样本妮维雅 soft rose 的红外光谱图

3. 同一品牌不同系列的润唇膏样本的分析

通过对选取曼秀雷敦（广东产）润唇膏系列的 13 个样本的红外光谱图进行分析，发现在官能团区吸收峰的位置基本相近，说明同一个品牌的润唇膏的基本成分是一样的。但在指纹区的吸收峰上有一些差异，这说明同一品牌、不同系列的润唇膏样本由于添加的成分不同，导致了红外光谱图的区别。比如，曼秀雷敦样本的 12、13 和 14，就可根据其在 892cm^{-1}处和 722cm^{-1}处是否有吸收峰加以区分，12 只在 892cm^{-1}处有吸收峰，13 只在 723cm^{-1}处有吸收峰，而 14 在 892cm^{-1}处和 723cm^{-1}处均有则吸收峰（见图 5 ~ 图 7）。

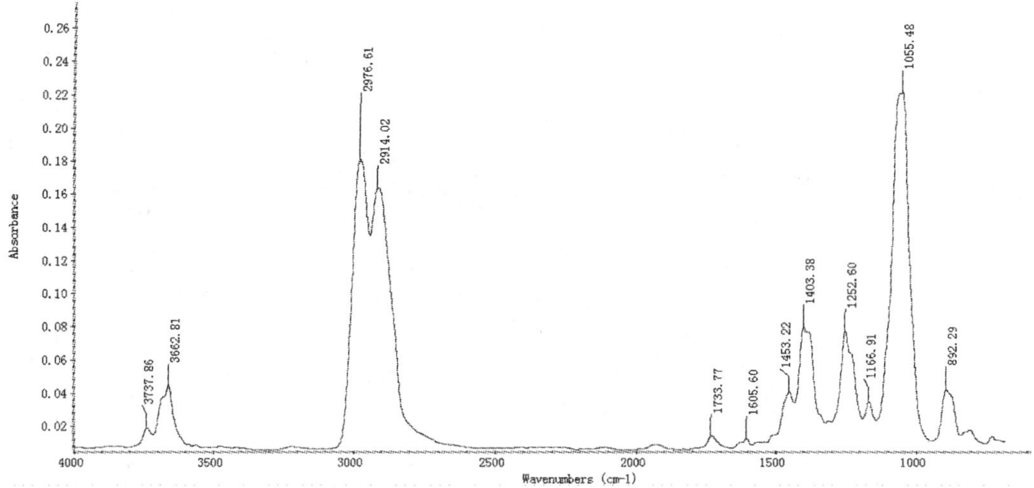

图5　12 样本（曼秀雷敦 Men Cool）的红外光谱图

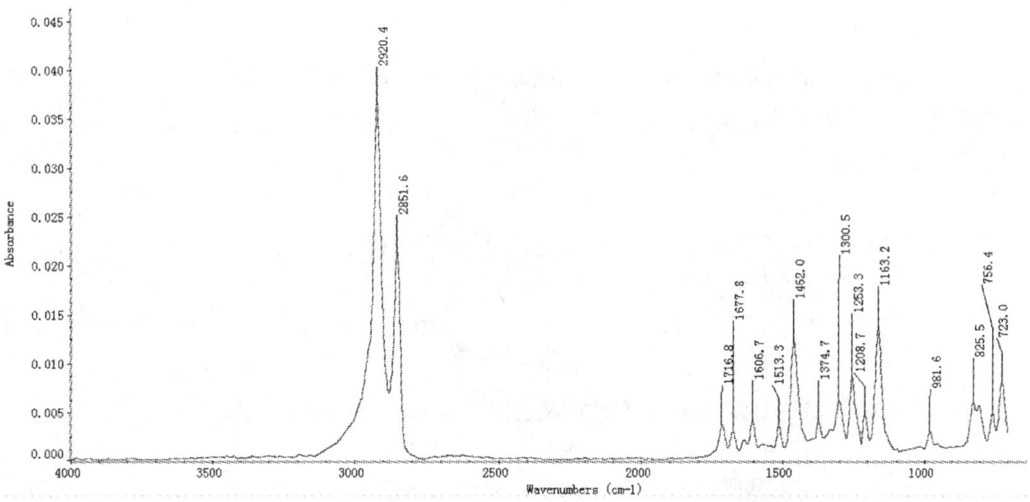

图6　13 样本（曼秀雷敦 lip balm sunscreen）的红外光谱图

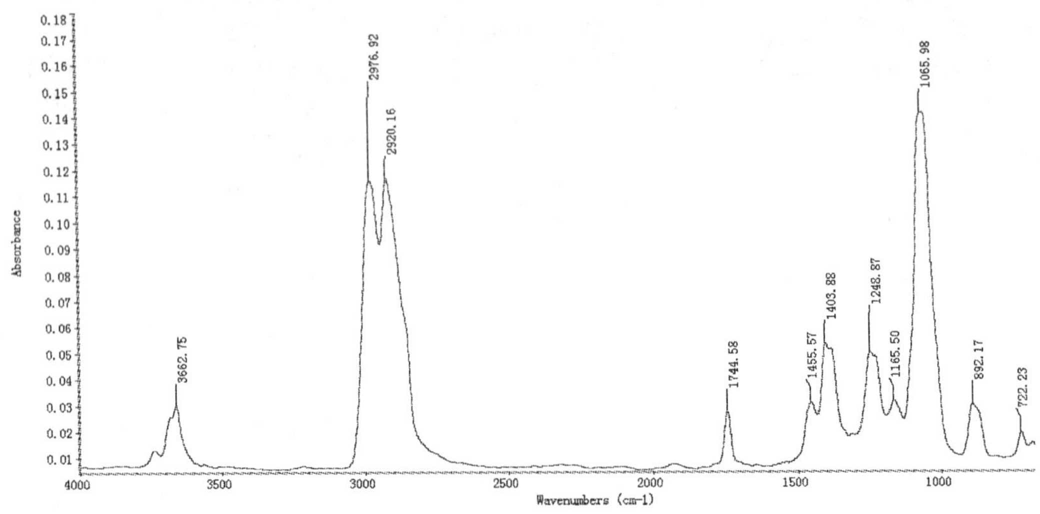

图7　14 样本（曼秀雷敦 lip pure natural）的红外光谱图

（三）重现性实验

对 2（雅芳 man daily performance）润唇膏样本，进行重复实验表明，该方法的重现性较好，5 次实验中相对峰高比的变异系数均在 10% 以内。

四、结　论

实验结果表明，利用傅立叶变换红外光谱法可以对不同品牌，同一品牌不同系列的润唇膏进行鉴别，该方法操作简便快捷，结果准确可靠，且不破坏检材，可以在实际办案中对现场提取的润唇膏进行检验。

参考文献

［1］白景瑞、藤进：《化妆品配方设计及应用实例》，中国石化出版社 2001 年版，第 132 ~ 135 页。

［2］Russel，L. W.；Welch，A. W. Analysis of Lipsticks，For. Sci. Int. 1984，25（2），pp. 105 ~ 116.

［3］O. P. Jasuja；R. Singh，Thin – Layer Chromatographic Analysis of Liquid Lipsticks by Department of Forensic Science. Punjabi University. Patiala，India；Journal of Forensic Identification，2005，55（1），pp. 28 ~ 35.

［4］曹建华、文国平：“微量唇膏检验”，载《第二届微量物证检验学术交流会论文汇编》，中国人民公安大学出版社 1987 年版，第 411 ~ 413 页。

［5］汪宝新：“口红的检验”，载《第二届微量物证检验学术交流会论文汇编》，中国人民公安大学出版社 1987 年，第 430 ~ 431 页。

［6］李重阳、李波阳、沙万中：“薄层色谱法鉴别口红”，载《刑事技术》1999 年第 2 期，第 21 ~ 23 页。

［7］姜红、路春清、鄢毅等：“口红 TLC 分析条件的优化”，载《公共安全化学研究论丛》（第一卷），中国人民公安大学出版社 2006 年版，第 109 ~ 113 页。

［8］D. J. Reul and W. A. Trinler，“A Comparison of lipstick Smears by high performance liquid chromatography”，*Journal of the Forens.* Sci. Soc（1980），pp. 20，111.

［9］D. J. Reuland W. A. Trinler，“A Comparison of lipstick Smears by high performance liquid chromatography Part Ⅱ", Journal of the Forens. Sci. Soc (1984), 24, pp. 509 ~ 518.

[10] 李继民、郝旺林、邹宁等:"二阶导数光谱法检验口红",载《中国刑警学院学报》1999 年增刊,第 75 ~ 76 页。

[11] 姜红、王洪波:"傅立叶变换红外光谱法检验口红的研究",载《刑事技术》2010 年第 4 期,第 20 ~ 24 页。

[12] 姜红、赵晶晶:"傅立叶变换红外光谱法检验唇彩的研究",中国刑警学院学报,2010 年第 4 期,第 55 ~ 57 页。

[13] 姜红编著:《化妆品物证分析》,化学工业出版社 2011 年版,第 157 ~ 165 页。

[14] 王岩、姚丽娟、陈星育:"傅立叶红外光谱法检验口红",引自《公共安全中的化学问题研究进展》,中国人民公安大学出版社 2010 年版,第 392 ~ 394 页。

[15] Choudhry. M. Y, "Comparison of Minute Smear of lipstick by Microspectrophotometry and scanning electron microscopy/energy - dispersive spectroscopy", *Journal of Forensic Science*, 2 (1991), pp. 366 ~ 375.

[16] 于晓娟、李国平、王玲惠:"应用扫描电镜、能谱仪鉴别口红",载《第四届全国微量物证检验学术交流会论文汇编》,警官教育出版社 1999 年版,第 145 ~ 147 页。

[17] 郝旺林、黄娟娟、赵彦军等:"用 SEM - EDS 鉴别不同品牌的口红",载《中国刑警学院学报》1999 年增刊,第 71 ~ 73 页。

[18] 何旭元、陈远斗、蔡湘雯:"基于空白 KBr 压片的红外光谱制样方法",载《湖南文理学院学报(自然科学版)》2006 年第 2 期。

微量物证在交通事故现场重建中的应用研究 *

刘 斌 **

一、引 言

随着汽车保有量的不断增加，交通事故发生的数量也呈现上升趋势，同时交通事故鉴定的需求也不断增加。这种现状促进了交通事故鉴定技术的发展，也给交通事故鉴定技术带来了新的挑战。交通事故鉴定属于综合性学科，其技术基于痕迹学、微量物证、法医学、车辆工程、道路工程、计算机技术、分析化学、机械零部件失效分析等。国内外学者对微量物证在交通事故鉴定方面的研究不断深入。[1][2]微量物证在交通事故鉴定中的作用很大，特别是在判断车辆之间及车辆与人之间是否发生接触方面，具有不可替代的作用。特别是逃逸案件的侦破，往往寄希望于微量物证的分析作用。

与交通事故鉴定有关的微量物证包括油漆、纤维、塑料、橡胶、玻璃、金属、油污、土壤等。本文从实际的鉴定工作经历出发，对于微量物证在交通事故鉴定方面的作用进行分析，并重点分析油漆、纤维在交通事故鉴定中的作用。油漆与纤维在判断车辆之间及车辆与人之间是否发生接触时所起到的作用较大，[3]本文将重点论述。本文提供了油漆、纤维等微量物证在现场重建中的具体事例，以此说明了微量物证在交通事故鉴定中的具体应用，并对证据解读做出了分析。

二、案例分析

在实际的鉴定工作中，遇到多起判断车辆与行人是否发生接触的案件。由于事发时车速较低，车辆表面未发现明显的可以判断与行人发生接触的痕迹，但经过对行人衣物的显微镜检验，发现了类似车漆的附着物，经过傅里叶红外光谱仪及扫描电子显微镜分析，可以确定行人衣物上的附着物与嫌疑车辆车漆为同种类油漆，对于案件的侦破与定性起到了很好的作用。

在车辆与行人接触的过程中，行人衣物上的纤维可能会转移到车辆表面。在激烈的碰撞过程中，车内驾乘人员衣物上的纤维会与车辆内饰件表面摩擦，可以造成塑料类车辆内饰件的表面高温熔化，并使衣物上的纤维与内饰件表面紧密结合。[4]这对判断驾驶员具有很强的证据作用。但在实际鉴定中需要注意的问题是：对于纤维的鉴定，主要依靠傅里叶红外光谱仪及偏振光显微镜，这两种仪器对于纤维的种类可以进行区分，但对于同种类纤维之间细微差别的区分能力很有限。本人在实际工作中遇到过一起驾驶员判断的鉴定，办案警方提供了车内 5 个人员的上衣及裤子，共计 10 件，均为深色。经过实际检验，10 件衣物的纤维种类可以分为棉纤维及涤纶两大类，不同衣物

---

* 基金项目：中国政法大学青年教师创新团队资助项目和证据科学教育部重点实验室（中国政法大学）开放基金（2011KFKT04、2012KFKT08）资助课题。

** 刘斌，博士，讲师。Email：rays_ liu@ 126. com。

纤维间的细微差别难以区分。再次对车内痕迹进行仔细分析，并结合衣物的显微镜检查，在一个嫌疑人的袖子上发现了与内饰板油漆类似的附着物，经过分析，该附着物与内饰板表面油漆为同种油漆；内饰板表面上的纤维与该嫌疑人袖子上的纤维为同类纤维，且纤维与内饰板表面紧密结合，可以判断为激烈碰撞过程中形成（具体见图1、2）。这种油漆与纤维互补的证据对确定驾驶员提供了确实的证据。

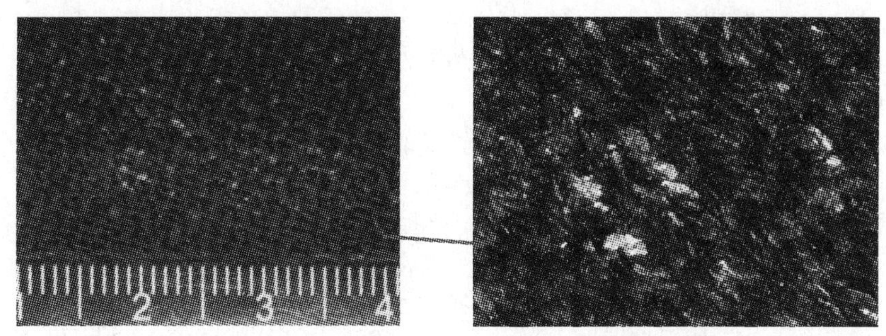

图1　嫌疑人XXX所穿上衣上提取的油漆状附着物

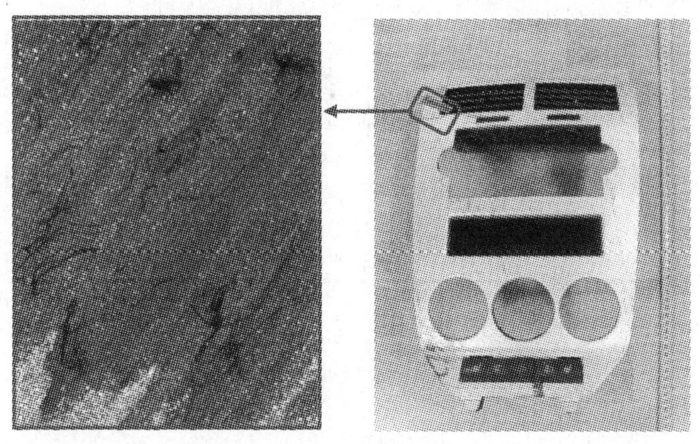

图2　肇事车辆中控板上的擦蹭痕迹及表面附着的纤维

三、微量物证的证据解读

对于油漆、纤维、塑料、橡胶等的微量物证鉴定结论中，如果检材与样本成分比对一致，其确切意义指的是两者的种类相同，进一步说指的是嫌疑车辆有肇事的嫌疑。如果嫌疑车辆外观痕迹特征和事故车辆外观痕迹特征相符合，再结合脱落零部件的整体分离鉴定、现场监控录像、嫌疑车辆运动过程分析等综合技术手段，才能确定嫌疑车辆肇事的事实。如果嫌疑车辆外观痕迹特征不明显，甚至在肉眼下难以观察清楚，这时提取微量物证一定要慎重。[5][6]

四、结　论

微量物证的提取与仪器分析要结合车辆碰撞的外观痕迹分析、运动状态分析。微量物证的提取是建立在对事故过程分析的基础之上的，只有对事故过程有了比较清晰的分析，才能确定要做的微量物证鉴定具体内容；而仪器分析过程相当于对最初事故过程分析的一个印证过程。仪器分析的过程依赖于尖端的仪器设备，看起来似乎是严肃而冷静的，但微量物证的提取过程与对微量物证报告的解读过程却是生动的，富于挑战性的。微量物证与车辆痕迹勘查的结合有利于交通事故鉴定技术的发展。

参考文献

［1］郝红霞、连园园、刘晓培等："国外微量物证检验研究进展"，载《证据科学》2011 年第 19 卷第 4 期，第 505 ~ 512 页。

［2］孙振文、权养科、孙玉友等："从 CTS 能力验证计划看纤维物证检验的发展趋势"，载《刑事技术》2011 年第 4 期，第 38 ~ 41 页。

［3］罗仪文、徐彻、杨旭等："纤维的检验及其新方法"，载《中国司法鉴定》2008 年第 6 期，第 64 ~ 67 页。

［4］何洪源："FPF 物证在交通事故现场重建中的证据作用"，载《中国人民公安大学学报（自然科学版)》，2010 年第 2 期，第 8 ~ 11 页。

［5］刘国民："交通事故微量物证检验失误原因之探讨"，载《中国人民公安大学学报（自然科学版)》，2011 年第 3 期，第 14 ~ 17 页。

［6］吴坚毅："道路交通事故现场中微量物证及提取"，载《广西公安管理干部学院学报》2001 年第 1 期，第 40 ~ 41 页。

摹仿签名笔迹的同一认定与探索

沈臻懿 *

一、案情简况

2010 年某月，某区人民法院受理原告杨某某诉被告燕锋（又名燕峰）民事纠纷一案。原告诉称其与被告曾有业务合作关系，2006 年 6 月 22 日，双方经多次友好协商后，自愿签订一份《还款补充协议书》，此后被告一直拖延、拒绝还款，原告经多次催讨无果后起诉至法院。法院依法受理该案后，被告在法庭质证中对原告提供的《还款补充协议书》落款处的"燕峰"签名笔迹真实性提出异议。为了明晰案件事实，该人民法院委托某司法鉴定中心对《还款补充协议书》落款处的"燕峰"签名笔迹真实性进行司法鉴定。

二、鉴定过程

（一）检材笔迹检验

受理该案鉴定后，司法鉴定人依照程序规范，对检材进行了分析与检验。送检的署期为"2006 年 6 月 22 日"、甲方为"杨某某"、乙方为"燕峰"的《还款补充协议书》为单页 A4 纸，系格式文书。正文部分为打印字迹，需检的"燕峰"签名笔迹位于《还款补充协议书》下方落款的乙方签字处。该签名笔迹由黑色墨水笔横向书写形成，书写速度一般，具备鉴定条件。目视观察可见"燕峰"二字为行书签名，字形结构匀称、连笔较多、笔力较为平缓（参见图 1）。通过倍率计与体视显微镜检验，该签名笔迹具有形快实慢的典型特点，虽连笔较多，但实则运笔较慢，笔画之间存在停滞、重起笔迹象（参见图 2）。例如，"燕"字中"艹"的连笔处；"峰"字中"山"的第三竖笔等。经显微检验，可检见该签名笔迹的书写较为呆板，缺乏正常连笔书写时应有的轻、重、疾、徐等节奏感（参见图 3）。签名笔迹中部分笔画连接部位存在拖、带痕迹，个别笔画还出现轻微的抖动弯曲现象（参见图 4）。对检材分析、检验后可以初步判断，该检材签名笔迹的笔力分布与书写速度不甚匹配，故需将检材笔迹与样本笔迹进行进一步比较检验。

---

* 沈臻懿，上海浦东人，华东政法大学司法鉴定专业博士研究生。基金项目：上海市教育委员会重点学科建设项目（司法鉴定 J51102）。Email：shenzhenyi1987@ yahoo. cn。

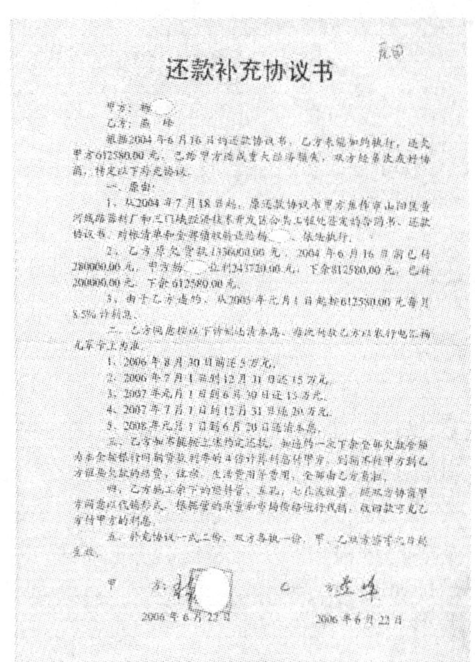

还款补充协议书

甲方：杨

乙方：燕 峰

[illegible]

一、原由：

[illegible]

二、[illegible]

1、2006年8月30日前还5万元。

2、2006年7月1日到12月31日还15万元。

3、2007年元月1日到6月30日还15万元。

4、2007年7月1日到12月31日还20万元。

5、2008年元月1日到6月30日还清本息。

[illegible]

甲 方：杨　　乙 方：燕峰

2006年6月22日　　2006年6月22日

图1　检材上的签名笔迹

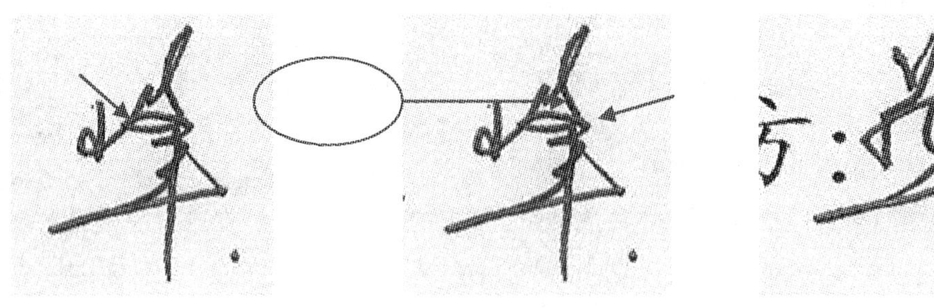

图2　形快实慢　　图3　笔力平缓　　图4　抖动弯曲

（二）样本笔迹检验

供比对检验的样本笔迹均为委托机关所提供，并由诉讼当事双方共同认可。由于该案当事人之一的燕锋又名燕峰，其在日常生活、工作中的签名笔迹既有“燕锋”、又有“燕峰”的写法。因此在提取比对样本时，不仅提取了署名为“燕峰”的签名笔迹，也同时提取了部分署名为“燕锋”的笔迹（参见图5）。比对样本上的燕峰（锋）签名笔迹中既有自然样本——多为其在另案中签署的庭审笔录、送达回证、民事诉状等法律文书上的签名笔迹，又有数量较为充足的实验样本。经司法鉴定人检验后可见，对比样本上的签名笔迹有一定书写速度，运笔较为自然流畅，具有轻、重、疾、徐之节奏感，充分显露出书写者的书写习惯，笔迹特征反映良好，具备鉴定条件。

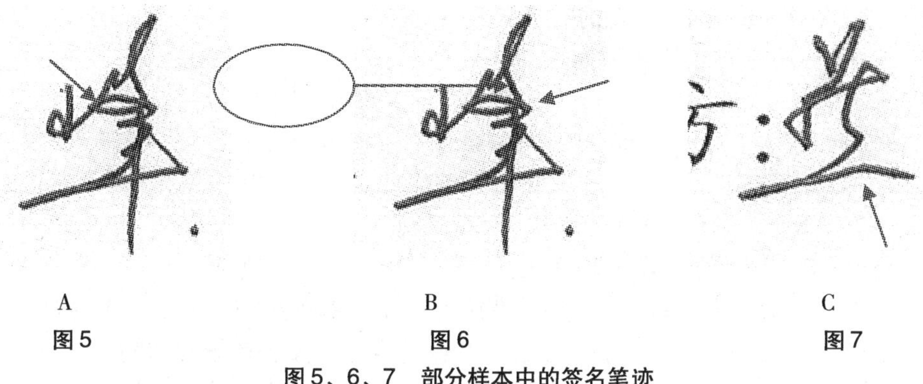

A 图5　　B 图6　　C 图7

图5、6、7　部分样本中的签名笔迹

（三）特征比较检验

司法鉴定人在对检材及样本分别检验的基础上，进一步对两者进行了比较检验，以确定检材笔迹与样本笔迹之间存在的特征符合点与差异点。检材签名笔迹与样本签名笔迹在外观形态、字形结构、字符间距、连笔形式、搭配比例、笔画运向等方面均较为接近。譬如："峰"字中"夆"的外观形态及笔画运向等。但深入比较检验后可以发现，检材签名笔迹与样本签名笔迹在笔力笔压、起收笔动作、运笔形态、连笔动作等细节特征上存在难以合理解释的差异点。例如："燕"字中"廿"的运笔力度，"灬"的运笔弧度；"峰"字中"山"的笔力分布，"夆"中第一、第二、第三横笔之间的连笔动作等。此外，检材笔迹在签名外侧的右下处多出了一小点，而该特征在样本中未能得到任何反映，样本笔迹在签名后并无多余的笔画动作（参见图8）。

检材	样本1	样本2

图8　检材笔迹与样本笔迹的特征比对情况

（四）综合分析评断

在上述比较检验所确定的特征符合点与差异点的基础上，司法鉴定人对检材及样本之间的特征组合进行了综合分析评断。结合客观检验的结果，司法鉴定人综合分析认为，检材笔迹与样本笔迹在外观形态、文字写法、字形结构以及笔画运行等特征上的符合点属于非本质性符合，系由摹仿所形成；而检材笔迹与样本笔迹在笔力分布、运笔形态、连笔动作等细节特征上的差异点属于本质性差异，差异点的质量反映了非同一人的书写习惯。最终，司法鉴定人作出检材中的"燕峰"签名笔迹与比对样本中的燕锋（峰）样本笔迹系非同一人所写的鉴定意见。

三、摹仿签名笔迹同一认定的启示与思考

物证类鉴定案件中，笔迹鉴定占到了相当一部分的比例。而摹仿签名笔迹鉴定，又是笔迹鉴定中的重要内容之一。由于摹仿签名笔迹鉴定中的检材量较少，其鉴定难度远超于其他类型的笔迹鉴定。鉴于摹仿签名笔迹鉴定的难度较大、鉴定要求较高等特点，司法鉴定人在鉴定过程中必须慎重对待。务必结合具体案情，全面、细致地对检材笔迹及样本笔迹进行分析与研究，从而去伪存真，深入探寻签名笔迹的真伪情况。

（一）全面了解案情，掌握案件信息

全面了解案件情况，是司法鉴定人实施鉴定工作的前提与基础。尤其在涉嫌摹仿签名的司法鉴定案件中，司法鉴定人更应当通过委托机关了解案件的性质、概况，当事人基本情况以及相互关系等信息。摹仿人实施的摹仿行为，其本身就是一种违背客观事实、制造假象骗局的违法行为。司法鉴定人在了解、分析具体案情的过程中，往往可以发现某些异常现象。如本案中的检材笔迹，肉眼观察其与样本笔迹在外观形态、文字写法上较为相似，但当事双方在法庭质证中却存在较大争议时，首先应当考虑检材笔迹是否存在摹仿的可能性。并在后续的客观检验过程中，进一步确定是否存有摹仿的迹象。

（二）奉行技术规范，遵循操作程序

笔迹鉴定实施过程中，司法鉴定人必须严格按照司法鉴定技术规范规定的程序及方法进行操作，不允许在检验过程中忽视规范操作、违反程序要求进行鉴定。检案实践中，部分司法鉴定人未能按照技术规范规定的步骤进行检验，在司法鉴定中忽略了检材与样本的分别观察、分析过程，直接将检材与样本进行比对检验，从而导致了较多鉴定问题的产生。尤其对于类似本案的摹仿签名案件，司法鉴定人更应当严格按照技术规范，循序渐进实施检验，才能更好地探究争议焦点背后蕴含的事实真相。奉行规范原则亦顺应了我国司法鉴定体制改革的必然趋势，有助于构建统一的技术标准规范，进一步完善司法鉴定意见的证明效力，树立起司法鉴定应有的社会公信力。

（三）深入研究检材，观察是否正常

司法鉴定人在分别检验阶段中，首先应当深入研究检材，确定检材笔迹书写是否正常，有无摹仿或者伪装的迹象存在。正常书写的签名笔迹自然流畅，运笔速度较快，具有轻、重、疾、徐之节奏感，笔画连接、转折、搭配以及照应关系等较为协调。而摹仿笔迹运笔平缓，缺乏快慢的节奏，笔力较轻，无明显的轻重变化，运笔连接与照应处与书写速度笔力互为矛盾，长笔画连笔处及复杂的运笔处可出现抖动弯曲，运笔过程中易呈现停顿及修饰重描现象。[1] 如本案中的“燕峰”二字，偏旁部首与笔画之间的照应关系不甚自然，连笔运转与实际书写速度不相吻合，笔画绕行动作存在停滞、抖动弯曲以及重起笔等现象。

（四）充分收集样本，使用原件检验

摹仿签名笔迹的鉴定与其他物证类司法鉴定一样，多采用特征比对法的方式进行鉴定。因此，全面、充分收集样本材料以待细致比对检验，也就成为了鉴定是否成功的必备条件。鉴定摹仿笔迹案件时，应当充分收集与检材笔迹书写条件、书写工具、

---

〔1〕 王伟平、刘承泉、熊平：“摹仿笔迹的检验”，载《中国司法鉴定》2005年第5期，第54页。

书写时间、书写速度等相近或者相同的样本笔迹，以便于司法鉴定人进行认真分析比对，把握检材与样本之间的本质特征。实践检案中，样本材料多由委托机关提供，如司法鉴定人根据鉴定工作的实际情况，需另行提取样本字迹时，可在委托机关的主持下，依法向相关人员进行提取。

摹仿签名笔迹的检材字数较少，能够利用的特征数量也屈指可数，检验时不能遗漏任何可能有价值的特征情况。而复印件在复制过程中不但会损失一些细小特征，还会增添因复印而形成的其他痕迹和疵点，从而导致运笔力度、书写节奏等细节特征会变形失真。[2] 这就要求司法鉴定人在鉴定摹仿签名笔迹时，必须使用原件进行检验。司法鉴定机构受理鉴定案件时，应当要求委托机关提供相应的原件，或者由司法鉴定人前往存有原件的主管部门对原件进行实地检验，以保证鉴定意见的证明效力。

（五）细致比对检验，确定特征异同

摹仿签名笔迹案件中，摹仿人的刻意摹仿行为，必然导致检材笔迹与样本笔迹在外观形态中极为相似。由于受到书写技能以及心理因素的制约，摹仿人通常只会注意摹仿他人签名笔迹的字形轮廓、明显的运笔方向以及连笔形势等特征，而对于笔力分布、起收笔的细节动作、没有连笔的笔顺、较为复杂的连笔动作等细节特征则容易被忽视。以至于将检材笔迹与样本标笔迹进行比对时，易给人以“形同实异、貌合神离”之感。因此，在对检材与样本进行比对检验以确定两者之间的特征异同时，应当对细节特征进行细致剖析，发现是否有本质差异点的存在。由于摹仿签名笔迹为少量字检验，特征数量较少、鉴定难度较大，实际检案中应借助现代化显微观察仪器，将字迹笔画中的反常现象予以放大检验。摹仿签名笔迹与样本字迹比较，往往是“同在明显处，异在细微处”，这就要求司法鉴定人在比较特征异同时，应当尽量选取较高质量的笔迹特征，如：笔力的大小及分布、运笔的弧度及方向、不连笔的笔顺等摹仿者较难摹仿的特征，以达到化少为多的检验效果。

（六）吃透摹仿笔迹，发现固有习惯

笔迹是书写人书写动力定型的客观表现，其书写活动方式一旦成为习惯，就难以轻易改变。摹仿他人笔迹，就要强行改变自身的不适应的那部分书写习惯方式。这种改变是主要靠注意控制来实现的，若注意分散，或未加注意控制，摹仿人自身的书写习惯便会自然流露。[3] 司法鉴定人在实际检案过程中，应当在吃透摹仿笔迹的基础上进行比较检验，从而在检材笔迹中发现摹仿人固有的书写习惯。着重观察样本签名笔迹中没有的，而检材签名笔迹中出现的多余动作，从而反映出摹仿人固有的书写习惯特征。例如，本案中，比对样本中被摹仿人在签名后并没有多余之笔画动作，而检材笔迹中却反映出书写者在签名后，在名字右下角处写有一小点，该顿点即可反映出摹仿人平日签名时的固有书写习惯。从而为判明检材笔迹是否为摹仿笔迹提供了参考依据。

（七）全面综合评断，判明摹仿事实

综合评断要求司法鉴定人把客体特征的符合点和差异点综合起来进行评价，不能

---

〔2〕 任玉苓、贾晓立：“摹仿签名笔迹检验1例”，载《刑事技术》2009年第3期，第76页。

〔3〕 贾玉文、邹明理：《中国刑事科学技术大全——文件检验》，中国人民公安大学出版社2002年版，第334页。

把二者的关系割裂。[4] 既要全面分析检材与样本之间异同点数量的多少，又要重视研究其质量的高低。尤其是摹仿签名笔迹案件，检材笔迹与被摹仿人的笔迹大同小异，两者之间的特征符合点往往多于特征差异点。符合点表现在容易摹仿的单字和笔画的明显特征上；差异点表现在不易摹仿的细节特征上。这种“形同实异”的表现，是摹仿笔迹与被摹仿人笔迹之间出现的一种必然现象。[5] 摹仿签名笔迹鉴定不同于其他一般类型的鉴定案件，要求司法鉴定人在综合分析评断时，全面考虑客体特征的异同点。舍弃因摹仿而形成的大同假象，准确判明细节特征中的本质性差异。防止将被摹仿人当作检材笔迹的书写人，从而导致错误鉴定意见的产生。例如，本案中检材笔迹与样本笔迹外观虽较为相似，但两者在笔力分布、起收笔动作、运笔转折、连笔动作等细节特征上存在本质性差异，反映了非同一人的书写习惯。

〔4〕 杜志淳：《司法鉴定概论》，法律出版社2010年版，第55页。
〔5〕 贾玉文：《文件检验学教程》，辽宁人民出版社1990年版，第103页。

信息综合分析法在交通肇事逃逸案件侦查中的应用

许哲峰 *， 王淳浩 **

引 言

道路交通事故信息综合分析法，是指通过对道路交通事故现场进行勘验检查并采用其他调查手段收集相关事故信息，再对收集到的事故信息进行综合分析（甄别、推理、判断等），确定事故信息与事故事实之间的直接联系和间接联系，为事故认定提供支持和帮助的一种方法。道路交通事故处理工作中，能否对事故准确认定取决于能否对交通事故信息进行及时收集并准确运用。道路交通事故信息综合分析法是一种科学、辩证地处理事故信息的方法，在准确认定事故方面常起到关键作用。本文借助一起实际案例，介绍了道路交通事故信息综合分析法在交通肇事逃逸案件侦查中的具体应用。

一、案件简介

2011 年 10 月 2 日 19 时 59 分，黄某驾驶黑色轿车沿广州绕城高速公路（原西二环高速公路）由西往东行驶至东行 195.3 公里路段，与行人陈某发生交通事故，造成陈某当场死亡。事故发生后，黄某驾车逃逸。

二、信息综合分析法在交通肇事逃逸案件侦查中的应用

（一）交通肇事逃逸案件中的事故信息及其作用

在交通肇事逃逸案件侦查工作中，有诸多信息可供利用，如交通违法信息、电子警察监控信息、治安卡扣信息、收费站、小区监控设备记录的信息、车辆登记信息以及其他社会信息。具体而言，可以利用交通监控设施记录的信息确定事故发生的准确时间、判定车辆的类型及颜色、推断车辆的使用性质；利用监控信息可以搜寻车辆行驶的线路和行驶范围；利用卡口信息、收费站监控信息可以准确确定逃逸车辆的号牌，有时可准确认定肇事车辆驾驶人。[1] 因此，将道路交通事故信息综合分析法应用于交通肇事逃逸案件侦查中尤为必要。

（二）道路交通事故信息综合分析法的具体应用

在上述案件中，经对事故现场勘验检查及调查访问，办案单位获取以下事故信息：①行人陈某头朝北脚朝南躺在由中央护栏起往南的第一行车车道内，头部、胸部损伤严重，已死亡。②现场提取了黑色破损机动车后视镜及其零部件碎片等现场遗留散落物，经勘验检查，后视镜外壳为黑色塑料材质，其内侧标有“06/8”字样（见图 1），

* 许哲峰，广州市公安局交通警察支队侦查大队副中队长。

** 王淳浩，北京市公安局公安交通管理局事故处物证鉴定高级工程师。

现场遗留的零部件碎片上标有英文字母“ichikoh”（见图2）。③报警人于事故发生后途径现场，因看到道路上躺有一人后而报警，故未看到事故发生过程；经查阅110接警记录，报警时间为当日20时06分，现场未发现目击证人。④中心现场所在地有监控录像拍摄点，经过调取并查阅视频资料，事故发生时间为当日19时59分26秒，并发现一从监控录像中无法辨别车辆号牌的嫌疑车辆（见图3）。

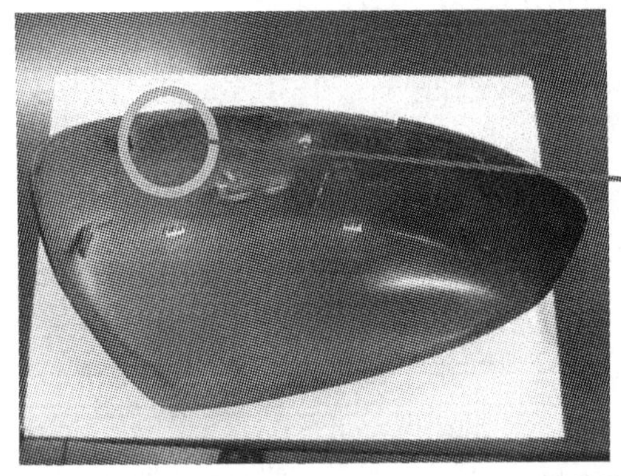

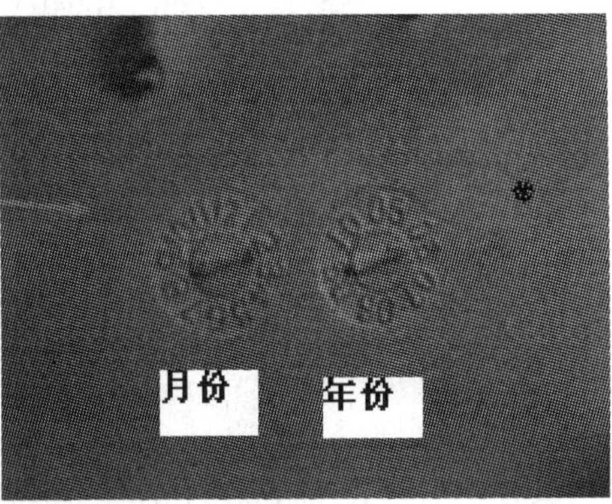

图1 散落物及特征字样

Figure 1 Debris and Characteristic Characters

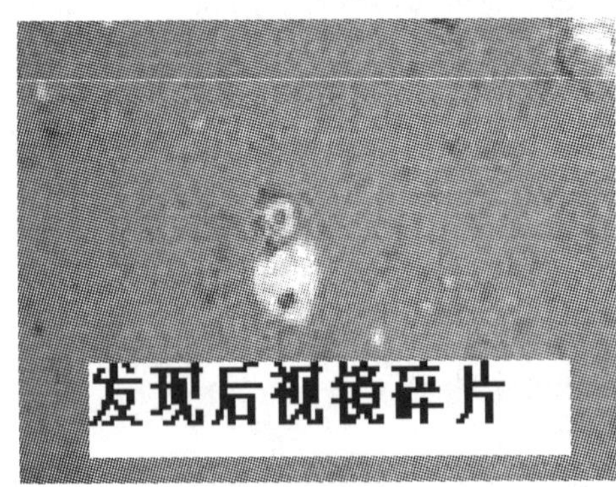

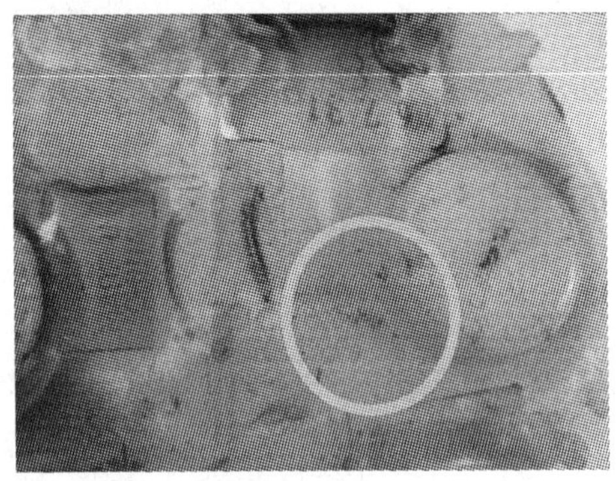

图2 现场提取的碎片及碎片上“ichikoh”英文字母

Figure 2 Fragment and English Letters ‘ichikoh’ Engraved in the Fragment

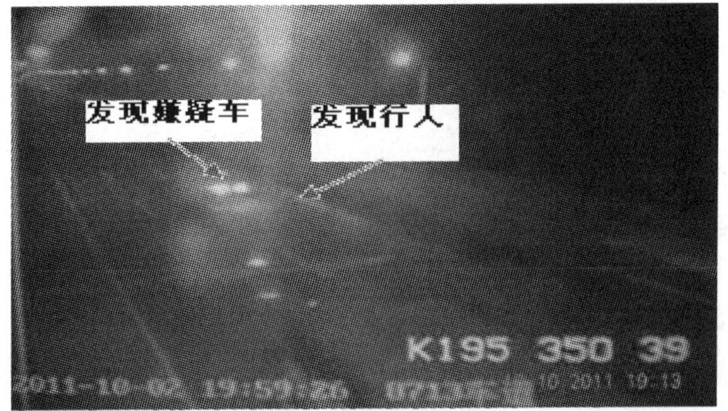

图3 监控录像发现嫌疑车，但无法辨别车辆号牌，时间为19时59分26秒

Figure 3 Video Data Containing Related Accident Information

据此，办案单位将侦查重点放在查找逃逸车辆上，并制定了侦查方案：①对提取的后视镜及碎片标识进行信息分析，确定嫌疑车辆类型；②调取事故发生路段各出入口的视频监控资料，对事故发生时间段内的录制的视频资料进行信息分析，排查嫌疑车辆；③根据排查情况，对信息进行综合分析，查找和确定嫌疑车辆。

1. 后视镜标识信息分析

车辆零部件上存在的标识能够反映出该部件所属品牌、生产日期等信息。根据提取的零部件碎片上标注的英文字母“ichikoh”，办案民警通过互联网对该关键信息查询，查得该部件为国内日系品牌；根据后视镜内侧标注的“06/8”字样，掌握到肇事逃逸车辆出厂日期为2006年8月或之后。据此判断：该肇事逃逸车辆为2006年8月份或之后出厂的黑色日系轿车。

2. 互联网汽车后视镜图库信息分析

考虑到国内日系车有“广州本田”、“广汽丰田”和“东风日产”三大品牌，办案民警利用互联网调取了上述三大日系品牌汽车后视镜外壳图库，经与现场散落的破损后视镜进行外观比对，结果显示：东风日产“轩逸”牌轿车所配置的后视镜与现场散落的后视镜外观一致（见图4）。据此，办案民警判断肇事逃逸车辆的品牌型号应是“轩逸”牌轿车。

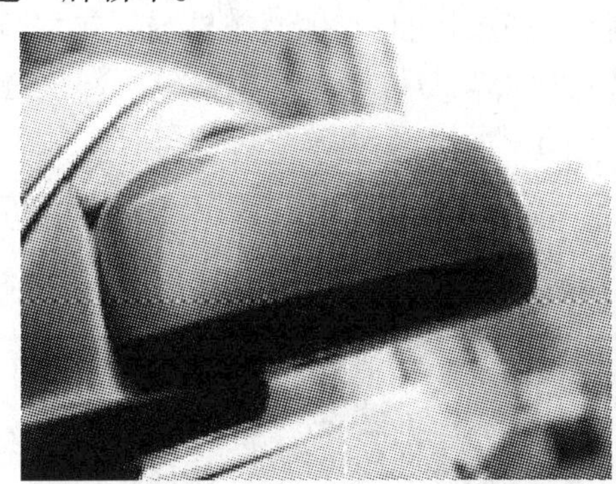

图4 东风日产”轩逸”牌轿车所配置的黑色后视镜与现场散落的后视镜外观比对

Figure 4 Appearance Match between Sample and Case Sample

3. 高速公路监控信息分析

根据事故发生地点距后方各入口和前方各出口的距离及事故发生时间段，办案民警调取了各入、出口相应时间段的视频监控资料。考虑到出口数量较多（9个，其中1个连接华南快速干线未设置收费站）、视频资料信息量较大，而入口数量少（5个），办案民警首先查看了距离事故发生地点最近入口（“和顺”站入口）的视频监控资料，排查出一号牌为“粤C669XX”的车辆为肇事嫌疑车辆（见图5）。视频显示，该车入口时间为当日19时56分35秒，考虑入口距事故发生地点的距离为2公里，经初步判断，该车从“和顺”站入口行驶3分钟至事故发生地点是可能的。

图5 “和顺”站入口监控排查出嫌疑车辆，时间为19时56分35秒

Figure 5 Video Data Containing Related Information of Suspect Vehicle

随即，办案民警登陆《全国公安交通管理信息查询系统》，查得如下信息：嫌疑车辆为黑色日产“轩逸”牌轿车，2006年8月23日出厂，车主为吴某，登记地址为珠海市香洲区某号。再登录《全国人口信息库》，掌握该车主暂住关联信息显示其地址在佛山市禅城区某号。

基于上述分析，办案单位及时掌握了车辆的准确信息，派员迅速驱车前往，于佛山市禅城区某号仓库内查获嫌疑车辆（见图6）。经对该车车体痕迹勘查，其左后视镜断离脱落且仍未修复。对事故现场提取的破损后视镜与该车左后视镜破损部位进行整体分离检验鉴定，两分离体颜色及材质相同，分离面、分离缘存在凸凹对应关系（见图7），可以对该车进行同一认定。[2]

图6 佛山查获嫌疑车辆

Figure6 Suspect Vehicle

图7 散落物断裂口与嫌疑车左后视镜支架断裂口吻合

Figure7 Physical Match Examination

经对吴某调查取证，吴某称：10月2日19时许其乘坐由黄某（吴某的丈夫）驾驶的该车从“和顺”站入口进入西二环高速公路往东行驶几公里后，在第一行车道内碰撞到不明物体，但其和家人因赶时间而未停车即驶离现场。再对黄某进行讯问，其供述与吴某的陈述一致。

至此，一起重大交通肇事逃逸案件，经过办案民警对事故现场进行细致的勘验调查，全面收集相关事故信息，经甄别、判断，利用信息综合分析法对其进行了准确的分析研判，在案发后36小时内即查获了肇事逃逸车辆及肇事者。

三、结论

道路交通事故信息综合分析法是侦破交通肇事逃逸案件的一种重要的技术方法，其核心在于对交通事故信息的收集、挖掘、甄别、判断及分析，为案件侦查提供侦查线索、划定侦查范围、排查嫌疑对象并判断、认定嫌疑对象。交通肇事逃逸案件侦查所涉及的信息非常广泛，公安机关要打破部门界限和信息壁垒，充分挖掘社会信息资源，整合多个部门的相关信息，实现信息共享，提高服务公安机关侦查办案的能力。这就要求：①侦查办案民警要牢固树立“信息主导警务”的理念，不断提高对事故信息进行深度挖掘、加工的水平，强化对信息的评估、分析和研判等工作，为正确决策提供强力支持；②侦查肇事逃逸案件不应囿于交通事故处理本身，要善于运用发散思维，在侦查空间上实施大范围的跳跃，通过对车辆零部件特征的分析，发现嫌疑车的重要信息，为缩小排查范围、快速破案奠定基础；③要充分利用现有社会信息资源为办案提供决策辅助，本案正是利用互联网汽车图库获得了嫌疑车辆的品牌型号，进而利用收费站监控系统确定嫌疑车辆，迅速侦破了案件。

参考文献

[1] 张新海：“交通事故动态分析法在肇事逃逸案件侦查中的研究与实践”，载《中国安全科学学报》2009 年第 6 期，第 122 ~ 128 页。

[2] 王淳浩：“整体分离痕迹检验在道路交通逃逸事故侦查中的应用”，载《道路交通管理》2011 年第 6 期，第 46 ~ 48 页。

三维伪彩色法及等高线圈法检验签字笔与印文的形成顺序研究

王 晶*

一、概 述

随着经济全球化的进一步发展，合同纠纷、经济补偿等民事案件中涉及对文件与印文形成先后顺序进行鉴定的案件日益增多。一份正常的文件或合同，在其形成时，必定是先书写或打印，后盖印印章的。但在实际工作中发现，通过改变印章盖印顺序进行诈骗、敲诈的案件不占少数。随着科技的发展，书写笔、打印设备以及印油的质量在不断提升，种类差异越来越小，特性逐渐趋同，朱墨时序的检验也成为了文件检验领域的难题之一。因此，不断地寻求科学准确的检验方法，尽快攻克这一技术难题，是当代文检技术人员的主要工作之一。

朱墨时序鉴定，又称印字先后顺序鉴定，指利用一定的仪器设备对文件系统要素中印迹（通常指印章印文和指印等）与文字（通常指各种书写工具形成的手写文字和打印、复印工具形成的印制文字）交叉部位的墨迹分布状态及理化特性进行检验和分析，从而判断两者形成的先后顺序。本文主要谈及笔者对签字笔与印文形成先后顺序的检验体会，与大家共同探讨。

二、研究对象

签字笔是圆珠笔的一种。圆珠笔是利用球珠滚动带出书写介质的书写工具的统称。按照圆珠笔的书写介质不同可分为三类，即圆珠笔油墨、水性墨水和中性墨水。签字笔是人们对水性笔墨水和中性笔墨水的一种习惯称呼。签字笔墨水主要由溶剂、着色剂、表面活性剂和其他添加剂等组成。黑色签字笔的着色剂主要是炭黑，炭黑是一种化学性能比较稳定的元素，一般不容易与其他物质发生化学反应；而蓝色签字笔的着色剂主要是染料，由于染料的粒子半径特别微小，很容易进入纸张纤维中，因此书写后的蓝色签字笔墨水字迹很耐磨，保存时间也较长久，但染料可溶于一些有机溶剂，在分析其与印文色料的交叉顺序时，我们也要有所考虑。

判断签字笔与印文形成的先后顺序时受印文色料成分的影响较大，目前根据其组成成分的不同，我们把印文色料分为印泥、印油、原子印油、光敏印油等，其组成成分及相应的印文特征如下：

（一）印 泥

印泥的主要成分是大红粉、涂料黄、银朱、重金石粉、白艳华、蓖麻油或氯化石蜡、苯酚、艾绒或木棉等。其中大红粉、朱砂是色素成分；蓖麻油、合成树脂是印泥

* 王晶，中国政法大学证据科学教育部重点实验室，主要从事文件检验方面的工作。Email：wangjing2012@cupl. edu. cn。

的连接料，在印泥中主要起调和、悬浮、转移色料和牢固印记的作用；重晶石粉、白艳华、滑石粉均为白色填料。

印泥印文是油溶性的，颜色稳定，不易褪色，可长期保存。印泥印文的立体感强，印迹较实，印文凸凹不平，显微镜下观察可见有红色颗粒状物质附着于纸张表面，同时有中淡边浓的挤墨现象。

（二）印　油

印油一般由染料、颜料、合成树脂、表面活性剂、植物油（或矿物油）以及高沸点溶剂等多种物质组成，合理地选择各种成分，是影响印油性能好坏的主要因素。

印油是水溶性的，其字迹较实，均匀，无疵点和色料堆积现象，但有洇散现象，印文边缘凸凹不平，有中淡边浓的挤墨现象。

（三）原子印油

原子印油包括渗透性和热固性两大类，目前国内使用的大部分都是渗透性原子印油。渗透性原子印油一般由颜料、合成树脂、表面活性剂、植物油、矿物油以及高沸点溶剂等物质组成。

原子印油印文不褪色，不扩散，保存时间长，印文字迹较均匀，无疵点和色料堆积，印文边缘较平整，无挤墨现象。

（四）光敏印油

光敏印油，全称为光敏平面橡胶渗透印油，是我国于20世纪末从日本引进的新型印油，因其制备工艺简单快速、印迹清晰、使用寿命长，在我国得到了迅速推广，司法鉴定中涉及光敏印油检验的案件也日益增多。光敏印油的主要染料为罗丹明B，是一种常见的工业污染物质。

光敏印油印文无压痕，色料平实、均匀、稳定，文字线条边缘平整，无挤墨现象。

三、仪器设备及检验方法介绍

（一）IDMH—Z780文件检验系统

IDMH—Z780是文件检验的常用仪器之一，由高倍体式显微镜、CCD、电脑及专业软件等组成。其中的图像处理软件具有将二维图像处理成三维图像，并用伪彩色实体图及等高线的形式表现出来的功能。

IDMH—Z780系统检验朱墨时序的原理是：利用视频数字CCD，将红、绿、蓝、温度、震动等多种光敏感传感器进行组合，对光谱照射下的检样“微痕迹和光谱反射率”等多种信息进行充分的提取，并通过等高线形态图的描述与分析方法实现。在判断朱文交叉先后顺序时，将传统的视觉图形直接变成全新的三维立体图形。正常条件下，由于朱墨交叉部位上存在先后顺序，导致“色料 ”在交叉部位上的分布方式和浓度上的差异，从而被CCD捕捉到其色料在交叉部位上的构成信息，软件根据其构成进行显现出来笔划的立体交叉形态，基本上可以通过“三维实体图形态描述”效果，直接进行判断。等高线的形态描述主要是作为实体图形态描述的一种有效补充，等高线所描述的形态是通过颜色的不同和闭合圈形态的不同来进行区分性的显示，并以此对色料浓度的状态进行细致而关键的描述。这种方式的描述突破了实体图的描述受色料成分及书写压力差别巨大的限制，更好地描述出交叉部位的边缘形态和表面形态的状态，使鉴定人员能够更加充分地掌握交叉部位的信息细节，从而得出更加客观的鉴定结果。

（二）3D 伪彩色图检验法

3D 伪彩色图检验法，主要是将笔画和印文交叉处的显微状态用软件自身配置的色彩图描述出来，根据色料的厚度或浓度的不同，其表现出来的颜色也不尽相同，由此来分析判断朱墨的先后顺序。总的说来是依靠对色料成份浓度的差异性进行细微描述，依靠色料浓度变化的状态再结合文检理论，从而得出最接近真实客观事实的结论。根据 3D 软件的原理与特性我们可以理解为：色料浓度越高，软件构成的 3D 的形态就越高，相反浓度越低，则 3D 形态就越低。

（三）等高线检验法

"等高线"是将物质关键点的基本信息作为描述对象，在形态上保持清晰的整体构成的同时，又对关键点和层次进行良好的描述，以数字图形的形式表现出来的一种图像。等高线在很多行业有着广泛的应用，并且表现出良好的应用价值。例如：地理、天气、地质等等。

IDMH—Z780 软件中的"等高线"主要是通过抓住色料浓度的"关键点"，勾勒出朱墨交叉处整体形态的重点，使色料形态的分布完整地展现出来。等高线检验法主要是作为 3D 伪彩色图检验法的一种有效补充，通过观察线圈颜色的不同和闭合形态的不同来进行区分性的显示，并以此对色料浓度的状态进行细致而关键的描述。

四、实验研究

1. 实验材料及样品制作：本次实验以晨光牌蓝、黑签字笔和红色速干印泥、传统印油、原子印油、光敏印油（品牌见表 1）为主要研究对象 。将蓝、黑两种签字笔分别与四种不同成分印油交叉制备实验样品，每种笔与每种印油制作成不同时序的两份材料，共计 16 份实验样本。

表 1　印油品牌

1	印泥	雪奥快干印泥
2	传统印油	得利牌印油
3	原子印章	永佳牌原子印油
4	光敏印章	利信牌光敏印油

2. 实验条件：运用3D 伪彩色图法进行检验前，需要通过预实验确定实验参数。经过多次实验摸索，确定 3－D 图采用双色阶显示模式，起始色阶值为 190，色阶宽度为 30。

3. 实验结果（表 2、表 3）：

（1）先书写后盖印。当先书写后盖印时，笔画书写在纸张上，所附着的媒介物保持不变，笔画自身比较完整，后盖印的印油覆盖在笔画之上，起到了叠加作用，因此交叉部位的 3－D 形态应该是高于其他部位的。具体表现是：交叉部位的表面色料密度较非交叉部位大，交叉部位等高线圈颜色近似且没有明显的界线。

（2）先盖印后书写。因为是先盖印的，当笔画经过已经盖印好印油的纸张时，字迹所附着的媒介物实际发生了改变，由于纸张和印油对墨水吸附能力的差异，造成了笔画自身的不完整，书写在印油上的笔画容易留下露白，交叉部位的部分区域实际上没有得到笔画和印油两种色料的叠加，而仅仅是印油的色料层，因此这些区域的3－D高度没有得到提升。具体表现是：交叉部位的表层色料密度与非交叉部位差异不大。等高线图的表现较为明显，交叉部位上得到两种色料叠加的地方和没有得到叠加的地方之间有明显的界限，由于没有得到笔画色料叠加的地方只有印油的色料，其线圈的颜色和密度与印油相似，而得到叠加地方的线圈颜色则与之明显不同。

表2 黑色签字笔与印文交叉顺序检验效果图

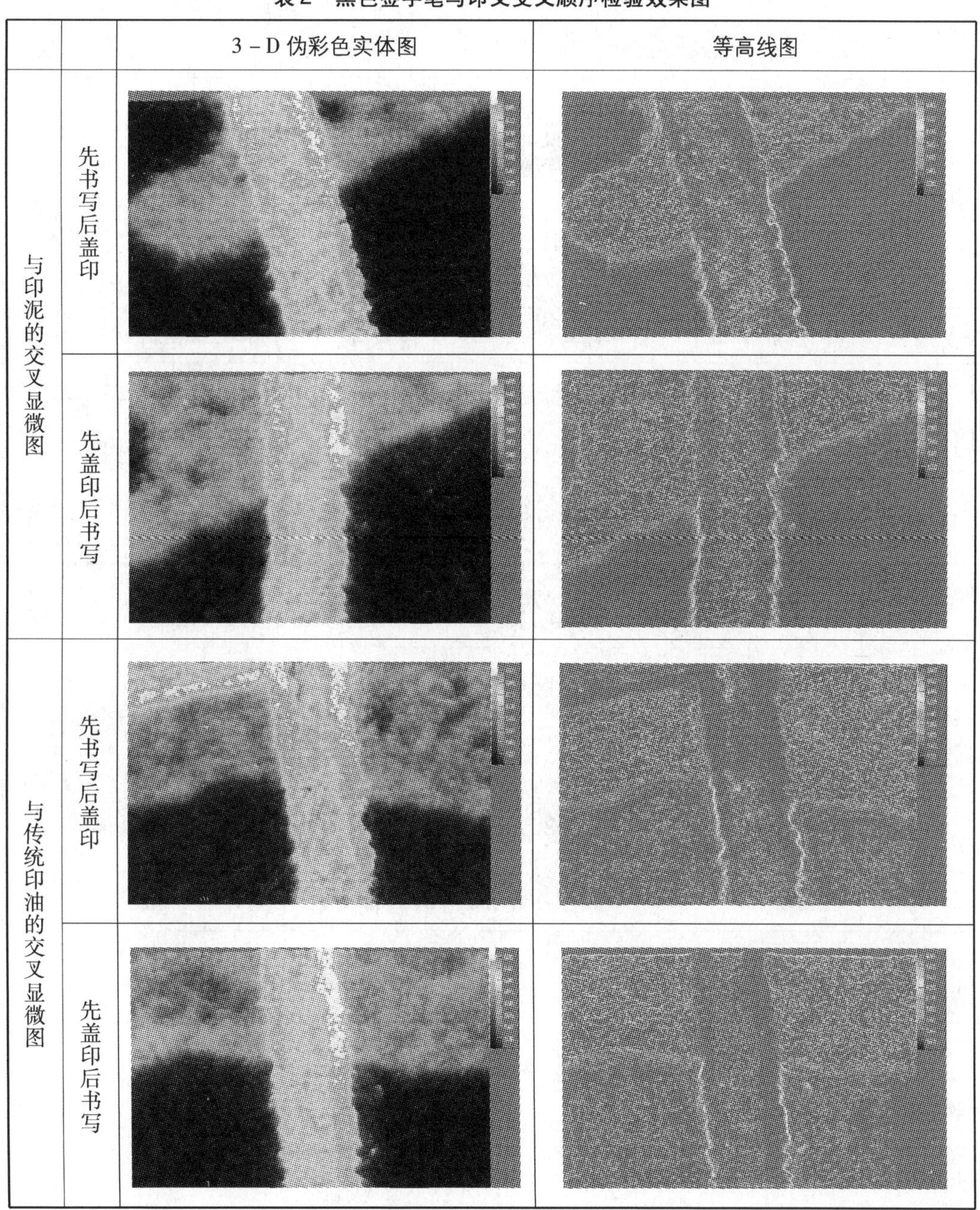

		3－D伪彩色实体图	等高线图
与印泥的交叉显微图	先书写后盖印		
	先盖印后书写		
与传统印油的交叉显微图	先书写后盖印		
	先盖印后书写		

续表

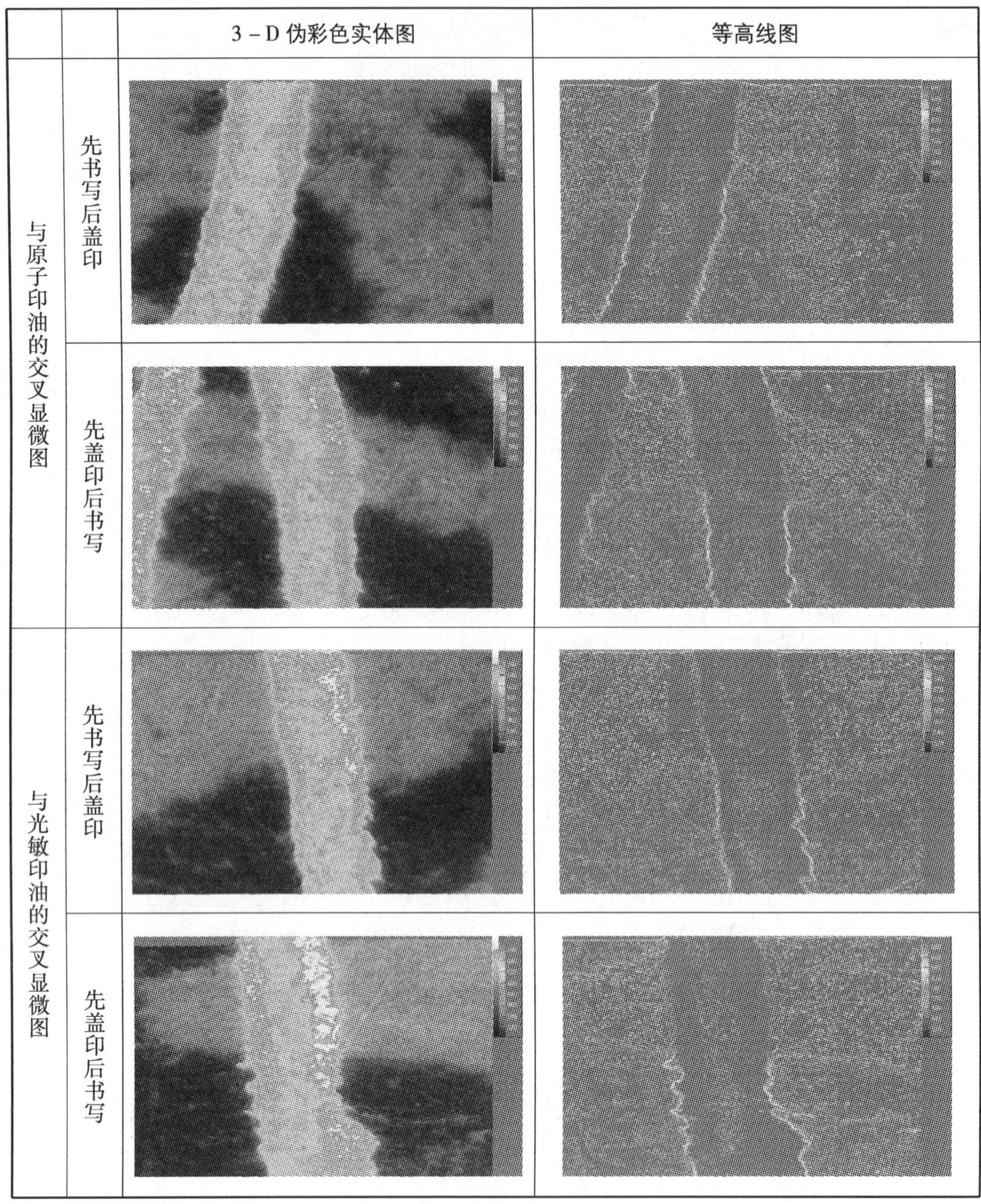

		3－D 伪彩色实体图	等高线图
与原子印油的交叉显微图	先书写后盖印		
	先盖印后书写		
与光敏印油的交叉显微图	先书写后盖印		
	先盖印后书写		

表 3　蓝色签字笔与印文交叉顺序检验效果图

		3－D 伪彩色实体图	等高线图
与印泥的交叉显微图	先书写后盖印	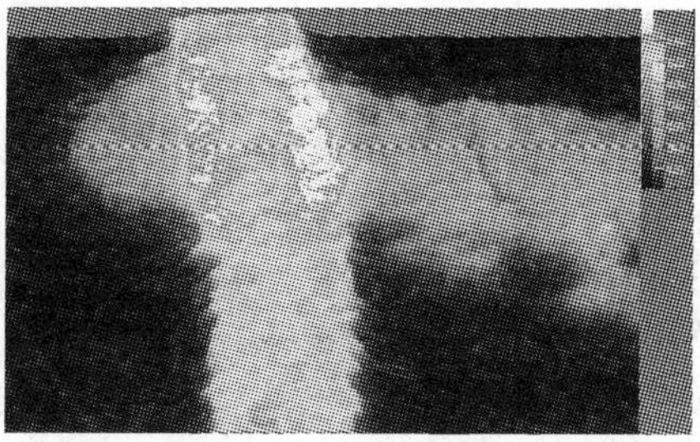	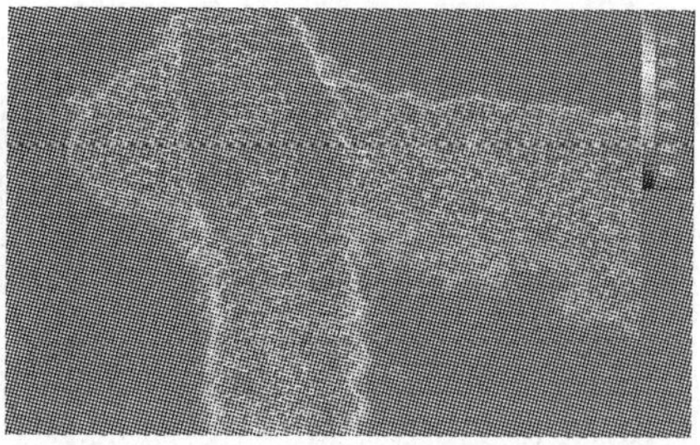
	先盖印后书写	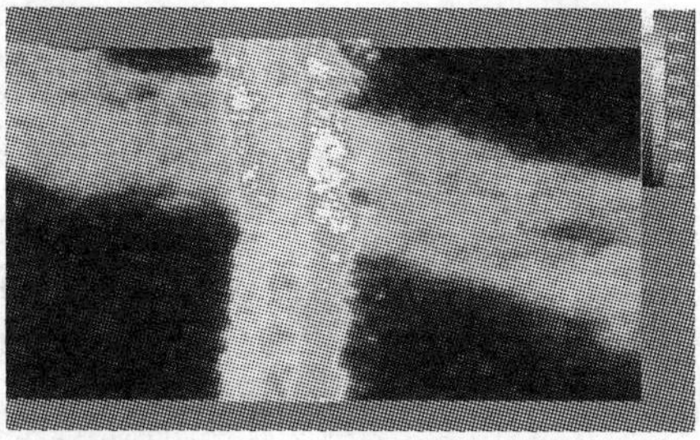	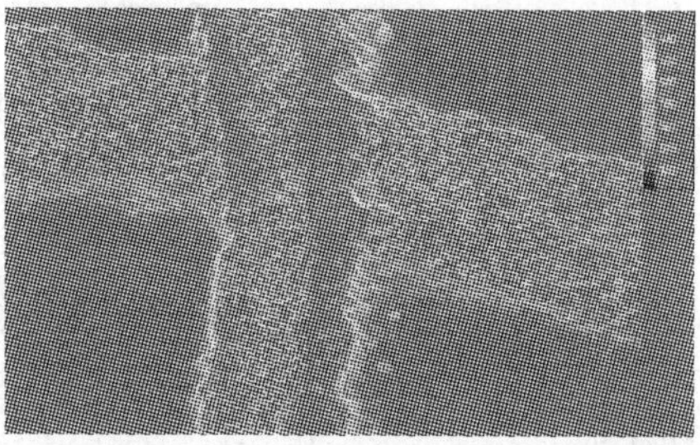
与传统印油的交叉显微图	先书写后盖印	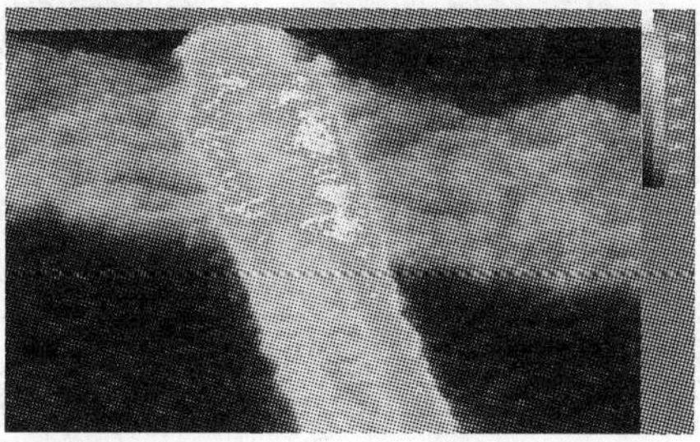	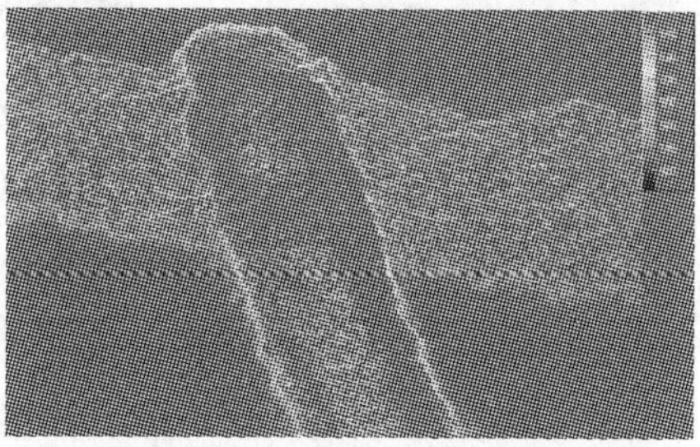
	先盖印后书写	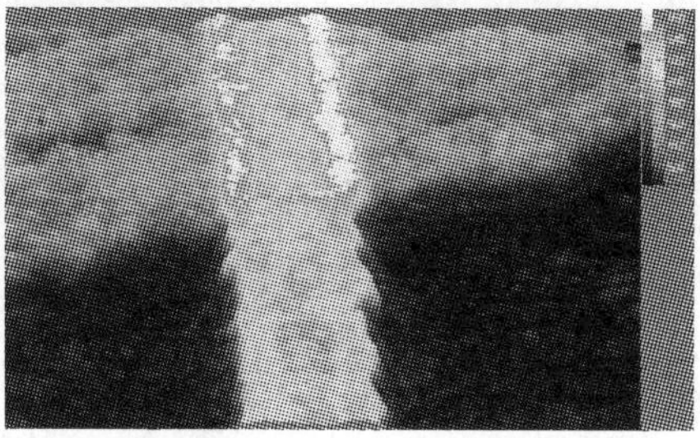	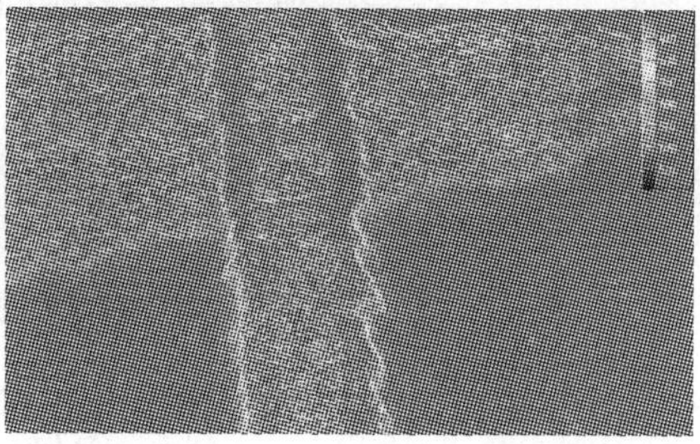

续表

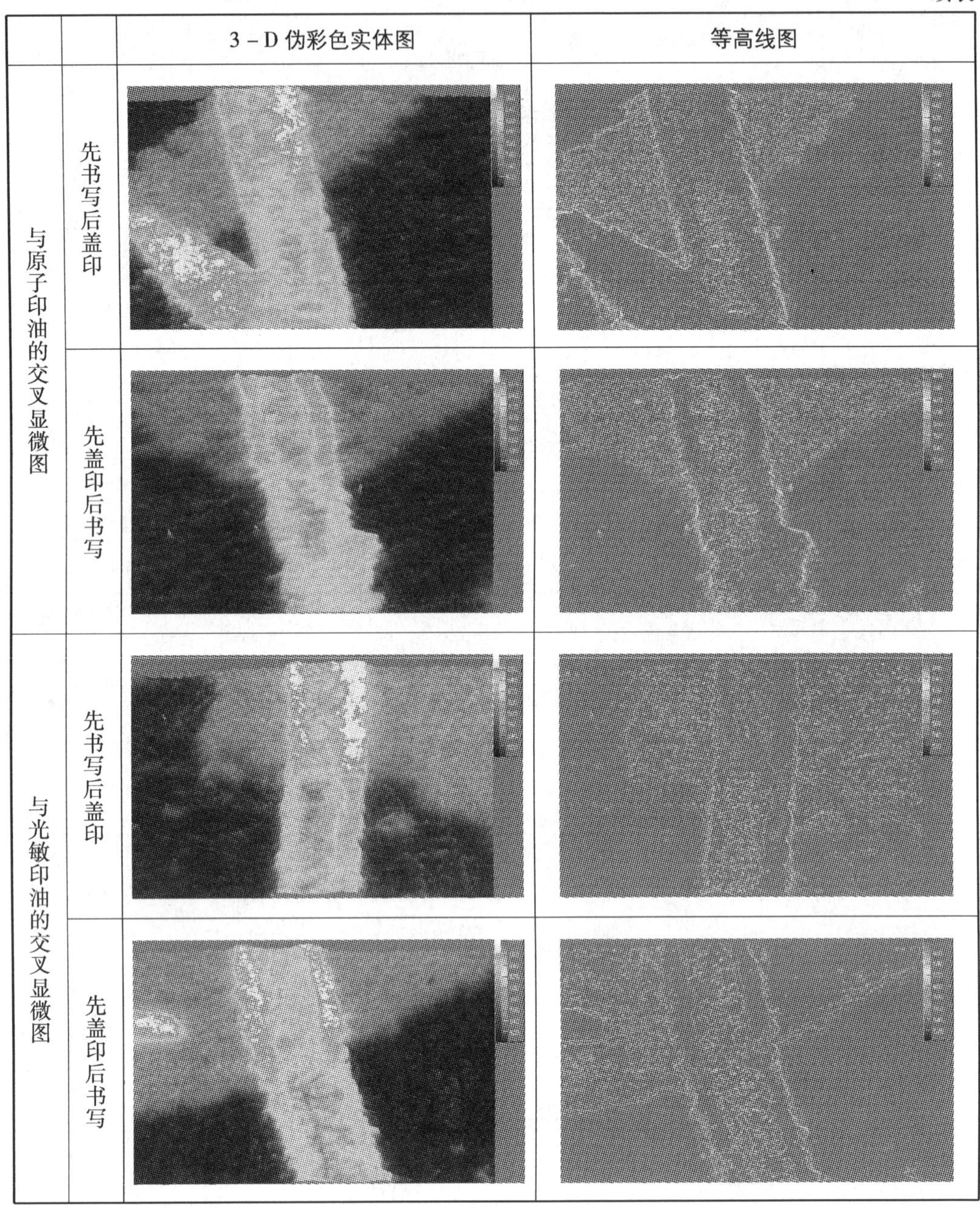

		3－D 伪彩色实体图	等高线图
与原子印油的交叉显微图	先书写后盖印		
	先盖印后书写		
与光敏印油的交叉显微图	先书写后盖印		
	先盖印后书写		

五、结 论

本文选取了4种不同品牌、不同成分的印油及晨光牌蓝色和黑色签字笔作为研究对象，制作了16份实验样品，运用IDHM－780系统中的3－D伪彩色图和等高线法对样品进行观察和检验，得出以下结论：

1. 3－D伪彩色图和等高线法在检验蓝色、黑色两种颜色签字笔与四种不同成分印油的形成顺序上具有良好的检验效果。通过分析交叉部位与非交叉部位3－D图色料的高度、密度的差异以及交叉部位等高线圈的颜色、闭合范围等特征，可以有效判断朱墨形成的先后顺序。

2. 不同品牌、不同成分的印油在运用3－D伪彩色图和等高线法进行检验时影响不大，尤其针对用显微法检验难度比较大的原子印油和光敏印油，其与签字笔的形成顺序从3－D伪彩色图和等高线图上都能够有所区分

3. 目前3－D伪彩色法和等高线法尚处于实验室研究阶段，能否运用到实际案件的鉴定中还需要进一步的实验研究和论证。这种方法具有应用在检验朱墨顺序鉴定的可行性，与显微观察法、荧光法、拉曼光谱法互相补充印证，能够增加对结论判断的科学依据。

最后，希望通过此篇文章给文检工作者提供一些技术支持，也期待今后能够在实际案件中发挥作用。

参考文献

［1］贾晓光、宋庆芳、罗顿："光敏印章盖印引文的检验"，载《政法学刊》2007年第3期，第98～100页。

［2］《朱墨时序鉴定规范》，司法鉴定技术规范，SF/2 JD020/007－2010，1。

［3］邹积鑫、陈跃、章晴、杨受东："光敏印油印迹主要染料成分定性及讲解规律研究"，www. docin. com/p－240569542. html。

蓝色印文与印刷文件朱墨时序的检验案例启示

王小怡 *

朱墨时序，是指印文与书写、打印或复写字迹形成的先后顺序，顺序的先后直接反映了文件要素的形成时序，是判断文件真伪的重要方面。朱墨时序鉴定是文件检验的组成部分，在司法实践中有着很大的鉴定需求。而蓝色印文，也称档案印文，采用蓝色的印油或印泥，多用于存档的文件，也有用于合同、名章的证明，但不多见。尤其是涉及蓝色印文与印刷文件文字的朱墨时序鉴定问题，在实践界更是少之又少。

2009 年 3 月，某事业单位送来一份档案文件，要求鉴定该档案文件的真伪。系统检验后发现，文件上的“副本”蓝色印文和真实的“副本”蓝色印文在概貌特征和细节特征上形成符合，印文是真实的。蓝色印文与文件末页印刷文字存在交叉点，那么该印文与文件的形成次序是否正常？和委托方进行深入交谈后，发现单位的“副本”蓝色印文保管松散，进出单位的人都有机会盖到该蓝色印文。档案文件的印刷方式是喷墨打印机打印，蓝色印文材质是光敏印文，在显微镜下观察，发现交叉点处的印文笔画和印刷文字均完整。为此我们要求委托方提供标称时间接近的档案文件样本和真实的“副本”印章，并用该印章制作了部分样本，结果发现先墨后朱情形下会有明亮的紫红色光泽出现，如下图。

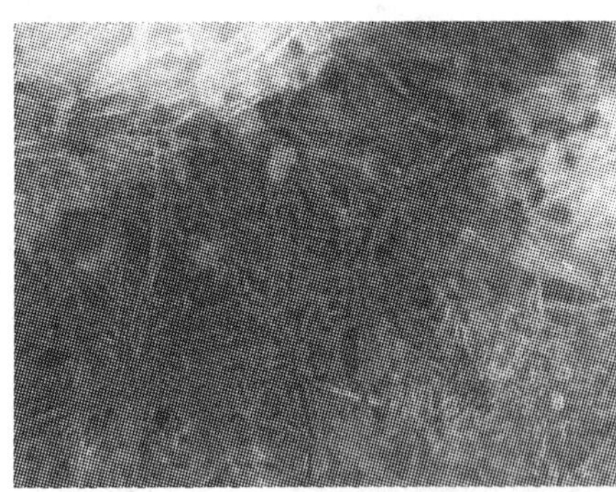
先墨后朱　文件的显微图片

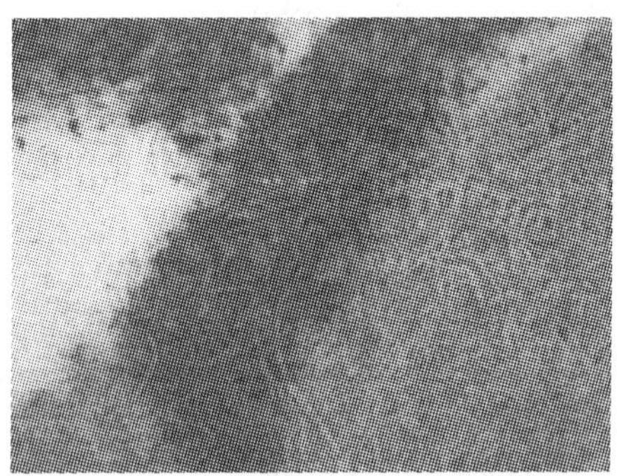
可疑文件的显微图片

2011 年 10 月，某建筑公司委托律师事务所送来一份造价合同书，要求鉴定该造价合同书的真假。该造价合同书的数额争议较大，建筑公司对这份造价合同没有印象，

* 王小怡，华东政法大学在读博士。Email：wangzixingcun@163.com。

而工程师本人也不记得盖印过这份合同。检验发现，造价工程师的个人私章系蓝色原子印章印文，和该文件的印刷文字有交叉点。有了上次检验蓝色印文的经验，我们对该造价合同的朱墨时序也进行了仔细的观察，最终确定文件的形成顺序是先盖章后打印。据工程师本人回忆，他有段时间办公室抽屉坏了，中间间隔了几个月才修该抽屉，没想到酿成大祸。

实际检案工作中，印文真伪鉴别和朱墨时序检验的案子中大概99%都是红色印文的相关检验，蓝色印文的检验案件很少。我们在这两起案件中，蓝色印文的真伪检验难度不大，但蓝色印文和印刷文件的朱墨时序判别却很棘手，因为这方面的检案经验不足。为此我们专门做了一系列和蓝色印文有关的实验，并让两起案件的当事人将印章提供给我们以供检验。受此启发，我们将案件处理过程中和实验中发现的蓝色印文和印刷文字交叉部位的一些规律进行总结，以便同行之间交流学习。

一、实验材料和方法

（一）实验材料

1. 印刷方式

（1）静电印刷文字。实验材料：第一类，原装墨盒，HPlaserjet2015 激光打印机、sharp 复印机；第二类，兼容墨[2]，canon 打印复印一体机。

（2）喷墨打印文字。实验材料：第一类，原装墨盒，HP5468 喷墨打印机、HP6000 喷墨打印机；第二类，兼容墨，EPSON 喷墨打印机。

2. 不同印文材料

（1）原子印油。实验材料：国产万次印油（蓝色 亚信牌）、进口万次印油（蓝色 上海长江刻字厂进口分装）。

（2）光敏印油。实验材料：国产光敏印油（蓝色 亚信牌）、进口光敏印油（蓝色 上海长江刻字厂进口分装）。

3. 用不用印文材料和不同的印刷文件分别制备先墨后朱和先朱后墨两种顺序的样本材料。

（二）实验方法

1. 显微检验

（1）体视显微镜。实验设备：DV4 体视显微镜、Lumar v12 荧光体视显微镜。

（2）三维立体显微镜。实验设备：Axio Imager Vario 材料纤维镜、ZEISS 3D 三维立体显微镜。

二、实验图片

显微观察图片如下所示：

---

〔2〕 兼容墨水也就是填充墨水（refill inks），其一般采用塑料瓶内装墨水，它也会分出 EPSON、COLOR、PHOTO 等产品种类。正规的此类兼容产品都带有详细的说明书和相应的填充工具，你可自行将墨水注入用过的原厂墨盒或兼容墨盒中反复使用。从种类上看，目前的填充墨水覆盖了各大厂牌的几乎全部型号的打印机墨盒。造价比原装墨盒低廉。

（一）静电印刷方式和各种印文

1. 激光打印，兼容墨

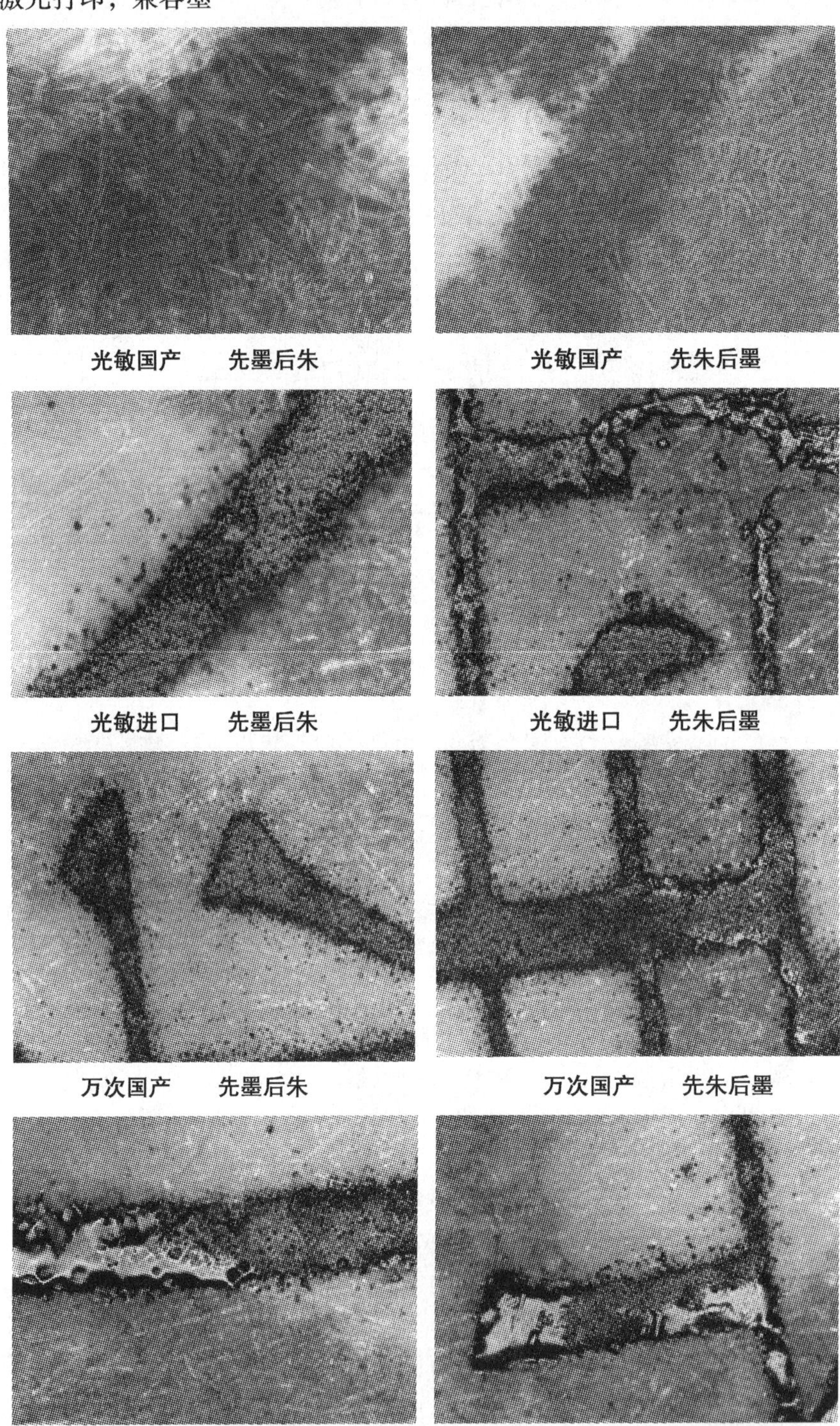

光敏国产　先墨后朱　　光敏国产　先朱后墨

光敏进口　先墨后朱　　光敏进口　先朱后墨

万次国产　先墨后朱　　万次国产　先朱后墨

万次进口　先墨后朱　　万次进口　先朱后墨

2. 原装墨盒，sharp 复印

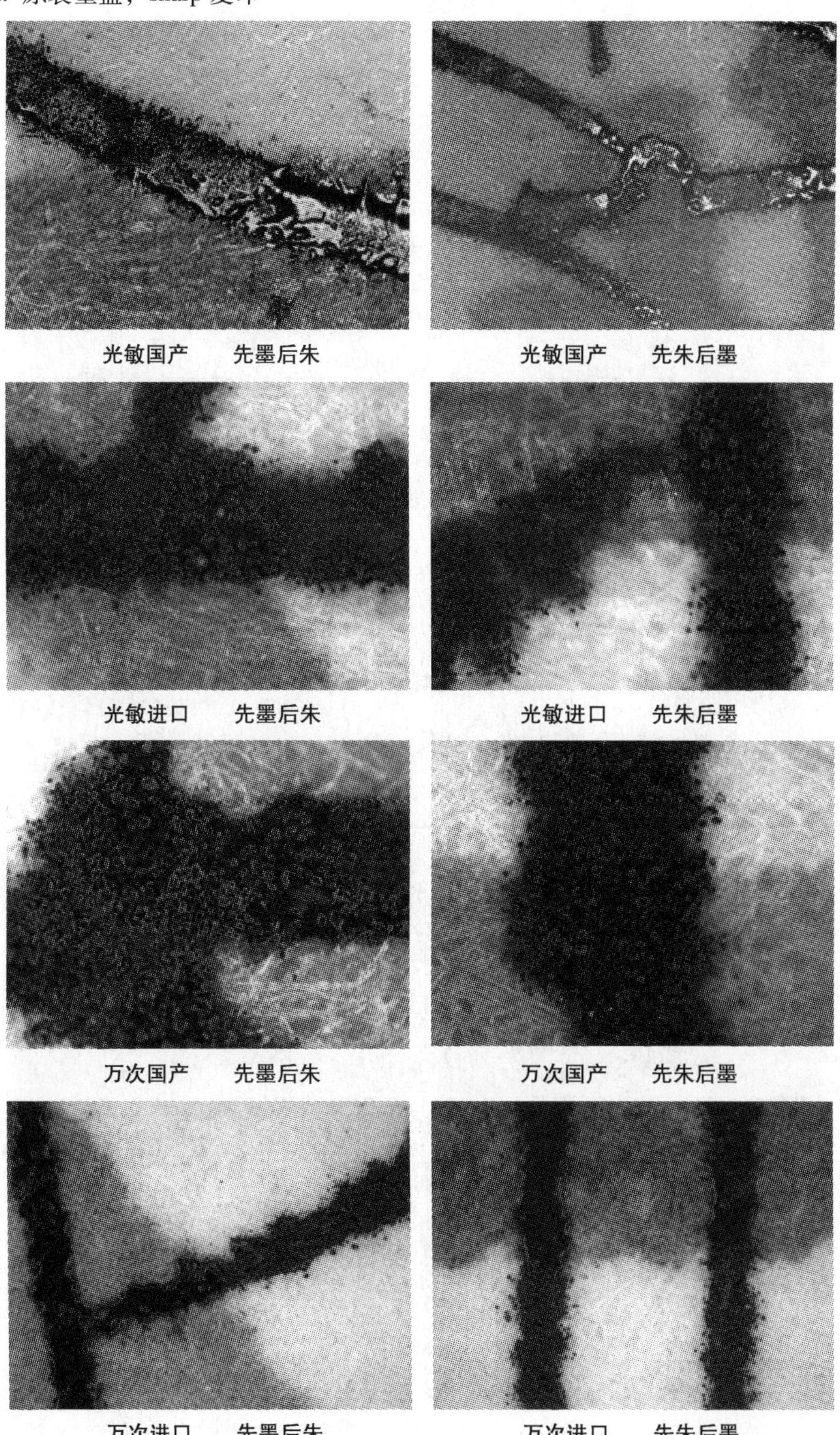

光敏国产　　先墨后朱　　　　光敏国产　　先朱后墨

光敏进口　　先墨后朱　　　　光敏进口　　先朱后墨

万次国产　　先墨后朱　　　　万次国产　　先朱后墨

万次进口　　先墨后朱　　　　万次进口　　先朱后墨

3. 原装墨盒，HP LaserJet 激光打印 2015

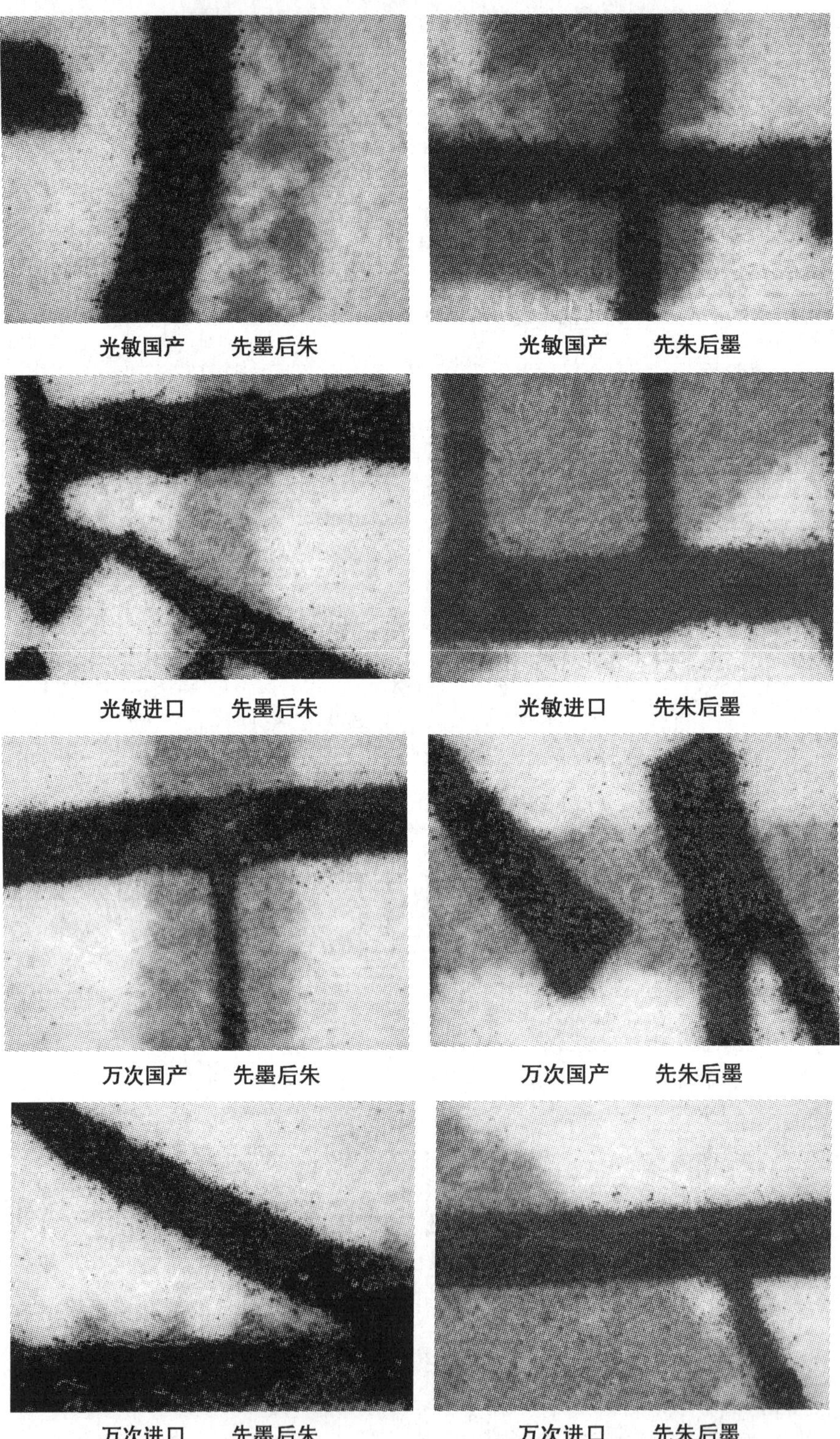

光敏国产　先墨后朱　　光敏国产　先朱后墨

光敏进口　先墨后朱　　光敏进口　先朱后墨

万次国产　先墨后朱　　万次国产　先朱后墨

万次进口　先墨后朱　　万次进口　先朱后墨

(二) 喷墨打印文件和各种印文

1. 兼容墨，EPSON 喷墨打印机

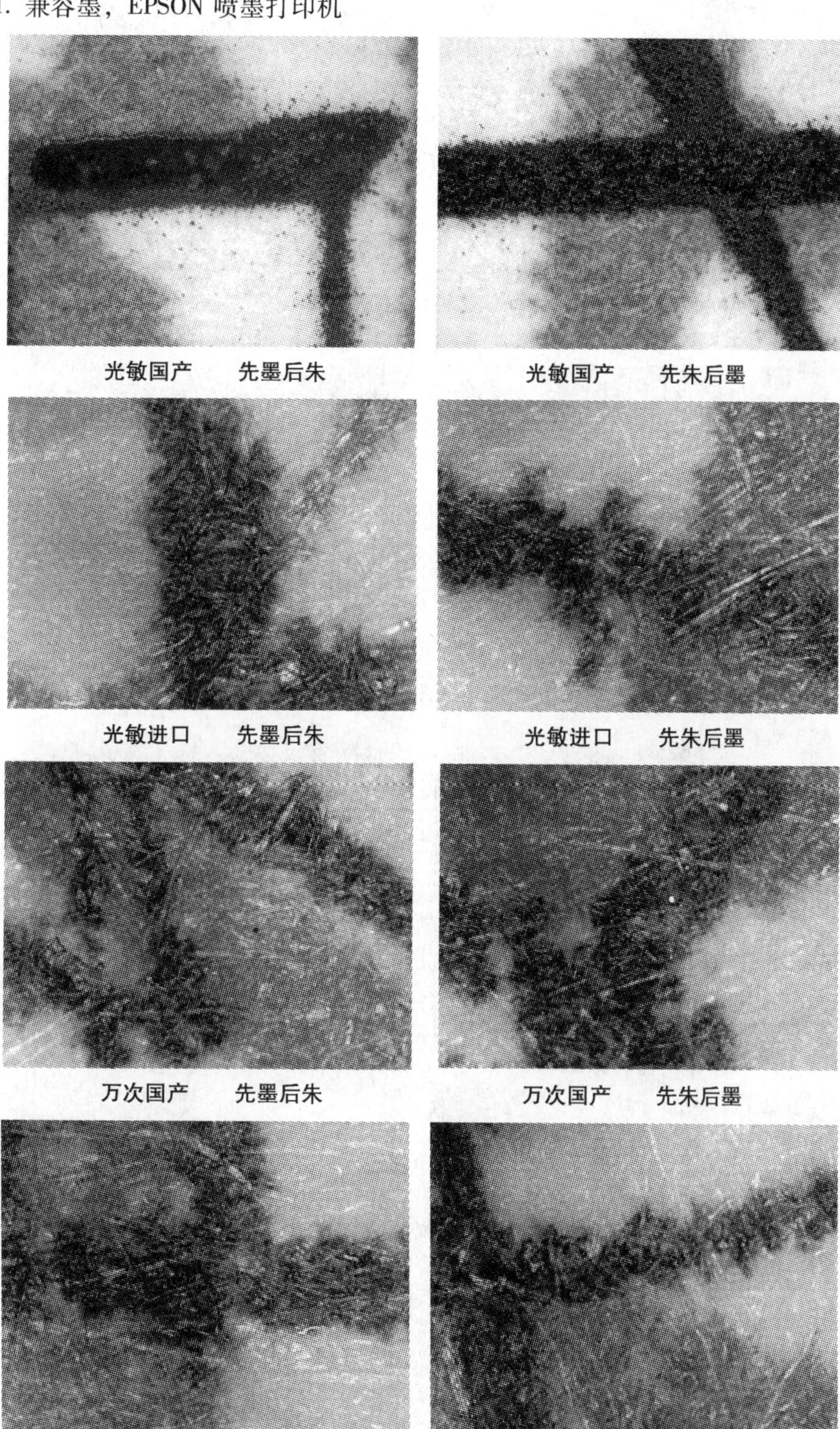

光敏国产　先墨后朱　　光敏国产　先朱后墨

光敏进口　先墨后朱　　光敏进口　先朱后墨

万次国产　先墨后朱　　万次国产　先朱后墨

万次进口　先墨后朱　　万次进口　先朱后墨

2. 原装墨盒，HP5468 喷墨打印机

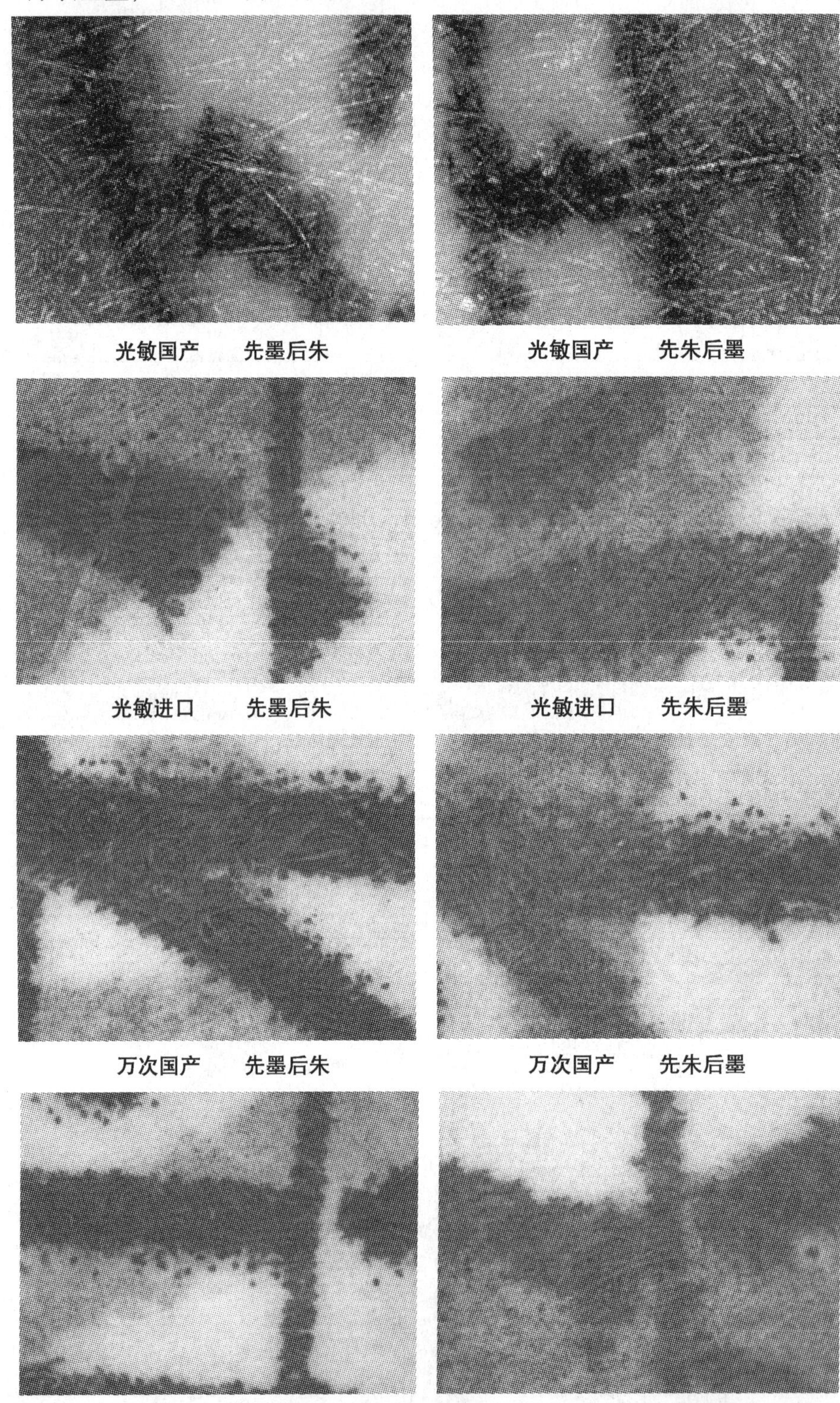

光敏国产　先墨后朱　　光敏国产　先朱后墨

光敏进口　先墨后朱　　光敏进口　先朱后墨

万次国产　先墨后朱　　万次国产　先朱后墨

万次进口　先墨后朱　　万次进口　先朱后墨

3. 原装墨盒，HP6000 喷墨打印机

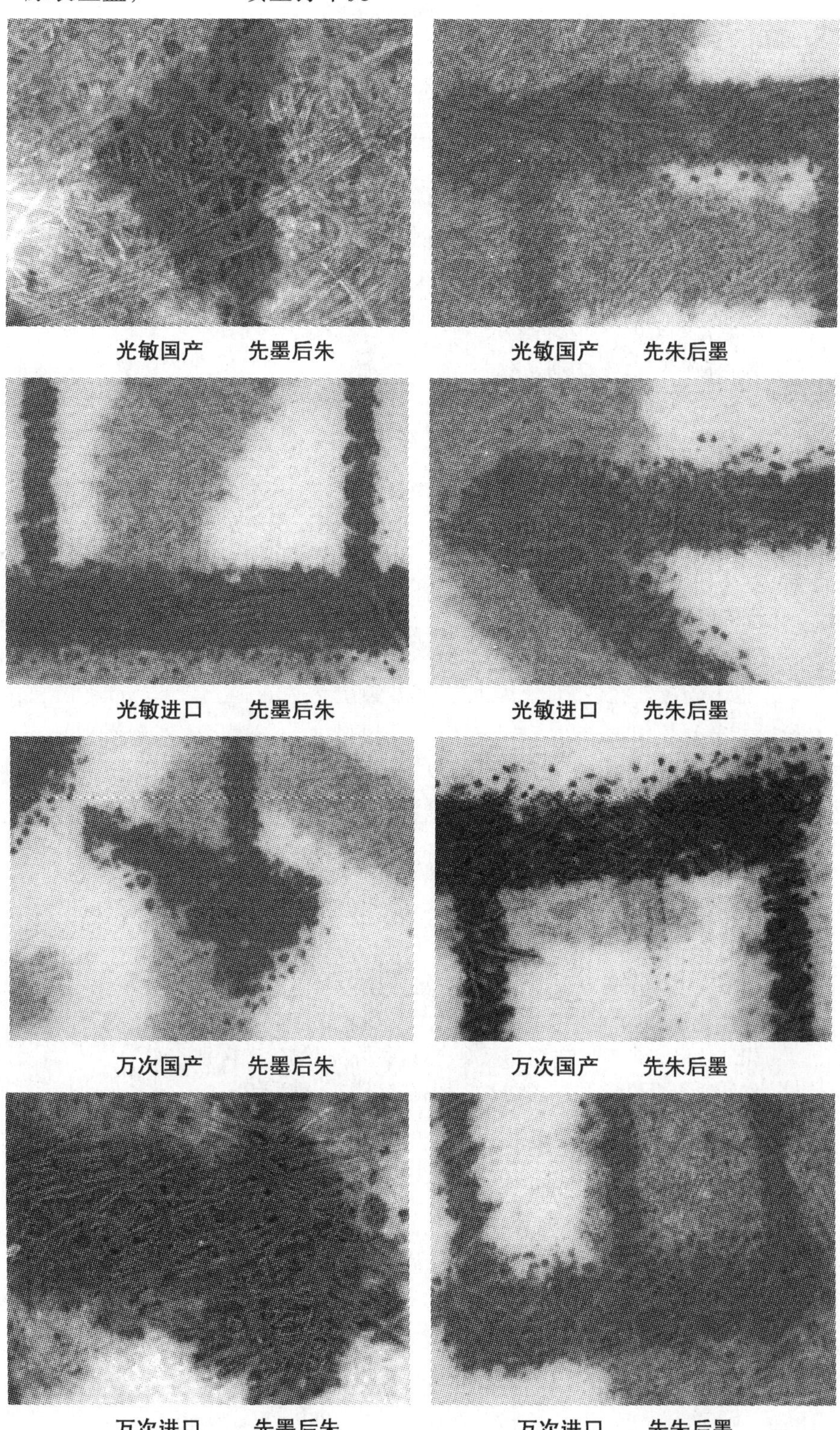

光敏国产　先墨后朱　　光敏国产　先朱后墨

光敏进口　先墨后朱　　光敏进口　先朱后墨

万次国产　先墨后朱　　万次国产　先朱后墨

万次进口　先墨后朱　　万次进口　先朱后墨

三、实验结论

（一）特征描述

印刷文件 印文种类	兼容墨 canon 打印复印一体机	原装墨盒 sharp 复印机	原装 HPlaserjet2015 激光打印机
光敏印 油国产	先墨后朱：交叉点上方有明亮的紫红色光泽 先朱后墨：交叉点处黑色印刷文字出现断笔现象 先朱后墨和先墨后朱在交叉点处的油墨聚集形态明显不同	先墨后朱：交叉点上方有浅淡的紫红色光泽 先朱后墨和先墨后朱在交叉点处的油墨聚集形态区别不明显	先朱后墨和先墨后朱在交叉点处的油墨聚集形态区别不明显
光敏印 油进口	先墨后朱：交叉点上方有明亮的紫红色光泽 先朱后墨：交叉点处黑色印刷文字出现断笔现象 先朱后墨和先墨后朱在交叉点处的油墨聚集形态明显不同	先墨后朱：交叉点上方有明亮的紫红色光泽 先朱后墨和先墨后朱在交叉点处的油墨聚集形态区别不明显	先朱后墨和先墨后朱在交叉点处的油墨聚集形态区别不明显
原子印 油国产	先朱后墨和先墨后朱在交叉点处的油墨聚集形态区别不明显	先朱后墨和先墨后朱在交叉点处的油墨聚集形态区别不明显	先朱后墨和先墨后朱在交叉点处的油墨聚集形态区别明显
原子印 油进口	先墨后朱：交叉点上方有明亮的紫红色光泽 先朱后墨：交叉点处黑色印刷文字出现断笔现象 先朱后墨和先墨后朱在交叉点处的油墨聚集形态区别不明显	先墨后朱：交叉点上方有浅淡的紫红色光泽 先朱后墨和先墨后朱在交叉点处的油墨聚集形态区别不明显	先朱后墨和先墨后朱在交叉点处的油墨聚集形态区别明显

印刷文件印文种类	兼容墨 EPSON 喷墨打印机	原装墨盒 HP5468 喷墨打印机	原装墨盒 HP6000 喷墨打印机
光敏印油国产	先墨后朱：交叉点处的黑色笔画和空白处的黑色笔画关泽区别不大 先朱后墨：交叉点处的黑色笔画有明显的变色现象，与空白处的黑色笔画颜色明显不同	先墨后朱：交叉点上方有明亮的紫红色光泽 先朱后墨：特征不明显	先墨后朱：交叉点上方有明亮的紫红色光泽 先朱后墨：特征不明显
光敏印油进口	先墨后朱：交叉点处的黑色笔画和空白处的黑色笔画关泽区别不大 先朱后墨：交叉点处的黑色笔画有明显的变色现象，与空白处的黑色笔画颜色明显不同	先墨后朱：交叉点上方有浅淡的紫红色光泽 先朱后墨：特征不明显	先墨后朱：交叉点上方有明亮的紫红色光泽 先朱后墨：特征不明显
原子印油国产	先墨后朱：交叉点处的黑色笔画和空白处的黑色笔画关泽区别不大 先朱后墨：交叉点处的黑色笔画有明显的变色现象，与空白处的黑色笔画颜色明显不同	先墨后朱：交叉点上方有浅淡的紫红色光泽 先朱后墨：特征不明显	先墨后朱：交叉点上方有明亮的紫红色光泽 先朱后墨：特征不明显
原子印油进口	先墨后朱：交叉点处的黑色笔画和空白处的黑色笔画关泽区别不大 先朱后墨：交叉点处的黑色笔画有明显的变色现象，与空白处的黑色笔画颜色明显不同	先墨后朱：交叉点上方有明亮的紫红色光泽 先朱后墨：特征不明显	先墨后朱：交叉点上方有明亮的紫红色光泽 先朱后墨：特征不明显

（二）规律总结

1. 实验收集的 24 份形成时序为先墨后朱样本中，有 14 份先墨后朱的实验样本在交叉点处出现了清晰的紫红色光泽。在 24 份形成时序为先朱后墨的实验样本中，交叉点处没有紫红色光泽的出现。因此交叉点处的紫红色光泽特征可以区分样本文件形成顺序正常与否的重要特征。

2. 静电印刷文件和印文的朱墨时序判断，除了正常文件形成时序下会出现的紫红色光泽外，还发现墨粉和印油物质的凝聚形态也可以作为判断文件朱墨时序的重要特征，但该特征的比对价值不高，12 份样本只有 3 份朱墨时序不同的样本可以用此特征进行区分，5 份朱墨时序不同的样本用交叉点处的紫红色光泽可以清楚区分，剩余 4 份实验样本单用显微镜观察的方法区分困难较大。

3. 喷墨打印文件和印文的朱墨时序判断，除了正常文件形成时序下会出现的紫红色光泽外，还发现在先朱后墨的文件形成时序下交叉点处黑色笔画的变色现象也可以作为判断朱墨时序的重要特征，但特征价值不高，12 份样本有 4 份朱墨时序不同的样本可以用此特征进行区分，另外 8 份朱墨时序不用的实验样本材料用交叉点处的紫红色光泽可以清楚区分。

参考文献

[1] 王世全：《印刷文件检验》，中国人民公安大学出版社 2001 年版。

[2] 贾玉文、邹明理：《中国刑事科学技术大全·文件检验》，中国人民公安大学出版社 2002 年版，第 1234 ~ 1235 页。

[3] 贾治辉：《文书检验》，西南政法大学教材编审委员会审定，法律出版社 2001 年版。

[4] 李江春、周茜、暴仁："朱墨时序检验的方法研究"，载《新疆警官高等专科学校学报》2008 年第 1 期。

[5] 胡爽、邹积鑫："文件朱墨时序的检验方法及其比较分析"，载《刑事技术》2007 年第 3 期。

[6] 胡向阳、姚慧芳："运用高倍显微镜判断朱墨时序的方法"，载《刑事技术》2008 年第 3 期。

法庭科学领域中油漆检验技术的进展

雷 蕾[1] 王元凤[1] 黄 威[2*]

公安部日前公布，2012 年年底全国机动车保有量已达 2.4 亿辆，18 个大中城市汽车保有量超过百万。[1]伴随着机动车数量的迅猛增长，是越来越多的道路交通事故。微量物证在确定交通事故中相互接触的事实，认定肇事车辆等方面起到极其重要的作用。在交通事故类案件中，常见的微量物证有油漆、纤维、塑料、橡胶等。针对这些微量物证，国内外已经形成了多种成熟而有效的分析方法来进行分析鉴定，如显微镜法、红外光谱法、拉曼光谱法、扫描电镜能谱法、裂解气相色谱法、薄层色谱分析法、显微分光光度法、原子发射光谱法等。[2]近年来，国内外学者又研究出了许多新的分析方法与技术应用与交通事故类案件中微量物证的分析，如飞行时间二次离子质谱法（Time - of - Flight Secondary Ion Mass Spectrometry，TOF - SIMS）、显微光谱成像（Microscopic Spectral Imaging，MSI）、X 射线光电子能谱分析法（X - Ray Photoelectron Spectroscopy，XPS）、X 射线衍射法（X - Ray Diffraction，XRD）、电感耦合等离子体质谱法（Inductively Coupled Plasma - Mass，ICP - MS）等。而对于某种特定的微量物证的鉴定，国内外学者还另辟蹊径地从不同的视角对传统的微量物证进行审视。如对于油漆类物证，国内有学者应用 MSI 法来对汽车多层漆片的横截面进行研究，有学者尝试应用扫描电镜法（Scan Electron Microscopy，SEM）检验漆膜厚度来鉴别同种颜色的汽车油漆；在国外，有学者应用高能量同步辐射 X 射线荧光光谱法（Synchrotron Radiation X - Ray Fluorescence Spectrometry，SR - XRF）鉴别汽车白色油漆碎片中所用无机颜料，通过其成分与含量来实现对不同油漆样品之间的区分。总体来说，国内外对于交通事故类案件中常见微量物证的研究处于不断发展状态，且国外发达国家的研究水平和先进程度高于我国。

一、国内相关研究

在我国，交通事故现场常见的微量物证主要有油漆、塑料和树脂、纤维、轮胎橡胶、汽车玻璃及法医物证。其中，最常见的微量物证为油漆和塑料树脂。我国对于微量物证的研究和应用较晚；但是，通过办案人员和相关研究人员不断的探索努力，在借鉴国外经验技术的基础上，我国也逐步发展了许多种微量物证的检验技术和手段，在实际办案过程中，一种分析技术方法可以应用于多种微量物证的鉴定。

---

* 雷蕾、王元凤，中国政法大学证据科学教育部重点实验室。基金项目：中国政法大学青年教师学术创新团队资助项目。

通讯作者：王元凤，博士，副教授，主要从事法庭科学等方面的研究。

黄威，公安部物证鉴定中心，北京 100038；Email：judie0505@gmail.com。

（一）红外光谱法

1. 红外光谱法在油漆检验中的应用

在我国，红外光谱法在微量物证分析中的应用起步很晚，1990 年，公安部第二研究所的张象喜介绍了显微傅立叶变换红外光谱法的仪器结构、特点，及其在高聚物材料、晶体物质、纤维、油漆分析、法庭科学和生物化学等领域中的应用。[3] 1991 年，李琼瑶等介绍了公安部第二研究所使用傅立叶变换红外光谱仪连接红外显微镜对刑事技术领域中从案件现场提取的油漆、塑料、纤维等微量有机物证进行结构分析并取得满意效果。[4]

随后，红外光谱法由于其具有定性快、检材用量少、结果准确度高等优点，逐步成为了截至目前最为常见的微量物证分析方法。路春清等应用傅立叶变换红外光谱仪分析、总结了汽车原厂漆、脱落原车漆和刮擦状油漆痕迹的检验结果及其影响，确定了 FT－IR 对交通肇事中油漆物证的分析方法，为科研和办案提供了可借鉴的依据。[5] 孙振文等采用衰减全反射红外光谱法（ATR－FTIR）研究 15 个厂家提供的 365 分油漆样品的罩光漆成膜物质，发现在所有油漆样品中，丙烯酸漆出现的频率最高，氨基漆出现的频率最低，在所有厂家中，使用丙烯酸漆的厂家最多，使用氨基氨脂混合漆的厂家最少，在一定程度上区分了不同汽车厂家的油漆样品，从而大大缩小了侦查范围，对于涉案车辆的快速侦破具有非常重要的作用。[6] 赵鹏程针对 90 种不同车型、不同颜色的汽车油漆样品进行了红外光谱分析及种类鉴别，发现实验所用油漆树脂成分大可分为三类，按样品量的多少依次为醇酸树脂、丙烯酸树脂和聚乙烯类，而对于相同种类油漆样品，可以通过比较其主要官能团的相对比值进行个体区分。[7] 陈涛等采集了 287 份汽车车身油漆样本，使用傅立叶变换显微红外光谱仪取得了 940 份油漆层光谱，对不同车型、颜色的汽车油漆的清漆层、面漆层、中涂层的光谱特征进行了分析，并对光谱相似度进行比较，结果表明，同车型不同颜色的清漆层光谱相似度达到 99.5%，部分相近车型的清漆层光谱高度相似；面层光谱因车型、颜色不同而差异较大，相似度在 70% 以下；中涂层的普通腻子光谱间的相似度在 83.33% ～96.91%，水基腻子光谱间的相似度在 70.12% ～96.44%；油漆中的金属成分会影响面漆层光谱的吸收特征；汽车油漆光谱随使用时间变化而发生变化。[8] 接着，他们又针对上述样品与得出的 940 份油漆红外光谱建立了汽车车身油漆红外光谱比对数据库，综合特征波峰法与相关系数法实现了车身油漆光谱的比对，并对不同车型油漆碎片进行了比对实验。[9] 王岩等用红外光谱分析法制备了常用的 18 大类塑料树脂红外标准光谱图 513 张，创建了塑料树脂红外标准谱库，对这些塑料树脂的中英文名称、中英文简称、商品名等信息进行整理归纳，建立了塑料树脂信息库，为快速检验、鉴定塑料树脂的种类、牌号、生产厂家、结构简式等相关信息提供了准确依据。[10]

2. 使用红外光谱法油漆检验时存在的问题

（1）部分研究的结论相互矛盾，仍需进一步确证。例如，对于汽车油漆所使用的树脂种类而言，有人发现丙烯酸树脂出现的概率最高，而有人却发现醇酸树脂出现的概率最高。这种结论的矛盾可能是由于研究年代存在差异而造成的，也可能是由于研究选样的地域不同而造成的。然而，不同种类树脂在油漆中出现的概率对于油漆证据价值的确定具有重要的意义。因此，仍需要进一步的全面研究准确总结出国内不同种类树脂在油漆中存在的情况。

（2）红外光谱分析结果相似度高，急需化学计量学的介入。许多研究结果表明，无论是清漆层、面漆层，还是中涂层，其红外光谱分析结果都具有较高的相似度。这非常不利于庭审人员解读基于红外光谱分析得到的鉴定意见。一方面，本质性的差异也许微弱的存在于相似度高的两个样品中，相关司法人员会误认为成分一致；另一方面，成分一致的两个样品会因非本质性差异的存在，而被相关司法人员误认为成分不同。因此，如何通过化学计量学，如何结合计算机技术，客观公正地呈现红外光谱分析结果，帮助相关司法人员对其进行正确的评价和解读，就成为我国微量物证分析人员需要攻克的另一个瓶颈。

（二）其他几种常见的分析方法

1. 拉曼光谱法

作为红外光谱法的最佳互补，拉曼光谱法也成为微量物证分析的常规手段之一。王志国介绍了拉曼光谱的发展过程和法庭科学领域应用的优点；简述了拉曼光谱与红外光谱相比的优点，并着重对国内外 FT - Raman 光谱在油漆、纤维、纸张等的检验鉴定应用现状进行了综述。[11]后来，王志国等又利用红外傅立叶变换拉曼光谱（NIR FT - Raman）技术对 13 个橡胶样品进行了扫描，并进行了较为详细的拉曼谱图解析，指出利用该方法检验橡胶具有速度快、无需制样等优势，能够成为与红外光谱互补的一种橡胶检验的新方法。[12]余静等对拉曼光谱在油漆鉴定中的研究和应用现状进行了综述，简要说明拉曼光谱用于油漆鉴定的特点，并对其应用前景进行了展望。[13]由于激光拉曼技术成熟的较晚，而且相关分析仪器在国内的普及度不高，所以使用拉曼光谱法鉴别交通事故类案件中的微量物证在司法实践中出现的频率较低。

2. 裂解气相色谱法

李玉兰等应用热裂解气相色谱/质谱法对国产 17 种不同牌号的油漆成膜物进行了分析，并采用"特征裂解产物"鉴定多种聚合物法，确定了各受试油漆的特征裂解产物，很适合交通事故现场提取物证的检验。[14]俞文采用裂解气相色谱分析法（PY/GC），对刑事案件中常见如油漆、橡胶、塑料、纤维等高分子聚合物微量物证进行比对检验，所采用的优化裂解色谱条件较为理想，可以有效解决实际案件中遇到的相关问题。[15]王岩等采用配以居里点裂解器的气相色谱仪，考察了升温程序和裂解时间等因素，最终确定了较理想的色谱分离条件和裂解条件，对常见的橡胶种类及同种类的橡胶制品进行了分析，达到了种类认定以及厂家、产地、牌号的认定，在法庭科学实验室具有实用价值。[16]由于裂解分析结果的重现性不好，所以依据裂解分析结果对相关微量物证进行检验的情况在国内司法实践中出现的概率也较低。

3. 扫描电镜/能谱法

扫描电镜/能谱法主要针对于物质中所含元素的种类及含量进行分析。它被广泛地应用于各类物证的无机成分检验中。另外，扫描电镜/能谱法在分析多层油漆时可以发挥更大的作用，即可获得油漆的层信息。裴茂清等介绍了低真空下扫描电镜/能谱分析技术在多层油漆检验中的应用，该方法在得到漆膜层数、每个分层厚度以及颗粒形态的同时，还可以得到分层油漆的元素成分信息，适合交通事故类案件中油漆物证的比对检验。[17]冷冷等应用扫描电子显微镜对不同厂家生产的 12 块蓝色油漆总厚度及分层厚度进行测量，并对所得数据进行 t 检验分析，发现在所有两两比对的 66 组样品对中，在置信度为 95% 时，用总厚度及分层厚度进行区分，区分率达到 100%，对颜色相近的汽车油漆进行了有效区分。[18] 扫描电镜/能谱法的不足之处在于，该方法一般不单独使用，而是要与其他检验手段相结合，最常见的是与红外光谱法相结合。先用红外光谱法分析微量物证的有机成分与种类，再辅以扫描电镜－X 射线能谱法检验无机成分，提高鉴别的准确度。蔡植海等讨论了红外光谱法、扫描电镜能谱法相结合检验汽车油漆物证的方法，可以对油漆样品进行比对分析，排除来源不同的油漆样品，找出来源相同的油漆样品。[19]

4. 近年发展的新型分析技术

近年来，由于办案的需要，我国法庭科学工作者和研究者们不断探索和创新，研究出了许多新的方法应用于微量物证的检验。李娉等运用显微光谱成像技术对收集了 12 个省市 623 个汽车漆片样本进行分层，并对截面结构相同或相似的油漆样本进行了区分，分析出漆层为两层及以上的油漆样本数占总数的 87.26%，截面结构相同或相似的油漆样本能够多层同时区分。[20] 孙振文等尝试将光谱成像技术应用于一起交通肇事逃逸案件中的显微物证比对检验中，将用红外光谱法不能区分的涉案纤维运用光谱成像技术成功进行了区分，取得了良好效果。[21] 史洪飞介绍了电感耦合等离子体质谱（ICP－MS）近年来在油漆、玻璃、泥土、书写材料等微量物证中的应用，并对这种技术在刑事技术领域的应用前景进行了分析和探讨。马栋等建立了车辆油漆的激光剥蚀电感耦合等离子体质谱分析方法，对 38 种车辆油漆样品分别测定其中所含金属元素种类和金属元素影响相对比值的差异，发现 38 种样品中有 30 种可直接依据所含金属元素种类的差异进行区分，其余 8 种依据元素响应值比值的差异进行区分，方法重现性良好，精密度小于 10%，适用于法庭科学对车辆油漆的检测。[23]

（三）相关技术发展状况综合分析

总体而言，我国微量物证检验工作虽然起步较晚，但发展并不缓慢，且已经逐步成为国内物证技术领域中非常重要的一个方面，在许多重大案件的侦破中发挥了重要的作用。尤其在交通事故类案件中，微量物证的运用已成为提供线索、排除嫌疑车辆以及认定事实的关键步骤。但是，从上述文献总结中，我们不难发现，现今我国微量物证检验工作仍存在许多问题。例如，实际操作过程中，对于分析方法的使用和研究仍处于单一化状态，即仅用一种方法来进行分析，容易产生假阴性或假阳性的分析结果。虽然红外光谱法结合扫描电镜/能谱法检验微量物证已经成为最常规的一种检验手段，但许多时候仅通过这两种手段是无法解决问题的。另外，研究者目前多数只注重研究如何通过有效的仪器分析方法来达到区分目的，即只注重数据的采集，却忽略了数据的后续处理。其实，得出的分析数据或者一张张谱图里面往往隐藏着大量的证据信息。如何处理和解析这些数据，如何挖掘出谱图中隐藏的丰富而有价值的信息，如何以合理的方式展示出鉴定意见，这已经变得越来越重要。实际上，有效的数据处理方法可以得到事半功倍的效果，可以在很大程度上帮助我们实现区分的目的。我国有些学者针对这个问题进行过一系列探索，如吴国萍等提出将红外光谱与化学计量学相结合，运用化学计量学的分析手段与理论解决微量物证红外分析中的技术难点具有非常大的作用与良好的应用前景。[24] 郝愫媛以微量油漆物证的傅立叶红外光谱作为研究对象，将适合高维化学量数据处理的模式识别方法 SIMCA 和 BP 人工神经网络算法应用与微量油漆鉴定中，得到了非常好的聚类效果与区分效果，在理论和实践上都具有重要意义。[25]但这方面的研究却没有得到普遍的重视。再者，我国法庭科学工作者目前只注重研究如何发现物证与分析物证，却忽略了对作为证据之一的鉴定意见的证据属性的研究与探索，如何展示证据、解读证据以及运用证据似乎并不在法庭科学工作者的考虑范围之内。

二、国外相关研究

在国外，各个国家的微量物证检验技术水平各有不同，其中欧美国家的微量物证检验工作起步最早、发展水平最高且应用较为成熟。例如，早在 1959 年，T. R. Harkins 等就应用红外光谱来区分油漆中的无机颜料。[26]综合而言，国外相关研究体现出以下两个特点：

（一）总体水平更先进

仅以油漆为例，在欧美国家，法庭科学工作者们对油漆物证的研究比我国深入和先进许多，分析操作方法也更加规范，他们甚至建立了系统而全面的作业指导标准。[27]美国 FBI 下属的材料分析科学工作组（SWGMAT）的油漆分组就制定了专门的《法庭科学油漆分析与比较指南》，对油漆分析比较中涉及的专业术语、分析方法、具体操作程序与注意事项都作了详细的指导。[28]不仅如此，他们还有专门的针对红外光谱法用于法庭科学油漆检验的标准指导。在对油漆物证检验分析方法的研究上，方法更加多样，研究角度更细致而深入。Suzuki 等利用傅立叶变换红外光谱和 X 射线荧光分析研究汽车油漆中的镍钛酸盐和铬钛，以期达到区分效果。[29] Flynn K 等利用红外化学成像技术分析多层油漆，发现该技术在很短的时间可以比对成千上万的光谱，且化学成像数据可以以直观和易于理解的方式来显示。[30] Yeonhee Lee 等将飞行时间二次离子质谱法（TOF－SIMS）应用于汽车油漆分析中，通过分析 73 份来自不同厂家、不同颜色的油漆样品的漆片表层所含元素相对丰度，将不同厂家生产的同种颜色的油漆区分开来，区分效果理想。[31] Yoshinori Nishiwaki 等应用高能量同步辐射 X 射线荧光光谱法（SR－XRF）鉴别汽车白色油漆碎片中所用 TiO_2 无机颜料中元素的种类与含量来实现区分目的。[32]

（二）综合手段更突出

国外法庭科学工作者一般不局限于一种分析手段，而是更关注多种分析方法的综合运用、研究和比较，并注重对获得的谱图数据进行后续处理，结合各种统计学方法，整理和转化分析数据，更科学而直观地展示研究成果，实现区分目的。D. Thorburn Burns 等比较了裂解气相色谱/质谱法与红外光谱法两种分析方法在分析油漆样品时的效果。[33] Diana M. Wright 等综合运用立体显微镜、傅立叶变换红外光谱法、扫描电镜能谱法、裂解气相色谱/质谱法等几种方法分析和区分 964 份建筑用油漆样品，区分效果非常好。[34] Janina Zieba－Palus 等将用红外光谱和元素分析无法进行区分的 36 个成分为苯乙烯丙烯酸氨基甲酸酯的汽车清漆层样本利用裂解气相色谱/质谱法（PY－GC/MS）法进行分析，并将谱图数据用似然率的方法进行处理和转化，既能将样品很好地区分，又有助于评价这类分析结果的证据价值。[35] Cytil Muehlethaler 等用红外光谱法与拉曼光谱法相结合分析 34 个红色油漆样本，得到谱图数据后尝试应用各种化学计量学方法处理数据，达到区分效果。[36] Pereira F 等采用能量色散 X 射线荧光光谱法结合使用数字成像和化学计量学的方法，检验经过加速老化的 17 种清漆和 10 种涂料的防水类别、级别和耐久性。[37] Erin McIntee 等将激光诱导击穿光谱技术应用于汽车油漆的鉴别中，并运用非参数性序列测试与参数性 Wald 测试处理数据，来比较两种方法对于样品的区分程度。[38] E. Manzanoa 等利用红外光谱法研究蛋白质类油漆粘合剂在紫外线的照射下随时间推移所产生的成分变化，并用主成分分析法（PCA）进行谱图数据的统计和区分。[39] Cyril Muehlethaler 等综合运用各种分析方法研究并区分同一厂家同种颜色不同批次的商业油漆间的差异，针对不同颜色的油漆采用不同的分析方法进行区分。[40]

当然，针对其他种类的微量物证检验方法，欧美国家同样比我国研究和探索得更深入，此处不做详述。由上述的文献综述可以看出，我国对微量物证工作的研究深度和实际运用细致、规范程度还不足以和欧美发达国家相媲美。就红外光谱法的应用与研究来说，相较于国外有详尽的指导标准、研究程度深入、综合多学科知识、注重谱图数据后续处理几方面来看，我国应用红外光谱法分析微量物证的实践工作中还有很大的提升与改进空间。

三、问题与展望

对于交通事故类案件中微量物证分析，现有的手段和方法已经很成熟；此外，近年来也出现了一大批新技术、新方法，有关的研究工作还在不断深入。总体而言，国内外交通事故类案件中常见微量物证的检验鉴定工作也逐步呈现以下四个发展趋势：

1. 对同一物证采用多种分析方法与技术手段进行检验；

2. 逐步建立不同种类微量物证样品库与数据库；

3. 更加注重分析结果的数据处理，以期得到更好的区分效果，例如引入化学计量学、模式识别等统计学方法对采集数据进行分析与归纳；

4. 更加注重证据的解读，证据的展示形式更加科学化，例如采用似然率或者引入贝叶斯理论展示证据，使得证据的内涵更为透明化。

对于油漆检验问题，论文前述的分析方法与技术均能实现区分的效果，但是有些方法非常复杂，或需要大体积样品才能得到明确的结论；或需要复杂而繁琐的前处理才能成就实验条件；或严重损耗样品，不利于后续的重复鉴定。某些方法的应用面较窄，仅仅适用于特殊类型特殊条件的样品，不具有普适性与可操作性；有些方法仅处于研究阶段，对于是否具有实用性与可靠性还有待商榷。因此目前，国内外对于交通事故类案件中常见微量物证的检验，最常规而可靠的方法即是傅立叶变换红外光谱法，该法具有定性快、检材用量少、结果准确度高等优点。

作为目前国内分析交通事故类案件中最常用的分析手段，红外光谱法虽然已经非常成熟有效且优点突出，而且通过这种方法所得到的鉴定意见也在认定交通事故事实与确定肇事车辆的过程中发挥着重大的作用；但在实际办案与检验工作中，仍然存在很多细节问题且并未得到重视，对于一些常见问题也并未寻求到有效的解决方法，对于红外光谱数据的应用也仅仅处于浅层次的看图比对阶段。总体而言，这些问题会直接导致鉴定意见的准确性与可靠程度的降低；此外，由于证据呈现的形式过于绝对，这使得检察官与法官在运用证据时存在僵化死板的状态，不利于法官对证据的自由裁量。可以说，现有的方法还存在数据处理、操作规范、适用范围、结论表述等多方面的问题，对现有微量物证检验方法进行全面梳理、细化和规范，是当前微量物证检验工作亟待解决的问题。如何提高微量物证的发现概率与提取的准确度？如何在已有的红外光谱分析方法的基础上运用其他科学方法（如统计学方法以及计算机技术等）提高微量物证的分析水平？如何将得到的分析结果以科学的方式解读出来，以使其作为证据可以灵活地在审判中使用？这些多维度的视角均触及油漆物证的完善问题。因此，我们不仅要注重开发新技术手段，实现创新，还要对已有的检验手段与证据呈现形式进行审视，使得现有分析方法，即红外光谱分析法可以更好地发挥作用，提高分析结果的准确度，提高证据的解读能力。

参考文献

[1] 城市跨入汽车“百万俱乐部”，http：//www. cusdn. org. cn/news_ detail. php？id =24656118.

[2] 权养科：“微量物证检验技术的发展趋势”，载《刑事技术》2009 年增刊。

[3] 张象喜：“显微傅立叶变换红外光谱法及其应用”，载《分析仪器》1990 年第 2 期。

[4] 李琼瑶、六品、李俊涛：“傅立叶变换红外显微镜及其在刑事技术中的应用”，载《仪器仪表与分析监测》1991 年第 1 期。

[5] 路春清、何洪源、贾艳超、张淑芳、陈占合：“交通肇事案件中油漆物证的傅立叶变换红外光谱分析”，载《中国人民公安大学学报（自然科学版）》2009 年第 1 期。

[6] 孙振文、权养科、陶克明：“汽车罩光漆的 ATR－FTIR 法检验”，载《刑事技术》2011 年第 3 期。

[7] 赵鹏程：“红外光谱法检验汽车油漆成膜物质的研究”，载《中国刑警学院学报》2012 年第 1 期。

[8] 陈涛、龙先军、魏朗、龚标、李春明：“汽车车身油漆红外光谱特征”，载《光谱学与光谱分析》2012 年第 7 期。

[9] 陈涛、龙先军、魏朗、龚标、李春明：“基于傅立叶红外光谱的汽车车身油漆比对”，载《光谱学与光谱分析》2013 年第 2 期。

[10] 王岩、纪雷、王英杰、刘心同、牛增元、杜恒清：“塑料树脂红外标准光谱库的创建与应用”，载《工程塑料应用》2005 年第 9 期。

[11] 王志国：“FT－Raman 光谱在法庭科学中的应用”，载《中国人民公安大学学报（自然科学版）》2002 年第 2 期。

[12] 王志国、汪聪慧、孙素琴、周群：“橡胶的傅里叶变换拉曼光谱法检验”，载《中国人民公安大学学报（自然科学版）》2002 年第 3 期。

[13] 余静、王琳琦、王继芬、武磊：“拉曼光谱技术在涂料鉴定中的应用进展”，载《现代仪器》2012 年第 3 期。

[14] 李玉兰、姚希：“热裂解气相色谱/质谱法分析油漆”，载《质谱学报》1998 年第 2 期。

[15] 俞文：“高分子聚合物微量物证的裂解气相色谱分析”，载《中国人民公安大学学报（自然科学版）》2004 年第 1 期。

[16] 王岩、邹宁、周晨：“裂解气相色谱法分析橡胶”，载《广东公安科技》2004 年第 1 期。

[17] 裴茂清、肖翔、郭海荣、冷泠：“SEM/EDX 在多层油漆检验中的应用”，载《广东公安科技》2010 年第 1 期。

[18] 冷泠、权养科、孙振文、陶克明：“SEM 检验漆膜厚度鉴别同种颜色的汽车油漆”，载《刑事技术》2010 年第 1 期。

[19] 蔡植海、蒋泽良、张亮、裴茂清：“显微红外光谱法和扫描电镜/能谱法检验汽车油漆物

证”，载《广东公安科技》2012 年第 3 期。

[20] 李娉、王桂强、权养科、俞涛、许可、李婷：“显微光谱成像技术在汽车油漆截面检验中的应用”，载《刑事技术》2011 年第 1 期。

[21] 孙振文、权养科、陶克明：“交通肇事案件中纤维物证的光谱成像检验”，载《刑事技术》2011 年第 6 期。

[22] 史洪飞：“电感耦合等离子体质谱在微量物证检验中的应用”，载《中国科技博览》2012 年第 8 期。

[23] 马栋、沈敏、罗仪文、卓先义、向平：“激光剥蚀电感耦合等离子体质谱技术检测车辆油漆金属元素”，载《中国司法鉴定》2010 年第 2 期。

[24] 吴国萍、蔡锡兰：“红外光谱结合化学计量学在微量物证分析中的应用”，载《江苏警官学院学报》2004 年第 4 期。

[25] 郝愫媛：《模式识别技术在法庭科学微量油漆物证鉴定中应用的研究》，山东科技大学 2004 年硕士学位论文。

[26] T. R. Harkins, J. T. Harris, O. D. Shreve, “Identification of Pigments in Paint Products by Infrared Spectroscopy”, *Analytical Chemistry*, 1959, 31 (4), pp. 541 ~ 545.

[27] Swgmat, “Forensic Paint Analysis And Comparison Guidelines” May 2000 Revision.

[28] Swgmat, “Standard Guide For Using Infrared Spectroscopy In Forensic Paint Examnations”.

[29] Edward M. Suzuki, Martin X. McDermot, “Infrared Spectra of U. S. Automobile Original Finishes. VII. Extended Range FT – IR and XRF Analyses of Inorganic Pigments in Situ—Nickel Titanate and Chrome Titanate”, *Journal of Forensic Sciences*, 2006, 51 (3), pp. 532 ~ 547.

[30] Flynn K, O Leary R, Lennard C, et al, “Forensic Applications of Infrared Chemical Imaging: multi—layered Paint Chips”, *Journal of Forensic Sciences*, 2005, 50 (4), pp. 832 ~ 841.

[31] Yeonhee Lee, Seunghee Han, Jung – Hyeon Yoon, Young – Man Kim, Sung – Kun Shon, Sung – Woo Park, “Application of Time – of – Flight Secondary Ion Mass Spectrometry to automobile Paint Analysis”, *Analytical Sciences*, 2001, 17, pp. 757 ~ 761.

[32] Yoshinori Nishiwaki, Seiya Watanabe, et al, “Trace Elemental Analysis of Titanium Dioxide Pigments and Automotive White Paint Fragments for Forensic Examination Using High – Energy Synchrotron Radiation X – Ray Fluorescence Spectrometry”, *Journal of Forensic Sciences*, 2009, 54 (3), pp. 564 ~ 570.

[33] D. Thorburn Burnsa, K. P. Doolan, “A comparison of Pyrolysis – Gas Chromatography mass Spectrometry and Fourier Transform Infrared Spectroscopy for the Characterisation of Automative Paint Samples”, *Analytica Chimica Acta*, 539 (2005), pp. 145 ~ 155.

[34] Diana M. Wright. Maureen J. Bradley, Andria Hobbs Mehltretter, “Analysis and Discrimination of Architectural Paint Samples via a Population Study”, *Forensic Science International*, 209 (2011), pp. 86 ~ 95.

[35] Janina Zieba – Palus, Grzegorz Zadora, Jakub M. Milczarek, “Differentiation and Evaluation of Evidence Value of Styrene Acrylic Urethane Topcoat car Paints Analysed by Pyrolysis – Gas Chromarography”, *Journal Of Chromatography A*, 1179 (2008), pp. 47 ~ 58.

[36] Cytil Muehlethaler, Genevieve Massonnet, Pierre Esseiva, “The Application of Chemometrics on Infrared and Raman Spectra as A Tool for the Forensic Analysis of Paints”, 209 (2011), pp. 173 ~ 182.

[37] Pereira F. Bueno M, “Evaluation of Varnish and Paint Films Using Digital Image Processing, Energy Dispersive X – ray Fluorescence Spectrometry and Chemomctric Tools”, *Journal of Coatings Technology and Research*, 2009, 6, pp. 445 ~ 455.

[38] Erin McIntee, Emilie Viglino, et al, “Comparative Analysis of Automotive Paints by Laser Induced Breakdown Spectroscopy and Nonparametric Permutation Tests”, *Spectrochimica Acta* Part B, 65

(2010), pp. 542 ~ 548 .

[39] E. Manzanoa, N. Navasa. et al, "Preliminary Study of UV Ageing Process of Proteinaceous Paint Binder by FT – IR and Principal Component Analysis", *Talanta*, 77 (2009), pp. 1724 ~ 1731.

[40] Cyril Muehlethaler, Geneviève Massonnet, et al, "Survey on Batch – to – batch Variation in Spray Paints: A Collaborative Study", *Forensic Science International*, 229 (2013), pp. 80 ~ 91.

人造指纹模具印痕的识别与检验方法

于遨洋 *

引言

指纹作为传统意义中的“证据之首”，对分析案情和鉴定犯罪人发挥着不可替代的作用，在生活中也作为识别人身的重要工具。近年来，越来越多的领域开始运用指纹自动识别技术识别身份，如指纹考勤、指纹社保、指纹银行、指纹商场、指纹接送幼儿等。然而，近期网络热卖的人造指纹膜，可以轻易混过指纹打卡机的检测，犯罪嫌疑人也可以采用相同的方法，在盗取他人指纹后，通过指纹制模，制成仿真指纹膜，从而在现场遗留非自身指纹，以干扰侦查方向，逃避侦查。因此，人造指纹膜等仿真品热销的背后，存在巨大的法律隐患。为了有效应对此类现象，一些刑事技术工作者开始着手研究人造指纹模具印痕的识别与检验技术，但由于时间和实验条件的限制，对于这个新问题的研究尚处于起步状态，研究成果主要是对工艺特征的分析，具有一定的局限性和不完整性，对指纹膜与真实指纹宏观特征和微观特征的分析尚属于空白阶段。随着指纹制模技术的发展，指纹膜与真实指纹的相似度不断增加，将二者区分出来的难度也在不断增大，如何综合运用工艺特征、宏观特征和微观特征等因素，高效而准确地确定指纹的真伪以及伪造指纹的方法，才能够从根本上维护指纹鉴定的科学性和可靠性，充分发挥指纹“人各不同，认定个人”的得天独厚的属性，以达到正确地刻画和锁定犯罪嫌疑人的目的。因此，深入探索人造指纹模印的特征，对于手印检验技术的发展和伪造指纹犯罪的预防和侦破具有重要意义。

一、理论综述

制模材料和方法是制作人造指纹膜的核心要素之一，理想的材料可以制成高质量的指纹膜，较好地反映指纹的形态和细节特点，目前，网络上销售的仿真指纹膜多采用先制指纹阴模，后灌指纹阳模的方法。首先，将手指按压在可塑性较好的柔软载体上，制成立体指纹，然后利用硅橡胶等材料进行灌模，待硅橡胶固化后将指纹模取出并修整，最终制成人造指纹模成品。

（一）硅橡胶的成分和性质

硅橡胶是一种兼具有机和无机性质的高分子弹性材料，其分子主链由硅原子和氧原子交替组成（—Si—O—Si—），如图 1 所示，侧链是与硅原子相连接的碳氢或取代碳氢有机基团，这种基团可以是甲基、不饱和乙烯基或其他有机基团，这种低不饱和度的分子结构使分子链的柔韧性大，分子链之间的相互作用力弱，形成了硫化硅橡胶

* 于遨洋，中国刑事警察学院讲师。Email：darkfish_ 2005@ qq. com，9148988@ qq. com。

柔软而富有弹性的特点。硅橡胶分为高温硫化硅橡胶和室温硫化硅橡胶，由于人造指纹模的制模通常在常温下进行，因此主要使用双组分室温硫化硅橡胶，这种硅橡胶流动性好，适于浇注成型，固化时不放热，收缩率小，不膨胀，无内应力，固化可在内部和表面同时进行，硫化比较彻底，可以保证人造指纹模的强度和对指纹特征的充分反映。

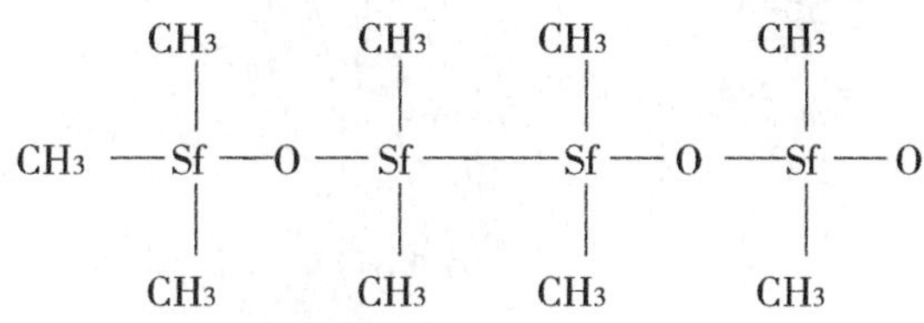

图1　硅橡胶的分子结构

（二）硅橡胶固化剂

硅橡胶固化剂，是针对液体硅橡胶凝的一种添加剂。能使液态硅橡胶凝固，使其产生交联反应凝固成为弹性的固体材料。固化剂种类很多，而且还在不断增加，已经使用的固化剂有硫黄、硒、碲、含硫化合物、金属氧化物、过氧化物、树酯、醌类和胺类等。一般的硅橡胶的固化剂的比例为2%～3%，这个比例一般是根据生胶的重量来计算的，少数时候还需要计算生胶中加入的其他添加材料的重量。

（三）指纹载体

常见的制作人造指纹模的载体有橡皮泥、石蜡和牙科打样膏。这三种材料中橡皮泥可塑性好但较软，易造成灌模过程中的细节损失。石蜡加热后具有一定可塑性，但在按压指纹的过程中表里层凝固速度不同，造成表层硬膜破坏，细节特征损失。牙科打样膏是一种牙齿粗翻模的材料，常温下比较坚硬，80℃左右软化可随意塑形，既能够很好地反映指纹细节，又能够随温度降低而增加硬度，从而避免灌模过程中的细节损失，是效果较好的指纹载体。

二、实验部分

（一）指纹模制作原理

利用液态硅橡胶流动性好、硫化快、注塑成型后能够较好地反映原物特征等特点，选其制作人造指纹模具。利用打样膏操作方便，具有较好的可塑性，能够完整地反映手指纹线特征的特点，选其作为制模打样的工具。在固化剂的作用下，液态硅橡胶固化成型，较好地复制了手指的纹线、皱纹等特征。液态硅橡胶通过固化成型，能够较好地反映手指的各项特征。制成的指纹模的柔软度、弹性、韧性均较良好，且硅橡胶指纹模有很好稳定性，能够长期重复使用。指纹模能够较好地模拟汗潜手印、油手印、血手印等多种手印，具有很强的适用性。

（二）指纹模制作过程

1. 实验材料

BW－ZK333型真空干燥箱（东莞博威仪器设备有限公司生产）、双组分室温硫化硅橡胶（RTV）、硫化物固化剂、打样膏、玻璃棒、蒸发皿、温度计等。

2. 制作步骤

（1）制作模具：将一块大小适中的打样膏放入70℃～80℃的热水中浸泡，待打样膏软化后取出，塑成大于手指表面积且表面平整的形状，选择指纹粗大清晰的指头垂直按压，用冷水浸泡，使打样膏上指纹硬化固定，如图2所示。

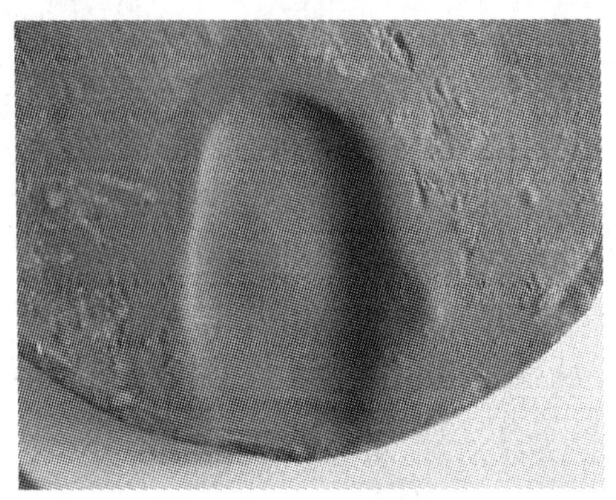

图2　制成的指纹阴模

（2）检查指纹阴模质量：要求纹线清晰连贯，边缘完整且无裂纹和裂痕。

（3）制作指纹胶：向蒸发皿中加入10ml液态硅橡胶，滴加3滴固化剂，用玻璃棒搅拌均匀后放入真空干燥箱，除泡2分钟。

（4）倒模：用玻璃棒适量蘸取蒸发皿内的调制好的指纹胶，将其均匀涂抹在制成的模具上，静置约3小时，待指纹胶完全固化定型后方可取下，如图3所示，用小刀对指纹模边缘进行适当修整，使其方便使用。

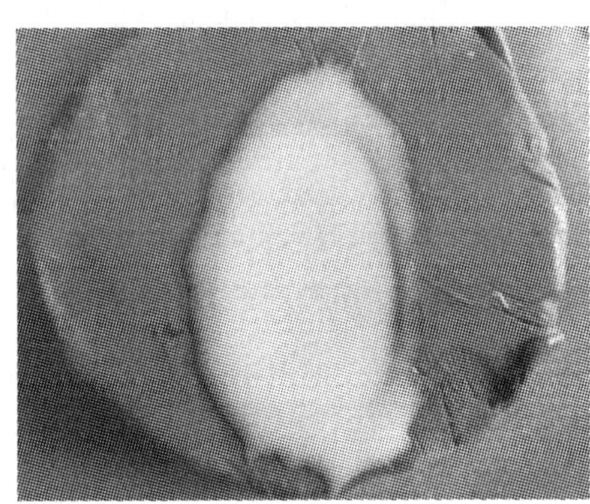

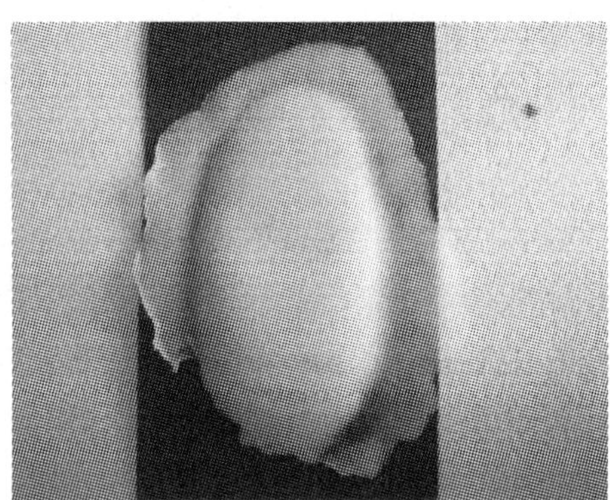

图3　指纹模倒模过程

3. 注意事项

（1）制作模具时，手指按压打样膏应用力均匀、大小适度，用力过大可能会造成部分纹线的粘连，中心花纹出现形变，影响指纹模的质量；用力过小可能会造成特征反映不全，还会使模具过浅，影响后期倒模时指纹胶的厚度，从而造成指纹模出现质量问题。

（2）制作指纹胶时，加入固化剂的剂量应适度，不可过多，否则会造成指纹胶过于黏稠，流动性差，还会在调制搅拌阶段造成大量气泡残留难以排除，进而影响制模效果。固化剂的剂量亦不可过少，过少会影响指纹胶的凝固时间，甚至无法凝固，由于市场上固化剂的浓度有差别，所以应先进行预实验，确定合理的浓度。

（3）倒模时，应从模具的一端开始引导指纹胶流动，使其均匀的覆盖在模具表面。同时，应注意指纹胶的厚薄应适度，以3mm为宜，过厚会影响指纹模的弹性，并且对后续捺印环节造成不便，影响指印的质量；过薄会影响指纹模的韧性，指纹模容易断裂。在倒模过程中，还要注意排除指纹胶中的气泡。

（4）倒模时还可以在指纹模具的两侧添加适当指纹胶，待其凝固后形成两个侧翼，用于固定在手指上，方便后期指纹模捺印指纹。

（三）油墨捺印样本制作

1. 实验材料

指纹捺印盒、益思牌普白A4复印纸、“502”胶、金粉、银粉、磁性粉、体视显微镜、扫描仪（BenQ Series 5560）等。

2. 手指平面捺印

将手指正面均匀接触捺印盒，使其正面全部着墨后，将其移印至A4复印纸上。[2]

3. 指纹模平面捺印

从制备的硅胶指纹模中选出乳突纹线最清晰，层次感最强的指纹膜，先将指纹膜黏附在对应的手指上，在捺印板附上油墨，然后用附着油墨的指纹膜在白纸上捺印指纹，蘸染一次油墨捺印两个指纹印痕，共蘸墨10次，捺印20个指纹模正面印痕。

（四）汗潜印痕的捺印及显现

1. 指纹模汗液指印痕与手指汗潜印痕的捺印

（1）手指直接捺印：用手指在瓷砖、玻璃、白纸三种客体上直接捺印汗潜指纹待用。

（2）指纹模捺印：将制作好的硅橡胶指纹模贴放在掌心片刻，使汗液充分黏附其表面，用以模拟真实手指表面的汗液附着，然后将其固定在指头上，如图4所示，分别在瓷砖、玻璃、白纸三种客体上捺印汗潜指纹模指印，每次捺印前要保证指纹模表面存在充分的汗液。

（3）分别为以上两种指纹进行标记，以区分两类指纹。

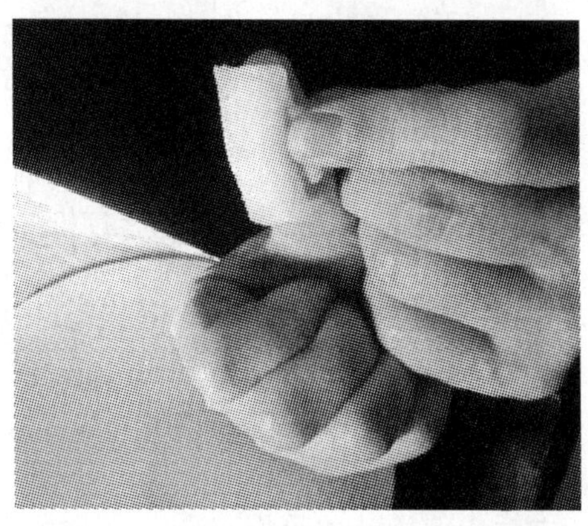

图4 指纹模捺印动作

2. 指纹模汗液指印痕与手指汗潜印痕的显现

分别用金粉、银粉对玻璃、瓷砖上的两种指印进行刷显；用滤纸贴附法对两种客体上的汗潜印痕进行“502”胶熏显，再用磁性粉染色。

三、结果与讨论

（一）油墨捺印样本比较

油墨捺印是反映指纹细节特征的较好方法，作为指纹的仿制品，指纹模的油墨印痕能够清晰地反映出指纹模上线条的细节特征，所以实验的观测讨论主要针对指纹与指纹模印痕的细节特征进行。

1. 指纹与指纹模平面印痕的宏观特征比较

手指纹线分分布均匀、连贯、粗细变化不大，且汗孔均匀分布于指头的纹线上，使得汗液也沿着纹线均匀地分布，捺印时手指满足用力均匀、无抖动，即可形成清晰完整特征反映明显的可用于识别、鉴定的指纹。对于指纹模捺印，从理论上讲，由于打样膏和液态硅橡胶的优良性质，人造指纹模的捺印指纹效果应与真实手指捺印的指纹效果一致。但是，在指纹模的制作过程与指纹的捺印过程中均会受到各种因素的影响，比如：用打样膏制作模具时，手指按压力量的大小，可能会造成手指纹线粗细与深浅的变化，中心纹线和某些细微特征也可能出现不同程度的变化；捺印时手指的用力角度与大小的不同，可能会造成伪造指纹汗液的堆积，边缘特征的变化等。

（1）纹线粗细的变化。据文献报道，男性指纹的平均密度小于 14.5 线/25mm^2，宽度在 1.78mm 左右；女性指纹的平均密度大于等于 15 线/25mm^2，宽度在 1.66mm 左右[1]。指纹的乳突纹线印痕和小犁沟清晰且均匀，犁沟与纹线宽度非常接近。在制作指纹模的过程中，留痕人在用手指按压打样膏时，会不可避免造成乳突纹线变宽，加之硅橡胶指纹模的硬度略小于乳突纹线，捺印过程中变形较大，通过观测，如图 5 所示，对于同一条乳突纹线的印痕，指纹宽度为 1.8mm，指纹模宽度为 2.8mm，宽度增加了 55.6%。

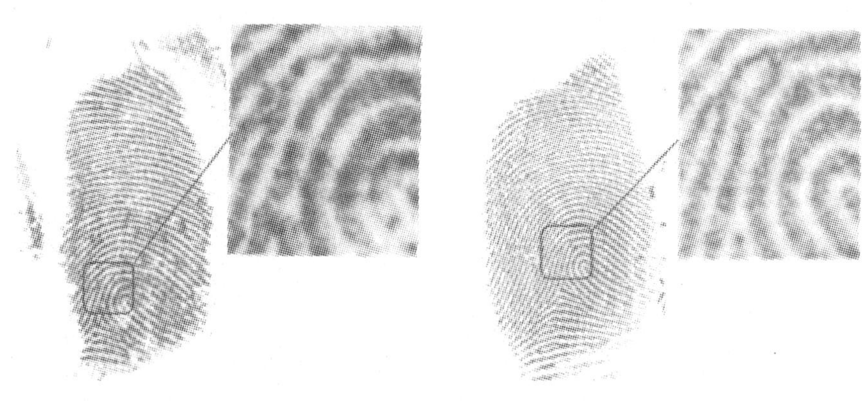

a 指指纹模印痕　　　　a 指指纹

图 5　指纹与指纹模印痕纹线对比

（2）墨迹浓淡变化。手指头的皮肤由表皮、真皮和皮下组织三层组成，最外层的表皮具有抗摩擦和抗损伤的作用，因此致密且具有一定非渗透性。硅橡胶与之相比，密度和渗透性较弱，因此更易黏附液体，如图 5 所示，从整体上看，在相同的着墨条件下，指纹模印痕墨迹比指纹更浓一些。

（3）局部缺损和纹线变形。用打样膏制作模具时，打印膏表面很难做到平整光滑，加之手指按压力量的分布不均匀，容易造成立体指纹的弧度和各部位高低与指头表面相比产生明显的差别。捺印留痕时，指纹模背面的平整程度也会影响指纹模对承痕体的压力分布。这两方面因素有时能够引起指纹模印痕的局部纹线缺损，有时能够造成局部纹线粗细、深浅和形态的变化，如图 5 所示，与指纹相比，指纹模印痕的中心花纹偏三角侧，出现了明显的花纹缺损和局部线条变形。

（4）印痕面积与捺印压力的矛盾。在指纹的捺印留痕中，印痕面积通常和捺印压力成正比关系，压力越大，该部位留痕面积就越大，这在图5 的 a 指指纹中有明显的反映。与指纹相比，指纹模印痕由于制模条件的限制，通常无法制成完整的指头三面印痕模型，在制作正面留痕印痕时，为控制指纹的变形，正面印痕的面积通常较小，因此，指纹模印痕虽能够反映出中介质较厚，线条宽度增加间距变窄的重压反映，但印痕面积却较小较窄，与压力的反映有明显的矛盾现象。

（5）模具轮廓印痕的有无。指纹在留痕的过程中，通常印痕外围干净整洁，而指纹模在制模过程中易形成不规则的边缘轮廓，如图5 中的 a 指指纹模印痕所示，在着墨后，容易在指纹外围出现弧形或不规则的轮廓印痕。

2. 指纹与指纹模平面印痕的微观特征比较

（1）线条光滑程度的差别。实验中，指纹的留痕人年龄为 30 岁，身体健康，发育正常，所留指纹及指纹模为青壮年纹线印痕。青壮年指纹线条光滑，连贯完整，中心纹线清晰，纹线受损后恢复较快，汗液分泌量大，汗孔开放呈圆形，呈完整的圆孔，显现条件较好。如图 6 所示，这些特点在指纹中有充分的反映。而相同部位制作的指纹模所留的印痕，纹线边缘不整齐，个别缺损严重，纹线出现断离现象。

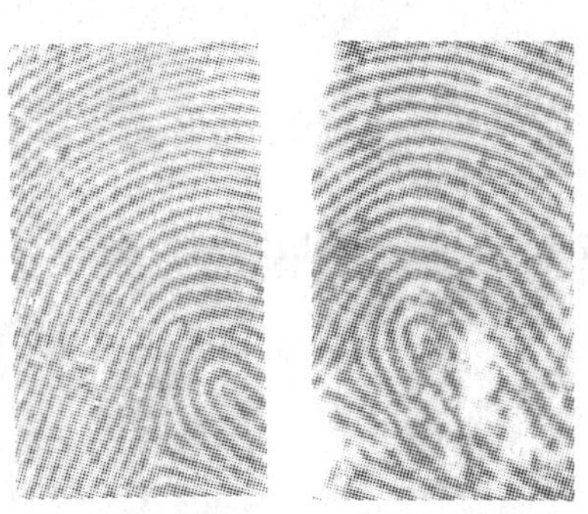

a 指指纹　　a 指指纹模印痕

图 6　指纹与指纹模印痕线条光滑度比较

（2）油墨疵点的有无。在油墨通过指纹或指纹模从捺印盒转移到纸张载体的过程中，作为转印过程中必然出现的缺陷—疵点，会在线条中有所反映。如图 7 所示，指纹由于线条细密，边缘光滑，犁沟与乳突纹线的高度差明显，所以着墨量少，疵点也很少，而指纹模边缘粗糙，线条宽大且凸凹线条间高度差不明显，因此容易出现周边带有放射状毛刺的疵点。

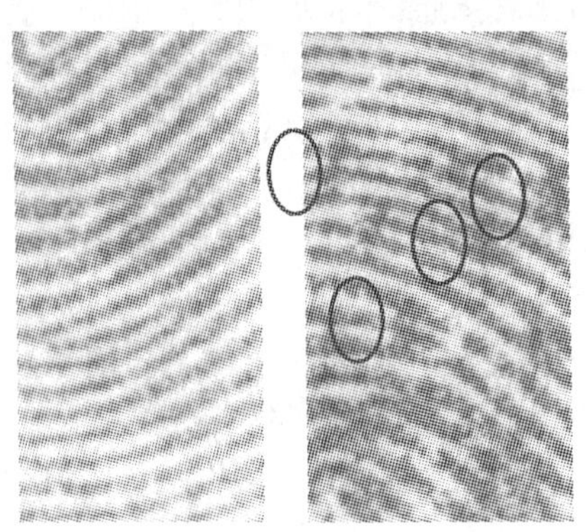

a 指指纹　　a 指指纹模印痕

图 7　指纹与指纹模印痕疵点

（3）细节特征的改变。同指同部位的指纹与指纹模上的细节特征改变是比较明显的，在实验中，如图 8 和图 9 所示，出现了多处起点终点与分歧结合互相变化的情况，小眼的形状发生明显改变，以及两条分离的线条间出现小桥的情况。这些都是制作指纹模的翻模和转印过程中，指纹信息损失的表现。

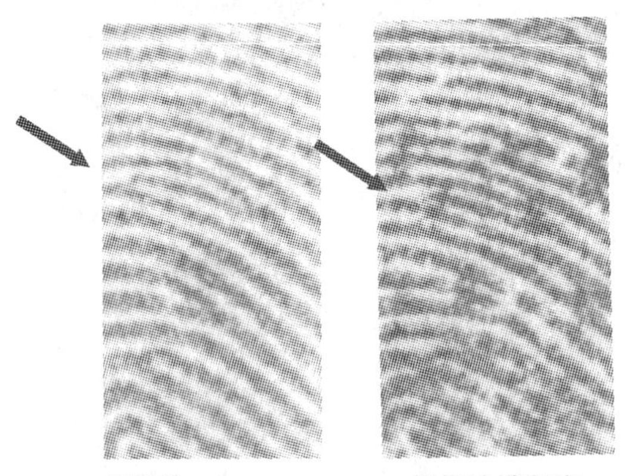

a 指指纹　　a 指指纹模印痕

图 8　指纹分歧在指纹模印痕中变成起点

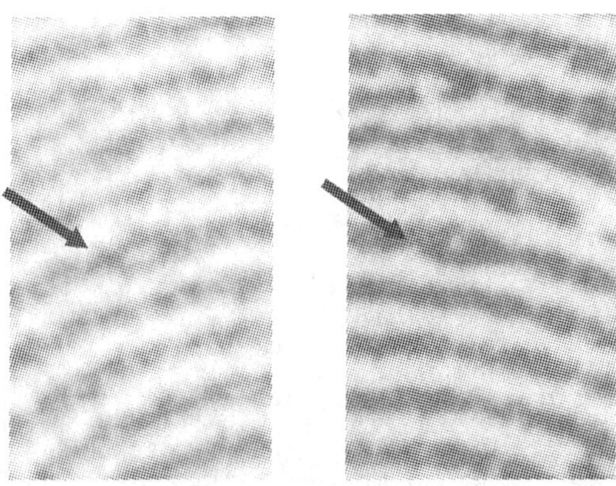

a 指指纹小眼　　a 指指纹模三角处印痕

图 9　指纹与指纹模印痕小眼的变化

（4）线条粘连的增加。与指纹相比，指纹模印痕的线条增粗，细节损失，疵点增加，这些因素导致一些相邻的线条间容易发生粘连的显现，从而改变花纹的结构，如图10所示，由于线条的粘连，导致两种印痕上三角区域的花纹形态发生了明显的改变。

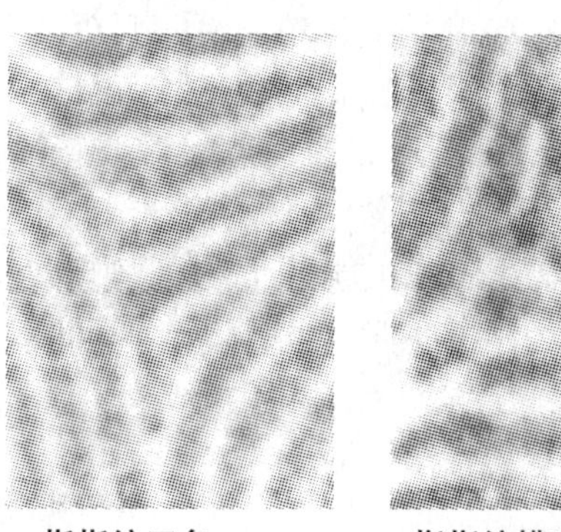

a 指指纹三角　　a 指指纹模三角处印痕

图10　指纹与指纹模印痕线条的粘连

（5）其他特征的差异。除了乳头纹线的细节特征差别，汗孔和印痕边缘线条端点在两种印痕间也有较明显的差别，如图11和图12所示，由于制模过程中，手指需用力按压打样膏，所以汗孔的形态能够在指纹模中反映出位置，但损失的形态细节比较严重，有时线条中的缺损与汗孔非常相似。另外，指纹的边缘纹线呈现出逐渐减弱、变细直至消失的状态，而指纹模印痕边缘纹线的止点非常明显，无明显的分界，几乎不存在指纹边缘的过渡现象，且指纹模印痕的边缘多平直、生硬，有时会出现明显的曲线。

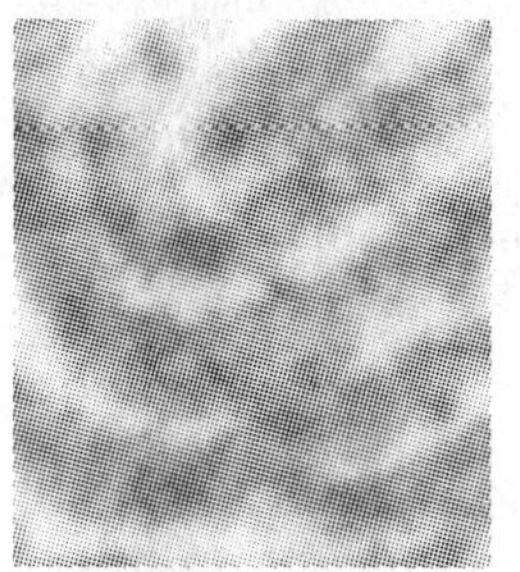

a 指指纹上的汗孔　　a 指指纹模印痕中的汗孔

图11 指纹与指纹模印痕汗孔的差异

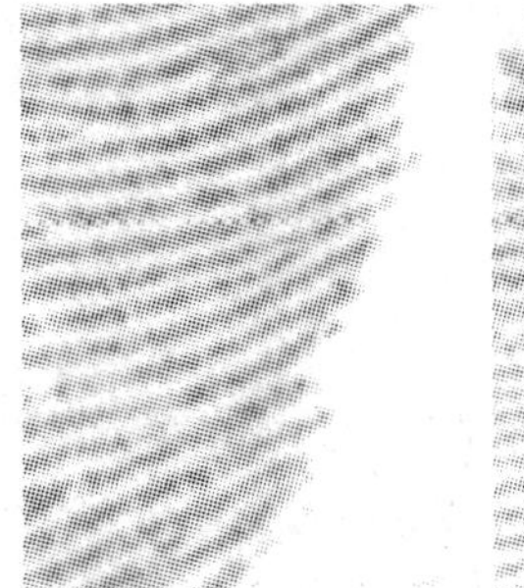

a 指指纹　　a 指指纹模印痕

图12　指纹与指纹模印痕边缘线条端点的反映

（二）汗潜印痕样本的比较

1. 粉末刷显法下汗潜指纹模指印与汗潜手指印的差别

粉末刷显现法属物理显现法，是利用固体粉末试剂吸附在手印纹线上，直接加染手印，其中固体粉末主要包括金粉、银粉、磁性粉等。[3]

（1）两种印痕的显现效果。粉末显现非渗透性客体上新鲜汗潜手印的效果优良，如图13所示，纹线清晰连贯，粗细均匀，过渡自然，细节特征明显，可用于检验、识别、鉴定、存档。对于新鲜的汗潜指纹模印痕，粉末的显现效果良好，纹线较为清晰连贯，粗细变化不大，过度略显生硬，由于粉末显现法不可避免地损失了细节特征，降低了特征的符合程度，因此在一定程度上掩盖了指纹模上特征信息的损失，实验中，指纹模印痕与指纹差别度降低，迷惑性增强。

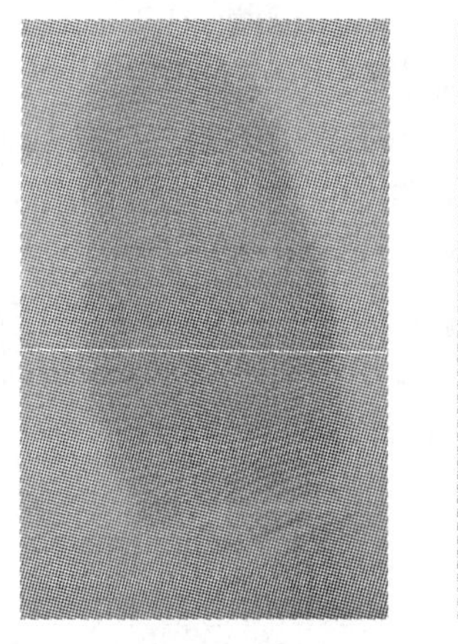

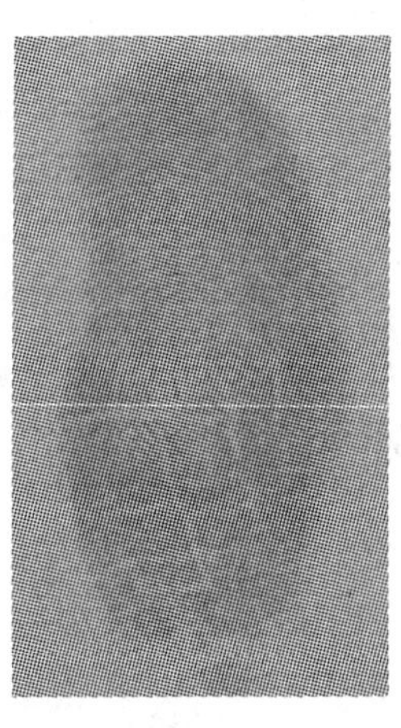

瓷砖上银粉刷显 a 指指纹　　瓷砖上银粉刷显 a 指指纹模印痕

图13　粉末法显现指纹与指纹模印痕

（2）两种印痕的差别。该方法显现出的指纹模指印与指纹间存在一定区别。首先，指纹模印痕的边缘存在介质挤压现象的特征，而指纹纹线过渡均匀，此类现象在一般情况下并不多见。在留下指纹模汗潜手印时，留痕力量的减弱也难以避免挤墨特征的出现，该特征能明显地将指印分割为明暗两部分，因此，该特征是粉末显现法条件下，区分两种指印的特征之一。其次，粉末显现法显现的指纹，粉末分布均匀，整体颜色深浅基本一致，非常自然，而指纹模印痕上的粉末分布并不均匀，出现了较多的深浅变化，整体看上去显得呆板。另外，印痕边缘纹线的形态差别与油墨印痕相同。

2. “502”胶熏显法下汗潜指纹模指印与汗潜手指印的差别

（1）两种印痕的显现效果。如图14所示，“502”胶熏显的非渗透性客体上的新鲜汗潜指纹，纹线清晰连贯，粗细均匀，过度自然，细节特征明显，可用于检验和鉴定。显现的指纹模指印显现效果一般，纹线基本清晰连贯，粗细有变化，过度显生硬，细节特征反映效果一般，与模糊指纹相似，迷惑性强。

瓷砖上502熏显a指指纹（磁性粉染色）　瓷砖上502熏显a指指纹模印痕（磁性粉染色）

图14“502”胶熏显法显现指纹与指纹模印痕

（2）两种印痕的差别。在此方法下，两种指印的区别较粉末显现法更加明显，首先，指纹模印痕的边缘的介质挤压现象，较粉末显现法更为明显，多数指印表面形成了明显的深浅不同的区域，如图15，该特征能够用于区别两类指印。其次，“502”胶熏显法显现磁性粉刷显染色的指纹，粉末分布均匀，整体颜色深浅基本一致，较为自然，而指纹模印痕的粉末分布较粉末刷显法不均匀，出现了更多的深浅变化，整体显得不够自然。

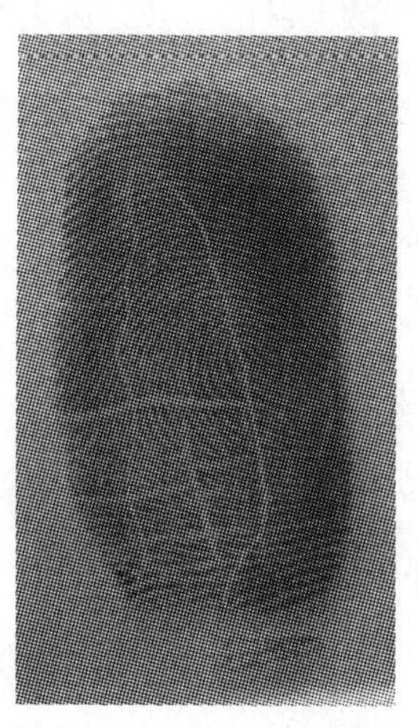

瓷砖上502熏显a指指纹（磁性粉染色）　瓷砖上502熏显a指指纹模印痕（磁性粉染色）

图15　“502”胶熏显法显现指纹与指纹模印痕的介质不均

三、结　论

油墨捺印指纹和指纹模印痕，能够在宏观和微观上产生差异，在指纹模印痕中，能够出现特征间的矛盾，以上差异和矛盾是区分二者的关键特征。

光滑非渗透性客体上的指纹和指纹模印痕，“502”胶熏显磁性粉染色的显现方法能够较明显地反映出两者的区别，进而区分两种指印。粉末刷显法虽然也能体现出两类指印的区别，但并不明显。

介质分布不均、疵点、纹线粗细、边缘轮廓、细节特征变化以及工艺特征，是识别指纹真伪的重要特征。

参考文献

[1] 倪萍雅等："指纹乳突纹线的性别差异初探"，载《刑事技术》2012 年第 2 期，第 1 ~ 4 页。
[2] 吕晓森：《痕迹检验学实验教程》，群众出版社 2009 年版，第 2 ~ 3 页。
[3] 罗亚平、史海青：《手印显现技术》，警官教育出版社 1999 年版，第 25 ~ 26 页。

Study on the Effect of the Applied Force on the Examination of the Writing and Sealing Sequence by Streamline Imaging of Raman Spectroscopy

Lian Yuanyuan[1,3], Liu Yao[2], Liu Jianwei[1], Wang Conghui[2], Liang Luning[2]*

It has been one of the tough problems for document examiners in China to determine the writing and sealing sequence. Because of the low examinable rate of traditional testing methods[1], it is difficult to get good results when determining the writing and sealing sequence , especially for the samples with thin imprint. To the end, document examiners have to seek a more simple and non - destructive way. Expanding the use of Raman spectral imaging technology into the determination of exemplars used for writing and sealing sequence, the samples can be examined with non - destructive approach. During the determination of writing and sealing sequence, there were many factors which could affect the results of the examination. In this paper, we studied on them through different applied force in writing and sealing, in order to obtain good results for the examination of writing and sealing sequence by streamline imaging of Raman spectroscopy.

1 Experimental

1. 1 Instrument

A Renishaw's inVia - Plus laser micro - Raman spectrometer was used. Table 1 shows its configurations and parameters in our experiment.

* Lian Yuanyuan, Female, a research worker of Fada Institute of Forensic Medicine & Science, Supported by Program for Young Innovative Research Team in China University of Political Science and Law (1000 - 10814344). Email: sophie028 @ cupl. edu. cn. Adress: LUGU Road 116, Shijingshan District, Beijing, China. Postcode: 100046. 1. Key Laboratory of Evidence Science (CUPL), China University of Political Science and Law, Beijing 100040;

2. The Institute of Forensic Science, the Ministry of Public Security, Beijing 100038;

3. Chinese People's Public Security University, Beijing 100038.

Table 1 Configurations and parameters of inVia - Plus laser micro - Raman spectrometer

	configurations	parameters
Raman Spectrometer	785nm helium - neon laser	250mW, air - cooled, 785nm Rayleigh filter
	laser attenuator	computer - controlled laser attenuator, from 0.000005% to 100%
	detector	Large area CCD detector
Microscope	Research - grade Leica microscope	color video camera, lens ×5, ×20 and ×50, 3D automatic platform of high speed
Software	Wire 3.2	instrument control , data collection, data analysis and image processing

1.2 Materials

A4 copy paper of Fule brand, glass slides of Fanchuan brand, double sides adhesive tapes, cardboard mat, blade, quick - drying stamp pad ink of Yaqili brand, BT - 550 blue gel pen of Baitong brand.

1.3 Experimental conditions

1.3.1 Experimental parameters of single - point scanning

Laser Name: 785nm line source, Output power: 1% 250mw,

Magnification of objective: ×50, Focus pattern: line focus,

Cumulative frequency: 3, Scanning time: 10s,

Wave range of scanning: Low -149.77 cm^{-1}

Centre 520 cm^{-1}

High 1107.65cm^{-1}

1.3.2 Experimental parameters of streamline scanning

Laser Name: 785nm line source, Output power: 10% 250mw,

Magnification of objective: ×50, Focus pattern: line focus,

Cumulative frequency: 1, Scanning time: 4s,

Wave range of scanning: Low -149.77 cm^{-1}

Centre 520 cm^{-1}

High 1107.65cm^{-1}

1.4 Experimental procedure

1.4.1 Sample preparation

First of all, to draw horizontal lines on an A4 paper with heavy force, moderate force and light force using blue gel pen, and to lay the paper aside under dry conditions at room temperature for 24 hours. Next, to seal the paper on each horizontal lines with heavy force, moderate force and light force using stamp pad ink, and to lay the paper aside under dry conditions at room temperature for 24 hours. Then, to draw vertical lines on stamps with heavy force, moderate force and light force using blue gel pen, and to lay the paper aside under dry conditions at room temperature for 24 hours. Finally, the exemplars for examination of writing and sealing sequence with different applied force were prepared. The cross section from stamp imprint and writing stroke in an exemplar was cut down as the testing samples by a blade, then the cross section was fixed on a glass slide using a double sides adhesive tape.

1.4.2 Instrument calibration

In order to ensure that the equipment was in good working condition, and had a high SNR (signal to noise ratio), the calibration should be performed on silicon before testing. The calibration parameters were as follows:

Laser wavelength: 785nm, Output power: 100% 250mw,

Magnification of objective: ×50, Cumulative frequency: 3,

Scanning time: 4s, Wave number of calibration peak: 520 cm – 1.

1.4.3 Distinguishing the type of materials by single – point scanning

The samples were placed under a microscope directly, and were focused under laser light the stroke of blue gel pen ink, the imprint of stamp pad ink and blank paper respectively. Then the parameters of single – point scanning were set, and the Raman spectra of different substances were collected, and these spectra were used as standard to fit the streamline images.

1.4.4 Showing the distribution of different substances by streamline scanning

The samples were placed under a microscope, and the center of the cross section of imprints and stroke was set in the middle of the vision field in a microscope. Then the focus was adjusted until a clear image. The examination range was selected and photos were taken under 5 times objective lens. After turning to the 50 times objective lens, the Raman spectra of different substances were collected.

1.4.5 Image Processing

According to the different Raman spectra from different substances, the images were fitted by wire3.2 software. Through defining each substance as different color, the distribution of different substance formed the pseudo – color images.

2 Results and discussion

2.1 Determining the Raman characteristic peaks of different substances by signal – point scanning

In our experiments, the Raman spectra of blue gel pen ink, stamp pad ink and paper were collected (see Figure 1 to Figure 3).

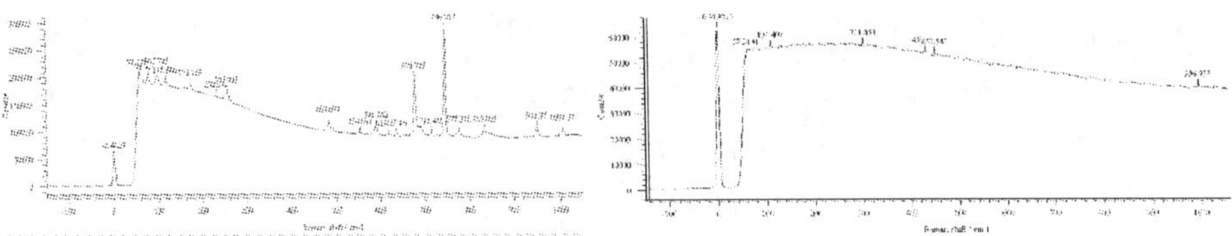

Fig. 1 Raman spectrum of blue gel pen Fig. 2 Raman spectrum of stamp pad ink

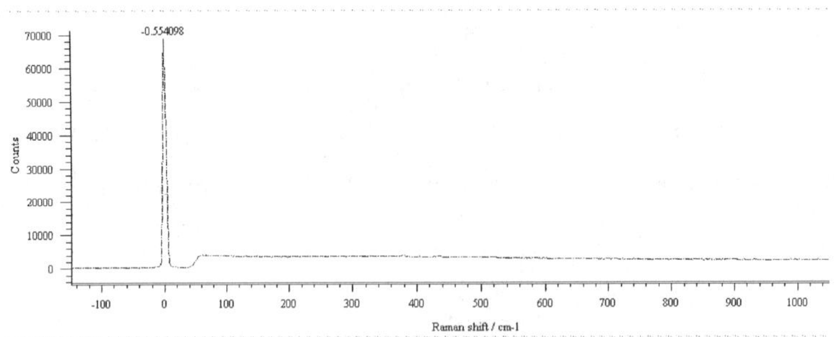

Fig. 3 Raman spectrum of paper used for the exemplars

We know that, as far as the blue gel pen ink is concerned, the intensity of laser reflection is weaker relative to intensity of its Raman signal and fluorescence background (see Figure 1). Comparing to Figures 1 – 3, we got the conclusion that the Raman peaks of blue gel pen ink at the range of 100 cm^{-1} – 1100 cm^{-1} was different from the Raman peaks of stamp pad ink and paper.

Figure 2 shows the stamp pad ink has hardly obvious characteristic peaks and the fluorescent background is high.

Figure 3 shows that the laser reflection of paper is strong, but the Raman signals of paper are nothing, and fluorescence background of paper is tend to be a straight line.

Comparing the Raman spectra of blue gel pen, stamp pad ink and paper with each other, it was evident that blue gel pen was 5 times higher than stamp pad ink in the intensity of Raman signal. The Raman spectrum of blue gel pen was different from another two. In a word, it has been possible to distinguish the distribution of the three materials by streamline imaging of Raman spectroscopy.

2. 2 The selection of light source

In order to get a better distribution of materials in streamline imaging of Raman spectroscopy, we had to examine the three materials under same light source. Meanwhile, the Raman spectra of the three materials were in high quality and were differentiated obviously. The Raman spectrometer in our experiments was equipped with light source at 532nm and 785nm of wavelength. The blue gel pen ink had good Raman spectra under the light source either at 532nm or at 785nm of wavelength. The paper used for experiment and the stamp pad ink had good Raman spectra only at 785nm of wavelength. Therefore, in the experiment, we selected at 785nm of wavelength as light source to do streamline imaging of Raman spectroscopy, under which the blue gel pen, paper and stamp pad ink had characteristic Raman information.

2. 3 The selection of output power of laser

The intensity of Raman signal is related to the number of laser photon irradiated on sample. The stronger of Raman signal, the more laser photon irradiated on sample, and the more power exchange between laser photon and sample molecule. When there is enough laser photon irradiated on the sample, the signal of the CCD will be saturated, and the Raman spectrum turns into a straight line. If the laser is strong enough, but the melting point or boiling point of sample is low, it is possible to make to evaporate or burn.

The main factor which affects the Raman signal intensity is the output power of laser. The higher of output power of laser, the stronger Raman signal. During the single – point scanning, low output power of laser was required, because it needed stay a period of time for the laser irradiation to excite Raman signals on the sample to be tested, and high output power of laser damaged sample. However, during the streamline scanning, high output power of laser was required, owing to the continuous movement of the automated platform. In the streamline scanning, the final Raman spectra of each point it were the sum of Raman signal of micro – points. To get better Raman spectra of points, sufficient Raman signals is needed. Long scanning time and high cumulative frequency lengthened the scan time.

Therefore, if we wanted to get better Raman spectra in short scanning time, we had to select low output power of laser in single – point scanning, and high output power of laser in streamline scanning.

2. 4 Determination of writing and sealing sequence

In our study, we classified test results of writing and sealing sequence into detected and undetected. Because the Raman signal intensity of blue gel pen was much stronger than the Raman signal intensity of stamp pad ink, the signal of stamp pad ink was detected only when the upper layer was stamp pad ink and thick enough. Otherwise, the signal of blue gel pen ink was detected preferentially. Therefore, it meant: strokes was covered by seals, and the edges of the strokes were not very smooth in writing at first sealing later. The seal imprint was covered by stroke in the cross section, so the edges of the stroke were very smooth in sealing at first writing later. The images are shown in Figure 4.

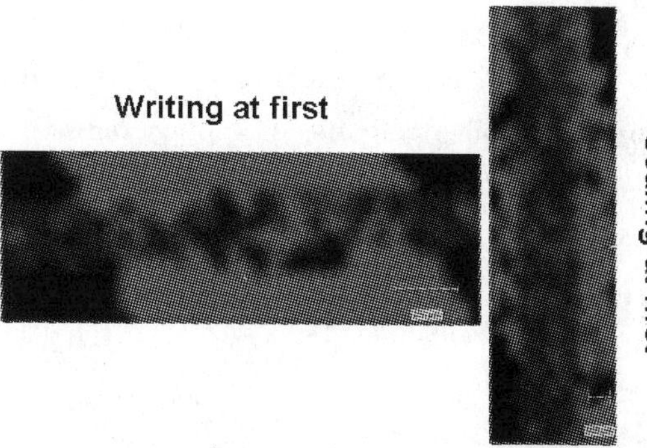

Fig. 4 Writing at first and sealing at first

In our experiments, the writing and sealing sequence samples which were formed with different applied force were examined by streamline imaging of Raman spectroscopy. Obviously, it has been difficult to judge the sequence under day light. After the use of streamline imaging of Raman spectroscopy, the writing and sealing sequence should be determined accurately. Examples are shown in Figure 5 to Figure 7.

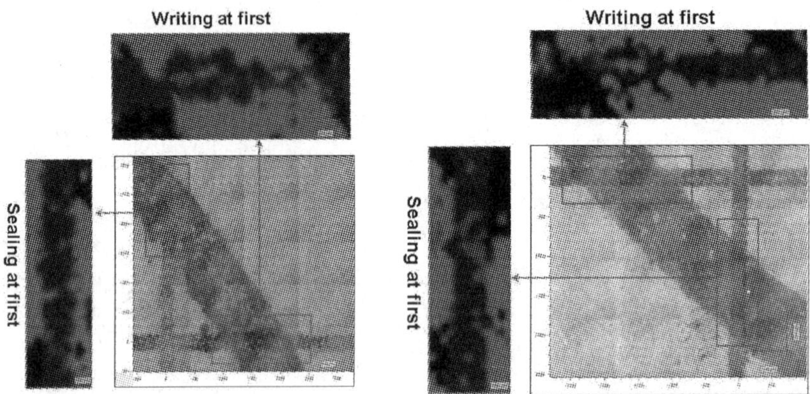

Fig. 5 The sample with heavy applied force both in writing and sealing

Fig. 6 The sample with moderate applied force both in writing and sealing

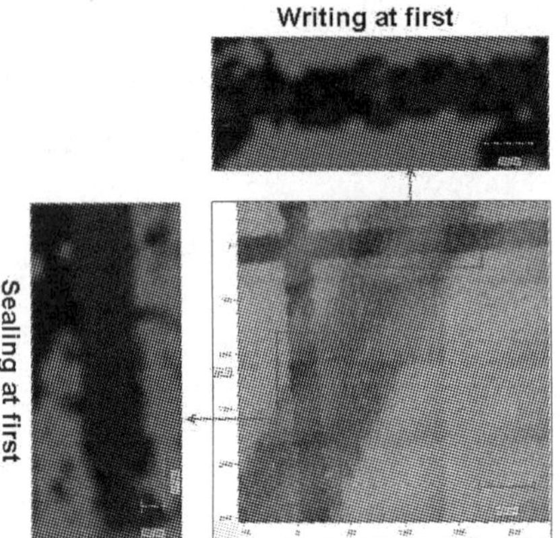

Fig. 7 The sample with light force both in writing and sealing

For the sample with light applied force (Figure 7), it was difficult to determine writing and sealing sequence. For the samples with heavy applied force and moderate applied force (Figure 5 to Figure 6), the results were satisfied. According to the classification criteria of the results above, their examination results of the experimental samples are listed in Table 2.

Table 2 Examinable ratio of samples obtained by different applied force

Stamp pad ink / Force intension	Writing at first sealing later			Sealing at first writing later		
	Sample number	Detected number	Detective percentage	Sample number	Detected number	Detective percentage
Heavy force	299	261	87.3%	299	261	87.3%
Moderate force	299	209	83.6%	299	209	83.6%
Light force	299	170	56.8%	299	170	56.8%

According to the interpretation of experiment results and examinable ratio, the conclusion would come out as follows: the intensity of applied force affected the result of writing and sealing sequence. Heavy force helps to the determination of writing and sealing sequence. If the force was too light, we might get an opposite result.

3 Conclusion

Experiments showed that writing and sealing sequence was able to be determined by streamline imaging of Raman spectroscopy. According to the characteristics reflected by writing and sealing sequence, it indicated that the applied force affected greatly on the experiment result of writing and sealing sequence. Heavy applied force was favorable to the determination of writing and sealing sequence. If the force was too light, opposite phenomenon might make us confused.

References

[1] Liu Jianwei, Li Shuyan, "Several Testing Methods of Written Order of Pen and Inkpad", *Chinese Journal of Forensic Sciences*, 2001, 3, pp. 36 ~ 38.

[2] Lian Yuanyuan, Li Wei, Liang Luning, Huang Jiantong, Liu Yong, "Research on Determination of Written Order of Black Pen Cross Strokes by Raman Mapping Spectroscopy", *Forensic Sciences and Technology* (*Chinese*), 2009, 3, pp. 14 ~ 17.

[3] Heng Hang, Ke Weizhong, Ji Kang, "Applications of Micro – Raman Spectroscopy on Ink Identification", *Spectroscopy Technology* (*Chinese*), 2007, 5, pp. 456 ~ 458.

[4] Xu Che, Tang Chun, Yang Yanyong, Pu Yumei, "Preliminary Study on Identification of Black Ball – pen Ink by Micro – Raman Spectroscopy", *Forensic Sciences and Technology* (*Chinese*), 2000, 4, pp. 244 ~ 245.

The Recent Development and Future Directions of Fingerprint Techniques

Ma Rongliang[1], Chen Jiang[2], Wang Jiachuan[3], Dong Limin[4] *

Fingerprint techniques is a mainstream in forensic science. Fingerprint evidence has been applied in crime investigation and in court for over a hundred years.[1-3] Nowadays with the rapid development of Automated Fingerprint Identification System (AFIS) fingerprint techniques have been widely used as one of the most important tools in crime investigation. Generally fingerprint techniques are divided into three categories: detection, identification and AFIS techniques.[1, 2] Fingerprint detection is developing latent (or invisible) fingermarks into visible ones by using physical, chemical, biological or combination methods; fingerprint identification is to compare the fingerprints collected from crime scenes and the suspects to decide if they are identical or not. AFIS is the application of information technology in fingerprint identification and it is virtually the information technology rather than fingerprint technology.

The advances of fingerprint techniques are slow compared to other more "modern" fields in forensic science, for instance, DNA and drug detection techniques. However, since around 2000 there is great development in fingerprint techniques, especially in fingermark detection techniques. Based on these observations we can draw the conclusion that fingerprint techniques will advance in the following areas:

First, pursuing more sensitive reagent is the eternal theme in fingermark detection techniques. Recently there are three types of reagents or techniques emerging in this direction: luminescent reagents, nanoparticles and immune technology.

Menzel et al. focused their research on the use of photoluminescent semiconductor nanocrystals (also referred to as nanocrystallites, quantum dots, nanoparticles, nanoclusters or nanocomposites), formed from compounds such as ZnS, CdS, CdSe, CdTe, InP, InAs, which yield intense luminescence with a lifetime in the desired range.[4, 5] Moreover, the absorption and emission can be tailored by adjusting the nanocrystal size. Basically, CdS nanoparticles

* 1. Institute of Forensic Science, Ministry of Public Security, Beijing 100038.
2. Longhua Branch, Bureau of Public Security, Shenzhen 518109.
3. Center for Forensic Science, Bureau of Public Security, Shenzhen 518000.
4. Center for Forensic Science, Bureau of Public Security, Shanghai 200083.
E-mail: rongliangma@yahoo.com.cn.

were used as the luminescence resources after CAF. Cadmium nitrite and sodium sulfate were added in the dendrimer solution to form the CdS/dendrimer nanocomposites. After that, exhibits with fingermarks already fumed by cyanoacrylate (CA) were dipped into a CdS/dendrimer nanocomposites solution for a number of hours (often left over night) to endure the possible reaction between the amino functionality of the dendrimer and the carboxylic acid of the fingerprint residue. An interesting observation was that this method was only effective on CA ester – fumed fingermarks, but ineffective when applied to unfumed fingermarks. This could be explained by the use of ethanol in the solution causing the fingerprint residues to be washed away. Moreover, to improve the binding of the fingermark to the dendrimer, Bouldin et al. used diimide to pretreat the fingermark to convert the carboxylic acid moieties of the fingerprint residue to esters that then reacted with the dendrimer amino groups to form amide linkages. [6] The effect of the reaction temperature of CdS/dendrimer nanocomposites with fingerprint residues was also considered and some positive results were acquired. In summary, the CdS/dendrimer nanocomposites improved the binding of nanoparticles with fingerprint residues and seemed an interesting direction in the powdering techniques, but the complexity of the operation, for example, long development time, also limited its further application. In addition, Jin et al. used CdS/PAMAM nanocomposites to develop sebaceous fingermarks on tinfoil and observed similar results. [7] Except luminescent reagent and nanoparticles immune technology is an emerging method for fingermark detection.

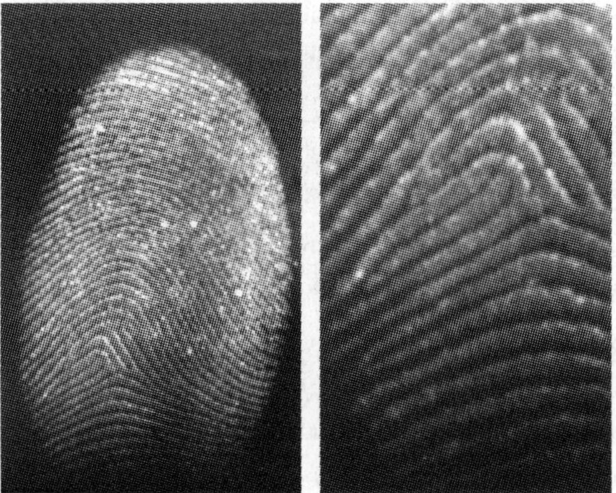

Fig. 1 Developed latent fingermark on PVDF using the aptamer – based reagent. Overall fingermark pattern (left) and a magnified section (right) show completely clear "valleys" of the fingermark, highlighting the lack of background interaction. [8]

Spindler used anti – L – amino acid antibodies conjugated to gold nanoparticles to facilitate the detection of latent fingermarks by interacting with amino acids present in fingermark residues. [9] This antibody – based system is particularly effective for the enhancement of aged and dried fingermarks on non – porous surfaces, an area unexploited by current techniques. Wood and coworkers detected latent fingermarks using aptamer – based reagents on the test substrate

(PVDF). [8-10] Some marks developed with this method showed level 1 and 2 features that are clearly visible. The definite potential of an aptamer – based reagent still need be fully explored in terms of use on surfaces more frequently encountered for fingermark detection, as well as its relative performance compared to conventional methods. However, it has been shown that an aptamer – based reagent is a novel technique capable of developing latent fingermarks with high selectivity and sensitivity (Figure 1). With the ability to create and modify aptamers to almost any target compound, theoretically aptamer – based reagents have enormous potential to detect various fingermarks. By targeting a variety of fingermark components, aptamer – based reagents would be possible for dealing with difficult fingermark cases. In addition, there is the potential to develop reagents that could provide "extra" information from fingermarks, such as the detection of drug residues or residues from the handling of explosives.

Second, fingermark detection on difficult surfaces always attracts the attention of forensic scientists, for example, fingermark detection on polymer banknotes, adhesive tapes and highly luminescent and patterned background.

Jones et al. used cyanoacrylate fuming/rohdamine 6g staining combined with vacuum metal deposition (VMD) techniques to detect fingermarks on Australian polymer banknotes. [11] Sufficient fingermarks with clear ridge details were detected using this method, especially for fresh fingermark. Australian polymer banknote is a notoriously difficult surface for fingermark detection. The coating of these banknotes is a modified polyurethane lacquer over patterned offset and intaglio printing and each of the denominations exhibited broadband luminescence.

Ma et al. applied a carbon – based suspension on the detection of fingermarks on the sticky side of adhesive tapes. Some organic solvents such as methyl ethyl ketone were also used to unravel the tangled tapes. A carbonic ink was also used on the detection of fingermarks on the tapes since carbonic ink is a carbon – based colloid solution. Clear fingermarks with enough ridges were developed by this method in several real cases. [12, 13]

Ma et al used upconverters to detect fingermarks on difficult surfaces with background luminescence and pattern interference. [14-16] Upconverter is a special material that emission light has a shorter wavelength or higher energy than the excitation light. The result shows that upconverter successfully developed clear fingermarks on surfaces that conventional techniques hardly work such as Australian Polymer banknotes (Figure 2).

Fig. 2 Fresh fingermarks (<5 h old) on an Australian five dollar polymer banknote developed with NaYF4: Er, Yb. Illuminated using 980 nmlaser light and imaged using a Rofin Poliview fitted with an IR blocking filter and using an exposure time of approximately 15s. [15]

Third, time – resolve (TR) and phase – resolve (PR) technology is effective for fingermark detection that conventional luminescence techniques cannot resolve. Usually TR and PR technology involves the use of complicated instruments such as pulsed lasers and imaging facilities. The time – resolved (TR) technique has been proposed to detect the luminescence of fingermarks for some time. [17-19] However, it is not a new technique but one developed by Murdock and Menzel in the 1990s. [20] TR spectroscopy is a method which utilizes the difference in luminescence lifetime between a substrate and a sample. [21] Luminescence lifetime is the average decay time of the luminescence emitted by a molecule after excitation with a short laser (or other light resource) pulse. [19] It has been extensively applied in biology, but not widely used in fingermark detection. So far the TR technique has been successfully applied to fingermark development with milli – , micro – and even nanosecond resolution (Figure 3). Generally the TR technique needs complex and expensive devices such as laser, CCD camera, image intensifier, programmable timing generator, and so on. This greatly limits the application of the TR technique, but it does have a significant advantage. It can address the issue caused by background luminescence interference.

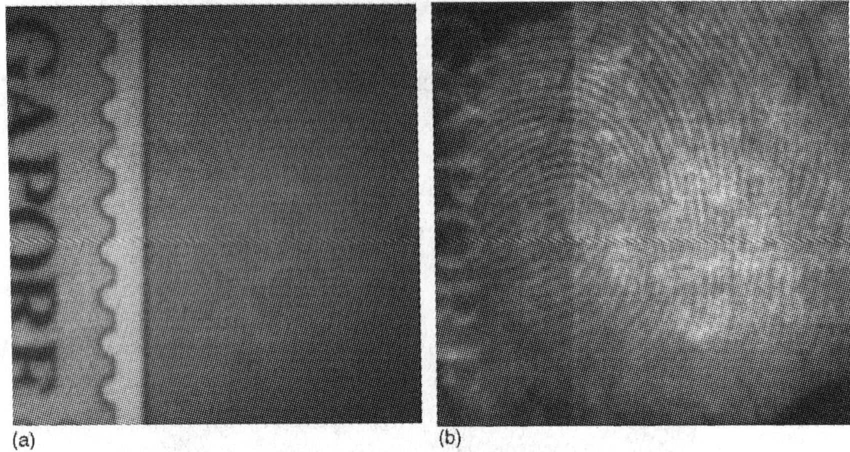

Fig. 3 The intensity image (a) and fluorescence lifetime image (b) of the blitz – green – treated finger mark samples on postcard substrate.[19]

A more complicated technique named the phase – resolved (PR) technique was also applied with the similar theoretical principle.[22, 23] The PR technique is based on the phase shift that occurs in luminescence emissions. In this method, the sample (fingerprint) is excited with an intensity – modulated laser. The luminescence emissions from the sample and the background will be phase shifted with respect to the excitation. Then the heterodyne technique is applied to acquire the frequencies of different emissions from the fingerprints and the background. The heterodyne signal obtained will be further processed to resolve the phase information by mixing it electronically with a square wave pulse. Finally, the fingerprint is "separated" from the background. The PR technique can image the luminescence emission even when the fingermark's luminescence lifetime is shorter than that of the background, which is not at all possible with the TR technique. Moreover, the PR technique offers better contrast for fingermark detection than the TR technique.[22] However, the PR technique also faces many of the same disadvantages as the TR technique, which limits its further application.

Fourth, chemical (or hyperspectral) imaging is the most powerful weapon that fingerprint expert have acquired. In fact chemical imaging techniques not only include infrared (IR) and visible and UV imaging, but also contain Raman, X – ray fluorescence imaging, etc.[24] When these images are obtained by the chemical imaging facilities, the component of the fingerprint residues can be acquired as well.[25] In theory the chemical imaging can even solve the most challenging problems in fingermark detection.

Infrared chemical imaging was first applied for fingermark detection on a variety of surfaces by Tahtouh and coworkers.[26 – 29] The fingermarks detected by this method usually should be treated before the application of chemical imaging. Several types of cyanoacrylate esters with strong absorption peaks in the infrared region were synthesized and applied for the fuming of fingermarks on various surfaces such as Australian polymer banknotes. The result showed that clear fingermarks with tertiary features were developed by this method on Australian banknote which was impossible to achieve with other techniques (Figure 4). After this work, advances have been achieved by chemical imaging in many areas in forensic science besides the application in fingermark detection, for example, trace evidence and document examination.

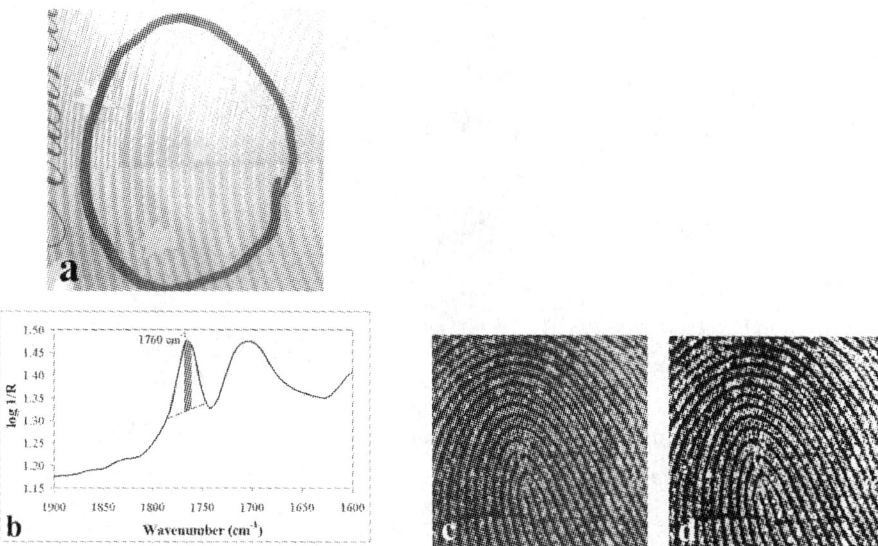

Fig. 4 Ethyl cyanoacrylate fumed mark on MYM5 note: (a) White light photograph of ethyl cyanoacrylate fumed mark on MYM5 note, (b) Infrared spectrum of fingermark ridge showing peak area at 1760 cm^{-1} used to generate image, (c) Monochrome representation of infrared chemical image, (d) Figure 5c with contrast and brightness adjustment. [30]

Fifth, it is a challenging issue on how to develop fingermarks on the exhibits that are polluted by bio – , chemical and nuclear hazardous materials. This issue was raised after the "Anthrax attack" that happened in the US right after the "911 attack".

Hoile et al. conducted research using a number of porous and nonporous items contaminated with viable anthrax spores and marked with latent fingermarks. The test samples were then subjected to a standard formulation of formaldehyde gas for decontamination. After decontamination latent fingermarks were recovered using a range of methods. It was found that the formaldehyde gas fumigation was effective at destroying viable spores, but also contributed to the degradation of amino acids leading to loss of ridge detail. Finally a new protocol for formaldehyde gas decontamination was developed which allows for the destruction of viable spores and the successful recovery of latent marks, all within a rapid response time of less than one hour. [31]

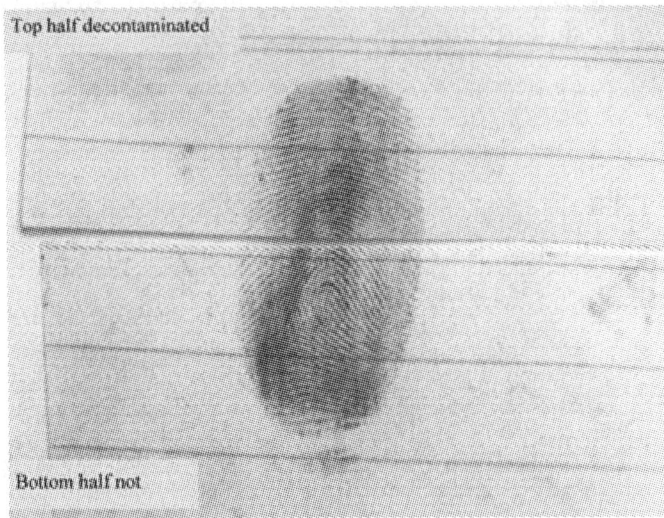

Fig. 5 Development of print using physical developer after decontamination treatment with formaldehyde (standard concentration). [31]

Sixth, the use of 3rd level characteristics in fingerprint identification remains a topic of interest. In fingerprint identification process usually the number of the 2nd level characteristics is used as the key criterion. Nevertheless, there is no solid standard on the numbers of 2nd level characteristics used as identification in some countries including China, US, Australia, etc. , but generally 7 or 8 2nd level characteristics is a conventional standard, even it is not declared by law. It is quite common that a fingerprint collected from crime scenes shows only 5 or 6 stable characteristics and under this situation many fingerprint experts resort the help of 3rd level characteristics. The 3rd level characteristics mainly includes sweat pores and the micro – shape of ridges. Some research groups have studied this 3rd characteristics and some preliminary result showed that the 3rd characteristics has the practical use in fingerprint identification. In fact there were some reports about the use of 3rd characteristics in real cases; the "cannabis leaf case" happened in Sydney, Australia is a famous example. [32] In this case, the fingermark expert only found seven 2nd level characteristics on the stamp of an envelope containing some cannabis inside. At that time, the High Court in New South Wales ruled that a person cannot be identified by fingerprint with less than 10 2nd characteristics. However, there were many sweat pores in the fingermark developed on the stamp. In the court the expert of Australian Federal Police showed 20 sweat pores plus seven 2nd level characteristics which both matched the suspect's fingerprint. Finally the jury accepted the identification using this 3rd level features and this also led that the NSW high court changed the regulation that fingerprint cannot be identified with less than ten 2nd level features.

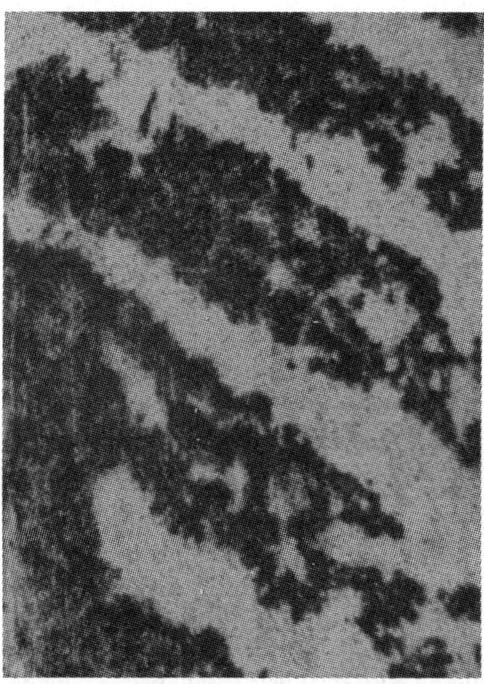

Fig. 6 Upconverter – developed fingerprint showing third level properties (magnification times: 50x).

Seventh, the application of more powerful AFIS will profoundly improve the efficiency of crime investigation and stimulate the research of fingermark detection techniques. Currently there is no national AFIS or central fingerprint database in China. Oppositely each province has its own AFIS and they come from 6 manufacturers that led to the inefficiency compared to a national database, such as the Integrated Automated Fingerprint Identification System (IAFIS) run by the FBI.

Automated Fingerprint Identification System (AFIS) is one of the fundamental projects built by China Police and also one of the most important scientific approaches for criminal investigation. AFIS has been applied universally in policing in China. Currently there are about 110 million suspects' fingerprints in the database of Chinese Police, together with about two million fingerprints from the crime scenes. In 2011 – 2012 over two hundred thousand criminal cases were solved using AFIS at provincial level in China. And more than twenty thousand criminal cases have been uncovered by cross – provincial assistance of AFIS (or national level) in China.

In order to solve the cross – provincial fingerprint searches the Ministry of Public Security (MPS, the Central Police of China) established an Assistant Fingerprint Search Platform (AFSP) in 2010. In the AFSP system the Provincial Police forward the request of fingerprint search to the AFSP and the AFSP people distribute the search task to all the other provinces. The people in other provinces will make the search and the result will be returned to the AFSP in different times according to the seriousness of the crimes. Finally the AFSP people will make statistics on all the results of cross – provincial hits and maintain the normal operation of this system.

However, the barriers among the seven manufactures still significantly affect the in – depth application of AFIS. To solve this trouble, the MPS also initiated the work of accreditation of the provincial AFIS. The aim of accreditation is to standardize the basic characteristics of fingerprints, strengthen the cooperation in criminal investigation using AFIS from different manufacturers, eliminate the barriers of different softwares and hardwares, and finally improve the information communication among different AFIS. The MPS promulgated a series of standards that all the Provincial AFIS have to comply with, for example, all the AFIS must have the input ports the permit the accredited livescan system to transfer fingerprint data, and must have the ports to be connected to the Central Management System and can be operated by operators in other provinces. Only when the above requirements are met can the AFIS pass the accreditation organized by MPS. The AFIS that does not pass this accreditation will be forbidden to sell, install and use within the Chinese Police.

The accreditation has two stages: the 1st stage is the software accreditation and the 2nd stage in the on – site test. In the 1st stage the software is tested for all the features in the laboratory and this stage has been completed now. Most of the AFIS manufacturers have passed the accreditation. In the 2nd stage, all the AFIS will be tested with the effectiveness of fingerprint check after being installed and updated in local Police. This 2nd stage work has started recently and will be completed in 2013.

The AFSP and the accreditation for AFIS can partially solve the difficulty of fingerprint search of cross – province and cross – manufacturer, but there remains the strong need to establish a NAFIS for China for crime investigation. MPS will eventually found the NAFIS and started the investigation for this huge project. MPS plans that there will be more than one hundred million people's fingerprints and more than ten million fingermarks collected from crime scenes in NAFIS' database. The daily search will be over twelve thousand and the equipment for live scan will be over fifty thousand. This huge project is under investigation now.

Reference

[1] C. Champod, C. Lennard, P. Margot and M. Stoilovic, *Fingerprints and Other Ridge Skin Impressions*, Boca Raton: CRC Press, 2004.

[2] M. Stoilovic and C. Lennard, *Fingerprint Detection and Enhancement.* 4th ed. , Canberra: National Centre for Forensic Study, 2010.

[3] R. E. Gaensslen and H. C. Lee, *Advances in Fingerprint Technology*, Boca Raton: CRC Press, 2001.

[4] E. R. Menzel, S. M. Savoy, S. J. Ulvick, K. H. Cheng, R. H. Murdock and M. R. Sudduth, "Photoluminescent Semiconductor Nanocrystals for Fingerprint Detection", *J. Forensic Sciences*, 2000, 45 (3), pp. 545 ~ 551.

[5] E. R. Menzel, M. Takatsu, R. H. Murdock, K. Bouldin and K. H. Cheng, "Photoluminescent CdS/Dendrimer Nanocomposites for Fingerprint Detection", *J. Forensic Sciences*, 2000, 45(4), pp. 770 ~ 773.

[6] K. K. Bouldin, E. R. Menzel, M. Takatsu and R. H. Murdock, "Diimide – enhanced Fingerprint Detection with Photoluminescent CdS/Dendrimer Nanocomposites", *J. Forensic Sciences*, 2000, 45 (6), pp. 1239 ~ 1242.

[7] Y. J. Jin, Y. J. Luo, G. P. Li, J. Li, Y. F. Wang, R. Q. Yang and W. T. Lu, "Application of Photoluminescent CdS/PAMAM Nanocomposites in Fingerprint Detection", *Forensic Science International*, 2008, 179 (1), pp. 34 ~ 38.

[8] M. Wood, P. Maynard, X. Spindler, C. Lennard and C. Roux, "Visualization of Latent Fingermarks Using an Aptamer – Based Reagent", *Angew. Chem. Int. Ed.*, 2012, 51, pp. 12272 ~ 12274.

[9] X. Spindler, O. Hofstetter, A. M. McDonagh, C. Roux and C. Lennard, "Enhancement of Latent Fingermarks on Non – Porous Surfaces Using Anti – L – Amino acid Antibodies Conjugated to Gold Nanoparticles", *Chem. Commun.*, 2011, 47, pp. 5602 ~ 5604.

[10] M. Wood, P. Maynard, X. Spindler, C. Roux and C. Lennard, "Selective Targeting of Fingermarks Using Immunogenic Techniques", *Australian Journal of Forensic Sciences.*

[11] N. Jones, M. Kelly, M. Stoilovic, C. Lennard and C. Roux, "The Development of Latent Fingerprints on Polymer Banknotes", *J. Forensic Identification*, 2003, 53 (1), pp. 50 ~ 77.

[12] 马荣梁、常柏年："如何提取及剥离胶带粘面的手印"，载《刑事技术》2000 年第 5 期，第 33 ~ 34 页。

[13] 马荣梁、常柏年："胶带粘面上的手印显现"，载《刑事技术》2000 年第 3 期，第 25 ~ 27 页。

[14] R. MA, *Novel Fingermark Detection Techniques Using Upconverters with Anti – Stokes Luminescence, in Centre for Forensic Science*, University of Technology Sydney: Sydney, 2012.

[15] R. Ma, E. Bullock, P. Maynard, B. Reedy, R. Shimmon, C. Lennard, C. Roux and A. McDonagh, "Fingermark Detection on Non – Porous and Semi – Porous Surfaces Using NaYF4: Er, Yb Up – converter Particles", *Forensic Science International*, 2011, 207 (1 ~ 3), pp. 145 ~ 149.

[16] R. Ma, R. Shimmon, A. McDonagh, P. Maynard, C. Lennard and C. Roux, "Fingermark Detection on Non – Porous and Semi – Porous Surfaces Using YVO4: Er, Yb Luminescent Upconverting Particles", *Forensic Science International*, 2012, 217, pp. e23 ~ e26.

[17] U. S. Dinish, Z. X. Chao, L. K. Seah and V. M. Murukeshan, "Nanosecond Resolution in Fingerprint Imaging Using Optical Technique", *International Journal of Nanoscience*, 2005, 4 (4), pp. 695 ~ 700.

[18] L. K. Seah, U. S. Dinish, W. F. Phang, Z. X. Chao and V. M. Murukeshan, "Fluorescence Optimisation and Lifetime Studies of Fingerprints Treated With Magnetic Powders", *Forensic Science International*, 2005, 152 (2 ~ 3), pp. 249 ~ 257.

[19] L. K. Seah, P. Wanga, V. M. Murukeshana and Z. X. Chao, "Application of Fluorescence Lifetime Imaging (FLIM) in Latent Finger Mark Detection", *Forensic Science International*, 2006, 160 (2 ~ 3), pp. 109 ~ 114.

[20] R. H. Murdock and E. R. Menzel, "A Computer Interfaced Time – Resolved Luminescence Imaging System", *Forensic Sci.*, 1993, 38, pp. 521 ~ 529.

[21] N. Akiba, N. Saitoh and K. Kuroki, "Fluorescence Spectra and Images of Latent Fingerprints Excited with a Tunable Laser in the Ultraviolet Region", *Forensic Sciences*, 2007, 52 (5), pp. 1103 ~ 1106.

[22] U. S. Dinish, Z. X. Chao, L. K. Seah, A. Singh and V. M. Murukeshan, "Formulation and Implementation of A Phase – Resolved Fluorescence Technique for Latent – Fingerprint Imaging: Theoretical and Experi-

mental Analysis", *Applied Optics*, 2005, 44 (3), pp. 297 ~ 304.

[23] U. S. Dinish, L. K. Seah, V. M. Murukeshan and L. S. Ong, "Theoretical Analysis of Phase – Resolved Fluorescence Emission From Fingerprint Samples", *Optics Communication*, 2003, 223, pp. 55 ~ 60.

[24] C. Roux, 2006.

[25] 王桂强："光谱成像检验技术"，载《刑事技术》2004 年第 1 期，第 7 ~ 12 页。

[26] M. Tahtouh, J. Kalman, C. Roux, C. Lennard and B. Reedy, "The Detection and Enhancement of Latent Fingermarks Using Infrared Chemical Imaging", *Journal of Forensic Sciences*, 2005, 50 (1), pp. 64 ~ 72.

[27] M. Tahtouh, J. R. Kalman and B. J. Reedy, "Synthesis and Characterization of Four Alkyl 2 – Cyanoacrylate Monomers and Their Precursors for Use in Latent Fingerprint Detection", *Journal of Polymer Science*, Part A: Polymer Chemistry, 2011, 49, pp. 257 ~ 277.

[28] M. Tahtouh, S. A. Scott, J. R. Kalman and B. J. Reedy, "Four Novel Alkyl 2 – Cyanoacylate Monomers and Their Use in Latent Fingermark Detection By Mid – Infrared Spectral Imaging", *Forensic Sci Int*, 2011, 207, pp. 223 ~ 238.

[29] M. Tahtouh, P. Despland, R. Shimmon, J. R. Kalman and B. J. Reedy, "The Application of Infrared Chemical Imaging to the Detection and Enhancement of Latent Fingerprints: Method Optimization and Further Findings", *Journal of Forensic Sciences*, 2007, 52 (5), pp. 1089 ~ 1096.

[30] M. Tahtouh, J. R. Kalman, C. Roux, C. Lennard and B. J. Reedy, "The Detection and Enhancement of Latent Fingermarks Using Infrared Chemical Imaging", *Journal of Forensic Sciences*, 2005, 50 (1), pp. 1 ~ 9.

[31] R. Hoile, W. S. J. and R. Claude, "Bioterrorism: Processing Contaminated Evidence, the Effects of Formaldehyde Gas on the Recovery of Latent Fingermarks", *Journal of Forensic Sciences*, 2007, 52 (5), pp. 1097 ~ 1102.

[32] D. Clegg, Personal Communication, 2005.

The Comparative Analysis of the Ballistic Impact Traces on the Plain – Woven Fabric

Yu Aoyang *

Introduction

In the crime scene investigation, the fabric is a common type of object with trace of bullet contact. When the investigator identified the holes on the fabrics are bullet holes, they could determine the case was a gun – related cases. As one of the most important technical examination in gun – related cases, bullet marks test is a mission of using traces, which are present on bullets and shells, and traces on the targets to determine the kinds of firing gun, the certain gun, and the nature and the process of the case. If the identified conditions bullet and cartridge cases can not find in the crime scene, trace of bullet contact on the target object becomes the only bullet marks. Currently, it is one of the difficulties to use trace of bullet contact on the subjects to determine the kinds of involved guns, especially the traces happened in the fabrics. Under normal circumstances, the determination kind of the bullets is an effective way to determine the involved kinds of firearms. If the criminal technical staff could use trace of bullet impact on the fabrics to determine the kinds of the bullets and combined with relationship between the bullet types and equipped firearms, they will greatly limit the scope of the investigation. If a bullet only can be launched in a certain firearm, the bullet types can directly determine the model of the gun.

Plain woven fabric is a modern textile material and has non – homogeneous anisotropy characteristics. Therefore, it is a kind of representative textile materials. In this paper, we choose the polyester plain woven fabric as the objects, six domestic representative firearms as launch firearm, shooting at the distance of 2 meters vertically. Observing the trace of bullet impact, comparing its morphological differences, analyzing the difference in the causes, initially establish the relations between the bullet holes morphology and bullets types, to provide an effective way for the use of the trace of the bullet impact to identify the type of firearm involved.

1 Theoretical analysis

1. 1 Researches of the related disciplines

* Yu Aoyang, Forensic Science Department National Police University of China, No. 83, Tawan Street, Huanggu District, Shenyang, Liaoning, P. R. China 110035. Forensic Science Department, National Police University of China, Shenyang, P. R. China. Email: 9148988@qq. com.

In the plain woven fabric, the warps and wefts of the spatial structure morphology and mating relationship with each other known as the structure, when the warp and weft density is not the same, this structure is called unequal support surface structure. The higher density of the warp or weft, the lower the tear strength is, while the higher anti – high breaking strength is, on the contrary, the lower density of the warp yarns or weft, the higher tear strength is, while the lower breaking resistance is. The lower density warps or wefts are broke firstly, while the higher density warps or wefts are tore firstly.[1] Relatively in our daily life, such equal support surface structure fabrics are not common, so the fabrics used in the experiments are the unequal support surface structure fabrics.

The terminal ballistic learn that the energy loss during the process of the bullet running through the textile, mainly from yarn elastic energy, kinetic energy of yarn breaking and the yarn kinetic energy. In the same fabric conditions, in the running throughout process, the bullet shape and bullet impact speed plays the decisive effect for the gain and release of the energy of the yarn. The weapons materials science research also shows that the impact of the bullet to the plain woven fabric, yarn material has the characteristics of anisotropic and orthogonal, a "diamond – shaped" will form in deformation zone in the plane of the fabric, the stress in the fabric was "cross" distribution, the shape of the impact zone are similar to the head of the bullet shape. The different head of the bullet shape affected the number of pulled yarn number in the impact zone, the blunter the bullet is, the more yarns are pulled out in the fabric. In addition, the axial rotation of the bullet will produce the strong friction on the pulled out yarn and the edge of the bullet holes, the friction effect is proportional to the rotation speed.

1.2 Theoretical derivation of the bullet holes form

Combination of materials science and ballistics research, we can derive the bullet holes formed by common bullets on the plain woven fabric of unequal support surface structure from a theoretical level, with the pulling yarn number, defect of bullet impact, the bullet holes shape, yarn end divergence as the indicators, according to the experimental results the variation of the curve in reference,[2] the bullet contact speed of 350m/s, on the base of the flat head and blunt ones classification, further divided into the low – speed pistol and high – speed pistol.

The characteristics of pointed rifle bullets are strong high – speed rotation, short period of time the bullets and fabric contact, less number of yarn gain energy, the warp and weft yarns produced only a very slight tear, then broke quickly, combined with the long bullets high – speed rotation, the yarn should be a serious defect, the yarn ends should be loose. Because the extent tear of longitude and latitude are similar, the stress was "cross" distribution, the shape of bullet holes are square and less yarns will be pulled.

[1] Liu Qin, Xie Guangyin, Xiong Yanli, "Research of Polyester Fabric Tensile and Tear Properties of Different Structure Plain Weave", *Progress in Textile Science & Technology*, 2009, 137 (1), pp. 70 ~ 71.

[2] Tan VBC, Lim CT, Cheng CH, "Perforation of High – Strength Fabric by Projectiles of Different Geometry", *International Journal of Impact Engineering*, 2003, 28 (2), pp. 207 ~ 222.

In the process of bullet holes formation by high - speed blunt pistol bullet, the contact period is short, the blunter bullet is, the more yarns were affected in the impact zone. The yarn slight tore and broke quickly. Friction caused by the bomb bullets rotation obviously defects the center of the hole and the yarn end fiber loose, the stress distribution form roughly the square round the bullet holes, the blunt bullet will pull more yarns out.

In the process of bullet holes formation by low - speed blunt pistol bullets, the contact period increased significantly. The Warp and weft yarns are tearing and breaking from the center to the periphery, and make the defect of bullet hole center becomes smaller, loose fibers of the yarn ends are significantly reduced.[3] Because of the mechanical property difference of the unequal support surface structure plain weave fabric warp and weft yarns, the stress distribution form the bullet holes roughly oval and the blunt bullets will pull out more yarns.

In the process of bullet holes formation by low - speed flat head pistol bullets, the contact period increased relatively.[4] The head of the bullet increases the contact area with the fabric, so it enhances the friction significantly. The annular edge of the flat head bullets play a strong shearing action to the yarns, the shearing force and the frictional force break and tear the fabric yarn along the rotational direction of the bullet, resulting in a larger defect formed by the bullet edge shear and accompanied by obvious pulling yarn phenomenon.

2 Test procedure

2. 1 Test equipment and materials

54 pistol, 59 pistols, 77 pistol, 79 - style micro submachine gun, 92 pistol, 9mm Police Wheel guns, 81 rifle (the parameters see Table 1), 51 pistol bullets, 59 pistol bullets, 64 pistol bullets, 92 pistol bullets, 9mm police wheel gun bullets, 56 - style rifle bullet (the parameters see Table 2), Digital camera, tape measure, tape, reading microscope, stereo-microscope.

Table 1 Parameters of firearms

Types of firearms	caliber (mm)	commencing speed (m/s)	Bullet equipped	effective range (m)
54 pistol	7.62	420	51 pistol bullets	50
77 pistol	7.62	318	59 pistol bullets	50
79 micro submachine gun	7.62	515	51 pistol bullets	200
81 rifle	7.62	750	56 rifle bullets	400

[3] Li yuchun, "Dynamic Response of Plain - woven Fabric Subjected to Ballistic Impact of A Flat Nosed Projectile", *Journal of Materials Science & Engineering*, 2010, 28 (3), pp. 380 ~ 384.

[4] Li Yuchun, Cheng Keming, Shen Wei, Liu Qiang, Mao Yiming, "Analysis on the Dynamic Response of Plain - Woven Fabric Under Ballistic Impact of Projectile", *Ordnance Material Science And Engineering*, 2010, 33 (1), pp. 30 ~ 35.

续表

Types of firearms	caliber (mm)	commencing speed (m/s)	Bullet equipped	effective range (m)
59 pistol	9	315	59 pistol bullets	50
92 pistol	9	350	92 pistol bullets	50
9mm Police Wheel guns	9	220	9mm wheel gun bullets	50

Table 2 Parameters of bullets

Types of bullets	caliber (mm)	Length (mm)	weight (g)	Shape
51 pistol bullets	7. 84	14. 90	5. 57	blunt
64 pistol bullets	7. 84	12. 34	4. 82	blunt
56 rifle bullets	7. 90	31. 46	7. 90	pointed
59 pistol bullets	9. 24	11. 18	6. 12	hemispheric
92 pistol bullets	9. 00	16. 34	7. 79	point domed
9mm wheel gun bullets	9. 00	12. 48	4. 40	flat

2. 2 Samples

Use the test firearms shot the polyester plain weave fabric vertically 2 meters away, 50 times per one. Exam the obtained sample with a magnification of 12 times stereoscopic microscope with top light and transmitted light irradiate on the inlet and transmitted light irradiates on the exit, in the lighting conditions, take pictures for the entrance and the exit holes of projectile vertically, and pictures from the side for the rolled yarns, and measure the data by the reading microscope and make statistics, eliminate overlapped bullet holes.

3 Results and discussion

3. 1 7. 62mm caliber bullet holes

Test firearms such as 79 – micro submachine gun, 54pistol, 77pistol, 81rifle are all 7. 62mm caliber guns produced in China, but with big difference between them. 79 micro submachine gun, 54 pistol and 77 – style pistol handgun are all equipped with the same shape as the blunt – head 7. 62mm projectiles, but these guns muzzle velocity varied, using a laser gun 2 meters from the muzzle, to measure the contact speed: 79 micro submachine gun's muzzle velocity is 500 m/s, 54 pistol's muzzle velocity is 405 m/s, 77 pistol's is 310 m/s, due to the different impact speed of different three guns, the bullet morphological holes are obviously different in plain weave polyester fabric.

79 micro submachine, high speed gun projectile impacts significantly on the fabric (see Fig. 1), the warp and weft yarns broke in the center of the bullet holes, the broken ends of fi-

bers spread out, in the center of the bullet holes obvious defected, length yarns in the bullet holes became shorter significantly, bullet holes were square, the visible soot appeared around the margin of bullet holes.

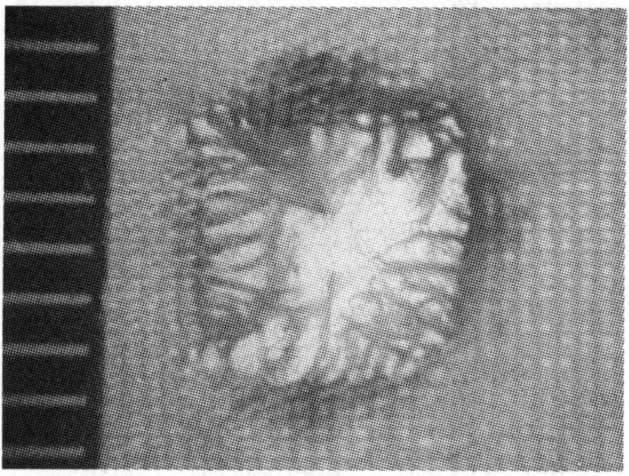

Fig. 1 The bullet holes of 79 micro submachine gun

The impact speed of 54 style pistols nearly 95 m/s slower than 79 micro submachine gun bullets, impact effect decreases significantly on the fabric (see Fig. 2). Bullet holes are similar to 79 micro submachine gun's bullet holes, but the defects decreases, and it is difficult to find the soot around the margin of the bullet holes.

Fig. 2 The bullet holes of 54 style pistols

Impact speed of 77 – style pistol is the minimum among the three guns (see Fig. 3). The low impact speed does not produce significant defect in the bullet hole center, the weft yarns broke, but the yarn ends intertwined due to the bullets pulling, so that the bullet hole became round, the broken yarns in the center intertwined, the soot are clear around the margin of the bullet hole.

Fig. 3 The bullet holes of 77style pistols

Test firearms, 81 rifle are equipped with the pointed – head 7. 62mm projectiles, the guns muzzle velocity is relatively high, using a laser gun 2 meters from the muzzle, to measure the contact speed is 720 m/s, due to the high impact speed and the pointed bullet form the obvious characteristics bullet holes.

Gun projectile shot by 81 rifle impacts significantly on the fabric (see Fig. 4), and most of the warp and weft yarns broke on the edge of the bullet hole. A few long yarns interwoven in the midpoint of each side of the square bullet holes, the four corners of the square bullet holes tore seriously, the near yarn obvious distorted, and the edge bullet holes charred and harden, the yarns rolled to the exit obviously.

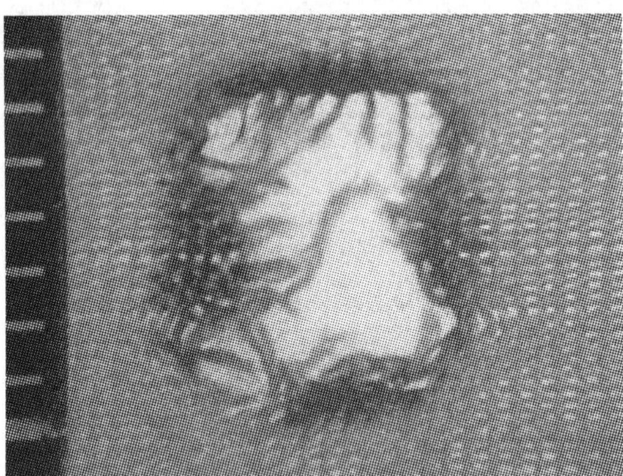

Fig. 4 The bullet holes of 81 style rifle

3. 2 7. 62mm caliber guns bullet holes

From the bullet holes shot by different kinds of guns, most of the shapes are square. In the case of the same bullet, the contact speed proportional to the degree of defect yarns of the bullet holes, the higher of the speed, the more obviously yarns around the bullet hole moved to the bullet impact zone in the strain, the yarn in the bullet impact zone continue to break, resulting in a more and more serious defect, the projectile velocity is lower, less defect, broken yarn intertwined under the bullets pulling, so the bullet holes become round. When the pointed bullets were used, bullet side tearing effect significantly enhanced, four corners of the square bullet holes were torn seriously into an acute angle, near yarns distorted.

The experimental results shows the yarn breaking are closely related to the projectile velocity, tearing action are closely related to the and bullet - shape, due to the elastic deformation of the yarn, measured by reading microscope, bullet hole diameter is about 6mm, and significantly less than the bullet diameter.

3. 3 9 mm caliber bullet holes

59 - style pistol equipped with 59 - style 9mm hemispheric bullet the guns muzzle velocity is 315m/s, using a laser gun 2 meters from the muzzle, to measure the contact speed is 308 m/s, the hemispheric bullet form the obvious characteristics bullet holes.

59 style bullets could pull more yarns (see Fig. 5). The broken yarns gather to the center of the bullet hole, most of the warp and weft yarns broke in the center of the bullet hole, the broken ends scatter obviously, and the bullet hole are circumference, with a thick soot around the margin.

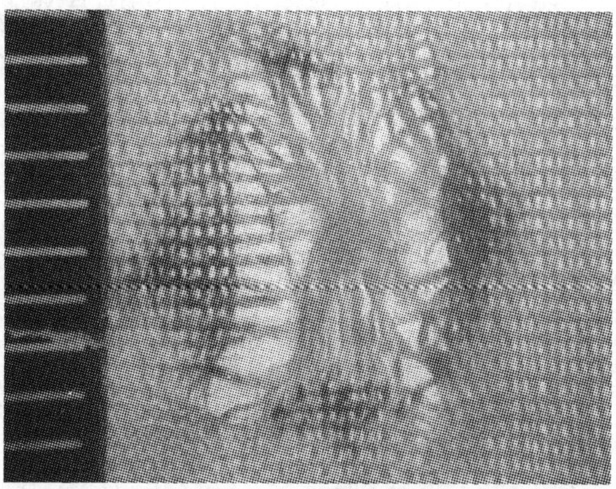

Fig. 5 The bullet holes of 59 style pistols

92 - style pistol equipped with 92 - style 9mm pistol bullet, with point domed head (the shape is the same as 9 × 19 mm "Parabellum" bullet) the guns muzzle velocity is 315m/s, using a laser gun 2 meters from the muzzle, to measure the contact speed is 322 m/s, the pointed domed bullet form the obvious characteristics bullet holes.

Bullets shot by 92 style pistol impacted the yarns showed obvious broken action (see Fig. 6). The broken ends are neat, reflect the snapping characteristic, parallel yarns defected obviously around the bullet hole margin, four corners of the bullet hole yarns completely broke, bullet hole shape are circumference, with a thick soot around the margin.

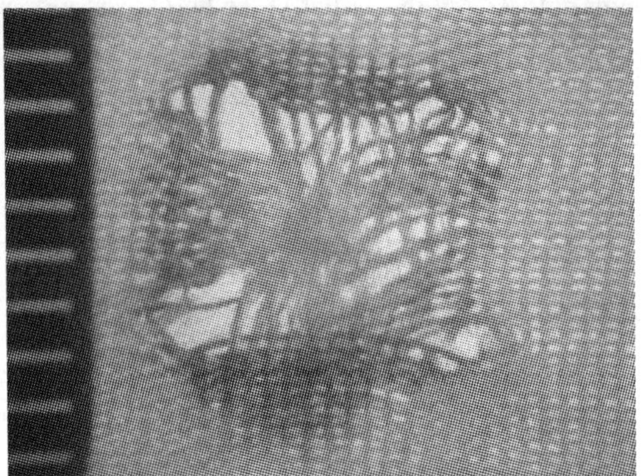

Fig. 6 The bullet holes of 92 style pistols

9mm police wheel gun equipped with 9mm flat wheel gun bullet, the guns muzzle velocity is 220m/s, flat bullet special shapes show obvious shearing action, the bullet hole characteristics are special.

The 9 mm police wheel gun flat bullet body's vertical edge produce shearing action, make the yarn internal stress is greater than the yarn broken failure threshold, yarns break. If the yarns of the across side of the bullet hole are all break, a small piece of fabric will separate from fabric (see Fig. 7). If only one side of the hole are break, a complete weave structure flake fabric will be formed in the center of the bullet hole. Bullet holes, which impacted by the flat bullet, show obviously defect on the fabric, and the ends of the yarns are neat, rectangular hole with slight soot around the margin.

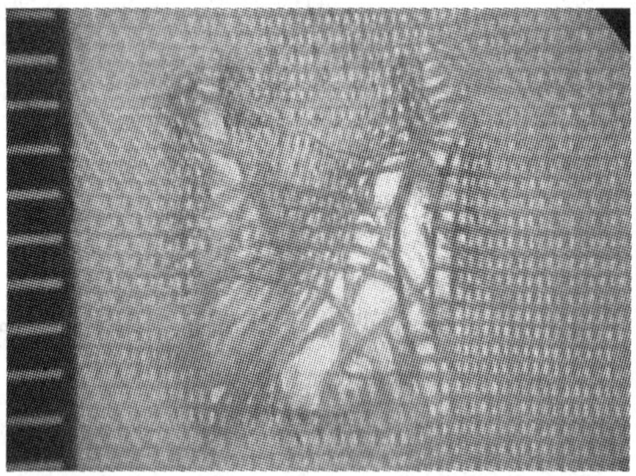

Fig. 7 The bullet holes of 9 mm police wheel gun

4 The exit shape

4. 1 The high speed bullets exits

In the experiment, the contact speed of high - speed bullet impact on the fabric are: 81 rifle is 720 m/s, 79 - micro submachine gun is 500 m/s, 54 - type pistol muzzle velocity of 405 m/s, significantly higher than the literature experimental[5] results in the curve of critical impact velocity (i. e. higher than 350 m/sec). Large difference between the impact speed of the different kinds of guns, so the rolled yarns at the bullet hole exit port form show obvious difference, reflected well by 79 micro submachine gun and 54 pistol which use the same kinds bullets. 81 rifle and two other firearms' bullet holes well represented the exit bullet holes form caused by the different shapes of the bullet.

Observe the bullet hole exit formed by high – speed 56 rifle pointed bullets under the transmitted light, the soot around the bullet hole margins in the edge is well ruled out (see Fig. 8). "Clover" – shaped bullet holes, small radius circle appears on four corners due to the tearing effect, yarns near the four corners pushing each other visibly, the center yarns long and sparse. Observed from the side of the bullet hole exit, the whole yarns shows "crown" shape, rolled clear, and each yarn are large bending (see Fig. 9).

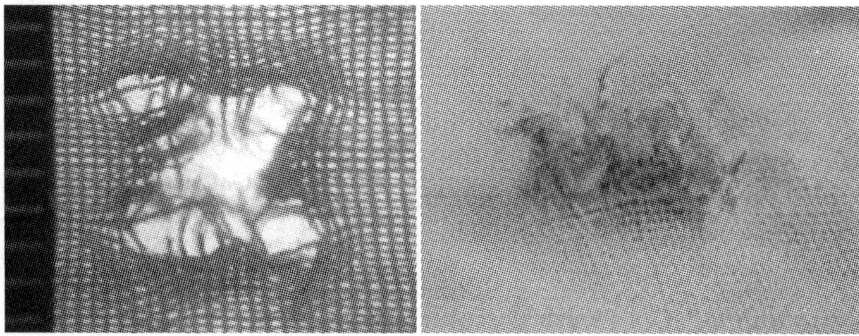

Fig. 8 The exit shape of 81 rifle pointed bullet hole

Fig. 9 Observed from the side of 81 rifle pointed bullet exit hole

Bullet holes formed by high speed blunt bullets fired for 79 micro submachine guns and 54 pistols, the form of exit bullet hole show the same characters and significant difference as well (see Fig. 10). The impact of high – speed 79 – micro submachine gun bullets forms a larger area of the rectangle defect in the internal of the bullet holes, very short broken yarns appears on the margin of the bullet holes yarn valgus, and no yarn in the center of the bullet hole. The lower speed bullet shot by 54 type pistols only form a smaller defect in the center of the bullet holes, the impact scattered fibers in the yarn into fluff shape, and the yarns show a high degree of transparency under the transmitted light. Observed from the side of the 79 micro submachine gun bullet hole exit (see Fig. 11), the whole valgus yarns are hollow cylindrical – shaped, yarns perpendicular to the fabric, no single bent yarn. The degree of the valgus yarns condition lessened clearly in the bullet hole formed by 54 – style pistol.

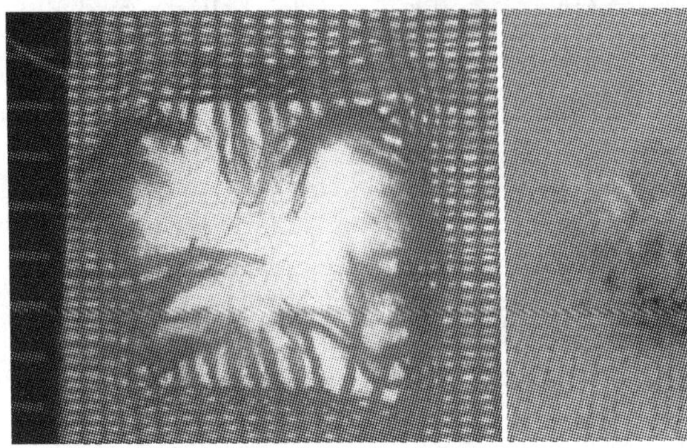

Fig. 10 The exit shape of 79 – micro submachine gun blunt bullet hole

Fig. 11 Observed from the side of 79 – micro submachine gun blunt bullet exit hole

4. 2 The low speed bullets exits

In the experiment, the contact speed of low – speed bullet impact on the fabric are: 92 pistol is 322 m/s, 59 – pistol is 308 m/s, 77 – type pistol muzzle velocity of 310 m/s and 9mm police wheel gun is 202 s/m, all lower than critical impact velocity (i. e. higher than 350 m/sec). Except the 9mm police wheel gun, all kinds of muzzle velocity are close to each other, and because they have the same speed, the different of the bullet holes exit would reflect the shape of the bullet. While because of the special speed and the bullet of the 9mm police wheel gun, the bullet holes exit of the certain pistol is special.

Bullet hole formed by pointed domed bullet 92 – style pistol, (see Fig. 12), the exit was "Four Mans Star" – shape, the internal yarns are relatively longer and to the center, and little yarns at the four corners, and more yarns in the center. Observed from the side, the ends of the yarn are neat and the overall shape is like the "pyramid" (see Fig. 13).

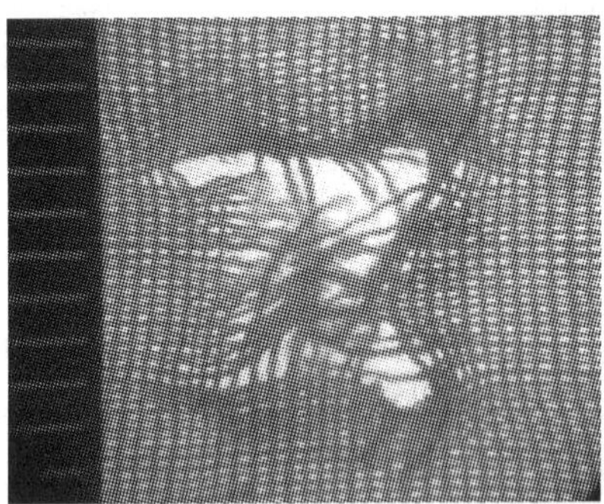

Fig. 12 The exit shape of 92 pistol point domed bullet hole

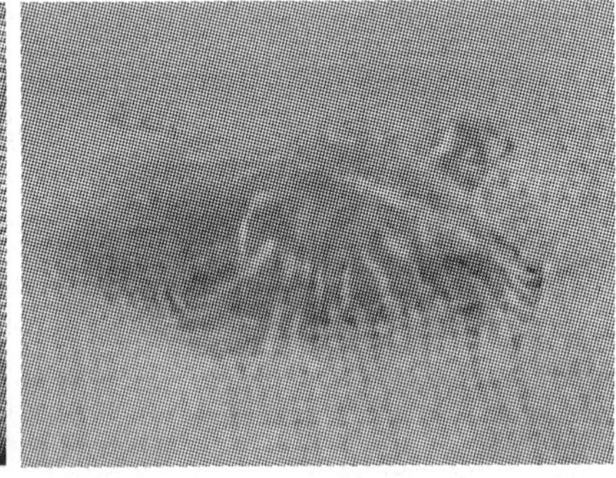

Fig. 13 Observed from the side of 92 pistol point domed bullet exit hole

Bullet hole formed by blunt domed bullet 64 – style pistol (see Fig. 14), the exit was square, no obvious defect in the center of the bullet hole, broken yarns are neat and intertwines in the center of the bullet hole, no reduction in the number of the yarns. Observed from the side, the yarn low – lying bunched in whole (see Fig. 15).

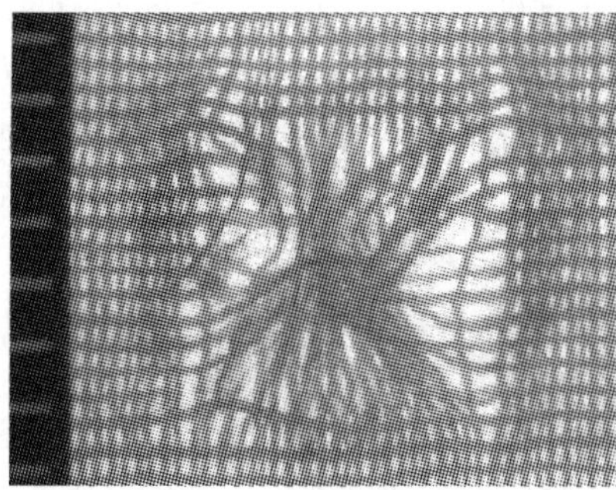

Fig. 14 The exit shape of 77 pistol blunt bullet hole

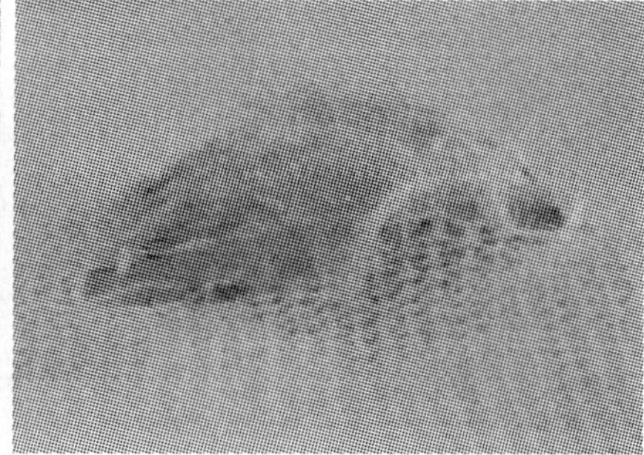

Fig. 15 Observed from the side of 77 pistol blunt bullet exit hole

Bullet hole formed by hemisphere bullet 59 – style pistol (see Fig. 16), the exit is rectangle, the yarns are bent torn due to the strong Hemispherical projectiles pulling, the maximum contact area with the fabric and the bullet of rotation friction, the four corners of the bullet holes are slight tear, a large of yarns defect in the center of the bullet hole, broken yarns are neat and intertwines in the margin of the bullet hole, no reduction in the number of the yarns. Observed from the side, the yarn low – lying bunched little in whole (see Fig. 17).

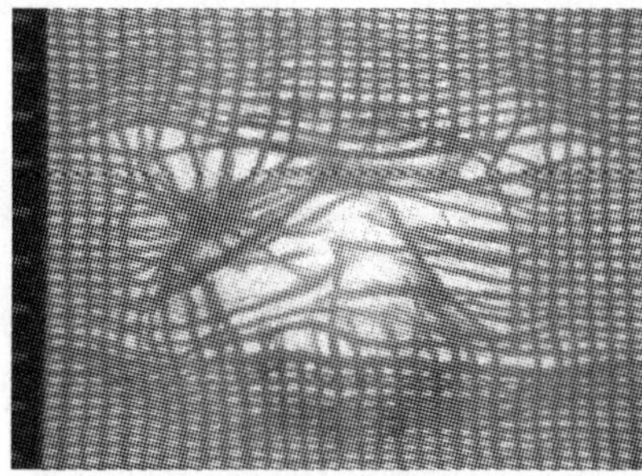

Fig. 16 The exit shape of 59 pistol hemisphere bullet hole

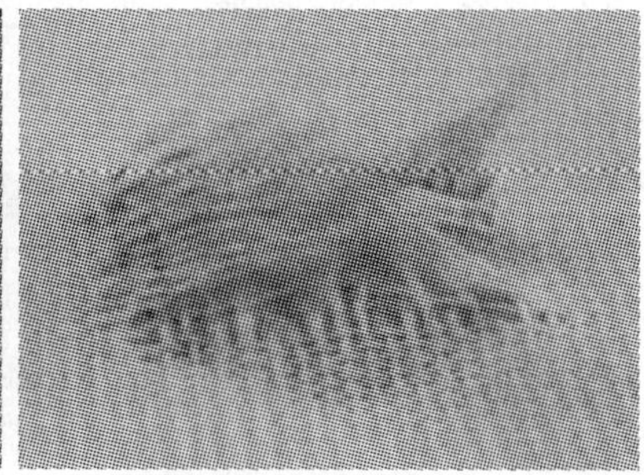

Fig. 17 Observed from the side of 59 pistol hemisphere bullet exit hole

Bullet hole formed by flat bullet 9mm wheel gun (see Fig. 18), the exit was rectangle, the yarns on the margin of the bullet hole broke firstly due to the shearing action of the edge of the bullet. Because the impact action are not high, yarns on the one side of the bullet hole break and release the energy, the other side of the yarn does not reach the fracture threshold is still connected. When the warp and weft yarn density of the fabric is not equal, in the low density direction, both sides of the yarns break severely, in the high density direction, the yarn is only broken at one side. In this condition, both sides of the bullet hole defect obviously, but the center yarns are dense. Observe from the side, the broken ends are neat, sloping shape in whole (see Fig. 19).

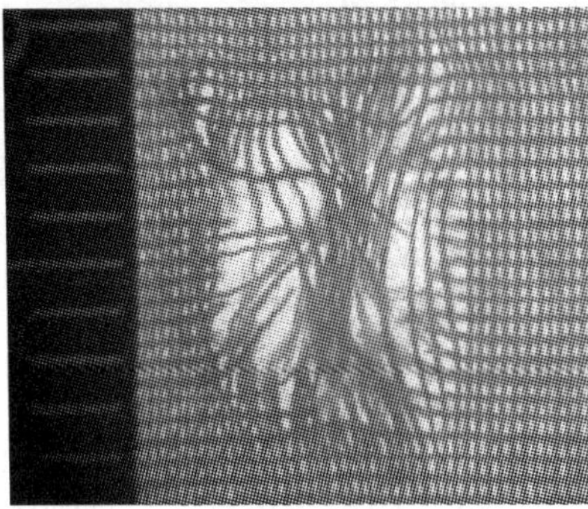

Fig. 18 The exit shape of 9mm wheel gun flat bullet hole

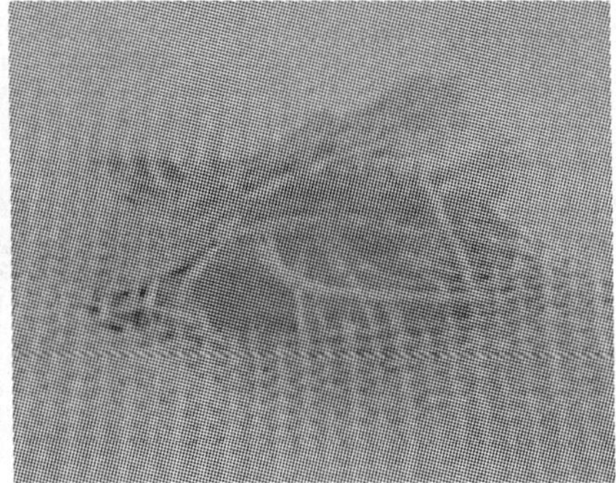

Fig. 19 Observed from the side of 9mm wheel gun flat bullet exit hole

By means of the observation of ballistic impact traces, the regulation of shape, which summarized by us, accord with theoretical analysis result in high degree and the influences of the ballistic impact trace, which reflect the relationship between bullet shape and impact speed, are clearly. In addition, the soot, stick on the edge of bullet hole, become different by the change of the model of gun and bullet. The reason for this situation is the change of gun propellant. The relativity of ballistic impact traces on the plain woven fabric and the kinds of the bullets , successfully control the number of influence factor and prove favorable situation for the analysis the relationship between bullet and ballistic impact traces.

5 Conclusion

The result of theoretical analysis and experimental observation shows that the ballistic impact trace has relevant relationship to the impact speed and the shape of bullet on the plain woven fabric.

Referring to the speed of bullet, the higher the impact speed is, the more defects could be appear in the center of bullet hole. More and more broken yarns are appeared, accompanied by the increased disassembly of yarns and serious yarn eversion of the bullet exit hole.

Referring to the shape of bullet, ends of fabric , broken by the pointed rifle bullet , gather in the central of the bullet hole intensively and the longer broken fabrics are quite few, which get close to the middle of each edge of bullet hole. Blunt bullet could contact more yarns at the moment of impact. Therefore, it may cause more serious defect or crispation. Flat head bullet could use its edge to shear yarns and break these yarn at the edge of bullet hole. The impact of flat head bullet has enough abilities to impact more pieces of fabric and make more defect.

With regard to different model firearm, shot bullets have obviously different to the collection of shape and speed. This phenomenon could prove enough requirement to distinguish the model of firearm and their bullet by the shape of ballistic impact traces on the plain woven fabric. In addition, the soot, stick on the edge of bullet hole, also have relativity to the kind of bulle.

建置情报导向犯罪现场数据库之研究

范兆兴 * 李承龙 ** 杨佳龙 ***

一、前 言

笔者从事第一线现场勘察（crime – scene investigation）工作多年，最常出勤勘察的案件以住宅窃盗案类为最高；从警政署发布网络上的2012年警政统计资料观察窃盗犯罪盛行率，发现民众遭受住宅窃盗犯罪威胁几率相当高，举例来说，以2012年我国台湾地区窃盗案件发生99 896件（统计数据来源包含重大窃盗与汽车、机车及普通窃盗）、移送检察官起诉窃盗嫌疑犯人数计38 637人，每名窃盗嫌疑犯平均犯下2.58件窃盗案件。对多数民众而言，警察侦破重大刑案等新闻话题，并无大感受；但是，对曾经遭受侵入住宅窃盗、心爱汽车或是平日代步机车被偷走的被害民众而言，最迫切的希望就是警方能迅速将小偷逮捕归案。

住窃案件多为陌生人犯罪，犯罪人多为经验老手，与被害人鲜少接触，现场所遗留迹证以及目击者信息较少，不易连结到嫌疑人，破案率相对低。又即便单一案件连结并逮捕犯罪人，但其通常不会将其犯案赃物藏于住处等地，无法直接搜索而查扣本案或其他案件相关赃物；在我国台湾地区现行“刑法”之一罪一罚法律架构下，嫌疑人通常仅就有直接证据案件加以承认（或全盘否认），未有更积极与进一步侦查作为，导致仅能就少数案件移送、起诉与审判，除无法发挥刑事司法系统发现真实的功能，犯罪人往往因刑度不高，未能发挥阻吓效果（施志鸿、杨诏凯，2012）。

施志鸿与杨诏凯（2012）认为连续住窃案件一具常业与连续性质，因此有犯案稳定、区域性、犯案手法固定、一定的销赃管道或模式等特性。因此笔者认为可引进案件连结（Case linkage）与地缘剖绘（Geographic profiling）等国外侦查技术，从勘察刑案现场开始→采集具有个化迹证（individual evidence）→分类嫌犯之作案手法（Modus operandi）→从地区警察分局端建置“刑案现场勘察报告数据库”（Crime Scene Investigation Report Database）搜寻相似作案手法之特定嫌疑人，并且在锁定嫌疑人后，持续掌握其模式与现场搜证等概念，提出连续住窃案件主动式侦查策略（proactive Investigation strategy）。

二、建置情报导向犯罪现场数据库之历程

从国内、外犯罪学（criminology）对于慢性犯罪人（chronic offender）研究发现，

* 范兆兴，警察大学犯罪防治研究所博士，现任台南市政府警察局刑事鉴识中心警务员，Email：a621227@gmail.com.

** 李承龙，现任台湾警察专科学校刑事警察科助理教授。

*** 杨佳龙，现任台湾警察专科学校行政警察科。警察大学犯罪防治研究所，台北，Email：a621227@gmail.com.

美国学者 Wolfgang 研究发现 6% 的犯罪人（如连续暴力犯罪）重复犯下 51.9% 的暴力犯罪案件；英国复制类似研究模式发现 6% 慢性犯罪人，犯下 49% 的犯罪案件。笔者从上述研究文献发现多数住宅窃盗犯罪者就是慢性犯罪人，惯窃从走出监狱第一步开始，负责第一线执法警察就准备接听民众报案，而我们鉴识人员（forensic specialists）就准备出勤进行现场勘察工作。

笔者自 2012 年 8 月至 12 月追踪辖区“剪断铁窗侵入住宅大盗”计 12 件窃案，经分析窃嫌作案手法（M. O）为“作案时段为深夜、从被害人住宅后侧使用破坏工具剪断铁窗（多为圆柱形）、作案时习惯穿棉质手套、现场地面仅留类似袜子印痕、窃取客厅被害人皮包内财物（容易得手有价值物品）及移动周边监视器”等签名特征（signature）犯罪手法。案经，项目小组将上述住宅窃盗案现场采获指纹经送验结果：为被害人所有或经输入指纹数据库比对未发现相符者。

为此，项目小组为有效解决侦办连续住宅窃盗之困境、建立智慧化与云端化之资源共享平台；让各个主官（管）经由计算机等数字设备监督、控管各类刑案侦办进度，以达科学化管理之目标。

有关建置符合地区特性之“情报导向犯罪现场数据库”之优点，如后：

1. 辖区警察分局各级主官（管）经由计算机等数字设备监督、控管各类刑案侦办进度，以达科学化管理之目标。

2. 各个侦查人员借由“情报导向犯罪现场数据库”之资源共享平台，掌握现场证物鉴验进度。

3. 建立“案件链接”科学化办案模式，举例而言，笔者于 2012 年 3 月中旬查获惯窃陈某某到辖区以“一字型螺丝起子”破坏住宅大门、行窃过程均穿戴手套，所幸笔者使用“鞋印线性特殊光源”在被害人卧室木质地板发现陈嫌所穿“LEINO”特殊字母之鞋印痕。案经，笔者比对“情报导向犯罪现场数据库”发现陈嫌分别涉及多起住宅窃盗，如照片 1。

4. 为因应刑事诉讼法之“交互诘问”与“无罪推定法则”制度，鉴识人员势必因案莅庭参与作证几率增高；藉由建置完善“情报导向犯罪现场数据库”与档案管理制度，届时侦查人员仅需透过具有“安全稽核机制”网络调阅承办案件之相关现场勘察及证物鉴识报告，将提升办公时效。

又从地缘剖绘技术适用连续侵入住宅窃盗案，分析潜在犯罪者地理环境脉络，搜集一系列的案发地点详加剖析，以推测歹徒的可能住处，甚至预估再度犯案的时段及位置的理论来观察。推动犯罪数据库之策略，可以整合已经开发完成各种数据库（例如指纹鉴验数据库、DNA 鉴验数据库）功效，并可另辟有别传统侦查模式的新兴侦查途径，相关具体概念如下（情报导向犯罪现场数据库之架构，详细情况如图 1 所示）：

1. 线索来源：运用迹证鉴定信息结合现场勘察所得犯罪模式等信息，藉以规划、建构本辖鉴识线索数据库。

2. 运用概念：提供侦查“以案锁人、以人追案”之功效。

3. 预期成效：扩充刑案侦破能量，达到证据充分、扩大侦破、羁押在所、防制再犯等四大面向。

4. 线索源数据库别：①指纹鉴验数据库，②DNA 鉴验数据库；③鞋印（现场、涉嫌人）数据库；④现场勘察犯罪模式分析数据库。

. 信息系统：①刑案知识库（前科素行与共犯结构），②刑案纪录表（已未破案件与其他犯罪手法分析）。

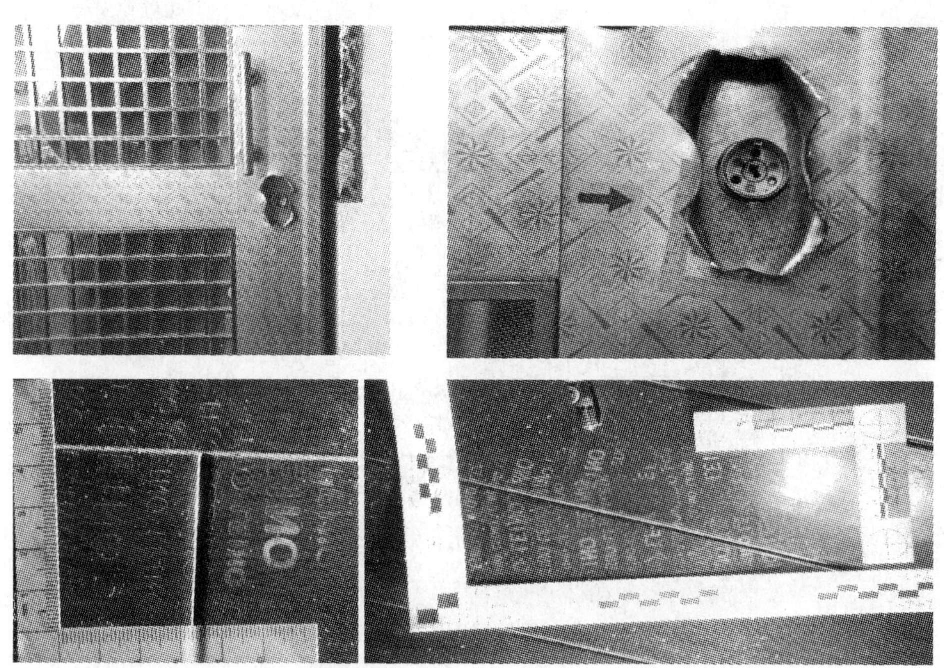

照片 1　笔者利用情报导向犯罪数据库侦破陈○○连续侵入住宅窃盗案

综上所述，鉴识科学可以广泛地定义为系运用各种自然科学知识与方法、以鉴定物证及重建犯罪现场以及提供信息与方向给执法人员的一门学科，其涵盖的范围广大。笔者即利用情报导向犯罪现场数据库，分析比对出专门侵入住宅之王姓窃盗集团作案手法（M. O）——“两人一组共乘窃取机车→作案时段为深夜（凌晨 2 时至 4 时）→挑选不同被害人机车至其他处所行窃”等签名特征（Signature）作案手法与 2013 年辖内吴某某等 7 件住宅遭侵入窃盗之作案手法相似，并利用现场鞋印以巧妙地连结王姓嫌犯与台南市多起住宅窃盗现场之鞋印相似，再使用追踪跟监侦查技巧，成功地逮捕王姓、许姓及黄姓嫌犯，如照片 2。

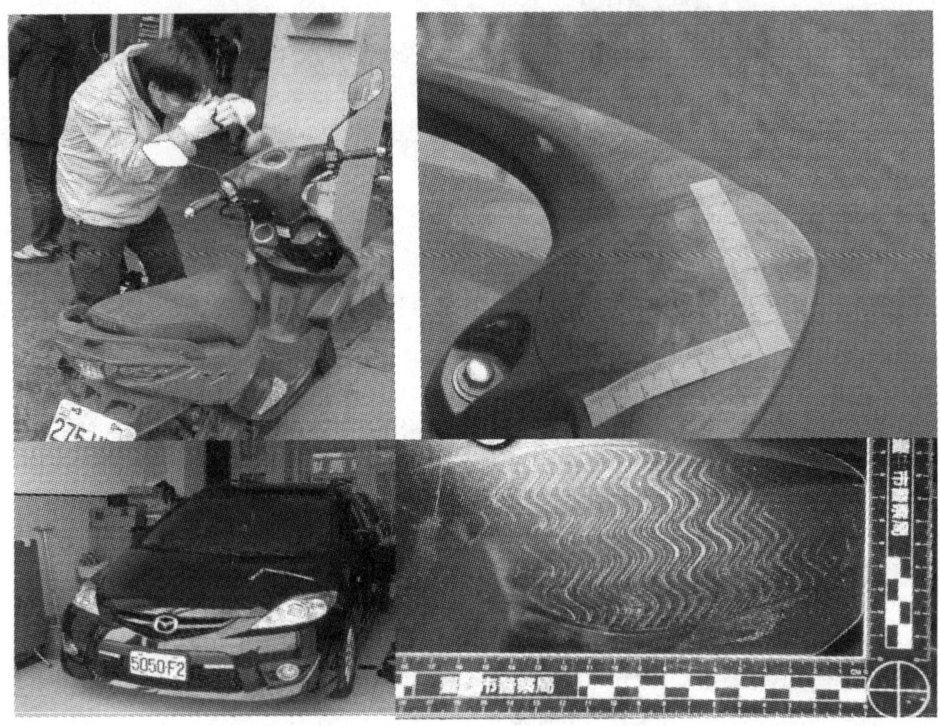

照片 2 笔者利用情报导向犯罪数据库侦破王姓连续侵入住宅窃盗集团

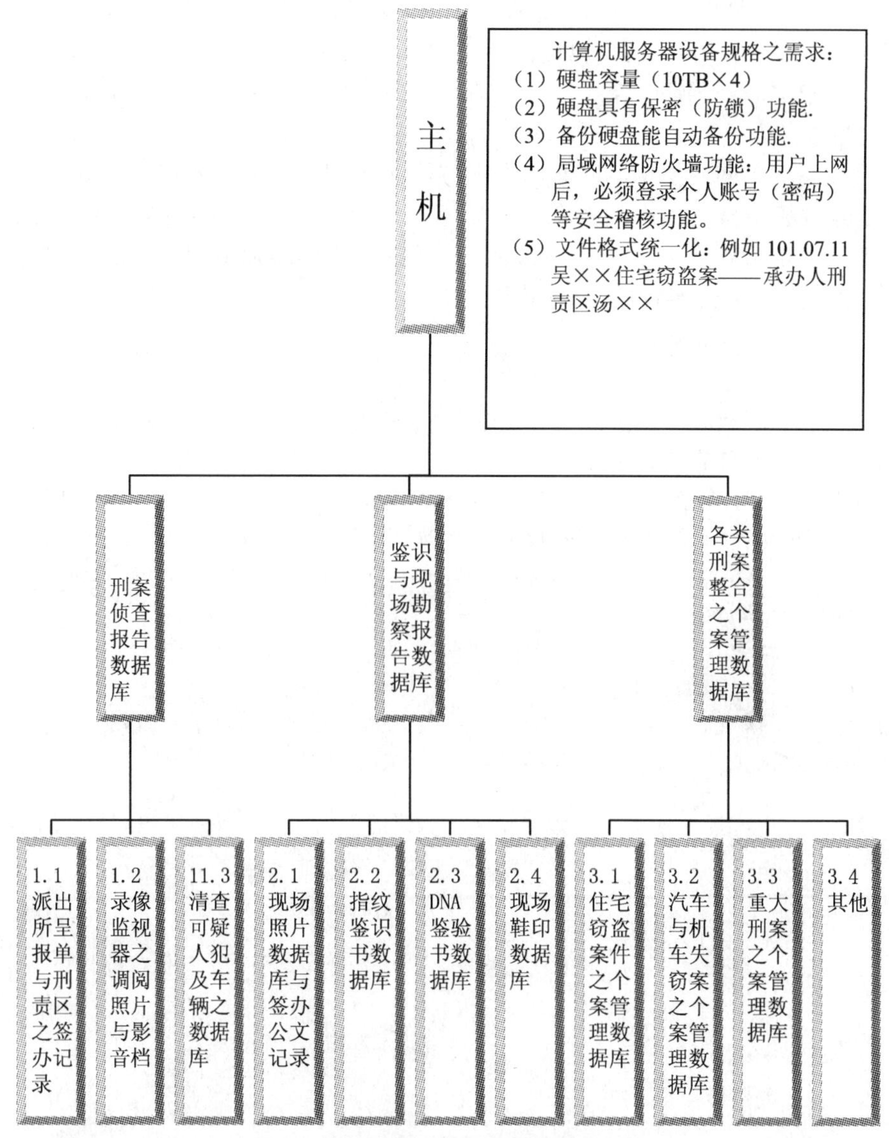

图1　情报导向犯罪现场数据库之架构

三、结语

“家”对每个人可说是“安全避风港”亦是“象征不容许外人侵入精神堡垒”，因此，对有住宅窃盗经历的被害人心理而言，在家无法获得安全感，夜晚就寝前仍需来回察看住家各个角落，才能勉强入眠；这种担惊受怕经验就如同个人的精神堡垒遭受强暴，将永远留下不可抹灭的创伤记忆。笔者曾经勘察一件住宅窃盗案，被害屋主的女儿，就亲身经历小偷从侵入大门到任意搜刮家中财物之后扬长离去完整犯罪过程；笔者从调查访谈被害屋主开始，就发现这名小女孩因害怕全身发抖，一直到完成现场勘察采证工作，准备返回实验室进行证物鉴识时，这名小女孩依旧是面容充满惊恐。这种被害经验、感受就会像感冒病毒在原本安静小区蔓延展开，就算未遭受小偷光顾的住户，也会对于居家环境是否安全产生疑虑，治安不好的印象逐渐扩大小区甚至区域层级。

此外，面对这种以现场迹证为基础，结合罪犯独特作案手法发展出“案件连结”侦查技术，面临下列几项挑战、瓶颈，值得未来有志研究犯罪剖绘学者持续关心议题：

1. 犯罪数据源正确性、发展自动检核刑案侦查报告数据库与鉴识及现场勘察报告数据库之检索技术。

2. 发展跨区、横向协调不同部门之标准作业流程，达到犯罪情资充分交流。由于侦查人员经常只为自己辖内的警察工作。不过，犯罪行为不可能仅在自己辖内发生，罪犯将越区至其他警察辖区犯案。侦查人员如果只分析辖内类似案件的犯罪行为，将无法与其他辖区的犯罪案件串并连结。

参考文献

[1] 施志鸿、杨诏凯：《连续住宅窃盗犯罪侦查思维——以主动式侦查模式为核心》，警察大学举办 2012 年台湾鉴识科学研讨会。

[2] Ribaux, O. & Zingg, C., “Intelligence - Led Crime Scene Processing, Part 2: Intelligence And Crime Scene Examination”, *Forensic Science International*, 2010, 199, pp. 63 ~ 71.

[3] Rossy, Q. & Ribaux, O., “Integrating Forensic Information in A Crime Intelligence Database”, *Forensic Science International*, 2012.

[4] Tonkin, M. & Bond, J., “Behavioural Case Linkage With Solved and Unsolved Crimes”, *Forensic Science International*, 2012, 222, pp. 146 ~ 153.

[5] Marie, M. & Roux, C., “The Use of Forensic Case Data in Intelligence - Led Policing: The Example of Drug Profiling”, *Forensic Science International*, 2013, 226, pp. 1 ~ 9.

鉴定人出庭作证相关问题及对策探讨 *

郭兆明 ** 常 林 ***

2012年《刑事诉讼法》（以下简称“新《刑诉法》”）和《民事诉讼法》（以下简称“新《民诉法》”）相继修订并发布，两部诉讼法都将鉴定人出庭作证提到了前所未有的高度，从要求到承担的后果均作了相应的规定，如均规定法院通知鉴定人出庭后，鉴定人如无正当理由拒绝出庭的，相关证据不予采纳。新《民诉法》第78条中还规定了支付鉴定费用的当事人可以要求返还鉴定费用。鉴定人出庭作证对案件审判及顺利解决具有积极意义，但从统计数据及笔者个人实际经验看，鉴定人出庭的案件占总案件的比例率很低，根据司法部司法鉴定管理局2008～2011年统计数据显示，出庭案件占所有受理案件总量的比例不足1%；2008～2011年，全国面向社会服务的司法鉴定机构共受理各类刑事和民事案件共2 697 187件，出庭的案件有47 682件，占该类型案件的1.77%。[1][2][3][4] 据江苏徐州市中级人民法院统计2004～2006年审理的案件中，通知鉴定人出庭作证的案件占所有鉴定证据案件的比例4%以内，刑事、民事、行政案件所占比例分别为1.49%，3.45%，3.13%。[5] 据河南省鄢陵人民法院2008～2010年共审理各类案件4105件，鉴定人出庭作证的案件仅有4件。[6] 由于鉴定人出庭的案件相对较少，多数法官和鉴定人都缺少相关经验，甚至有些鉴定人和法官到退休都未曾经历过鉴定人出庭的案件，尤其是中小城市的基层法院。就笔者所在机构而言，出庭最多的当属法医临床鉴定中医疗纠纷鉴定、损伤程度鉴定案件，以及文书鉴定案件。就诉讼案件类型而言，涉及人身伤害或死亡的刑事案件，涉及医疗纠纷、标的额度较大的民事诉讼案件，出庭率较高。有关出庭作证方面目前在全国层面尚无专门性规范文件，不同法院、甚至同一法院不同法官针对鉴定人出庭质证掌握的规则也不尽相同，因此有必要汇总并分析目前在鉴定人出庭作证方面存在的问题，并制定相关规范，以确保鉴定人出庭作证效果和该项规定顺利实施。

一、鉴定人出庭作证相关问题

目前针对司法鉴定人出庭作证的研究更多是从制度架构层面分析，从实践过程中总结的具体问题进行分析的文献相对较少。笔者根据文献及经验大致罗列了以下具体问题：

1. 通知程序的多样化。法律条款中只是规定法院应通知鉴定人，但在通知形式和时间方面并无规定，因此通知程序方面存在多样化的问题。主要表现在①通知方式多样化，口头、书面通知均存在，且多数法官是在确定了开庭时间后才通知鉴定人出庭，

* 本文系科技部十二五支撑项目司法鉴定关键技术子课题（项目号：2012B02－2）研究成果。

** 郭兆明，副主任法医师，中国政法大学讲师。Email：gzmng@ sina. com。

*** 常林，中国政法大学证据科学研究院院长。

事前就开庭时间多未征求鉴定人意见。甚至有的法官确定开庭时间后不允许鉴定人改期。②通知时间随意性。有的法院在开庭前1周通知，笔者曾遇到法院在开庭前2天通知出庭的情况。新《刑诉法》中目前规定为开庭前3日应送达出庭通知，但笔者感觉给出的时间偏短，鉴定人出庭作证不同于一般证人，一般证人只需要把自己的客观感受陈述即可，而鉴定人需要重新分析案件材料、汇总可能的问题并准备相关材料和文献等工作，部分案件出庭可能在鉴定文书出具半年，甚至一年以后，留给鉴定人准备材料的时间过短不利于法庭质证效果。

2. 鉴定人拒绝出庭问题。鉴定人拒绝出庭时有发生，据江苏徐州市中级人民法院统计，2004~2006年，民事案件通知鉴定人出庭作证而实际到庭作证的比例为39.44%。究其原因大致有以下几种：①以未支付出庭费用为理由的，目前缺少相关统计数据，但笔者考虑该因素可能是主要因素之一。该因素也是目前争议较大的方面，有些专家学者认为出庭费用已包含在鉴定费之中，不应当再收取出庭费，但实践过程中，尤其是外地案件，交通费就远高于鉴定费，更别提误工费、食宿费等。如出庭费用问题不能顺利解决，一定程度上还会阻碍出庭率。②鉴定人畏惧出庭，主动拒绝出庭的，也是主要因素之一。③其他原因，如工作繁忙、路途遥远等。④拒绝出庭的追责机制缺乏，助长鉴定人主动拒绝出庭的比例。大部分鉴定人还是能够积极应对出庭请求，也能够配合法庭审判工作，如何更大程度地激发鉴定人出庭的积极性，需要管理部门研究和制定相关措施。

3. 出庭的鉴定人指定问题。按照目前法律法规中的规定，同一鉴定事项通常应至少2人共同出具报告，从出庭作证的本意而言，应当由出具报告的鉴定人同时出庭来说明和解释。但实践中存在以下几种情况：①机构指定其中1个鉴定人作为代表或本案全部鉴定人参加；②机构指定非本案鉴定人代表参加；③机构指定本案鉴定人和其他非本案鉴定人员共同出庭。对第一种形式从法律层面没有问题，但如果鉴定人之间有不同意见的，应全部出庭并分别询问。第二种情形应当不允许，除非诉讼参与人、法官、鉴定机构等均同意。第三种情形中非本案鉴定人员应不允许参加出庭过程，包括费用承担方面也不应考虑。一般情况下，只有本案的鉴定人即报告中签字的鉴定人才有资格出庭作证，其他人员应当属于无权出庭。

4. 出庭收费、收费标准及方式等。“出庭费是否应当收”，“收费标准如何界定，应当包含哪些费用”，“谁来收取费用”，“什么时候收取”，这些方面均应当有统一规定，但实践中只有极少数地方可能有参照规定，如青海省黄南州中级人民法院出台的《关于统一委托鉴定、拍卖和通知鉴定人出庭支付费用标准的通知》中规定：“通知鉴定人出庭作证，鉴定人在指定日期出庭作证所发生的误工补贴可暂以每天或每次100~150元为标准，异地出庭交通费、住宿费按照国家机关工作人员出差标准支付”。2012年浙江省物价局、浙江省司法厅发布《关于进一步规范司法鉴定出庭作证费的通知》（浙价服（2012）295号）规定：司法鉴定人出庭作证费标准统一为本地（设区市行政区域内）500元/人·次：外地（设区市行政区域外）700元/人·次，司法鉴定人赴外地出庭作证的住宿费、交通费参照我省机关事业单位工作人员差旅费标准另行收取。在实践过程中也存在鉴定人出庭，但未能收到出庭费的情况。其实费用承担主体不明也是出庭费用得不到保障的主要原因，民事案件出庭申请通常由鉴定不利的一方申请，该费用到底是垫付还是最终就由申请方支付，在法律层面无相关规定。刑事案件出庭，目前多数法院遵循由法院承担的原则，也有一些由申请人承担，对刑事案件出庭费承担如何把握也值得思考，既要保障庭审顺利进行，同时也要防止出庭申请权被滥用。

5. 多个鉴定人出庭作证顺序问题。在多个鉴定人出庭作证顺序方面也比较混乱，有些法院按照证人作证的规则要求鉴定人分别询问，来看多个鉴定人之间是否有差异，或者说防止串供，有些法院要求鉴定人同时出庭接受询问。第一种方式一般情况下应该不适用于鉴定人，除非多个鉴定人意见不一致，才适用分别询问方式。因为鉴定意见是鉴定人集中讨论和决定的，是集体的智慧，通过分别询问的方式不利于鉴定人出庭效果的实现，也没有任何实质意义。

6. 承诺如实作证程序。新《刑诉法》第211条中规定“证人、鉴定人作证前，应当保证向法庭如实提供证言、说明鉴定意见，并在保证书上签名”，但在《民诉法》中尚无此方面的规定，因此在实践过程中各个法官掌握如实作证承诺书签署方面也不太一致。从法律层面应当有签署如实作证承诺书的程序，既是从法律层面也是从道德层面对鉴定人进行约束。

7. 鉴定人在出庭作证时就座位置的尴尬问题。由于鉴定人出庭作证一直未得到法院的重视，因此在目前法庭中根据未设置鉴定人出庭作证的就座位置，尤其是法庭较小的，笔者与所在单位的同事可以说在许多位置上都坐过，与原告、被告、法官或旁听人员一起落座，甚至与犯罪嫌疑人一起落座，能够单独设置鉴定人出庭位置的极少。所以司法行政管理部门应向法院提出建议，确保鉴定人的最基本尊严，在法庭中专门设置鉴定人出庭的位置，并保证一些基本的设施，如桌子和椅子，以确保法庭审判顺利进行。

8. 质询鉴定人的顺序问题。在法庭质证过程中，通常是由申请方先进行询问，再由另一方询问，第三人及法官如有必要也可以询问；有的法院遵循原告、被告、第三人、法官（民事案件）的顺序。实践中也存在支付出庭费用方询问后，法官不允许另一方发问的情况，原因是其未支付出庭费用。当然，这个问题也值得商榷，其实还是费用负担的问题。为了提高出庭效果，出庭费应当作为诉讼费，根据审判结果、责任比例情况进行分配，既保证了法庭审判的完整性，又保证了鉴定人的权益。

9. 专门知识人员出庭问题。专门知识的人或者称专家辅助人出庭其实在2001年《最高人民法院关于民事诉讼证据的若干规定》中已有表述，只是这次在新《刑诉法》和《民诉法》中明确表述和规定了相关条款。但目前就专门知识人员出庭问题还缺少相关配套程序和制度方面规定，专门知识人员在法庭中的地位如何定位，专门知识人员的发言或意见是否可作为证据使用，专门知识人员的意见能否否定司法鉴定意见，谁有资格可以做专门知识人员出庭等问题均无定论，应该说专门知识人员出庭有利于促进司法鉴定的发展，但如何得当使用非常关键，如果混乱发展可能结果会适得其反。2001年《最高人民法院关于民事诉讼证据的若干规定》出台专家辅助人规定以后之所以未能得到推广，一个非常重要的原因就在于缺少相关配套规定。

10. 人身安全问题。鉴定人出庭作证的人身安全有时难以保证，尤其鉴定结果对其不利的一方，鉴定人被当事人谩骂或威胁时有发生，甚至发生个人鉴定人被当事人打击报复的问题。

11. 法官驾驭庭审能力的问题。法官是法庭的裁判者和负责人，法官庭审掌控能力非常关键，法官应具有绝对的权威，有时当事人反复询问同样问题，或者当事人在庭审中大吵大闹，法官能否及时制止很重要，其次法官庭审的节奏把握也是庭审顺利进行的关键。但在目前的法治环境下，有些法官惧怕被投诉、信访，往往不会主动制止当事人的一些不良行为，也助长了当事人对庭审的干扰。

二、鉴定人出庭作证相关对策

鉴定人出庭作证之所以出现这么多的问题，分析其原因主要是缺少相关出庭的统一规定或程序，各地法院或不同法官掌握各异；司法鉴定管理部门也缺少有关鉴定人出庭作证配套的制度或程序，导致出庭作证的工作无法顺利执行。目前在网络中能够查阅到极个别地方出台了相关规则，如：《北京市高级人民法院北京市司法局关于司法鉴定人出庭作证的规定》（京高法发［2008］133 号）、《青海省高级人民法院关于鉴定人出庭作证若干问题的规定》（青高法［2011］106 号），以及安徽省高级人民法院安徽省司法厅《安徽省司法鉴定人出庭作证规则》、安徽省黄山市中级人民法院和司法局、广西梧州市司法局。应该说在国家层面缺少相关完善法律法规或制度程序是产生诸多问题的根本原因。有关部门应尽快出台完善的配套制度和措施，确保鉴定人出庭作证工作能够顺利开展。在此提出以下建议供参考。

通知程序方面。鉴于鉴定人出庭作证需要提前准备相关材料和文献等，法院应在开庭日前 5 个工作日送达出庭通知书。当然，也可以先行口头通知再补送书面通知。通知中应指明需要出庭的鉴定人姓名、鉴定文书编号、被鉴定人姓名、出庭事由、到庭时间、地点，通知出庭联系人、联系方式。此外，非本案鉴定人应不能受委托出庭作证，除非诉讼各方、法官、鉴定人、鉴定机构均同意。

出庭费用方面。鉴于出庭费用方面存在争议，建议相关部门尽快明确出庭费相关规定，确定是否应当收，收费标准。但笔者认为应当收取出庭费用，费用标准可由各省、直辖市或自治区发改委相关部门协同司法行政管理部门共同出台，公安机关、检察机关鉴定人属于国家公务员，其出庭属于工作职责范围，可不收取出庭费用。费用方面应考虑误工费、食宿费、交通费等，误工费标准应考虑职称、开庭质证的时间等因素，费用是按天、按次还是按小时计算也比较重要。民事案件、行政案件出庭费收取方面应由法院在开庭前先行预收，由申请方先行垫付，最终费用的承担按照审判结果分配；刑事案件出庭费应当由国家设立专项经费予以保障，由专项经费支付。如果申请方拒绝预交和支付出庭费用的，鉴定人有权拒绝出庭作证，且不影响该案件正常审理。

鉴定人拒绝出庭方面。一方面，尽量出台措施激励鉴定人积极参与出庭作证，另一方面，应尽快出台在什么情况下可以拒绝出庭或不出庭，不能到庭出庭的应考虑通过其他方式对质疑进行答复，如远程视频、书面回复等形式，尽可能保证相关的质疑得到及时、合理的解释和说明。如有下述情况，鉴定人可以不出庭作证，例如，①两名以上的司法鉴定人共同作出一致鉴定意见，已有一名司法鉴定人出庭，并向人民法院提交了其他鉴定人书面授权委托书的；②司法鉴定人因自然灾害、意外事件等不可抗力无法出庭的；③司法鉴定人因突发疾病、重病或者行为不便等难以出庭的。再者，鉴定人无正当理由拒绝出庭的，应从国家层面出台鉴定机构和鉴定人的惩罚措施，根据不同原因出台各层次惩罚措施，尤其司法鉴定行政管理部门应出台配套的惩罚机制和措施。

鉴定人在法庭中位置及人身安全保障方面。今后，鉴定人出庭作证可能常态化，有条件的法院应在法庭中设立专门鉴定人席位，鉴定人席位应独立于原告、被告和法官等，体现其独立性、公正性职业特点。如法院条件有限，应考虑在一些空间较大的法庭设置鉴定人出庭席位，毕竟出庭的案件还是占比较小的比例，遇有需要出庭的案件可调整到该法庭。设立专门席位也一定程度上可以保障鉴定人的人身安全。另外，从人身安全保障方面还应考虑在鉴定人身份核实环节，不应要求鉴定人提供家庭地址，只需提供鉴定人工作单位、执业资质、职称和职务即可，涉及鉴定人个人隐私的内容不应提供。对于涉黑案件的鉴定人出庭作证，除对鉴定人保护外，还应对鉴定人家庭及近亲属进行保护。鉴定人保护机制的建立可以让鉴定人无所顾忌地参加出庭作证，也有利于出庭作证的顺利实施。

鉴定人出庭质证顺序方面。鉴定意见是由鉴定人集体讨论形成，出庭作证的人可以是其中 1 个或全部鉴定人，如果由多个鉴定人出庭的也应当同时出庭，不应分别询问，因为分别询问没有任何的法律意义。除非，鉴定书中已明确表述某鉴定人的不同意见，分别询问才有意义。目前阶段为了防止出现此类情况，鉴定人在出庭前应提前询问法官具体的质证流程和要求，如果多人出庭是分别询问应予以告知，要求同时出庭。

专门知识人员出庭方面。专门知识人员出庭参与法庭证据质证环节还是具有很大的积极意义的，应当鼓励更多专业人士参与庭审，但是应当出台相关配套规定确保立法本意得到准确实施，如果混乱发展势必会导致庭审的混乱，进而干扰法庭审判。笔者建议：一是成立专家辅助人协会（或其他名称），形成技术自律组织；同时从法律法规层面出台配套规定，规定应体现专门知识人员资质要求、专门知识人员的意见法律属性及证据价值、专门知识人员出庭规范、专门知识人员权利义务、惩罚机制等。

法官驾驭庭审能力方面。法官的驾驭能力直接决定着庭审效果和进展，因此法官的关键作用应从各方面进行加强，首先，从制度层面，应保证法官在法庭上的绝对权威，能够通过各种手段对干扰法庭庭审进展的行为进行制止。其次，法官应加强鉴定人出庭方面的培训，熟悉各项流程，提高庭审驾驭能力。再次，应规定庭审中对鉴定人质证的内容及范围进行限定，通常包括：司法鉴定人、司法鉴定机构的主体资格和执业资质；司法鉴定人从事本专业的资历和业绩；鉴定材料的来源；鉴定意见依据的鉴定资料；鉴定使用的技术方法（仪器设备、技术标准、技术规范等）；鉴定的实施程序；鉴定意见得出的依据，分析论证的逻辑性和充分性；与鉴定意见有关的其他争议情况。与鉴定意见无关的内容应当及时制止，如果当事人、律师对鉴定人进行诱导性发问也应当予以制止，鉴定人也有权拒绝回答的权利。最后，为了能够达到更好的出庭效果，建议由法官向申请鉴定人出庭作证的一方要求必须提交质询提纲，目的是让鉴定人能够更有针对性地准备相关材料。

鉴定人出庭作证能力方面。出庭作证是一项要求较高的技术能力，除了要求有扎实深厚的专业功底，还要求有良好的表达能力和应变能力，因此鉴定人应当专门培训此方面的内容，提高出庭作证能力，以适应未来出庭作证的需要。出庭作证能力应作为司法行政部门或行业协会、鉴定机构定期培训的内容和强制要求。出庭作证能力的加强可以减少鉴定人对出庭作证的畏惧感，建立自信。其实，鉴定人出庭作证的启动因素是当事人、法官等对鉴定意见理解存在异议，从法律意义上分析既是法庭证据质证的需要，其实也是一种救济途径。应从正反两方面分析出庭作证需求的增加，正面的考虑可以讲是当事人的法律权利得到贯彻和实施，反面的考虑是鉴定人出具的鉴定意见书还不能完全满足各方面的需求（无理需求除外），说明我们鉴定工作还需要不断完善和改进，不断适应法庭审判对司法鉴定的工作要求，应该说这是最基础的工作。我倒是更希望主动要求鉴定人出庭作证的数量不断下降，因为这才是我们鉴定工作做得很好的客观体现。

总之，鉴定人出庭作证的加强是社会法制建设进程中必然要求，其积极意义是显而易见的，通过鉴定人出庭作证可以更好地诠释鉴定意见书中的内容，做到释疑解惑，有利于法院审判，有利于息诉息访。当然，在目前阶段鉴定人出庭作证还有许多问题亟待解决，有些问题已经明显阻碍鉴定人出庭作证，比如出庭费用问题，希望有关部门尽快制定配套的规定和措施，确保鉴定人出庭作证工作能够得到顺利的实施。

参考文献

[1] 李禹："2008 年度全国法医类、物证类、声像资料类司法鉴定情况统计分析"，载《中国司法鉴定》2009 年第 4 期，第 77～79 页。

[2] 李禹、王奕森："2009 年度全国'三大类'司法鉴定情况统计分析"，载《中国司法鉴定杂志》2010 年第 4 期，第 S9～S11 页。

[3] 李禹、陈璐："2010 年度全国法医类、物证类、声像资料类司法鉴定情况统计分析"，载《中国司法鉴定》2011 年第 4 期，第 91～94 页。

[4] 李禹、党凌云："2011 年度全国法医类、物证类、声像资料类司法鉴定情况统计分析"，载《中国司法鉴定》2012 年第 3 期，第 124～127 页。

[5] 刁国民："对证人、鉴定人出庭作证的调查报告"，http://xzzy.chinacourt.org/public/detail.php?id=3323，访问时间：2013 年 6 月 19 日。

[6] 乔瑞锋、闫青山："关于对证人、鉴定人出庭作证情况统计分析"，http://www.hncourt.org/public/detail.php?id=108579，访问时间：2013 年 6 月 19 日。

[7] 何杰："鉴定人出庭作证——控辩式庭审模式的必然选择"，载《昆明师范高等专科学校学报》2005 年第 3 期，第 55～57 页。

[8] 叶亿培："当前我国司法鉴定人出庭率低的原因及相关制度的完善"，载《广西社会科学》2007 年第 5 期，第 84～87 页。

[9] 陈一鸣："关于司法鉴定人出庭作证的探讨"，载《临床精神医学杂志》2007 年第 5 期，第 344 页。

证人证言收集中的认知访谈技术

姜丽娜 * 罗大华**

在国外的司法实践中，认知访谈技术作为一种侦查的手段，主要用于收集证人证言。在我国，讯问犯罪嫌疑人的策略是我们探讨得较多的，而关于如何有效地收集证人证言，人们却较少关注。而事实上，侦查中所获得的证人证言的数量、质量与询问的方式有很大的关系。证人证言是诉讼中运用较为广泛的证据之一，对认定案件事实具有极其重要的价值。大量研究和实践表明，人们对证人证言具有较大的依赖性，特别是诚实证人的证言，被采信的概率较大。然而，在司法实践中，因采信错误的证人证言造成的冤假错案时有发生，甚至成为错判案件最常见的原因，而这与传统的询问方式不无关系。传统的询问方式存在着一些普遍的错误，比如在收集证人证言的过程中，所提出的问题没有结构的一致性，所有的问题几乎都是以非常直接的方式进行的，经常打断证人的陈述等。司法实践中，需要一种有效的方式来收集证言，在这种情况下，认知访谈技术逐渐地进入了人们的视野。

一、认知访谈的原理及原则

（一）认知访谈的原理

认知访谈技术最早是由美国的吉斯尔曼和弗希尔（Geiselman & Fisher，1984）提出的，是一种提高回忆的方法。认知访谈技术建立在心理学关于记忆和证人表现的研究结论的基础之上。认知访谈强调两个过程，一是记忆的过程，二是交流的过程。在收集证言的过程中，证人会努力地回忆这些信息，并与询问者交流这些信息，因此，成功的访谈依赖于这两个过程。访谈者的任务是通过提问来引导证人回忆相关的信息。弗希尔和吉斯尔曼认为，认知访谈技术应该基于下述观点：

第一，记忆痕迹通常非常复杂，而且包含了各种各样的信息；

第二，提取线索的有效性依赖于它与记忆痕迹中所贮存信息的交叉程度，这就是编码特异性原则；

第三，各种提取线索都可以介入任何特定的记忆痕迹；

第四，如果一条提取线索是无效的，那就再寻找另一条线索。[1]

至今为止，认知访谈技术是被广泛承认的收集证人证言的有效方法。从认知访谈

---

* 姜丽娜，浙江金华人，讲师，研究方向：法律心理学、证据法学，Email：jln0507@163.com。本研究为国家社会科学基金项目（12CFX055）；教育部人文社科研究青年基金项目（12YJCZH085）的部分研究成果。

** 罗大华，杭州电子科技大学人文与法学院，杭州，310018；中国政法大学证据科学教育部重点实验室，北京100088。Email：jln0507@163.com。

〔1〕［英］M.W. 艾森克、M.T. 基恩：《认知心理学》，高定国、肖晓云译，华东师范大学出版社2004年版，第345页。

的理论提出以来，学者们就投以极大的热情，认知访谈技术也不断地得到发展和改进。

（二）认知访谈的原则

最初认知访谈的形式包括四个原则：一是重构事件的情境；二是报告每一个细节，包括那些看起来琐碎和似乎无关的；三是按不同的时间顺序来报告事件；四是从不同的角度来描述事件，比如从另一个当事人的角度。[2]

1. 重构事件的情境

重构事件的情境包括证人在案件发生前、发生时和发生后所体验到的心境、背景和经历。当应用这项技术时，询问者鼓励证人从心理和物理环境两个层面来重构案件发生时的相关情况，以激发回忆的线索。重构事件情境的原因在于事件不是在真空的状态中发生的，而是证人所经历的，假如仅让证人回忆其中的一部分可能不会产生细节的回忆。因此，重构事件的情境对于唤起证人当时的感受非常的重要。询问者在询问的过程中要给予证人必要的说明和便于联想的提示，在每次说明之后要有适当的停顿，以使证人有足够的时间去重构事件。

例如："我将会帮助你尽可能多地回忆。我希望你去思考我所说的每一件事情。闭上眼睛或者是看着墙壁可能会帮助你。现在我希望你回到事件发生的当天。想想那天…你做了什么…天气怎么样…想想事件发生的地点…在你的头脑里画出一幅图。想想那个地方是怎么样的…想想那里都有些什么…想想那里有些什么颜色和气味。你当时有什么感觉？现在想想当时都有哪些人？…发生了什么事情？…如果你准备好了，请你用你自己的方式和速度告诉你所记得的一切。"[3]

有时候人们不能回忆相关事件不是因为相关事件的痕迹已经消逝了，而是因为不能找到有效的线索。比起外部环境，我们的记忆更多地受心理感受的影响。重构事件使得证人重新体会当时编码的情况，以使回忆最大化。

2. 报告每一个细节

让证人报告每一个细节的原因在于我们通常会编辑我们的回忆或总结我们的感受来符合我们认为的应该与案件相关的信息，这样做会使得我们忽略很多细节，而这些细节可能对于调查来说是很关键的。运用这项技术时，询问人员应当向证人说明不要编辑任何与事件有关的细节，即便这些细节被他们认为是不重要的、无关的。

例如："有些人会隐瞒一些信息，因为他们不太确定这些信息是否是正确的或者你可能会认为我已经知道了这些信息。请不要遗漏任何的事情。我对你所记得的任何事情都很感兴趣，甚至是你认为不重要的事情，请全部告诉我。"[4]

关于对事件的记忆被认为是以一系列编码表征的方式被储存的，被记忆的并不是事件的精确的复制，而是以多种交互作用的编码保存这些经历。所以，会存在一些能引起人们回忆的，但是却被人们认为是不重要的线索。另外，证人通常会认为询问者是了解案件情况的，他们只对重要的、能够完全回忆的信息感兴趣。这样就导致很多

---

〔2〕 Gayla Swihart, "the Utility of the Cognitive Interview as A Credibility Assessment Tool", *B. A. the University of British Columbia*, 1996, p. 7.

〔3〕 Dando, C. J. & Milne, R. , The Cognitive Interview Chapter in : In R. N. Kocsis (Ed.), Applied Criminal Psychology: A Guide to Forensic behavioural Sciences, 2009, pp. 6 ~ 17.

〔4〕 同注〔3〕。

信息被隐瞒。询问者向证人说明让其报告每一个细节，可以降低证人报告信息的主观标准，这样就有希望通过一些看起来不重要的、不全面的线索来激发一些不能回忆的信息。

3. 按不同的时间顺序来报告事件

改变报告事件的顺序是基于有多条途径可以达到记忆编码这一假说。改变报告事件的顺序，可以使证人关注事件的不同部分，从不同的顺序对事件进行回忆可以填补证人记忆的空白。心理学的研究表明，证人采用一种途径无法有效地获得信息，并不能说明信息不在人的记忆中，这时候应该鼓励证人采用别种途径来获得有效的线索。很多时候证人在一次提取失败后，往往会认为自己已经忘记了，不愿做新的尝试。这时，询问者应该鼓励证人采用其他的途径进行回忆，其中改变报告事件的顺序就是一种非常有效的方法。

例如："以你自己的顺序来回忆事件是非常自然的。我将会尝试做一些可以使人们回忆得更多的方式。我想请你用倒叙的方式告诉我发生了什么？你所记得的发生的最后一件事是什么…之前发生了什么…这之前又发生了什么（这一说明可以重复，有必要的话，可以用至证人回忆出事件的最初情节）。"〔5〕

怀顿和莱昂纳德（Whitten & Leonard，1981）的研究发现采用倒叙的方式进行回忆比顺序和随机回忆更有效，回忆的错误率也更低。〔6〕其他的一些研究也发现采用倒叙的方式进行回忆比顺序的方式收集到更多的细节。

4. 从不同的角度来描述事件

从不同的角度来描述事件可以使证人回忆出更多的细节。采用这项技术的目的是在前三项技术都不能获得有效的线索时，能激起相关的记忆编码。

例如："试着从另一个知道事件的人的角度来回忆事件。想想他在哪？他看到了些什么？"〔7〕

许多的研究表明，改变角度进行回忆，得到了一些新的信息。

上述四个原则构成了认知访谈技术的核心。许多的实证研究都证实采用认知访谈的方法能够收集到更全面更准确的信息。吉斯尔曼等（Geiselman et al.，1986）的研究发现采用认知访谈技术能收集到更多更准确的信息，而错误信息和虚假信息的数量并没有增多。〔8〕吉斯尔曼和帕蒂娜（Geiselman & Padilla，1988）以儿童为被试，对认知访谈与传统访谈进行了比较，结果发现采用认知访谈的方式收集到的准确的证言增加了21%，而错误的证言和虚构的证言都没有增加。〔9〕

---

〔5〕 Dando, C. J. & Milne, R., The Cognitive Interview Chapter in : In R. N. Kocsis (Ed.), Applied Criminal Psychology: A Guide to Forensic behavioural Sciences, 2009, pp. 6 ~ 17.

〔6〕 Whitten, W. B. & Leonard, J. M., "Directed Search Through Autobiographical Memory", *Memory and Cognition*, 1981, 9 (6), pp. 556 ~ 579.

〔7〕 同注〔6〕。

〔8〕 Geiselman, R. E., Fisher, R. P., MacKinnon, D. P. & Holland, H. L., "Enhancement of Eyewitness Memory With the Cognitive Interview", *American Journal of Psychology*, 1986, 99 (3), pp. 385 ~ 401.

〔9〕 Geiselman, R. E. & Padilla, J., "Interviewing Child Witnesses With The Cognitive Interview", *Journal of Police Science and Administration*, 1988, 16 (4), pp. 236 ~ 242.

二、认知访谈技术在司法实践中的运用

目前，许多国家（如美国、英国、加拿大、澳大利亚等）都已采纳认知访谈技术作为收集证人证言的方法。实践也证明无论在数量方面还是在质量方面，采用认知访谈技术收集证人证言都比传统的方法收集证人证言更有效。

在国外，相关的侦查人员需要接受认知访谈的培训。例如，美国的 FBI 等机构都有专门的认知访谈培训。在英国，所有的侦查人员都要求接受认知访谈的培训。在英格兰和威尔士，从 1992 年起，就开始给每一名侦查人员发放认知访谈手册。英国、美国、加拿大等国家的法庭对于运用认知访谈技术收集到的证人证言几乎是没有什么争议的，新入职的警察和专门的询问者都要接受认知访谈培训，这样才能确保询问者采用正确的方法去收集证言，因为采用不当的方法可能会带来适得其反的作用。

但是凯贝尔、米尔勒和瓦格斯塔夫（Kebbell, Milne & Wagstaff, 1999）的调查显示，在实践中几乎没有侦查人员是完全使用认知访谈技术的。为什么实践中认知访谈的这种优势并没有显现出来？原因在于不是所有的询问者都真正掌握了认知访谈技术。在国外的司法实践中，对询问者进行相关访谈培训的力度还不够。例如，英国的侦查人员要接受一周的询问课程的学习，其中关于认知访谈的培训平均下来也就两天。而在国内几乎没有关于认知访谈技术的任何培训，相关的司法工作者对于认知访谈技术还是非常陌生的，因此，在实践中也就根本谈不上对认知访谈技术的运用。

总之，到目前为止，认知访谈技术是提高证人回忆数量和质量最有效的方法之一。但是，实践中询问者有时候会不使用或不完全使用认知访谈技术去收集证言。而在我国，由于相关知识的缺乏，在实践中，几乎没人采用认知访谈技术收集证人证言。借鉴国外的研究成果，学习不同学科的研究方法，并将这些成果和方法运用于实践，必将收到意想不到的效果。

三、认知访谈技术的改进

认知访谈理论的逻辑依据包括记忆的复杂性，以及回忆可以通过多条途径实现。认知访谈一直被认为是收集证言的有效方式，但是在现实生活中，证人会经历更多的焦虑和面对更多的困惑。为了解决这些问题，吉斯尔曼和弗希尔（Geiselman & Fisher）改进了认知访谈技术。改进后的认知访谈技术包括原始的四个程序，增加了访谈过程中的对话成分。改进后的认知访谈技术更多地关注询问者的行为，有学者提出了 13 种询问者在询问过程中应当掌握的技巧，具体见下表。

访谈者技巧[10]

（1）与证人建立融洽的关系	（2）积极倾听
（3）鼓励证人自发的回忆	（4）采用开放式的问题
（5）答复后适当的停顿	（6）避免打断证人的陈述
（7）要求证人描述细节	（8）鼓励证人重视访谈
（9）鼓励证人想象	（10）重构原始情境
（11）采纳证人的观点	（12）问适当的问题

---

〔10〕 Dr. Jenny Wilson, The Cognitive Interview, Hopelive. hope. ac. uk/criminology/LevelH/. . . /cognitive_ interview. ppt.

(13) 遵循认知访谈的程序

从上述内容我们可以看出改进后的认知访谈技术关注于三个核心的观点，一是知识的表达，二是记忆恢复的过程，三是交流的技巧。[11] 并对访谈者提出了更高的要求。弗希尔（Fisher）等人于1987年进行了实验研究，比较了改进前后的认知访谈技术在收集证人证言方面的差异，结果发现改进后的认知访谈技术比原始的认知访谈技术多收集到40%的准确信息，而在错误信息和虚构信息方面，两者没有差异。[12] 1989年，弗希尔等人在真实的案件中运用了此项技术，结果发现询问者在经过改进后的认知访谈技术培训后比原先多收集到47%的信息。[13] 另外，斯坦因和麦蒙（Stein & Memon, 2006）的研究[14]也支持了这一结论。

四、对认知访谈技术的评价

应该说，自认知访谈技术提出以来，这种方法还是受到了司法工作者的关注，并在一定程度上被人们所接受。但关于认知访谈技术的争论也是存在的，主要集中在以下两点：

（一）关于认知访谈技术的效果问题

认知访谈技术是建立在记忆与认知的相关原理之上的，学者们提出了许多有价值的观点，从理论上来分析，这种方法确实能收集到更多有用的信息。究竟实际效果如何呢？关于认知访谈技术效果的问题，多是心理学工作者进行相关的实验研究来加以检验的，实验的结果证实认知访谈是一项有价值的技术。但是，不少人对于心理学的研究存在着如下的质疑：①心理学实验多选取学生为被试，被试的代表性如何？②实验室环境与现实案件的环境是不同的，能否将实验室的研究结论推广到现实案件中？

应该说，这些质疑都是颇有道理的，上述问题是心理学研究受攻击的主要原因，我们没法回避这些问题。在现实中，采用真实案例研究的方法来探讨侦查人员对认知访谈的使用情况是非常少见的。有学者将仅有的几个真实案件中采用认知访谈技术收集证人证言的结果与实验室中采取认知访谈技术收集的证人证言的结果进行了比较，结果发现两者并没有显著的差异。这从一个侧面也说明了心理学关于采用认知访谈技术收集证人证言的研究具有一定的价值。我们认为，在实践中，相关司法人员可以尝试采用认知访谈技术收集证人证言，并在实践中不断地完善这项技术。

（二）关于认知访谈技术的培训问题

如前所述，在接受认知访谈技术收集证人证言的国家，都要求对相关人员进行认知访谈技术的培训。而在国外的司法实践中，关于认知访谈培训也并没有相关的规范，以致认知访谈技术的培训并没有达到很好的效果。在国外司法实践中，许多的侦查人员也并没有完全地采用认知访谈技术。

---

〔11〕 Dando, C. J. & Milne, R., The Cognitive Interview Chapter in: In R. N. Kocsis (Ed.). Applied Criminal Psychology: A Guide to Forensic Behavioural Sciences, 2009, pp. 6 ~ 17.

〔12〕 Finsher, R. P., Geiselman, R. E. & Raymond, D. S., "Critical Analysis Of Police Interview Techniques", *Jounal of Police and Science Administration*, 1987, 15 (3), pp. 177 ~ 185.

〔13〕 Finsher, R. P., Geiselman, R. E., & Amador, M., "Fiedl Test of the Cognitive Interview: Enhancing the Recollection of Actual Victims and Witnesses of Crime", *Journal of Applied Psychology*, 1989, 74 (5), pp. 722 ~ 727.

〔14〕 Stein, L. & Memon, A., "Testing the efficacy of the Cognitive Interview in A Developing Country", *Applied Cognitive Psychology*, 2006, 20 (5), pp. 597 ~ 605.

认知访谈技术涉及多学科的知识，特别是心理学的知识，要求相关的侦查人员有深厚的理论功底。关于认知访谈的培训由谁来做？应当培训多久？这些都需要我们在实践中不断摸索。只有侦查人员真正地掌握了认知访谈技术，才能更有效地收集证言。

当前司法鉴定委托程序中存在的问题及若干建议

——以北京司法鉴定委托的情况为视角

李 冰 [*] 刘建伟 [**]

目前，随着社会经济生活的活跃、科学技术的发展和人民法律意识的不断提高，在为数众多、类型广泛的民事诉讼中，当事人申请对专门性问题进行司法鉴定以证明自己主张的情况越来越普遍。鉴定意见正逐步成为法院处理相关专业类诉讼案件中一类不可或缺的证据形式。

委托——作为开启司法鉴定程序的初始环节有着非常重要的地位。从法院角度来看，对外委托司法鉴定工作是法院完成审判任务的一项极为重要的辅助手段，也是实现司法公正、效率的重要保证；从司法鉴定机构角度来看，接受委托是实施司法鉴定活动的开始，其重要性无须多言。但就目前情况来看，在司法鉴定委托工作中仍存在诸多问题和不足（这里既有法院的原因也有司法鉴定机构的因素），这些问题不仅影响到法院民事诉讼程序的顺利进行，也极易引发当事人对司法鉴定和法院裁判权威性的质疑，造成涉诉信访、反复投诉等不和谐现象。本文将从司法鉴定的实践出发，探讨司法鉴定委托工作中存在的各种问题，并提出几点个人拙见，以供参考。

一、当前司法鉴定的委托模式

根据《北京市高级人民法院关于委托司法鉴定工作的若干规定（试行）》、《北京市高级人民法关于委托司法鉴定和拍卖工作的若干规定》等相关文件的规定，对于需要进行司法鉴定的案件，法院办理时遵循的一般工作流程是：由当事人向法院提出鉴定申请（个别情况由法院依职权决定）——→法院经审查后认为确有必要进行鉴定的，依据法定程序确定鉴定机构——→由法院向相关鉴定机构出具委托函、提交经过当事人质证后的鉴定材料、办理委托事宜——→鉴定机构鉴定并直接向申请人收取费用（对于需要进行现场勘验的，法院组织双方当事人到场并负责协调监督）——→鉴定机构向法院出具鉴定意见报告，由法院向当事人送达并组织质证——→必要时法院通知鉴定人出庭作证或根据需要进行补充鉴定或重新鉴定。

其中，上述环节中，鉴定机构的选定较为复杂，凡属法医类、物证类、声像资料类鉴定的案件，先由当事人在法院的主持下协商在北京市司法局印制的《国家司法鉴定人和司法鉴定机构名册（北京市）》的范围内选择司法鉴定机构。当事人选择一致

* 李冰，中国政法大学证据科学研究院讲师、工程师，法学硕士。
** 刘建伟，中国政法大学证据科学研究院副教授、高级工程师，博士。
中国政法大学证据科学教育部重点实验室，Email：Lbgmm@126.com。

的，委托该机构进行司法鉴定；当事人一方放弃选择或一方当事人经正式传唤不到的，则由另一方当事人单方选择；双方当事人均表示放弃选择的，可由具体承办人提出建议，经双方当事人同意后确定；当事人不同意协商或选择不一致的，由承办人填写《委托司法鉴定移送表》，将相关材料报送高院，由高院在名册范围内随机确定鉴定机构。[1]

二、当前司法鉴定委托模式存在的问题

自2005年2月28日《全国人民代表大会常务委员会关于司法鉴定管理问题的决定》（下称《决定》）出台后，全国法院系统都撤销了原有的司法鉴定职能，随后根据最高人民法院的指示，各地法院纷纷成立了司法辅助办公室（或称为对外委托服务办公室等）从事对外委托的工作。法院大部分司法鉴定工作都将由专门的司法辅助办公室独立负责完成。这一决定对避免“自审自鉴”的问题，提高审判人员的办案效率，减轻审判人员的工作量起到了积极的作用，笔者也是持赞同观点的。但反观实践中出现的种种问题，笔者又不禁产生了些许疑惑。

由于法院对外委托司法鉴定工作中存在三方主体，即法院、鉴定机构和当事人，因此，一项高效优质的司法鉴定工作的完成是离不开此三方的通力协作、密切配合的。然而，审视目前的司法鉴定工作，除体制设计等方面的原因外，上述三方也均或多或少地存在一些问题。

1. 个别承办法官出具的委托函载明的委托事项、鉴定范围不明确。例如对文件物证是否存在伪造事实进行鉴定，由于其文件物证中所包含的内容信息往往是多样的，既有打印字迹、手写字迹，还有盖印印文，纸张等信息，如果没有明确说明针对哪一项进行鉴定，仅以一句“对文件物证是否存在伪造事实进行鉴定”为委托事项，这会使鉴定人产生困扰，不得不再行联系重新确定鉴定事项，造成诉讼时间成本的浪费。

2. 委托方与鉴定机构的沟通、配合不够。其主要表现为：

（1）在法院进行委托鉴定的时候，司法辅助办公室的送检人大多数情况只负责送来鉴定材料，而对于相应的案情则不甚了解，而必要的案情了解是鉴定人获取相关鉴定信息非常重要的途径。可能有些法官认为：“我只需要你来做鉴定，其他事情你不需要了解”，这种认识是狭隘的。如张三诉李四民间借贷纠纷，张三提交的证据为一张借条，其上内容为李四借其5万元于2个月之内归还。张三主张该借条上所有字迹均为李四书写，而李四否认，称其没有借过张三的钱更没有见过该借条。现在争议的焦点就集中在该借条的真伪问题上，需要进行笔迹鉴定。这种情况下，通过鉴定整张借条的字迹是否为李四书写就可以解决。如果该案在送检的时候仅要求鉴定李四的签名真伪并且没有交代相应的案情（如借条是谁提供的、提供方称借条上字迹是谁写的），送检的样本又很有限，而签名鉴定属于少量字迹检验，往往鉴定的难度更大，在样本不够充分的情况下很有可能得不出明确性的鉴定结论，这会直接影响案件事实的查明。由此可见，在委托过程中充分地掌握案情对于鉴定人来说是非常必要的。

（2）在委托的过程中还容易造成信息对接错位。从委托鉴定开始，承办法官把需要鉴定的材料转到司法辅助办公室，再由司法辅助办公室送到鉴定机构，最后由鉴定

---

〔1〕 北京市朝阳区人民法院：《关于司法鉴定适用中存在的问题的调研报告》。

机构审查材料并受理过程中，如果发现送检的材料不充分、需要补充鉴定材料的情况时，鉴定机构通常都是将信息反馈给送检人（即司法辅助办公室），再由司法辅助办公室反馈给承办法官。这个过程中司法辅助办公室实际充当了“中间人”的角色，在信息的反馈上或多或少地会出现偏差。容易给司法鉴定工作造成不便。

3. 部分法官对待司法鉴定观念上有误区，不够重视。在案多人少的结案压力下，部分承办人放松了对自己的要求，自认为审鉴分立后鉴定问题均应由鉴定机构解决，案件一移送了事，不能真正做到事必躬亲，努力提高效率。[2]

三、完善当前司法鉴定委托的若干建议

法院撤销鉴定部门的主要目的是为了避免“自审自鉴”的问题，最大限度地保障司法的中立性、公正性。但其实际上只是在形式上体现了司法鉴定的中立性质。在实践中，审判部门并不是独立于法院之外的，即使司法鉴定的委托工作由司法辅助办公室来做，也不能阻断审判法官与司法鉴定有所联系，并且，审判法官与司法鉴定机构或司法鉴定人之间有必要的互动是有利于司法鉴定工作顺利进行的，所以，不能单纯地认为只有阻断审判法官与司法鉴定的联系就是达到了所谓的“公平、中立”；综上，笔者认为，法院成立司法辅助办公室的初衷是正确的，但在实践中其与司法鉴定机构及司法鉴定人之间的工作交接上仍然存在不少问题，值得商榷。

（一）法院方面

法官应加强与鉴定人以及当事人之间的协调沟通、加强对当事人的诉讼指导。

对于鉴定工作，法官还应着重在以下几个方面对当事人释明：①释明配合义务。在委托鉴定前和委托鉴定过程中，应视情况向当事人释明其配合义务，包括配合向鉴定机构提供材料、配合出现场、应鉴定机构的要求配合交费等。并告知当事人如拒不配合影响鉴定进行或鉴定结果的将承担相应法律责任。②释明司法鉴定风险。在司法鉴定过程中，应告知当事人鉴定意见并非必然是决定性证据，案件的裁判结果与鉴定意见之间不具有法定相关性，从而帮助当事人客观理性地对待鉴定意见。

（二）司法鉴定机构方面

在受理案件时，鉴定人应当场告知委托人委托的鉴定事项是否具备鉴定条件，如不具备鉴定条件，应充分说明理由；如需补充鉴定材料后才可继续进行鉴定的案件，应及时告知情况；如当场确定不了能否受理，应事后尽快答复。以确保司法鉴定机构与委托单位的交接工作高效有序地进行。

另外，还应注意在受理案件时鉴定人应主动的询问与案件有关的信息，特别是涉及鉴定内容的相关信息，如果委托人对案情不了解，鉴定人可以与案件的承办法官联系询问相关案情。主动地了解案情不仅对鉴定工作的顺利开展起着关键的作用，还对鉴定人对鉴定意见的把握起着重要的辅助作用。

（三）委托的案件属于信访、上访、缠诉等矛盾争议较大的案件时，法院与鉴定机构应通力配合

近年来，信访、上访、缠诉案件数量不断攀升，笔者在此不去讨论其内在社会原因，而是想从司法鉴定委托程序角度来谈如何降低这类案件的受理风险。

---

〔2〕 北京市朝阳区人民法院：《关于司法鉴定适用中存在的问题的调研报告》。

首先，这类案件的矛盾争议都比较大，这就意味着双方当事人对法院的判决、鉴定机构的鉴定意见有着更高的期望值，而一旦结果没有达到当事人的心理预期，当事人双方很有可能将矛盾转嫁给法院或鉴定机构甚至鉴定人。所以，法院在受理此类案件时，更应做好委托前的准备工作；在委托鉴定时，法院应该如实详尽地告知鉴定机构该案的实际情况，便于后续开展鉴定工作时，鉴定机构与法院就有关问题进行沟通了解。而实践中，往往有委托方出于某种顾虑，刻意回避或有所隐瞒案件的特殊、复杂程度等真实情况。这些做法都不利于真正解决矛盾，反而可能增加鉴定的风险。

其次，这类案件往往引起的社会关注大，如果处理不好，极易引发更大范围的社会纠纷。所以在委托这类案件时，笔者认为应建立起“三方共同监管”的模式：法院——司法鉴定机构——主管司法局，法院将案件委托给司法鉴定机构后，鉴定机构应如实上报给主管司法局备案，在鉴定中或鉴定完结时，法院——司法鉴定机构——主管司法局三方都应对案件情况进行充分的沟通，如遇到突发情况，三方应相互配合，共同化解矛盾。

最后，司法鉴定委托的工作繁琐复杂，不仅仅是法院一己之力就能做好的，还需要鉴定机构及其他方面的鼎力配合，一个司法鉴定的好的开端一定是从好的委托程序开始。程序公正是现代诉讼价值的取向，是实现司法公正最高价值目标的重要环节。司法鉴定委托作为司法鉴定程序〔3〕中的一个重要环节，其直接关系到鉴定所涉各方权利的实现，程序的公正成为司法鉴定制度公正的逻辑起点和价值核心。

---

〔3〕 完善的鉴定程序立法应当包括以下内容：①鉴定的启动程序：涉及诉讼过程中，由谁在什么时候启动鉴定程序的问题。②鉴定的实施程序：应对鉴定事项的明确性、送检材料的标准、司法机关的监督权以及完成鉴定的期限等加以界定。③鉴定结论的提交审查程序：主要涉及鉴定结论的形式要件以及鉴定人出庭接受法官和当事人询问的程序。④补充鉴定及重新鉴定程序，应对补充鉴定、重新鉴定的申请权、决定权，重新鉴定对鉴定机构的要求以及对次数的限制等作出规定。

刑事强制医疗程序的司法实践状况以及存在的问题

——以北京首例精神病强制医疗已决案为分析对象

连 洋*

本案例是网络上公开报道的："某地首例强制医疗已决案"，之所以选择这个案例作分析是因为它经历了一审终结和二审复议即一个完整的强制医疗程序过程，而且，虽然它仅只是强制医疗案例之一，但由于它是今年新法实施后该地的首例强制医疗案件，所以该地法院对其的审理慎之又慎，故此，在这样一个十分慎重，严格遵守程序下的审理更能反映出我国法院系统在实践中适用强制医疗程序的智慧和遭遇的尴尬。现将本案实际运行状况分析如下：

案情简介：2012 年 11 月 30 日，王某（化名）在某市地铁某线某站，将在站台边候车的李某（化名）推下站台，致李某被进站列车碾轧经鉴定为重伤，后王某经鉴定为完全无刑事责任能力人。2013 年 1 月 7 日，侦查机关作出撤销案件的决定，并于 1 月 11 日某区检察院移送强制医疗意见书。某区检察院于 2013 年 2 月 17 日向某区法院申请启动强制医疗程序，同日，某区法院向某区司法局法律援助中心送达提供法律援助通知书，某区法院于 2013 年 3 月 13 日不公开但开庭审理此案，并于 2013 年 3 月 17 日宣布对王某决定强制医疗。王某的法定代理人申请复议，上一级法院于 2013 年 4 月 1 日受理此案，于 2013 年 4 月 25 日作出维持某区法院强制医疗决定的复议意见。

参与案件的机关和人员：某区公安局、某安康医院、某区检察院、某区法院、某中级人民法院、被告人王某及其法定代理人、某区司法局受某区法院委托指派的法律援助律师。

下面笔者将本案在整个刑事诉讼中的程序分别展开讨论，从案件的程序进展和各机关的处理方式来简要分析案件处理中有效的方法和出现的问题。

一、侦查阶段

由于本案发生在地铁之中，侦查工作由某区公安局进行，侦查阶段公安机关对被告人王某进行讯问，但讯问期间王某反映自己患有精神分裂症，因此，安康医院处对王某进行了精神病鉴定，经鉴定王某确系精神病患者，是在控制能力和意识能力丧失的情况下实施了危害行为，此外，通过走访王某的亲属得知王某确系精神病患者，且正处于治疗期，但此前一个月左右王某自己把药丢了，所以就停药了。基于此，某区公安局于 2013 年 1 月 7 日作出撤销案件的决定，并于 1 月 11 日向某区检察院移送强制

* 连洋，中国人民公安大学 2011 级刑事诉讼法硕士研究生。Email：lianyang2692@163.com。

医疗意见书。

案件在侦查阶段主要牵扯以下三个问题。

（一）确认是否具有精神病问题

公安机关在办理刑事案件中会有专门人员对犯罪嫌疑人进行精神病的鉴定，因此，王某是否具有精神病在公安机关办理案件之初就开始着手委托机关对其进行了鉴定，并于 2013 年 1 月 6 日经法定程序鉴定依法不负刑事责任。第二天即 1 月 7 日，王某被释放，同时，安康医院对其采取保护性约束措施。

本案中，笔者就已经收集的资料来看，公安机关的一些合理做法是值得立法者借鉴的：先对其刑事犯罪进行审查，看其是否属于刑事案件；确定案件性质后对其进行精神病鉴定，在鉴定的同时走访其亲属搜集其他证明其患有精神病的证据材料，如其父母提供的其成长经历、病发状况，治疗情况等等，这些合理的做法，一方面，体现了公安机关的全面收集证据，不轻信单一鉴定意见的思维；另一方面，先判断刑事案件后判断是否属于精神病强制医疗案体现了公安机关很好地区分两种程序的程序意识。唯一的不足之处在于：对鉴定意见的判断，仅根据书面意见就直接采信而没有直接对鉴定意见进行必要的询问。

（二）关于临时保护性约束措施

刑事诉讼法规定，侦查机关对患有精神病的犯罪嫌疑人可以采取临时保护性约束措施。但具体什么程度？由谁来采取？时间的长短？法律都没有明确的规定，实践中得靠公安机关自己去摸索。本案的做法是：由安康医院对其采取临时性约束性措施，并且在安康医院采取，时间是 1 月 7 日到 3 月 17 日（决定强制医疗日）共计 70 天。

从笔者收集到的资料看，本案相对合理的做法有：由安康医院来对精神病人采取临时保护约束措施而不是直接由办案机关采取，一定程度上有利于更好地保证精神病人的合法权益。采取措施的场所在安康医院也有利于对精神病人进行必要的治疗。但其弊端主要有：临时约束措施的手段有哪些，是否与当事人的病情严重程度相吻合，措施采取的时间不受限制一定程度上侵害了其合法权益，律师在该阶段是否允许介入，其近亲属能否去看望他都没有规定。

（三）刑事案件与强制医疗程序的转化问题

强制医疗程序产生的前提是被申请人的行为已经触犯刑法，符合实施暴力行为，危害公共安全或者严重危害他人人身安全的行为。那么强制医疗程序启动的前提首先是刑事诉讼程序，公安机关先期如果没有确实的证据证明被申请人（此时是犯罪嫌疑人）确属无责任能力精神病人的话，必须先以刑事案件予以立案，那么就涉及刑事程序与强制医疗程序的转化问题，本案中某区公安局于 2013 年 1 月 7 日撤销案件，并于 1 月 11 日制作强制医疗意见书送交某区检察院。就本案而言，笔者认为公安机关做得好的地方有：能够及时地将刑事程序与强制医疗程序予以区分并在停止刑事程序后的短时间内启动强制医疗程序，从而避免了因无限期的过度延长羁押期限而侵害被申请人的合法权益。但有待完善的地方有：法律对撤销案件和启动强制医疗程序之间的时间间隔没有明确规定，容易导致因无限制的延长等待转换期而侵害被申请人合法权益，另外，公安机关制作的强制医疗意见书所包含的内容也应该有一个统一的指导规范，公安部的适用刑事诉讼法的规范中明确规定了强制医疗意见书应该具备的必备内容有：

案发状况以及案发时发现病人的情况、使病人符合强制医疗的条件以及相关的证据材料以及该病人依法不负刑事责任的鉴定意见。

二、审查起诉阶段

某区公安局于2013年1月11日向某检察院移送强制医疗意见书，某区人民检察院于2013年2月17日向某区法院申请启动强制医疗程序。在审查起诉阶段，本案主要关注的焦点主要有以下两个：

1. 核实证据，决定是否申请强制医疗。本案的某区检察院的任务就是接收并核实公安机关强制医疗意见书的内容，如果确实属实而且符合刑事诉讼法规定的强制医疗程序启动所具备的所有条件，那么就在此基础上制作强制医疗申请书，如果经审查案件虽然属实但有些条件还未满足刑事诉讼法要求的启动条件，则退回公安机关补充侦查或者自行补充证据，以求达到启动的条件后再申请启动强制医疗程序。由于本案是强制医疗程序的首例案件，所以公安机关在收集证据方面比较细致，检察院在审查起诉阶段也比较慎重，所以检察院在收到案件1个多月后才向法院送达强制医疗申请书。但本案有个问题就是，基于保障被申请人合法权益防止其被较长时间羁押的原则，检察机关在申请启动强制医疗程序的时间上是否应作出一定限制。

2. 指派人员支持出庭。刑事诉讼法规定刑事强制医疗程序的启动需要法院组成合议庭进行审理，在庭审中法律还规定应当通知被申请人及其法定代理人、诉讼代理人、法律援助律师到场，那么，检察机关作为申请启动该程序的机关当然需要派员出庭支持该程序的启动（《人民检察院刑事诉讼规则（试行）》已经明确规定强制医疗案件，检察院应当派员出庭）。笔者想强调的是检察官出庭的人数上是否应该也延续普通程序中的至少2名或以上的检察官，而且检察官在法庭中的称谓是不是也不能是公诉人而应该改为申请人（当然相对应的被强制医疗人也应该称为被申请人）。

三、庭审阶段

强制医疗程序中，案件的中心环节是审理阶段，因为所有的证据材料包括鉴定意见等都需要在法庭上进行展示质证，并且需经过被申请人方和申请方出庭进行辩驳论证，最终由法院组成的合议庭做出是否强制医疗的决定。因此，可以说前边的侦查、审查起诉阶段等等准备的材料都是为了庭审而进行的，所以，庭审才是本程序的核心和中心环节。而就笔者所触，审判环节最大的漏洞在于：审判权被架空了。

刑事强制医疗程序设置的目的之一是为了将是否被强制医疗的决定权由行政机关变更为司法机关，从而由更中立的机关更好地保障被强制医疗人的合法权益，防止权力滥用。而在本程序中涉及的判断标准有两个即医学标准和法学标准，我们知道精神病是一种医学上的疾病，但患有此病的病人由于涉及犯罪而被司法机关进行审判，因此，判断被申请人是否患有精神病是否属于完全无刑事责任能力人既涉及医学的鉴定与判断，又涉及法学上的认定和判断，两环紧紧相扣。本案中虽表面上看没有出现混乱，某区法院最终采纳了安康医院的鉴定意见，认定申请人宋某确系完全无刑事责任能力精神病人，但实际上隐含着法院的法学判断标准一定程度上被精神病专家的医学判断所左右。

法院在审理强制医疗案件中，争议的核心主要牵扯两个问题：一是对精神病的鉴定；二是对是否有继续危害社会的可能。对于“是否有继续危害社会的可能”的判断，法官可以根据被申请人案发前的表现、案发后的行为并综合参考其家属、邻居、亲朋好友对其平时状况的反映进行判断，这样的判断合乎常人的思维，法官也能够实实在在地操作。而对于其“是否具有精神病和是否属于完全无责任能力人”，法官的根据则主要依靠鉴定医师的鉴定意见，而这样的结果使法官的审判权被架空了。

法官的判断之所以会被精神病医师的鉴定意见所架空是因为：①逻辑上的依赖性。法官判断精神病人是否是完全无刑事责任人的前提是根据精神病专家鉴定其有精神病，然后才根据此进行行为时是否也有病、是否控制能力辨认能力完全丧失的法学判断，但试想如果精神病专家鉴定其是限制责任能力人，那么法官会怎么判呢？是否会据此判断行为人行为时只是控制辨认能力减弱而未丧失，最终作出构成犯罪应负刑事责任的判决。②知识上的匮乏性。法官缺乏专门的精神病知识，对精神病的鉴定意见无法有效地辩驳和论证，但我们知道，精神病鉴定的判断依据没有什么客观标准而主要依据医师对病人的主观分析，这种非客观标准的判断本来就充满着不可知性，所谓仁者见仁智者见智，不同的医师很可能根据自己的判断标准作出不同的结论，而面对这种结论法官也无法真实地辨别。③实践上的不可操作性。据笔者实际考察法院在处理控方提供的鉴定意见时一般会基于以下两方面的考虑给以直接采纳不去重新鉴定：其一，如果否定，那么法院将面临着重新鉴定，一旦鉴定意见和原来的不一致，到底是采纳先前那个呢还是采纳后边这个，为什么要选择它，万一错了最后案件被翻过来法院是要承担责任的；其二，鉴定意见一般在案件送至法院之前就已经过公安机关或者检察机关出具了，如果法院要推翻公检机关的鉴定，势必造成整个案件推倒重来，否定了公检的成果，违背三机关互相配合原则，同时也得罪了检察机关这个监督机关，因此在没有确信把握之前，法院是不会重新鉴定的。④被申请方的辩护职能失灵。被申请人的法定代理人、诉讼代理人以及援助律师在被申请人被鉴定的时候不在场，无法针对鉴定医师的鉴定过程进行监督和批判，加之其本身就缺乏精神病的知识，对于开庭审理过程中的鉴定意见无法形成有效的辩驳和论证，导致的结果也往往是尴尬地接受鉴定意见。

综上，整个庭审过程仿佛是医师鉴定意见在操控着，而主审的法官、参审的律师、诉讼代理人等都没有对鉴定意见形成有效的反驳和对抗，这样的庭审模式直接导致的结果就是：审判活动被虚化，法庭的司法监督作用无从体现，被申请人的合法权益无法保障。虽然强制医疗程序涉及医学判断，但毕竟我们处理的是犯罪与否是否需要负刑事责任问题，它是一个法律问题，法律问题的处理必须依靠司法机关和司法程序，如果一个国家的司法程序被其他程序操控，那么这个国家的法律人还有何尊严，有何行业优越感，还有什么值得被人们所尊重的权威，依法治国目标还如何实现……

因此，笔者建议，是否在庭审中考虑引进专家证人和精神病专家人民陪审员。

四、决定阶段

刑事强制医疗程序最终的结果是法院以“决定”而非“判决”的方式作出，决定的特点是一经作出立即生效不得上诉，可以复议但复议期间不停止决定的执行。本案的决定在2013年3月17日作出，王某直接从临时保护约束措施的羁押场所转向了强制医疗场所进行治疗。但法院在作出强制医疗决定之前，被申请人王某的家属已经与被害人李某达成了赔偿协议并取得了被害人谅解。

笔者注意到一个问题：如果被申请人家属能够与被害人达成调解协议并取得其谅解，那同未赔偿未达成谅解协议的家属比较而言，他们的效果或者利益在哪即是什么在促进被申请人家属希望与被害人达成调解协议，如果说普通刑事案件中被告人与被害人达成和解协议有利于法院在法定幅度范围内从轻判决的话，那么强制医疗程序中的和解协议的达成并不会产生让被申请人强制医疗期限的缩短，因为治疗是一个过程，它需要根据病人的具体情况而定，不可能限定具体的期限。

虽然我国并没有建立起来“辩诉交易”制度，但从目前的刑事调解特点来看，一定程度上有着辩诉交易的精神内涵，因为真正促成双方愿意进行和解的原因是利益的交换：即刑期和赔偿的交换。但强制医疗程序中却天生的不存在这样一种利益交换机制，不可能因为家属赔偿了就缩短精神病人的强制医疗期限。

因此，笔者认为法律应该明确强制医疗程序中受害人如果在强制医疗阶段未获得被申请人的赔偿那么其可以另行提起民事诉讼索要赔偿，因为根据法律规定精神病人造成的损害他的法定代理人或者监护人是负有赔偿责任的。

五、执行阶段

本案被告人王某于2013年3月17日当天即从临时保护约束场所转移至强制医疗场所进行强制治疗。据笔者了解，王某的临时性保护约束场所和强制医疗的场所其实都在安康医院，只不过二者不是同一间房子而已。从安康医院的执行活动中，笔者发现以下两个问题比较突出：

1. 混押。本案的被执行人王某是一个经过强制医疗程序送交强制执行的人员，而与其在一起接受治疗的人还有许多，他们大多是原来新刑事诉讼法实施前治安案件中关押的精神病人，将王某与这些人关在一起笔者认为有所不妥：他们涉嫌的罪名、适用程序、治疗的措施都是不同的，此外关押的缘由、决定的机关、是否受检察机关监督都是不同的，将如此不同的两种人混押在一起显然是不妥的（当然我们的安康医院资源有限，这样做也是现实的无奈之举）。

2. 新刑事诉讼法实施前已经在押的精神病人处理问题。笔者从安康医院了解到现在安康医院关押的精神病人很多，他们绝大多数都是新法实施以前就送进来进行治疗的，其中很多人都是涉嫌危害治安或者刑事犯罪被送进来的，笔者想到，就这样的一个群体来看，如果继续这样对他们关押是否有：无正当理由非法关押之嫌。因为他们毕竟都不是经过法院通过强制医疗程序决定送交执行的，而大部分都属于公安机关直接决定送交执行的（安康医院是一个公安机关的执行场所，所以新法实施前对精神病人的强制医疗是由公安自己决定自己执行的，没有外部的监督）。当然这涉及一个新旧法衔接问题，涉及新法是否有溯及力问题。从社会实际和运行成本来看，司法机关没有那么大财力将安康医院关押的所有病人都通过强制医疗程序决定是否关押，但毕竟新法实施前关押在安康医院的精神病人的合法权益应该受到保障，否则会损害法律面前人人平等的宪法原则：新法实施后精神病人的合法权益有了保障，新法实施前的精神病人则仍旧处于无监督无保障状态。因此，如何妥善处理新法的溯及力问题直接关系到宪法的基本原则和新法适用前安康医院已经关押的精神病人的合法权益保障问题。

六、复议程序

刑事强制医疗程序是一审终局的，一审法院作出决定立即生效，上一级的法院只有复议权，而没有二审权，本案中王某的家属申请了上一级法院复议，复议的原因是：家属给予被害人所有赔偿并取得了被害人的谅解、家属有能力看护好精神病人并给予他最好的治疗，希望法院对精神病人予以释放，现就本案复议情形和遇到的问题加以阐释：

首先，关于本案的复议：某中级人民法院于2013年4月1日受理本案复议。在复议期间中级人民法院的法官通过查阅某区法院的案卷，了解案件情况与证据，并且通过联系被执行人的家属（申请复议人），并且亲自去安康医院会见王某和其主治医师了解情况，最终于2013年4月25日作出维持原决定的复议决定。复议中本案的焦点问题主要有两个：一是某区法院的决定是否正确，二是被执行人王某是否仍然具有危害社会的可能。通过对案件的了解，本案被执行人王某在对其采取临时保护措施期间仍旧具有幻听、臆想并且伤人情形，虽然在送交强制治疗期间病情有所好转，但只是刚刚稳定仍需阶段性的持续治疗，且其本人在意识清醒时也同意继续接受治疗，故此，复议法院决定维持某区法院的决定继续对其进行治疗。

其次，复议法院在对案件进行复议时遇到的窘境。具体表现如下：

第一，性质定位上。刑事强制医疗程序复议的性质定位：因为复议本来就是一个行政特征的程序，但本案是司法机关在当事人参与下的复议，那么又具有了司法特征。因此，强制医疗程序的复议时一个兼具行政与司法性质的复议。但这个复议与行政复议和普通二审程序的区别在哪呢？

第二，具体操作中：

1. 是否组成合议庭。法律只规定法院在审理强制医疗案件中应该组成合议庭，但组成合议庭只是规定在审理程序中，并没有说复议程序中是否也应该组成合议庭？本案为了慎重起见，复议法院决定参照二审由3个审判员组成了复议的合议庭。

2. 是否开庭审理。行政机关的行政复议一般是不开庭审理，只是书面审即可，而且，本程序中即使复议法院想开庭审理也无法操作，因为如果开庭那么就意味着检察院应派员出庭，那按照对等性原则是应该由中级人民法院的对应检察院出庭，但本案件在原审法院已经生效开始执行了，二审法院对应的检察院没有接触本案的资料，而且一个生效的判决，检察院何必要出庭应诉呢？又不是审判监督程序再审的案件。而如果是要原审检察院派员出庭，那岂不是有诉讼不对等之嫌，怎么能中级人民法院对应基层检察院呢？如果检察院不派员出庭，缺乏当事双方的对抗与辩驳，这样的开庭审理并没有什么实质效果，法庭审理形同虚设。

3. 复议庭审模式怎么走？已经生效的决定再走诉讼模式不是相当于二审了吗？鉴于复议并不是二审程序，没有对应的检察院出庭复议，此外，当事双方对于强制医疗三要件中的案件的事实，是否是精神病人都没有争议，仅对第三个要件即是否具有继续危害社会可能有争议，所以中级人民法院并没有采取开庭审理模式而是采用书面复议模式。不过并非所有的案件都是事实争议清楚的，都无需开庭审理的，因此，立法是不是应该考虑复议的具体模式了。

4. 当事人各方的称谓。由于本案是一个特别程序，所以关于本案复议期间原审当事人的称谓颇为头疼，因为原审检察院是申请人，而复议阶段被执行人的家属是申请人，而二者申请的请求又是不同的，法律没有明确的称谓用于他们。某中级人民法院暂且将其归类为：原审检察院为原申请机关，被执行人的家属为复议申请人、被执行人为原审被申请人。

5. 复议期限是多久。法律只规定强制医疗程序的作出期限是1个月，但对于复议期限则没有规定，但复议期限没有规定是否意味着我们可以无限制地复议下去，当然不是，那样情形下如果被执行人确系应该释放的人员，这样的久拖不决岂不侵害了其合法权益，因此，本案中级人民法院参照了原决定的1个月期限将复议期限也限定在1个月内。

6. 如果复议后释放被执行人，是上一级法院自己直接作出决定还是责令原法院作出决定。对于维持原决定的决定比较简单，而要是改变原决定即复议决定将被执行人予以释放怎么办？法院只规定了原审法院才有权决定是否强制医疗，对于复议法院是否具有此权力法院没有规定，仅仅是在后边执行的时候提到如果执行期间被执行人已不具有社会危害性，那么想要改变原审决定必须报原决定法院予以作出，如此，可不可以说上一级法院在复议期间原审的决定已经在执行，而要作出改变的决定，也必须由原审法院决定而不是上一级法院，即由上一级法院作出责令原审法院改变原决定而不是由上一级法院直接作出改变的决定。

当然上述的讨论仅仅是以点概面，不能完全说清楚或者反映强制医疗实践操作中的瓶颈，但鉴于笔者能力所限只能将自己所能够了解的东西反映出来，期望能对强制医疗程序改善提供些许帮助。

参考文献

[1] 李娜玲："刑事强制医疗程序适用对象之研究"，载《法学杂志》2012年第10期。

[2] 冯仁强、张曦、李益明："强制医疗中的法律问题探析——以精神病强制医疗程序为视角"，载《河北科技大学学报》2012年第6期。

[3] 汪海燕、王迎龙："我国刑事强制医疗程序研究"，载《江淮论坛》2012年第5期。

[4] 秦宗文："刑事强制医疗程序研究"，载《华东政法大学学报》2012年第5期。

[5] 刘文："强制医疗程序探究"，载《医学与法学》2012年第3期。

[6] 陈卫东、程雷："司法精神病鉴定基本问题研究"，载《法学研究》2012年第1期。

[7] 朗胜主编：《中华人民共和国2012刑事诉讼法修改与适用》，新华出版社2012年版。

[8] 陈卫东、程雷：《2012刑事诉讼法修改条文理解与适用》，中国法制出版社2012年版。

司法鉴定风险防范问题研究

刘建伟 *

一、前　言

随着社会的进步和人民法律意识的提高，目前在诉讼过程中对于证据的要求越来越高。鉴定意见作为我国法定证据之一，发挥着越来越大的作用。但随着多次重复鉴定、鉴定意见相互矛盾冲突情况的发生，人们也逐渐开始透过“科学的光环”审慎地对待司法鉴定意见这种科学证据，渐渐认识到尽管鉴定意见有种种其他证据形式无法替代的特殊功能，甚至在某些案件的事实认定上具有决定性的作用，鉴定人也多是各方面的专家，但它与其他任何的言词证据一样，也存在着许多虚假的可能性。因而，大家对司法鉴定的神秘感和信任感降低，代之以来的是逐日增多的关于鉴定意见的质疑和对司法鉴定工作的投诉。近几年来，关于对鉴定意见的异议和投诉不断见诸网络和报端，大大影响了司法鉴定工作的科学性和严肃性，也为我们司法鉴定人提高鉴定风险防范意识敲响了警钟。本人拟初步对司法鉴定风险防范进行一定的论述，以期得到广大同行的共鸣，起到抛砖引玉之目的。

二、司法鉴定风险防范的必要性

（一）我国法律法规对司法鉴定人法律责任有着明确的规定

鉴定人是以其提供的专业知识以及在其专业范围内的经验法则、专家意见等，来帮助发现案件的真相的。司法鉴定人所从事的鉴定活动虽然是以科学技术为指导的科技实证活动，但同时也是一个由主观性支配的有意识的取证活动。在司法鉴定实践中，并非没有司法鉴定人因故意或过失不履行法定或约定义务、因错鉴等给当事人造成损害情况的可能。并且，随着对鉴定需求的大量增加，出现错误鉴定的机率也就会大大增加。于是，司法鉴定人的责任就凸显出来，成为一个不容忽视的问题。司法部《司法鉴定人登记管理办法》第 28 ~31 条对司法鉴定人的法律责任有明确的规定：司法鉴定人有违反本法规定的，可由省级司法行政机关依法给予警告，并责令其改正；或给予停止执业 3 个月以上 1 年以下的处罚；情节严重的，撤销登记；构成犯罪的，依法追究刑事责任；司法鉴定人在执业活动中，因故意或者重大过失行为给当事人造成损失的，省级司法行政机关应当责令其停止司法鉴定活动，并处以违法所得 1 ~3 倍的罚款，罚款总额最高不得超过 3 万元。其所在的司法鉴定机构依法承担赔偿责任后，可以向有过错行为的司法鉴定人追偿。司法鉴定人因违法鉴定或鉴定行为过错应负的法律责任，可能只承担 1 项，也可能同时承担多项，这取决于司法鉴定人鉴定行为的性质。司法鉴定人员会因不当的执业行为而需承担刑事、民事、行政以及诉讼法责任等

* 刘建伟，博士，副教授、高级工程师，硕士生导师。中国政法大学证据科学教育部重点实验室，北京，100040。Email：liujianwei@ cupl. edu. cn。

法律责任，所以有必要对司法鉴定工作加强风险防范措施。

（二）司法鉴定技术本身的局限

这是由司法鉴定的科学属性决定的。司法鉴定是鉴定人运用科学技术或者专门知识对诉讼涉及的专门性问题进行鉴别和判断并提供鉴定意见的活动。因而进行鉴定所运用的知识、方法和技术需要依赖于其他科学技术的发展。一方面，司法鉴定技术与当代科学技术的发展水平是相适应的，解决的专业问题不会超过现有科学技术能够认识的范畴。如在赵作海一案中，1998 年案发当时，由于鉴定技术的限制，骨头中的 DNA 检测技术还不过关，所以没有检测出 DNA，而在 2010 年由于技术水平的提升，鉴定人员在被害人的骨头中提取出了 DNA，从而为案件最终判决提供了重要证据。另一方面，用于司法鉴定的鉴定技术必须是成熟的科学技术，必须得到广大同行的认可。那些停留在实验室阶段的技术或未经验收的科研成果是不能用于司法鉴定工作的。如果监管不严，就会造成误鉴。如文件制成时间的鉴定之所以是一个世界性难题，并不是因为缺乏精密的分析仪器，而是作为检验对象的文件材料往往受到许多因素的影响和制约。如书写工具、文件存放情况、文件所处环境的温湿度等，均能使文件材料随时间发生很大变化，因而到目前为止，对文件材料进行的书写时间检验只能停留在实验室阶段，在司法鉴定实践中，还没有一个完美、成熟、系统的方法能准确地鉴定出某文件具体书写时间。

（三）司法鉴定工作市场化的影响

随着“2.28 决定”的颁布实施，司法鉴定工作逐渐发生重大变化。突出的表现就是面向社会服务的司法鉴定机构像“雨后春笋”般发展起来。司法鉴定工作市场化的结果就是对经济利益的追逐。当经济利益与公正鉴定的目标相冲突时，如果没有一定的政策相制约，必然就会引起司法鉴定市场的混乱，动摇司法鉴定意见的证据效力，也必然会使司法鉴定的权威荡然无存。如有地方司法鉴定机构为了经济利益，存在不具备受理文件制成时间鉴定的技术能力而超范围收案、不具备鉴定条件的根据案情来确定最后的鉴定意见等情况，严重地影响了司法鉴定工作的科学性和严肃性。网络上大量的关于司法鉴定的异议和投诉多和鉴定人的中立性有关。

（四）案件当事人法律意识和维权意识的提高

随着社会的进步，普法工作的拓宽，人民群众的法律观念逐渐提高。这一方面有助于人民群众依法维护自己的各项权利，另一方面也使得司法鉴定机构及鉴定人努力提高鉴定质量。这是积极的方面。然而，随着社会诚信体系的缺失，相关部门在处理投诉、上访等行为时原则性不强，使得一些无效投诉中当事人本不应该得到保护的非法利益得到了保护，这使个别当事人尝到了甜头，热衷于投诉、上访，有的甚至发展成“鉴闹”，使得面向社会服务的鉴定机构几近沦为弱势群体。近年来鉴定机构、鉴定人被当事人聚众围堵、围攻的事件屡见不鲜，甚至有当事人住在鉴定机构办公场所多日的事件发生。

三、当前司法鉴定工作中存在的问题

司法鉴定在实践中暴露出一些问题，概括如下：

（一）从事司法鉴定的鉴定人的专业资质认定标准的缺失

司法鉴定人作为专家，正是因为其具有一般人所不掌握的专业知识和技能，也正是其自身的专业技能，才保障了司法鉴定意见的科学性。为了保持鉴定人具备必要的专业能力，除了强化准入标准外，还应该定期对司法鉴定人员的技术能力进行考核，否则，鉴定质量控制之目标将难以实现，司法鉴定活动的“可信程度”也会大打折扣。一旦司法鉴定意见出现失误，则不仅会增加诉讼成本，影响到诉讼裁决，而且可能酿成冤假错案，损害司法权威。如在鉴定实践中，有些从事文件制成时间鉴定的鉴定人并不一定具有相应的专业知识，只是经过简单的培训获得了司法鉴定人资格。如果将案件的文件物证交由这些鉴定人进行文件制成时间的鉴定，鉴定的准确性如何保障?不言而喻。可见，制定统一的司法鉴定人专业资质认定标准不仅可保证司法鉴定意见的证据效力，而且也是减少重复鉴定、多重鉴定，解决司法鉴定意见采信难的有效对策之一。

（二）进行司法鉴定的技术方法标准的缺失

司法鉴定技术方法标准的缺失是当前司法鉴定工作面临的重大问题，各家鉴定机构往往各自为战，纷纷采用自制方法标准进行鉴定。既没有经过论证，也没有得到行业认可，极大地影响了司法鉴定工作的严肃性。表现在：

1. 我国尚未建立统一的司法鉴定的技术方法标准

技术方法是实施司法鉴定的技术依据，应优先选择使用国际、区域、国家标准的技术方法。这些方法是通过统一验证的最可靠的技术方法。进行司法鉴定时，应当优先选择国际、区域、国家标准、行业标准或者司法部批准使用的技术规范。若无上述标准时，应采用经过统一验证的比较成熟和完善的技术方法，如相关技术组织、有关书籍期刊发布的或由设备制造商制定的技术方法。如果没有相关的国际标准、国家标准或公认的行业标准，司法鉴定机构也可以自行制定相应的技术方法，即非标准方法，但应保证自制非标准方法的有效性。司法鉴定机构自行制定的非标准方法，经确认后，可以作为资质认定项目。自制非标准方法的确认应遵照省级以上司法行政机关的规定进行。自制的非标准方法须有相关技术单位验证其可靠性或者经有关主管部门核准后，由司法鉴定机构负责人批准和委托人接受，并将该方法进行文件规定。利用司法鉴定的相关技术方法得出的鉴定意见应具有可验证性和可重复性。所谓可验证性和可重复性，就是其他鉴定人使用相同的技术方法得到一致的结果。但在司法实践中，我国还没有统一的司法鉴定技术方法标准，每个鉴定机构往往都持有自己的秘密武器，出于种种目的，自制的方法常以技术秘密为由不予公开，从而不利于对鉴定意见进行检验监督，这样既剥夺了法律赋予当事人应有的权利，也使一些鉴定机构、鉴定人的行为失去了监督。同时，在当前检验方法有限的情况下，一些错案得不到及时的纠正。

2. 现有司法鉴定的一些技术方法存在一定的局限性

现有司法鉴定的技术方法绝大多数是科学的、可行的，能够满足司法鉴定的需要。但随着社会分工的日益细化，司法鉴定的客体日趋复杂，也有一些技术方法显示出一定的局限性，不能满足当前形势下实际办案、法庭诉讼等对此提出的需求，这就需要广大鉴定人员对此进行更加深入的研究，最大可能地减少在检验时的限制条件，扩大适用对象，以利于操作。如在文件制成时间领域，无论是通过确定构成文件有关要素等的形成时间上限方法确定文件最早可能形成的时间，还是通过对文字色料书写在纸张上以后随时间变化规律的发现，在与已知时间文件比较后得出文件相对制作时间的方法，都存在较大的局限性，并且只能解决某种色料形成文件一部分时间内的时间鉴定问题，而不能对文件的绝对时间或未有限定条件的文件制成时间作出准确的鉴别。如在已有的方法中，主要是针对圆珠笔油、蓝黑墨水、红色印油等文件制成时间的鉴定，而对打印、复印、碳黑墨水等形成的文件则无能为力。

3. 实践中有些鉴定机构无限扩大某些鉴定方法的适用对象和应用范围，司法鉴定工作缺乏科学的、实事求是的态度

一般情况下，一种鉴定方法只有在特定的条件下针对一定的检验对象使用，其科学性才能得到保证，得出的鉴定意见才能客观、准确。而那种无限扩大使用对象和应用范围的做法，其科学性无从谈起。例如，文件制成时间的鉴定多数依靠一些物理、化学的方法，如薄层色谱法、分光光度计法、热分析法、傅立叶红外光谱法等，这些仪器和方法有的针对某种墨水的检验效果较好，有的在文件形成的某一阶段有较好的检验效果。并且，在运用这些方法时，都必须与同种色料、纸张及相同保管条件下的已知样本作比对，才能得出较为准确的鉴定意见。但是，在这个鉴定项目上，有的鉴定机构、鉴定人员无限扩大某些鉴定技术方法的应用范围，夸大检验结果，并仍然口口声声称采用了科学的鉴定方法。这与以往的在鉴定意见上有分歧不同，这是一种在检验工作中缺乏科学的、实事求是的态度，是对法律和当事人的不负责任。有时，也是利益驱动使然。所以，应当坚决克服那种以为随便使用了某种科学的技术方法，就可以不考虑被检对象的具体情况和是否具有可比条件，就一定会得出科学结论的错误观点。

（三）司法鉴定的受理环节亟待进一步完善

“严谨的收案是成功鉴定的一半”。案件受理阶段，是整个鉴定过程中鉴定人能够获取信息的最佳阶段。在这个环节中，为什么进行鉴定、进行什么样的鉴定、鉴定意见作出会有哪些法律后果都是我们需要了解的。同时需要鉴定的检材是否具备鉴定条件、用于比对的样本是否充分、案情资料是否翔实都影响着最后的鉴定意见是否客观准确，因而在收案环节一定要给予高度重视。实践证明，一些久鉴不决或重复鉴定的案件往往都是由于收案时没有严格把关所致。我们曾经受理过一起重新鉴定的案件，之前经过省部两级司法鉴定机构的鉴定，均对检材中的签名进行了认定。后法院委托到笔者所在单位仍然要求对签名的真伪进行鉴定。笔者在受理案件时详细询问了双方当事人的争议焦点是什么，获悉一方当事人除了否定签名的真实性之外，还对材料本身的真实性存在疑议，从而帮助委托人确定了除鉴定签名真实性外还应对文件物证本身的真实性进行鉴定的鉴定要求。通过进一步检验，发现签名确为被鉴定人书写，但整个文件物证是在原有被鉴定人书写的收条上添加了一些字迹内容后变造形成的，因而整个文件物证的真实性是存在问题的。这就避免了为“违法行为提供合法证明”的后果。鉴定意见出具后，法院很快就进行了判决，除了驳回原告的无理要求外，还对造假者给予了处罚，取得了很好的法律效果和社会效果。

（四）司法鉴定人员法律知识亟需进一步加强

司法鉴定是鉴定人对诉讼中涉及的专门性问题进行鉴别和判断并提供鉴定意见的活动，因而具有法定性。表现在司法鉴定机构必须依法成立；鉴定人资格必须依法取得，并施行鉴定负责制；司法鉴定的启动和鉴定程序必须依法进行；作为司法鉴定活

动的产品的鉴定意见是法定诉讼证据之一。这就要求司法鉴定人一定要掌握相应的法律知识。但长期以来，大多数司法鉴定人只注重专业技术的培训而忽视了法律知识的学习，“重技术轻程序”的思维在一定范围内普遍存在。他们不懂得“毒树之果”的危害，导致辛辛苦苦作出的鉴定意见最后未被法院采信，既影响了诉讼效率，还使鉴定意见的权威性受损。如某医疗纠纷案，当事人诉某医科大学附属医院存在医疗过错，委托某鉴定机构进行医疗事故鉴定，鉴定意见作出后患方对某鉴定人提出回避，原因是该鉴定人毕业于这所大学，怀疑存在一定的利益关系，后法院不得不重新委托鉴定。本案中鉴定人如懂得一些法律知识的话，鉴定前主动提出回避，就不会是这个结果了。再如，《司法鉴定程序通则》要求在整个鉴定过程中要有不少于两名的鉴定人参与，包括外出调查取证。某鉴定机构在进行文件鉴定时，因只有一名鉴定人带领一名没有鉴定资格的鉴定助理去工商局调查取证，后被当事人投诉导致鉴定意见未被采信。可见相关法律法规知识的掌握对鉴定人至关重要。此外，新《刑事诉讼法》、《民事诉讼法》强化了鉴定人出庭的义务，尤其是民诉法更是规定如鉴定人无正当理由拒绝出庭的，除鉴定意见不被采信外，还应退还已收鉴定费用。这些规定，鉴定人都应及时学习，并在鉴定实践中加以注意。

四、司法鉴定的风险防范对策

（一）加强司法鉴定人的素质培养

司法鉴定之所以要求由具有专门知识的人来进行，是因为鉴定人所接受的专业训练是鉴定工作的基础与保障，使之能完成非专业人士不能完成的工作，并做出合理的鉴定意见。鉴定人的专业理论知识与技术水平在保证鉴定的科学性上起着重要的作用，鉴定人科学的工作态度，经验的丰富程度也直接影响着鉴定的科学性。

加强鉴定人的素质培养，一方面，应严格控制司法鉴定人的准入标准。鉴定人应当受到过相应专业训练，具有鉴定所需要的专业知识，拥有从事司法鉴定业务的职业资格。全国人民代表大会常务委员会《关于司法鉴定管理问题的决定》第 4 条明确了关于司法鉴定人从业的条件；司法部《司法鉴定人登记管理办法》第 13 条规定，司法鉴定人的准入条件主要包括学历要求或者专业技术要求，除特殊行业以外，经验型鉴定或技能型鉴定需从事相关工作满 10 年，高级专业技术职称或具备大学本科相关专业学历从事司法鉴定工作满 5 年者，方可申请从事司法鉴定工作。这一制度初步解决了司法鉴定人的资格条件问题，并用法律明确固定我国采用的是“固定资格”的司法鉴定人“事前”资格审查制度。

另一方面，提高司法鉴定人的专业技术能力，建立司法鉴定人的职业资质认定规则。由具备相应的专业知识、不以营利为目的的“第三方技术服务组织”，每 5 年对司法鉴定资格申请者分别从技术、法律和程序层面进行考核和实际检案的能力验证，从而认定司法鉴定人的执业资质。

（二）引入先进的仪器设备进行司法鉴定

许多鉴定项目，仅仅依靠鉴定人自身的专门知识无法完成，还必须借助实验室和相关仪器设备。因此，鉴定机构的实验室、相关仪器设备等是否具有良好的技术条件，往往直接关乎能否进行鉴定以及能否得到准确、科学的鉴定意见。司法鉴定专业不是固定不变的，而是逐渐发展进步的。随着现代科学技术的迅速发展，各种精密的仪器和先进的方法不断出现，要求我们司法鉴定工作者必须始终关注科学的前沿，时刻准备将科研的最新成果移植到司法鉴定工作中来，提高司法鉴定意见的客观化，为我国司法鉴定事业作出自己应有的贡献。

（三）把好案件受理关

在案件受理环节，一方面要对检材的状况、条件进行严格评估，看其是否具备鉴定条件；另一方面要对样本的数量、质量进行审查，以足以反映被鉴定客体特征为标准来决定是否能满足出具鉴定意见的条件。如目前用于鉴定文件制成时间方法、手段，绝大多数需要比对样本确定文件物证的相对形成时间。因此，样本的选择对鉴定意见的准确出具有至关重要的作用。样本材料必须满足两方面要求，其一，用于比对检验的样本材料须经双方当事人共同确认方可用于鉴定；其二，用于比对的样本材料的纸张、色料及保存条件应与检材的纸张、色料及保存条件相同，得出的结论才科学可靠。为此，最高人民法院司法行政装备管理局于2008年发布《关于对外委托文件制成时间鉴定有关事项的通知》（法司［2008］12号），该通知第2条规定："由于检材与样本在纸张、墨水、油墨、保存环境等方面的不同都会对鉴定结果产生决定性影响，鉴定机构自备的样本不可能满足与送检材在纸张的种类及颜色，墨水、油墨的色料及染料的主要成分，保存环境的温度、湿度等方面相同。因此，不能使用鉴定机构的自备样本进行文件制成时间鉴定。"

此外，还应详细了解案情，找出矛盾双方争执的焦点，调整鉴定要求，理清鉴定思路，以切实解决案件专业问题为出发点进行鉴定，充分发挥司法鉴定专业的魅力。

（四）使用成熟、可靠的司法鉴定技术方法

由于种种原因，我国司法鉴定很多专业还未建立统一的鉴定技术标准。在这个问题上，我们可借鉴美国关于科学技术方法的采信标准，在以下几个方面综合考虑：①该技术方法是否在权威行业出版物上发表并被同行肯定；②该技术方法是否已在实验室或者实践中获得检验，并被证明是正确的或者可行的；③该技术方法是否存在客观标准控制检验过程，如果有，在司法鉴定中的使用是否符合标准；④该技术方法的出错率是否确定；⑤该技术方法是否已被同领域大部分人所接受。

就目前司法鉴定实务而言，在相关的较完善的理论研究成果及标准出台之前，可采用司法鉴定界在实务工作中常采用的一个不成文规则，即鉴定理论和方法必须是各专业统编高校教材和各权威行业期刊中介绍过的，以此作为判断技术方法科学性、先进性的最低标准。那些未经论证并得到同行认可的自制方法或科研过程中使用的单位经过专家论证的技术方法不应用于实际鉴定工作中来。随着全国刑事技术标准化委员会的成立，会有越来越多的标准出台，相信对我国的司法鉴定工作会有很大的促进。

（五）熟悉相关的法律法规

从事司法鉴定的鉴定人，一定要对与司法鉴定有关的法律、法规、规章制度有着深入全面的了解。由于我们做出的鉴定意见是法定的证据之一，所以就有必要熟悉三大诉讼法关于司法鉴定方面有关的规定；由于我们从事的司法鉴定活动必须严格按照相关的规范进行，所以必须掌握《司法鉴定程序规则》、《司法鉴定文书规范》、《司法鉴定收费办法》《司法鉴定投诉处理办法》等法律法规的有关内容，了解司法鉴定人的权利义务，应承担的法律责任，积极履行司法鉴定人出庭作证义务等。

综上所述，我们看到，司法鉴定风险防范对策基本围绕国家实验室认可委员会（CNAS）评价法庭科学实验室的5个重要的技术要素，即人、机、料、法、环来展开，将司法鉴定工作分为5个要素，司法鉴定主体（人）、司法鉴定仪器（机）、司法鉴定客体（料）、司法鉴定技术方法（法）和司法鉴定实验室（环），通过分别完善5个环节的相关规则，来对司法鉴定工作的风险进行防范。因此，积极开展实验室认证认可为我们防范司法鉴定工作的风险提供了有力保障。

司法鉴定主体的选择权

潘 溪*

司法鉴定活动中涉及的选择权利主体主要包括当事人、司法机关和司法鉴定人及鉴定机构，对于在鉴定中各种主体分别拥有不同的选择自由，首先体现在鉴定的启动阶段，在鉴定过程的科学操作和结论形成过程中同样面临各种选择，甚至在质证、采信、应用和排除鉴定意见中同样涉及自由选择的权利。

一、鉴定活动中当事人的选择权

司法活动中的当事人不必然成为鉴定活动的当事人，只有参与鉴定活动的申请、质疑、选择过程，才涉及本文所指的当事人在鉴定活动中的选择权。总体来说，当事人在鉴定活动的过程中可能涉及的选择主要包括是否申请鉴定、申请哪家鉴定机构、是否申请回避和重新鉴定等问题，客观上还可能存在当事人对自己掌握的鉴定证据材料进行取舍的问题。

（一）选择申请司法鉴定

是否申请鉴定是当事人的权利。往往涉及鉴定是在司法实践过程中针对当事人双方争议的专门性或者技术问题提出的，这一问题的提出常出现在双方交换证据或者庭审的过程中。现实中存在两种容易被忽视的误区：一是过分依赖鉴定，对案件事实没有意义的争议、无需通过技术检验即可得出结论的问题等没有必要的鉴定的提出，不仅造成司法资源的浪费、增加当事人的诉累，也降低了司法部门的法律权威。二是当事人由于对法律和鉴定常识的缺乏，无从知晓可以通过申请鉴定解决现实问题。所以审判机关在案件诉讼过程中应当告知当事人可以就有关问题提请鉴定，同时对于当事人的申请进行适当引导，比如对于假证假章中大小规格显然不符，常人肉眼即可辨别的问题，即可由审判人员作出裁决。我国目前的鉴定申请程序通常是由当事人在诉讼过程中提出，法官作出是否委托送检的裁决，所以还存在司法机关不同意启动鉴定程序时当事人的申请鉴定权利问题。不管是基于客观正义的角度还是尊重当事人的选择自由，都应当允许就专门问题直接提请司法鉴定机构进行鉴定，并且在没有正当排除事由情况下，法院应对于该鉴定意见予以同样的对待，即是否认可和采信与法院送检情况采用同样标准。这里同样也涉及重新鉴定的申请和启动问题，对于司法机关是否启动重新鉴定应当采用一定的标准，这一问题本文在效率角度有专门的论述，但是对于当事人来讲，是否申请重新鉴定或者补充鉴定应当也是自主选择权利的一个方面。

（二）选择司法鉴定机构

当事人在鉴定活动中的自由的另外一个重要体现在于对于鉴定机构的选择权，但

* 潘溪，南京师范大学讲师，南京师范大学司法鉴定中心主任助理。

是这一方面的选择权应该是有所限制的。常见的处理方式是由法院提供可以解决专门鉴定问题的鉴定机构名单，由申请鉴定的一方提出选择哪家鉴定机构，对方当事人如果不同意，可以采用协商解决或者摇号选择的办法确定。有学者提出的鉴定法律专家建议稿也肯定了这一点，指出“当事人对鉴定主题选任的合意优先于法官依职权指定鉴定主体”。〔1〕选择鉴定机构和鉴定人的同时自然涉及回避问题，应当“割断鉴定人与诉讼结果之间的直接利害关系，保证鉴定意见的客观性”，〔2〕我国法律对鉴定人的回避制度有明文规定，各地鉴定规章中也有对于限制鉴定机构和人员与当事人非正常接触的规范。如何避免鉴定人在鉴定活动中徇私，在鉴定机构选择之初和鉴定进行中都应当考虑回避问题，这一问题在医疗事故、医患纠纷问题的鉴定活动中尤为突出。除了立法和制度规范外，各地目前纷纷成立的司法鉴定行业协会也应该对该问题有所作为。

二、鉴定活动中审判人员的选择权

审判人员在鉴定活动中主要存在对于鉴定机构的选择，对于鉴定意见的采信和排除等方面的选择权利。法官在诉讼过程中处于事实裁判者的地位，所以对鉴定机构的选择和对鉴定意见证明力的判断有着绝对的地位和权力。

（一）选择鉴定机构

司法鉴定公平所面临的一个最初问题可能就是对于鉴定人和鉴定机构的选择问题，“而这一问题的焦点又在于分配这种权利时，如何实现对当事双方的平等对待，而不至于使双方权利失衡”。〔3〕大陆法系国家奉行的是职权主义的鉴定制度模式，鉴定人作为法官的专家助手，所以一般对于鉴定人的选任都基于法官的职权。比如《德国刑事诉讼法典》规定，由法官决定需要聘请的鉴定人及人数，而控辩双方无此项权利。〔4〕《意大利刑事诉讼法典》也规定“法官可主动裁定进行鉴定，在鉴定中说明理由，任命鉴定人，概要地说明调查对象，指出要求鉴定人到场的日期、时间和地点。”〔5〕我国对于鉴定机构的选择通常存在两种模式，一个是合意、一个是指定。前文已经述及作为司法鉴定的利益涉及的当事人具有一定的公平选择权，基于双方当事人的协商确定的共同一致选择鉴定机构或者鉴定人的方式有其实质上的优越性。但是双方不能够形成合意的情况下，鉴定机构的选择问题又回到了事实审判者——法官面前。对于法官启动司法鉴定的职权，有学者认为应当区分鉴定范围对待，认为“法院启动鉴定程序指派、聘请鉴定人鉴定的范围，应当……结合职权主义诉讼模式的特点和鉴定制度改革的方向，合理地界定鉴定的范围，并通过实体性和程序性的规定，共同约束法官在鉴定方面的权力。其鉴定范围可分为强制启动鉴定程序的范围、裁量启动坚定程序的范围和限制启动坚定程序的范围”，〔6〕而对不同范围的鉴定项目程序通过立法给予法

---

〔1〕黄维智：《鉴定证据制度研究》，中国检察出版社2006年版，第274页以下。

〔2〕郭华：“论鉴定委托权的合理配置”，载范方平主编：《建构统一司法鉴定管理体制的探索与实践》，中国政法大学出版社2005年版，第265页。

〔3〕汪建成：《理想与现实——刑事证据理论的新探索》，北京大学出版社2006年版，第246页。

〔4〕李昌珂译：《德国刑事诉讼法典》，中国政法大学出版社1995年版，第21页。

〔5〕黄风译：《意大利刑事诉讼法典》，中国政法大学出版社1994年版，第77页以下。

〔6〕郭华：《鉴定结论论》，中国人民公安大学出版社2007年版，第202页。

官不同程度的裁量权。我们认为，我国的鉴定机构选择和鉴定人选任过程中，法官应当首先为当事人双方提供符合法律要求的鉴定机构名单供双方合议，这种名单应当符合某一项鉴定的技术和规范要求外，法官也应当基于效率和鉴定水平作出初步筛选，比如综合考虑地理位置、鉴定时限等因素。在当事人双方合议不成的情况下，法官有权指定鉴定机构，针对不同类别的鉴定范围法官可以采用任意指定或者摇号指定的方式确定。

（二）司法鉴定意见是否采信

鉴定意见是证据的一种，作为证据必然面临是否被法官所采信的抉择，因为鉴定意见本身只是对案件审理中的一个问题得出的、带有鉴定人推理或者主观判断的、存在相对但不是绝对科学认识的证据。鉴定意见的专业性和科学性“都不足以使鉴定意见获得与裁判者做出的事实认定同样的终局性的效力”，所以，“从各国立法情况来看，基本都将鉴定意见置于与其他证据形式同等的地位，交由法官或陪审员依照自由心证原则加以衡量”。[7] 法官作为审判者对鉴定意见证据的选择有天然的权力，作为自由心证的主体，法官对于鉴定意见的采信和排除不仅是一项权力，更加是一种责无旁贷的审查义务。但是由于鉴定意见所涉及的专门问题的特殊性，法官在对鉴定意见进行审查时也容易存在轻率或者武断评价的问题。“法律设计的自由心证证据证明力规则、鉴定意见客观存在分歧的事实，以及鉴定人和事实审理者自身的弱点，使得事实审理者在选择鉴定意见上出现任意性。”[8] 具体采用的审查方式和态度，应该考虑三个方面的因素：首先是鉴定活动的法律性形式要件审查，对于鉴定机构和鉴定人的资质，鉴定案件是否涉及回避制度、鉴定的流程是否符合法律规定等法定规则进行审查；其次是鉴定流程的科学性形式要件的审查，这要求法官借助一定的专业科学知识，或者通过书面咨询和庭审质证让鉴定人举证来进行，主要审查鉴定实验检验过程是否符合科学的形式标准和操作规范；最后，应当结合案件的其他证据和相关材料进行审查，鉴定意见本身的正确性存在一定的概率，所以案件的其他证明材料或者已知的、无争议的事实同样可以是排除鉴定意见的依据。

三、鉴定活动中鉴定人的选择权

司法鉴定人的选择权利主要体现在对于选择科学方法、结论表述与内心确信、出庭质证等方面的讨论，其中也分别对应鉴定人在鉴定活动中的各项义务，除此之外，鉴定人是否可以兼任律师和其他鉴定机构兼职从事鉴定活动，也是鉴定人是否存在选择权的讨论问题。高等院校中从事司法鉴定的人员分为专职鉴定人员和兼职鉴定人员两大类，其中兼职人员可能同时承担教学、科研和司法鉴定的多重任务，虽然其自身有着技术水平和科研能力的优势，但是鉴定活动越来越体现的职业化和专业化给这些鉴定人带来了冲击。

（一）选择科学鉴定方法

司法鉴定人对于鉴定的方法有选择权，鉴定人作为掌握专门知识的技术专家，对于运用何种技术手段解决鉴定问题有自身的经验和技能。同时，对于同类的委托鉴定

---

〔7〕 汪建成：《理想与现实——刑事证据理论的新探索》，北京大学出版社2006年版，第244页。

〔8〕 郭华：《鉴定结论论》，中国人民公安大学出版社2007年版，第61页。

事项，可能存在多种不同的方法得以检验鉴定。这就造成在检验或者鉴定过程中，鉴定人可能面临多种途径并要从中选择一种或者几种来解决专门问题。例如，对于测定一份书写字迹的形成时间，针对不同种的墨迹材料可以采用诸如：离子迁移测定法、文字墨迹化学褪色程度测定法、溶解测定法、墨水成分测定法等方法[9]等，具体采用何种具体测定方法，将由鉴定技术人员通过对于检验材料的技术筛选比对，初步分析后采用具体的检验方法，而这个科学技术方法的选择不应当由当事人或者法官指定，只应当由具备鉴定资质的鉴定人员作出选择。

（二）鉴定意见的表述方式

鉴定人在鉴定过程中对于鉴定意见要署名并对其负责，所以鉴定意见的表述应当依据鉴定人基于科学检验后对检验结果的分析判断，在这个基础上鉴定人形成自己的内心确信，把这个确信的内容以鉴定意见的方式表达出来。所以，司法鉴定人员基于自身对于科学方法和专门知识的掌握，对检验过程和具体检验材料的了解，做出的检验结论应当符合自身的检验实际情况，而不是简单地回答“是”或者“否”的问题。针对检验要求，鉴定人员应当拥有按照实际检验效果得出符合客观情况的检验结论的权力。实际工作中，一些当事人甚至法官可能对鉴定意见提出较为苛刻的要求，或者要求鉴定人精确地回答委托事项中的问题，这并不是实事求是的做法。

（三）出庭接受质证问题

对于一个司法鉴定意见存在质疑，法官或者当事人能否要求鉴定人员出庭解释，答案当然是肯定的。但是，鉴定人是否有出庭质证的选择权，是一个值得讨论的问题。笔者认为，并不是所有的司法鉴定案件都必须鉴定人员出庭作证接受质疑，司法鉴定人员对于鉴定意见的出庭质证应当以一定的方式享有选择的权利。首先，无选择的出庭质证是对鉴定资源的极大浪费，同时鉴定人员出庭产生的差旅、住宿和出庭费用也加大了当事人的支出。其次，一部分鉴定意见的质疑可以通过口头或者书面回答等方式解决。如果是对于鉴定文书中存在的非关键问题、本质问题，比如涉案的双方当事人名称表述错误，日期笔误等，完全可以通过电话沟通、书面发函的方式解决。最后，对于鉴定中涉及法定程序的问题和科学程序的问题应当分别对待。鉴定人员的专门知识决定其对鉴定活动过程中的操作步骤环节符合科学程序的标准和要求，如果这方面存在疑问，鉴定人应当出庭解释。

（四）司法鉴定人员兼职问题

有些鉴定人员由于种种原因可能存在在不同鉴定机构兼职的情况，类似问题法律已经给出了明确的界定。一个鉴定人员不可以同时在两家或者两家以上的鉴定机构担任鉴定人，从事鉴定活动。我国《司法鉴定程序通则》对此有明确规定。这样规定有利于规范鉴定市场秩序，明确鉴定机构和鉴定人员职责，保证鉴定人员的职业责任心。

实践中还存在鉴定人员是否可以同时从事律师职业的问题。一般认为，对于同样案件，一个自然人不可以同时作为代理律师和司法鉴定人，法律虽然没有明文规定，但是，我国《司法鉴定程序通则》（司法部 2007 年 7 月 18 日审议通过）第 20 条规定：“司法鉴定人本人或者其近亲属与委托人、委托的鉴定事项或者鉴定事项涉及的案件有

---

〔9〕 参见贾治辉主编：《文书检验》，法律出版社 2000 年版，第 292 页。

利害关系，可能影响其独立、客观、公正进行鉴定的，应当回避。”可以参照适用。司法鉴定的特征之一就是要求鉴定人员独立、中立，所以以往公检法机关的鉴定机构和鉴定人员不再从事司法鉴定，但是律师与司法机关工作人员的身份存在着明显差异，不能进行简单的类比就认为律师绝对不可以兼任司法鉴定人。实际上，公检法机关代表国家行使司法行政职能，国家在诉讼特别是刑事诉讼活动中是一方，所以剥夺了其中立性。而律师如果不代理特定案件，则不代表任何一方，与司法鉴定活动没有自身利害关系，不管从法律规定还是诉讼资源的角度考虑，都不应当一概排除在司法鉴定人队伍以外。由于律师有从事法律实务的经验，有庭审质证的经历，如果具备相应的鉴定人员资质条件，反而更能够得出有针对性的、有利于解决纠纷的司法鉴定意见。所以，除了涉及自己代理的案件，司法鉴定人应当允许兼任律师。

参考文献

1. 黄维智：《鉴定证据制度研究》，中国检察出版社 2006 年版。

2. 郭华：“论鉴定委托权的合理配置”，载范方平主编：《建构统一司法鉴定管理体制的探索与实践》，中国政法大学出版社 2005 年版。

3. 汪建成：《理想与现实——刑事证据理论的新探索》，北京大学出版社 2006 年版。

4. 李昌珂译：《德国刑事诉讼法典》，中国政法大学出版社 1995 年版。

5. 黄风译：《意大利刑事诉讼法典》，中国政法大学出版社 1994 年版。

6. 郭华：《鉴定意见论》，中国人民公安大学出版社 2007 年版。

7. 贾治辉主编：《文书检验》，法律出版社 2000 年版。

对被羁押人员死因鉴定机制的思考

宋方明 *

以“躲猫猫死”“做梦死”“喝水死”等为代表的一系列羁押场所死亡事件的报道和传播，引发国人对被羁押人员死亡的高度关注。本文尝试性创新被羁押人员的死因鉴定机制，以期能够妥善处置羁押场所的死亡事件，这对于化解社会矛盾、彰显公平正义、构建和谐社会都具有一定的意义。

一、“被羁押人员”范围的确定

在我国，羁押不是一个严格意义上的法律概念，[1] 羁押的本质是在一定期限内，以在专门场所关押的方式，剥夺嫌疑人或被告人的人身自由，以保证一定法律秩序的强制措施。[2] 从我国现行刑事诉讼立法来看，羁押似乎只是拘留或逮捕（法定刑事强制措施）的必然结果和状态，好像是相对特定的；但在刑事司法实践中，能够带来限制人身自由的必然结果和状态的强制措施，又不限于刑事拘留或逮捕。[3] 羁押概念的不特定及开放性，使得能够对羁押场所和被羁押人员的概念进行学理解释。

有学者认为，羁押场所这个概念的外延，应该涵盖公权力机关依法限制公民人身自由的一切场所，包括：依法设置的固定羁押场所，如监狱、看守所、拘留所、强制戒毒所等；侦查机关依法设立的审讯室等；侦查机关在侦查阶段设立的临时羁押地点；采取拘传、取保候审和监视居住等限制公民人身自由的强制措施的场所；纪检、监察等部门对有关涉案人员进行调查的“双规”、“双指”场所；等等。[4] 本文所指的被羁押人员就是上述场所关押的人员。他们的相同之处在于都处在公权力机关管控之下，一旦发生死亡案件，极容易引发当事人家属的激愤和猜疑，进而有可能引发公共舆情甚至群体性事件。

二、检察机关相应检察职责的界定

（一）检察机关负责对被羁押人员死亡事件进行检察监督

尽管有学者指出，一切公权力机关限制人身自由的场所都应被纳入法律监督的范围内，[5] 但检察机关的法律监督需要依法进行，需要在现行的法律法规授权的范围内

---

* 中国政法大学证据科学教育部重点实验室，北京，100088，Email：sfm7863@gmail.com。

本文系中国政法大学博士创新实践活动基金项目“在押人员死亡调查检验制度初探”（2012BSCX20）阶段性成果，项目负责人为中国政法大学博士研究生宋方明。

〔1〕 石经海：“我国羁押制度的法文化考察”，载《法律科学》2008 年第 3 期。

〔2〕 隋光伟：“羁押属性及其适用原则”，载《当代法学》2004 年第 3 期。

〔3〕 参见石经海：“论羁押制度的内核”，载《中国刑事法杂志》2009 年第 2 期。

〔4〕 参见刁振娇：“羁押场所非正常死亡事件的宪法反思”，载《法学》2010 年第 7 期。

〔5〕 参见刁振娇：“羁押场所非正常死亡事件的宪法反思”，载《法学》2010 年第 7 期。

开展监督，因此是一种有限的监督。[6] 根据《监狱法》第55条、《看守所条例》第27条、《劳动教养管理工作执法细则》第60条等，[7] 监狱、看守所等监管场所[8]发现被监管人员死亡，应立即向承担监管场所检察任务的检察机关报告，即监管场所承担着立即报告职责。相应地，检察机关也应立即做出反应。根据最高人民检察院《关于监管场所被监管人员死亡检察程序的规定（试行）》，检察机关接到监管场所发生被监管人员死亡报告后，应当立即受理，并且派员及时介入，展开审查、调查，掌握情况，对被监管人员死亡的处理工作全程进行法律监督。而对未明文列入检察监督范围的其他羁押场所，其日常工作并不在检察机关检察监督之下，但是一旦发生被羁押人员死亡事件，如果涉嫌存在国家机关工作人员渎职犯罪的，则仍应由检察机关负责立案查处。

（二）检察机关负责对被羁押人员涉嫌非正常死亡的进行检验鉴定

2005年，全国人大常委会《关于司法鉴定管理问题的决定》（以下简称《决定》）的出台，揭开了我国司法鉴定领域改革大幕，与人民法院和司法行政部门鉴定机构被撤销的命运不同，检察机关鉴定机构“根据侦查需要设立”而得以保存，其为检察机关对羁押场所的案件侦查应该责无旁贷地提供技术协助。根据《监狱法》第55条、《看守所在押人员死亡处理规定》第9条、《劳动教养管理工作执法细则》第60条等，监管场所发生非正常死亡的，人民检察院应该立即检验，对死亡原因作出鉴定。根据《人民检察院法医工作细则（试行）》的规定，被监管人员非正常死亡的尸体是检察机关法医进行检验鉴定的主要内容之一。另外，发生在其他羁押场所（如侦查机关的讯问室、纪检部门的“双规”场所等）的非正常死亡事件，有可能涉嫌体罚虐待、刑讯逼供、滥用职权等违法乱纪行为，这也需要检察机关鉴定机构查明死因，并为渎职侵权检察部门侦办案件提供线索、指明方向。

三、检察机关鉴定机构的状况和处境

（一）检察技术部门和检察机关鉴定机构之间的关系

检察机关鉴定机构隶属检察技术部门，二者之间是管理与被管理的关系，检察技术部门另外还承担着检察信息化工作及综合管理工作，有相当多的非技术鉴定人员。具有检察技术部门单位建制是检察机关设立鉴定机构的基础条件，此前，市级检察院以上及部分基层检察院均设置有检察技术部门，但根据《决定》的规定，[9] 并不是所有检察技术部门都具备设立鉴定机构的条件。人民检察院设立鉴定机构是以有能力开展鉴定业务的检察技术部门为基础，实行“一套人马、两块牌子”，而不是在检察技术部门之外再设立一个司法鉴定机构。

---

〔6〕参见周伟：“监管场所被监管人死亡若干问题研究”，载《中国刑事法杂志》第2011年第4期。

〔7〕《拘留所条例实施办法》第47条、《公安机关强制隔离戒毒所管理办法》第38条、《司法行政机关强制隔离戒毒工作规定》第62条等都作出类似规定，要求发生所内死亡事件后向人民检察院报告。

〔8〕监管场所是检察机关内部通行叫法，是狭义的羁押场所，指明文规定属于刑罚执行检察监督范围的羁押场所。相应地，被监管人即指关押在前述监管场所的人员。

〔9〕《决定》第5条规定：“法人或者其他组织申请从事司法鉴定业务的，应当具备下列条件：（一）有明确的业务范围；（二）有在业务范围内进行司法鉴定所必需的仪器、设备；（三）有在业务范围内进行司法鉴定所必需的依法通过计量认证或实验室认可的检测实验室；（四）每项司法鉴定业务有三名以上鉴定人。”

（二）检察机关鉴定机构的基本现状

全国各级检察技术部门都或多或少地存在着人员流失、检验鉴定设备匮乏、知识更新不及时等问题，其中尤以专业人员不足为掣肘。最高人民检察院为此于2009年出台了《关于检察机关鉴定资源整合及相关工作的指导意见》，借以改善检察机关司法鉴定资源缺乏、鉴定人分散的状况，并积极探索建立了检察技术部门“上下一体、横向联动”的工作机制，但这毕竟是为了各地市检察机关鉴定机构顺利登记注册的一时权宜之策，长此以往并不利于鉴定工作的展开。截至2013年5月，全国检察机关完成审核登记的鉴定机构310家、鉴定人4831人，其中法医鉴定人1451人（包括已经调离检察技术部门的兼职法医鉴定人111人）。〔10〕相比较全国3640〔11〕家检察院，这意味着平均每家检察院拥有不到1名法医鉴定人，基层检察院鉴定机构基本丧失殆尽。

（三）对被羁押人员死因鉴定工作的窘境

近年来，被羁押人员死亡持续成为公众和媒体关注的焦点，成为新的社会矛盾触点，敏感性很强，被羁押人员的死因鉴定工作就成了重中之重。出于自身条件的限制，根据《人民检察院刑事诉讼规则（试行）》第248条规定“必要的时候，也可以聘请其他有鉴定资格的人员进行”，再加上社会鉴定资源的蓬勃发展，于是，处于窘境之中的检察技术部门，往往将此项业务推向社会。这尽管避免了死者家属因羁押场所与检察机关关系密切而对检察机关死因鉴定信赖力不够的影响，但另一方面，完全由社会鉴定机构承担又面临检察监督缺位、侦查与鉴定脱节等问题，毕竟社会鉴定机构属营利化运行，且缺乏现场勘验、调查取证等的业务优势和职权优势。

四、日本的检视官制度对我们的借鉴

在日本，死因鉴定的法医学解剖分为司法解剖与行政解剖，前者主要负责他杀、伤害致死、过失致人死亡、交通肇事逃逸及其他怀疑涉及刑事犯罪死亡的尸体检验；后者主要适用于经检视后认为死亡与犯罪无关但死因不明确者，如突然病死、灾害死亡、自身过失导致死亡、明确的自杀或死因不明的急性死亡和事故死亡尸体的检验。除在少数大城市（东京、大阪、横滨、神户四地）设置了监察医务院承担行政解剖职责之外，日本死因鉴定的法医学解剖均在大学的法医学教室进行，而不由警察机关承担，并以法律条款加以规定。由于实施法医解剖的医师不隶属于警察部门也不承担现场尸体勘验的任务，且日本医学院校的法医学教室一般在每日10时至15时进行尸体解剖，为了不影响及时办案，日本设置了检视官制度，检视官就成为警方负责现场勘查、尸表检验、区分案件性质、决定是否实施解剖、与解剖医师沟通协调等工作的重要角色。在日本，检视官由具有刑事侦查经验的警官在接受法医学知识培训后担任。解剖前，检视官会向执刀法医详细介绍尸体的现场检视和调查走访情况，同时提出希望明确的主要问题；检视官全程参与解剖过程，同时记录各种重要的阴性和阳性发现，在需要时也会协助进行一些解剖操作；解剖结束后，执刀法医会向检视官通报解剖所见、初步可以确定的死因、死亡时间等，检视官会将这些信息及时转达给检察官及案件承

〔10〕数据来源于最高人民检察院检察技术信息研究中心。

〔11〕数据截至2011年12月，《中国法律年鉴（2012年）》，中国法律年鉴社出版，第1068页。

办警署，并对下一步的工作进行安排布置。[12]

五、我国检察机关移植日本检视官制度的设想

（一）我国检察机关移植日本检视官制度必要性之探讨

1. 内部环境决定检察机关死因鉴定工作应充分利用社会资源。对比中日两国司法鉴定体制现状，与日本警察机关不设法医鉴定机构相比，我国公安机关法医鉴定力量雄厚，人员齐整、设备先进、经费充足，可谓“兵强马壮”，甚至四级公安机关鉴定机构绝大多数都能够独立进行法医学解剖检验，及时出具鉴定意见，遇见复杂疑难案件商请上级公安机关法医配合，可以说，我国公安系统不存在移植日本检视官制度的土壤。反观我国检察机关，自身鉴定资源则显得“捉襟见肘”，案源较少导致人员流失、设备落后且投入较少。尽管目前检察机关上下正在积极进行司法鉴定实验室建设，但就法医学鉴定来说，检验设备动辄几百万乃至上千万的投资，还需要每年不菲的试剂耗材和运营维护费用，这对本就经费不充裕的各级检察机关来说无疑雪上加霜，搞实验室建设最忌一哄而上、重建轻用、重建轻管等现象。另外，检察机关本身尸检案源不多的现实，达不到锻炼专业人才的需求，这在法医病理学检验上尤显突出，与其他法医学检验（如DNA检验、毒化检验等）不同，后者更多地依赖于设备、试剂及实验方法，而法医病理学检验更注重鉴定人在长年累月的众多切片观察中所积累的经验和能力，对病理人才的培养好比“太极十年不出师”，是不能一蹴而就的，对检察机关鉴定机构来说，法医病理学检验明显是其薄弱环节。综上所述，为谨慎、稳妥、及时、准确地处理被羁押人员的死因鉴定工作，应该创新工作机制，积极利用社会资源尤其是高校、医院资源，避免重复投资、盲目建设。

2. 外部环境要求检察机关死因鉴定工作应积极利用社会资源。目前我国司法鉴定体制的不完善，存在着侦查机关“自侦自鉴”与社会鉴定追求利益的权力博弈，造成现实中司法鉴定行业普遍存在着信任危机。纵观国外司法鉴定机构之设置，以及从长远社会发展规律来看，应当确立司法鉴定机构及所属鉴定人的中立性，一般意义上，中立性至少要求与公权力机关没有任何隶属关系，从而使鉴定人能够排除各种行政、人为等因素干扰，独立、公正地开展鉴定工作。但是，从现阶段我国基本国情出发，将司法鉴定机构完全与侦查机关绝缘有点不切实际，司法鉴定中立化是一个长期的过程，盲目鼓吹不能解决任何问题，现阶段应积极打造权威性社会鉴定机构，确保其中立性，这对于提高司法鉴定公信力、解决实践中突出问题、化解矛盾纠纷等，都具有重要意义。比如2008年贵州瓮安李某的死因鉴定，家属已然对公安机关内设鉴定机构失去信任，如果及时由中立的社会权威鉴定机构进行鉴定，也许不会出现那么严重的后果。[13] 现阶段，检察机关的死因鉴定工作应体察民众的诉求，变革死板的工作机制，积极利用社会鉴定资源，提高鉴定意见公信力，促进司法鉴定的公开与公正，这样有

---

〔12〕 参见霍塞虎：“日本法医尸体检验制度的现状与展望”，载《中国司法鉴定》2012年第5期；唐泽英：“日本法医解剖法律制度及特点”，载《中国司法鉴定》2012年第5期；张维东：“日本的检视官制度”，载《中国法医学杂志》1997年第1期。

〔13〕 2008年6月，贵州瓮安县初二女学生李某被发现死于河中，家属不能接受警方做出的“溺水死亡”鉴定报告，邀约百余人打着横幅在瓮安县城游行，随后当地群众陆续加入，游行队伍先后冲击多家政府机关，整个过程持续近7个小时，形成一起严重的“打砸抢烧”群体性突发事件，被称为“瓮安事件”。

利于理性合法地化解利益矛盾、满足死者家属的利益诉求，避免“重复鉴定”、“久鉴不决”、“涉鉴上访”等现象甚至群体性事件的发生。

3. 检察职责要求检察机关法医对社会鉴定机构进行必要的配合和监督。实践中，一旦发生被羁押人员死亡案件，检察技术人员（不单是法医，还有痕迹、刑事照相等人员）立即赶赴羁押场所进行勘验和检查，并针对发现的问题对相关人员和场所进行调查，这使得具有专业优势的技术人员在某种程度上具有了侦查属性，且该属性在被羁押人员死因鉴定案件中尤显突出，这是社会鉴定人员所不能比拟且亟需配合的。在进行法医学解剖及后续法医学检验时，考量鉴定机构及鉴定人员的选择是否合理、仪器设备是否先进、鉴定流程是否恰当等专业问题时，检察机关法医更有发言权，有理由做好对社会鉴定机构的配合角色。检察机关法医还有必要起到勘验现场[14]与法医检验、侦查机关与鉴定机构之联系纽带的作用，更好地发挥二者合力，公正、准确、及时地完成尸体检验任务。另外，出于检察职责的要求，更由于社会鉴定群体尚未达到——认识到其对社会的责任超出了自身的利益——的高度，检察机关法医应该对社会鉴定机构整个鉴定过程加以必要的监督，所谓监督，并不是对检验结果的实体控制，而是着重过程控制和质量控制，例如，委托鉴定时听取羁押场所和死者家属双方的意见，对鉴定人询问并商讨检验方案，检验过程确保标准操作程序、遵循最优方法，根据具体情况随时矫正检验方案，确保检材提取正确、全面及检材保管措施妥当，监督检验方法和器具符合相关技术规制，保证检验设备及技术原理稳妥可靠等。

（二）我国检察机关移植日本检视官制度可行性之探讨

1. 检察机关法医队伍有自己的专业优势。与日本检视官都是“半路出家”不同，我国检察机关法医鉴定人一般都是“科班出身”，并且根据资格准入要求，至少都具备5年以上相关工作经验，[15] 这省却了进行法医学专业知识培训的过程。况且，检察机关法医曾经负责工伤事故检验鉴定的繁重任务，有着丰富的尸体检验、现场勘查和案件侦查经验，只是由于20世纪90年代《刑法》与《刑事诉讼法》的相继修订施行，更加突出检察机关的法律监督地位，强化其查办国家工作人员犯罪的职能，检察机关法医一直负责的工伤事故检验鉴定才全部移交公安机关，这也是造成检察机关法医鉴定案源下降、人员流失的主要原因之一。[16] 另外，身为司法机关中的一员，检察机关法医更注重法律知识的学习和证据意识的培养，实际鉴定及侦查中更注重程序上的公正，与之相对应，社会鉴定群体更注重鉴定结果的准确，二者能够互相弥补、相得益彰。

2. 检察机关法医队伍有自己的利益诉求。根据对2011年中组部会同最高检联合下发的《检察官职务序列设置暂行规定》的解读文件中可以得知，检察技术人员作为内设的综合管理机构工作人员，不再任命检察官职务，这对广大检察技术人员来说无异

---

〔14〕 必须承认尸体现场勘验应该不是法医鉴定人的职责，这是为了规避先入为主的预断，但具有法医知识的技术人员参与现场勘验对尸体解剖工作非常有利，便于鉴定人结合尸体检验结果分析案情。

〔15〕 现实中，目前检察机关大部分法医鉴定人的资格准入，都是根据《人民检察院鉴定人登记管理办法》第8条第2款之要求：“具有与所申请从事的鉴定业务相关的专业执业资格或者高等院校相关专业本科以上学历，从事相关工作5年以上”。

〔16〕 参见张阿众：“天津市检察机关2000～2011年法医现状的调研探析”，2012年8月中国法医学会全国第十五次法医临床学学术研讨会资料。

于当头一棒，无疑会加剧技术人才由检察技术部门向检察业务部门的内部流失。最高人民检察院《检察人才队伍建设中长期规划（2011～2020年）》中，专门提出了检察技术人才分别设置或实行单独职务序列的要求，在此时机下，在检察机关创建“检视官”制度，对广大法医来说是正当其时。要抓住检察人员分类改革的有利时机，依靠检视官制度，参比警官序列，推进检察机关法医的职称、职级制度改革，大力改善其待遇，适时建立符合检察工作需要、适应未来发展要求的科技职称评定体系，增强检察机关法医的职业认同感和荣誉感，减少人才流失。此外，在称谓上，相比公安机关法医能够以“警官”代称而言，没有检察官资格的检察机关法医可以冠以“检视官”，避免一些称谓上的尴尬。

3. 目前的工作机制揭示检视官制度的可行性。根据新《刑事诉讼法》第144条的规定，“为了查明案情，需要解决案件中某些专门性问题的时候，应当指派、聘请有专门知识的人进行鉴定。”所谓“指派”是指由侦查机关内设的鉴定机构中的鉴定人进行鉴定；所谓“聘请”是指由侦查机关委托外部的鉴定人或专家独立或协助完成鉴定。根据《人民检察院鉴定规则（试行）》的相关规定，人民检察院各业务部门委托鉴定都需要检察技术部门统一协助办理，具备鉴定条件的，受理并完成鉴定，不具备鉴定条件的，为对外委托鉴定提供协助。其意义在于，专业人士更能从鉴定工作的专业性角度，听取委托方相关的案情介绍和具体的委托要求，对委托鉴定事项所提供的鉴定材料进行核对审查，协助联系社会鉴定机构，办理相关委托鉴定手续。实践中，针对被羁押人员死亡案件，许多地方检察机关法医在进行完现场勘验、尸表检验后，对其他的诸如法医学解剖、病理学检验、毒化检验和DNA检验等主要依靠社会资源进行，这与日本的检视官制度正好不谋而合，我们要做的，只是把这种工作机制以制度的形式固定下来，加以保障。

六、我国检察机关检视官制度之建构

为更好地应对被羁押人员的死因鉴定工作，根据检察机关现有的法医鉴定人员和检验设备情况，在检察机关内部尝试建立并实行检视官制度，套用警官序列施以职级、职称待遇。检察机关鉴定机构接受案件侦办部门委托后，立即派遣至少2名以上检视官，赶赴羁押场所进行现场勘验、尸表检验等工作，协助相关侦查工作，并协助委托、聘请具备实力的社会鉴定机构及人员，向其通报现场检视及调查情况，提出具体的亟需明确的问题，共同拟定法医学解剖及后续法医学检验方案，检视官对鉴定全程给予配合并监督，在侦查期限内督促社会鉴定机构及时完成各项检验报告。然后，综合分析现场勘验、走访调查、医疗资料、尸表检验、尸体解剖、病理学检验、毒化检验乃至DNA检验等结果，确定被羁押人员死亡原因。必要情况下，在检察机关邀约和主持下，举行专家会鉴，共同对疑难复杂案例的死亡原因进行分析、讨论。最后，以检察机关鉴定机构名义出具鉴定意见，鉴定书中对利用社会力量完成的检验部分进行标注说明。

笔者认为，检视官制度不仅仅是一种职级、职称待遇，更主要的，是一种工作机制的创新。在我国现有国情和司法鉴定体制下，尝试移植日本检视官制度，充分发挥并利用检察机关内、外鉴定力量的各自优势，不失为一种解决目前被羁押人员死因鉴定困境的良好途径，能够彰显检察机关深入推进社会矛盾化解、社会管理创新、公正廉洁执法三项重点工作。

试论法庭科学与司法公正的捍卫

王小怡 *

一、司法公正是构建和谐社会的必然要求

（一）司法公正的基本内涵

司法，是国家权力通过法律适用形式在社会纠纷解决领域进行的活动，是国家“为当事人双方提供不用武力解决争端的方法”。[1] 广义上的司法包括审判、侦查、检察等国家权力运作行为以及调解、仲裁等“准司法”活动，[2] 而狭义的司法仅指审判。本文所指的司法是指狭义上的司法。

古往今来，正义总是被视为人类社会的根本价值目标以及人类评价是非的基本标准，而公正则是法律领域“正义”的表现形式，法与正义自法律诞生之日起就是司法永恒的主题和至高的价值追求。公正是人类普遍追求的一种价值，指人们在社会关系中，谋求公平地分配权利和义务，合理地处理各种利益关系，以及为维护社会全体成员的共同利益，协调成员间的社会关系所应遵循的伦理准则。“司法公正是人类进入文明社会以来，为解决各类社会冲突而追求或持有的一种法律思想和法律评价。”[3] 正如当代著名法学家、新分析法学派的代表人物哈特说的那样：在对法律调整进行道德评论方面，公正是一个“占有最为显赫之地位”的概念。[4]

因此，如何实现司法公正就是我们实现和谐社会所必须要实现的价值目标。司法公正有很多项标准，概括起来可以包括下列五个方面，一是司法的结果公正，即裁判在认定事实和适用法律方面的正确性。司法结果公正，是人们对司法的基本价值要求，是司法公正的首义。二是司法过程的公开性和透明化，这是司法的基本标准和要求。三是裁判过程的公正和形象公正，即看得见的正义。包括裁判机构和人员的地位中立以及对当事人诉讼参与权充分的保证。四是司法审判的自治性。五是司法的效率性。正如波次纳所说：公正在法律中的第二意义是指效率。[5] 这5项标准的概括实现都离不开一点，即要以事实认定的正确性为基础。而案件中的事实是由证据来证明的，调查显示民事诉讼中63%的案件的关键证据都是以鉴定意见书和检验报告书的形式来体现的。由此可见法庭科学在案件审判中的关键作用。

---

* 王小怡，华东政法大学司法鉴定专业博士。Email：wangzixingcun@163. com。

〔1〕 英国法学家金斯伯格在《公正的概念》中谈到这是法治的含义之一。参见张文显：《当代西方法哲学》，吉林大学出版社1987年版，第206页。

〔2〕 孙国华主编：《法学基础理论教程》，人民法院出版社1991年版，第288页。

〔3〕 孙国华、唐仲清：“公正理念论”，载《依法治国与司法改革》，中国法制出版社1999年版。

〔4〕 郑成良：《法律之内的正义》，法律出版社2002年版，第3页。

〔5〕 梅启勇：《论司法公正》，武汉大学2004年硕士学位论文，第6页。

（二）司法公正与和谐社会

“司法公正是法律公正的全权代表和集中体现，从依法治国的意义上讲，如果一个社会中没有了司法公正，那么这个社会也就根本没有公正可言了。”〔6〕按照亚里士多德的看法，所谓法治就是指“已成立的法律获得普遍的服从，而大家所服从的法律又应该是本身制订得良好的法律”。〔7〕和谐社会的内涵必然包含民主法治与公平正义。而司法公正作为司法活动的准则，同时也是司法存在的主要意义。所以，司法公正是社会主义法治社会的根本标准之一，是文明社会的重要组成要素。在一个成熟的社会体制中，公民与法律直接发生关系一般都发生在与司法机关之间，因此对大多数人来说，司法即是法律，而司法的公正代表的是法律的公正，也是法治社会的最后一道底线。司法公正不仅意味着司法机关的司法活动要坚持正当平等的原则，还意味着司法机关的裁判应当体现公平正义的精神。

具体来说，司法公正与和谐社会的关系可以概括为以下几点：其一，司法公正是维护法律权威的必要条件。美国学者博登海默也指出，法律体系建立的意义不仅仅在于制订和颁布良好的科学的法律，还在于被切实执行。其二，司法公正是促进依法行政的必要条件。富勒提出“法治的实质必然是在对公民发生作用时，政府应忠实地运用已曾公布并应由公民遵守和决定其权利和义务的规则，如果不是指这个意思，那就什么意思也没有。”依法行政是法治社会的必然要求，只有公正的司法才能树立法律的权威，才能对行政权构成足够的监督力量。其三，司法公正是促进社会和谐的根本条件。法律具有对人民行为的指引作用，而审判结果对社会的影响则是指引作用的集中体现。正如培根所指出的：“一次不公的（司法）判决比多次不平的举动为祸尤烈，因为这些不平的举动不过弄脏水流，而不公的判决则把水源败坏了。”〔8〕正如一个彭宇案的判决让中国司法饱受诟病，也一度使人们将助人为乐视为洪水猛兽。因此，公正的司法应该能够消除社会主体在冲突发生时对诉讼的不良预期，抑制寻衅滥讼现象的发生；同时，也可以减少被诉主体应诉的心理障碍，使其运用法律手段维护自己的合法权益。

（三）我国司法公正的现状分析

司法不公是我国司法体制改革过程中所面临的一个主要方面，如何从制度上和根源上遏制司法不公是我们必须加以研究的重要问题。而司法鉴定是法庭科学的重要组成部分，是司法活动的一种，也是证据的一种表现方式，其客观性和科学性直接影响到案件事实的认定，法官也往往据此作出审判结论，进而影响到司法公正，因此如何从法庭科学的角度预防司法不公，是本文所要解决的主要问题。

从法理学上讲，法律是法治的最高准则，而法院是法律帝国的首都，法官则是帝国的王侯。〔9〕我国的司法公正所面临的第一个障碍是司法的行政化。我国受政治文化传统和司法传统的制约，我国现行的司法体制带有明显的行政化色彩。法院与行政机关之间关系错综复杂，并且执行严格的行政管理模式，上下级法院之间还存在着权威

〔6〕何家弘：“司法公正论”，载《中国法学》1999 年第 2 期，第 14 页。

〔7〕［古希腊］亚里士多德：《政治学》，商务印书馆 1965 年版，第 199 页。

〔8〕［英］培根：《培根论说文集》，水天同译，商务印书馆 1983 年版，第 193 页。

〔9〕［美］德沃金：《法律帝国》，李长青译，中国大百科全书出版社 1996 年版，第 361 页。

的行政控制和行政权力。司法机关实际上长期处于行政化的管理状态。法院管理的行政化，不仅使法院和法官丧失了独立的司法主体地位，也使法院的司法权全面走向了行政化道路，使行政权长期在司法系统处于主导化的地位：主导审判过程、主导审判方向、主导法官办案、主导最后裁判。这种行政化的无边际性延伸，不仅使法官丧失了本应有的中立立场和消极地位，而且造成法官的司法活动掺入大量利益因素。司法的非独立性严重影响了司法公正的实现，同时对司法鉴定也造成了恶劣影响。第二个障碍则是司法的权威性无法得到保障。在我国长期存在着权大于法、钱大于法的现象，这固然有地方权力对司法的不当干预这一因素，但也是法院监督体制不健全以及司法人员素质不均等原因共同作用的结果。因此，适当引入媒体监督，整合法院内部监督、检察监督、地方党委和行政监督各项力量，形成合力，也是预防司法腐败，树立司法权威性的最佳做法。而法庭科学手段的合理运用，对于树立司法权威，合理解决争端，预防司法腐败具有十分重要的作用。第三个障碍则是司法效率的低下。在我国司法审判实践中，当庭宣判的比例十分之低，更有甚者开庭半年之后都没有判决结果，这与美国95%以上的民事案件在进入开庭审理之前通过庭前和解或其他当事人之间协商的方法就得到了解决的现状形成了鲜明的对比。[10] 因此，改革司法机制，树立迟到的正义是非正义的这一观点，提高司法效率是实现司法公正的必由之路。

二、法庭科学对实现司法公正的重要作用

（一）法庭科学的内涵

司法事实认定中的科学技术、法庭科学、裁判科学、法庭科学技术等词语含义大体相当，泛指一切在司法事实认定之中所使用的科学技术，外延非常广泛。除法医学之外，法庭科学包括指纹检验、微量物证分析、枪弹检验、文件检验、声纹鉴定、痕迹检验、爆炸与纵火现场物证鉴定等，其外延不仅包含科学证据，还泛指法庭上使用的一切科学技术，其涵义较为模糊。

法庭科学（Forensic Science）[11] 是“应法律的需要而适用的科学，任何科学分支只要被用于解决法律纠纷，就可以被视为法庭科学。”法庭科学是以一般科学原理和技术的发展为前提的，当代自然科学和社会科学的飞速发展是法庭科学赖以发展和成熟的根本动力。法庭科学的出现大约始于20世纪20年代，最初的法庭科学可以说是刑事技术的代名词。直到20世纪中叶，随着美国法庭科学学会（American Academy of Forensic Science，1948）和国际法庭科学协会（International Association of Forensic Science）的成立，法庭科学的内涵才开始明确。从字面上看，“法庭科学”似乎仅指在法庭上应用的科学，但发生在法庭上的活动并不仅仅是“法庭”所指的空间领域以内的活动，其活动内容溯及庭审之前法庭空间之外的全部诉讼活动。作为为法庭审判提供证明服务的活动，是裁判者认定案件事实、解决纠纷的重要手段。

司法事实认定中的法庭科学，主要体现在以大陆法系的鉴定结论和英美法系的专家证言为代表的各类证据中，同时也体现在以质证、认证为核心的整个事实认定程序之中。

---

〔10〕 白绿铉：《美国民事诉讼法》，经济日报出版社1996年版，第61～86页。

〔11〕 孙立群：《司法鉴定制度改革研究》，法律出版社2002年版，第30～31页。

现行法学界，通常把“科技证据”定义为通过科学、技术手段所获得的证据，是运用科学技术原理和方法发现、收集、保全以及揭示其证明价值的或本身就具有科学技术特性的一切具有查明案件事实真相的证据。鉴定结论和专家证言（专家证人）一般被公认为大陆法系和英美法系科学证据的主要形式。

法庭科学是科学证据的一系列学科的总称，法庭科学是一个科学群。广义的法庭科学除了物证技术学、法医学外，还包括更具专业性的多种内容，如犯罪侦查学、遗传学、司法人类学、司法精神病学、毒理学、昆虫学、可疑文献检验学、火器、DNA分型、影像学、法学、法庭工程学和计算机学等。随着世界科学技术的迅猛发展，法庭科学的内容也会随之发生变化，法庭科学的学科群是开放性的。科学技术的发展给人类生活的方方面面都带来了深远的影响，其中科学原理和技术在诉讼领域的应用，促使了法庭科学的诞生。

（二）法庭科学在司法中的应用

科学证据是法庭科学为法律服务的重要载体和表现形式，是诉讼活动中自然属性和社会属性的桥梁，是沟通科学和法学的桥梁。一方面，作为科学证据母体的法庭科学是以一般科学原理和技术为基础的。无论是自然科学、社会科学，还是行为科学、应用科学，都具有科学的基本特性，在能够用客观性、系统性和可检验性保证其可靠性的同时，也决定了它的专业性，非本专业的人士都是门外汉。另一方面，为了发现案件的真相或阐明事件，裁判者在很多时候都需要属于科学的专门知识和技能，需要把属于科学支配的领域交给科学去承担。专家对科学专门知识和技能的运用和解读，为科学知识实现为法律服务的目的提供了可能性。由于科学证据是为司法证明服务的，因此也要受到证据法程序、价值、时效等多种因素的制约。总之，科学证据是在一定法律制度规范下的科学运用的结果。科学技术越来越多地运用于诉讼领域，越来越多地为诉讼证明服务，是自然科学和其他社会科学侵入司法证明过程的一种表现，也是证据法学向新证据学再向证据科学发展过程中的一股重要的推动力量。将科学证据放在证据科学大背景下进行解读，将其定位为证据法学和法庭科学的桥梁，一方面有利于证据科学的研究，另一方面也能更好地理解科学证据的交叉特性。法庭科学是以科学原理和技术的存在和发展为基础的，它的科学性、多元性、学科互涉性、开放性和发展性决定了科学证据首先应该具有科学的本质特征，其次它也是多元的、是开放的、是随着科学技术的发展变化而变化的。证据法是一个价值平衡的产物，科学证据在诉讼中的应用不但要符合证据的属性，还要满足证据法的价值要求。同时，对科学证据的研究不应再仅仅局限于与此相关的证据规则，还应该关注其在发现、收集、保存、检验鉴定以及对其他证据进行证明或解读的过程中的问题；不应该将眼光仅仅局限在科学证据在审判中的应用，而应将其延伸至包括审前和审后在内的整个司法证明过程；不应再仅仅从刑事诉讼的角度研究科学证据，而应该扩大至从科学技术的可靠客观性来研究。

（三）存在的问题

法律作为社会关系的调整器，作为调控社会的一种手段，作为评价社会事实的一种制度机制，其任务便是对社会其他领域的调整。法律不可能远离其他专业，而独自生活在自己的世界中，这样便失去了其存在的价值。然而这在法律领域便形成了悖论，因为法律人缺乏对于其他科学领域的了解。这一点在司法领域体现得尤为明显，因为司法活动相对立法活动来说更加频繁，对于涉及相关专业内的立法，可以由相关专业中的人参加并在立法过程中表达出相关领域的意见，但司法活动不同，司法活动更加频繁，并且作为案件事实审理者的法官或英美法系中的陪审团是不可能拥有相关专业的知识的，像案例中所讲到的情况是十分常见的，并且也不可能让法官仅凭借法律知识去解决科学争论。这时法律便安排出了相应的制度解决渠道，如英美法系的专家证人和大陆法系的鉴定结论、专家证人制度和鉴定制度的安排，使得事实审理者能够根据专家对于某一事实问题的看法作出裁判。但作为事实审理者的法官和陪审团，本身既无能力认定和评价专业领域内的事实问题，又何来能力去理解用专业技术所做出的事实认定和判断呢？事实审理者并未跳出专业隔阂的困惑，他们仍然被排除在专业领域之外，不过就是将相应的事实认定权部分地让渡给专家证人和鉴定人罢了。然而这种让渡本身既缺乏理论上的正当性，又与司法独立的理念相悖，同时这种让渡缺乏相应的监督。对于专家证言和鉴定结论事实审理者没有能力进行判断，并且碍于科学技术的权威，实践中他们只能被动地接受。专家证人和鉴定人在实际上行使着事实认定权，却不用为错判而负责。并且科学技术越来越广泛的应用于司法事实认定之中，似乎这一趋势有增无减，因此目前司法制度的安排令人担忧。

伴随着上述理论困境，司法实践中出现了大量的假鉴定、重复鉴定、矛盾鉴定的现象，司法鉴定也逐渐成为社会关注的焦点。

三、以科学捍卫公正是法庭科学的目标

（一）法庭科学与司法公正的对立统一关系

公正是证据制度的首要价值。证据制度之所以构成司法公正的基石，就在于其规制证据的使用，以减少误用、滥用和人为操纵，保证案件事实得到公正的认定。公正作为证据制度的首要价值，意味着当多元价值发生冲突时，其他价值应当让位于公正价值。作为法律的总目的，正义把真理作为实现自己的手段。但在具体的案例中，司法人员如果一味追求真实，则很可能会过度侵犯人权，降低诉讼效率，从而反过来影响法律的正义。科学证据并不是为了无条件地发现真实，而是在正当程序下发现真实。这就是科学证据的法律目的。

（二）如何以法庭科学来捍卫司法公正

急剧发展的现代科技在给这个世界带来飞速增长的物质福利的同时，也给人类的安全和自由带来了威胁。以科学技术为载体的科学证据在诉讼中的应用也面临着涉嫌侵犯人权、违背伦理的挑战。如测谎试验、催眠证据、法庭科学 DNA 数据库的建立、监听证据、强制采样等，都与公民隐私权、身体健康权、人身自由等一系列基本人权之间存在着冲突。此外，各国司法实践中对科学证据的滥用也因为冲击了伦理道德的要求而遭到了科学界的普遍质疑和反对。如美国临床和实验催眠学会对美国警方 20 世纪 80 年代滥用催眠术来获取言词证据的做法提出了强烈的抗议。一系列科学证据在诉讼中的运用丰富和充实了传统的非法证据排除规则的内容。对科学证据运用的规制，其核心就是谋求使用科学证据发现案件真实与保障人的基本权利不因此而被任意侵犯这二者之间的平衡。也会强迫被采样人按手印或签名。强制采样还会侵犯公民的身体权。在强制采样过程中人体血液、毛发等被强制与人体分离，侵犯了被采样人身体的

完整性。在用麻醉药物对人体进行催眠以获得言词证据的时候，麻醉药物也会对人体健康造成一定损害。

综上，我们可以看出用法律保障法庭科学的良性发展、以法庭科学引导司法公正是可以得到和谐发展的。但是如何在法律层面上来规范法庭科学，仍然是摆在我们面前的问题。简单来说，就是在法庭科学的使用、鉴定意见的采纳、法庭科学的科学性监督等环节要展开合理的规划，并要有权力部门对此进行合适的管理和协调，这涉及司法权、行政权的双重管理，并和质量监督部门密切相关。在物证大行其道的今天，用科学捍卫公正，以法庭科学的良性发展来帮助解决诉讼中的事实性问题，是符合法治要求和社会进步发展的举措。法庭科学发展的目标就是司法公正的实现。两者相辅相成，不可偏颇。

论司法鉴定中的科学问题

张凤芹 *

引 言

司法鉴定是鉴定人运用科学技术或专门知识对涉及诉讼的专门性问题进行检验鉴别和判断并提供鉴定意见的活动。具有合法律性和合科学性的双重特征。是依照法律规定的科学实证活动。[1] 司法鉴定的任务在于在法律规定的前提下，依据科学知识和技术手段来协助揭示案件事实及内在相关因素间的本质联系。司法鉴定突出体现了符合法律规定的科学证据的角色。然而，科学的探究性、认识的有限性以及案件隐藏的未知性，使司法鉴定的科学性的本质呈现出不成熟的一面。如何客观地审视司法鉴定的科学问题，是一个关于鉴定理论基础和鉴定认识基础的问题，它将迫使我们反思司法鉴定的科学理论价值和评价体系。从而，体现科学证据的严肃性。

本文的目的仅在于让我们更贴近司法鉴定的实相，来审视和反思司法鉴定的内涵与其所承担的使命间的距离。从而，重新审查什么是司法鉴定的科学性的理念。

随着司法鉴定质量规范化体系的建立与建设步伐的深入，在一定的法律制度背景下，司法鉴定的真实到底是什么，与我们所期待的揭示案件事实的目的之间是什么样的关系，或许，我们应试图架设一些桥梁，以使司法鉴定更平实地进入我们的视线。而这正是，司法鉴定的质证中的核心本质。科学与现实的融合，应是合理性。

一、司法鉴定的基本属性特征是符合法律规定前提下的科学的得当性

司法鉴定结论为什么存在？是因为，司法鉴定结论揭示了案件事实的内在联系，具有证明力。因此，司法鉴定的最终使命是通过科学的方式来展现证据，以证明案件事实要素间的内在关系，以揭示事实的本质。

从需要层面上看，对司法鉴定的基本要求是很明晰的。司法鉴定的对象是某一专门领域中的专业性问题。司法鉴定人的要求是专业人员具有专家型素质。司法鉴定的方法是运用科学的理论、方法、技术手段，检验、论证、说明案件中某一事实的内在本质关系。司法鉴定的总体要求是符合法律规定。司法鉴定中的科学属性不是科学研究、不是科学探索、不是科学探究，是该领域内已被公认的具有相对确定性的东西，因此具有非常典型的代表性、确定性、肯定性的特点。

司法鉴定的最重要的方面是科学性，它是司法鉴定的生命力，它决定了司法鉴定的客观真实性和准确性。司法鉴定的另一面是鉴定的案件材料提供上的有限性和层次

---

* 张凤芹，中国政法大学证据科学研究院副教授，从事法医学鉴定研究工作，副主任法医师，Email: fengqinzh@ cupl. edu. cn。

〔1〕 杜志淳、闵银龙：《司法鉴定概论》，法律出版社 2010 年版，第 8 页。

差别性，因此，鉴定材料本身具有不同程度的局限性，限制了对其科学性实现可能的展现程度。司法鉴定的内在要求，在实践中强烈要求统一限定的规范性，以保证鉴定的科学性的良好体现。这在某种程度上，已被纳入到科学的范畴，即科学的程序和技术要求。

司法鉴定的科学性需要展现出来，需要的是对鉴定结果的论证、说明。其基本要求是站得住脚的理论基础，得到行业广泛认可的方法和技术手段，符合分析判断逻辑关系的分析推理和说明。

因此，鉴定的科学性在鉴定意见或者鉴定结论中的体现，是得当的表述意见。什么叫做得当呢？这确是个巨大的问题。也是本文的焦点。那就是科学的价值体系中的核心。科学价值体系的构建基础是什么呢？应该是得当性。

二、科学证据的实质不仅是指系统的知识和科学方法，而是如何确定和确定什么是科学知识与科学方法

关于科学的观点有很多的不同层面的定义。一般认为科学是指系统的知识，科学是指科学方法。亚里士多德认为科学研究是从观察到一般原理，再返回到观察的活动，科学重要的功能在于解释，科学的解释是从有关事实的知识到有关事实原因的知识。罗素认为凡是诉诸人类理性而不是诉诸权威的一切确切的知识，称之为科学。康德认为科学是按照一定原则而建立的一个完整的知识体系的学问。1987 年《中国大百科全书 哲学卷》对科学解释为以范畴、定理、定律形式反映现实世界多种现象的本质和运动规律的知识体系。1989 年《辞海》将科学定义为关于自然、社会和思维的知识体系。《韦伯氏大字典》定义科学为确定事物的原理或本质，进行观察、研究和实验取得的系统知识。英国著名哲学家皮尔逊认为“科学的统一仅仅在方法，不在它的材料。”卡尔普尔科学哲学观点，科学是能被证伪的，科学是对世界的理论解释的过程。

科学证据中的科学，或者指科学知识，或者指科学方法。科学与法律分属不同的文化，存在诸多矛盾，当科学走入法庭，法庭需要判断是否源于科学知识，是否是真正的科学，由法律确定何为科学知识，由法官决定科学专家证言的质量。科学证据的实质是如何和确定何为科学知识和科学方法的复杂的与科学哲学相关的问题。〔2〕

三、司法鉴定的科学性的本质来源于潜在的一组命题的假设，是一定社会时期社会利益的法律制度与社会价值判断体系的结合

司法鉴定的本质特征来自于人们对司法鉴定的期待与需要。由此，司法鉴定本质中的科学内涵是源于潜在的一组命题的假设的提出。

1. 司法鉴定是一种思维判断模式的展现
2. 司法鉴定是一种解决问题方式的体现
3. 司法鉴定是科学的体现
4. 司法鉴定是当前价值判断的体现
5. 司法鉴定是解决矛盾冲突的当前社会价值理念的体现
6. 司法鉴定是法律制度思想的体现
7. 司法鉴定是某一领域知识与科学技术手段的系统性体现

---

〔2〕 刘晓丹：《论科学证据》，中国检察出版社 2010 年版，第 6～9 页。

8. 司法鉴定是人类对未知的一种合理性的解释

……诸如此类。

司法鉴定的目的是为了解决案件或事件内在相互关系而产生的，是一定社会法律制度下的、一定价值观念下的具体体现。在本质理念上渗透着现实法律理论和社会价值判断体系的结合。

四、司法鉴定具有强烈的现实性和时空情境性，是对一组因素关系的判断结果。而科学则是假设的相对单纯的因素组合环境下的关系运作关系

1. 司法鉴定是实务要求决定的，也就是说司法鉴定的环境要素可能是残缺不全的，这限制了司法鉴定中科学性的展现程度

基于实务处理的需要，司法鉴定应运而生。只要能够合理地解决问题，就完成了司法鉴定的使命。因此，这充分体现了司法鉴定的实践性是其显著的特征，也是司法鉴定存在的价值所在。它不应是科学探究和科学验证理论层面的。科学是实验室诞生的，是在限定条件下的假设关系组合体。然而，司法鉴定是问题层面的，它所处的环境更为复杂，因此是多维角度的概念，是一组因素的判断结果。

2. 司法鉴定的科学内涵常常是不同层面的、深浅不一的

通常，司法鉴定的材料基本上是不够完善的，无法清晰地完整地再现一个事实。司法鉴定发生的，通常是基于上述部分环境要素的基础，需要进行一个方向的推断。因此，司法鉴定潜藏着不科学的风险，是从司法鉴定产生的基础决定的。因此，可以得出，司法鉴定是有限条件下的科学的展现。而这个有限条件，却深深地决定着司法鉴定的科学性问题的内涵。也就是，是什么层面上的科学性问题。

3. 司法鉴定的科学性在很大程度上需要通过科学的逻辑展现出来

亦即司法鉴定是通过符合科学的手段推演出来的主观判断。司法鉴定的本质是对假设的验证和揭示的过程。

司法鉴定中的科学性体现在很多方面，如：思维逻辑模式是科学的，基础理论是科学的，揭示和验证的方法是科学的，环境背景条件符合科学要求等。而逻辑性的作用常常是非常显著的，这是司法鉴定的科学性得以展现的最直接和最重要的、不可或缺的部分。

在法医学司法鉴定意见的论证方面，常见的一种思维判断模式是：确定一个结果或称损害后果，再者是否成立损伤性依据，然后论证两者之间建立因果关联或不构成因果关联的证据间的证明能力和证明力。因此，从思维角度这是一种论证的关系，从明面上可以明朗地呈现因素与现象间的关系。

同时，我们还会发现，在这个呈现层面之下，是内心确信的方面。在专业技术领域里，依然存在严密的原因与结果之间的关系模式。因此，鉴定人需要做的，仅仅是严谨地将之呈现出来。当然，首先需要的是该领域中的有代表性的概念、术语及逻辑关系形式，其存在的本质是内心确信。因此，我们可以得出这样一个结论，鉴定是通过符合科学的手段推演出来的主观判断。

当然，为了达到符合科学性的条件，我们需要进行设定，例如，设定材料的种类、范围、特点和基本要求，设定呈现材料的程序和要求，设定验证的方式、方法、理论和条件，设定数据的基本要求，设定分析数据的基本模式和条件，设定意见呈现得出

的产生方式（逻辑形式），设定基本概念、术语和意见分类方式，等等。由此可见，一个鉴定意见的得出，本质上确实是基于一组基本的假设。这些假设的存在价值在于产生另一组表面上与之没有相关性的另一组假设。因此，司法鉴定的本质是对于假设的验证和揭示的过程。

举例说明：关于难免流产的鉴定。我们的思维模式多为：损伤是什么，确定损伤吗，损伤严重程度是什么，足以引起这个结果吗？再者，损害依据是什么，能验证这个损伤的存在吗，即两者的内在一致性存在吗？在多大程度上得出这样的判断，而又在多大程度上否定这样判断的存在？业内目前的认识层面与之是否一致，若一致，则基本结论可以做出；若不一致，则是否不适宜做出这样的意见。再次的问题是，如何呈现这样的判断与推理过程，有所保留，还是原样推出，还是在此基础上的进一步推断。这就是三种形式的鉴定意见。

其实，实质上，我们常常处在一个多因素的网中，内在的联系常常不是单一的，就是说，会出现这样的境状：那么关键的问题是如何取舍我们的内在判断。

五、司法鉴定的科学的标准是什么

对鉴定意见的抉择，本质上是源于有没有判断标准。比如：法律的标准是什么？刑事严、民事宽的思想？因果关系成立的基本要求、事实或诊断认定的基本要求、诊断依据判定的基本要求？还比如：专业领域的判断标准、学术领域的标准等等。总而言之，至少有5个层面：法律层面、事实层面、学术层面、认定领域层面和社会效果层面或者叫做平衡（和谐）层面等。

社会效果这个层面常常被看得很轻，但应该是至关重要的。因为，它决定了我们的判断模式是否应予调整的问题，这是鉴定的核心问题。

确实，在所有的问题中，那个潜在的有关科学的标准一次又一次地展现出来，它不断地呼唤着我们去认出它来。然而，我们往往成为门外的过客。这样的价值判断，一次次地在案件中呈现着，它在说明着关系平衡的本质和关键在哪里。

因此，我们应该安静下来，清晰后，就可以看到这个有关科学的标准，同时，是不是存在着一个又一个别样的状况存在，能够更好地带来关系的和谐呢？这虽然属于认识领域的问题，但确实是司法鉴定的内在核心。作为鉴定人应予以足够的重视，而不应让自己一次次地成为盲者，司法鉴定中的盲者。

很多时候，这些没有展现出来。于是，我们一次次地争论，乃至厌烦。

关于难免流产的例子，一种观点认为：缺乏客观真实的认定依据。需要进一步探究，以试图揭示与查明什么。科学，确实是对事物本质关系的认识。那么，一个鉴定人的职责是什么？是依据手里的鉴定资料，做出所及领域的专业分析，以说明事物内在的本质关联吗？还是，对现有材料做出一个专业推断。

是否能够做出明确的鉴定结论，表面上是专业领域的问题，而实质上是社会价值系统的问题。社会价值系统的杠杆是否得当。因此，科学的标准应当来源于它所服务的使命，实现社会对得当的追求。

在这个案例中，我们常常可以看到自己这样的样子：我说它是不合理的，应予处罚。理由是：诊断可以成立的依据，如：技术的、标准的、法律的规定等等。而诊断不成立的依据目前缺乏。其实是支持诊断不成立的依据，没有进行进一步的寻找。这就成了，居于一定的先有理论，符合这个理论的依据聚集，就自然构成了这个理论的一个验证例子。

第二种情况是与此截然不同的，诸如此类，还有很多很多。这就是说，我们如何居于一种共识的社会价值体系理念基础上，运用科学技术手段和科学方式，展现在具体案件的司法鉴定中。

六、司法鉴定中的科学

司法鉴定中的科学是不同层次、不同层面的，其差别决定于两个方面，社会对这个问题的认识和接纳程度，科学研究的深度，专业领域达成共识的深度，现实层面的技术手段呈现的广度和深度，社会法律环境的支持与接纳程度，社会影响效果等等。凡此种种是当前社会对科学的接纳度。

无论怎样的科学展现的样态，都须符合社会的认可能力，因此，司法鉴定中的科学是因需要而诞生的。这就是司法鉴定中的所谓的科学证据的本质样貌。

那么，什么是司法鉴定的需要形式呢？那就是，社会的质疑的深度。有多大的质疑，就有多大的需求形式，要通过人们认可的思维模式展现出来，那才叫做科学。

科学，真的能够独立存在吗？不存在。其实，是你的思维方式，是否能够被对方理解并认可的问题。司法鉴定中的科学，就是获得最大范围与程度的质疑的认同。

再论新刑诉法背景下专家辅助人制度的完善

朱晋峰 * 宫 雪 **

庭审过程中，由诉讼各方当事人对鉴定意见的有关问题进行质询、加以抗辩，发现其存在的不足是鉴定意见证据能力和证明力的有效保障。然而，正是因为诉讼双方当事人及裁判法官缺乏相应的专业知识，所以才聘请能够解决案件中的专业问题的鉴定人进行鉴定，因此，又迫使庭审各方对鉴定人出具的鉴定意见进行质证、审查、认证，显然强人所难。因此，在司法实践中，可能出现，一方面无论是理论界还是实务界都强调鉴定人应当出庭作证，新刑诉法第 187 条〔1〕也规定了鉴定人应当出庭作证，否则将承担鉴定意见不得作为定案根据的程序性后果；另一方面，即使鉴定人出庭，如果不借助于其他任何人的帮助，控辩双方也难以对鉴定意见进行有效质证，法官也难以对其进行有效认证。据此，为充分实现对鉴定意见的质证，有必要确立专家辅助人制度，以弥补控辩双方和法官在专业知识方面存在的不足。而所谓“专家辅助人，又称为专家技术顾问，是指在诉讼活动中受当事人和司法人员委托就鉴定结论涉及的专门问题进行说明和评价的掌握特定科学技术和专门知识的人。”〔2〕

一、专家辅助人制度具有重要意义

在司法实践中，鉴定意见在刑事诉讼中的地位凸显，已经有逐渐取代被告人口供，成为“证据之王”的趋势。在庭审各方普遍缺乏专业知识的情形下，允许双方聘请其信任的专业技术人员，帮助其对鉴定意见进行质证，在司法实践中就显得十分必要，且在我国实践中具有可行性。在科学证据受到推崇的新形势下，如何防止“伪科学”证据或“冒牌专家”的司法意见进入法庭，即如何设定“守门人”的职责，已成为我国司法鉴定法律制度改革的核心问题。〔3〕

---

* 朱晋峰，司法部司法鉴定科学技术研究所《中国司法鉴定》编辑部编辑，主要从事刑事诉讼法学、证据法学、司法鉴定制度研究。Email：zhujinfeng_ 1987@163. com。

** 宫雪，华东政法大学博士研究生。

〔1〕 新《刑事诉讼法》第187条第3款规定：“公诉人、当事人或者辩护人、诉讼代理人对鉴定意见有异议，人民法院认为鉴定人有必要出庭的，鉴定人应当出庭作证。经人民法院通知，鉴定人拒不出庭的，鉴定意见不得作为定案的根据。”另外，对于鉴定人不出庭的规制，除新《刑事诉讼法》对其进行了规定之外，有关行政法规也有规范，如2005年9月30日国务院批准实施的《司法鉴定人登记管理办法》第22条规定：“司法鉴定人应当履行下列义务……（六）依法出庭作证，回答与鉴定有关的询问……”。对于鉴定人无故不出庭的，《司法鉴定人管理办法》第30条规定：“司法鉴定人有下列情形之一的，由省级司法行政机关给予停止执业3个月以上1年以下的处罚；情节严重的，撤销登记；构成犯罪的，依法追究刑事责任……（四）经人民法院依法通知，非法定事由拒绝出庭作证的……”。

〔2〕 卢建军：“司法鉴定结论使用中存在问题及解决途径——兼论我国诉讼专家辅助人制度的建构和完善”，载《证据科学》2010年第6期。

〔3〕 常林：“谁是司法鉴定的‘守门人’？——《关于司法鉴定管理问题的决定》实施五周年成效评析”，载《证据科学》2010年第5期。

（一）有助于进一步强化鉴定人出庭作证

判断鉴定意见是否具有证据能力，关键是在庭审上控辩双方通过对作出鉴定意见的人进行质询，发现鉴定程序中可能存在的各种问题，从而为法官是否最终认定、采信鉴定意见提供依据。但是，在实践中鉴定人普遍不出庭作证。其有一项重要原因就是控辩双方对鉴定意见难以进行有效质证。2005 年通过的《关于司法鉴定管理问题的决定》第 11 条规定："在诉讼中，当事人对鉴定意见有异议的，经人民法院依法通知，鉴定人应当出庭作证。"对此，2012 年 3 月 14 日通过的新刑诉法也作了类似的规定。可见，鉴定人出庭作证的前提必须是当事人对鉴定意见提出了异议。然而，鉴定意见是鉴定人对案件中的专门性问题，依据其所掌握的专业性知识，所得出的结果。因此，在庭审过程中的鉴定意见，无论是在其鉴定技术规范方面，还是在鉴定程序方面，都无法提出"专业"的不同异议，或者虽然提出有关异议，也有可能因为不涉及核心内容而被法庭驳回鉴定人出庭的申请。据此，在诉讼过程中，也就无法保障鉴定人出庭，也无法对其鉴定意见证据能力和证明力进行审查。如果允许控辩双方聘请具有专门知识的人，帮助其对意见进行质询，必然会改变目前当事人无法提出实质异议的情形，鉴定人出庭作证的现状也会得到有效改观。

（二）有助于进一步保障鉴定意见的真实性

鉴定是一个运用科学技术知识的过程，而"科学知识的运用依赖于专家，专家是人，因而具有多重属性。作为拥有专门知识的人，一方面专家可以正确运用自己掌握的科学知识和经验，对事实认定者感到不明确的数据进行合理的拼合或解释，帮助事实审理者理解证据或确定争议事实。另一方面，专家也可能误用科学原理和技术方法而形成错误的判断，误导事实认定者（包括法官、陪审团成员）作出错误的判断"。[4] 由控辩双方聘请具有专门知识的人对鉴定意见中可能存在的问题进行询问，可以及时辨清鉴定意见中可能存在的不足，从而帮助法庭对案件中专门性事实问题的认定是建立在有证据能力的鉴定意见基础之上的。特别是在关键鉴定人制度下，对定罪量刑起关键性作用的鉴定意见的真实性，[5] 将直接保障诉讼结果的公正。

（三）有助于进一步保障法官对鉴定意见的认证与采证

在没有专家辅助人的情况下，控辩双方无法对鉴定意见进行有效质证，从而对法官采信鉴定意见的活动，无从认证，可能引发法官随意认定鉴定意见的情形。例如，对于不符合资格的鉴定人出具的鉴定意见予以认定，或者对于违反法律程序出具的鉴定意见予以认定等。在鉴定意见对案件的定罪量刑起关键作用的情形下，这种随意认定鉴定意见证据能力的做法，势必会影响案件的公正审理。然而，"由专门知识的专家辅助人在庭审上代表辩方与控方的鉴定人针对鉴定结论进行对质和辩论，不仅可以切实解决专业垄断、暗箱操作的问题，达到真正意义上的去伪存真，而且能够制约法官

---

〔4〕 常林："谁是司法鉴定的'守门人'？——《关于司法鉴定管理问题的决定》实施五周年成效评析"，载《证据科学》2010 年第 5 期。

〔5〕 例如，在法医伤残鉴定中，鉴定人出具的被害人是构成轻微伤还是轻伤的意见，其最终将决定侦查机关是否立案侦查，检察院是否起诉，法院是否将被告人定罪处理。

对证据取舍的任意性，弥补法官专业知识的不足，帮助法官确认证据”。[6]

（四）有助于与域外法制的交流，促进法的国际对话

“为确保鉴定结论的准确从而避免诉讼中法院基于不准确的鉴定结论而作出错误的裁判，各国一般均在法律程序上设置相应的抗辩和审查机制，而在审查和抗辩中除了普通的质证和审查以外，相关专家的参与越来越得到法律的认可。”[7] 例如，在当事人主义的英美法系国家中，控辩双方可以各自聘请对案件中的专门性问题具有专业知识的人，以专家证人的身份向法庭提供专家证言，同时，也可以对对方专家提出的证言进行反驳。在大陆法系国家中，虽然鉴定人被视为法官辅助人，但其在诉讼法典中也多规定了“专家证人参加诉讼的程序规则，即为了证明过去的事实、情况需要询问具有特别专门知识的人员时，适用关于证人的规定”[8]。英美法系和大陆法系国家有关专家辅助人制度的这些立法和司法实践，为我国在刑事诉讼中完善专家辅助人制度提供了借鉴。另外，在国际法律交流日益频繁的今天，我国专家辅助人制度的构建将无疑促进我国与域外法制的交流，也有助于与国际公约、地方公约等的契合。

专家辅助人制度其实在我国民事诉讼程序中早已有之，并且在域外诉讼中已经成为帮助控辩双方进行质证的有效手段，最为重要的是刑诉法对专家辅助人制度的探索，这都无疑表明，在我国刑事诉讼中最终确立专家辅助人制度具有现实可行性，且存在充分的基础，只不过立法者应当进一步明确专家辅助人的资格、诉讼地位、权利义务以及专家辅助人出庭的程序等，以切实保障鉴定意见的证据能力能够得到充分认证。

二、专家辅助人制度的现实困境

专家辅助人早在2002年4月1日生效的《最高人民法院关于民事诉讼证据的若干规定》中就已经有所体现，其第61条规定：“当事人可以向人民法院申请1至2名具有专门知识的人员出庭就案件的专门性问题进行说明。人民法院准许其申请的，有关费用由提出申请的当事人负担。审判人员和当事人可以对出庭的具有专门知识的人员进行询问。经人民法院准许，可以由当事人各自申请的具有专门知识的人员就有关案件中的问题进行对质。具有专门知识的人员可以对鉴定人进行询问”。随后，新刑诉法和有关司法解释对专家辅助人予以了进一步明确。可见，专家辅助人制度在我国并不是一项新型制度，但就目前有关法律和司法实践来看，该制度的运行还可能存在一定的阻碍。这主要是指目前专家辅助人制度缺乏完善的立法性规定。

首先，立法抽象，属原则性规定，缺乏实践可操作性。2012年新修改并已于2013年1月1日起实施的新刑诉法仅仅在第192条进行了规定：“公诉人、当事人和辩护人、诉讼代理人可以申请法庭通知有专门知识的人出庭，就鉴定人作出的鉴定意见提出意见。”由该法律条文可以看出，新刑诉法对于专家辅助人的规定较为简陋，缺乏必要的操作性规范。根据立法传统，在刑诉法制定出来之后，公检法基本会制定自身的操作规范。如2012年11月5日由最高人民法院审判委员会第1559次会议通过的《最

---

〔6〕 许明：“试论完善鉴定结论审查机制的新对策——设置专家辅助人制度”，载《法制与社会》2009年第1期。

〔7〕 周士敏：“试论建立审查鉴定结论的新机制——设置专家辅助人质证制度”，载《人民检察》2003年第4期。

〔8〕 黄学贤：“行政诉讼中的专家辅助人制度及其完善”，载《法学》2008年第9期。

高人民法院关于适用〈中华人民共和国刑事诉讼法〉的解释》第217条规定："公诉人、当事人及其辩护人、诉讼代理人申请法庭通知有专门知识的人出庭，就鉴定意见提出意见的，应当说明理由。法庭认为有必要的，应当通知有专门知识的人出庭。申请专门知识的人出庭，不得超过二人。有多种类鉴定意见的，可以相应增加人数。有专门知识的人出庭，适用鉴定人出庭的有关规定。"2012年12月3日公安部部长办公会议通过的《公安机关办理刑事案件程序规定》已于2013年1月1日起实施，其第244条规定："犯罪嫌疑人、被害人对鉴定意见有异议提出申请，以及办案部分或者侦查人员对鉴定意见有疑义的，可以将鉴定意见送交其他有专门知识的人员提出意见。必要时，询问鉴定人并制作笔录"。2012年10月16日由最高人民检察院第十一届检察委员会第八十次会议通过的《人民检察院刑事诉讼规则（试行）》第440条规定："公诉法人对鉴定意见有异议的，可以申请人民法院通知鉴定人出庭作证。"三机关的司法解释和有关规定，除最高院司法解释对申请专家辅助人的条件和人数进行了规定之外，其余的解释和规定均没有突破新刑诉法的界限，仅仅停留在原则性规定上面，这势必会影响专家辅助人制度的良性运行。

其次，对于专家辅助人的资格没有明确。无论是新刑诉法，还是两高司法解释、公安机关办理刑事案件的程序规定，都只是表明当事人可以申请有"专门知识的人"出庭对鉴定人的鉴定意见提出意见，但是对于"专门知识的人"的资格没有提出明确的要求。该"专门知识的人"是否应当像鉴定人一样具备某种特定的资格证书？在与双方当事人、鉴定人等有某种利害关系的情况下，是否可以继续担任有"专门知识的人"？有"专门知识的人"是否可以像英美法系的专家证人一样？等等。诸如此类，新刑诉法和司法解释都没有给予特别的规定，这势必会导致在司法实践中，双方对于"专门知识的人"的聘请无所适从，也会对法官对"专门知识的人"的资格的审查造成严重困难。有关部分对此应当从"专门知识的人"的资格要件的正反两方面予以完善。

再次，对于"专门知识的人"的诉讼地位没有明确，致使其权利义务缺位。在理论界和实务界对有"专门知识的人"进行探讨过程中，虽然都将其称为专家辅助人，但是在法律上却没有赋予其一个正式的身份，而是与其他一些有"专门知识的人"混同，如最高人民法院司法解释第87条规定："对案件中的专门性问题需要鉴定，但没有法定司法鉴定机构，或者法律、司法解释规定可以进行检验的，可以指派、聘请有专门知识的人进行检验，检验报告可以作为定罪量刑的参考"。这里的有"专门知识的人"显然与本文所探讨的有"专门知识的人"（专家辅助人）不是同一概念。即使我们将本文探讨的有"专门知识的人"称之为专家辅助人，但这也不表明法律赋予了其特定的诉讼地位。诉讼地位的不明确最终将导致专家辅助人在诉讼过程中的权利义务的缺位，从而影响其功能作用的充分发挥。

最后，立法对于专家辅助人出庭的具体程序没有加以规定，可能致使实践运行受阻。专家辅助人作为帮助诉讼各方对鉴定人的鉴定意见进行审查、认证的一项制度，其应当与鉴定人一样出庭，在法庭之上对鉴定人进行质询，并同时接受鉴定人的对质、对方当事人和律师、法官的询问。因此，立法应当有特定的程序对专家辅助人出庭的行为进行规制，包括程序的启动与决定、申请事由的审查、专家辅助人出庭程序、费用的负担，等等。这是公安、司法机关运行专家辅助人制度的前提要件。然而，无论是处于上位法的新刑诉法，还是对于司法实践发挥重要作用的司法解释和其他有关规定，均未对专家辅助人出庭的有关程序加以规定，这就足以造成实践对专家辅助人的运行产生障碍，极易造成地方各自立法、做法不一的现象产生，甚至可能致使专家辅助人制度沦为虚置。

综上所述，虽然专家辅助人制度在新刑诉法中得以确立，对于控辩双方对自己缺乏专业判断能力的鉴定意见进行有效质证，以及法官对鉴定意见进行正确的确立具有重要的意义。但是无论是从立法完善、资格、地位，还是从具体运行程序来看，专家辅助人制度还显然难以达到发挥其应有效果的状态，在实践中也必然会遇到上文所述的诸如此类问题。对此，有关部门应当采取适当措施对该制度进行完善，确保其良性运行。

三、专家辅助人制度的完善

对于专家辅助人制度在我国的完善，笔者认为，首先应当予以解决的就是专家辅助人的资格问题、诉讼地位问题，以及专家辅助人的权利义务和出庭程序等问题。

（一）专家辅助人资格

鉴定人与专家辅助人有本质区别，前者是接受公安、司法机关的聘请或者委派，对案件中的专门性问题，运用其专业知识对其进行判定的人；后者是对前者向法庭提供的证据——鉴定意见的真实与否，是否存在瑕疵等问题，帮助控辩双方对其进行质证的人。因此，两者在资格条件、资格限制方面也存在不同。对于鉴定人的资格条件，在2005年全国人大常委会颁布的《关于司法鉴定管理问题的决定》（以下简称《决定》）中，立法者就已经予以了明确。但是，对于专家辅助人的资格限制，无论是在《决定》中还是在《民事诉讼法》中都没有加以限制。

据此，有学者认为，“在具体实施过程中应当根据不同的委托人来限定专家辅助人的不同资格。对于当事人委托的专家辅助人，一般只有实质要件的要求，即其只要具有一定的科学技术知识或专家知识即可；而对司法人员委托的专家辅助人应当借鉴司法鉴定制度中的‘鉴定权主义’原则，既要做实质要件的要求也要做形式要件的要求，由鉴定专家名册中的人员担任”。〔9〕本文认为，该观点不能成立。理由是：专家辅助人是帮助控辩双方当事人对鉴定意见进行审查的人员；司法人员委托的、对鉴定意见进行审查的人员在我国不能称之为专家辅助人，〔10〕只能说是机关内的技术辅助人员。因此，也就不存在对专家辅助人的资格予以区别对待的情形。

对于专家辅助人的资格应当与其在诉讼中的职责相适应，本文认为，专家辅助人

---

〔9〕新《刑事诉讼法》第187条第3款规定：“公诉人、当事人或者辩护人、诉讼代理人对鉴定意见有异议，人民法院认为鉴定人有必要出庭的，鉴定人应当出庭作证。经人民法院通知，鉴定人拒不出庭的，鉴定意见不得作为定案的根据。”另外，对于鉴定人不出庭的规制，除新《刑事诉讼法》对其进行了规定之外，有关行政法规也有规范，如2005年9月30日国务院批准实施的《司法鉴定人登记管理办法》第22条规定：“司法鉴定人应当履行下列义务……（六）依法出庭作证，回答与鉴定有关的询问……”。对于鉴定人无故不出庭的，《司法鉴定人管理办法》第30条规定：“司法鉴定人有下列情形之一的，由省级司法行政机关给予停止执业3个月以上1年以下的处罚；情节严重的，撤销登记；构成犯罪的，依法追究刑事责任……（四）经人民法院依法通知，非法定事由拒绝出庭作证的……”。

〔10〕如果司法人员要委托专门知识的人对鉴定意见进行审查，可以将该具有专门知识的人员吸收为陪审员。

是帮助当事人对鉴定意见进行质证的人，其必然具有一定的倾向性。其对于鉴定意见中存在的错误的证明，无须达到案件事实清楚、证据确实充分、排除合理怀疑的证明标准，而只要使得法官确信该鉴定意见的证据能力和证明力可能存在疑问即可。因此，本文认为，我国的专家辅助人的资格可以参考意大利刑诉法的有关规定。《意大利刑事诉讼法典》第 222 条通过排除法的方式规定了四种人不得充任技术顾问：①未成年人、被禁治产人、被剥夺权利的人、患有精神病的人；②被禁止包括暂时禁止担任公职的人、被禁止或者暂停从事某一职业或技艺的人；③被处以人身保安处分或防范处分的人；④不能担任证人或者有权回避作证的人、被要求担任证人或译员的人。[11] 虽然专家辅助人与鉴定人不同，但两者在专家技术知识的掌握方面存在一定的类似，由于目前我国鉴定人资质管理还比较混乱，尤其是在“三大类”以外的鉴定人资质还不足以应对司法实践对其的要求。对此，本文认为，在结合国外有关专家辅助人资格的基础之上，考虑我国司法实践情形，有必要从积极和消极要件两个层面来确定专家辅助人的资格。

首先，积极要件，即专家辅助人必须具备对该鉴定意见进行质证的专门性知识。至于专家辅助人是否应同鉴定人一样，必须取得某方面的专业资格，必须在司法行政部门登记，本文认为，对此没有必要加以规定。因为专家辅助人，尤其是辩护方委托的专家辅助人，是对鉴定意见可能存在的问题进行质询，只需要使得法官产生“该鉴定意见可能存在瑕疵，不具备证明该专门性问题的资格”的疑问即可。因此，作为一种否定性证明方式，专家辅助人无须取得特定的专业资格条件和在相关部门予以备案，但必须具备对该专门性问题的专业技能。

其次，消极要件，即当该专门性人才具备某些条件的情况下，其不得作为专家辅助人对鉴定意见进行质询。至于哪些具体情形，本文认为，可以包含以下五方面：①未成年人、限制刑事责任能力人、被剥夺政治权利的人；②在服刑期限内的犯人，以及被采取强制措施的人；③被禁止从事该专业领域的人员，包括在一定时期内禁止从事该专业领域的人员，在该期限内不得作为辅助人；④在诉讼过程中，没有作为其他诉讼参与人参与诉讼；⑤其他存在不得作为专家辅助人的情形。最后一条为兜底条款，一方面，可以赋予法官一定的自由裁量权，予以灵活掌握；另一方面，有助于立法者通过修订法律或者颁布司法解释的方式，对其进行进一步完善。

当然，对于专家辅助人是否具备相应的资格，法官具有审查权。对于不符合专家辅助人资格条件的，法官应当对要求当事人撤换。此外，专家辅助人还应当遵循回避原则，即该专家担任专家辅助人可能与其自身利益有关联的，应当予以回避。如出具鉴定意见的鉴定人与该专家辅助人具有亲戚、同事等关系，或者鉴定意见的处理与专家辅助人有利益关联的，该专家都应当排除在专家辅助人范围之外。

（二）专家辅助人诉讼地位

在明确了专家辅助人具备什么条件方可帮助当事人对鉴定意见进行质询的情况下，我们有必要对其在诉讼中的地位予以明确。因为只有在立法上明确其诉讼地位之后，才能赋予其特定的权利义务。关于专家辅助人的诉讼地位，在理论界存在多种不同的

---

〔11〕《意大利刑事诉讼法典》，黄风译，中国政法大学出版社 1994 年版，第 77 页。

观点。

有学者认为，专家辅助人“由于其要么是帮助当事人共同行使当事人在法庭对鉴定结论的质询权，要么是帮助司法人员完成对鉴定结论的审查权，决定了他在诉讼活动中不想有独立的主体地位，仅是一种附属性的诉讼参与人”。[12] 还有学者认为，“专家辅助人的身份具有二重性。一方面，具有当事人的证人身份，审判人员和当事人可以对出庭的具有专门知识的人员进行询问。经人民法院准许，可以由当事人各自申请的具有专门知识的人员就有关案件中的问题进行对质。另一方面，又具有类似于当事人的律师身份，这特别体现在，‘具有专门知识的人员可以对鉴定人进行询问’。”[13] 此外，在新刑诉法颁布之前、征询意见的草案中，立法者也对专家辅助人的诉讼地位进行了规定：“公诉人、当事人和辩护人、诉讼代理人可以申请法庭通知有专门知识的人作为证人出庭，就鉴定人做出的鉴定意见提出意见”。可见，刑诉法草案将专家辅助人作为“证人”对待。

本文认为，上述观点都存在一定瑕疵。首先，专家辅助人是以自己的专业性知识帮助当事人对鉴定人进行质询，就如同律师以自己的法律专业向当事人提供法律帮助一样，不能因为是当事人聘请的，就认为其具有附属性。其次，任何一个诉讼参与人在诉讼活动过程中，只具有一项诉讼职能，承担一项诉讼职责，而不可能同时履行两项或两项以上的诉讼职能。因此，认为专家辅助人具有身份二重性的观点存在一定的不足。最后，认为专家辅助人的身份是证人的观点，本文认为，也存在缺陷。因为证人是在诉讼过程中，就自己所感知的案件事实向公安、司法机关提供证言的人。证人所了解的事实，必须是在案发过程中所知晓的。证人的身份具有不可替代性和优先性。但专家辅助人并不是以自己所感知的案件事实，而是以自己的专业技术知识对鉴定人进行发问。两者在知晓案件事实的时间上、作证的方式和内容上都存在显著区别，并且如果具有专门知识的人，同时又知道案件具体情况的，应当作为证人，而排除专家辅助人的身份。

据此，本文认为，刑事诉讼中的专家辅助人是独立的诉讼参与人，具有独立的诉讼地位。专家辅助人以其专门性知识，对鉴定意见中的问题向鉴定人发问，揭露其中存在的不足，独立的行使诉讼权利，承担相应的诉讼义务，并不依附于当事人而存在。当然，专家辅助人的职能具有一定的倾向性，一般是从有利于委托方当事人的利益角度出发，帮助其揭露对其不利的鉴定意见中存在的问题，证明对其有利的鉴定意见成立，但应当在法律规定的范围之内进行。

---

〔12〕 新《刑事诉讼法》第187条第3款规定：“公诉人、当事人或者辩护人、诉讼代理人对鉴定意见有异议，人民法院认为鉴定人有必要出庭的，鉴定人应当出庭作证。经人民法院通知，鉴定人拒不出庭的，鉴定意见不得作为定案的根据。”另外，对于鉴定人不出庭的规制，除新《刑事诉讼法》对其进行了规定之外，有关行政法规也有规范，如2005年9月30日国务院批准实施的《司法鉴定人登记管理办法》第22条规定：“司法鉴定人应当履行下列义务……（六）依法出庭作证，回答与鉴定有关的询问……”。对于鉴定人无故不出庭的，《司法鉴定人管理办法》第30条规定：“司法鉴定人有下列情形之一的，由省级司法行政机关给予停止执业3个月以上1年以下的处罚；情节严重的，撤销登记；构成犯罪的，依法追究刑事责任……（四）经人民法院依法通知，非法定事由拒绝出庭作证的……”。

〔13〕 常林：“司法鉴定与案结事了”，载《证据科学》2008年第2期。

（三）专家辅助人权利义务

专家辅助人在诉讼活动过程中具有独立的诉讼地位，与此相对应，鉴定人也应该享有与之相适应的权利和义务。具体表现在以下几方面：

1. 专家辅助人的权利。为方便专家辅助人能够顺利履行自己的职责，辅助诉讼顺利进行，其享有的权利应当包括：①了解与鉴定事项有关的案件事实的权利，以帮助其能对鉴定所涉及的问题有所了解，如专家辅助人有权了解鉴定人对检材的选取、鉴定方法、鉴定标准等有关内容。这是专家辅助人就鉴定人出具的意见提出意见的前提，也是帮助聘请其作为专家辅助人的当事人对鉴定意见进行有效质证的前提。②对鉴定意见进行质询的权利。即专家辅助人对于鉴定人出具的鉴定意见有权提出异议、自己的看法，当然鉴于专家辅助人在一定意义上仅仅是当事人的技术顾问，其主要是针对可能影响鉴定意见客观性、真实性的内容予以质询。③与鉴定人进行对质的权利。在庭审中，如果鉴定人出庭的，则专家辅助人可以就鉴定意见中的有关问题与鉴定人进行对质、辩论。④获得相应报酬的权利，专家辅助人出庭可能会产生相应的费用，包括误工费、车旅费、食宿费等，对于这些费用，专家辅助人可以获得相应的补偿。⑤拒绝接受委托的权利，“如果委托事项违法，委托人利用专家辅助人提供的服务从事违法活动或者委托人隐瞒事实以及侮辱专家辅助人的人格和声誉时”，[14] 专家辅助人可以拒绝接受委托，或者终止已经接受的委托。⑥专家辅助人在诉讼过程中享有的其他权利，包括知晓开庭时间、地点权、发表意见权，等等。

2. 专家辅助人的义务。具有独立诉讼地位的专家辅助人，在诉讼中除享有特定的权利以外，也承担着一定的义务，以督促其认真履行职责、帮助当事人对鉴定意见进行质证。主要包括：①帮助当事人对鉴定意见的专业性问题提出质询的义务。当事人聘请专家辅助人的目的就是揭露不利己的鉴定意见存在的问题，使得对案件具有裁判权的法官对鉴定意见的证据能力和证明力产生疑问的心证，从而获得利己的诉讼利益。②接受法官和对方当事人、专家辅助人等的询问的义务。专家辅助人除可以对鉴定人进行质询之外，还必须接受双方和法官对他本人的询问，如其是否具有该专业方面的知识、是否与对方当事人具有某种特定的关系，等等。③保证其所依据的科学技术、知识具有真实性、客观性的义务，而不是随意自行编造的。虽然专家辅助人是当事人聘请的，理应为聘请他的当事人的利益付出最大的努力，但是作为技术专家，其对鉴定意见提出的任何质询都应当建立在确实、可信的技术基础之上的，而不能一顾为了当事人的利益，运用自行编造虚假的或者是已经被证明错误的技术，歪曲事实。④保守在诉讼活动过程中所知晓的国家秘密、个人隐私及商业秘密等。专家辅助人应当于审判期日参与庭审，在法庭之上对鉴定意见进行质询，因此势必会对案件涉及的国家秘密、个人隐私、商业秘密有所了解，为保障这些利益，专家辅助人应当保密。⑤专家辅助人应遵守的其他义务，包括按时到庭的义务、恪尽职守的义务等。

专家辅助人所享有的权利和承担的义务是与其独立的诉讼地位相适应的，都是为了帮助辅助人能够顺利和督促其履行职责，对鉴定意见进行质询，帮助法官和当事人对其中的疑问予以澄清。

---

〔14〕 陈斌、王路：“论我国刑事诉讼中的专家辅助人及其制度构建”，载《湖北社会科学》2011 年第 1 期。

（四）专家辅助人出庭程序

在明确了专家辅助人的资格、诉讼地位和权利义务以后，建构专家辅助人制度，还必须明确其出庭的具体程序，包括启动、时限、费用的承担、出庭方式等。

1. 专家辅助人的启动。专家辅助人在诉讼职能上，与辩护人具有一定的相似性，因此，专家辅助人的启动程序也与辩护人制度具有一定的类似。在一般情形下，专家辅助人应当由当事人自行聘请或委托；如果法院对鉴定意见存有疑问，需要具有专业知识的人帮助其解决的，可以通过吸收其为专家陪审员的方式将其纳入诉讼程序之中。不过，对于控辩双方当事人，尤其是辩方当事人，如果在经济上存有困难、无力聘请专家辅助人的，法庭应当通过法律援助的形式，为其聘请专家辅助人，具体情形可以参见指定辩护的适用情形。

2. 启动专家辅助人程序的理由和时间。首先，聘请专家辅助人的理由必须是对鉴定意见中的专门性问题存有疑问，并且可能影响其证据能力和证明力的判断。对此，法庭应当对其理由进行审查，如果理由成立的，应当予以准许；如果当事人提出的理由无根据的，如仅对鉴定提出异议，但是，无法说明理由的，法庭则不应当允许，防止其故意拖延诉讼等不正当目的实现。

其次，启动专家辅助人程序的时间，本文认为，在双方当事人知晓在诉讼过程中存有鉴定意见这一证据之后，当事人就可以聘请专家辅助人帮助其对鉴定进行质询。此外，我国《刑事诉讼法》第159条规定：“法庭审理过程中，当事人和辩护人、诉讼代理人有权申请通知新的证人到庭，调取新的物证，申请重新鉴定或者勘验。”可见，在庭审过程中，如果当事人认为对于诉讼过程中的专门性问题，如果确实需要委托专家辅助人对其鉴定意见的证据能力和证明力进行质询的，也可以再行委托。

3. 专家辅助人费用的负担与出庭程序。首先，专家辅助人出庭作证的目的是为了帮助当事人，对不利于自己的鉴定意见可能存在的问题进行质询，以使法庭作出有利于他的最终判决。因此，对于专家辅助人的费用，应当同律师费用一样，由委托辅助人的当事人自行负担。对于法庭根据法律援助，为当事人聘请的辅助人，其费用应当由国家财政予以负担。其次，专家辅助人的出庭程序关键在于明确专家辅助人是否可以参与庭审，进行旁听。本文认为，专家辅助人仅仅是对鉴定中涉及的技术性问题对鉴定人进行质询，并不涉及其他事实问题。辅助人参与庭审可以帮助其对鉴定所涉及的案件事实有更清晰的认识，从而有助于其对鉴定意见证据能力向鉴定人进行质询。因此，本文认为，专家辅助人可以参与庭审，进行旁听。

4. 专家辅助人提供的书面意见。虽然刑诉法规定鉴定人应当出庭作证，但是在司法实践中，或是由于鉴定人权利保障不到位，或是由于立法缺乏强制性规定等原因，鉴定人出庭作证比例极低，出现较多的往往是鉴定人仅向法庭提供书面鉴定意见。这极大影响法庭对鉴定意见证据能力的审查判断。与此相对应，专家辅助人是否可以不出庭，而仅仅向法庭提供书面质询意见？本文认为，根据前文所述强制关键鉴定人出庭作证的精神，对于在一些重要案件中，鉴定意见对定罪量刑起决定性作用的，然而专家辅助人的质询意见又对鉴定意见的证据能力和证明力的认定起决定性作用的，专家辅助人应当出庭进行质询。对于其他的质询，可以由专家辅助人提出书面质询意见，至于其具体情形，可以参照关键鉴定人出庭作证的具体情形。

四、余论：司法实践可能遇到的阻碍

虽然本文对专家辅助人的完善提出了相应的对策，但是我们依然要直面专家辅助人制度在司法实践的实际运行过程中可能遇到的实际阻碍。

第一，新《刑事诉讼法》已经颁布，并已经于2013年1月1日起实施，加之公检法三机关的司法解释和有关规定也已经制定完毕和生效，那么对于明确专家辅助人的资格、诉讼地位和权利义务、出庭程序等内容，应当以何种立法形式出现，在此存在障碍，因为我们不可能在新刑诉法和有关解释仅仅生效半年之际就对其进行修改。

第二，对于专家辅助人的资格和对其资格审查问题，也存在一定的障碍。这里最为关键的就是鉴定人能否担任专家辅助人？如果能够担任专家辅助人，那么是否会对有关司法鉴定的立法中所规定的统一受理等内容造成侵蚀？作为鉴定人所依靠的鉴定机构是否要对鉴定人作为专家辅助人的案件进行监管？如果鉴定人不能担任专家辅助人，当事人如何选任有“专门知识的人”？如何对其掌握知识的水平、专业技能进行评价，从而选取一个能够真正帮助自身对鉴定意见进行质询的人？另外，法官对于有“专门知识的人”的审查如何把握？法官对于专家辅助人的出庭是否会同对待证人、鉴定人一样，持消极态度？

第三，当事人和有“专门知识的人”的趋利化障碍。人具有趋利性，这是一个亘古不变的真理。一方面，当事人具有极强的胜诉愿望，这是其趋利性的本质在诉讼中的体现。无论当事人参与诉讼的目的，还是聘请律师、代理人，或是专家辅助人的目的，都是基于胜诉的愿望，为了获取有利于自身的诉讼结果。因此，从该角度来看，当事人当然会聘请为自己的胜诉而付出极大努力的、有“专门知识的人”参与诉讼，必然会拒绝为了实体公正、司法公正而置当事人利益不顾，使得当事人败诉的专家辅助人。另一方面，专家辅助人，作为具有某种专业知识的人必然也具有趋利性。其之所以愿意担任专家辅助人，除部分是基于司法公正、法律援助、社会正义等目的，还有很大部分专家辅助人是希望通过帮助当事人对鉴定意见进行质证，而获取相应的经济利益。据此，在专家辅助人和当事人之间就形成一种自然而然的默契，当事人为胜诉聘请专家辅助人，并给予其一定经济利益；专家辅助人为获取相应、甚至高昂的经济利益，而不顾事实，甚至歪曲事实，帮助当事人获取相应的诉讼利益，也为自己赢得更大的“市场价值”。据此，专家辅助人和当事人的趋利性也有可能致使该制度的运行产生如同英美法系国家专家证人制度相同的困境：专家辅助人费用的高昂，造成诉讼在富有者与贫穷者之间的不平等；诉讼效率的低下，当事人为胜诉，双方聘请大量的专家辅助人，如此反复，增加诉讼成本和当事人、法院的诉累，等等。

第四，专家辅助人运行的体制障碍问题。我国的司法体制是在职权主义的基础之上，吸收当事人主义的合理化内核，同时又具有我国传统司法体制的影子。因此，可以说，我国目前的鉴定制度也具有上述三种不同的司法文化因素。实际上，我国的鉴定人制度与大陆法系国家的法官辅助人、技术顾问制度具有一定的相似性，而专家辅助人制度却有英美法系国家的专家证人制度的精神。虽然两大法系的法律体制在不断地融合、相互借鉴，但也只是某些方面的融合，不可能是制度的简单叠加，我国刑事诉讼将两种截然不同的制度放在同一司法体制下，是否会产生相反的效果？这也是我们在运行专家辅助人制度过程中可能会遭遇的现实性阻碍。

综上所述，仅仅依赖法官和控辩双方的能力难以对鉴定意见的证据能力和证明力进行充分审查。相反，专家辅助人制度的设立则可以有效弥补各方专业知识的不足，而对涉及专门性知识的鉴定意见的证据能力和证明力进行判定，以保障案件事实的正确认定。这也在国内外立法活动中得到了实践。当然，对于专家辅助人这一新兴制度，立法者应当在法律中对专家辅助人的资格、诉讼地位、权利义务以及出庭程序等予以明确，以确保该制度的良性运行。